To

Love Giles and Nancy

17 August 2023

THE INDIAN SAPPERS AND MINERS

GENERAL SIR BINDON BLOOD, G.C.B., G.C.V.O.,

Chief Royal Engineer and formerly Commandant,
Bengal Sappers and Miners.

(By permission of Vandyk, 41, Buckingham Palace, Road London, S.W.1.)

THE INDIAN SAPPERS AND MINERS

BY

LIEUT.-COLONEL E. W. C. SANDES
D.S.O., M.C., R.E. (*Ret.*)

LATE PRINCIPAL, THOMASON CIVIL ENGINEERING COLLEGE, ROORKEE, INDIA,

AND AUTHOR OF
"IN KUT AND CAPTIVITY," "TALES OF TURKEY," "THE MILITARY ENGINEER IN INDIA," VOLS. I AND II, AND "THE ROYAL ENGINEERS IN EGYPT AND THE SUDAN."

The Naval & Military Press Ltd

Published by

The Naval & Military Press Ltd
Unit 5 Riverside, Brambleside
Bellbrook Industrial Estate
Uckfield, East Sussex
TN22 1QQ England

Tel: +44 (0)1825 749494

www.naval-military-press.com
www.nmarchive.com

TO MY BROTHER OFFICERS

OF

THE INDIAN SAPPERS AND MINERS

IN

THE GREAT WAR, 1914–18

FOREWORD

By Lieut.-General Sir J. R. E. Charles, K.C.B., C.M.G., D.S.O., late Chief Royal Engineer and Colonel, K.G.V's O. Bengal Sappers and Miners.

IN recording the development of the engineer arm of the Indian Army the author has traced its evolution against the background of nearly two centuries of warfare both in and outside India. This period began about the middle of the eighteenth century, when the East India Company first found it necessary to safeguard its hold on its trading posts on the coasts by engaging in war against the French and against the rulers of inland Indian states. The opening chapters of this history give most interesting descriptions of the Mysore, Maratha, Burma, Nepal and other wars which succeeded each other so rapidly that there was hardly one year in the century preceding the Indian Mutiny when the troops of one or other of the Presidency Armies were not engaged in fighting.

The record begins with the story of the formation of the first unit of "Pioneers" in 1759 during the siege of Madras; it was composed of European volunteers. At that time, the engineers consisted of a Corps of European officers only, who served in one or other of the three Presidency Armies. Troops were placed under their orders for actual operations, and their training had to be acquired by bitter experience in the field. It was not until nearly the end of the eighteenth century that the maintenance of Corps of Pioneers in peace-time became a recognized necessity, and even then, their officers were drawn from infantry units and were without any technical qualifications.

The raising, and not infrequently the subsequent disbandment, of Pioneer units seems to have been a very haphazard affair during the Mysore and Maratha Wars. They were apparently regarded as units necessary only in war and of no particular peace-time value. It is, therefore, not surprising that, at the completion of any particular campaign when military budgets were subjected to close scrutiny, units considered to be redundant should have been disbanded.

The seniority of the three Corps of Sappers and Miners has been the subject of some controversy. Their predecessors went under various titles in which the word "Pioneers" generally occurred. It must be recollected that, from the earliest days of its formation, the Indian Army was organized on a Presidency basis; there were, in fact, three armies, each with its own Commander-in-Chief, recruited from the provinces of Madras, Bombay and Bengal. The first record we have of the formation of an Indian Pioneer unit was the raising of two volunteer companies of Madras Pioneers in 1759. The first unit of Bengal Pioneers was formed on a temporary basis in 1764; but it was not until 1803 that the Corps of

Bengal Pioneers was officially brought into being at Cawnpore. The first unit of Pioneers to be raised in the Bombay Presidency was the " Pioneer Lascar Company ", which was authorized in 1777. The question of seniority is fully discussed in Chapter II of this history, and it would be out of place for the writer to record an opinion on the subject. The vicissitudes of the titles and strengths of the three Corps seem to have been left entirely to the decision of the Commanders-in-Chief of the Presidency Armies.

The unification of titles was gradually achieved, and the title of " Sappers and Miners " was adopted for the Bengal Corps in February, 1819, when the Bengal Sappers and Miners came into being with headquarters at Allahabad, from which the Corps moved to Cawnpore two years later. The Bombay Sappers and Miners received that designation in August, 1820; but it was not until May, 1831, that the 1st Battalion of Madras Pioneers was re-designated Sappers and Miners. Although most of the new Corps was stationed at Bangalore, seven years elapsed before that cantonment was recognized as its permanent headquarters.

The half-century which included the first and second Afghan Wars was a period of almost continuous activity for the Sappers and Miners. The few redeeming features of the disastrous First Afghan War included such achievements by the Sappers as the blowing in of the Kabul Gate at Ghazni in July, 1839, and the gallant defence of Jalalabad nearly three years later by Broadfoot. It is typical of the British love for improvisation that Broadfoot, who was not an engineer officer, was called upon in 1840 to raise an irregular unit of Sappers, although three Corps of Sappers and Miners were already in existence. Broadfoot's Sappers made a great name for themselves and were eventually incorporated in the Bengal Sappers after some two years of independent existence.

The Sikh wars, which followed, gave little scope for the Sappers and Miners other than the bridging of the rivers of the Punjab and the siege operations at Multan; but the policy of starving the three Corps of experienced engineer officers still persisted with deplorable results when the Indian Mutiny broke out in May, 1857.

This black page in the history of the Bengal Army unfortunately records the defection of a portion of the Bengal Sappers. On reading the account given in this history, one is struck by the fact that a high proportion of the Corps as a whole remained loyal. Life in Roorkee was, at first, very uneasy; but there was no open mutiny and recruit training was proceeding normally again by September. The behaviour of the men who took part in the blowing in of the Kashmir Gate at Delhi, and in the relief of Lucknow, went far to erase the stain of mutiny from the Bengal Sappers.

The assumption by Her Majesty Queen Victoria of the Government of India in 1858 led to a general reorganization of the military forces in that country. Amongst many other reforms, the Presidency Engineers disappeared and the officers were amalgamated with the Royal Engineers in 1862. It was not, however, until twenty-three years later that the three Corps of Sappers and Miners came to be officered exclusively by Royal

Engineers. In the meantime, the lack of a proper engineer organization persisted, and poor equipment, combined with lack of proper transport, considerably impeded the work of the Sappers and Miners during the Second Afghan War, which broke out in November, 1878. All three Corps participated in this laborious campaign, towards the end of which the 2nd Company of the Bombay Sappers earned undying glory by their gallant stand at Maiwand.

One very important happening in this war was the appointment of Major Bindon Blood to the command of the Bengal Sappers in Afghanistan. This officer, whose name was to become a family one in the Royal Engineers, saw so clearly the deficiencies in organization and equipment of the Sappers he commanded that, on the termination of the war, he concentrated his energies on an all-embracing scheme for the reorganization of the Sappers and Miners in India. It took five years of hard work before his efforts were rewarded by the publication of an Indian Army Order which brought into being the organization which substantially held the field until the outbreak of the Great War in 1914.

The outstanding overseas expedition after the Mutiny was that to Abyssinia in 1867, which is of special interest in view of the campaign against the Italians in that country during 1940 and 1941. It was a war against nature rather than against man, and was essentially an engineer war in which both the Madras and Bombay Sappers and Miners played very important parts.

Other overseas expeditions took place from time to time in almost every country from Africa to the Far East, the most important ones being to Somaliland and Egypt and to China. The adaptability of all three Corps of Sappers and Miners, chiefly the Madras and Bombay Corps, was an important feature of these expeditions. One notable episode was the gallantry of the Madras Sappers and Miners at Mc.Neill's Zareba outside Suakin in 1885, when they helped to retrieve what was nearly a major disaster.

The author has written a remarkable *résumé* of all the expeditions on the North-West Frontier of India from 1849 onwards, together with a graphic account of the terrain and of the Pathan tribes who inhabit it. This gives the reader who has never served there a good idea of the dangers and hardships of campaigning in those parts. The North-West Frontier was an admirable training ground for the Sappers and Miners who, though they figured in very few of the expeditions until 1891, formed part of every force employed in expeditions subsequent to that date. During the latter period, three officers gained the distinction of the Victoria Cross for gallantry in action; one of these, the late Lieut.-General Sir Fenton Aylmer, in addition to his outstanding leadership, was really the pioneer of extemporized suspension bridges, built largely of locally available materials. Improvisation of this sort was the order of the day, for little attention was paid to the needs of engineers in up-to-date equipment until the Great War. The only bridging equipment available consisted of pontoons and, though the N.W. Frontier was well known to be a country of deep gorges, mountain torrents and occasionally sizable rivers, no provision was made in peace-time for standard suspension or other bridges.

The North-East Frontier saw numerous, if small, expeditions between 1860 and 1913. The best-known of these was that to Tibet in 1904, which was commanded by a Sapper, Major-General Macdonald. The physical difficulties to be overcome in crossing mountain ranges whose passes rose to as much as 17,000 feet, and finally the crossing of the Tsanpo River with locally extemporized bridging equipment, required immeasurable energy and not a little ingenuity. It was indeed fortunate that Captain (now Major-General) Sheppard commanded the 3rd Company, Bengal Sappers and Miners, which formed part of the force; his physical endurance is well known to his contemporaries, whilst his boundless energy, not to mention the charmed life he then seemed to bear, contributed in no small measure to the success of this remarkable campaign.

The history of the Sappers and Miners in the Great War is a record of gallantry, of the surmounting of obstacles, and of successful achievement in the face of discouragement and sometimes of failure. It reflects in some measure the experiences of their Indian comrades of the other arms; but there is no doubt that long years of fighting under the conditions of the North-West Frontier of India, and of other war theatres in undeveloped countries, had created almost a genius for improvisation which stood the Indian Sappers in good stead, certainly during the opening stages of the war, and especially in France and Iraq.

In every theatre, the Indian Sappers were woefully deficient in modern weapons, transport and technical equipment; but everywhere, they accepted the inevitable and made the best of it, emerging triumphant. In France especially, the conditions of trench warfare made terrific demands on troops unaccustomed to shell-fire, ill-clothed and faced with a climate such as is not encountered in any part of India. Few people realize how gallant was the defence made by the Indian Corps in France in 1914–15: the writer was there himself and can testify to the fact that, in spite of one or two minor failures, the gallantry of the Indian troops was no small factor in the successful resistance which prevented the Germans from breaking through the British line during the first winter of the war. In this successful defence, the Sappers and Miners played, one is tempted to say, the leading part. Two companies of the Bengal and two companies of the Bombay Sappers were almost continuously in the line. They built obstacles, organized defences, carried out one major attack and a host of minor raids, and heartened their comrades in the infantry by example and resourcefulness, but at a terrible cost in officer casualties, particularly in the Bombay companies, which lost three hundred per cent of officers before New Year's Day, 1915.

The story of the war in Iraq is most graphically unfolded from a landing at Basra with a strictly limited objective to the eventual conquest of the whole country. It is a story beginning with high hopes, subsequently dashed to the ground by the disaster of Kut, and finishing with the final victory over the Turks. Here, the main task of the Sappers was that of making and improving communications and, as in France, it was made infinitely harder by the lack of proper equipment, particularly for floating bridges. Again we see the genius for improvisation overcoming difficulties arising from the refusal of the Government of India to make adequate preparation for war necessities in peace-time.

It is not too much to say that the technical skill of the British officers, ably seconded by the work of their well-trained and gallant Indian Sappers, was a decisive factor in the success of the operations, for it ensured the continuous mobility of the other arms beside whom they fought.

In Egypt and Palestine, the campaign developed from a purely passive defence of the Suez Canal to the capture of Jerusalem and eventually of all Palestine and Syria. The Sappers again played an important part in improving communications and producing water in an arid theatre of operations. By the time the advance started from the Canal, it had been realized that modern warfare demands modern technical equipment. It was consequently possible to provide railways, pipe-lines and adequate pumping plant without which the advance across the Sinai Desert would have been quite impossible.

The East African campaign was remarkable for the very small numbers of engineer troops employed. Four Sapper and Miner railway companies were eventually used and made possible General Smuts' advance after the initial failures of these operations.

Most of the limelight of the Great War was directed on the European and Middle Eastern Theatres. Little enough has been written about the operations against the Turks north of Aden. The protection of that fortress on the main line of communication with India, Australia and New Zealand was essential to the free movement of our ships sailing on those routes. The climatic conditions in and around Aden were terrible; but in spite of some local setbacks, the troops in its garrison maintained the integrity of the fortress in the face of several determined attacks, and indeed, carried out many minor offensives. Two field companies of Sappers and Miners found themselves taxed to the utmost in surmounting the difficulties due to the heat and the lack of water which faced the garrison, whilst the 23rd Bombay (Fortress) Company covered itself with glory when it formed the rearguard during the retreat from Lahej in July, 1915. The 5th Bengal Company had, time and again, to act as infantry, and showed the value of the excellent peace-time training it had undergone.

A period of almost continuous unrest on the North-West Frontier of India, culminating in the Third Afghan War in 1919, kept the Sappers busy on their normal tasks of maintaining the communications and water supply of the expeditions of which they formed part. Following on the Afghan War came an extensive rising in Waziristan. This caused the Government of India to reconsider its frontier policy. In shaping this new policy, Lord Rawlinson, then Commander-in-Chief in India, urged the building of roads through tribal territory which would accelerate the movement of troops by the use of mechanical transport, and incidentally, would provide remunerative work for the tribesmen and divert their thoughts from raiding. This policy was finally adopted in 1922 and was maintained until the outbreak of the World War in 1939. The writer helped in the initiation of this policy, and it was interesting to watch the gradual introduction, after 1921, of mechanical road-making tools in the many expeditions which culminated in the extensive operations in Waziristan and the Mohmand country during the last decade before the World War. The Government of India had at length realized the necessity for equipping their technical troops with road-making and water-supply plant of modern design.

In 1932–33, far reaching changes were made in the organization of the technical troops in the Indian Army. For reasons which are not easy to understand, the Government of India decided to disband the Pioneer regiments *in toto* and to expand the Sappers and Miners. Whilst this change was to the advantage of the latter, it was carried out at the expense of losing a number of well-trained Pioneer battalions who had built up fine traditions for themselves in numerous hard-fought campaigns.

The story of the Sappers and Miners does not end with this volume. During the six or seven years succeeding the outbreak of the recent World War, the three Corps were expanded to between 20,000 and 30,000 men each, and took part in every campaign other than in France and Germany. Between 1943 and 1946, the three Corps were gradually merged into the Corps of Royal Indian Engineers. Though they have lost their old identity and their Royal Engineer officers, we can be sure that the traditions which they have built up over the last two centuries will survive and will help them to hold their heads as high in the future as they have in the past.

RONALD CHARLES.

October 19th, 1947.

PREFACE

MORE than nine years have elapsed since I began to write this book—years of anxiety, war and scarcity. My earlier histories were finished more quickly, for the writing of Volume I of *The Military Engineer in India* begun in June, 1930, occupied little more than 2½ years, and Volume II only 1½ years, while *The Royal Engineers in Egypt and the Sudan* was completed in 2 years.

In August, 1935, three months after commencing *The Royal Engineers in Egypt and the Sudan*, I was asked by the Commandant, K.G.V's O. Bengal Sappers and Miners, to write a history of his Corps; but as it seemed to me that the Q.V.O. Madras Sappers and Miners and the Royal Bombay Sappers and Miners should be included because all three Corps had shared in so many campaigns, I proposed instead that I should write a combined history for the three Corps. This was approved by the Commandants in May, 1936, and having finished *The Royal Engineers in Egypt and the Sudan* in April, 1937, I began to supplement the information about the Sappers and Miners which I had collected originally for Volume I of *The Military Engineer in India*.

The first words of *The Indian Sappers and Miners* were penned in February, 1938, when the dark cloud of Nazi Germany loomed, ominous and menacing, on the political horizon. During periodical visits to London from Weymouth before and after that date, I collected so much information from the India Office and the R.E. Corps Library at the Horse Guards that, with the addition of copious notes from many ex-Sapper and Miner officers, I was able to continue writing without interruption until March, 1940, when the World War was already six months old. By then, all sources of information had dried up. Historical work seemed so incongruous that it was impossible to concentrate on it. The India Office records had left London, the R.E. Library had gone to Chatham, the War Office was "otherwise engaged," and all R.E. officers on the active list had scattered to secret destinations. Although fifteen, out of twenty-five, chapters had been written and typed, the prospect of finishing the history seemed remote.

In March, 1940, therefore, I informed the Commandants that I must postpone completion until the circumstances were more favourable, and thereafter, for four years, I served voluntarily as an Assistant C.R.E., Works Department, until obliged to retire once more on account of age. Thus it was not until March, 1944, that I could resume the history at Chapter XVI, and then only because I had amassed so much information before the war that there was no need to visit London or Chatham for further research. The handicaps were still severe. The Historical Section of the Committee of Imperial Defence had moved from the Thames

Embankment to Lancashire, and then to Wales; many retired officers were still busy on war work, and the addresses of serving officers were not shown in the *R.E. List*; the Commandants in India were engrossed in the war against Japan; and Weymouth, like other places on the south coast, was a favourite target for German bombers. After " D Day ", I made better progress. Chapter followed chapter at regular intervals of from two to three months, and now at length, in August, 1947, I have reached the end of the road. The journey has been long and difficult, but I have been helped by many willing hands.

My particular thanks are due to three ex-Royal Engineers who have acted throughout as readers of the typescript—Major-General Sir Theodore Fraser, K.C.B., C.S.I., C.M.G., on behalf of the Madras Corps, Major-General S. H. Sheppard, C.B., C.M.G., D.S.O., for the Bengal Corps, and Brig.-General G. H. Boileau, C.B., C.M.G., D.S.O., for the Bombay Corps. Also to Major-General S. G. Loch, C.B., C.S.I., D.S.O., late R.E., who was a reader for the Madras Corps until March, 1940. Without their constructive criticism, valuable suggestions and graphic reminiscences, this history could not have been produced in its present form. My acknowledgments are due also to many other serving or retired Royal Engineers for notes of their experiences with the Indian Sappers and Miners both in peace and war, and to Dr. H. N. Randle and the staff of the India Office Library and the Librarian of the R.E. Corps Library for facilities accorded to me in consulting books and records. Brig.-General Sir James Edmonds, C.B., C.M.G., late R.E., has often helped me with information from the Historical Section of the Committee of Imperial Defence, and I have been assisted throughout by successive Secretaries of the Institution of Royal Engineers, first the late Lieut.-Colonel E. V. Binney, D.S.O., R.E. (retd.), then the late Colonel H.M. Fordham, O.B.E., M.C., late R.E. (acting Secretary), and latterly, Brigadier C. C, Phipps, C.B.E., M.C., late R.E. The Commandants, Sappers and Miners, have answered many queries and have lent me their Annual Records. The laborious task of preparing an Index has been undertaken by Colonel F. C. Molesworth, late R.E., who compiled the Indices of my previous books on India and Egypt. A draft for the Signals' Appendix was written by Brig.-General H. S. E. Franklin, C.M.G., C.B.E., D.S.O., late Indian Army and Royal Corps of Signals, in place of the late Major-General S. H. Powell, C.B., late R.E., Col.-Commandant, Indian Signal Corps, who had agreed to prepare it. I am indebted to Miss M. Wilkins, P.C.T., A.C.T.S., for the accuracy and rapidity of her typing not only of this history but also of that on Egypt and the Sudan and the second volume on India, and to Captain A. C. Jenner, R.E., for fairing my sketch maps in the same finished style which he showed in *The Royal Engineers in Egypt and the Sudan.*

To avoid the inconvenience of frequent reference to several large folding maps, or to a great number of small maps grouped in a bulky end-pocket or in a separate cover, I have included in each chapter the appropriate maps for the operations described. This system proved satisfactory in *The Royal Engineers in Egypt and the Sudan.* Three general maps, however, are given at the end of the volume, Map No. III being especially useful as showing the entire North-West Frontier of India. All the 47 sketch maps are my own work. The labour has been great; but I think it has been justified by the resulting facility in finding the locations of any places mentioned. The maps are sufficiently to scale to give accurate information. Some are repeated in subsequent chapters. The spelling of names accords with that shown in the *Imperial Gazetteer of India.* As all sources of information are given throughout in footnotes, a separate bibliography is not included. Nine Appendices at the end of the volume afford detailed information which could not be incorporated appropriately in the general history.

Greatly to my regret I have been unable, through lack of space, to describe the splendid record of the Indian Sappers and Miners in the field of sport. A volume might be written on the achievements of Sapper and Miner officers in pursuit of big game in every part of India and Burma and even in Africa, on duck-shooting and pig-sticking in the Ganges *khadir*, tournament polo and racing, and rowing at Kirkee. Many have excelled as sportsmen, but none more than the eminent soldier whose picture forms the frontispiece of this volume.

I have tried to produce a readable narrative which will appeal to any student of Indian history, whether soldier or civilian. The field has been so vast that compression has been unavoidable, especially in the later chapters; but I hope that it has not been carried too far, and that it will not obscure the picture of how much the modern Dominions of India and Pakistan owe to men of their new armies who fought as gallantly in the recent World War as in the Great War, the frontier campaigns, and the scores of small expeditions I have described.

Ubique. Quo Fas et Gloria ducunt.

So runs the motto of the Corps of Royal Engineers. It might well be the motto also of the late Indian Sappers and Miners, for duty and glory led them indeed to the ends of the earth.

E. W. C. SANDES.

Faircross,
Weymouth.
August 19*th*, 1947.

CONTENTS

CHAPTER I

PIONEERS IN SOUTHERN INDIA, 1759–1809

CHAPTER II

PIONEERS IN WESTERN, CENTRAL AND NORTHERN INDIA, 1777–1809

CHAPTER III

THE NEPAL AND THIRD MARATHA WARS, 1814–1819

CHAPTER IV

THE FIRST BURMA WAR, THE CAPTURE OF BHURTPORE AND MINOR CAMPAIGNS, 1824–1838

CHAPTER V

EARLY OVERSEAS EXPEDITIONS, 1762–1857

CHAPTER VI

THE FIRST AFGHAN AND FIRST CHINA WARS AND CAMPAIGNS IN SIND AND GWALIOR, 1838–1843

CHAPTER X

THE SECOND AFGHAN WAR, 1878–1880

CHAPTER XI

OVERSEAS EXPEDITIONS AND THE THIRD BURMA WAR, 1867–1889

CHAPTER XV

EXPEDITIONS ON THE NORTH-EAST FRONTIER, 1860–1913

CHAPTER XVI

THE GREAT WAR: FRANCE AND BELGIUM, 1914–1915

CHAPTER XVII

THE GREAT WAR: IRAQ, 1914–1916

CHAPTER XVIII

THE GREAT WAR: IRAQ AND IRAN, 1917–1918

CHAPTER XIX

THE GREAT WAR: EGYPT AND PALESTINE, 1914–1918

CHAPTER XX

CHAPTER XXI

CHAPTER XXII

CHAPTER XXIII

OPERATIONS IN IRAQ AND IRAN, 1919–1922, INCLUDING THE ARAB REBELLION

CHAPTER XXIV

PROGRESS IN WAZIRISTAN, OPERATIONS NEAR PESHAWAR AND IN BURMA, AND THE REORGANIZATION OF THE SAPPERS AND MINERS, 1922–1932

CHAPTER XXV

PRELUDE TO THE WORLD WAR, 1933–1939

APPENDIX A

APPENDIX B

APPENDIX C

APPENDIX D

APPENDIX E

APPENDIX F

APPENDIX G

APPENDIX H

APPENDIX I

ILLUSTRATIONS

PLANS AND MAPS

SKETCH MAPS

GENERAL MAPS

THE INDIAN SAPPERS AND MINERS

CHAPTER I

PIONEERS IN SOUTHERN INDIA, 1759–1809

THE INDIAN SAPPER AND MINER was a descendant of the Pioneer, who was created in the process of time from the civilian artisan or labourer. Towards the end of the 17th century, when the East India Company was struggling to retain a precarious footing on the coasts of Hindustan and its servants were housed in fortified settlements at Surat, Bombay, Madras, Masulipatam and Hugli, military engineering was confined to the construction and repair of primitive defences designed to safeguard the garrisons and merchandise. Any man who could wield a spade was required to do so, and the direction of the work was entrusted to the captains of the Company's ships, or occasionally to hired adventurers who prided themselves on a smattering of mathematics or some experience in European wars. " Our business is Trade, not Warr," wrote the Directors,[1] " and wee question not but the Commanders of our ships, and others you have with you, will continue the carrying on of the work to make it answer our ends without sending an Engineer from hence, those sort of men being alwaies found very expensive."

In 1685, Job Charnock, the founder of Calcutta, rashly planned to raid Chittagong from his settlement at Hugli as a counterblast to Mughal threats, and the Directors thought fit to address a letter to Madras in which they discussed " the Duty of a Soldier in Intrenchment Work." " In the expectation of our fortifications at Chyttegam," they wrote,[2] " wee doe much depend upon the prudence of our Vice-Admirall and all our Captains of Sea and Land forces, that they will by perswasion, their own example, and some little rewards, encourage our Seamen and Soldiers to work hard upon our fortifications, untill they are finished ; for untill a City or an Army be intrenched, out of danger of the Enemy, no man ought to think himself too good, to give his helping hand, although after the danger is over, such worke is only propper for Pioneers, or such as you call Cooleys." Here, then, is the first mention of the Indian Pioneer, a common labourer, unfitted for war.

For the protection of the early factories, it was necessary to enrol British and Indian guards, and these, though ill-disciplined and badly armed, may be considered as the origin of the Army in India. In 1665, the island of Bombay was handed over to the East India Company by King Charles II,[3] who had secured it in 1662 on his marriage to Catherine of

[1] *Public Despatches from England*, Vol. I, Dec. 12th, 1677.
[2] *General Letter*, Court to Fort St. George, Jan. 24th, 1685.
[3] The other early factories in India were founded on the following dates : Masulipatam, 1611 ; Surat, 1612 ; Madras, 1640 ; Hugli, 1651. Calcutta was not founded until 1690.

Braganza. With it went volunteers from among the King's troops who were garrisoning the island. The Company was thus enabled to recruit in Bombay a small but organized military body, and by 1708 the Madras and Bengal Presidencies had followed suit and possessed units of European soldiers and others of half-castes or natives under their own officers. The war with France brought larger European forces to India than had ever existed there; but as neither side could obtain reinforcements from home, each was obliged to increase its native contingents to carry on the struggle. In 1757, shortly before the Battle of Plassey, Clive began to organize his native troops into regular battalions with a nucleus of British officers and non-commissioned officers; and as, by that time, the Company's soldiers had become more accustomed to take the initiative in the field, an increasing need was felt for engineer soldiers on whom some reliance could be placed. Accordingly, it became the custom to form temporary companies of European or Indian Pioneers for particular operations and to break them up when they were no longer required. History does not relate how the men were selected; but presumably they were expert diggers and hewers, who, after some experience in the field, could act as instructors to other volunteers.

Although each Presidency had a cadre of Engineer officers, employed chiefly in the construction or demolition of fortresses, there were no regular engineer units as we know them today. The gap was filled by the temporary Pioneer companies. For instance, in January, 1759, during the siege of Madras by the French under Count Lally, Captain John Call, M.E.,[1] the Chief Engineer on the British side, finding that the infantry could not cope with the damage to the masonry bastions, recommended the formation of a Pioneer company, composed of volunteers from British units, to carry out the necessary repairs. This European company was commanded by Lieutenant Meyer, assisted by Ensign West, and included 6 sergeants, 6 corporals and 88 privates. In addition, two native Pioneer companies were formed on the same plan.[2] Before the end of the siege, the European unit had proved its worth. "Nor must I forget to observe," writes Call,[3] "that a few raw men, taken from the Pioneer Company, greatly outdid the boasted miners of the French, who were to blow whole bastions into the air; for, after the breaching battery was erected, those men, without having seen anything of the kind before, and without any previous preparations of stanchions or tools, carried a gallery 95 feet in length under the enemy's battery, where two chambers were made and loaded with 250 lbs. of powder each. This work was executed within a few feet of the enemy. They saw and dreaded, but could not interrupt it, though we lost many men." After the siege, the survivors of the company were set to destroy the enemy's works and completed the task

[1]M.E. = Madras Engineers. B.E. = Bengal Engineers. Bo.E. = Bombay Engineers. M.I. = Madras Native Infantry. B.I. = Bengal Native Infantry. Bo.I. = Bombay Native Infantry. Similarly for Native Cavalry (Cav.) and Artillery (Art.).

[2]*The Military History of the Madras Engineers and Pioneers*, by Major H. M. Vibart, Royal (late Madras) Engineers (1881), Vol. I, p. 33.

[3]*Ibid.*, p. 40.

within a fortnight. Their work done, they returned to their regiments, well satisfied, no doubt, with the 8 annas a day extra pay which they drew while acting as Pioneers.

At the end of 1760, when Lally was besieged in Pondicherry by a force under Lieut.-Colonel Eyre Coote, a Pioneer Company of 50 Europeans and 100 lascars helped to dig the trenches and raise a siege battery; and in 1761, a party of 36 European Pioneers and 40 lascars under Ensign Ware accompanied an expedition against the French at Mahé, on the western coast.[1] In the same year, Colonel John Caillaud, laying siege to Vellore, was assisted by a Pioneer Company of 60 Europeans under Captain Abraham Bonjour. These men were allowed double pay during the operations, and it was agreed that this should be the standard rate in future. After taking part in a campaign against the Spaniards in the Philippines, a company of European Pioneers helped in the reduction of Madura in 1764 by enclosing that fortress with a ring of redoubts and a deep ditch. It is probable that, in all these operations, the European Pioneers were reinforced by bodies of Native Pioneers or lascars.

The next appearance of temporary Pioneers was during the siege of Tanjore in 1771 by a force under Colonel Joseph Smith. Engineering was in a bad way, for the cadre of Madras Engineers, headed by Lieut.-Colonel Patrick Ross, had suffered heavily. On October 20th, Smith wrote: "Colonel Ross is again abroad.[2] Montresor is much indisposed from a musket ball that went through his hat and grazed his head. Captain Campbell is wounded through both thighs. Lieutenant Geils, a very active young gentleman, is shot in the head, and Lieutenant Bonneveaux in the arm. In short, scarce one in that corps has escaped, and only Mr. Maule remains."[3] On the 27th, after Tanjore had capitulated, Smith reported as follows:—"I was under the necessity of forming a Pioneer Company of Europeans from the different corps, which was commanded by Captain Wolf during the siege. A body of Miners was also formed under Lieutenant Barrow. Both these small corps were indefatigable in their duty and showed the utmost spirit and activity on every occasion."

Tanjore was besieged again by Colonel Smith in 1773, and on that occasion Patrick Ross had the services of a European Pioneer Company under Lieutenant Fletcher, assisted by a detachment of Miners. Five years later, some European Pioneers and Miners took part in the siege and capture of Pondicherry by Major-General Hector Munro and afterwards accompanied an expedition against Mahé.[4] The fortifications of both these French settlements were demolished. At Mahé, the first explosion took place on the birthday of H.M. King George III, and by September, 1778, the defences were in ruins. These few examples of the work of the European Pioneers are sufficient to show that such units, though ill-trained

[1]See the *Sketch Map of the Carnatic, Mysore, Malabar and Travancore in* 1795, included at the end of this chapter.

[2]Col. Ross, the Chief Engineer, had been wounded on Oct. 7th.

[3]Lieut.-Col. George Maule, M.E., was killed in Aug., 1793, when Chief Engineer at the siege of Pondicherry.

[4]The Pioneer officers at Mahé were Lieuts. Abbot and Johnson and Ensigns Baillie, Bannerman and Mullick, M.I.

and poorly equipped, were found to be indispensable in fighting the French and their Indian allies.

Haidar Ali, the ruler of Mysore, was furious at the capture of Mahé, for he was accustomed to receive stores and French recruits for his army through that place. Indeed, his onslaught on the Carnatic in 1780, which started the Mysore Wars that were continued after his death[1] by his degenerate son, Tipu Sultan, may be attributed partly to this fact. His attitude towards his son is shown by the following strange compact, extracted from Tipu in 1770 and discovered in 1799 among the archives at Seringapatam :—[2] " I, Tippoo, will not do any one thing without the pleasure of your blessed Majesty, Lord of Benefits : if I do, let me be punished in whatever manner may seem fitting to your auspicious mind. If, in the affairs of the Sircar (Government), I should commit theft, or be guilty of fraud, great or small, let me, as the due punishment thereof, be strangled. If I be guilty of prevarication, or misrepresentation, or deceit, the due punishment thereof is the same strangulation. Without the orders of the Presence, I will not receive from anyone Nuzzers (presents), etc., neither will I take things from anyone forcibly : if I do, let my nose be cut off and let me be driven from the city. If, excepting on the affairs of the Sircar, I should intrigue with any person, or be guilty of deceit, let me, in punishment thereof, be stretched on a cross."

A brave and capable soldier and administrator, though savage and relentless, Haidar Ali succeeded in welding his forces into a formidable army that obliged the Company to take stock of their resources. Defence behind walls gave place to operations in the field, and forces were required which included all arms. The day of the amateur engineer drew to a close, and with it the era of the temporary Pioneer. In the temporary units, discipline was lax and *esprit de corps* non-existent. The officers were often strangers to their men. Such a system was doomed to extinction; and thus, to counter the threat from Mysore, the trained engineer soldier made his appearance in the Indian Army, being known first as the " Pioneer " and later as the " Sapper and Miner."

In June, 1780, Haidar Ali marched from Seringapatam into the Carnatic plain at the head of 80,000 men, advancing on Madras from the south-west while Tipu led a division into the country further north. A brief campaign, which may be called the First Mysore War,[3] ended in September with the annihilation of a force under Colonel Baillie near Pollilur and the discredit of Major-General Hector Munro, the Commander-in-Chief in Madras ; but the disaster to Baillie infused new vigour into the process of reformation already started in the Company's armies, and inspired Lieutenant Joseph Moorhouse[4] of the Madras Artillery, then Commissary of Stores and in charge of the labourers in Fort St. George, to propound a

[1]Haidar Ali died in 1782.

[2]*Historical Sketches of the South of India*, by Col. Mark Wilks, Vol. II, Appendix I.

[3]Some historians allude to the subsequent campaign in 1781–4 as the First Mysore War.

[4]Joseph Moorhouse was commissioned as an Ensign in 1768 and was promoted Lieut. in 1772, Capt. in 1780 and Major in 1786. On March 7th, 1791, shortly after his promotion to Lieut.-Col., he was killed during the siege of Bangalore. A monument was erected to him in St. Mary's Church in Fort St. George.

scheme for raising two regular companies of Native Pioneers in replacement of his "Mamooty Men."[1] The proposal was approved by the Madras Government in the following order, dated September 30th, 1780:—"The Honourable the President and Select Committee are pleased to direct that two companies of Pioneers be raised as soon as possible by the Commissary of Stores, each company consisting of 2 Sergeants, 3 Corporals, 5 Havildars,[2] 5 Naiks[3] and 100 Black Pioneers. The Havildars to be paid 3½ Pagodas per month,[4] the Naiks 2½ pagodas, and the private Pioneers to have 2 Pagodas per month, paid by rolls signed by the Commissary of Stores to the Army. The Pioneers to be clothed in blue jackets, and to be armed, 50 of each company with light pistols and 50 with pikes 6 feet long. When these Pioneers are raised, they are to be employed with the Army to clear and mend roads, etc., instead of mamooty men, for whom no charge is then to be made. The stoppages from the above corps to be the same as those made from the Sepoy Corps for half-mounting,[5] and they are to be supplied with the same articles, the jackets only to be blue instead of white."

The formation of these two Pioneer companies was a notable achievement,[6] but it was soon found that there were serious anomalies in administration. For instance, while the Pioneers were under the orders of the Commander-in-Chief and were officered in peace-time from the Artillery or Infantry, they were often commanded, in time of war, by Engineer officers who had had no part in training them and were under the orders of the Governor. Naturally, this was far from pleasing to the Pioneer officers, or to the Engineers who superseded them at short notice. The Engineers, indeed, were loud in their complaints; but nearly half a century elapsed before their sentiments were ably expressed by Lieutenant Edward Lake of the Madras Corps. "During the whole of the wars that have hitherto been carried on in India," writes Lake in 1825,[7] "the Company's Engineer Officers have never had a man employed under them who understood beforehand any one of the duties which he was required to execute. Now, if we were told that the Artillery of any Power consisted of a body of officers, with an establishment of guns and stores, and sufficiently instructed in the theory of their duties, but who, instead of having a permanent Corps of skilful Gunners under their orders, were only supplied with men to fight their guns on the day of battle; and that they were under the necessity of teaching these men how to load and fire, and to perform all the other necessary manœuvres of Artillery, in the presence of the enemy; every military man would naturally laugh at such an arrangement as the height of

[1]*Madras Consultations*, Sept. 28th, 1780. *Momaty* or *Mamuti*, a digging implement like a short hoe.

[2]*Havildar*, an Indian sergeant.

[3]*Naik*, an Indian corporal.

[4]About sixpence a day. 1 *pagoda* = 45 *fanams* = 3,600 *cash* = 3½ *rupees*.

[5]*Half-mounting*. The articles of clothing furnished annually by the Commandant himself.

[6]A lead had been given to the Madras Government by Bombay, where a company of "Pioneer Lascars" had been raised by Major Nilson, the Chief Engineer, in Dec., 1777. (See Chapter II.)

[7]*Journals of the Sieges of the Madras Army*, by Lieut. Edward Lake, M.E., pp. 236, 237.

absurdity, and one that must lead to the certain loss of every action in which the fire of Artillery was of the least importance. Yet, absurd as it may appear, such is a correct picture of what has hitherto been the actual state of the Engineer Department of the Company's Armies. The only men generally available for the duties of that Department have been the Pioneers, and as these men have never been employed in military works of this description, excepting upon actual service, it has been the hard fate of the Engineer officers to be obliged to teach them everything that was to be done, either when exposed to fire, or at least when in the presence of the enemy, and thus to waste those precious moments, when skill, energy and activity were most wanted, in the irksome and laborious drudgery of superintending a multitude of little details, which in other services would be the duty of a private, or, at the utmost, a corporal of Sappers. It is a fact that, in our sieges, the Officer of Engineers in person has often had to teach a Pioneer how to make a gabion or fascine, and to stand over him in the execution of the work. The confusion, the difficulties, the loss of time, and the consequent loss of lives which have attended, and which must necessarily attend, such an imperfect mode of proceeding, may easily be conceived. Even in the first and simplest operations of an irregular siege, these difficulties have always been sufficient to exhaust the bodies, if they could not subdue the spirit, of the Engineer Officers. What prospect of success, therefore, could an Engineer have had in the execution of a sap under close musketry fire without Sappers, and the execution of mines without Miners ? "

" It may be said," continues Lake, " that the Pioneers, after having been employed in several successive sieges, must necessarily have acquired some portion of that skill in which they were at first deficient. In reply I need scarcely suggest that the knowledge thus acquired by some individuals out of a large body, without any systematic instruction beforehand, must necessarily be of a most imperfect nature ; and if there be no regular practice afterwards to perpetuate it, it must of course evaporate and become lost to the Service for ever. And, after all, what did the Pioneers actually do, or what did they learn, in those sieges ? Were they in the habit of crowning the counterscarp by sap ? No ! Did they ever work across a dry ditch, or fill up a wet one, under fire ? Never ! Did they ever breach an enemy's scarp revetment by mining ? Never ! And yet these are the duties of Engineer Soldiers. Poor, indeed, would the Sapper and Miner be considered in Europe whose skill, like that of our most experienced Native Pioneers, extended no further than the making of a fascine and a gabion, and having some notion of the nature of a battery. By these observations, I am far from wishing to depreciate that respectable body of men. It has been their misfortune, not their fault, that they have been constantly called upon to perform duties in the field of a most difficult nature for which they were not qualified, like other soldiers, by previous exercise and instruction. So far from blaming them, every Engineer, who has witnessed their exertions, must admit that they deserve great credit for having shown so much zeal under such very discouraging circumstances.

PRIVATE, MADRAS PIONEERS, 1780.
(Coat, blue with black facings; shirt and drawers, white; *pagri*, black.)

But the opinions of those officers of the Army who maintain that the present Pioneers have always been a perfect model of a Military Working Corps, and equal to all the wants of the Service, cannot be too highly reprobated."

From the foregoing remarks, it is evident that when Lieut.-General Sir Eyre Coote, the Commander-in-Chief in India, arrived in Madras in November, 1780, to direct the operations of the Second Mysore War against Haidar Ali, the newly formed Pioneer companies could have differed very little, except in outward appearance, from the " Mamooty Men " of the First Mysore War. Nevertheless, they marched with Eyre Coote and came through the campaign in a creditable manner, being present at the relief of Wandiwash and the battles of Porto Novo, Pollilur, Sholinghur and Virakandalur. One company, under Lieutenant John Innes, M.I., took part in the relief of Vellore and the siege of Chittur. The other, or a portion of it, under Lieutenant N. S. W. Abbott, M.I., served in November, 1781, with Colonel John Braithwaite's force at the siege of Negapatam, a Dutch settlement in Tanjore.[1] War had been declared against Holland, and expeditions were sent against many Dutch settlements including Trincomalee in Ceylon.[2] As regards the operations against Mysore, the campaign of 1781 closed with Eyre Coote victorious over Haidar Ali, who began to evacuate the Carnatic. The defeat of the Mysore Army at Sholinghur on September 21st, 1781, is commemorated as one of the battle honours of the Q.V.O. Madras Sappers and Miners.[3]

The remainder of the Second Mysore War calls for little remark. It was an era of small manœuvre and counter-manœuvre. Some Madras Pioneers were present at an engagement at Arni in June, 1782. A campaign on the west coast by Major-General Mathews began well but ended in a surrender to Tipu at Bednore in May, 1783.[4] Three companies of Madras Pioneers, under Ensign James Cunningham, M.I., were on active service in various parts, and a detachment accompanied a force under Colonel Ross Lang to the southern districts of Dindigul and Coimbatore. During April and May, 1783, Lang reduced the forts of Karur, Aravakurichi and Dindigul.[5] Later, under Colonel William Fullarton, H.M. 98th Regiment, the operations became more extended. On August 12th, 147 Pioneers were engaged in the capture of the fort at Panjalamkurichi in the Tinnevelly District in the extreme south, where they removed a stout hedge in front of a breach and thus cleared a way for the stormers. Fullarton next proceeded to attack the mountain stronghold of the Poligar[6] of Sivagiri and took it on September 2nd after the Pioneers had cut a road for a distance

[1]Three months later, Col. Braithwaite met with disaster. He was overwhelmed by Tipu Sultan, and his entire force killed or captured. There is no record that any Pioneers were included in this force.

[2]Early expeditions overseas are dealt with in Chapter V.

[3]The honours " Sholinghur " and " Carnatic " were awarded to the Corps under G.O. 250, dated April 26th, 1889.

[4]A detachment of Bombay Pioneers, under Capt. J. C. Sartorius, Bo. E., assisted Gen. Mathews in the siege and capture of Mangalore in Feb., 1782. (See Chapter II.)

[5]*Historical Record of the Q.V.O. Madras Sappers and Miners*, Vol. I, p. 6.

[6]*Poligar*. A local chieftain of S. India.

of 3 miles through dense forest.[1] During October, 1783, the forts of Kamalum, Chaklagiri and Anaimalai were reduced; and in the following month, Palghat fell and Fullarton occupied Coimbatore. The Pioneers excelled themselves on the march from Anaimalai to Palghat, filling up ravines for the passage of guns, felling and removing large trees and making a passable track, though fever sapped their strength and rain fell unceasingly for a fortnight. Meanwhile, Major-General Stuart was being assisted by 284 Pioneers under Lieutenant Mitchell, M.I., in a siege of the French settlement at Cuddalore; but this operation was abandoned when news arrived of the conclusion of peace between England and France. Mangalore fell to Tipu after a gallant defence by Colonel Campbell, and the Second Mysore War ended with the signature of a treaty on March 11th, 1784. Unsatisfactory and inconclusive, the situation was bound to result in a renewal of hostilities; and within the next few years, the Company was engaged once more in a struggle against Tipu Sultan and the warriors of Mysore.

Although the engineering operations of the Second Mysore War were of no great importance, they emphasized the value of Pioneers in offensive warfare and drew from Colonel Fullarton a recommendation that the establishment should be increased "not only for expertness and despatch in the preparation of a siege but to facilitate the rapid movement of your armies." So convinced was Fullarton that an adequate contingent of Pioneers was necessary in the field that on February 4th, 1784, anticipating that hostilities would continue for some time, he had ordered Captain John Byres, M.E., to raise a body of 200 to 300 men in addition to the units already serving under Cunningham, and Byres had succeeded in recruiting 160 men. The termination of the war, however, denied these recruits the chance of proving their worth. Nevertheless, Fullarton's initiative, and the subsequent efforts of other officers, had their effect during the next twenty years. The complacent fortress engineer was transformed gradually into the daring field engineer, and with that change, the embryo Pioneer developed into a soldier, equal to most of the engineering demands of primitive warfare.

An amusing picture of camp life during the early Mysore Wars is given by Captain Innes Munro. "The preparations for war," he writes,[2] "carry nothing hostile in their appearance, ease and comfort being far more studied upon these occasions than despatch. It would be absurd for a captain to think of taking the field without being attended by the following enormous retinue, viz., a dubash,[3] cook and boy; and as, in these times, bullocks are not to be had, he must assemble fifteen or twenty coolies to carry his baggage, whom with an horse-keeper and grass-cutter, and sometimes a dulcinea and her servants, complete his train, having

[1] *The Military History of the Madras Engineers and Pioneers*, by Major H. M. Vibart, R.(M.) E., Vol. I, p. 201.

[2] *A Narrative of the Military Operations on the Coromandel Coast*, by Capt. Innes Munro, H.M. 73rd Regiment (1789), p. 186, *et seq.*

[3] *Dubash* or *Dobashi*. Man of two languages, i.e., an interpreter, but generally a head servant or butler.

occasionally the assistance of a barber, washerman and ironer, in common with the other officers of his regiment. It might be thought improper on such occasions as that of taking the field, to allow a captain a palanquin, although I have known many of them permitted to enjoy this luxury at very important seasons, which of course must add nine bearers to his suite. His tent is furnished with a good large bed, mattress, pillows, etc., a few camp stools and chairs, a folding table, a pair of shades for his candles, and six or seven trunks with table equipage; his stock of linens (at least twenty-four suits); some dozens of wine, brandy and gin; tea, sugar and biscuit; an hamper of live poultry and his milch-goat. A private's tent holding the overplus of his baggage is also requisite. When an officer has company to dine with him in camp, he never provides plates, knives and forks, glasses or chairs for them; it being the invariable custom for each guest to send his servant thither with these articles, who lays them down upon the table wherever he sees a vacant place. . . . In place of messing together, as in Europe, each officer keeps a cook; and in this manner entertains half a dozen friends in his turn."

So much for the officers. Now for the rank and file and camp followers. "In addition to the superabundant multitude of attendants," continues Munro, "every sepoy in the Army carries with him to camp his whole family, be they ever so numerous. The wife shares the hardships of war with her husband in the most cheerful manner, and follows him wherever he goes. Besides, a sepoy's station in life is reckoned so far respectable and elevated above the common rank, that he is looked up to for support and protection by all his needy relatives. There is not so much excuse for suffering all the coolies and other followers to be attended by their wives and children, which is also the case. . . . The sepoys are surprisingly active upon their posts, and pay the most implicit attention to orders, which are given in English but afterwards explained to them in their own language. . . . Should it happen to rain during the night, every servant thinks himself fully entitled to take shelter in his master's tent. You may imagine how much their disgusting habits must blast all the enjoyment of life, the captain being obliged to repose in a closed tent, surrounded by twenty or thirty of these blacks, lying compactly upon the floor. Some gentlemen get so enraged upon these occasions as to disperse them with a smack of the whip. . . . Orders being issued for the army to march, the officers' coolies are sure to come the night before to solicit sometimes a whole month's wages in advance, and the officer must of course yield. The dubash, being always the domestic paymaster, deducts his own fees and immediately concerts another plan with the coolies. All then retire until the general beat in the morning, when, breakfast over, the baggage is mounted upon the coolies' heads. The officers' foot-boys sling their brandy bottle, a tumbler and an earthen pot of cool water, carrying also a camp-stool or chair lest master should soil his small clothes by sitting upon the ground. All the drums of the army strike up the march and the whole line moves off. While the country continues open, the army is not much interrupted in its march; but if it should be obliged to pass through a narrow defile, a scene of general confusion commences, and the mob, bursting through the line, become at once a solid wedge. Here the cattle are lamed, the carriages broken down, and the soldiers and coolies almost squeezed to death. The enemy appears, and the coolies throw down their loads, and they and their families betake themselves to the hills and woods."

In this curious blend of confusion, hardship, indolence and chicanery, luxury on the one side and poverty on the other, the Pioneer was born in the Indian Army. Is it surprising that his development was slow and uncertain? The wonder is that he ever became a disciplined and trained soldier; and when trained, that he could cope, even partially, with the appalling conditions of service in the field.

The Madras Army was so exhausted by the long campaign against Tipu that a period of recuperation was essential before the struggle could be resumed. Not an Engineer took the field between 1784 and 1790, although some Pioneers served in the Guntur District in September, 1788, and a detachment of 80 men joined a force operating in the Sivaganga District of Madura and was present at the capture of Kollargudi, Ranamangulam and Kaliakoil in May and June, 1789. At the end of 1789, Tipu invaded Travancore and thus forced the Company to embark on the Third Mysore War. The operations started in May, 1790, with a campaign by Major-General Medows in the Coimbatore and Dindigul Districts; but the results were so poor that Lord Cornwallis, the Governor-General, decided to assume command in person, and arriving in Madras towards the end of the year, advanced on Bangalore in February, 1791, at the head of a large army. He counted on assistance from a Bombay army under Major-General Sir Robert Abercromby,[1] and from the forces of Hyderabad and certain Maratha states. Owing, perhaps, to the representations of Colonel Fullarton, Cornwallis had a respectable, though still inadequate, contingent of Pioneers with his army. On February 11th, 1790, before Medows took the field, a capable youngster in the person of Lieutenant W. Dowse, M.I.,[2] had been posted to the command of the Madras Pioneers on the Coromandel Coast, and on June 7th, the establishment of that Corps had been increased to 5 companies, each consisting of 1 sergeant, 4 havildars, 4 naiks and 90 privates, the whole to be under a Lieutenant assisted by an Ensign.[3] At the same time, a scale of equipment was laid down.[4] In September, 1790, after the campaign under Medows had been in progress for several months, Dowse was superseded by Lieutenant

[1]Younger brother of Lieut.-Gen. Sir Ralph Abercromby, who was killed in the siege of Alexandria in 1801. (See *The Royal Engineers in Egypt and the Sudan*, by the present author, p. 12.)

[2]William Dowse was commissioned as an Ensign in 1782. He was promoted Lieut. in 1789, Capt. in 1798, Major in 1804, Lt.-Col. in 1808, and Col. in 1814. He died at Bangalore in 1814.

[3]The name of the officer appointed as Ensign is not recorded, but he was probably Ensign J. H. Stokoe, B.E.

[4]For each company, 60 hatchets, 40 billhooks, 48 pickaxes, 6 picks, 10 felling axes and 28 *mamutis*—an equipment designed more for clearing undergrowth than digging trenches.

W. C. Lennon, M.E.,[1] because of Lennon's "activity and experience in his profession." Thus Dowse, the peace-time Infantry commander, gave place to a war-time Engineer commander; but he remained as second-in-command and led contingents of Pioneers with success in many battles and sieges in Southern India.

The beginning of March, 1791, found Cornwallis facing Bangalore, which he had to capture or mask before he could advance against Seringapatam. The lay-out of the place was typical of the Indian cities of those days—a town or *pettah*, encircled by a wall and ditch, and adjoining it, a huge masonry fortress into which the inhabitants could retire for protection. No attempt will be made to describe the general military operations of the Third Mysore War nor any other campaign,[2] for this narrative is concerned only with the exploits of Pioneers or Sappers and Miners. Accordingly, it must suffice to record that Cornwallis gained possession of the Bangalore *pettah* on March 7th, and that, on the 21st, his storm troops crossed the wide ditch of the fortress with scaling ladders, clambered through a breach and occupied the place after a hand-to-hand fight in which the enemy lost 1,000 killed. Two detachments of Madras Pioneers, under Lennon and Dowse, took part in the siege and assault, losing 24 killed, 25 wounded and 3 missing, a higher casualty list than that of any unit except H.M.'s 36th Regiment. It is interesting to note that a temporary company of European Pioneers was formed for the siege of Bangalore and served in subsequent operations. It consisted of detachments of 1 sergeant, 1 corporal and 10 privates from each regiment or corps, the whole being under Ensign Macpherson of H.M.'s 52nd Regiment.

After taking Bangalore, Cornwallis marched on Seringapatam, and having been reinforced by an army from Hyderabad, defeated Tipu at Arakeri on May 15th, 1791, in a battle in which some Madras Pioneers were engaged. Meanwhile, Abercromby, with 9 battalions of the Bombay Army, had been moving inland from Tellicherry and on May 15th lay only 40 miles west of Seringapatam; but when almost within sight of the capital, Cornwallis was brought to a halt by lack of transport and supplies and was obliged to retreat on Bangalore, while Abercromby retired to the western coast. Foiled in his main object, Cornwallis then proceeded to lay siege to several strongholds near Bangalore, and thus maintained the morale of his men and gave useful occupation to his Engineers and Pioneers. A detachment of the army took several small

[1]William Caulfield Lennon was commissioned as an Ensign in 1782, and became a Lieut. in 1786. He was promoted Capt. in 1793, Major in 1802 and Lt.-Col. in 1806. He retired in 1810 and died in 1835. Interesting correspondence, dated 1790, between Lennon and the Chief Engineer regarding the equipment, organization and duties of the Madras Pioneers in the Third Mysore War appears in the Mackenzie Collection of Manuscripts, Vol. LXIX, in the India Office.

[2]Such operations have been recorded in many histories. A framework of the operations in every war in which the Indian Army has been engaged from the foundation of the East India Company to the present day, with special reference to military engineers and engineering, is contained in *The Military Engineer in India*, Vol. I, by the present author, published by the Institution of Royal Engineers in 1933. That work gives, in concise form, many of the episodes in the history of the Pioneers and Sappers and Miners which are elaborated in this volume.

forts during July, and on September 17th, with the assistance of some Pioneers, captured Ramandroog.[1] North of Bangalore lay Nandidroog, 3 miles in circumference, perched on a precipitous, granite mountain 2,000 feet high, and with a single, strongly defended line of approach. This fortress, though deemed to be impregnable, was captured on October 18th with prodigious exertion after a number of guns had been hauled to adjacent heights by men and elephants. In an order issued on the following day, Cornwallis remarked :—" Although the services of the Pioneers are less brilliant than those of the troops, they are of peculiar value in all such operations, and His Lordship thinks himself called upon, in justice to Lieutenant Dowse and all the N.C.O.s and men of the Pioneer Corps,[2] as well as to Ensign Stokoe of the Engineers,[3] who assisted with so much ability in directing their labours, to declare that their behaviour on this occasion has deserved his highest commendation."

The next objective was Savandroog, west of Bangalore, whither Lieut.-Colonel Patrick Ross, M.E., the Chief Engineer, was sent with orders to direct the engineering work in person. Savandroog lay on a great mountain surrounded by malarial jungle. The main fortifications were in two parts, separated by a chasm, and below them was a continuous line of ramparts. Ross, and a party of Pioneers under Dowse, reconnoitred the place at the end of November, 1791, and, on December 10th, marched with an attacking force from Bangalore. The first obstacle was a belt of dense bamboo through which the Pioneers had to cut a road to the positions selected for the siege batteries. This was a work of almost incredible labour, and in many places the men were obliged to drag the guns over high rocks. On the 17th, the artillery opened fire. For a time it did little damage to the massive walls on the heights ; yet a practicable breach was made at last, and on December 21st, to the strains of " Britons, strike Home," the stormers poured through. Once again the services of the Pioneers were recognized by the Governor-General. " His Lordship desires it may be particularly signified to Lieutenants Macpherson and Dowse, who conducted the European and Native Pioneers that were employed in carrying the scaling ladders and breaking open the gates, that he considers their behaviour highly meritorious." The reduction of Savandroog was followed by the capture of Hutridroog (Ootradroog) on December 24th, when the Pioneer contingents under Macpherson and Dowse were employed on similar duties. There can be little doubt that the experience gained in these small sieges was invaluable in preparing the men for the major operations at Seringapatam.

On January 22nd, 1792, the Bombay Army of 9,000 men under Abercromby started again from the west coast towards Mysore.[4] Three days later, the Madras Army of 22,000 men under Cornwallis, joined at

[1]Also known as Ramanghur.

[2]A detachment of 100 men.

[3]Ensign Joseph H. Stokoe, was commissioned in the Bengal Infantry in 1783, but was soon transferred to the Bengal Engineers. He was promoted Lieut. in 1794 and died in the Straits of Malacca in 1801.

[4]A corps of Bombay Pioneers (probably 2 companies) under Lieut. W. Brooks, Bo.E., accompanied this force. (See Chapter II.)

Savandroog by 18,000 cavalry from Hyderabad, prepared to deliver the main thrust at the capital. Cornwallis arrived before Seringapatam on February 6th, and without waiting for Abercromby, attacked in three columns under cover of darkness. The Chief Engineer with the Madras Army was Lieut.-Colonel Patrick Ross, M.E., and with the Bombay Army, Major J. C. Sartorius, Bo.E.[1] To facilitate the control and execution of the engineering work, the Madras Pioneers were formed into three detachments, led respectively by Lieutenants Lennon and Dowse and Ensign Stokoe, and these were distributed among the columns. With the Right Column (Major-General Medows) was the detachment under Lennon, and with the Centre Column (Lord Cornwallis) that under Dowse. The detachment under Stokoe marched with the Left Column (Lieut.-Colonel Maxwell). Engineer officers, with crews of gun-lascars carrying scaling ladders, accompanied each body of Pioneers, and were instructed, after the manner of those days, that " the ladders were not to be left carelessly in the enemy's works."

Seringapatam stood on a large island in the Cauvery River. At the west or upstream end was a vast quadrangular fortress; and at the downstream end, a *pettah* or town, and a palace and garden known as the Lal Bagh. The intervening space was occupied by scattered buildings and a garden called the Daulat Bagh. Across the river to the north, a wide area was enclosed by a " Bound Hedge," a formidable obstacle of thorny shrubs; and the defences were further strengthened by a redoubt (the Idgah) within the western flank, another (the Karighat) on a hill outside the eastern flank, and several within the enclosure. The river was fordable in places, but had a rapid current and a rocky bottom.[2]

The attack launched by Cornwallis from the north did not develop according to plan. The Right Column assaulted the Idgah Redoubt, instead of masking it and pushing on, and losing touch with the Centre Column, wandered eastwards as far as the Karighat Hill, where it was out of the fight. The Centre Column succeeded in crossing the northern branch of the Cauvery and occupied the eastern portion of the island; but the delay caused by the mistake of the Right Column gave Tipu an opportunity to realize the situation, and he withdrew into the fortress, which he prepared to defend. The advantage of surprise being lost, Cornwallis decided to resort to a deliberate siege. A company of European Pioneers was formed from H.M.'s 76th Regiment and placed under the command of Macpherson; and on February 16th, with the arrival of the Bombay Army, a contingent of Bombay Pioneer Lascars became available also for general engineering duties.

It fell to Lieut.-Colonel Patrick Ross, M.E., as Chief Engineer, to propose the method of attack, and after some discussion, he recommended siege operations against the northern face of the fortress and the diversion of water from the northern branch of the river by means of a dam. The

[1]The cadre of Engineers comprised 12 officers from the Madras Corps, 6 from the Bengal Corps, and 6 from the Bombay Corps.

[2]See the plan entitled *Siege of Seringapatam in* 1799, included in this chapter. This shows also the defences in 1792.

European and Native Pioneers were placed under his orders as a distinct unit for the duration of the operations, and an Engineer Park was established near the Bound Hedge. The Pioneers then dug a parallel within breaching distance of the north face and another within 600 yards of it, while the troops already on the island improved their entrenchments opposite the east face. These works were completed on February 23rd, after a sortie by the enemy had been repulsed. Tipu, however, was already suing for peace, and on March 19th, 1792, signed a treaty under which he paid a heavy indemnity and ceded one-half of his kingdom to the Company and its allies. Thus ended the Third Mysore War, which shook but did not shatter the power of an unscrupulous ruler. Tipu had put into the field an army of 18,000 cavalry, 50,000 infantry, 100,000 irregulars and many guns. His losses had been heavy, but he was still formidable.

The Madras Pioneers played an inconspicuous though creditable part in the first siege of Seringapatam.[1] During the preliminary advance, they cut passages for the troops through the Bound Hedge; and later, when a portion of the Centre Column seemed to be isolated from the remainder on the island, Dowse tried, though unsuccessfully, to recross the river to report the situation to Cornwallis. Thousands of gabions, fascines and pickets were prepared and stored in the Engineer Park, and parallels were dug or repaired as occasion required. The Pioneers, in fact, did much towards ensuring success in a great undertaking.

In June, 1792, Dowse and his men took the field with a force assembled in Madura to punish the Poligar of Sivagiri, and returned to Trichinopoly in August after Sivagiri had been occupied and the country reduced to submission. Their work during this small expedition enhanced the reputation which they had earned in the Third Mysore War and induced Colonel John Braithwaite,[2] commanding the troops on the Coromandel Coast, to put forward proposals for an increase in their establishment. Towards the end of the year, Braithwaite recommended that there should be three bodies of Pioneers, one for each division of the Madras Army, and each consisting of two companies. Each company was to be commanded by a Lieutenant or Ensign and to comprise 1 sergeant, 1 jemadar, 6 havildars, 6 naiks, 122 privates, 2 bhistis and 12 artificers—a total of 150 men excluding the British officer. The existing establishment of 5 companies, with a total strength of 2 British officers, 5 sergeants and 490 Indian other ranks, would be increased to 6 companies, with a total strength of 6 British officers, 6 sergeants, 6 jemadars and 804 Indian other ranks, and the monthly cost of maintenance would be raised from 1,814 to 3,098 pagodas.[3] The financial aspect of these proposals frightened the Government, and after much discussion the scheme was shelved; but in June, 1793, four months after France had declared war, preparations were begun for the siege of Pondicherry, and Braithwaite returned to the charge, recommending that "that very useful Pioneer

[1]Their services during the campaign were recognized by the grant of the honour "Mysore" to the Madras Sappers and Miners under G.G.O. 378 dated April 26th, 1889.
[2]Col. Braithwaite had been released by Tipu on the conclusion of peace in 1784.
[3]Equivalent to Rs. 6,349 and Rs. 10,843 respectively.

Corps should be augmented by 150 men, i.e., brought up to a strength of 600."[1] This was approved on July 11th in the following terms :—" The Honourable the President in Council is pleased to direct that the Pioneers on this establishment be considered a separate Corps, the Officers to be supplied from the Infantry and to rise in the list of the Army in like manner. That it consist of 1 Lieutenant-Commandant, 3 Lieutenants, 1 Assistant Surgeon and 6 Companies, each to consist of 1 Sergeant, 1 Jemadar, 3 Havildars, 3 Naiks and 100 Privates. That 8 Pakhalis[2] be allowed to the Corps, 1 Conicopoly[3] and 1 Assistant Conicopoly. That the Lieutenant-Commandant be upon the same footing with regard to off-reckonings[4] as the Commandants of Corps of Native Cavalry."[5]

For the siege of Pondicherry by Colonel Braithwaite, the Madras Pioneers, who numbered 612 of all ranks, were reinforced by Lieutenants O. Grose and C. Armstrong, M.I. Dowse remained in command of the Corps. The Government Order of July 11th had stipulated that the Pioneers were to be officered from the Infantry, and it seems that the custom of detailing an Engineer to lead the Corps in the field had been abandoned because Infantry officers with sufficient knowledge and experience were available and Engineers were scarce. Nevertheless, it was still considered necessary to recruit temporary European Pioneers, and the Madras Pioneers were assisted at Pondicherry by two parties, each of 1 British officer and 34 other ranks, formed from the 1st European Battalion. Siege operations began on August 10th. The Chief Engineer, Lieut.-Colonel George Maule, M.E., was killed on the 15th; but his successor, Captain Elisha Trapaud, M.E., employed the Pioneers to such advantage in digging approaches and raising batteries that the garrison of Pondicherry surrendered on August 24th. Dowse then proceeded to destroy the defences, and by June, 1794, with the help of 3,000 coolies, he had filled in the ditch of the Fort and levelled the ramparts " so that a body of horse might charge into the place." Afterwards, he marched the Pioneers into the Baramahal District to demolish several hill-forts ceded by Tipu at the end of the Third Mysore War.

In July, 1795, England being at war with Holland, two companies of Madras Pioneers, under Dowse, sailed with an expedition against the Dutch settlements in Ceylon, where they were joined later by two more companies. Another company, under Lieutenant W. P. Heitland, M.I.,[6] accompanied an expedition against the Dutch at Manila in the Philippine Islands. These and other adventures overseas are described in Chapter IV: for the present it is sufficient to record that they brought Dowse a

[1] *Historical Record of the Q.V.O. Madras Sappers and Miners*, Vol. I, p. 10.

[2] *Pakhali*. The carrier of a *pakhal* or leather water-bag. A *bhisti*.

[3] *Conicopoly*. An Accountant, or Accounts Clerk.

[4] *Off-reckoning*. An allowance formerly made to British officers from the money appropriated for clothing for the men.

[5] Monthly rates of pay were authorized as follows (converted from pagodas, fanams and cash into rupees) : Sergeant, Rs. 35 ; Jemadar, Rs. 25½ ; Havildar, Rs. 9½ ; Naik, Rs. 8 ; Private, Rs. 7. These were liberal for those days.

[6] William P. Heitland was commissioned as an Ensign in 1782, and promoted Lieut. in 1790, Capt. in 1798 and Major in 1806. He retired in 1807 after seeing much service in the field in command of Pioneers.

Brevet-Captaincy in April, 1797, and fostered in his men a spirit of daring and enterprise which carried them successfully through the ordeal of the final war against Tipu Sultan.

The intrigues of the ruler of Mysore had been, for several years, a thorn in the flesh of the Madras Government. Tipu was known to have invited French assistance in a plan to attack the British possessions in India and to be well aware of the formidable preparations made by France in the Mediterranean. Frenchmen dominated the court at Hyderabad, and the Madras Army was scattered in the Carnatic, Ceylon and the Philippines. Tipu, having concluded an offensive and defensive alliance with the French, tried to lull the Company into a sense of security by declaring in April, 1798, that " his friendly heart was disposed to pay every regard to truth and justice and to strengthen the foundations of harmony and concord between the two nations."[1] This, however, did not deceive Lord Mornington,[2] the Governor-General, who issued orders on June 20th for the assembly of the Company's armies on both the Coromandel and Malabar coasts, not only to guard the Carnatic, but to checkmate any designs for the landing of a French force at Mangalore. Passing soon from the defensive to the offensive, Lord Mornington directed Lieut.-General George Harris, the Commander-in-Chief in Madras, to select a base and mobilize an army for an invasion of Mysore in co-operation with an army from Bombay and another from Hyderabad State, which had been relieved of French domination. Harris proceeded to carry out his orders, though seriously hampered by lack of transport and money. The Pioneers, under Dowse, were employed during October in repairing roads and constructing boats for the passage of the Palar River, and were joined on December 11th by Lieutenants H. M. Cormick and W. Davis, M.I. At the same time, the establishment was increased from 6 to 8 companies, each of 1 Sergeant, 1 Jemadar, 3 Havildars, 3 Naiks, 1 Pakhali and 100 Privates, with 1 Sergeant-Major attached. Early in 1799, in consequence of the war against Mysore, the establishment was increased again to 10 Companies, and the strength of the Corps was authorized as 2 Captains, 1 Captain-Lieutenant, 1 Lieutenant, 1 Assistant Surgeon, 1 Sergeant-Major, 10 Sergeants, 11 Jemadars, 30 Havildars, 30 Naiks, 1,000 Privates and 10 Pakhalis. All being ready, Harris started from Vellore at the beginning of February, 1799, at the head of a " Grand Army " of 15,000 men, and on the 20th, joined hands with the Hyderabad Army, 16,000 strong. The Bombay Army, of 6,000 men, under Lieut.-General James Stuart, marched from Cannanore on February 21st, and by March 2nd had reached Periapatam, 50 miles west of Seringapatam.

The advance of the Grand and Hyderabad armies into Mysore resembled the migration of the Israelites from Egypt. Slowly and ponderously, an amazing multitude of men and animals laboured up hill and down dale and across the barren plains in rolling clouds of dust and unimaginable

[1] *A View of the Origin and Conduct of the War with Tippoo Sultaun* (1800), by Lieut.-Col. Alexander Beatson, p. 10.

[2] Richard Colley Wellesley, later Marquis Wellesley, was the elder brother of Col. Arthur Wellesley, who became the Duke of Wellington.

din and confusion. In a phalanx, two miles wide and seven miles long, 31,000 soldiers toiled onwards with 116,000 bullocks, 5,000 elephants and camels and 150,000 followers. On the front and flanks rode the cavalry: in the centre were the guns, transport and non-combatants, surrounded by battalions of sweating and choking infantry. "In India," writes Ensign Rowley on March 23rd,[1] "every supply must be conveyed by the invading Army. The Bazar, or market, of General Harris' Army equals in extent, and in variety of articles exposed for sale, that of a populous city. The followers of the Army are so numerous that on a moderate calculation they may be considered to exceed the number of fighting men in the proportion of five to one. Herds of cattle and flocks of sheep conceal the soil. The route of the troops is marked by the gleaming of their arms, and that of the battery train by a long, slow-moving, inky line. On a nearer view, the scene is sometimes laughable. Here, a laden, ill-bred bullock, taking fright, scampers off, plunging and kicking: twenty others follow his example, and broken pots and pans strew the plain. The drivers abuse their cattle and each other. Sometimes an alarm of the Looties'[2] approach occasions a worse disorder. Men, women and children scamper in all directions, and leave their unconcerned charge to its fate." The duties of the small detachments of Pioneers who accompanied this rabble were varied and onerous. On them devolved the chief responsibility for clearing a passage for the heavy artillery through jungle and across broken and barren country. They earned their pay by the sweat of their brows.

On March 15th, 1799, the Grand Army was in the neighbourhood of Bangalore, and six days later, at Karkanalli. Meanwhile, on March 6th, Tipu had struck at the weaker Bombay Army at Sidasir, near Periapatam, and had been defeated by General Stuart. Four companies of Bombay Pioneers, under Captain-Lieutenant Bryce Moncrieff, Bo.E., took part in this battle.[3] Foiled in his attempt, Tipu hastened back to check the Grand Army under General Harris, and encountered it at Malavalli on March 27th. Again, he attacked with great fury, but was forced to retire after suffering heavy casualties. The Madras Pioneers, under Dowse, were present at this battle and lost a few men; but according to Ensign Rowley, the affair was little more than a confused skirmish. There is no record that any engineering work was carried out. Although an easy route to Seringapatam was now available along the northern bank of the Cauvery, Harris decided to cross the river at Sosili and follow the southern bank, where he could join hands with Stuart, and this sound strategy brought him, on April 5th, to a strong position, about two miles west of the capital. The Hyderabad troops occupied a chain of advanced posts in front. Beyond these, and skirting the left flank, lay a winding canal, 15 yards broad.[4] Clumps of trees within the position afforded an abundant supply of timber for siege works. Half

[1] *Journal of the Second Siege of Seringapatam* by Ensign G. Rowley M.E., appearing in *Professional Papers of the Madras Engineers*, Vol. IV, 1856, p. 121.

[2] Mysore irregular cavalry.

[3] The strength of the Bombay Pioneers was 416 of all ranks. Bryce Moncrieff was commissioned as an Ensign in 1791, resigned in 1793, rejoined in 1794, was promoted Captain-Lieutenant in 1796, and died in Bombay in 1802. (See Chapter II.)

[4] See the plan entitled *Siege of Seringapatam in* 1799, included in this chapter.

a mile beyond the canal was a dry channel called the Little Cauvery; and a short distance beyond again, the southern branch of the Cauvery itself, overlooked by the massive ramparts and bastions of Seringapatam.

As the enemy held a large wood, known as the Sultanpettah Tope, situated beyond the canal on the right front of the Madras Army, the first operation was to dislodge them from that shelter and from the banks of the canal. This was accomplished on April 6th, and the Engineers and Pioneers then fortified the line of the canal and strengthened the posts established on either flank. On the right was the Sultanpettah Post; on the left, Shawe's Post. The canal line thus became the first parallel for the siege. The Chief Engineer, Colonel William Gent, M.E., moved his headquarters to a position on the bank of the canal close to the Sultanpettah Tope, and employed the European and Native Pioneers in felling timber and making fascines, gabions and ladders.

Next, in accordance with the usual custom, Gent was ordered to prepare plans of attack, and on April 13th, submitted alternative schemes. He proposed either to attack the north-west angle of the fortress by the joint operations of two forces, one on the north bank and the other on the south bank of the Cauvery; or, assuming that a part of the island had already been taken, to attack the south-west angle, below which lay the Periapatam Bridge, by which the stormers might cross the river. He favoured the latter scheme, and was supported in his opinion by Colonel John Sartorius, Chief Engineer of the Bombay Army, and by every other Engineer officer present. Nevertheless, on the recommendation of Major Alexander Beatson, M.I.,[1] the Surveyor-General with the Army, General Harris decided to attack the north-west angle, and arrangements were made accordingly.

The Bombay Army arrived on the south bank on April 14th, and as provisions were running low, Harris issued orders on the 17th that the attack should be launched without delay. Meanwhile, the Bombay Army had crossed to the north bank, taking up a position with its left on the ruined Idgah Redoubt. On the 17th, it occupied the riverside village of Agrar, near which Dowse and his Madras Pioneers dug a battery after nightfall to enfilade the western face of the fortress.[2] This battery was designed for six 12-pounders and two howitzers, and was located according to surveys made in 1792; but daylight revealed that these had been inaccurate, and in consequence the battery had to be rebuilt further eastwards. It is remarkable that this work on the north bank was carried out by the Madras Pioneers instead of by the Bombay Pioneers, who were with the Bombay Army on that bank. On the south bank, Harris cleared the enemy from the line of the Little Cauvery and established on it a post called Macdonald's Post, which he connected to Shawe's Post in rear by a communication trench. The enemy having retreated to an entrenched position near the Cauvery itself, the Engineers and Pioneers occupied the

[1]Some details of the remarkable career of Major (afterwards Maj.-Gen.) Alexander Beatson are given in *The Military Engineer in India*, by the present author, Vol. I, pp. 173–4.

[2]The position was known as Hart's Post.

bed of the Little Cauvery, where they established a depot of tools and siege materials.

The Engineers, under Colonel Gent, were organized in four "brigades," commanded respectively by Captains Colin Mackenzie and George Johnstone, and Capt.-Lieutenants James L. Caldwell and John Blair, M.E. Mackenzie's brigade was attached to the Bombay Army, and the others were detailed for duty in rotation with the Madras Army. A temporary company of one hundred European Pioneers was formed as usual by selecting men from all the British units, and was placed under the command of Lieutenant Farquhar of H.M.'s 76th Regiment. These preparations having been completed, operations to eject the enemy's forces from the south bank were begun on April 20th. Supported by the fire of two guns placed in front of the Sultanpettah Post on the right flank, a successful attack was launched against a powder-mill in advance of the left flank near the river, and this post was connected by a parallel with Macdonald's Post. The front line was then within 800 yards of the western face of Seringapatam.

During the night of April 20th–21st, the European and Madras Pioneers worked furiously on the construction, near the powder-mill, of a battery for four 18-pounders and two howitzers to enfilade the northern face and bombard the north-west bastion,[1] and finished their task in six hours. The battery came into action on the 22nd and silenced the opposing artillery. After dark, the Pioneers constructed a similar enfilading battery on the north bank, near Agrar, in replacement of the one incorrectly sited, and the combined fire of the two batteries rendered the north-west bastion almost untenable. The excavation of zigzag approach trenches from the parallel between the powder-mill and Macdonald's Post was taken in hand on the night of the 24th–25th. By the 26th, the trenches extended to within 400 yards of the north-west bastion, and another battery had been constructed and brought into action. Two days later, the first breaching battery for six guns was marked out on the river bank, which the approach trenches had almost reached; and on the 27th the troops stormed the river defences and drove the enemy across the Periapatam bridge to the island. During the next few days, the Engineers and Pioneers strengthened the enfilading batteries. In addition, they constructed a second breaching battery for five guns on a site close to the first battery. On the 29th, Lieutenant Farquhar of the European Pioneers, and Captain John Norris, M.E., crossed the greater part of the river in an attempt to ascertain whether it was fordable; but they were discovered by the enemy before they could reach the far bank. They were able to report, however, that the water was shallow and the rocks smooth, and that, as far as they had gone, a crossing was practicable. A few more guns were mounted, and all was ready for the final bombardment and storm of Seringapatam.

At sunrise on May 2nd, 1799, the two breaching batteries, mounting 11 guns, opened fire at a range of about 400 yards on the massive curtain near the point of the north-west bastion, while 24 smaller guns and

[1]This battery, strengthened by two more guns, was used later as a breaching battery.

howitzers engaged the enemy's artillery and swept the ramparts with shot and shell. In the midst of this inferno, the European and Madras Pioneers, under the direction of Captain G. Johnstone, M.E., and others of the 2nd Brigade of Engineers, began to prolong the zigzag approaches from the rear of the six-gun breaching battery and reached the river bank opposite the breach on May 3rd. Scaling ladders and fascines were then brought up and stored under cover. Before daybreak on the 4th, the troops intended for the assault were massed in the trenches—10 picked companies of British Infantry, 3 companies of Native Infantry, and 2 companies of Hyderabad Infantry; in all, about 2,500 European and 1,900 Native soldiers. They were divided into two columns, with instructions to capture the breach together and then turn right and left. Captain J. L. Caldwell, Lieutenant B. Sydenham and Ensign G. Rowley, M.E., of the 3rd Brigade of Engineers, were detailed for the assault, and detachments of European and Madras Pioneers were allotted to each column. The assaulting troops were commanded by Major-General David Baird[1] and were supported by several battalions under Colonel Arthur Wellesley.

Throughout the morning, the stormers waited impatiently in the trenches, while the guns roared and the breach across the river was shrouded in rolling clouds of dust. At last, at one o'clock, General Baird mounted the rear of the trench, and drawing his sword, shouted "Men, are you all ready?" "Yes," came the answer. "Then forward, my lads"; and on the word, the troops raced for the river under a storm of bullets and rockets. Slipping, falling, gasping, sweating and bleeding, they laboured through the rock-strewn bed, and scaling the debris of the breach, planted their colours on the crest within seven minutes of leaving their positions. Many were killed or wounded in the river; more, in the breach; but, undaunted, the remainder divided and fought their way along the ramparts. The column working along the northern face had a desperate struggle at a traverse which barred the way. Tipu headed his troops in person and twice repulsed the storming party with heavy loss. Both Farquhar of the European Pioneers, and Cormick of the Madras Pioneers, were killed; but Dowse survived, and with the infantry, helped to drive the Mysoreans towards the entrance to an inner line of fortification. There, jammed in a gateway, the enemy were shot down in hundreds, and among them their leader, Tipu. A similar massacre took place at the eastern gateway of the fortress, where the fugitives were caught between the burning gate and the British bayonets. Captured guns, turned on the enemy, added to the shambles. Within two hours, all resistance had ceased except at the Palace. Seringapatam was won.

The smoking ruins, soaked with the blood of ten thousand slain, presented a melancholy spectacle. Baird marched to the Palace and took possession of it without much difficulty. Enormous armaments were seized—more than 900 guns, 99,000 muskets, 500,000 cannon balls and

[1]In 1801, General Baird commanded the Indian contingent sent to Egypt to assist the British against the French. The contingent made a remarkable desert march from the Red Sea to the Nile. (See *The Royal Engineers in Egypt and the Sudan*, by the present author, pp. 16, 17.)

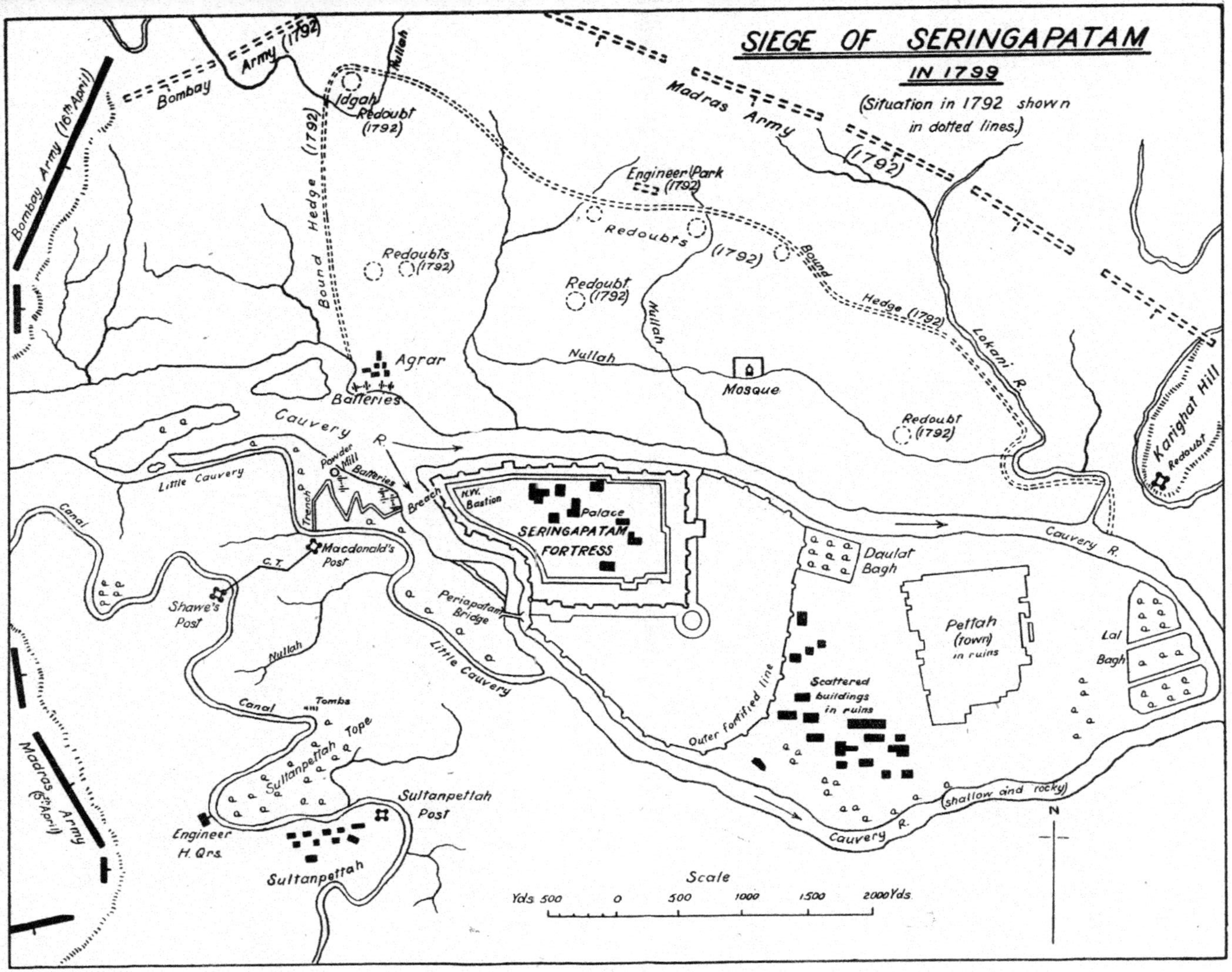

SIEGE OF SERINGAPATAM
IN 1799
(Situation in 1792 shown in dotted lines.)
Bombay Army (16th April)
Bombay Army (1792)
Idgah
Redoubt (1792)
Nullah
Bound Hedge (1792)
Redoubts (1792)
Agrar
Batteries
Madras Army (1792)
Engineer Park (1792)
Redoubts (1792)
Redoubt (1792)
Nullah
Mosque
Bound Hedge (1792)
Lokani R.
Redoubt (1792)
Karighat Hill
Redoubt
Cauvery R.
Little Cauvery
Powder Mill
Batteries
Trench
Breach
N.W. Bastion
Palace
SERINGAPATAM FORTRESS
Canal
Macdonald's Post
C.T.
Shawe's Post
Periapatam Bridge
Little Cauvery
Nullah
Canal
Tombs
Tope
Sultanpettah
Sultanpettah Post
Engineer H. Qrs.
Sultanpettah
Madras Army (5th April)
Daulat Bagh
Pettah (town) in ruins
Lal Bagh
Outer fortified line
Scattered buildings in ruins
shallow and rocky
Cauvery R.
N
Scale
Yds 500 0 500 1000 1500 2000 Yds

200 tons of gunpowder; vast treasure also—thousands of costly muslins, cambrics and shawls, and jewels and gold to the value of £1,500,000. The sight of Tipu's throne of solid gold, 8 feet long and 5 feet wide, raised high from the ground on the back of a golden tiger, and with silver steps leading up to it, filled the troops with amazement. While order was being restored, and the prisoners collected and removed, the Pioneers were employed in the mournful duty of burying the dead. They had been in the thick of the fight, and had been fortunate to escape with 8 men killed and 37 wounded. On May 5th, 1799, their services were recognized by General Harris in a complimentary order which ran as follows:—[1] "In thus publicly expressing his sense of their good conduct, the Commander-in-Chief feels himself called upon to notice, in a most particular manner, the exertions of Captain Dowse and his Corps of Pioneers, which, during the present service, has been equally marked by unremitting labour, and the ability with which that labour was applied." The Madras Pioneers fully deserved the battle honour "Seringapatam" which was awarded to their descendants, the Q.V.O. Madras Sappers and Miners.

The Fourth Mysore War was followed by much guerilla fighting against the scattered remnants of Tipu's army, and by minor campaigns against rulers of small states who had been his subjects and saw in his defeat and death an opportunity to gain their independence. Such operations had started before the fall of Seringapatam with the despatch of an expeditionary force, including a section of Madras Pioneers, to reduce the country north of Rayakottai in the Salem District. Another expedition, including 106 Pioneers under Lieutenant E. B. Bagshaw, M.I., marched from Trichinopoly towards Coimbatore in March, 1799, and took the forts of Karur on April 5th and Aravakurichi on the 10th. In June, 1799, a Maratha freebooter named Dhundia Nagh, who had gathered around him a gang of desperadoes after his release from the dungeons of the Mysore capital, began to raid isolated posts and molest convoys, and it became necessary to hunt him down. During the operations which ensued in the region of Bednore and Honalli, a party of Pioneers, working under the direction of Capt.-Lieutenant John Baird and Ensign William Garrard, M.E., had an interesting experience in ferrying a column of troops across the Tungabhadra. As the river was in full flood and no suitable boats were available, they constructed a barge of raw hides, stretched on a bamboo framework, and fitted it with a mast, sail and rudder. In this peculiar craft, Garrard transported piecemeal across the river not only the troops but their artillery, and so ensured the capture of Honalli. Dhundia then fled into Maratha territory, where, for a time, he ceased to give trouble.

In August, 1799, Lieutenant W. Davis, M.I., was on service with a detachment of Madras Pioneers at Manjarabad, 75 miles north-west of Seringapatam; but it was not until April, 1800, that the defiant attitude of the Raja of Bullum, whose capital was at Arakeri near Manjarabad, gave

[1] G.O.C.C., dated May 5th, 1799.

the Pioneers another opportunity. A detachment then accompanied a force sent from Seringapatam by Colonel Arthur Wellesley, and assisted in the capture of Arakeri on April 30th. This expedition was of no great importance, but it had a tragic result for the Pioneers, for it entailed the loss of their commander, Captain Onslow Grose, M.I., who was attached temporarily to the Corps. The enemy had barricaded the approaches through dense jungle, and while trying to place some ladders at one of these barriers, Grose was shot dead. He was a very popular officer, with a keen sense of humour and a ready wit. There is a tale that, being singularly averse to correspondence, he was warned on one occasion that all communications to Headquarters must be made officially and in writing. Soon afterwards, while he was entertaining a few friends to dinner, including some of the Headquarters' Staff, a donkey strayed in front of his tent and began to bray. Up rose Grose, and addressed the intruder with becoming gravity. "I presume, sir," said he, "that you come from Headquarters. If so, please note that I receive no verbal communications whatever. Anything which you may wish to say to me, sir, I beg you will commit to paper."

Dhundia Nagh was soon on the war-path again, and accordingly, in June, 1800, Wellesley took the field against him with a force of two cavalry and three infantry brigades, to which was attached a body of Madras Pioneers under Captain W. P. Heitland, M.I. The Pioneers—possibly two companies—were distributed throughout the force. Fifty men preceded the heavy transport to repair the road, twenty accompanied a cavalry regiment, and the remainder marched with the advanced guard or main body. Wellesley was at Harihar on June 16th, but could not complete the crossing of the Tungabhadra till the 24th. Capturing the fort of Ranibennur (Rani Bednore) on the 27th, he marched to Savanur, 80 miles south of Belgaum, where the Pioneers helped to build a redoubt on the river bank. He took the fort of Kundgol by surprise on July 14th and captured Dummal on the 26th, the Pioneers being thanked for their services in the latter affair. After a fight at Manoli on July 30th, the campaign ended with the defeat and death of Dhundia near Konagal,[1] on September 10th. The Pioneers were not present at Manoli nor at the final action near Konagal; but the operations in which they took part gave them further experience of jungle warfare and impressed upon Heitland and his superiors the need for a pontoon train in a country so intersected by rivers. The hardships endured by the Pioneers, and the strenuous nature of their labours, may have contributed towards the grant by Government of an increased scale of pay and field allowances which was sanctioned on July 1st, 1800, while the operations were still in progress.[2] This must have had a beneficial effect on recruitment.

Towards the end of 1800, the Pioneers were engaged in an expedition despatched to the Wynaad District of Malabar to deal with a chieftain

[1]About sixty miles north of Bellary.

[1]Converted into rupees, the new monthly scale of pay, exclusive of stoppages for clothing, was as follows :— Jemadar, Rs. 24½ ; Havildar, Rs. 10½ ; Naik, Rs. 8¾ ; Pioneer, Rs. 8 The field allowances (*batta*) were Rs. 7, 3½, 3½ and 2 respectively.

known as the Pychy Raja, and under Heitland, assisted by Davis, acquitted themselves well, though they suffered severely from malaria. Those who remained fit for duty afterwards joined an expedition under Colonel Agnew against the savage Poligars of the Tinnevelly jungles, where some Pioneers under Bagshaw, assisted by Lieutenant L. Gordon, M.I., were already engaged. Bagshaw and his men had an unpleasant experience at Panjalamkurichi, the stronghold which Colonel Fullarton had taken in 1783. On April 22nd, 1801, while engaged in strengthening the outposts and batteries around this mud fort, which had been assaulted without success, they were rushed by the enemy, and as they were unarmed and unprotected by any covering party, they were compelled to retreat with great speed. During this retirement, they were nearly shot down by our own troops in mistake for the enemy. Heitland and some more Pioneers arrived from Wynaad on May 22nd, and on the following day the fort was captured, though not without heavy casualties. The Pioneers, and some companies of infantry, then destroyed the defences.

On July 25th, Heitland was incapacitated by a wound, and consequently was unable to superintend the work of cutting a broad road through dense jungle towards the fort of Kaliakoil (Calicoil), which was the next important objective. The Pioneers toiled heroically—on August 4th they progressed a distance of 580 yards—but owing to strong resistance by the enemy, only 5½ miles had been completed by August 30th and Kaliakoil was still nearly a mile distant. The force then retreated and attempted to reach the place by other routes, and this change of plan proving effective, Kaliakoil fell on October 1st. The labour undergone by the Pioneers in this brief campaign was extremely severe and was performed frequently under the close fire of a concealed enemy; yet little time for recuperation was given to them, for the Raja of Bullum became refractory once more, and Heitland and Davis, with a detachment of Pioneers, were despatched from Seringapatam on January 5th, 1802, with a force under Colonel Wellesley, and were present at the capture of Arakeri on the 16th. Afterwards, the Pioneers filled up the ditches of the fort, destroyed the defences of 25 villages, and opened roads through the forests and down several passes leading to Malabar.

In 1800, the authorized establishment of the Corps had been increased from 10 to 14 companies, but now a further increase was sanctioned. Detachments had proved so useful in the small campaigns of 1801 and 1802 that an order was issued on January 28th, 1803, authorizing an increase of the establishment to a total of 16 companies. These were to be formed into 2 battalions, each of 8 companies, and each company was to comprise 1 Jemadar, 3 Havildars, 3 Naiks, 1 Pakhali and 100 Privates. "In this country," remarked the Commander-in-Chief, "the services of the Pioneers always repay their expenses in war by the additional facility which they give to the movements of an army; and in peace, by the useful labour which they perform. They have completed a number of useful works since their formation—filled up ditches and levelled walls at Seringapatam and formed roads in the Baramahal,

Southern Division, Ceded Districts and Mysore." The new formations were completed in March, 1803. Captain W. P. Heitland was appointed to command the 1st Battalion, with Captain John Brown, Captain William Davis and Lieutenant Robert Barclay as his assistants; while the command of the 2nd Battalion was given to Captain John FitzPatrick, assisted by Captain Edward B. Bagshaw and Lieutenant John Grant. These officers came from battalions of the Madras Native Infantry.

The 2nd Battalion served in the Wynaad District during December, 1803, and in the Javadi Hills and Chittur between August, 1804, and March, 1805; and at the end of 1805, 3 companies were again in the Wynaad, employed in fortifying posts and erecting buildings under the direction of Ensign John Blakiston, M.E. Meanwhile, Bagshaw had succeeded Heitland in command of the 1st Battalion, to which he was appointed on January 22nd, 1805.[1] The Madras Pioneers saw no further active service in Southern India until the outbreak of an insurrection in Travancore at the end of December, 1808, when four companies under Captain T. Smithwaite, with Lieutenants A. N. Bertram and G. Patterson, M.I., were detailed for duty. Four columns invaded Travancore, and the Pioneers marched with one of these from Trichinopoly, through Palamcottah, to attack the northern section of a line of defence at Arumbuli. On February 10th, 1809, Bertram and a detachment of Pioneers took part in the escalade and capture of one of two redoubts covering an entrance through the defences, and afterwards helped to carry the remainder of the works and to destroy them. On the 17th, one company under Patterson was engaged in a successful action against a large body of the enemy. A number of villages were occupied, and the campaign ended in the beginning of March with the surrender of Trivandrum and the flight of the Dewan of Travancore into the mountains to the north.

The fighting in Travancore was the last of any importance in Southern India in which the Madras Pioneers were concerned. Their achievements

[1]The complete list of Commandants of the Madras Pioneers is as follows :—

(i) *Corps of Pioneers.*
1790–1801. Lieut. W. Dowse.
1802. Lieut. W. P. Heitland.

(ii) *Battalions of Pioneers.*
(*a*) *1st Battalion*
1803–04. Capt. W. P. Heitland.
1805–08. Capt. E. B. Bagshaw.
1809–12. Capt. R. Hughes.
1813–14. Capt. E. W. Snow.
1814–15. Capt. A. N. Bertram.
1816–19. Capt. R. McCraith.
1820–24. Capt. W. Milne.
1825. Lt. F. H. Wheeler and Capt. F. Crowe.
1826. Capts. Crowe, Wheeler and J. Sinclair.
1827–31. Capt. W. Murray.
(*b*) *2nd Battalion*
1803–09. Capt. J. FitzPatrick.
1810–19. Capt. T. Smithwaite.
1820–24. Capt. E. Richardson.
1825–31. Capt. E. Cadogan.

(iii) *Corps of Pioneers.*
1831. Major E. Cadogan.
1832–33. Capt. W. Murray.

All these officers belonged to the Madras Native Infantry.

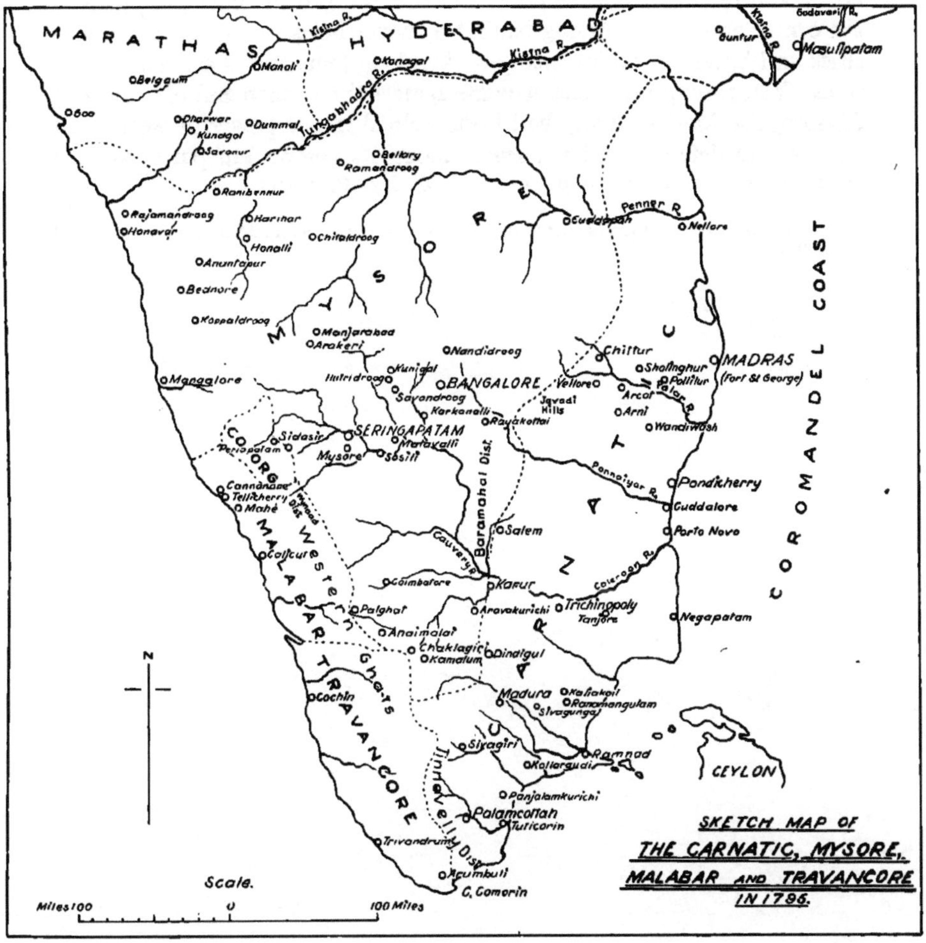
MARATHAS
HYDERABAD
Kistna R.
Godavari R.
Guntur
Masulipatam
Kistna R.
Manoli
Konagal
Belgaum
Goa
Tungabhadra R.
Dharwar
Dummal
Kunagol
Savonur
Bellary
Ramandroog
Ranibennur
Rajamandroog
Honavar
Harihar
Honalli
Chitaldroog
Anuntapur
Bednore
Koppaldroog
MYSORE
Cuddapah
Penner R.
Nellore
Manjarabad
Arakeri
Nandidroog
Chittur
Shollinghur
MADRAS
(Fort St George)
Pollilur
Mangalore
Hulridroog
Kunigal
Savandroog
BANGALORE
Vellore
Arcot
Palar R.
Javadi Hills
Arni
Karkanelli
Rayakottai
Wandiwash
SERINGAPATAM
Sidasir
Periapatam
Malavalli
Mysore
Sosile
COORG
Cannanore
Tellicherry
Mahé
Wynaad Dist.
Ponnaiyar R.
Pondicherry
Cuddalore
Porto Novo
Baramahal Dist.
Salem
Calicut
MALABAR
Western Ghats
Cauvery R.
Coimbatore
Karur
Coleroon R.
Palghat
Aravakurichi
Trichinopoly
Tanjore
Negapatam
Anaimalai
Chaklagiri
Dindigul
Kamalum
CARNATIC
COROMANDEL COAST
N
Cochin
Madura
Kalliakoil
Ranamangulam
Sivaganga
TRAVANCORE
Sivagiri
Ramnad
Kollarqudi
CEYLON
Tinnevelly Dist.
Panjalamkurichi
Palamcottah
Tuticorin
Trivandrum
Acumbuti
C. Comorin
Scale.
Miles 100
0
100 Miles
SKETCH MAP OF
THE CARNATIC, MYSORE,
MALABAR AND TRAVANCORE
IN 1786.

in the early Maratha Wars, in conjunction with their brethren, the Bombay Pioneers, are described in the next chapter, which deals with operations in Western, Central and Northern India. When hostilities re-opened in the south with the campaign in Coorg in 1834, the Madras Pioneers had become Sappers and Miners ; and after Coorg, peace reigned in the peninsula until the Moplahs devastated Malabar in 1921.[1] The tide of war ebbed and receded from the jungles of the south to the hills and plains of the centre and north, leaving behind it, nevertheless, many racial animosities and bitter memories, many broken kingdoms and shattered reputations. Yet, through the long struggle against the French and the rulers of Mysore, the Madras Army had been welded into a powerful weapon of offence and defence, and not least among its component parts was the industrious and experienced Corps of Madras Pioneers.

[1]A small Moplah rebellion occurred in 1889, but no Sappers and Miners were employed in quelling it.

CHAPTER II

PIONEERS IN WESTERN, CENTRAL AND NORTHERN INDIA, 1777–1809

THE reorganization of the Bengal Army, initiated by Clive after the Battle of Plassey, was followed by a remodelling and strengthening of the Bombay Army which showed that the East India Company intended to emerge as a political and military power on the western coast and was preparing for the possibility of a conflict with the Maratha Confederacy. For the moment, Baroda was friendly; but the other important States—Gwalior, Poona, Indore and Berar—were secretly or openly hostile. Consequently, the time-honoured custom of parsimony in military affairs was abandoned and in 1765 the Europeans of the Bombay Army were formed into 15 companies of infantry and 3 companies of artillery. Three years later, the army comprised a regiment of 3 battalions of European infantry and a Sepoy Corps of 2 battalions, in addition to artillery. The strength of the Sepoy Corps was raised to 4 battalions in 1770 and 7 battalions in 1778. In its later stages, this expansion was fostered by the enterprise of Mr. William Hornby, who became Governor of Bombay in 1771 and Commander-in-Chief, in addition, in 1774. Hornby saw, in the dissensions of the Maratha States, an opportunity for casting aside the rôle of a purely mercantile body and putting to the test the military and political capacity of the Company. The new attitude of the Bombay Government was shown clearly by the rapid increase in military strength. "A soldier," said the Council in 1770,[1] "should be as attached to, and careful of, his musket as his mistress," and in this apt simile, disclosed their ambitions.

Experience gained in military operations by Lieut.-Colonel Thomas Keating, Bo.E., against the Marathas in the island of Salsette and elsewhere in 1774–75, and difficulties encountered in fortifying Salsette, led to a scheme for the separation of the Bombay Engineers from the Bombay Artillery, proposed on August 2nd and ratified by a General Order on December 9th, 1777; but meanwhile, Ensign Charles Henry Wittman,[2] a young German serving in the Bombay Infantry, had become so impressed by the shortage of skilled labour and supervision that he made the startling proposal that the Bombay Government should recruit from Germany an entire company of military artificers to replace the civilian artisans whom he despised, and thus indirectly paved the way for the advent of the Bombay Pioneer Lascar, the Bombay Pioneer, and finally the Bombay

[1] "The Bombay Engineer Officer in 1800," by Arthur Vincent, appearing in *The R.E. Journal*, Vol. XLII, 1928, p. 260.

[2] Wittman (or Witman, or Whitman) was commissioned in 1775, but had probably served already as a subordinate during the operations under Colonel Keating. He became a Brevet-Capt in 1784 and died in 1788.

Sapper and Miner. Possibly, he had in mind the company of "Soldier Artificers" added in 1772 to the garrison of Gibraltar. The ink flowed so freely from his pen that his thesis cannot be recorded in full, but a précis will show his general line of argument.[1]

Wittman started by remarking that, in the army of every German prince, each battalion of artillery had a company of artisans who acted as armourers in the field and worked in the arsenals and foundries in time of peace. He proceeded to enlarge on the defects of Indian artificers: they were clumsy, idle, weak, incapable of understanding verbal instructions, cowardly and unfitted to take their place in the ranks in an emergency. Many of the tasks that might fall to their lot in a siege were quite beyond their powers. He contrasted them with German artisans, who could fight when necessary and earn their keep in the arsenals. He could recruit these men on the same pay as that allowed for the Indian artisans, ranging from Rs. 10 to Rs. 16 per mensem. "The company," he wrote, "might consist of 100 privates, or more if necessary, all versed in some business. The non-commissioned officers should be masters or very able workmen in different trades. I could also engage experienced officers, well versed in every branch of the artillery. . . . The company might be kept constantly complete by recruits from Europe which I could send annually to London by means of agents established in Germany. Exclusive of their utility to the Company, these artificers would be of great convenience to the place; and as many of them would bring their wives and children, they might in time produce a race which would be at once useful inhabitants and add considerably to the strength of the place in case of a siege."

On February 13th, 1776, the President laid these military and eugenic proposals before the Bombay Council, who were pleased to grant Wittman a free passage to Europe in order that he might lay his scheme before the Directors, adding that he should be informed that the Brigadier-General (in command of the garrison) considered that some Miners would be a very useful addition to the German Artificer Company.[2] Wittman sailed for England and launched his recruiting campaign; but his efforts met with little success, for in three years he secured only 25 men,[3] and although these were allotted passages to India, there is no record that they ever reached Bombay. Nevertheless, he had sown good seed by his representation in 1776 that a body of trained engineer soldiers was a necessary adjunct to a cadre of engineer officers. His contempt for the local civilian artisan blinded him to the possibility of recruiting and training men from among the martial races of India and caused him to seek them in Europe.

The credit for realizing that suitable men might be recruited in Western India should be accorded to Major Lawrence Nilson of the Bombay

[1] *Bombay Public Diary*, No. 69 of 1776. Letter from Ensign Wittman dated Feb. 11th 1776, appearing in the *Bombay Gazetteer*, Vol. XXVI, Part II, Section II, pp. 425–30.

[2] *Bombay Government Consultations*, Feb. 13th, 1776. *Public Diary* No. 69 of 1776.

[3] Court to Bombay. Letter dated May 27th, 1779. *Public Department Courts' Letters*, Vol. X of 1778–82.

Engineers, who succeeded Lieut.-Colonel Thomas Keating as Chief Engineer in October, 1776.[1] At the end of November, 1777, Nilson made an application that he should be permitted to raise a company of Pioneer Lascars, consisting of 1 Sarang, 4 Tindals and 100 "Private Men," to work under the direction of the Engineer Corps, and this was considered by the Bombay Council on December 7th in conjunction with the general question of the establishment of Artillery Lascars. The Council then fixed the latter at 5 companies, each of 100 men, and it was resolved that, as a body of Pioneer Lascars was indispensable, a company should be raised by the transfer of 60 supernumerary Artillery Lascars and the recruitment of 40 additional men. The unit was to be under the orders of the Chief Engineer.[2] A General Order appeared on December 13th, 1777, authorizing the establishment of a Pioneer Lascar Company under these conditions, and thus the Bombay Army obtained the services of an engineer unit nearly three years before the formation of the first two companies of Madras Pioneers by Lieutenant Joseph Moorhouse of the Madras Artillery. The 18th Field Company, Royal Bombay Sappers and Miners, claimed its descent from this small unit of Bombay Pioneer Lascars.[3]

The First Maratha War, begun in 1774 with the operations under Keating in Salsette and continued in 1775 in the region of Baroda, was resumed in 1778 with the despatch of an expedition under Colonel Egerton, a "bed-ridden commander," against Tukoji Rao Holkar of Indore and Mahadji Sindhia of Gwalior. This mad project ended in disastrous failure. In December, a small column toiled up the ghats and advanced slowly towards the Maratha armies near Poona; but on January 11th, 1779, Egerton gave the order to retire, and his men were only saved from annihilation by the conclusion of the humiliating Treaty of Wargaum[4] on January 13th. It is believed that a detachment of 50 Pioneer Lascars shared in this unfortunate venture[5] and perhaps helped to fortify the village of Wargaum, where the troops made a final stand and repulsed several attacks.

Meanwhile, Brig.-General Goddard was making a wonderful march across India with 6 battalions from Bengal, and hearing of the fiasco at Wargaum, hastened to Surat, which he reached on February 6th. After months had been spent in political negotiations, he was reinforced from Bombay, and as Baroda was hostile, he sent Lieut.-Colonel Hartley to capture Dabhoi.[6] That place fell on January 19th, 1780, and Ahmadabad on

[1]Lieut.-Colonel Keating resigned after being tried by court-martial and acquitted on account of his alleged misdirection of the operations in Salsette and Baroda in 1774–5. He had been Chief Engineer since 1764. (See *The Military Engineer in India*, by the present author, Vol. I, pp. 181–83.)

[2]*Bombay Government Consultations*, Dec. 7th, 1777. *Public Diary* No. 72 of 1777.

[3]*A Brief History of the Royal Bombay Sappers and Miners*, p. 1.

[4]Also spelt "Wargaon" and "Wadgaon" or "Vadgaon."

[5]A Bombay General Order, dated March 31st, 1778, authorized the recruitment of 50 extra Pioneer Lascars to replace a like number proceeding to the Maratha War under Colonel Egerton.

[6]The names of all places mentioned in this Chapter appear in Maps I or II at the end of this volume or in the Sketch Map included in Chapter I.

February 15th, detachments of Pioneer Lascars taking part in both sieges. Under Major David Spaeth, Bo.E., as Chief Engineer, they built a battery at Dabhoi; and at Ahmadabad, where Spaeth was mortally wounded, they filled up a ditch for the passage of the Bombay Grenadiers in the final assault. Goddard then turned southwards to deal with Sindhia and Holkar, but the Marathas avoided encounter. The rainy season over, he laid siege to Bassein, and the Pioneer Lascars under Captain Theobald, a temporary Bombay Engineer,[1] were present when the town and fort were captured on December 11th, 1780.

In January, 1781, Goddard began an advance on the Maratha capital at Poona; but when he reached Khopuli at the foot of the Bhor Ghat, he found the defile held by 4,000 men with many guns and heard that Holkar was at the top with 15,000 horse. Nevertheless, he ascended the ghat under cover of darkness and captured two defended posts, the second of which, called the Darwaja or gate of the defile, was taken chiefly through the enterprise of the Pioneer Lascars[2] and some Bengal Grenadiers who climbed the heights on one side of the road, advanced along them, and assisted the attack by flanking fire. The column reached Khandala at the head of the ghat, where it maintained a precarious footing until the middle of April. Then, harassed by large bodies of Marathas, it retreated to Panvel near Bombay, fighting an action at Chauk[3] on April 21st in which the Pioneer Lascars lost a few men. Minor hostilities continue until March, 1782, and the First Maratha War ended with the Treaty of Salbai, signed in May, 1782, but not ratified until February, 1783.

The Pioneers in Bombay and Madras received some attention in 1782 through the representations of a certain Major George Burghall, formerly attached to the Madras Engineers,[4] for the following letter, dated January 25th, reached Bombay from London on September 5th:—

> " Major George Burghall, late of our Corps of Engineers at Fort St. George, having submitted to our consideration a plan proposing sundry improvements in the mode of fortification at present adopted in India, and that an Inspector and Director of Fortifications throughout India should be appointed, also that a Corps of Miners and Pioneers should be established at each of our Presidencies, we enclose a copy thereof and direct that you take the opinion of the Commander-in-Chief at your Presidency on its utility and expediency, whose report thereon must be forwarded to England by the first ship."

[1]Capt. Theobald does not appear in any list of the Bombay or Bengal Engineers. It can only be supposed that he was attached to the Bombay Corps. (See *The Military Engineer in India*, by the present author, Vol. I, p. 194.)

[2]In *A History of the Marathas*, Vol. II, p. 436, Grant Duff states that 200 " Pioneers and Lascars " were present, but some of these may have been Artillery Lascars.

[3]Chauk is midway between Khandala and Panvel.

[4]Major Burghall does not appear in any list of the Madras Engineers. He came to India in 1763, when he joined the Bengal Artillery from the Royal Artillery with the rank of Capt.-Lieut., and was dismissed from the Bengal Army in 1765. (See *List of the Officers of the Bengal Army*, 1758–1834, by Major V. C. P. Hodson, Part I, p. 251.) During the next three years he applied for appointment to the Madras Engineers, or as Lieut.-Governor of St. Helena, or as a Major in the Bombay or Bengal Armies. However, having influence at Court, he was appointed in 1769 as Principal Engineer at Fort Marlborough in Sumatra. Thence he gravitated apparently to Madras.

The report must have been adverse, for no more was heard of Burghall's scheme. Except in the opinion of the Engineers themselves, the Pioneer Lascars of Bombay, and the Pioneers of Madras, were adequate for the field operations of the period. In Bengal, for many years, each regiment of infantry had had some artificers or Pioneers on its establishment, and in September, 1776, 4 companies of artificers—garrison troops sometimes called "Pioneers"—had been raised and added to the army. There are indications, however, that temporary companies of Bengal Pioneers were formed for field service when occasion demanded, as in the Madras Army.

The campaigns against the Marathas in the eighteenth century involved little field engineering, for these warlike people were merely a nation of mounted freebooters with a following of wretched mercenaries. "The Mahratta[1] guns are of all sorts and dimensions," writes Major Dirom in 1793,[2] "and having the names of their gods given to them, are painted in a most fantastic manner. Many of them, held in esteem for the services they are said to have already performed for the State, cannot now be dispensed with, although in every respect unfit for use. The Mahratta infantry is composed of black Christians, and despicable poor wretches of the lowest caste, uniform in nothing but the bad state of their musquets. Few are provided with either ammunition or accoutrements. They are commanded by half-caste people of Portuguese or French extraction who draw off the attention of spectators from the bad clothing of their men by the profusion of antiquated lace bestowed on their own. The Mahrattas do not appear to treat their infantry with more respect than they deserve as they ride through them without ceremony on the march and on all occasions evidently consider them as foreigners. On a marching day, the guns and infantry move off soon after daylight, but rarely together: the bazaars and baggage move nearly about the same time. The guns and tumbrils, sufficiently unwieldy without further burden, are so heaped with stores and baggage that there does not seem to be any idea of its ever being necessary to unlimber and prepare for action on the march. There are sometimes a hundred or a hundred and fifty bullocks, in a string of pairs, to one gun. The chiefs remain upon the ground, without tents, smoking their hookahs, till the artillery and baggage have got on some miles: they then follow, each pursuing his own route, attended by his principal people, while the inferiors disperse to forage and plunder over the country."

Who that has trekked in the wilds of India will not recognize the scene? The awaking crowd, the confusion of packing and loading, the early start, the creaking of over-laden carts, the straining bullocks, the departure of the *sahib* on duty or shikar and his return at nightfall to bath, dinner and bed in a new camp. India, the true India of ravine, swamp and jungle changes little. Its mountains and plains, sad and majestic, repel the puny

[1]This spelling of the name, i.e., "Mahratta" as opposed to "Maratha," though incorrect according to the *Imperial Gazetteer of India*, is the original one which is still used in the names of Maratha regiments of the Indian Army. Accordingly, it will be adopted in referring to such units.

[2]*A Narrative of the Campaign in India which terminated with the War with Tippoo Sultan in* 1792, by Major Dirom, p. 10.

efforts of man to mar their natural beauties with modern invention, and vast tracts remain much as they were when Sindhia and Holkar marched across them.

Having pacified the Marathas, the Bombay Government was free to help Sir Eyre Coote in the Second Mysore War and embarked a force under Major-General Mathews for service in Malabar. Sailing from Bombay on December 12th, 1782, Mathews took the fortress of Rajamandroog by storm on December 18th, reduced Honavar on January 5th, 1783, and before the end of the month was in possession also of Bednore. Mangalore fell on March 9th and afterwards, by rashly depleting the garrison of Bednore, Mathews was able to capture many neighbouring hill forts. By this time, however, Tipu was on his way from the east with a large army, and after a gallant resistance, Mathews was forced to capitulate at Bednore on May 3rd. Only Honavar and Mangalore held out, though Cannanore and other places were recaptured by the Company before the conclusion of peace with Tipu in March, 1784.

A detachment of Pioneer Lascars sailed with Mathews[1] and took part in the siege of Mangalore in March, 1783, under Captain J. C. Sartorius, Bo.E., as Chief Engineer.[2] They were reinforced in December by a small party under Captain D. B. Christie, Bo.E.[3] In January, 1786, a similar party was despatched by ship with other troops on a "secret mission," led by Sartorius, to survey Malabar or Mysore.[4] This was during the period of recuperation which preceded the Third Mysore War. In February, 1789, the Bombay Government took action on an order issued by the Directors in September, 1785, regarding the reduction and standardization of the Presidency armies and curtailed the establishment of the Bombay Pioneer Lascars to 1 company of 1 Sarang, 4 Tindals and only 56 Lascars;[5] in October, 1791, however, the establishment was increased during the Third Mysore War and so remained until it was reduced once more to a single company after the return of the Bombay Army from Seringapatam in 1792.[6]

There is little to record of the doings of the Bombay Pioneer Lascars in the Third Mysore War. On December 10th, 1790, a small detachment was in action at Calicut when Colonel Hartley routed a Mysore force;[7] and it is believed that a strong contingent was with the Bombay Army under Sir Robert Abercromby when it set out from Tellicherry towards Periapatam on February 22nd, 1791, in the first attempt to join hands with the Madras Army under Lord Cornwallis at Seringapatam, for under a

[1]Bombay General Order, Dec. 7th, 1782.

[2]*A Brief History of the Royal Bombay Sappers and Miners*, p. 2, and Bombay General Order, July 7th, 1785, confirming promotions made by Sartorius during the siege.

[3]Bombay General Order, Oct. 26th, 1783. The party consisted of 1 Tindal and 25 Lascars.

[4]Bombay General Order, Jan. 23rd, 1786.

[5]Bombay General Order, Feb. 5th, 1789, giving extracts from the Hon. Company's letter of Sept. 26th, 1785, received on July 19th, 1786.

[6]*A Brief History of the Royal Bombay Sappers and Miners*, p. 2.

[7]Under a Bombay General Order of April 6th, 1790, a detachment of 1 Sarang, 1 Tindal and 25 Pioneers was detailed to embark at Bombay with other troops under Col. Hartley.

General Order published on October 21st, 1791, three months before Abercromby advanced again towards Seringapatam, Lieutenant (afterwards Major-General) William Brooks,[1] Bo.E., was appointed " Captain of the Pioneers in the Field," under Major Sartorius as Chief Engineer, a post which he held until he left for Bombay on April 25th, 1792, after the conclusion of the war. During the first siege of Seringapatam, the Pioneer Lascars under Brooks were with the Bombay Army on the north bank of the Cauvery, and it is presumed that they assisted the Madras Pioneers in the preparations for attack.

Before the arrival of Brooks, the Pioneer Lascars were under the temporary command of Ensign Bryce Moncrieff, Bo.E., who now appears on the scene as a victim of the Government's wrath, for a letter, signed " B.M.," had appeared on October 8th, 1791, in a newspaper called the *Argus*, criticizing the Government and General Abercromby for their conduct of the early part of campaign, and it was clear that Bryce Moncrieff had written it in a fit of exasperation at his supersession by Brooks. " Although Mr. Bryce Moncrieff does not acknowledge being the author of the said letter," wrote the Bombay Council,[2] " yet he does not deny it but says that whenever he wrote his opinion it was in confidence to a particular friend, by which it is evident that he has corresponded by his private letters upon the public affairs of the Company ; and as he has not thought proper to retract or make any apology or atonement for expressions tending to the hurt and dishonour of the Commander-in-Chief, the Board is of opinion that he has behaved himself with contempt and disrespect towards the Hon. the Governor-General in Council of Bengal. The Hon. the President in Council has therefore resolved that Practitioner Engineer Moncrieff be suspended the service until the pleasure of the Hon. Company is known in order to deter others from such dangerous practices. The Hon. the President in Council is of opinion that Mr. Moncrieff's writing this libel was occasioned by pique and disappointment in not being confirmed in the office of Captain of Pioneers, which the Hon. the President deemed an unnecessary expense." It is pleasant to record that Bryce Moncrieff afterwards regained the good opinion of the Government so completely that in 1797 he was selected to command a Corps of Bombay Pioneers which the Government had decided to raise.

A remark appears in the small volume entitled *A Brief History of the Royal Bombay Sappers and Miners* that in 1797 the Corps (of Pioneer Lascars) was expanded to a Pioneer Corps of 4 companies of 100 men into which the whole of the original company of Pioneer Lascars was absorbed. The authority for this statement is not given ; but a careful study of the Bombay General Order, dated March 5th, 1797, which authorized the change, gives the impression that the Pioneer Corps was a new body. The establishment was to be separate. The officers were to be drawn from the Line, though an Engineer was to be the first

[1]Sometimes spelt Brookes.
[2]Extract from *Bombay Public Consultations*, published in Bombay General Order, Nov. 21st, 1792.

Commandant. The men, though unarmed, were to have a distinctive uniform. They were to be paid as Infantry and to be subject to Army discipline. Subsequently, they were given a place in the Army List, after the Bombay Infantry and before the Marine Battalion. The General Order ran as follows:— "The Commander-in-Chief now delivers in the plan for the establishment of a Corps of Pioneers, agreeable to the minutes of our last meeting. Agreed that the Commander-in-Chief be requested to issue the necessary orders for carrying into execution the plan that has been approved of for establishing a Corps of Pioneers. *The Plan.*—The Hon. the President in Council having been pleased to approve of the institution of a Pioneer Corps, as proposed in the Commander-in-Chief's minute of the 24th ultimo, General Stuart now delivers, agreeable to the last para. of that minute, the following detail for that establishment. That the Corps consists of one officer of the rank of Captain as Commandant, two subalterns, one assistant surgeon, and four companies, each to consist of 1 Sergeant, 1 Jemadar, 3 Havildars, 3 Naiks and 100 Privates. . . . That the full pay of the natives of every description in this Corps be the same as that of the corresponding situations in the Native Infantry. The Corps of Pioneers, when raised, to be considered a separate establishment, and the officers to be supplied from the Line, but to rise in the list of the Army as before. The officers and privates of the Pioneer Corps to be subject to the articles of war in the same manner as the regular regiments. . . . The Pioneers are to carry no arms, but to be furnished with working tools of such description as are suited to natives of their service. General Stuart begs leave to recommend Captain Moncrieff of the Engineers as Commandant of the Pioneer Corps, and that he be accordingly instructed to raise men for this service with the utmost expedition. To assist him in the accomplishment of this object it will be necessary to appoint two subaltern officers to the new Corps. The Pioneer Corps is to be distinguished by the following uniform:— dark green jackets, with black cuffs and collars and white lace and blue turbans for the men. For officers: a dress in conformity with the above." In a General Order, dated April 5th, 1797, the Government added that the Pioneers (i.e., the Pioneer Lascars) hitherto attached to the Corps of Bombay Engineers were to be incorporated in Captain Moncrieff's Corps and to join it immediately.

Now the importance of these orders lies in the fact that although, according to the Indian Army List, the Corps of Royal Bombay Sappers and Miners was raised at Bombay in 1820, designated "Engineers" in 1829, the "Engineer Corps" in 1830 (when the Corps of Pioneers raised in the last decade of the 18th century was absorbed into it) and "Bombay Sappers and Miners" in 1840, some officers contend that it can claim an unbroken line of descent from the Pioneer Lascars raised in 1777 and should accordingly be the senior of the three Corps of Indian Sappers and Miners by virtue of priority of foundation. They point out that the Army List shows the Madras Corps as raised in the form of two Pioneer companies in 1780 and the Bengal Corps as Bengal Pioneers in

1803. Why, they ask, should the Bombay Corps be shown as originating as Sappers and Miners in 1820 instead of as Pioneer Lascars in 1777, or at least as Pioneers in 1797?

This somewhat controversial matter has been the object of investigation by several Royal Engineer officers of the Bombay Corps, including Captain G. H. W. O'Sullivan before 1890, Captain A. G. Bremner in 1903 and later, Major G. A. J. Leslie and Captain W. Bovet in 1913–14, and Major M. Rawlence after the Great War. In 1923, after examining records in Bombay, Simla and London, Rawlence submitted a draft case to Army Headquarters, but could not pursue the matter further. Subsequently, a decision was given that as no evidence had been produced to show that the Pioneer Lascars or Bombay Pioneers were *combatant* troops, no action could be taken. Although a digest of the services of the Bombay Sappers and Miners from 1820 to 1895 had been prepared in the latter year by O'Sullivan, Rawlence had much difficulty in finding copies of many of the older General Orders, for almost all the Bombay Army military records had been destroyed in a fire at the Command Offices in Poona in 1907 and others of a purely regimental character, mostly prior to 1820 in date, had been used before 1890 by an economical subaltern to manufacture targets for the Sappers' rifle range! Certain points, however, stand out in the available records.[1] The Pioneer Lascars of 1777, and the Pioneers of 1797, were unarmed in peace, though they may have carried arms in war: for instance, it is recorded that the Pioneer Lascars supported the attack in the Bor (or Bhor) Ghat in 1781 by flanking fire. The records seem to show that the Pioneer Lascars had an unbroken existence from 1777 to 1797;[2] but they indicate also that the General Order authorizing the immediate recruitment of the Bombay Pioneers was issued one month *before* the order for the absorption of the Pioneer Lascars into that Corps and that consequently the Corps was, as the Government stated, a separate establishment.

While on the intricate subject of the origin of the Royal Bombay Sappers and Miners it may be well to remark that, under a General Order of December 23rd, 1799, a Corps of "Engineer Lascars" (2 Tindals and 30 Lascars), claimed as the ancestor of the 17th Field Company, was raised by Major-General Robert Nicholson, Engineer-in-Chief and Commander-in-Chief, and that these men were clothed and paid like other Lascars (5 companies) employed in the Stores Department. They wore red jackets with black facings. This small body survived until 1820, when, in a General Order dated August 28th, the Government directed that the establishment of Engineer Lascars should be *increased* forthwith to a specified strength, designated "Sappers and Miners," and trained under an Engineer Officer. Accordingly, the entry in the Indian Army List which indicates that the establishment *originated* in 1820 appears to be

[1]The evidence which Major Rawlence collected is with the Bombay Corps at Kirkee.

[2]In addition to the Bombay General Orders already quoted, others dated April 1st, April 24th and May 10th, 1785, and Jan. 28th and Oct. 22nd, 1789, refer to Pioneer Lascars and deal mostly with pay and allowances.

incorrect, although the Engineer Lascars were called then, for the first time, "Sappers and Miners."

As regards the companies of Bombay Pioneers raised in 1797, these and others added to them were amalgamated with the Sapper and Miner companies in 1830, though still classed as "Pioneers," and the establishment so formed was designated the "Engineer Corps." The question then arises as to whether the Royal Bombay Sappers and Miners can claim descent through the Bombay Pioneers, who were contemporaries before 1830 of some of their original companies evolved from the Engineer Lascars; but as this narrative is concerned only with historical fact, no opinion will be expressed on the evidence which has been given. The unravelment of the tangled skein may be left to others.

The entire Corps of Bombay Pioneers, consisting of 4 companies under Captain-Lieutenant Bryce Moncrieff, Bo.E., sailed from Bombay on April, 9th, 1797, to improve road communications in Malabar[1] and remained in the south-west for several years. Reinforcements were sent to them on four occasions during 1797.[2] On January 16th, 1799, the establishment was increased by 50 men per company for the invasion of Mysore; but on November 27th, after the fall of Seringapatam, it was reduced to normal strength.[3] The Pioneers, 416 strong, marched from Cannanore on February 21st, 1799, with the Bombay Army under Lieut.-General Stuart and fought at Sidasir on March 6th. During the siege of Seringapatam, they worked mostly on the northern bank of the Cauvery under the direction of Colonel J. C. Sartorius, the Chief Engineer of the Bombay Army; but they could not have been in the final assault as they lost only 2 killed and 26 wounded throughout the operations. Nevertheless, their performance in the Fourth Mysore War brought them an increase of pay in June, 1801, "in appreciation of special service and in consideration for general fidelity and gallantry."[4]

Their work in Mysore having been finished, three companies of the Corps under Bryce Moncrieff, assisted by Ensign E. F. Frissel, Bo.I., returned in January, 1800, to Malabar to resume the roadmaking operations interrupted by the war, while the fourth company proceeded to the Kanara District, further north.[5] So much surveying was demanded that Bryce Moncrieff was absent from his command for long periods[6] during which he was assisted by Lieutenant Monier Williams, Bo.I.[7] However, with Lieutenant W. F. Henderson, Bo.I., as his subaltern, he was present with part of the Corps at the relief of Manatana (Montana), near Cannanore, in August, 1800. "Captain Moncrieff's zeal and activity, always conspi-

[1]Bombay General Order, April 7th, 1797, ordering embarkation of the Corps on April 8th.

[2]Bombay General Orders, April 23rd, July 27th, Aug. 20th and Nov. 8th, 1797.

[3]Bombay General Orders, Jan. 16th and Nov. 27th, 1799.

[4]Bombay General Order, June 18th, 1801.

[5]Bombay General Order, Jan. 20th, 1800.

[6]Bombay General Order, March 30th, 1800.

[7]Bombay General Order, June 26th, 1800. Lieut. Monier Williams had been posted to the Bombay Pioneers and was still with them in 1803. (See Bombay General Order Jan. 7th, 1803.)

cuous," wrote Sartorius,[1] "calls on this occasion for the commanding officer's most public notice, and it has given him great satisfaction to observe his report of Lieutenant Henderson's exertions and the officers with him at Montana in strengthening their post and their conduct in defence of it." Bryce Moncrieff seemed destined for a distinguished career, but his health failed and he died in Bombay on January 10th, 1802. Captain-Lieutenant William Cowper, Bo.E., who succeeded him as Commandant, resigned a few weeks later, and on March 3rd, 1802, the appointment was given to Captain John Johnson, Bo.E.[2] In Johnson, the Bombay Pioneers found a worthy successor to Bryce Moncrieff, for he was an experienced soldier and engineer. Commissioned in May, 1785, he had served with a Maratha force in the siege of Dharwar in 1790 under Lord Cornwallis in the Third Mysore War, in the siege of Cochin in 1796, and in the siege and capture of Seringapatam in 1799. The Second Maratha War, which was soon to begin, afforded him new opportunities for the display of natural ability and leadership.

At this time, the ruling Princes of the Maratha States were Baji Rao, the Peshwa or Prime Minister and nominal head of the Maratha Confederacy, whose dominions stretched along the western coast to north and south of his capital at Poona; Daulat Rao Sindhia[3] of Gwalior, whose territory lay north of that of the Peshwa and extended as far as Delhi; Jaswant Rao Holkar[4] of Indore in Central India, whose possessions were intermingled with those of Sindhia; Raghuji Bhonsla, Raja of Berar, whose domains extended eastwards from his capital at Nagpur to Cuttack on the Bay of Bengal; and Fateh Singh, the Gaikwar of Baroda, a small State in Gujarat in Western India.[5] As the Nizam of Hyderabad had been defeated by the Marathas in 1795, Marquis Wellesley, the Governor-General, had decided in 1798 that he must support the Nizam against further Maratha aggression. Dissension then developed among the Marathas, for Sindhia aspired to be head of the Confederacy and allied himself to the weak and vacillating Peshwa. This excited the enmity of Holkar, who defeated Sindhia and Baji Rao at Poona in 1802. Baji Rao appealed to Marquis Wellesley, and it was agreed under the Treaty of Bassein, ratified on December 31st, 1802, that the Peshwa should be restored to his throne. The deed was done with proper ceremonial by a force under Colonel Arthur Wellesley. Sindhia, foiled in his ambition, then turned to the Bhonsla Raja of Berar and planned with him to march on Poona or invade Hyderabad; but Marquis Wellesley promptly ordered Sindhia to separate his army from that of Berar and retire across the Narbada, and when he found that his ultimatum was ignored, declared war on August 3rd, 1803. Baroda was friendly, and Holkar of Indore, hating both the British and Sindhia, had retreated northwards after threatening Hyder-

[1]Provincial Order, dated Aug. 8th, 1800, by Col. J. C. Sartorius, late Bo.E.
[2]Bombay General Orders, Jan. 17th and March 3rd, 1802.
[3]Successor to Mahadji Sindhia.
[4]Successor to Tukoji Rao Holkar.
[5]Gujarat is the territory on the western coast, north and east and west of the gulf of Cambay, where the Gujarati language is spoken.

abad. Such were the political events leading up to the Second Maratha War, a struggle which resolved itself into two distinct campaigns—one by Colonel Arthur Wellesley and other commanders against the combined forces of Sindhia and Berar operating in Central India, and the other by Lieut.-General Gerard Lake in the north opposed to Sindhia's main army which was commanded by a Frenchman, Perron.

An interesting description of the ruler of Gwalior and his followers is given by an anonymous writer in 1803.[1] "We were fortunate enough," he says, "to meet Scindia returning from the chase, surrounded by all his chiefs and preceded or followed by about 700 horse. Discharges of cannon announced his approach. First came light-armed horse; then some better clad with the quilted pashauk, and one in a complete suit of armour; then a few elephants, among them the hunting elephant of Scindia from which he had dismounted. Then came, slowly prancing, a host of fierce, haughty chieftains on fine horses, showily caparisoned. They darted forward and took their proud stand behind and around us, planting their long lances on the earth and reining their eager steeds to see, I suppose, our salaam. Next, in a common native palkee, its canopy crimson and not adorned, came Scindia himself. He was plainly dressed, with a reddish turban and a shawl over his vest, and lay reclined, smoking a small gilt or golden hookah. We stood up in our howdah and bowed, and he half rose in his palkee and salaamed in rather a courteous manner. At this there was a loud cry from all his followers, who sung out his titles and the honour he had done us, and all salaamed themselves profusely. I looked down on the chiefs under us and saw that they all eyed us haughtily. They were armed with lance, scymitar and shield, creese and pistol, and wore, some shawls, some tissues, and some plain muslin or cotton. They were all much wrapped up in clothing, and wore, almost all, a large fold of muslin, tied over the turban top, which they fasten under their chin and which looks warlike and is a very important defence to the sides of the neck." These were the warriors against whom the Company's troops were pitted in the Second Maratha War, the opponents of the Madras, Bengal and Bombay Pioneers in many a siege and battle.

To enable him to cross the flooded rivers of the Deccan in the rainy season, Colonel Arthur Wellesley had ordered boats and pontoons from Bombay, but unfortunately none reached him. However, a pontoon train was formed in Bombay on May 20th, 1803,[2] and placed under the command of Lieutenant (afterwards Lieut.-General) Samuel Goodfellow, Bo.E., with orders to join Wellesley. It is believed that the pontoon train set out towards the interior on June 6th;[3] but after a few miles had been covered, the carriages broke down in the torrential rain and the small unit returned to headquarters, though it was able to proceed later to Gujarat to help Colonel Murray in operations conducted in that province. In July, a second and successful attempt was made to send it to the Deccan;

[1] *Sketches of India for Fireside Travellers at Home*, pp. 260, 264, quoted in *The East India Military Calendar*, Vol. III, pp. 68, 69, f. n.
[2] Bombay General Order, May 20th, 1803.
[3] Bombay General Order, June 5th, 1803, authorized the assembly of the unit.

yet it was found to be unsuitable for the rapid movements of a campaign against the elusive Marathas. It was outdistanced by the troops, and consequently Wellesley had no pontoons at the Battle of Assaye, when they would have been of inestimable value to him. In a memorandum on basket-boats and the construction of floating bridges, written before he started northwards from Mysore, Wellesley had shown himself an authority in such matters.[1] His engineers were instructed in the best methods of stretching cables across a river, attaching boats to them, cross-bracing the bridge and laying the superstructure. If Wellesley had not become the Duke of Wellington, he would have excelled as an Engineer-in-Chief.

Early in August, 1803, after despatching a force under Colonel Stevenson north-eastwards to watch the enemy's movements and safeguard Hyderabad from invasion, Wellesley advanced from Poona with about 10,000 regular troops and a large body of native horse to besiege Ahmadnagar. This walled town was assaulted and captured on August 8th, and the fort outside it, on the 12th. Wellesley thus secured at the outset a success of great political value, for Ahmadnagar was the principal stronghold of Sindhia in the Deccan. Six companies (653 men) of the 1st Battalion of Madras Pioneers, under Captain W. P. Heitland, M.I., took part in the siege, and it is recorded that " the activity and address of the Corps were the admiration of the Army."[2] Captain John Johnson, Bo.E., was mentioned with Heitland for his excellent work, but in his dual capacity as Commandant of the Guides[3] and Chief Engineer and not as Commandant of the Bombay Pioneers.

Vibart states that two companies of " Pioneers " (202 men) accompanied the force under Stevenson[4] but does not show them as " Madras Pioneers," though the Q.V.O. Madras Sappers and Miners claim them as such.[5] On the other hand, the Royal Bombay Sappers and Miners believe that the two companies with Stevenson were Bombay Pioneers from Kanara and Malabar, for they state that the Bombay Pioneers participated with the Madras Pioneers in the special monetary reward allotted after the campaign.[6] No Bombay Pioneers were present at the siege of Ahmadnagar, where Johnson was Chief Engineer in virtue of being the senior engineer officer in the field; but they may have been with Stevenson under the temporary command of Lieutenant Monier Williams, Bo.I., who remained with the Corps until March, 1807. If the two companies with Stevenson were Bombay Pioneers, where were the two remaining companies of the 1st Battalion, Madras Pioneers, the whole of which was on service under Heitland? The available records give no information on the subject.

[1]Memorandum by Col. Arthur Wellesley, dated March 27th, 1803, quoted in *Wellington Despatches*, by S. J. Owen, pp. 618, 619.

[2]*The Military History of the Madras Engineers and Pioneers*, by Major H. M. Vibart, R. (M.) E., Vol. I, pp. 374, 377.

[3]The Corps of Guides was employed chiefly in reconnaissance and surveying.

[4]*The Military History of the Madras Engineers and Pioneers*, by Major H. M. Vibart, R. (M.) E., Vol. I, p. 375.

[5]*The Roll of Honour of the " Queen's Own " Madras Sappers and Miners*, p. 13.

[6]*A Brief History of the Royal Bombay Sappers and Miners*, p. 3.

At the siege of Ahmadnagar, the Madras Pioneers did not see much fighting, for their losses were small. Their chief employment was the construction of batteries, regarding which Blakiston remarks :—[1] " During the night (August 9th–10th) a battery of four iron 12-pounders was erected within about 400 yards of the walls and opened at daybreak. The celerity with which batteries are erected by the English in India would astonish the regular stagers of Europe. Nearly three times the number of hands allowed by the German, Müller, are allotted to the work ; and instead of a regular ditch being made in front of the parapet, as soon as the gabions are placed the working party is set to fill up the coffre[2] as fast as possible by getting soil from any place where it can be most easily obtained. For this purpose, a certain portion of the party is employed in digging where the soil is loosest, and the rest are posted in chains extending thence to the battery to pass the baskets of earth as fast as they are filled. In this manner, the coffre is generally filled in less than two hours. The most expert of the engineering department are then employed in laying the embrasures and picketing the fascines. The battery is thus completed two or three hours before daybreak. The platforms are laid, and the battery is given up to the Artillery in time for them to run their guns in and open at daybreak."

By capturing Ahmadnagar, Wellesley prevented Sindhia from advancing on Poona and confined him to the alternative of raiding Hyderabad, which Stevenson manœuvred to frustrate. On August 29th, 1803, Sindhia being at Jafarabad, Wellesley decided that the time had come for a general action and marched to Aurangabad, but afterwards moved southwards to the Godavari to prevent Sindhia from crossing that river. Marching from Jafarabad, Stevenson stormed the fortress of Jalna[3] on September 2nd and with the co-operation of Wellesley, caused the Maratha army to retire northwards towards the Ajanta Pass. On the 21st, Wellesley made a plan with Stevenson for a combined attack from opposite directions, but this scheme failed because Stevenson was misled by his guides ; and when, on September 23rd, Wellesley came suddenly upon the Maratha army of 40,000 men encamped on a small peninsula formed by the junction of the rivers Kaitna and Jua, he had lost touch with Stevenson. Realizing, however, that delay would be fatal, he launched his 4,500 men to the glorious action of Assaye and carried the enemy's position, though at the cost of nearly 2,300 casualties. The story of that desperate battle is well known. Sindhia and Berar lost 115 guns and left 1,200 dead on the field when they fled to the north. The Madras Pioneers were in the thick of the fight ; their casualties amounted to 71 men, and Heitland had his horse shot under him. For this battle and others, the honour " Assaye " was granted to their descendants, the Q.V.O. Madras Sappers and Miners.[4]

[1] *Twelve Years' Military Adventure in Three Quarters of the Globe, or Memoirs of an Officer*, by Major J. Blakiston, M.E., Vol. I, pp. 134–36.

[2] *Coffre.* The space between and within gabions, which were wicker-work, cylindrical, bottomless baskets filled with earth.

[3] Jalna is about 35 miles east of Aurangabad.

[4] All units present at Assaye, except the Madras Pioneers, were granted, in addition, the badge known as the " Assaye Elephant." (See G.O.G.G., dated Oct. 30th, 1803, other official documents of 1811–12, and correspondence of 1923–25, included in Case 16, Historical Records, Q.V.O. Madras Sappers and Miners, Bangalore.)

No Bombay Pioneers, except Johnson acting as Chief Engineer, were present at the Battle of Assaye: but if two companies of that Corps were with Stevenson, who joined Wellesley on the day after the battle, they may have accompanied him in a short pursuit of the enemy towards the Ajanta Pass. Meanwhile, the Madras Pioneers under Heitland were engaged in burying the dead and collecting the trophies of victory. Blakiston records that they were so much impressed by the gay colours of several Maratha standards that they gave them to their wives to use as petticoats "from which ignoble purpose," he adds, "they were rescued to hang as memorials of British prowess in the church of Fort St. George and perhaps from the dome of St. Paul's."[1]

Streaming through the Ajanta Pass, the Marathas met reinforcements at Burhanpur, and proceeding westwards along the Tapti, turned southwards and again threatened to enter Hyderabad; so Wellesley, after moving to the Ajanta Pass on September 30th, returned towards Aurangabad and camped about 30 miles north of it. Then, by despatching Stevenson to capture the fortress of Asirgarh, he caused Sindhia and Berar to withdraw north-eastwards while he watched the passes into Hyderabad. Stevenson crossed the Tapti, entered Burhanpur on October 16th and advanced thence on Asirgarh. With him must have marched the Madras and Bombay Pioneers, for it is recorded that he was fully equipped for a siege.

Asirgarh fell to Stevenson on October 21st, 1803, and the last of Sindhia's possessions in the Deccan having then been wrested from him, Wellesley resolved to deal with the Raja of Berar. On November 11th, Sindhia sued for peace and a truce was granted, but he soon broke his word and consequently hostilities were resumed. The result was a decisive victory for the British on November 29th against the combined forces of Sindhia and Berar at the Battle of Argaon,[2] where the Maratha forces, totalling 30,000 men, were routed with the loss of 38 guns and quantities of ammunition and stores. A detachment of the 2nd Battalion, Madras Pioneers, in addition to the 1st Battalion under Heitland, was present at this action,[3] and possibly also a detachment of Bombay Pioneers.

After his victory at Argaon, Wellesley moved eastwards to lay siege to Gawilgarh, and on December 6th was within striking distance of it. This fortress was situated on a lofty peak in a range of mountains and was divided into two parts by a deep gorge. Three lines of approach were available, but two of these could not be made suitable for the passage of guns and wheeled transport. The third road wound for nearly 30 miles through mountains and jungles before debouching on high ground to the rear or north of the fortress. However, as a result of a reconnaissance by Captain John Johnson, Bo.E., and Ensign J. Blakiston, M.E., Wellesley decided that this was the best line of approach for the main body of the attacking troops, and accordingly despatched Stevenson along it on

[1] *Twelve Years' Military Adventure in Three Quarters of the Globe, or Memoirs of an Officer*, by Major J. Blakiston, M.E., Vol. I, p. 175.

[2] 50 miles south-east of Burhanpur.

[3] *The Military History of the Madras Engineers and Pioneers*, by Major H. M. Vibart, R. (M.) E., Vol. I, p. 381.

December 7th with a strong force, including all the Pioneers and a siege train, while he himself advanced directly on the fortress. The Madras and Bombay Pioneers laboured for four days to make the road practicable for guns. " The exertions of the army," writes Blakiston,[1] " in cutting a road through the mountains were such as to call forth the warmest applause of the General. The Pioneers, as usual, performed their task in the most efficient manner. But the conduct of Captain Johnson of the Engineers was the theme of admiration from the General downwards. Indeed I think he was, without exception, the best officer I ever served with. To great natural and acquired talents he joined a zeal and an ardour in his professional duties which I never saw equalled. Having no one to assist him in the duties of an engineer, he was compelled to live constantly in the trenches during the siege ; but a strong constitution enabled him to get over it without injury. I was not quite so fortunate ; from having been nearly a fortnight without ever going to bed, and most of that time without entering a tent, while the thermometer was upwards of 100 degrees in the shade during the day and down as low as freezing point at night, I was seized, as soon as the siege was over, with a dysentery."

After darkness had fallen on December 12th, Stevenson erected two siege batteries facing the rear of Gawilgarh, while Wellesley constructed another to breach the front. This was a most arduous task, for the twelve-pounder guns had to be hauled up steep slopes by tackle fastened to trees. A heavy fire was opened on the 13th and, on December 15th, Stevenson assaulted and captured the rear or outer fort in which he was joined by Wellesley. Together, they crossed the deep gorge, rushed the main defences, and Gawilgarh was in their hands. The victorious troops hoped to find immense treasure, but in this they were disappointed for all valuables had been removed. The Europeans got out of hand and, not content with the great slaughter of the recent fighting, began to shoot down their prisoners and even to threaten their officers. It is said that, out of a garrison of 8,000 Marathas and Rajputs, none escaped except those who threw themselves from the lofty bastions. After all firing had ceased, Blakiston witnessed a scene which made his blood run cold. Hearing groans in one of the larger houses, he entered and found a room full of young and beautiful native women, many dying but most of them already dead. They had been cut to pieces by their husbands and fathers before the latter sallied forth to sell their lives as dearly as they could. Order having been restored in the fortress, Wellesley marched away to subdue Berar, while Stevenson remained at Gawilgarh for a time to keep Sindhia in check and then evacuated the fortress. A veritable mausoleum, it fell slowly to ruin, and its last remains were dismantled in 1858.

While Wellesley and Stevenson were operating in the Deccan, subsidiary campaigns had been in progress in neighbouring territories. On October 14th, 1803, in Orissa near the Bay of Bengal, Lieut.-Colonel G. W. R. Harcourt had carried the fortress of Barabati, close to Cuttack. The

[1]*Twelve Years' Military Adventure in Three Quarters of the Globe, or Memoirs of an Officer*, by Major J. Blakiston, M.E., Vol. I, p. 232.

GAWILGARH.

Field Engineer with this force was Lieutenant J. T. Blunt of the Bengal Engineers, under whose direction was a detachment of Madras Pioneers commanded by Lieutenant George Shepherd, M.I.[1] Harcourt wrote that the Pioneers had contributed greatly to his success. "Without them," he remarked on October 22nd,[2] "I do not think it would have been practicable for me to have brought up the 12-pounders and my heavy stores, and I still have much need of their services to bring up the remainder of the heavy guns and to accompany the detachments it will be necessary to send out to settle the country completely. I intend to employ the Pioneers in opening direct communication on the only practicable road from Nagpur."

Another minor campaign was fought in Gujarat near the western coast where Broach was stormed and captured by Colonel Murray on August 29th, 1803, in the course of operations designed to protect the loyal Gaikwar of Baroda from the vengeance of Sindhia. The Field Engineer was Captain John Cliffe, Bo.E., and it is possible that some Bombay Pioneers were present because Lieutenant David Prother, Bo.I., had been appointed Commandant of Pioneers in Gujarat in the spring of 1802 with a force which stormed the fortress of Kaira.[3] The capture of Broach completed the occupation of Sindhia's possessions in the west; but it did not conclude the work of the Bombay Pioneers in that region, for one company went on field service to Gujarat on April 27th, 1805, and remained at Baroda until February 8th, 1806, after the Second Maratha War had ended. This company was one of two which had returned to Bombay from Malabar during the winter of 1804–5, the other company proceeding to Poona in March, 1805, to join the Poona Subsidiary Force, a permanent garrison sanctioned under the Treaty of Bassein.[4] On December 1st, 1806, three companies of the Bombay Pioneer Corps proceeded from Bombay to Salsette for road work. In March, 1807, Lieutenant Peter De La Motte, Bo.I., succeeded Captain Monier Williams as Commandant of the Bombay Pioneers, and in the following July orders were issued that the Corps should be reduced to one company with the Poona Subsidiary Force and that another, serving in Gujarat under Major Alexander Walker, Bo.I., should be abolished when no longer needed there.[5] Accordingly, in August, 1807, two companies still employed in Salsette, and a detachment at Surat, were disbanded.[6] Thus, within a few years of the termination of the Second Maratha War, the Bombay Pioneer Corps was reduced to a single permanent company which, in May, 1809, was

[1]Lieut. G. Shepherd (or Sheppard) did not belong to the Madras Engineers as shown in the *Historical Record of the Q.V.O. Madras Sappers and Miners*, p. 18. He was an officer of the Madras Native Infantry, serving in the Madras European Regiment. (See *The Military History of the Madras Engineers and Pioneers*, by Major H. M. Vibart, R. (M.) E., Vol. I, p. 391.)

[2]*The Military History of the Madras Engineers and Pioneers*, by Major H. M. Vibart, R. (M.) E., Vol. I, p. 391.

[3]*East India Military Calendar*, Vol. I, p. 304. Kaira is 25 miles south of Ahmadabad.

[4]*A Brief History of the Royal Bombay Sappers and Miners*, p. 3. Under Bombay General Order, March 8th, 1805, the movement was ordered to take place a few days later. No British officer was to remain in command of these Pioneers at Poona, who were to work under the orders of the O.C. Subsidiary Force.

[5]Bombay General Order, July 25th, 1807.

[6]Bombay General Orders, Aug. 5th and 21st, 1807.

stationed under Captain De La Motte with the Subsidiary Force at Poona.[1]

Reverting to the final events of the Second Maratha War, it is sufficient to record that the loss of Cuttack and the fall of Gawilgarh decided the Bhonsla Raja of Berar to sue for peace, and that on December 17th, 1803, he concluded with the Company the Treaty of Deogaon under which he ceded much territory. Sindhia followed suit on December 29th, when he signed the Treaty of Surji Arjangaon and relinquished all territory between the Ganges and Jumna and south of the Ajanta Hills, though he was allowed to reoccupy Asirgarh, Burhanpur and some tracts in Gujarat and elsewhere. Wellesley marched in triumph to Poona, and there we will leave him to follow the course of events in Hindustan, the northern territory where Lieut.-General Gerard Lake had been carrying all before him, aided in every venture by the newly formed Corps of Bengal Pioneers.

There is evidence that in Bengal and Oudh, as in Central and Southern India, temporary companies of Pioneers were formed for special service before a regular establishment was authorized. For instance, in November, 1764, after Major Hector Munro had routed the Mughal army at Buxar, a company of Pioneers marched from Benares with a force detailed for the reduction of Chunar.[2] At this time, each regiment of Bengal Infantry had a few artificers and pioneers on its establishment; but in September, 1776, four companies of artificers were raised, officered from the Bengal Engineers and added to the Bengal Army.[3] These artificer units, however, were non-combatant, and being quartered in the forts guarding the Company's settlements in Bengal, they were not readily available for field service.[4] The unsettled condition of the country at the end of the 18th Century demanded a better provision of engineering labour. The Mughal Empire had fallen to ruin, torn to shreds by the Marathas, who still held Delhi, though driven from the Punjab. Each petty Raja had his fort and maintained a rabble of Arab soldiery to prey on his weaker neighbours. In the Punjab lived the warlike Sikhs under Ranjit Singh: in the Himalayas, the Gurkhas, eager to raid the fertile plains. The Bengal Army could no longer sit behind its fortifications, guarding what it had won. It had to take the field and to be prepared to lay siege to many fortresses. Thus, in 1803, when Sindhia and Berar were about to throw down the gauntlet, the Bengal Pioneer was born in Northern India just as the Madras and Bombay Pioneers had come into existence in Southern and Western India to meet earlier emergencies.

On July 28th, 1803, a General Order was issued in Calcutta for the raising of a Corps of Bengal Pioneers at Cawnpore to consist of 3 companies, each of 75 men. Lieutenant Thomas Wood, B.E.,[5] was directed

[1] *East India Military Calendar*, Vol. II, p. 401.

[2] *The Services of the Bengal Native Army*, by Lieut. F. G. Cardew, p. 27. Chunar is 20 miles south-west of Benares.

[3] *History and Digest of Service of the 1st K.G.O. Sappers and Miners*, p. 4.

[4] Two Artificer Companies were serving in the Hugli Forts in 1800.

[5] The entry in the Indian Army List under the head of "King George V's Own Bengal Sappers and Miners" shows Thomas Wood as a Captain. This is incorrect. Lieut. Thomas Wood was promoted Captain on April 15th, 1806. It is possible, however, that he may have been given local rank as Captain in 1803.

to recruit the necessary personnel, a task in which he was highly successful although he had had more experience in topographical surveying than military duty, resembling in this respect his elder brother, Colonel Sir Mark Wood, Bart., late B.E.,[1] who had become Surveyor-General in 1787 and resigned in 1793. Thomas Wood was commissioned in 1785 and died in Calcutta as a Colonel in 1834, but during that long period he saw no active service of any importance except in the Second Maratha War. His connection with the Bengal Pioneers was brief, for it had been stipulated that the Corps should be officered from the Bengal Infantry, and accordingly he handed over charge as soon as possible to Lieutenant John Swinton, B.I., a man whose amazing courage and fine leadership had already brought him into prominence.

John Swinton had been commissioned in 1799 and had joined the 12th Bengal Native Infantry in 1801 after serving for one year in the 11th.[2] Early in 1803, he served as an Assistant Engineer under Thomas Wood in the "Mud War," so called because certain mud forts in the Doab[3]—Sasni, Bijagarh and Kachaura—were besieged and captured. At Sasni, in January, Swinton built the siege batteries and was wounded in the foot during preparations for the assault. At Bijagarh, he led a party of only 12 Europeans in storming an outwork and narrowly escaped destruction when the enemy blew up a magazine. After the surrender of Kachaura, he captured an outlying fort when reconnoitring with only 21 native soldiers. It was natural that Wood should recommend his daring assistant for the post of Commandant of the Pioneers, and so we find John Swinton in charge of the new Corps during the campaign under General Lake. At Laswari, Gwalior, Delhi, Dig, Bhurtpore, Komona (where he was again wounded) and Ganouri he maintained his reputation in the field. In the Nepal War of 1814–16 and the siege of Hathras, he continued a brilliant career, lame, battle-scarred but still indomitable. On January 13th, 1825, he was invalided with the rank of Lieut.-Colonel and died in the following September. So passed John Swinton, the father of the Bengal Sappers and Miners.

Lieut.-General Gerard Lake, with a "Grand Army" of 10,000 men, set out from Cawnpore on August 7th, 1803, to take Aligarh, where Sindhia's forces under M. Perron were then concentrated. With him marched the three small companies of Bengal Pioneers under Swinton, with Thomas Wood as senior Engineer. The fort at Aligarh had inner and outer lines of defences, and the whole was surrounded by an immense wet ditch. Consequently, as Lake had no bridging equipment, he decided to assault where a causeway crossed the ditch to the gateway of an island outwork, and on September 3rd, the Pioneers erected two batteries to breach the walls near the gate. At dawn on the 4th, the stormers rushed across under heavy fire, and after the gate had been demolished by a 12-pounder shot, charged along a road to a second gate, which they carried easily. The

[1] *The Military Engineer in India*, by the present author, Vol. II, pp. 188, 195.
[2] The career of Lieut.-Col. John Swinton, B.I., is described in the *East India Military Calendar*, Vol. III, pp. 415–18. In 1804 he was transferred to the 21st B.N.I.
[3] *Doab.* (Lit. "Two Rivers.") The fertile territory between the Ganges and the Jumna.

island work defending the main entrance being now in their hands they had next to gain the fortress itself. Dashing across another causeway, they seized a third gateway, and then, turning left, charged for some distance until they found themselves opposite the final gateway leading to the interior. There they were obliged to halt under a withering fire until some hero managed to force an entrance through a small wicket gate, and followed by others, opened the main gate to the assaulting troops. The defenders jumped by hundreds into the ditch; some escaped, but more than 2,000 were slain. And who was the hero of the wicket gate who won Aligarh for the British? According to Sir John Philippart, he was John Swinton.[1] With Swinton was Lieutenant William Forrest, B.I.,[2] who served under him in many battles and sieges. The only Engineer officer present was a young subaltern of the Bengal Corps, Lieutenant H. W. Carmichael-Smyth. Truly, an extraordinary state of affairs, for any failure in the engineering arrangements might have jeopardized success.

Having taken Aligarh, Lake marched for Delhi where another Frenchman, Louis Bourquin, had replaced Perron in command of Sindhia's army, and on September 11th, 1803, finding Bourquin with 19,000 soldiers and 100 guns in a position near the city, he lured him from his trenches by a clever stratagem and routed him with only 4,500 men. Bourquin lost 3,000 men and 86 guns in the Battle of Delhi, and he and other Frenchmen surrendered. Lake entered the Mughal capital on September 16th, but left it a few days later for Muttra, where he arrived on October 9th and made a treaty with the Raja of Bhurtpore. Marching thence for Agra, he took that place on October 14th. These operations resulted in the dispersal of all Sindhia's forces in the field except a remnant under a French adventurer, Dudrenec, which Lake annihilated on November 1st, 1803, at Laswari, about 80 miles south of Delhi. With the exception of Holkar, all the Maratha leaders had then been subdued. The Bengal Pioneers, under Swinton assisted by Forrest, took a creditable part in the movements and battles of this campaign and gathered experience which was valuable in the last phases of the Second Maratha War.

Jaswant Rao Holkar, noting that the British had left him severely alone while they dealt with his neighbour, Sindhia, conceived the idea that they were afraid of him. He took up a position near Ajmer and tried to induce Sindhia to join him, becoming at length so truculent that Lake, who was near Jaipur, was ordered to drive him southwards while Sindhia and the Gaikwar attacked him from Gujarat, Malwa and the Deccan. The campaign began well. Lake forced Holkar to retire to Kotah and captured Rampura on May 15th, 1804; but afterwards he withdrew to Agra and Cawnpore, leaving detachments under Colonels Don and

[1]*East India Military Calendar*, Vol. III, p. 416. The Hon. J. W. Fortescue in *A History of the British Army*, Vol. V, p. 51. gives the honour to Major McLeod, H.M.'s 76th Regt.

[2]William Forrest joined the 2nd Bengal Native Infantry as an Ensign in 1799. He was promoted Lieut. in the same year, Capt. in 1808, Major in 1823 and Lieut.-Col. in 1824. He was posted to the Bengal Pioneers before the siege of Aligarh after serving as an Assistant Engineer in the sieges of Sasni, Bijagarh and Kachaura in company with Swinton and under the command of Lieut. Thomas Wood, B.E. (See *East India Military Calendar*, Vol. III, pp. 29–31.)

Monson to hold the passes from Hindustan into Malwa. Monson, however, was not content with passive defence, and when he found that Holkar had retreated almost to Ujjain, he followed to Kotah. Advancing still further, he was soon in a dangerous situation and only saved himself by retiring to Agra, harassed by the enemy and losing all his guns, ammunition and baggage.[1]

This unfortunate affair lowered British prestige and allowed Holkar to return to Hindustan to sow the seeds of dissension. The Raja of Bhurtpore prepared to break his treaty and join him. Sindhia began to waver. However, Lake took early and effective action to retrieve his strategic error of losing contact with the enemy, and marching again from Cawnpore on September 3rd, advanced towards Muttra on October 1st to deal with Holkar's cavalry and then onwards to Delhi to relieve the garrison under Major-General J. H. Fraser which was besieged by Holkar's infantry and artillery. On Lake's approach, the Marathas decamped from Delhi towards Dig, 30 miles west of Muttra. Holkar himself crossed the Jumna with his cavalry to raid the Doab, so Lake went after him with his mounted troops and surprised and defeated him at Farrukabad on November 17th. Meanwhile, Fraser had marched for Dig with the remainder of Lake's army, including the Pioneers,[2] and had defeated the enemy in a battle outside that place. On December 13th, he was joined by Lake, who then made preparations for a siege.

The town of Dig, belonging to the Raja of Bhurtpore, was surrounded by a large mud wall and a ditch, the defences running up to a rocky peak at the south-west corner called the Shah Burj, in front of which was a fortified castle. Within lay a square citadel with rounded bastions and a deep ditch. A small redoubt and a dozen batteries blocked the only line of approach, which ran between a lake and a swamp. Several days of heavy fighting ensued before Lake was close enough to breach the defences of the Shah Burj, but he captured that peak and the castle on December 23rd, though not without desperate street-fighting. By Christmas morning, Dig was in his hands and it seemed that the campaign in Hindustan had ended in victory as had the war in the Deccan. Lake was jubilant, and in a despatch dated December 26th, paid a tribute to Swinton and the Bengal Pioneers. "My Lord," it ran, "my despatches of the 24th and 25th instants will have informed your Lordship of the complete success of our operations against the town and fort of Deeg. The Corps of Pioneers, under the orders of Captain Swinton, command my warmest praise for the cheerfulness with which they performed their laborious duties and particularly for the alacrity they displayed on the night of the 22nd instant. Too much praise cannot be bestowed on Captain Swinton, who, on this and every former occasion, has been most zealous and active. I am sorry to add that this excellent officer is severely wounded, as is Lieutenant

[1]The retreat was perpetuated by a native doggerel :—" *Ghore par Hauda! Hathi par Zin! Dauro! Dauro! General Monseen.*" (Literally : " On the horse, the howdah! On the elephant, the saddle! Run! Run! General Monson:")

[2]See correspondence entitled *Recovery of Battle Honours, Deig*, 1803, at the headquarters of the K.G.V's O. Bengal Sappers and Miners at Roorkee.

Forrest of the same Corps, whose conduct was equally meritorious." Swinton had been hit in the thigh by a cannon ball and lamed for life, and Forrest had received no less than 23 wounds and had lost an arm; but they and their men had the satisfaction of knowing that their efforts were appreciated, and that, by their work in constructing batteries and digging trenches at Dig and carrying ladders in the assault, they had contributed towards the success of the operations.

Determined to punish the Raja of Bhurtpore for harbouring Holkar's army at Dig, Lake now marched for Bhurtpore, where he arrived on January 2nd, 1805. This city was some 8 miles in circumference and enclosed by a mud wall of great height and thickness with round bastions mounting scores of guns. Around it was a wide ditch, full of water. A citadel, with still more formidable defences and a larger ditch, lay towards the north-eastern end, and surrounding the whole, a belt of jungle and swamp.[1] Lake erected his batteries and opened fire, not realizing apparently that his small guns would be useless against the mud bastions and ignoring the fact that he had no means of crossing the flooded ditch. His attempt was pure bluff, and the bluff was called. On January 9th, he advanced against the south-west angle, where no practicable breach had been made. Most of the troops were unable even to cross the ditch, and after making many attempts and suffering severely, they withdrew to their trenches. On the 16th, when a breach had been made further south, the stormers found that they could not ascend it because the defenders had stockaded the crumbling debris. Then Lake called on his engineers, who contrived a frail bridge of bamboos and inflated skins for the passage of infantry in single file, and on January 21st, a gallant band of eleven British volunteers under Sergeant John Shipp tried to cross the ditch under heavy fire. The attempt failed for the bridge was too short. The troops, tired and half-starved, began to lose heart. Reinforced by a Bombay division, Lake resorted to deliberate methods, sapping to the ditch, making a new breach and placing supporting and enfilading batteries. On February 20th, he assaulted again in three columns. Now, however, he could not induce his soldiers to press home the attack. Finally, on February 21st, John Shipp led a forlorn hope against the fortress; but the men were hurled down again and again in vain efforts to scale the crumbling walls. Then Lake abandoned hope, for he had suffered more than 3,000 casualties in a few weeks, and drawing off 6 miles to the north-east, devoted himself for a time to minor operations against Holkar. Bhurtpore stood majestic, battered, but inviolate.

A scapegoat had to be found, and it was discovered, by adroit manœuvre, in the Corps of Engineers. No one knows the identity of the Commanding Engineer. He was not Lieut.-Colonel George Prole, B.I., who acted occasionally as an Engineer, nor Captain John Johnson, Bo.E., nor Capt.-Lieutenant William Cowper, Bo.E. These were employed elsewhere. Possibly he was Capt.-Lieutenant Thomas Robertson, or one of four

[1]A plan of Bhurtpore in 1826 is included in Chapter IV. In 1805, the defences were less elaborate.

Lieutenants, Thomas Wood, Henry Carmichael-Smyth, Richard Tickell and Robert Smith, all of the Bengal Engineers and all serving against the Marathas in 1805. Neither is it known who commanded the Bengal Pioneers, for Swinton did not rejoin until after the siege and Forrest was in hospital. The Pioneers were worked almost to death in their customary occupations of sapping, constructing batteries and preparing materials for siege operations; but they were sheep without a shepherd and had no chance to distinguish themselves. " As we had no regular Corps of Sappers and Miners in those days," wrote Lake in July, 1805, " it is hardly fair to assume the apparent want of skill of our Engineers as showing them deficient in scientific and professional knowledge." Perhaps, in that phrase, he touched upon the chief cause of the failure at Bhurtpore—the lack of trained engineer soldiers under trained engineer officers—though he himself was primarily to blame for attacking with an inadequate force, deficient in artillery, experienced engineers and siege equipment, and without proper reconnaissance and a well conceived plan of operation.

After the echoes of Bhurtpore had died away, Lake followed Holkar to the Punjab, where the Marathas hoped to join hands with the Sikhs. In December, 1805, Holkar was at Amritsar and Lake on the River Beas. The Bengal Pioneers, under Swinton, were with the army under Lake. Holkar concluded a treaty which restored to him the whole of his lost dominions, and Lake marched back to Oudh—a sorry end to a war which began in a blaze of splendour and glorious achievement. The Bengal Pioneers reached Muttra in February, 1806, and there for a moment we will leave them to outline some minor operations in which the Madras Pioneers had been concerned.

While Lake was fighting Holkar, two companies of Madras Pioneers had assisted in the reduction of a couple of hill forts lying about 80 miles north-west of Aurangabad. They marched from Poona in August, 1804, with a force under Lieut.-Colonel Wallace, and on October 8th were close to Chandor.[1] This fort was perched on the precipitous summit of a mountain 1,600 ft. high to which the only approach was by a narrow path winding upwards through a series of fortified gateways. At the base lay the usual walled town or *pettah*. If strongly held, the place might have been impregnable; but on October 10th, Wallace surprised the Arab garrison in the *pettah*, and as the enemy forgot to carry any provisions with them when they fled up to the fort, they decided to surrender forthwith. The Field Engineer at the capture of Chandor was Captain John Johnson, Bo.E. Later, on October 21st, Wallace was facing the hill fort of Galna. This stronghold was less formidable than Chandor and gave no trouble, for the garrison surrendered on the 26th after the walls had been breached by artillery fire. The Madras Pioneers were employed chiefly in clearing tracks for the movement of siege guns. Some operations under Colonel Doveton in February, 1805, in Khandesh and Berar gave experience to a detachment of the Corps which had joined the Poona Subsidiary

[1]*The Military History of the Madras Engineers and Pioneers*, by Major H. M. Vibart, R. (M.) E., Vol. I, p. 394.

Force, but they call for no particular remark. The part played by the Madras Pioneers in the later stages of the Second Maratha War was a minor one; the Corps had already fought at Ahmadnagar, Assaye, Argaon and Gawilgarh and was needed for work in Southern India. After the war had ended, two companies under Lieutenant F. Bowes, M.I., served in Central India with a force which occupied Sironj, north of Bhopal, in March, 1810, during operations against Pathan marauders, and one company remained in that neighbourhood until the end of 1810 with a brigade detailed to guard the Berar frontier.

The Bengal Pioneers acquired a reputation during the struggle against Sindhia, Holkar and Bhurtpore sufficient to justify a substantial increase in their establishment, and in consequence, the strength of the Corps was raised in 1808 from 3 companies of 75 men to 8 companies of 90 men, each with two British sergeants and a few miners. The Corps was placed on the same footing as the Infantry and designated the "Corps of Pioneers or Sappers."[1] A company of Miners was recruited for field service, particularly in sieges, and was placed under the command of an officer of the Bengal Engineers,[2] but the Pioneer companies were still officered from the Infantry. The Bengal Pioneer of 1809 wore a green tunic, with facings of the same colour, adorned with yellow lace and black buttons. On his head was a tall black hat, built up on a bamboo framework to resemble the headgear of the British soldier, and on his legs, the loose white trousers which had been authorized in 1808 in substitution for short white drawers. The private was shod with *chapplies* (sandals) and the Indian officer wore high boots. The accoutrements were of black leather.

In 1809, the Madras Pioneers were by far the largest of the three Pioneer Corps in India, having no less than 16 companies. The Bengal Corps had 9 companies including the Miner Company, but the Bombay Corps only one permanent company. As the arena of warfare had shifted from Southern to Central and Northern India this would appear to be a bad distribution of strength; but it should be remembered that the Madras Pioneers were peculiarly adapted by training, temperament and religion for service overseas and consequently their maintenance on a high establishment was justified. It is difficult to explain the stringent reduction in the establishment of the Bombay Pioneers except on the ground of economy. The need for a large establishment of Bengal Pioneers was evident: the general turbulence of the northern peoples, and the attitude of the Sikhs and Gurkhas in particular, demanded no less. The Bengal Corps, however, should have been commanded by Engineer officers, as the Bombay Corps had been for many years; but unhappily, Engineers were scarce. Swinton was an exceptional man and no general inference can be drawn from his success, nor from that of Heitland. Within the next twenty-five years, the principle was recognized throughout India that the only proper leader and instructor of the engineer soldier is the engineer officer.

[1] *The Services of the Bengal Native Army*, by Lieut. F. G. Cardew, p. 114.
[2] *History and Digest of Service, K.G.O. Bengal Sappers and Miners*, p. 3.

CHAPTER III

THE NEPAL AND THIRD MARATHA WARS, 1814–1819

APART from expeditions overseas, the Company's armies in India saw little field service between the end of the Second Maratha War in 1806 and the outbreak of hostilities against the Gurkhas in 1814. Lord Minto, as Governor-General, was opposed to any policy of territorial annexation or intervention in the internal affairs of native states; but after he had been relieved from the anxieties engendered by Napoleon's dreams of conquest in Asia, he despatched successful expeditions against the insular possessions of the French and Dutch in the course of which his military subordinates gathered valuable experience. However, the cessation of action in India itself had the unfortunate result of encouraging certain nations to adopt a more defiant attitude; and thus it fell to Lord Moira,[1] who succeeded Lord Minto in October, 1813, to complete the fabric of British dominion by undertaking campaigns to which by nature he was opposed, and to carry them through in the face of many difficulties and disappointments.

When Lord Minto assumed office in 1807, British suzerainty extended effectively over six of the leading native states—Mysore, Travancore, the Maratha principalities of Baroda and Poona, Hyderabad, and in the north, Oudh; but in Central India the Marathas of Gwalior, Indore and Nagpur were resentful and suspicious and looked eagerly for a chance to avenge their recent defeats. Westward lay the Rajput states, weak, disunited and an easy prey to the freebooters who swarmed into them for plunder or for service as mercenaries. These marauding bands increased and multiplied, the principal being known as "Pindaris." One of the Pindari leaders, Amir Khan by name, gathered an army of 30,000 men in Rajputana; another, Chitu, raided the country at the head of 10,000 horse; all used torture to compel the inhabitants to reveal hidden treasure and left behind them a trail of wanton destruction and outrage. The great Maratha chiefs would not interfere with them because of their possible value as future allies against the British, a concession which the marauders acknowledged by sparing the Maratha districts.

In the Punjab, Ranjit Singh, bent on extending his conquests south of the Sutlej, advanced to Ambala in 1808 at the head of an army of Sikhs; and though he retired in the following year and undertook to abstain from such encroachments in future, he continued to drill and arm his men on the British model. The Pindaris, with Maratha support, and the Sikhs under Ranjit Singh, were dangerous neighbours; but there was a third power which threatened war in the north. The spirit of conquest was strong in the Gurkhas, who treated the British Government with contempt

[1]Afterwards the Marquis of Hastings.

and refused to give up any of the territory which they had won while extending their kingdom of Nepal westwards along the Himalayas to the Sutlej. In the region of Calcutta, the Burmese appeared near Chittagong and boasted that they would invade Assam. Such was the precarious situation which called forth renewed military efforts on the part of the Company.

While the Bengal and Bombay Pioneers prepared to take the field in Northern and Central India, the Madras Pioneers found ample occupation not only in Southern India but in Réunion, Mauritius, and Java. Their establishment was revised in October, 1810, so that each of the two battalions had 7 British officers, 8 Indian officers and 748 Indian other ranks.[1] "Recruit Boys" and "Pension Boys" made their first appearance in 1813, when thirty of each class were enlisted for each battalion.[2] In the same year, the establishment of British officers was again under revision and was fixed at 2 Captains and 6 Subalterns for each battalion, together with an Assistant-Surgeon.[3] An Adjutant, for each battalion, was added in December, 1814. Many officers of the Madras Infantry found congenial employment in the Corps, which afforded excellent opportunities for active service.[4] A detachment was in the field in the Southern Maratha Country from August, 1812, to May, 1814, with a force which assembled at Bellary under the command of Lieut.-Colonel William Dowse, M.I., whose exploits as a leader of the Madras Pioneers in the Mysore Wars have been recorded in these pages. This was the last service of an honourable career, for Dowse died in Bangalore on June 27th. Early in 1815, two companies of Madras Pioneers were employed with the Hyderabad Subsidiary Force; and towards the end of that year a detachment served in the Kurnool District, near the Hyderabad border, and was present when the fort of Gooty, 70 miles east of Bellary, was occupied on December 15th.

Meanwhile, important changes had taken place in the Bombay Pioneers, for on July 12th, 1812, the Governor-in-Council had announced that he had decided to increase the establishment of that Corps to four companies, including the one attached to the Poona Subsidiary Force.[5] Each company was to comprise 2 British officers, 2 Indian officers, 2 Sergeants and 99 Indian other ranks,[6] and the Corps was to be commanded by a Captain-Commandant with an Assistant-Surgeon in medical charge.

[1]Under G.O.G., Oct. 12th, 1810, the establishment was authorized as 3 Captains, 4 Subalterns, 8 Jemadars, 24 Havildars, 24 Naiks and 700 Privates, in addition to an Assistant-Surgeon, a Sergt.-Major, several Sergeants and 9 Pakhalis. The establishment of Privates had been fixed at 700 in June, 1809. (See *Historical Record of the Q.V.O. Madras Sappers and Miners*, Vol. I, pp. 21, 23.)

[2]G.O.G., Feb. 23rd, 1813. The Recruit Boys were the sons or near relatives of old soldiers and could be enlisted at the minimum age of 11 years. The Pension Boys were admissible at any age and were mostly the sons of deceased native officers or soldiers.

[3]G.O.G., Nov. 3rd, 1813.

[4]The names of Capts. R. Hughes, E. W. Snow and A. N. Bertram and Lieuts. E. Richardson, T. G. Prendergast, G. M. Steward, A. Stewart, H. Massey, C. Wilson and F. W. Morgan are mentioned in *The Military History of the Madras Engineers and Pioneers*, by Major H. M. Vibart, R. (M.) E., Vol. I, p. 486.

[5]B.G.O., July 12th, 1812.

[6]1 Captain, 1 Subaltern, 1 Subadar, 1 Jemadar, 2 Sergeants, 4 Havildars, 4 Naiks, 90 Privates and 1 Bugler.

This General Order was followed by another, dated July 17th, giving the views of the Commander-in-Chief in Bombay on the future status and conditions of service of the Pioneers.[1] "The Corps," wrote the Governor-in-Council, "will be raised to the same Honourable Level with the other Corps of the Hon. Company's regular army. The same consideration which attaches in every situation to the character of soldiers in the Service will attach to the Pioneers, and they will be allowed the same pay, clothing, tents and medical assistance as received by the corresponding ranks in the Native Infantry, so they will be entitled under the existing regulations of the Service to the benefits of the Pension establishment on being disabled by wounds, or on being worn out by length of service, as a reward for their courage and fidelity. While these advantages are held out to the Pioneer Corps, the Commander-in-Chief considers it proper and necessary that they should be at the same time fully apprised of the duties expected from them both in peace and war, and desires that these duties be explained to them. In time of peace, they will be employed in making, clearing and repairing roads, in the construction and repair of fortifications, in the demolition of dismantled forts and other works, and in giving assistance in magazines. In time of war, they will be employed as Pioneers in making, clearing and repairing roads for the Troops, Artillery and Baggage of the Army, and, as they will also be employed at sieges, in carrying on the approaches, making the Places of Arms, Parallels, etc.; while it will be a further essential part of their duty to cut down materials and prepare from them Fascines, Gabions, Pickets, etc. The Commander-in-Chief desires it may be at the same time explained to the men that no degrading work, or work unusual for Pioneers to perform, will at any time be exacted from them. The existing rules for recruiting Native Corps of the Line, in Height and Age, are applicable to Recruits to be entertained in the Pioneers, and the greatest care must be taken that no men are admitted into the Corps but such as from age, strength and activity are capable of undergoing its most laborious duties. Age, 22 years. Height, 5 feet 3 inches. All recruits enlisted at the Presidency are to be approved of by the Adjutant-General on the regular approving days."

Captain Peter De La Motte, Bo.I., Commandant since March, 1807, was retained in command of the Bombay Pioneers and raised Nos. 2 and 3 Companies, the ancestors of the 19th and 20th (Field) Companies of the Royal Bombay Sappers and Miners.[2] No. 1 Company remained in the Deccan with the Poona Subsidiary Force, and it is probable that No. 4 Company was formed from the men of the temporary unit which had served in Gujarat in 1807 and was under orders for reduction when no longer needed there. After 1812, the Bombay Pioneers were officered entirely from the Infantry, the last Bombay Engineer to serve in the Corps being Lieutenant Robert Gordon, who left it in that year. Among the Infantry officers who served with the Pioneers were Lieutenants R. Pottinger, T. D. Morris and M. L. Gallway; and in 1815–16, Lieutenant

[1] B.G.O., July 17th, 1812.
[2] *A Brief History of the Royal Bombay Sappers and Miners*, p. 4.

J. D. Crozier commanded a company in minor operations under Lieut.-Colonel East in Kathiawar and Baroda. For the most part, the work of the Pioneers was laborious and uninspiring. " The Pioneers at the Presidency to clean certain wells at Colaba " runs a typical Bombay Order of May 24th, 1815. They were considered apparently as the " general utility " men of the garrison, and in the estimation of the Government, were little superior to the Pioneer Lascars of the previous century.

We turn now to the Bengal Army in which 8 companies of a " Corps of Pioneers or Sappers," under Captain John Swinton, B.I., had been created in 1808 from a nucleus of 3 companies of Pioneers raised at Cawnpore in 1803. This expansion was well justified, for the Bengal Pioneers had proved their value in the Second Maratha War and the abortive siege of Bhurtpore, and also in the reduction of the fortresses of Komona and Ganouri after a local rebellion in the Delhi region in 1807.[1] Another formation, the " Company of Miners " raised at Cawnpore in 1808 for deliberate siege operations, occupied a peculiar position in the Bengal Army, for although it was commanded on service by Engineer officers, it had no official connection with either the Corps of Engineers nor the Corps of Pioneers or Sappers; it was merely an adjunct of the Artillery[2] and worked in co-operation with the siege train. The Company of Miners did not take the field in the Nepal War of 1814–16 because there was no prospect of mining, but it shared in operations near Rewah[3] in Central India in 1813–14. A detachment of the Corps of Pioneers or Sappers took part in February, 1812, in the reduction of the fortress of Kalinjar[4] (where Lieutenant R. C. Faithful of the Pioneers was wounded when the first assault was repulsed) and part of the Corps served at Rewah.[5] These minor operations afforded little training for hill warfare, but they accustomed the troops to fire. The bitter experiences of the Nepal War, the siege-work at Hathras, and the incessant marching and fighting of the Third Maratha War, completed the education of the Bengal Pioneers.

The kingdom of Nepal extended from the frontier of Bhutan to the River Sutlej and bordered for 700 miles on British territory or that of friendly states. Little was known of it or its chief inhabitants, the Gurkhas. The latter were said to be hardy and brave, though badly armed. They could muster some 16,000 soldiers with a few antiquated guns, and every man carried his own supplies. They relied chiefly on shock tactics with the *kukri*, a heavy, curved knife. Their country was precipitous, densely wooded and without roads. Against these mountaineers, Lord Hastings[6] put into the field on November 1st, 1814, an army totalling more than

[1]The Bengal Pioneers lost Lieuts. J. Du Feu and T. K. Ramsay, B.I. (both wounded, the latter mortally), during the siege of Komona in Oct. and Nov., 1807. They suffered no casualties in the reduction of Ganouri.

[2]Letter, dated Simla, Aug. 7th, 1909, from Mr. G. W. de Rhé-Philipe (an expert in Indian military records) to the Adjutant, 1st K.G.O. Sappers and Miners, included in the " Restoration of Battle Honours " file at the Corps Headquarters at Roorkee.

[3]Rewah is about 80 miles south-west of Allahabad.

[4]Kalinjar is about 25 miles south-east of Banda in Central India.

[5]*The Services of the Bengal Native Army*, by Lieut. F. G. Cardew, p. 112.

[6]Lord Hastings was Commander-in-Chief of the Bengal Army in addition to being Governor-General in India.

30,000 men—an unwieldy, inexperienced, unsuitably equipped and, for the most part, badly led force, encumbered by elephants, baggage, siege guns and all the other paraphernalia of warfare in the plains. Two of his divisional commanders were utterly incompetent: one was also a madman or a coward. Fortunately, the junior officers and rank and file made up in gallantry what they lacked in experience and so retrieved some of the worst errors of their leaders.

Lord Hastings planned to invade Nepal at four points. While the 1st Division under Major-General David Ochterlony marched from Ludhiana in the Punjab and attacked the western extremity of the frontier, the 2nd Division under Major-General Robert Gillespie was to advance from Saharanpur, seize Dehra Dun and capture the hill fortress of Jaitak. Simultaneously, the 3rd Division under Major-General John Wood was to move from Gorakhpur, through Butwal, to Palpa, and the 4th Division, under Major-General Bennet Marley, was to march from Patna to occupy the Gurkha capital of Katmandu.[1] The main body of the enemy under Amar Singh Thapa, the best of the Gurkha generals, was known to be guarding the western extremity, and the general idea was that Ochterlony and Gillespie should close in upon it from west and east, while Wood cut its line of communication and Marley seized its base. The scheme was sound, though based on a misconception of the enemy's probable movements. It was thought that Amar Singh, if engaged closely by Ochterlony and with his communications threatened by Wood, might retreat into the arms of Gillespie and there meet his fate. Actually, he remained in his exposed position and fought Ochterlony to the end. Thus, in the first phase of the Nepal War, there was only one division that counted—that of Ochterlony.

The campaign opened with the occupation of Dehra Dun by Gillespie on October 22nd, 1814. With him were the 5th and 6th Companies of Bengal Pioneers under Lieutenant J. Elliot and Ensign R. Ellis, B.I. The Gurkhas retired into the fort of Kalanga, situated on a steep hill in densely wooded country about 5 miles from Dehra. The trace of the work was irregular, following the form of the ground, and the walls were unfinished; but as every approach was heavily stockaded, preliminary reconnaissance was most difficult and the details of the assault could not be planned. To avoid the delay of siege operations which might jeopardize his proper co-operation with the other advancing divisions, Gillespie decided to attack as soon as possible and sent forward his Pioneers under Lieutenant G. R. Blane, B.E., to construct a battery some 600 yards from the fort. By the evening of the 30th, Elliot and Ellis had finished this work and had mounted in it ten small guns and howitzers brought up by elephants.[2] Gillespie then divided his force into four columns and a reserve, allotting to each column a small party of Pioneers with ladders. On October 31st, he attacked under cover of his guns. Unfortunately, two of the columns went astray in the jungle and he was obliged to assault with less than half

[1]See the *Sketch Map of Nepal and the Ganges Valley* included in this chapter, and also, *Sketch Map of Northern India*, Map I, at the end of this volume.

[2]*Narrative of a Five Years' Residence in Nepaul*, by Capt. Thomas Smith, Vol. I, p. 223.

his strength. "The whole of his combinations went to pieces," remarks Sir John Fortescue.[1] An embarrassing situation for any commander!

The Bengal Pioneers, with scaling ladders, accompanied a dismounted squadron which carried an outlying stockade and rushed up to the walls of the fort. The Gurkhas counter-attacked and swept them away with the *kukri*. Then the infantry came up with more Pioneers, and desperate attempts were made under a heavy fire to plant the ladders against the walls. Ellis was killed while placing the first ladder: Elliot was badly wounded. The troops retreated, leaving the ladders among some huts which soon caught fire. Gillespie pushed forward his guns, and with his usual bravery, headed the next assault in person, only to fall dead with a bullet through his heart while waving his men forward. "There is reason to believe," writes an anonymous officer,[2] "that could the ladders have been found in the last assault their application would have been attended with success." The order to retire was given, and Colonel S. Mawbey, now in command, realizing that the situation was hopeless, withdrew the shaken troops to Dehra Dun, where they awaited the arrival of a siege train. No less than 743 officers and men had been killed or wounded, and as most of these were British, the political and moral effect of the failure was deplorable.

On November 7th, Mawbey renewed the attack on Kalanga, though with no better success, so he sent for Captain H. W. Carmichael-Smyth, B.E., to superintend the engineering work and set the Pioneers to cut off the water-supply to the fort while he bombarded the place with the siege guns which had reached him. However, the Gurkha garrison, now reduced from 600 to 150 men,[3] had no intention of standing a siege, and evacuating Kalanga on November 30th, escaped into the jungle. Mawbey occupied the fort, where the spectacle of the dead and wounded lying on every side testified to the stubborn nature of the defence. On December 20th, Major-General G. Martindell arrived to take command. He occupied Nahan, the capital of the Sirmur State, and on December 27th, made a futile attempt to capture the fortress of Jaitak overlooking the town. Fifty Bengal Pioneers marched with each of the two columns detailed for the assault. Martindell then established siege batteries in commanding positions, and changing his tactics, contented himself with a blockade which lasted till the spring of 1815. His division became a mere holding force in a subsidiary area. The labours of his Pioneers were thrown away, and the companies might almost as well have been in garrison in Cawnpore.

Eight companies of the Bengal Pioneers or Sappers, under Captain John Swinton, B.I., were distributed among the four divisions invading Nepal. Ochterlony, on the left flank, had the 3rd and 4th Companies; Gillespie, as we have seen, had the 5th and 6th Companies; the 8th Company marched with Wood; and, on the right flank, Marley had the 1st, 2nd and 7th Companies under Swinton himself. The 4th Division

[1] *A History of the British Army*, by the Hon. J. W. Fortescue, Vol. XI, p. 129.
[2] *A Memoir of Major-General Sir R. R. Gillespie, K.C.B.*(1816), p. 233.
[3] *History of the Bengal Artillery*, by Major F. W. Stubbs, Vol. II, p. 9.

under Marley was the most powerful of the four columns,[1] and it is probable that three companies of Pioneers were allotted to it because its objective was the strongly defended Gurkha capital. Nevertheless, if the primary aim of the operations was, as it should have been, to defeat and destroy the enemy's army in the field rather than to occupy his capital, the bulk of the Pioneer strength should have been with Ochterlony and Gillespie on whom the brunt of the fighting was likely to fall.[2]

The operations of the 3rd and 4th Divisions, under Generals John Wood and Marley, make a sorry tale. Wood advanced slowly from Gorakhpur, and on January 3rd, 1815, captured a Gurkha position at Jitpur, near Butwal, though at a heavy cost: then, losing heart, he withdrew his division and resorted to a passive defence of Gorakhpur, varied only by occasional demonstrations or reconnaissances. The 8th Company, Bengal Pioneers, was forced to share in this travesty of war. Still worse was the conduct of General Marley. Soon after he started from Patna he heard that the Gurkhas had overwhelmed some frontier posts ahead of him, and bringing his division to a halt, refused to enter the hills. He was reinforced, but would not budge; and finally, on February 10th, without a word of warning, he disappeared from camp and thus provided the sole instance of desertion by a British general in the field. His successor, Major-General George Wood, who arrived on February 20th, infused no life into the 4th Division. He made a demonstration along the edge of the foot hills, declared that the fever-season was too near for serious operations in the forest, and camped without seeing a Gurkha. One may imagine the disgust of John Swinton and his Pioneer companies. Three of the four operations included in first phase of the Nepal War proved lamentable failures. It is a relief to turn from such tragic displays of ineptitude to the battles of the 1st Division and the experiences of the 3rd and 4th Companies of Bengal Pioneers or Sappers in the fierce struggle against Amar Singh Thapa.

In October, 1814, General Ochterlony advanced from Ludhiana up the left bank of the Sutlej, while Amar Singh concentrated at Arki, a few miles west of the site of Simla, and occupied advanced posts on high ridges to his front. Range after range of forest-clad mountains, each fortified and strongly held, barred the progress of the 1st Division, the principal Gurkha positions being at Nalagarh, Ramgarh and Malaon. Ochterlony brought up his heavy artillery and bombarded Nalagarh, which surrendered on November 5th. A track had been cut through the jungle by the 3rd and 4th Companies of Bengal Pioneers and a fascine battery raised within a furlong of the defences. Elephants hauled the

[1]The original strengths of the four columns were as follows :—1st Division, 5,993 ; 2nd Division, 3,515 ; 3rd Division, 4,494 ; 4th Division, 7,989. (See "Early Indian Campaigns," by Major H. Biddulph, R.E., appearing in *The R.E. Journal*, Vol. XVIII, July–Dec., 1913, pp. 169–78.)

[2]Capt. Thomas Smith, in his *Narrative of a Five Years' Residence at Nepaul*, Vol. I, pp. 217–19, gives the distribution of the Pioneers as follows :—1st Division (Ochterlony) 265 ; 2nd Division (Gillespie) 133 ; 3rd Division (Wood) 90 ; 4th Division (Marley) 276. These figures indicate that 3 Companies were with the 1st Division and only 1 company (over-strength) with the 2nd Division ; but too much reliance should not be placed on the accuracy of the narrative in question.

eighteen-pounder guns into position. " To transport the heavy guns over a road so rough and steep appeared to many an impracticable undertaking " writes an eye-witness,[1] " and it certainly would have cost much time and labour had not the strength and docility of the elephant been put into requisition. The eighteen-pounders were dragged from the camp by working parties of the troops, each followed by one, or where there was room, by two elephants. This animal, as the nature of the impediment required, sometimes applying his proboscis to the circumference of the carriage wheels, would at once lift and push it forward; sometimes twisting the same trunk round one of the spokes, he would raise the wheel out of a hollow or over a projecting piece of rock; and when the ground became tolerably even, a sign from the driver made him lay his forehead to the gun carriage in order to hurl it along. By this means, the battery train arrived in perfect order and opened on the morning of the 4th. The walls being constructed of the best stone and mortar, two eighteen-pounders played about twenty-four hours on an angle of the front before a practicable breach could be effected. The enemy, besides keeping up a constant fire, showed their determination to stand a storm by piling heaps of large stones on the ramparts. A battery of 6-pounders was now directed against these preparations. The shot, shivering and dispersing the stones, not only cleared the ramparts but drove their own missiles among the besieged like showers of grape. The Commandant then sent two Bramins to the General to treat for a capitulation. Many of the garrison had stolen out and made their escape, but one hundred fighting men were taken and conveyed to Lodiana."

" Of Nallaghur and these hill-forts in general," continues this anonymous writer, " it may be remarked that they derive almost their whole importance from their position. They are not constructed according to any principles of science. Their form is made to suit the spot on which they are built. After the Indian manner, the walls are high, with a parapet and round towers, rather than bastions, at the corners, the whole having many loopholes. The shot of their heaviest artillery weighs only about four pounds: but their most serviceable engine of defence is a sort of swivel, called Gingall. One of these, not exceeding double the size and weight of a musket, is easily carried, and a single person can work it. The Goorkas have many in all their posts; and throwing balls which weigh three or four ounces to a great distance, they do far more execution than cannon."

After the fall of Nalagarh, Amar Singh advanced from Arki and concentrated at Ramgarh. This position was more formidable than Nalagarh, and the Pioneers spent a whole month in constructing roads for the passage of heavy guns towards it. Meanwhile, the 6-pounders were brought up by pairs of elephants, one carrying the gun and the other the carriage. The Pioneers were assisted by hundreds of native stone-cutters. They felled trees, blasted rocks, cleared undergrowth, eased gradients and built parapet walls, while the Field Engineer, Lieutenant Peter Lawtie, B.E.,

[1] *Military Sketches of the Goorka War in India in the Years* 1814, 1815, 1816. (1822), pp. 4, 5.

carried out daring reconnaissances during one of which he and his party were nearly overwhelmed. The Gurkhas covered the Ramgarh ridge with stockades built on commanding points. These defences were constructed very rapidly in the following manner. One party cut down small timber with their *kukris* while another levelled the site with picks and shovels. Inner and outer lines of stakes were then driven into the soil along the selected perimeter and branches woven into each line, the intervening space being filled in with stones and earth. A strong stockade was thus erected almost as quickly as a British unit could pitch its tents, and Ochterlony, wherever he moved, was faced always with the unpleasant necessity of attacking fortified positions. Twice he issued orders for the assault of Ramgarh. Twice he countermanded them on the strength of Lawtie's reports. In the end, he abandoned the idea of a direct assault and struck at Amar Singh's lines of communication with Arki and Bilaspur, a movement which caused the Gurkha leader to draw back his left to cover his main position at Malaon, though he still clung to Ramgarh with his right.

By the middle of January, 1815, Ochterlony had turned the Malaon ridge, and moving towards Bilaspur, cut Amar Singh off from Arki and forced him to evacuate Ramgarh and retreat to the heights of Malaon. He then proceeded to clear the Malaon ridge by a series of small operations in which Lawtie distinguished himself[1] and in one of which Lieutenant R. Armstrong and two sergeants of the Bengal Pioneers, with Ensign G. Hutchinson of the Bengal Engineers, gallantly served a 6-pounder gun after the whole detachment had been killed. At last, Amar Singh stood at bay within the defences of Malaon itself. On April 16th, he launched a desperate counter-attack against Deothal, a position which he had lost. The Gurkhas, match-lock in left hand and *kukri* in right, hurled themselves against our troops but were mowed down by rifle and gun fire before they could use their knives. Nevertheless, our casualties were considerable, the Pioneers alone losing 13 men including Lieutenant H. Bagot, B.I., who was mortally wounded. In this action, Ochterlony was entrenched and the Gurkhas in the open.

The end was near. The Pioneers continued their road-making operations towards Malaon and threw up defences of the Gurkha type against counter-attack. The siege guns were dragged into position, and on May 11th, 1815, after a bombardment lasting for three days, Amar Singh surrendered to superior force. For his services in this campaign, Ochterlony was made a baronet and received the K.C.B. By his clever strategy, his careful consolidation of every step and his effective employment of heavy artillery, he had retrieved the honour of his country.

The labours of the Pioneers would have been lightened if the infantry had afforded more assistance. On this subject, the anonymous writer already quoted compares the Bengal Army with that of ancient Rome and remarks that to the Roman legionaries the spade and pickaxe were as familiar as the sword and pilum "I am certain," he adds,[2] "that were

[1]Unfortunately, Lieut. Peter Lawtie, B.E., died at Ratnagarh on May 4th, 1815, and the Bengal Army thereby lost a most promising young officer.

[2]*Military Sketches of the Goorka War in India in the Years* 1814, 1815, 1816, pp. 53–56.

the whole of the seapoys enlisted on the condition of their learning to employ these ignoble instruments, their usefulness would be much increased. The seapoys comprising the present Corps of Pioneers are of the same classes with those in the Infantry regiments, who pretend that any kind of manual labour degrades them. The assumptions of vanity and laziness are too extensively admitted in the Bengal Army. An Army of ten thousand Romans could never be seen lying inactive and discontented, waiting for two hundred people to prepare the road for them. Without requiring the bribe of extra pay and public thanks to pull a rope, all the men off duty would have done their best and, though not expert Pioneers, they might perhaps accomplish that work, say of a week, in one day and thereby save a great deal of time to the General and much expense to the State." This criticism of the Bengal Army was amply justified. In the Gurkha army, every soldier was a Pioneer, for he could hew and dig as efficiently as he fought.

The first phase of the Nepal War came to an end with the Gurkhas subdued only in the west. Elsewhere, they were triumphant and boasted of their victories, particularly over the British troops. The capture of Almora by a small column operating in Kumaon added somewhat to British prestige, but the Government at Katmandu was in no mood to ratify the treaty prepared after Ochterlony's triumph. It was necessary to drive home the lesson of Malaon, and Ochterlony was selected for the task. Early in February, 1816, he took the field in the eastern area of operations at the head of four brigades for a rapid and concentrated attack on the Gurkha capital. The 1st Brigade, under Colonel W. Kelly, H.M.'s 24th Regiment, was to enter Nepal by Hariharpur; the 2nd, under Lieut.-Colonel O. Nicolls, H.M.'s 66th Regiment, was to penetrate by Ramnagar; the 3rd and 4th, under Ochterlony himself, were to advance through Makwanpur on Katmandu. The distribution of the Bengal Pioneer units is not recorded; but it is certain that the 1st, 2nd and 7th Companies, previously with General Marley's division, were included in the expedition, and possibly also the 8th Company, which had been in the Gorakhpur District with General John Wood. The 3rd and 4th Companies in the Punjab, and the 5th and 6th Companies in Kumaon, were far from the scene of action. In command of the Pioneers with Ochterlony was the redoubtable John Swinton.

The 3rd and 4th Brigades moved northwards from the Patna area towards the Chariagati Pass, fortifying every camp, collecting supplies, and leaving nothing to chance. At the foot of the pass, Ochterlony halted to reconnoitre. He found that the enemy's defences were most elaborate. Every path was stockaded, and every hill fortified and piled with stones ready to be hurled down upon his troops. Further reconnaissance, however, disclosed an unguarded and circuitous route by means of which the summit of the range was reached by the 3rd Brigade on February 11th. The enemy then abandoned the pass and the 4th Brigade ascended it. The march of the 3rd Brigade is described in picturesque manner by Lieutenant John Shipp, leader of a forlorn hope at Bhurtpore in 1803. "Had

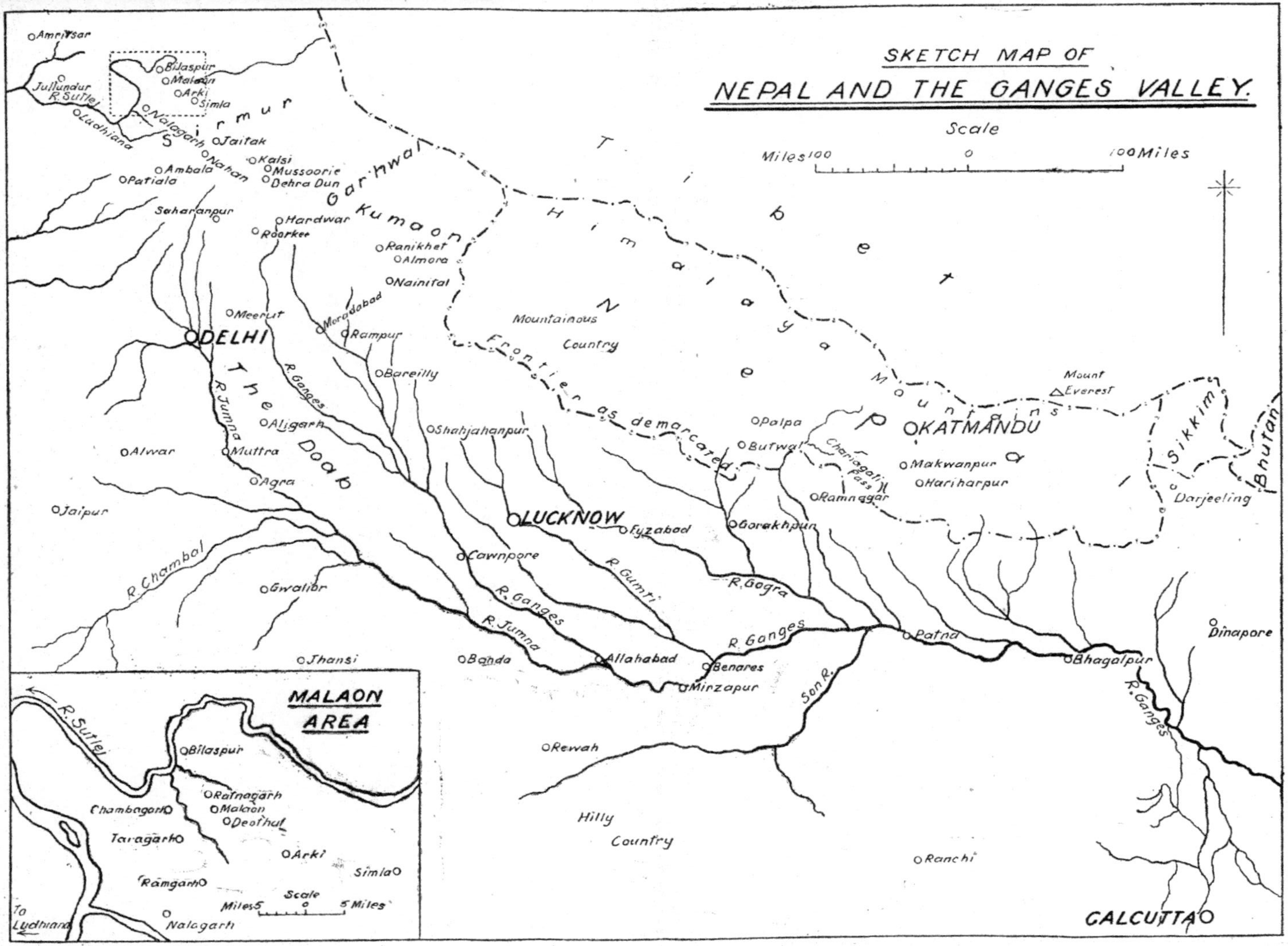
SKETCH MAP OF
NEPAL AND THE GANGES VALLEY.
Scale
Miles 100
0
100 Miles
Tibet
Himalaya Mountains
Nepal
Mountainous Country
Frontier as demarcated
Mount Everest
KATMANDU
Sikkim
Bhutan
Darjeeling
Palpa
Butwal
Chariagali Pass
Makwanpur
Hariharpur
Ramnagar
Gorakhpur
Amritsar
Jullundur
R. Sutlej
Ludhiana
Bilaspur
Malaon
Arki
Simla
Sirmur
Nalagarh
Jaitak
Nahan
Kalsi
Mussoorie
Dehra Dun
Ambala
Patiala
Garhwal
Kumaon
Saharanpur
Hardwar
Roorkee
Ranikhet
Almora
Nainital
Meerut
Moradabad
Rampur
Bareilly
DELHI
The Doab
R. Ganges
R. Jumna
Aligarh
Muttra
Agra
Alwar
Jaipur
Shahjahanpur
LUCKNOW
Fyzabad
R. Gumti
R. Gogra
Cawnpore
R. Chambal
Gwalior
Jhansi
Banda
Allahabad
Benares
Mirzapur
Son R.
Patna
Bhagalpur
Dinapore
Rewah
Hilly Country
Ranchi
CALCUTTA
MALAON AREA
Chambagarh
Taragarh
Ratnagarh
Malaon
Deothal
Ramgarh
Nalagarh
Scale
Miles 5
0
5 Miles
To Ludhiana

the enemy been aware of our nocturnal excursion," he writes,[1] " they might have annihilated us by rolling rocks and stones upon our heads. Our march became more and more tardy, and the ascents and descents more and more difficult and intricate. The soles of both my boots had long refused to bear me company any further. The dawn began to break through the cerulean chambers of the east, the faithful moon still lingering on the tops of the western hills, loth to bid us farewell. Our gallant General walked every yard of this critical march, encouraging his men. Having got all the men up, except the rearguard, the Pioneers went to work with their pickaxes, some making a road, the others felling trees. This accomplished, the guns were our next object. Having cut a good deal of the prominent part of the hill away and laid trees on the ascent as a footing for the elephants, these animals were made to approach it, which the first did with some reluctance and fear. He looked up, shook his head, and when forced by his driver, he roared piteously. But the moment some little alteration had been made, he seemed willing to approach. He then commenced his examination and scrutiny by pressing with his trunk the trees that had been thrown across; and after this he put his foreleg on with great caution. The next step for him to ascend was a projecting rock, and the next against a tree, but this he did not like. Here his driver made use of the most endearing epithets, such as " Wonderful, my life "—" Well done, my dear "—" My dove "—" My son "—" My wife "; but all these endearing appellations, of which elephants are so fond, would not induce him to try again. Force was at length resorted to and the elephant roared terrifically but would not move. Something was then removed: he seemed satisfied and in time ascended the stupendous ghaut. On reaching the top, his delight was visible. He caressed his keeper and threw dirt about in the most playful manner. Another elephant followed, and having accomplished their task, they embraced each other. . . . Their drivers then made them salaam to the General, who ordered them five rupees each for sweetmeats, and they immediately returned thanks by another salaam."

The Bengal Pioneers in the Nepal War were employed from February 10th to February 18th, 1816, as John Shipp remarks, in making a practicable path for elephants and guns up the precipitous ravine and steep hill-side by which the 3rd Brigade reached the summit. With great labour, they constructed a long flight of steps formed of tree-trunks. One elephant climbed a part of this ladder with a 6-pounder gun on his back, but losing his balance, fell to the bottom and was killed. The remainder ascended unloaded, and the guns were hauled up by men. In some places, the heavier guns were dragged up by luff tackles fastened to posts wedged into the rocks on either side, a preventer rope being belayed on a third post in the centre at the head of the ascent. While the infantry manned the tackles to the strains of light music from a regimental band, a subaltern sat perched precariously on the floundering gun to

[1] *Memoirs of the Extraordinary Military Career of John Shipp, late a Lieutenant in His Majesty's 87th Regiment*, p. 172, *et seq.*

direct the operations. The ladder was a most creditable piece of rapid work and enhanced the reputation of John Swinton and his Pioneers.[1]

Having concluded their labours in and near the Chariagati Pass most of the Bengal Pioneers rejoined the army advancing across the uplands. Swinton was with Ochterlony when Makwanpur was captured after a stiff fight on February 27th. The enemy suffered severely, but their wounded received every attention from the British doctors. John Shipp records[2] that some of these unfortunates believed that their lives were being prolonged only that they might be put to a more cruel and lingering death. Indeed, one man, whose leg had been amputated, thought that this merely confirmed the rumour that all Europeans were cannibals and asked when the other leg would be taken off because he would prefer to destroy himself unless it was done soon. These wounded, when discharged from hospital, became the most ardent emissaries of peace and friendship between their people and the British.

The war was drawing to a close. Colonel Kelly had occupied Hariharpur and Colonel Nicolls had rejoined Ochterlony. Katmandu was within easy grasp. The Gurkhas, however, were tired of fighting, and the Treaty of Sagauli, signed on March 3rd, 1816, brought hostilities to an end. It was agreed that Sikkim and the lowlands bordering on British territory should be evacuated by Nepal, and that the provinces of Garhwal and Kumaon, and the district of Dehra Dun, should be handed over to the British, who thus acquired the sites of Simla, Mussoorie, Naini Tal, Almora and Ranikhet. The Bengal Army had learnt the need for caution in hill warfare, and the Bengal Pioneers the value of field defences. The price had been heavy, but the experience was invaluable. Since the unhappy days of 1814–16, the Gurkhas have been our trusted allies, and, enlisted in the Indian Army, have fought loyally and gallantly in all parts of the Empire and far beyond its boundaries.

After the conclusion of the Nepal War the Bengal Army refrained from military adventures until the Government decided in February, 1817, to reduce the fortified town of Hathras, between Agra and Aligarh, where a landowner named Dayaram was in open defiance of authority. Lord Hastings wished to crush Dayaram before turning his attention to the Pindaris, and accordingly sent three divisions, under Major-Generals D. Marshall, R. Donkin and T. Brown against him. Marshall was in supreme command and had, as his Chief Engineer, Major Thomas Anburey, B.E., a future Commandant of the Bengal Sappers and Miners.[3] Eight companies of Bengal Pioneers or Sappers under Captain John Swinton, B.I., were included in the force, and also two companies of Miners, who marched as

[1] *Considerations on Tactics and Strategy*, by Col. G. Twemlow, p. 48, quoted in *History of the Bengal Artillery*, by Major F. W. Stubbs, Vol. II, p. 33.

[2] *Memoirs of the Extraordinary Career of John Shipp, late a Lieutenant in His Majesty's 87th Regiment*, p. 199.

[3] The other Bengal Engineers at the siege of Hathras were Capt. H. W. Carmichael-Smyth and R. Tickell, Lieuts. W. Morton and J. Taylor, and Ensigns A. Irvine and G. Hutchinson.

usual with the siege train.[1] On February 12th, no less than 6 regiments of cavalry, 9 battalions of infantry, and about 100 guns were in position around Hathras. It was evident that the Government had no intention of risking a second Bhurtpore.

The town of Hathras was walled and surrounded by a deep ditch 28 to 50 feet wide, and some 700 yards from it lay a powerful fort enclosed by a ditch about 110 feet wide and 36 feet deep, parts of which were flooded to a depth of 6 feet. Marshall decided to reduce the town before he attacked the fort, but as a preliminary he opened negotiations with Dayaram in order to secure a bloodless surrender if possible. These negotiations lasted for four days. While they were in progress the enemy allowed our engineers to reconnoitre freely, except between the town and the fort, and even to walk up the glacis and look down into the ditch, possibly with the idea of inducing them to change their minds when they saw the strength of the defences. However, the conversations led to no result, so the Pioneers, having already prepared the necessary fascines and gabions, helped in the construction of four siege batteries from which fire was opened on February 22nd with 24-pounder and 18-pounder guns, 8-inch howitzers, 10-inch, 8-inch and 5½-inch mortars and a battery of 32-pounder Congreve rockets. "The Congreve rocket," writes John Shipp,[2] "is a most destructive instrument of death; its enormous, shaking tail carries everything before it; and when it explodes, it kills some yards around and sets fire to houses right and left." Before dawn on the 24th, Captain R. Tickell, B.E., went forward under a screen of blank cartridge fire to examine the breaches and ditch; but after he had plumbed the ditch with a 6-pounder shot and found that it was 24 feet deep, he advised against an immediate assault.[3] This was fortunate because the enemy evacuated the town shortly afterwards and retreated into the fort, which Marshall then proceeded to besiege. New battery positions were selected, the batteries constructed and armed, and approach-trenches pushed forward. Anburey ran a parallel from the south-east corner of the town to skirt the southern face of the fort, and from February 27th to March 1st the Pioneers laboured with large working parties of infantry in excavating this trench and preparing more battery positions.

On the morning of March 2nd, after the garrison had been warned to evacuate all women and children, a general bombardment was opened on Hathras Fort from 42 mortars, 24 heavy guns and howitzers, a number of light guns, and the rocket battery. "I never saw implements of destruction so accurately thrown," remarks John Shipp.[4] "Some of them were scarcely five inches above the walls of the Fort. The

[1]Detailed Report on the Engineer Operations during the Siege of Hathras, by Major (temp. Lt.-Col.) Thomas Anburey, B.E., forming pages 105 to 152 of a manuscript file at Roorkee entitled "Major-General Cameron's Report on the Defence of the Fort of Allahabad, June, 1802." See also a Journal by Major Anburey in a file at Roorkee entitled "Siege Diaries, 1817–25," pp. 9 to 24. A second company of Miners had apparently been added to the original unit raised in 1808.

[2]*Memoirs of the Extraordinary Military Career of John Shipp*, p. 219.

[3]*History of the Bengal Artillery*, by Major F. W. Stubbs, Vol. II, p. 52.

[4]*Memoirs of the Extraordinary Military Career of John Shipp*, pp. 222, 223.

system of shelling had been so improved in the twelve years that had elapsed since the siege of Bhurtpore that instead of one shell in five minutes from a single battery it was by no means extraordinary to see twenty in one minute. The roaring Congreves ran along the bastion's top, breaking legs and arms with their shaking tails. Nothing could be more grand to the eye, or more affecting to the sympathizing heart, than this horrid spectacle." Fires broke out in many places, and at 5.30 p.m. a magazine containing 150 tons of gunpowder blew up with a shattering roar which was heard at Delhi, 100 miles away. The cries of buried men, women and children came from the smoking debris around a crater 83 feet in diameter. Our guns ceased fire but soon reopened in reply to shelling from the fort under cover of which Dayaram and a few of his men escaped. Before midnight, Hathras surrendered. The scene within the walls of the fort defies description. The charred and disfigured bodies of 400 men and 80 horses, with 700 prisoners, remained to represent the original garrison of 1,400. The number of women and children killed is unknown. Only 9 days were occupied in reducing the town and fort and only 17 casualties were incurred, thus exemplifying the economy of overwhelming force. The Pioneers remained for a time to destroy the defences and then returned to their peace stations. They had added yet another proof, to the many already on record, of their coolness under fire and their skill in their work,[1] attributes which were soon to be tested in the prolonged and intricate series of campaigns known as the Third Maratha War.

Since the close of the Second Maratha War, Rajputana and Central India had been ravaged by Pindari freebooters, encouraged and sometimes helped by the Maratha chiefs. Jaswant Rao Holkar of Indore had been succeeded in 1811 by his son, Malhar Rao Holkar, a child only six years of age; and in 1816 a Regent, named Appa Sahib, had been appointed at Nagpur to manage the affairs of the imbecile Mudaji, the successor of Raghuji as Bhonsla Raja of Berar. These changes, and the resulting political confusion, led to a gradual concentration of British forces in the Deccan and a corresponding reduction elsewhere which was most welcome to the Pindari raiders. At length, the Government was obliged to take action against the Pindaris, even at the risk of a general conflagration involving the Maratha states; and although it seemed probable that the first theatre of war would be the Narbada Valley, it was recognized that, after the expulsion of the Pindaris, the operations might extend to any part of Malwa or the Deccan. The latter province was occupied by forces which could be reinforced easily from Madras and Bombay. Campaigns to the north and east of Malwa could be undertaken by the Bengal Army, and to the west, by the Bombay Army.

Given a free hand, Lord Hastings made every preparation during the rainy season of 1817 to surround the Pindaris in Malwa by a huge army of 114,000 men sub-divided into a Grand Army of 4 divisions (44,000 men) which he himself would command, and an Army of the Deccan of 7 divisions (70,000 men) under Lieut.-General Sir Thomas Hislop.

[1]*East India Military Calendar*, Vol. I, pp. 395, 396.

Excluding irregular troops, Hastings and Hislop had 13,000 British and 74,000 Indian soldiers with 282 guns. Opposed to them at first were 15,000 mounted Pindaris with a few guns, and 22,000 Pathan mercenaries with 200 guns; and later, when the Maratha states joined in the fray, a further 130,000 cavalry and 76,000 infantry with 369 guns. The Divisional Commanders in the Grand Army were Major-Generals T. Brown, R. Donkin, D. Marshall and Sir D. Ochterlony, and in the Army of the Deccan, Major-Generals Sir T. Hislop (Army Commander in addition) and Sir W. Keir, Brig.-Generals J. Doveton, L. Smith, Sir J. Malcolm and Sir T. Munro, and Lieut.-Colonel J. W. Adams.

The plan of campaign was simple, though its execution proved difficult. The Pindaris were to be enclosed in a cordon of divisions facing inwards while the ring was kept by an outer cordon facing outwards. Unfortunately, however, the Maratha states refused to be mere spectators. The vast encircling movement planned against the Pindaris by columns operating from Bengal on the north and east, from Gujarat on the west and from the Deccan on the south, all driving inwards on Hindia in the Narbada Valley, had to be modified to meet a new situation. The Peshwa, Baji Rao, had been coerced by a rigorous treaty in June, Appa Sahib of Berar and Holkar of Indore were quiet, but Sindhia of Gwalior was restive. Accordingly, when Hastings marched to battle with the Grand Army in the autumn of 1817 he went straight for Gwalior where, on November 5th, he forced Sindhia to sign a treaty. On the same day, however, the perfidious Baji Rao threw off his disguise, sacked the British Residency at Poona and declared himself an enemy. Appa Sahib followed suit, and thus the British were confronted at once by the armies of Poona and Berar as allies of the Pindaris.

Most of the Pioneer units in India joined one or other of the armies. At the end of August, 1817, 4 companies of the 1st Battalion of Madras Pioneers under Captain R. McCraith, M.I., marched from Secunderabad (near Hyderabad) to join the 1st Division of the Deccan Army under Hislop, and on September 20th the remaining 4 companies moved through Ajanta to establish a crossing at the junction of the rivers Purna and Tapti for the 2nd Division under Doveton.[1] On October 23rd, 3 companies of the 2nd Battalion under Captain T. Smithwaite, M.I., marched from Bellary to join the Reserve Division under Munro and were reinforced later by another company.[2] The remaining 4 companies of the 2nd Battalion joined the 4th Division under Smith. Thus, Hislop, Doveton, Munro and Smith each had 400 Madras Pioneers. Meanwhile, the Bombay Pioneers under Captain Peter De La Motte, Bo.I., were able to supply one company, then at Poona, to assist the 4th Division under Smith, and another company, at Hoshangabad on the Narbada, for attachment to the Gujarat Division under Keir. The remaining two companies were held in reserve temporarily at Bombay[3]

[1]See the *Sketch Map of Central India* included in this chapter, and also General Map II at the end of this volume.
[2]*Historical Record of the Q.V.O. Madras Sappers and Miners*, Vol. I, p. 25.
[3]*A Brief History of the Royal Bombay Sappers and Miners*, p. 4.

but soon took the field. The Bengal Pioneers or Sappers were scattered far and wide. At Delhi were the headquarters and three companies under Captain John Swinton, B.I. One company was divided between Karnal and Ludhiana; another, the 4th, was at Cawnpore, another in Kumaon, and another in Garhwal. The 2nd Company, under Lieutenant J. A. Currie, B.I., with Lieutenant T. R. Fell, B.I. attached, was with the Nagpur Subsidiary Force, which became the 5th Division of the Deccan Army under Lieut.-Colonel Adams.[1] On mobilization, all the Bengal Pioneer companies except the 2nd were distributed among the Centre, Right, Left and Reserve Divisions of the Grand Army which assembled at Cawnpore, Agra, Kalinjar and Rewari.[2] The Company of Miners was attached to the Centre Division under Brown.

Little serious fighting or technical work for the Engineers or Pioneers was involved in the rounding up of the Pindari gangs under their leaders Chitu, Karim Khan and Wazil Muhammad. Karim and Wazil, fleeing from the Deccan Army in the direction of Gwalior, were headed towards the north-west, overtaken by Marshall's Left Division of the Grand Army, and turned back by Donkin's Right Division. Retreating some distance, they encountered a part of the Deccan Army and fled to the south-west. Meanwhile, Chitu had been defeated by Donkin. The pursuit of the Pindaris could not be resumed until the end of 1817 when several columns took up the chase in the region of Jawad, west of Gwalior State. Chitu joined forces with Holkar of Indore, and Karim and Wazil were invited to join Sindhia of Gwalior; but after Holkar had been subdued there was no hope for the Pindaris, and in January, 1818, they were hunted backwards and forwards until finally dispersed by Adams near Kotah. Karim and Wazil surrendered. Chitu escaped to the Deccan and in 1819 was killed by a tiger in the Malwa jungles. The Pindari Campaign would hardly be worthy of description were it not that in its earlier stages it was the match that lighted the fire of the Third Maratha War.

The fate of Chitu in the Malwa jungles was not uncommon in the days when tigers were plentiful and sportsmen few. Many of the Company's officers had narrow escapes and the discursive John Shipp records an instance. "A captain," he writes, "once told me that he had just discharged his last barrel when a large tiger appeared. The captain stared: the tiger grinned. Then the captain, being a funny fellow, thought of a stratagem to put his grinning neighbour to flight, and turning his back to the animal and looking at him through his legs, he ran off backwards. He positively declared that the moment the tiger saw this strange metamorphosis he took to his heels; but I will not vouch for the verity of this tale." Neither will we.

It is impossible to record in a few pages the movements, battles and

[1]Letter, dated Aug. 2nd, 1909, from Mr. G. W. de Rhé-Philipe to the Adjutant, K.G.O. Bengal Sappers and Miners, included in the "Restoration of Battle Honours" file at Roorkee.

[2]Kalinjar is about 75 miles south-west of Allahabad; Rewari about 50 miles south-west of Delhi. As 23 companies of Pioneers, Miners and Gun-Lascars took the field with the Bengal Army, it can be assumed that all the Bengal Pioneers were included.

sieges undertaken during a period of nearly two years by eleven divisions operating, sometimes independently, in an area larger than Great Britain. A complete and detailed account can be found in Lieut.-Colonel Valentine Blacker's great volume of 494 quarto pages, published in 1821 and entitled *Memoir of the Operations of the British Army in India during the Mahratta War of* 1817, 1818 *and* 1819.[1] The present narrative must be confined to the part taken by the Madras, Bengal and Bombay Pioneers in some of the principal battles and sieges which gave them so many opportunities for the display of courage, initiative, skill and endurance.

In the Third Maratha War, the experiment was repeated of recruiting a temporary engineer unit. The 2nd Division of the Deccan Army under Doveton had not only 4 companies of Madras Pioneers but a company of 80 European and Indian Sappers and Miners, regarding which Lieutenant Edward Lake writes in 1825 :—[2] "Recently, a few recruits, trained at Chatham, have been sent out to Bengal, where a permanent Corps of Sappers and Miners has been raised and a large increase made in the Engineer Corps. The sister Presidencies have not, as yet, shared in these benefits, although the principle has been established and the necessity of improvement, in time of war at least, acknowledged; for, during the last campaign in the Deckan (the Third Maratha War) Lieutenant Davies, the Senior Engineer of the Madras Establishment with Sir Thomas Hislop's army, was allowed (as a temporary measure) to recruit 30 Europeans and 50 Pioneers for this Service, who were denominated "Sappers and Miners." These men, it must be observed, who only volunteered for the inducement of increased pay, were, when they joined that Officer, wholly ignorant of the duty they were to be employed on, and the European part of them were so far from feeling that *Esprit de Corps* which should be the mainspring of a soldier's actions that they at first seemed to look on their duty as a degrading one. Nevertheless, they were brought to a state of considerable efficiency by the exertions of their Commanding Officer."

Lake then proceeds to discuss the shortcomings of the Pioneers, the Engineer Department and the Siege Train.[3] "The Madras Pioneers, who, with the exception of the temporary Sappers and Miners, were the only men at the immediate disposal of the Engineers for the duties of that department, possess in a peculiar degree every necessary physical qualification; but being never, except in times of actual warfare, employed in Military Works, at least of this description, their instruction in these duties commences at the very moment that practised men are required. Another war finds them as ignorant as before, or perhaps replaced by a fresh set of men: and the trenches again become the school of instruction

[1]More concise accounts are given in *Summary of the Mahratta and Pindaree Campaign during* 1817, 1818 *and* 1819 (1820) by an anonymous writer, and in *A History of the British Army* (1923) by the Hon. J. W. Fortescue, Vol. XI, pp. 163–254. The sieges are well described in *Journals of the Sieges of the Madras Army in the Years* 1817, 1818 *and* 1819 (1825), by Lieut. Edward Lake, M.E.

[2]*Journals of the Sieges of the Madras Army in the Years* 1817, 1818 *and* 1819, by Lieut. E. Lake, M.E., pp. 18, 19.

[3]*Ibid.*, pp. 19 and 28–31.

for the most simple works of a siege. . . . The Battering Train and the Engineer Department of the Deckan Army were utterly disproportionate to its strength. The Train with the 1st, 2nd and 3rd Divisions consisted only of two 18-pounders and two 12-pounders, two 8-inch mortars and two 8-inch howitzers. The Engineer Department with these divisions was similarly constituted. A few scaling ladders, intrenching tools for 50 men, with two or three platform carts containing small stores, formed the Engineer Park. None of the peculiar tools or implements required in Mining, or in the Sap, were provided, nor was there any equipment of Pontoons or of other stores for the Military Passage of Rivers. These, although thought indispensable in Europe, have never been supplied in India. In other divisions, composed partly of Bengal and Bombay troops, the Battering Train and Engineer Department, although very imperfect, were more respectable . . . In the 4th, 5th and Reserve Divisions the Engineers had to depend for all seige operations solely on the Pioneers. The progress of the troops was delayed by numerous streams which intersect this part of the Deckan, and the aid of the Engineer Department to overcome these obstacles was only called for in one instance when they were sent forward in September, 1817, to prepare means for throwing the advanced division over the Taptee; but as there were no Pontoons and no timber, a flying bridge was the only resource."

These few remarks give some indication of the difficulties under which the Pioneers laboured. They had no proper equipment for the siege operations which occupied so much of their attention, and their equipment even for field operations left much to be desired.

The first serious battle of the Third Maratha War, and one of particular interest to all Bombay Sappers and Miners, was fought at Kirkee, their present headquarters, on November 5th, 1817. The British force engaged was small, but the political effect of the resultant victory was far-reaching, and for that reason the battle deserves more attention than it has received from some historians. In October, 1817, Mountstuart Elphinstone, the Resident at Poona, found himself in an unpleasant situation. He distrusted the Peshwa, Baji Rao, and was wont to declare he had never heard a single word of truth from any Maratha except one man whom he always suspected, and him he never believed.[1] Finally, having ascertained that Baji Rao was massing troops to threaten the Subsidiary Force Brigade stationed at Poona, he ordered the brigade to march out to the Kirkee Ridge, some 6 miles north-east of the city. Thither it moved on November 1st. As the nearest supporting force was General Smith's 4th Division on the Godavari at least 70 miles away, Elphinstone summoned a battalion from Sirur, 30 miles distant; but before it could arrive, Baji Rao advanced on the Residency outside Poona. Elphinstone then joined the brigade at Kirkee, and Baji Rao sacked and burned the Residency and thus started the war.

As David advanced to meet Goliath, so the Poona Brigade, under Lieut.-Colonel Burr, marched boldly down from its post at Kirkee to encounter

[1] *Summary of the Mahratta and Pindaree Campaign* (Anonymous), p. 68, f. n.

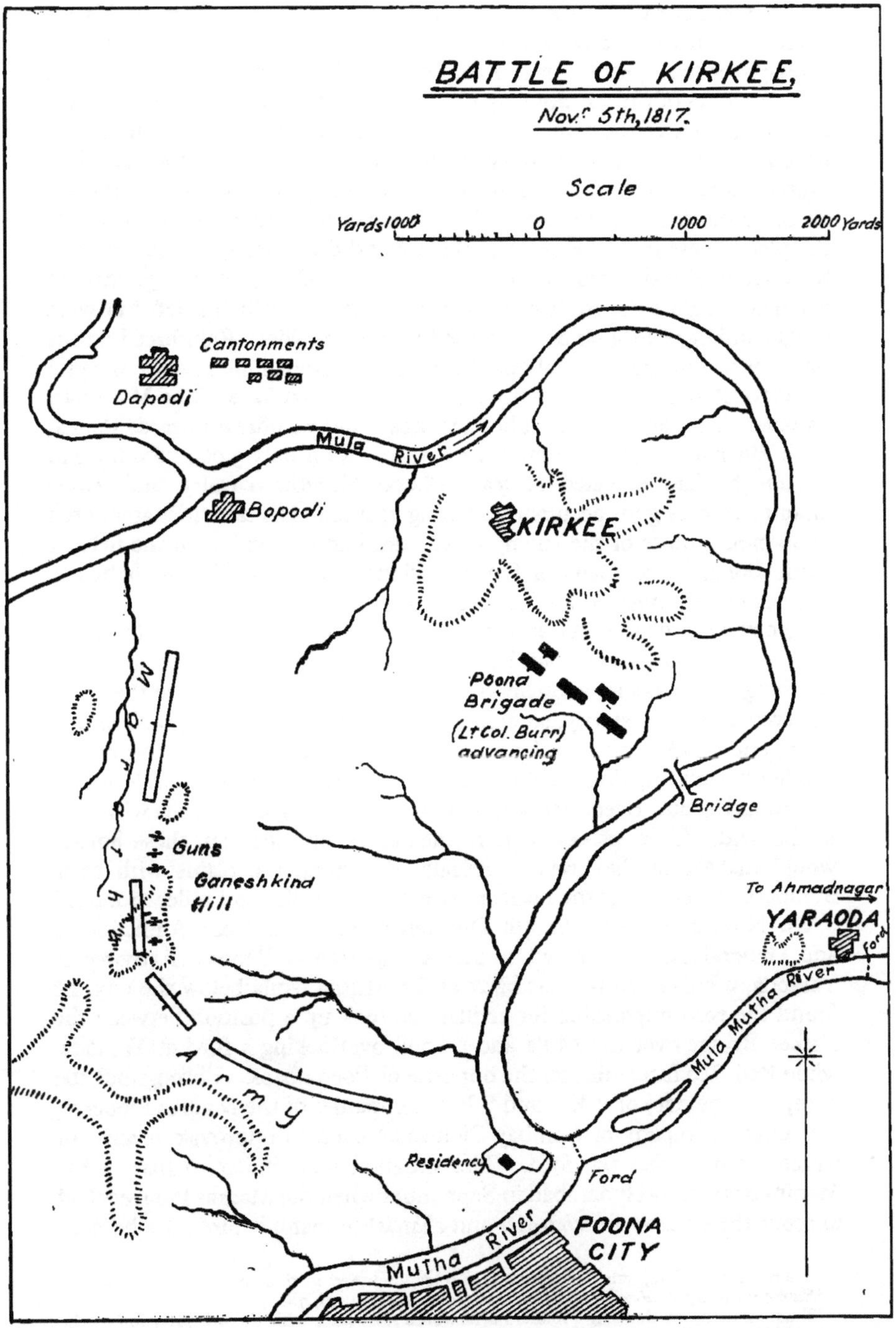
BATTLE OF KIRKEE,
Novr 5th, 1817.
Scale
Yards 1000
0
1000
2000 Yards
Cantonments
Dapodi
Mula River
Bopodi
KIRKEE
Poona Brigade (Lt Col. Burr) advancing
Bridge
Guns
Ganeshkind Hill
To Ahmadnagar
YARAODA
Ford
Mula Mutha River
Residency
Ford
POONA CITY
Mutha River

the Maratha army. On the right, near Kirkee, was the 1st Bombay Native Infantry; in the centre, a wing of the 103rd Foot; on the left, near a bridge over the Mula River, the 7th Bombay Native Infantry; in support, six companies of the 6th Bombay Native Infantry, and in reserve at Kirkee, two companies of the same regiment. Kirkee lies in a bend of the Mula, which joins the Mutha tributary at Poona to form the Mutha Mula.[1] The Maratha army almost spanned the Mula peninsula, with its artillery grouped on and around the Ganeshkind Ridge in the centre. As Burr moved across the plain, these guns opened a heavy fire and the Maratha horse swarmed forward far ahead of most of their infantry. A body, 6,000 strong, charged diagonally across the front in an attempt to turn the British left but were caught in boggy ground and repulsed with heavy loss. Reinforced on his right by two irregular battalions, Burr then continued his advance in spite of demonstrations by the enemy's horse against that flank. The Marathas, however, had had enough. They lost heart and withdrew towards Poona, while Burr returned in triumph to Kirkee. With only 3,000 infantry and 4 guns he had defeated at least 18,000 Maratha cavalry and 8,000 infantry with 14 guns occupying a strong position. His casualties amounted to 86 men; those of the enemy to 500 dead and wounded on the field of battle alone. A company of Bombay Pioneers took part in this fight but was not closely engaged and suffered no casualties.

The repulse of the Maratha cavalry was a fine achievement, for these soldiers were born to the saddle. "They can make their horses do almost anything" remarks an anonymous writer.[2] "They likewise use the spear with remarkable dexterity, sometimes at full gallop. Grasping their spears short, and quickly sticking the point in the ground, they turn their horses suddenly round it, thus performing, as on a pivot, the same circle round and round again. Every Maratha brings his own horse and arms with him in the field. If troops could be frightened by appearances, these hordes would dishearten the bravest, actually darkening the plains with their numbers and clouding the horizon with dust for miles and miles around."

On November 13th, the 4th Division marched in from Ahmadnagar and General Smith resolved to attack Baji Rao at Poona. Arriving at Yaraoda, a village on the left bank of the Mutha Mula below the city, he found the ford impassable for artillery so took up a position between the Kirkee Bridge over the Mula and a knoll overlooking a ford at Yaraoda, while Baji Rao faced him on the opposite or Poona bank. Throughout the 15th, detachments of "E" and "F" Companies of the Madras Pioneers, and Burr's company of Bombay Pioneers,[3] tried to improvise means for passing guns across the ford. The situation was similar to that at the Manjra River near Hyderabad in September when the Madras Pioneers had to scour the country for *charpais* and *chattis*[4] to manufacture rafts because

[1]See the Sketch Map entitled *Battle of Kirkee*, included in this chapter.

[2]*Summary of the Mahratta and Pindaree Campaign*, pp. 77, 78.

[3]This company of Bombay Pioneers afterwards took part with the 4th Division in the relief of Satara. It was then transferred to the Reserve Division (Munro) and assisted in the capture of many hill forts.

[4]String bedsteads and earthenware jars.

they had no pontoons, basket-boats or other materials.[1] However, on November 16th, though opposed by the Peshwa's infantry, a brigade forced the passage of the Yaraoda ford and established itself some two miles east of the city.[2] During the night, Baji Rao fled southwards, and on the 17th, Smith crossed by another ford and entered Poona. After the fall of Poona, the Peshwa became a hunted fugitive with rapidly dwindling forces: he was troublesome but no longer dangerous.

Baji Rao's misfortune did not deter Appa Sahib of Nagpur, who rose against the British on November 25th, 1817, and on the following day sent a force of 3,000 Arab mercenaries to attack the British Residency, which lay below the twin hills of Sitabaldi to the west of the city. The Nagpur Subsidiary Force Brigade, of 1,600 men with 4 guns, held the hills and the Residency and repulsed a resolute assault. During the following night, a company of the 1st Battalion, Madras Pioneers[3]—probably under orders to join General Doveton's 2nd Division—fortified the smaller hill-top with a breastwork of bags of grain, but the Arabs returned to the attack and captured the hill on the 27th. Appa Sahib, with a total of 18,000 men and 36 guns, then closed in on the other hill and the Residency, but his troops were put to flight by a series of gallant cavalry charges and the Battle of Sitabaldi ended in a victory for the British, though at a cost of 364 casualties.

While Appa Sahib entered into negotiations, Doveton's division was summoned to Nagpur, where it arrived on December 12th, with three more companies of the 1st Battalion, Madras Pioneers, in addition to a temporary company of Sappers and Miners composed of 34 volunteers from the Madras European Regiment and 33 from the Madras Infantry.[4] Doveton took up a position at Sitabaldi: Appa Sahib, anxious to surrender, lay in camp south of the city. His Arabs, however, would not lay down their arms until he had settled their arrears of pay, so Doveton attacked on December 16th. The 2nd Division routed the Nagpur army, but the Arabs and some Hindustanis took refuge in the citadel, where they prepared to stand a siege. On December 19th, with 64 captured siege-guns, Doveton began his approach from Sitabaldi along the southern bank of a large reservoir, consolidating his position as he moved forward. It was fortunate that on this occasion he had the services of temporary Sappers and Miners, for on the 20th the Madras Pioneers refused to bring forward materials until the Sappers had entrenched themselves in advance and thus provided their sole instance of misbehaviour under fire.[5] They were unaccustomed to the conditions, and strangers to

[1]*Summary of the Mahratta and Pindaree Campaign during* 1817, 1818 *and* 1819, pp. 81, 82.

[2]The Madras Pioneers lost 5 men wounded and the Bombay Pioneers 1 man.

[3]When the war started, the 2nd Company, Bengal Pioneers or Sappers, under Lieut. J. A. Currie, B.I., was with the Nagpur Subsidiary Force ; but when Nagpur was attacked, this unit was with the 5th Division of the Deccan Army under Colonel Adams in Western Malwa, far from the scene of operations.

[4]*Europeans*, 3 Sergeants, 3 Corporals, 28 Privates. *Natives*, 3 Havildars, 2 Naiks, 28 Privates. (See *Journal of the Sieges of the Madras Army in the Years* 1817, 1818 *and* 1819, by Lieut. E. Lake, M.E., p. 42.)

[5]*Historical Record of the Q.V.O. Madras Sappers and Miners*, Vol. I, p. 26. In spite of the temporary lapse of the Madras Pioneers, the honour " Nagpore " was awarded later to the Q.V.O. Madras Sappers and Miners.

Lieutenants Thomas Davies and J. W. Nattes, the Madras Engineers in charge. After siege batteries had been constructed and armed, the guns opened fire and breached one of the gates of the citadel, and on December 24th, Doveton ordered an assault.

The attack on Nagpur was made at three points and ended in failure. In the main assault, Davies led the European Sappers and Miners, 5 companies of Native Infantry, and a detachment of Madras Pioneers carrying tools and ladders, up the debris of the breached gateway only to be checked at the top by a murderous fire. He, Nattes, and many of the Sappers, fell severely wounded and the remaining troops ran for cover. Doveton then decided to await the arrival of a proper siege train; but meanwhile, the Arabs decided to surrender, which they did on December 29th in return for a gratuity of Rs. 50,000. The European Sappers and Miners were highly praised in dispatches. "This particular arm," wrote Doveton, "only requires an adequate increase to render the most essential service in the public interest." Sir John Fortescue condemns the attack on Nagpur as the most wantonly foolish enterprise to be found in the annals of the British Army in India;[1] but he admits, nevertheless, that it resulted in the reduction of another of the great Maratha powers to a state of abject dependency. Little was to be feared from the Gaikwar of Baroda; Sindhia of Gwalior had been bound by a treaty, and the Peshwa driven from the field. Now that the Bhonsla Regent of Berar had been subdued, Lord Hastings was free to leave his subordinates to disperse the remnants of the Pindaris and to concentrate his attention for the moment on Holkar of Indore.

The tame ending to the siege of Nagpur may be explained by the light-hearted and casual manner in which the Marathas were accustomed to attack or defend fortified places. Edward Lake records the following account of the siege of a town by the Marathas in 1815:—[2] "The besieging army consisted principally of horse and about four guns which were drawn out in the open plain about fifty yards asunder. The besiegers had a Portuguese who levelled each gun himself and appeared to have the direction of the attack. They fired about once in a quarter of an hour; and if by chance a shot struck any part of the wall so as to raise a dust, the air resounded with acclamations in praise of the Portuguese, who seemed in no small degree flattered thereby. The siege was brought to a conclusion in a curious way. A small party of Europeans were pitched near the place about three weeks after, and five or six of them stole out of camp at night to assist the besiegers and fired the guns so fast that the town was found evacuated next morning. Two of the Europeans were wounded in this frolic."

After the fall of Nagpur, Holkar defied the British and, joined by the fugitive Pindari, Chitu, announced that he would march on Poona to retrieve the fortunes of Baji Rao. Accordingly, Lord Hastings directed

[1] *A History of the British Army*, by the Hon. J. W. Fortescue, Vol. XI, p. 196.

[2] Extract from *Journals of the Sieges of the Madras Army in the Years* 1817, 1818 *and* 1819, by Lieut. E. Lake, M.E., quoted in *The Military Engineer in India*, by the present author, Vol. I, p. 202.

that the 1st and 3rd Divisions of the Deccan Army, under Hislop and Malcolm, should be sent against him in the position which he had taken up at Mehidpur in the Indore State. The Maratha left rested on the River Sipra, their right was covered by a deep ravine, and they had 63 guns. Nevertheless, Hislop and Malcolm, with only 9,000 men and 18 small guns, crossed the river by a ford on December 21st, 1817, assaulted the position, and routed 30,000 Maratha horse and foot, who suffered 3,000 casualties and lost all their guns. Holkar's artillerymen stood to their guns until bayonetted and inflicted more than 700 casualties on the British, but his infantry and cavalry fled as soon as the guns were carried and were pursued and cut down in scores by our cavalry. Four companies of the Madras Pioneers,[1] under Captain R. McCraith, M.I., were present at the Battle of Mehidpur and worked for many hours in deep water to make the fords of the Sipra practicable for the artillery. Their labours were described as so highly meritorious and useful that the honour "Mahidpore" was awarded subsequently to their descendants, the Q.V.O.Madras Sappers and Miners. Thoroughly cowed by his defeat, Holkar of Indore signed a treaty on January 1st, 1818, and took no further part in the war.

After his overthrow at Poona, Baji Rao was pursued by the 4th and Reserve Divisions of the Deccan Army under Brig.-Generals Smith and Pritzler, the latter having succeeded Brig.-General Munro in command of the Reserve Division. The Peshwa eluded both these divisions until they had been reformed into a flying column under Smith to follow him and a siege column under Pritzler to reduce his forts. Eventually, Smith came up with the Marathas at a place called Ashti in the Sholapur District south-east of Ahmadnagar and in a purely cavalry action on February 20th, 1818, gained a complete victory over them. He killed the Maratha general, Gokla, captured the titular Raja of Satara, and put Baji Rao to flight once more. The battles of Kirkee, Sitabaldi, Nagpur, Mehidpur and Ashti decided the war. It remained only to keep Sindhia, Holkar, the Bhonsla and the Gaikwar in subjection while exterminating the Pindaris and reducing a large number of forts in Western and Central India, and accordingly the greater part of the Grand or Bengal Army returned to its cantonments with the exception of a force under General Marshall which captured the fortresses of Dhuma (Dhamoni) and Mandla (Mandala)[2] in March and April. Detachments of the Bengal Pioneers or Sappers were present at these affairs, and also the Bengal Company of Miners,[3] but it may be remarked that, except in the sieges of Chanda and Asirgarh, the Bengal Pioneers saw little fighting in the Third Maratha War.[4] This was inevitable because the divisions of the Grand Army to

[1] "B," "E," "F" and "G" Companies of the 1st Battalion, totalling 315 men with 4 British officers. (See "Early Indian Campaigns and the Decorations Awarded for them," by Major H. Biddulph, R.E., appearing in *The R.E. Journal*, Vol. XVIII, July–Dec., 1913, pp. 227–35.)

[2] Between Balaghat and Jubbulpore in the Central Provinces.

[3] *History and Digest of Service of the 1st K.G.O. Sappers and Miners*, p. 1.

[4] Some Bengal Pioneers or Sappers may have been present at the reduction of Jawad by Gen. Brown on Jan. 29th, 1818, as Brown commanded a Bengal Division and Pioneer casualties are mentioned.

which they were attached were intended primarily to hold the ring while the Deccan Army dealt with the Marathas and Pindaris.

A process of "mopping up" was carried out by the Deccan Army during the remainder of 1818 and early in 1819 in which dozens of hill-forts in Khandesh, the Konkan and the Deccan were besieged and captured. These ancient strongholds of feudal times were often located on steep mountains with precipitous tops of basaltic rock which were so unscalable that the defenders did not trouble to build any large fortifications other than gateways over the flights of steps which led upwards, through clefts or gullies, to the summit. Some of the mountains had a natural supply of water from springs, and their garrisons could hold out almost indefinitely if provided with sufficient food. The garrisons of others had to carry water to the summit from a stream at the base, where they lived in a walled town or *pettah* forming their first line of defence. Artillery fire was most ineffective against these natural fortresses, and a besieging force was commonly faced with the alternatives of a surprise assault or a prolonged blockade. The one was hazardous in the extreme: the other entailed a dreary vigil under a burning sun and was seldom attempted.

Some of these hill fortresses were very powerful, such as Vasota on a peak 3,000 feet high in the Western Ghats, or Trimbak on a large mountain in the Nasik region topped by sheer precipices. The garrisons of these places were prepared to put up a stout resistance, but those of the smaller forts often preferred to surrender when summoned. The Madras Pioneers were present at the reduction of most of these forts and the sieges also of many fortified towns. They took part in the relief of Nalgonda in Hyderabad in December, 1817, the capture of Gadag, Dambal and Hubli in the Dharwar District of Bombay in January, 1818, and of Badami in the Bijapur District on February 17th, 1818; also in the capture of Thalner (Talnair) on the Tapti north of Aurangabad on February 27th, of Singarh, south of Poona, on March 2nd, and of Jeypur, Purandhar and Vazirgarh, a few miles still further south, between March 12th and 16th. They were present at the surrender of Gokak on March 9th and the siege of Belgaum from March 20th to April 10th, 1818, and at the reduction of Ankai-Tankai (Unkye-Tunkye) in Khandesh on April 3rd and of Vasota, near Satara, on April 7th; also at the siege of Rajdair, north-east of Nasik, on April 11th/12th, and of Trimbak on April 23rd/24th, after the fall of which 17 other forts in Khandesh surrendered without resistance.[1]

Continuing the tale of the exploits of the Madras Pioneers, it may be recorded that they served in the siege of Sholapur from May 10th to 15th, 1818, and were present when the surrender of Pavagarh[2] on August 8th completed the reduction of the Peshwa's territories. They were present with a company of Bengal Pioneers at the siege of Chanda, south of Nagpur,

[1]It is probable that detachments of the Madras Pioneers were present when the surrenders were received. In his *Memoir of the Operations of the British Army in India*, p. 322, Lt.-Col. Blacker gives the names of the forts as follows (adopting the peculiar spelling of the period):—Haruss, Wajeerah, Bowleyghur, Cownye, Eyewattah, Achlah, Marundah, Rowlah, Towlah, Caheenah, Caldher, Hatghur, Ramsey, Kumeirah, Bapeirgun, Gungurrah and Tringlewarree.

[2]A hill fort in the Panch Mahals District of Bombay.

TRIMBAK
The north face.

from May 10th to 20th, in which Lieutenant T. R. Fell of the Bengal unit was severely wounded while planting a standard on a breach, a feat which is commemorated on a memorial tablet in Winchester Cathedral. They fought in the siege of Malegaon, north of Aurangabad, from May 8th to June 13th, in which Lieutenant T. Davies, M.E., was killed and Lieutenant J. W. Nattes, M.E., mortally wounded. On November 30th, 1818, they were present at the surrender of Amalner in Eastern Khandesh, and from January 6th to 11th, 1819, at the siege of Jilpi Amnair on the Tapti, where three companies under Captain R. McCraith, M.I., made a road for guns through a difficult pass. A detachment took part in the siege of Nowa on the Godavari from January 8th to 31st, 1819, and another in operations under Maj.-General Keir in February. Several companies were present at the siege of Asirgarh from March 17th to April 19th, 1819, and of Koppal, west of Bellary, from May 8th to 13th.[1] The Madras Pioneers were indeed ubiquitous in the Third Maratha War and no force of any size was complete without them.

As regards the services of the Bombay Pioneers after the expulsion of the Peshwa from Poona, it may be mentioned that while the Baroda Company with the Gujarat Division took part in the operations in Malwa after the Battle of Mehidpur, including the reduction of Amalner, and also in the siege and capture of Asirgarh, the Poona Company assisted the Reserve Division in the reduction of 22 forts including Singarh, Purandhar, Vasota and Sholapur.[2] The remaining two companies, stationed normally in Bombay, sent detachments to assist in the reduction of no less than 33 forts in Khandesh, the Konkan and neighbouring districts.[3] It is evident that the Bombay Corps under Captain Peter De La Motte, Bo.I., formed a valuable source for the supply of small bodies of engineer troops to many columns operating in the western littoral.

The brief siege of Trimbak, a fortress situated about 26 miles south-west of Nasik, is typical of some of the operations in which the Madras

[1]The record of these services will be found in greater detail in the *Historical Record of the Q.V.O. Madras Sappers and Miners*, pp. 26–28, and in *The Military History of the Madras Engineers and Pioneers*, by Major H. M. Vibart, R. (M.) E., Vol. I, pp. 517–579.

[2]The names of the remaining 18 forts are thus given in the *Brief History of the Royal Bombay Sappers and Miners*, p. 5 :— Wazeerghur, Pandanghur, Kamalghur, Kalunjah, Chundun, Wundun, Wyratghur, Seedasheerghur, Machendraghur, Baltee, Seraolee, Islampur, Wanghy, Walwa, Kundulghur, Mussoor, Wassantghur and Kola. On modern maps these appear as Vazirgarh, Padavgarh, Kamalgarh, Kenjalgarh, Chandan, Wandan, Vairatgad, Sadashivgarh, Machhindragarh, Baltis, Shirala, Urun-Islampur, Vangi, Valva Kundal, Masur, Vasantgarh and Kola. It is possible that some Bombay Pioneers were present at the reduction of Chakan, north-west of Poona, on Feb. 26th, 1818.

[3]In the *Brief History of the Royal Bombay Sappers and Miners*, p. 5, the names of these forts are given as follows :—Lohghur, Kurnalla, Chanderghur, Myputghur, Pallee, Gunga, Byghur, Lingunia, Takoonah, Toongah, Ouchilgurh, Songhur, Koaree, Zella, Raighur, Kangooree, Katellaghur, Ragh, Muchee, Boorup, Gowsilla, Essapur, Muddunghur, Ramghur, Palghur, Anjanweil, Rassulghur, Seedghur, Bhugwantghur, Deoghur, Campta, Acheera and Newtee. In modern spelling these are : Lohogarh, Karnala, Chandragarh, Mahipatgarh, Parli, Ghangarh, Bhairongad, Lingana, Tikona, Tung, Uchel, Songhar, Korigarh, Rezala, Raigarh, Kangori, Kotilgarh, Rajmachi, Manranjan, Borap, Gosale, Yisapur, Mandangarh, Ramgarh, Palgad, Anjanvel, Rasalgarh, Sidhgarh, Bhagvantgarh, Devagarh, Kamte, Achra and Nivati. At Raigarh, in particular, the Bombay Pioneers excelled themselves in making roads for heavy guns and mortars up the mountains (see the Memoir of Major Peter De La Motte, Bo.I, appearing in the *East India Military Calendar*, Vol. II, p. 401).

and Bombay Pioneers took part. On April 22nd, 1818, a column marched from Nasik while Lieutenants Davies and Nattes, M.E., went ahead to reconnoitre. With the main body was a temporary company of Sappers and Miners (27 Europeans and 47 Indians) and four companies of Madras Pioneers. When Davies approached the fort, the enemy evacuated the *pettah* near the base, and gaining the crest through a northern gateway, opened fire on him and his party. Trimbak looked almost impregnable. The perpendicular scarp varied from 200 to 400 feet in height and the only assailable points were two gateways, that on the southern side being the principal one and more easily reached than the northern gateway to which the only means of approach was by a long, narrow and precipitous flight of steps. The head of the stairway was defended by two towers flanking the gate; otherwise, the northern face was unfortified, though there were some isolated towers on conspicuous points. The defences around the southern gateway were more elaborate. At the foot of the scarp on the northern side were some ruined houses, and half a mile from it, the *pettah* or town.

Davies recommended an attack on the northern gate, giving as his reasons that there was only one line of works to be destroyed by artillery fire and that the ruined houses and *pettah* below the cliffs would afford cover. The easier approach to the southern gate was impracticable for heavy guns. Accordingly, it was decided that, after the enemy's artillery had been silenced, a battery for heavy guns should be erected between the *pettah* and the northern face to cover an advance to the ruined houses, where a 6-pounder battery could be placed to breach the northern gate on the heights above. Supported by the artillery, the stormers might then be able to climb the stairway without heavy loss, while the attention of the garrison was diverted by a feint against the southern gate.

At 4 p.m. on April 23rd, after all tools and materials had been collected in the *pettah*, a detachment including some Sappers and Miners and 30 Madras Pioneers marched round to the southern side to construct a battery for two 6-pounders, and at sunset a working party of 30 Sappers and Miners, 80 Madras Pioneers and some infantry and lascars advanced from the *pettah* towards the northern face to build the battery for heavy guns. This was extremely difficult because the ground was solid rock, and to gain sufficient elevation for the guns it was necessary to raise the wheels instead of sinking the trails. However, the remainder of the Sappers and Miners and 400 Pioneers arrived at midnight, and before dawn the battery was completed and armed. By nightfall, the ruined houses had been occupied, though under heavy musketry fire and showers of stones, and finally, when his enemies were almost at the gate, the Kiladar of Trimbak decided to capitulate. His offer was gladly accepted, and the garrison of 530 men was allowed to march out with all the honours of war.

Such tame surrenders were common, and their causes sometimes ludicrous. For instance, Rajdair was given up because the garrison, having set fire to the Kiladar's house after they had discovered that certain trivial

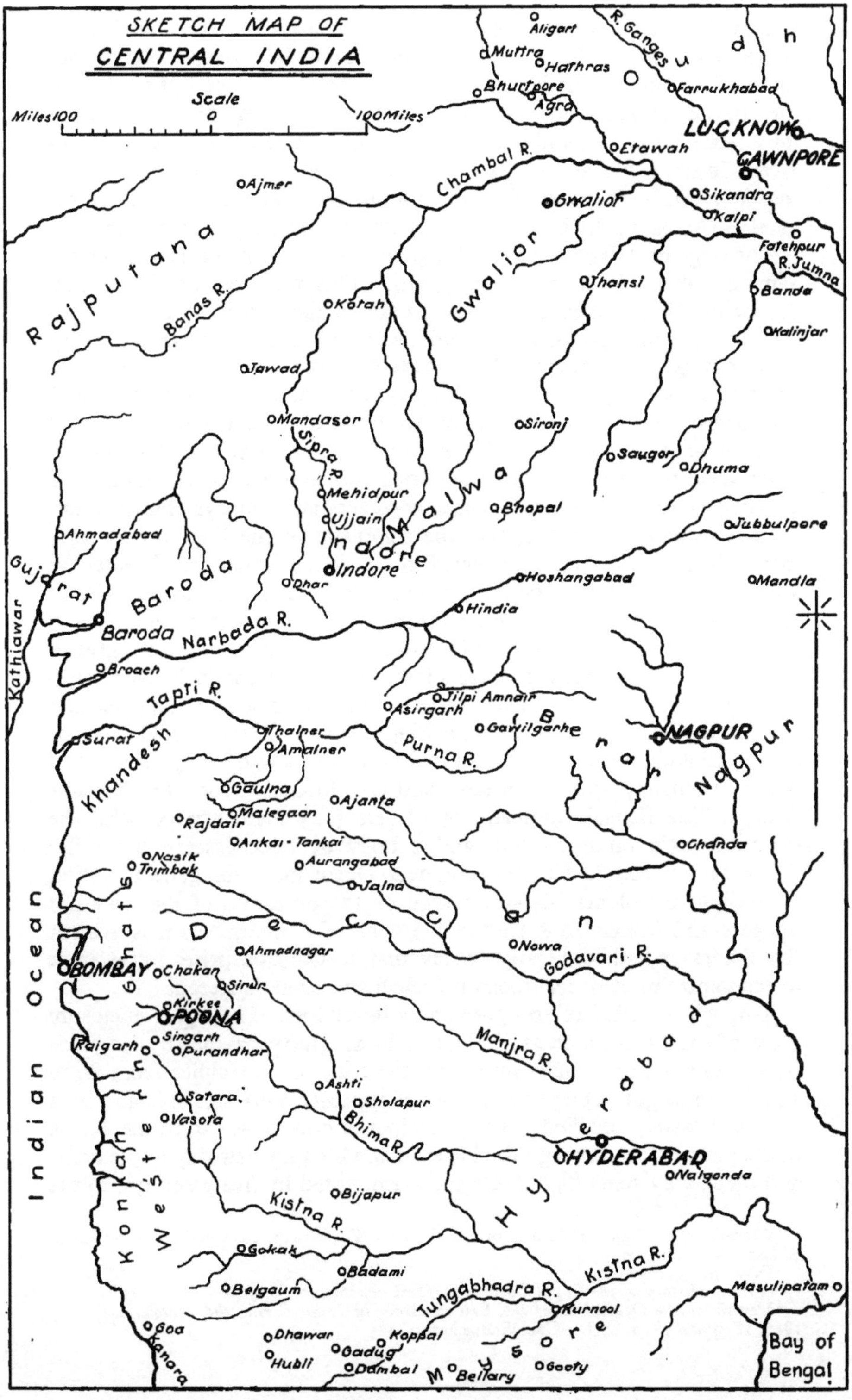
SKETCH MAP OF
CENTRAL INDIA
Scale
Miles 100
0
100 Miles
Aligarh
Muttra
Hathras
Bhurtpore
Agra
R. Ganges
O u d h
Farrukhabad
LUCKNOW
CAWNPORE
Etawah
Chambal R.
Ajmer
Gwalior
Sikandra
Kalpi
Fatehpur
R. Jumna
Banda
Kalinjar
Rajputana
Banas R.
Kotah
Gwalior
Jhansi
Jawad
Mandasor
Sipra R.
Sironj
Saugor
Dhuma
Mehidpur
Ujjain
Malwa
Bhopal
Jubbulpore
Ahmadabad
Indore
Indore
Gujarat
Baroda
Dhar
Hoshangabad
Mandla
Kathiawar
Baroda
Narbada R.
Hindia
Broach
Tapti R.
Jilpi Amnair
Asirgarh
Berar
Gawilgarh
NAGPUR
Nagpur
Surat
Khandesh
Thalner
Amalner
Purna R.
Gaulna
Ajanta
Malegaon
Rajdair
Ankai - Tankai
Chanda
Nasik
Trimbak
Aurangabad
Jalna
Deccan
Nowa
Godavari R.
Ahmadnagar
Indian Ocean
BOMBAY
Chakan
Sirur
Kirkee
POONA
Singarh
Raigarh
Purandhar
Manjra R.
Hyderabad
Ashti
Sholapur
Satara
Vasota
Bhima R.
HYDERABAD
Nalgonda
Western Ghats
Konkan
Bijapur
Kistna R.
Gokak
Badami
Kistna R.
Belgaum
Tungabhadra R.
Masulipatam
Kurnool
Goa
Dhawar
Koppal
Mysore
Gadug
Hubli
Dambal
Bellary
Gooty
Kanara
Bay of
Bengal

arrears of pay had not been settled, became so alarmed by the spread of the flames that they decided that the besiegers might help them to extinguish the conflagration! Trimbak was reputed to be the strongest of all the hill forts in the Konkan. The losses in an assault might have been very heavy, for a storming party climbing up to the northern gate would have had to ascend in single file, and under a deluge of stones, a flight of steps so steep that it would be necessary for each man to hoist himself upwards by his hands.[1] Actually, the British lost only 22 men and captured 25 guns.

The siege of Asirgarh furnishes a good example of an operation against a more elaborately fortified stronghold. This place lay on the eastern border of Khandesh in one of the passes leading from the Deccan into Hindustan, and Doveton's and Malcolm's divisions of the Deccan Army were sent against it because the Kiladar had given asylum to the fugitive Appa Sahib of Nagpur. By March 17th, 1819, the British force in front of Asirgarh comprised 5 regiments of cavalry and 14 battalions of infantry with 46 guns; and by April 3rd, when the siege was in progress, it reached a strength of 15,000 men with the arrival of 4 battalions and a battering train of 16 heavy guns, howitzers and mortars from Saugor. It is remarkable, therefore, that the command of the Engineer Department should have been entrusted to a young subaltern, Lieutenant John Coventry, M.E., assisted by five other junior engineers. Under Coventry's orders was a large contingent of Pioneers consisting of about 1,000 men drawn from all three Presidencies. These included the greater part of the 1st Battalion, Madras Pioneers, under Captain R. McCraith, M.I., 3 companies (300 men)[2] of the Bengal Pioneers or Sappers, and the Baroda Company of the Bombay Pioneers under Lieutenant C. F. Hart, Bo.I.[3] In addition, Coventry had the services of a temporary Sapper and Miner Company (34 Europeans and 45 Indians) from the Madras Army. The Bengal Company of Miners (125 men) arrived with the battering train on April 3rd, and a body of 1,000 lascars and other followers was attached to the Engineer Department for general duties. According to Colonel Blacker, a total of 13 companies of Pioneers and Sappers and Miners took part in the siege of Asirgarh,[4] so it is evident that the lesson had been learned at last that in such enterprises any attempt to economize in engineer troops is foolish and even dangerous.

Asirgarh consisted of an upper and a lower fort. The upper enclosure crowned the top of a hill 750 feet high and was 1,100 yards long by 600 yards wide. The masonry walls rose from the edge of a precipice from 80 to 120 feet in height. Only two avenues of approach were available and both were elaborately fortified. The principal approach was from the *pettah* in the plain below, through the lower fort, which lay half way to the crest, and thence, by steep flights of steps surmounted by five gateways, to the

[1] *Journals of the Sieges of the Madras Army in the Years* 1817, 1818 *and* 1819, by Lieut. E. Lake, M.E., p. 107.
[2] *Ibid.*, p. 154.
[3] *A Brief History of the Royal Bombay Sappers and Miners*, p. 5.
[4] *Memoir of the Operations of the British Army in India during the Mahratta War of* 1817, 1818 *and* 1819, by Lt.-Col. V. Blacker, p. 425.

west gate of the upper fort; but there was another, though circuitous, approach to a gateway at the south-east angle without traversing the lower fort. The fortress was heavily armed and strongly held, and as it had an ample supply of water, it could not be blockaded.

The attack began on the western side under the burning rays of a tropical sun. Doveton occupied the *pettah* on March 18th, 1819, and the Pioneers began to throw up batteries to breach the walls of the lower fort. On the 20th, the guns opened fire and an assault was planned for the following day, but it was abandoned after a British magazine had exploded. Coventry then recommended an attack on the eastern side of the upper fort, and the Pioneers prepared roads by which the guns were hauled with extreme difficulty to positions opposite the northern and eastern faces. By April 7th, a practicable breach having been made in the eastern face, all was ready for an assault, but the Kiladar did not await the attack. Following the example of Trimbak, he entered into negotiations, and on April 9th, was allowed to evacuate the place while Doveton hoisted the Union Jack over the walls. The garrison lost only 138 men, but the British casualties amounted to 311, including 16 Madras Pioneers; yet the political effect of the victory was so far-reaching that it may be said to have put the *coup de grâce* to the intrigues of the Maratha Confederacy.

The fall of Asirgarh marked the virtual end of the Third Maratha War, though a few minor operations were still required to complete the subjugation of the country. In May, 1819, General Pritzler besieged and captured the mountain fastness of Koppal,[1] where two companies of the 2nd Battalion, Madras Pioneers, under Captain T. Smithwaite, M.I., assisted in making roads and building batteries and subsequently carried bamboo ladders in the assault.[2] Gradually, the whole of Central India and the Deccan settled down to an era of peace and order unknown since the zenith of the Mughal domination. The protection afforded by Great Britain shadowed the ancient houses of the Rajput States, and her rule was undisputed from Cape Comorin to the Sutlej. The Pioneers had made their contribution towards securing these happy results, and thereafter they were prominent in every expedition and siege until they handed over their well-earned laurels to their successors, the Sappers and Miners.

[1]Koppal or Koppaldroog, west of Bellary, should not be confounded with another Koppaldroog, south of Bednore in Kanara. (See Sketch Map in Chapter I.)

[2]As regards scaling ladders, Lt.-Col. Blacker remarks (p. 234) that attempts to design jointed ladders adaptable to varying heights had failed, and that a one-piece bamboo ladder up to 35 feet in length, bound throughout with spun yarn, had been adopted. It was very light, yet strong enough to carry a soldier on every rung if placed correctly at a slope of 2/1.

CHAPTER IV

THE FIRST BURMA WAR, CAPTURE OF BHURTPORE AND MINOR CAMPAIGNS, 1824–1838

MANY reorganizations and changes took place in the three Corps of Pioneers after the conclusion of the Third Maratha War. Recruiting for the Madras Pioneers was suspended in July, 1819, in the interests of economy, and the two battalions fell much below strength. As in Bengal, an experiment was in progress with a small Corps of " Sappers and Miners," the formation of which had been ordered on March 24th, 1818. This Corps, consisting of one European and two Native Companies, was to be officered from the Madras Engineers ; but whereas the Bengal Corps was supplied with trained non-commissioned officers from Chatham, no such assistance was given to the Madras Corps, and perhaps in consequence of this handicap, the experiment failed. The Sapper and Miner companies never exceeded a combined strength of 50 Europeans and 32 Indians and died a natural death in May, 1821, without seeing any active service. They could not compete against the experienced and well-paid Pioneers, whose battalion establishment had been revised once more in 1818 and fixed at 9 British officers, 8 Indian officers and 748 Indian other ranks, in addition to an assistant-surgeon, a sergeant-major and a number of artisans and followers.[1]

Employment with the Madras Pioneers was most popular with the British officers of the Madras Infantry. In fact, there were so many candidates for vacancies that the situation drew a strongly worded protest from an anonymous writer. " Of late years," wrote " Carnaticus " in 1820,[2] " we have to complain of the strange want of officers in every part of the Native Army. We find, in 1818, the officers of the Madras Native Army not averaging above five actually doing duty with each battalion. It must be understood that officers attached to the Pioneers receive an extra allowance of about 135 rupees monthly ; but such an occupation for officers is altogether unseemly and would be much better transferred to respectable non-commissioned officers. . . . Whilst every other corps in the army laboured under the greatest want of European officers, the Corps of Pioneers had many claimants because there was something to gain by it,

[1]In Jan., 1818, when the currency of the Madras Presidency was changed from pagodas, fanums and cash to rupees, annas and pies, the monthly rates of pay of the Madras Pioneers were as follows :—Jemadar, Rs. 24/8/0 to Rs. 42/0/0 ; Havildar, Rs. 10/8/0 ; Naik, Rs. 8/12/0 ; Pioneer (Private) Rs. 7/13/4. In addition, all ranks usually drew certain field allowances called *batta*. The new establishment authorized in 1818 for each battalion was 2 Captains, 5 Lieutenants, 1 Ensign, 1 Adjutant, 1 Assist-Surgeon, 1 Sergt.-Major, 8 Jemadars, 24 Havildars, 24 Naiks, 700 Privates and 99 artisans and followers.

[2]*Summary of the Mahratta and Pindaree Campaign during* 1817, 1818 *and* 1819 (Anonymous), p. 311.

and the channel in which that branch of patronage ran always succeeded in keeping the Pioneers complete with officers to the detriment and prejudice of the army at large."

This attack on his Department caused the Quarter-Master-General much annoyance, and he recommended to Major-General Sir Thomas Munro, the Governor and Commander-in-Chief, in a letter dated January 18th, 1821, that recruiting for the Pioneers should be resumed at once because their services were indispensable to him. Sir Thomas agreed, and in forwarding the recommendation to the Government on January 30th, he remarked that as no inland navigation existed, and as communication by road between the coast and the interior led through certain passes which were difficult to keep open, he considered that the services of the Pioneers were necessary for clearing and repairing these roads and also for the construction and repair of military buildings, which would be expensive if executed by civilian labour. The Government approved these recommendations, and recruiting for the Madras Pioneers was resumed in the spring of 1821.[1]

Then Major T. F. De Havilland, M.E.,[2] a keen reformer who was acting as Chief Engineer, began his *magnum opus*—a stupendous memorandum to Sir Thomas Munro on the status, employment, administration and organization of the Engineers, Pioneers and Sappers and Miners in the Madras Army, which, when submitted to the Governor on November 23rd, 1821, covered 172 closely-written pages of manuscript and had no less than 206 paragraphs. A few extracts will suffice to show the general nature of De Havilland's proposals :—[3]

"The continuance of the Corps of Engineers in the condition of a mere skeleton, composed of officers only, having no soldiers under their immediate command, may be attributed chiefly to the fact that the Corps of Pioneers had existed long before the present Corps of Engineers. . . . The Engineer Department, being in itself imperfect and dependent on others, an Engineer officer takes the field under every possible disadvantage. He not only goes thither soldierless but he is scarcely allowed assistance of any kind. No preparation seems necessary for his Department. If he asks for Stores, he will get them 'there'—for Men, they will be drawn from the Line if any be required in aid of the Pioneers—for Artificers, they will be furnished from other Departments or he will be authorized to pick them up from among the Camp followers or in native villages. If he suggests the expediency of materials for a Pontoon train, he is told they *may* not be necessary. . . . It will be admitted that the inconveniences of the present system would be remedied in *personnel* at least if the Pioneers formed a constituent part of the Engineers. . . . The Pioneer Officer

[1]*Historical Record of the Q.V.O. Madras Sappers and Miners*, Vol. I, p. 30.

[2]See *The Military Engineer in India*, by the present author, Vol. I, p. 228. De Havilland is mentioned also in Vol. I, pp. 171 and 200 and Vol. II, pp. 89 and 171, of the same work. See also *The Royal Engineers in Egypt and the Sudan*, by the present author, pp. 16, 17, 464 and 465, for De Havilland's services in Egypt in 1801.

[3]A printed copy of the memorandum of Nov. 23rd, 1821, is in the R.E. Museum at Chatham and extracts from it are given in *The Military History of the Madras Engineers and Pioneers*, by Major H. M. Vibart, R. (M.) E., Vol. II, pp. 3–25.

already receives the double pay of his rank, while the whole Corps is always on full *batta*. These extra allowances are bestowed on the Pioneer Officer who may neither have studied his profession nor have any pretensions to it. . . . In the late campaign, Captains of Pioneers performed their duties under the directions of junior Engineers. It was found necessary to raise a small corps of Sappers and Miners, and these came untaught, unlearnt, to the Engineers. They had to be organized and brought into action, as it were, in one and the same moment by a young Officer aided by a few still younger. . . . The recent formation of a regular Corps of Sappers and Miners in Bengal strengthens the argument that it is most essential that the Corps of Engineers should have soldiers, both European and Native, permanently attached, and I express a hope that they may form a constituent and integral part of the Corps though I am aware that in Bengal the Corps of Sappers and Miners is only *attached* to the Engineers. . . . I would also submit that the Sappers and Miners should bear arms and be regarded in every respect as Soldiers, and when encamped, should not be pitched in the rear of the Quarter-Master-General's Department in the condition of public followers as the Pioneers now are. It is absurd that *any* Corps in the army should require others to protect it. The arms should be the *Fusee* and Bayonet with a light Pouch, the same as the Foot Artillery carry, except that a Lance and Pistol might be preferred for the front rank. . . . As there does not appear to me a necessity for both Engineer men and Pioneer men, I may show how the latter may be dispensed with in the Quarter-Master-General's Department in case your Honour in Council should deem it expedient to transfer them to the Engineers. It does not appear that taking the Pioneers away from the control of the Quarter-Master-General would impede the service."

In addition, De Havilland suggested that his proposals would prevent the Quarter-Master-General from interfering in engineering matters, and he recommended that the Pioneers should be removed from the control of that officer and incorporated in a " Regiment of Engineers " which might comprise one European company, another of " Men of Colour " and eight native companies.

The Quarter-Master-General was naturally much annoyed and asserted that he could not perform his duties properly without the aid of the Pioneers. " The Chief Engineer," he wrote, " may still maintain that the Pioneer officers have neither studied the profession of engineering nor have any pretensions to it, but it is almost farcical to talk of science when speaking of the construction of roads or opening of passes. It is a fact that the best road-maker now in England is a *ci-devant* purser of a ship.[1] The Chief Engineer's proposal is evidently that the Corps to which he belongs should engross every duty and service of a scientific nature. These lofty pretensions of the Corps of Engineers are nothing new ; and when they assumed in the French service the proud title of Corps of Genius (Corps du Génie) they showed the extent to which they were inclined to push their exclusive claims to all scientific requirements. I beg leave to

[1]Mr. J. L. McAdam, the inventor of the macadam process, who died in 1836.

inform them that the word 'Engineer' is derived, not from Genius, but from the word 'Engine'."

This acrimonious letter and other correspondence were forwarded to the Court of Directors with the result that in 1823 orders were issued that one of the two battalions of Madras Pioneers should be disbanded forthwith and the remaining battalion officered from the Corps of Engineers. No action, however, seems to have been taken to carry these orders into effect, possibly because of the threatening clouds over Burma. A General Order by the Governor-General in Council was published on August 12th, 1824, directing that the Pioneer establishments throughout India should be transferred to the appropriate Engineer Corps as soon as practicable; but on the representation of the Governor of Madras that sufficient Engineers were not available at the moment to officer the Pioneers, and that he anticipated most beneficial results from the eventual conversion of one of the battalions into Sappers and Miners provided that some non-commissioned officers could be sent from Chatham, the Court agreed to postpone the reorganization and both Pioneer battalions were allowed to remain as they were. Thus, at the outbreak of the First Burma War, the Madras Pioneers still consisted of two battalions, officered entirely from the Infantry and under the control of the Quarter-Master-General. Nevertheless, De Havilland had sown good seed, and the results were reaped in a sweeping reform which was initiated in 1831.

In Bengal, until 1818, the eight existing companies of Pioneers or Sappers under Major John Swinton, B.I., were considered to be sufficient for the engineering demands of the army if assisted during siege operations by the Company of Miners. In March, 1818, however, it was decreed that, as in Madras, a Corps of Sappers and Miners should be formed, and shortly afterwards a draft of British non-commissioned officers, trained at Chatham, was sent to India and posted to it. The new corps was to consist of six companies, officered from the Bengal Engineers, whose establishment was to be increased correspondingly, and on February 19th, 1819, the Bengal Sappers and Miners came into being at Allahabad.[1] The Corps was commanded at first by Captain (afterwards Lieut.-General) Richard Tickell, B.E., who had been appointed Adjutant; but an official Commandant was soon provided in the person of Major (afterwards Major-General Sir) Thomas Anburey, B.E., though the latter does not appear to have assumed charge until 1821. Apart from British officers, the Bengal Sappers and Miners had a total strength of 816 Indian ranks, with an Assistant-Surgeon, a Sergeant-Major and 38 British non-commissioned officers, and each company contained 120 men.[2] Selected men from the 4th and 8th Companies of the Bengal Pioneers provided a nucleus for each company, and the remainder were obtained by recruitment. The two denuded companies of Pioneers were replenished from the Company of Miners, which then ceased to exist. The Sappers and Miners were clothed at first as Pioneers; but in September, 1819, they were provided

[1]G.O.G.G., Feb. 13th, 1819, and G.O.C.C., Feb. 19th, 1819.
[2]*History and Digest of Service of the 1st K.G.O. Sappers and Miners*, p. 5.

with a uniform resembling that of the Royal Sappers and Miners in England. This consisted of a red tunic with blue collar and cuffs, ornamented with gold braid for officers and yellow braid for other ranks, blue trousers with a broad red stripe, a blue *paggari* (turban) with a yellow fringe (gold for officers) and a red *kullah* (centre cap). At a later date, the trousers were replaced by pyjamas and blue *puttees*.[1]

An allusion to the Bengal Sappers and Miners appears in a letter written by Ensign George Thomson, B.E., on August 29th, 1819, soon after his arrival in India. " The new Corps which is established at Allahabad," he writes,[2] " is intended to be on the same principles as the establishment at Chatham, only on a larger scale as we have 700 men instead of 200. As the Government wishes the juniors of the Corps to pass through it, I think it better to be some months with it before I apply for any appointment. Cawnpore, where I now am, will probably not be marked in the maps you have, as it was a place of no consideration before the cantonments, which are the largest in India, were built there. When built, it was meant for a frontier station, but the rapidity of Lord Lake's conquests soon changed it from a frontier to a central station."

On June 4th, 1821, the headquarters of the Bengal Sappers and Miners were transferred to Cawnpore, where the Bengal Pioneers were stationed, and nine days later Lieut.-Colonel Thomas Anburey, B.E., arrived to assume command. No military operations were in prospect, and the companies were employed chiefly on road construction in Central India. The haphazard nature of the administration is shown by the fact that for some time after Thomson arrived at Asirgarh in January, 1821, with a detachment of Sappers, he was unable to start work because he had received no instructions. Mails took three weeks to reach him from Allahabad because the *dak*-runners would not travel by night for fear of tigers on the road. A year later, he was still engaged on road-making between Asirgarh and Nagpur in command of two companies of Bengal Sappers and Miners and a detachment of Bengal Pioneers. Other companies were employed on road work between Nagpur and Calcutta and in the neighbourhood of Saugor, and several Maratha fortresses were dismantled. On March 30th, 1824, Thomson writes :—" A few days after my arrival at Nagpore I received an order appointing me Adjutant of the Sappers and Miners and directing me to join the headquarters at Cawnpore. On arrival, I was laid up with fever. However, I got over it in two months. Soon after I was able to work, about 500 of the Sappers were ordered in for practice. I was the only officer with them, and you may suppose I had sufficient employment in drilling so many men and teaching them sapping and mining." As Thomson was then a subaltern of less than six years' service it seems that, before the First Burma War, the Bengal Sappers and Miners received little training in their profession and earned their pay chiefly as road-labourers supervised by non-commissioned officers sent from Chatham at great

[1]*Lectures on the Regimental History of the K.G.O. Bengal Sappers and Miners. Instructional Circular* No. 16 of 1927, compiled by Major L. V. Bond, R.E., p. 4.

[2]Letter quoted in the Obituary Notice of Col. George Thomson, C.B., late R. (Bengal) E., appearing in *The R.E. Journal*, Vol. XVI, 1886, pp. 77–84.

expense. It is remarkable, therefore, that they did so well in the siege of Bhurtpore in 1826. However, in numbers at least, the Bengal Army had a respectable establishment of engineer soldiers on the outbreak of hostilities against Burma, for the six companies of Sappers and Miners under Anburey were supported by eight companies of Pioneers under Swinton. Two additional companies of Bengal Pioneers were added to the establishment during the summer of 1824, making a total of ten companies in all. The chief deficiency was in Engineer officers.

Meanwhile, there had been important changes in the establishment of engineer units in the Bombay Army. Experience gained in the Third Maratha War had shown that the four existing companies of Bombay Pioneers under Captain Peter De La Motte, Bo.I., could not meet the demands of all the small columns operating in Khandesh and the Konkan, and accordingly, under a General Order which appeared on December 16th, 1819, the Corps was augmented to six companies, each of one hundred men. In May, 1820, De La Motte was transferred to the 3rd Bombay Cavalry on promotion to Major and was succeeded as Commandant by Captain George Challon, 3rd Bombay Infantry. The Pioneers had recently done execllent work under De La Motte, having demolished eighteen hill forts and marched 600 miles during January, 1820, and the endurance of their leader is proved by the fact that when he embarked for England on furlough in February, 1822, his 23½ years of service in India had included only one month's leave![1] A further increase in the strength of the Bombay Pioneers was soon approved, for their establishment was raised on May 6th, 1822, from six to eight companies and they were recognized officially as a battalion,[2] though the companies were still scattered in Bombay, Poona, Baroda, Kaira, Sholapur and other stations. It may be noted, however, that the term " battalion " was applied to the Corps in 1821 before this expansion was sanctioned.[3] The Pioneers continued to be officered from the Bombay Infantry.

Prior to the raising of the Bombay Pioneers to battalion strength, a company of Sappers and Miners had been added to the Bombay Army. As mentioned in Chapter II, Major-General Robert Nicholson, Chief Engineer and Commander-in-Chief in Bombay, had been authorized on December 23rd, 1799, to enlist 2 *tindals* (overseers) and 30 lascars to perform certain garrison duties with the assistance of lascars from the Artillery and Commissariat Departments. These recruits were designated " Engineer Lascars " and were clothed in red uniforms with black facings. On August 31st, 1820, a Bombay General Order appeared in the following terms :—" The Hon. the Governor in Council is pleased to direct that the number of Engineer Lascars be forthwith increased to a complete Company

[1] *East India Military Calendar*, Vol. II, p. 401.

[2] Under B.G.O., dated May 6th, 1822, the establishment of the battalion was authorized as follows :—1 Capt.-Commandant, 1-2nd Captain, 8 Lieutenants or Ensigns, 1 Adjutant, 1 Assist.-Surgeon, 2 Native Doctors, 1 Subadar-Major, 7 Jemadars, 1 Sergt.-Major, 8 Sergeants, 8 Havildar-Majors, 32 Havildars, 40 Naiks, 800 Privates, 8 Buglers and 8 Bhistis or Pakhalis, together with a number of artificers.

[3] In B.G.O. dated Oct. 5th, 1821, Capt. Challon is mentioned as commanding the " Battalion of Pioneers."

of the undermentioned strength,[1] to be designated in future ' Sappers and Miners ' and to be trained under an Officer of Engineers." Captain Thomas Dickinson, Bo.E., was appointed to command the company and was joined later by Lieutenant T. B. Jervis, Bo.E., as Company Officer. Both officers sailed with the unit on January 5th, 1821, for service in Arabia.[2] The formation of this Sapper and Miner Company did not affect the establishment of Bombay Pioneers ; and the General Order of the Governor-General in Council, published on August 12th, 1824, which directed that all Pioneer formations in India should be transferred to the Engineer Corps, was held in abeyance in Bombay as in Madras. Thus, at the beginning of the Burma War in 1824, the Bombay Army had eight companies of Pioneers under Captain Challon and one company of Sappers and Miners under Captain Dickinson.

We come now to the events leading up to the outbreak of hostilities against the Kingdom of Ava. Past experience had taught the Company that the Burmese were a very peculiar people who responded readily to flattery, and for many years they had been accustomed to supply it on a lavish scale. In 1695, for instance, the Governor of Fort St. George addressed to the King of Burma a petition through which he hoped to obtain important political concessions by a gross exaggeration of the usual ornamental style of Eastern correspondence. " To His Imperial Majesty," wrote Nathaniel Higginson, " who blesseth the noble city of Ava with his Presence, Emperour of Emperours, and excelling the Kings of the East and of the West in Glory and Honour, the clear firmament of Virtue, the fountain of Justice, the perfection of Wisdom, the Lord of Charity and Protector of the Distressed ; the first mover in the Sphere of Greatness, President in Council, Victorious in War ; who feareth none and is feared by all : Center of the Treasures of the Earth and of the Sea, Lord Proprietor of Gold and Silver, Rubys, Amber and all precious Jewells, favoured by Heaven and honoured by Men, whose brightness shines through the World as the light of the Sun, and whose great name will be preserved in perpetual memory ; I humbly pray your Majesty's fountain of goodness to continue your wonted favours to the Right Honourable English Company and to permit our Factors to buy and sell under such Priviledges as your Royal bounty shall please to grant, whereby I shall be encouraged to send my Shipps to your Majesty's Port."[3]

Although such grovelling effusions may have been effective in maintaining amicable relations and furthering trade, they encouraged a predatory people to extend their conquests and to hold the East India Company in the most utter contempt. Having wrested the southern province of Tenasserim from Siam in 1766, the Burmese turned their attention to the coastal region of Arakan and by 1793 were within measurable distance of Calcutta. A rabble of Arakanese, known as Maghs, fled before them to-

[1] 1 Captain, 1 Lieutenant, 2 Sergeants, 2-1st Corporals, 2-2nd Corporals, 1 Subadar, 1 Jemadar, 4 Havildars, 8 Naiks, 120 Privates, 2 Buglers, 2 Bhistis.

[2] *Digest of the Services of the Bombay Sappers and Miners* (1895), compiled by Major G. H. W. O'Sullivan, R.E., p. 2. (See Chapter V.)

[3] *Our Burmese Wars and Relations with Burma*, by Col. W. F. B. Laurie, pp. 4–5.

wards Chittagong and were tamely handed back to them on demand. The King of Ava naturally concluded that the British were afraid of him and became more insolent and contemptuous. The influx of Maghs continued, and their occasional retaliatory raids into Arakan were made a pretext by the Burmese for a constant menace of war. During the Third Maratha War, they planned an invasion of Assam and demanded the cession of Chittagong, Dacca, Murshidabad and Cossimbazar, and their general attitude is shown by the following letter from the Burmese Governor of the island of Ramree, off the Arakan Coast,[1] to the British Magistrate at Chittagong :—[2] " His Majesty has appointed me Governor of Ramree. Understand what kind of personage I am. Four provinces are under my orders. The Mugs belonging to your territory have injured and despoiled my country and have received protection in your territory. The King of Ava has ordered me to demand those Mugs. It is not well to detain those ungrateful people with their ears bored. The sovereigns of many countries have, through fear of the King, delivered up their territories to him, which His Majesty governs like gold and silver. It is not proper to be at enmity, but the English Government does not try to preserve friendship. There will be a quarrel between us and you like fire. Consider what I have written. I was formerly a chief in the army. The King, witnessing my bravery, made me Governor of Ramree. It is useful to have great abilities. I am Governor of Ramree. Therefore I write to you to restore the Mugs. Understand this."

Frequent missions and negotiations served only to increase the contempt in which the Court of Ava held the British. By 1822, through the prowess of Maha Bandula, their best general, the Burmese were in possession of both Assam and Manipur. Bandula had announced that he would shortly take Calcutta, and that a pair of golden fetters, which he carried with him, were destined for the limbs of the Governor-General ! Gold was the symbol of excellence throughout Burma. The " White Elephant of Ava " ruled his subjects with " golden " hands. Perfumes were said to be agreeable to the " golden " nose, and suppliants prostrated themselves before the " golden " feet. Pride and ambition drove the Court of Ava at last to decisive action which provoked war. On September 24th, 1823, a Burmese force landed on the British island of Shahpuri, south of Chittagong, and shortly afterwards two columns advanced upon Sylhet from Assam and Manipur. The column from Assam was driven back, but that from Manipur maintained its footing east of Sylhet, and thus, after all protests had been ignored, the Governor-General was forced to declare war against Burma on February 24th, 1824. The declaration was received with some relief in Bengal for Bandula had declared that, after he had taken Calcutta, he would march on England !

The main invasion of the country was entrusted to Brig.-General Sir Archibald Campbell, K.C.B., late 38th Foot, who was placed in command

[1]See the *Sketch Map of Burma in* 1824 included in this Chapter and also Maps I and II at the end of this volume.

[2]Extract from a translation of a letter, dated April 24th, 1817, appearing in *Documents Illustrative of the Burmese War*, by H. H. Wilson, p. 3.

of 11,500 men,[1] with 42 guns, drawn chiefly from the Madras Army because the Bengal native troops disliked serving overseas.[2] The Madras and Bengal contingents met at the Andaman Islands on May 2nd and entered the Rangoon River on the 10th, the rainy season having been selected as it was thought that water-transport would be easy while the rivers were in flood. The Burmese, however, had been careful to remove all boats and supplies, and accordingly Campbell was tied for a long time to Rangoon, where his troops rotted in a pestilential climate.

The Pioneers with this expedition were drawn wholly from the Madras Presidency, the 1st Battalion, under Captain W. Milne, M.I., sailing from Madras on April 16th with a strength of 552 of all ranks. The other officers were Captain F. Crowe, Lieutenants F. H. M. Wheeler, J. W. Moncrieff, J. Macartney and A. A. Campbell (Adjutant) and Ensigns J. W. Smyth and W. C. Macleod, all of the Madras Infantry.[3] The men were so eager for foreign service that a detachment which had been recalled from Hyderabad marched 25 miles a day for 15 consecutive days in the hottest season of the year.[4] On joining the expedition the Pioneers came under the control of the Chief Engineer, Captain John Mackintosh, M.E.,[5] who was assisted by Lieutenants Edward Lake, George Underwood and Arthur Cotton, M.E., and at the Andamans they met the engineers of the Bengal contingent, Captain (afterwards General Sir) John Cheape and Lieutenants Henry de Budé, James Crommelin, Joseph Tindal, William Dickson and Frederick Abbott, B.E.

The flotilla was convoyed by a number of warships, including the little *Diana*, the first steam vessel ever employed in British warfare, and ascending the Rangoon River on May 11th, 1824, without serious opposition, approached Rangoon and dropped anchor. The town was seen to be surrounded by lofty palisades and to extend for about half a mile along the left bank. Upstream and downstream of it were unprotected suburbs, and inland, some two miles to the north, a golden pagoda towered above the swampy jungle. On the right bank, opposite the town, was the village of Dala. A few dilapidated brick houses among a multitude of huts, and a solitary hull upon the stocks in a small dockyard, completed the drab picture of Rangoon in 1824. "The huts are built of wood or bamboo,"

[1]Of these, nearly 5,000 were British.

[2]Three Bengal battalions had mutinied at Barrackpore near Calcutta in Nov., 1823, when warned for service. (See *Frontier and Overseas Expeditions from India, Vol. V, Burma*, pp. 44, 45.)

[3]This list is given in the *Historical Record of the Q.V.O. Sappers and Miners*, p. 31; but according to the *East India Registers* in the late India Office, in which the regimental lists show officers serving with the Pioneers although there is no separate list for the Pioneers, the following were with the Madras Pioneers in 1824:—Capts. W. Milne and J. S. Trotter and Lieuts. F. H. M. Wheeler, J. W. Moncrieff, J. Macartney and A. A. Campbell. Lieuts. C. Daviniere and A. Milne appear in 1825; but Capt. F. Crowe and Ensigns J. W. Smyth and W. C. Macleod are not mentioned. Possibly they were only attached. Crowe may have replaced Trotter; he was Commandant of the 1st Battalion in Burma in 1825–26, *vice* W. Milne.

[4]*Historical Record of the Q.V.O. Madras Sappers and Miners*, p. 31.

[5] Capt. J. Mackintosh, M.E., was invalided on Aug. 11th, 1824, and died in Mauritius on Oct. 22nd. He was succeeded as Chief Engineer by Capt. J. Cheape, B.E., who acted as such until the arrival of Capt. A. Grant, M.E. Grant was Chief Engineer until he died at Prome on May 20th, 1825. Lieut. George A. Underwood M.E., was then appointed to the vacant post.

LANDING AT RANGOON, MAY 11TH, 1824.

writes Snodgrass,[1] "and the floors, being raised some feet above the ground, would contribute to their dryness and healthiness were not the space beneath a receptacle for dirt and stagnant water from which pestilential vapours ascend. Herds of meagre swine infest the streets by day, and at night are relieved by packs of hungry dogs. One object alone attracts universal admiration: the lofty Shoedagon (Shwedagon) Pagoda, rising in splendour and magnificence. It stands at the summit of an eminence, 75 feet above the road. In shape it resembles an inverted speaking trumpet, 338 feet in height and surmounted by a cap made of brass, 45 feet high. The whole is richly gilded."

The flotilla arrived off Rangoon at 2 p.m. and was fired on by a Burmese battery which was promptly silenced by a couple of broadsides from the *Liffey*. Some of the transports opened fire with their carronades, "but I believe," says Doveton,[2] "they more frequently fired off their sponges and rammers than shot and shell." It was soon evident that a show of resistence was being made by the Burmese only to allow them to remove their belongings to the jungle, and accordingly, under cover of advanced parties from the British regiments, the expeditionary force landed in three detachments and Campbell was soon in full possession. He found a mere shell of a town, deserted, filthy and emptied of all boats, cattle, provisions and valuables. Some of the troops dispersed in search of plunder, and many of the British soldiers, discovering a store of liquor, became riotously drunk. Unhappily, this was by no means unusual, for a dram of brandy was the common reward for good work. Indeed, a whole bottle was sometimes promised by an officer to the first man over a stockade in an assault.[3] Order was restored at length and the Shwedagon Pagoda and other positions garrisoned. The discipline of the force on this occasion was not creditable, but it should be remembered that the British rank and file had been reared in a hard and rough school. By their courage and resource in action, they redeemed their occasional lapses in sobriety, and they inspired the Indian troops in every critical situation.

No transport being available in Rangoon, Campbell was obliged to postpone his intended advance up the Irrawaddy. On May 28th he drove the enemy from some stockades a few miles from his camp and proceeded on June 2nd to attack a powerful position at Kemmendine, three miles upstream.[4] The Burmese stockades were built of teak logs or large bamboos, planted vertically in the ground and connected by longitudinals of timber or bamboo. Heavy timber stockades were reserved chiefly for the defence of large towns or important positions. The enclosures were roughly rectangular in plan, and the stockades varied in height from 10 to 20 feet. The garrison fired from platforms or earthen banks on which *jingals* (small cannon) were mounted. Outer and inner ditches were added, and around the whole was an abattis of trees felled in an outward direction,

[1]*Narrative of the Burmese War* (1827), by Major Snodgrass, pp. 12–15.
[2]*Reminiscences of the Burmese War in* 1824–5–6, by Capt. F. B. Doveton, p. 21.
[3]*Ibid.*, p. 251.
[4]See the *Sketch Map of Burma in* 1824, included in this chapter.

securely anchored, and with branches sharpened. Bamboo spikes, planted in the long grass outside the abattis and in the outer ditch, completed the obstacles. There was, however, one weak point in the design. The exit at the rear was always so narrow that if the stockade were carried by escalade there was no escape for the garrison and they were massacred to a man. The Burmese neither gave nor expected quarter, and if wounded, would shoot in the back any soldier who passed them as they lay. Consequently, it was rarely possible to take any prisoners.

The first attack on Kemmendine on June 3rd, 1824, was unsuccessful. It was a combined naval and military affair in which an absurdly small detachment of only 15 Madras Pioneers accompanied one of the two land columns.[1] "The formidable stockade of Kemmendine was constructed directly across the road," writes Doveton.[2] "It was determined to ply the enemy with Congreve rockets and shrapnell, and in the meantime our flank companies were ordered to clear the way for the column. . . . The crack of firearms was soon heard in front and increased to a regular and continued fire, and at length some of our men were seen emerging from the thick underwood. They told us that in the absence of scaling ladders it would be impossible to force an entrance. Our casualties were rapidly increasing, but all in vain; the obstacle was as unyielding as ever though every effort had been applied to tear down a portion of the palisades, the height and strength of which exceeded anything we had looked for. The most sanguine could not deny the necessity for retreat, at all events until the construction of scaling ladders—which might have been made by the Pioneers in half an hour—would enable us to renew the attack. How the force happened to be unprovided with ladders I cannot say. The fault must rest, I conceive, with the Superintending Engineer, though scaling ladders are a munition of war seldom called for." The columns returned to Rangoon, weary, hungry and spattered with mud, blood and powder. About 80 men had been killed or wounded, partly by misdirected fire from the warships. The lack of scaling ladders and the ineffectiveness of round shot against the stockades were the chief causes of this reverse. Ever afterwards, larger detachments of Madras Pioneers were included in the storming parties and were supplied plentifully with ladders.

On June 10th, all the available Pioneers under Milne took part in a second advance against Kemmendine. On this occasion Campbell had 3,000 men supported by warships and heavy artillery, and after capturing an outlying stockade on June 11th, occupied Kemmendine, which the enemy had evacuated. He then withdrew to Rangoon after detaching garrisons for Kemmendine and the stockade; but unfortunately he allotted no Pioneers to the garrison of the stockade to bury the Burmese dead—the usual task of the Pioneers after a battle—and in consequence sickness and disease, already rampant, began to claim more victims. The enemy retired from the vicinity of Rangoon and concentrated at Danubyu (Donabyu) about 50 miles up the river; but they began to reassemble

[1]*Frontier and Overseas Expeditions from India, Vol. V., Burma*, p. 24.
[2]*Reminiscences of the Burmese War in* 1824–5–6, by Capt. F. B. Doveton, pp. 52–63.

around Rangoon at the end of the month and accordingly Campbell determined to capture a fortified post at Pagoda Point, situated upstream of Kemmendine at the junction of the Hlaing and Panhlaing branches of the Rangoon River. He planned to approach it himself by water with 800 men while Brig.-General W. MacBean marched with 1,200 men to Kamayut on the Hlaing to cut the Burmese communications. The Madras Pioneers accompanied MacBean, and after bridging a creek, carried and placed their ladders in assaults on several stockades, refusing on one occasion to wait for a covering party. No less than seven stockades were escaladed in half an hour, and at least 800 Burmese were killed. Campbell, meanwhile, had taken three stockades at Pagoda Point[1] and had occupied that position, so the result of the combined operations was most satisfactory.

Conditions in Rangoon itself were deplorable. The place was one vast hospital in which the wretched victims of dysentery, scurvy and malaria gasped in the sweltering heat as they lay in dilapidated huts or on the damp ground where leeches and mosquitos added to their sufferings. In the water-logged soil, it was difficult even to bury the dead. " Altogether," remarks Sir John Fortescue,[2] " there were elements in this Burmese expedition of 1824 which provoke comparison with the worst epidemics of yellow fever in the West Indies." Campbell did his best to maintain the morale of his force by constant activity. On July 19th, he organized and dispatched a small expedition to Kyaikkalo (Kaiklu), 13 miles to the north, and on August 4th, another more successful one to Syriam, on the Pegu River east of Rangoon, where the Burmese held an old Portuguese fort and a pagoda. Four days later, he sent a small force across the river to Dala, and on August 20th, a larger force to the southern province of Tenasserim, where Tavoy and Mergui were occupied in due course. As a detachment of the Madras Pioneers assisted in the capture of two stockades at Dala, it is probable that some Pioneers accompanied all these expeditions, though the fact is not recorded. Little happened during September. The enemy reappeared at Pagoda Point, Dala and Syriam and, reinforced by a battalion of elaborately tattooed warriors, who were known as " The King's Invulnerables " and relied on charms, spells and opium to give them courage, they annoyed our outposts by night attacks, sniping and yelling. Rain fell unceasingly, accoutrements rotted in the humid atmosphere, and men died by scores and were buried in shallow and watery graves.[3]

When the monsoon began to abate, hostilities were resumed. On October 5th, 1824, a detachment of 40 Madras Pioneers under Milne marched with a column of Indian troops towards Kyaikkalo and helped *en route* to capture a stockade at Tadagale. On the 7th, after storming a succession of breastworks, the column arrived in front of the Kyaikkalo stockade and proceeded to assault, but it soon recoiled before an accurate

[1]An illustration entitled " Storming a Stockade at Pagoda Point " appears opposite p. 254 in *The Military Engineer in India*, Vol. I, by the present author.

[2]*A History of the British Army*, by the Hon. J. W. Fortescue, Vol. XI, p. 292.

[3]During the first year of the war, while 3½% of the troops were killed in action, 45% died of disease. The total loss during the war amounted to 72½% of the troops engaged.

and heavy fire at close range. " Several of the Pioneers with the ladders were knocked down, together with the leading officers," writes the Column Commander.[1] " Consequently, from the awful and destructive fire and the loss of their commanding and leading officers, the men were seized with panic and lay down." Moncrieff and A. A. Campbell were the Pioneer officers wounded in these operations, and Campbell succumbed to his injuries.[2] The other ranks lost 5 killed and 7 wounded. Milne rallied his men and earned the praise of the Column Commander by procuring transport for the wounded after the troops had retreated. On the 9th he had the satisfaction of destroying the Kyaikkalo defences after reinforcements had occupied the place without opposition. The spectacle of the crucified and horribly mutilated bodies of 28 sepoys and Pioneers, who had perished on the 7th, infuriated the troops to such an extent that thereafter they could not be induced to give quarter to any Burman.

Meanwhile, another small force, including a detachment of Madras Pioneers under Wheeler, was ascending the Hlaing River to attack the fortified village of Tantabin. This place was captured on October 7th, and on the 8th, a powerful stockade upstream of it. The stockade was of solid timber, 15 feet high, with a continuous firing-platform, 8 feet above the ground, on which were wooden guns, iron *jingals*, and piles of wooden shot. The Pioneers received a fine tribute for their work at Tantabin. " I cannot close my report," remarked the Column Commander,[3] " without mentioning the very meritorious services of Brevet-Captain Wheeler and the detachment of Pioneers. Their prompt and ready zeal in situations of difficulty and danger was not less conspicuous than their indefatigable exertions in performing other parts of their laborious duty, and the very gallant style in which they repeatedly dashed forward with the scaling ladders was as honourable to themselves as it was a gratifying mark of faith and confidence in the troops employed." The occasion was unimportant and the casualties small; but this tribute to the services of the Madras Pioneers is quoted as typical of many earned by that Corps during the First Burma War.

The Burmese now began to lose confidence, and the " Lord of All the Golden Umbrellas " issued orders from his capital at Ava recalling from Assam and Arakan the armies which were threatening Bengal. Campbell sent a small expedition eastwards to Martaban and improved the defences of his position at Rangoon extending from the town to the Shwedagon Pagoda with an outpost on the river bank at Kemmendine. By the end of November, 1824, 50,000 Burmese under Maha Bandula were grouped around the position. They were massed chiefly before the pagoda; but

[1]Report from Brig.-Gen. H. F. Smith to the D.A.G., dated Oct. 10th, 1824, quoted in *A Narrative of the First Burmese War*, 1824–26, by G. W. de Rhé Philipe (1905), p. 149. This book contains all the important official reports and despatches and a number of biographical notices of officers.

[2]It appears that the vacancy caused by the death of Lieut. A. A. Campbell was filled by Lieut. J. A. Campbell, an officer slightly junior to him in the Madras Infantry.

[3]Report by Major T. Evans, 38th Regt., to Brig.-Gen. Sir Archibald Campbell, dated Oct. 11th, 1824, quoted in *A Narrative of the First Burmese War*, by G. W. de Rhé-Philipe, p. 159.

the line of their bivouacs in the forest, stretching from the river above Kemmendine to the Pazundaung Creek below Rangoon, could be traced by the smoke of their camp fires. They appeared also at Dala opposite Rangoon. Still without land transport and lacking proper food for his men, Campbell was restricted to a passive defence.

The Burmese attack on Rangoon was launched on December 1st. Heralded by snake-like fire-rafts formed of strings of platforms carrying earthen pots filled with petroleum and cotton and designed to wrap themselves around ships, Bandula pushed his infantry towards Kemmendine and made a series of resolute attacks, all of which were repulsed by our troops aided by fire from the warships. During the next few days, Campbell replied with some local counter-attacks, though he was careful not to drive the enemy out of reach. Then Bandula resorted to deliberate methods and began to dig towards the Shwedagon Pagoda, the key of the British position. The Burmese advanced from the forest and within two hours had vanished into the ground. Working in pairs, a spearman digging while a musketeer stood on guard, they excavated a series of holes which they connected afterwards by trenches to form a properly traversed parallel. Each night they dug a new parallel, and by December 7th, they had sapped almost up to the Shwedagon stockades. Glimpses of the tops of golden umbrellas indicated the movements of Burmese generals along the parallels. Finally, Campbell made a sortie in four columns and drove the Burmese back into the jungle, killing large numbers and capturing 240 small guns. Bandula then abandoned his attempt on Rangoon and withdrew to Kokine, some 4 miles to the north, where he stockaded himself with great skill. The Madras Pioneers were prominent in the defence of Kemmendine and the Shwedagon Pagoda and in a raid on the enemy at Dala, and Wheeler who was temporarily in command, was signalled out for special praise.

Bandula fared no better at Kokine than at Rangoon, for Campbell attacked him on December 15th and drove him towards Danubyu. "When it is known," wrote the British Commander-in-Chief,[1] "that 1,300 British infantry stormed and carried by assault the most formidable intrenched and stockaded works I ever saw, defended by upwards of 20,000 men, I trust it is unnecessary for me to say more in praise of men performing such a prodigy. Future ages will scarcely believe it!" Making due allowance for Campbell's habitually magniloquent style of correspondence, it must be admitted that on this occasion his eulogy was well merited. He brought to notice the services of Cheape and Underwood of the Engineers but omitted any mention of the Madras Pioneers, whose officers were prominent in the attack. Wheeler, Macartney and J. A. Campbell were all severely wounded.[2]

As a result of the fighting at Rangoon and Kokine the offensive passed to the British, and Campbell determined to undertake his long postponed project of an advance on Prome. He tried to induce

[1]Despatch from Brig.-Gen. Sir Archibald Campbell, K.C.B., to the Secretary to the Government of India, dated Dec. 16th, 1824.
[2]Lieut. J. A. Campbell, M.I., died on March 25th, 1825, in Rangoon.

the Siamese, the hereditary enemies of the Burmese, to demonstrate towards Toungoo on the Sittang River, but in this he was unsuccessful. Their leading chief, a gentleman who was pleased to describe himself as " the splendid hero and renowned warrior, of great dignity and riches, the high-caste prince," replied in a non-committal strain, and accordingly it became clear that the banks of the Irrawaddy must be the sole line of operations. While preparations were in hand, a small force was sent to Syriam to dislodge some of the enemy who had reoccupied the fort and pagoda at that place. This was accomplished on January 11th and 12th, 1825, with the help of a party of Pioneers who lost Ensign W. C. Macleod and four men wounded while bridging a creek. A column sent to Tantabin to dislodge a Burmese outpost had no Engineers nor Pioneers with it. All was now ready for the advance up the Irrawaddy; but before we pass to the final phases of the First Burma War it may be advisable to outline the operations in two secondary theatres in which engineer units other than the Madras Pioneers took the field and tried to achieve the impossible.

Unaware of the appalling difficulties of the country, the Government of India had decided to dispatch columns from Assam and Chittagong to join Sir Archibald Campbell during his advance up the Irrawaddy. It was intended that a force of two brigades, under Brig.-General Thomas Shuldham, should march in an easterly direction from Sylhet[1] in Assam through Cachar and Manipur, and turning south-eastwards, should meet Campbell before he reached the Burmese capital at Ava near Mandalay. Another force of three brigades, under Brig.-General J. W. Morrison, was to proceed southwards from Chittagong as far as the town of Arakan, the capital of the province of that name, whence it was to strike eastwards across the mountains and descend into the Irrawaddy Valley in the region of Minbu and Minhla, about 100 miles north of Prome.

The Cachar Column consisted of 7,000 men and included 4 companies of Bengal Pioneers under Major John Swinton, B.I. It set out from Sylhet at the end of January, 1825, and moved 70 miles eastwards to the village of Banskandi in Cachar, traversing for the last 20 miles a track prepared by the Pioneers. During February, with the assistance of working parties of troops and coolies, the Pioneers extended this track for a further distance of 40 miles through dense forest towards the mountain ridges beyond, but torrents of rain soon made it impassable for guns and transport.[2] Hundreds of bullocks and scores of camels and elephants died in vain attempts to carry supplies to the head of the column, and towards the end of March the expedition was recalled and the Pioneers returned to Bengal. Within the next three months, some irregular troops under native leadership, accompanied by Lieutenant R. B. Pemberton of the Bengal Pioneers, penetrated into and through Manipur and drove the Burmese

[1]Sylhet is on the Surma River about 125 miles north-east of Dacca. (See Map I entitled *Sketch Map of Northern India,* at the end of this volume. Map II, entitled *Sketch Map of Southern India and Burma,* will be found useful for general reference.)
[2]*Documents Illustrative of the Burmese War,* by H. H. Wilson, p. 49.

into the jungles beyond,[1] but this expedition was small, mobile and suitably equipped. It is deplorable that the services of four regular companies of Pioneers, directed by an experienced leader such as Swinton, should have been wasted in the ill-conceived and abortive expedition under Shuldham.

The Arakan Column of 11,000 men under Brig.-General Morrison met with initial success, though it failed to reach the Irrawaddy. Six companies of Bengal Pioneers (649 men) under Captain John Wilkie, B.I., marched with it from Chittagong on January 1st, 1825, and were reinforced by 3 companies of Magh (Arakanese) Pioneers, recruited for the occasion, and an " Extra Pioneer and Pontoon Train."[2] The train was commanded by the Field Engineer, Lieutenant George Thomson, B.E., working under the direction of Captain (local Major) J. A. Schalch, B.I., who had been a Superintendent of Canals in Lower Bengal. Thomson had joined the improvised Pioneer and Pontoon Train in Calcutta, where he drilled 150 natives recruited as pontoniers. " A dirtier set of coolies I never saw," he wrote on October 23rd, 1824;[3] " Major Schalch, whose department I am in, is expected to have these men and 72 pontoons ready next month. He has made the whole over to me." On December 14th, Thomson left Calcutta for Chittagong as Field Engineer, Commandant of the " temporary Pioneers in charge of the Pontoon Train," and Surveyor to the Arakan Column. No Madras Pioneers served in Arakan—a matter on which some misapprehension has arisen since a unit called " A " Company, 1st Battalion, Madras Artillery Pioneers, is shown in an official publication as part of the Pioneer establishment with the force.[4]

Morrison followed a coastal route instead of moving inland, even though this involved crossing numerous estuaries, and marching through Cox's Bazar, reached the Arakan border on February 1st, 1825. He continued southwards to the mouth of the Mayu River, north of Akyab, where he arrived on February 22nd, but there he was delayed for several weeks in crossing five miles of water. On February 23rd, he lost Major Schalch, mortally wounded during an unsuccessful naval attack on some stockades up the Kaladan River towards the town of Arakan.[5] After crossing the Mayu estuary, the troops concentrated gradually, and the pontoon train bridged several affluents of the Kaladan while the Pioneers prepared a road. Through their efforts, Morrison was able to advance on Arakan on March 26th at the head of three columns and a reserve in which were included 2 companies of Bengal Pioneers, 3 companies of Magh Pioneers and three companies of " temporary Pioneers." On the 28th, Captain P. B. Fitton, B.I., of the Bengal Pioneers, was severely wounded in an unsuccessful attack on the town; but Arakan

[1] *Documents Illustrative of the Burmese War*, by H. H. Wilson, p. 49.
[2] *Frontier and Overseas Expeditions from India, Vol. V., Burma*, p. 46.
[3] Letter quoted in the Obituary Notice of Col. George Thomson, C.B., late R.(B)E., appearing in *The R.E. Journal*, Vol. XVI, 1886, pp. 78–84.
[4] *Frontier and Overseas Expeditions from India, Vol. V., Burma*, p. 46. This unit was actually " A " Coy., 1st Battalion, Madras Artillery, under Capt. J. Lamb, and was not a Pioneer formation. (See *History of the Bengal Artillery*, by Major F. W. Stubbs, p. 140.)
[5] Arakan, the former capital, is now known as Myohaung.

was taken by assault on April 1st, 1825, and the subjugation of the entire province was thus completed.

So far, Morrison had done well under most trying conditions. Now his luck deserted him, for he was completely baffled in trying to find a way from the Arakan Province into Burma. A small column set out for the An (Aeng) Pass and struggled to within one march of the Burmese frontier only to find its way barred by impassable roads and a vigilant enemy. Morrison remained in Arakan until September, 1825, when the remnants of his force were withdrawn. By then, four out of every five British soldiers had died of disease and the Indians also had suffered very severely. Morrison himself succumbed on his voyage to England. The utter impossibility of sending a large force to Burma, except by sea, seemed to require no further proof.

The four companies of Bengal Pioneers in this unfortunate expedition had the consolation of receiving some recognition of their services. " To Captain Wilkie, more especially, and to the officers of the Pioneers generally," wrote Morrison on April 2nd,[1] " the advance of the division may be mainly attributed. A road of nearly 150 miles in length has been completed by the labour of the Pioneers under their judicious directions, many morasses rendered passable, and innumerable *nullahs* bridged. I much fear the continued exposure to the sun will for some time deprive the division of the benefit of Captain Wilkie's services, who persevered in doing his duty till success crowned our efforts, though suffering from severe indisposition."

We return now to the main theatre of war where Sir Archibald Campbell, after nine months at Rangoon, was able in February, 1825, to commence his long-postponed advance on the Burmese capital. His shortest route to Ava was by Pegu and Toungoo, a distance of less than 400 miles ; but he had insufficient land-transport for this route and accordingly chose the line of the Irrawaddy. At the same time, he invited the Siamese to co-operate by moving on Toungoo, which, needless to say, they did not do. The first objective was Prome. Campbell divided his striking force into three columns ; one, of 2,738 men under his personal command, to march northwards to Tharrawaw (Sarawah) on the Irrawaddy above Danubyu ; another, of 1,169 men under Brig.-General W. Cotton, to proceed by ship up the Panhlaing channel and force a passage past Danubyu on the main stream ; and a third, of 780 men under Major R. Sale, to move westwards against Bassein and afterwards rejoin the other columns at Henzada opposite Tharrawaw.[2] Nearly 4,000 men had to be left as a reserve in Rangoon because of the lack of transport and food in the Irrawaddy Valley.

On February 13th, 1825, Campbell set out for Tharrawaw, and three days later, Cotton sailed for Danubyu. With Campbell were four companies of Madras Pioneers (257 men), and it is probable that the remaining

[1]Despatch from Brig.-Gen. J. W. Morrison, dated Arakan, April 2nd, 1825, quoted in *A Narrative of the First Burmese War*, 1824–26, by G. W. de Rhé-Philipe, pp. 222–231.

[2]This proved to be impossible. Sale never succeeded in reaching Henzada though he occupied Bassein.

companies of the 1st Battalion were with Cotton.[1] The latter captured a few stockades at the village of Panhlaing and on the morning of March 6th his flotilla anchored below Danubyu; but there he was held up by Bandula and suffered a repulse when he attempted to carry the place by storm. The news was caried to Campbell, who had reached Tharrawaw and rashly continued towards Prome, and he hurried back to help Cotton. Arriving again at Tharrawaw, Campbell was faced with the problem of crossing the Irrawaddy with no other craft than a few small canoes; but here the Madras Pioneers under Captain F. Crowe came to his aid, and by building bamboo rafts, enabled the entire column, with artillery, baggage and stores, to be ferried across to Henzada in five days and nights of unceasing labour.[2] On the 21st, Campbell was able to resume his march southward, though with great difficulty for it is recorded that on the following day the Pioneers had to cut a path for nearly ten miles through grass and reeds from 10 to 20 ft. in height.[3] However, Danubyu was in sight on February 24th. The defended enclosure measured about 1 mile by ½ mile and was held by 15,000 Burmese under Bandula with 150 small guns. On the perimeter was a stockade of teak beams 16 ft. high, and behind this, brick ramparts. A wide ditch, studded with spikes and nails, surrounded the stockade, and outside it were lines of smaller stockading. Encircling the whole, except on the river face, was an abattis some 30 yds. broad, and the defences were completed by two strong outworks on the downstream side.

Campbell might well have hesitated to attack such a stronghold with only 3,900 men including the force under Cotton, but he was bold and resourceful and knew the value of the offensive in savage warfare. Cotton's flotilla ran the gauntlet of the Burmese guns on the 27th, when Bandula made an unsuccessful sortie with seventeen war-elephants, gorgeously caparisoned and loaded with "King's Invulnerables" and other fantastic warriors. On April 1st, Campbell opened fire and on the following day marched unopposed into Danubyu, which the Burmese had evacuated under cover of darkness after Bandula had been killed by a rocket. An object of interest to the troops was Bandula's observation post on the river face, a hugh banian tree with lopped branches supporting three platforms on which small guns were mounted. The fall of Danubyu opened the way to Prome, and Campbell occupied that place on April 25th. A small column, including some Madras Pioneers, was then detailed to explore north-eastwards towards Toungoo and was absent on this duty during most of May; but the monsoon put an end to further operations and brought in its train the usual epidemic of malaria. On August 18th, 1825, no less than 133 Madras Pioneers were in hospital in Prome out of a total of 542. This was a much higher proportion than in any infantry unit and

[1] *A Narrative of the First Burmese War*, 1824–26, by G. W. de Rhé-Philipe, p. 292, and casualty list on p. 304. The companies were now far below their normal strength. There is no evidence that any Pioneers accompanied Sale.

[2] *Narrative of the Burmese War*, by Major Snodgrass, p. 159.

[3] *Ibid.*, p. 162.

was explained by the fact that the work done by the Pioneers was harder and more exhausting than ordinary garrison duty.

The Court of Ava spent the rainy season in collecting troops and negotiating for peace. "If you wish for peace," wrote the golden-footed monarch, "you may go away; but if you ask either money or territory, no friendship can exist between us. This is the Burmese custom!" At the same time he began to encircle Prome with 70,000 men whom he had collected at Myede (Meaday), forty miles further north, so Campbell decided to resume the offensive and prepared in November, 1825, to drive the Burmese from a powerful position at Napadi on the left bank of the Irrawaddy a few miles above Prome. The enemy were distributed in three bodies: one on the Napadi hills in the centre, another on the left flank at Sinbaik, about ten miles to the east and separated from Napadi by a belt of forest, and the third on the right flank beyond the Irrawaddy. All were powerfully stockaded, particularly at Napadi. On December 1st, Campbell feinted at the Burmese right and centre and overwhelmed the isolated force at Sinbaik. A detachment of Madras Pioneers took part in this fight and one of their officers, Lieutenant J. W. Smyth, M.I., was dangerously wounded. Campbell next attacked the Burmese centre on the Napadi hills and on December 2nd drove the enemy from a strong position of great depth and captured all their guns and stores. There remained only the force on the right bank, and this was routed with great slaughter on December 4th. Madras Pioneers were with the attacking troops both at Napadi and across the Irrawaddy. Thus ended the last offensive undertaken by the Burmese army in the First Burma War.

The next objective was Myede, which Campbell approached by a detour eastwards. His men, racked with malaria and decimated by cholera, toiled in deluges of rain for many miles through elephant grass 15 feet high. He entered Myede unopposed on December 19th, but left it as soon as possible for it was thickly strewn with unburied Burmese dead. Rejoined by the flotilla and a division under Brig.-General Cotton, he arrived opposite Malun, below Minhla, on the 27th. Cotton had been delayed in his advance along the river bank by a large ravine which his Pioneers had to bridge.[1] The Burmese commander at Malun asked for an armistice and actually signed a treaty of peace; but when Campbell saw that the object of these manœuvres was merely to gain time for further fortification, he attacked the Malun stockades on January 19th, 1826, and soon had possession of them. "I ordered the construction of batteries and the landing of heavy ordnance from the flotilla to commence immediately after midnight," he wrote in his report on the operations.[2] "His Lordship in Council will be enabled to appreciate the zeal and exertion with which my orders were carried into effect under the direction of Lieut.-Colonel Hopkinson, commanding the Artillery, and Lieutenant Underwood, the Chief Engineer, aided by that indefatigable Corps, the 1st Battalion, Madras

[1]Despatch from Brig.-Gen. W. Cotton to Brig.-Gen. Sir Archibald Campbell dated Dec. 19th, 1825.

[2]Despatch from Major-Gen. Sir Archibald Campbell to the Secretary to Government, Secret and Political Department, dated Jan. 20th, 1826.

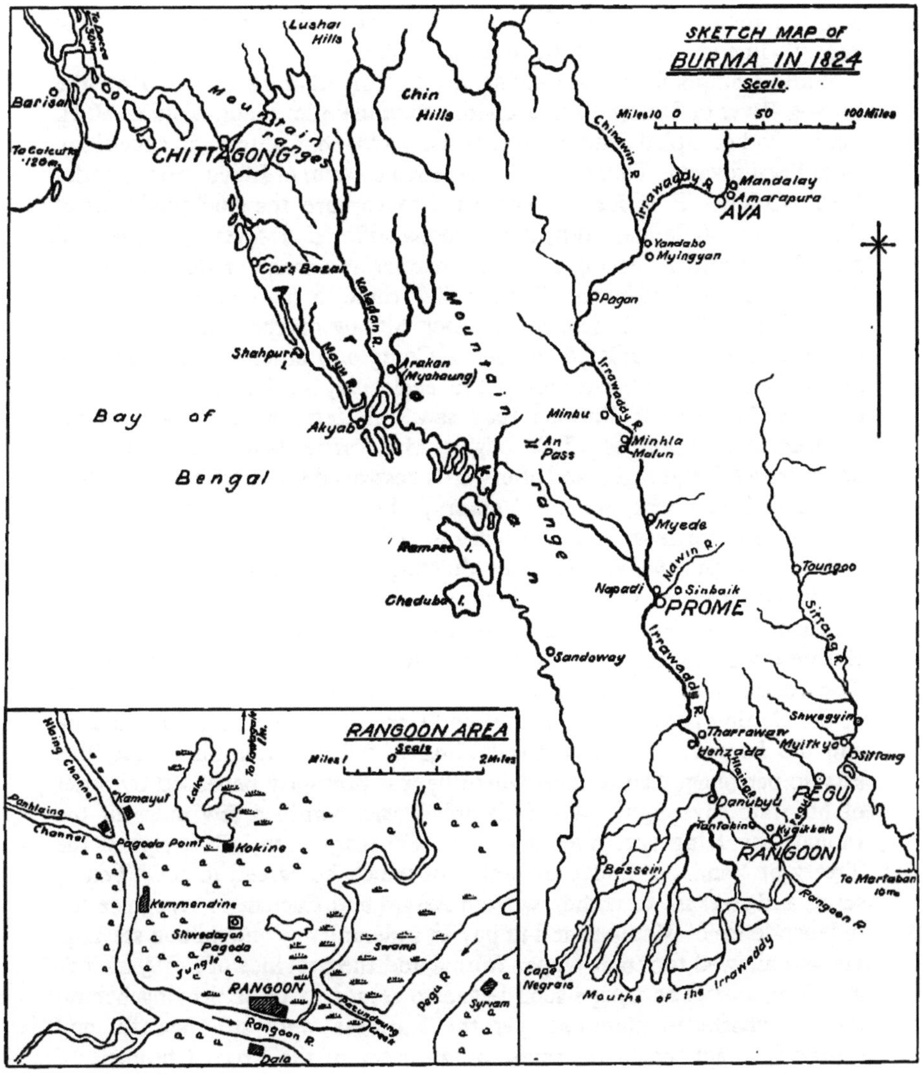
SKETCH MAP OF
BURMA IN 1824
Scale
Miles 10 0 50 100 Miles
Lushai Hills
Chin Hills
Mountain ranges
CHITTAGONG
Barisal
To Calcutta 120m
Cox's Bazar
Kaladan R.
Mayu R.
Shahpuri I.
Arakan (Myohaung)
Akyab
Bay of Bengal
Mountain range
Arakan
An Pass
Ramree I.
Cheduba I.
Sandoway
Chindwin R.
Irrawaddy R.
Mandalay
Amarapura
AVA
Yandabo
Myingyan
Pagan
Minhu
Minhla
Melun
Myede
Nawin R.
Napadi
Sinbaik
PROME
Toungoo
Sittang R.
Shwegyin
Tharrawaw
Henzada
Myitkyo
Sittang
PEGU
Danubyu
Kyaikkalo
RANGOON
Bassein
To Martaban
Rangoon R.
Cape Negrais
Mouths of the Irrawaddy
RANGOON AREA
Scale
Miles 1 0 1 2 Miles
Hlaing Channel
Panhlaing Channel
Kamayut
Lake
Pagoda Point
Kokine
Kemmendine
Shwedagon Pagoda
Jungle
Swamp
RANGOON
Pegu R.
Syriam
Rangoon R.
Dala

Pioneers, under the command of Captain Crowe, when I state that by ten o'clock the next morning I had eight and twenty pieces of ordnance in battery on points presenting a front of more than one mile on the eastern bank of the Irrawaddy, which corresponded with the extent of the enemy's line of defence on the opposite shore."

While Campbell was advancing on Malun, fighting occurred on the Sittang River in Eastern Burma where a column under Lieut.-Colonel H. H. Pepper had occupied Shwegyin on January 3rd, 1826, during an expedition from Pegu towards Toungoo. Pepper sent a column of Indian troops under Lieut.-Colonel E. Conry downstream to capture the stockaded port of Sittang, but on January 6th, these troops suffered a severe repulse and retired in disorder, leaving their commander and many of their comrades dead on the field of battle. Pepper then came to the rescue, and with a force of British and Indian troops, took Sittang on the 11th. The sight of the naked and mutilated corpses of Conry and other soldiers, hanging by the heels from a beam within the enclosure, so infuriated our men that they killed every Burman they saw. A detachment of 25 Madras Pioneers under Lieutenant J. Woodgate, M.I., carried ladders in the assaults on January 6th and 11th,[1] and afterwards destroyed the defences of Sittang. Another detachment, under Captain J. Leggett, M.I., accompanied a column sent northwards in February to relieve the garrison of Myitkyo.

The First Burma War was now drawing rapidly to a close. Campbell continued his victorious advance up the Irrawaddy, and at Pagan (Paghamyu) on February 9th, 1826, with only 1,300 men, defeated 10,000 Burmese who called themselves "The Retrievers of the King's Glory." The commander of these heroes bore the formidable titles of "Prince of the Setting Sun" and "Prince of Darkness," but to the British rank and file he was, of course, the "King of 'ell." After his defeat, this satanic personage fled to Ava, where he was promptly beheaded by order of his irate sovereign. When Campbell was within a few miles of the capital, the King surrendered and on February 24th, 1826, signed the Treaty of Yandabo[2] under the terms of which he agreed to cede Tenasserim and Arakan, to withdraw from Assam and Cachar, to recognize the independence of Manipur and to pay an indemnity of one million sterling. He was allowed to retain Upper Burma and the province of Pegu, including Rangoon. The troops soon began to return to India, leaving behind them a chastened country; yet the Burmese were still boastful and arrogant, a fact which is proved by an entry in the Royal Chronicle of Ava. This records that the British were permitted to advance as far as Yandabo "from motives of piety and regard to life," but that afterwards, as they were in distress, "they petitioned the King of Ava, who generously sent them money and ordered them out of the country!" The

[1]Report by Lieut.-Col. H. H. Pepper dated Jan. 14th, 1826, quoted in *A Narrative of the First Burmese War*, 1824–26, by G. W. de Rhé-Philipe, pp. 374–379. On these occasions the scaling ladders were designed to allow men to ascend two abreast. (See *Reminiscences of the Burmese War in* 1824–5–6, by Capt. F. B. Doveton, p. 343.)

[2]Yandabo is just north of Myingyan on the Irrawaddy and about half-way between Pagan and Ava.

Madras Pioneers received many compliments on their work in Burma, and the honour " Ava " was granted subsequently to the Corps.

The long and uncertain course of the First Burma War encouraged rebellion in the newly subjugated territories of India, and particularly at Bhurtpore, where one Durjan Lal usurped the throne and defied the Government at the head of 25,000 Jat, Rajput and Pathan malcontents. The Resident at Delhi was forbidden to march against him; but in October, 1825, it was recognized that strong measures were necessary and accordingly an army of some 30,000 men was mobilized for the reduction of Bhurtpore under the personal direction of Lord Combermere,[1] the Commander-in-Chief in India. The force comprised two infantry divisions under Major-Generals Thomas Reynell and Jaspar Nicolls, two cavalry brigades, a powerful siege train and a full complement of engineer troops, and it included a good proportion of British units.[2] The Chief (or Principal Field) Engineer was Lieut.-Colonel (local Brig.-General) Thomas Anburey of the Bengal Engineers, who was assisted by 15 other officers of the same Corps.[3] Anburey had at his disposal six companies of Bengal Sappers and Miners and two companies of Bengal Pioneers. These engineer units marched from Cawnpore on October 30th to join the main concentration at Agra. The siege of Bhurtpore was a purely Bengal Army affair. No engineer formations from Bombay or Madras were concerned in it.

The defences of Bhurtpore had grown since Lake failed to penetrate them in 1805.[4] The outer line, 8 miles in perimeter and with 9 gates, consisted of 35 semi-circular bastions and massive curtains of mud in which palisades of tree trunks were buried, and dominating the town within this enclosure was a lofty citadel with a double line of masonry towers and curtains of great height. The whole was enclosed by a dry watercourse adapted as a ditch, and the citadel had a still wider and deeper ditch. Except on the south-west side, a belt of jungle approached to within 600 yards of the outer line. The nature of the fortifications was such that round shot or shell had little effect on them: the mud walls crumbled, the buried timber was exposed and shattered, and the debris formed a mountain of dust and splintered beams in which men sank to their armpits. It devolved upon the engineers to find a way of entry, and this they did by mining on a scale unprecedented in Eastern warfare. " Every day's experience," writes Blacker,[5] " shows that most men, however vulgar, are capable of being made good soldiers as far as acting

[1]Formerly Maj.-Gen. Sir Stapleton Cotton.

[2]Lord Combermere had 8 regiments of cavalry, 18 battalions of infantry, 112 siege guns and 50 field guns.

[3]Capts. R. Smith, J. Taylor, J. Colvin and C. J. C. Davidson; Lieuts. W. N. Forbes, A. Irvine (Brigade-Major), E. Swetenham, E. J. Smith, H. de Budé, J. Thomson, J. Tindal, B. Y. Reilly and G. T. Greene; and Ensigns H. Goodwyn and A. H. E. Boileau. Tindal was killed and Taylor, Colvin, Forbes, Irvine, de Budé and both Smiths were wounded. Thomson (Adjutant), Reilly, Greene, Goodwyn and Boileau were attached to the Sappers and Miners under Anburey as Commandant, and Davidson accompanied the Engineer Park. The remainder were Field or Assistant Field Engineers.

[4]See the plan entitled *Bhurtpore in* 1826, included in this chapter.

[5]*Memoir of the Operations of the British Army in India during the Mahratta War of* 1817, 1818 *and* 1819, by Lieut.-Col. V. Blacker, p. 331.

well in a body is deserving of that character ; yet how few can be selected from any walk of life capable of independent action. The more, therefore, an individual is left to his own resources, so in proportion is the possession of courage necessary. The more the mind has leisure to contemplate danger, the more it is likely to be appalled. The solitary fate of the Miner, who meets his antagonist and his death in the grave of his own digging, has nothing parallel above ground." Gasping and sweating in ill-ventilated galleries, and in constant peril from heavy falls of earth, the Bengal Sappers and Miners burrowed day by day and week by week through the water-logged soil beneath the outer ditch and ramparts of Bhurtpore and charged and fired the mines which demolished them. To these brave men should be accorded the chief credit for enabling Lord Combermere to retrieve the errors of Lake and capture the mightiest fortress in India.

The six companies of Bengal Sappers detailed for Bhurtpore had each been reinforced by a Jemadar and 44 other ranks and were followed by an Engineer Park with 286 carts loaded with entrenching and mining tools and thousands of fascines and gabions. Their first duty, however, was not concerned with trench work nor mining. On December 10th, while Lord Combermere was proceeding to his positions encircling part of the fortress, he sent forward a strong party to seize a lake called the Moti Jhil, lying about two miles to the north-west, the water of which was impounded on the Bhurtpore side by a long *bund* or embankment containing several sluices. He had heard on the previous evening that the bund was being cut in order to flood the land to the west of the fortifications and accelerate the filling of the ditches with water. A daring reconnaissance by Lieutenant A. Irvine, B.E., disclosed that a sluice had been opened and that water was already pouring through a masonry drain towards Bhurtpore, though the bund itself had been cut only down to water level. Irvine then took two companies of Sappers and five companies of Native Infantry to the site, and in two hours, by sinking a boat across the drain and adding brushwood, completely stopped the flow. The enemy had dug a canal across the plain to carry the water onwards to the outer ditch of Bhurtpore, but the bulk of the water was overflowing into the jungle *en route* and little had reached the place. Nevertheless, if both the sluice and cut had been open, there is no doubt that the inner and outer ditches would have been filled within a few hours to a depth of many feet and mining would have been impossible. It was discovered later that the canal discharged through an archway into the outer ditch between the Khumbir Gate and a salient south of the Govardhan Gate, and that thence the water found its way through a subterranean masonry duct to the citadel ditch.[1] The result of Irvine's initiative and resource was that throughout the siege the outer ditch remained almost dry and thus a most formidable obstacle lost half its value.

On December 11th, Anburey reconnoitred the north-east face of

[1]Entry dated Dec. 10th, 1825, on p. 290 of a manuscript file at Roorkee entitled *Siege Diaries, 1817–25, Bhurtpore, Allygurh, Delhi, etc.* This file contains the original reports of the Engineer Department.

THE BREACH IN THE NORTH-EAST BASTION AT BHURTPORE IN 1826.

Bhurtpore and recommended an attack from that side; and accordingly, being unable to invest the huge fortress completely, Combermere concentrated his infantry in an arc six miles long around the north-east defences and held the remainder of the circumference with cavalry and fortified posts. The siege train arrived, further reconnaissances were made, and the preparation of siege material in the Engineer Park was pushed forward. By the 18th, 54 bamboo single-ladders of 30 feet length and 2 double-ladders of 36 feet length were ready, together with a number of *sal*-wood ladders.[1] Anburey was able to report on December 22nd that his preparations were complete, and the attack was begun by the occupation of Baldeo Singh's Garden, some 600 yards from the north-east angle between the Jangina and Surajpur Gates, and of the village of Kadam Kandi, lying a similar distance from a prominent feature known as the "Long-necked Bastion." These posts were connected by a trench to form a first parallel, and siege batteries were mounted in front of them and opened fire on the 24th. A second parallel was completed on the following day within 250 yards of the Long-necked Bastion, and additional batteries opened fire on the 26th. So energetically did the Sappers, Pioneers and infantry dig and build that by January 4th, 1826, the north-east angle alone was under the fire of 78 siege pieces and a sap was being run along the counterscarp of the great ditch. Assistance was given by large numbers of native *beldars* (diggers), but these men, though highly paid, were most unreliable under fire. Five mines were being sunk in the counterscarp under the cover of parties of Gurkhas, and three breaches had been made in the scarp—one in the curtain north of the north-east angle, another in the bastion of that angle, and a third in the Long-necked Bastion.

Stirring tales are recorded of the exploits of the mining parties. On the night of January 6th–7th, after three mines had been charged under the counterscarp of the north-east angle, a party of Engineers and Sappers and Miners broke into the ditch and rushing across it began to dig into the scarp under a rain of fire-balls from the defenders. Irvine, Taylor, Colvin, Thomson and Sub-Conductor H. Richardson took part in this affair; but the outstanding figures were those of Jemadar Bajur Singh, Havildar Muhammad Ali and Sepoys Ganga Prasad, Hussain Baksh and Galim Singh of the Bengal Sappers whose conduct brought them promotion on the field. Charges were placed in the scarp and a long canvas hose stuffed with powder (a *saucisson*) was laid across the ditch and lighted. The hose, however, had become wet and the fire seemed to have been extinguished before it reached the scarp. Bajur Singh then dashed across to relight the train; but while he was blowing his slow-match, the charges exploded. The heroic Jemadar was so badly injured that he died within a few hours, and all to no purpose because the small charges had little effect on the massive bastion above them.

The defenders now began to countermine. An entry in the Siege Diary of January 9th, 1826, runs:— "One of the enemy having shown

[1]These were found to be unwieldy and unsatisfactory.

himself in the mouth of the mine in the scarp from which our Miners were obliged to retreat on the 7th, it was determined to repossess ourselves of our own gallery and therefrom make a lodgment in that of the enemy. For this duty, Sub-Conductor Richardson with a party of ten men of the Sappers and Miners (volunteers) under Captain Taylor stepped out and the attempt was crowned with success. Our own gallery was regained; but finding a light in that of the enemy and hearing many voices, it was deemed likely to prove successful to load the passage the enemy had made between their gallery and ours, by which means the enemy's gallery and passage to their mine would be completely destroyed. Both mines were sprung, and it cannot be doubted that many, if not all, their miners in the gallery were killed. The assistance afforded by Sub-Conductor Henry Richardson being highly creditable and gallant, he was immediately promoted to the grade of Conductor and permitted to remain attached to the Corps of Sappers and Miners."

Mining in the counterscarp of the Long-necked Bastion was started on January 11th, and later also in the scarp, where two charges, each of 1,200 lbs., were exploded on the 13th, though without making a practicable breach. The Siege Diary of January 14th records that Sepoys Ramnad of the 1st Company and Pirkhan of the 6th Company, Bengal Sappers and Miners, crossed the ditch in broad daylight and by evening were reported to have driven two galleries for a distance of 30 feet into the bastion. Breast-works of sandbags and *chevaux-de-frise* were then erected across the ditch to guard the entrances. Meanwhile, several galleries were being driven under the ditch itself at both the north-east angle and the Long-necked Bastion, and although some of these had to be abandoned owing to falls of earth, others were carried across and far under the bastions and curtains. The longest gallery was 279 feet in length, and the hired miners who worked in it suffered severely from lack of air. The atmosphere, indeed, was so foul that lights would not burn in it. Mine after mine was charged, and after several had been exploded in the counterscarp to enable the stormers to descend into the ditch, Anburey was satisfied that an assault was possible.

On January 16th, a great mine was exploded under the Long-necked Bastion, and on the following day the Sappers and Miners charged the greatest of all, one of 10,000 lbs. under the north-east angle. Its explosion was to be the signal for the storm. At 8 a.m. on January 18th, 1826, the train was fired. "The massive bastion trembled from level to summit," writes Stocqueler,[1] "and gradually rising from its firm foundation and increasing in bulk as it rose, seemed almost to precipitate its overwhelming mass upon our heads. Still it rose on high, and still it distended in one gigantic cloud of dull hue, in graceful, silent sublimity, high into the blue vault of heaven. There it stood many seconds like a tower connecting earth and sky, then slowly dissipated its particles upon the breeze of the morning." Earth, timber and the mangled bodies of men showered on the stormers, and many were killed or injured by gabions overturned by the force of the explosion, Anburey himself being struck in the shoulder;

[1] *The Old Field Officer*, by J. H. Stocqueler, Vol. I, p. 137.

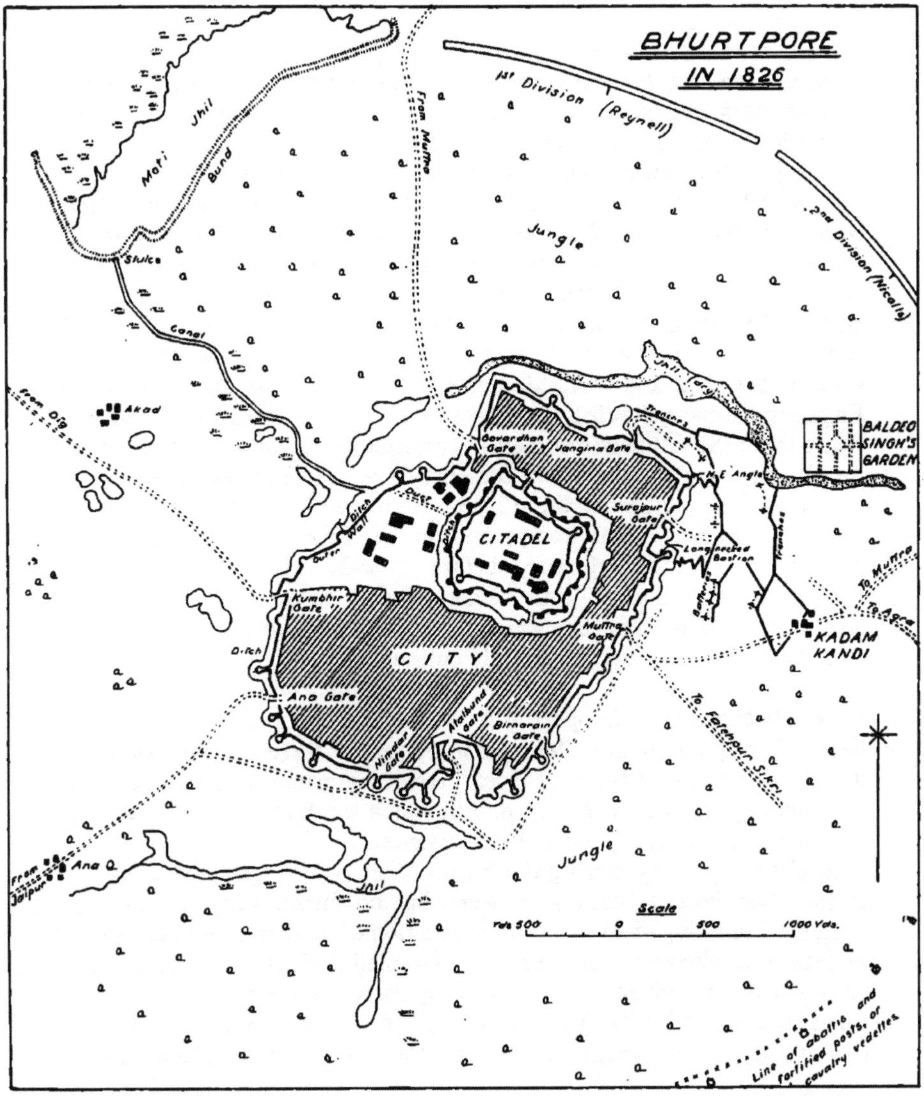
BHURTPORE
IN 1826
1st Division (Reynell)
2nd Division (Nicolls)
Moti Jhil
Bund
Sluice
Canal
From Muttra
Jungle
Jhil (dry)
BALDEO SINGH'S GARDEN
From Dig
Akad
Trenches
Govardhan Gate
Jangina Gate
N.E. Angle
Surajpur Gate
Outer Wall
Ditch
CITADEL
Long-necked Bastion
Kumbhir Gate
Muttra Gate
To Muttra
To Agra
KADAM KANDI
Ditch
CITY
Ana Gate
Atalbund Gate
Birnarain Gate
Nimdar Gate
To Fatehpur Sikri
From Jaipur
Ana Q
Jhil
Jungle
Scale
Yds 500 0 500 1000 Yds.
Line of abattis and fortified posts, or cavalry vedettes

but the troops dashed forward, and while General Reynell assaulted the north-east angle and General Nicolls the Long-necked Bastion, smaller columns forced an entry at other points. The 1st Company, Bengal Pioneers, under Captain D. D. Anderson, B.I., carried and planted ladders for a column escalading a re-entrant angle of the Long-necked Bastion, but the 7th Company under Lieutenant A. Arabin, B.I.,[1] did not use its ladders in an assault further north. After the columns had gained the crest they swept along the ramparts and carried all before them, and with the surrender of the citadel, the victory was complete. Some 14,000 of the enemy perished during the siege and assault, though the British loss did not exceed 1,000 men. The spoils included 200 guns and enormous treasure; but the chief value of the capture of Bhurtpore lay in the restoration of British prestige which had suffered so much by Lake's failure in 1805. Incidentally, it established for ever the reputation of the Bengal Sappers and Miners, whose first honour is "Bhurtpore."[2] "It would be difficult," wrote Lord Combermere,[3] "to appreciate fully the science, devotion and fortitude evinced by the officers and men of the Engineer Corps, including the Corps of Sappers and Miners," and with that tribute the Sappers returned in triumph to Cawnpore after they had put the finishing touches to the destruction of the Bhurtpore defences.

There was a curious tradition in connection with this great fortress. It had been predicted that it would never be taken by an enemy until a *Kumbhir* or crocodile appeared before its walls. When, therefore, the defenders learnt that an army under a leader named Combermere was advancing against them they were much perturbed and some of them lost heart.[4] The coincidence is certainly curious.

It is advisable now to trace some of the reorganizations and changes in the establishments of Sappers and Miners and Pioneers which occurred between 1824 and 1838. The most important of these was the disappearance of the Pioneers from all three Presidency armies and their replacement by Sappers and Miners, a reform which was bound to come with the advance of engineering and military science.

In February, 1825, during the Burma War, two companies were added to each battalion of Madras Pioneers, but no further change took place until the beginning of 1831 when the question of reorganization, postponed in 1824, was taken up after the arrival of a small draft of non-commissioned officers from Chatham.[5] In a Minute dated February 7th, 1831, the Commander-in-Chief in Madras opposed the scheme formulated in 1823 that one of the two battalions of Madras Pioneers should be disbanded and

[1]Both Capt. Anderson and Lieut. Arabin were serving temporarily with the Pioneers. Arabin had already served with them in 1823 and 1824, and re-joining the Corps in Nov., 1826, was posted to the 7th ("Hill") Company. He was Adjutant from July, 1829, to June, 1832.

[2]G.G.O., April 9th, 1832.

[3]G.O.C.C., Jan. 19th, 1826. Later, an anonymous writer expressed his opinion that "a more efficient body than the Bengal Sappers and Miners it would be impossible to conceive." (See *East India United Service Journal*, Vol. III, July–Dec., 1834, p. 259.)

[4]"My Recollection of an Indian Battlefield," by Capt. M. Power, appearing in *The R.E. Journal*, Vol. XVI, July–Dec., 1912, pp. 125–136.

[5]1 Sergeant, 1-2nd Corporal and 8 Sappers, R.E.

the other officered from the Madras Engineers and transferred from his control to that of the Chief Engineer. " They have now been in existence for a great number of years," he wrote,[1] " and have shared in every active service. The escalade of every fortified post must depend on the gallantry of the Pioneers, and no substitute can be furnished to carry scaling ladders where it is so necessary to preserve the European soldier for actual conflict." His representations had some effect, for although a General Order was published on May 24th, 1831, directing that the 1st Battalion of Pioneers should be converted into a Corps of Sappers and Miners with an Engineer Commandant and an Adjutant and such other officers as might be available from the Engineers,[2] the 2nd Battalion was untouched and remained for a time at the disposal of the Commander-in-Chief for Pioneer duties.

The newly formed Corps of Madras Sappers and Miners consisted of 8 companies, each of 80 men.[3] Of these, 4 companies were stationed in Bangalore and one in Madras. Captain A. Lawe, M.E., was appointed as Commandant[4] and had as Adjutant, Lieutenant E. Lawford, M.E., and as Company Commanders, Lieutenants S. Vardon, J. H. Bell and F. Ditmas and 2nd Lieutenants J. C. Shaw, H. Watts, J. P. Power and T. Smythe, M.E. It is presumed that Lawford commanded a company until another officer was appointed to complete the establishment. The Corps was placed under the control of the Chief Engineer, except for discipline and interior economy, and was to have a distinctive uniform. Thus the Madras Army was provided at last with a body of engineer soldiers under professional leadership.

The end of the 2nd Battalion of Madras Pioneers, however, was not long delayed, for in December, 1833, the Directors ordered the reduction of the Madras Sappers and Miners or Madras Pioneers, " whichever they might be called " to one battalion, and naturally the Pioneers had to go. Accordingly, on February 1st, 1834, the 2nd Battalion was absorbed into the Sappers and Miners, and with that absorption the Corps of Madras Pioneers disappeared from the Indian Army, leaving behind it a record which will never be forgotten. A small revision of the Sapper and Miner establishment was authorized on February 3rd, 1837, when the Corps was placed under the direct control of the Commander-in-Chief; and a further revision was sanctioned on December 26th, 1837, under which the number of companies was reduced from eight to six, each of 120 men, and

[1]Minute by Lt.-Gen. Sir George Walker, G.C.B., quoted in *Historical Record of the Q.V.O. Madras Sappers and Miners*, Vol. I, p. 37.

[2]The Corps of Madras Sappers and Miners continued to be officered solely from the Madras Engineers until 1839 when some Infantry Officers were posted to it owing to a scarcity of Engineers. From 1839 to 1879, there were always a few Infantry Officers on the establishment.

[3]The Corps establishment was as follows :—1 Capt.-Commandant, 8 Subalterns, 1 Adjutant, 1 Sergt.-Major, 1 Q.M.S., 8 Sergeants, 8 Jemadars, 1 Havildar-Major, 24 Havildars, 24 Naiks, 640 Privates, and a number of Recruit and Pension Boys, artificers and followers.

[4]Capt. Lawe was Commandant until March, 1833, when he was succeeded by Capt. G. A. Underwood, M.E. Lieut. T. T. Pears, M.E., became Commandant in July, 1838, after Capt. J. T. Smith, M.E., had officiated from January to July.

the rank of Subadar was introduced.[1] On February 15th, 1838, Bangalore was selected as the permanent headquarters of the Corps,[2] and thereafter the Madras Sappers and Miners were recognized as an important and indispensable part of the Indian Army.

The Bengal Pioneers suffered a fate similar to that of their brethren in Madras. On November 28th, 1833, the disbandment of the Corps of Bengal Pioneers or Sappers and its incorporation with the Bengal Sappers and Miners were decreed in a General Order by the Governor-General. The order was carried into effect in February, 1834, when 31 Indian officers, 57 Indian non-commissioned officers, 422 privates and 7 buglers were absorbed into the Sappers and Miners.[3] Thus the Corps so ably commanded by Swinton ceased to exist. In spite of the sudden influx of Pioneers, the establishment of Bengal Sappers and Miners still remained as six companies, each of 140 men.[4] The headquarters of the Corps were located at Bhurtpore until May, 1826, when they were transferred to Aligarh, and in November, 1830, to Delhi. Lieut.-Colonel T. Anburey, B.E., the Commandant during the siege of Bhurtpore, handed over charge to Captain H. De Budé, B.E., in May, 1828. Captain T. Warlow, B.E., followed De Budé in January, 1834, and Captain G. Thomson, B.E., became Commandant in March, 1837.

The small establishment of engineer troops in the Bombay Presidency led a chequered existence after the First Burma War. On December 4th, 1826, orders were issued for the raising of a second company of Sappers and Miners. The two companies were to form a "Corps"[5] and to be officered from the Bombay Engineers, non-commissioned officers being drawn from the European regiments in Bombay if any could be found with "an insight into the practice of Sapping and Mining as conducted under Colonel Pasley at Chatham." In 1829, the strength of each company was reduced to 50 men. The Corps was transferred from Bombay to Ahmadnagar and became known as the "Bombay Engineers," while its headquarters assumed the curious title of "The Engineer Institution."[6] In 1830, the headquarters were moved to Sirur, and in 1837, came to rest at Poona.[7] After 1829, the men were clothed in red instead of the green which distinguished the Pioneers. The increase in the establishment of Sappers and Miners was followed by a decrease in the strength of the Pioneers, who, on September 28th, 1830, were reduced from eight to six companies

[1]The reduction was carried out under G.O.C.C. dated March 20th, 1838.

[2]In May, 1834, the headquarters had been transferred from Madras to Mercara in Coorg.

[3]*History and Digest of Service of the 1st K.G.O. Bengal Sappers and Miners*, p. 7.

[4]The establishment consisted of 916 Indians of all ranks.

[5]The authorized establishment was 2 British officers, 15 British Warrant and N.C.O.s, 20 British Privates, 4 Indian officers, 20 Indian N.C.O.s, 200 Indian Privates, 1 Native Doctor, 2 Buglers, 2 Bhistis and 32 Artificers.

[6]G.G.O. dated Dec. 24th, 1829.

[7]With the exception of a five-years transfer to Karachi (1843–48) the headquarters have remained always near Poona. For many years they were south of the site of the old polo ground to the east of the city, the field-works' ground being on the site of the Lloyd Polo Ground. On Oct. 28th, 1869, they were moved to a cantonment at East Kirkee which was known as "New Jhansi" until the name was abandoned because of confusion with Jhansi in Gwalior State.

and incorporated on November 1st with the Sappers as an " Engineer Corps " having a Commandant, an Adjutant and a Quartermaster from the Bombay Engineers. Any Pioneer disliking the " fatigue and exertion " of service with the Sappers was allowed to take his discharge. Training was simplified because a draft of R.E. non-commissioned officers (2 sergeants and 6 corporals) had arrived from Chatham at the beginning of the year. The " Engineer Corps "[1] was caught in 1834 in the general scheme of retrenchment in all the Presidencies, and the establishment was reduced on June 20th from eight to four companies, with a total strength of 452 Indian soldiers of all ranks, the two Sapper companies forming No. 1 Company and the six Pioneer companies providing Nos. 2, 3 and 4 Companies.[2] Lieutenant A. C. Peat followed Lieutenant S. Slight as Commandant of the Sappers and Miners in 1828; but in November, 1830, Captain C. Waddington became Commandant of the Engineer Corps and held that appointment until he was succeeded by Captain C. W. Grant in January, 1835. All these officers were Bombay Engineers. In November, 1835, orders were issued that the three companies of Pioneers in the Engineer Corps were to be disbanded; but fortunately these instructions were cancelled in December, and thus the Bombay Sappers and Miners were saved from virtual extinction.

With the end of the siege of Bhurtpore, India sank into the tranquillity of the overawed. Between 1829 and 1832, some desultory fighting occurred in Assam and Central India and against a sect called the Wahabis near Calcutta, and preparations for a siege of Jhansi at the end of 1838 provided some diversion for several companies of Bengal Sappers and Miners. As the Rani of Jhansi had rebelled, a mixed force under Major-General Sir Thomas Anburey, late B.E., was sent against her. However, she was not disposed to fight, and Anburey marched unopposed into her capital. In the west, the Bombay Sappers and Miners were occupied with routine duties and training. In the south alone was there any opportunity for field service. A detachment of Madras Pioneers took part in minor operations in Kolhapur near Belgaum in 1827,[3] and a company of Madras Sappers and Miners was concerned in 1834 in operations in the Kimedi District of Madras. Some Madras Sappers and Miners served also in the Gumsur District in 1836 and in Kurnool in 1839.[4] A more serious test was provided by the brief campaign in Coorg in 1834 when five companies of Madras Sappers laboured in the forest-clad and mountainous regions near the Kanara coast. At the beginning of April, a force of 6,000 men set out in four columns to subdue the Raja of Coorg by converging on his capital. Captain G. A. Underwood, M.E., was in command of 300 Madras Sappers

[1]The term " Engineer Corps " fell into disuse after 1836.

[2]4 Subadars, 4 Jemadars, 20 Havildars, 20 Naiks, 400 Privates and 4 Buglers with 4 followers (*Bhistis*). The actual Sapper strength was unaltered as the two original Sapper companies had only 50 men each. The Pioneer strength, however, was much reduced.

[3]In 1824, a detachment under Lieut. T. Clendon, M.I., had served at Kittur near Belgaum.

[4]A Memorandum by Lt.-Col. T. T. Pears, M. E., on the crossing of the Tungabhadra in basket boats during the Kurnool operations appears in *Professional Papers of the Madras Engineers*, Vol. IV, pp. 100–106.

with the eastern column; Lieutenant F. Ditmas, M.E., commanded 200 with the northern column, and Lieutenant J. H. Bell, M.E., a further 200 with the western column. No Sappers accompanied the fourth column. The eastern column entered the capital on April 6th without difficulty, but the northern column met with serious opposition and lost 166 men in an unsuccessful assault on a stockade. In this affair, 17 Madras Sappers were killed or wounded. The western column also had some fighting in the mountains, and the Sappers lost a few men. However, the Raja surrendered on April 10th and hostilities came to an end.

A special silver medal was awarded for the campaign in Coorg to Havildar Chokalingam of the Madras Sappers and Miners, who served with the western column. A Court of Enquiry was assembled in September, 1834, "to ascertain the claims of certain Native soldiers reported conspicuous for gallantry," and as the resulting report made it appear that Havildar Chokalingam "had satisfactorily established pretensions to eminent bravery" he was given an honorary medal and an increase for life of one-third of his pay.[1]

Owing to the huge expense of the First Burma War, the East India Company was obliged to put quality before quantity, and the reorganizations effected before the outbreak of the First Afghan War were designed to produce a more efficient army. The Pioneer had to go because he was insufficiently skilled in military engineering and the use of arms and could no longer compete, in peace-time, with civilian labour. Yet his successor, the Sapper and Miner, was open to some criticism, as is shown by the following letter from an anonymous subaltern of the Madras Sappers which appeared in June, 1836, in the *East India United Service Journal*. "Your readers," he writes, "are aware that the Sappers and Miners are at present but old friends with a new face. Their duties are utterly undefined. Imperfectly organized, they are nondescript in equipment, character and occupation. They are maintained to perform certain duties in time of war, for which, strange to say, they are imperfectly, or not at all, prepared in time of peace. I believe economy to be one motive; but it arises also out of the greater error which would confound the duties of Sappers and Miners with those of Pioneers. The Corps of Pioneers in this Presidency has always maintained a character for gallantry and usefulness in the field; but they have invariably been called upon to perform, not the duties of Pioneers, but of Sappers and Miners. Trenches and batteries and shafts and mines have been executed. But were they, in any one instance, properly or expeditiously executed? Alas! the history of Indian sieges points with a fatal meaning often to complete failures. How, indeed, could it be otherwise when far more discipline and training are required to form a Sapper than any other soldier? Though I am aware that my opinion may appear abrupt, *I consider the Corps of Pioneers to have been a useless institution*. In a country where the peasant's labour is cheaper than that of the soldier, to give military organization to a body of men who are merely to make roads and break stones is certainly a work of supererogation."

[1]G.O.C.C., Oct. 15th, 1834.

Criticism, however unpalatable, is often valuable and may result in much-needed reform ; but some of the opinions expressed by this young officer cannot be accepted. Who, reading the history of the Indian wars, will admit that the Pioneers were altogether incapable and useless ? Their work in Mysore, Nepal, the Maratha territories and Burma was hard and exacting. They hacked their way through miles of jungle, prepared siege material and built batteries, carried ladders in every assault, and after the fighting was over, destroyed the enemy's fortifications and buried the dead. Many became Sappers and Miners, and the experience which they had gained was handed down to the three new Corps and enabled the latter to add to their reputation in Afghanistan, Sind, the Punjab and overseas. Their status was humble, their rewards were few ; but their record proves that their maintenance was justified and that they served the East India Company well and truly.

CHAPTER V

EARLY OVERSEAS EXPEDITIONS, 1762–1857

ALTHOUGH the Directors of the original East India Company never tired of declaring that their business was trade, not war, their sphere of influence extended so far that they were obliged, from time to time, to despatch expeditions overseas to protect their outlying settlements and trade-routes against the Portuguese, Spanish, Dutch or French. During the 16th century, the Portuguese were in the ascendant, for the British had not yet entered the arena; they enjoyed a monopoly of commerce in the East, and their ships sailed on every sea from the Persian Gulf to the Malay Archipelago. But after Sir Francis Drake had visited the Spice Islands in 1579 during his famous voyage round the world, both the British and Dutch began to plan an assault upon the Portuguese supremacy in that area. The British East India Company, founded in 1600, was outdistanced by a Dutch company in the race for trade. The Dutch captured Amboyna from the Portuguese in 1605, and having gradually ousted them from the other Spice Islands, deprived them of Malacca in 1641. Foiled in the Malay Peninsula and Archipelago, the British consoled themselves by developing their commerce with India and extending it westwards to the Persian Gulf, where they had taken the island of Hormuz from the Portuguese in 1622.[1]

The Malay Archipelago, comprising Sumatra, Java, Borneo, the Spice or Molucca Islands and other territories, remained a Dutch preserve except for British settlements at Bencoolen on the west coast of Sumatra and, until 1682, at Bantam in Java. Trade languished in Bencoolen and drunkenness was rife. "Could we once hear that Sobriety was become as fashionable on the West Coast as hard drinking," wrote the Directors in 1717–18,[2] "we should entertain strong hopes that your new settlement at Marlborough[3] would give a better reputation to the Coast for health. It is said that a little tea, boiled in water, kept till cold and so drank, would contribute to the health of those who used it. . . . It is a wonder to us that any one of you lives six months to an end if half the liquors he charges are really guzzled down." They pointed to the accounts which showed that in a single month their nineteen employees at Bencoolen had consumed, or otherwise disposed of, 144 dozen bottles of claret, 42 gallons of madeira, 24 dozen bottles of beer, and the equivalent of at least 8 large casks of *arrack* and *toddy*, so it seems that their protests were justified.

[1]Sketch Maps of the Malay Archipelago, and of Southern Persia and Eastern Arabia, are included in this chapter.

[2]Indian Office Records. Letter Book No. 16. Despatches to Bencoolen, dated Feb. 6th, 1717, and March 14th, 1718.

[3]Fort Marlborough at Bencoolen.

Meanwhile, the French had staked their claim in the field of eastern trade by founding Pondicherry in Southern India in 1674 and Chandarnagar on the Hugli in 1690. A few years later, their influence began to decline and they abandoned several of their factories, but their position was strengthened in 1721 when they added Mauritius to their possessions east of Madagascar, where they were already in occupation of Réunion. These islands formed valuable stepping-stones to their maritime base at Pondicherry, and from 1746 to 1760 they made full use of them to harry British shipping while England and France were at war. Then came the fall of Pondicherry and the virtual collapse of French power in India and of French aspirations further east, leaving England the sole challenger of Holland in the Malay Archipelago.[1] From a trading corporation owning isolated towns, forts and factories, the East India Company had blossomed into a ruling power controlling vast territories and searching diligently for foreign markets.

The first occasion on which Pioneers from India were employed overseas was after the outbreak of war with Spain in 1762. In July and August of that year a squadron carrying a mixed force of 1,670 men sailed from Madras and came to anchor off Manila in the Philippine Islands on September 23rd.[2] Great booty was expected, and as dishonesty was rife and the expedition a combined affair of the King's and Company's armies, the naval and military commanders,[3] both King's officers, thought well to safeguard themselves before they started by addressing to the Madras Council the following peculiar statement:—[4] "Our intentions are most upright. Your Agent may certainly join with ours in taking an Inventory and Account of the whole Booty and Plunder. We want to secrete nothing from you, but we adhere to our first Determination to allow you only a Third of the said Booty and Plunder." The Council assembled and prepared a protest, but before it could be delivered the ships had sailed. The force for the invasion of the Philippines was curiously constituted, for in addition to a battalion of British and another of Indian infantry and some artillery, it had a contingent of 200 "foreign deserters," a company of Portuguese half-castes and another of African ex-slaves; but to readers of this narrative the most interesting item will be a detachment of 60 Pioneers, Europeans recruited temporarily from British units at Fort St. George on the plan adopted during the defence of that stronghold against the French in 1759.[5]

Although the garrison of Manila consisted of 800 Spanish troops and some thousands of half-castes and natives, the fortifications were incomplete and in bad repair, and consequently, after the troops had landed and bombarded the town for a few days, it was taken by assault without much difficulty on October 6th, the Pioneers being well to the fore with their

[1]The chief events of this period are outlined in *The Military Engineer in India*, by the present author, Vol. I, Chapters IV to VII.
[2]*Frontier and Overseas Expeditions from India*, Vol. VI, p. 308.
[3]Rear-Admiral Samuel Cornish and Brig.-Gen. William Draper.
[4]*Madras Consultations*, Vol. XVI, July 31st, 1762.
[5]See Chapter I.

entrenching tools and siege materials.[1] The conquest proved a barren one, for the place was ransomed and evacuated in March, 1764, after news had arrived of a treaty of peace between England and Spain. It is worthy of record that Indian mounted infantry were employed in the operations. " To keep the enemy's horse in awe," runs the official report,[2] " General Draper thought proper to mount fifty sepoys upon the horses that were found straggling there." After their return to Madras in July, 1764, the European Pioneers were employed in throwing up redoubts around the city of Madura and were present at the surrender of the native garrison of that place in October. Presumably, the Pioneers were then disbanded. The results of the expedition were meagre—a trophy in Fort St. George and several files added to the Government records—yet the venture may have provided some useful experience in the transport of Indian troops by sea.

Nearly twenty years later, a regular unit of Indian Pioneers was despatched for the first time on foreign service. This was on the occasion of the combined naval and military expedition in 1782 against the Dutch at Trincomalee in Ceylon. Rear-Admiral Sir Edward Hughes and Major-General Sir Hector Munro had recently laid siege to and captured Negapatam in Southern India, and the Admiral sailed thence for Ceylon on January 2nd with a squadron carrying a composite battalion of Indian infantry (529 men) and one of the two newly formed companies of Madras Pioneers under Lieutenant N. S. W. Abbott, M.I.[3] A landing was effected near Trincomalee on January 5th and Trincomalee Fort was stormed and captured ; but the greater part of the garrison escaped to Fort Ostenburg, which commanded the entrance to the harbour. On the 7th, as siege operations against Fort Ostenburg were probable, the Admiral directed that a body of temporary Pioneers should be raised by obtaining volunteers from the infantry,[4] and accordingly three small companies were formed, each consisting of a Sergeant, a Jemadar, 3 Havildars, 3 Naiks and 44 Privates and placed under the command of Abbott assisted by Ensigns J. Bryne and J. Wright, M.I.[5]. If the regular company of Madras Pioneers was at full strength (110 Indian ranks) Abbott had then at his disposal no less than 263 Pioneers, while the infantry establishment was depleted to a total of 376 men. It seems that Admiral Hughes relied on his marines and sailors for infantry work.

After the heights near Fort Ostenburg had been reconnoitred by the Chief Engineer, Major Thomas Geils, M.E., Hughes got possession of a hill near the defences. Geils was then sent to the Dutch Governor with a summons for surrender. The enemy omitted to blindfold him, so after

[1]The capture of Manila is described in *The Military History of the Madras Engineers and Pioneers*, by Major H. M. Vibart, R. (M.) E., Vol. I, pp. 63–71.

[2]Report to the Madras Government, dated Dec. 25th, 1762.

[3]It is stated in *Frontier and Overseas Expeditions from India*, Vol. VI, p. 278, that the original strength of the Madras Pioneers was 200 (i.e., 2 companies), but this is improbable as only 2 companies existed in 1782.

[4]These volunteers were drawn chiefly from the detachments of the 9th and 23rd Madras Infantry serving in the composite battalion which was formed by detachments of volunteers from four battalions.

[5]*Frontier and Overseas Expeditions from India*, Vol. VI, p. 278.

he had returned with a refusal, he suggested that he should be sent back with a second summons in order, as he put it, that he might be more exact in his observations on the defences![1] This was done on January 10th; but as the Governor still refused to surrender, Hughes assaulted the fort on the following day and took it at a cost of 63 casualties. The marines and sailors re-embarked and the squadron sailed for India, leaving a small military garrison at Trincomalee, which was reinforced in May and July. However, in August, 1782, a French squadron under Admiral Suffrein appeared off the place and the British garrison was obliged to surrender to superior force. The fate of the Madras Pioneers is not recorded; but it is presumed that they had already returned to the Carnatic, where they were urgently needed in the struggle against Mysore.

Madras Pioneers served again in Ceylon in 1795 when another expedition was sent to capture the Dutch settlements because Holland had allied herself with France against England. Convoyed by several warships, a force of about 3,000 men under Colonel James Stuart sailed from Madras and Negapatam for Trincomalee and landed near that town on August 3rd. Two companies of Madras Pioneers[2] under Lieutenant W. Dowse, M.I. were included and were present at the surrender of Trincomalee Fort on August 26th after a short bombardment. This was followed by the reduction of Fort Ostenburg on August 31st, and of Batticaloa on September 18th. Stuart then sailed northwards, and with a small force including some Pioneers, occupied Jaffna[3] near the Palk Strait on September 28th. During October, Mullaittivu, Manar and Kalpitiya[4] fell to small detachments, and with the arrival of large reinforcements, including two additional companies of Madras Pioneers, the expeditionary force under Stuart reached a strength of nearly 6,500 men.[5]

Colombo was the next objective, and by February 6th, 1796, Stuart had concentrated his main body at Negombo, 20 miles to the north. Then he marched southwards through densely wooded country and had little difficulty in occupying the town of Colombo on the 11th and the fort on the 15th. The Dutch garrison of 3,000 men with 260 guns capitulated without being attacked, and as all the remaining Dutch possessions were included in the terms of surrender, the whole of the coastal area of Ceylon passed into British hands. The littoral was firmly held, but the interior of the island continued under the dominion of the King of Kandy, whose bellicose subjects caused much trouble. In consequence, it was

[1]*The Military History of the Madras Engineers and Pioneers*, by Major H. M. Vibart, R.(M.)E., Vol. I, p. 165.

[2]2 Sergeants and 119 Indian ranks.

[3]Known also as Jaffnapatam.

[4]Ceylon appears in outline in Map II at the end of this volume. Mullaittivu and Batticaloa are on the east coast, 55 miles and 65 miles north and south respectively of Trincomalee. Jaffna is in the extreme north. Kalpitiya and Manar on the west coast are respectively 85 and 140 miles north of Colombo. Kandy is in the centre of the island.

[5]These two companies were part of a contingent of 300 Madras Pioneers which had embarked at Madras on Aug. 26th, 1797, with other troops under Major-Gen. Sir James Craig, for an expedition against the Spaniards at Manila in the Philippines. The expedition was abandoned, however, owing to the threatening attitude of Tipu Sultan, and the troops disembarked after a few days.

necessary to maintain a strong garrison for several years, and by special request a half-company of Madras Pioneers was allowed to remain in the island. In September, 1797, it was joined by two companies[1] under Lieutenant J. Fitzpatrick, M.I., and served in Ceylon until 1802 when the island became a Crown Colony after the Peace of Amiens.[1]

In 1795, while two companies of Madras Pioneers under Dowse were labouring in the unhealthy jungles of Ceylon, another company, under Lieutenant W. P. Heitland, M.I., was attached to a small force of 400 British Infantry which had been sent against the Dutch settlement at Malacca in the Malay Peninsula. Sailing from Madras on July 23rd, the expedition occupied Malacca without resistance on August 18th and remained there until the close of the year, when a force was organized for the capture of Amboyna and other Dutch possessions in the Spice Islands of the Malay Archipelago. This was a more ambitious affair, and 1,100 British and Indian infantry, with a detachment of artillery and a half-company[2] of Madras Pioneers under Heitland, were detailed for the task. Convoyed by five warships, the transports sailed from Malacca on January 6th, 1796, and arrived on February 16th at Amboyna, where the troops landed and took possession. The squadron then sailed for the Bandas and annexed that group of islands. During the summer and autumn, reinforcements were sent from Madras to the garrisons of Malacca, Amboyna and the Banda Islands, and it appears that these troops must have included at least one company of Madras Pioneers, for it is recorded by Vibart that two companies were stationed in the Spice Islands until peace was concluded with Holland in 1802.[3] One of these companies supplied a detachment of 20 men under Lieutenant J. Wissett, M.I., which accompanied a small expedition against Ternate, one of the Spice Islands, in April, 1801. Ternate was occupied before the end of June, though not without stubborn resistance from the Dutch. However, under the terms of the Treaty of Amiens, all the Dutch possessions, except Ceylon, were restored to Holland in 1802, so the labours of the Pioneers and other troops in the Malay Archipelago were thrown away.

We come now to the expedition to Egypt in 1801, which provided the first instance of the employment of Indian troops outside Asia. Arrangements had been made in January of that year to despatch from Trincomalee a force under Colonel Arthur Wellesley with orders to evict the French from Batavia in Java and from the island of Mauritius; but at the last moment the destination of the expedition was changed to the Red Sea, and Wellesley was ordered to drive the French from any ports in which they might be found and afterwards to co-operate with the army under Major-General Sir Ralph Abercromby in expelling them from Egypt. The assistance of a contingent of troops was promised from the Cape of Good Hope. The transports proceeded to Bombay, where the chief command

[1]Ceylon was not finally pacified until 1819; but no Pioneers served in the island after 1803, when a detachment accompanied a force which occupied the capital at Kandy.
[2]The remaining half-company was left in garrison at Malacca.
[3]*The Military History of the Madras Engineers and Pioneers*, by Major H. M. Vibart, R.(M.)E., Vol. I, p. 282.

was transferred from Colonel Wellesley to Major-General Sir David Baird[1], under whose orders more than 7,000 British and Indian troops sailed during February and March. The ships were despatched in small convoys as soon as ready, and their commanders were directed to call at Mocha and Jidda on the eastern coast of the Red Sea, to concentrate at Quseir on the western coast further north, and finally to disembark the troops at Suez for the march to Cairo. These plans, however, were upset by the monsoon which made it impossible for the ships to reach Suez; and although Baird, while at Mocha, tried to collect camels for the alternative scheme of marching to the Nile from Quseir instead of Suez, he had no success. His ships were scattered far and wide. Seventeen of his transports foundered on the Red Sea reefs, and others returned in a sinking condition to India; and when he landed at Quseir on June 8th, he found himself almost alone in a cluster of mud hovels on a bare and utterly inhospitable coast.

While awaiting the arrival of the transports, Baird occupied himself in collecting 5,000 camels for the desert march of 120 miles to Qena (Kena) on the Nile, whence he intended to proceed downstream to Cairo. On June 19th, when a portion of the 5,200 men who completed the journey by sea had arrived at Quseir, he began to push them forward in small detachments. The undertaking required most careful organization, and as the water-supply was bad and scarce, a heavy responsibility devolved on a very inadequate cadre of Engineer officers. Of these, there were only four—Captain Howard Elphinstone, R.E., from the Cape; and from India, Lieutenants Thomas De Havilland, M.E., and Samuel Goodfellow, Bo.E., and Ensign George Steell, B.E.[2] Included in the force was a company of Madras Pioneers[3] under Captain J. Fitzpatrick, M.I.,[4] which had been serving in Ceylon. This unit had embarked at Trincomalee in December, 1800, with the original force under Wellesley and was delayed for many weeks in Bombay while the transports were being prepared for the voyage across the Indian Ocean. It is stated in the *Historical Record of the Q.V.O. Madras Sappers and Miners*[5] that the company reached Quseir on June 8th; but this is improbable because Baird himself, one of the first to land, only arrived on that day. According to an official publication,[6] the Madras Pioneers landed in Quseir during the early part of July with detachments of the 61st and 80th Regiments and the Bengal Horse Artillery. If that is so, their absence must have been felt keenly, for there was much work to

[1]Col. Wellesley then became second-in-command; but as he was in bad health, he relinquished the appointment and returned to Mysore.

[2]In *The Military History of the Madras Engineers and Pioneers*, Vol. I, pp. 355–356, Major H. M. Vibart remarks that a Lieutenant and two Ensigns of the Bengal Engineers accompanied the expedition; but according to the Prize Rolls for Egypt, 1801, Ensign Steell was the only Bengal Engineer present. He and De Havilland were attached to General Baird's staff.

[3]1 Jemadar, 4 Sergeants and 88 Indian other ranks.

[4]Major Vibart states (Vol. I, p. 361) that he had been unable to ascertain the name of the officer who commanded the Pioneers. According to the Prize Rolls for Egypt, 1801, it is clear that the officer was Capt Fitzpatrick.

[5]Vol. I, p. 15.

[6]*Frontier and Overseas Expeditions from India*, Vol. VI, p. 13.

be done in the desert and they must have been among the last of the detachments to march along the route to Qena.

Reconnaissance had shown that water was obtainable in small quantities at a few places between Quseir and Qena, either from existing wells or by digging; but the difficulties of supply were increased by the fact that most of the *mussacks* (water-skins), collected for the transport of water on camels, leaked badly, and the liquid itself was so brackish that it caused dysentery among the troops and followers. Yet by dint of careful staff-work, all the problems of supply in the desert were solved. How meticulous, and even grand-motherly, that staff-work was may be judged from some of the copious instructions issued to the commanders of detachments before they set out. Here is a sample :— " You will proceed on the evening of the 20th to the New Wells, distance about 11 miles. Be careful not to pass them. . . . On your arrival there, which will be about 11 o'clock at night, you should not allow your men to keep each other awake, as a good night's rest will enable them to march the next night with more alacrity. In the morning, half a pint of wine should be given to each man, and their rice, which they must cook for that day and the following. The men's canteens should be filled with *congee* (gruel) or the water in which the rice has been boiled; and just previous to their marching, another half-pint of wine should be issued to them to mix with their *congee*. . . . Be extremely careful that your *mussacks* are not damaged, particularly in lifting them on and off camels, which ought to be done with a tent pole. . . . On the evening of the 21st you will proceed half-way to Moilah, which is 34 miles from the wells. Therefore, if you start at 5 p.m. and march till midnight, you will have marched 17½ miles (at 2½ miles an hour), or half-way to Moilah. You will halt there and in the morning issue half a pint of wine per man and the rice cooked the preceding day. . . . Two gallons of water for each man is sent with you. You will, in the morning, issue a gallon per man and fill the canteens before you march. On the evening of the 22nd you will proceed to Moilah, where you may halt one day and night if your men are much fatigued, and on the following evening you will proceed to the wells about 9 miles beyond Moilah. Your next march is half-way to Legaitha. Then to Legaitha, where you will find water and provisions. . . . Your two next marches will carry you to Ghenna (Qena). . . . You will endeavour to conciliate the camel-men. . . . At Moilah and Legaitha you will issue spirits to your men as your wine must be used only on marching days. You have with you one gallon of wine for each European soldier. You will endeavour to dissuade your men from drinking a great quantity of water which has been found very hurtful and weakening." It will be seen that little was left to the initiative and common-sense of the detachment commanders, though it should be remembered that these officers had had no previous experience of marching in the Red Sea littoral.

Early in July, parties of the troops were still plodding along the desert route, while others had not yet even landed at Quseir; but the bulk of the force had reached Qena and was camped on the right bank of the Nile.

Baird had been in correspondence with Major-General J. H. Hutchinson, who had succeeded to the command of the British army in Egypt after the death of Sir Ralph Abercromby, and had informed him that he had disembarked at Quseir instead of at Suez; but while he was awaiting a reply he heard that the French had agreed to surrender Cairo, and thinking that the Indian contingent would no longer be needed in Egypt, he prepared to retrace his steps to Quseir, whence he hoped to be able to start on the expedition originally planned against Mauritius. On July 10th, however, he received orders from Hutchinson to procure boats and proceed forthwith to Cairo and thence to Rosetta on the Mediterranean coast near Alexandria, which the British army was already approaching on its return march from Cairo. Accordingly, he despatched his stores downstream in boats and set out at once for the Egyptian capital, where his force was concentrated by August 27th on Rhoda Island after a journey of 500 miles. The Indian soldiers were much admired by the populace. "The Turks," writes Wilson,[1] "were astonished at the novel spectacle of men of colour being so well disciplined and trained. Indeed, the general magnificence of the establishment of the Indian army was so different from what they had been accustomed to see in General Hutchinson's that the contrast could not fail to be striking. Never were finer men seen than those which composed this force." It is gratifying that a company of Madras Pioneers was included in a contingent which earned such high praise.

Leaving Cairo on August 29th, and still confident of seeing active service against the French at Alexandria, the Indian troops resumed their journey downstream, and preceded by Baird, arrived in Rosetta on the 31st. Then, to their bitter disappointment, they learnt that the French had capitulated and that they were to halt at Rosetta.[2] The war in Egypt had ended before they had seen a shot fired! Four days later, Hutchinson made a triumphal entry into Alexandria, and afterwards, having handed over command to Lord Cavan, sailed for England. Baird now expected, with some justification, that his troops would be allowed to return at once to India, for his transports were already collecting at Suez and their hire was costing the East India Company £40,000 a month. In this, he was again disappointed. Orders came from England that his contingent was to remain for a time as part of the garrison of Alexandria; and it was not until May 7th, 1802, after news had arrived of the Treaty of Amiens, that he was able to commence his march to Suez by way of Cairo. The Indian contingent reached the capital on the 11th, and crossing the desert by easy stages in successive detachments, concentrated in Suez on the 25th. The whole fleet put to sea on June 5th, and before the end of July the Pioneers were home in Madras.

General Baird was thanked by the Government of India in a despatch dated February 8th, 1802. "Although," wrote the Governor-General in

[1] *History of the British Expedition to Egypt*, by Lieut.-Col. R. T. Wilson, Vol. II, p. 39.

[2] An outline of the operations of the British Army in Egypt, from the landing at Abu Qir on March 8th to the occupation of Alexandria on Sept. 3rd, 1801, is given in *The Royal Engineers in Egypt and the Sudan*, by the present author, pp. 10–18.

Council, "the rapid progress of the British arms precluded the troops under your command from participating in the glory of those operations which terminated the conquest of Egypt, you omitted no exertions to render your approach useful to the common cause." In July, 1802, the honour "Egypt" was bestowed on the Madras Pioneers; and more than three-quarters of a century later, in January, 1879,[1] the addition of the badge of "The Sphinx" was granted by Queen Victoria to the Queen's Own Madras Sappers and Miners in further recognition of the services of the small unit of Madras Pioneers in the Egyptian campaign of 1801. The award of this badge was especially gratifying as no other Indian regiment was honoured in like fashion.

It is remarkable that until 1811 the Pioneer units employed in overseas' expeditions from India came exclusively from Madras. There is no record that prior to that date a single Bengal or Bombay Pioneer left the country. What is the explanation of this curious state of affairs? The Bengal Pioneers under Swinton were brave and enterprising; the Bombay Pioneers, adventurous and accustomed to war; yet neither took any part in the expeditions before 1811 to the Malay Archipelago, Ceylon, Egypt and Mauritius. As regards the expeditions to Malaysia, the Directors were probably influenced in some degree by the fact that the Madras Pioneers were more numerous and experienced than their brethren in the north; and as for the expeditions to Ceylon and Mauritius, there could be no doubt that preference should be given to the Madras Corps for geographical reasons. It is evident also that the Bombay Pioneers could not conveniently be sent eastwards to Malaysia, and that there was no urgent need to dispatch them to Mauritius or Ceylon. But what of Egypt? In that expedition the transports were overhauled and provisioned in Bombay, the headquarters of the Bombay Pioneers, and yet not a man of that Corps was embarked for service. Making due allowance for the fact that the Egyptian Expeditionary Force of 1801 was assembled originally in Ceylon for operations in Java and Mauritius, and was therefore an affair chiefly of the Madras Army, it must be admitted that the exclusion of all Bombay Pioneers is difficult to understand.

There were potent reasons for the preference given to the Madras Pioneers, and one of these was their lack of caste prejudice. The men were of low caste and humble origin. Muhammadans, Hindus, Adi Dravidians and Christians were accustomed to live together, work together, and eat the same food from the same cooking-pot. The modern Madras Sapper and Miner, a man of much the same stock as the Pioneer of former days, used to smoke his pipe and drink his beer in the canteen. He regarded service in the Corps as a family tradition; and being humorous, intelligent and quick to imbibe new ideas, he fraternized easily with the British soldier. An Inspecting Officer once asked a Madras Sapper what caste he belonged to. "Sapper caste, sir," replied the man. On another occasion, a senior officer addressed the Corps in high-flown Urdu, and then, noticing the blank faces of the men, asked a Subadar to translate the speech into a

[1]G.G.O. No. 23, dated Jan. 14th, 1879.

language which they could understand. Thereupon, the Subadar rendered the speech in English! In a word, the Madras Sapper was more anglicized than his counterpart in Bengal or Bombay and consequently fitted more easily into an expedition which included British troops.

The Bombay Pioneers did not allow caste restrictions to interfere seriously with military duty. Their class composition, however, was very mixed, like that of the Bombay Army generally. There were Marathas from the Konkan; Tamils, Telegus and low-caste Hindus from various districts; Muhammadans from the Deccan, and a sprinkling of Brahmans and Rajputs from Oudh. The Marathas, who formed the bulk of the Corps, had the roving spirit of their ancestors, the corsairs of the western coast, and for that reason did not object to crossing the ocean; but the Brahmans and Rajputs did not always see eye to eye with them, and caste difficulties were liable to arise. In addition, the establishment of Bombay Pioneers was so small that it could not meet the demands of overseas' expeditions without prejudice to the engineering requirements of the Bombay Presidency. The Corps had neither the strength, homogeneity nor adaptability of the Madras Pioneers, though the men were good fighters and fair artisans.

The Bengal Pioneers were recruited for the most part from the martial races of Oudh and the Punjab, and comprised Muhammadans, Sikhs, Jats, Rajputs and Hindus who were of higher social status or caste than the Bombay Pioneers, though perhaps inferior in those respects to the rank and file of the Bengal Cavalry and Infantry because they were prepared to dig as well as fight. Nevertheless, they were soldiers first and artisans afterwards, reversing the character of the Madras Pioneers. Skilled craftsmanship, so beloved by the Madrasi, did not appeal to them, and though physically powerful, they appreciated the value of manual labour only when it was applied to the art of war. Their occasional employment as road labourers in time of peace must have been abhorrent to them. They were gallant and well-disciplined, though not overburdened with intelligence; but they were not so well suited as the Madras Pioneers to meet the strange conditions of service in foreign countries. Many of the Hindus were strict observers of caste and consequently required special food and special arrangements for cooking and eating it. Some even carried the holy water of the Ganges to drink. The most serious obstacle, however, to the employment of Bengal Pioneers in overseas' expeditions arose from the aversion, which they shared with the entire Bengal Army, to being transported across the sea, a process known to them as "*kala pani*."[1] The cause of this aversion has been a matter of considerable discussion. In the case of the Hindus it was understandable, for to cross the "*khara pani*" or salt water might entail caste defilement. The Sikhs, though subject to no such risk, may have sympathized with this attitude. But what of the Muhammadans? Their feelings may perhaps be summed up in the phrase "*Main bulunteer hun, lekin main jane ko nahin mangta*"[2] which

[1]In more modern times, the term *kala pani* (literally "black water") was usually taken to imply only penal transportation to the Andaman Islands.

[2]"I am a volunteer, but I don't want to go."

was reputed to be common among the few volunteers forthcoming. Superstitition had full play in men who were stationed far from the sea and did not come of a maritime stock, and the average Muhammadan, enlisted for local service in Northern India, saw no reason to undertake duties in foreign lands from which Hindus were excused. To sum up, the Bengal Pioneer was rigid in his insularity. He preferred to remain in his own country and to fight under conditions which were familiar to him and against enemies whose methods he could understand. In his proper surroundings, he was equal to any emergency and ideal for the work he had to do.

Operations against the French settlements in Mauritius and Réunion, which had been postponed in favour of the expedition to Egypt in 1801, came under consideration during the next few years. Nelson's victory at Trafalgar gave the British the command of the Atlantic and Mediterranean, but not of the Indian Ocean; and French privateers from Mauritius, Réunion and the small island of Rodriguez[1] continued to harry the Company's shipping and disorganize their trade. Accordingly, Rodriguez was seized and occupied in August, 1808, as an advanced base, and from it the coast of Réunion was successfully raided. The Government then resolved to gain complete possession of Réunion and Mauritius and in May, 1810, despatched from Madras a mixed force of about 3,500 men which was joined by two companies of Madras Pioneers (200 men) under Lieutenant J. B. Scouler, M.I., from the port of Quilon in Travancore. The expedition reached Rodriguez on June 20th, and after some delay, sailed thence for St. Denis, the capital of Réunion. The French Governor of that town is described as a "mild man," and true to that description he made only a brief resistance to the troops who landed east and west of him, for on July 7th he surrendered not only St. Denis but the whole island. A detachment was sent to Mauritius and succeeded in gaining a foothold on the islet of La Passe outside an important harbour, but it was forced to surrender after a powerful French squadron had defeated the British in a desperate naval action. The Pioneers were not involved in this mishap, for they were hard at work in Réunion.

Well aware of the necessity of wresting Mauritius from the French as soon as possible, the Government of India then took strong action and during November, 1810, assembled at Rodriguez a force of some 10,000 men, under Major-General John Abercromby,[2] including two companies of Madras Pioneers, one under Scouler from Réunion and the other under Lieutenant C. Swanston, M.I.,[3] from Madras. The fleet and transports sailed for Mauritius, and on November 29th, the troops landed without opposition about 12 miles from St. Louis, the capital on the west coast. Owing to the natural protection afforded by reefs, the French had neglected he fortifications of the town, and consequently Abercromby was able to

[1]Réunion (Ile de Bourbon), Mauritius (Ile de France) and Rodriguez lie respectively 450, 550 and 950 miles east of Madagascar.

[2]Son of Major-Gen. Sir Ralph Abercromby, who was killed in Egypt in 1801.

[3]Lieut. Swanston was attached to the Engineer Department soon after his arrival in Rodriguez, leaving Scouler in sole charge of the Pioneers.

advance without serious opposition, though hampered by dense jungle through which the guns were dragged with great difficulty. The Pioneers laboured in extreme heat to cut the necessary tracks and suffered much from thirst. At noon on the 30th, Abercromby was within six miles of St. Louis, and on December 1st, the French commander proposed terms of capitulation. These having been accepted, the whole island passed into British possession on December 3rd, together with a large number of ships and many heavy guns. The expeditionary force was thanked by the Governor-General in Council[1] and the honour " Bourbon " was awarded to all the infantry units engaged ; but because the Pioneers mustered only two companies, the distinction was withheld from them, a decision for which there seems little justification. They had already returned to India, leaving behind them Lieutenant Swanston, who remained in Mauritius until August to survey the island and its harbours.

The activities of the Government of India in 1810 were not confined to the despatch of expeditions to Réunion and Mauritius, for it was known that Napoleon had incorporated in the French Empire the Dutch settlements in the Eastern seas and that he hoped to make Java a base for attacks on British shipping. Batavia, the capital, was strongly fortified, and an entrenched camp had been made at Cornelis, six miles inland. In 1811, therefore, after the capture of Mauritius, an important expedition was sent to Java in which the Madras Pioneers were fortunate enough to see further active service. The force was commanded by Lieut.-General Sir Samuel Auchmuty and comprised about 5,300 British and 6,600 Indian troops, among whom were 3 companies of Pioneers (300 men) under Captain T. Smithwaite with Lieutenants R. McCraith and G. Shepherd and Ensigns W. Stuart and N. McLeod, M.I.[2] Sailing from Madras in two convoys during the latter half of April, the expedition was brought to full strength at Malacca on June 1st by a division from Bengal which included 4 companies of Bengal Pioneers under Lieutenant W. C. Baddeley, B.I.,[3] and proceeding past Singapore, reached the southern point of Borneo on July 20th. Meanwhile, the Chief Engineer, Lieut.-Colonel Colin Mackenzie, M.E., had gone ahead with Lieutenant John Blakiston, M.E., to reconnoitre for a landing place in Java. On July 11th, they were in sight of the lofty

[1]G.O.G.G., dated Feb. 11th, 1812.

[2]Other Pioneer officers who served in Java in 1811 were Lieuts. R. Home and V. Hughes and Ensign W. J. Darby, M.I. These appear in the Prize Rolls.

[3]Under G.O.C.C., dated Dec. 24th, 1810, volunteers were called for from the Bengal Pioneers to form 3 companies for service in Java comprising 4 British officers, 6 Sergeants, 3 Jemadars (as Subadars), 3 Havildars (as Jemadars), 12 Naiks (as Havildars), 12 Privates (as Naiks), 3 Buglers and 273 Privates. Total 316. Also 6 Bhistis and 6 Lascars. (Lieut. F. G. Cardew in *The Services of the Bengal Native Army*, p. 110, shows the strength as 361, but his authority is not quoted.) The volunteers were to be drawn from all eight companies of Pioneers (about 40 % of each company), the units being at that time distributed as follows :—1st and 7th Coys. at Ludhiana, 4th and 5th at Karnal, 2nd at Kotah, 3rd at Jhansi, 6th at Meerut and 8th at Muttra. However, under G.O.C.C., dated March 19th, 1811, the O.C. Barrackpore was directed to form the Pioneer details assembled near Calcutta for foreign service into 4 *companies* under Lieuts. W. C. Baddeley, J. Elliot and R. C. Faithful and Ensign R. Ellis, B.I., and on April 8th, Ensign J. A. Currie, B.I., was appointed Adjutant of the " Corps of Volunteer Pioneers." The date of embarkation of the units is not recorded, nor is there much on record of their services in Java. (See the file at Roorkee entitled " Restoration of Battle Honours.")

mountain of Cheribon and a small fort below it which was typical of the Dutch settlements on the coast. Continuing to Batavia Bay, they landed on the 14th with an escort of thirty men. They were dressed as seamen, and it is recorded that Mackenzie, who stood 6 feet 2 inches, cut a ridiculous figure in a suit lent to him by the very short commander of his ship. However, the reconnaissance proved satisfactory, and after cruising back along the coast to Cheribon and beyond, Mackenzie returned to the fleet and guided it to an anchorage off Chillingching, 10 miles east of Batavia, where the expedition landed on August 5th. Owing to sickness, the force had dwindled to about 9,000 men. Opposed to it were 13,000 native troops under General Janssens in the fortified camp at Cornelis with an advanced detachment at Weltevreden between Cornelis and Batavia.

On August 8th, Auchmuty occupied Batavia without opposition, and then, turning towards his main objective at Cornelis, defeated the enemy at Weltevreden on August 11th in an action in which the Madras Pioneers under Smithwaite and McCraith took a prominent part.[1] Three days later, the army was concentrated before Cornelis. So formidable were the defences of that place that the engineers began regular siege approaches; but Auchmuty was pressed for time and could not await the completion of the works, and consequently he decided to risk an assault as soon as his artillery had made practicable breaches. On the 22nd, the day on which the guns opened fire, the enemy made a sortie, in repelling which Shepherd was killed and McLeod mortally wounded, so it is evident that the Madras Pioneers were in the thick of the fight. In the final assault on Cornelis, on August 26th, the Madras and Bengal Pioneers accompanied the main attack under Colonel Robert Gillespie against the enemy's right. General Janssens made a spirited resistance, but his batteries were silenced one by one, and redoubt after redoubt fell to the invaders. Although he attempted a last rally at Fort Cornelis, his men could not withstand the British bayonets and broke and fled in all directions, pursued by our cavalry for a distance of fifteen miles. Over 6,000 prisoners were taken, and many thousands of the enemy were killed or wounded. The victory was overwhelming and complete.

After the defeat of his army, Janssens fled eastwards, passing through Cheribon only two days before it was occupied by a British detachment. Sumarang fell on September 12th, after an engagement at Jatty in which the cocked-hatted squadrons of a peculiar chieftain called the "King of Solo" were charged and put to ignominious flight by two British officers, one of whom was Blakiston. Two companies of Madras Pioneers witnessed this feat of arms. On September 17th, 1811, the whole of Java was surrendered to the British, and military operations came to an end with the exception of minor expeditions against rebellious chiefs in Sumatra, Borneo and Celebes in which no Pioneers were concerned. The acquisition of Java checkmated French designs in the Malay Archipelago; but

[1]The operations in Java in 1811–12 are described in some detail in *The Military History of the Madras Engineers and Pioneers*, by Major H. M. Vibart, R.(M.)E., Vol. I, pp. 453–479.

FORT CHERIBON. A DUTCH SETTLEMENT IN JAVA IN 1811.

the island did not remain long under British control, for it was returned to Holland in August, 1816. After the conclusion of the main operations, a detachment of Madras Pioneers under Stuart was left in Java until June, 1813, and when it was ordered back to Madras, four non-commissioned officers of the 1st Battalion were retained in the island and remained there until 1814 to assist in the formation of a Colonial Corps of Pioneers.

The scene now shifts from the Malay Archipelago to Arabia. For several years after the conquest of Java the Government of India was occupied so fully with the internal troubles which culminated in the Third Maratha War that it had no inclination to embark on expeditions overseas; but by 1819 the internal situation had improved considerably and it was possible to make a determined attempt to extinguish in the Persian Gulf the piracy which was interfering so seriously with the expansion of trade in a westerly direction. The chief objective was the stronghold of the Joasmi pirates at Ras al Khaimah on the Arabian coast within the entrance to the Gulf. This place had been attacked and captured in November, 1809, by a small expeditionary force from Bombay in which no Pioneers were included; but soon after the return of that force to India in 1810, the pirates had resumed their evil calling. The second and larger expedition which was despatched to Ras al Khaimah at the beginning of November, 1819, gave the Bombay Pioneers their first experience of service overseas, and as such it is worthy of notice. The force comprised about 1,600 British and 1,400 Indian infantry, a company of artillery and the 3rd Company, Bombay Pioneers,[1] and arrived on November 17th under the command of Major-General Sir W. Grant Keir, at Qishm Island in the Strait of Hormuz. It came none too soon, for large pirate fleets had been reported recently to be cruising off the western coasts of India. Sailing from Qishm, the troops landed in boats at Ras al Khaimah on December 3rd and formed up across the isthmus which connects the small peninsula, on which the town lies, with the neighbouring and remarkably arid country. Across the isthmus ran a high wall flanked by four towers, and along the shore in front of the town were batteries and entrenchments.

On December 4th, 1819, Grant Keir began his advance along the isthmus in the face of a strong resistance, and after nightfall the Pioneers and working parties dug two batteries within 300 yards of the south-western tower. On the 6th, the guns opened fire from these positions and silenced the Arab artillery, and more guns having been mounted and brought into action, the troops moved forward on December 9th to the assault. As the enemy had made several sorties during the preceding days, hard fighting was expected, but the town and its defences were found to be deserted and not a shot was fired. The Arabs had escaped under cover of darkness. Ras al Khaimah having been occupied, Grant Keir proceeded to capture an adjacent hill-fort and returned on December 26th, after the Pioneers had destroyed the defences. Hostilities were brought to an end on January 8th,

[1]According to the *Brief History of the Royal Bombay Sappers and Miners*, p. 6, an entire company of Bombay Pioneers (probably the 3rd Company) was included in General Keir's force. It may be noted, however, that only half a company is mentioned in *Frontier and Overseas Expeditions from India*, Vol. VI, p. 249.

1820, by the signature of treaties with the chiefs of Ras al Khaimah and other places on the Persian Gulf, and by the middle of March the Pioneers were back in Bombay with a mention in despatches to their credit.

But although the operations in 1819 served to suppress piracy in the Persian Gulf, they were not so effective in Eastern Arabia, where a fierce and turbulent tribe, called the Bani bu Ali, rose in June, 1820, and murdered the pilot of a British ship which had called at Ras al Junaiz[1] to deliver a letter of protest from the Government of Bombay. A small punitive expedition was therefore sent from Bombay at the beginning of October, and after calling at Muscat in the Gulf of Oman, sailed southwards to Sur, where it landed and marched 35 miles inland against the tribal capital at Balad Bani bu Hasan. The force consisted of only 380 Indian infantry with some 2,000 local irregulars and was utterly inadequate for the task. It was attacked and almost annihilated on November 8th when close to the capital. Most of the British officers, and two-thirds of the sepoys, were killed, for the Arabs gave no quarter. The survivors, including many wounded, escaped to Muscat, whence they were taken to Qishm at the entrance to the Persian Gulf.

News of this disaster having reached India, the Bombay Government took immediate steps to retrieve British prestige in Arabia and organized a mixed force of about 6,000 British and Indian troops, under Major-General Lionel Smith, which sailed from Bombay on January 11th, 1821. Included in this force was a recently formed company of Bombay Sappers and Miners under Captain T. Dickinson, Bo.E., assisted by Lieutenant T. B. Jervis, Bo.E.,[2] and with it sailed also the 3rd Company, Bombay Pioneers, which had served in 1819 in the Ras al Khaimah Expedition. Disembarking at Sur on January 27th, the troops began their march into the interior and reached Balad Bani bu Hasan on March 2nd after repulsing an attack on February 10th. The Bani bu Ali at once advanced to give battle in the open. Ignoring the showers of grape from the British guns, they surged forward with broad-sword and shield, striving with desperate fanaticism to find weak points in the line of bayonets. Some won through and played havoc at close quarters with their swords; but the bayonets triumphed in the end, and when the attack had been beaten off, 500 of the Bani bu Ali lay dead or dying. The casualties on the British side amounted to only 29 killed and 173 wounded—a small price to pay for British honour. The fort at Balad was occupied after a short bombardment and the troops marched back to Sur, where they embarked for Bombay. By a General Order, dated February 11th, 1831, all the units engaged in this expedition, including the Bombay Sappers and Miners and Pioneers, were permitted to bear on their colours and appointments the name "Beni Boo Ali" which headed the list of honours held later by the Royal Bombay Sappers and Miners.

After the expeditions to Arabia, many years elapsed before an engineer unit from Bombay proceeded again on foreign service. The Madras

[1]Called also Ras al Hadd.
[2]See Chapter IV.

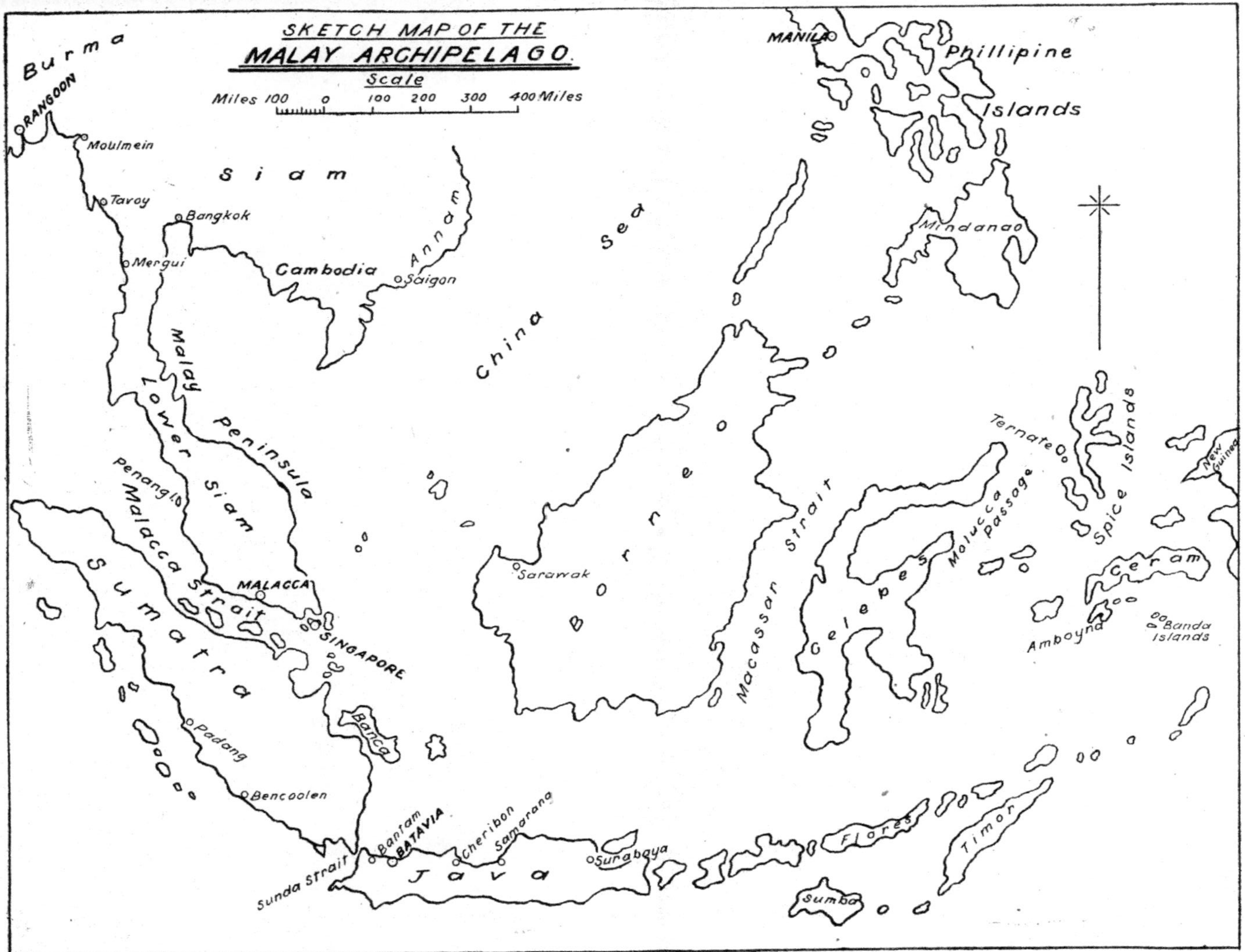

SKETCH MAP OF THE
MALAY ARCHIPELAGO.
Scale
Miles 100 0 100 200 300 400 Miles
Burma
RANGOON
Moulmein
Siam
Tavoy
Bangkok
Mergui
Cambodia
Annam
Saigon
China Sea
Malay Peninsula
Lower Siam
Penang I.
Malacca Strait
MALACCA
SINGAPORE
Sumatra
Padang
Bencoolen
Banca
Sunda Strait
Bantam
BATAVIA
Cheribon
Samarang
Surabaya
Java
Borneo
Sarawak
Macassar Strait
Celebes
Molucca passage
MANILA
Phillipine Islands
Mindanao
Ternate
Spice Islands
New Guinea
Ceram
Amboyna
Banda Islands
Flores
Sumba
Timor

Pioneers voyaged no further than Burma, and no attempt was made to induce the Bengal Pioneers to cross the " salt water." A period of internal reorganization followed the conquest of Ava and the reduction of Bhurtpore. Nevertheless, trouble was brewing in the Malay Peninsula, where the Dutch had ceded the Straits Settlements—Penang, Malacca and Singapore—in exchange for the British possessions in Sumatra. An obstreperous chieftain known as the Panghooloo of Nanning became dissatisfied with British rule and refused to obey a summons to Malacca. Accordingly it was decided in 1831 that he should be reduced by force of arms. True to their traditional policy of economy in military matters, the authorities at Malacca despatched an expedition of less than 200 native soldiers against a State which could put 1,500 armed men into the field. The little force set out on August 5th, and made its way through dense jungle towards the Panghooloo's capital, well-named Taboo, which lay about 22 miles to the north-west. Three weeks later, it was back in Malacca after failing to reach its objective and narrowly escaping annihilation on the return journey. The Panghooloo then overran the country and blockaded the British settlement.

The Government of India now awoke to the gravity of the situation and despatched reinforcements from Madras under Lieut.-Colonel C. Herbert. They amounted to about 1,500 men and included " C " and " G " Companies of the Madras Sappers and Miners under Lieutenant J. H. Bell, M.E., with 2nd Lieutenants H. Watts and T. Smythe, M.E. Bell and Watts, with " C " Company, arrived at Malacca at the end of January, 1832, and Smythe, with " G " Company, on February 9th. This was the first occasion of the employment of Madras Sappers and Miners on field service.

" C " Company began to cut a road through the jungle towards Taboo and to clear the forest to a width of 80 yards on either side.[1] They were assisted by gangs of natives and protected by covering parties of Indian infantry. The progress of the work was accelerated after the arrival of " G " Company at the front on February 26th, but nevertheless it remained very slow. Several men were injured by falling trees while removing obstacles erected by the Malays. Others were pierced by pointed bamboo stakes concealed in the undergrowth, and a few fell victims to snipers. As the advance continued, the resistance stiffened. The Sappers were present at the assault and capture of many stockades in the forest—at Sangipatti on March 17th, Kalama on March 25th and Bakti si Barsu on May 25th—and dozens of unoccupied stockades were seized by the rapid and unexpected advance of small detachments. On only one occasion did the enemy take the offensive, and then they were repulsed with heavy loss. The Panghooloo became alarmed when the expedition was nearing Taboo and asked for an armistice. He was allowed to enter the British camp to negotiate with a Dutch intermediary but insisted on a preliminary exchange of upper garments as a customary and mutual

[1] *The Military History of the Madras Engineers and Pioneers*, by Major H. M. Vibart, R.(M.)E., Vol. II, p. 77.

assurance that no treachery was contemplated. The result was grotesque. On the one side stood the portly Dutchman tightly swathed in the linen *badjoo* of the Malay; on the other, the diminutive Panghooloo sinking under the weight of a huge coat. Terms were arranged, garments handed back, and the Panghooloo took his departure. However, as soon as it became clear that the proposal for an armistice was merely a ruse to gain time, Herbert resumed his advance. On June 14th, the main defences of Taboo were in sight, and on the following day the Sappers took part in a general assault which resulted in the capture of the place. Two breastworks and eight stockades were carried by storm. For once, Taboo belied its name, and the Panghooloo fled into the jungle with the remnant of his followers.

News of this success was slow in reaching India, for in July, 1832, a large reinforcement of Sappers and Miners embarked at Madras for Malacca. This comprised the Corps Headquarters and "A" and "F" Companies (328 men) under Captain A. Lawe, M.E., with Lieutenants E. Lawford and F. Ditmas and 2nd Lieutenant W. H. Horseley, M.E.[1] These Sapper units got no further than Penang and were back in Madras at the end of August. After the companies had returned to India, Bell remained for a time in Malacca to advise Colonel Herbert on matters of defence and did not reach Madras until the beginning of December, 1832. The Panghooloo of Nanning surrendered in March, 1834, and Malacca was then able to settle down at last to an era of peace and prosperity under the British flag. So ended another little expedition which gave useful experience in jungle warfare.

During the next few years, the Madras Sappers and Miners saw active service in various parts of Southern India, but they did not proceed overseas until the outbreak of hostilities against China in 1840. The Bengal and Bombay Sappers and Miners were then fully engaged in the First Afghan War, and for that and other reasons were not available. Consequently, the engineer units for the First China War were supplied by the Madras Corps, and three complete companies, with detachments from others, were despatched to the Far East, where they did well under novel conditions. Very distant or exceptionally large expeditions, however, such as those to China in 1840 or Burma in 1852, can be described more conveniently in later chapters, and accordingly we pass to the last expedition of moderate dimensions undertaken before the Indian Mutiny, the excursion to Southern Persia in 1856 to punish the Shah because he had violated his treaty obligations by occupying Herat in Western Afghanistan at the instigation of Russia.

Two courses were open to the Indian Government to bring the Shah to reason: either to march a force through Afghanistan to expel the

[1] In addition, a certain Capt. A. Roberts is mentioned in the *Historical Record of the Q.V.O. Madras Sappers and Miners*, Vol. I, pp. 39 and 228; but according to the *Indian Army List*, 1760–1834, by Dodwell and Miles, and the *List of Officers of the Corps of Royal Engineers*, by Capt. T. W. J. Connolly, R.E., there was no such officer in the Madras Engineers. He is not mentioned by Major H. M. Vibart in *The Military History of the Madras Engineers and Pioneers*, Vol. II, p. 81.

Persians from Herat, or to send an expedition by sea to the Persian Gulf to invade Persia from Bushire or further north. The latter plan having been approved,[1] a division comprising about 2,300 British and 3,400 Indian soldiers, under Major-General F. Stalker, was organized in India and was joined at Bombay on October 18th, 1856, by two companies of Bombay Sappers and Miners. These units were the 2nd Company under Captain C. T. Haig, Bo.E., and the 4th Company[2] under Captain J. Le Mesurier, Bo.E., and with them went the Corps headquarters under Captain W. R. Dickinson, Bo.E.,[3] with Lieutenant H. F. Hancock, Bo.E., as Adjutant. War was declared on November 1st, and a fleet of seven steamships, towing thirty sailing vessels, carried the 1st Division to the Persian Gulf, where the island of Kharag was occupied on December 4th and a landing completed on December 9th a few miles south of Bushire. Stalker immediately advanced on that city and captured it on the 10th after taking the old fort of Rishahr (Rashir) by storm. The two companies of Bombay Sappers and Miners, now joined by 2nd Lieutenant H. R. Meiklejohn, Bo.E., were praised for the valuable assistance they rendered in these operations.

Reconnaissance inland disclosed the fact that an army of 4,000 Persians had collected at Shiraz, and as it was evident that the 1st Division was too weak to venture far from the coast, a 2nd Division was formed in India in the middle of January, 1857, under Brig.-General Henry Havelock and the command of the entire force in Persia was entrusted to Major-General Sir James Outram.[4] The latter reached Bushire on January 20th, followed gradually by the 2nd Division, and marching on February 3rd with three brigades against a Persian concentration at Borazjan on the road to Shiraz, halted on the 5th near the village of Khush-Ab, where good water was available. He advanced further on the 6th; but on the 7th, as food was scarce and the enemy seemed to be retiring into the mountains, he decided to return to Bushire and moved back to some wells near Khush-Ab. Encouraged by this retrograde movement, a body of 8,000 Persians took up a position dominating the British camp; but Outram attacked them on the 8th and they fled, leaving 700 dead on the field.

After the victory at Khush-Ab, the British force resumed its march to Bushire, which it reached on February 10th, though in a deplorable condition. Rain was falling in torrents, and the mud was so deep that the men's boots were dragged from their feet. The troops had covered 46 miles in 41 hours to meet the enemy, a further 20 miles over most difficult country during the night after the battle, and after a rest of 6 hours, another 24 miles to Bushire. The 2nd and 4th Companies of Bombay Sappers took part in the battle and the strenuous marching which preceded and followed it.

[1]In this expedition the Indian Government acted under the direction of the British Government.

[2]The 4th Company had returned from Karachi to Poona in the spring of 1856.

[3]Capt. Dickinson had been appointed Commandant in succession to Major J. Hill, Bo.E., who was nominated as Commanding Engineer to the expedition. Hill resumed the post of Commandant in Oct., 1857. (See *Digest of the Services of the Bombay Sappers and Miners* (1895), by Major G. H. W. O'Sullivan, R.E., p. 20.)

[4]The same Havelock and Outram who afterwards became famous at Lucknow in the Indian Mutiny.

The Persian Government published their own version of Khush-Ab. They said that their brave soldiers had won a great victory and had pursued the British to within a few miles of Bushire. There they had fought heroically for four hours, twice breaking the British squares, and had only relinquished their efforts when both sides had been forced to abandon their guns in the mud. They stated further that their troops had lost only 500 men while the British casualties amounted to 1,000 killed and wounded, and thus they attempted to minimize the political effects of a severe defeat.

Preparations were now made for the invasion of Southern Persia by an expedition to Mohammerah at the junction of the Karun River with the Shatt al Arab Estuary below Basra. The force collected at Bushire amounted to 1,500 British and 2,400 Indian soldiers and included the 2nd Company, Bombay Sappers and Miners (109 men) under Haig[1] and "B" Company, Madras Sappers and Miners (124 men) under Brevet-Major A. M. Boileau, M.E., with 2nd Lieutenants H. N. D. Prendergastand H. J. G. Gordon, M.E., and Lieutenants P. A. Brown, M.E.R.,[2] and F. R. Fox, M.I. "B" Company had embarked at Coconada[3] on January 19th and reached Bushire just in time to join the expedition to the head of the Persian Gulf. Starting on March 19th, the transports and escorting warships entered the Shatt al Arab and were in sight of Mohammerah on the 24th. Boileau and other officers then reconnoitred the neighbourhood of the enemy's defences to ascertain whether it was possible to erect a battery on a swampy island, and when this proved impossible, they approached to within close range of the Persian batteries in a small canoe, towing a raft on which mortars were mounted, and moored the raft behind the island so that the gunners could bring effective fire to bear. Two days later, the warships entered the Karun River and silenced the enemy's guns. It is recorded that on this occasion the Madras Sappers were aboard the S.S *Hugh Lindsay* and helped the men of the 64th Regiment to fire the ship's carronades.[4]

The troops landed and advanced through date-groves intersected by irrigation channels, which the Sappers and Miners bridged rapidly with palm-trees. Mohammerah was occupied on March 27th after 13,000 Persians and Arabs had fled northwards up the Karun, and thereafter the Sappers were employed in destroying batteries, making roads, building landing-stages and erecting huts in the pestilential heat of Lower Mesopotamia. There was so much work to be done at Mohammerah that they could not accompany the expedition up the Karun River to Ahwaz which resulted in the capture of that town on April 1st. Three days later, the Ahwaz Column was back in Mohammerah and news was received of a treaty of peace concluded in Paris on March 4th. The troops then began to

[1] *Frontier and Overseas Expeditions from India*, Vol. VI, p. 236. As only 109 Bombay Sappers were included, it is assumed that they formed a single company and that the unit was the 2nd Company.

[2] Madras European Regiment.

[3] North of Masulipatam on the east coast of India.

[4] *The Military History of the Madras Engineers and Pioneers*, by Major H. M. Vibart, R.(M.)E., Vol. II, p. 284.

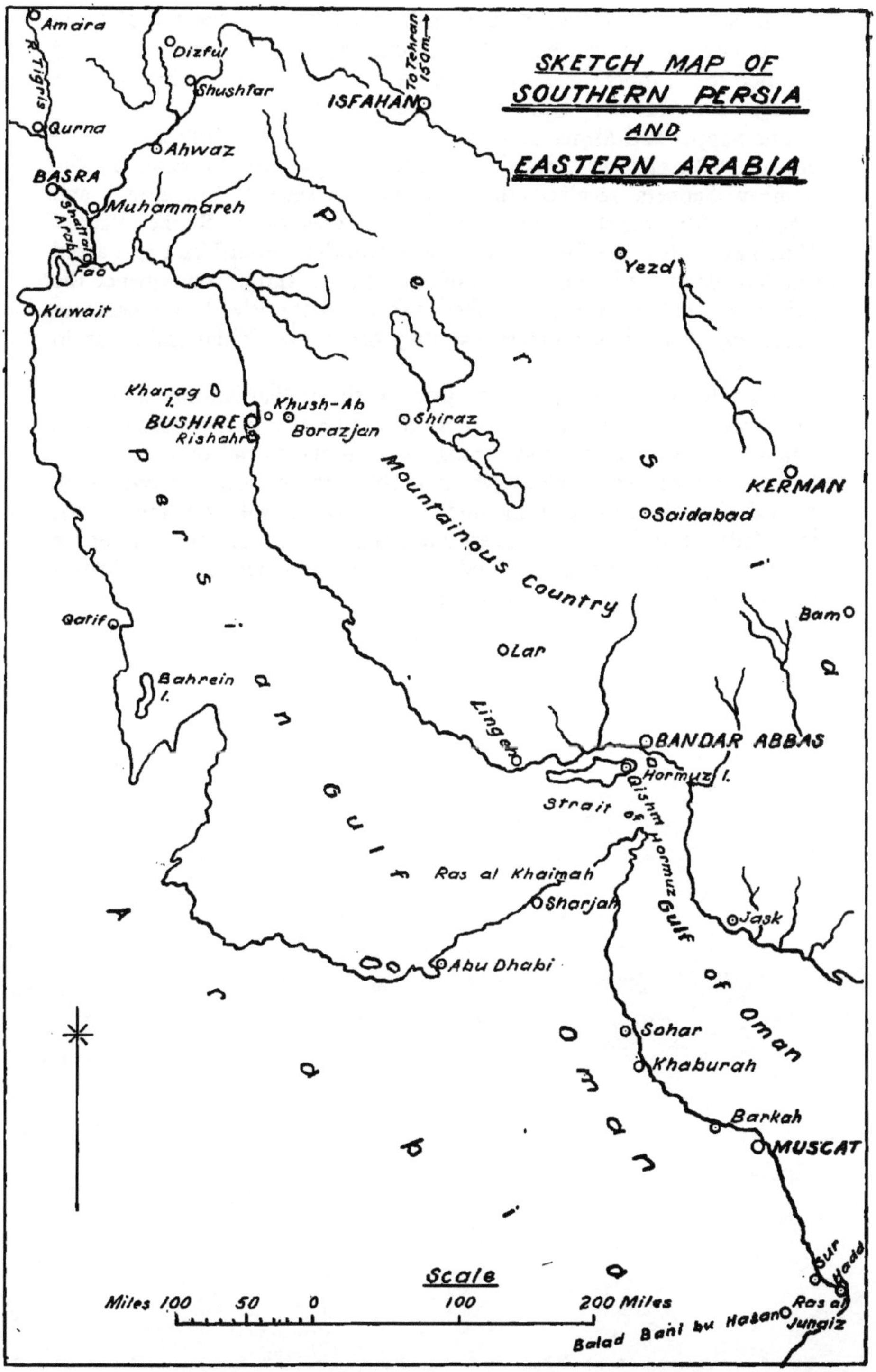
SKETCH MAP OF
SOUTHERN PERSIA
AND
EASTERN ARABIA
Amara
R. Tigris
Qurna
BASRA
Shatt al Arab
Fao
Kuwait
Dizful
Shushtar
Ahwaz
Muhammareh
ISFAHAN
To Tehran 150m.
Yezd
Kharag I.
BUSHIRE
Rishahr
Khush-Ab
Borazjan
Shiraz
Mountainous Country
KERMAN
Saidabad
Bam
Lar
Lingeh
BANDAR ABBAS
Hormuz I.
Qishm
Strait of Hormuz
Qatif
Bahrein I.
Persian Gulf
Persia
Ras al Khaimah
Sharjah
Jask
Abu Dhabi
Gulf of Oman
Sohar
Khaburah
Barkah
MUSCAT
Oman
Arabia
Sur
Hadd
Ras al Junaiz
Balad Bani bu Hasan
Scale
Miles 100 50 0 100 200 Miles

return to India ; " B " Company reached Bombay on June 1st, 1857, in time to take part in the Central India Campaign of the Indian Mutiny, and the Bombay Sappers and other troops followed them. Thus a brief though successful campaign came to a sudden end.

The Sapper and Miner units were highly praised for their work. The honour " Persia " was awarded to both Corps,[1] and in addition, the Bombay Sappers received the honours " Reshire," " Bushire " and " Khoosh-Ab " for their exploits in the early operations. By the treaty of March 4th, 1857, the Shah undertook to withdraw from Herat and avoid interference in the internal affairs of Afghanistan, and in consequence the British vacated Bushire in October, 1857, and the island of Kharag in February, 1858, thus proving that they had no territorial ambitions in Persia.

This tale of fifteen expeditions prior to the Indian Mutiny illustrates the diverse conditions under which the Company's forces marched and fought in foreign lands, and through it runs the thread of Pioneer and Sapper and Miner activities which enabled those forces to cope with natural obstacles and novel methods of warfare. It will be admitted that the Madras and Bombay Pioneers and Sappers deserved much credit for the success of the operations and the resulting enhancement of British prestige and expansion of British trade.

[1]G.O.G., dated Sept. 14th, 1858, and June 18th, 1861.

CHAPTER VI

THE FIRST AFGHAN AND FIRST CHINA WARS AND CAMPAIGNS IN SIND AND GWALIOR, 1838–1843

THE FIRST AFGHAN WAR was a tragedy in which thousands of brave men were sacrificed to redeem the errors of commanders equally brave though often incompetent and always under autocratic civilian direction. Politically the war was disastrous, and morally, unjustifiable. It dragged its weary course through a sombre welter of misrepresentation, unscrupulousness, and intrigue. Politics determined the whole form and shape of the operations. Politics forbade a direct thrust at Kabul and decreed instead a circuitous approach down the Indus, through the Bolan Pass to Quetta, through the Khojak Pass to Kandahar, and so by Ghazni to the capital.[1] The abandonment by the Persians of the siege of Herat made the invasion of Afghanistan an act of aggression destitute of any adequate pretext, and Lord Auckland, the Governor-General, had no proper excuse for his attempt to depose Dost Muhammad, the Amir of Afghanistan, in favour of the exiled monarch, Shah Shuja. However, against the advice of the Commander-in-Chief but with the support of Mr. William Macnaghten as Political Envoy, Auckland launched a cumbrous, inexperienced and unsuitably equipped army into a barren and mountainous region, arctic in winter, torrid in summer, unapproachable except through narrow defiles and peopled by fierce and treacherous tribes. He invited catastrophe and he achieved it.

The full history of this deplorable war has been told so often that it is unnecessary to trace it in detail in these pages.[2] Engineering interest centres on the exploits of the Bengal, Bombay and Madras Sappers and Miners concerned in it, and on the achievements of a famous irregular Corps known as "Broadfoot's Sappers" which had a brief but glorious existence. The crossing of the Indus, the blowing in of the Kabul Gate at Ghazni and the defence of Jalalabad are feats which will live for ever in the annals of Indian warfare.

The assembly of an "Army of the Indus" for the invasion of Afghanistan having been decided upon, orders were issued in August, 1838, to Captain George Thomson, B.E., then Commandant of the Bengal Sappers and Miners at Delhi, directing him to make all preparations for an Engineer

[1] See Maps I and III at the end of this volume.

[2] A very complete and readable account is given in *A History of the British Army*, by the Hon. J. W. Fortescue, Vol. XII, pp. 1–280. *History of the War in Afghanistan in 1838–42*, by Sir J. W. Kaye, and *The Afghan War and its Causes*, by Maj.-Gen. Sir Henry M. Durand, are also excellent, and most of the important despatches are given *verbatim* in *Memorials of Affghanistan*, by J. H. Stocqueler. More concise accounts appear in *Frontier and Overseas Expeditions from India*, Vol. III, pp. 271–466, and in *The Military Engineer in India*, by the present author, Vol. I, pp. 267–279. See also the article by Col. F. C. Molesworth, late R.E., entitled "Afghan Wars", appearing in *The R.E. Journal*, Vol. XLIII, 1929, pp. 595–614.

Department with the army in the field. He was informed that no wheeled transport would be allowed and that all tools and stores must be carried on camels; and further that, in adapting everything to camel transport, he must arrange for the carriage only of indispensable tools and stores which were not likely to be obtainable in Afghanistan.[1] Accordingly, he prepared two lists—one for the equipment of an Engineer Park and the other for that of the 2nd and 3rd Companies, Bengal S. & M.,[2] under Captain Edward Sanders, B.E., which were detailed to join the army at Ferozepore. The tools and stores were packed at Delhi by Lieutenants H. M. Durand and E. J. Brown, B.E., assisted by Conductor Richardson, and three pairs of wooden tool-racks, adapted to the camel pack in common use, were made for the essential tools of each company.[3] The remaining equipment, including that of the Engineer Park, was packed in wide strips of sacking, sewn together at right angles so that the lappets could be folded over and the whole tied with rope. It was impossible to devise any practicable method of carrying on camels the immensely long bamboos needed for scaling-ladders, and consequently these had to be loaded on carts drawn by bullocks and many of them were damaged by the jolting caused by bad roads. Owing to the difficulty of transporting ammunition in large quantities, the siege train was limited to four 18-pounder guns, two 8-in. mortars and two 5½-in. mortars, and Thomson was warned that he must be fully prepared for mining operations. He arranged, therefore, that 10,000 lbs. of powder for this purpose should be carried by the Artillery Park; but even without this burden the transport needed for the Engineer Department amounted to 178 camels and 8 bullocks.[4] The tools, particularly the pickaxes, were far too heavy. A body of 300 temporary Pioneers (*beldars*) was recruited to assist the infantry in digging. On September 13th, Thomson was appointed as Chief Engineer,[5] and the Sapper and Miner officers and Assistant Field Engineers of the Engineer cadre under his command were Captain E. Sanders and Lieutenants J. Anderson, H. M. Durand, J. L. D. Sturt, N. C. Macleod, J. S. Broadfoot and R. Pigou, B.E.

The Army of the Indus consisted at first of 16,000 men under Major-General Sir Willoughby Cotton; but after the Persians had withdrawn from Herat it was reduced to a brigade of cavalry, a few batteries of artillery, two companies of Bengal Sappers and Miners and three brigades of infantry, the infantry commanders being Colonel R. H. Sale, Major-General W. Nott and Lieut.-Colonel A. Roberts.[6] Cotton was ordered to march from Feroze-

[1] "Notes on the Field Equipment of the Engineer Department with the Bengal portion of the Army of the Indus," by Lieut. H. M. Durand, B.E., appearing in *Professional Papers of the Corps of Royal Engineers*, Vol. VI, 1843, pp. 1–11.

[2] Bengal Sappers and Miners.

[3] Each tool-rack held 10 pickaxes, 10 shovels, 10 *phaorahs*, 2 axes and 2 saws, and the camel load of 2 racks was 4 cwts. 48 lbs., exclusive of the pack saddle.

[4] Engineer Park, 110 camels and 8 bullocks; Sapper equipment, 28 camels; tents 14 camels; Q.M. stores, 4 camels; spare, 22 camels.

[5] Obituary Notice of Col. George Thomson, C.B., late R.(B).E., appearing in *The R.E. Journal*, Vol. XVI, 1886, pp. 78–84. Capt. E. Swetenham, B.E., was appointed Commandant of the Bengal Sappers and Miners at Delhi, *vice* Thomson, on Nov. 9th, 1838.

[6] Father of Field-Marshal Earl Roberts.

pore down the Sutlej and Indus to join a Bombay Division under Major-General T. Willshire which included the 1st Company, Bombay S. & M.,[1] under Captain A. C. Peat with 2nd Lieutenants C. North and W. F. Marriott Bo.E.[2] A mixed force of British and Sikhs was assembled to operate in the Khaibar Pass, and some attempt was made at Ferozepore to organize and train 6,000 irregulars in the service of Shah Shuja, who was to lead the way into Afghanistan. The supreme command was allotted to Lieut.-General Sir John Keane, Commander-in-Chief in Bombay, who was expected to assume charge when the Indus was reached.

Shah Shuja headed the advance from Ferozepore on December 2nd, 1838, and Cotton followed on the 10th in five columns. Troubles arose at once. A host of 50,000 followers, and almost as many camels, impeded the army. One brigadier had no less than 60 camels for his personal belongings. The supply depots along the route, which had been provided by the Political Department, failed to yield more than half-rations. Drivers deserted, animals were stolen, the troops became weak and dispirited; and thus, long before the first Afghan was seen, the efficiency of the force was impaired. However, the Indus was reached at last, and marching into Rohri on January 24th, 1839, Cotton prepared to cross the river in the wake of Shah Shuja's following who had been ferried across to Sukkur. He was delayed for a time by the necessity of demonstrating towards Hyderabad to reduce opposition to the advance of the Bombay Division through Sind; but a bridge was ready on February 3rd, and 4,000 camels crossed it on the 5th, followed by the Artillery Park and a solitary elephant on the 9th. The siege train was ferried to the right bank on the 13th, and by February 18th the entire Army of the Indus, with all its transport and supplies, had effected the passage of the mighty river without accident.

The story of the engineering preparations for this feat may now be recorded.[3] On October 12th, 1838, at Delhi, Thomson had been ordered to prepare a scheme for the transport of the army, and especially of its cavalry, artillery, baggage and animals, across the Indus at Rohri and had submitted a project based on the very meagre information available. He suggested that both branches of the river, formed by the island of Bukkur between Rohri and Sukkur, should be bridged for the passage of troops, field artillery and camel transport if sufficient and suitable boats could be obtained, but that the siege train should be ferried across. Subsequently, information was received which encouraged the hope that a large number of boats would be available, and orders were sent to Lieutenant J. D. Cunningham, B.E., the Political Officer at Ferozepore, to purchase deodar timber and collect boats. Orders were sent also to the Political Agent at Shikarpur,

[1]Bombay Sappers and Miners.

[2]*Digest of the Services of the Bombay Sappers and Miners*, by Major G. H. W. O'Sullivan, R.E., p. 6. Under G.G.O., dated Oct. 30th, 1838, the 1st Company, Bombay Sappers and Miners was ordered to join the force detailed for " service in Sind."

[3]A full account of these preparations, and of the actual bridging of the Indus between Rohri and Sukkur, is contained in a report by Lieut. H. M. Durand, B.E., entitled " Passage of the Indus by the Bengal portion of the Army of the Indus ", appearing in *Professional Papers of the Corps of Royal Engineers*, Vol. IV, 1840, pp. 92–105.

near Sukkur, to collect as many boats as possible. The 2nd and 3rd Companies, Bengal S. & M., the Engineer Park and presumably the contingent of temporary Pioneers, marched from Delhi on October 24th and joined the infantry concentration at Karnal on the 30th. Three weeks later, Thomson visited Ferozepore to ascertain the progress made in collecting materials for bridging the Indus at Sukkur and the number of boats secured for the transport of the Engineer Department down the Sutlej and Indus and subsequent incorporation in the bridge. Then he received his first insight into the methods under which the military operations would be conducted. He was informed that the political authorities at Ferozepore had commandeered 25 boats, and all the timber collected by Cunningham, in order that the Governor-General might cross the Sutlej in proper state to visit Shah Shuja! Also that the remainder of the boats, 105 in all, had already been allotted to Shah Shuja's contingent and to the medical services and commissariat. Realizing that it was useless to protest, Thomson bought some rafts and prepared to march with the Sapper companies to Sukkur, leaving a detachment under Sturt to dismantle the Governor-General's bridge when it was no longer needed and to follow with the boats, rafts and material. He assumed that the Political Agent at Shikarpur would have collected a large number of boats at Sukkur, and on December 2nd he marched from Ferozepore. When near Bahawalpur, however, he heard that hardly any boats were moored at or near Sukkur, and consequently, on January 2nd, 1839, he sent Sanders forward to Shikarpur to make enquiries. The result was the discovery of only five boats upstream of Sukkur; and when the Sappers crossed the Indus above that place on January 11th and 12th, they had only these boats and 10 others which arrived in the nick of time with Sturt from Ferozepore. It seems that Captain Alexander Burnes, the British Envoy to Sind, had asserted that in his opinion a bridge at Sukkur was neither practicable nor necessary, and hence no serious effort had been made to carry out the orders from Delhi. On January 13th, the Sappers marched into Sukkur. The Army of the Indus was approaching, and to transport it and its supplies across the river seemed beyond the power of human ingenuity.

The Indus at Sukkur makes a sudden bend and forces its way through a rocky barrier in two channels, one on either side of the island of Bukkur, the width of the eastern channel (on the Rohri side) being about 190 yards at the upstream end of the island, where the current is rapid, and increasing steadily towards the downstream end. The western or Sukkur channel averages about 100 yards in width and has a slow current. Thomson found that the passage of troops across the island was possible only at the upstream or downstream ends because the remainder of the area was obstructed by fortifications, and accordingly, for the sites of his floating bridges, he selected the downstream end, where he hoped to obtain good holding for his anchors and a suitable approach on the Rohri bank. The spans were estimated at 367 yards and 133 yards respectively, which would be easy to bridge with trained men and sufficient boats and material;

but the 2nd and 3rd Sapper companies—270 men with 14 sergeants—were unaccustomed to such work, and no timber or rope, and only 8 boats, had yet arrived. However, on January 14th, Thomson began to bridge the narrow western channel while local rope-makers manufactured 500 cables of coarse grass and local carpenters prepared pyramidal anchors of wooden cribwork loaded with stones. Until good timber could be floated down from Ferozepore, the Sappers were compelled to use split palm-trees both for road-bearers and decking, and even nails had to be manufactured. Yet a bridge of 19 boats, each about 30 feet in length, was completed over the western channel in four days. Attention was then turned to the more difficult eastern channel. As an intimation was received at this time that the boats allotted to the medical and commissariat services would be made over to the engineers, the situation began to look more cheerful. Gradually, these craft arrived and were supplemented by others obtained locally, and by January 27th, three days after the Army of the Indus had marched into Rohri, the eastern bridge had 30 boats in position. Further progress was then checked for a time by a shortage of boats, and the incomplete structure was nearly carried away in a flood in which floating trees were washed down on to the anchor cables and severed many of them; but work was resumed on the 29th after the arrival of more boats, and on February 3rd, after sixteen days of unceasing labour and anxiety, the eastern bridge of 55 boats[1] was finished. Two days later, the camel transport began to stream across and was followed by the army itself on its return from the demonstration southwards, and thus a stupendous obstacle was surmounted and the seemingly impossible achieved. "It was truly a beautiful sight," wrote the correspondent of the *Englishman*,[2] "to see the different corps with their bands playing, followed by long strings of camels and camp followers, wending their way over the bridge. The glittering of their arms in the sun, the Fort of Bukkur with its picturesque battlements frowning over the bridge, and the ancient towns of Rohree and Sukkur overhanging the mighty stream, formed altogether a delightful picture." Towards the end of the month, the eastern bridge was dismantled so that its boats might be used as ferries during the flood season; but in this operation the Bengal Sappers had no concern for they were then marching to Afghanistan with an army which was destined to suffer terribly in that inhospitable land.

Some 15,000 soldiers and 65,000 followers were massed near Shikarpur on February 20th. They depended wholly on their commissariat for food and were equipped only for service in the plains of India. Seven columns left Shikarpur on consecutive days and discovered that the promised depots of supplies along the desert route to Dadhar did not exist. Led by the Bengal Sappers and Miners, they toiled onwards; and when Thomson was told that the cavalry might have to turn back, he replied that the engineers would go forward whether or not the cavalry followed. The

[1]Most of these boats were larger than those in the western bridge, being from 40 to 60 feet in length. In all, about 120 boats were collected for bridging and rafting in addition to those from Ferozepore.

[2]*Memorials of Affghanistan*, by J. H. Stocqueler, p. 21.

exhausted men and animals stumbled into Dadhar on March 10th, and after resting for six days, threaded the stony defiles of the Bolan Pass and arrived in the mud village of Quetta on the 26th with only ten days' rations in hand and Kandahar still 147 miles away. Ordered by Keane to halt at Quetta, Cotton hesitated to place his force on reduced rations, for a suggestion that the sepoys might receive half a pound of mutton instead of a pound of flour daily had met with a blank refusal from all except the Sappers and Miners.[1] However, urged by Thomson, Cotton was induced at last to issue orders that the troops should receive half-rations and the followers quarter-rations, so that when General Keane joined the army at Quetta on April 6th, the supplies were not completely exhausted and a further advance was still possible.

Leaving a garrison at Quetta under Nott, Keane marched for Kandahar on April 7th, 1839, and four days later the Sappers and Miners were preparing a practicable road through the Khojak Pass. By April 13th, three parallel tracks were ready, one for camels, another for wheeled transport and artillery and a third for bullocks, ponies and men, but they were very narrow and the gradients unusually steep. A hurried attempt was then made to thrust the army through the defile. Guns and carriages overturned, and thousands of animals became jammed so tightly between the vertical walls that the losses in transport were paralysing. The Bengal Army entered Kandahar on April 26th incapable of moving another mile. The Bombay Army under Willshire fared better and reached Kandahar in good fettle on May 4th. Owing, however, to the general disorganization of the transport and the necessity of accumulating supplies, it was not until June 27th that the combined armies under Keane could resume the march on Kabul after leaving a garrison at Kandahar.

At the head of 7,800 fighting men, still on half-rations, Keane plodded onwards through Kalat-i-Ghilzai towards the fortress of Ghazni where, according to Macnaghten, he might expect no resistance. Because of that assurance and the scarcity of draught-cattle, Keane had committed the serious mistake of leaving his 18-pounder guns at Kandahar, and consequently, when he came in sight of Ghazni on July 21st with only two days' rations and a single day's artillery ammunition in hand, he found himself in an unpleasant predicament. He could hardly believe that the place was empty, though Captain Burnes, his Political Officer, had informed him to that effect. Thousands of Ghilzais had shadowed him all the way from Kandahar, and now he learnt that beyond Ghazni lay an Afghan force under Dost Muhammad, the ruler of the country. In this dilemma he consulted Thomson who, after reconnoitring with Peat, asserted that the army must either mask Ghazni and advance to fight the Afghans or carry the fortress by a surprise assault after the engineers had blown in the Kabul Gate on the north-eastern side. Mining was impossible because the walls were surrounded by a wet ditch or watercourse. Escalading was impracticable because there were few ladders and those available

[1] *The First Afghan War*, by Maj.-Gen. Sir Henry Marion Durand, K.C.S.I., C.B., late R.(B.)E., p. 137.

GHAZNI IN 1839.

would not reach the crest of the parapet. The fortifications could not be breached by artillery because the heavy guns had been left at Kandahar. There was therefore no alternative to a desperate attempt to force an entrance through a gateway.

" Captain Thomson's report was very clear," wrote Keane.[1] " He found the fortifications equally strong all round ; and as my own opinion coincided with his, I did not hesitate a moment as to the manner in which our approach and attack should be made. At daylight on the 22nd July I reconnoitred Ghazni in company with the Chief Engineer and the Brigadier Commanding the Artillery for the purpose of making all arrangements for carrying the place by storm, and these were completed in the course of the day. Instead of the tedious process of breaching, for which we were ill prepared, Captain Thomson undertook, with the assistance of Captain Peat of the Bombay Engineers, Lieutenants Durand and Macleod of the Bengal Engineers and other officers under him (Captain Thomson), to blow in the Cabool Gate (the weakest point) with gunpowder, and so much faith did I place in the success of this operation that my plans for the assault were immediately laid down and the orders given."

The demolition of the Kabul Gate and the storm of Ghazni may best be described by quoting extracts from the reports of the engineers concerned in the operations or summarizing their several accounts. We begin with a memorandum by the Chief Engineer which was submitted to the Governor-General with the official despatch from the Commander-in-Chief.

" The accounts of the fortress of Ghuznee," writes Thomson,[2] " were such as to induce H. E. the Commander-in-Chief to leave in Kandahar the very small battering train then with the army, there being a scarcity of transport cattle. When we came before it on the morning of the 21st July, we were very much surprised to find a high rampart in good repair, built on a scarped mound about 35 feet high, flanked by numerous towers and surrounded by a *fausse-braye*[3] and wet ditch. The garrison was stated to be 3,000 to 4,000 strong, and on the approach of the army a fire of artillery was opened from the body of the place and of musketry from the neighbouring gardens. The works were evidently much stronger than we had been led to expect. We had no battering train, and to besiege Ghuznee in form, a much larger one would have been required than the army ever possessed. The great command of the parapets, from 60 to 70 feet, with the wet ditch, were unsurmountable obstacles to an attack either by mining or escalading. The engineers, with an escort, went round the works ; but the garrison were on the alert and kept up a hot fire. The

[1]Despatch dated Ghazni, July 24th, 1839, from Lieut.-Gen. Sir John Keane, K.C.B. to the Governor-General, quoted in *Memorials of Affghanistan*, 1838–42, by J. H, Stocqueler, pp. 28–35.

[2]" Memorandum of the Engineer Operations at the taking of Ghuznee in July, 1839," by Capt. George Thomson, B.E., Chief Engineer to the Army of the Indus, appearing in *Professional Papers of the Corps of Royal Engineers*, Vol. IV, pp. 3–6, and in *Memorials of Affghanistan*, 1838–42, by J. H. Stocqueler, pp. 37–39.

[3]*Fausse-braye.* A low parapet built outside a higher one to provide a second tier of fire. See the plan of Ghazni in 1839, included in this chapter.

only tangible point for a *coup-de-main* was the Cabool gateway. The road to the gate was clear, the bridge over the ditch unbroken, there were good positions for the artillery within 300 yards of the walls on both sides of the road, and we had information that the gateway was not built up, a reinforcement from Cabool being expected. The result of this reconnaissance was a report to H.E. the Commander-in-Chief that the only feasible mode of proceeding was a dash at the Cabool gateway, blowing the gate open by bags of powder. His Excellency decided upon the attempt, the camp was moved that evening to the Cabool road, and the next morning, the 22nd, Sir John Keane in person reconnoitred the proposed point of attack, approved the plan, and gave orders for its execution."

"It was arranged," continues Thomson, "that an explosion party consisting of three officers of Engineers—Captain Peat and Lieutenants Durand and Macleod—3 sergeants and 18 men of the Sappers in working dresses, carrying 300 lbs. of powder in 12 sandbags, with a hose 72 feet long, should be ready to move down to the gateway at daybreak. At midnight the first battery left camp, followed at intervals by the other four. Those to the right of the road were conducted to their positions by Lieutenant Sturt, those to the left by Lieutenant Anderson. The ground for the guns was prepared by the Sappers and Pioneers. The artillery was all in position and ready by 3 a.m. on the 23rd; and shortly after, at the first dawn, the party under Captain Peat moved down to the gateway, accompanied by six men of H.M.'s 13th Light Infantry and supported by a detachment of the same regiment which extended to the right and left of the road when they arrived at the ditch and endeavoured to keep down the fire from the ramparts.[1] Blue lights were shown by the enemy, but luckily they were not thrown down. The explosion party marched steadily on, headed by Lieutenant Durand; the powder was placed, the hose laid, the train fired, and the carrying party had retired to tolerable cover in less than two minutes. So quickly was the operation performed that not a man of the party was hurt. As soon as the explosion took place, Captain Peat, although hurt by the concussion because his anxiety prevented him from keeping sufficiently under cover, ran up to the gate with a small party of the 13th Regiment and ascertained that it was completely destroyed. There was some delay in getting a bugler to sound the advance, and this was the only mistake in the operation. The assaulting column, consisting of four European regiments[2] commanded by Brigadier Sale, and the advance (party) under Lieut.-Colonel Dennie guided by Lieutenant Sturt, moved steadily through the gateway in a domed building which, opening on one side, rendered everything very obscure and made it difficult to find the outlet

[1]The detachment was a strong one and comprised 18 officers, 28 sergeants, 276 rank and file and 7 buglers. It might have been required to assault and capture the outer works. The advantage of surprise was lost because Keane had imparted his plans to Macnaghten, who promptly passed them on to Shah Shuja, so that they became the common talk of the camp, where Afghan spies abounded.

[2]Actually, 4 regiments, less 1 company each, were detailed for the assaulting column. The column was followed by a reserve of 3 native infantry battalions under Brig. Roberts.

into the town.[1] They met with little opposition ; but a party of the enemy, seeing a break in the column owing to the difficulty of scrambling over the rubbish in the gateway, made a rush, sword in hand, and cut down a good many men, wounding the Brigadier and several other officers. These swordsmen were repulsed and there was no more regular opposition, though a good deal of desultory fighting took place. The whole of the works were in our possession before 5 a.m. We lost 17 men, 6 Europeans and 11 natives, killed, and 18 officers, 117 Europeans and 30 natives wounded ; total, 182. Of the Afghans, more than 514 were killed in the town and about 100 outside by the cavalry, and 1,600 prisoners were taken."

So runs a rather prosaic account of a gallant exploit which is almost as famous as the blowing in of the Kashmir Gate at Delhi in the Indian Mutiny. Thomson could supply no details of the actual demolition because he was not with the explosion party ; but in a letter written a few weeks later he gives plans of the gateway and its approaches and some information about the effects of the explosion. " We were aware," he remarks,[2] " that the wicket was open from seeing men pass in and out ; yet we were not at all certain that the gateway itself had not been partly blocked up, for there was information that the other gates had a quantity of large stones piled against them. It was uncertain also whether there was not an inner gate, and had there been one, 300 lbs. of powder would probably have cleared both away.[3] A second party of Sappers, with 300 lbs. more, was ready in case any obstacle was met. However, the archway in which the second gate had been formerly[4] was found built up, the arch being cracked, and an opening had been made to the right in which were fastenings for a gate but none hung. The turn in the passage prevented the fragments of the gate from being blown clear, and they were much in the way of the assaulting column. The gate was so completely destroyed that its construction could not be ascertained ; but it had a strong frame with rather weak planking, as the light in the guardroom[5] was seen through the joints by Lieutenant Durand when he laid the powder. The piers of the arch outside the gate were shattered, and the flat roof of the short passage leading from the gate to the domed portion of the building was blown off."

[1]See the plan of the Kabul Gate, Ghazni, included in this chapter with a plan of Ghazni in 1839. A detailed plan of the fortress in April, 1880 (by Lieut. C. Hoskyns, R.E.), appears in a report on Ghazni by Bt. Major E. M. Larminie, R.E., included in *Professional Papers of the Corps of Royal Engineers*, Vol. VI, 1881, pp. 173–176.

[2]Letter from Capt. George Thomson, E.I.C. Engineers, to Col. Pasley, R.E., dated Kabul, Aug. 15th, 1839, appearing in *Professional Papers of the Corps of Royal Engineers*, Vol. IV, pp. 1–2.

[3]Capt. Peat remarks in his report attached to the official despatch that Col. Pasley recommended a charge of 60 to 120 lbs. for blowing open such gates, but 300 lbs. was used because it was feared that the enemy might have taken alarm and built up the gateway with masonry. He adds that it was found afterwards that they had actually tried to shore up the gate with beams. The charge of 300 lbs. proved excessive and produced debris which obstructed the stormers.

[4]This archway was the original exit from the domed building and was immediately opposite the entrance gateway.

[5]Presumably, the domed portion of the building was occupied by a guard.

In a letter from Kabul to his brother John of the Bengal Engineers,[1] Thomson gives his personal experiences in the storming of Ghazni. "To sound the advance if the explosion was effective," he writes,[2] "I sent a European bugler, thinking him more sure than one of our own. That was a mistake, for the Sappers were as cool as possible, and when called for, the bugler had disappeared. Seeing the explosion, and not hearing the bugle, I got very anxious, so I left the Brigadier (Sale) and ran down[3] to see what was the matter. There was a domed building inside the gate, with a passage (15 to 20 feet long) roofed over between, so everything was pitch dark inside.[4] However, I told the advance (4 companies of Europeans) to push on. As soon as they got in, I had the 'Advance' sounded by Sale. It was while the rear of the advance (party) was struggling out of the gateway, which was choked with beams and rubbish, that forty Afghans made a rush down from the ramparts above. The cover of my cap was cut through, but I was not touched. One of the Europeans, who fell across my leg, was killed, and before I could get clear of him, a dead Afghan fell across me. The Afghans cut down the rest of the light company of the European Regiment and then commenced on the head of the main column, wounding Sale and several officers and men. I felt exceedingly uncomfortable while struggling to get clear of the bodies above me and the timber under me, while sabres and bayonets made a most unpleasant clashing about my ears."

The assaulting troops had assembled at two ancient towers erected by Mahmud of Ghazni alongside the road leading north-eastwards to Kabul. The Explosion Party and the Advance Party under Dennie took up a position at the nearest tower about 1,000 yards from the Kabul Gate, and the main body under Sale at another tower a further 600 yards distant. The Kabul road runs along the south-eastern slope of a high ridge terminating in the fort or citadel, and opposite the two pillars is the site of the ancient city of which no trace now exists. Keith Jackson describes these pillars as tapering brick structures about 100 feet high and 12 feet in diameter at the base, the lower half being hexagonal in plan with projecting corners and the upper half a circular column crowned by a Muezzin's gallery;[5] but according to Lieut.-Colonel C. L. B. Duke, M.C., R.E., who visited Ghazni in April, 1938, this description is inaccurate. The upper columns and galleries have disappeared, but the lower portions still stand and they

[1]There were several pairs of brothers in the Bengal Engineers, such as Robert and Edward Smith, George and John Thomson, John and Alexander Boileau, Joseph and Alexander Cunningham, Edward and Alexander Fraser, Charles and George Newmarch, William and Salisbury Trevor, Duncan and Robert Home, and Henry and Elliot Brownlow. Many of these served in the Bengal Sappers and Miners.

[2]Letter dated July 29th, 1839, quoted in the Obituary Notice of Col. Geoge Thomson, C.B., late R.(B.)E., appearing in *The R.E. Journal*, Vol. XVI, 1886, pp. 78–84.

[3]The assaulting column had moved forward to high ground overlooking the bridge which carried the approach road over a watercourse supplying the flooded ditch. The road then ascended in a winding fashion between loopholed towers of the *fausse-braye* and reached the Kabul Gate in a deep recess between two high bastions of the main fortifications.

[4]This reconnaissance was probably made from the *fausse-braye*. It is unlikely that Thomson had time to ascend to and enter the gateway and then return to Sale and the main body.

[5]*Views in Affghaunistaun*, by Sir Keith Jackson, p. 11.

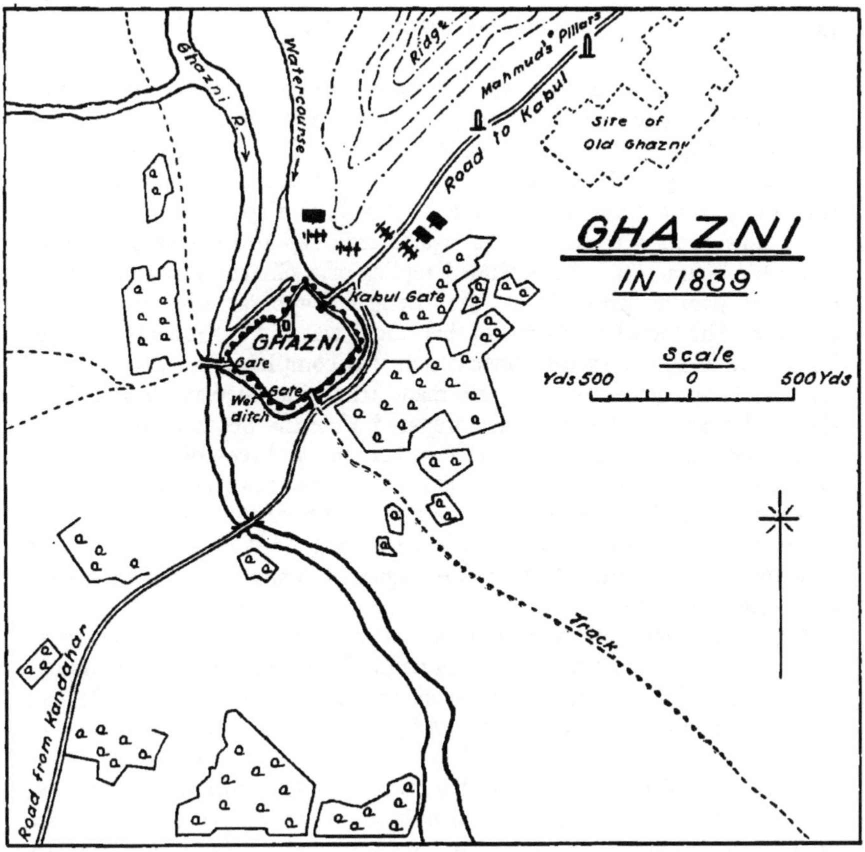
GHAZNI
IN 1839
Scale
Yds 500
0
500 Yds
Ghazni R.
Watercourse
Ridge
Mahmud's Pillars
Road to Kabul
Site of
Old Ghazni
Kabul Gate
GHAZNI
Gate
Gate
Wet
ditch
Track
Road from Kandahar

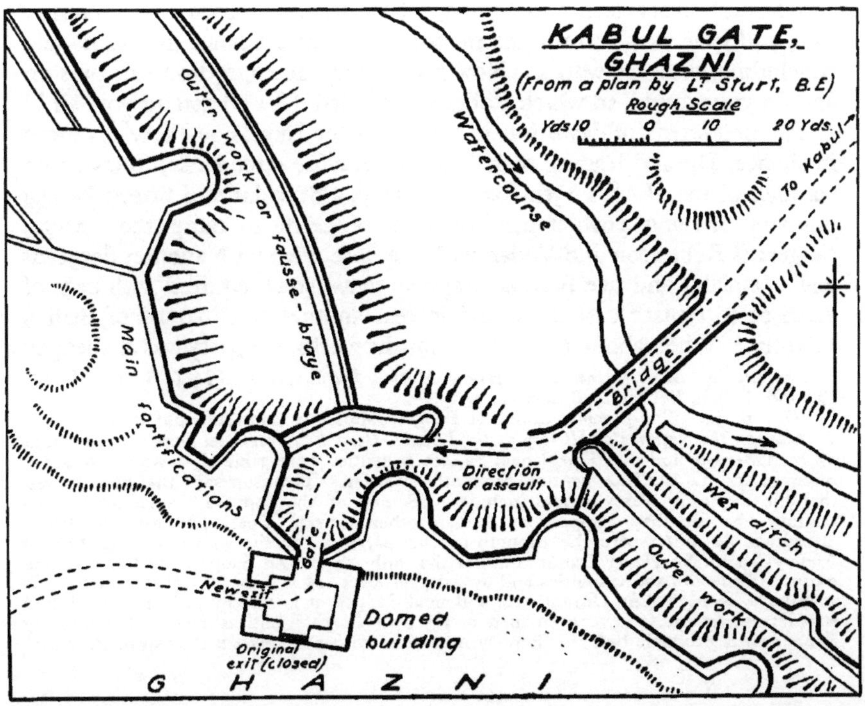
KABUL GATE,
GHAZNI
(From a plan by Lt Sturt, B.E)
Rough Scale
Yds 10
0
10
20 Yds.
To Kabul
Watercourse
Outer work or fausse-braye
Main fortifications
Bridge
Direction
of assault
Wet ditch
Outer work
Gate
New exit
Domed
building
Original
exit (closed)
G H A Z N I

are not hexagonal. Each tower rests on a rough masonry plinth about 8 feet high and the plan is a nine-pointed star with an overall diameter of 24 feet. The faces of each projecting point are 4½ feet wide and form a right angle at the apex. The masonry is of thin bricks laid in mud and strengthened by layers of timber at intervals. Within is a spiral staircase. Each tower now bears a pyramidal corrugated iron cap and has an inscription in Arabic characters. An intended replica of a Ghazni Tower was built on the parade ground of the Bengal Sappers and Miners at Roorkee. The foundation stone of this edifice was laid by General Viscount Kitchener in 1907 and the construction was completed in 1911; but unfortunately the lower portion was made triangular in plan, having been designed from a rough drawing, prepared after the Second Afghan War, which gave the impression that the plan was a three-pointed star. In 1913, the tower was crowned with a small dome, and in 1924–26, a colonnade was built around it to commemorate the services of the Corps during the Great War. This was opened by Field-Marshal Sir W. Birdwood in 1927. The tower and colonnade bear the names of many who fell or earned distinction in battle.

After this digression we come to the adventures of the Explosion Party itself. Thomson had offered the command of this detachment to Durand; but the latter, knowing that Peat was his senior and expected to be selected, had declined and asked only that he might be allowed to place the powder and fire the train. Accordingly, Peat was notified in orders as the commander of the party. An attack of jaundice had left Durand so weak that he could hardly walk, and in this condition he considered that his chance of survival was small. He called up two sergeants of the Bengal Sappers and Miners, Robertson and Vivian, whom he had chosen to accompany him, and gave them careful instructions for their guidance in case he fell, concluding with the words "Now remember. If I am dropped, pass on and do your duty," to which Robertson replied "I understand you, sir."[1]

The first streak of dawn was in the sky as the Explosion Party advanced in silence, Durand leading with Macleod in close attendance, followed by six men of the H.M.'s 13th Light Infantry, a Subadar and fifteen Bengal Sappers carrying powder-bags or bags of earth to tamp the charge, Sergeants Robertson and Vivian with the hose, Peat with another Sergeant and a Jemadar and five Bombay Sappers to assist as required with bags of earth or to replace casualties, and in rear another small squad of British infantry.[2] When about 150 yards from the works, the party was challenged

[1] *The Life of Major-General Sir Henry Marion Durand, K.C.S.I., C.B.*, by H. M. Durand, C.S.I., Bengal Civil Service, p. 53.

[2] *Ibid.*, p. 54. The precise number of Bengal Sappers is uncertain, but it is stated in *Lectures on the Regimental History of the K.G.O. Bengal Sappers and Miners* (p. 21) that 15 men were included. The Bengal Sapper casualties were 3 killed, 2 wounded and 1 missing, and 12 I.O.M.s were subsequently awarded. Thomson says that he arranged that the Explosion Party should include "18 men of the Sappers"—presumably including the Bombay Sappers (5 Indian other ranks). Peat, Durand and James Broadfoot do not record the strength of the party; and the writer of *The Life of Major-General Sir Henry Durand* implies that only 12 Bengal Sappers started with the party. In view of the casualties and awards, however, 15 is a more probable figure. It may have been 18. As Durand was a Bengal Sapper, it is certain that all the selected powder-carriers must have been men of his own Corps; and as Peat was a Bombay Sapper, it is probable that the Bombay men were with him towards the rear of the party.

and then fired upon. Blue lights flared on the battlements and a general fusillade began, but the fire of the covering party disturbed the enemy's aim to such an extent that there were no casualties. Durand pushed on across the bridge, through the *fausse-braye* and up the winding road to the Kabul Gate, while Peat halted in a sally-port of the *fausse-braye* after posting the rear party of infantry in a position to repel any attack of swordsmen. Under the superintendence of Durand, Subadar Devi (Debi) Singh of the Bengal Sappers and Miners laid the first bag containing the end of the powder-hose; the other powder-carriers followed, and finally those with the earth for tamping the charge. Each man, having deposited his bag, retired under the direction of Macleod along the foot of the massive walls, where he was screened from fire.[1]

Meanwhile, Durand and Sergeant Robertson were uncoiling the hose towards a sally-port to the right of the gateway, laying it close to the wall. The enemy tried to interfere by hurling down stones and clods of earth, but these did no serious damage because most of them bounded clear of the attackers. Most fortunately, the end of the hose just reached to the shelter of the sally-port, the existence of which was unknown when the hose was prepared, for the length had been designed only to give Durand a slender chance of escape if he was forced to flash the train with a pistol to save it from being seized and extinguished by the enemy. At first, the port-fire would not light, and Durand was occupied for some time in trying to ignite it by blowing on the quick-match and port-fire held together. Even then, when he had succeeded, the port-fire went out when laid on the ground. The garrison redoubled their efforts with musketry, stones, bricks and earth. Then Durand drew his pistol, and telling Robertson to run, prepared to flash the train and probably die in the explosion. Robertson, however, refused to leave him and begged him to give the port-fire another chance. He did so, and it burned steadily at last. The roar of the guns was deafening, the rattle of musketry incessant, and after calling several times to Peat and receiving no answer, Durand and Robertson retreated some distance and lay down to watch the flame of the ignited train run up to the gateway. A heavy report and a column of fire and smoke showed that the charge had exploded and that the way was open to the stormers; but no bugle call rang out and no troops advanced, and after sending Robertson back with an urgent message, Durand made for the nearest covering party of infantry to obtain a bugler. The subaltern with the infantry refused to allow the " Charge " to be sounded without orders from his Major and could not say where the latter might be found. The men cursed Durand because, they said, a bugle call would only draw more fire on them. In desperation, and unaware that Peat had been stunned and his bugler killed, Durand then made for the head of Dennie's advance party, and in so doing tripped over a tomb and fell heavily. And as he lay almost helpless on the ground he became aware that Sale's buglers with

[1] *The First Afghan War and its Causes*, by Maj.-Gen. Sir Henry Marion Durand, K.C.S.I., C.B., late R.(B.)E., p. 178.

the main body were sounding the retreat, not the advance, and that for some unknown reason the attack seemed to have failed.

It is now time to follow the adventures of Peat, the leader of the Explosion Party. Peat had lost touch with Durand and did not know that the latter was lighting the train in a sally-port near the gate. Disquieted by the long delay, he left the sally-port in the *fausse-braye* and ran up to the gateway to investigate. As he neared the gate, the charge exploded and he was thrown violently to the ground, but recovering his senses, he forced an entrance through the debris into the passage beyond and saw, facing him, on the opposite side of the domed building, another archway built up with masonry. This, he assumed, still blocked the way. He did not know that the opening had been closed because it was unsafe, nor that the road inside the domed building turned sharply to the right and made its exit through a new archway where no light showed. Afghan swordsmen appeared, and Peat decided to return to report to Thomson, but failed to reach him. Thomson, who had requested Dennie with the advance party to press forward, found Peat badly injured and with Macleod in attendance, lying under the shelter of a small tomb by the roadside and asked him what had happened. Peat replied that he had been inside the demolished entrance but had been unable to see a clear way through the domed building. Brigadier Sale overheard this dialogue, and whether by his orders or not, his bugler sounded the retreat and others repeated the call. Hence a mistake which might have had most disastrous consequences.

When Durand heard the call, he staggered to his feet and, badly shaken by his fall, limped slowly back towards the head of the assaulting column. On his way he met Lieutenant James Broadfoot, B.E., a brother of the famous Captain George Broadfoot, M.I.,[1] who had been sent forward by Thomson to ascertain the cause of the delay. James Broadfoot shouted, "Has it failed"? and Durand answered "No, no," so Broadfoot ran back to Sale whose bugles pealed out the advance whilst Dennie's four companies were pushing through the Kabul Gate.[2] Broadfoot then joined the main column headed by Sale and Thomson and was soon involved in the hand-to-hand fight in the gateway. Lieutenant Marriott, Bo.E., was wounded in this struggle while trying to rejoin the main column from the advance party. Some Sappers with felling axes under Lieutenant Wemyss, Bo.E., and others with two scaling ladders under Lieutenant Pigou, B.E., were also with the column. Once within the walls the assaulting troops carried all before them, and many of the Afghans leaped to their death from the ramparts rather than face the British bayonets. Thus the strongest fortress south of Kabul fell to the Army of the Indus on July 23rd, 1839.

Ten Engineer officers were engaged in the assault and capture of Ghazni—Captain G. Thomson and Lieutenants J. Anderson, H. M. Durand,

[1]George Broadfoot was not then in Afghanistan; but William Broadfoot, of the 1st European Regiment, the second of the three brothers, was in the assault on Ghazni as a volunteer from Shah Shuja's force. James, the youngest, was killed near Kabul on Nov. 2nd, 1840, and William perished in Kabul a year later.

[2]Extracts from the diary of Lieut. James Broadfoot, B.E., quoted in "Sieges and the Defence of Fortified Places", by Col. Sir E. T. Thackeray, V.C., K.C.B., late R.E., appearing in *The R.E. Journal*, Vol. XX, July–Dec., 1914, pp. 239–258.

J. L. D. Sturt, N. S. Macleod, J. S. Broadfoot and R. Pigou of the Bengal Corps, and Captain A. C. Peat and Lieutenants W. F. Marriott and F. Wemyss (senior) of the Bombay Corps. All volunteered for the Explosion Party, though only Peat, Durand and Macleod were selected. The British non-commissioned officers were Sergeants Robertson, Vivian and another. The Bengal and Bombay Sappers volunteered almost to a man, though few could be taken. Peat was subsequently awarded a Brevet-Majority and a C.B., but there was no suitable decoration in those days for Durand and Macleod. The Indian ranks fared better, and in 1839 the following received the newly established Indian Order of Merit, 3rd Class :—[1] Subadar Devi Singh and Sepoys Bisram Singh, Kalu Beg, Sheikh Rajab, Gurdial, Qadir Bakhsh and Dayal Singh of the 2nd Company, Bengal S. & M. ; Sappers Bhik, Baldan, Ganesh (1), Ganesh (2), Shiv (or Sheo) Rattan and Shiv Sahai of the 3rd Company of the same Corps ; and Jemadar Bhawani Singh, Naik Ganga Singh and Sappers Sheikh Amir, Suraj Singh, Sital Singh (2) and Ram Purshad of the 1st Company, Bombay S. & M. The names of the Bengal Sappers are engraved on the Ghazni Tower at Roorkee.

In a complimentary order, dated July 23rd, 1839, Sir John Keane remarked that he could hardly do justice to the gallantry of his troops. " The scientific and successful manner," he wrote, " in which the Kabul Gate, of great strength, was blown up by Captain Thomson, in which he was most ably assisted by Captain Peat in the daring and dangerous enterprise of laying down powder in the face of the enemy, reflects the highest credit on their stern and cool courage." He then acknowledged in general terms the work of the other Engineers and of the Sappers and Miners.[2] After Durand's death in January, 1871, an obituary notice appeared in *The Times* which was considered by some people to attach excessive importance to his part in blowing in the Kabul Gate, and Lord Keane of Ghazni (formerly Sir John) wrote that the credit was due entirely to Thomson though Durand had performed his part with coolness and self-possession. James Broadfoot, however, states in his notes on the siege that while the credit for planning the demolition and the assault was due to Thomson as Chief Engineer, that for successfully carrying out the instructions should be given to Durand. A careful perusal of the available records leads inevitably to the conclusion that the services of Durand were not adequately recognized by Government. Neither Thomson nor Peat were the outstanding figures in the demolition of the Kabul Gate. The leader in that heroic exploit was Durand.

Keane made a triumphant entry into Kabul on August 7th, 1839, and

[1]The 3rd Class was the normal award. The 2nd Class was awarded to a holder of the 3rd Class. The 1st Class was given only for deeds which would now be recognized by the award of the Victoria Cross. The Sappers and Miners who received the 3rd Class for Ghazni were the first soldiers to be so honoured.

[1]It may be noted here that the honours " Ghuznee, 1838 " and " Affghanistan, 1839 " were granted to the Bengal Sappers and Miners under G.O.G.G. dated Nov. 19th, 1839. These honours were shown in the Army List until Jan. 1st, 1859. Thereafter, they were omitted because they were adjudged to have been forfeited in consequence of the mutiny in 1857 of the greater portion of the 2nd and 3rd Companies who had won them.

forced Shah Shuja upon the Afghan nation. A veil may well be drawn over the inefficiency which thereafter affected both the civil administration under Macnaghten and the army itself. On September 18th, the Bombay Division under Willshire marched southwards for Kandahar and Quetta, and on October 16th, Keane started for Peshawar with a force composed mostly of cavalry but including also the 2nd and 3rd Companies, Bengal S. & M. (less a detachment of 20 men left in Kabul and another at Kalat-i-Ghilzai) and half the 1st Company, Bombay S. & M. A British brigade was left to garrison Kabul, and Shah Shuja undertook to hold Ghazni and Girishk.[1] Keane, fighting his way through the Khaibar Pass, relieved the garrison of Ali Masjid, and after he had reached Peshawar, the Bombay Sapper half-company under Macleod helped to take provisions back to Ali Masjid and earned praise for resisting a heavy attack.[2] Willshire arrived in Quetta at the end of October and later sent a detachment including the other half-company of the Bombay Sappers under Peat to capture Kalat. This was accomplished rapidly and successfully on November 13th, and, as a result, permission was accorded on August 6th, 1841, for the Bombay Sappers and Miners to bear the word "Khelat" on their appointments. The honours "Ghuznee, 1838," "Affghanistan, 1839" and "Khelat" were sanctioned officially for the Corps in February, 1877.[3]

Major-General Nott made himself secure in Kandahar, though he could not prevent the recapture of Kalat, and the command of the small garrison at Kabul devolved on Major-General Cotton under the dictatorship of the Political Envoy. Durand, the senior engineer in Kabul, was unable to induce the autocratic and contemptuous Macnaghten to take proper steps to strengthen the position. The only ray of hope was the voluntary surrender of Dost Muhammad. At the end of 1840, Cotton left for India and was succeeded in April, 1841, by Major-General W. G. K. Elphinstone, an invalid. On October 20th, 1841, Brigadier Sale marched with a brigade for Gandamak on relief by another brigade under Brigadier Shelton. Sale reached Gandamak on the 30th after some fighting with the Ghilzais in the Jagdalak Pass, but not with his whole force, for while at Tezin he had sent back some artillery, infantry and three companies of the corps known as "Broadfoot's Sappers," and these retraced their steps to Kabul when transport became available.[4]

On November 2nd, 1841, the storm broke over Kabul. The story of the siege and the ghastly retreat through the Khurd Kabul and Jagdalak defiles is too well known to need repetition. Of 16,000 people—men, women and children—who marched from the capital in the bitter cold of January 6th, 1842, only one, Dr. Brydon, rode six days later into Jalalabad, whither

[1]Girishk, on the Helmand, had been occupied while the army was at Kandahar.

[2]*Digest of the Services of the Bombay Sappers and Miners*, by Major G. H. W. O'Sullivan, R.E., p. 7, and *The First Afghan War*, by Maj.-Gen. Sir H. M. Durand, pp. 218–219. Macleod was a Bengal Sapper, but he may have been acting for Marriott who had been wounded at Ghazni.

[3]G.O.C.C., dated Feb. 24th, 1877.

[4]The road from Kabul to Jalalabad is shown in the *Sketch Map of North-Eastern Afghanistan, Kabul–Jalalabad Area*, which is included in Chapter X.

Sale had retired from Gandamak in spite of orders to return to Kabul. Nott had tried without success to send help from Kandahar. Macnaghten and Burnes had been murdered. Elphinstone and many others were prisoners. Then Ghazni fell, and Kalat-i-Ghilzai and Jalalabad were besieged. Nott alone was left to uphold British honour. " The conduct of the thousand and one politicals," he wrote, " has ruined our cause and bared the throat of every European in this country to the sword and knife of the revengeful Afghan and bloody Beluch." One gleam of sunshine penetrated the universal gloom. The little garrison of Kalat-i-Ghilzai held out until they were relieved on May 26th, 1842, and in that gallant band were 23 Bengal Sappers and Miners.[1]

The history of Broadfoot's Sappers, and the adventures of that corps, culminating in the defence of Jalalabad, now demand attention. During Keane's advance to Kabul, Captain George Broadfoot of the 34th Madras Native Infantry was serving as a Commissariat Officer in Lower Burma; but letters written from Afghanistan by his brothers, William and James, inspired him to apply for a transfer to the seat of war and he was ordered to raise an irregular regiment of Sappers for Shah Shuja's force and proceed with it to Kabul. He left Tenasserim in the summer of 1840, landed at Calcutta and journeyed up country. On August 20th, the Bengal Sappers and Miners provided him with a stiffening of 3 British non-commissioned officers, 4 Indian officers and 20 Indian non-commissioned officers as Jemadars and Havildars, and 20 sepoys as Naiks.[2] He expected to receive at Kabul some Hazara Pioneers recruited further west by his brother William, but he was still at Delhi in October, 1840, busily engaged in gathering men for the new corps. These were a motley crowd of Hindustanis, Gurkhas, Pathans from Peshawar and the Yusufzai and Hazara Districts, and Afghans from Kabul and beyond. Though many were desperate characters, they were moulded into good soldiers and taught the rudiments of field engineering by the Sappers and Miners. Broadfoot saw to their physical welfare and comfort and punished their moral delinquencies with an almost ferocious severity which they understood and respected.[3]

The march of Broadfoot's Sappers to Kabul was impeded by a large amount of treasure and baggage and a contingent of 600 *zenana* ladies for Shah Shuja. By the middle of May, 1841, however, the column had

[1]Among these men was Sapper Hanuman Singh, who had been wounded at Bhurtpore in 1825. Later, he served with distinction in the Sikh Wars and the Indian Mutiny and retired in 1870, after 46 years' service, with the rank of Subadar-Major. His medals are in the Officers' Mess at Roorkee. (See " Some War Medals of the Bengal Sappers and Miners," by Lieut. P. C. S. Hobart, R.E., appearing in *The R.E. Journal*, Vol. XX, July–Dec., 1914, pp. 73–80.)

[2]Among these was Havildar Ganga Singh, who had served in the First Burma War and was one of the Explosion Party at Ghazni. Later, he shared in the defence of Jalalabad and fought in the Sikh Wars. He retired as a Subadar-Major in 1857 with over 40 years' service. His 3 decorations and 8 medals are in the Officers' Mess at Roorkee. It may be noted, however, that in a Corps Order dated Delhi, Sept. 15th, 1840, 3 British N.C.O.s, 2 Havildars, 1 Naik and 36 Sepoys were transferred with effect from Sept. 1st as volunteers for Shah Shuja's Force, and the name of Ganga Singh is not included. Nevertheless, he certainly joined the draft. Half the men came from the 5th Company.

[3]*Memoirs of Major-General Sir Henry Havelock*, by J. C. Marshman (1870), p. 87.

reached Peshawar, and early in July it arrived in Kabul. Broadfoot was then reinforced by the Hazara Pioneers and proceeded to organize his Sappers into six companies. " Bengal sepoys are good troops " he wrote later. " My corps, Sappers, 600, is :— 300 Hindoostanees (brave), 200 Goorkhas (braver), 100 Afghans and Hazaras (heroes)."[1] As assistants he had Lieutenants S. G. G. Orr and F. C. Cunningham, 23rd Madras Native Infantry—" my two Mulls "[2] as he called them—and also Sergeant-Major F. W. Kelly and Sergeants I. M. Bruen and W. Dadd. The corps had few tools, and not a man was ever furnished with uniform.[3]

Broadfoot soon obtained an insight into the administrative chaos at Kabul. On October 7th, he was ordered to prepare to march with one company as part of a force under Lieut.-Colonel T. Monteath which was to precede the main body of Sale's brigade on its return to India. As all his tools had gone with two other companies towards Ghazni, he set the local artisans to make others in the bazaar and visited Monteath to ascertain the nature of the work which the Sappers might have to perform. Monteath could tell him nothing, having received no orders whatever except that he was to move towards Jalalabad, so Broadfoot went next to General Elphinstone who was non-commital and sent him with a note to the Envoy. Macnaghten returned him to the General: the General returned him to Macnaghten. The Envoy then became peevish, denounced the General as fidgety, and remarked that he expected no serious opposition. As for Broadfoot and his Sappers, said he, twenty men with pickaxes would suffice, for their only duty would be to pick stones from under the gun-wheels. " Are those your orders ? " asked Broadfoot. " No, no," answered the Envoy, " only my *opinion*, given at the General's request and yours. The General must decide the number of sappers and tools to go." Back to Elphinstone went the infuriated Broadfoot and was told by that perplexed and ailing officer to follow his own judgment. An insolent staff officer entered and advised the General to wash his hands of the Envoy, Broadfoot and the Sappers, and with these remarks ringing in his ears, Broadfoot went back to Macnaghten. The Envoy lost his temper. He would commit himself to nothing and informed Broadfoot that if he thought that Monteath's movement was likely to bring on an attack, he need not go at all, for he was not wanted ; and even if he *were* wanted, there were others who might be preferable. Thoroughly disgusted, Broadfoot set out with Monteath as ordered. A severe reprimand was sent after him for taking with him all the tools and stores he could collect in Kabul. This message was crossed on the road by a demand from Broadfoot for more tools, the necessity for these having already arisen. The demand was so large that it could not be met fully, but the tools and stores which Broad-

[1] *The Career of Major George Broadfoot, C.B.*, by Major W. Broadfoot R.E., p. 40.

[2] An abbreviation of " Mulligatawnies " as they came from Madras. Lieut. F. C. Cunningham had two brothers in the Bengal Engineers—Lieut. J. D. Cunningham and Lieut. (afterwards Maj.-Gen. Sir) Alexander C. Cunningham. The latter was the grandfather of the Col. A. H. Cunningham (late R.E. and Bengal Sappers and Miners). Lieut. S. G. G. Orr was a younger brother of Lieut. C. A. Orr, M.E., who served in Afghanistan with " C " Company, Madras Sappers and Miners.

[3] *The Career of Major George Broadfoot, C.B.*, by Major W. Broadfoot, R.E., p. 169.

foot succeeded in collecting were mainly instrumental afterwards in saving the besieged garrison of Jalalabad and were used also by the regular Sapper and Miner companies of General Pollock's relieving army in the final advance to Kabul.

Monteath marched to Butkhak on October 9th, 1841, and repulsed an attack on his camp, regarding which Broadfoot writes " I had proof here of the value of our Afghan troops. These men are of a bolder race than the Indians and require a sterner discipline. Their commander must be feared, though he must know their prejudices and provide for their wants." Sale arrived with reinforcements, and Broadfoot was joined by Lieutenant Colin Mackenzie, 48th Madras Native Infantry. On October 12th, " Fighting Bob" Sale fought his way over the Khurd Kabul Pass, and the remaining five companies of Broadfoot's Sappers having arrived with other troops, he marched over the Taraki and Haft Passes to Tezin, whence, on the 26th, he sent back half a mountain battery, some infantry and three of the Sapper companies[1] to Khak-i-Jabar. He stated that he required their transport for the use of the remainder of his brigade, but his action put them in a dangerous situation until other transport could reach them from Kabul. Continuing through the Tezin defile, Seh Baba and Katasang, Sale camped at Jagdalak, and on October 29th, started for the Jagdalak Pass.

A company of Broadfoot's Sappers was at the tail of the rear guard and was in action even before leaving camp. The main body outdistanced the baggage and rear guard during the ascent of three miles, and the Ghilzais fell upon the transport and demoralized the troops. The Sapper company was picketing the heights when this occurred, but five Sapper orderlies followed Broadfoot, Cunningham, Sergeant-Major Kelly and two infantry officers in a charge which checked the swordsmen and saved several hundreds of men and most of the baggage from destruction. Nevertheless, Sale lost 120 men in this affair. Heavily encumbered with sick and wounded he entered Gandamak, as already related, on October 30th and prepared to defend the place, but on November 10th came an urgent appeal from Macnaghten that he should return forthwith to Kabul. Sale then called a Council of War which, by a majority, endorsed his decision against a return because of the number of sick and wounded and the insufficiency of transport, food and ammunition.[2] The dissentients were Broadfoot and a few other brave soldiers. Sale marched from Gandamak on the 11th, on which day Cunningham, Sergeant-Major Kelly and 30 Sappers destroyed Mama Khel Fort, and on the 12th he reached Jalalabad. " A daring general," writes Archibald Forbes,[3] " would have fought his way back to Cabul. A prudent general would have remained at Gundamuk. The occupation of Jellalabad was the expedient of a weak general." To

[1] " Early Indian Campaigns," by Major H. Biddulph, R.E., appearing in *The R.E. Journal*, Vol. XVIII, July–Dec., 1913, pp. 285–302. Major Biddulph estimates their combined strength at 240 men, but according to Broadfoot it was about 300. At Kabul, the companies were commanded by Lieut. W. Bird, 30th M.N.I.

[2] Despatch from Maj.-Gen. R. Sale, dated Jalalabad, April 16th, 1842, appearing in *Memorials of Affghanistan*, by J. H. Stocqueler, pp. 215–221.

[3] *The Afghan Wars*, 1839–42 *and* 1878–80, by Archibald Forbes, p. 69.

which Durand adds[1] that " to throw his brigade into Jellalabad, a place of no military strength or importance, without magazines and in utter disrepair, served no conceivable purpose except to betray weakness." Here we may leave Broadfoot and his three companies and revert to Kabul, whither the other three companies had found their way from Kahk-i-Jabar and had joined hands with the small detachment of 20 Bengal Sappers and Miners included in the 4,500 troops under Elphinstone.

" I had 300 Sappers at Kabul," wrote George Broadfoot later.[2] " They were very fine troops which had been sent back from Tezin. When the force marched, they were ordered to bridge the watercourses near the cantonment *and were not allowed to take their arms.* These were left under a guard in the cantonment. The men were kept at the bridges till night, when the enemy rushed into the cantonment and seized the arms. Thus, by gross mismanagement, were these men delivered up helpless to slaughter. Some have made their way through all: most of them perished in the passes. They were transferred from one strange officer to another, but clung together to the last, and no small number reached Jugduluk, to perish in the last fatal march from that place." Archibald Forbes, however makes the following remarks :—[3] " It was not until two o'clock of the following morning that the rear-guard reached bivouac at the end of the first short march of six miles (from Kabul). The soldiers and camp followers froze to death in numbers. . . . Already defection had set in. One of Shah Shuja's regiments, *and his detachments of Sappers and Miners,* had deserted bodily, partly during the march, partly in the course of the night." Forbes was not present and does not quote his authority. It is possible that a number of Broadfoot's Sappers returned to their kinsmen and co-religionists among the enemy ;[4] but it is evident from Broadfoot's writings that the accusation of wholesale desertion is unfounded and that most of the men perished with the detachment of 20 Bengal Sappers and Miners in the retreat.

On November 12th, 1841, Sale entered Jalalabad and took possession of a quadrilateral enclosure about a mile and a quarter in circuit, buried amid houses and gardens, without a ditch, and with low and crumbling mud walls topped by small towers or bastions. After repulsing an attack, he set Broadfoot to repair the wretched defences with the tools brought from Kabul, which included 330 pickaxes and 390 shovels. On January 9th, 1842, he received an order from Elphinstone to retire to

[1] *The First Afghan War and its Causes,* by Maj.-Gen. Sir H. M. Durand, K.C.S.I., C.B., p. 360.

[2] *The Career of Major George Broadfoot, C.B.,* by Major W. Broadfoot, R.E., pp. 126, 127.

[3] *The Afghan Wars,* 1839–42 *and* 1878–80, by Archibald Forbes, pp. 107, 108.

[4] Some officers believe that one of the three companies was composed of Gurkhas. If so, it is most unlikely that these men, Hindus, would desert to the Afghans, who are Muhammadans. Both Gurkha companies were not in the retreat from Kabul because at least one of them was still with Broadfoot in the final advance under Gen. Pollock. The available evidence seems to indicate that the three companies in the retreat were the " Hindustani " units, which included men from the frontier. Broadfoot would naturally keep with him his best units—the Afghan and Hazara Company and the two Gurkha companies. It may be noted that in his despatch dated April 16th, 1842, Gen. Sale refers to the Afghan Sappers in Jalalabad during the siege.

Peshawar, but he preferred to remain inactive in Jalalabad; and when Broadfoot implored him to fight his way through the Khaibar in order to refit and return with reinforcements, he declined to move and turned his transport animals loose for the Afghans to seize. The whole country rose from Gandamak to the mouth of the Khaibar, and a force from Peshawar under Brigadier Wild, which succeeded in rescuing the small garrison of Ali Masjid, was obliged to retire afterwards to the plains.

"On January 13th," wrote Sale,[1] "I received the melancholy intelligence of the disastrous retreat of our troops from the capital. Almost at the same time it became known to us that the brigade from Hindoostan had been forced back upon Peshawur. . . . Our works had in the meantime been completed. They consisted in the destruction of an immense quantity of cover for the enemy, raising the parapets to six or seven feet high, repairing and widening the ramparts, extending the bastions, retrenching three of the gates, covering the fourth gate with an outwork, and excavating a ditch ten feet deep and twelve feet in width round the whole of the walls. The place was thus secure against the attack of any Asiatic enemy not provided with siege artillery. But it pleased Providence, on the 19th February, to remove in an instant this ground of confidence. A tremendous earthquake shook down all our parapets, injured several of the bastions, cast to the ground all our guard houses, demolished a third of the town, made a breach in the Peshawur face and reduced the Cabool Gate to a shapeless mass. The troops turned with indefatigable industry to the reparation of the walls. . . . The report of Captain Broadfoot will meet with attentive perusal.[2] His fertility in resource obviated great difficulties in procuring iron, timber and charcoal, and to the foresight of his arrangements we owe our having had a very ample supply of tools. The Corps under his command performed, from Bootkhak, the duties equally of good sappers and bold light infantry soldiers, and the Afghan, Huzaree and Eusifzye portion of it have been singularly faithful in time of general defection."[3]

In this despatch, Sale makes no mention of the Council of War which he convened on January 26th, 1842, as a result of a letter from Shah Shuja inquiring when Jalalabad would be evacuated. The members, in addition to himself, were Captain Macgregor (Political Officer), Colonels Dennie and Monteath (Infantry), Captain Oldfield (Cavalry), Captains Abbott and Backhouse (Artillery) and Captain George Broadfoot. Captains Henry Havelock and H. Wade (Staff) were also present. Macgregor asked whether the others agreed with Sale and himself that they should treat with Shah Shuja for the evacuation of the country, giving and receiving hostages and insisting on a safe conduct to Peshawar.

[1]Despatch from Maj.-Gen. R. Sale, dated Jalalabad, April 16th, 1842, appearing in *Memorials of Affghanistan*, by J. H. Stocqueler, pp. 215–221.

[2]This report gives full details of the work of the Sappers and infantry working parties at Jalalabad. It is dated April 16th, 1842, and appears in *Memorials of Affghanistan*, by J. H. Stocqueler, pp. 224–228, and (with diagrams) in *Professional Papers of the Corps of Royal Engineers*, Vol. VI, pp. 12–18.

[3]Apparently the Afghan and Hazara Company was not among the three sent back to Kabul.

An excited debate followed. It is a truism that " a Council of War never fights," but Broadfoot himself was strongly against capitulation. Although ridiculed, he maintained that they could hold out till relieved. He denied the value of hostages. Sale remarked that an Afghan hostage could be executed if the enemy attacked, and Broadfoot replied by asking whether Sale would do this if the enemy, before their faces, hanged two British women prisoners for every Afghan put to death. Finally, Broadfoot threw on the ground the paper of proposed terms and the meeting broke up. When the Council met on the following day, however, he argued the items of the proposed treaty one by one and made some impression, though all but two of the members remained against him. A resolution to treat for the abandonment of Jalalabad was carried, but Broadfoot procured some modifications in the proposals before they were sent to Kabul. When the answer was received, the Council reassembled and, after further deliberation, again adjourned. Most of the members were won over gradually to Broadfoot's view. Another letter was despatched on February 13th which left Sale free to act as he thought best. This was fortunate because news arrived at the same time that relief operations would be attempted. All idea of surrender was then relinquished, and thus Broadfoot saved the garrison of Jalalabad from disgrace and possibly annihilation.[1]

During the early part of the occupation, the three companies of Broadfoot's Sappers were assisted in constructional and repair work by H.M.'s 13th Light Infantry, and in demolitions by the 35th Bengal Native Infantry. All worked for seven hours daily. The Artillery prepared their battery positions unassisted. Some 1,300 camp followers helped as required and on January 15th, 1842, were organized for defence purposes, those who were unarmed being detailed to bombard the enemy with stones. After the repulse of their attacks on November 14th and December 1st, 1841, the Afghans showed little enterprise until the arrival of Muhammad Akbar, a son of Dost Muhammad. Then they established a rigorous blockade and on February 21st and 22nd, 1842, harried Sale's foraging parties outside the walls. Throughout the remainder of the siege, skirmishes occurred almost daily. On March 11th a sally was made by a detachment under Dennie to defeat a suspected attempt of the enemy to drive a mine. Broadfoot records that two of his companies were closely engaged, and that Orr, Cunningham, Kelly and Bruen were conspicuous when the Sappers repulsed a charge of cavalry while retiring into Jalalabad.

Skirmishing occurred on a larger scale on March 24th, on which occasion Broadfoot was severely wounded while commanding a mixed detachment of Sappers and the 13th Regiment. A body of Afghans rushed from a ravine and began to occupy a fortified post vacated by the Sappers while covering the retreat of the garrison's grass-cutters, so Broadfoot

[1]The Minutes of the Proceedings of the Council of War at Jalalabad are given in a pamphlet entitled " The Defence of Jalalabad," a copy of which is in the R.E. Corps Library at Chatham. A Memorandum of the Proceedings, prepared by George Broadfoot, appears in *The Career of Major George Broadfoot, C.B.*, by Major W. Broadfoot, R.E., pp. 67–77, with remarks by Capt. Henry Havelock. A graphic account of the meetings is given in *The First Afghan War and its Causes*, by Maj.-Gen. Sir H. M. Durand, K.C.S.I., C.B., pp. 390–401.

returned to the post with Orr and the Sappers and then, almost single-handed, charged the enemy beyond. The Afghans fled back to the nullah under a heavy fire from the Sappers; but while Broadfoot was scrambling up the parapet to rejoin his men, he was shot through the hip, and had it not been for the skill of Dr. John Forsyth, the Corps Surgeon, he would probably have died. The command of Broadfoot's Sappers then devolved on Orr, who led them in a sally on April 7th[1] which drove the besiegers away only nine days before the arrival of the "Avenging Army" from Peshawar.

Every soldier in the garrison of Jalalabad—2,596 in all—received a silver medal, and the regiments of the British and Company's armies were granted the honour of carrying upon their colours and appointments a mural crown superscribed "Jellalabad." Shah Shuja's units, however, were held to be those of a foreign state, and consequently Broadfoot's Sappers were not deemed eligible for the honour "Jellalabad" awarded on April 30th, 1842. After the Shah's death on May 6th, the status of his forces was changed and Broadfoot's Sappers were recognized as belonging to the Bengal Army, and accordingly they received the honour "Cabool, 1842" for the final advance. This was awarded on November 8th. The Bengal Sappers and Miners afterwards claimed that an order had appeared on April 5th, two days before the end of the siege of Jalalabad,[2] incorporating some of Broadfoot's Sappers in their Corps, and that, in consequence, Broadfoot's Sappers were eligible for the honour "Jellalabad" and therefore the Bengal Sappers and Miners also. Indeed, until 1859, the honour appeared in the Army Lists among those gained by the Bengal Sappers, though apparently without proper authority. It was then excluded because of certain events in the Indian Mutiny. Attempts were made between 1904 and 1907 to secure its restoration, but they met with no success for Army Headquarters maintained that no Broadfoot's Sappers were incorporated officially in the Bengal Sappers and Miners until the beginning of 1843.[3]

With the "Avenging Army" of 8,000 men under Major-General Sir George Pollock which marched into Jalalabad on April 16th, 1842, was the 5th Company, Bengal S. & M.,[4] under Lieutenant J. R. Becher, B.E., and a semi-civil Corps of Pioneers (150 *beldars*) raised at Ali Masjid by Mr. F. Mackeson, a volunteer. These, with the three companies of Broadfoot's Sappers, formed an adequate cadre of engineer troops, and the way seemed open to Kabul; but owing to transport difficulties and political restrictions it was not until August 20th that the advance could be resumed.

[1]In this operation, Col. Dennie was killed. The Sappers had 2 sergeants, 1 corporal, 1 bugler and 5 privates wounded.

[2]The Jalalabad medal bears the date April 7th, 1842, as the termination of the siege.

[3]See the "Restoration of Battle Honours" file at Roorkee, and in particular a note by Mr. G. W. de Rhé-Philipe, dated Sept. 23rd, 1907.

[4]According to the *History and Digest of Service, 1st K.G.O. Sappers and Miners* (p. 9) the 4th Company was also with Gen. Pollock's army. This seems to be incorrect. The location of the 4th Company is uncertain, but it received the honour "Cabool, 1842." According to a G.G.O. dated June 6th, 1842, the 3rd and 6th Companies were sent to the Army of Reserve at Ferozepore and the 6th Company afterwards went to Afghanistan, presumably on the line of communication.

Pollock was permitted by Lord Ellenborough[1] to "strike a severe blow at the enemy," and Nott "to retreat from Kandahar by way of Ghazni," and the result was a race for the capital. Operations in the Shinwari Valley, in which the 5th Company participated, had served to keep the "Avenging Army" in good fettle during the enforced halt. On August 23rd, Pollock arrived with the advanced guard in Gandamak and learnt that the enemy were holding the neighbouring village and fort of Mama Khel, so he sent for Broadfoot's Sappers, who were with Sale some fifteen miles in rear. The Sappers marched all night, and on arrival, tired and hungry, were pushed immediately into the fight and carried the village. While some of them, under Broadfoot's direction, kept up a covering fire, the remainder escaladed a bastion topped with thorns and routed the defenders. By this time, most of the men were completely exhausted, yet a few of the strongest climbed still further and occupied the village of Kudi Khel. "A Sapper ran at the enemy with his bayonet," writes Broadfoot,[2] "followed by myself and the only other man on the spot. The Afghans, supposing a large force was on them, fled over walls and housetops. The alarm spread and the camp was abandoned." The 5th Company, Bengal S. & M., was not with Broadfoot's Sappers, but it took part, nevertheless, in the operations around Mama Khel and Kudi Khel on August 24th, 1842.

Pollock halted for a fortnight at Gandamak and then advanced through Surkhpul towards Jagdalak, the posts of honour at the head and tail of the column being assigned to Broadfoot's Sappers. In the vanguard, behind Broadfoot's Sappers, marched the 5th Company. Both units distinguished themselves on September 8th when they stormed the enemy's *sangars* in the Jagdalak Pass. "Seldom have soldiers had a more arduous task to perform," wrote Pollock, "and never was an undertaking of the kind surpassed in execution." On the 11th, the army entered the Tezin defile, where lay 1,500 of Elphinstone's dead, and by the morning of the 13th, it was climbing the Haft Kotal. Sixteen thousand Afghans held the surrounding heights, and groups of these charged down sword in hand; but they could not stand against the British bayonets and were soon in flight towards Kabul. Cunningham and a party of Sappers captured a 24-pounder howitzer. According to Marshman, the finest sight of the day was Broadfoot and the diminutive Gurkhas of his Corps pursuing the enemy from crag to crag and climbing heights which seemed inaccessible.[3] In the Khurd Kabul Pass, the remains of the victims of the retreat lay in heaps for three or four miles. Indeed, as one officer remarked, the entire march of 77 miles from Gandamak to the capital was over the bodies of a massacred army. On September 15th, 1842, Pollock made a triumphant entry in Kabul, where Nott joined him two days later from Kandahar.

In Sir William Nott's division there were detachments of both the Bengal and Madras Sappers and Miners, a fact which leads us to a brief outline of

[1]Lord Ellenborough had succeeded Lord Auckland as Governor-General on Feb. 28th, 1842.

[2]*The Career of Major George Broadfoot, C.B.*, by Major W. Broadfoot, p. 137.

[3]*Memories of Major-General Sir Henry Havelock, K.C.B.*, by J. C. Marshman, p. 128.

the part played in the campaign by the Madras Corps. "C" Company, Madras S. & M., under Lieutenant T. F. V. Outlaw, 26th M.N.I., with Lieutenant C. A. Orr and 2nd Lieutenant A. J. M. Boileau, M.E., arrived at Karachi from Belgaum on December 4th, 1840. It moved up country, and passing alone through the Bolan Pass, though with only 46 muskets, reached Quetta in March and until October was employed chiefly on road construction.[1] It then returned to Sibi and Dadhar and came under the command of Captain R. Henderson, M.E. In the middle of April, 1841, most of the company went back to Quetta and remained there for the next five months; but a small party consisting of Havildar Amarabathi, 1 Naik and 28 Sappers, was attached to a force under Major-General R. England marching to join Nott at Kandahar and was in action on April 29th at Haikalzai beyond Pishin and again in the Khojak Pass. From Kandahar the detachment proceeded with a column under Brig.-General G. P. Wymer to the relief of Kalat-i-Ghilzai. This was accomplished on May 26th, and afterwards the Madras Sappers, and the 23 Bengal Sappers of the garrison, destroyed the defences before retiring to Kandahar.

The two detachments of Sappers and Miners, now amalgamated under Major E. Sanders, B.E., as Field Engineer, set out for Kabul on August 10th, 1842, with Nott's division. They were present on August 30th at a battle 40 miles south-west of Ghazni, and when Nott arrived before that place on September 5th, they prepared mines to breach the walls. After the garrison had capitulated, fourteen mines were exploded with good effect, destroying some of the walls and breaching others, and all the gateways and principal buildings were set on fire.[2] Thus Nott set his mark on Ghazni as Pollock did later on Kabul. The march was then resumed, and after a few skirmishes on the road, the division joined Pollock in the capital. The Sapper detachments quitted Kabul with the remainder of the army and shared in the adventures of the return journey to Peshawar and finally to Ferozepore. Thence the Madras Sappers marched to Sukkur and proceeded in boats down the Indus to Hyderabad, where they rejoined "C" Company on March 24th, 1843, in time to take part in the final battle of the campaign in Sind. Jemadar[3] Amarabathi and his 29 men had completed a circuit of a large part of Afghanistan and were praised for their zeal and industry.[4]

While the "Avenging Army" was in Kabul, a column under Major-General K. H. McCaskill was sent northwards into Kohistan to disperse an enemy concentration at Istalif. This was accomplished on September 29th, when Broadfoot was wounded in the hand while leading his men in the

[1]From March to July, 1841, "C" Company worked on the Quetta-Kalat road with the exception of a detachment under Orr which went to Nushki in May and returned in June.

[2]Report by Major E. Sanders, B.E., dated Ghazni, Sept. 9th, 1842, appearing in *Memorials of Affghanistan*, by J. H. Stocqueler, p. 264.

[3]Amarabathi had received well earned promotion.

[4]The work of this detachment is described in *The Military History of the Madras Engineers and Pioneers*, by Major H. M. Vibart, R.(M.)E., Vol. II, pp. 185–189, and in the *Historical Record of the Q.V.O. Madras Sappers and Miners*, Vol. I, pp. 50–51. Monthly details the work of "C" Company as a whole are given in *Professional Papers of the Madras Engineers*, Vol. II (1859), pp. 150–153, where a statement appears by Major R. Henderson, M.E.

attack. McCaskill then destroyed Charikar, still further north, and returned to Kabul. Pollock now determined to retire as rapidly as possible to India, but not before he had impressed the Afghans with the power of British arms by burning the principal bazaar in the capital. This act of retribution was carried out by Captain F. Abbott, B.E., the Commanding Engineer, and the troops left Kabul on October 12th, 1842, in three divisions, with the first of which were Broadfoot's Sappers and the 5th Company, Bengal S. & M. There was some fighting on the return journey, but by November 6th the entire army was encamped near Peshawar, and when it crossed the Sutlej on December 17th to receive a grand official welcome from Lord Ellenborough at Ferozepore, Broadfoot's Sappers, 375 strong, were at its head. Honours were showered on the various commanders; but, as Fortescue remarks,[1] the peoples of the East were not deceived, and particularly the Baluchis of Sind and the Sikhs of the Punjab. These turbulent folk saw in the result of the First Afghan War nothing but the defeat and dishonour of the Government of India and they acted accordingly. Dost Muhammad was released and regained his kingdom. There was little to show for the sacrifice of 20,000 lives and the waste of fifteen millions sterling.

The end of Broadfoot's Sappers was in sight. Orders had been issued in June, 1842,[2] that, on arrival at Ferozepore, Shah Shuja's troops should be distributed among units of the Bengal Army, the Sappers supplying two additional companies for the Bengal Sappers and Miners; but these orders were modified by others on January 5th, 1843, which decreed that the Sappers, except Gurkhas or those required for the two companies, were to be discharged. The men detailed for the companies were to march with Broadfoot from Ferozepore to Delhi, where they would be made over to Captain B. Y. Reilly, B.E., the Commandant of the Bengal Sappers and Miners. All the Gurkhas of Shah Shuja's force, including those of Broadfoot's Sappers, were to be left at Ferozepore.[3] These instructions were duly carried out. Cunningham and Orr departed to take up new appointments, and Broadfoot said good-bye to his Gurkha Sappers and marched with most of the others to Delhi, which he reached on January 31st. There, on his way to a civil post in Lower Burma, he handed over charge of the men who had served him so well and who became in March, 1843, the 7th and 8th Companies of Bengal S. & M.[4] Twenty of these soldiers were subsequently awarded the Indian Order of Merit, 3rd Class, for their work in Afghanistan.[5]

[1] *A History of the British Army*, by the Hon. J. W. Fortescue, Vol. XII, p. 277.

[2] G.O.C.C., June 27th, 1842.

[3] Some of the Gurkhas were posted forthwith to the Sirmur and Nasiri battalions. Others were detailed to form two companies which were added to the Nasiri and Kumaon battalions.

[4] G.O.C.C., March 11th, 1843. Some of the Afghans, however, refused to leave Broadfoot and accompanied him as a bodyguard to Burma and served later in the First Sikh War

[5] G.O.C.C., April 20th, 1843. The names are as follows :— Subadars Ganga Singh, Ranjit Singh and Dallu ; Jemadars Aslam Khan, Chhabba, Ganga Ram and Ram Bakhsh ; Havildars Aziz Khan, Mata Din, Madho, Man Phul Singh and Ram Charan ; Naiks Madho and Burhan Khan ; Sepoys Nihal Khan, Alam Shah, Baz Gul, Bahadur and Arjun ; and Bugler Sheikh Shabrati. The names are on the colonnade of the Ghazni Tower at Roorkee.

The scene now shifts temporarily to the Far East, where the Madras Sappers and Miners were fully compensated for the minor part they played in the First Afghan War. After Keane had occupied Kabul in 1840, the British Government turned their attention to affairs in China and required the Government of India to furnish the necessary troops for the First China War, a long and disjointed struggle occasioned by the wholesale destruction of British property in an attempt by the Chinese to stop the importation of opium by British merchants. The " Opium War " was really a naval expedition to which India supplied some 4,000 soldiers. Three battalions of British infantry, some artillery, and a composite battalion of Indian infantry (volunteers) were found by Bengal; but the greater part of the Indian contingent came from Madras and included " A " and " B " Companies, Madras S. & M., under Captain T. T. Pears, M.E., who acted also as Chief Engineer. The other Sapper and Miner officers were Brevet-Captain F. C. Cotton, Lieutenants W. I. Birdwood, J. W. Rundall, J. G. Johnston, H. W. Hitchens, and J. C. Shaw and 2nd Lieutenants J. Ouchterlony, M.E., with Lieutenant R. A. Doria and Ensign Clerk, M.I. No Bengal or Bombay Sappers served in the campaign.[1]

Singapore, the *rendezvous* of the " Eastern Expedition," was reached early in May, 1840. The fleet sailed northwards at the end of that month, and after blockading the entrance to Canton, landed the troops on the island of Chusan on July 5th and occupied Tinghai.[2] The expedition remained for several months in Chusan under most unhealthy conditions while the Madras Sappers strengthened the position and fortified a height known as the " Joss House Hill." Pears returned on duty to India, and until September, 1841, the command of the Sappers devolved on Cotton. Early in January, 1841, a force proceeded southward and captured Chuenpi and Taikoktow, two of the Bogue forts in the Canton Estuary; whereupon the Chinese opened negotiations, and as a result, the British evacuated Chusan and occupied Hongkong on January 26th. Towards the end of February, however, the negotiations having failed, the British attacked and captured others of the heavily armed Bogue forts guarding the waterway to Canton, an operation in which " A " Company participated under Birdwood.[3] Major-General Sir Hugh Gough then arrived from Madras as Commander-in-Chief, and on May 24th, 1841, took the powerful forts defending Canton itself. The Chinese saved the city from occupation by starting negotiations, and when a portion of a ransom had been paid, Gough withdrew his troops to Hongkong. Warm approval was accorded

[1]A full account of the First China War is given in *The Chinese War*, by Lieut. John Ouchterlony, M.E., a volume of 522 pages published in 1844. A précis of this account is included in *The Military History of the Madras Engineers and Pioneers*, by Major H. M. Vibart, Vol. II, pp. 132–184. See also *Frontier and Overseas Expeditions from India*, Vol. VI, pp. 362–399, and *A History of the British Army*, by the Hon. J. W. Fortescue, Vol. XII, pp. 302–326.

[2]See *Sketch Maps of China*, included in Chapter XII.

[3]The subsequent destruction of some of these forts is described in an article entitled " Memorandum regarding the Demolition of the Bogue Forts in the Canton River," by Lieut. J. G. Johnston, M.E., appearing in *Professional Papers of the Madras Engineers*, Vol. II, pp. 102–103. The demolition is described also in a letter from Lieut.-Col. G. Phillpotts, R.E., appearing in *Professional Papers of the Corps of Royal Engineers*, New Series, Vol. II, 1852, pp. 93–94.

to the work of "A" and "B" Companies in the operations around Canton which ended on June 1st; but the companies were unfortunate in losing the services of Rundall, who was dangerously wounded. It must be admitted that the Chinese, though masters of subterfuge, offered little resistance to the invaders of their country. As soldiers they could not compare with the Marathas or Mysoreans against whom the Madras Sappers had fought in the past.

The war in China was resumed after the failure of negotiations in August 1841, and as Peiping (Peking) was considered to be out of reach, an advance was planned against Nanking on the Yangtze Kiang. On August 26th, Amoy was occupied without resistance, the Madras Sappers under Cotton[1] being employed in disembarking the guns. The fleet then sailed northward for Chusan Island to recapture Tinghai, which the Chinese had strengthened with enormous batteries mounting hundreds of small guns. Powerful defences at "Joss House Hill" were carried on October 1st by an assault led by Pears, who had recently returned from India, and after Tinghai had fallen, preparations were made to capture Chinhai on the Ningpo River about 50 miles from Chusan. This was accomplished on October 10th. The enemy had obstructed the river with wreckage and piling; but while most of the troops attacked on the right bank, a naval contingent on the left bank, accompanied by 30 Madras Sappers under Cotton, carried the lofty ramparts of the town by escalade. "The scaling ladders," wrote Sir Hugh Gough, "were brought up on most difficult and rugged heights by the great exertions of the Madras Sappers and were gallantly planted under the direction of Captain Pears, who was the first to ascend." The Chinese suffered heavy casualties at Chinhai, and with the surrender of Ningpo on October 13th, the campaign of 1841 came to an end. A detachment of Madras Sappers continued the destruction of the Bogue forts outside Canton and then went into winter quarters at Hongkong. Other detachments settled down at Chusan, Chinhai, Ningpo and Amoy. The enemy had been defeated but were by no means demoralized. "The red-bristled barbarians are wildly careering in the Celestial waters," wrote a Chinese general to his Emperor, "but the lightnings of the Empire have cleared them from the coast." "Most right," replied that august monarch. "Let our servants, however, be merciful."[2]

Hostilities recommenced in March, 1842, when the Chinese attacked Ningpo and were repulsed. Reinforcements arrived from India, including "F" Company and details of "C," "D" and "E" Companies, Madras S. & M., and Gough proceeded to make the preliminary moves for his advance on Nanking. On March 15th, the Sappers assisted in driving the enemy from a position at Tsu-ki, a few miles from Ningpo. The offensive was then taken against Chapu (35 miles from Hangchow) which was captured on the 18th after some of the Tartar defenders had put up a desperate resistance in a Joss House. Detachments of Sappers were included in the three columns engaged, and Pears distinguished himself

[1] 5 British officers and 184 Indian ranks.
[2] *Six Months with the Chinese Expedition*, by Lord Jocelyn, p. 134.

by breaching an outer wall with a 50-lb. bag of gunpowder. After the fall of Chapu, the fleet withdrew to Woosung, and ascending the river of that name, landed the expeditionary force near Shanghai, which was occupied without resistance on June 19th. Much plunder was obtained by the troops and sold by them to Chinese buyers below the ramparts. However, after four days of rest and diversion, Shanghai was evacuated, and the expedition, now mustering 9,000 bayonets, prepared to start on its voyage up the Yangtze Kiang to Nanking. The Engineer Department and the Sapper and Miner companies were formed into a distinct command under Pears, one company being posted to each of the three brigades under Gough. Sailing up the great river, the warships and transports anchored off Chinkiang-fu on July 19th, and on the 21st, the troops disembarked to fight in extreme heat the heaviest and most costly engagement of the war.

Although the Tartar garrison of Chinkiang-fu offered a stubborn resistance, the defences were carried successfully by assault, Johnston being one of the first two men on the walls. Some interesting details of the blowing in of an outer western gate by the Sappers are recorded by Pears. Unknown to them, the western gateway gave access only to an outwork from which an inner gateway led under the main fortifications into the interior. The outer gateway had massive folding doors about 5 inches thick. " The means at hand for forcing the gate," writes Pears, [1] " consisted of three powder bags each containing 58 lbs. of powder. Having frequently to carry the bags some distance, the mode that has been hitherto adopted has been to make the bags with a strong loop at the top and appoint two men to carry each by means of a stick 6 feet long. This stick, upon which the box containing each bag is slung, is notched at one end, and having a spike at the other is found most convenient in fixing the bag against doors or walls by letting the loop pass into the notch, placing the bag against the door, and propping it up as closely as the thickness of the bag will allow. . . . . . A smart fire having been opened on the ramparts, the explosion party advanced across the bridge, one sepoy carrying each bag and prop, the former on his head, the latter in his hand. It was ascertained that the doors were barricaded within to a height of about 3 feet 6 inches by bags of earth or stones, so I resolved to apply three bags, two placed side by side, fixed with props which were gently raised so as to admit a portion of the third which was laid lengthways, resting partially upon and between the heads of the others and the doors. Thus placed, the centre of the charge was a few inches above the line to which the doors appeared barricaded within. The match was applied, and in a few seconds the explosion took place. The 3rd Brigade then pushed through the passage effectually prepared for them. The arch remained perfect, whereas the two massive doors were blown completely out of their places and lay at a distance of 19 feet. In conclusion I am bound to express my acknowledgments for the great assistance rendered to me on this

[1] " Report on the Destruction of the Gates of Chin-Keang-Foo," by Major T. T. Pears, C.B., M.E., appearing in *Professional Papers of the Madras Engineers*, Vol. II, pp. 104–105.

occasion by Lieutenant and Adjutant Rundall of the Engineers and Conductor Almond of the Sappers and Miners."

In this account, Pears makes no mention of a circumstance which might have converted the blowing in of the western gate at Chinkiang-fu into a tragedy. It seems that, while he was preparing the demolition, the 2nd Brigade had gained an entrance by escalading, or through other gateways, and that Johnston, with some of the Madras Sappers and 55th Regiment, entered the outwork by the inner gateway, reached the outer gateway, and began to drag away the barricade on the inside of the gate. However, finding the task laborious, and imagining from a cessation of firing outside that the 3rd Brigade had withdrawn to try elsewhere, they desisted and marched away. Hardly had they passed through the inner gateway when the explosion occurred and the 3rd Brigade surged through behind them. Johnston had been removing the barricade on one side of the gate at the very time when Pears was laying his charge on the other side ![1]

The troops proceeded to clear the ramparts and occupy the town, a process hindered only by a final rally by some of the Tartars and by occasional street fighting during the ensuing night. Numbers of the enemy cut their wives' throats, broke their children's backs, and then committed suicide. Chinkiang-fu ran with blood: its whole aspect was hideous beyond description. Gough made haste to leave it and continue his advance on Nanking. The victory was decisive, for it closed the navigation of the Yangtze Kiang and the principal canals and severed the Chinese Empire in two. On August 9th, 1842, the troops landed at Nanking, and on August 29th the Treaty of Nanking brought the First China War to a close. The Emperor agreed to pay an indemnity of 21 million dollars, to cede Hongkong, and to make other concessions including the opening to foreign trade of the ports of Canton, Amoy, Foochow, Ningpo and Shanghai. The units of the British expeditionary force then began to return to India, and among them all the Madras Sappers and Miners except " F " Company, which remained at Hongkong under Hitchens until October 1846.[2] For their services in China, " A," " B " and " F " Companies were permitted to bear upon their appointments a Golden Dragon wearing an Imperial Crown and also the word " China."[3] Pears was awarded a C.B., and he and Cotton received brevet promotion. Among the Indian ranks, Subadar-Major Komarasami was promoted to the 1st Class of the Order of British India.[4] The Madras Sappers and Miners were said to have borne a gallant part on every occasion when the enemy was in the field throughout the whole war.[5]

Before concluding with an outline of the Sapper work in the Sind and

[1] *The Chinese War*, by Lieut. J. Ouchterlony, M.E., pp. 378–380.

[2] 7 British officers, 5 Indian officers and 278 Indian other ranks of the Madras Sappers and Miners embarked at Hongkong in Dec., 1842, for the return voyage to India.

[3] G.G.O., Sept. 22nd, 1843.

[4] When the Order of British India was instituted on May 25th, 1838, 34 Indian officers, including Subadar Chokalingam of the Madras Sappers, were admitted to the 1st Class. At the same time, 33 Indian officers were admitted to the 2nd Class, and among these was Subadar Komarasami.

[5] G.O.C.C., March 10th, 1843.

Gwalior campaigns, which came hard on the heels of the First Afghan War, it may be well to describe as briefly as possible some of the changes in the administration, organization and equipment of all three Corps of Sappers and Miners which occurred during and after the period covered by this chapter. While the struggle against Afghanistan was in progress, the headquarters of the Bengal Corps were at Delhi. Working pay for the men was introduced on June 30th, 1841, during the tenure of Captain E. Swetenham, B.E., as Commandant.[1] The Bengal Sappers and Miners then comprised only six companies, each of 100 men; but in 1843 the 7th and 8th Companies were formed from Broadfoot's Sappers, and on March 21st, 1844, the 9th and 10th Companies were added to the establishment.[2] It has been mentioned already that in February, 1834, the "Pioneer" disappeared from the Bengal Army. Nevertheless, in September, 1847, he made a brief reappearance in the Bengal Sappers and Miners.[3] For reasons of economy, an order was then issued that the Corps should be remodelled into three companies of Sappers (300 men) and seven companies of Pioneers (700 men), a step which amounted to a division into first and second line troops. The Sappers were to be selected and highly paid men, officered by Engineers and clothed in red: the Pioneers, less skilled men on lower rates of working pay, officered from the Infantry and dressed in green. Vacancies in the Sappers were to be filled by men chosen from the Pioneers, and promotion was to be separate in the two branches. The change was duly carried out, and the "Bengal Sappers and Miners" became the "Bengal Sappers and Pioneers."[4] So they remained until March, 1851,[5] when a reversion to the original name was authorized. The Corps was then raised to a strength of twelve companies of Sappers and Miners[6] to be officered as soon as possible by Engineers and clothed in red uniforms with blue facings. All young Engineer officers were to be posted to it for a period of twelve months after their first arrival in India. The headquarters were transferred from Delhi to Meerut in 1845, to Ludhiana in 1847, back to Meerut in 1852, and finally to Roorkee in December, 1854.

As regards the Bombay Sappers and Miners, it will be recollected that in 1834 the two small Sapper companies and six Pioneer companies of the so-called "Bombay Engineer Corps" were remodelled into one company of Sappers and three of Pioneers, each of 100 men.[7] In 1837, the designation

[1]Capt. E. Swetenham assumed charge on Nov. 9th, 1838, when Capt. G. Thomson went to the Afghan War. The succeeding Commandants were as follows:—Capt. P. W. Willis (1841–43); Capt. B. Y. Reilly (1843–47); Brevet-Capt. H. Siddons (1847–49); Capt. J. A. Weller (1849–52); Brevet-Major. J. R. Western (1852–54); Major J. A. Weller (1854–56) and Capt. E. Fraser (1856–57). All were officers of the Bengal Engineers. The ranks shown are those on assumption of office.

[2]The personnel for the 9th and 10th Companies was obtained by transferring an increased establishment of 25 men per company sanctioned on Nov. 27th, 1843.

[3]G.O.C.C., Sept. 30th, 1847.

[4]G.O.C.C., Oct. 20th, 1847.

[5]G.G.O., March 20th, 1851.

[6]The newly formed 11th and 12th Companies were composed of Pontoniers. (See a Note dated Aug. 4th, 1905, by Gen. Sir Frederick Maunsell, K.C.B., Col.-Commandant, R.E., in the "Restoration of Battle Honours" file at Roorkee.)

[7]G.G.O., June 20th, 1834 (see Chapter IV).

" Engineer Corps " was discontinued, but the establishment remained unaltered until September, 1840, when the three Pioneer companies were converted into Sappers and Miners and the Corps was clothed in red uniforms with blue facings and khaki *pagris*.[1] In spite of the excellent services rendered by the Bombay Corps in Afghanistan, Sind and elsewhere,[2] no increase was made in the establishment until December 1855[3] when it was expanded to five companies of Sappers and Miners, each of 100 men, under Brevet-Major John Hill, Bo.E.[4] The headquarters of the Corps remained at Poona except during the period from January 1843 to April 1848, when it was at Karachi.

Turning now to the Madras Sappers and Miners, it will be remembered that the establishment of that Corps was reduced in December, 1837, from eight to six companies, though the strength of each company was increased at the same time from 80 to 120 men.[5] Four companies were normally employed on civil engineering work under the Revenue Board while the other two were undergoing instruction in military duties at the headquarters at Bangalore.[6] This system not only produced a large number of expert artificers but ensured that each company was a fully equipped unit capable of independent action. So efficient did the Madras Sappers prove themselves in Afghanistan, China, Sind and Burma that in September, 1854, the strength of the Corps was increased from six to nine companies and in November, 1857, to twelve companies. Until 1845, when Lieutenant J. W. Rundall, M.E., was Commandant,[7] the headquarters except on field service, were at Bangalore; but in that year they were moved to Mercara in Coorg, and in 1855 to Dowlaishweram in the Godavari District, before coming permanently to rest in Bangalore in March, 1865. The uniform of the men was a red tunic with blue facings, blue trousers with a red stripe, and on their heads a species of shako.

Although the Sappers and Miners in all three Presidencies were trained soldiers, their arms and their instruction in musketry left much to be desired. Until 1843, the Bengal Sappers carried the " fusil "[8] and bayonet, but in January, 1844, they were re-armed with the " Sapper carbine." The Bombay Sappers also carried the fusil and bayonet until issued with the Brunswick rifle at the end of 1844. From 1838 to 1845, some of the Madras Sappers were armed with fusils and " bayonet knives " and others with pistols; in 1846, however, all received the Sapper carbine though they

[1] G.O.C.C., Sept. 14th, 1840.

[2] In Nov., 1840, the 4th Company was sent to Aden and was the first Sapper and Miner unit to land there. It remained in Aden until Jan., 1843.

[3] G.G.O., Dec. 18th, 1855.

[4] Capt. A. C. Peat succeeded Capt. C. W. Grant as Commandant in 1838. He was followed by Brevet-Capt. F. Wemyss (1843–45); Capt. W. G. Hebbert (1845–47); Brevet-Capt. H. J. Margary (1847–49); Major W. B. Goodfellow (1849–54); Capt. W. Kendall (1854–55); Brevet-Major J. Hill (1855–56) and Capt. W. R. Dickinson (1856–57). All were Bombay Engineers.

[5] G.G.O., Dec. 26th, 1837.

[6] G.O.C.C., Feb. 15th, 1838.

[7] The list of Commandants of the Madras Sappers and Miners prior to the Indian Mutiny is as follows (excluding officiating officers):—Capt. A. Lawe (1831–33); Capt. G. A. Underwood (1833–38); Lieut. T. T. Pears (1838–44); Lieut. J. W. Rundall (1844–52) and Lieut. J. Carpendale (1852–57). All belonged to the Madras Engineers.

[8] A light musket introduced in 1826.

were allowed no practice with it on the range.[1] They were valued for their engineering skill rather than their military strength.

The inadequacy of the fusil and bayonet-knife was proved by the Madras Sappers and Miners during a campaign in which the Government of India became involved immediately after the Afghan and China Wars. Desiring to gain control of the Indus, Lord Ellenborough deliberately provoked a war against the Amirs of Sind and sent Major-General Sir Charles Napier to that country as a kind of military dictator. This forceful and outspoken commander had no illusions about his task. " We have no right to seize Scinde," he wrote,[2] " yet we shall do so ; and a very advantageous, useful and humane piece of rascality it will be : " and afterwards, the accomplished deed was commemorated in *Punch* by the famous couplet :— " *Peccavi ! I've Scinde,*" *said Lord Ellen so proud : Dalhousie, more modest, said,* " *Vovi, I've Oudh.*"[3] Napier arrived in Sukkur on October 5th, 1842, and in December proclaimed the annexation of part of Northern Sind. For the subjugation of the Amirs he had a force of about 8,000 men, including more than half of " C " Company, Madras S. & M., under Captain R. Henderson, M.E., with Lieutenants T. F. V. Outlaw, M.I., and C. A. Orr, M.E., and 2nd Lieutenant A. J. M. Boileau, M.E. A detachment of 30 Sappers was absent with the Army under General Pollock in Kabul. The Chief Engineer with the force in Sind was Major C. Waddington, Bo.E., who was assisted by Lieutenant T. Studdert, Bo.E. ; but the only representative of the Bengal Engineers was Lieutenant E. J. Brown, a Political Officer. No Sappers and Miners from Bengal or Bombay took part in the operations.[4]

Unwilling to resort to war if he could secure the submission of the Amirs by a display of power, Napier decided to raid and destroy the

[1]The Brunswick rifle gradually ousted the Sapper carbine in the Bengal and Madras Corps, but was replaced in 1866 in all three Corps by the Lancaster rifle. This gave way in 1875 to the Snider carbine (.577). All Corps received the Martini-Henry rifle (.450) in 1888, the Lee-Metford (.303) in 1900 and the Lee-Enfield (.303) in 1909. The *fusil* was a smooth-bored, flint-lock musket : calibre, about 16 bore : weight, 8 lbs., length overall, 53 in., length of barrel, 37 in., bayonet of triangular cross-section, length of blade, 11¾ in. The *Sapper carbine* was of similar type : calibre, .753 in., weight, 8 lbs. 6 oz., length overall, 48 in., length of barrel, 32 in., sword bayonet, length of blade, 22½ in. The *Brunswick rifle* (E.I.C. pattern) had a two-grooved bore (1 turn in 30 in.) : fired by percussion cap, calibre, .704 in., length overall, 46½ in., length of barrel, 30 in., heavy, dagger-shaped bayonet, length of blade, 22 in. The *Lancaster rifle* (known also as the " R.E. Carbine ") was oval-bored : calibre .577 in., brass-mounted. The fusils, Sapper carbines and Brunswick rifles of the East India Company bore on the lock-plate a Lion Rampant carrying a Crown.

[2]*The Life and Opinions of General Sir C. Napier*, by Sir W. Napier, Vol. II, p. 218.

[3]The authorship of this brilliant couplet is now generally accorded to Michael John Barry, then on the staff of *Punch*. Barry was regarded in his day as the equal in wit of Douglas Jerrold (1803–57). The authorship, however, was claimed both by *Punch* and Thomas Hood (1799–1845), editor of the *Comic Annual*. A speaker in the House of Commons debate on the Kandahar question in 1880 referred to the unexampled brevity of the despatch received after the final victory in Sind in 1843, evidently believing that the first half-line of the epigram was Lord Ellenborough's actual report.

[4]It may be remarked, however, that some Bombay Sappers and Miners saw active service soon after the end of the Sind Campaign. This occurred when the 3rd Company under Lieut. G. B. Munbee, Bo.E., with Lieut. W. D. Graham, Bo.E., took part at the end of 1844 in the storming of the fortress of Panalla, north of Belgaum, by a force under Maj.-Gen. De la Motte. Major A. C. Peat, Bo.E., of Afghanistan fame, was present on that occasion.

fortress of Imamgarh, some eight marches distant to the south-east, and for this purpose organized a small flying column which included Henderson and Boileau with a detachment of 30 Madras Sappers. The troops crossed the waterless desert on camels and arrived before Imamgarh on January 12th, 1843, to find the place deserted. As the masonry walls and towers were solidly built and at least 40 feet in height, the demolition presented a difficult problem, nor could it have been executed had there not been in the magazines of the fort many tons of gunpowder. On January 13th, under the direction of Waddington, the Sappers drove seven experimental mines under the northern curtain and charged each with 34 lbs. of country powder. These were exploded with little effect, so two towers were mined and the charges increased to 300 lbs. of country powder or 100 lbs. of European powder. Assisted by howitzer fire, the demolition of Imamgarh then proceeded satisfactorily. On the 15th, the last twelve of a total of twenty-four mines were exploded and all that remained was to destroy the powder still in the magazines. A truly magnificent explosion was produced by 7,000 lbs. placed in a single room, and an even more spectacular result by 4,000 lbs. collected within an outer gateway.[1] On January 16th, the flying column left the smouldering ruins of Imamgarh and a few days later rejoined the army on the Indus.

The fate of Imamgarh, however, had so little effect on the Amirs that war became inevitable. Matters came to a head in February, 1843. The Amirs demanded that Colonel James Outram, the Resident at Hyderabad, should leave that city, and because he refused to do so, attacked the Residency with 8,000 men on February 15th when Napier, with less than 3,000 men at his immediate disposal, was still some 35 miles to the north-east. Outram put up a gallant defence and then joined Napier, who advanced on February 17th, 1843, to attack the Sindians at Miani, a few miles from the capital. Unknown to him, the enemy were strongly posted in and beyond the dry bed of the Fuleli River, a small tributary of the Indus, and had both their flanks resting on patches of jungle. They numbered about 20,000 men, and Napier was obliged to launch a frontal attack with only 1,600 bayonets.[2] Nevertheless, after parking his strictly limited transport, he advanced in échelon of regiments with half of " C " Company, Madras S. & M., under Henderson, covering the flank of his artillery on the right. To his surprise he was held up by a large force of hostile infantry in the bed of the Fuleli, and the Sappers were crowded out of the line by a block caused through the change in direction of a high wall which skirted the forest or *shikargah* on the right. The British infantry came under heavy fire from the river bed, and for a time there was a check

[1]The destruction of Imamgarh is described in detail in a journal of the engineering operations compiled by 2nd Lieut. A. J. M. Boileau, M.E., which appears in *Professional Papers of the Madras Engineers*, Vol. II, pp. 145–148.

[2]In an article entitled " Account of the Battle of Meeanee, with a Plan," appearing in *Professional Papers of the Corps of Royal Engineers*, Vol. IX, pp. 25–34, Major C. Waddington, Bo.E., stated that Sir Charles Napier had 3,000 men. Napier himself, however, contradicted this statement and asserted that he had only 1,700 men, including officers. (See " Explanation of the Battle of Meeanee," by Maj.-Gen. Sir W. Napier, appearing in the same publication, Vol. X, pp. 66–70.)

and considerable confusion. An outflanking movement on the right was stopped by gun-fire through a breach in the wall which had been enlarged by the Sappers. More guns came into action against the enemy in the river bed, the cavalry charged their right, and the infantry and Sappers advanced and finally leapt down into the nullah and ended the battle with the bayonet. On February 19th, Napier marched unopposed into Hyderabad, and on March 12th he proclaimed the annexation of the whole of Sind.

As regards the part played by the Madras Sappers and Miners in the Battle of Miani, Henderson writes :—[1] " We had to make a practicable road for the artillery across several irrigation canals. The final advance was that of the whole line to the bank of the Foolaylee, where the enemy were in great force and a desperate conflict ensued. The enemy having fired a volley, threw down their matchlocks and with sword and shield rushed up the bank and penetrated into the ranks of the infantry; but they could not stand against the murderous fire of the British musketry and at last they fell in heaps, while those that took to flight were pursued by our cavalry. Whilst this was going on towards the left, the Sappers assisted in getting the guns into position in broken ground to the right, in which direction the enemy were rushing into the Shikargah to turn our position, and many approached so close under cover of the wall as to annoy the artillery greatly. Those of the Sappers who were armed immediately fired over the wall at the enemy, and those with working tools commenced destroying the top of the wall to get a better fire over it. This had the desired effect, and the artillery poured such a destructive fire in the direction of the Shikargah that the enemy abandoned their intention and the rout was complete. They fled in all directions, pursued by our cavalry. The infantry crossed the river and the guns followed. . . . After the battle our men were ordered to destroy the enemy's ammunition and gun-carriages. I desire to record the valuable assistance I received from Lieutenant Outlaw and 2nd Lieutenant Boileau, who encouraged the men by their own personal example. The men behaved with great gallantry; but most of them were called upon to take part in a severe action without arms to defend themselves, as they merely carried their working tools. I would also remark that the bayonet-knife at the end of the fusil, with which the men were partially armed, appears to be a most inefficient weapon, if not a great encumbrance, as it was found almost impossible to make it penetrate the clothes generally worn by the enemy. I beg to annex a memorandum prepared at the desire of Major-General Sir C. J. Napier of the manner in which I became possessed of one of the enemy's standards, which I beg permission to present to the headquarters of the Corps, and also take the opportunity of recommending to his notice Jemadar Tonderoyen as well deserving of promotion."

In this report, Henderson makes no mention of hand-to-hand fighting by the Sappers, but Sir Charles Napier alludes to it in a letter written five

[1]Article entitled " Correspondence and Journals connected with the Operations of the Army in Scinde from 1840 to 1844," by Capt. R. Henderson, M.E., appearing in *Professional Papers of the Madras Engineers*, Vol. II, pp. 142–153. Excellent plans of the battles of Miani and Hyderabad are included in this article.

years later. " At the battle of Meeanee," he remarks,[1] " Subadar Tonderoyen led his company most gallantly down into the bed of the Fullailee. He followed Major Henderson, his commanding officer, who for that action received the Companionship of the Bath. At this time, the part where these two brave men led was about the most dangerous part of the field. I saw with admiration the boldness of the behaviour of the company and its commander, and the Subadar was at his side on all occasions. If I am entitled to the Red Ribbon of the Bath, he is to the Order of Merit." Yet although Henderson received brevet promotion in addition to a C.B., the services of Subadar Tandavarayan (Tonderoyen) were never recognized by Government.

The enemy's losses at Miani were computed at 6,000 men. About 1,000 dead lay heaped in the Fuleli alone, and Napier records that 400 bodies were counted at another spot within a semi-circle of 50 paces' radius. It must have seemed to him that no further resistance need be expected from the Amirs of Sind. Yet such was not the case. Mirpur or Eastern Sind still remained defiant, and its ruler, Sher Muhammad, known as " The Lion," proceeded to collect 20,000 men at Dabba, close to Hyderabad, to challenge the 5,000 soldiers whom Napier could now put into the field.

The decisive action known as the Battle of Hyderabad was fought at Dabba on March 24th, 1843. Sher Muhammad was strongly entrenched in two parallel water-courses with his right flank resting on the village of Dabba and the Fuleli River, but Napier's cavalry turned his left, and the infantry broke through and drove him in utter rout from the position. " C " Company, Madras S. & M., brought almost up to full strength[2] by the arrival of the detachment under Jemadar Amarabathi from Afghanistan, took part in the fight, though it was not closely engaged. On March 22nd, part of the company made a ramp for the descent of the artillery into the dry bed of the Fuleli, and on the morning of the 24th marched at the head of the advanced guard to prepare ravines for the passage of guns. After three miles had been covered, Napier located the enemy in position. Waddington, the Commanding Engineer, having made a daring reconnaissance, Napier formed for the attack. " C " Company, under Henderson, was divided into two sub-divisions to help the men of the Heavy Battery in moving, unlimbering and limbering up their two 8-inch howitzers.[3] The weapons soon opened fire, and re-opened later at closer range with more satisfactory results, though opposed by eleven hostile pieces. They had to cease fire, however, when the infantry advanced to the assault. Henderson then went forward with the infantry, and Outlaw and Boileau followed with the Sapper company after it was decided that the howitzers should proceed no further. The enemy fled in all directions, leaving hun-

[1]Letter dated July 14th, 1849, quoted in *The Military History of the Madras Engineers and Pioneers*, by Major H. M. Vibart, R.(M.)E., Vol. II, p. 198, and in *Historical Record of the Q.V.O. Madras Sappers and Miners*, Vol. I, pp. 53, 54.

[2]14 men of the right half-company did not receive the medals awarded for Hyderabad or Meeanee-Hyderabad.

[3]Report by Major R. Henderson, M.E., dated Hyderabad, April 20th, 1843, appearing in *Professional Papers of the Madras Engineers*, Vol. II, pp. 143–145.

dreds of dead, and the Sappers returned in due course to the Heavy Battery and marched with it to camp. After resting during the 25th on the field of battle, "C" Company was attached to a column which occupied Mirpur and Umarkot, east of Hyderabad, and on April 11th it was back in the capital having covered 200 miles in 16 days with the thermometer at 110°. From that time until March 25th, 1844, when it sailed from Karachi, detachments were employed on various public works in Lower Sind.[1]

Referring to the experiences of the Madras Sappers and Miners in Sind, Henderson writes[2] :—"In the brief space of five weeks, the men under my command were called upon to take part in two battles—one of which was perhaps the most severe ever fought in India—when two-thirds of them were without arms to defend themselves. Surely this is a convincing proof that the Corps should be fully armed." According to Sir Charles Napier, "C" Company acquitted itself nobly at Miani, and its labours during the desert marches, though exceeding those of any other troops, were undergone with spirit.[3] For these services, the Madras Sappers received in 1854 the well-earned honours, "Meeanee" and "Hyderabad."[4]

Although the Bengal Sappers and Miners took no part in the campaign in Sind, they were on field service elsewhere within a few months of the defeat and flight of Sher Muhammad. The occasion was the Gwalior Campaign, which was undertaken because it had become necessary to quell an army of 40,000 Maratha insurgents who had taken charge of the affairs of the Gwalior State after the death of the Maharajah early in 1843. Lord Ellenborough knew that he must soon fight the Sikhs of the Punjab and wished to forestall a combination of the Sikhs and Marathas against him. He tried the effect of a threatening gesture by concentrating near Gwalior a powerful "Army of Exercise," and, when that failed, sent the two wings of an "Army of Gwalior" under the Commander-in-Chief, General Sir Hugh Gough, to attack the rebels from Agra in the north and Jhansi in the south. These formations advanced in December, 1843. With the Right Wing, of more than two divisions under Gough himself, marching southwards from Agra, were the 3rd, 4th and 7th Companies, Bengal S. & M.;[5] and with the Left Wing, under Major-General Sir John Grey, marching northwards from Jhansi, the 1st Company. Major E. J. Smith, B.E., accompanied the Right Wing as Chief Engineer, and the

[1]At the same time, orders were issued that Madras Sapper companies were to serve in Aden. "D" Company was sent there in April, 1844, "E" Company in Nov., 1845, and others later, each for a 3-years tour of service. From Nov., 1845, until April, 1852, there were always two companies in Aden.

[2]"Statement of the Services of 'C' Company, Madras Sappers and Miners in Scinde," by Capt. R. Henderson, M.E., appearing in *Professional Papers of the Madras Engineers*, Vol. II, p. 149.

[3]General Order by Maj.-Gen. Sir C. J. Napier, dated Karachi, March 25th, 1844.

[4]G.O.G.G., April 11th, 1854.

[5]According to the *History and Digest of Service of the 1st K.G.O. Sappers and Miners* (p. 9), the 5th Company was also present. No mention, however, is made of the 5th Company in the award of battle honours.

Engineer officers with the Sapper companies were Lieutenants W. Abercrombie (Brigade-Major), T. Renny-Tailyour, S. Pott and C. B. Young and 2nd Lieutenants J. D. Campbell, W. D. A. R. Short and J. E. T. Nicolls, B.E. On the staff of Lord Ellenborough, who accompanied the Right Wing, were Major E. Sanders, B.E. (killed at Maharajpur) and Captain H. M. Durand, B.E. (Political Officer). The Left Wing had only Lieutenant J. H. Maxwell, B.E., in command of the 1st Company.

On December 23rd, 1843, Gough and the Governor-General crossed the Chambal and advanced on Gwalior with 6,000 men and 30 guns. Five days later, they came upon an army of 18,000 Marathas entrenched in two positions in front of the villages of Maharajpur and Chaunda. Gough attacked the Maharajpur position and a bloody fight ensued. The Maratha gunners stood to their weapons till bayoneted, and the infantry fought with the courage of desperation, but the trenches were carried by a frontal assault and afterwards the main position at Chaunda, more than a mile distant. The enemy suffered very heavy casualties and lost 56 guns and all their ammunition. On the British side, nearly 800 men were killed or wounded; but the Sappers escaped lightly as the companies were not closely engaged. Nevertheless, it was through their efforts during the advance, in bridging nullahs and clearing tracks through eight miles of difficult country, that Gough was able to bring his artillery into action.

On the same day that Maharajpur was fought, the Left Wing under Grey defeated 12,000 Marathas at Panniar, 12 miles south-east of Gwalior. After the enemy had attacked Grey's cumbrous baggage train, he assaulted them in a position which they had taken up on high ground four miles to the east, and routed them in a fight in which the 1st Company, Bengal S. & M., was conspicuous. When the baggage was attacked, the 1st Company was sent forward with the Buffs and a battalion of Indian infantry to reconnoitre some hills to the right. It discovered the enemy beyond the crest and immediately assaulted the centre of the position, though unsupported and far outnumbered. Under a heavy fire from the Maratha artillery, it carried this part of the position and captured eleven guns and a standard.[1]

The Battle of Panniar not only ended the Gwalior Campaign but established an enduring link between the Buffs and the Bengal Sappers and Miners. Until the Indian Mutiny the latter bore upon their appointments the honours "Maharajpoor" and "Punniar,"[2] and it is probable that the acquisition of two such distinctions in a single day is unique in the annals of the Indian Army. The campaign was brief, but it gave some valuable experience to the four companies of the Bengal Corps who fought in it before they took the field in the fierce struggle against the Sikhs of the Punjab.

[1]Despatch from Gen. Sir Hugh Gough, dated Dec. 30th, 1843.

[2]G.O.C.C., Jan. 5th, 1844, and G.O.G.G., Jan. 14th, 1844. According to Gen. Sir Frederick Maunsell, honours gained by particular companies of the Bengal Sapper and Miners were assumed to belong to the Corps in general without official sanction

CHAPTER VII

THE SIKH, SECOND BURMA AND SECOND CHINA WARS, 1845–1860

AFTER the death of Ranjit Singh in 1839, the Punjab sank into a state of chronic revolution. Rival competitors for the throne arose in succession and each came to an untimely end. At length, when the Sikh Army had become the real master, the Sikh Government at Lahore incited the Khalsa or military order to challenge British supremacy in the hope that this would lead to the overthrow of military domination. In November, 1845, the Sikhs began to move southwards from their capital, and on December 13th an army of about 50,000 men with 100 guns, under Sirdars Lal Singh and Tej Singh, crossed the British frontier on the Sutlej near Ferozepore and thus precipitated the First Sikh War. The British were not taken by surprise, for the garrisons at Ferozepore, Ludhiana, Ambala and other stations near the frontier[1] had been increased gradually until they totalled 32,000 men with a reserve of 10,000 at Meerut, and shortly before the outbreak of hostilities the Governor-General, Lieut.-General Sir Henry Hardinge,[2] had formed these troops into an " Army of the Sutlej " under the leadership of the Commander-in-Chief in India, General Sir Hugh Gough. This army included four infantry divisions,[3] three cavalry brigades and a number of batteries, though it was deficient at first in engineers. It moved towards Ferozepore when war was declared on the day of the Sikh invasion.

The 1st and 6th Companies, Bengal S. & M., had been stationed at Ferozepore since March, 1845,[4] so that these units were available immediately for local defence duties ; but no steps were taken to reinforce the Engineer Department of the army from the Corps headquarters at Meerut until after the proclamation of war, and consequently no Sappers and Miners were engaged in the first battle of the campaign which was fought on December 18th at Mudki, 18 miles south-east of Ferozepore. On this occasion, Gough made a frontal attack on the Sikh trenches while his cavalry turned the enemy's left flank. After a day of confused fighting and heavy loss, he emerged victorious with the capture of 17 guns ; but the Sikhs under Lal Singh made an orderly retreat to a stronger position at Ferozeshah, 8 miles nearer to Ferozepore, while another Sikh army under Tej Singh threatened a division under Major-General Littler at Ferozepore. The Governor-General, who was in the field, then tendered

[1]See *Sketch Map of the Punjab in* 1849 included in this chapter, and also Map I at the end of the volume.

[2]Sir Henry Hardinge succeeded Lord Ellenborough as Governor-General in July, 1844.

[3]The Divisional Commanders were Maj.-Gens. Sir Harry G. Smith, W. R. Gilbert, Sir J. M'Caskill and Sir J. Littler.

[4]*History and Digest of Service of the 1st K.G.O. Sappers and Miners*, p. 11.

his military services to Sir Hugh Gough as second-in-command, and Gough had no alternative but to accept. The Battle of Mudki has little engineering interest except that it saw the baptism of fire of Captain Robert Napier, B.E., afterwards Lord Napier of Magdala, who had been for no less than 17 years in civil employment.[1]

Before Lord Ellenborough vacated the appointment of Governor-General he had wisely made provision for the transfer of an army across the Sutlej in the event of hostilities, bearing in mind, no doubt, the difficulties which had arisen in the passage of the Indus at Sukkur in 1839. Under his direction, there had been built in the Bombay Dockyard in 1843 a flotilla of 60 boats, of which 11 were armed with 12 pr. carronades and all were provided with the necessary baulks, chesses, cables, anchors and other gear for bridge construction. These craft were about 47 feet in length and 12 feet in beam and were designed to be spaced in a bridge at 26 feet central intervals.[2] The baulks rested on, or were fastened to, the gunwales; they overlapped, and each spanned a boat and one adjacent waterway. Provision was made for two separate roadways, complete with ribands and rack-lashings. Under the superintendence of officers of the Indian Navy, the flotilla was towed to Karachi and thence 'tracked' up the Indus to Sukkur. Confidential instructions were given in February, 1845, to Major George Broadfoot, M.I., Agent for the North-West Frontier,[3] that he was to pretend that the boats, though adapted for military purposes, were to be used for the transport of grain from Ferozepore to Sukkur.[4] Broadfoot requested that the boats should be sent on to Ferozepore, where 54 of them arrived safely, with crews of lascars, during September and October and were handed over to Major Frederick Abbott, B.E. Abbott transferred them to the charge of 2nd Lieutenant (afterwards General Sir) Alexander Taylor, B.E., who was ordered to use them for the instruction of the 1st Company, Bengal S. & M., in bridging and watermanship. The boats were moored in a creek of the Sutlej at Kunda Ghat about two miles from Ferozepore City, and there Taylor set to work to train the men; but on December 10th he received orders through Lieutenant A. G. Goodwyn, B.E., that he was to sink the boats and fall back on Ferozepore and accordingly he holed and abandoned them, though he removed the small stores.[5] As this occurred only three days before the Sikhs crossed the river, it was fortunate that the sunken boats were not discovered. There were in Ferozepore sufficient Pasley pontoons, complete

[1]Obituary Notice of Field Marshal Lord Napier of Magdala, appearing in *The R.E. Journal*, Vol. XX, 1890, pp. 61–67.

[2]Article entitled " Some Account of the Passage of the Sutlej by the British Army in February, 1846," by Capt. H. Yule, B.E., appearing in *Professional Papers of the Corps of Royal Engineers*, Vol. X (1849), pp. 177–186. This article gives a detailed account of the bridging operations and includes several plates.

[3]Major George Broadfoot, M.I., late commander of " Broadfoot's Sappers," became Agent for the N.W. Frontier on Nov. 1st, 1844, on transfer from Burma.

[4]Letter dated Feb. 20th, 1845, from the Private Secretary to the Governor-General to Major George Broadfoot, quoted in *The Career of Major George Broadfoot, C.B.*, by Major W. Broadfoot, R.E., pp. 283–286.

[5]*General Sir Alex Taylor G.C.B., R.E. : His Times, His Friends and His Work*, by A. C. Taylor, Vol. I, p. 44.

with wagons, to form 14 rafts, but these would not have sufficed to bridge the Sutlej for the passage of a large army.

The invading Sikhs crossed the river by utilizing a type of craft known as a *chappu*—a shallow and roughly triangular "tray," about 45 feet long and 18 feet wide, with a high prow. These craft were most useful as ferry boats, though ill adapted for bridging. Nevertheless, the enemy often constructed *chappu* bridges by dovetailing the boats together stem to stern, leaving no waterway whatever, and superimposing a roadway of rammed earth and brushwood on massive baulks resting on trestles in the boats. On a bridge of this type, General Pollock's army, with its elephants and heavy guns, crossed the Sutlej safely in December, 1842, for the triumphal entry into Ferozepore after the Afghan War ; but such a bridge was possible only in a very sluggish current and was liable to destruction if the water level rose a few inches. Most of the *chappus* on the Sutlej were in Sikh hands when the invasion occurred, so it was fortunate that the British had received the flotilla from Bombay.

On December 21st, 1845, Gough marched to attack Lal Singh at Ferozeshah,[1] expecting that he would soon be joined by Littler from Ferozepore. Littler, however, was engaged in evading Tej Singh and did not appear until early in the afternoon. Gough wished to attack without him, but was forbidden to do so by Hardinge, who suddenly resumed the rôle of Governor-General. When Littler arrived, the British force of 18,000 men with 69 guns advanced against the far more powerful Sikh army entrenched around the village of Ferozeshah. Littler's division on the left was repulsed, but those under Gilbert and M'Caskill made some progress, though subjected to a heavy bombardment.[2] The reserve under Sir Harry Smith was then thrown in and fought a way through where Littler had failed. The British force, however, suffered terribly and was in great confusion when darkness fell. It spent a miserable night in extreme cold and under artillery fire from a part of the position still held by the enemy. The remaining trenches were carried easily at dawn after most of the defenders had withdrawn ; but hardly had the position been won when Tej Singh appeared from Ferozepore with 30,000 fresh men and 100 guns and opened fire. The exhausted British troops formed to meet him, the cavalry charged, and Tej Singh retreated, and thus the final victory rested with Gough, though at a cost of 2,877 casualties.[3]

There was no scope for engineering in this hand-to-hand struggle ; but the 6th Company, Bengal S. & M., was present with Littler's division and thus secured the honour "Ferozeshah." The 1st Company under Taylor was part of the small garrison left by Littler in Ferozepore. Among

[1]The correct name is "Pheru" or "Pheru Shah," called after Bhai Pheru, a fakir. To Punjabis, the Battle of Ferozeshah is still "*Pheru da larai.*"

[2]The cannonade was heard by Capt. H. Yule, B.E., from a distance of 115 miles to the south-east, and there is evidence that it was heard by natives at Roorkee nearly 190 miles distant.

[3]A good account of all the battles of the First Sikh War, with excellent maps on a large scale, appears in an article entitled "Campaign of the Sutlej, 1845–46," by Col. G. G. Lewis, C.B., late R.E., in *Professional Papers of the Corps of Royal Engineers*, Vol. X, pp. 156–166.

those killed on the first day of the battle was Major George Broadfoot, M.I., who was riding at the time with the Governor-General and his Staff. When opposite the southern face of the Sikh position, Broadfoot was wounded through both thighs and thrown from his horse. Gallant as ever, he remounted, but was immediately shot through the heart and fell dead.[1] He was buried with full military honours, and on March 2nd, 1846, his death was recorded as a public calamity in both Houses of Parliament. On his tombstone at Ferozepore is an inscription to the effect that he was "the foremost man in India." So passed an outstanding figure in the history of the North-West Frontier.

After Ferozeshah, Tej Singh retreated across the Sutlej by a ford at Sobraon, 20 miles north of the battlefield, and then proceeded to bridge the river at that place. Gough, having been reinforced from Meerut, moved up from Ferozepore on January 12th, 1846, to keep the enemy under close observation pending the arrival of his heavy artillery. He made no attempt to prevent the Sikhs from recrossing the river in large numbers at Sobraon for he hoped to trap them in a bend of the river after destroying their bridge. The enemy began to prepare a formidable position in this bend, with supporting works on the high right bank beyond the bridge. Meanwhile, the 1st Company of Bengal Sappers at Ferozepore was preparing to bridge the Sutlej further downstream, for Taylor had received orders to march out to the river at Kunda Ghat, raise his sunken boats and resume the interrupted training of his men. Great was his delight when he found that the 54 boats from Bombay had not been injured by a fortnight's immersion, and that the small holes in their bottoms were easy to repair. After a time he was joined by Major F. Abbott, B.E., and other officers with the 2nd, 7th and 8th Companies, for the entire Bengal Corps under Major B. Y. Reilly, B.E., had received orders to join the Army of the Sutlej.[2] Training in bridging then proceeded with great energy in the quiet backwater near Ferozepore, using not only the Bombay boats but 28 pontoons and a few *chappus*. A site for a bridge was selected near the mouth of the creek, where the banks were sound and the width about 200 yards, although this location involved the subsequent crossing of a fordable channel beyond. All carronades were removed from the boats and stacks of bridging material prepared. The Sappers were also practised in ferrying operations in case it should be necessary to transport a large covering force across the river.

While these engineering preparations were in progress, a Sikh army crossed the Sutlej upstream to threaten Ludhiana and the British communications with Ambala, and a force under Sir Harry Smith defeated it at Aliwal on January 28th, 1846. On this occasion, the enemy numbered 18,000 men with 67 guns. They offered a determined resistance in a position with their backs to the Sutlej; but Smith, with only 12,000 men and 32 guns, turned their left and rolled up their line and finally drove them across the river with great slaughter. In this battle, the Bengal Sappers and

[1] *The Career of Major George Broadfoot, C.B.*, by Major W. Broadfoot, R.E., p. 400.
[2] G.O.C.C., Dec. 13th, 1845.

Miners were represented only by one half of the 6th Company, and consequently the Corps was not awarded the honour "Aliwal."[1] Although there was no regulation on the subject, it was decided later that, to validate a claim for a battle honour, at least one complete company must have been present.[2] The names of the Bengal Engineers with the half-company at Aliwal are uncertain because it was customary to award clasps to officers who were not on the battlefield. For instance, Lieutenants R. Strachey and R. Baird Smith and 2nd Lieutenants G. P. Hebbert and Alexander Taylor, B.E., were granted the clasp "Aliwal" for military services;[3] yet it is certain that Taylor was not present for he was then with his flotilla of boats near Ferozepore. Similarly, Taylor received the clasp awarded for the Battle of Ferozeshah although he was at that time in Ferozepore Cantonment.

The brilliant victory at Aliwal had great moral effect, and the Sikhs retreated everywhere across the Sutlej except at Sobraon, whither Sir Harry Smith marched to assist Gough in assaulting the strong position on the left bank. This was two miles in length and powerfully entrenched.[4] Massed batteries were placed to sweep its flanks from positions across the river. It was held by 30,000 regular troops under Tej Singh with 70 guns, and against them Gough could bring only 16,000 men with artillery which was mostly of smaller calibre. Though the prospect was not alluring, Gough decided to attack, and the battle opened on February 10th, 1846, with a heavy bombardment. A first attempt on the enemy's right was repulsed, but was renewed after other attacks on the centre and left had been pressed strongly. The Bengal Sappers and Miners came forward and made openings through the Sikh entrenchments near the river which enabled the British cavalry to pass through and charge the enemy's batteries and infantry.[5] The Sikhs began to fall back towards their bridge, but discovered to their dismay that the river had risen and the structure of flat *chappus* had been swept away. There was then no escape. Under a hail of grape, they were driven into the rushing waters, where some 10,000 perished miserably. The Sikh army had been taught an unforgettable lesson, though at a cost of nearly 2,400 casualties.

Among the assaulting troops at Sobraon were the 2nd, 3rd, 4th, 5th,[6] 6th and 7th Companies, Bengal S. & M., under Major B. Y. Reilly, B.E., working under the direction of the Chief Engineer, Lieut.-Colonel (local Brigadier) E. J. Smith, B.E.[7] Captain Robert Napier, B.E., was present on the Staff, as in the earlier battles at Mudki and Ferozeshah, and

[1] Granted under G.O.C.C., Dec. 12th, 1846, to all other corps engaged.

[2] Letter dated Aug. 7th, 1909, from Mr. G. W. de Rhé-Philipe, included in the "Restoration of Battle Honours" file at Roorkee.

[3] "Early Indian Campaigns and the Decorations awarded for them," by Major H. Biddulph, R.E., appearing in *The R.E. Journal*, Vol. XIX, Jan.–June, 1914, pp. 37–46.

[4] The Sikh defences at Sobraon are described in an article entitled "Some Remarks explanatory of a Plan and Sections of the Sikh Intrenchment at Sobraon," by Brevet-Major W. E. Baker, B.E., appearing in *Professional Papers of the Corps of Royal Engineers*, New Series, Vol. I (1851), pp. 24–27.

[5] Despatch from Gen. Sir Hugh Gough, dated Feb. 13th, 1846.

[6] The 5th Company was with General Gilbert's division.

[7] Lieut.-Col. A. Irvine, B.E., had arrived as Chief Engineer but had refused to supersede Smith until after the battle.

25 Engineer Officers in all received the clasp for Sobraon though some were absent from the actual battlefield. The honour "Sobraon" rightly appears among those held by the Bengal Sappers and Miners, for the Sapper units took a prominent part in the later stages of this decisive battle. The campaign had lasted only two calendar months ; yet it had included four major actions in which 200 guns were captured from the enemy, and it had cost the Army of the Sutlej nearly 7,000 casualties.

The bridging operations carried out by some of the Sapper companies near Ferozepore enabled Gough to pursue the routed Sikhs beyond the Sutlej and make a triumphal entry into their capital. On the evening of February 8th, two days before the battle, the 2nd and 7th Companies received orders to march with Major Abbott from their bridging camp at Kunda Ghat to join Gough in the attack on the Sobraon position, and accordingly they left at once for the front. On the 9th, the remaining two companies—the 1st and 8th—were warned to be ready to bridge the river on the night of the 10th–11th. It was fortunate that Captain Henry Yule, B.E., who was in command of these companies, had secured the services of 126 local boatmen for he was told that his first task would be to ferry across to the right bank 6 regiments of native infantry, 5 troops of irregular cavalry and a troop of horse artillery. For this operation he prepared 14 pontoon rafts, manned by the 1st Company under Lieutenant A. D. Turnbull, B.E., and 7 *chappus* with small crews of boatmen. Next, he selected 28 of the best Bombay boats for bridge construction and allotted them to the 8th Company and the remaining 98 boatmen.[1]

At dawn on February 10th, 1846, the distant roar of artillery told the Sappers at Kunda Ghat that the battle at Sobraon was in progress, and in the afternoon they heard of the British victory. During the ensuing night the covering troops arrived and were ferried safely across. Every Sapper was then turned on to bridge building, and by the evening of the 11th a bridge was almost finished. Hundreds of Sikh corpses, floating down from Sobraon, bumped against the boats and often blocked the waterway between them. The 1st and 8th Companies had worked for 36 hours with only 3 hours' rest, and although the 2nd and 7th Companies, who now rejoined from Sabraon, were too exhausted to help, a bridge of 21 boats with a single roadway of tamarisk brushwood and earth was opened to traffic on the morning of the 12th. During the intervals between the passage of troops, the pressure of camels, carts, ponies, elephants and camp followers at the bridge-head was beyond the conception of all but those who had already seen the baggage of an Indian army. The bridge had no stern anchors, so the dressing of the boats was never perfect. Several animals fell into the river because there were no side-screens or rails and the baulks were warped and easily displaced. Nevertheless, eight 24-pounder guns were man-handled across on the 13th after the elephant teams had been unharnessed. By the evening of the 14th, a second bridge had been con-

[1] "Some Account of the Passage of the Sutlej by the British Army in February, 1846," by Capt. H. Yule, B.E. (*Professional Papers of the Corps of the Royal Engineers*, Vol. X, p. 182.)

THE SUTLEJ BRIDGE AT NAGAR NEAR FEROZEPORE IN MARCH, 1846.
The bridge has two separate roadways.

From a drawing by Lieut. H. Yule, B.E.

structed 70 yards downstream ; and by February 19th, the entire Army of the Sutlej with its transport and camp followers, comprising 100,000 men, 68,000 animals and 40 heavy guns, had crossed the river and was advancing on Lahore.

The bridging operations of the Bengal Sappers and Miners, however, did not end with this remarkable achievement, for a new and better site for a bridge was selected at Nagar, 9 miles upstream, whither the four companies marched on February 20th after dismantling the upper bridge at Kunda Ghat. As the width at the new site was 233 yards, and consequently 27 boats were needed to span it, it was decided that a double-roadway bridge should be constructed according to a design prepared in Bombay. Wooden cleats were fixed to the gunwales to hold the crooked baulks in position, and work started with the building of a long causeway on the low right bank. On the 25th, a single roadway was opened to traffic over the Nagar bridge, and the lower bridge at Kunda Ghat was dismantled and the boats tracked upstream. The second roadway over the Nagar bridge was ready on March 1st, tamarisk brushwood covered with stable-litter and earth being used for the surface. This bridge was dismantled by Turnbull[1] on March 27th after the Army of the Sutlej had recrossed the river on its return from Lahore.

By a treaty concluded in the Sikh capital, the Khalsa Army was reduced in strength and all Sikh territory on the British side of the Sutlej was given up. The Sikhs also relinquished Kashmir. During the summer of 1846, many of the Sapper and Miner companies were stationed in the conquered districts. At Lahore were the 8th and 9th Companies, and in the Jullundur *doab*[2], the 3rd, 4th and 5th Companies. The 2nd and 7th Companies formed part of the Ferozepore garrison, and the 1st, 6th and 10th Companies[3] returned to the new Corps Headquarters at Ludhiana. The work of the Bengal Sappers and Miners in the First Sikh War consisted chiefly of bridging the Sutlej and preparing tracks for the passage of heavy guns across *nullahs*, but none the less it was of great importance in securing a rapid decision in the field.

In view of the system under which the Bengal Sappers and Miners were officered in peace, it is remarkable that the Corps did so well in war. A glance at the Army List for the year 1846 will show that, as regards Engineer officers, the Bengal Sappers had then only a Major as Commandant, a Captain as second-in-command, a Lieutenant as Adjutant, and fourteen 2nd Lieutenants who had recently arrived in India. There was not a properly qualified Company Commander in the whole Corps, unless the second-in-command be considered as such. It is true that a few specially trained Infantry officers were available, though not so many as in the Madras and Bombay Corps, but apparently these did not proceed

[1]Capt. H. Yule, B.E., had left Nagar on March 2nd after handing over charge of the bridge to Lieut. A. D. Turnbull, B.E.

[2]*Doab*. The area between two rivers. In this case, the area between the Sutlej and its tributary the Beas.

[3]The 9th and 10th Companies (formerly Broadfoot's Sappers) saw nothing of the war. They did not join the Army of the Sutlej until March 22nd, 1846, when it was at Lahore. (See *History and Digest of Service of the 1st K.G.O. Sappers and Miners*, p. 11.)

with the companies on service. Instead, selected Bengal Engineers were drafted at the last moment from civil employment and thrust upon men who were strangers to them. The only explanation of the undoubted success of this extraordinary system is that the excellent British non-commissioned officers, who were attached permanently to the units, stepped in and saved the situation, acting as wise counsellors and intermediaries until the officers could learn their new duties and gain the trust and confidence of the rank and file. Financially, the system was highly economical, for in time of peace the Engineer officers were paid mostly by the Civil Government; but from a military standpoint the system was deplorable and even dangerous.

Soon after the conclusion of the First Sikh War there was trouble at the hill fortress of Kangra, about 65 miles north-east of Jullundur. The Sikh commandant refused to surrender under the terms of the Treaty of Lahore, and consequently it was decided that a small force with a siege train should be sent against him. This was no easy matter as there was no road from the plains of the Jullundur District to Kangra, a distance of 40 miles through mountainous country. Colonel Henry Lawrence, the Resident at Lahore, said that a month would be needed to make a path for the passage of 18-pounder guns to Kangra; but Major Robert Napier undertook to do it in a week, and in a week it was done. This feat was performed in April, 1846, under the direction of Napier as Chief Engineer, by two companies of Bengal Sappers and Miners (probably the 4th and 5th) under Lieutenants H. Drummond and J. H. Dyas, B.E., assisted by working parties from the Artillery and gangs of native labourers. When the track had almost reached Kangra, a deputation from the garrison came out to discuss terms and were invited to watch the heavy guns being brought up the final hill. At dawn there appeared a couple of elephants slowly pulling an 18-pounder, tandem fashion, with a third pushing behind. Other guns followed, and when the last had reached the crest the deputation took their leave. The display impressed the Sikhs so greatly that within a very short time a white flag was raised on the ramparts and the garrison marched out in tame surrender.[1] Thereafter, until the outbreak of the Second Sikh War, one of the companies of Bengal Sappers in the Jullundur *doab* was always stationed at Kangra.

A brief respite was secured by the Treaty of Lahore and another concluded in December 1846; but when the Earl of Dalhousie succeeded Lord Hardinge as Governor-General in January 1848, the partial autonomy granted to the Punjab was already proving a failure and the country was ripe for revolt. The Second Sikh War originated as a local rebellion in the distant fortress of Multan on the Chenab River after the murder of two political officers on April 18th, 1848, by Diwan Mulraj, the Sikh Governor. Lord Dalhousie hoped to localize the effects of this rebellion by entrusting to the Sikh Government the task of quelling it, but the scheme failed because the Sikh troops sent to Multan were disloyal to their masters. Lieutenant

[1]Obituary Notice of Lieut.-Gen. W. A. Crommelin, C.B., late R.(B.)E., appearing in *The R.E. Journal*, Vol. XVII, 1887, pp. 9–14.

Herbert Edwardes, a young political officer, then swept across the Indus from the Derajat at the head of a body of Pathan irregulars, and with the aid of a Sikh force under General Van Cortlandt of the Sikh service, and a Bahawalpur State force under Lieutenant E. J. Lake, B.E.,[1] defeated Mulraj in two battles and drove him into Multan. The British Resident at Lahore afterwards took the situation in hand and despatched a division under Major-General W. S. Whish in two columns down the Ravi and Sutlej. This force reached Multan on August 19th and joined the irregulars under Edwardes, Van Cortlandt and Lake and a body of very disaffected Sikhs under a Sirdar called Sher Singh.

The defences of Multan were strong. It was common knowledge that a siege train would be needed to breach the walls and a large cadre of engineer troops to conduct the necessary siege operations. Fortunately, the services of Major Robert Napier, B.E., were available as Chief Engineer, and the Government was able to supply him with an adequate Staff and five companies of the reconstituted Corps of "Bengal Sappers and Pioneers"[2] from Ludhiana. These units comprised the 1st, 2nd and 3rd Companies of Sappers and the 2nd and 3rd Companies of Pioneers, the whole being under Brevet-Captain Henry Siddons, B.E., Commandant of the Corps.[3] No Madras Sappers and Miners were present at Multan, nor indeed in any of the battles of the two Sikh Wars, and the Bombay Sappers did not appear at Multan until the second phase of the siege operations. The first phase was entirely a Bengal affair. Marching from Ludhiana on July 13th at 24 hours' notice, the Bengal Sappers and Pioneers passed through Ferozepore and arrived on August 2nd at Bindri Ghat, a wharf near Adamwahan which lies opposite Bahawalpur on the Sutlej. There they employed the interval until the arrival of the siege train on August 15th in practising field works for the first time since the winter of 1844–45.[4] There also they learnt that with Van Cortlandt's contingent of 2,100 Sikhs before Multan was a body of 260 so-called "Pioneers" who might help them in trench digging. The Bahawalpur contingent of 7,600 men under Lake had no engineer troops, nor had the contingent of 5,800 irregulars under Edwardes.

The first problem confronting Napier was to transport his engineering stores and the ammunition for the siege train some 200 miles down the Sutlej from Ferozepore. Remembering the 54 bridging boats at that place, which might serve for the purpose though ill adapted to carry freight, he sent for Alexander Taylor and invited him to undertake the task. Taylor

[1]Lieut. E. J. Lake, B.E., though acting as a political officer, was appointed to the command of the Bahawalpur force on June 29th, 1848.

[2]Formerly the Bengal Sappers and Miners.

[3]The total strength was 12 British officers, 5 Indian officers and 413 British and Indian other ranks. Major H. Biddulph, R.E., in his article "Early Indian Campaigns and the Decorations awarded for them." (*The R.E. Journal*, Vol. XIX, Jan.–June, 1914, p. 100, states that a detail of the 5th Company of Pioneers was also present. This, however, is not mentioned by Capt. Siddons in his official report.)

[4]"The Siege of Mooltan," by Major H. Siddons, B.E., appearing in *Corps Papers of the Royal Engineers and E.I.C. Engineers*, Vol. I (1849–50), Paper XLI, pp. 419–460. This article has numerous plans, illustrations and appendices and gives a detailed account of the siege operations.

accepted the offer eagerly and asked for Sergeant Bates of the Bengal Sappers as an assistant. On July 30th, the flotilla, accompanied by Napier, started on its long journey to Bindri Ghat, and after many hair-breadth escapes on the flooded river, reached its destination in sixteen days. Taylor then landed his cargo of stores and ammunition and very nearly lost the whole consignment when the current undermined the river bank. However, on the evening of August 29th, escorted by the Sappers and Pioneers, Napier and Taylor marched with the stores and ammunition for Multan. At dawn on the third day of fearful heat, the fortress came in sight, lying still and pale as a cloud on the horizon, and as no one knew the direction of Whish's camp, Taylor volunteered to reconnoitre and rode alone towards the north-east. After covering three or four miles of difficult country intersected with irrigation channels, he sighted the camp and had just turned to gallop back and report when thirty horsemen burst upon him and gave chase. A furious race ensued until Taylor plunged into the escort of Sappers with the convoy and wheeled round to watch the fight; but great was his surprise to see that his pursuers had halted, and still greater when he saw Lieutenant J. E. Cracroft, B.I., the Quarter-Master of the Sappers, ride out of their midst. They were actually a detachment sent by Whish to guide the convoy to camp! A few hours later, Taylor handed over the ammunition and was placed in charge of the Engineer Park. Diwan Mulraj was invited to surrender Multan, and on September 5th Whish fired a salute from his 24-pounders as a reminder that a reply was due. The answer came in the shape of a 14 lb. shot. Mulraj had spoken. The siege had begun.

At a Council of War on September 6th, Napier came forward with two schemes. Either General Whish might try to take Multan by a *coup-de-main* by advancing to within battery distance of the Khuni Burj or "Bloody Bastion" at the southern angle,[1] breaching it and then launching his whole force to the assault, or he might march round to the northern side, where the citadel lay, and attack by regular approaches. Napier himself preferred the northern attack, though he remarked that the besieging force was scarcely strong enough to invest Multan and at the same time to guard its own communications. Lake then suggested a regular approach against the Khuni Burj, and this was the plan finally approved. It was arranged that a trench should be run from Herbert Edwardes' camp in a north-easterly direction for a distance of one mile to a point called Ram Tirut and used as a first parallel from which to advance on the city and the network of gardens, ravines, canals, mosques and huts around it. Nearly 3,000 men, including the Sappers and Pioneers, started digging at dawn on September 7th, and by the 9th several batteries had been established within a mile of the Khuni Burj and half that distance from some outlying works; but the peculiarities of some of the 13,000 irregulars interfered with proper progress, for although the Pathans were ready and willing to fight anyone anywhere and in any way, and would dig trenches for themselves in furtherance of that laudable object, nothing would induce them to put a

[1]See the sketch entitled *Multan in* 1848–49 included in this chapter.

spade into the ground for the defence of others. The Sikhs were little better, so the available trench diggers were reduced to the 5,800 British and Indian regulars. It was found, however, that the British soldiers could not work under a burning sun, and consequently all the regular troops dug during the night and the irregulars were allowed to excavate a separate trench system by day under the direction of Lieutenants C. Pollard and F. R. Maunsell, B.E. It was fortunate that Napier had the assistance of such able officers. " A finer body of men than the Engineer staff at Mooltan," wrote Herbert Edwardes, " was never collected in any Indian Army."[1]

The advanced camp occupied by the irregulars under Edwardes and Lake was within range of the enemy's guns in the Khuni Burj, and the officers' tents were favourite targets. " Major Napier came over one night," writes Edwardes. " We sat under the awning of my tent with our feet on a table. Lake was fast asleep in bed under the same awning. Presently a shot buried itself, hissing, in the sand by Napier's side ; then another ripped its way past me. A third fell at the head of Lake's bed and his servant immediately turned the bed round. Lake asked sleepily " What's the matter ? " " Nothing, Sahib," replied the Bearer. " Only a cannon-ball." So Lake went to sleep again. Five minutes later, another shot fell at his feet. Again the good Bearer shifted his master's bed and again Lake murmured "What's the matter *now ?* " and was told, " Another cannon-ball. Nothing more " ; on which he said " Oh ! " and returned calmly to the land of dreams while Napier and I finished our conversation." As an example of coolness under fire, this would be hard to equal, but of such stuff were the Bengal Engineers made. These were the men who led the Bengal Sappers in war.

Early in the siege there was much skirmishing while the enemy was being dislodged from houses and gardens outside the walls ; but the advance continued steadily, and on September 13th, covered by light batteries in rear, the Sappers and Pioneers began to build a breaching battery on a high mound called Mandi Awa within 600 yards of the Khuni Burj. Then an event occurred which changed the whole aspect of affairs. Sher Singh and his following of 4,000 Sikhs treacherously went over to the enemy. It was evident that the rebellion at Multan was about to develop into a general conflagration involving the entire Sikh nobility, army and nation, and accordingly General Whish wisely decided to raise the siege temporarily and take up a defensive position until reinforced. He retired some five miles southwards to Suraj Kund to await the arrival of a division which was ordered immediately from Bombay. The first step in this retrograde movement was the withdrawal of the guns and ammunition, which was done after nightfall on the 14th ; but by some oversight, no orders were issued to the Engineers, who had established an advanced depot of tools and stores near the breaching battery. Napier had been wounded, and had it not been for the gallantry of Alexander Taylor, who returned unescorted and retrieved the contents of the depot, the army might have lost much of its siege equipment.

[1] *A Year on the Punjab Frontier*, by Major Herbert Edwardes, Vol. II, p. 513.

Though thwarted by the duplicity of an ally, Whish had no intention of abandoning the siege, and the five companies of Bengal Sappers and Pioneers continued their preparations. On October 2nd, 1848, they marched to Shujabad, 20 miles south of Multan, and during the next two months accumulated an immense store of material, returning to Suraj Kund on December 19th with 12,000 gabions and 8,000 fascines besides many ingenious appliances invented by Taylor. During their absence, a detachment of 40 men of the 6th and 7th (Pioneer) Companies arrived at Suraj Kund, and took part in an action on November 7th when Mulraj was driven from a position which he had occupied near the camp.[1] Colonel John Cheape, late B.E., also arrived as Chief Engineer.[2] On December 21st, the 1st and 4th Companies of the Bombay Sappers and Miners under Major Walter Scott, Bo.E., appeared on the scene with a Bombay Division under Brigadier-General the Hon. H. Dundas, raising the strength of the force under General Whish to a total of nearly 16,000 men. The 1st Company was commanded by Lieutenant William Kendall, Bo.E., and the 4th Company by Lieutenant John Hill, Bo.E.[3] Thus, for the second phase of the siege of Multan, Cheape had no less than 7½ companies of Sappers and Miners or Pioneers[4] and an ample supply of equipment and stores. The operations were resumed at once, and it will be convenient to trace their course before dealing with the battles of the Second Sikh War which had already begun on the Chenab River in the region of Wazirabad.

On Christmas Day, Whish reoccupied part of the trench system south of Multan which he had evacuated in September. The Bombay Division under Dundas came up, and on December 27th the whole force attacked the southern suburbs in three columns. On the left, a Bombay column under Dundas drove the enemy from the Maya Temple, a mound called Sidi Lal ki Bed and a garden known as the Baghi Bagh.[5] A centre column advanced against Ram Tirut and afterwards dislodged the enemy from the mound at Mandi Awa and from a defended post called Angirabad lying in the suburbs between the Khuni Burj and the Delhi Gate. Field guns were then brought into action on the tops of the two mounds. A company of Bombay Sappers was included in each of these columns and took part in the fighting. Meanwhile, a column of Bengal troops on the right advanced

[1] *The Services of the Bengal Native Army*, by Lieut. F. G. Cardew, p. 235.

[2] Colonel Cheape became Chief Engineer on Nov. 30th, 1848.

[3] See the *Digest of the Services of the Bombay Sappers and Miners*, by Major G. H. W. O'Sullivan, R.E., p. 13. The Company Officers were as follows :—

1st Company.—2nd Lieut. J. A. Fuller, Bo.E. and Lieut. H. P. B. Berthon, Bo. Art. (attached).

4th Company.—2nd Lieuts. J. T. Walker and J. W. Playfair, Bo.E.

The units embarked at Bombay for Karachi on Oct. 13th, 1848. According to Major O'Sullivan, however, and to the *Brief History of the Royal Bombay Sappers and Miners* (p. 11), the 4th Company was commanded by Lieut. Cowper. This is incorrect. No officer of that name served with the Bombay Division at Multan. 2nd Lieut. Alexander Cowper, Bo.E., who became Commandant of the Bombay Sappers and Miners in 1859, was then an Executive Engineer at Shikarpur in Upper Sind, but he was junior to both Hill and Walker.

[4] 18 British officers, 13 Indian officers and 777 British and Indian other ranks. (See the Abstract of the British Force at Mooltan, Appendix F, p. 450, of "The Siege of Mooltan," by Major H. Siddons, B.E., appearing in *Corps Papers of the Royal Engineers and E.I.C. Engineers*, Vol. I.

[5] See the sketch map entitled *Multan in* 1848–49.

against the citadel, and gaining possession of some lofty brick-kilns, occupied the fortified posts of Wazirabad and Shamastabriz and the palace and garden of Am Khas. These gains were consolidated by the Bengal Sappers and Pioneers under Siddons while the rebels fled through the Delhi Gate into the City. Thereafter, the Bengal and Bombay forces formed the " Right and Left Attacks " respectively, the one against the citadel and the city as far south as the Delhi Gate, and the other against the southern defences of the city, including the Khuni Burj.

The occupation of the city being the first objective, a powerful breaching battery was established within 120 yards of the Khuni Burj, and others to play on that bastion and the Delhi Gate, and the fire from these guns soon brought the walls down in crumbling masses. A chance shot into the citadel on December 30th pierced a mosque, and a large magazine within its walls blew up with a terrific explosion. An immense volume of smoke arose and spread slowly outwards. " At a vast height," writes Edwardes, " the heavy cloud stood still like some great tree. Its shadow fell as night over the camp below. All action was suspended and every eye was turned up in awe to watch the strange vision sink and disappear."[1]

Siddons reconnoitred the main breach at the Khuni Burj before dawn on January 2nd. He reported that it was practicable ; and as it was assumed that the breach at the Delhi Gate would also be negotiable, a general assault was ordered. Napier was to guide the Delhi Gate column and Alexander Taylor the Khuni Burj column. Among the officers and men detailed to storm the Delhi Gate breach were Lieutenants P. Garforth, C. Pollard and F. R. Maunsell, B.E., with the 2nd (Sapper) and 3rd (Pioneer) Companies of the Bengal Corps, and also a ladder party of the 3rd (Sapper) Company under Lieutenant W. S. Oliphant, B.E.[2] The Bengal troops approached the ditch, ready for the assault, but discovered that the breach was still impracticable and that no proper footing could be obtained for the scaling ladders. Nothing remained but to retire to the shelter of the suburbs to await news of the success or failure of the assault on the Khuni Burj. Happily, this attack was completely successful. The infantry of the Bombay Division carried everything before them. Whish and the Bengal troops came round from the Delhi Gate in support, and by dusk the whole of Multan City, except the Lohari and Daulat Gates below the citadel, was in British hands. The Tak, Haram, Bakhar and Delhi Gates were cleared of obstruction and opened on the following day. The Bombay Sappers and Miners suffered heavily in the operations on January 2nd, for although only 10 men were killed, Hill, Fuller and no less than 52 Indian ranks were wounded or were injured in the explosion of a powder magazine near a gateway which they were opening. The Bengal Sappers and Pioneers escaped lightly with a few wounded, including Garforth and Taylor.

[1] "Sieges and Defence of Fortified Places. Siege of Mooltan, 1848," by Colonel Sir E. T. Thackeray, V.C., K.C.B., late R.E., appearing in *The R.E. Journal*, Vol. XX, July–Dec., 1914, pp. 248–258. This article is a valuable précis of the official report by Major Siddons already quoted.

[2] *History and Digest of the 1st K.G.O. Sappers and Miners*, p. 13.

The city having been occupied, the attack was next directed against the citadel, and batteries were placed to breach the walls. On January 5th, the Bengal Sappers and Pioneers moved into the Am Khas garden in order to be near their work, which consisted chiefly of sapping and battery construction. During the next few days, they were concerned in many daring exploits. For instance, Lieutenant J. H. Maxwell, B.E., accompanied by Sapper Sahadat Singh of the 1st (Sapper) Company, went forward before dawn on the 6th and measured the depth of the citadel ditch outside the Daulat Gate of the city. On the same day, the distance to the ditch and its width were measured under heavy fire by Havildar Hussain Baksh and Sapper Brij Lal of the 3rd (Sapper) Company. On one occasion, when a sap was being driven in ground overlooked by the enemy, the " sap-roller " of brushwood, which was used as a protection for the diggers, escaped and rolled away. Sapper Asan Singh immediately jumped out of the trench, and although wounded, tied a rope to the roller by means of which it was pulled back. Three days later, the gabions in a trench burst into flame and Naiks Shiv Din and Baldan climbed out and removed them under a heavy matchlock fire at close range. Again, Havildar Chathu of the 3rd (Sapper) Company volunteered with four men to measure the height of the citadel wall, and though injured by a stone at the first attempt, tried again and arrived within five feet of the wall, where he was shot in the leg and had to be removed to safety by his men. Most of these brave soldiers were subsequently awarded the Indian Order of Merit.[1]

The approach to the citadel was pushed energetically through the city by the Bombay Sappers and Miners as well as by the Bengal Sappers and Pioneers from the Am Khas, but the Bengal Sappers had the more important task. On January 16th, 1849, they began to sink mine-shafts, and two days later exploded several mines under the counterscarp to provide an easy descent into the ditch, which was about 28 feet wide and 20 feet deep. The numerous batteries were advanced closer and closer to the walls and dealt satisfactorily with the escarp and the fortifications above.[2] On the 21st, the Bombay Sappers exploded a mine of 1,600 lbs. under the counterscarp, and during the following night, free access to the interior of the citadel having been opened by both attacks, arrangements were made for an assault. This, however, proved to be unnecessary. On January 22nd, 1849, Mulraj hoisted the white flag and marched out with the 3,800 soldiers remaining from the original garrison of perhaps 10,000 men. Thus ended an important siege in which the expenditure of ammunition was second only to that of Bhurtpore in 1826. The Sapper casualties were not heavy—18 killed and 34 wounded (including 7 British officers) in the Bengal Corps, and 12 killed and 52 wounded (including 2 British officers) in the Bombay Corps. Yet in view of the fact that the total casualty list

[1]*Lectures on the Regimental History of the K.G.O. Bengal Sappers and Miners*, by Major L. V. Bond, R.E., p. 11. Under G.G.O. April 14th, 1849, the 3rd Class of the Order was awarded to 2 Havildars, 2 Naiks and 3 Sappers (Sepoys). Naik Baldan was promoted to the 2nd Class because he already held the 3rd Class for gallant conduct in blowing in the Kabul Gate at Ghazni in 1839. Siddons received a Brevet-Majority.

[2]Some of these batteries were elevated on piles of fascines to obtain a better field of fire.

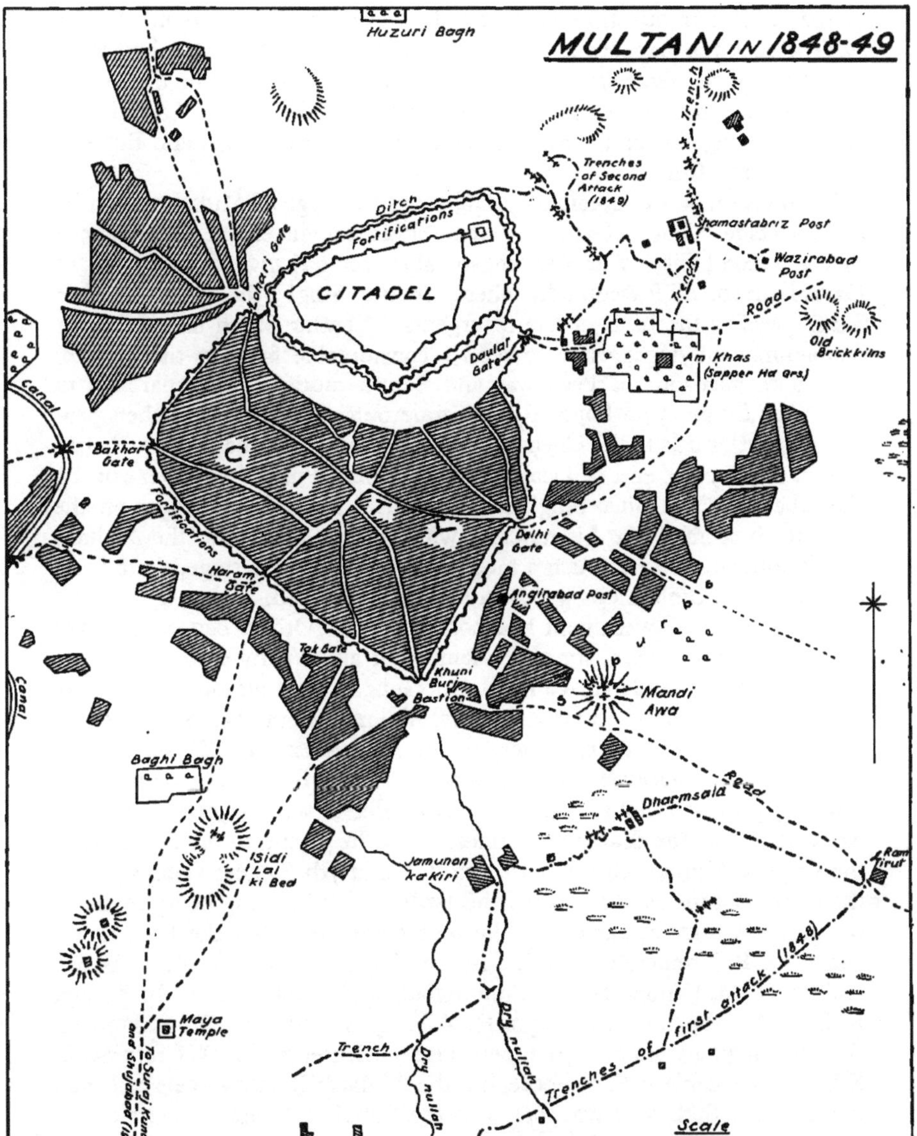
MULTAN IN 1848-49
Huzuri Bagh
CITADEL
Fortifications
Ditch
Lohari Gate
Daulat Gate
Trenches of Second Attack (1849)
Shamastabriz Post
Wazirabad Post
Trench
Road
Old Brickkilns
Am Khas (Sapper Hd Qrs.)
Canal
Bakhar Gate
CITY
Fortifications
Delhi Gate
Haram Gate
Angirabad Post
Tak Gate
Khuni Burj Bastion
Mandi Awa
Baghi Bagh
Dharmsala
Road
Ram Tirut
Sidi Lal ki Bed
Jamunan ka Kiri
Maya Temple
To Suraj Kund (4m) and Shujabad (lam)
Trench
Dry nullah
Dry nullah
Trenches of first attack (1848)
Scale
Yds.100 0 500 1000 Yds.

of the regular troops amounted to only 1,192 killed and wounded, it is evident that the Sappers and Miners and Pioneers at Multan had their fair share of the fighting and were thus compensated in some degree for their absence from the earlier battles of the Second Sikh War. "Mooltan" appears among the battle honours held by both the Bengal and Bombay Sappers and Miners.[1]

We revert now to September 1848, when the siege of Multan was in its earliest stage. The defection of Sher Singh convinced the Government that a Second Sikh War was unavoidable, for a rising had occurred in Hazara, north of Rawalpindi, where Chattar Singh, the father of Sher Singh, was at the head of the insurgents. Chattar Singh induced Dost Muhammad of Afghanistan to send a considerable force to the Punjab. The Sikh garrisons of Peshawar and Bannu mutinied and marched to join Sher Singh, who lingered for a time outside Multan and then proceeded northwards to the Chenab to meet his father. Attock fell to Chattar Singh, and by the end of October the Northern Punjab was over-run by the rebels. When Sher Singh marched his army into Ramnagar on the Chenab, it seemed that his junction with Chattar Singh and the Afghans was imminent, and had such a meeting occurred at this stage, there is no knowing what dimensions the war might have reached.

However, the Government had not been idle. Orders had been issued on October 13th, 1848, for the assembly of an "Army of the Punjab" under the Commander-in-Chief, Lord Gough; and although this army included the infantry division under Major-General W. S. Whish at Multan, the other two divisions, under Major-Generals W. R. Gilbert and Sir J. T. Thackwell, with a cavalry division and eleven batteries of artillery, provided Gough with a striking force of some 16,000 men. The weak point was the dearth of engineer units, for owing to the demands of the siege of Multan only the 4th, 5th, 6th and 7th Pioneer Companies of the Bengal Corps were available, the 1st Pioneer Company being required for garrison duty at Lahore. The four companies took the field under Major G. B. Tremenheere, B.E., assisted by Captains J. Glasfurd, B. W. Goldie, H. M. Durand and A. Cunningham and Lieutenants C. B. Young, R. Baird Smith, A. G. Goodwyn, H. Yule, T. S. Irwin and W. E. Morton, B.E. A bridging train of 28 pontoons under Lieutenant W. A. Crommelin, B.E., was available at Ferozepore, but the flotilla of Bombay boats collected for the First Sikh War was far down the Sutlej at Multan. Some of the most efficient officers and the best trained companies of the Bengal Sappers and Pioneers were also at Multan.

Early in November 1848, Sher Singh was holding the fords of the Chenab at Ramnagar with 30,000 men and 28 guns, awaiting the arrival of the armies under Chattar Singh and Dost Muhammad. He retreated across the river when Gough advanced from Lahore, though he kept some outposts on the left bank. There followed, on November 22nd, an unsatisfactory cavalry battle at Ramnagar[2] of which the 4th and 6th Pioneer

[1]The award was made under G.G.O. dated April 26th, 1853.
[2]See the *Sketch Map of the Punjab in* 1849 included in this chapter.

Companies were interested spectators. Decimated by artillery fire and hampered by quicksands, the British cavalry was compelled to retire after many gallant and successful charges. The Sikhs proved to be no mean swordsmen. "Their propensity to aim cuts at the back of the head," writes an eye-witness,[1] "was so manifested on the 22nd of November that it became an object of consideration to the officers of the army to provide some defence, however slight, for the precious *caput*. Some officers wrapped rolls of linen cloth round the back of the shako, the folds of which hung down their backs, affording some protection. The officers of the Head-Quarter Staff imitated the example of the noble Commander-in-Chief, who carried a head-piece made of leather, partly resembling a helmet, partly like a jockey-cap. The leather edge hanging down behind from many of these fantastic caps gave them the appearance of those hats so peculiar to the fraternity of coal-heavers. The cap was ornamented by a white linen cover, forming a defence against the solar rays."

On the whole it may be said that the Second Sikh War afforded little opportunity for engineering. It was a war of movement; of fierce bombardment, cavalry shock action and infantry duels. The Sappers and Pioneers bridged rivers and ramped *nullahs*, but there their activities ended. Usually, they marched with the heavy artillery, acting as an escort and helping it across difficult country, and in battle they supported the infantry. No defensive positions were ever needed because Gough always assumed the offensive. For these reasons, the Second Sikh War does not call for much detailed description in these pages and a general outline of the operations should suffice.

On the arrival of his siege train on November 27th, 1848, Gough prepared to cross the Chenab to attack Sher Singh in his position opposite Ramnagar. He detached the 3rd Division under Thackwell, accompanied by the 5th and 7th Pioneer Companies and a pontoon train under Crommelin, and sent it upstream with orders to cross the river by two fords some twelve miles distant, and then, turning left, to march downstream against Sher Singh's left flank while the main body tried to force a passage at Ramnagar. The fords were reconnoitred by Lieutenant C. S. Paton, B.E., but as they were found too difficult to negotiate against strong resistance, Thackwell continued up the left bank of the Chenab to Wazirabad, where Lieutenant John Nicholson, B.I.,[2] had collected 17 boats with the assistance of Baird Smith and Yule. It was soon found that the pontoon train could not keep up with the troops. "The creeping, snail-like pace which characterized the movement of the pontoon train," writes Edward Thackwell,[3] "considerably impeded the rapid advance of the column by the occasional long halts necessary to enable it to close up." Accordingly, it was sent back with the 7th Company to a position about six miles upstream of the main body, where it proceeded to bridge the Chenab and enabled a brigade to cross the river to reinforce Thackwell.

[1] *Narrative of the Second Seikh War*, by E. J. Thackwell, pp. 59, 60.
[2] The hero of the Siege of Delhi, who was then a political officer in the Punjab.
[3] *Narrative of the Second Seikh War*, by E. J. Thackwell, pp. 73, 74.

The latter forded the Chenab at Wazirabad on the night of December 1st–2nd, the 5th Pioneer Company assisting in ferrying the guns to the right bank, and he then descended rapidly on the left of the Sikh position. At this juncture, Sher Singh showed considerable strategical ability. Withdrawing most of his troops facing Gough at Ramnagar, he advanced to meet Thackwell; but he was defeated on December 3rd at Sadulapur in a battle in which the 5th Pioneer Company and the personnel of the pontoon train participated. Afterwards, he retreated northwards, with Thackwell in pursuit. On December 8th, Gough crossed the Chenab by an excellent bridge of local boats, constructed at Ramnagar by Young, and joined hands with Thackwell.

There was then a pause in the operations, for Gough wished to await news of the fall of Multan before risking a general action against Sher Singh; but when he heard on January 10th, 1849, that Chattar Singh had occupied Attock and was moving down to effect a junction with Sher Singh, he realized that he must act without delay. Accordingly, he marched towards Rasul on the left bank of the Jhelum, near which Sher Singh had occupied a position with 30,000 men and 62 guns. Included in the British force were the 4th and 7th Companies of the Bengal Pioneers under Tremenheere and a detachment of the 5th Company.[1] On January 13th, Gough advanced through very difficult and broken country to reconnoitre the enemy's position, and arriving at the village of Chilianwala at 2 p.m., prepared to camp. But Sher Singh was determined to force a decision. He opened a heavy bombardment which was promptly returned, and thus Chilianwala, the " evening battle fought by a brave old man in a passion," developed unexpectedly on the bank of the Jhelum. The Bengal Pioneers were engaged in it and consequently earned the honour " Chillianwalla " for their Corps,[2] though this distinction was forfeited with others in 1859. The extent of the Sikh position rendered a frontal attack unavoidable and the advance was through dense scrub jungle. Nevertheless, the right flank was rolled up and the enemy were pressed slowly back to the Jhelum with the loss of 7,000 men while the British casualties amounted to less than 2,400. Nowhere, except at Sobraon, remarked Gough, had he seen so many dead Sikhs.

Yet the hard won victory at Chilianwala was by no means decisive. It is true that Sher Singh retreated, but only for a distance of three miles to a second position near Rasul, where he was reinforced at last by Chattar Singh. Gough dared not renew the attack until his 1st Division appeared on the scene from Multan, and meanwhile the combined Sikh armies began to move eastwards towards Gujrat to threaten his communications. On February 13th, Brigadier Cheape arrived from Multan as Chief Engineer to the army and marched with it on the 15th towards Ramnagar, news having been received that the Sikhs were in a position covering the sacred city of Gujrat. Five days later, reinforced by most of the 1st Division under

[1]List III in the " Statement as to Honorary Distinctions desired by Indian regiments, 1909," included in the " Restoration of Battle Honours" file at Roorkee.
[2]G.G.O., April 26th, 1853.

Whish, Gough changed direction eastwards and approached the enemy whose position was reconnoitred by Cheape, Napier and other Bengal Engineers. The information which they supplied enabled Gough to distribute to the best advantage the guns which decided and ended the Second Sikh War.

The Battle of Gujrat took place on February 21st, 1849. "This fight," writes Alexander Taylor,[1] "will stand upon record as the most extraordinary engagement we have ever fought in India. It was nothing but a cannonade and not more than four regiments engaged ever fired a shot, yet the overthrow was most complete. We made no charges, but brought a heavy fire of artillery on the enemy, and in one hour the result of the action was decided." The Sikhs were drawn up to the south of the city, and against their 60,000 men Gough could oppose only 20,000; but while the Sikhs had only 29 guns, Gough had no less than 96 and consequently possessed an overwhelming superiority in weight of metal. He advanced his right and his heavy guns. The artillery broke down all resistance and inflicted enormous loss, the infantry seized their opportunity, and by one o'clock the Sikhs were streaming in flight across the plain, pursued by the cavalry. On February 22nd, Major-General Gilbert was despatched with two divisions to follow the enemy northwards. The famous "battle of the guns" had decided the war.

The Bengal Sappers and Pioneers under Siddons were represented at Gujrat by the 2nd and 3rd Sapper Companies and the 2nd, 3rd, 4th, 5th, 6th and 7th Pioneer Companies, and the Bombay Sappers and Miners under Kendall by the 1st Company. Some extracts from the report of the Chief Engineer will serve to show the nature of the duties performed by the officers and men of the Bengal units. "Major Napier, attended by Lieutenant Greathed," wrote Cheape,[2] "and Major Tremenheere, attended by Lieutenant Glover, were employed on the 21st, the former with the right, the latter with the left column of attack, and were very useful for their previous examination of the ground. Captain Western, and Lieutenants Goodwyn, Crommelin and Taylor accompanied me. . . . I have gratification to report the zealous manner in which Captain Cunningham and Lieutenant Paton performed the duty of bringing up the fleet of boats from Ramnagar and placing them so as to enable the portion of the army on the other side of the Chenab to co-operate and come up.[3] Captain Siddons, commanding the Sappers and Pioneers, was attached to the heavy guns with a portion of his Corps, the remainder being detached by companies to the different divisions. Such duty as was required of them I need hardly say was effectively performed, and I trust that it may not be out of

[1]Letter from Lieut. A. Taylor, B.E., quoted in *General Sir Alex Taylor, G.C.B., R.E.*, by A. C. Taylor, Vol. I, p. 92.

[2]Report by Brig. J. Cheape, late B.E., dated Feb. 26th, 1849, appearing in *Narrative of the Second Seikh War*, by E. J. Thackwell, pp. 345–347. The Bengal Engineer officers mentioned here are Majors R. C. Napier and G. B. Tremenheere; Capts. J. R. Western, H. Siddons and A. C. Cunningham; Lieuts. A. G. Goodwyn, W. A. Crommelin, A. Taylor and C. S. Paton and 2nd Lieuts. T. G. Glover and W. W. H. Greathed.

[3]See "A Contemporary Account of the Battle of Gujarat," by the late Maj.-Gen. Sir Alex Cunningham, appearing in *The R.E. Journal*, Vol. XLI, March–Dec., 1927, p. 624.

place to mention the gallant behaviour and unwearied exertion displayed by these men throughout the present service." As regards the Bombay Sappers and Miners, Brigadier-General Dundas reported[1] that they were kept prepared for any duty that might be required, such as making ramps in nullahs for the passage of guns, but that the ground was so favourable for the movement of troops that their services were not utilized. For their part in this battle and the campaign as a whole, both the Bengal and Bombay Sappers were awarded the honour "Goojerat" with the addition of the word "Punjaub."[2]

Included in the force under Major-General Gilbert which pursued the remnants of the Sikh army to Rawalpindi were the 1st, 2nd and 3rd Sapper Companies of the Bengal Corps and the 1st Company, Bombay Sappers and Miners. The bridging train under Crommelin laboured in rear of the army, and the 5th and 6th Pioneer Companies of the Bengal Corps joined the troops *en route*. Sher Singh, Chattar Singh and all their followers surrendered at Rawalpindi on March 14th, 1849, and Gilbert then made for Peshawar. He was too late to prevent the Afghans from cutting the floating bridge across the Indus at Attock, and consequently on March 18th the Sapper units were engaged in collecting and repairing the damaged boats and building a narrow bridge.[3] The pursuit was resumed, however, on March 19th; and two days later, while the Afghans fled through the Khaibar Pass, Gilbert entered Peshawar and brought the Second Sikh War to a close. On March 29th, 1849, Lord Dalhousie proclaimed the annexation of the Punjab. "That which Alexander attempted," wrote Gough, "the British Indian Army has accomplished."

After the war, the Sappers and Pioneers were distributed throughout the conquered territory. The 1st Company, Bombay S. & M., remained in Peshawar until November, 1849, when it moved to Karachi under Lieutenant J. G. Fife, Bo.E., and in the following May to Poona, whither the 4th Company had already returned from Multan. One or more companies of the Bengal Sappers and Pioneers were quartered in most of the principal stations—the 2nd (Sappers) in Peshawar, the 1st (Sappers) in Attock, the 5th (Pioneers) in Rawalpindi, the 6th (Pioneers) in Jhelum, the 4th and 7th (Pioneers) in Wazirabad, the 3rd (Sappers) and the 1st and 3rd (Pioneers) in Lahore, and the 2nd (Pioneers) at the Corps headquarters in Ludhiana.[4] During 1849 and 1850 the entire Bengal Corps was employed in building cantonments and making roads and bridges for the development of the vast resources of the country and for defence against the Afghans and the frontier tribes with whom the British were now brought for the first time into close and not too welcome contact. The great public works inaugurated in the Punjab after the close of the Second Sikh War were on a scale recalling the engineering feats of the ancient Romans, and

[1]Report by Brig.-Gen. H. Dundas, C.B., Commanding Bombay Column, Army of the Punjab, dated Feb. 22nd, 1849, appearing in *Narrative of the Second Seikh War*, by E. J. Thackwell, pp. 371–373.

[2]G.G.O., April 2nd, 1849, and G.G.O., April 26th, 1853.

[3]The history of subsequent bridging at Attock is given in *The Military Engineer in India*, by the present author, Vol. II, pp. 64–66.

[4]*History and Digest of Service of the 1st K.G.O. Sappers and Miners*, p. 15.

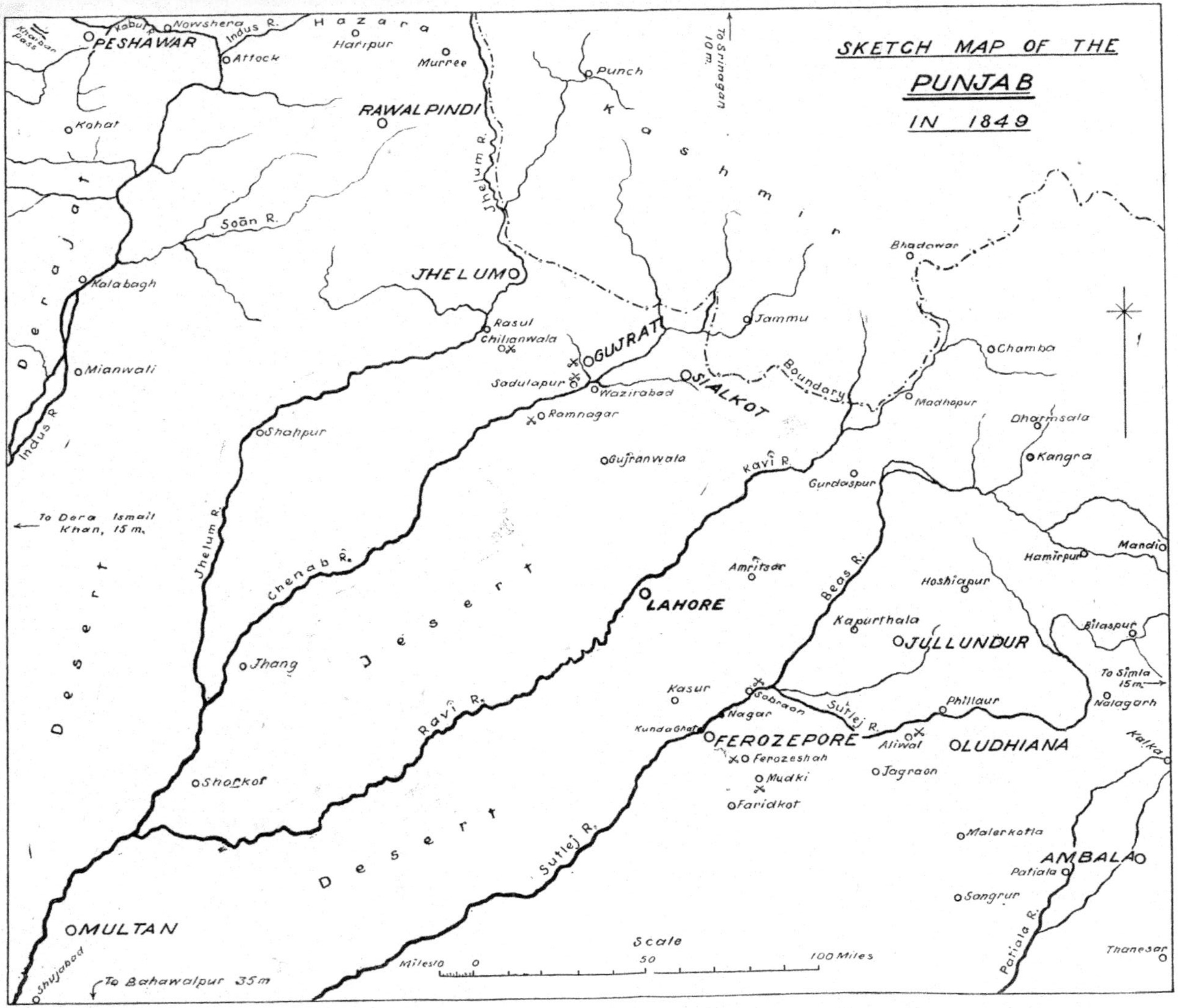
SKETCH MAP OF THE
PUNJAB
IN 1849
PESHAWAR
Khaibar Pass
Kabul R.
Nowshera
Indus R.
Attock
Hazara
Haripur
Murree
RAWALPINDI
Kohat
Soān R.
Derajat
Kalabagh
Mianwali
Indus R.
JHELUM
Jhelum R.
Punch
To Srinagar 10 m.
Kashmir
Rasul
Chilianwala
GUJRAT
Sadulapur
Wazirabad
Ramnagar
SIALKOT
Jammu
Boundary
Bhadawar
Chamba
Madhopur
Dharmsala
Kangra
Gujranwala
Ravi R.
Gurdaspur
Shahpur
To Dera Ismail Khan, 15 m.
Jhelum R.
Chenab R.
Desert
Amritsar
LAHORE
Beas R.
Hoshiapur
Hamirpur
Mandi
Kapurthala
JULLUNDUR
Bilaspur
To Simla 15 m.
Nalagarh
Jhang
Kasur
Sobraon
Nagar
Kunda Ghat
FEROZEPORE
Sutlej R.
Phillaur
Aliwal
LUDHIANA
Kalka
Ferozeshah
Mudki
Faridkot
Jagraon
Shorkot
Ravi R.
Desert
Sutlej R.
Malerkotla
AMBALA
Patiala
Sangrur
Patiala R.
Thanesar
MULTAN
Shujabad
To Bahawalpur 35 m
Scale
Miles 10 0 50 100 Miles

unfortunately they attracted back to civil employment Robert Napier, Alexander Taylor and many other Bengal Engineers whose services might have been of inestimable benefit to the Sapper units during the period of comparative peace and reorganization which preceded the Indian Mutiny.

While the Bengal and Bombay Sappers were earning fresh laurels in the Sikh Wars, they were watched with envious eyes by the Madras Sappers, who had seen no active service since 1844. The Madras soldiers, however, were given their opportunity in 1852 on the outbreak of the Second Burma War. No Bombay troops were employed in Burma, partly on account of their distance from the scene of operations and partly because they had already served in Afghanistan, Sind and the Punjab; and as regards the Bengal troops employed, these included no Bengal Sappers and Miners because none of the twelve companies of that Corps[1] was stationed in or near Bengal and there was ample work for all of them in developing the Punjab and fighting the Afridis and Mohmands across the border. Thus, the engineering operations in Burma became the prerogative of the Madras Sappers and Miners, who maintained in that land of golden pagodas, jungle, swamp, heat and pestilence the excellent reputation which they had established in 1824–26.

The events which led to the Second Burma War are outside the scope of this narrative. Burmese truculence was shown in many ways. British merchants were insulted, and the reparation demanded was, as some wag remarked, "the price only of four or five golden spittoons in the palace of Ava." At length the British seized a Burmese vessel, the Burmese opened fire, and in the spring of 1852, the war began. Every preparation had been made for such an eventuality. Tests of the effect of artillery fire on stockades had been carried out near Calcutta and the troops trained in escalading. Experiments undertaken to ascertain the charge required to demolish a stockade had shown that 200 lbs. of powder would suffice.[2] The equipment of the troops, and their commissariat, transport and medical services, had been carefully scrutinized. On the outbreak of war, the engineer units were provided with scaling ladders and tons of explosive, and a fleet of steamers was chartered to navigate the Irrawaddy during the best season of the year. There was, indeed, little resemblance between the well organized and concentrated offensive of 1852–53 and the haphazard and scattered operations of 1824–26.

The Burma Expeditionary Force of 5,800 men was commanded by Major-General H. Godwin and comprised a Bengal Brigade and a Madras Brigade with artillery and engineers. Escorted by an armed flotilla, the Bengal Brigade, with General Godwin, arrived off the mouth of the Rangoon River on April 2nd, 1852, and continuing eastwards, captured Martaban on the 5th[3] When the Burmese Governor of Rangoon first heard that the

[1]Under G.G.O., dated March 20th, 1851, the "Bengal Sappers and Pioneers" had become once more the "Bengal Sappers and Miners" with a strength increased from 10 to 12 companies, of which 3 companies were to be always at the headquarters at Ludhiana.

[2]*The Second Burmese War*, by W. F. B. Laurie, p. 21.

[3]See the *Sketch Map of Lower Burma in* 1852 included in this chapter. Also Map II at the end of the volume.

squadron had been sighted he wrote to the King of Ava, somewhat prematurely, that the foreign soldiers were already his prisoners. "Please cut me some thousands of spans of rope to bind them," he added. His chagrin may be imagined therefore when Godwin returned to the mouth of the Irrawaddy and, joined by the Madras Brigade, ascended the river, landed his troops on the right bank and marched on April 12th against Rangoon. Four companies of the Madras Sappers and Miners were included in the force. "A" and "B" Companies under Lieutenant B. Ford, M.I., had embarked at Madras about March 23rd, and after taking part in the reduction of Martaban with the Bengal Brigade, were joined at the mouth of the Rangoon River on April 8th by "C" and "E" Companies under Brevet-Captain J. W. Rundall, M.E., who arrived with the Madras Brigade.[1] With Rundall were 2nd Lieutenants G. Dennison, E. R. Blagrave[2] and J. O. Mayne, M.E., and Sub-Conductor Almond. Other Madras Engineers who served with the companies in Burma were Lieutenant J. Carpendale and 2nd Lieutenants R. F. Oakes, H. J. Rogers, J. G. Ryves, H. Vaughan, J. Mullins and T. E. Gahagan. It is remarkable that no less than ten subalterns of the Madras Native Infantry served with the four companies, these being Lieutenants B. Ford, H. Mackintosh, G. M. Carter, F. J. Wilson, V. I. Shortland, W. G. Farquhar, A. M. Harris, H. Allen, G. I. R. Furlong and E. S. Daniel.[3] Thus the number of engineers by profession barely exceeded the number of those by adoption; and yet, such was the keenness of the infantry officers that the efficiency of the companies does not seem to have suffered. Each Sapper company took the field with five officers—a very liberal allowance, though justified in view of the probable casualties through sickness.

Rangoon was found to have changed considerably since 1824. The golden Shwedagon Pagoda was now included within the northern defences of a new and strongly fortified town, built upstream of the old town, some distance from the river bank, and held by 20,000 men with a number of guns. Godwin did not advance directly towards it, as the enemy had anticipated, but marched inland on April 12th by a circuitous route designed to bring him opposite the eastern face of the Pagoda, the key of the position. On his way he had to deal with an outlying work known as the White House Stockade, and this he did in two columns supporting a storming party of the 51st Regiment and some Madras Sappers under Rundall, accompanied by the Chief Engineer, Major H. Fraser, B.E.[4] Most of the Sappers marched with ladders in rear of the

[1]*The Military History of the Madras Engineers and Pioneers*, by Major H. M. Vibart, R.(M.)E., Vol. II, pp. 212, 213. Major Vibart states definitely that the two companies present at the reduction of Martaban were commanded by Lieut. Ford, M.I. and that Capt. Rundall arrived later with the other two companies. It is stated, however, in the *Historical Record of the Q.V.O. Madras Sappers and Miners*, Vol. I (p. 60) that Rundall led and Ford followed. It is probable that Vibart is correct for Rundall would naturally accompany the Madras Brigade.

[2]2nd Lieut. E. R. Blagrave, however, did not receive the medal awarded for the campaign, so it is presumed that he was invalided at once.

[3]*Historical Record of the Q.V.O. Madras Sappers and Miners*, Vol. I, p. 60.

[4]As his assistants during the campaign, Major Fraser had the following Bengal Engineers :— Lieuts. C. B. Young, H. Drummond, G. A. Craster, W. S. Trevor, J. D. Campbell, A. Fraser and E. C. S. Williams. Many of these afterwards rose to high rank. Major Fraser himself was a most capable engineer and rebuilt Rangoon and other towns.

left flank of the right column, and after the artillery had bombarded the stockade, they came under such heavy musketry fire as they moved up to the front that they were obliged to ground their ladders and return the fire. Resuming their advance, those with the storming party reached the stockade and planted four ladders. One of these was raised by three Sappers after four of their comrades had been shot down in the attempt. Followed by Rundall, Fraser then led the stormers up the ladders and the stockade was carried, though not without considerable loss. The heat was so terrific that the exhausted troops could do no more. They rested during the remainder of the day, and on the 13th, assisted by the Sappers, disembarked and hauled to camp four 8-inch howitzers intended for the bombardment of the Pagoda.

At dawn on April 14th, Godwin resumed his advance on the Shwedagon Pagoda. The howitzers came into action, and in due course a storming party rushed forward under a heavy fire, and entering through a gate, captured in succession the terraces of the wonderful structure. During this operation, Naik Muniah and Private Ramasami of " A " Company, Madras S. & M., volunteered to carry tools across a bullet-swept zone to the advanced troops. They succeeded in doing so, and each was subsequently awarded the Indian Order of Merit (3rd Class) for gallantry. Both Rundall and Ford were wounded. This action gave the British possession not only of the Shwedagon Pagoda but all Rangoon, since the enemy fled in wild confusion from the city to the jungle and disappeared northwards. Godwin was fortunate to capture Rangoon with the loss of only 149 men, for the defences were powerful and intricate. Behind a deep and flooded ditch lay an abattis of felled trees ten yards broad and including a palisade. In rear of this obstacle was a stockade formed of a triple row of tree trunks placed vertically and connected by horizontal timbers, and behind the stockade an earthen backing 45 feet thick at the base. Artillery was powerless against such fortifications.

Apart from defeating some attempts by the Burmese to recapture Martaban, the next undertaking was the despatch of a small expedition westwards against Bassein. A party of 67 Madras Sappers under Ford accompanied a force of about 900 men under Godwin himself which left Rangoon on May 17th, 1852, voyaged up the Bassein River, and captured Bassein on the 19th. A detachment, including a ladder party of Sappers under Ford, then advanced on a stockade south of the town and came under point blank fire from the defenders. The ladders were planted, and Ford and another officer led the men up them and dropped down into the enclosure, across which they pursued the enemy. The Burmese, unable to escape quickly through the single exit usually provided in such works, then turned about and showed fight; but Naik Muttuvirapan of the Madras Sappers, who was leading at the moment, charged them without hesitation, shooting one and bayoneting two others, and for this exploit was awarded the Indian Order of Merit (3rd Class). Ford and the remainder of the Sapper party were highly commended for their gallant conduct on the same occasion.[1]

[1]G.O.G.G., June 5th, 1852.

Another detachment of the Corps under Mackintosh left Rangoon on June 3rd with a small expedition detailed to capture Pegu. They assisted in storming the Pegu Pagoda, and having destroyed the defences, returned to Rangoon. Pegu was handed over to a friendly tribe, the Talaings, but these people were driven out by the Burmese within a week. In July, a naval flotilla reconnoitred up the Irrawaddy to Prome and cleared the delta of the enemy. Nothing then remained but to pacify the conquered territory, recapture Pegu, and extend the operations up the Sittang river as far as Toungoo, that place and Prome having been fixed as the northern limits of the offensive. However, despite the loss of the Rangoon coast, the Golden Monarch of Ava was still defiant, so Lord Dalhousie visited Rangoon on July 27th, 1852, to examine the situation. The result was that on August 13th the army of about 20,000 men in Burma was reorganized into two divisions, a Bengal Division under Brigadier-General Sir John Cheape, late B.E., who had hitherto held a Staff appointment under General Godwin, and a Madras Division under Brigadier-General S. W. Steel.[1] Orders were issued at the same time for an advance on Prome. The Madras Sappers were employed during August in fortifying the upper and second terraces of the Shwedagon Pagoda at Rangoon and preparing emplacements on them for a number of field guns which were ordered from India. The Pagoda was thus converted into an impregnable citadel dominating Rangoon and the surrounding country.

All arrangements having been completed for the voyage up the Irrawaddy, Godwin started from Rangoon with a force of three battalions and some artillery to which a company of Madras Sappers and Miners under Allen was attached. The Sappers embarked on September 26th and landed near Prome on October 9th after a few skirmishes on the way. The enemy opened a desultory fire from the Prome defences; but when the troops advanced on the following morning to attack the fortified pagoda they found that the Burmese commander, known as Bandula,[2] had evacuated it and withdrawn eastwards with all his men to meet large reinforcements. Godwin then returned to Rangoon, leaving Cheape in command at Prome. Cheape was gratified soon afterwards to receive the surrender of Bandula who preferred to give himself up rather than obey an order from the King of Ava to appear at court in the dress of a woman to answer for his defeat. November passed with a few skirmishes and night attacks. Carpendale, Mackintosh, Allen and the Sapper Company were employed in roadmaking, fortifying the position and fighting an epidemic of cholera. On November 12th, Rundall died in Prome from liver trouble and the command of the Madras Sappers and Miners in Burma devolved on Carpendale.

After the occupation of Prome, and before the main body of the army moved forward from Rangoon, Godwin accompanied an expedition of 900 men under Brigadier-General M. McNeill to Pegu. A detachment of 70 Madras Sappers and Miners under Shortland and Harris embarked

[1] *Frontier and Overseas Expeditions from India, Vol. V., Burma*, p. 92.
[2] This Bandula was a son of the Bandula of the First Burma War. (See Chapter IV.)

PROME IN 1853.

with the remainder of the troops on November 19th and disembarked below Pegu before dawn on the 21st after preparing the river bank for the landing of two 24-pounder howitzers.[1] They helped the infantry to clear a track for a distance of two miles through high grass and jungle for the advance of the guns, and then, under a burning sun, joined in a successful assault on a main gateway and afterwards on a golden pagoda which towered above the town. A garrison of 500 men having been installed in the pagoda, Godwin retired with the remainder to Rangoon. This was a serious error. His departure was followed immediately by the reappearance of the Burmese, who invested the pagoda and prevented a small reinforcement from reaching it. The only Engineer officer present was Lieutenant J. D. Campbell, B.E., and he had no sand bags for the construction of hasty defences. Nevertheless, he was equal to the occasion, for with Harris and the Madras Sappers he erected barricades of bags of rice and barrels of pork or biscuits and thus provided some protection.[2] On November 27th the enemy attacked the pagoda on all sides and repeated the operation on December 4th and 6th, after which they resorted to daily bombardments. The siege was raised on December 14th when a force of 1,100 men under Godwin arrived from Rangoon, while a column which included some Madras Sappers cleared the country between Rangoon and Pegu. Godwin then pursued the enemy towards Shwegyin with a force which included 30 Madras Sappers under Harris, but lack of supplies soon forced him to give up the chase. Leaving an adequate garrison in Pegu, he returned to Rangoon, where, on December 20th, 1852, he issued a proclamation announcing the annexation of the Pegu Province.

Meanwhile, the scattered troops of the disgraced and captive Bandula had resumed hostilities at Prome. On several occasions they attacked outlying posts, and on the night of December 8th–9th they launched a series of daring assaults on Prome itself during which the Madras Sappers under Carpendale were in support of the infantry on some heights to the south. Sir John Cheape, however, had little difficulty in repelling these attempts because Prome had been well fortified by the Sappers. "We cannot omit to bring to notice," remarks Laurie,[3] "the admirable conduct of a small body of the native army—men who, although they had been broken down by disease, had rendered the most valuable service previous to this night attack in the construction of breastwork, battery, abattis, parapet, bridge and road. Yes, it will be read now and hereafter with admiration, that the small body of Madras Sappers at Prome worked as subjects of the British Indian Government should work—with the right spirit of soldiers."

Shortly after their repulse, the Burmese around Prome disappeared into the jungle and were seen no more. They had heard that a revolution

[1] *Pegu. A Narrative of Events during the Second Burmese War*, by Lieut. F. W. B. Laurie, p. 103.
[2] *Ibid.*, p. 372.
[3] *Ibid.*, pp. 152, 153.

had broken out in distant Ava and had consequently stampeded northwards to claim their share of the probable loot! The main operations of the Second Burma War thus came to a sudden and surprising end, and nothing remained but to march through outlying districts such as the Sittang Valley, round up dacoits, and settle the terms of peace. The task of "showing the flag" on the Sittang was entrusted to a force of some 2,100 men under Brigadier-General S. W. Steel which embarked at Rangoon on January 4th, 1853, and included a company of 70 Madras Sappers under Shortland and Harris with Lieutenant A. Fraser, B.E., as Field Engineer. The expedition proceeded by ship to Martaban but could not start its march into the interior until January 14th. Desperately hard work soon fell to the lot of the Sappers. From the 21st to the 23rd, they were employed in hacking a passage through dense jungle. On the 24th, they built a bridge of Burmese canoes across a wide creek which, it was said, a Napoleon or a Wellington would have crossed with delight. The column reached the town of Sittang on February 3rd and Shwegyin on the 10th. A detachment of 900 men, including 50 Sappers under Shortland, was then pushed forward up the left bank of the Sittang River through broken and forest-clad country, where the heat was terrific and the mosquitoes unbearable, and crossing the river on February 22nd, marched unopposed into Toungoo having covered 240 miles from Martaban in 39 days. Thereafter, a detachment of Madras Sappers and Miners always formed part of the Toungoo garrison.

With Toungoo and Prome in their hands, the Government turned their attention to the suppression of large gatherings of dacoits on the Irrawaddy. At the beginning of February, 1853, a naval expedition had been severely handled by a dacoit leader named Myat-Tun, who had collected 7,000 men in the jungles west of Danubyu, so Cheape went down to Henzada, 35 miles north of Danubyu, and marched thence on February 22nd with 1,000 infantry, a few cavalry and guns and 70 Madras Sappers under 2nd Lieutenant J. Mullins, M.E., with 2nd Lieutenant W. S. Trevor, B.E., attached. Cheape believed that he could reach Myat-Tun's stronghold within four days and consequently took only eight days' rations with him; but finding on the 26th that he had been misinformed, he returned to the Irrawaddy at Zalun, re-embarked his troops, and proceeded downstream to Danubyu, where he arrived on March 3rd to find that Myat-Tun had recently burned and wrecked the entire town. Having replenished his supplies he set out westwards on March 7th with the Sappers immediately in rear of the advanced guard, and after covering seven miles, camped behind a belt of jungle bordering a creek 130 yards wide beyond which the enemy were in position. Early on the 8th, the Sappers began their preparations for transporting the force across the creek. A number of empty barrels had been sent up from Rangoon to Danubyu, where the Sappers had made barrel piers for two rafts and had loaded them, with other materials, on to carts. These carts having arrived, a site was selected for a bridge and the rafts were assembled, though under a considerable fire from muskets and jingals. Two hours after daybreak, the crossing began. A covering party was ferried across, cables were carried over and fixed to trees, and the rafts were pulled backwards and forwards along them so that by midnight the whole column had reached the far bank.

On the following day, after the morning mists had cleared, the troops broke camp and toiled for hours under a glaring sun along a path which eventually led back to their starting point. They had no maps, and their Burmese guide pretended that he had lost his way. Another attempt brought them to a village called Kyontani, where the Sappers spent the whole of March 10th in bridging a creek only 50 yards wide and dismantling the structure after the troops and baggage had crossed. The bridge was made from the two cask rafts, an old boat and some planks and canvas. Ferries were arranged for the guns. The fact that a whole day was occupied in this small undertaking shows the exhausted condition of the men. Little progress through the jungle was made on the 11th because the enemy had felled dozens of trees across the road. The Sappers laboured till dusk in clearing away the smaller obstructions and cutting a path round the larger ones. Provisions soon began to run short and the troops were placed on half-rations. At last, Cheape decided for the second time that further progress was impossible. On March 12th he led the force back to Kyontani, where some of the Sappers collected materials for huts and others, under Trevor, marched with a detachment to Danubyu to obtain provisions. The force remained at Kyontani for the next four days, suffering from malaria and ravaged by cholera. So far as their weakness would allow, the Sappers occupied themselves in building stockades and huts.

Provisions having arrived, the Sappers set out with an advanced party on March 17th to clear the road which had again been obstructed by felled trees. They were sniped continually and took part in storming a stockade. The main body followed on the 18th, but the march was peculiarly difficult and the rate of advance only one mile in two hours. On the 19th, after a mile had been covered, the enemy were found to be holding a stockaded rampart, 1,200 yards in length, which lay beyond a creek running parallel to the road. The only approach was by a narrow causeway, flanked by dense jungle, commanded by two captured naval guns, and broken in one place by a pit in which sharpened stakes had been planted. A turning movement was impossible because one flank rested on an impassable morass and the other on a belt of abattis. Two assaults failed. Several officers were shot down and the troops could make no headway. In this dilemma Cheape decided to force an entrance with the aid of the point blank fire of a 24-pounder howitzer, and in order that it might be brought into action the Madras Sappers cut a track through the jungle along most of the face of the stockade under a heavy fusillade from loopholes only 50 yards distant. By this exploit, Mullins, Trevor and their men enabled the gunners to drag forward the heavy weapon and bring it into action at 25 yards' range. A third column of assault was then formed to which Trevor and Ensign G. J. Wolseley, H.M. 80th Regt. (afterwards Field-Marshal Lord Wolseley) were attached. As they advanced, the guns were again fired and Wolseley fell wounded, but Trevor succeeded in making his way unobserved into the work by creeping along the slope of the causeway. Alone, he then proceeded to shoot down the enemy's gunners with his revolver and thus enabled the stormers to rush along the top of the causeway and carry the defences at the point of the bayonet.[1] The majority of the 4,000 defenders, including Myat-Tun himself, escaped into the jungle. Their headquarters, the adjacent village of Kyaukazin, was found to be deserted. After destroying that place, Cheape started for Danubyu, and, on March 24th, the expedition re-embarked and voyaged up the Irrawaddy to Prome. The British casualties in the operations against Myat-Tun were only 140 killed and wounded, but 100 victims were claimed by cholera.

The Madras Sappers escaped lightly, though they worked usually in a very exposed position at the head of the column, protected only by a few skirmishers as there was no space for a larger body until the jungle had been cleared. Carrying arms in addition to tools, and piling and unpiling them frequently, was found to be so exhausting that they placed their weapons in a cart and often took part in assaults armed only with felling axes and Burmese swords (*dhas*). Never did representatives of their famous Corps have more strenuous work. Through their exertions, and those of their comrades in previous operations in Burma, the Madras Sappers and Miners gained the honour "Pegu," which was awarded in 1855.[2]

No treaty was signed on the conclusion of the Second Burma War. Instead, on June 30th, 1853, Lord Dalhousie issued a Proclamation of Peace naming a parallel of latitude 48 miles north of Toungoo and 6 miles north of Myede as the location of the British frontier. In January, 1854, a party of Sappers was involved in a fight when some dacoits attacked a detachment engaged in marking this boundary, so it is evident that for many months the outlying districts were in a very unsettled condition. It was not until the beginning of 1856 that "A," "B," "C" and "E" Companies said goodbye to the Land of the Golden Pagodas and returned to Madras to receive the congratulations of their comrades.

Four years later, "A" Company, Madras S. & M., was on field service in China with "K" Company, which had been raised during the Indian Mutiny. The Treaty of Nanking had been ignored by the Chinese. Another agreement concluded at Tientsin in 1858, after the occupation of Canton, had suffered a like fate. The Chinese barred the mouth of the Paiho, the waterway to Peiping (Peking) and repulsed a naval attempt to force an entrance, so the British Government decided in 1860 to send an expeditionary force of two infantry divisions and a cavalry brigade against them in co-operation with the French and directed the Government of India to assist. The chief command was entrusted to Lieut.-General Sir Hope Grant with Major-Generals Sir John Michel and Sir Robert Napier (late B.E.) as Divisional Commanders. Napier, fresh from his triumphs at

[1]Memoir of Maj.-Gen. W. S. Trevor, V.C., late R.(B.)E., appearing in *The R.E. Journal*, Vol. VII, Jan.–June, 1908, pp. 79–85.
[2]G.G.O., Feb. 2nd, 1855.

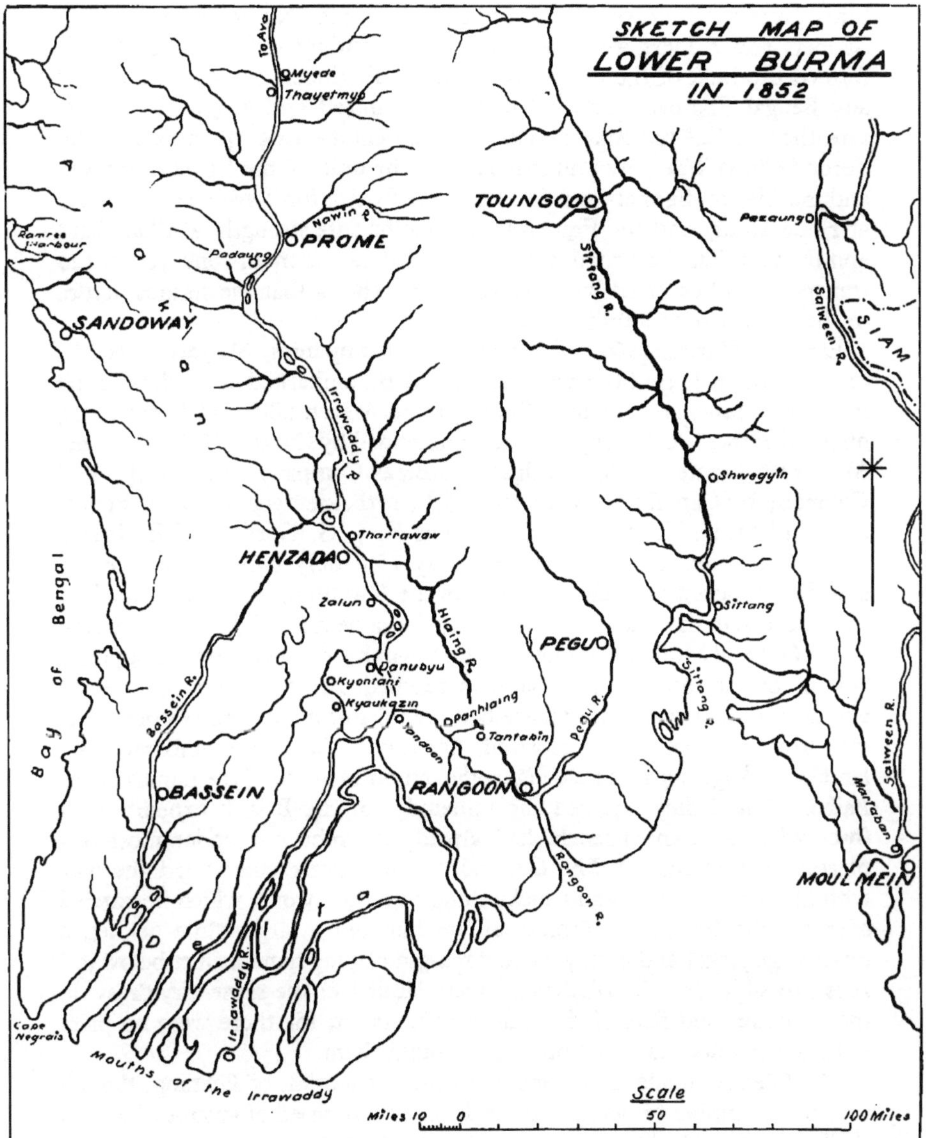
SKETCH MAP OF
LOWER BURMA
IN 1852
To Ava
Myede
Thayetmyo
Nawin R.
Ramree Harbour
Padaung
PROME
SANDOWAY
Arakan
Irrawaddy R.
Tharrawaw
HENZADA
Zalun
Danubyu
Kyontani
Kyaukazin
Yandoon
Panhlaing
Tantabin
Hlaing R.
PEGU
Pegu R.
RANGOON
Rangoon R.
Bassein R.
BASSEIN
Bay of Bengal
Delta
Irrawaddy R.
Cape Negrais
Mouths of the Irrawaddy
TOUNGOO
Sittang R.
Pezaung
Salween R.
SIAM
Shwegyin
Sittang
Sittang R.
Martaban
Salween R.
MOULMEIN
Scale
Miles 10 0 50 100 Miles

Lucknow and in Central India, superintended at Calcutta every detail of the supply and equipment of the 2nd Division, and to this may be attributed largely the success of his operations in China. No Bengal or Bombay Sappers and Miners were included in the contingent from India which formed the bulk of the force. No Bombay Engineers served with it, nor any Bengal Engineers other than Napier himself and Major W. W. H. Greathed, B.E.,[1] his Aide-de-Camp. The engineering operations of the Second China War were undertaken solely by units of the Royal Engineers and the Madras Sappers and Miners. The British force was to concentrate at Hong Kong, and the French force, one half its strength, at Shanghai; and the fact that the British alone numbered 14,000 men, conveyed in 120 transports and escorted by 70 ships of war, shows that the serious nature of the enterprise was fully realized.

Early in March, 1860, "A" and "K" Companies, Madras S. & M., under Captain J. H. M. Shaw-Stewart, M.E., embarked at Madras in the transport *Statesman*, reaching Singapore on March 28th and Hong Kong on April 27th. "A" Company was commanded by Captain H. F. Dakeyne, M.I., with Lieutenant A. F. Filgate, M.E., as Company officer, and "K" Company by Captain N. Swanston, M.I., with Lieutenants M. E. Foord, M.I. and D. H. Trail, M.E. Lieutenant H. J. G. Gordon, M.E., joined "A" Company at Hong Kong on May 16th only two days before the expedition started for Talienwan Bay in the Kwantung Peninsula, north of the entrance to the Gulf of Pechihli. At the same time, the French division under General Montauban moved from Shanghai to Chefoo on the opposite side of the entrance.[2] The Sappers reached Talienwan on June 16th,[3] and during their stay at that place had the misfortune to lose Gordon, who was drowned when a boat capsized. On July 24th, they re-embarked and landed on August 7th at Pehtang, some ten miles north of the mouth of the Paiho. There they rejoined the remainder of the British expeditionary force who, with the French, had already disembarked under most unpleasant conditions. "The General," writes Fortescue,[4] "led the way with his trousers, boots and socks slung over his sword, which he carried over his shoulder, and nothing left on him but a large white helmet, a dirty serge jacket and a very narrow margin of grey flannel shirt below it." It is probable that the Madras Sappers landed in the same airy dress on the shelving mud flats of that inhospitable coast, for there were no piers until the engineer units found time to build them.

The Chinese made no resistance to the occupation of Pehtang, though they left a number of percussion land-mines composed of groups of buried shells which might have caused serious loss had they not been discovered. The quarters allotted to the Sapper companies were found to contain the rotting carcases of animals placed there by the enemy in the hope of causing

[1]The three Corps of Company's Engineers existed as such until they were amalgamated with the Royal Engineers on April 1st, 1862. Hence the letters "B.E."

[2]See the *Sketch Maps of China* included in Chapter XII.

[3]Their strength was then 8 British officers (including an asst. surgeon) and 245 Indian ranks.

[4]*A History of the British Army*, by the Hon. J. W. Fortescue, Vol. XIII, p. 408.

an epidemic, so the men had first to clean and disinfect the rooms. Afterwards, they were employed in building piers and wharves and making a road through the marshes around the town to facilitate the transit of guns and baggage to a main causeway which led south-westwards for a distance of five miles to Chinese entrenchments guarding Sinho. By landing at Pehtang, Hope Grant avoided the necessity of forcing a passage up the Paiho past the powerful Taku Forts at the mouth of that river.

The allied forces marched from Pehtang towards Sinho on August 12th, 1860, after reconnaissances had shown that the ground to the right of the causeway was passable in spite of heavy rain. " A " and " K " Companies were attached to the 2nd Division (Napier), which moved with the cavalry by that route in order to operate against the enemy's left flank, while the 1st Division and the French marched along the causeway. A detachment of " K " Company under Trail worked at the head of the 2nd Division to improve the track for the first two miles, but even so the guns often sank to their axles in the swamp and several wagons had to be abandoned. Firmer ground was then reached and Napier deployed his division for battle, while the 1st Division and the French followed suit on either side of the causeway; but the manœuvre was unnecessary, for the enemy abandoned their two positions covering Sinho and fled up the Paiho or towards Tangku. Hope Grant then occupied Sinho and bivouacked near it.

On August 13th, the allied forces marched eastwards down the Paiho to within two miles of Tangku. An Engineer Brigade was formed under Lieut.-Colonel G. F. Mann, R.E., consisting of the 10th and 23rd Companies and one half of the 8th Company, R.E., with the 1st Division, and " A " and " K " Companies, Madras S. & M., with the 2nd Division.[1] After dark, a detachment of Sappers under Trail approached Tangku with some Royal Engineers and infantry and dug a trench within 400 yards of the defences, and at dawn on August 14th the 1st Division and the French advanced to the attack between the Paiho and a causeway, the 2nd Division being in reserve. The Madras Sappers were well to the front. Filgate was in charge of a party with bamboo scaling ladders, and Swanston of another with powder bags. Parties of Royal Marines were also present with pontoons. None of this equipment was needed, however, because the Chinese abandoned the mud walls and trenches of Tangku after they had been heavily bombarded and crossed to the south bank of the river by a bridge of boats. The capture of Tangku placed Hope Grant and Montauban in a very strong position in rear of the group of Taku Forts defending the entrance to the Paiho.

The principal Taku Forts were four in number, two on the north bank commanding two others on the south bank, and Hope Grant decided to attack the nearest fort on the north bank which took in reverse the defences of the other and larger northern fort at the river mouth and also enfiladed the sea defences of the main southern fort opposite to it. In

[1]As arranged at Hong Kong on April 20th, 1860, the 10th Company was allotted to the 1st Division and the 23rd Company to the 2nd Division, while the Sappers and Miners and the detachment of the 8th Company were detailed to form an " Engineer Reserve." See *Overseas Expeditions from India*, Vol. VI, Appendix C, pp. 443, 444.)

shape, the fort was almost square, with sides about 200 yards in length, and in the centre an enormous earthen mound carrying large brass guns. The walls were surrounded by three wet ditches, the outer one broad and shallow and the inner ones each about 24 feet wide and 6 feet deep, with the intervening spaces and the berm covered with abattis, sharpened stakes and iron spikes. Alarm bells were concealed in the abattis. The surrounding country was intersected by canals and ditches, and the river entrance obstructed by rows of booms, hawsers, piles and stakes. Altogether, the Chinese had excelled themselves in preparations for a passive defence, and the first problem confronting Hope Grant was how to approach within striking distance. With this object in view, the engineer units were employed, during August 18th and most of the 19th, in preparing small bridges to carry the artillery over the canals and ditches and to enable the troops to advance on a broad front. After dark, these bridges were placed in position by a party of Madras Sappers under Dakeyne and Filgate, while others dammed the source of the water-supply to the canals. On the 20th, Trail and Lieutenant F. Hime, R.E., traced the positions for five batteries selected by Napier, and Swanston, Dakeyne and Foord, with two Sapper companies, dug three of the batteries during the ensuing night. These works were armed with some of the heavy guns which had just begun to arrive at the front. Meanwhile, the Royal Engineer companies and French engineers were bridging the Paiho with local boats at a spot near the 1st Division camp where the width was about 270 yards.

The assault on the north-western Taku Fort was launched on August 21st, 1860, by 2,500 British and 1,000 French after the Chinese artillery had been silenced and one of their magazines exploded. The 1st Division was in reserve, and the 44th and 67th Regiments of the 2nd Division led the assault, closely followed by the Madras Sappers. The latter, who were detailed to accompany the stormers, were formed into four sub-divisions—a pontoon party under Lieutenant (afterwards Lieut.-General Sir Gordon) Pritchard, R.E., a ladder party under Lieutenant Hime, R.E., an obstacle party under Lieutenant Trail, M.E., and an explosion party under Lieutenant F. W. R. Clements, R.E.[1] To cross the succession of ditches and obstacles was a most arduous and dangerous task, especially as the defenders threw missiles of all sorts including round-shot and pots filled with lime. According to Pritchard,[2] "A" and "K" Companies and the 23rd Company, R.E., paraded before dawn in front of the supports with escalading ladders joined together and mounted on wheels to form bridges. "The attack commenced soon after 6 a.m.," he writes. "The English pontoon bridge, carried by Royal Marines, was met by so heavy a fire that half the carriers were disabled and construction rendered impracticable.

[1] "Sieges and Defence of Fortified Places. The War in China, 1860; Capture of Pekin," by Col. Sir E. T. Thackeray, V.C., K.C.B., late R.E., appearing in *The R.E. Journal*, Vol. XXII, July–Dec., 1915, pp. 257–264. Also "Reports on the Taking of the Forts on the Peiho and the Advance on Pekin in 1860," by Lieut.-Col. G. F. Mann, R.E., appearing in *Professional Papers of the Corps of Royal Engineers*, New Series, Vol. XI (1862), pp. 1–11.

[2] Extracts from a letter by Lieut. G. P. Pritchard, R.E., quoted in "Deeds of the Royal Engineers," appearing in *The R.E. Journal*, Vol. XXV, Jan.–June, 1917, pp. 201–214.

Sir Robert Napier asked if I could cross the ditch with escalading ladders alone. . . . I placed the ladders across the wet ditches, and the Sappers, jumping into the bottom of the ditch, supported the ladders in the centre by holding their hands over their heads. The men were up to their armpits in water. Then, with our bamboo ladders, we ran along the rungs of the escalading ladders, crossed the ditch, and entered the fort. Sir R. Napier afterwards said to me 'Well done, Pritchard! This is the first time I have seen a bridge with living piers.' The French, on our right, succeeded in crossing by means of their ladder bridges. At 8.30 a.m., this fort, the key of the whole position, was in our hands."

There are certain discrepancies in the various accounts of the storming of the north-western Taku Fort. For instance, Sir Hope Grant writes as follows in his official report:—[1]" A detachment of Royal Marines carried a pontoon bridge for crossing the wet ditches, and Major G. Graham, R.E.,[2] conducted the attack. The French pushed on to the salient next the river, crossed the ditch and established themselves on the berm from whence they endeavoured to escalade the walls. This, however, they were unable to effect. The efforts of the Sappers to lay down the pontoon bridge were unavailing, no less than fifteen of the men carrying it being knocked over in one instant and one of the pontoons destroyed. At this juncture, Sir R. Napier caused two howitzers to be brought to within fifty yards of the gate to create a breach, where our storming party, joined by the 67th which had crossed partly by the French bridge and partly swum over, forced their way in by single file. At the same time, the French effected their entrance. The ground inside the fort was literally strewn with the enemy's dead and wounded."

In his private journal, however, Sir Hope Grant remarks:—[3] "Our marines now brought up the pontoons to form a bridge, but sixteen of them were knocked over. The French were more successful. By means of scaling-ladders carried by Chinese coolies, they constructed a way across the ditch. The Chinamen jumped into the water up to their necks and supported the ladders upon their hands and shoulders to enable the men to get across. . . . At last my A.D.C., Anson, succeeded in clambering across to a drawbridge which had been hauled up, and with his sword cut the supporting ropes. In this operation he was nobly aided by Lieut.-Colonel Mann of the Royal Engineers. The bridge fell and afforded our men a means of crossing." It would appear that the Marines acted as carriers for the Sapper pontoon party under Pritchard, and that the Sappers who leapt into the water to form the living piers which so much impressed Napier were imitating the example of the Chinese coolies in the adjacent French assault. Filgate was praised for making a causeway under heavy fire across a canal outside the fort, and Trail for being one of the first men to enter the place. Napier himself had his field glass shot out

[1]Despatch from Sir Hope Grant dated Aug. 24th, 1860, included in *Incidents in the China War of* 1860, by Capt. H. Knollys, pp. 253–257.
[2]Afterwards Gen. Sir Gerald Graham, V.C., G.C.B., G.C.M.G.
[3]*Incidents in the China War of* 1860, by Capt. H. Knollys, pp. 87, 88.

of his hand, his sword hilt broken, three bullets through his coat and another in his boot.[1]

The north-western Taku Fort having been taken, Hope Grant advanced on the north-eastern fort, 1,000 yards distant, at the entrance to the Paiho. This was surrendered without resistance, and afterwards also the two forts on the southern bank and a fortified post near them. The construction of these works was very peculiar. The walls consisted of massive piles interlaced with straw ropes and covered with rammed layers of stiff clay, and each enclosure had one or more raised battery positions on mounds within it. After the 1st Division had started for Tientsin on August 30th, followed by the 2nd Division on September 1st, a detachment of "K" Company under Foord remained at the mouth of the Paiho to demolish the southern forts under the direction of Trail while the French dealt with those on the northern bank. Thereafter, mining and demolition proceeded steadily until the conclusion of peace.[2] Hope Grant occupied Tientsin and started for Peiping as soon as the weather permitted, while "A" Company, Madras S. & M., rejoined the 2nd Division which was detailed to remain temporarily in garrison at Tientsin. Passing through Yangtsun, the 1st Division reached Hosiwu on September 16th, and two days later, in company with the French, drove 30,000 Chinese from a strong position outside Changkiawan. This victory was followed by another on September 21st at Palichow, some five miles beyond Changkiawan, where 70,000 Chinese were routed and pursued towards Peiping. No Madras Sappers and Miners were present at Changkiawan, and the only representative of the Corps at Palichow was Shaw-Stewart himself who had joined the army ahead of his men. Tungchow fell in due course and became a base for the final advance on the capital. The siege train having arrived on pontoon rafts on October 6th, escorted by "A" Company with Dakeyne, Swanston and Filgate, the allied armies moved round the north-eastern corner of Peiping, in almost unbearable heat, the British to occupy a large suburb north of the city and the French to bivouac in the gardens of the magnificent Summer Palace to the west. Three days later, an ultimatum was presented to Prince Kung, in the absence of the Emperor, requiring the surrender on October 13th of the Anting Gate of the city, but meanwhile the Engineer Brigade constructed breaching batteries near the north-east angle in case the demand was refused. However, at the last moment the gate was thrown open and the allied troops marched in. As the Chinese had murdered, or treated with most revolting barbarity, many of the British and French subjects in their hands, Hope Grant decided to retaliate by destroying the Summer Palace. This was taken in hand by the engineer units on October 18th, and by the evening of the following day the palace buildings lay in smoking ruins.

The Madras Sappers and Miners took little part in the final military operations of the Second China War because the 2nd Division, to which

[1]Obituary Notice of Field Marshal Lord Napier of Magdala appearing in *The R.E. Journal*, Vol. XX, 1890, p. 65.

[2]*Military History of the Madras Engineers and Pioneers*, by Major H. M. Vibart, R.(M.)E., Vol. II, p. 429.

they were normally attached, was holding the line of communication from Tientsin. Lord Elgin, afterwards Governor-General of India, entered Peiping in state on October 24th, 1860, to sign a Treaty of Peking which was in most respects a ratification of the treaty concluded at Tientsin in 1858.[1] On November 7th, " A " Company, Madras S. & M., left Peiping with the 2nd Division and five days later they were in Tientsin. The weather had become bitterly cold, with a north wind, hail and snow. Gunboats took them down the Paiho, and, joined by " K " Company, they boarded the transport *Statesman* at the mouth of the river. On November 17th, *en route* for Hong Kong, they watched the China coast sink below the horizon. As the Governor of Madras remarked, on their return to their native land, they had well sustained the ancient reputation of their Corps. Their services in China were recognized by the award of the honours " Taku Forts " and " Pekin, 1860."[2]

On the whole it may be said that the Second China War was a well planned and well executed undertaking. No mistake occurred to mar its general outline, and in the short space of three months the enemy were defeated thrice, their strongest forts taken and their capital occupied. The cost was great, but the ultimate return still greater, for the British secured complete freedom of action for their merchants, and respect and protection for all their subjects resident in the Far East.

[1]The convention of 1860 included the installation of a British Ambassador at Peiping, the payment of an indemnity of eight million taels, and the cession of territory on the mainland opposite Hong Kong.

[2]In addition, the services of Capt. Shaw-Stewart, M.E., were recognized on Feb. 15th, 1861, by the award of a Brevet-Majority.

CHAPTER VIII

THE INDIAN MUTINY: ROORKEE, MEERUT AND DELHI, 1857

THIS is a story, not of the Indian Mutiny as a whole, but of the part played by the Bengal Sappers and Miners in the events which culminated in the recapture of Delhi in September, 1857. The history of the disaster which tore the Bengal Army to shreds and gave the death blow to the East India Company has appeared in scores of books and hundreds of official reports, and the engineering operations and the exploits of individual engineers have been outlined in *The Military Engineer in India*. Some space is devoted in Volume I of that work to the experiences at Roorkee, Meerut and Delhi of the Bengal Sappers and Miners, and to the assistance given at Delhi by certain irregular formations recruited from the Punjab; but much remains to be told, and accordingly an attempt will be made to describe in greater detail how and to what extent the Mutiny affected the Bengal Corps, and how some of the men remained true to their salt, and by their heroism and endurance, redeemed the misguided actions of their mutinous comrades.

In May, 1857, the Bengal Sappers and Miners consisted of 12 companies with an establishment of 16 British officers, 23 Indian officers and 1,279 Indian other ranks.[1] The Corps had been commanded for eleven months by Captain Edward Fraser, with Lieutenant F. R. Maunsell as Adjutant and Lieutenant M. G. Geneste as Interpreter and Quartermaster. At the headquarters in Roorkee were the 1st Company (2nd Lieut. A. McNeile), 2nd Company (2nd Lieut. D. Ward), 3rd Company (2nd Lieut. H. A. L. Carnegie), 4th Company (2nd Lieut. W. F. Fulford), 7th Company (2nd Lieut. F. L. Tandy), 8th Company (probably 2nd Lieut. R. C. B. Pemberton with 2nd Lieut. W. Jeffreys), 9th Company (probably 2nd Lieut. E. Jones), 10th Company (2nd Lieut. E. T. Thackeray), 11th (Pontonier) Company (2nd Lieut. J. G. Forbes) and 12th (Pontonier) Company (2nd Lieut. G. Newmarch). At Attock was the 5th Company (2nd Lieut. P. Murray), and at Peshawar the 6th Company (2nd Lieut. E. W. Humphry).[2] All these officers were Bengal Engineers, for the last representative of the Bengal Infantry had recently reverted to regimental

[1]The establishment of Indian ranks comprised 12 Subadars, 11 Jemadars, 39 Havildars, 89 Naiks, 23 Buglers and 1,128 Sepoys. Total 1,302. (See *History and Digest of Service of the 1st K.G.O. Sappers and Miners*, p. 25.)

[2]The Corps records of this period are very incomplete, but the names of the Company Commanders have been decided after a careful examination of the Corps Orders from Oct. 19th, 1856, to May 12th, 1857, contained in a file at Roorkee. The establishments of the 5th and 6th Companies were as follows:—*5th Company*, 1 Subadar, 3 Havildars, 4 Naiks, 20 Buglers and 70 Sepoys. Total 80. *6th Company*, 1 Subadar, 1 Jemadar, 4 Havildars, 7 Naiks, 3 Buglers and 99 Sepoys. Total 114.

employment.[1] Some 50 British non-commissioned officers or privates were attached to the Corps as instructors.

The list of officers is most surprising. At the head of 1,318 soldiers was a Captain of less than 13 years' service though with considerable experience in the field.[2] His Adjutant was a subaltern of 11 years' service who had fought in the 2nd Sikh War; but his Quartermaster, a subaltern of 6 years' service, had had no war experience. And what of the remainder? Not another officer had more than 4 years' service and several had only recently arrived from Chatham. For instance, Jones reported his arrival on February 15th, 1857, when he was ordered to "make himself acquainted with the duties of Orderly Officer," and Carnegie, Thackeray and Forbes did not appear on the scene until March 3rd within eleven weeks of the beginning of the mutiny. The services of 2nd Lieutenant J. U. Champain, B.E.,[3] happened to be available in Roorkee because he had joined the staff of the Thomason Civil Engineering College as Acting Assistant Principal[4] under Captain R. Maclagan, R.E., on December 15th, 1856, after handing over the command of the 11th Company. However excellent these young officers might be, they must have been sadly handicapped by lack of experience. They had to rely on Fraser, Maunsell, Geneste and the senior British non-commissioned officers for guidance in matters affecting the religious or caste prejudices of their men. They required the services of Geneste as "Interpreter." They had been too short a time in the country to know their men and to recognize the first signs of an undercurrent of discontent. To these facts may be attributed to some extent the depredations effected by the Indian Mutiny in the ranks of the Bengal Sappers and Miners. The fault lay in the absurd system of attempting, through reasons of economy, to carry on the administration of the Corps in time of peace with a regimental staff of only three qualified officers assisted by a dozen inexperienced youngsters.

Caused partly by suspicions that defilement would ensue from the use of the Government cartridges and flour, the unrest in the Bengal Army spread up-country and culminated in a serious mutiny at Meerut on Sunday, May 10th, 1857, when the 3rd Light Cavalry galloped to the gaol and released 1,200 prisoners, among whom were some of their comrades who had been manacled and severely sentenced for refusal to obey orders. Two regiments of Bengal infantry then broke loose in the cantonment, murdering Europeans and burning houses in company with the riff-raff of the bazaar. The British garrison prepared for action, but the 3rd Light Cavalry escaped towards Delhi and, reaching that city early on the 11th, proceeded to repeat on a larger scale the atrocities of Meerut. The terrible news was telegraphed to the Punjab. The Indian regiments at Delhi rose and murdered their British officers, and a general massacre of Europeans

[1]Lieut. F. Staples, 58th B.N.I., reverted on March 8th, 1857, after bringing to Roorkee, from the Punjab, the 7th, 8th and 9th Companies. This movement was sanctioned on Dec. 11th, 1856, and the units arrived on March 3rd, 1857.

[2]Capt. E. Fraser, B.E., had served in both the Sikh Wars and in the 2nd Burma War.

[3]Afterwards Col. Sir J. U. Bateman-Champain, K.C.M.G.

[4]The Assistant Principal, Lieut. G. T. Chesney, B.E., was absent at Ambala and proceeded thence to Delhi.

followed. In the confusion, however, a party of twelve men and women, including Lieutenant Philip Salkeld, B.E., escaped from the Main Guard near the Kashmir Gate and arrived at Meerut a week later, starved, exhausted and almost naked. These were some of the early events of which, for a time, the Sappers in Roorkee remained blissfully unaware. All was peace and quiet in the little station on the left bank of the Ganges Canal. The Corps Orders of May 11th contained no hint of the coming storm. Newmarch was detailed in the ordinary way for duty as Orderly officer for the 12th. Jones, Forbes and Carnegie were enjoying themselves on leave at Mussoorie,[1] and only eleven officers of the Corps were present in Roorkee.

Before daybreak on May 12th, a message was delivered to Captain Fraser, the Commandant, which contained most disturbing news and orders. "It was on the 12th at daybreak," writes Brevet-Major R. Baird Smith, B.E., Superintendent of Canals,[2] "that I received the intimation of the Meerut mutiny and massacre. When I went to the porch of my house to mount my horse for my morning ride I found Medlicott, our geological professor,[3] sitting there looking oppressed with some painful intelligence. He told me that, about an hour before, Fraser had received an 'express' from the General at Meerut[4] ordering him to proceed with the regiment by forced marches to that place as the native regiments were in open revolt and had left the cantonment with their arms. I immediately suggested the Ganges Canal route instead of forced marches, and as Fraser at once agreed, I had boats equal to the transport of 1,000 men ready within 6 hours, and the Corps, 713 strong, started the same afternoon and got to Meerut, 60 miles off, in about 24 hours. Just as they were starting, another express came to say that two companies were to be left for the protection of Roorkee, so that finally about 500 men moved. I sent off the same morning an express to the Commandant of the little Ghoorkhas at Deyrah to tell him I thought his Corps would be ordered down too, and begging him to march on Roorkee where I would have another fleet ready for him in a day or two. He came with his almond-eyed Tartars, in due course, and off they went too."

It seems that on May 14th, Major C. Reid, Commandant of the Sirmur Battalion of Gurkhas at Dehra Dun, had received orders to march to Meerut, and having been warned by Baird Smith, was able to start at once for Roorkee where 50 boats were available. Traversing the Mohan Pass, he reached the village of Kheri (28 miles) on the morning of the 15th.

[1]Fulford, Jones, Forbes and Carnegie had been granted 30 days' leave on April 28th, but Fulford was present in Roorkee on May 11th.

[2]Letter from Major Baird Smith to Mr. C. E. Norton, dated Roorkee, May 30th, 1857, included in an article entitled "Baird Smith Papers during the Indian Mutiny," appearing in *The R.E. Journal*, Vol. XIX, Jan.–June, 1914, pp. 231–259. The original Baird Smith Papers are in the R.E. Museum at Chatham. At the outbreak of the Mutiny, Major Baird Smith was Superintendent of Canals, North-West Province, with his headquarters in the Canal Foundry Workshops at Roorkee.

[3]Mr. H. B. Medlicott was Professor of Geology at the Thomason College, Roorkee.

[4]The message was sent by Major Waterfield, A.A.G. to Maj.-Gen. S. H. Hewitt, G.O.C. Meerut District. It may have been in the form of a telegram, but it is more probable that it was a letter carried by a mounted messenger as the mutineers always cut the telegraph wires.

There he received another message from Baird Smith telling of a Sapper mutiny at Meerut and urging him to hasten onwards to Roorkee to prevent a similar catastrophe at that place. Accordingly, he resumed his march, and before dawn on the 16th, when within 3 miles of Roorkee on the Saharanpur Road, he was handed yet another message from Baird Smith begging him to proceed direct to the point of embarkation below the Roorkee Bridge instead of to the cantonment by way of the Ganeshpur Bridge, as otherwise the Bengal Sappers might imagine that the march of the Gurkhas was a hostile movement against them and mutiny forthwith. Reid acted upon the suggestion. He pretended that he had lost his way and told the messenger to procure a guide from the nearest village to lead him straight to the boats, and thus he arrived and embarked his men without causing undue alarm, though some disloyal Sappers appeared near the boats and tried unsuccessfully to poison the minds of the Gurkhas before they embarked.[1] The wretched story of bone-dust having been mixed with the Government flour was circulating in the Sapper Lines, and there was a vague fear among the men remaining in Roorkee that the British intended to surprise, disarm and destroy them.

Another account of the first news of the Mutiny and the departure of most of the Bengal Sappers for Meerut comes from the pen of 2nd Lieutenant E. T. Thackeray. "At about 8 o'clock on the morning of May 12th," he writes,[2] "two or three of the officers were standing outside their quarters looking at a pony when Lieutenant Ward rode up and called out 'Have you heard the news? We are to march to Meerut this afternoon.' Shortly afterwards, a parade of the whole Corps was ordered. Nine officers,[3] 50 British non-commissioned officers[4] and 500 out of 700 sappers were put under orders to march. We marched down to the landing-stage and embarked at about 6 p.m. At this time, none of us, with the exception of the Commandant, were aware of the state of affairs at Meerut. We thought that a local riot had occurred, and we expected to be away for about a week. On the morning of the second day, we saw a European driving along the left bank of the canal in a buggy. He was, I think, an overseer in the Irrigation Department. We hailed him to ask the state of things at Meerut, but he did not stop. He shouted, 'They're cuttin' throats in Meerut like mad, and burnin' 'ouses' and drove on in the direction of Roorkee. On the afternoon of the 14th we disembarked from the boats and marched (next morning) to Meerut which was about 8 miles distant from the canal."

The first Corps Order issued by Fraser on receipt of the intelligence

[1] "Letters and Notes made during and since the Siege of Delhi in 1857," by Col. Charles Reid, C.B., appearing in the *Journal of the United Service Institution of India*, Vol. 34, 1905, pp. 265–289. See also *A History of the Sepoy War in India in* 1857–1858, by J. W. Kaye, Vol. III, p. 176, *Richard Baird Smith*, by Col. H. M. Vibart, p. 4, and *Biographical Notices of Officers of the Royal (Bengal) Engineers*, by Col. Sir E. T. Thackeray, V.C., K.C.B., p. 104.

[2] Extract from "Two Indian Campaigns," by Col. Sir E. T. Thackeray, V.C., K.C.B., appearing in "A Subaltern in the Indian Mutiny," in *The R.E. Journal*, Vol. XLIV, 1930, pp. 451, 452.

[3] Thackeray includes Assistant Surgeon Turnbull, who was in medical charge.

[4] Actually, the number of B.N.C.O.s was 45.

from Meerut was worded as follows:—[1] "Roorkee, Tuesday, 12th May, 1857. Agreeably to orders received from Divisional Head Quarters, the Corps will immediately proceed to Meerut, embarking at the Roorkee Cattle Ghat, where boats have been provided by the Canal Department. The whole of the available men of the Corps will parade for this purpose at 1 p.m. and be marched down to the Ghat. The following Guards will remain behind:—1 Native Officer, 1 Havildar, 2 Naiks, 40 Sepoys and 73 Recruits. . . . Mr. Conductor Smith will remain in charge of the Magazine. . . . All reports of the Detachment (at Roorkee) will be made to Lieutenant Drummond,[2] Superintendent, 1st Division, Ganges Canal." Subsequently, the movement of two companies was countermanded, but no written order by Fraser to that effect can be traced.

The Bengal Engineers who embarked with the Sappers and Miners on May 12th were Fraser, Maunsell, Geneste, McNeile, Ward, Tandy and Thackeray, and in addition, Champain from the Thomason College. Those who remained for a time with the two companies detailed to garrison Roorkee were Newmarch, Pemberton, Jeffreys and Fulford. Baird Smith states that only *six* companies embarked at 2 p.m. on the 12th,[3] but this must be incorrect unless some of these were composite units. Ten companies were stationed at Roorkee, and consequently *eight* companies must have started for Meerut. As the total strength of the whole Corps of twelve companies was 1,302 Indian ranks, it is remarkable that, before the detachment of two companies, only 713 men paraded out of a normal establishment of 1,085 in the ten companies at Roorkee; but it should be remembered that the leave season had started and that some men may have been in hospital or employed on work outside the station. A Corps Order of May 28th shows that representatives of the 1st, 3rd, 7th, 8th, 9th, 10th, 11th and 12th Companies were serving on that date in Meerut, but no order published at Meerut makes any mention of personnel of the 2nd and 4th Companies. The 5th and 6th Companies, as already indicated, were absent in the Northern Punjab. Accordingly, it is fair to assume that, on May 12th, Fraser paraded all the available officers and men of the ten Sapper and Miner companies at Roorkee, and that, when ordered at the last moment to leave two companies behind, he detailed the 2nd and 4th Companies to remain at Headquarters and formed the remaining eight companies into six units under McNeile, Ward, Tandy, Thackeray, Champain and Geneste, the last named acting as Company Commander in addition to his duties as Interpreter and Quartermaster. Maunsell, the Adjutant, would then be available as second-in-command, and the force (about 500 strong) would be adequately officered. As Fulford remained in Roorkee it is probable that his company (the 4th) did not move. Ward, on the other hand, left his company (the 2nd) in order to join the expedition to Meerut, and it seems that the command of that unit must have been

[1]The original order can be seen in the file at Roorkee entitled "Corps Orders, S. & M. Commenced 19th Oct., 1856. Finished 12th May, 1857."

[2]Lieut. Henry Drummond, B.E., an officer of 13 years' service who had served in the 1st Sikh and 2nd Burma Wars.

[3]"Baird Smith Papers" in *The R.E. Journal*, Vol. XIX, Jan.–June, 1914, p. 238.

taken over by Pemberton, assisted by Jeffreys.[1] Newmarch, as Orderly Officer on May 12th, could not leave the station; but he lost no time in following the eight companies to Meerut for he was on duty there on the 17th.[2] It is hoped that these remarks may throw some light on the difficult problem of the two "missing" companies of Bengal Sappers after the outbreak of the Indian Mutiny.

Before dealing with the tragic events at Meerut which followed the arrival of Fraser and his men, it will be convenient to describe the steps taken in Roorkee to safeguard the small European community and allay the suspicions and fears of the Bengal Sappers remaining in the station. Baird Smith, though not yet in military command, assumed charge, and with the assistance of Lieutenant G. Baillie of the Bengal Artillery, began to prepare mountings for some old Sikh guns which he had in the Canal Foundry Workshops. During the night of May 13th–14th, one of the barracks occupied by 30 British soldier students of the Thomason College was set on fire, and although the Sappers and Miners came from their lines and helped cheerfully to subdue the flames, there could be little doubt that some of them had been guilty of incendiarism. In consequence, Baird Smith arranged that the station should be patrolled at night by a party of British officers and that an armed guard of soldier students should be mounted at the Canal Foundry Workshops, which he selected as a place of refuge. On the 15th, he was ordered to assume military command and to despatch to a concentration of troops at Ambala one of the two Sapper companies at Roorkee, together with an Engineer Park. While this movement was being arranged, it became advisable to collect ammunition for the defence of the Workshops. In the magazine of the Sapper lines were 200 stands of spare arms, quantities of ammunition and 211 barrels of powder; but the removal of these munitions to the Canal Foundry Workshops, under the eyes of the Sappers and Miners, was an undertaking requiring the greatest tact. As a first step, Baird Smith sent Drummond and Lieutenant H. Bingham, a veteran instructor of the Thomason College,[3] to take up their quarters in the Sapper lines, hoping that, as both these officers had served in the Corps and were respected by the men, their presence would help to prevent trouble. After Drummond and Bingham had moved to the lines, carts were sent to Conductor James Smith, in charge of the magazine, with orders that the arms, ammunition and powder should be loaded into them. The first set of carts was loaded and despatched without difficulty, a few Sappers looking on unconcernedly; but when the loading of a second set was begun, numbers of the

[1]2nd Lieut. W. Jeffreys, B.E., had actually been struck off the strength of the Corps. Under a Corps Order, dated May 11th, he was appointed to the Department of Public Works and directed to make over charge of his company to Lieut. Geneste. This order never came into effect, but the fact that it was issued on the day *following* the mutiny at Meerut shows the unexpected nature of the news received on the 12th.

[2]Corps Orders, dated May 17th, 1857, appearing in the file at Roorkee entitled "Corps Orders, Delhi. From 15th May, 1857, to 8th August, 1857."

[3]Lieut. Bingham was headmaster of the military and civil subordinate students at the Thomason College, working under Capt. R. Maclagan, B.E., as Principal. He had served for 20 years with the Bengal Sappers and Miners as a non-commissioned or warrant officer.

men rushed excitedly from their barracks and stopped the work. The carts remained outside the quarterguard, near the magazine, until the following day, when the Sappers allowed them to proceed to the Workshops after Baird Smith had visited the lines and discussed the matter amicably with them.[1]

Owing to news of the massacres at Delhi, and to the uncertain attitude of the Sappers in Roorkee and the presence of marauding bands around the place, Baird Smith collected the entire European community in the Canal Foundry Workshops on the evening of May 16th. Besides Eurasian women and children, the little gathering included the wives of six British officers or non-commissioned officers and their five children. For defence purposes there were available the 30 soldier students and perhaps 60 clerks or other civil employees who were fit to bear arms. At Maclagan's suggestion, the Sappers and Miners were placed in charge of the empty College buildings, and Baird Smith explained to them that he relied on their loyalty for the protection also of the whole cantonment. A Sapper guard under Fulford was stationed in the entrance hall of the College. It might be thought that these signs of trust and confidence would have quieted and pacified the men; but the fact that they flew to their arms on the first approach of the European night patrol showed that they were still in a very excitable state. Baird Smith kept them under close observation, and as a precautionary measure, mounted the old Sikh guns to sweep the roads leading to the Workshops.

May 18th was a day of intense anxiety. About noon a sepoy of the Corps arrived in the Sapper lines from Meerut. His coming was followed by great agitation among the men and much lamentation by the women. He had told the men that their comrades at Meerut had been trapped by the British and utterly destroyed by artillery fire. When this rumour was reported to Baird Smith by Drummond and Bingham he gave them a letter from Maunsell, written on the 16th, in which no mention was made of any such catastrophe and instructed them to return to the Sapper lines and translate it to the men, which they accordingly did. The Sappers appeared to be to some extent reassured; but it was evident that a crisis was approaching and that at any moment a general mutiny might occur.

While Drummond and Bingham were arguing with the men of the 4th Company and other details remaining in Roorkee—about 190 in all—Pemberton and Jeffreys, with the 2nd Company and the Engineer Park, had reached the village of Sikandarpur, a few miles along the Saharanpur Road, on their way to join the Commander-in-Chief's force then assembling at Ambala for an advance on Delhi in conjunction with a column from Meerut. There they were overtaken by the same messenger who had spread alarm in Roorkee, and the men of the 2nd Company insisted on returning at once to Headquarters. Protests by Pemberton having proved

[1] "Report of the Proceedings at Roorkee during the Disturbances of 1857 and 1858," by Lieut.-Col. R. Baird Smith, C.B., appearing in the "Baird Smith Papers," published in *The R.E. Journal*, Vol. XIX, Jan.-June, 1914, pp. 236–252. This report gives a detailed account of the events at Roorkee.

unavailing, the return march began after dark.[1] The men maintained a perfectly inoffensive demeanour towards the two British officers and the three non-commissioned officers with the detachment, but they were determined to have their own way. A mounted man carried the news of this latest complication to Baird Smith, who sent out a party to watch for the approach of the returning Sappers. If they intended to attack him they would probably march direct to the Roorkee Bridge over the Ganges Canal. Great was his relief when he learned at about midnight that the men had turned off the main road and were making for the Ganeshpur Bridge leading to their lines. Before reaching the lines, the mutinous Sappers advised Pemberton, Jeffreys and the British non-commissioned officers to join the other Europeans in the Workshops, and they did so. Drummond, Bingham and others in the Sapper lines had already proceeded to the Workshops on the advice of certain well-disposed native officers and men of the 4th Company, who escorted them as far as the College buildings to see that they came to no harm. It is presumed that Fulford was at this time in the Workshops with Maclagan and others of the College European staff. Every preparation was made to resist a sudden assault under cover of darkness. The men were at their posts on the walls: the women and children, congregated in the model room.

Then the situation changed dramatically. Before dawn on May 19th, a report reached Baird Smith that the Sappers and Miners were fleeing from their lines and making for the open country in the belief that the British were about to attack them. Their conduct confirmed Baird Smith in the opinion which he had already formed that their mutinous attitude was the result of fear rather than disaffection to the State, and he lost no time in sending a strong party of Europeans under Maclagan to clear the lines and re-establish order. Maclagan found only 50 sepoys and a few native officers in the lines.[2] The mutineers had decamped after maltreating their loyal comrades and were making their way to Delhi or across the Ganges towards Moradabad, where many of them were caught and disarmed. A few rejoined at Roorkee so that the eventual number in the Sapper lines rose to 2 Indian officers, 13 Indian non-commissioned officers and 69 sepoys and buglers. These men were reinforced, during May and June, by 40 others who had deserted at Meerut on May 16th after the Sapper mutiny at that place. Several who had been wounded in that affair made no attempt to conceal the fact when they were treated in the Roorkee Hospital. They did not regard their conduct in a serious light and seemed to have joined the rebel cause for the sake of excitement and possible plunder.[3] The growing establishment at Roorkee provided

[1]According to the *History and Digest of Service of the 1st K.G.O. Sappers and Miners*, p. 25, the strength of the company which countermarched from Sikandarpur was only 42 Indian ranks, including 2 Indian officers and 6 Indian N.C.O.s. The fact that this company was so much below strength supports the contention that Fraser probably amalgamated the other companies to form six units of suitable strength for the journey to Meerut.

[2]These included the 42 Indian ranks of the 2nd Company who had marched back with Pemberton and Jeffreys from Sikandarpur. The men in question served afterwards at the siege and capture of Delhi and the capture of Lucknow, and elsewhere in Oudh or Rohilkhand.

[3]*A Year's Campaigning in India*, by Capt. J. G. Medley, B.E., p. 140.

small drafts from time to time for the Engineer Department in the siege of Delhi and afterwards for the operations at Lucknow and elsewhere.[1]

Little remains to be told of the events at Roorkee. Fulford, Bingham and Conductor Smith left the station about May 26th with a small detachment of men of various companies and a supply of Engineer stores to join the force then marching from Meerut to Delhi. Baird Smith devoted himself to suppressing rebellion in the surrounding districts and strengthening the defences of the Canal Foundry Workshops. Maclagan produced a new periodical—*The Roorkee Garrison Gazette*—of which only 50 copies were ever printed. Pemberton commanded the loyal Bengal Sappers and Miners and participated, with a few infantry officers, in leading patrols as far afield as Muzaffarnagar. The *beldars* (diggers) of the Ganges Canal establishment had shown such an excellent spirit throughout the critical period that Baird Smith formed two companies from them, each 100 strong, and after arming one company with carbines and the other with spears, used them for police work. On June 27th, when he started for Delhi to take up the post of Chief Engineer of the besieging army, he was followed from Roorkee by a contingent of 600 unarmed *beldars* under Lieutenant H. A. Brownlow, B.E.,[2] escorting a large convoy of stores supplied by the Canal Foundry Workshops for the Engineer Park. Towards the end of August, Pemberton also left for Delhi. The command of the Sappers in Roorkee then devolved on Jeffreys until Baird Smith returned, a very sick man, on September 29th.[3] With his return, normal life was resumed in the little station. The training of recruits proceeded in the Sapper and Miner lines. The European community reoccupied their bungalows and tried to forget the dark days in the Canal Foundry Workshops.

We revert now to the afternoon of May 14th, 1857, when the main body of the Bengal Sappers and Miners, formed by Fraser and Maunsell into six units or companies under Geneste, NcNeile, Ward, Tandy, Thackeray and Champain, disembarked at Sardhana, on the left bank of the Ganges Canal some eight miles from Meerut, and prepared to march to that place. The journey downstream had involved much strenuous rowing and frequent repairing of canal-locks by Ward,[4] but the men were in good fettle though somewhat tired and rather anxious. At three o'clock in the morning they marched into Meerut where they were received in a manner that was utterly incomprehensible to them. They knew nothing of the recent rebellion, murder and arson except what they may

[1]According to the *History and Digest of Service of the 1st K.G.O. Sappers and Miners*, p. 25, the following Indian other ranks (deserters) rejoined at Roorkee during May and June from Meerut:— 4 Havildars, 6 Naiks, 1 Bugler, 29 Sepoys. Total 40. The following loyal ranks rejoined from leave, furlough or command:— 1 Subadar, 1 Jemadar, 3 Havildars, 1 Naik, 22 Sepoys. Total 28. A statement in the "Restoration of Battle Honours" file at Roorkee shows that the strength of the Corps at Roorkee on May 30th, 1857, was 56 Indian ranks.

[2]Lieut. H. A. Brownlow was Superintendent, Eastern Jumna Canal, and was stationed at Saharanpur.

[3]Baird Smith was suffering so acutely from scurvy and the effects of a wound that he was obliged after a few weeks to proceed to Mussoorie to recuperate.

[4]*Biographical Notices of the Royal (Bengal) Engineers*, by Col. Sir E. T. Thackeray, V.C., K.C.B., p. 253.

have gathered from the reply of the fugitive overseer on the canal bank, which many of them could not have understood. They were escorted into Meerut by the Carabineers and 60th Rifles and found the Artillery standing to their guns—a sinister reception. Then they remembered the corpses of natives which they had passed on their voyage down to Sardhana. Was this to be their fate also? They were unaware that the men had fallen victims to marauders of their own race and thought it must be the work of the British. For the most part loyal and veteran soldiers, they were bewildered and exasperated to be treated almost as criminals. It is well to view the situation as it must have appeared at the moment to the average man in the ranks. There may be extenuating circumstances even in mutiny, however deplorable the crime.

At dawn on May 15th, two of the Sapper companies were sent from their camp to the outskirts of Meerut, one under Thackeray to demolish walls alongside the Delhi Road in the northern part of the city and the other under Ward to dig trenches at another place. The remaining four companies were to parade in camp under Fraser himself. The European garrison had good reason to distrust all native troops, and this sentiment had its effect on Fraser. Although he had promised the Sappers that they should keep and guard their ammunition, he seems to have decided later that it would be safer to store it in a bomb-proof magazine, and accordingly he issued an order that this should be done. To remove the ammunition was equivalent to disarming the men. The Sappers objected strongly to the measure and resolved to resist it. Maunsell, the Adjutant, was aghast when he read the order, for he was fully aware of the temper of the men. He sent a note at once to Fraser to warn him of danger,[1] but the Commandant was adamant and nothing could shake his determination. The parade was held. Without offering any explanation, Fraser ordered the men to load the ammunition into some carts which had been provided. Protests from the men were met by an angry reply from Fraser and the loading began; but it was not until the carts had started to move away that the storm broke. An Afghan sentry with loaded carbine rushed forward and shot Fraser in the back. A gallant havildar tried to protect him and was killed also. Fire was opened on Maunsell, but he managed to escape unharmed. A general stampede to the open country followed. The mutinous Sappers were pursued by some Carabineers and a troop of Horse Artillery, and fifty were annihilated in a small wood among some sandhills where they made a stand. The remainder fled towards Delhi or made their way slowly back to Roorkee, where some of them rejoined the Corps.

"Yesterday was a day of fearful excitement," writes Brig.-General Archdale Wilson on May 17th.[2] "About 3 p.m. or a little later, the alarm was given that the Sappers had mutinied and were going off. I immediately sounded the assembly, sent for two Horse Artillery guns with a squadron

[1]This note was found subsequently in Fraser's pocket.

[2]Letter from Brig.-Gen. Archdale Wilson, dated Meerut, Sunday May 17th, 1857, in an article entitled "The Mutiny, Day by Day," appearing in the *Journal of the United Service Institution of India*, Vol. XLIX, 1920, pp. 272, 273.

of Carabineers to follow me, and sent on a party of the 3rd Cavalry to watch the fugitives. I went down to the Sapper lines and found they had shot Fraser, their Commanding Officer, and with the exception of about 150 who were employed on picquet and as a working party at another part of the cantonment, had run off with their arms. The guns having come up, followed by the Dragoons, I went after them. After a six mile ride, we came up with a party of fifty, posted in a small *tope*. The Dragoons could not get at them except by dismounting, but we at last destroyed every one of them. They had shot their Commanding Officer in a deliberate, cold-blooded manner, and I therefore neither offered nor gave quarter. The fellows fought manfully for their lives to the very last man. Yesterday morning, I would have trusted the Sappers as I would a European regiment. Today, I can trust no native regiment, not even the Goorkhas."

It cannot be too strongly asserted that this disastrous outbreak was the result of *panic* rather than treachery. Maunsell and every other officer in the Corps formed that opinion. Indeed, Maunsell was so convinced that the men were still loyal to the Government that he allowed two havildars to follow the fugitives to Delhi to induce those who had not been concerned in the murder of Fraser to return under a promise of pardon. Unhappily, the two volunteers were caught by mutineers who were strangers to them. One was allowed to go back to Meerut. The other—a brother of the gallant havildar who had tried to save Fraser—was condemned to death and tied to the mouth of a cannon, but he managed to escape during a sudden alarm and afterwards rejoined the Corps.

The rigid discipline of the Bengal Sappers is illustrated by the wording of the laconic order which was the sole announcement of the tragedy. It runs as follows :—[1] " Meerut, 15th May, 1857. *After Orders.* Captain Fraser, Engineers, having been murdered by a Sepoy of the Corps, is struck off the strength of the Corps from this date, and all reports will be made to Lieutenant and Adjutant F. R. Maunsell who has assumed command. 2nd Lieutenant J. U. Champain is appointed to act as Adjutant from this day." Thus wrote Maunsell shortly after witnessing a foul murder and narrowly escaping a similar fate.

During the morning of May 15th, as already stated, Thackeray, Quartermaster-Sergeant W. T. Stuart, 3 Sergeants and 90 men were engaged in the northern part of Meerut City in dismantling some walls alongside the Delhi Road. The men were in high spirits and laughed and joked with Thackeray and the other Europeans. Soon after three o'clock, however, the sound of bugles was heard from the direction of the cantonment, 1½ miles distant, and a native trooper of the 3rd Light Cavalry, fully armed, galloped along the road, shouting and pointing in the direction of Delhi. He told the Sappers that their comrades in the cantonment were being killed by the British and invited them to desert. " I turned to look towards the men," writes Thackeray,[2] " and saw that many of them had laid

[1]The order appears in the file at Roorkee entitled " Corps Orders, Delhi. From 15th May, 1857, to 8th August, 1857."

[2]Extracts from letters from 2nd Lieut. E. T. Thackeray, B.E., quoted in " A Subaltern in the Indian Mutiny," by Lieut.-Col. C. B. Thackeray, R.A., appearing in *The R.E. Journal*, Vol. XLIV, 1930, pp. 455, 456.

down their pickaxes and shovels and had run to the piles of muskets from which they commenced taking their arms. Before an order could be given, they were running along the road, following the trooper in the direction of Delhi. I ordered the bugler to sound the assembly, and by dint of threats and expostulation, and with the aid of the European sergeants, I succeeded in inducing 36 men to fall in. It is a wonder they did not shoot us. I ordered the little detachment to march to the lines, and before proceeding far we were joined by 28 men who at the first bugle call had been undecided. Others joined us, and I marched in fifty-four, thirty-six escaping, who were, I believe, afterwards killed. We met a troop of Carabineers. The officer told me that the rest of the men had fled, shooting poor Fraser. I saw the body of the havildar who had tried to save the Commandant. He was lying on his face on the ground, the back part of his head having been blown away by a shot from behind. Lieutenant David Ward had been sent out with a party of Sappers by Captain Fraser to execute some entrenching work on one side of the station. This party remained faithful and Lieutenant Ward brought them back to the lines, where they were disarmed."[1]

It seems that, on their arrival in the lines, the two detachments under Thackeray and Ward were formed up by Maunsell preparatory to being dismissed from parade in the ordinary way. At that moment Maunsell heard a shout " Look out, sir " from Quartermaster-Sergeant Stuart, and turning round, saw that one of the men was fingering his carbine. Instantly, he rapped out the order " Fours left. Quick March," and before the men realized the object of the manœuvre they were in the Artillery lines where the guns were in position and manned. They were then disarmed without resistance. Shortly afterwards, several Indian Officers of the Corps emerged from an adjacent building in which they had taken refuge when the other companies had mutinied and fled. They were profuse in their professions of loyalty and condemnation of the outbreak. It is satisfactory to record that the two detachments were afterwards rearmed and performed invaluable service on the march to Delhi and during the siege. Together, they formed the equivalent only of one strong company of 5 Indian officers and 124 Indian other ranks, to which 45 British non-commissioned officers and privates were attached.[2] This was all that was left of the Bengal Sappers and Miners who had marched into Meerut that morning 500 strong.

At sunset on May 17th, Edward Fraser was buried with military

[1]On the following morning some of these men asked to be allowed to go out to bury their comrades killed by the Carabineers after the murder of Fraser. Ward accompanied them, and they did him no harm in spite of the gruesome spectacle of their slaughtered brethren.

[2]According to the *History and Digest of Service of the 1st K.G.O. Sappers and Miners*, p. 25, the numbers were as follows :— 3 Subadars, 2 Jemadars, 6 Havildars, 7 Naiks, 3 Buglers and 108 Sepoys. Total 129. The Muster Roll of June 1st shows that the numbers of British N.C.O.s and privates were :— 1 Sergt.-Major (E. Ovens), 1 Q.M.S. (W. T. Stuart), 6 Sergeants, 16 1st-Corporals, 15 2nd-Corporals, and 6 Privates. Total 45. Among the N.C.O.s was Sergeant John Smith who had rejoined the Corps from the Department of Public Works on July 8th, 1856 ; and among the Privates, No. 400 Private Frank Burgess (alias Joshua Burgess Grierson) who had joined from England on Dec. 14th. Burgess was promoted to 2nd-Corporal on June 20th. Of these two, more anon.

honours in the cemetery behind St. John's Church. The officers and men of his Corps paraded at full strength at the Artillery Hospital and followed the coffin to the grave. A British firing party under a Captain was furnished by the 60th Rifles.[1] Fraser was the first officer of his Corps to fall in the Indian Mutiny. A memento of him—his mess-jacket—may be seen in the R.E. Museum at Chatham.

The British non-commissioned officers of the Sappers and Miners at Meerut were employed every night on picket duty in the churchyard and cemetery, and the Indian soldiers provided working parties day and night in various parts of the station. A typical Corps Order is that of May 18th:—"All available men to parade immediately for work under 2nd Lieut. Tandy to open the communication from No. 19 Compound, Artillery Lines, to the School of Instruction. Europeans will parade for picket duty, as last evening, at 5 p.m. under 2nd Lieut. McNeile. All available men to parade for work at 5 p.m. under 2nd Lieut. Tandy as in the morning." The number of British officers available for duty was increased on May 19th by the arrival of Jones, Forbes and Carnegie from the hills. Maunsell had then nine subalterns under his orders. Philip Salkeld, the Bengal Engineer who escaped from Delhi, was on duty in Meerut in charge of the defence of the School of Instruction, but he was not at that time attached to the Sappers and Miners. Night work was discontinued on May 21st, and thereafter half the men paraded for work at 6 a.m. and the other half at 1 p.m. By May 25th, the European garrison was securely entrenched and the civil population quiet. The Sappers and Miners were the only Indian troops in the place. The whirlwind of the Mutiny had passed onwards to Delhi.

General Sir George Anson, the Commander-in-Chief in India, now began his advance southwards from Ambala after ordering a column from Meerut, and a small siege train from Ludhiana, to meet him at Baghpat near Delhi. He marched to Karnal; but there he died of cholera, and the command of the force devolved on Major-General Sir Henry Barnard. The Meerut column was commanded by Brig.-General Archdale Wilson, who had succeeded Major-General Hewitt. It included all the Bengal Sappers and Miners with the exception of Assistant-Surgeon Turnbull, who was detailed to remain at Meerut in charge of the sick in hospital and the heavy kit of the Corps.[2] Parading at sunset on May 27th, the Sappers joined the other troops assembled behind the Artillery Barracks and formed up as baggage guards on either flank; and in this humble position, led by their Europeans, they marched with the column for Delhi. Once more, though still under suspicion, they were armed soldiers, and no men were more fully determined than they to wipe out the memory of their recent lapse.

[1]Station Order, Meerut, dated May 17th, 1857. The Burial Register of St. John's Cemetery records the interment of 31 victims of the Mutiny, but the graves of only 11 can now be distinguished. None of these bears the name of Capt. Fraser, B.E.

[2]Station Order, Meerut, dated May 21st, 1857. Under this Order, only 30 British N.C.O.s of the Sappers and Miners were to accompany the force marching to Delhi, but it appears that eventually all the N.C.O.s were allowed to go.

Reaching the bank of the Hindan River near Ghaziuddin-Nagar[1] on May 30th, Archdale Wilson found a body of mutineers from Delhi at a place where a suspension bridge spanned the shrunken stream. He camped near the river, and the Sappers took their share of protective duty by supplying a picket of 20 men and patrolling the left flank. Fourteen Engineer officers passed the morning in a single-fly tent in which the heat was so intense that they wrapped wet towels round their heads and sheltered them as well as they could under the only table they possessed. At three o'clock, the fight began. McNeile, Carnegie, Geneste, Thackeray, and 50 Sappers doubled for two miles under a burning sun and showers of grape. The mutineers were driven off but returned on the following day, when they were again repulsed. The Sappers were employed in making a sandbag battery and guarding the guns, and for the remainder of the halt on the Hindan they supplied a picket at the bridge-head.[2] Fulford arrived in camp on June 2nd with a small detachment from Roorkee and some Engineer stores. With him came Bingham of the Thomason College and the estimable and popular Conductor Smith, generally known as the "Miscreant." Salkeld had accompanied the column from Meerut and was now engaged in surveying the river bank with Jones of the Sappers.

On the evening of June 4th, the force marched north-westwards to join General Barnard's column at Alipur; but 10 Europeans, 20 sepoys and all the artisans of the Sappers remained behind under Salkeld to destroy the Hindan Bridge and then overtake the rear-guard. The rest marched with the baggage in front of the heavy guns. On June 7th, the Meerut and Ambala columns met, and at 3 a.m. on the 8th, Barnard advanced towards the enemy entrenched at Badli-ki-Serai, only 4 miles from Delhi. Champain, Ward and Fulford were with one of the columns of attack and McNeile, Carnegie and Thackeray with another. Each party had a Sapper detachment of 15 Europeans and 50 sepoys, and the remainder of the Corps under Maunsell accompanied the heavy artillery which had been reinforced from Ludhiana. The mutineers were routed with the loss of 13 guns. "Many of the enemy got inside a strong-walled sort of village and fired at our men" writes Thackeray.[3] "Our little party of Sappers burst open the doors and rushed in. We had orders to destroy all the villages on the way which had harboured the rebels. No quarter was given." Pushing on rapidly, Barnard reached and cleared the famous Delhi Ridge, behind which he camped after picketing the crest. There we may leave the remant of the Bengal Sappers and Miners for a time to describe briefly the steps taken in the Punjab to remedy the deficiency of Engineer troops for the siege of Delhi.

One of the first to realize that the wreck of the Bengal Sappers and

[1]Now Ghaziabad.

[2]Corps Order, Camp Ghazioodeen Nugger, June 2nd, 1857. The strength was 1 British officer and 10 British and 22 Indian other ranks by night, and 1 Indian officer and 33 Indian other ranks by day.

[3]Letter from 2nd Lieut. E. T. Thackeray, B.E., to Miss Henrietta Shakespear, dated Camp Delhi, June 20th, 1857, quoted in "A Subaltern in the Indian Mutiny," by Bt.-Col. C. B. Thackeray, R.A., appearing in *The R.E. Journal*, Vol. XLIV, 1930, pp. 462, 463.

Miners would create serious difficulties was Lieutenant J. G. Medley, B.E., then stationed at Dera Ghazi Khan on the Indus in charge of the defences of some frontier posts. During March, 1857, he had commanded a small unit of 58 "Punjab Sappers and Miners" in an expedition against the Buzdars inhabiting the hills to the north.[1] This unit was maintained by the Punjab Government as part of the Punjab Irregular Force ("Piffers") and as it was called the "1st Company" there may have been others of a similar nature. Early in June, Medley suggested to the Punjab Government that he should march with the company to join the Irregular Army then being raised by General Van Cortlandt, late of the Sikh service, in the Hissar District west of Delhi, and in reply he was ordered to send the company but to remain himself in Dera Ghazi Khan. It is not recorded whether the unit moved as directed, but shortly afterwards Medley wrote again and proposed that he should raise some new companies of Punjab Sappers of different castes, hoping that he would be allowed to take these to Delhi. Again he was disappointed, and several weeks elapsed before he was able to secure his transfer to the besieging army.[2]

It is probable that Medley's proposals, and others of a like nature, induced Mr. Robert Montgomery, the Judicial Commissioner at Lahore under Sir John Lawrence, to initiate the recruitment of men for service as Pioneers at Delhi. The Punjab Government had given employment on their roads and canals to a fierce, lawless but industrious people in an effort to uplift them from crime. These men were known as Mazbhi Sikhs, a portion of the depressed and outcaste tribes who had been admitted to Sikhism although they could never attain its full status. In 1850, a corps of Mazbhi Sikh Pioneers had been formed from such men as had served in the Sikh Army, and, after a somewhat chequered career, had come to rest at Madhopur, the growing headquarters of the Bari Doab Canal, where many of the original men, and a number of new recruits, were working in 1857 under the control of the Superintendent of Canals, Lieutenant J. H. Dyas, B.E. With the approval of Lawrence, Montgomery decided to use these Mazbhis as engineer soldiers, and on June 19th, 1857, he wrote the official letter which resulted eventually in the birth of the 24th Sikh Pioneers of the Punjab Irregular Force.[3] He ordered Dyas to call for 240 Mazbhi volunteers to be formed into three companies and to proceed at once to Delhi.[4] The volunteers were to be, if possible, men with previous military experience.[5] They were to be given an advance of one month's pay. Dyas was authorized to select a good officer from among his assis-

[1] *Campaigns on the North-West Frontier*, by Capt. H. L. Nevill, D.S.O., R.F.A., p. 38.

[2] *A Year's Campaigning in India*, by Capt. J. G. Medley, B.E., pp. 6 and 27.

[3] *The History of the Sikh Pioneers (23rd, 32nd, 34th)*, by Lieut.-Gen. Sir George MacMunn, K.C.B., K.C.S.I., D.S.O., Col.-Commandant, R.A., p. 19. The 24th Sikh Pioneers, P.I.F., became later the 32nd Sikh Pioneers, Bengal Army, and until 1933 were the 2/3rd Sikh Pioneers.

[4] The establishment of Indian ranks in each company was to be 1 Subadar, 1 Jemadar, 5 Havildars, 5 Naiks and 80 Sepoys.

[5] One hundred such men were obtained who had served under Ranjit Singh in the Sikh Army. See an article entitled "The Genesis of the 32nd Sikh Pioneers," by Col. H. R. Goulding, Indian Volunteer Forces, appearing in the *Journal of the United Service Institution of India*, Vol. XLIX, 1920, pp. 145–150.

tants; but he was informed at the same time that Lieutenant H. W. Gulliver, B.E., Executive Engineer at Amritsar, hoped that he would be chosen. In conclusion, Dyas was asked how soon the men would be ready to start and by what date they could reach Ludhiana. Montgomery added in a demi-official letter that the companies should be despatched, if possible, on the evening of the day after the receipt of the official letter, and that the selected commander should tell the men that they must reach Delhi in from ten to twelve days by covering thirty miles each night. Gulliver would be awaiting orders at Amritsar. The companies should march by way of Phillaur, where they would receive their arms and equipment.

Dyas acted with the greatest promptitude. He replied on the 20th that the Mazbhis would cross the Beas on June 23rd and arrive at Phillaur on the 25th. Then, assisted by Lieutenant D. C. Home, B.E., and Sergeant Robson, both of the Canal service, he enlisted the volunteers, and, as he and Home were unable to leave Madhopur, he arranged that Sergeant Robson should be placed in temporary command of the units. Robson marched with the three companies on June 21st and reached Phillaur five days later. There he handed over command to Gulliver, who had arrived with Ensign John Chalmers[1] as his Adjutant. The Mazbhis were then armed, equipped and drilled, and marching from Phillaur, arrived in Karnal on July 5th.[2] With 150 carts and 200 camels, they set out once more and finally reached Delhi on July 9th after a fight in which Sergeant Robson was wounded.

The three original units were soon reinforced by others, for Home had already been ordered to raise two more companies. " On July 3rd " writes Lieutenant A. M. Lang, B.E., from Lahore,[3] " an order came for Gustavinski[4] to take down 200 Mazbhi Sikhs to join the Sappers (at Delhi). I certainly don't envy him. I wouldn't go down in that way for anything." The two additional companies left Lahore under Ensign Gustavinski on July 11th, and, joined by Home, were armed at Phillaur and reached Delhi by forced marches on August 20th. The British officers appointed at one time or another to the " Punjab Sappers " (as the Mazbhi Sikh Pioneers came to be known) were Lieutenants H. W. Gulliver, D. C. Home and J. St. J. Hovenden, B.E., and temporary Ensigns J. Chalmers, L. T. K. Gustavinski, H. J. Nuthall, C. Anderson, T. Righy, J. Stevenson and F. Knowles, all of the Department of Public Works.[5] In addition, 27

[1]Mr. J. Chalmers, Assistant Engineer and Deputy Superintendent of Canals at Lahore, had been given a temporary commission.

[2]The strength of the three companies was then 2 British officers, 1 Sergeant, 16 Indian officers, 30 Indian N.C.O.s, and 240 Sepoys.

[3]" The Diary and Letters of Arthur Moffatt Lang, 1st Lieut. Bengal Engineers. India, 1857 to 1859," appearing in the *Journal of the Society for Army Historical Research*, Vol. IX, April, 1930, p. 87. Lieut. A. M. Lang, B.E., was officiating Executive Engineer, D.P.W., Lahore Division, and stationed at Mian Mir (now Lahore Cantonment).

[4]Mr. L. T. K. Gustavinski was a probationary Assistant Engineer on the Bari Doab Canal who was given a temporary commission as Ensign. Later, he obtained a commission in the 95th Foot and afterwards transferred to the Bengal Staff Corps.

[5]Messrs. Nuthall, Anderson and Righy were Assistant Engineers in the Irrigation Department under Baird Smith.

British non-commissioned officers were posted to the Corps, though only eight of these were serving with it at the end of the siege.

The engineer officers at Delhi had no great opinion of the Punjab Sappers, however useful their services might be when labour was scarce. Lang evidently considered that it was derogatory to march with them; and towards the end of the siege he wrote "The Punjab Sappers—raw, undisciplined dogs—trusting to the dark, the thick cover and scattered position, took to skulking from bullets and work by hiding in the grass. . . . It is a great bore having to instruct these raw Sikh recruits in the duties of sappers. However fine a corps the Punjab Sappers may be some day, they are undisciplined, stupid recruits now." Thackeray describes them as "wretched, low-caste men, enticed from their country by the hope of plunder to work on the construction of the batteries before Delhi."[1] He admits that they were good trench-diggers but maintains that they were useless for any more complicated work. The truth is that the bulk of these so-called Sappers had had no military training whatever. A few had fought in the Sikh wars: a few had accompanied Nicholson's Movable Column when John Nicholson was restoring order in the Punjab: but the remainder were mere *beldars* or road coolies, thrust into military service in an emergency. Nevertheless, they afterwards rendered good service at Lucknow, and without their help the remnant of the Bengal Sappers and Miners at Delhi would have been utterly incapable of coping with the fortification of the British position on the Ridge, the clearing of undergrowth, and the building of batteries for the siege and assault.

The Bengal Sappers had other and more humble helpers than the men from the Punjab. Writing in 1908, Major-General Warrand, a survivor of the Bengal Engineers at Delhi, remarks[2] that eventually the labour available for the works amounted to about 120 trained Bengal Sappers and Miners, 800 Punjab Sappers ("Mazbhi Pioneers") and a body of 1,000 labourers recruited locally on high pay by the Chief Engineer, Lieut.-Colonel Richard Baird Smith, B.E. Four additional companies of Punjab Sappers (two of Mazbhi Sikhs and two of Jat Sikhs) were recruited during August and were sent to Delhi in September to reinforce those commanded by Gulliver and Home. Warrand makes no mention of the 600 beldars, or "Roorkee Pioneers" as they may be called, who arrived under Henry Brownlow, though according to Miss A. C. Taylor[3] these were distinct from Baird Smith's 1,000 road coolies, who may be known, for convenience, as the "Delhi Pioneers." Also, Warrand omits to mention that the Punjab Sappers did not reach a strength of 800 until late in September, *after* the capture of Delhi. Both sets of Pioneers were unarmed

[1] "A Subaltern in the Indian Mutiny." (*The R.E. Journal*, Vol. XLV, 1931, p. 227.) It may be interesting to record that according to *Allen's Indian Mail* of April 28th, 1858, much ill-feeling developed in the Punjab Sappers after the siege and capture of Delhi owing to the recruitment of Jat Sikhs in addition to Mazbhi Sikhs. At Fatehgarh in 1858, the Jats, being of superior caste, petitioned that a space might be left between them and the Mazbhis on parade. This was refused, and in consequence 104 out of 130 Jat Sikhs took their discharge.

[2] "Reminiscences of the Siege of Delhi, 1857," by Maj.-Gen. W. E. Warrand, late R.E., appearing in *The R.E. Journal*, Vol. VII, Jan.–June, 1908, pp. 9–18.

[3] *Life of General Sir Alex Taylor*, by A. C. Taylor, Vol. I, p. 230.

and both were loyal and enduring. Of the Delhi Pioneers, Warrand writes:—" Their aid was invaluable in relieving the fighting men from digging in such fearful heat; and though without arms and untrained, they rendered the most essential service. In spite of many casualties, they worked cheerfully under fire. With the passive courage so common to natives, as man after man was knocked over, they would stop a moment, weep a little over their fallen friend, lay his body in a row along with the rest, and then work on as before."[1] These brave men, under one or two British officers and a number of British non-commissioned officers,[2] formed a solid support to the Bengal and Punjab Sappers.

Some description, however brief, must now be given of Delhi and its surroundings.[3] When General Barnard occupied the Ridge on June 8th, 1857, he established a chain of posts along the portion nearest to the city, a most difficult proceeding because the surface was rocky and there was little earth. On the right, towards Delhi, was " Hindu Rao's House " with an outpost at " Sammy House "; then in succession, the " Observatory," the " Mosque," and on the extreme left, " Flagstaff Tower." These were connected by a road along the crest. Between the Ridge and the Jumna were bungalows and walled gardens or waste areas covered with jungle and intersected by ravines leading to the river. More than half-way along one large ravine lay " Ludlow Castle," and at its outfall, the palace known as " Kudsia Bagh." On the river bank upstream of the Kudsia Bagh was " Metcalfe House," and downstream, closer to the city, the " Custom House." The fortifications of Delhi were about seven miles in circuit. The northern front, nearly one mile in length, extended from the Water Bastion near the river, past the Kashmir Bastion and Gate, to the Mori Bastion only a few hundred yards from the southern end of the Ridge. This front was the objective of the British attack. The western front ran from the Mori Bastion by the Kabul Gate, the Burn Bastion, the Lahore Gate and the Garstin Bastion to the Ajmer Gate, while the southern front stretched thence to the Jumna. At about the middle of the eastern or river front stood the King's Palace (Delhi Fort) with gigantic battlements enclosing many beautiful buildings, and from its north-east face projected the Salimgarh outwork overlooking a bridge of boats. The city wall averaged 16 feet in height and was surmounted by a loop-holed parapet and surrounded by a wide ditch. Major Robert Napier, B.E., had improved the defences only a few years earlier. The streets of Delhi were mostly narrow and winding. Near the Kashmir Gate was St. James' Church; and

[1]In his despatch, dated Delhi, Sept. 17th, 1857, Baird Smith adds the following tribute to the Pioneers:—" Under Lieut. Bingham they have proved to be a most useful and fearless body of men. Though designed for works only, and being unarmed and only rudely organized for the occasion, they have shown perfect readiness to work under fire and have taken their turn in the most exposed and dangerous positions it has been necessary to occupy."

[2]At the end of the siege, no less than 19 British N.C.O.s were serving with these corps of labourers. Mr. William Willcocks, a Conductor and acting Assistant Engineer, Irrigation Department, served as Adjutant of the Pioneers at Delhi under Lieut. Bingham as Commandant. He was the father of Sir William Willcocks, the famous engineer, and of General Sir James Willcocks, who commanded the Indian Corps in France in the Great War.

[3]See the Sketch Map entitled *Delhi in* 1857, included in this chapter.

between that edifice and the King's Palace, a College and a Magazine. Outside the Kabul Gate lay the suburbs of Kishanganj and Paharipur and the village of Sabzi Mandi, all close to the southern end of the Ridge. Some protection to the right and rear of the British position on the Ridge was afforded by the Delhi or Western Jumna Canal, and further back, by the Najafgarh Jhil drainage-channel which passed under an aqueduct of the canal and thence to the Jumna, though it was necessary for proper defence to destroy the bridges over these channels. Such were the circumstances in which, with less than 4,000 men and 55 guns, Barnard sat down in the terrific heat of June to besiege 9,000 trained soldiers, and as many more irregulars, supplied with twice as many guns and unlimited ammunition and occupying a stronghold which he could not encircle.

The cadre of Engineers, including that of the Sappers and Miners, consisted at first of only 18 officers under Major John Laughton, B.E., and the Engineer Brigade could muster no more than the remnants of the Bengal Sappers, formed into three small units or companies, each of 42 men, and supported by 450 unarmed Delhi Pioneers.[1] The available equipment was 600 *phaorahs*,[2] 300 pickaxes and some tools from the local bazaars, which furnished also the only engineering materials. However, with the arrival of the Punjab Sappers, and the Roorkee Pioneers with their Engineer Park, the situation improved. Captain Alexander Taylor, B.E., joined on June 28th, and the inexperienced Major Laughton returned to his Irrigation work in the Punjab on the following day. On July 3rd, Baird Smith arrived from Roorkee to become Chief Engineer in a cadre of 22 officers which rose in time to 32. He was only 38 years of age, and Taylor, his second-in-command, only 31. In addition to many of the officers already mentioned, Lieutenants W. W. H. Greathed, C. T Stewart, J. F. Tennant, E. Walker, G. T. Chesney, Aeneas Perkins and C. S. Thomason of the Bengal Engineers served at Delhi. Lieutenant J. T. Walker was the only representative of the Bombay Engineers. There were no Madras Engineers, nor Bombay or Madras Sappers and Miners. Baird Smith, Taylor, Greathed, Gulliver, Stewart, Maunsell and Home had served in the Sikh Wars, but none of the others had war experience and some had been engaged for years in building roads and digging canals. As these were obliged to study Pasley's *Siege Operations* before they could undertake the duties required of them, it is remarkable that they succeeded so well and made so few mistakes.

The Engineer Mess was in a small bungalow in the old cantonment below the Ridge. Some of the officers slept on the floor, others in the verandahs, others again on an old billiard table which was used during the day as a dining table. A small room was utilized by Maunsell as the head-quarter office of the Sappers and Miners when not too obstructed by

[1] *Two Indian Campaigns*, by Col. Sir E. T. Thackeray, V.C., K.C.B., late R.(B.)E. p. 23. It may be noted, however, that according to a detailed statement in the "Restoration of Battle Honours" file at Roorkee a total of 237 Indian ranks of the Bengal Sappers, of all companies except the 6th, were at Delhi on June 10th; but this total included only 2 men of the 2nd Company, 16 men of the 4th, and 6 men of the 5th Company. The authority is not given.

[2] Native digging implements.

sleeping officers. The heat was overpowering, the flies insatiable, and when the rains began, they brought with them fever, cholera and dysentery. "Everything is stagnant," wrote Hodson on September 5th[1] "except the hand of the destroying Angel of Sickness. We have 2,500 in hospital, of whom 1,100 are Europeans out of a total of 5,000." Yet the Engineers kept up their spirits. They played football and racquets, fished, bathed and even indulged in instrumental music, and at all times and in all circumstances they showed the indomitable courage and remarkable power of leadership which were their heritage.

There was nothing spectacular in the Sapper and Miner work at Delhi until the blowing in of the Kashmir Gate in the assault. Working parties of Bengal and Punjab Sappers, and Roorkee and Delhi Pioneers, went out daily to dig trenches, construct or repair batteries, clear undergrowth or demolish buildings and bridges. Others laboured in the Engineer Park, preparing fascines and gabions and all the varied paraphernalia of siege warfare. The full story of the daily tasks performed from June 8th to within ten days of the assault is recorded in Baird Smith's *Journal of the Siege Operations at Delhi in* 1857, the original of which is in the R.E. Museum at Chatham.[2]

No sooner had the posts along the Delhi Ridge been garrisoned on June 8th than hordes of mutineers poured from the city and attacked them, supported by artillery fire from the Mori and Kashmir Bastions. The Bengal Sappers were sent to superintend the building of two batteries ("Salkeld's" and "Wilson's") near Hindu Rao's House. These were enlarged, and another ("Maunsell's") added, and all three opened fire on June 11th after a second attack had been repulsed. On the 12th, the whole position was assaulted by the enemy and nearly captured, and on the 13th, another attempt was made. Far from besieging Delhi, the British were themselves besieged.

On the morning of June 12th, 60 Bengal Sappers under Geneste, who were working in the batteries on the Ridge, made a gallant charge and drove the mutineers away from their vicinity. Metcalfe House was occupied the same evening as an advanced post, and thereafter the Sappers and Pioneers were employed on defence work in that locality in addition to building and repairing batteries and cutting brushwood in the area between the house and the Ridge for the manufacture of fascines and gabions. A daring plan for a general assault on Delhi was prepared by Greathed, Chesney and Maunsell, but it was abandoned after the arrangements had been upset by a mistake by one of the units concerned. On June 15th, the enemy attacked the Ridge unsuccessfully for eight hours and afterwards began to erect a battery in Paharipur. However, they were cleared from that suburb by a sortie in the course of which a party of 40 Bengal Sappers under Fulford and Jones, with Perkins as Field Engineer, demolished the battery. This

[1]Lieut. W. S. R. Hodson, Bengal Cavalry, the founder of Hodson's Horse.

[2]A printed copy of Baird Smith's Journal, with a continuation to Sept. 23rd compiled from official documents, appears in a paper entitled "Journal of the Siege Operations against the Mutineers at Delhi in 1857," edited by Col. H. M. Vibart, which is included in *Professional Papers of the Corps of Royal Engineers*, Vol. 23, 1897, pp. 87–130.

episode drew attention to the dangerous situation on the right flank, and a new battery was traced near Hindu Rao's House to deal with reverse fire and sweep the ground towards the city. Not a spadeful of earth was procurable anywhere near the site, the soil being pure rock. The work was begun by the infantry; but on the night of June 18th–19th the infantry parties were reinforced by 30 Sappers and 150 Delhi Pioneers, and on the next night by smaller parties, and thus the battery was brought into action on the 22nd after the repulse of another attack.[1]

Attention was directed also to demolition work in rear of the British position. On the night of the 21st–22nd, a party of Bengal Sappers under Salkeld destroyed the bridge near the "General's Mound" carrying the Grand Trunk Road over the Najafgarh Jhil Drain, using 325 lbs. of powder in three charges, and on the following night Maunsell and Jones demolished two remaining bridges. Thus, when the rebels launched a general attack on the 24th, the rear of the position was safe and they were repulsed with very heavy loss. Forbes then began demolitions in Sabzi Mandi. Thackeray continued them, while Champain with 200 Delhi Pioneers commenced the construction of "Champain's Battery" on the Ridge. As the rebels were reported to be attempting to fill the ditch of the King's Palace with water from the Delhi Canal, Champain set out with 20 Sappers on June 27th to divert the flow. This he accomplished by cutting the canal bank above the Pulchadar Aqueduct and so allowing the water to fall into the Najafgarh Jhil Drain. Parties under Forbes, McNeile and Tandy prepared a defensible post in Sabzi Mandi, and on the 28th, the day on which Alexander Taylor arrived from the Punjab, Stewart attempted to blow up one arch of the empty aqueduct.

Demolitions continued steadily. On July 8th, five days after Baird Smith had become Chief Engineer, a Sapper and Pioneer party under Geneste and Champain, accompanied by Chesney, marched up the Najafgarh Jhil Drain with a small column and destroyed a distant bridge, and on the 9th a small party under Carnegie, with Stewart as Field Engineer, dismantled two bridges over the Delhi Canal while McNeile and Jones completed the demolition of the aqueduct. These numerous demolitions were a heavy strain on the small band of Bengal Sappers and their amateur assistants, the Delhi Pioneers. Then came Gulliver and his 300 Punjab Sappers, and Henry Brownlow and his 600 Roorkee Pioneers, and the scarcity of labour was eased. With the breaking of the monsoon on July 27th, all serious danger to the position on the Ridge was removed. Brig.-General Archdale Wilson was now in chief command as Major-General Barnard had died and his successor Major-General Reed had been invalided. Bingham had been appointed to command the Corps of Pioneers;[2] the size of the Sapper and Pioneer working parties had been

[1]As a recompense for working under fire, 3 annas a day working pay was authorized for all Sappers and Miners, and 2 annas for Pioneers, with effect from June 8th. This was sanctioned in a Field Force Order of June 24th.

[2]Corps Order dated July 11th, 1857. The Corps presumably included both the Roorkee and Delhi Pioneers. Ensign Henry Righy, though originally posted to the Punjab Sappers, was appointed to the Delhi Pioneers on Aug. 25th, 1857, and served under Bingham. On Dec. 8th, 1857, after the conclusion of the operations at Delhi, Bingham handed over the command of the Corps of Pioneers to Lieut. J. F. Tennant, B.E.

trebled or quadrupled; Gulliver and Fulford had dispelled fears that the rebels were mining under the picket at Metcalfe House; extensive clearances had been made in Sabzi Mandi; and unhappily, Jones had died, on the 24th, from wounds received on the 18th. These were some of the events during the latter half of July. The casualties among the British non-commissioned officers with the Sappers and Pioneers had been very heavy. Out of forty-five who left Roorkee on May 14th, ten had already died of disease, one had been killed and nine wounded, and of the remainder hardly any were really fit for duty. The officers had escaped more lightly, but nevertheless the Engineer Department was severely handicapped.

At the beginning of August, some attempts were made by the Engineers and Sappers to destroy the bridge of boats below the Salimgarh outwork by which rebel reinforcements were reaching Delhi from across the Jumna. "Yesterday afternoon," writes Lang on August 4th,[1] "I was on duty from three till sunset at the mouth of the Najafgarh Jhil cut constructing a heavy raft of big casks and trees for the destruction of the bridge of boats, but I am anything but sanguine as to the usefulness of it. We sent down two infernal machines[2] yesterday; one struck on an island and exploded in fine style; the second, I believe, reached the bridge but didn't explode." As regards this failure, Lang adds on August 8th:—"I am certain that our Khits[3] *and our Sappers* are in constant communication with the enemy. When the first infernal machine was started, none knew of the project but Engineer officers and a few Sappers. Yet on that day not a grass-cut[4] crossed the bridge. All were sent to forage on this side, and men evidently waited for these things and knew how to handle them." Now there may have been a few traitors among the Bengal Sappers and Miners still serving under Maunsell, but it is safe to say that the majority of the men were completely loyal. They ignored frequent taunts hurled at them during the rebel assaults and laboured to the end under the fire of rebel guns mounted by their former comrades. The men who had deserted at Roorkee and Meerut formed an invaluable addition to the mutineers for they constructed and repaired their defensive works. For instance, on one occasion after our artillery had dismounted the enemy's guns and demolished the face of a bastion, an assault was planned for the next morning; but at dawn the bastion appeared stronger than ever and heavier guns had been mounted on it. This was the work of the well-trained Bengal Sappers who had joined the mutineers.[5]

Brig.-General John Nicholson arrived on August 7th with his Movable Column and other reinforcements from the Punjab, raising the strength of the force before Delhi to more than 8,000 regulars and 3,000 irregulars.

[1] "The Diary and Letters of A. M. Lang, 1st Lieut., Bengal Engineers," appearing in the *Journal of the Society for Army Historical Research*, Vol. IX, 1930, p. 201. Lang had arrived in Delhi from Lahore on July 27th.

[2] Each fire-raft carried a barrel of powder in which a cocked pistol was buried so that any shock would fire the charge.

[3] *Khitmagars*. Indian servants who wait at table.

[4] Grass cutters. Men sent to cut grass for fodder.

[5] *The Campaign in India*, by Capt. G. F. Atkinson. Note relating to an illustration (No. 17) entitled "Sappers at Work in the Batteries."

New life was infused into the force, and Nicholson marched out and defeated a rebel army at Najafgarh on the 25th. The engineer working parties now consisted of as many as 60 Bengal or 150 Punjab Sappers, and 450 or more Pioneers. The batteries on the Ridge were connected by covered ways or trenches and the position became impregnable. Preparations were begun for the assault and capture of Delhi, which would be possible after the arrival of a great siege train then on its way from Ferozepore. Meanwhile, the Bengal Sappers under Maunsell received a small addition to their strength. It seems that permission had been given on May 16th to 2nd Lieutenant Patrick Murray, B.E., to march from Attock with one half of the 5th Company in order to join Nicholson's Movable Column, and this he did with 36 Indian ranks[1] who fought subsequently in two of Nicholson's actions against the rebels in the Punjab. On the arrival of the Movable Column at Ambala, however, the *Purbias*[2] of the Sapper half-company—about five-sixths of its strength—came under suspicion and were disarmed and sent back to Attock, so the unfortunate Murray reached Delhi on August 14th with only four Afghans and two Sikhs in charge of the entrenching tools of the detachment![3]

The Engineer Park, under Henry Brownlow[4] assisted by Conductor James Smith, soon became the scene of immense and unceasing activity, for the work of providing sufficient siege material was enormous. Large areas of the British camp presented the somewhat anomalous spectacle of an army engaged apparently in basket-making. The scale on which fascines as well as gabions were manufactured may be gathered from the fact that during the final operations no less than 1,500 camels were employed nightly to carry fascines to the sites of the siege batteries. Experiments were made in the Engineer Park in the erection of various types of batteries. Under the superintendence of the Bengal Sappers, the Punjab Sappers were trained in battery construction, laying gun-platforms, making field magazines and marching working parties on to their tools. The Pioneers were exercised in digging trenches. Dozens of gun-platforms and scores of scaling-ladders were manufactured in addition to 100,000 sandbags, 10,000 gabions and a similar number of fascines. Time-scales for the loading and unloading of carts and transport animals were prepared, and every conceivable arrangement made to avoid delay. "During the ten days preceding the assault," writes Brownlow,[5] I lived in my boots, eating and sleeping when and where I could, living on bread, milk, eggs, tea, quinine and chlorodyne, and doing as much work as I could with my *kamarband* pulled very tight round my poor stomach." By September

[1]*History and Digest of Service, 1st K.G.O. Sappers and Miners*, p. 25. The strength was 1 Subadar, 2 Havildars, 1 Naik, 1 Bugler and 31 Sepoys. Total 36.

[2]*Purbias*. Men from the *Purab* or East. In the Punjab, these were emigrants from Oudh or Rohilkhand and therefore likely to have friends among the rebels. The Purbias of the 5th Company served loyally in 1858 against the Yusufzais on the N.W. Frontier.

[3]"The Diary and Letters of A. M. Lang," appearing in the *Journal of the Society for Army Historical Research*, Vol. IX, 1930, p. 206.

[4]Lieut. P. Salkeld had handed over charge of the Engineer Park to Lieut. H. A. Brownlow on July 10th after the latter had arrived from Roorkee.

[5]Extract from Lieut. H. A. Brownlow's diary quoted in *Life of General Sir Alex Taylor*, Vol. I, p. 291.

1st, the supply of labour in the Engineer Park and elsewhere had improved greatly. Pemberton arrived from Roorkee, bringing with him a reinforcement of Bengal Sappers which, with previous small drafts, brought the Corps at Delhi up to a total strength of 21 Indian officers and 440 other ranks, formed into 8 small companies.[1] These, with at least 500 Punjab Sappers under Gulliver and Home and thrice that number of Pioneers under Bingham, formed a respectable Engineer Department, though many of the men were sick and incapable of heavy work.

The siege train having reached Delhi on September 4th, arrangements were made to put into operation a plan of attack evolved by Baird Smith and Taylor as a result of daring reconnaissances made by the latter in the area between the Ridge and the river. The front selected was the northern line between the Water Bastion and the Kashmir Gate, and as this was out of range from the Ridge, it was obvious that breaching batteries must be built to face it. The first step was to gain control of the ground on which the batteries would be located. On the night of September 5th–6th, Thackeray and some hundreds of Pioneers occupied the large ravine skirting the enclosure wall of Ludlow Castle and stocked it with sandbags for battery construction. The Castle itself was seized on the following night. Then, covered by some light batteries near Sammy House, Maunsell, Home, Medley and all the available Sappers and Pioneers began the construction of a powerful Battery No. 1, to the north of the Mori Bastion, to engage the enemy's guns on the city walls and cover the building of the breaching batteries nearer the river. This work was started during the afternoon of the 7th and continued with desperate energy throughout the night. "At three o'clock in the morning," writes Medley,[2] "the place presented a scene of awful confusion. Sappers, pioneers, artillerymen and infantry, all mixed up together with an inert mass of carts, guns and bullocks. Men and officers worked like horses. Nevertheless, with all our exertion we had only one gun ready for the Moree when day began to dawn, the other five platforms being still incomplete."

From dawn onwards, the Sappers and Pioneers and infantry working parties laboured under heavy fire; but although seventy men were killed during the next few hours, they enabled No. 1 Battery to fire its first salvo and, in the course of the morning, to silence the Mori Bastion. With No. 1 Battery in action, it was possible to begin the construction of the breaching batteries, Nos. 2, 3 and 4. Taylor, Greathed, Lang and Thackeray had already traced the two separate sections of No. 2 Battery near Ludlow Castle and, on the night of September 8th–9th, the Sappers and Pioneers began to dig the right section. No. 3 Battery, constructed by Home, was located inside an office building of the Custom House within 140 yards of the walls. The platforms were ready before dawn on the 10th,

[1]According to the Muster Roll of Sept. 1st, 1857, appearing in the file at Roorkee entitled "Corps Orders, Delhi. From 15th May, 1857, to 8th August, 1857," the 1st, 3rd, 4th, 7th, 8th, 9th, 10th, 11th and 12th Companies were present, and their combined strength was 21 Indian Officers, 34 Havildars, 68 Naiks, 3 Buglers and 335 Sepoys. Total 461 Indian ranks.

[2]*A Year's Campaigning in India*, by Capt. J. G. Medley, B.E., pp. 76, 77.

but the demolition of the masonry in front, and the mounting of the heavy guns, were attended with so many casualties that the battery did not open fire until the morning of the 12th. Meanwhile, Battery No. 4, to the north-west of the Kudsia Bagh, had come into action on the night of the 10th–11th, and Battery No. 2 followed suit on the 11th. A party of Bengal Sappers and Miners was afterwards posted to each battery for repair work.

The mutineers replied to the British dispositions by establishing an advanced battery near the Kabul Gate which enfiladed Batteries Nos. 1 and 2 with fearful effect. "At 1 p.m.," writes Lang on September 11th,[1] "I went with twelve Sappers and sixty Pioneers to No. 2 Right to make the traverses and epaulments longer. The enfilade fire from the right-rear was dreadful; the gun-wheels, carriages, trails, platform ribands and traverses were struck again and again. Six Sappers and I on the parapet got lots of grape plugged at us; all missed, but men in the batteries were hit." And on the 12th, he continues:—"We are worked to the very limit of human power. As I come into my tent after a night out, my eyes are closing themselves and my senses quite foolish! I fling myself down with the sun up and am too tired to sleep but restlessly. Again, in excited dreams, I set parties to work under a hot fire, howl at them, urge them on, grape pouring in, and guns drowning one's voice. We are fighting close up now, hurrying on the most rapid of sieges, working recklessly under fire without approaches or parallels. Our big, smashing guns roar out together in salvoes and crash into the crumbling walls."

On the evening of September 13th, several breaches could be seen, but it was not known whether they were practicable. The point was settled through daring reconnaissances undertaken by Lang, Medley, Greathed and Hovenden, and Brig.-General Archdale Wilson then decided to assault at daybreak on the 14th. All the Engineers fit for duty, except Baird Smith,[2] assembled at 2 a.m. in their little Mess behind the Ridge to study their orders and make their final preparations. There were to be four columns of attack and a reserve, each including about 1,000 regulars. The main attack on the left was allotted to Brig.-General John Nicholson, with Alexander Taylor to direct the assault. It was formed in two columns; No. 1 under Nicholson himself, with Taylor, Lang, Medley and Bingham (Pioneers), was to storm a breach in the Kashmir Bastion, while No. 2 under Brig.-General W. Jones, with Greathed, Hovenden, Pemberton and Gustavinski (Punjab Sappers), was to assault a breach in the Water Bastion near the river. Column No. 3 under Brig.-General G. Campbell, with Home, Salkeld, Tandy, Murray and Nuthall (Punjab Sappers), had orders to storm the Kashmir Gate after the Engineers had blown it in. Column No. 4 under Colonel C. Reid, with Maunsell and Tennant, was to help the cavalry to guard the right flank, and advancing from Hindu Rao's House through the suburbs, enter the city through the Kabul Gate. A con-

[1] "The Diary and Letters of A. M. Lang," appearing in the *Journal of the Society of Army Historical Research*, Vol. X, 1931, pp. 74, 75.

[2] Baird Smith had been wounded in the ankle on Aug. 12th and his health was bad, but nevertheless he was with Brig.-Gen. Archdale Wilson on the roof of Ludlow Castle during the assault.

tingent of 1,200 Kashmir irregulars was attached to this column. The Reserve under Brig.-General J. Longfield, with Brownlow, Thackeray and Ward, was directed to support the main attack. It was hoped that Columns Nos. 1 and 2 would be able to sweep westwards along the walls to the Kabul Gate, whence they would penetrate into the city with No. 4 Column by way of the Chandni Chauk and meet No. 3 Column at the great Jama Masjid. The Reserve would halt in the open space inside the Kashmir Gate. The plan was sound in conception, and at the beginning, it was faultless in execution. Only the failure of No. 4 Column to reach the Kabul Gate, a failure due to the cowardice of its irregulars, prevented Archdale Wilson from securing an overwhelming victory.

It will be noticed that there were few Sapper and Miner officers in the assault—none with No. 1 Column, only Pemberton with No. 2, Tandy and Murray with No. 3, Maunsell with No. 4, and Thackeray and Ward with the Reserve. No record seems to exist of the distribution of the Indian ranks of the Bengal and Punjab Sappers among the various columns, but Thackeray remarks that the Engineers were accompanied by Sappers with powder-bags when they paraded with their columns at 3 a.m. It is presumed, accordingly, that a strong party of Sappers, with powder-bags, scaling-ladders and tools, was attached to each column.[1] The Engineers were detailed to their columns in order of seniority without regard to their previous service, and as Geneste, Champain, Carnegie, Fulford, McNeile and Forbes were on the sick list, the cadre of Sapper and Miner officers was much depleted.[2]

Soon after dawn on Monday, September 14th, the British guns ceased fire and Nicholson gave the order to advance. Skirmishers ran forward, and instantly the walls of Delhi blazed with musketry. A detachment with ladders and powder bags then pushed on to demolish the Kashmir Gate. It was led by Home and Salkeld and consisted of 3 British non-commissioned officers, 14 Bengal Sappers, 10 Punjab Sappers and a British bugler. When the limit of cover had been reached, the actual Explosion Party, of all the Europeans and 8 Bengal Sappers, rushed in two small squads towards the gate. Duncan Home describes what followed :—[3] " Sergeants John Smith and Carmichael,[4] all the Sappers[5] and myself arrived at the Cashmere Gate untouched a short time in advance

[1]Lieut. Bingham, O.C. Pioneers, who was with No. 1 Column, was mentioned in despatches for bravery " in command of a party of Sappers in the assault."

[2]The following Bengal Engineers were also on the sick list :— Lieuts. C. T. Stewart, W. E. Warrand (severely wounded) and H. W. Gulliver, and 2nd Lieut. C. S. Thomason. Also Lieut. J. T. Walker of the Bombay Engineers (severely wounded). Out of a total of 936 officers and men in the Engineer Department, 214 were ineffective through sickness. Four officers and 40 men had been killed and 18 officers and 67 men wounded. (*Journal of the Siege Operations at Delhi in* 1857, by Lieut.-Col. R. Baird Smith, B.E.)

[3]Report by Lieut. D. C. Home, B.E., quoted in " A Subaltern in the Indian Mutiny," by Brevet-Col. C. B. Thackeray, R.A., appearing in *The R.E. Journal*, Vol. XLIV, 1931, pp. 604, 605. This report appears also as an Appendix to *The Royal* (*Bengal*) *Engineers*, by Col. Sir E. T. Thackeray, V.C., K.C.B., together with Baird Smith's order for the operation and his official report on it. A good description is given by Miss A. C. Taylor in her *Life of General Sir Alex Taylor*, G.C.B., R.E., Vol. II, pp. 13–17.

[4]Sergeant A. B. Carmichael had joined the Bengal Sappers and Miners at Delhi on Aug. 2nd, 1857, after employment on the Hindustan-Tibet Road beyond Simla.

[5]The Sappers of the leading party, four in number.

of the remainder of the party under Lieutenant Salkeld, having found the palisade gate on the outside of the ditch and the wicket of the Cashmere Gate open, and three planks of the bridge across the ditch removed. As Sergeant Carmichael was laying his powder bag (containing 25 lbs.) he was killed by a shot from the wicket. Havildar Mahdo was, I believe, also wounded about the same time. Lieutenant Salkeld, carrying the slow match to light the charge, now came up with a portion of the remainder of the party, and with a view to enable him to shield himself from the fire from the wicket which was very severe (and the advanced party having deposited the powder bags) I slipped down into the ditch. Lieutenant Salkeld being wounded in the leg from the wicket, handed over the match to Corporal Burgess, who was mortally wounded while completing the operation. Havildar Tillok was at the same time wounded while assisting Corporal Burgess into the ditch; Sepoy Rambeth (elsewhere Ram Heth) was also killed at the same time. As I was assisting Lieutenant Salkeld into the ditch I think he was wounded a second time. The charge having exploded blew in the right (proper right) leaf of the gate,[1] on which I caused the regimental call of the 52nd Regiment to be sounded as the signal for the advance of the storming party. I caused the bugler (Hawthorne) to sound the call three times, after which the column advanced to the storm and the gate was taken possession of by our troops."

The accounts of this heroic deed are to some extent conflicting, and the lists of the names of those who participated in it do not always agree. A memorial erected outside the Kashmir Gate in 1876 by Lord Napier of Magdala gives the names of the Explosion Party as Lieutenants Duncan Home and Philip Salkeld (mortally wounded), Sergeants John Smith and A. B. Carmichael (killed), Corporal F. Burgess (killed), Bugler Hawthorne, 52nd Foot, Subadar Toola Ram, Jemadar Bis Ram, Havildars Madhoo (wounded) and Tillok Singh (mortally wounded) and Sepoy Ram Heth (killed). On this memorial the name of Sepoy Jahub Singh, who was mentioned by Home for gallantry, does not appear. On the other hand, Jemadar Bis Ram, though named on the tablet, is not mentioned by Home, and the name of Sepoy (some say Havildar) Ajudhia Pershad Pathak,[2] who was present, is omitted altogether. The correct list of the Indian ranks, as given by the Commandant, K.G.O. Bengal Sappers and Miners, in 1932 is as follows:—Subadar Toola (Tula Ram), Jemadar Bis Ram, Jemadar Ramteroz (elsewhere Havildar Ramtaroy or Ramtarai or Ramdulari), Havildar Mahdoo (Madhoo), Havildar Tilok Singh (Tillok or Tiluk Singh), Havildar (elsewhere Naik) Harpal Singh, Havildar (some say Sepoy) Ajudhya Pershad Pathak, Naiks Devi Deen (Debi Singh), Sheik Abdulla (Sheik Abdul) and Nihal Khan; and Sepoys Ram Heth (Heth Ram), Thakurdin Tiwari, Ramsaful Upadhya and Sahib Singh (the "Jahub Singh" of Home's report).

[1]In *The Tale of the Great Mutiny* (p. 387) Mr. W. H. Fitchett writes:— "As a matter of fact, it was only the wicket gate which was blown in. Lord Roberts has told how, in the after part of the day, he crept through the wicket."

[2]A coloured portrait of Subadar Ayodhya (Ajudhia) Patak Bahadur, I.O.M., Bengal Sappers and Miners, 1841–1876, a Brahman of Oudh and the last survivor of the Explosion Party at Delhi, appeared on the Bengal Sappers' Christmas Card in 1938.

THE BLOWING IN OF THE KASHMIR GATE, DELHI, SEPTEMBER 14TH, 1857

From the original drawing by Eyre Crowe, A.R.A.

A graphic description comes from the pen of Sergeant John Smith, who was at the rear of the party when it went off at the double from Ludlow Castle, preceded by skirmishers of the 60th Rifles. The infantry halted and opened fire while the demolition party continued towards the Kashmir Gate. According to Sergeant Smith, Home and the bugler led, and a few paces behind them came Salkeld with the three British non-commissioned officers and nine Bengal Sappers carrying twelve bags of powder. When Smith reached the gateway, Sergeant Carmichael had already been killed and Home and Bugler Hawthorne had jumped into the ditch. " I placed my bag," he writes,[1] " and then Carmichael's bag, arranged the fuse and reported ' All ready ' to Lieutenant Salkeld who held the slow match. In stooping down to light the quick match he put out his foot and was shot through the thigh from the wicket, and in falling had the presence of mind to hold out the slow and told me to fire the charge. Burgess was next him and took it. I told him to fire the charge and keep cool. He turned round and said, ' It won't go off, sir ; it has gone out, sir,' not knowing that the officer had fallen into the ditch. I gave him a box of lucifers, and as he took them he let them fall into my hand, he being shot through the body from the wicket also, and fell over after Lieutenant Salkeld. I was then left alone, and keeping close to the charge, seeing from where the others had been shot, I struck a light, when the port-fire in the fuze went off in my face, the light not having gone out as we thought. I took up my gun and jumped into the ditch, and when I had reached the ground the charge went off. I stuck close to the wall and by that escaped being smashed to pieces. I put my hands along the wall and touched someone. It was Lieutenant Home. . . . As soon as the dust cleared a little I saw Lieutenant Salkeld and Burgess, covered with dust, lying in the middle of the ditch. I called the bugler to help me remove Lieutenant Salkeld under the bridge as his arms were broken, but Lieutenant Salkeld would not let us remove him so I put a bag of powder under his head and with the bugler's puggery bound up his arms and thigh. I left the bugler to look after him and did what I could for Burgess. I got some brandy from Lieutenant Home and gave to both, also to a Havildar (Tillok Singh) who had his thigh shot through. Lieutenant Home got out of the ditch, leaving me in charge of the wounded, and went to the front after the Rifles had gone in and the 52nd followed them. I then went to the rear for three stretchers. One was taken from me, and I had to draw my sword and threaten to run anyone through who took the other two. I put them into the ditch and with the bugler's assistance got Lieutenant Salkeld into one and sent him with him, and with the assistance of a Naik, got Burgess into the other and sent the Naik with him, I being scarcely able to walk. After assisting to clear away the gate and make the roadway again, I went to the front."

Corporal Burgess died almost at once, and Salkeld lingered only two days.[2] Within a few weeks, Home also was gone—killed by the accidental

[1] *A Story of the Sepoy War in India*, by J. W. Kaye, Vol. III, pp. 674–675.

[2] A memorial to Philip Salkeld exists in the form of a masonry bridge about 1½ miles from Sturminster on the road to Dorchester. It was built in 1864 by his friends and has tablets in each parapet inscribed " Salkeld, 1857, Delhi." (See *The R.E. Journal*, Vol. LI, 1938, p. 1.)

explosion of a mine at the empty fortress of Malagarh. The Victoria Cross was awarded to Salkeld shortly before his death and also to Home, Smith and Hawthorne, and there is little doubt that Carmichael and Burgess would have received it also if a posthumous award had then been permissible. The Indian ranks were rewarded with the Indian Order of Merit, promotion and grants of land, and never were distinctions better earned.

It is unnecessary to describe in detail the operations of the various columns in the assault and capture of the northern fortifications of Delhi, for there is little on record about the exploits of the Sappers and Miners. Columns Nos. 1 and 2 stormed the breaches in the Kashmir and Water Bastions and fought their way along the walls to the Burn Bastion, where they were checked and John Nicholson mortally wounded. No. 3 Column pushed through the shattered Kashmir Gate and penetrated to the Jama Masjid, near which Tandy was killed, but afterwards it retreated to St. James' Church. No. 4 Column was held up altogether, and Maunsell was dangerously wounded. For several hours, many of the troops in Delhi were somewhat out of hand. After dark, however, a detachment of Sappers and Miners constructed a battery at the College to bombard the King's Palace and Salimgarh. Another under Lang began a house to house advance from the Kabul Gate to avoid street fighting and continued the process on the 15th. The operations on the 16th were marked by the capture of the Magazine between the Kashmir Gate and the King's Palace, and here it was that Thackeray earned the Victoria Cross although he did not receive it until 1862. The mutineers had tried to recapture the place and set fire to some thatched sheds against one of the walls. The conflagration spread rapidly towards the magazine, and while Major Renny of the Artillery stood on a blazing roof and threw shells with lighted fuses among the enemy, Thackeray on the same roof extinguished the flames with bags of water before they could reach the powder below. Both officers were under close fire from the walls and houses around, and both rightly received the coveted Cross. After the Magazine had been saved, the Sappers and Miners under Lang built a battery there for the bombardment of Salimgarh.

So few Bengal Engineers were now available to lead the Sapper companies that the activities of the Corps were sadly restricted. Greathed, Maunsell, Chesney, Hovenden, Medley, Brownlow, Perkins, Pemberton, Home, Murray and Champain had been wounded since the assault began. Salkeld and Tandy were dead, and Baird Smith seriously ill. Only Taylor, Lang, Thackeray and Ward were fit for duty. By the 17th, however, these four had been reinforced by Geneste and Forbes from the sick list, and by the slightly wounded quartette, Pemberton, Home, Murray and Champain, the last of whom had been on the sick list during the actual assault. On the 16th, as Taylor was completely exhausted, Home acted as Chief Engineer of the force in spite of his wound; while Ward, a 2nd Lieutenant of 3 years' service, was the senior Bengal Sapper and Miner officer on duty. The Punjab Sappers were commanded by a temporary Ensign, Chalmers, with three others to assist him—Nuthall, Knowles and Righy. Gustavinski and Anderson had been wounded. The veteran Bingham had

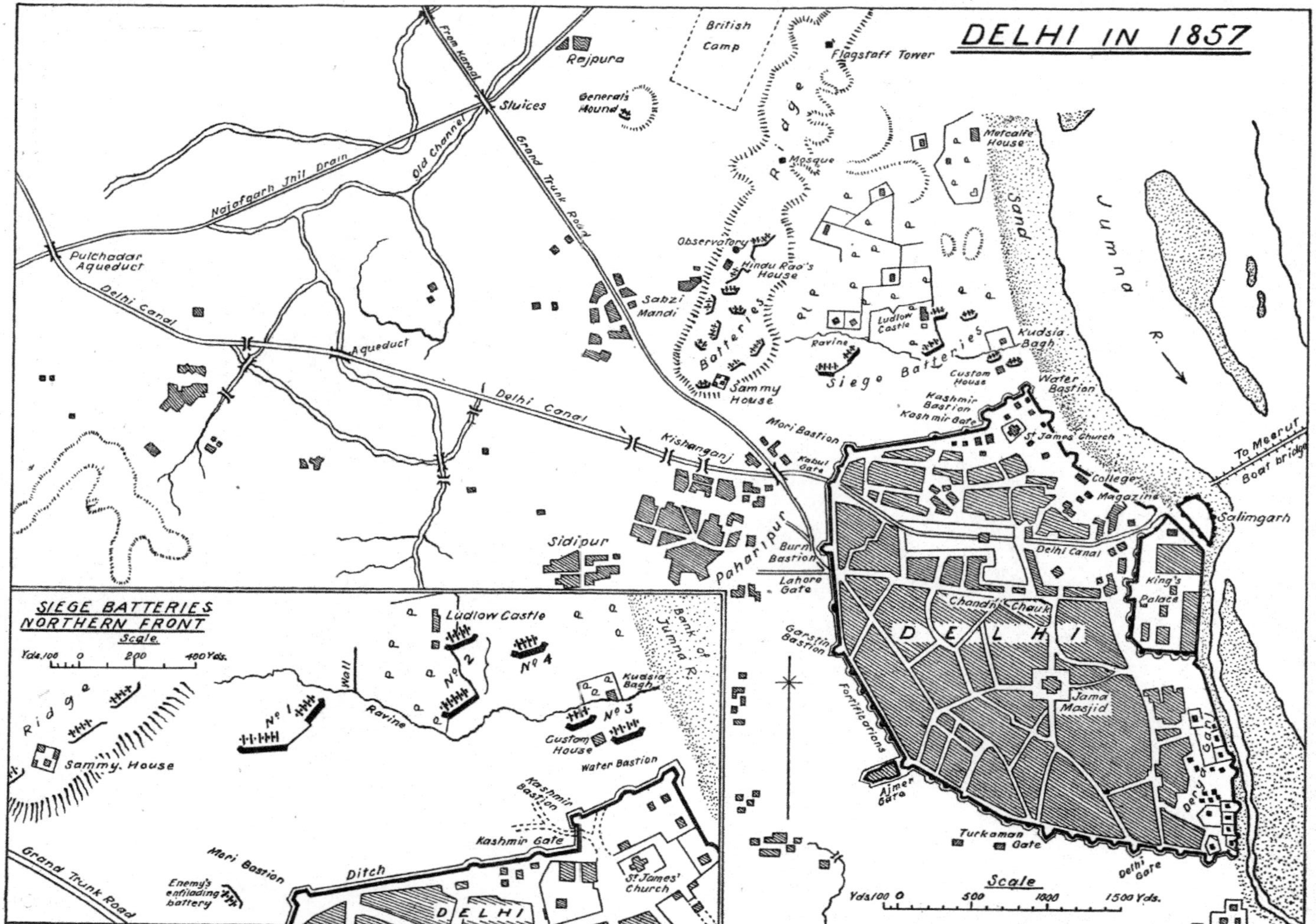
DELHI IN 1857
British Camp
Flagstaff Tower
Rajpura
Sluices
General's Mound
From Karnal
Grand Trunk Road
Najafgarh Jhil Drain
Old Channel
Pulchadar Aqueduct
Delhi Canal
Aqueduct
Ridge
Mosque
Metcalfe House
Sand
Jumna
R.
Observatory
Hindu Rao's House
Sabzi Mandi
Batteries
Ludlow Castle
Ravine
Kudsia Bagh
Siege Batteries
Sammy House
Custom House
Water Bastion
Kashmir Bastion
Kashmir Gate
St James' Church
Mori Bastion
Kishanganj
Kabul Gate
College
Magazine
To Meerut
Boat bridge
Salimgarh
Paharipur
Burn Bastion
Lahore Gate
Delhi Canal
Sidipur
King's Palace
Chandni Chauk
D E L H I
Garstin Bastion
Fortifications
Jama Masjid
Ajmer Gate
Turkaman Gate
Delhi Gate
Scale
Yds/100 0 500 1000 1500 Yds.
SIEGE BATTERIES
NORTHERN FRONT
Scale
Yds.100 0 200 400 Yds.
Ludlow Castle
Bank of Jumna R.
No 4
No 2
No 1
No 3
Wall
Ridge
Ravine
Kudsia Bagh
Custom House
Water Bastion
Sammy House
Kashmir Bastion
Kashmir Gate
Mori Bastion
Ditch
St James' Church
Enemy's enfilading battery
Grand Trunk Road
DELHI

come through unscathed and was still at the head of the Delhi and Roorkee Pioneers.

Lang and some Bengal Sappers assisted in the capture of the Burn Bastion on September 19th and the occupation of the Lahore Gate on the 20th. On the following day, Home blew in the southern gate of the King's Palace, and with the capture of that stronghold, all resistance came to an end. The Engineer Brigade moved from a temporary camp near the Metcalfe House estate to another in Derya Ganj, south of the King's Palace. On the 23rd, Baird Smith handed over charge to Taylor and set out for Roorkee. Two-thirds of his cadre of Engineers had been killed or wounded since the beginning of the siege. Geneste and Fulford died in 1858 from the effects of exposure and overwork, and Baird Smith himself succumbed in 1861. The Sappers and Pioneers had suffered nearly 300 casualties during the operations out of a total casualty list of about 1,000 killed and 3,000 wounded or missing. Such was the price of victory.

Although the fall of Delhi assured the ultimate suppression of the Indian Mutiny, there was much to be done at Lucknow and elsewhere. Columns set out from Delhi to sweep the *doab* between the Jumna and Ganges. One under Colonel Greathed, which included Home and Lang with 50 Bengal Sappers, and also Lieutenant Stevenson, B.I., with 2 companies of Punjab Sappers,[1] marched on September 24th and four days later defeated a rebel force at Bulandshahr. Then it started for Malagarh, where the gallant Home was blown to pieces on October 1st while examining a charge which had failed to explode. Thackeray and Humphry,[2] with two companies of Punjab Sappers, marched with a column under Brig.-General Showers towards the Bikaner desert and blew up many forts. The unfortunate Humphry afterwards set out with another column, and during a fight at Narnaul on October 16th, was wounded in no less than seventeen places.

Most of the Bengal and Punjab Sappers and the Roorkee and Delhi Pioneers remained for a time at Delhi under Taylor to repair and strengthen the damaged fortifications, but the battered walls around the Kashmir Gate were left untouched as a memento of the assault. Few officers were fit for work, and Geneste, Medley and Carnegie were invalided to the hills. Gradually, the Sappers and Pioneers moved south-eastwards to assist in the operations at Lucknow, and by the end of February, 1858, almost all had gone. So ended the siege of Delhi, an episode which is without parallel in the military history of India.

[1]Lang alludes to these as the 10th and 11th Companies, yet there is no record that more than nine companies of Punjab Sappers came to Delhi.

[2]Lieut. E. W. Humphry, B.E., O.C. 6th Company, Bengal S. & M., at Peshawar, had recently arrived in Delhi.

CHAPTER IX

THE INDIAN MUTINY: CAWNPORE, LUCKNOW AND CENTRAL INDIA, 1857–1859

WHEN Delhi was recaptured in September, 1857, operations against the rebel forces in Oudh had been in progress for several months. The massacre of British women and children on July 15th at Cawnpore after the surrender of the small garrison under Major-General Sir Hugh Wheeler on June 27th, had shocked the civilized world. Brig.-General Henry Havelock had marched into the city from Allahabad, crossed the Ganges, defeated the rebels at Unao and Bashiratganj, retired to Mangalwar, advanced once more towards Lucknow, gained two further victories at Bashiratganj, recrossed the river to Cawnpore and routed the rebels at Bithur. The Ganges at Cawnpore had been bridged by Captain W. A. Crommelin and Lieutenant G. E. Watson, B.E., thus enabling a large force under Havelock, accompanied by Major-General Sir James Outram, to cross on September 20th for another advance on Lucknow.[1] Meanwhile, the small garrison of the Lucknow Residency under Colonel J. Inglis had been besieged since July 1st, and the five engineers present—Major J. Anderson, Captain G. W. W. Fulton and Lieutenants G. Hutchinson and J. J. McLeod Innes, B.E., and Lieutenant J. C. Anderson, M.E.—had performed prodigies of valour in countermining and the construction of hasty defences. Major Anderson died, Fulton was killed, but the three survivors continued the work and thus helped to preserve the garrison from destruction and the women and children from butchery.

On September 25th, Havelock and Outram fought their way into the Residency at the head of 3,000 men, and Outram, assuming the command which was his by right of seniority, proceeded to extend the defences under the advice of Colonel Robert Napier, late B.E., his Chief of Staff. Captain W. A. Crommelin and Lieutenants L. Russell and D. Limond, B.E., of Havelock's force, with Lieutenants Hutchinson, Innes and Anderson of the original garrison and six Assistant Engineers, devoted their energies chiefly to countermining, in which they were remarkably successful.[2] On November 12th, a powerful force under General Sir Colin

[1]The ferrying and bridging operations are described in a "Memorandum on Three Passages of the River Ganges during the Rainy Season of 1857," by Capt. W. A. Crommelin, B.E., appearing in *Professional Papers of the Corps of Royal Engineers*, New Series, Vol. VIII, 1859, pp. 106–115.

[2]The defence of the Lucknow Residency is described fully in *Lucknow and Oude in the Mutiny*, by Lieut.-Gen. McLeod Innes, V.C., late R.(B.)E., pp. 97–180. See also *The Military Engineer in India*, by the present author, Vol. I, pp. 348–355, and official reports by Maj.-Gen. Sir John Inglis, K.C.B., Maj.-Gen. Sir James Outram, G.C.B., Major W. A. Crommelin, C.B., B.E., and Lieuts. J. C. Anderson, M.E., and G. Hutchinson, B.E., appearing in Paper IX of *Professional Papers of the Corps of Royal Engineers*, New Series, Vol. X, 1861, pp. 48–66. For the relief operations under Havelock and Outram see "Sieges and the Defence of Fortified Places," by Col. Sir E. T. Thackeray, V.C., K.C.B., appearing in *The R.E. Journal*, Vol. XXII, July–Dec., 1915, pp. 17–24 and 97–105.

Campbell, marching from Cawnpore, reached the Alam Bagh enclosure south of Lucknow City. It was composed of troops from the column under Colonel Greathed which had started from Delhi on September 24th and of reinforcements from Calcutta and elsewhere including the 23rd Company, R.E., under Captain A. J. Clerke with Lieutenants W. O. Lennox, V.C., E. D. Malcolm, G. D. Pritchard and R. Harrison, R.E., and "C" Company, Madras S. & M., under Lieutenant C. Scott, M.E., with Lieutenant F. M. Raynsford, M.I., 2nd Lieutenant W. H. Burton, M.E., and Ensign D. S. Ogilvie, M.I. The 23rd Company and "C" Company marched together to Bani Bridge, 18 miles south of Lucknow, and having repaired the bridge, joined the main body at Bantara, south of the Alam Bagh. There they found Lang and two companies of Punjab Sappers from Greathed's column which had come under the command of Colonel Hope Grant. Thus, for the relief of Outram and Havelock in Lucknow, Sir Colin Campbell had the services of two regular and two irregular units of engineer troops. As there were no Sappers and Miners in the original garrison of the Residency,[1] nor in the strong reinforcement brought by Havelock and Outram, the Sapper and Miner history of the Mutiny in Oudh begins with the concentration of troops for the relief operations under Sir Colin Campbell.

Most of the Bengal Sappers and Miners remained in Delhi until December, 1857, to repair the damage caused during the siege and to convert the King's Palace—known thereafter as "Delhi Fort"—into a strong citadel with suitable accommodation for a British garrison. They were assisted by the Delhi Pioneers, and by the Roorkee Pioneers until the latter returned to their canal work. Meanwhile, the Punjab Sappers supplied companies to various columns engaged in sweeping the *doab* between the Jumna and Ganges. Two companies under Stevenson (B.I.), and a detachment of 50 Bengal Sappers under Lang, were with Colonel Greathed's column when it drove the enemy from Bulandshahr, destroyed Malagarh and, on October 5th, retook Aligarh. Three days later the column was diverted towards Agra, and arriving there on the 10th, routed 7,000 mutineers in a surprise encounter. Forbes joined Lang on October 14th, and on the 20th the column, now under Colonel Hope Grant, proceeded on its way to Cawnpore, leaving Forbes and all the Sappers at Mainpuri[2] to blow up the fort and afterwards rejoin the main body. Hope Grant marched into Cawnpore on October 26th to reinforce the army assembling under Sir Colin Campbell for the advance on Lucknow.

In 1857, the city of Lucknow, about five miles in length and three in width, lay mostly on the right or southern bank of the River Gumti.[3] It was bounded on the south and south-east by a canal leading into the river near La Martinière College. South of the College was a celebrated

[1]Major Anderson's head accountant, however, was ex-Sergeant-Major Casey, late of the Bengal Sappers and Miners.

[2]25 miles west of Fatehgarh. Important places such as Fatehgarh are shown in Map I at the end of this volume.

[3]See the sketch map entitled *Lucknow in* 1858, included in this chapter.

palace, the Dilkusha. The city itself was squalid and densely populated, but there were a number of large buildings and gardens in a more open area at the north-east corner in a loop of the Gumti. A so-called "stone" bridge (actually of brick masonry) spanned the river at the centre of the northern face and carried a road leading to the cantonments of Mariaon and Mudkipur. Further downstream, an iron bridge provided a crossing for another road to Mariaon, and also for the Cawnpore-Fyzabad Road which ran past the Alam Bagh, south of the city, crossed the canal by a bridge at the Char Bagh, traversed the city, and emerged by the Residency. Near the stone bridge was the old Machhi Bawan Fort, and to the east of the iron bridge, the Residency and its subsidiary buildings. Still further eastwards stretched a line of palaces and large houses—the Chattar Manzil, Kaisar Bagh, Imambara, Hazratganj, Begum Kothi, the Hospital and, a little to the south, Banks' House. North-east of this line, in the bend of the river, lay the Moti Mahal, Shah Najaf, Kadam Rasul and Sikandar Bagh, and between these and the line of palaces, the Kurshid Manzil or Mess House and the European Barracks. North of the Gumti were the walled enclosures of the Badshah and Hazari Baghs.

The problem confronting Sir Colin Campbell was to fight his way round from south to north with only 5,000 men while hordes of mutineers threatened his left flank from the palaces and enclosures bordering the city. This was a difficult and dangerous undertaking, but he accomplished it successfully on November 17th, 1857. After an historic meeting with Outram and Havelock outside the Residency, he evacuated the women and children and, by dawn on the 22nd, had returned to the Dilkusha Palace where he was safe from attack. On November 27th, he set out for Cawnpore with part of his force and all the non-combatants, leaving Outram to hold a position at the Alam Bagh with about 4,000 men. The universal rejoicing which followed the relief and evacuation of the Lucknow garrison was marred only by the death of the gallant Havelock on November 24th.

The part played by the engineer units in these rapid manœuvres was a minor one. The mutineers were taken by surprise: they had prepared no elaborate works of defence. The plan of attack was based on proposals sent from the Residency by Outram, and the troops advanced from the Alam Bagh on November 14th in the direction of the Dilkusha Palace instead of towards the Char Bagh as Havelock and Outram had done in the first attempt. The Dilkusha was soon occupied, and the Madras Sappers and Miners cut openings in the boundary walls for the passage of troops and guns towards La Martinière.[1] The latter was captured without much difficulty, and Lang and Burton hoisted the Union Jack on the tower. On the 16th, Sir Colin attacked the Sikandar Bagh enclosure, the 23rd Company, R.E., and "C" Company, Madras S. & M., being with the advanced guard. Two companies of Punjab Sappers were with the main body with orders to improve communications and assist the heavy artillery. The Sikandar Bagh was taken by assault and the mutineers within it were

[1] *The Military History of the Madras Engineers and Pioneers*, by Major H. M. Vibart, R.(M.)E., Vol. II, p. 374.

THE RESIDENCY, LUCKNOW, AT THE END OF THE SIEGE.

exterminated. " Some of our Sappers were at work making ramps up which we pulled the heavy guns," writes Lang.[1] " The infantry were lying under shelter ready for a rush, ' Pandy '[2] all the while keeping up no end of a fire from the walls. While I was working I saw the 4th Punjabis yelling and shouting as they charged straight at the building.[3] Down we dropped the ropes and rushed along too. Up sprang the 93rd and 53rd, and cheering and shouting ' Revenge for Cawnpore,' on we went, some at the breach in one of the corner towers and some over a loopholed mud wall straight for the gate. Axes and muskets soon smashed the gate, and then, didn't we get revenge ! Right and left of the gateway, Pandies lay in heaps, three or four deep. They made but little stand. The bodies of 1,840 Pandies have now been buried."

" Between the Sikandar Bagh and Shah Najaf," continues Lang, " the ground is open, Kadam Rasul standing on the right on a mound. I was ordered on from the Sikandar Bagh with some Madras Sappers and heard that the 93rd had taken the European Barracks and the 2nd Punjabis the Kadam Rasul. Our guns, heavy and light, were playing on the white dome of the Shah Najaf and had been for two or three hours. Anyhow, to advance to the Shah Najaf was our order—93rd, 1st Madras Fusiliers, Peel with one 24-pounder and his sailors,[4] and some Madras Sappers. Within 20 to 30 yards of the wall, Peel's gun opened to make a breach and our poor fellows were being knocked about dreadfully. An hour of this work cost us no end of lives, and the gun was being withdrawn and the troops moved back when, by luck, another breach was found and in went the 93rd. . . . At daybreak (17th) I went to the European Barracks where I found Stevenson and Pritchard with Sappers and three companies of the 93rd. The barrack itself we held, but the enclosure walls on the south and east were held by the enemy and from their loopholes they kept up a deadly fire. We worked hard at closing all the openings with sandbags, shutters, etc. After some hours I was ordered off on another work. The Mess House (Kurshid Manzil) was to be taken. Forbes with 20 Sappers was to throw a bridge over the moat, and I with 10 Sappers was to lay *mussacks* (skins) of powder at the doors and blow them in. I arranged my *mussacks*, powder-hoses and quick-matches and then we watched the reconnoitring. Forbes with some men, and Powlett (58th B.I.) with others, went in unopposed. Our troops then carried the Moti Mahal, and cheers from house to house, gun to gun, and regiment to regiment down the road conveyed the news that the junction was effected. Outram, Havelock, the two young Havelocks and Napier and Russell (engineers)—the two latter wounded—had met Sir Colin. How we all did cheer ! That night, all the right bank of the Gumti from the Residency to the Dilkusha was ours."

After the meeting, " C " Company under Scott made a battery outside

[1] " The Diary and Letters of A. M. Lang, 1st Lieut., Bengal Engineers," appearing in the *Journal of the Society for Army Historical Research*, Vol. X, 1931, p. 138.

[2] The rebels were commonly known as " Pandies " because the first to be executed at Barrackpore, near Calcutta, was named Mangal Pande.

[3] A small building containing the entrance gateway to the enclosure.

[4] A naval contingent from H.M.S. *Shannon* under Capt. Sir William Peel, R.N.

the Moti Mahal from which a heavy bombardment was opened on the 18th on the Kaisar Bagh while Lang and Pritchard prepared a screened way from the Chattar Manzil to the Moti Mahal. During the 19th and 20th, the evacuation of non-combatants proceeded under cover of this bombardment, all being hurried along behind the screens, down a lane to the Sikandar Bagh and thence to the Dilkusha, whither they were followed by the troops. On the 21st and 22nd, Lang and some Sappers made a demonstration of bridge construction to deceive the enemy, and afterwards the engineer units moved to the Alam Bagh. "C" Company then marched down the Cawnpore Road to Bani Village, which they put in a state of defence, but later they returned to the Alam Bagh to join the garrison under Outram. Meanwhile, the 23rd Company, R.E., and the two Punjab Sapper companies proceeded with the troops under Sir Colin Campbell to Cawnpore, escorting an enormous caravan of sick, wounded, women and children. Thus ended the rescue of the Lucknow garrison in which the Madras Sappers were closely engaged and the Punjab Sappers took some part.

A continuous concentration of troops on Cawnpore was now resumed both from the Punjab and Calcutta, and three movable columns operated in the *doab*. A column under Brig.-General Seaton, to which Thackeray and three companies of Punjab Sappers were attached, moved southwards from Delhi with a large convoy; it defeated three rebel forces and met another column under Brig.-General Walpole moving northwards by a circuitous route. By the beginning of December, most of the Delhi Engineer Brigade under Taylor had arrived in Agra, and on December 8th the headquarters and some companies of Punjab Sappers set out for Aligarh to join Seaton's column, leaving the Bengal Sappers temporarily at Agra. A third column, under Sir Colin himself, advanced from Cawnpore against the enemy around Fatehgarh, and after routing them, occupied that city on January 2nd, 1858, and was joined there by the other columns. A company of Punjab Sappers then marched with a force under Walpole to the Ramganga River beyond Fatehgarh, where several small engagements were fought. On January 7th, the Engineer officers of the East India Company's Army present in Fatehgarh were Taylor, Greathed, Gulliver, Brownlow (E.P.), Lang, Humphry, Murray, Fulford, Thackeray and Forbes, and the Engineer units comprised a detachment of Bengal Sappers under Murray, and the 3rd, 6th, 7th and 8th Companies of Punjab Sappers under Gulliver, assisted by Stevenson.[1] The garrison included not only the 23rd Company but also the 4th Company, R.E., under Major L. Nicholson with Lieutenants P. H. Scratchley, C. E. Wynne, G. Swetenham and W. Keith, R.E., this unit having arrived recently from Calcutta.[2] Lieut.-Colonel H. D. Harness, R.E., commanded the Royal Engineer companies under the orders of Brig.-General Sir Robert Napier,

[1]Engineer Brigade Order, dated Camp Fatehgarh, Jan. 7th, 1858, included in the volume at Roorkee entitled "Order Book, Engineer Brigade. Commenced 13th Dec., 1857. Finished 10th April, 1858."

[2]The 11th and 21st Companies, R.E., had also arrived in India but were not present during the operations in Oudh.

the Chief Engineer, who was with Outram at the Alam Bagh. The Engineer Department was reinforced on January 13th by the arrival of four small companies of Bengal Sappers and Miners (about 200 men) from Agra under Champain as officiating Commandant, with Pemberton, McNeile, Ward and Carnegie.[1] A small detachment of the Corps assisted the 4th Company in demolishing some of the defences of the adjacent town of Farrukhabad.[2] The Punjab Sappers were not entrusted with any technical work; for instance, after the 23rd Company, R.E., and detachments of the Bengal and Punjab Sappers, while on the march to Fatehgarh at the end of December, had destroyed the fort of Tattia on the Fatehgarh-Agra Road, Lieutenant Lennox, R.E., reported that "the Punjaub Pioneers, being uninstructed, were simply used as coolies: the Bengal Sappers, however, were employed in mining."[3]

The Engineer Department marched for Cawnpore on February 3rd, the Royal Engineer companies being under Lieut.-Colonel Harness, R.E., and the Indian companies under Captain Alexander Taylor, B.E., who had arrived from Delhi. Champain was officiating as Commandant of the Bengal Sappers and Miners, Gulliver commanded the Punjab Sappers, and a contingent of Delhi Pioneers was led by Lieutenant E. O. B. Horsford, B.I. On February 7th, the Engineer units joined the army under Sir Colin Campbell at Cawnpore and marched on the following day with the Engineer Park towards Lucknow. On the 11th they were at Unao, on the 12th at Nawabganj, on the 13th at Bani Bridge, and on the 14th they entered Sir James Outram's camp at the Alam Bagh.[4] The Engineer Brigade for the recapture of Lucknow was a curious blend of British and Indian soldiers. "Major Nicholson has evidently always done regimental duty" writes Lang. "He is more like a strict little Adjutant than an Engineer officer, fond of smart drills, pipeclay, *et hoc genus omne*. I fancy the 'Delhi' style of the Bengal and Punjab Sappers perplexes him; our scorn of appearances and drill, our absolute sway over our men. I expect he will soon ask me to doff my peacock feather plume from my helmet! Perhaps he may ask me to doff also my loose khaki tunic and jack boots and my black pouches and belts and request me to wear red and Russia leather and gold lace and other pomps, a more glittering but not half so soldierly set of harness."

The Alam Bagh had been held by Sir James Outram since November 27th, 1857. It was a walled garden about a quarter of a mile square, with a battery outside each corner, and formed the chief defence of the right front of the British position opposite which some 90,000 rebels were ensconced in the southern suburbs of Lucknow. The old and dilapidated fort of Jalalabad, two miles to the south-east, guarded the right flank, and field works and abattis protected the front and left flank. The British force was

[1]Engineer Brigade Order, dated Camp Fatehgarh, Jan. 13th, 1858.
[2]Report by Lieut. Scratchley, R.E., appearing in *Professional Papers of the Corps of Royal Engineers*, New Series, Vol. VIII, 1859, pp. 44–48.
[3]Report by Lieut. Lennox, R.E., appearing in *Professional Papers of the Corps of Royal Engineers*, New Series, Vol. VIII, 1859, p. 56.
[4]Corps Orders, Feb. 2nd–13th, appearing in the volume at Roorkee entitled "Order Book, Engineer Brigade. Commenced 13th Dec., 1857. Finished 10th April, 1858."

encamped across the Cawnpore-Lucknow Road behind this defensive line. For three months, Outram had clung tenaciously to his isolated position. During this period, the rebels attacked him repeatedly, and he defeated them on six occasions—December 22nd, January 12th and 16th, and February 15th, 21st and 25th. The defences were designed by Lieutenants G. Hutchinson and C. N. Judge, B.E., and their construction was carried out by "C" Company, Madras Sappers and Miners, under Lieutenant C. Scott with 2nd Lieutenant W. H. Burton, M.E., and by infantry and civilian working parties under seven Assistant Field Engineers.[1] Until the arrival of the army under Sir Colin Campbell, "C" Company was the only engineer unit at the Alam Bagh. The Madras Sappers were employed day and night in battery construction, trench digging, improving communications and providing obstacles. "Their skill as workmen, their industry, their cheerful alacrity and general good conduct," wrote Outram, "commanded the respect of all who saw them."

The enemy displayed so much initiative and aptitude in digging zigzag approaches towards the Alam Bagh that it was thought that they were working under the direction of mutinous Bengal Sappers; and Lang records that on February 14th, after the arrival of the Engineer Brigade from Cawnpore, he observed hundreds of mutineers labouring on their main defensive line under the superintendence of red-coated havildars who were apparently experts for they were hectoring and driving the men. Every available man of the Engineer Brigade was soon employed in and around Jalalabad Fort in making gabions, fascines, barrel-piers for bridging the Gumti, and scaling-ladders and other material for the assault on Lucknow, and in practising the rapid construction of batteries and field magazines. Experiments in the demolition of walls were carried out, and it was found that a barrel of powder, wheeled forward on a hand-barrow and fired by a hose, fuse and quick-match, would create a breach 12 feet wide in a wall 2½ feet thick. Large numbers of coolies were engaged for work under Pemberton in the Engineer Park. The Engineer Brigade camp was pitched outside the Jalalabad Fort and contained more than 3,000 officers and men of the 4th and 23rd Companies, R.E., "C" Company, Madras Sappers and Miners, the Bengal Sappers and Miners, the Punjab Sappers and the Delhi Pioneers. On February 24th, 1858, the strength of the Bengal Sappers under Maunsell in the Alam Bagh position amounted to 11 British and 16 Indian officers, and 30 British and 205 Indian other ranks.[2] The 4th and 23rd Companies, R.E., mustered 232 officers and men, and the strengths of "C" Company, the Punjab Sappers and the Delhi Pioneers were 107, 776 and 754 respectively. It is evident that

[1] Capt. C. Oakes and Lieuts. Hon. A. Fraser and A. Tulloch, B.I., Ensign Ogilvie, M.I., and Messrs. J. May and J. Tait.

[2] Corps Order dated Feb. 24th, 1858. On this date the strength of the whole Corps of Bengal Sappers and Miners was 11 Lieuts., 1 Assist. Surgeon, 1 Conductor, 1 Q.M.S., 24 Sergeants, 24-1st Corporals, 24-2nd Corporals, 61 Privates, 2 Native Doctors, 9 Subadars, 11 Jemadars, 34 Havildars, 18 Naiks, 8 Buglers, 365 Sepoys and 326 Recruits. Of these, 1 Lieut., 1 B.N.C.O., 1 Subadar, 69 I.O.R.s, and 249 Recruits were at Roorkee. Only 2 B.N.C.O.s, 1 Subadar, 13 I.O.R.s and 3 Recruits remained at Delhi. Apart from the 262 officers and men at the Alam Bagh, the remainder were mostly in the 5th Company at Attock and the 6th Company at Peshawar.

Brig.-General Sir Robert Napier lacked neither men nor material for his operations as Chief Engineer in the final offensive against the mutineers in Lucknow.

On March 2nd, 1858, Sir Colin Campbell began his advance from behind the Alam Bagh position. Including Outram's division he had an army of about 19,000 men with 120 guns, which, when reinforced later by a column under Brig.-General T. H. Franks[1] and a Nepalese contingent from the south-east, reached a total of 31,000 men with 164 guns. Napier reconnoitred the ground and recommended that Lucknow should be attacked from the east. The city was not surrounded by a wall, but many commanding buildings on the outskirts had been prepared for defence and three elaborate lines of earthworks thrown up. Rejecting the possibility of attack from the west, the enemy had concentrated their efforts during the preceding three months on fortifying the southern and eastern faces. Their first or outer line of earthworks extended along the canal bounding the southern face from the neighbourhood of the Char Bagh to the River Gumti. As far as Banks' House the line was weak; but from that building to the river it consisted of massive ramparts with numerous bastions and batteries. The second line ran northwards from the Imambara to the Gumti; and the third, at right angles to it, covered the front of the main citadel, the Kaisar Bagh, and its mosque. In the two previous advances on Lucknow, the British forces had been too small to operate simultaneously on both banks of the river. It seems that the mutineers did not realize the altered circumstances. Though they held the left bank with mobile troops, they prepared no defences on that side. This was their undoing. By despatching a strong force across the river, Sir Colin Campbell was able to bring enfilade and even reverse fire to bear on their first and second lines and thus to render them untenable in face of a powerful frontal attack, a happy result which was secured by the bridging exploits of the Royal Engineers, Sappers and Pioneers.

Sir Colin began his operations on March 2nd, 1858. Moving up from behind the Alam Bagh position and circling round the Jalalabad Fort, he made straight for the Dilkusha Palace, which he secured with trifling loss. Then, in drenching rain, he encamped in the Dilkusha Park between the palace and the river. On the morning of March 3rd, the greater part of the Engineer Brigade and Engineer Park marched from Jalalabad Fort to the gardens of a house called the Bibiapur near the Dilkusha. "From the top of the house," writes Thackeray,[2] "we got our first view of Lucknow. We could see the Martinière, an enormous building which had been used as a college, about a quarter of a mile from the Dilkusha. The enemy's first line of entrenchments looked very formidable, and we were told that they had two more with ramparts twice as thick and ditches twice as deep. The quantity of labour they had expended was enormous. Streets a mile

[1] Brig.-Gen. Franks had defeated the rebels at Chanda, Hamirpur, Sultanpur and Dhaurahra. At Sultanpur, on Feb. 22nd, 1858, Lieut. J. J. McLeod Innes, B.E., gained the Victoria Cross.

[2] "A Subaltern in the Indian Mutiny," appearing in *The R.E. Journal*, Vol. XLV, 1931, p. 425.

long had every house loopholed and guns pointing up many of them. The bridges were all mined."

On March 3rd, while detachments of the 23rd Company, R.E., and the Punjab Sappers constructed a battery in front of the Dilkusha, a party from the 4th Company, R.E., staked out a ford across the Gumti and the Delhi Pioneers prepared the banks for bridging. At sunset on March 4th, the 4th Company and a detachment of the 23rd Company under Major Nicholson, R.E., with 120 Punjab Sappers under Lieutenant J. F. Tennant and 2nd Lieutenant R. G. Smyth, B.E., began to build two barrel-pier bridges near the Bibiapur camp within 1½ miles of the Martinière. Each bridge was to be 102 feet in length, the remainder of the width of the river being traversed by causeways extending from the left bank. Unfortunately, the first bridge was found to require 135 feet of barrel-piering because the causeway was not sufficiently long. "There was some mess about the cask bridges," writes Lang. "They tried to make two but had not enough material." On the morning of the 5th, a strong bridge-head was provided for the first bridge, and by the evening, 4 companies of Punjab Sappers and Delhi Pioneers had completed the second bridge and its causeway though exposed to considerable fire from guns at the Martinière and on the left bank.[1] Soon after midnight, a force of 7,000 men under Outram, including the 4th Company, R.E., under Nicholson and 200 Punjab Sappers under Hovenden and Nuthall, began to cross the bridges and march northwards towards Ismailganj on the Lucknow-Fyzabad Road. It was hoped that the operation would be completed before it was discovered by the enemy, but when day broke, the greater part of Outram's force was still on the wrong side of the river. Sir Colin rode down in person to direct the crossing. The more phlegmatic Outram, having done all he could, sat down on a fallen tree and lit a cheroot. Throughout the day a stream of men, animals, guns and baggage surged across the swaying structures, and at dusk, when the troops were far northwards, the baggage was still crossing. As the bridges were under bombardment from the Martinière it was decided that they should be moved out of range as soon as possible, and accordingly the lower bridge was dismantled after dark by a party of the 23rd Company, R.E., under Lennox, assisted by 100 Punjab Sappers, and towed more than one mile downstream, where it was re-erected on March 7th. The upper bridge was shifted to the same spot on the 8th.

While these operations were in progress, "C" Company Madras Sappers and Miners, was engaged in making fascines in Jalalabad Fort, and the Bengal Sapper and Miner companies were relegated to similar work behind the lines at Bibiapur. An Engineer Brigade order of March 7th runs :—"The Commandant, Bengal Engineers (Bt. Major A. Taylor) will supply the following working parties tomorrow. Bengal Sappers at gabion making, 121 men. Delhi Pioneers at cutting brushwood, 300 men : ditto in Park, 300 men." The orders of this period show also that most of

[1] "Reports on the Engineering Operations at the Siege of Lucknow in March, 1858," by Maj.-Gen. Sir R. Napier, K.C.B., Col. Harness, C.B., and Lieut.-Col. Lennox, V.C., R.E., appearing in *Professional Papers of the Corps of Royal Engineers*, New Series, Vol. X, 1861, pp. 67–88.

the British officers of the Bengal Sappers were employed in command of units of the Punjab Sappers, and accordingly the conclusion is formed that for a time the Bengal Sapper companies were kept purposely in the background. The Madras Sappers well deserved to be in the front line from the outset, and the loyal Bengal Sappers also after their excellent work at Delhi; yet the chief assistants of the Royal Engineers were the newly formed Punjab Sappers.

On March 8th, a party of Punjab Sappers under Ward made a battery near the Dilkusha to bear on the Martinière, while another under Fulford constructed a battery at the north-east corner of the Muhammad Bagh. These and other batteries opened on the 9th, when Outram, moving westwards along the Fyzabad road on the left bank, captured the Badshah Bagh and began to sweep with his guns the rear and flank of the enemy's first and second lines across the Gumti. At 2 p.m., a mixed brigade of the main attack occupied the Martinière without resistance, being assisted by two companies of Punjab Sappers under Lang and two companies of the same Corps under Thackeray and Forbes. The Sappers then made roads across the rebel trenches, loop-holed the outer wall of the Martinière garden, and fortified an adjacent village. The brigade continued its advance and before sunset had captured the enemy's first line beyond the canal from the neighbourhood of Banks' House to the river. This was accomplished easily for the position had been rendered untenable by the enfilade fire of one of Outram's batteries on the left bank. After all resistance had ceased, several companies of Punjab Sappers and Delhi Pioneers cut a road through the ramparts. Banks' House was taken by assault on the morning of the 10th, and Taylor then constructed batteries near it to bombard the Begum Kothi, while Outram's guns, near the Badshah Bagh, played on the Kaisar Bagh and Imambara. Thus the first and most formidable line of fortifications was captured with little loss.

During the night of March 9th–10th, the 23rd Company, R.E., under Clerke, with 100 Bengal Sappers under Champain, a company of Delhi Pioneers under Ensign E. C. Garstin, B.I., and all the available boatmen, moved one of the barrel-pier bridges upstream to a point just above the end of the rebel first line. "C" Company, Madras Sappers, was sent forward on the 10th to put Banks' House in a state of defence, and the Royal Engineers and Punjab Sappers bridged the canal with beams collected from the Martinière estate, to which the Engineer Brigade camp was moved from Bibiapur.

Important progress was made on the 11th. The Sikandar Bagh having been occupied without resistance, the Kadam Rasul and Shah Najaf were seized after a daring reconnaissance by Medley, Lang and Carnegie. "Seeing from the Sikandar Bagh that the two posts were very quiet and that no fire was coming from them," writes Medley,[1] "Lang proposed that we should go and reconnoitre. So with four of our native Sappers, Lang, Carnegie and I got well away into some cover, and creeping up, revolvers in hand, found ourselves close to the Kadam Rasul. There

[1] *A Year's Campaigning in India*, by Capt. J. G. Medley, B.E., pp. 172–177.

appeared to be no one there, so we were soon in the little building and looking down into the garden of the Shah Najaf which also appeared to be abandoned. We did not like, however, to capture that place with four men as there might have been rebels inside the mosque, so we went back to the Sikandar Bagh to ask for men to go and take the Shah Najaf. The Colonel ordered a detachment of 100 Europeans, with 50 of our Sappers, to accompany us, and we broke open the doors of the Shah Najaf and found the place evacuated. We set the Sappers to work to make it defensible, and at my suggestion 100 more men were thrown into it. . . . About dark, Lang and Carnegie were relieved by Champain with a working party of 50 Bengal Sappers and he told us that there had been a severe struggle on the left and that Major Taylor was amongst the wounded. Lang and Carnegie then went off to camp and Champain and I made ourselves comfortable for the night. About eight o'clock, the officer commanding the European detachment with us came up and said he had orders to withdraw his men to the Sikandar Bagh, but Champain and I decided to remain and defend the place with 50 native Sappers, who were nearly all Purbias. The Europeans marched off and we posted our sentries. It was a large place for so few men to hold on a dark night within 200 yards of the enemy and I was not sorry when we were marched back safely very early in the morning having received an order to that effect."

The severe struggle reported on the left took place when the Begum Kothi, the first of the main line of palaces, was taken by assault. Taylor led one of the columns, and as the two other columns were headed by Maunsell and Scott with parties of men carrying powder bags and tools[1] it is evident that both the Bengal and Madras Sappers and Miners were closely engaged on this occasion. A diversion on the left bank was made by Outram, who seized the iron bridge and thus turned the enemy's second line. The Nepalese contingent also was making its presence felt and was preparing to fight its way through the city from south to north. On the 12th, Sir Colin Campbell started a house-to-house advance from the Begum Kothi. The procedure adopted was to direct a heavy fire from the sand-bagged windows or loopholed parapets of adjacent houses on to the building to be attacked. The Sappers then blasted small openings through the walls and these were enlarged with pickaxes and crowbars to admit parties of infantry. By the evening of March 13th, the line of great buildings as far as the outskirts of the Imambara had been occupied, and the Imambara, Kaiser Bagh, Moti Mahal and Kurshid Manzil were under a concentrated fire of artillery.

The operations culminated on March 14th, 1858, in the capture of the Imambara and Kaisar Bagh. "I was ordered down with a strong working party in company with several other Engineers" writes Medley.[2] "We marched at daylight, carrying scaling ladders, powder bags, crowbars, etc., and found ourselves at length behind a wall with only the breadth

[1]Memorandum by Lieut.-Col. Lennox, V.C., R.E., attached to the "Report on the Engineering Operations at the Siege of Lucknow," by Maj.-Gen. Sir R. Napier, K.C.B.
[2]*A Year's Campaigning in India*, by Capt. J. G. Medley, B.E., pp. 178–181.

of the road between us and the Imambara enclosure. A battery of heavy guns was making a breach in the place at a distance of about 30 yards, and the enemy were lining the top of the wall and all the neighbouring houses and keeping up a hot fire. As the breach would not be practicable for some time, I sat down and had a cheroot. At length, about nine o'clock, we got the order to advance and in another minute were scrambling through the breached walls. The building was full of an extraordinary assortment of ornaments. . . . The Sikhs and 10th Foot poured out through the gateway into the road and we found we had turned the second line of entrenchments and saw the rebels rushing away towards the Kaisar Bagh. Then began a series of skirmishes as ' Pandy ' was driven out of one building after another. Meanwhile, the Sappers were busy in loopholing the parapets and breaking open doors. At length we found ourselves in the Chini Bazar close to the Kaisar Bagh and behind the enemy's third line of works, and I really do not think there were fifty men with us. The enemy, seeing our small numbers, came round on both flanks, but we rushed at them and they fled, and our Gurkhas, charging along the third line entrenchments, cleared them out very speedily. As soon as more men had come up, an advance was made to the Kaisar Bagh through the large court of the great mosque on our left, and the whole place was soon in our possession. An immense amount of plunder was obtained by the troops."

Captain W. O. Lennox, V.C., and Lieutenant F. E. B. Beaumont of the Royal Engineers, with Lieutenant W. W. H. Greathed, B.E., Lieutenant C. Scott, M.E., and Ensign Ogilvie of the Madras Sappers, distinguished themselves in the capture of the Imambara and Kaisar Bagh. The original storming party consisted of 100 Sikhs followed by a detachment of Bengal Sappers, under Lieutenant E. P. Brownlow, B.E., with powder bags and another of Royal Engineers, under Captain A. J. Clerke, R.E., with scaling ladders and tools. Behind these detachments came 200 infantry, and in rear, the party of Bengal or Punjab Sappers, under Medley and Lang, with more ladders and tools, and a working party of Madras Sappers under Scott and Burton. During the attack, the Moti Mahal and Kurshid Manzil were occupied by troops moving up from the European Barracks which had been vacated by the rebels, and also from the Sikandar Bagh. A detachment of the 23rd Company, R.E., dismantled one of the barrel-pier bridges at the end of the enemy's first line above the Martinière and began to move it upstream to a position near the Sikandar Bagh, where it was rebuilt. On the 16th, after Sir Colin Campbell had occupied the Chattar Manzil and adjacent buildings, a brigade from Outram's force crossed the river by this bridge and drove the enemy from the Residency, the iron bridge, the Machhi Bawan and the stone bridge. Every vital point was then in British hands, and within the next five days the recapture of Lucknow was completed. The victory was marred only by a sad fatality which had occurred on the 17th when Clerke, Brownlow, 14 men of the Royal Engineers and 30 Punjab Sappers were killed or fatally injured by the accidental explosion of some gunpowder.

The operations at Lucknow were neither so arduous nor so dangerous as those at Delhi, and through the mishandling of the cavalry most of the mutineers managed to escape. "I would rather go through five Lucknows than another Delhi," remarks Lang in his interesting diary. Nevertheless, the Madras and Bengal Sappers and Miners, and the Punjab Sappers and Delhi Pioneers, took a prominent part in a very unpleasant form of warfare—street fighting in a densely populated area—and helped Sir Colin Campbell to complete his conquest in the remarkably short period of fifteen days.

After the recapture of Lucknow, the engineer units, and large parties of infantry, were employed for a time in fortifying and preparing accommodation in certain buildings selected as barracks, levelling those portions of the city which interfered with defence, cutting roads through the city, and constructing military posts at the Residency, the iron bridge and the Machhi Bawan near the stone bridge.[1] The chief clearances were along the main line of palaces, where every building within 300 yards of the Kaisar Bagh was demolished. On March 29th, an order appeared proclaiming the dissolution of the Engineer Brigade. A division under Major-General Hope Grant was detailed to garrison Lucknow, while the remainder of the army, with the exception of a force under Brig.-General Lugard which was to march southwards, was formed into a movable column under Brig.-General Walpole to advance northwards to effect the conquest of Rohilkhand. On March 31st the various engineer detachments left their camp between the Martinière and Banks' House. The 23rd Company, R.E., under Lennox, the Bengal Sappers and Miners with Maunsell, Champain, McNeile, Murray, Forbes, Bingham and Assistant Surgeon Turnbull, "C" Company, Madras Sappers and Miners, with Scott and Raynsford, and five companies of Punjab Sappers, with Gulliver, Gustavinski and Chalmers, joined Walpole's column and, marching with it on April 7th up the left bank of the Ganges, were present at the abortive assault on Roya Fort a fortnight later which induced Sir Colin Campbell to proceed northwards to take command in person. The remaining three companies of Punjab Sappers, under Hovenden assisted by Stevenson and Nuthall, the 4th Company, R.E., under Nicholson, and a contingent of Delhi Pioneers, were kept in Lucknow to help Brig.-General Napier in defence work.

To attempt to describe the intricate movements of the various columns sweeping Oudh and Rohilkhand during the summer of 1858 and the succeeding winter is beyond the scope of this narrative. The Roorkee Column under Brig.-General Jones, which included 103 Bengal Sappers and Miners, occupied Bareilly on May 6th after actions at Boginwala on the Ganges and at Nagina[2] and was joined there by Walpole's force and other troops under the Commander-in-Chief. Jones was then sent to relieve Shahjahanpur and afterwards helped to drive a force of rebels

[1]Reports on these defence measures and their progress, by Brig.-Gen. Napier, Lieut.-Cols. Nicholson and Lennox and Majors Crommelin and Greathed, appear in *Professional Papers of the Corps of Royal Engineers*, Vol. IX, 1860, pp. 17–38. The fortification of the three posts was entrusted to Greathed.

[2]22 miles south-east of Roorkee.

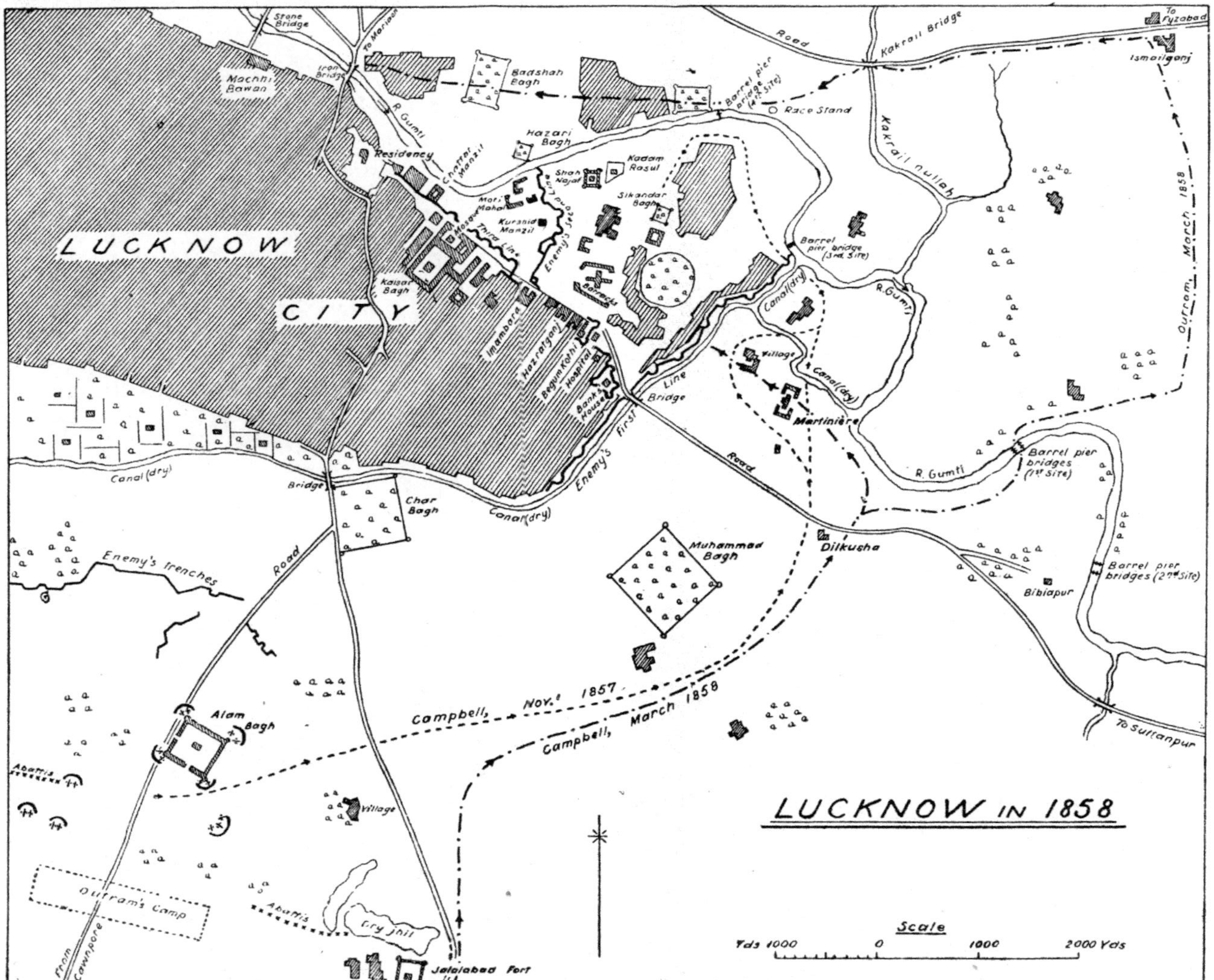
LUCKNOW IN 1858
LUCKNOW CITY
Stone Bridge
To Mariaon
Iron Bridge
Machhi Bawan
Badshah Bagh
R. Gumti
Hazari Bagh
Residency
Chattar Manzil
Shah Najaf
Kadam Rasul
Moti Mahal
Mosque
Kurshid Manzil
Sikandar Bagh
Third Line
Enemy's Second Line
Kaisar Bagh
Barracks
Imambara
Hazratganj
Begum Kothi
Hospital
Bank House
Enemy's First Line
Bridge
Barrel pier bridge (4th Site)
Race Stand
Road
Kakrail Bridge
To Fyzabad
Ismailganj
Kakrail nullah
Outram, March 1858
Barrel pier bridge (3rd Site)
R. Gumti
Canal (dry)
Village
Martinière
Barrel pier bridges (1st Site)
Barrel pier bridges (2nd Site)
Bibiapur
To Sultanpur
Dilkusha
Muhammad Bagh
Char Bagh
Canal (dry)
Enemy's trenches
Alam Bagh
Campbell, Nov.r 1857
Campbell, March 1858
Abattis
Village
Outram's Camp
Dry Jhil
Jalalabad Fort
From Cawnpore
Scale
Yds 1000 0 1000 2000 Yds

across the border of Rohilkhand into Oudh and defeat them at Mohamdi. On June 9th, the Bengal Sappers from Lucknow marched from Bareilly with the 23rd Company, R.E., arriving in Roorkee on June 18th, some 13 months after they had started in boats down the Ganges Canal. Towards the end of July, the companies present at headquarters under the command of Maunsell were the 1st and 8th (Humphry), 2nd (Ward), 3rd (Murray) and 7th (Thackeray).[1] Champain, Forbes and Jeffreys were under orders to join the Department of Public Works. Two companies under Maunsell took part, during the winter of 1858–59, in actions under Brig.-General Colin Troup at Maholi and Biswan near Sitapur and another at Aliganj near Fatehgarh. At this time, the 4th, 5th and 6th Companies were at Peshawar, and the 4th Company had recently been converted into a wholly Pathan unit.[2] It seems that although the authorized establishment of the Corps was 12 companies, only 8 companies were actually in existence as a result of the ravages of the Indian Mutiny.

Meanwhile, "C" Company, Madras S. & M., had been actively employed in Oudh to the east and south-east of Lucknow. The unit was present at many actions between April and November, 1858, including those at Nawabganj, Fyzabad, Sultanpur, Daudpur and Dhundikera. At Sultanpur it excelled itself in bridging. From December 6th, 1858, to January 17th, 1859, it served on the Rohilkhand frontier beyond the Gogra River and returned to Madras in February, 1859, though unhappily without Scott who had been killed two months earlier while reconnoitring a fort. The Punjab Sappers reverted to infantry duty: since the spring of 1858 they had been known officially as the 24th Punjab Regiment. The Delhi Pioneers were disbanded and returned to their villages. Thus the engineer units which had done so well at Lucknow were scattered far and wide or ceased to exist. The war in Oudh and Rohilkhand was finished. The Bengal Sappers and Miners subsequently received the honours "Delhi, 1857" and "Lucknow," while the latter was awarded also to the Madras Corps.[3]

We come now to the exploits of the Madras and Bombay Sappers and Miners in Central India. Fortunately, the Mutiny hardly affected the Bombay Army and left the Madras Army untouched. All serious trouble was confined to the provinces of Malwa and Bundelkhand, north of the Narbada River, though there was some unrest in Rajputana. The risings in Malwa were dealt with promptly and effectively by the Resident at Indore, Colonel H. M. Durand, late B.E., the hero of Ghazni. A column under Major-General Woodburn was despatched from Poona on June 8th, 1857, and was joined at Aurangabad on July 5th by "B" Company, Madras S. & M., which had returned recently from Persia. This unit was commanded by Captain (Brevet-Major) A. J. M. Boileau, M.E., whose company officers were Captain P. A. Brown, Madras Fusiliers, Lieutenant F. R. Fox, M.I., and 2nd Lieutenants H. N. D. Prendergast and H. J. G.

[1]Corps Order dated July 24th, 1858, appearing in a volume at Roorkee entitled "Corps Orders, Sappers and Miners. 24th July, 1858, to 13th March, 1859."
[2]Corps Order dated Sept. 17th, 1858. The order came into effect on Oct. 1st, 1858.
[3]G.O.G.G., Oct. 11th, 1860.

Gordon, M.E. The Deccan Field Force, as it was called, marched from Aurangabad on July 7th and relieved Asirgarh on the 25th and Mhow on August 2nd, the Sappers being employed in clearing the road and ramping nullahs. Meanwhile, the command of the force had devolved on Brig.-General C. S. Stuart, of the Bombay Army, under the direction of Durand as Political Officer. During the monsoon, " B " Company strengthened the defences of Mhow, but from October 24th to 31st it was engaged in the siege of the fortress of Dhar, 40 miles to the west,[1] where it made roads and constructed batteries. The garrison evacuated the place during the night of October 31st–November 1st, and as it was believed that Dhar contained much treasure, " B " Company made extensive excavations, though with little success.[2] Marching thence towards Nimach, Durand and Stuart captured the village of Guraria near Mandasor on November 24th, the Madras Sappers under Brown[3] being especially useful in preparations for the assault in which they took an active part. Prendergast was severely wounded in this affair. " B " Company then marched back through Mehidpur and Ujjain to Indore, whither Durand returned on the conclusion of the brief campaign in Malwa. He had been eminently successful in suppressing Holkar's mutinous Marathas and their sympathizers in Mhow.

Operations were now directed against rebel forces in Bundelkhand. It was planned that a Bombay division under Major-General Sir Hugh Rose should advance north-eastwards from Mhow through Jhansi to Kalpi on the Jumna, while a Madras division under Major-General G. C. Whitlock moved northwards from Jubbulpore on Banda. The thrust by Sir Hugh Rose was designed to relieve the pressure in Oudh and, aided by Whitlock, to shepherd the rebels northwards from Central India to the banks of the Jumna, where they would be crushed between the southern and northern armies. Sir Hugh marched from Mhow with the 2nd Brigade (Brig.-General Charles Steuart[4]) on January 6th, 1858, and sixteen days later was facing the fortress of Rahatgarh, west of Saugor. With him were " B " Company, Madras S. & M., and also the 2nd Company, Bombay S. & M., under 2nd Lieutenant H. R. Meiklejohn with 2nd Lieutenant J. Bonus, Bo.E., and the 5th Company of the same Corps under 2nd Lieutenant W. G. D. Dick with 2nd Lieutenant C. A. Goodfellow, Bo.E. Like " B " Company, the 2nd Company had returned recently from Persia. Though Rahatgarh was taken without difficulty, the short siege of only six days duration afforded opportunities for the Sappers to show their daring and enterprise. On January 26th, for instance, after Major Boileau, the Field Engineer, had called for volunteers to reconnoitre the ditch, Subadar Silavay, Jemadar Appavu and Privates Chinnatambi, Appasami and Savathiyan of " B " Company advanced under heavy fire in broad

[1]See the *Sketch Map of Malwa and Bundelkhand* included in this chapter.
[2]*Recollections of the Campaign in Malwa and Central India*, by Assist.-Surgeon J. H. Sylvester, p. 33.
[3]Major Boileau was acting as Field Engineer, with Prendergast as his Assistant.
[4]Brig.-Gen. Charles Steuart, late 14th Light Dragoons. The 1st Brigade was commanded by Brig.-Gen. C. S. Stuart, late 1st Bombay Fusiliers.

daylight, jumped into the ditch, took the requisite measurements and returned in safety.[1] The three Sapper units were employed as usual in improving communications, raising protective works and constructing batteries, and on the 30th, when a breach had been reported as practicable, it was examined under a close fire by Corporal Linahan, Lance-Naik Pichamuttu and Private Savathiyan of "B" Company. Rahatgarh Fort, however, was evacuated by the garrison. The Sappers mined and destroyed it and the whole force under Steuart marched to Saugor; which was relieved on February 3rd.

On February 10th, 1858, having already destroyed two forts near Saugor, the three Sapper and Miner companies marched 28 miles eastwards to the fort of Garhakota, demolished part of the defences, and returned on the 13th to Saugor. It was not until February 27th that Sir Hugh Rose, tired of awaiting the arrival of the division under Whitlock, began his advance on Jhansi. Meanwhile, the 1st Brigade, marching from Indore through Guna, had reached the neighbourhood of Chanderi. There is little to record of Sir Hugh's progress northwards with the 2nd Brigade. He forced the Madanpur Pass on March 3rd and crossed the Betwa on the 19th. The Madras and Bombay Sappers destroyed several forts, and the 21st Company, R.E., with the 1st Brigade, did likewise. On March 21st, the 2nd Brigade was before Jhansi, where it was joined three days later by the 1st Brigade from Chanderi. The Saugor Division under Whitlock was still far away to the south-east.

From an engineering point of view the chief interest of the campaign in Central India lies in the siege and assault of Jhansi, for there the Sappers and Miners were in the forefront of the battle and no longer mere adjuncts of the fighting forces. The place consisted of the usual fort and city. The latter had a perimeter of about 4½ miles and was surrounded by a high masonry wall with numerous bastions carrying heavy guns. It lay amidst tanks and trees on an inhospitable plain from which sprang a number of bare hills of granite. The huge fort, within its western boundary, towered above the city on a hill with precipitous sides. It was heavily fortified and amply supplied with embrasures and loopholes and was practically unassailable except from within the city. A large mound, over which the southern face of the city defence line ran, enabled the defenders to flank or enfilade long stretches of the wall. Some 600 yards outside this face was a line of rocky hills nearly as high as that on which the fort stood, but none of these was held by the enemy. As the garrison numbered some 12,000 men it might be thought that Jhansi was impregnable. Yet it had one fatal weakness. The fort, the key of the position, could not resist a siege for it had no water-supply and its storage tanks were empty. If the city defences were carried, Jhansi was doomed. This, of course, was unknown to Sir Hugh Rose, and it says much for his daring that he was prepared to attack the city, and afterwards attempt to reduce the fort, with a force consisting of only two brigades.

[1] *Historical Record of the Q.V.O. Madras Sappers and Miners*, Vol. I, p. 71, and *The Military History of the Madras Engineers and Pioneers*, by Major H. M. Vibart, R.(M.)E., Vol. II, p. 330.

An attack on Jhansi offered serious difficulties. The walls of the fort could not be breached except from the south, which was commanded by a bastion of the city wall on the mound. Batteries located on the southern line of rocky hills would be too distant. Consequently, it was obvious that the capture of the bastion on the mound must be the first objective, for this would lead to the occupation of the southern area of the city and facilitate an approach to the fort from the east. Accordingly, after Sir Hugh had invested the city with his cavalry, Major Boileau, his Chief Engineer, began to establish batteries on the southern hills to breach the city wall near the mound (left attack) and also further eastwards (right attack). The first of these batteries opened fire on March 25th, and by the 30th a practicable breach had been made to the west of the mound. A timber retrenchment of the breach was destroyed with red-hot shot, but the expenditure of ammunition in this and other bombardments was so great that it became evident that the city would have to be taken chiefly by escalade—an uninviting prospect. Arrangements for the assault were almost complete when a Sapper outpost on one of the hills announced that a rebel army was approaching. This proved to be a force of 20,000 men, under the infamous Tantia Topi, moving southwards to relieve the garrison. Without hesitation Sir Hugh advanced to meet the rebels and in a brilliant action on the Betwa River on April 1st, 1858, repulsed them and took all their guns. In this battle, Prendergast was again severely wounded and Fox shot eight men with his own hand.

Orders were issued that Jhansi City should be stormed at dawn on April 3rd. The 1st Brigade on the left was to attack the breach near the mound and attempt an entry by escalade further west, being assisted in both projects by the 21st Company, R.E. The 2nd Brigade on the right was to escalade at two points, and as this formation included "B" Company, Madras Sappers, and the 2nd and 5th Companies, Bombay Sappers, its fortunes may be followed in some detail. Brown of the Madras Sappers directed the attack, which was made in two columns on either side of an important gate in the city wall. The ladder party on the extreme right was led by Meiklejohn and the other by Dick,[1] both of the Bombay Sappers. They were accompanied by Bonus of the same Corps and Fox of the Madras Sappers. While the 1st Brigade carried the breach near the mound without difficulty and gained an entrance also by escalading, the ladder parties of the 2nd Brigade suffered a severe check. Under a devastating fire, the Madras and Bombay Sappers ran forward and planted three ladders against a wall nearly 30 feet in height, and led by Meiklejohn, Dick and Bonus, the 3rd Europeans swarmed up them. As Meiklejohn reached the top, he was dragged across the wall by the enemy and cut to pieces. Dick, bayoneted and shot through the head, fell dead at the foot of

[1]Maj.-Gen. Porter, in his *History of the Corps of Royal Engineers*, Vol. I, p. 495, states that one party was led by Meiklejohn and Dick and the other by Bonus and Fox; but Lieut. J. B. Edwards, R.E., who was present at Jhansi, remarks that Meiklejohn commanded one party and Dick the other. (See the Journal by Lieut.-Col. Fenwick and Major Edwards, R.E., appearing in *Professional Papers of the Corps of Royal Engineers*, New Series, Vol. X, 1861, pp. 33–38. This Journal includes an excellent plan of Jhansi.)

another ladder. Fox, wounded in the neck, fell also. Bonus was struck in the face by a stone and hurled down. The frail bamboo ladders, overloaded with men, broke and precipitated them to the ground. Thus the first attempt ended in complete disaster. Other ladders were brought forward only to be thrown down as soon as placed, and for a time the attack could make no headway; but at length the stormers gained a footing from eight ladders and, rushing along the walls, made contact with the left attack and swept into the city.

Street fighting continued for several days, the Sappers assisting the infantry by knocking holes in the roofs of houses and dropping live shells into the rooms. It is said that five thousand of the enemy perished. On April 5th, the fort was found to be empty, and with its occupation all serious resistance ceased. The Rani of Jhansi, a noted leader in the rebellion, had already fled. The Sappers and Miners, though closely engaged, did not lose many men,[1] but the casualties in officers were formidable. Before the battle of the Betwa there were six British officers of the two Corps. Now, Boileau had only Gordon of the Madras Sappers and Goodfellow of the Bombay Corps. Meiklejohn and Dick were dead, Prendergast, Bonus and Fox wounded, and Brown on the sick list.

After halting for three weeks at Jhansi, the Central India Field Force began to move on April 25th, 1858, towards Kalpi on the Jumna. "B" Company, Madras S. & M., under Gordon, and the 2nd Company, Bombay S. & M., under Bonus, marched north-eastwards with it, but the 5th Company under Goodfellow proceeded no further. The heat was terrific. Metal articles became so hot that it was painful to touch them. Every march was a nightmare. The troops toiled onwards, parched by thirst and suffocated by dust. Yet on May 7th, they were capable of routing 20,000 rebels at Kunch. Three times during the battle Sir Hugh Rose collapsed through heat-stroke, and the men fell out by scores. At Kalpi, still far distant, the Rani of Jhansi, Tantia Topi and other rebel leaders lay in wait, but beyond the Jumna was a British force under Colonel Maxwell advancing to join Sir Hugh. The Sapper companies were present at a small action on May 12th after remaining behind for two days to destroy a fort, and at length, on May 15th, they reached Galaoli on the Jumna, about 6 miles downstream of Kalpi. Until the 23rd, there was constant guerilla warfare on the right bank of the river, culminating in the repulse, with the aid of Maxwell, of a powerful attack by Tantia Topi on Galaoli. The Sappers worked day and night at roadmaking and hauling heavy guns across nullahs, and when Kalpi was occupied after the victory at Galaoli, they were completely exhausted.

Tantia Topi, the Rani and other rebels then made for Gwalior, where they won over Sindhia's troops to their side and again defied the Government. Accordingly, on June 6th, Sir Hugh set out for that place. The thermometer now stood at 130° in the shade. At Gwalior, on the 16th, the force was joined by Brig.-General Robert Napier, who shortly afterwards received command of the 2nd Brigade. Sir Hugh gave battle and drove

[1] "B" Company, Madras S. & M., lost only 4 killed and 9 wounded.

the enemy from the cantonment at Morar, both " B " and the 2nd Companies sharing in the fight. By this time, " B " Company could muster no more than 45 men. After reconnoitring Gwalior, the Commander-in-Chief moved part of his force some 20 miles westwards to effect a junction with a brigade from Rajputana and then proceeded to clear the rebels from several outlying positions. To facilitate the operations against the city and fort, " C " Company was employed in bridging a canal. " So long as they were supplied with their dram," writes Sylvester,[1] " they worked as merrily as English navvies." Gwalior was taken by assault on June 19th, 1858, and with its fall the hopes of the mutineers were irretrievably shattered.

A few Sapper and Miner companies, other than those already mentioned, fought in the Indian Mutiny in subsidiary theatres of war, but space does not permit more than a brief outline of their experiences. " L " Company,[2] Madras S. & M., under Lieutenant D. S. P. Campbell with Lieutenant J. J. Eager, both of the Madras Infantry, joined the division under Major-General G. C. Whitlock assembling at Jubbulpore in February, 1858, and moving northwards, reached Damoh on March 4th after Sir Hugh Rose had left Saugor for Jhansi. The division was destined to act merely as a barrier against the escape eastwards of the rebel forces defeated by the Commander-in-Chief, and when Jhansi fell it was marching through Panna towards Chhatarpur, 70 miles south-east of the Rani's capital. " L " Company took part in two skirmishes west of Banda on April 9th and 17th and a battle at Banda on the 19th, and was present in December, 1858, at the surrender of Karwi (south-east of Banda) and an action on the Panwari Heights near that place. The unit had much hard marching but little serious fighting.

In Rajputana, the 3rd Company, Bombay S. & M., under Lieutenant C. T. Haig, Bo.E., with 2nd Lieutenants C. Hancock and E. P. Gambier, Bo.E., took part in the siege and capture of Kotah from April 22nd to 30th, 1858. Hancock died of wounds on May 15th and was replaced by 2nd Lieutenant G. L. C. Merewether, Bo. E. The unit was present at the battle of Sanganer, near Jaipur, on August 7th, and an engagement on the Banas River on the 15th, and a detachment fought at Sikar, north of Jaipur, in February, 1859. The company then returned to Poona by way of Mhow. The 1st Company, Bombay S. & M., saw no active service, but the 4th Company under Lieutenant C. A. Goodfellow, Bo.E. was sent from Bombay in September, 1859, to join a force operating in Kathiawar, and Goodfellow was awarded the Victoria Cross for gallantry during the assault of the coastal fortress of Beyt on October 6th. In 1864, both the Madras and Bombay Sappers and Miners were granted the honour " Central India."[3]

The officers and men of the Madras, Bengal and Bombay Sappers and Miners received many individual honours and rewards for their services

[1] *Recollections of the Campaign in Malwa and Central India*, by J. H. Sylvester, p. 184.
[2] " L " Company was formed in Nov., 1857, from detachments of " A " and " E " Companies.
[3] G.G.O., Jan. 6th, 1864.

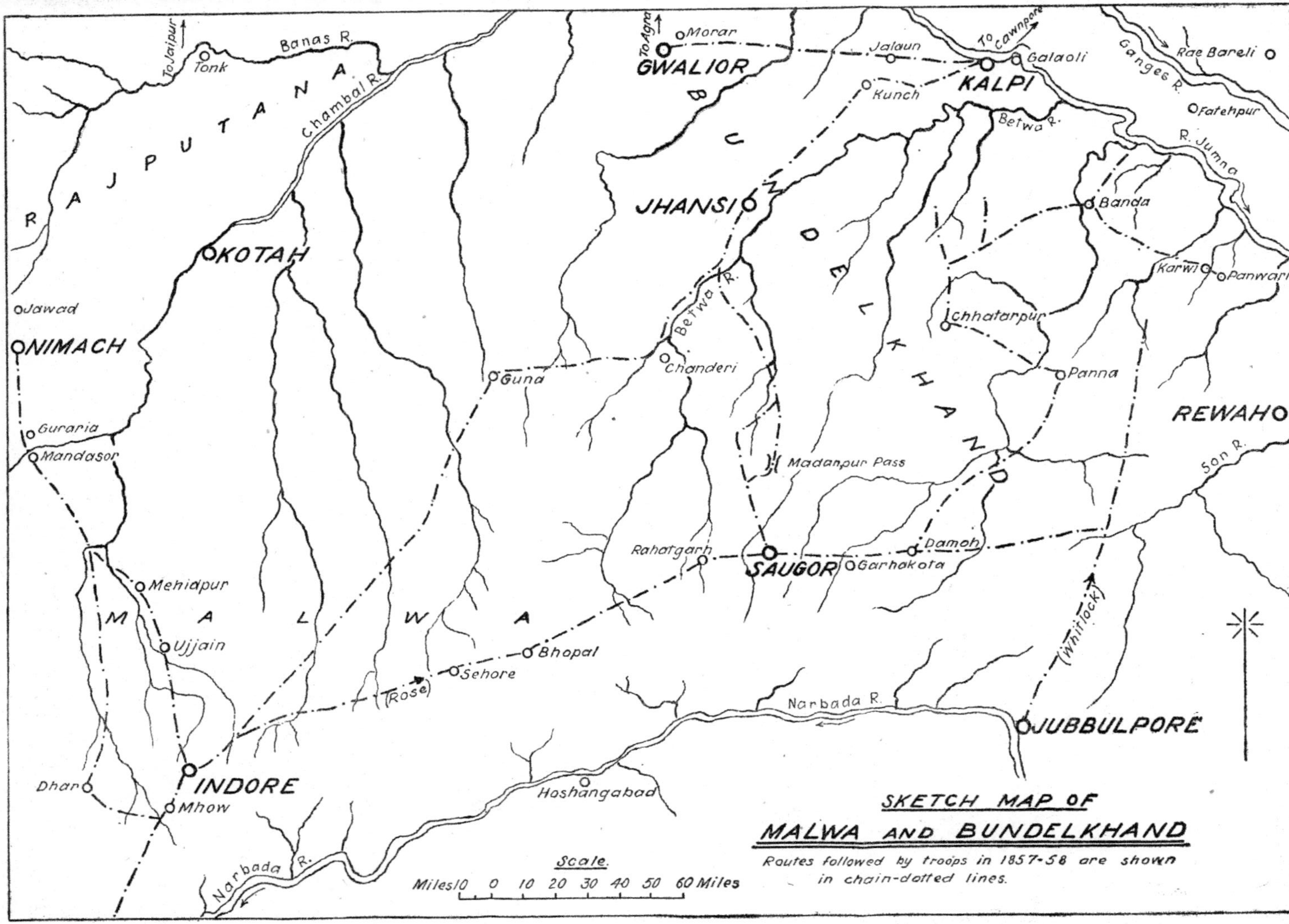
SKETCH MAP OF
MALWA AND BUNDELKHAND
Routes followed by troops in 1857-58 are shown in chain-dotted lines.
Scale.
Miles 10 0 10 20 30 40 50 60 Miles
RAJPUTANA
MALWA
BUNDELKHAND
To Jaipur
Tonk
Banas R.
Chambal R.
Jawad
NIMACH
Guraria
Mandasor
KOTAH
Mehidpur
Ujjain
Dhar
INDORE
Mhow
Narbada R.
To Agra
Morar
GWALIOR
Jalaun
Kunch
KALPI
To Cawnpore
Galaoli
Ganges R.
Rae Bareli
Fatehpur
R. Jumna
Betwa R.
JHANSI
Banda
Karwi
Panwari
Chhatarpur
Panna
REWAHO
Son R.
Chanderi
Guna
Madanpur Pass
Rahatgarh
SAUGOR
Garhakota
Damoh
Bhopal
Sehore
(Rose)
(Whitlock)
Narbada R.
JUBBULPORE
Hoshangabad

in the Indian Mutiny, but a complete record of these distinctions cannot be given here. Slowly but surely the last embers of the revolt were extinguished in the main theatres of operations. Brig.-General Robert Napier, who succeeded Sir Hugh Rose, led the Central India Field Force south of Gwalior against Tantia Topi and other rebels, destroyed many forts, and pursued Tantia until that desperado was run to earth in April, 1859. The Nana Sahib, the assassin of Cawnpore, was never taken. The Rani of Jhansi had been killed near Gwalior in June, 1858. Thus, after a struggle lasting more than two years, the great rebellion was quelled. Such a contest had never before been seen in India. At one time it threatened to wreck the work of a century, and it left behind it untold bitterness and misery. Nevertheless, it will ever remain an epic of British heroism and of the fidelity of many Indian soldiers under great temptation.

CHAPTER X

THE SECOND AFGHAN WAR, 1878–1880

APART from minor operations on the Indian frontiers and larger expeditions overseas to China, Abyssinia and Malaya, the Indian Mutiny was followed by a long period of comparative inactivity. On November 1st, 1858, Her Majesty the Queen had assumed the government of the country. Afterwards, the Honourable East India Company passed gradually into the pages of history. It was necessary to create a new Bengal Army and to effect a general reorganization of all the forces. On April 1st, 1862, the Madras, Bengal and Bombay Engineers were amalgamated with the Royal Engineers, the officers being granted royal commissions though remaining on their separate lists for promotion.[1] The post-Mutiny measures of reorganization did not seriously affect the Sappers and Miners until 1862, when the Madras Corps was reduced from twelve to ten companies.[2] The Bengal Corps suffered a similar reduction in 1863,[3] but the strength of the Bombay Corps remained unaltered at five companies. Three years later,[4] a scheme was prepared to improve the quality and supply of British non-commissioned officers for the Sappers and Miners by establishing three "skeleton" companies of Royal Engineers in India, one in each Presidency, and allowing each Commandant to select men for his Corps from the appropriate company.[5] These Royal Engineer units came into being on May 1st, 1868, as the 41st (Bengal), 42nd (Madras) and 43rd (Bombay) Companies, and thus, for the first time, the Royal Corps gained a permanent representation on Indian soil. Meanwhile, the financial and other attractions of employment in the Political or Public Works Departments continued to interfere with the peace-time recruitment of engineer officers for the Madras and Bombay Sappers and Miners. In 1865, for instance, all the officers of these Corps, with the exception of the Commandants, belonged to the infantry; and ten years later, there were still three infantry officers serving with the Bombay Sappers and no less than nine with the Madras Sappers.[6] The Bengal Sappers did not lack engineer officers, for the prospect of frequent service against the tribes on the North-West Frontier was always alluring to the adventurous spirit. By 1885, however, all three Corps were officered entirely from the Royal Engineers.

[1] A Madras Engineer, for instance, became a Royal (Madras) Engineer and was shown as R.(M.)E. In practice, however, the letter in brackets was often omitted. It will be omitted in future in this narrative.

[2] G.O.C.C., dated Jan. 30th, 1862. "L" and "M" Companies were broken up in July, 1862.

[3] The establishment was reduced to 10 companies on Aug. 24th, 1863.

[4] G.G.O., dated Nov. 20th, 1866.

[5] Two companies of Royal Engineers were formed at Chatham to train and supply men to the "skeleton" companies in India.

[6] Madras and Bombay Army Lists, 1865 and 1875.

Prior to the Second Afghan War, the Sappers and Miners progressed in efficiency, though they laboured under great difficulties because they were overshadowed at Army Headquarters by other branches of the service. " Before the amalgamation with the Royal Engineers," writes an officer of that period, " the Sapper Corps were much neglected by the authorities of the Army in India. No Commander-in-Chief, except Lord Napier of Magdala, took any trouble about them, and it was not until 1885 that their organization was at last assimilated to that of the Corps at home and they were given a reasonably permanent staff of officers and modern equipments of the tools, etc., necessary for their efficiency in the field. Cases occurred in which officers were appointed to them who could not otherwise be conveniently disposed of and were quite unfitted for their positions." Happily, the records of the three Corps prove that such cases were infrequent, but it is obvious that for many years after the Indian Mutiny the star of the Sappers and Miners was not in the ascendant. Better times came when Lord Napier was appointed Commander-in-Chief of the Bombay Army in 1866. He showed in Abyssinia what Indian Sappers and Miners could do, and as Commander-in-Chief in India from 1870 to 1876 he continued to watch over their interests and instituted an enquiry into their organization and equipment which laid the seeds of future reform.

The great upheaval of 1878–80 was needed to press home the point that engineer troops cannot do themselves justice without proper equipment and a suitable organization. " The Sappers and Miners," writes an anonymous author in 1881,[1] " are said to be simply native infantry battalions and, except for the superior scientific attainments of their British officers and non-commissioned officers, rather inferior ones. The companies are not units. They are weak, usually unaccustomed to much skilled labour, often kept at Headquarters unemployed, and subject to constant transfers. The officers commanding have little authority over them except when on detachment. The worst evil of the present system is that it tends to make the Commandant of the Sappers independent of his senior professional officer, the C.R.E. As there is never likely to be more than one company of Sappers with a brigade on active service, the *company* should be the unit, the O.C. Company being *solely* responsible for the dress, pay, equipment, discipline, transport and general efficiency of his men. If the company is the unit in time of war, it should be so also in time of peace ; otherwise, when it is sent on service, a complete change is made in its government and in the responsibilities of its commander at a time when change is least to be desired. The company should be able to supply strong working parties so that it should be at least 200 strong. . . . The C.R.E. with any body of troops should have command of all the skilled labour. Accordingly, the Sapper company or companies should be under his command. The native officers and men should not be transferred from one company to another but remain as much as possible in

[1]Abstract from a pamphlet entitled " Principles upon which the Indian Sappers and Miners should be organized," appearing in *The R.E. Journal*, Vol. XI, 1881, p. 180.

their own companies. The more the companies are accustomed to skilled work in time of peace the better. Instead, therefore, of being kept in one place and drilled as an infantry battalion they should be stationed in peace-time wherever their services could be most effectively used and where they would be learning work that would be useful to them in war."

While there are many objections to the system of scattered and independent companies advocated by this writer—among them the loss of *esprit de corps* which the abolition of the Corps system would entail—it is true that some of his criticisms were amply justified. For example, a General Order published in August, 1879, during the Afghan War, ran as follows :—[1] " When on field service, the Corps of Sappers and Miners is a distinct body under the command of its own officers appointed by the Corps of Royal Engineers. Commanding Officers of Engineers in the field have no power to interfere with the interior economy of companies of Sappers for which the officers belonging to the Corps are alone responsible to its Commandant. When any work is required from the Sappers and Miners attached to a force, orders will be issued to the regimental officer in charge by the officer commanding the division, brigade or detachment to which the Sappers and Miners are attached. The Engineer Department has no control over the Sappers, but the services of the Sappers, as of other troops, can at any time be placed at the disposal of the Commanding or Field Engineer for the carrying out of any specific work, and whilst so employed, the officer commanding the Sappers will receive orders regarding such work from the staff of the superior Engineer authority." This order was found to be prejudicial to efficiency and harmony. During the Afghan War there were instances of Field Engineers being sent to execute work on which, unknown to the Commanding Royal Engineer, the Sappers were already engaged. At Kabul in 1880, the Sapper officers messed separately from the other Royal Engineers. The Commandant of Sappers was denied access to the General Officer in chief command and received his orders through the Quartermaster-General. It is a fine tribute to the tact of the Sappers and Miners and the Engineer Department that there were few instances of jealousy or misunderstanding. The system, however, was unworkable, and an improvement was made in September, 1882, when it was directed that on field service the Sappers and Miners should be under the orders of the Commanding Royal Engineer, though their own officers should still be responsible for their interior economy.[2] An extensive reorganization in 1885, to which a reference will be made later, placed the Sapper companies at last on a proper footing.

On January 1st, 1877, an Imperial Assemblage was held at Delhi to proclaim Her Majesty Queen Victoria as Empress of India, and among the 17,000 troops on parade were the 5th, 6th, 9th and 10th Companies of Bengal Sappers and Miners. The ceremony was well timed for trouble was already brewing on the North-West Frontier and it was evident that war against Afghanistan could not long be delayed unless Amir Sher Ali, the

[1] " Occasional Notes, " in *The R.E. Journal*, Vol. IX, 1879, p. 168.
[2] S.G.O., dated Sept. 14th, 1882.

son and successor of Dost Muhammad, abandoned his friendship with Russia. Far from so doing he became gradually more intractable and truculent towards the British, and in October, 1878, turned back a mission under General Sir Neville Chamberlain and Major Cavagnari which was on its way to Kabul. In consequence, war was declared against him on November 20th, 1878, and immediate steps were taken to invade his country in three columns. The Peshawar Valley Field Force of four infantry brigades, a cavalry brigade and several batteries under Lieut.-General Sir Samuel Browne, V.C., was to advance through the Khaibar Pass by the shortest route to Kabul, while a Kurram Valley Column of six battalions with cavalry and guns under Major-General Frederick Roberts, V.C., was to proceed towards Kabul by a circuitous route leading over the Peiwar and Shutur Gardan Passes, and a Kandahar Column of one division with powerful artillery under Lieut.-General Donald M. Stewart was to enter Southern Afghanistan by way of Quetta, where it would be reinforced by a division under Major-General M. A. S. Biddulph.[1] A division under Major-General F. F. Maude, V.C., was detailed as a reserve for the Peshawar Valley Field Force, and another in Sind, composed of Bombay and Madras troops under Major-General J. M. Primrose, was formed into a reserve for the Kandahar Column, or " Quetta Field Force " as it was sometimes called.

Although the Second Afghan War may be divided for convenience into two phases, it consisted actually of two distinct campaigns separated by the conclusion of a treaty. During the first phase, which began on November 20th, 1878, with the entry of the Peshawar Valley Force into the Khaibar, and ended with the signature of the Treaty of Gandamak on May 26th, 1879, no less than fourteen companies of Sappers and Miners were in the field. With the Peshawar Valley Force were the Headquarters and four companies of Bengal Sappers under Captain W. North, R.E., Brevet-Colonel F. R. Maunsell, R.E., the Commandant, having been appointed as Commanding Royal Engineer. These companies were the 2nd, 3rd, 6th (Telegraph) and 8th under Lieutenants J. C. Campbell, H. Dove, W. F. H. Stafford and H. P. Leach, R.E., respectively.[2] The Company Officers were Lieutenants Hon. M. G. Talbot (3rd), A. R. Ancrum (6th) and R. V. Phillpotts, R.E. (8th). Captain B. Lovett, R.E., was Brigade Major, Lieutenant S. H. Exham, R.E., Adjutant, Lieutenant G. W. Bartram, R.E., Superintendent of Park, and Lieutenant E. Blunt, R.E., Instructor in Telegraphy. The 2nd and 3rd Companies had been stationed in Peshawar : the 6th and 8th came from Roorkee. The Bengal units were soon reinforced by three companies of Madras Sappers and Miners from Bangalore —" B," " E " and " K "—under Major C. Sim, R.E. These reached Jamrud at the foot of the Khaibar between January 9th and 23rd, 1879, and worked chiefly on the line of communication. The officers with " B "

[1]See Map III at the end of this volume.

[2]In an official report dated Aug. 27th, 1879, Capt. North mentions that Lieut. C. Maxwell, R.E., O.C. 1st Company, was present, but he does not record the presence of the unit and gives no account of its work. Lieut. L. C. Jackson, R.E., joined the 6th Company in Afghanistan in April, 1879.

Company were Lieutenants W. D. Conner, F. W. T. Attree and R. A. Wahab, R.E.; with "E" Company, Captain F. H. Winterbotham, M.I., and Lieutenants W. D. Lindley and A. C. MacDonnell, R.E.; and with "K" Company, Lieutenants C. C. Rawson, P. B. Poulter and R. E. Hamilton, R.E.

The Kurram Valley Column under General Roberts was sadly deficient in engineer troops, for Lieut.-Colonel Aeneas Perkins, R.E., the Commanding Royal Engineer, had at his disposal only the 7th Company, Bengal S. & M., under Lieutenant P. T. Buston, R.E.[1] The Adjutant was Lieutenant J. Burn-Murdoch, R.E. It seems either that Roberts did not want more engineer units or that the difficulties of the Peiwar and Shutur Gardan Passes were much underrated.

The Kandahar Column, on the other hand, was amply supplied. Under Lieut.-Colonel R. H. Sankey, R.E., as Commanding Royal Engineer of the whole force, with Lieut.-Colonel W. Hichens, R.E., as Commanding Royal Engineer with Biddulph's division, there were collected gradually four companies of Bengal Sappers and two companies of Bombay Sappers. The Bengal units were the 4th, 5th, 9th and 10th Companies under Captain P. Haslett (with Lieutenant H. J. W. Jerome), Lieutenant E. S. Hill, Lieutenant M. C. Barton and Captain L. F. Brown, R.E., respectively, and the Bombay units, the 2nd and 5th Companies under Lieutenants T. Rice Henn and E. H. Bethell, R.E. Lieutenant G. Turner Jones, R.E., acted as Company Officer with the 2nd Company. Colonel Sankey had Captain A. Le Messurier, R.E., as Brigade Major and Lieutenant J. D. Fullerton, R.E. as Adjutant. A large number of Royal Engineers served with one or other of the three invading forces as Field Engineers, political officers, staff officers or railway engineers. That the Afghan War was no petty frontier affair is shown by the fact that 171 Engineer officers earned the Afghan medal during the first phase.

On the evening of November 20th, 1878, Sir Samuel Browne despatched the 2nd Brigade from Jamrud under Brig.-General J. A. Tytler to move by a circuitous route to a position in rear of Ali Masjid Fort, 13 miles up the Khaibar Pass, and before dawn he sent the 1st Brigade under Brig.-General H. T. Macpherson to occupy some heights overlooking it. A few hours later, he started with the remainder of the Peshawar Valley Force to make a direct attack on Ali Masjid, and at 10 a.m. on the 21st his leading troops were on the Shagai Ridge within striking distance. Neither Tytler nor Macpherson had any Sappers and Miners with their brigades, and both being delayed by natural obstacles, Browne decided to attack without their assistance. Ali Masjid was held by 4,000 Afghans with 24 guns, and Browne met with most determined resistance. At one time, indeed, his position was critical, but Maunsell saved the situation by pushing up a company of Sappers to cover the withdrawal of some scattered troops who had failed in an assault. "On November 21st," writes North,[2]

[1]The 7th Company was commanded for a time by Lieut. C. H. Bagot, R.E.

[2]Report by Capt. W. North, R.E., Commanding Bengal Sappers and Miners, dated Roorkee, Aug. 27th, 1879, appearing in *Professional Papers of the Corps of Royal Engineers*, Vol. 4, 1880, pp. 159–162.

" the 2nd, 3rd, 6th and 8th Companies were considerably below strength owing to sickness. The 6th and 8th proceeded from Jamrud with the vanguard, the 2nd and 3rd being ordered to improve the road near the mouth of the pass. The advanced companies were employed throughout the day in improving the way and rendering it passable for artillery: also in dragging up the guns. I am justified in reporting very highly on the Sappers' work on this day. For the night of the 21st, when the force was bivouacked in front of the Ali Masjid position, the Sappers took picquet duty on the left flank, and in the morning they were the first troops to enter the fort which was only being evacuated by the last of the enemy as they entered." The 8th Company led the way.[1] The Sappers drove off enemy stragglers and Afridi plunderers and then resumed their road-making operations. During the next two days, they accompanied the advanced guard up the Khaibar and, using gun-cotton, made eight miles of road passable for the Horse Artillery. This work, however, and the problems of the steep descent from Landi Kotal to Landi Khana, delayed them to such an extent that although the main body began to arrive in Dakka (Loe Dakka) on November 23rd, the 6th and 8th Companies did not reach that place until the 26th and the 2nd and 3rd Companies until the 27th. The Sappers were then employed in strengthening Dakka Fort, making defensible posts, repairing roads, and building two boats for use in the advance. The fall of Ali Masjid completely disorganized Sher Ali's plans. He fled to Russian Turkestan and instructed his son Yakub Khan to treat with the British. Striving to conceal his discomforture, he wrote a bombastic letter in which he announced that, with the aid of the Almighty, his " lion-devouring " warriors had defeated the British;[2] but he omitted to add that his lion-devourers had afterwards evacuated Ali Masjid and retreated in disorder through the Khaibar.

Leaving the 2nd Brigade at Dakka, Sir Samuel Browne occupied Jalalabad on December 20th, 1878, with the 1st and 3rd Brigades, the 4th Brigade having been detached to garrison Ali Masjid. At Jalalabad, the 3rd and 6th Companies of Bengal Sappers were engaged in constructing fortified posts, demolishing the enemy's defences, building sheds and improving communications, and after being joined on December 29th by the 2nd Company from Dakka, they built a large work called Fort Sale and a trestle bridge across the Kabul River.[3] The 2nd Company had been delayed at Dakka in attempting, with the aid of the 8th Company, to open an alternative route to India leading through Michni on the Kabul River, north-east of the Khaibar. Campbell and Leach constructed 15 miles of road at a ruling gradient of 1 in 5, but the project was soon abandoned and the 2nd Company started for Jalalabad while the 8th Company returned to join the garrison of Dakka.

For several months, the 1st Division under Sir Samuel Browne remained at Jalalabad engaged in punitive operations against adjacent hostile gather-

[1]*History and Digest of Service of the 1st K.G.O. Sappers and Miners*, p. 37.
[2]Letter from Sher Ali to the Governor of Herat quoted in *The Second Afghan War*, by H. B. Hanna, Vol. II, p. 149.
[3]The bridge was built under the direction of Lieut. G. W. Bartram, R.E.

ings. The 2nd Division under Maude in the Khaibar region was similarly occupied. On January 20th, 1879, the 2nd and 3rd Companies of Bengal Sappers marched to Ali Boghan, 7 miles downstream of Jalalabad, to open a new route along the river bank.[1] They were joined, on February 19th, by the 8th Company from Dakka and laboured near the Kabul River until March 19th when they returned to Jalalabad. This was the largest undertaking by the Bengal Sappers during the first phase of the campaign and involved about 8 miles of difficult road-making in hard rock. On April 12th, Sir Samuel Browne advanced with his main body and camped at a place called Safed Sang,[2] some 3 miles from Gandamak. He was followed by the Bengal Sappers who remained at Safed Sang, employed on bridging and defence and road work, till the end of hostilities except when accompanying minor expeditions. The problems which confronted the engineers in Afghanistan may be exemplified by the story of the building of a trestle bridge, 185 feet long, over the Murki Khel Nullah at Safed Sang by Lieutenant W. Peacocke, R.E. On May 6th, Peacocke began the work with one carpenter. On the 9th he had three carpenters, but not a single nail was procurable and the only tools were an auger and three hand-saws. Some Bengal Sappers then arrived from Jalalabad and the bridge was finished on the 16th.

The services of the 6th Company under Stafford were seldom available for engineering work for the unit was employed chiefly on the extension of the military telegraph system under the direction of Colonel Maunsell as Commanding Royal Engineer. Beginning operations at Jalalabad, Stafford completed the laying of 40 miles of ground line to Dakka on January 25th, 1879, and within another three weeks had replaced it by aerial line. This was reeled up when a Government civil line reached Jalalabad on March 10th. Afterwards, the military line was extended to Fatehabad and finally to the Safed Sang Camp, whither it was followed by the civil line.[3]

In December, 1878, General Maude with the 2nd Division was having much trouble on the line of communication through the Khaibar. He sent two small expeditions against the Zakka Khel Afridis of the Bazar and Bara Valleys, and a detachment of the 8th Company had some useful experience in demolishing the towers of the enemy's walled villages. These were of stone, solidly built and about 40 feet in height, and the only access was by a rope ladder to a door near the top. Towards the end of January, 1879, another expedition, formed of columns from Jamrud, Ali Masjid and Basawal,[4] was led into the Bazar Valley by Maude himself. The Madras Sappers and Miners had now appeared on the scene, and a detachment of

[1]Report by Maj.-Gen. F. R. Maunsell, C.B., late C.R.E., 1st Division, appearing in *Professional Papers of the Corps of Royal Engineers*, Vol. IV, 1880, pp. 131–134.

[2]Another place of the same name exists on the Logar River south of Kabul.

[3]The work of the Field Telegraph Train is described in detail by Maj.-Gen. F. R. Maunsell in a report dated Aug. 11th, 1879, appearing in *Professional Papers of the Corps of Royal Engineers*, Vol. IV, 1880, pp. 137–144. The development of military telegraphy in India from 1867 to 1880, and its relationship to the civil system, are described by the same officer in an article entitled "Memoranda on the Military Telegraph Train in India," appearing in *The R.E. Journal*, Vol. XI, 1881, pp. 39–41.

[4]Basawal lies on the Kabul River between Jalalabad and Dakka, over 11 miles upstream from Dakka.

FRONTIER TOWER DEMOLITION, KHAIBAR PASS.

" B " Company marched with the Ali Masjid Column and, joined by another of " E " Company, reached China, the most important village, on January 26th, and having destroyed many towers, returned to Ali Masjid on February 4th. It was during this expedition that Lieutenant (afterwards General Sir) Reginald C. Hart, R.E., won the Victoria Cross for saving the life of a wounded soldier.[1] Other punitive expeditions followed. The 8th Company took part in one against the Shinwaris at Maidanak, 14 miles south-west of Basawal, on March 18th and was present when a column from Basawal defeated the same tribe in a fight at Deh Sarak near Maidanak. On March 17th, before the fight at Maidanak, Captain E. P. Leach, R.E., a Survey officer, gained the Victoria Cross for covering the retirement of a Survey party.[2] There were few expeditions which were unaccompanied by Sappers and Miners. A Bengal company was attached to a column under Brig.-General H. T. Macpherson which co-operated at the beginning of April with another under Brig.-General C. J. S. Gough when the latter defeated 5,000 Ghilzais from the Laghman Valley who were threatening Fatehabad on the road to Kabul.[3] These examples will suffice to show that the Sappers and Miners got their full share of the fighting.

The Madras Sappers and Miners rendered invaluable service on the long and difficult line of communication. Leaving " B " and " E " Companies at Ali Masjid, " K " Company moved to Dakka on March 18th, 1879, and on the following day to Basawal. Rawson, in command, must have been something of a wit for he erected at a road junction below Landi Kotal a sign-post one of whose arms bore the words " To Madras." After the campaign, he revealed his sense of humour also in the " Bailswamy " trophy presented by " K " Company to the R.E. Officers' Mess at Roorkee. This trophy is in the form of a silver inkstand bearing the figure of a Brahminy Bull and the curious inscription " Bailswamy," presumably to commemorate a joke which Rawson had enjoyed with the Bengal Sappers. " Swamy " is a common ending of Madrassi names; and as for the " Bail," an explanation may be found in the enormous cost of transporting to the front a bullock belonging to " K " Company. An article in *The Pioneer* of February 23rd, 1879, runs as follows :— " The K. Company of Madras Sappers have now with them at Landi Kotal their bullock, used for carrying water for the sepoys. The railway fare of this useful animal from Bangalore to Jhelum was Rs. 2,000 or Rs. 3,000 as he was provided with a truck to himself. Such bullocks are worth only Rs. 60 or Rs. 80 each, at which price serviceable animals could have been bought at Jhelum." It may be added that in many cases Government

[1]A graphic account of this exploit is given by Maj.-Gen. Sir Louis Jackson, K.B.E., C.B., C.M.G., late R.E., in an article entitled " Memories of Afghanistan in 1879," appearing in *The R.E. Journal*, Vol. LII, 1938, pp. 97–108.

[2]*History of the Corps of Royal Engineers*, by Maj.-Gen. W. Porter, Vol. II, p. 48. See also " Deeds of the Royal Engineers, " in *The R.E. Journal*, Vol. XXV, Jan.–June, 1917, pp. 9–20, which gives the gazettes of all Victoria Crosses awarded to military engineers in India from 1857 to 1897. The Victoria Cross was instituted on Jan. 29th, 1856.

[3]See the *Sketch Map of North-Eastern Afghanistan, Kabul-Jalalabad Area*, included in this chapter.

paid Rs. 1,000 for the railway transport of an officer's charger from Madras to the north when the animal was worth no more than Rs. 200, for the regulations required that certain officers should bring their chargers with them.

On March 26th, 1879, "K" Company moved to join the Bengal units at Jalalabad and was with the reserve when Gough defeated the Ghilzais near Fatehabad.[1] "B" Company advanced up the Khaibar to Landi Kotal. Until April 12th, "K" Company worked on the Jalalabad-Fatehabad road; but on the 14th it proceeded to Gandamak, where it remained in the Safed Sang Camp till the close of the operations. Meanwhile "E" Company moved forward to Basawal. At the end of April, "B" Company marched to Landi Khana and began to build a defensive post between that place and Dakka, after completing which it went back to Landi Kotal. The Madras Sappers commenced their return march to India on May 31st. "K" Company left Gandamak on that date and, joined by the other companies *en route*, reached the railhead at Jhelum on July 4th and Bangalore on July 29th.

It had seemed that the Afghan War was finished. The Treaty of Gandamak, signed by the new Amir, Yakub Khan, on May 26th, 1879, had brought the operations of the Peshawar Valley Field Force to an end, and all that remained was to face the hardships and difficulties of the withdrawal through the Khaibar. These were indeed formidable. "The march of Sir Sam Browne's force from the breezy upland of Gandamak down the passes to Peshawar," writes Archibald Forbes, the War Correspondent,[2] "made as it was in the fierce heat of mid-summer through a region pervaded by virulent cholera, was a ghastly journey. That melancholy pilgrimage, every halting place in whose course was marked by graves, dwells in the memory of British India as the 'death march'." On Maunsell devolved the task of arranging for the rafting down the Kabul River of an immense quantity of stores from Jalalabad to Dakka, a distance of 40 miles. He arrived from Gandamak with Major H. F. Blair, R.E., on June 2nd and set a company of Bengal Sappers to work on the construction of rafts, using timber from demolished buildings. In all, 225 rafts were put together under the superintendence of Blair, mostly of *mussacks*,[3] though some were of timber and others of barrels or earthenware pots. The first rafts were despatched downstream on June 4th, and by the 13th some 900 tons of stores and 885 officers and men, including 339 sick, had been transported to Dakka by small parties of Sappers.[4] This, remarks Maunsell, was the most interesting engineering operation of the campaign.[5] From Dakka onwards, none could avoid the hardships of the journey

[1] *Historical Record of the Q.V.O. Madras Sappers and Miners*, Vol. I, p. 110 and *The Military History of the Madras Engineers and Pioneers*, by Major H. M. Vibart, Vol. II, p. 500.

[2] *The Afghan Wars*, 1839–42 *and* 1878–80, by Archibald Forbes, pp. 180, 181.

[3] 7,000 skins were used to form 184 *mussack* rafts.

[4] "Report of Rafting Operations," appearing in *Professional Papers of the Corps of Royal Engineers*, Vol. IV, 1880, pp. 153–157.

[5] Report by Maj.-Gen. F. R. Maunsell appearing in *Professional Papers of the Corps of Royal Engineers*, Vol. IV, 1880, pp. 132–135.

overland, but the rafting operations by the Bengal Sappers beyond Dakka eased the problem of pack and wheeled transport through Landi Khana, Landi Kotal and Ali Masjid. By the middle of June 1879, all the Madras and Bengal Sapper companies, except one Bengal unit dropped at Landi Kotal,[1] were encamped at Peshawar, sadly depleted by sickness but with the satisfaction of having done credit to their respective Corps. The Madras companies soon started for Bangalore, while the Bengal units remained in Peshawar.

We revert now to November 1878 to follow the fortunes of the 7th Company, Bengal S. & M., with the force under General Roberts in the Kurram Valley. Roberts advanced simultaneously with Sir Samuel Browne and, crossing the frontier at Thal, marched towards a formidable Afghan position on the Peiwar Kotal.[2] While the 7th Company under Lieutenant P. T. Buston, R.E., repaired and strengthened a fort near the foot of the ascent, Roberts reconnoitred the approaches to the position which was four miles in length and held by 4,000 men with 24 guns. The attack was planned for December 2nd. After a night march, the British turned the Afghan left on the Spingawi Kotal and the enemy fled precipitately from the Peiwar position when their rear was threatened. Roberts then advanced to Ali Khel and, on December 8th, reconnoitred the great Shutur Gardan Pass, the main obstacle between him and Kabul. Transport difficulties, however, forbade further progress until the line of communication was improved, and as such improvement could not be secured during the winter with only one company of Sappers and a single battalion of Pioneers (the 23rd Bengal Infantry), Roberts was obliged to content himself with operations southwards against the Mangals of Khost whose fort at Matun[3] he occupied on January 6th, 1879. He passed the remainder of the winter and early spring in the Kurram Valley.

As regards the experiences of the 7th Company, Buston writes :—[4] " When the war started, we were ordered down from Murree to Rawalpindi to join a column under General Roberts and were given fifty mules for transport although most of our equipment was adapted for camels. The mules had rough straw saddles and there was no means of fixing the packs on them, for we had only *kajawas*[5] to take our picks and shovels and boxes of explosives. We had to place the packs one on each side of the mules and usually they did not balance. Nevertheless, I had to hustle the animals along and in due course we arrived at Thal. My Company Commander being on furlough, Lieutenant C. H. Bagot, R.E., was sent from Roorkee to take command, and on the very day of his arrival General Roberts came to inspect the unit. Many of the mules were found to have sore backs and the General was furious. Owing to sickness, the company

[1]*Official History of the Anglo-Afghan War*, 1878–89 *and* 1879–80, p. 62. This large volume, with many maps, gives a complete account of all the operations.

[2]*Kotal.* A pass, or dip in a ridge.

[3]See Map III at the end of this volume.

[4]Notes by Brig.-Gen. P. T. Buston, C.B., C.M.G. D.S.O., late R.E., sent to the author on Sept. 2nd, 1937.

[5]Receptacles for tools, etc., designed to balance on either side of the camel-pad on which they are slung.

could muster only 90 men, and when we started on the march and had to make roads across nullahs, we could not compete with the Pioneers who could produce a working party of 400 men or more. The result was a certain amount of friction between the C.R.E. and our Company Commander. After the attack on the Peiwar Kotal and the defeat of the Amir, we settled down in the Kurram Valley to make roads. I had with me an old Kohistani in charge of the coolies' tools, and I employed his son, a small boy, to buy poultry from the local villagers. After the war I took this lad with me to Roorkee and some years later he enlisted in the Corps and served with the 4th Company. Eventually he became Subadar Abdulla Khan Bahadur, I.O.M." Most of these remarks show the inadequate equipment and unsuitable organization of the Sapper companies. The reforms of 1885 were badly needed.

The operations in Southern Afghanistan during the first phase of the war were exacting but of a subsidiary nature. The original Kandahar Column, as already stated, comprised the 1st (Multan) Division under Lieut.-General D. M. Stewart, and to it was added later the 2nd (Quetta) Division under Major-General M. A. S. Biddulph. The 4th, 9th and 10th Companies, Bengal S. & M., were included in the 1st Division and the 5th Company in the 2nd Division, but the 10th Company was soon transferred to the 2nd Division. Advancing from Quetta, Biddulph entered the Pishin Valley on November 22nd, 1878. On December 12th, the 2nd Division was concentrated near the Khojak Pass, while the 1st Division under Stewart, who had assumed the chief command, was beginning to arrive at Dadhar below the Bolan Pass. Stewart then directed Biddulph to proceed through the Khojak towards Kandahar while he surmounted the Ghwazha Pass in the Khwaja Amran range and joined the 2nd Division beyond the Khojak at Takht-i-Pul.[1] This was accomplished, though with great difficulty, and the two divisions occupied Kandahar without opposition on January 8th, 1879. Very heavy work fell to the lot of the Bengal Sappers. The roads were execrable and the problems of transport stupendous. For supply purposes it was necessary to provide a camel and its attendant for every man in the ranks, and the mortality among the animals was so great that 1,500 fresh camelswere needed every week to maintain 12,000 camels in the field.[2]

From Kandahar, the 1st Division under Stewart continued north-eastwards to Kalat-i-Ghilzai and occupied that fortified town on January 21st, returning soon afterwards to Kandahar. Meanwhile, the 2nd Division marched westwards to Girishk on the Helmand River, where it remained until it was recalled to Kandahar on February 23rd. The retirement of the 2nd Division was the signal for hostilities by the Alizais who attacked it on the Kushk-i-Nakhud River on the 28th and were severely punished. Biddulph reached Kandahar on February 28th and the 2nd Division was then broken up, Biddulph and most of his troops, accompanied by the 5th and 9th Companies of Bengal Sappers,[3] returning to India by the Thal-

[1]See the *Sketch Map of Southern Afghanistan and Baluchistan*, included in this chapter.
[2]*Kandahar in* 1879, by Major A. Le Messurier, R.E., p. 85.
[3]The 5th and 9th Companies, Bengal S. & M., reached Roorkee in June, 1879.

Chotiali route leading to Dera Ghazi Khan, and Stewart with the 1st Division and attached troops remaining at Kandahar. During these operations, a portion of the composite Reserve Division of Madras and Bombay troops, under Major-General H. M. Primrose, had been pushed up from Sind on to the line of communication between Sukkur and Quetta. With it were the 2nd and 5th Companies of the Bombay Sappers. The 2nd Company, with Lieutenants T. Rice Henn and G. Turner Jones, R.E., had joined the Reserve Division in December, 1878, after returning from Malta and Cyprus and was employed until April, 1879, on roadmaking in in the Bolan Pass and Nari Valley. The 5th (Bombay) Company, under Lieutenant E. H. Bethell, R.E., also worked in the Bolan Pass and in the Harnai and Pishin Valleys in the Quetta region.[1]

The most important engineering operations undertaken by the Bengal Sappers and Miners during the first phase of the campaign in the south consisted of road-making by the 5th and 9th Companies in the Khojak and Ghwazha passes beginning on December 12th, 1878, and bridging on the Helmand River by the 5th and 10th Companies at the end of January, 1879. Barton, who commanded the 9th Company, writes :—[2] "We were the first company to move from Roorkee and marched from Khairpur on the Indus[3] to Sibi to open up a possible route that way. The heat was great and we had a very trying march. The numerical weakness of the company became evident, for owing to sickness there were few men available for road-making after the necessary guards had been furnished. Our equipment was designed for cart and camel transport, and loading and unloading were most laborious. After reaching Quetta, my company and the 5th (Lieutenant E. S. Hill, R.E.) were employed on the Khojak and Gwaja (Ghwazha) passes.[4] The road from Chaman to Kandahar presented no difficulties and there was little opposition." It may be remarked, however, that the work of improving the track through the Khojak Pass was exceedingly difficult. For instance, at one place the Sappers and Pioneers had to construct a ramp or slide for guns which sloped at 30° for a distance of 150 yards and very steeply for another 400 yards.

As regards the bridging operations on the Helmand by the 10th Company of Bengal Sappers, assisted by the 5th Company, Le Messurier records in his diary :—[5] "Read Brown's report.[6] Material was originally intended to have been for 150 yards of bridge, but this was reduced to 50 yards. Twelve pontoons and twelve chess-carts with spare stores were despatched by rail from Roorkee to Multan, but this was further reduced at Multan to one raft of two pontoons. The raft, with twelve extra chesses,

[1]*Digest of the Services of the Bombay Sappers and Miners*, by Major G. H. W. O'Sullivan, R.E., pp. 42, 43.

[2]Notes by Col. M. C. Barton, D.S.O., late R.E., sent to the author on Sept. 15th, 1937.

[3]70 miles east of Jacobabad.

[4]According to the *History and Digest of Service of the 1st K.G.O. Sappers and Miners*, p. 33, the companies employed on the Ghwazha Pass were the 4th and 9th. The 4th afterwards accompanied the advance to Kalat-i-Ghilzai from Kandahar and in March, 1879, returned to the Khojak Pass for road work.

[5]"Diary of Major Le Messurier, Brigade Major, R.E., with the Quetta Column," appearing in *The R.E. Journal*, Vol. IX, 1879, pp. 180–182.

[6]Capt. L. F. Brown, R.E., O.C. 10th Company, Bengal Sappers and Miners.

tools and spare rope, was conveyed from Sukkur to the Helmand on two equipment wagons and three carts. The river near Girishk was from 80 to 300 yards wide with a velocity of 4½ miles an hour and a hard bottom with plentiful boulders. Borstan[1] was selected as the crossing place, there being two channels with islands between; but as there was not sufficient material, a flying bridge was made of the pontoon raft, and another of a boat found in a village. The work was completed in three hours on January 31st, and by 2 p.m. the troops and baggage had crossed."

In his book, *Kandahar in* 1879, Le Messurier gives many interesting descriptions of Afghanistan. As the troops approached Kandahar he writes " I have never seen such a country. Plain after plain as void of vegetation as it is possible to be, and the mountain ridges more and more rocky and rough, with a howling desert of sand on the left leading to goodness knows where. The climate, though bitterly cold, is most invigorating. Your hands are not merely chapped but chopped into gashes: the air so dry that, touch what you will, it crackles with electricity: an appetite at all times, but little thirst. The horses seem all right, but the camels die by hundreds." At Kandahar he adds " Haslett, Barton and Hill, with their companies of Sappers, have commenced knocking down partition walls, filling in debris, and executing works necessary for the different departments to be located in the citadel. I have sent to the Editor of *The R.E. Journal*, plans of the city, with sections of the walls." He remarks that the dress of the Engineer and Sapper and Miner officers was decidedly irregular. Some helmets had spikes: others had not. Sankey wore a corduroy suit with field boots and carried a sword with an inlaid handle. Le Messurier himself favoured brown boots with canvas tops and was armed with a cavalry sabre. The Sapper and Miner officers had helmets with wadded khaki covers, khaki blouses, and trousers and boots of different patterns.[2] Comfort, in fact, was preferred to smartness, and Sankey set the fashion.

The conclusion of peace at the end of May, 1879, was followed by the instalment of Major Cavagnari as British Resident at Kabul, but on September 3rd the smouldering fires of Afghan hostility burst into flame and Cavagnari and his small escort were murdered. Energetic measures were taken immediately for the re-establishment of British influence by a second invasion of Northern Afghanistan and at the same time the evacuation of troops from the southern area was stopped. Major-General Sir Frederick Roberts, V.C., with a force of one cavalry and two infantry brigades and subsidiary troops, was directed to advance on Kabul from the Kurram Valley, while a division under Major-General R. O. Bright marched through the Khaibar to join him. Lieut.-General Sir Donald Stewart was ordered to hold Southern Afghanistan with a third division based on Kandahar.

[1] 8 miles downstream of Girishk.

[2] Khaki, with blue facings, had been introduced in 1859 as the hot weather dress of the British Officers and N.C.O.s of the Madras Sappers and Miners. The helmets in that Corps were then of felt with a twisted *paggri* of red cloth. Cork helmets were introduced in 1870. In 1877, the full dress of the Indian ranks of the Madras Sappers was altered to a dark blue turban, scarlet tunic of cloth with blue facings and dark blue trousers with a red stripe, but the working dress was a dark blue cotton turban and tunic and black cotton trousers.

Units of the Sappers and Miners were allotted to each formation. Roberts retained the 7th Company of Bengal Sappers, now under Lieutenant C. Nugent, R.E., with Lieut.-Colonel Aeneas Perkins, R.E., as Commanding Royal Engineer. The 8th Company, which had entered the Kurram Valley in the latter half of October and fought in the Zaimukht territory north of Thal in December, was not included in his command and consequently he was again deficient in engineer troops. Bright, in the Khaibar, was allotted the 2nd, 3rd and 6th Companies of Bengal Sappers from the Peshawar and Rawalpindi Districts, and also the 5th Company which had been stationed in Roorkee since its return from Kandahar. The Commanding Royal Engineer was Lieut.-Colonel D. Limond, R.E. Major E. T. Thackeray, V.C., R.E., of Indian Mutiny fame, succeeded Colonel F. R. Maunsell as Commandant of the Bengal Corps on September 20th, 1879, and left Roorkee for the front with the 5th Company on October 5th.[1] With the Kandahar Force (afterwards called the Southern Afghanistan Field Force) were Lieut.-Colonel W. Hichens, R.E., and the 4th and 10th Companies of the Bengal Sappers; and on the line of communication through the Bolan Pass, the 2nd Company, Bombay Sappers, under Lieutenant T. Rice Henn with Lieutenant G. Turner Jones, R.E., and the 5th Company under Lieutenant E. C. Spilsbury, R.E. The two Bombay units were soon reinforced by two others—the 3rd Company under Lieutenant G. H. W. O'Sullivan with Lieutenant M. J. Slater, R.E., and the 4th Company under Lieutenant H. O. Selby with Lieutenant W. Coles, R.E.—and the four Bombay companies then came under the command of Lieut.-Colonel J. Hills, R.E., with Lieutenant J. D. Fullerton, R.E. as Adjutant.[2]

Three companies of Madras Sappers and Miners, under Major Ross Thompson, R.E., were sent to work on the line of communication of Bright's force in and beyond the Khaibar. These were "A" Company under Lieutenant C. H. Darling with Lieutenants W. D. Lindley and R. A. Wahab, R.E., "C" Company under Lieutenant A. R. F. Dorward with Lieutenants L. Langley and G. E. Shute, R.E., and "I" Company under Lieutenant A. E. Dobson with Lieutenants C. B. Henderson and T. Digby, R.E.[3] "A" Company set out from Bangalore on October 3rd, followed on the 5th by "I" Company, and "C" Company sailed from Rangoon on November 16th. By December 25th, 1879, all the Madras companies had reached Landi Kotal, a place well known to Lindley and Wahab who had served there with "B" Company in the first phase of the war.

Meanwhile, Major-General Sir Frederick Roberts had reached Kabul. The leading troops of the 1st Division, Kabul Field Force, which he commanded, secured the Shutur Gardan Pass on September 11th, 1879, and on the 24th a column under Brig.-General T. D. Baker advanced towards Kushi where the whole division was concentrated by October 1st.

[1] *History and Digest of Service of the 1st K.G.O. Sappers and Miners*, p. 33.

[2] *Digest of the Services of the Bombay Sappers and Miners*, by Major G. H. W. O'Sullivan, R.E., p. 43.

[3] *Historical Record of the Q.V.O. Madras Sappers and Miners*, Vol. I, p. 111.

Nugent and Buston, with the 7th Company, Bengal S. & M., had assisted the passage of the division over the Shutur Gardan Kotal by making a road up a very steep ascent for a distance of three miles.[1] Beyond Kushi, where Yakub Khan surrendered himself to Roberts, the way was barred by a powerful army in the Sang-i-Nawishta defile north of Charasia, but Roberts routed the enemy there on October 6th and three days later was encamped on the Siah Sang heights outside Kabul. The general situation was now very serious, for although the capital was at Robert's mercy he was threatened by an army of 60,000 Afghans under Muhammad Jan. General Bright, with the 2nd Division, was unable to reinforce him owing to lack of transport on the Khaibar route and there was every prospect that the Kurram route would soon be closed by snow. Roberts decided to occupy the great Bala Hissar fortress of Kabul. Buston relates that the 7th Company was employed for some time in clearing the place; but the project was abandoned after some explosions had occurred within the fortress and Roberts occupied instead the Sherpur cantonment, a walled enclosure to the north of the city below the Bimaru heights. The 7th Company strengthened the defences of the enclosure and added to those on the heights above.

On December 14th, learning that Muhammad Jan was advancing, Roberts took the offensive but was overpowered by numbers and obliged to retire into Sherpur, where he was closely invested by 100,000 Afghans. " Two columns were sent out," writes Buston,[2] " one under Brig.-General T. D. Baker and the other under Brig.-General H. T. Macpherson. I accompanied Macpherson with 25 Bengal Sappers, and Lieutenant Charles Nugent, R.E., who had commanded the 7th Company since we left the Kurram Valley, led a similar detachment with Baker. There was a large army of malcontents in a certain valley and it was intended that Baker should drive them in one direction and Macpherson take them in another, and that a force from Kabul should then meet them and shut them in. As we were going along with Macpherson we heard gunfire and, turning in that direction, came across numbers of dead Afghans and some of our own. We learned that our cavalry and artillery from Kabul had met a large body of the enemy in an area intersected by small irrigation channels and that some of our guns had been abandoned and our cavalry defeated. We ourselves experienced little opposition, the enemy fleeing to the hills, and we made our way back safely to Kabul though sniped continually in the retreat. Afterwards, we were shut up in Sherpur for several months. We occupied barracks in the cantonment, and the 7th Company had a section of wall to defend."

[1]*Official History of the Afghan War of* 1878–79 *and* 1879–80, Section V, p. 32. In an article entitled " Notes on the Operations in the Kurram Valley, 1878–79," appearing in the *Journal of the United Service Institution of India*, Vol. X, 1881, pp. 7–14, Lieut. M. Martin, R.E., remarks that the engineer troops (7th Company and 23rd Punjab Native Infantry (Pioneers)) were inadequate and suffered from being under multiple control. He admits, however, that there was little to be done beyond road-making and occasional hutting.

[2]Notes by Brig.-Gen. P. T. Buston, C.B., C.M.G., D.S.O., late R.E., sent to the author on Sept. 2nd, 1937.

The Afghans attacked the cantonment repeatedly, and before dawn on December 23rd, 1879, they launched a grand assault. "The darkness faded," writes Hanna,[1] "but still the vast mob rushed on, wave after wave, filling the air with deafening cries of *Allah-i-Allah* as they hurled themselves upon the defences. With only their naked hands to tear down the obstructions, not one succeeded in getting within the walls. The Engineers had done their work too well. For seven hours the enemy hurled themselves upon the abattis and under a murderous fire tore at the tough telegraph wires which held the heavy logs together. Great heaps of dead testified to the spirit by which they were inspired. That night, every man in Sherpur knew that the siege was at an end."

The repulse of this assault was followed by a successful counter-attack. "Following in the wake of the 9th Lancers and 5th Punjab Cavalry" writes Hensman,[2] "came the Sappers with every engineer officer in camp, their orders being to blow up and burn all villages and forts lately occupied by the enemy. In the villages some fanatics remained, and these were blown up in their houses by the mines laid by the engineers." It was during these operations that Captain J. Dundas, V.C., and Lieutenant C. Nugent, both of the Royal Engineers, lost their lives in an accident attributable indirectly to the parsimony of the Government in the matter of engineer equipment. Buston writes[3] "There were two empty fortified villages which the 7th Company was ordered to demolish. Nugent took one half-company and I the other. I was just going away after exploding my mines when a messenger arrived from the other half-company to say that Nugent and Dundas had been killed. All that we could do in those times was to load a mine with powder, thrust into it a tin trough which we filled with powder, insert a quick-firing fuse, light it and run. Presumably, on this occasion the fuse must have lit the powder before the officers could get away. Our limited supply of Bickford's fuse was almost exhausted, and as we could get none from India we had to make a substitute by soaking cotton thread in gunpowder. This, of course, burned very unevenly." Thus, two valuable lives were sacrificed to effect an infinitesimal saving in the military budget.

While Sir Frederick Roberts was hard pressed in Kabul, General Bright had been trying to reach him by the Khaibar route. The 2nd and 6th Companies, Bengal S. & M., arrived from Jalalabad at the Safed Sang camp near Gandamak on October 30th, 1879, and joined a column under Brig.-General C. J. S. Gough, V.C., which set out with Bright on November 2nd to meet another column marching from Kabul under Brig.-General H. T. Macpherson. The 6th Company had recently extended the military telegraph line from Landi Kotal to Gandamak. It was commanded by Lieutenant W. F. H. Stafford, R.E., with Lieutenants A. H. Randolph and E. C. Stanton, R.E., as Company Officers. The 2nd Company was under Lieutenant J. C. Campbell, R.E. Lieut.-Colonel

[1] *The Second Afghan War*, by H. B. Hanna, Vol. III, pp. 244–247.
[2] *The Afghan War*, 1878–80, by H. Hensman, p. 255.
[3] Notes by Brig.-Gen. P. T. Buston, C.B., C.M.G., D.S.O., late R.E., sent to the author on Sept. 2nd, 1937.

D. Limond, R.E., was Commanding Royal Engineer, and Major E. T. Thackeray, V.C., R.E., commanded the Bengal Sappers. Passing through Surkhpul on November 4th and Jagdalak on the 5th, Bright and Gough met Macpherson at Katasang on November 6th and established a new line of communication with Kabul, through Lataband, replacing the Kurram route. The line, however, was subject to constant raids and consequently was in urgent need of protection, so Gough posted detachments at Jagdalak Fort, on the Jagdalak Kotal and at Pezwan,[1] and on November 9th, accompanied by Thackeray and the 5th Company under Lieutenant E. S. Hill, R.E., which had just arrived from Roorkee, returned with Bright to Gandamak. Meanwhile, the 2nd Company improved the road and the 6th Company extended the telegraph line to Pezwan. Orders were now given that the 2nd Company at Jagdalak Fort should strengthen that post and the Kotal post, and that the 6th Company should work on the Pezwan post. At Gandamak, Hill and Maxwell with the 5th Company prepared a hutted camp under the direction of Thackeray and North. They were joined early in December by the 3rd Company under Lieutenant H. Dove, R.E., but that unit was sent forward immediately to the Jagdalak Kotal to help the 2nd Company.

On December 13th, Gough was ordered by Bright to advance with his brigade to occupy Pezwan, Jagdalak Kotal and Jagdalak in strength, which he did on the 14th. The same night, however, he received orders direct from Roberts to march at once to Kabul; but as he was warned that the Ghilzais would probably rise and that the enemy in front of Sherpur numbered 30,000, he reported to Bright that in his opinion the operation was too dangerous. Bright concurred, so the brigade remained in occupation of the three posts. Gough inspected the Kotal post, which was 150 yards west of the road and some four miles from Jagdalak Fort, and placed Thackeray in command of the garrison with orders to strengthen the defences as rapidly as possible. The post lay 6,300 feet above sea level and the descent to Jagdalak ran through a defile. On December 15th, Thackeray set the 2nd and 3rd Companies to build traverses in the Jagdalak Kotal post and to dig pits for storing water, and during the afternoon the 5th Company, with North, Hill and Maxwell, passed through on its way to Jagdalak Fort.

The garrison on the Kotal amounted to about 1,400 men. At sunset, the Ghilzais began to invest the place and attacked it unsuccessfully during the night. The telegraph line had been cut, but communication with Jagdalak Fort and Pezwan in either direction was maintained during the day by heliograph. Skirmishing never ceased, but this did not deter Thackeray from making several reconnaissances. On one occasion, after he had walked alone from the Kotal to Jagdalak Fort because he wished to discuss the situation in person with Gough, the General insisted that he should have a horse and a mounted escort for his return journey. Work on the defences at Jagdalak Kotal continued on the 16th, and on the 17th the

[1]Pezwan lies on the Surkhpul-Jagdalak road, 4 miles west of Surkhpul and at the foot of the ascent to the Jagdalak Kotal.

3rd Company under Dove took part in a successful fight and the 2nd Company under Campbell destroyed a village. The enemy retaliated with a night attack. As a convoy was about to pass through to Jagdalak Fort, it became necessary to drive the enemy from some *sangars* which they were building on the heights overlooking the road. This was accomplished on December 19th by Thackeray and the 3rd Company, while Campbell with the 2nd Company and some Gurkhas, held the Kotal post. During a Ghilzai counter attack in the afternoon, the convoy passed safely through; but scarcely had Thackeray returned to the Kotal post than the enemy, descending from the heights, opened a heavy fire which they maintained for several hours.

After the convoy had reached Jagdalak Fort, Gough was in a position to advance if necessary to Kabul. On the 20th, he received another peremptory order from Roberts to march without delay and consequently he set out on the 21st with a column which included the 5th Company of Bengal Sappers. He anticipated strenuous opposition, but the unexpected happened. Picking up the Lataband detachment on his way, he entered the Sherpur Cantonment on December 24th, 1879, without firing a shot. The Afghans, repulsed by Roberts, had raised the siege.

On the afternoon of December 23rd, a determined attack was made on the Jagdalak Kotal post where Thackeray had now only the 2nd and 3rd Companies of Bengal Sappers and a weak company of Punjab Native Infantry. The other engineer officers present were Campbell and Gordon (2nd Company), Dove and Randolph (3rd Company) and Blunt (Signals). About 2 p.m. the enemy approached in great force along the crest of a ridge north-east of the post. Some gathered close under a corner of the defences while others built *sangars* on the principal spurs and opened a plunging fire directed chiefly against the east face held by the 2nd Company. They kept up incessant cries of " Allah " and called on the Mussulman sepoys to desert. At about 4 p.m. Thackeray was seriously wounded while directing the fire from the east face. " He was standing exposed, giving his orders to his Adjutant, Lieutenant Gordon," writes a brother officer.[1] " It was pointed out to him that an Afghan at close range was taking deliberate aim at him, but he paid no attention. The Enfield bullet lodged in his right forearm, shattering the bone, but during the remainder of the attack he continued to direct the operations from the mess and hospital tent which was protected by boulders and brushwood. The danger of the desertion of Muhammadan sepoys to the enemy added greatly to his anxieties with his experiences in the Mutiny ever present in his mind." Gradually, the enemy enveloped the post until they were firing into it from almost every side, but the defenders, now commanded by Dove, were unshakable. All assaults were checked by well directed volleys, and before midnight the tribesmen, numbering 3,000 men, relinquished the attack and retreated.[2] The 2nd and 3rd Companies remained at the Kotal until

[1]Memoir of Col. Sir E. T. Thackeray, V.C., K.C.B., late Royal (Bengal) Engineers, appearing in *The R.E. Journal*, Vol. XLII, 1928, pp. 315–330.

[2]A full account of the defence of the Jagdalak Kotal post is given in " Memorandum on the Operations of the Bengal Sappers and Miners at Gandamak and Jagdalak, " by Lieut.-Col. E. T. Thackeray, V.C., R.E., appearing in *Professional Papers of the Corps of Royal Engineers*, Vol. VI, 1881, Paper VIII, pp. 153–172.

January 10th, 1880, when they moved forward to Lataband to improve the road. At the same time, the 6th Company advanced from Pezwan to Jagdalak Fort and formed part of the garrison of that post until August 10th when they marched for Peshawar.

Thackeray was sent back to India, his wound being a very severe one and aggravated by a piece of his *poshtin*[1] carried in with the bullet. Within a few months, he was invalided to England and did not resume his appointment at Roorkee until 1881. The command of the Bengal Sappers and Miners in Afghanistan devolved in consequence on North who held it until the arrival in Kabul of Captain and Brevet-Major Bindon Blood, R.E., fresh from the Zulu War.[2]

The arrival of the 5th Company, Bengal S. & M., in Kabul with Gough's brigade on December 24th, 1879, was very welcome to the hard-pressed 7th Company, and after the latter had returned from a small expedition into Kohistan, the two units were fully occupied in defence work. Assisted by working parties of infantry and local labourers, they demolished every house and wall within 1,000 yards of the Sherpur enclosure. In addition, they made roads and bridges, improved the fortifications, prepared barracks for occupation, and built forts and blockhouses on the heights around. At one time, under the direction of Lieut.-Colonel Perkins, the Commanding Royal Engineer, they and their helpers had in hand 10 forts, 17 defensible posts, several trestle bridges, 4,000 yards of entrenchment, 45 miles of road, and quarters for 8,000 men. However, after the arrival of Major Bindon Blood on March 16th, 1880, the British officers found some time for relaxation without prejudice to their professional duties. "Some of us clubbed together and got a few couple of hounds up from the Peshawar Vale Hunt," writes Sir Bindon,[3] "and after the snow melted we ran a drag. We also played polo on a natural ground which our sappers extended and made good, and had a race meeting and frequent tent-pegging. We had a lesson in tent-pegging from the body-guard of a chief who visited us. I saw them take out ordinary round tent-pegs as cleanly as we did the

[1] *Poshtin.* Sheep-skin overcoat.

[2] Gen. Sir Bindon Blood, G.C.B., G.C.V.O., Col. Commandant, R.E., whose portrait forms the frontispiece of this volume, was born on Nov. 7th, 1842, and was appointed to the newly created post of Chief Royal Engineer of the Corps of Royal Engineers on Oct. 16th, 1936, when nearly 94 years of age. His very distinguished record is remarkable for the fact that it includes high military appointments attained after service spent mostly with engineer units. Commissioned on Dec. 19th, 1860, he proceeded to India in 1871 after 8 years' service at Aldershot with the R.E. Train and joined the Bengal Sappers and Miners with whom he was destined to spend 17 years of regimental soldiering. His earlier active service included the Jowaki campaign 1877–78, Zululand 1879 (Brevet-Major), Afghanistan 1880 and Egypt 1882 (Brevet Lieut.-Colonel). Returning to India in 1885 after service at home, he spent the next 21½ years there except for 9 months in South Africa. His reputation, both as a soldier and a *shikari*, now stood high. In 1885, he was Chief Staff Officer with the Chitral Relief Force and received a K.C.B. Afterwards, he held a brigade command for two years. In 1897–98, he commanded the Malakand and Buner Field Forces and was promoted Major-Gen. in 1898. Then followed the command of the Meerut District until he was called upon in 1901 to command columns during the South African War as a Lieut.-Gen. He was promoted General on Dec. 13th, 1906, retired on Nov. 7th, 1907, and was appointed Col. Commandant, R.E., on July 9th, 1914. He died on May 16th, 1940, at the age of 97 years.

[3] *Four Score Years and Ten*, by Gen. Sir Bindon Blood, G.C.B., G.C.V.O., Representative Col. Commandant, R.E. (1933), pp. 211, 212.

usual flat soft-wood pegs." The officers of the 2nd and 3rd Companies on the Lataband route to Katasang and Jagdalak could not share in the diversions of their more fortunate brethren in the capital.

Meanwhile, "A," "C" and "I" Companies, Madras S. & M., under Ross Thompson were busily engaged further down the line of communication to India. The fact that they were on field service in Afghanistan excited the envy of the other units of their Corps, though "D" and "G" Companies had had the consolation of serving in August and September, 1879, against insurgents in the Rumpa District of the Godavari Delta north of Madras.[1] The work of "A," "C" and "I" Companies in Afghanistan was hard and often uninteresting, but it was always of the highest standard; and when Sir Frederick Roberts presented Afghan medals to the troops at Bangalore on July 26th, 1882, he remarked that the road-making of the "Queen's Own" Sappers and Miners in the Khaibar was justly praised by everyone who had occasion to travel through that historic defile.[2] On arrival at Landi Kotal on December 25th, 1879, "A" Company under Darling was employed at first on defence work but soon moved onwards to Basawal. "I" Company under Dobson advanced to Jalalabad where it bridged three channels of the Kabul River and improved the defences of Fort Sale; and though the bridge could not be finished by Dobson because he was despatched with half the company on a small expedition against raiders near Batikot,[3] it was completed on February 27th by the other half-company under the direction of Lieutenant R. H. Brown, R.E.[4]

At the beginning of 1880, "I" Company had its headquarters at Jalalabad, "A" Company at Basawal and "C" Company at Landi Kotal.[5] A detachment of "C" Company, with Dorward and Shute, marched on January 15th with a force moving to get in rear of 5,000 Mohmands who had crossed the Kabul River and were threatening Dakka. The Sappers ferried 600 men across the river on skin rafts and destroyed a village. On January 21st, "A" Company took part in another expedition to Batikot, afterwards moving north-westwards to join "I" Company in making a road over the Siah Koh Range beyond Jalalabad to afford access to the Laghman Valley. A few days later, "C" Company came up from Landi Kotal to Jalalabad to bridge the river and continue the road-making in the Siah Koh Range begun by "A" and "I" Companies which had been ordered away on an expedition into the Laghman Valley. "C" Company afterwards returned with "I" Company to Jalalabad to make a new road along the river between that place and Basawal, while Ross Thompson, with "A" Company, reconnoitred and improved part of a

[1] *Historical Record of the Q.V.O. Madras Sappers and Miners*, Vol. I, pp. 114, 115. Lieut.-Col. F. A. Howes, R.E., commanded the two companies, "D" Company being under Lieut. C. C. Rawson and "G" Company under Major A. F. Hamilton, R.E.

[2] "Occasional Notes," in *The R.E. Journal*, Vol. XII, 1882, p. 200.

[3] Batikot is on the Jalalabad-Basawal-Dakka road, 20 miles from Jalalabad.

[4] "Construction of Bridges over the Kabul River near Jalalabad," by Capt. R. H. Brown, R.E., appearing in *Professional Papers of the Corps of Royal Engineers*, Vol. VIII, 1882, pp. 143–156.

[5] *Military History of the Madras Engineers and Pioneers*, by Major H. M. Vibart, R.E., Vol. II, p. 508.

mountain track between Jalalabad and Katasang and rejoined the main line at Jagdalak, the furthest point reached by Madras Sappers and Miners in the war.

"C" and "I" Companies were employed during March and April 1880 on the river road between Jalalabad and Basawal, and "A" Company, then at Gandamak, was sent in April on two expeditions eastwards one of which led them into the Hisarak Valley, 15 miles south-east of Jalalabad.[1] It is recorded that "C" and "I" Companies suffered severely from the constant work and exposure in the extreme heat of the Kabul Valley. At the beginning of June, "I" Company was detailed for another expedition into the Laghman Valley and, as a result of the hardships endured, Dobson died a few weeks later. "I" Company, now under Henderson, returned to Gandamak, and "C" Company was sent to Jalalabad to make rafts to convey the sick and stores downstream to Dakka as all the troops were under orders to leave Afghanistan. In July, the Madras Sappers marched through the Khaibar to Peshawar and thence to Jhelum, where they entrained for Bangalore. They had accomplished harder and more continuous work than any other troops on the line of communication to Kabul, and in addition had proved in many small skirmishes that they could give a good account of themselves against the tribesmen of the North-West Frontier.

While these events were occuring in the north, the force under Lieut.-General Sir Donald Stewart in the south had not been idle. A brigade had advanced from Kandahar in September, 1879, and leaving a garrison at Kalat-i-Ghilzai, had rejoined the division in November. For the remainder of the winter, calm prevailed around Kandahar. The 4th and 10th Companies, Bengal S. & M., under Captains P. Haslett and L. F. Brown, R.E., and the 2nd, 3rd, 4th and 5th Companies, Bombay S. & M., under Lieutenants T. R. Henn, G. H. W. O'Sullivan, H. O. Selby and E. C. Spilsbury, R.E., with Lieut-Colonel J. Hills, R.E., in command, worked on the line of communication through Quetta under the direction of the Commanding Royal Engineer, Lieut-Colonel W. Hichens, R.E. In February, 1880, all the Bombay Sapper companies were under orders to proceed to the Nari Valley, north of Sibi, to make a road to facilitate the construction of a projected railway from Sukkur through Quetta to Kandahar; two companies were to go at once to the valley, and the others as soon as their road-making in the Bolan Pass was finished.[2] These movements were duly carried out, and the 4th Company saw some fighting with a force sent to open the Chappar Rift beyond Harnai.[3]

On March 29th, 1880, the Ghazni Field Force, as Sir Donald Stewart's command was now called, started on a notable expedition from Kandahar to Kabul, its place being taken in the Kandahar area by a Bombay Division

[1]A detachment of the 6th Company, Bengal S. & M., was present also in the Hisarak Valley under Lieut. Stafford, R.E.

[2]"Occasional Notes," dated March 1st, 1880, appearing in *The R.E. Journal*, Vol. X, 1880, p. 56.

[3]*A Digest of the Services of the Bombay Sappers and Miners*, by Major G. H. W. O'Sullivan, R.E., p. 44.

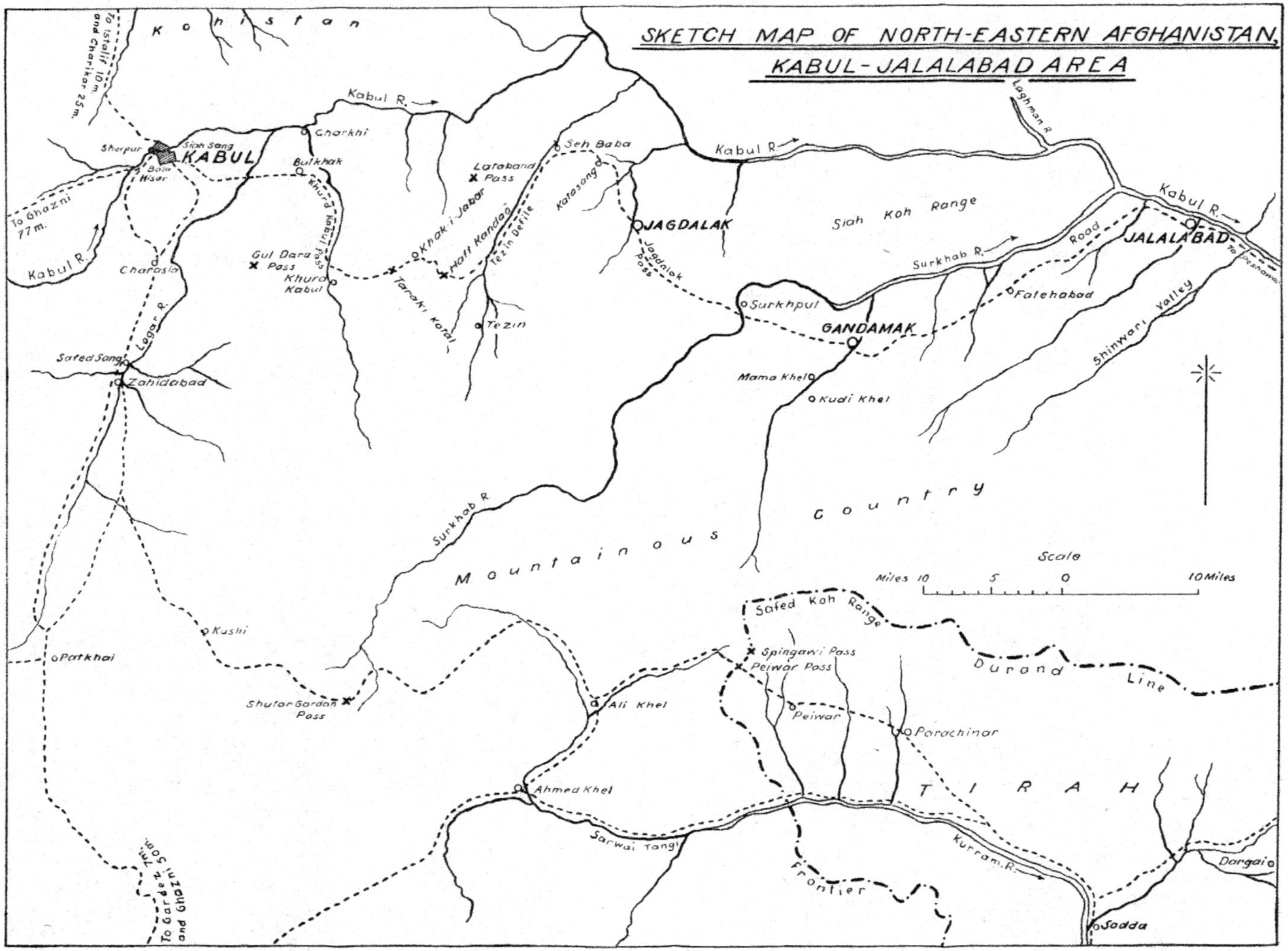

SKETCH MAP OF NORTH-EASTERN AFGHANISTAN, KABUL-JALALABAD AREA

under General Primrose. Though Stewart had only two brigades, he experienced no opposition until he was far beyond Kalat-i-Ghilzai. Then, gangs of marauders began to swarm on his flanks and he had great difficulty in procuring supplies. An Afghan army appeared also, and marching parallel with him, threatened his right. On the morning of April 19th, he found his way barred by 16,000 of the enemy holding a range of hills at Ahmad Khel, 23 miles south of Ghazni, and consequently prepared for action ; but scarcely had his guns opened fire when the Afghans charged furiously down on him. The scene that followed baffles description. Hordes of Ghazni swordsmen drove in the cavalry, and regardless of loss from gunfire at almost point blank range, engaged the infantry in hand-to-hand combat. Every man of the reserve had to be thrown into the fight before the tide could be turned, and an hour elapsed before the enemy took to flight with the cavalry in hot pursuit. At first, the 4th and 10th Companies of Bengal Sappers were in reserve, but when the onslaught of the fanatic swordsmen was pushed with desperation they reinforced the left of the firing line. The Company Commanders, Haslett and L. F. Brown, were justly commended for their services on this occasion.[1] Stewart marched on to occupy Ghazni on April 21st and soon afterwards joined Roberts in Kabul, where he assumed the chief command. The 4th and 10th Companies then moved with the other troops into the Logar Valley, south-east of the capital, and resumed their usual occupation of making roads.[2]

Under arrangements made with the newly installed Amir, Abdur Rahman Khan, the successor of Yakub Khan, Stewart next prepared to lead the army back to India, but hardly had the troops begun to move when the whole situation was altered by news of a disaster at Maiwand, west of Kandahar. With the consent of the Commander-in-Chief, Roberts telegraphed to Simla on July 30th proposing that he should lead a force of nine regiments of infantry and three of cavalry, with three mountain batteries, from Kabul to Kandahar and in reply was authorized to do so. Accordingly, he set to work at once to organize the column. " I wished," he writes,[3] " that the force should be composed, as far as possible, of those who had served with me throughout the campaign ; but as some of the regiments (more especially the native corps) had been away from their homes for two years and had had more than their share of fighting, I considered it right to consult their commanders before detailing the troops. With the exception of three, who thought that their regiments had been long enough away from India, all eagerly responded to my call. The strength of the force placed at my disposal consisted of 9,986 men with 18 guns divided into three brigades of infantry and one of cavalry and three batteries of mountain artillery. There were besides over 8,000 followers

[1] " Occasional Notes," dated Aug. 2nd, 1880, appearing in *The R.E. Journal*, Vol. X, 1880, p. 189.

[2] The 4th and 10th Companies had obtained proper mule-saddles from the Ordnance Department and had made others, so that their equipment was easily carried. Noting this, the 5th and 7th Companies in Kabul obtained similar saddles and thus became more mobile.

[3] *Forty-one Years in India*, by Field Marshal Lord Roberts of Kandahar, V.C., G.C.B., G.C.S.I., G.C.I.E., Vol. II, pp. 339–340.

and 2,300 horses and gun-mules. There was no wheeled artillery."

Roberts set out from Kabul on August 8th, 1880, and traversed the whole distance of 321 miles to Kandahar in 23 days. It is unnecessary to describe this fine and daring feat. The story has been written many times. Any operation undertaken to relieve a British force in danger has always attracted particular and sometimes excessive notice—as, for instance, the relief of Mafeking—and Roberts' march from Kabul to Kandahar received the widest publicity; but though arduous and dangerous, it was less so than Stewart's previous advance from Kandahar to Kabul, which passed almost unnoticed in the press. There is a curious feature, however, in the composition of Roberts' force which warrants attention in these pages. In spite of his statement that he wished to include men who had served with him throughout the campaign, Roberts did not invite the 7th Company, Bengal S. & M., to accompany him; neither did he ask for the services of the 4th or 10th Companies which had recently traversed the route with Stewart, nor of the 5th Company which had done well under Gough. In fact, incredible though it may seem, *no Sappers and Miners whatever were included in the Kabul-Kandahar Field Force.* Those who, like the author, had the privilege of knowing Sir Bindon Blood will realize that as Commandant of the Bengal Sappers at Kabul he would never have refused an invitation on the grounds that his men had been absent from India for a long period. It is true that Roberts had been advised that for political reasons it was desirable to eliminate units in which the Pathan element preponderated, and it is possible that he considered that the 23rd Pioneers would suffice to overcome any engineering obstacles, but the Bengal Sappers and Miners felt their omission very keenly and particularly so when they noted that the only engineering establishment taken was a small Field Park, hurriedly improvised by and commanded by Captain W. G. Nicholson, R.E.,[1] an officer of great energy and capability but with little experience of India and none whatever of the Sappers and Miners. It may be that Nicholson, whose service had been spent chiefly on the home establishment, was apt to compare the Sappers and Miners unfavourably with the British companies to which he was accustomed. This was natural; but it was most unfortunate for the Sappers and Miners, for Nicholson was *persona grata* with Roberts.

The trouble in Southern Afghanistan which brought Roberts to the rescue had begun with the advance of Ayub Khan on Kandahar from the direction of Herat in June, 1880, at the head of 20,000 men. On July 4th, General Primrose sent a brigade under Brig.-General G. R. S. Burrows westwards towards the Helmand River to assist a force under the Wali of Kandahar in checking Ayub, and with it marched a detachment of 41 Indian ranks of the 2nd Company, Bombay S. & M., under Lieutenant T. R. Henn, R.E., with Sergeant Heapy and 1st Corporal Ashman, R.E.[2] When Burrows arrived on the Helmand, the Wali's troops deserted, and

[1]Afterwards Field-Marshal Lord Nicholson of Roundhay, G.C.B.

[2]The 2nd Company had proceeded to Kandahar in April, 1880, after working in the Bolan Pass and Nari Valley with other companies of Bombay Sappers and Miners.

the brigade was obliged to retreat to Kushk-i-Nakhud to replenish supplies.[1] On the 27th, Ayub was reported at Maiwand, about 12 miles to the north-east, so Burrows moved to the attack. He soon found himself in a critical position. Outnumbered and outflanked, the Indian regiments on his left gave way and rolled in a great wave on to the right. The artillery and the Bombay Sappers alone stood fast, fighting the Ghazis with the greatest coolness and stubbornness, but meanwhile the torrent of panic-stricken sepoys and fanatical Ghazis from the left had engulfed and swept away H.M.'s 66th Regiment, the backbone of the defence. Henn and his half-company of Bombay Sappers and Miners earned undying fame at Maiwand, for they did not give an inch until the artillery had retreated after abandoning two guns. They were the last to leave the field. Henn and 14 of his men afterwards joined a party of the 66th and some Bombay Grenadiers and with them made a most determined stand in a small enclosure at a place called Khig. Though the Afghans shot them down one by one, they fired steadily until only eleven of their number were left, and this small party then charged out into the masses of the enemy and so perished. Henn was the only officer in that gallant band and he led the final charge.

The foregoing account is based on that given by Major G. H. W. O'Sullivan, R.E., in the small volume entitled *A Brief History of the Royal Bombay Sappers and Miners*. Brig.-General A. G. Bremner, who served for many years with the Bombay Corps, remarks that O'Sullivan was positive that his account of Maiwand was correct for he had confirmed every detail. "The story as I know it is as follows" writes Bremner.[2] "The Bombay Sappers were posted near a battery of Bombay Horse Artillery and so were somewhat detached from the firing line. When the retreat started there appears to have been much confusion which eventually developed into something worse. The Sappers seem to have been the last to leave their original position and to have covered the withdrawal of the Artillery. This was confirmed by a Gunner officer in Kirkee who informed me that his unit had a report on the action which was apparently confidential. He added that he doubted whether the Sappers held on for the benefit of the Artillery for he believed that they were fully occupied with their own particular fight. His impression was, however, that the Artillery were aware that the Sappers were covering them and consequently did not retire until the holding of their original position was no longer of any value. Be that as it may, it is clear that the Sappers held on until the withdrawal of the Artillery and that at that time all others were retiring. I could never discover exactly what happened to them in the retreat until some of them joined a party of the 66th and Grenadiers near Khig. Several attempts were made to rally detachments of the troops. Small parties were wiped out or broken up until only one remained, that of the 66th,

[1]A letter from Lieut. T. R. Henn, R.E., describing the experiences of his detachment in the advance and retreat, appears in *The R.E. Journal*, Vol. X, 1880, p. 254.

[2]Notes by Brig.-Gen. A. G. Bremner, C.M.G., late R.E., sent to the author on March 5th, 1938.

Grenadiers and Sappers at Khig. Also, I could never ascertain whether there were any stragglers from that party."

Not until midday on July 28th did the last exhausted survivors of Burrows' brigade reach Kandahar. Out of 2,500 fighting men, nearly 1,000 had been killed, and General Primrose had only 4,300 men to man the miles of city wall when Ayub Khan invested the place. Of the Bombay Sappers who did not perish at Khig, a party of about a dozen men marched into Kandahar as a formed body. Others, mostly wounded, arrived on camels, wagons or limbers. Subadar Hassan Khan, a survivor, has stated that he reached the city on a camel at 10 a.m.[1] In the general confusion none of the men could say how he came to be separated from Henn, but all agreed that in the end a small party marched in as a military body. One of this party added that, when a few men had collected together, they decided that it was improper to straggle into the city and accordingly fell in under the senior Sapper to make a suitable entry. Thus, even in defeat the discipline of the Corps held good.

Lieut.-Colonel John Hills, R.E., bears witness also that Henn and his half-company of Bombay Sappers were the last to leave the line of battle at Maiwand. " Henn made his men stand up and fire a volley at the crowd of Ghazis and regulars pouring down upon them " he writes. " Then he gave the order to retire steadily. He had been wounded in the arm some time before this, but remained with his men to the last. He followed the line of retreat of the 66th towards the wall of the first garden across a large nullah, and in a small water-channel in that garden he and the remnant of his men took their stand with some of the 66th and Grenadiers, and here he fell, using a rifle until shot through the head. Around the place were found, lightly buried, Henn and 14 Sappers,[2] 23 men of the Grenadiers and 46 men of the 66th." A marble monument to Thomas Rice Henn can be seen in St. Patrick's Cathedral in Dublin and a memorial window in Rochester Cathedral. The inscription on the monument records that " having led into action a detachment of the Bombay Sappers and Miners he perished gloriously on the fatal field of Maiwand on July 27th, 1880, covering with a small but indomitable band—eleven in number—the retreat of the entire British brigade."[3]

The survivors of Henn's detachment joined the remainder of the 2nd Company under Lieutenant G. Turner Jones, R.E., in Kandahar and

[1]Account of the service of Subadar Hassan Khan, O.B.I., Bahadur, sent to the author on Sept. 24th, 1937, from Kirkee. This account was given by the Subadar himself.

[2]These 14 Bombay Sappers and Miners were among the following 15 who were killed at Maiwand :— Havildar Muhammad Khan, Naik Siuram Wanjari, Bugler Shaikh Abdulla and Privates Biru Nikam, Shaikh Pir Bakhsh, Govindrao More, Ramji Talekar, Siurattan Singh, Jangu Narsu, Rama Powar, Ambuji, Balnak Yesnak, Poshuti Piraji, Ithu Damu and Chocnak. Sergt. Heapy and 1st Corporal Ashman, R.E., were also killed at Maiwand.

[3]A detailed description of the monument is given in an article entitled " The late Lieutenant Henn, R.E." appearing in *The R.E. Journal*, Vol. XII, 1882, p. 171. In *The R.E. Journal*, Vol. X, 1880, pp. 280, 281, a letter appears from Henn's father quoting others from brother officers in which they discuss the final stand at Khig and remark that General Primrose had reported erroneously when he wrote that the stand was made by men of the 66th Regiment alone. The omission of Henn's name by Primrose is discussed also by " A Layman " in *The R.E. Journal*, Vol. XI, 1881, pp. 13, 14, and it is shown not only that Henn was one of the final eleven but that he was the only British officer present.

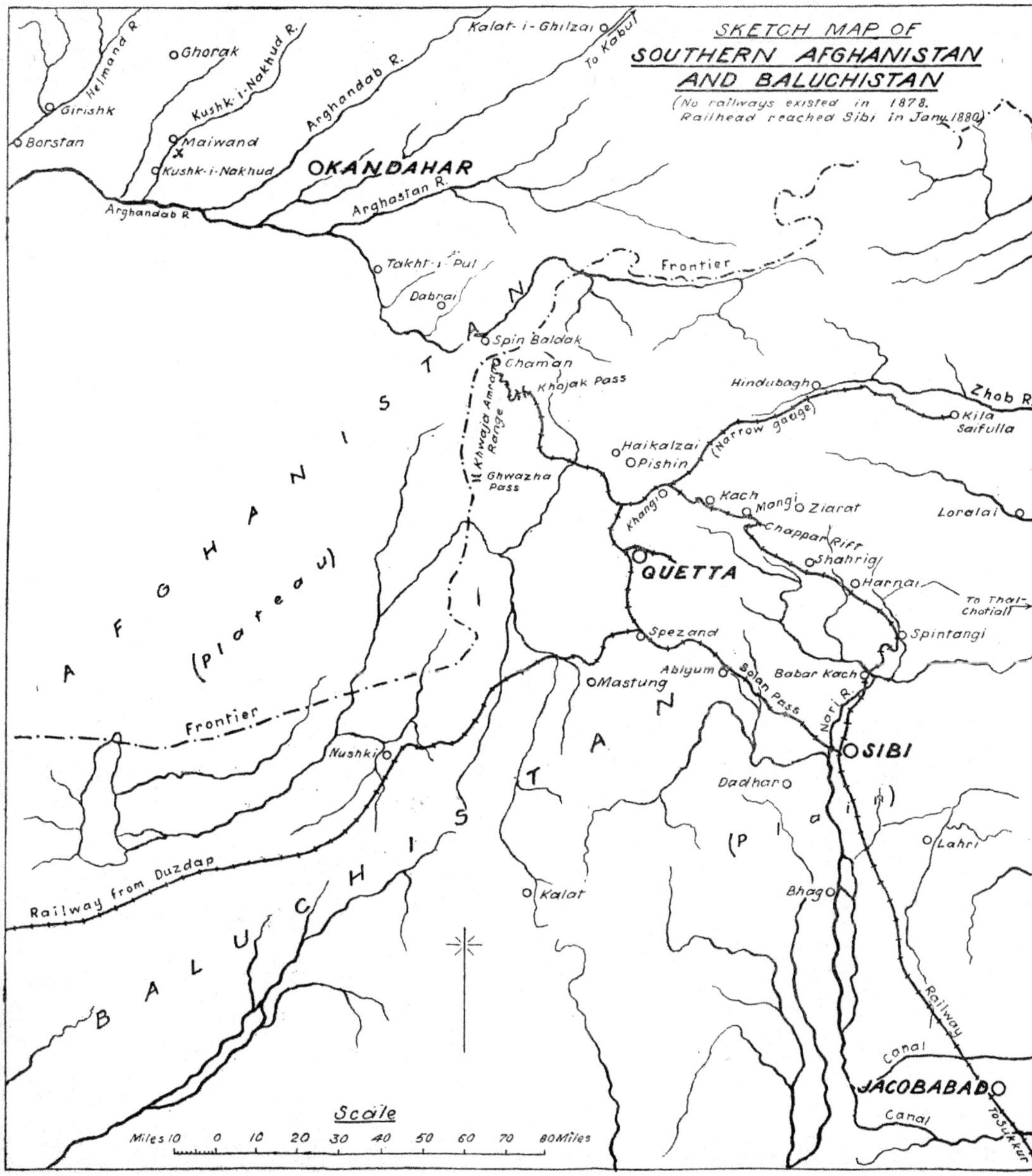
SKETCH MAP OF
SOUTHERN AFGHANISTAN
AND BALUCHISTAN
(No railways existed in 1878.
Railhead reached Sibi in Jany. 1880)
Helmand R.
Ghorak
Kushk-i-Nakhud R.
Kalat-i-Ghilzai
To Kabul
Girishk
Borstan
Maiwand
Kushk-i-Nakhud
Arghandab R.
KANDAHAR
Arghastan R.
Takht-i-Pul
Dabrai
Frontier
Spin Baldak
Chaman
Khojak Pass
Khwaja Amran Range
Ghwazha Pass
Hindubagh
Zhob R.
Kila Saifulla
(Narrow gauge)
Haikalzai
Pishin
Khangi
Kach
Mangi
Ziarat
Loralai
Chappar Rift
Shahrig
Harnai
To Thal-Chotiali
QUETTA
Spezand
Spintangi
Ablygum
Babar Kach
Mastung
Bolan Pass
Nari R.
SIBI
AFGHANISTAN
(plateau)
Frontier
Nushki
Dadhar
(Plain)
Lahri
Railway from Duzdap
Kalat
Bhag
BALUCHISTAN
Railway
Canal
JACOBABAD
To Sukkur
Scale
Miles 10 0 10 20 30 40 50 60 70 80 Miles

assisted them in demolitions undertaken to secure a better field of fire. On August 8th, Ayub Khan opened a general bombardment and occupied all the outlying suburbs, using the village of Deh Khoja as an advanced artillery position. The garrison replied with a few sorties during one of which, on August 12th, Lieutenants G. Turner Jones and E. A. Waller, R.E., earned recommendations for the Victoria Cross though they did not receive that honour. " From the parapet," writes Brig.-General Brooke, " I witnessed a grand piece of gallantry by two young R.E. officers who, under a galling fire, returned from cover and carried into safety a wounded sepoy. One of the men who was with them was killed."[1] Soon afterwards, Brooke himself perished in an unsuccessful attempt to carry Deh Khoja in the course of which the 2nd Company did sterling work. Roberts marched triumphantly into Kandahar on August 31st, and, forestalling by a few days a force from Quetta under Major-General Sir R. Phayre which included the 3rd, 4th and 5th Companies of the Bombay Sappers,[2] immediately attacked Ayub Khan's army on the surrounding hills and routed it with the loss of all its guns and equipment and 1,000 killed.

The Battle of Kandahar ended the Second Afghan War. Turner Jones and 38 men of the 2nd Company were present as part of a force under Brig.-General Burrows which was with the heavy artillery in support.[3] They were too exhausted, as were most of the Kandahar garrison, to take an active part in the operations. Afterwards, Roberts led part of his army from Kandahar to India, leaving a garrison under Major-General Hume to hold the city. Meanwhile, Stewart had almost completed his withdrawal from Northern Afghanistan, and the frontier demarcated under the Treaty of Gandamak was resumed. In due course, the Bombay Sappers units left Kandahar, the 2nd Company in October 1880[4] and the 3rd, 4th and 5th Companies in the spring of 1881, and after several punitive operations, Kandahar was evacuated and the Amir Abdur Rahman was left securely seated on his throne in Kabul. The Madras Sappers and Miners were awarded the honour " Afghanistan, 1878–80," the Bengal Corps the honours " Ali Masjid," " Charasiah," " Kabul, 1879," " Ahmad Khel " and " Afghanistan, 1878–80," and the Bombay Corps the honours " Kandahar, 1880 " and " Afghanistan, 1878–80." Never were distinctions better earned.

Some four years after the conclusion of hostilities came the great Sapper and Miner reorganization which was the embodiment of many years of hard work. The drafting of the Army Order introducing it was rightly entrusted to Lieut.-Colonel Bindon Blood, R.E., the newly appointed Commandant of the Bengal Corps, who had initiated it and had overcome powerful opposition to it by certain officers at Army Headquarters. " I got back to Roorkee (from Afghanistan) in September, 1880," writes Sir

[1]Letter from Brig.-Gen. H. F. Brooke quoted in *The R.E. Journal*, Vol. XI, 1881, p. 36.

[2]Gen. Phayre reached Kandahar on Sept. 3rd, 1880.

[3]Article entitled " The Battle of Kandahar," appearing in *The R.E. Journal*, Vol. XI., 1881, pp. 3–6

[4]" Occasional Notes " in *The R.E. Journal*, Vol. XI, 1881, p. 16.

Bindon Blood,[1] " At this time I paid Simla a short visit to arrange for personal consultations with the other two Sapper Corps about a scheme for the radical reorganization of all three Corps. This reorganization, which was urgently required, had been mooted many years before and was now regarded with interest by the Indian military authorities in consequence of experience gained in the war. . . . I was transferred home in May, 1883, but returned early in 1885. On arrival I was posted for duty to Simla, arriving just in time to put the finishing touches to the reorganization of the Corps of Sappers and Miners in India on which I had been so much employed during my previous service in that country. I had the help of a first-class staff whom I was allowed to select from the Corps of Royal Engineers and Indian soldiers of various ranks."

According to Lieut.-General Sir Fenton Aylmer, V.C., the Bengal Sappers and Miners were not well organized when he joined the Corps in 1883. " The technical education of the Indian ranks in trades was most indifferent, " he writes.[2] " The companies were really only superior Pioneers. On field service, the working parties available were very weak, though the equipment and its carriage had been excellently worked out by Maxwell and Martin. Among Royal Engineers in other employment, the Corps was unjustly regarded as a refuge for the inefficient. The fault, however, was in the organization and not in the British officers. There were few inducements for an officer to remain in the Corps since the Company Commanders got no regular staff pay. The Bombay Corps was in much the same condition. It was Bindon Blood who was really responsible for the excellent reorganization of the three Corps in 1885, and Barton for increasing the trades' efficiency of the Bengal Corps."

The Special Indian Army Order (No. 174) which authorized the reorganization was published on December 16th, 1885. The Madras and Bengal Sappers and Miners were each to have 6 Service companies, numbered 1 to 6, and 2 Depot companies, lettered " A " and " B." " A " Company was to include 2 Pontoon Sections, 2 Telegraph Sections, 2 Field Printing Sections and 1 Submarine Mining Section ; it was to be, in fact, a specialist unit, though without prejudice to the general training of the whole Corps in bridging and telegraph work. The Bombay Sappers and Miners were to have 4 Service companies and 1 Depot company, and a " Superintendent of Instruction and Park and Train " was authorized. Each of the other Corps had already a " Superintendent of Instruction " and a " Superintendent of Park and Train." The most important feature, however, of the reorganization of 1885 was the official recognition of the principle that the *company* and not the battalion should be considered as the basic unit of engineer troops, and consequently that it should be ready always for independent movement or action and capable of rapid expansion for war. This principle had been observed to some extent by the Madras Corps for many years; but in the Bengal and Bombay Corps there had been

[1] *Four Score Years and Ten,* by Gen. Sir Bindon Blood, G.C.B., G.C.V.O., Representative Col. Commandant, R.E., pp. 229, 255.

[2] Notes by Lieut.-Gen. Sir Fenton J. Aylmer, V.C., K.C.B., Col. Commandant, R.E., sent to the author on June 19th, 1932.

a tendency to stress the battalion formation in spite of the fact that it was impracticable in the field.

The establishments of the Madras and Bengal Corps were each fixed in 1885 at 20 British officers, 43 British warrant or non-commissioned officers, 24 Indian officers, 112 Indian non-commissioned officers, 16 Buglers and 1,200 Sepoys, designated for the first time "Sappers." All the British officers were to be Royal Engineers, and the Commandants were not to be below the rank of Major. A revised engineer equipment was specified, and each company was to have with it always its full service equipment. Such were the more important provisions of the reorganization. Alterations occurred, of course, after the metamorphosis which resulted from the lessons of the Second Afghan War. In 1903, for instance, some eight years after the three Presidency armies were combined into a single " Army in India," the Madras companies were renumbered 9 to 14 and the Bombay companies 17 to 22. During the Great War of 1914–18, each Corps was expanded enormously to meet the exceptional though temporary demands, and in 1932–33 each received into its ranks large numbers of men from the disbanded establishment of Pioneer regiments. But the main provisious of the reorganization of 1885 held good, and no subsequent reform was more beneficial to the Indian Sappers and Miners than that originated by the late Sir Bindon Blood to whom the three Corps owed the deepest gratitude for his persistence and foresight.

CHAPTER XI

OVERSEAS EXPEDITIONS AND THE THIRD BURMA WAR, 1867–1889

FOR several years after the Indian Mutiny, there was little chance of active service for the Sappers and Miners except on the North-West Frontier. In 1867, however, the expedition to Abyssinia gave certain units of the Madras and Bombay Corps unique opportunities for the display of initiative and endurance under most arduous conditions. The success of the expedition depended largely on the work of the engineer companies, and the campaign in Abyssinia was in fact an " engineer war," carefully planned and skilfully conducted by a celebrated engineer in the person of Lieut.-General Sir Robert Napier, then Commander-in-Chief in Bombay. Though the armed resistance was small, the natural obstacles were stupendous as the Italians found in 1896 and again in 1935. Storm, pestilence, famine and thirst were the real enemies on the stony track, nearly 400 miles long, which led through incredibly mountainous country from the arid coast of the Red Sea to the heights of Magdala.

King Theodore of Abyssinia had imprisoned and ill-treated a number of Europeans and it was necessary to rescue them and punish him. Napier, on appointment as Commander-in-Chief of the expedition, was under no illusions as to the magnitude and difficulty of his task. He deprecated any attempt at misplaced economy and asked for 12,000 fighting men with a very large amount of transport, including 3,000 native carriers, and so high was his reputation that he was given almost a free hand. For three months before he embarked, he supervised every detail of mobilization, supply and equipment. Transports were chartered, a field telegraph improvised, signalling apparatus prepared, a searchlight provided, and condensers supplied for converting salt water into fresh. The manufacture of 5,000 Snider breech-loading rifles, and of mountain guns adapted to mule carriage, was commenced in England, and railway material was collected in India. Every contingency was foreseen, and rightly so for this was a campaign in almost unknown country against a warlike people provided with artillery.

The expeditionary force amounted to about 14,000 men selected almost entirely from the Bombay Army. " The troops to be employed should know each other and their commander " wrote Napier.[1] From the Bengal Army came only two regiments of Indian cavalry and two battalions of Indian infantry, one of which was the 23rd Punjab Pioneers. No Bengal Sappers and Miners were included. The whole force comprised four and a half regiments of cavalry, seven batteries and a company of artillery, four battalions of British and ten of Indian infantry, and eight companies of

[1]Minute by Sir R. Napier, dated Sept. 5th, 1867, quoted in *The Royal* (*Bengal*) *Engineers*, by Col. Sir E. T. Thackeray, V.C., K.C.B., p. 211.

engineers. Attached to it were a Bengal Cooly Corps of 2,000 men, a Bombay Army Works Corps of 1,000 men and many thousands of followers. No less than 205 sailing vessels and 75 steamships were needed to transport the 62,000 men and 55,000 animals of the expedition, with their equipment and supplies, from India to the Red Sea.[1]

Thirty officers of the Royal Engineers served in Abyssinia under Napier. With Lieut.-Colonel H. St. C. Wilkins, R.E., as Commanding Royal Engineer, were the 10th Company, R.E., from England under Major G. D. Pritchard, R.E., with Lieutenants J. L. Morgan and A. R. Puzey, R.E., "G," "H" and "K" Companies of the Madras Sappers and Miners under Major H. N. D. Prendergast, V.C., R.E., and the entire Corps of Bombay Sappers and Miners (1st, 2nd, 3rd and 4th Companies)[2] under Captain A. R. MacDonnell, R.E. "G" Company, Madras S. and M., was commanded by Lieutenant R. F. Morris, R.E., with Lieutenants M. Protheroe, M. I., and J. N. Mainwaring, R.E., "H" Company by Lieutenant J. Pennycuick, R.E., with Lieutenant C. Cunningham, R.E., and Cornet R. Dalrymple, 19th Hussars, and "K" Company by Captain H. R. Elliott, M.I., with Lieutenants F. H. Bird, M.I., and W. H. Coaker, R.E.[3] Captain M. E. Foord, M.I., was Adjutant. The 1st Company, Bombay S. & M., was commanded by Captain S. C. Newport, Bo.I., the 2nd by 2nd-Captain N. G. Sturt, R.E., the 3rd by Captain G. B. Leslie, Bo.I., and the 4th by Lieutenant F. S. Leacock, Bo.I.[4] Lieutenant G. L. C. Merewether, R.E., was Adjutant to the Bombay Corps. Lieutenant W. H. Coaker, R.E., was transferred from the Madras Sappers to the 4th Company, Bombay Sappers, on arrival in Abyssinia, and in January, 1868, Lieutenant W. Osborn, R.E., joined the 1st Company and afterwards acted for a time as Adjutant. In view of the fact that the Bombay units were under-staffed, and commanded mostly by infantry officers, it is greatly to their credit that they did so well during the campaign, for the brunt of the work in the advance to and withdrawal from Magdala fell on them. Captain C. J. Darrah, R.E., was in charge of the railway work, Lieutenant A. Le Messurier, R.E., of the water-supply, and Lieutenant O. B. C. St. John, R.E., of the telegraph construction and operation, in all of which the Sappers and Miners were concerned from time to time.

On September 16th, 1867, a reconnoitring party including Lieut.-Colonel Wilkins with Captains W. W. Goodfellow and K. A. Jopp, R.E., set out from Bombay and, after examining the port of Massawa in the Red Sea on October 2nd and finding it unsatisfactory, proceeded southwards to Annesley Bay[5] where the small water-supply from the Haddas

[1]*Frontier and Overseas Expeditions from India*, Vol. VI, p. 69.

[2]The 5th Company had been broken up and distributed among the other companies to raise them to war strength. (See *Digest of the Services of the Bombay Sappers and Miners* (1895), by Maj. G. H. W. O'Sullivan, R.E., p. 32.)

[3]*The Roll of Honour of the Queen's Own Madras Sappers and Miners*, pp. 33, 34.

[4]*Digest of the Services of the Bombay Sappers and Miners*, by Major G. H. W. O'Sullivan, R.E., pp. 32, 33.

[5]Annesley Bay and other places mentioned are shown in the *Sketch Map of Northern Abyssinia* included in this chapter.

River seemed fairly promising. They selected Malkatto, near the village of Zula on the western shore of the bay, as a suitable landing place for the expeditionary force. Zula, as the maritime base came to be known, was an uninviting spot. The plain between it and the mountains was covered with thorny scrub. The climate was hot and enervating. No stone was available for building, and the beach shelved so gradually that ships could not approach close in shore. Nevertheless, the decision was made, and on October 21st the advanced brigade of the expedition began to arrive. With it were the 3rd and 4th Companies, Bombay S. & M., which had embarked at Bombay on October 3rd, and also the 1st Company from Aden. Meanwhile, the reconnoitring party had selected a line of advance inland to Kumayli, at the foot of the mountains 12 miles distant, and thence up a series of deep gorges past Lower Suru and Upper Suru to Senafé, a place only 63 miles from Zula yet 7,400 feet above it. By the middle of November, the route to Senafé had been fully examined and the 1st Company was at work under the direction of Jopp in the Suru defile. On December 4th, the 2nd Company landed with the leading (Sind) brigade of the main body under Major-General Sir Charles Staveley and was sent shortly afterwards to the Suru defile to help the 1st Company.

There was ample work of every description in and near Zula for the 3rd and 4th Companies of Bombay Sappers and for the 23rd Punjab Pioneers and the men of the two labour corps, but the most urgent project was the building of a long pier for unloading ships. A filling of coral, transported across the bay in native boats, was enclosed between walls of brushwood fascines which were afterwards reinforced by masonry walls, and thus by degrees a stone pier to carry a line of tramway was run out 300 yards into the sea. By the end of November, the pier was nearly finished and a number of wells near the Haddas River had been cleared of silt. A large shed had been built, and a flume was being erected on trestles to convey fresh water from the condensers of a ship moored alongside an artificial island formed some 200 yards from the shore. These and other works were executed in sweltering heat and clouds of dust and in an atmosphere poisoned by the decaying carcases of many transport animals which had died of thirst after being deserted by their Arab and Levantine attendants.

The hard-pressed Bombay Sappers and Miners were reinforced during December by "G," "H" and "K" Companies of the Madras Corps under Prendergast. "K" Company had left Calicut in the steamship *John Bright* (1,000 tons) on November 26th and disembarked at Zula on December 6th, followed on the 12th by "G" and "H" Companies. The 10th Company, R.E., arrived also after a long voyage from England, but being composed of telegraphists, signallers, well-borers and photographers it took little part in the major engineering operations.[1] Sir Robert Napier landed on January 7th, 1878, and made his final preparations. A

[1]Report on the Abyssinian Expedition by Lieut.-Col. St. Clair Wilkins, R.E., Commanding Engineer, appearing in *Prof. Papers of the Corps of Royal Engineers*, New Series, Vol. XVII, 1869, pp. 140–149. This report describes in considerable detail the work of the R.E. officers and engineer units.

group of Royal Engineer officers, headed by Darrah, started to build a 5 ft. 6 in. gauge railway towards Kumayli, assisted at first by some of the Sapper companies but later by the 23rd Punjab Pioneers and 2nd Bombay Grenadiers. The progress was slow because expert platelayers were scarce. The rails sent from India were of five different types, and many were bent and useless. The sixty wagons provided were without springs or grease-boxes, and their cast-iron bearings lasted less than a month. The six locomotives were fit only for the scrap heap. The railway authorities in Madras, Bombay and Sind had apparently seized the opportunity to get rid of unserviceable material. By February 22nd, only 6 miles of line had been laid; but Kumayli was reached before the end of the campaign, and the early discovery of good water in wells dug along the railway route eased the problem of water-supply at the base. The line was of great value in forwarding troops and supplies to the mountains during the advance to Magdala, and in evacuating them after the operations had ended.[1] "G" and "H" Companies, with Colonel Wilkins, had the misfortune to be tied to the Zula-Kumayli area throughout the campaign, so they never saw a shot fired; but their work, and that of the railway personnel, was of the highest importance, for on it depended the welfare of the expedition. After the completion of the stone pier, both "G" and "H" Companies dug many wells and assisted in building a pile pier and a number of sheds for stores, and detachments of "G" Company erected a telegraph line to beyond Kumayli and excavated an unlined well 85 feet deep. The companies were engaged also on land reclamation work.

The engineering problems on the route from Kumayli to Senafé were formidable. Three miles after entering the Kumayli gorge the track began to ascend steeply. The mountains closed in till, at Lower Suru, 10 miles from Kumayli, the precipices on either side were only a few yards apart.[2] "The Suru defile," writes Wilkins, "occupied the labours of two companies of Sappers[3] and two companies of Beloochees (27th Bombay N. Infantry) for three months. The road when completed had a breadth of about 10 feet and was constructed on the principle of ramping over boulders and obstacles instead of attempting their removal by blasting. The boulders were found to be of the toughest description of granite." However, under the direction of Jopp, Sturt and Coaker, the track was made suitable for the transport of guns and supplies to the advanced base at Senafé on the tableland. According to Goodfellow, this was the hardest and most uninteresting work undertaken by the Sappers and Miners during the campaign, and Sturt, commanding the 2nd Company, was said to have been much indebted to his Subadar, Saye Erappa, for preventing the men from becoming disheartened when the 3rd and 4th Companies, and "K" Company of the Madras Sappers, passed them *en route* to the front. Sturt

[1]The railway operations are described in a report entitled "The Abyssinian Railway," by Lieut. T. J. Willans, R.E., appearing in *Prof. Papers of the Corps of Royal Engineers*, New Series, Vol. XVIII, 1870, pp. 163–176.

[2]An illustration entitled "The Devil's Staircase, Suru," appearing opposite p. 400 of *The Military Engineer in India*, Vol. I, by the present author, shows the nature of the Suru defile.

[3]The 1st and 2nd Companies, Bombay S. & M., joined later by the 4th Company.

adds that the 2nd Company laboured in the Suru defile from December 22nd to January 27th when the task was finished.[1]

Supplies were collected gradually at Senafé, and when Napier arrived there on January 29th, 1868, he decided to advance without delay on Magdala. King Theodore was known to be moving with a large army from Debra Tabor[2] to the capital, making a road for his heavy guns as he went. Beyond Senafé the route was easy for 37 miles to Adigrat; but thence to Antalo, a further 91 miles, the track led through waterless uplands destitute of supplies and almost impassable for wheeled traffic. The entire expeditionary force was now reorganized into two divisions and a Zula Brigade, the 1st Division, composed of two brigades and a "Pioneer Force," being selected to advance on Magdala and the 2nd Division to hold the line of communication from Senafé to Antalo. Two companies of Bombay Sappers and Miners, with two companies of Pioneers and some cavalry and infantry, were detailed to form the "Pioneer Force" and were ordered to proceed two marches ahead of the remainder of the division to improve the road. Napier, with the 1st Division, reached Adigrat on February 6th and established a permanent post at that place. On February 26th, he continued his advance towards Antalo, and, passing through Adabaya, Dongolo and Agula, halted at Buya near Antalo on March 2nd. The Antalo camp lay in desolate and undulating country, covered with coarse grass and dotted with a few deserted villages. After establishing a depot, Napier set out again on March 12th and, surmounting the Alaji Pass, completed a journey of about 70 miles to LakeAshangi on March 18th.

Beyond this lake, a most difficult stretch was encountered between Mussagita and Lat, where the track ascended in steep zigzags to the village of Adiwoka in the Womberat Mountains and afterwards skirted the hillside at a height of 10,000 feet above sea-level. The "Pioneer Force" was sent forward on March 20th to make this route passable for guns and transport and succeeded so well that the striking force reached Lat, 73 miles from Antalo, on the 22nd. Here it was divided into three brigades, and orders were given to proceed without baggage in two échelons. The 3rd Brigade, which included the Sappers and Miners, was detailed to prepare a road to Magdala suitable for elephants, for these unweildy animals had been brought from India to pull the heavy guns. Passing through Marawa and climbing 3,000 feet to Wandach (10,900 feet), the leading troops reached Muja on March 26th and on the following day descended 3,000 feet into the Takkaze Valley. Then came a climb to Santara, 56 miles from Lat, where a halt was made for two days at an elevation again exceeding 10,000 feet. The troops suffered severely from heat and cold, for the shade temperature varied between 110° and 20°F. Nevertheless, they were in good spirits. Magdala was only 40 miles distant, though separated from them by a maze of gigantic chasms and heights. At Santara,

[1]Memoranda dated Aug. 18th and Sept. 24th, 1869, from Maj. W. W. Goodfellow and Capt. N. G. Sturt, R.E., appearing in a file at Kirkee entitled "Recommendations of Indian Officers, Bombay Sappers and Miners, for reward for special service in Abyssinia, 1869."

[2]Debra Tabor is 100 miles W.N.W. of Magdala.

ON THE ROAD TO MAGDALA.
The ascent to Adiwoka village beyond Lake Ashangi in Abyssinia.

the 3rd Brigade was broken up and distributed among the others, the Sappers and Miners joining the 1st Brigade.

The Sapper units at Santara were " K " Company of the Madras Corps and the 2nd, 3rd and 4th Companies of the Bombay Corps. Prendergast and MacDonnell were in command. After helping the 1st and 2nd Companies in the Suru defile and working subsequently near Upper Suru higher up the gorge, " K " Company had marched from Senafé on February 28th as an escort to a convoy of two 8-inch mortars with a quantity of ammunition and forty elephants. It reached Antalo on March 13th and started for Lat on the 18th, six days after Napier, so it did not overtake him until the halt at Santara. The 1st Company, Bombay S. & M., got no further than Antalo and consequently saw no fighting. It left the Suru defile in December to work on the road between Upper Suru and Senafé, and at the end of January moved towards Adigrat, where it remained until it had completed the Senafé-Adigrat section. During March, it erected a line of telegraph from Adigrat to Antalo and worked also on the road. The 2nd Company left the Suru defile at the end of January to accompany the advance to Magdala ; but as it was not in the " Pioneer Force " it is presumed that it was employed behind the leading troops to improve the road. The 3rd and 4th Companies were included in the " Pioneer Force " and consequently bore the brunt of the work of preparing a way to Magdala.

From Santara on the Wadela plateau, Napier could study the panorama of precipitous heights and deep valleys lying between him and his objective. Behind him lay the gorge of the Takkaze or Upper Setit River, which he had recently crossed : in front, the chasm in which flowed the Jedda, a tributary of the Blue Nile. Beyond the Jedda rose the lofty Talanta plateau, and in the distance, in a fork between the Bashilo tributary and its confluent, the Kulkulla, he could discern the group of flat-topped mountains of which Magdala is the key. A direct advance being impossible, Napier decided to move south-westwards to cross the Jedda lower down and reach the Talanta plateau by the road made by Theodore when he marched from Debra Tabor. This he accomplished on April 4th. He was delayed for several days on the plateau owing to lack of supplies, but the Sappers and Miners were fully employed not only in repairing the road but in making scaling ladders, 27 feet long, from the poles of dhoolies, using pick-helves as rungs. The advance was resumed on April 9th and the Talanta tableland crossed. From its southern edge, Napier was now able to see in greater detail the flat-topped peaks of Fahla and Selassie, 10 miles distant, which screened the Magdala peak from view. Fahla was the outpost of the mountain group held by Theodore with some 30,000 men and 30 guns.

On April 10th, Napier descended into the Bashilo gorge and crossed the river beyond which his outposts were already established. Two routes led thence up to the Arogi plateau between Fahla and Selassie, one by a valley and the other by Theodore's road up an adjacent spur. From the Arogi plateau, a single track continued along the slope of Selassie, crossed the

Islamgi plateau and ascended to the top of Magdala, 9,200 feet above sea-level. The road to Magdala in 1868 was therefore under fire first from Fahla on the right, then from Selassie on the left, and lastly from Magdala in front. The main attack was directed up the Fahla spur while a subsidiary force moved up the Arogi valley, the Sapper and Miner companies ascending the spur with the 1st Brigade. When the valley force began to debouch on to the Arogi plateau, the Abyssinians, mistaking a mountain battery for transport, attacked it with 6,000 men but were driven back by the 1st Brigade and retreated to the Selassie position. " K " Company, Madras S. & M., and the 2nd, 3rd and 4th Companies, Bombay S. & M.,[1] took a prominent part in the Battle of Arogi in which the enemy lost 700 killed and 1,200 wounded. The casualties on the British side were trifling.

King Theodore now tried to make terms, but Napier demanded unconditional surrender and the release of all European captives. To this ultimatum Theodore replied that " a warrior who has dandled strong men in his arms like infants will never suffer himself to be dandled in the arms of others," so hostilities were resumed after a short truce. The garrison of Selassie, 20,000 strong, surrendered without a blow on April 11th, and on the following day Theodore wrote apologizing for his missive and asking for permission to send Napier a peace offering of 1,000 cattle. The Abyssinian monarch handed over his captives; but as he did not make a formal surrender of himself and his army, Napier attacked Magdala on April 13th, 1868, covered by the fire of all his artillery. " Magdala, in its natural inaccessibility, is much stronger than either Selassie or Fahla," writes Willans.[2] " It is guarded by two scarps, the upper varying from 20 to 70 feet in height and the lower a perpendicular wall of solid rock in some places 250 feet high. The only entrances are from Islamgee by the Kokilbir gate and on the south side by the Kaffirbir gates : the former by a rugged and inaccessible path, the latter by one which is even more precipitous. . . . The defences were rendered more formidable by the outworks being commanded by a second line of stockades. The great drawback was the want of water, for there were few wells on the top of the hill."

About 4 p.m., in a violent thunderstorm, the assaulting troops advanced towards the Kokilbir Gate, preceded by a storming party consisting of a detachment of the 10th Company, R.E., under Pritchard, " K " Company, Madras S. & M., under Elliott, and H.M.'s 33rd Regiment. The 3rd and 4th Bombay Sapper companies followed in rear.[3] Covered by artillery and rifle fire, the stormers rushed up the path, but as there were no powder-bags to hand they had to force the gate with crowbars. It appears that Pritchard had arranged for a supply of powder in *mussacks* (skins) but had been ordered to leave it behind, and when he sent back for it he

[1]The strength of the Bombay Sappers and Miners at Arogi was 337 men.
[2]Article entitled " Sketch of Magdala and the surrounding country," by Lieut. T. J. Willans, R.E., appearing in *Prof. Papers of the Corps of Royal Engineers*, New Series, Vol. XVII, 1869, pp. 150–153.
[3]*The Military History of the Madras Engineers and Pioneers*, by Maj. H. M. Vibart, Vol. II, p. 463.

learnt that the *mussacks* had been taken away to carry water. He had some powder in small barrels, but it is fortunate that he did not attempt to use it because, when the gate had been battered down, it was found that there was a massive barricade of stones in rear and the effect of an explosion outside the gate would have been to blow the stormers over the cliff.[1] The Royal Engineers and Madras Sappers working in the gateway were under close fire from loopholes and suffered nine casualties including Elliott and Dalrymple slightly wounded. In the meantime, ladders had been brought up by men of the 10th Company, R.E., and the 3rd and 4th Companies, Bombay S. & M., who had been detailed to carry them,[2] and Pritchard, with Le Messurier and a party of the 33rd Regiment, effected an entrance by escalade over the wall to the right of the gate. The defenders of the gate then fled, and the stormers still outside were able to remove the barricade of stones and enter through the gateway. Pritchard, though slightly wounded, continued to lead his men. An undefended gap in the inner defence line having been discovered, the storming party was soon in the heart of the fortress, where the garrison surrendered at once. Theodore was found dead. He had shot himself when he realized that all was lost. Thus, at a small cost,[3] Magdala fell to Napier and the Union Jack was planted on its crest.

Victory having been attained, it was essential that the troops should cover the greater part of the return journey to the coast before the rains broke, and consequently Napier sent off his guns and elephants on April 15th and gave orders that Magdala should be evacuated by 4 p.m. on the 17th. At that hour, the work of dismantling the fortress and destroying the captured ordnance was begun by the engineer units. The gateways were demolished with gunpowder, and the stockaded defences razed to the ground. All the buildings within the fortifications were burnt and, being of wickerwork with thatched roofs, they made a fine conflagration. The smoke of blazing Magdala darkened the sky. On April 18th, the last of the British forces having crossed the Bashilo and camped on the Talanta plateau, the final preparations were made for the march northwards. Napier declared the campaign to be finished and issued a complimentary order to his troops. On April 26th, the force reached the Takkaze; but already the line of communication between Senafé and Kumayli had been interrupted by rain, and it was evident that the retirement was to be a race against time. As the transport animals weakened and died, the pace decreased, but the rearguard reached Antalo on May 12th along a rain-swept track marked by the Bombay Sapper companies.

[1]Extracts from a report by Maj. Pritchard, R.E., are given in "Sieges and the Defence of Fortified Places. Capture of Magdala, 1868", by Col. Sir E. T. Thackeray, V.C., K.C.B., late R.E., appearing in *The R.E. Journal*, Vol. XXII, July–Dec., 1915, pp. 281–284. Others appear in the article by Lieut. Willans already quoted.

[2]Memorandum by Capt. G. B. Leslie, Bo.I., dated Feb. 7th, 1870, appearing in a file at Kirkee entitled "Recommendations of Indian Officers, Bombay Sappers and Miners, for reward for special service in Abyssinia, 1869."

[3]The casualties during the campaign were chiefly from sickness. The British troops lost 379 ranks invalided and the Indian troops 570 ranks, but the followers lost 6,056 men of whom 512 died.

The damage in the Suru defile beyond Senafé was so serious that Captain W. Chrystie, R.E., was sent from Adigrat to take charge of the repair work. When he arrived in Upper Suru on May 2nd, he found that long stretches of the road had been scoured away and that at the Devil's Staircase below Upper Suru, and also in the Lower Suru defile, the track had been obliterated completely. The 1st and 2nd Bombay Sapper companies, with some infantry and labour gangs, were moved to the scene of the disaster and repaired the road roughly with large stones rolled down from the hillsides, but hardly had they finished when, on May 19th, a terrific thunderstorm broke over the gorge. Every watercourse became a foaming torrent. In the main gorge, the flood rose with such rapidity that seven men were swept away before they could run a few yards to safety, and at the Devil's Staircase a cart was deposited on a rock 22 feet above the bed. Next morning, the narrow parts of the defile were found to be a succession of precipices and pools. The ramps for the roadway had gone, and at one place in the Lower Suru gorge, where the width was only four feet between vertical cliffs, there was a perpendicular drop of 18 feet to a pool 14 feet deep. This was the route down which Napier had shortly to lead his army with its heterogeneous collection of guns, wagons, elephants, horses, mules and donkeys.

It was fortunate that a brigade including "K" Company, Madras S. & M., arrived in the nick of time at Senafé and was able to make the gorge passable for pack transport by strenuous labour on May 20th and 21st. During the next ten days, the road was prepared for wheeled transport by ramping the vertical drops with rocks and stones covered with sand, and thus, on June 1st, Napier was able to pass through and reach Kumayli and Zula. Nine days later, he embarked for England, and his troops for England or India. Most of the Madras and Bombay Sappers and Miners reached Bangalore or Kirkee before the end of the month, but the 3rd Company landed at Aden. The units received many tributes to their energy and endurance and earned for their respective Corps the honour "Abyssinia."[1] Zula reverted to its pristine desolation, and the railway buildings and piers were left to rot on the inhospitable coast of Annesley Bay.

A silver drum, one of the spoils obtained at Magdala, was shared between the 10th Company, R.E., and the Madras Sappers, and the half allotted to the Sappers was packed in a tightly fitting tin case and sent in a wooden box to England to be made into a cup; but about two months later, a letter was received stating that the box had been opened by the Customs' officials and had been found to be empty. Eventually, however, it appeared that the silver of the half-drum was so tarnished that it had been mistaken for the tin covering and that the trophy was safe, though the open box had lain for weeks in a shed.

Sir Robert Napier was raised to the peerage for his services in Abyssinia. "Never was a campaign more dependent upon the exertions of a single man," wrote his son, Colonel H. D. Napier, in 1927.[2] "The Commander-

[1]Awarded under G.O.G. dated Nov. 30th, 1869.

[2]*Field Marshal Lord Napier of Magdala, G.C.B., G.C.S.I.*, by Lieut.-Col. Hon. H. D. Napier, C.M.G., p. 255.

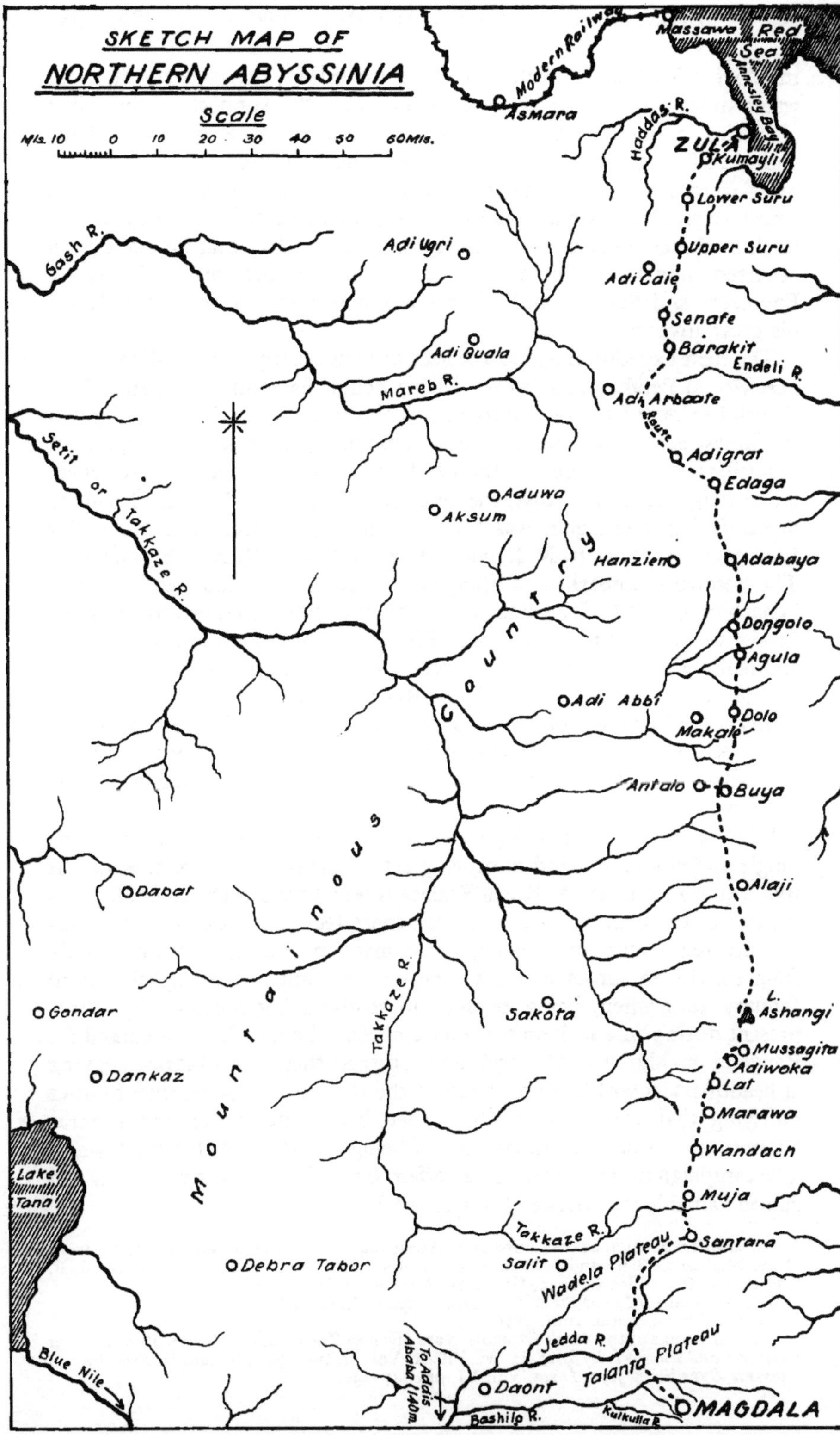
SKETCH MAP OF
NORTHERN ABYSSINIA
Scale
Mls. 10 0 10 20 30 40 50 60 Mls.
Modern Railway
Massawa
Red Sea
Annesley Bay
Asmara
Haddas R.
ZULA
Kumayli
Lower Suru
Upper Suru
Adi Ugri
Gash R.
Adi Caie
Senafe
Barakit
Endeli R.
Adi Quala
Mareb R.
Adi Arbaate
Route
Setit or Takkaze R.
Adigrat
Edaga
Aduwa
Aksum
Hanzien
Adabaya
Dongolo
Agula
Mountainous Country
Adi Abbi
Dolo
Makale
Antalo
Buya
Dabat
Alaji
Takkaze R.
Sakota
L. Ashangi
Gondar
Mussagita
Adiwoka
Dankaz
Lat
Marawa
Wandach
Lake Tana
Muja
Takkaze R.
Santara
Debra Tabor
Salit
Wadela Plateau
Jedda R.
Talanta Plateau
To Addis Ababa (140m.
Blue Nile
Daont
MAGDALA
Bashilo R.
Kulkulla R.

in-Chief calculated the value of every mule-load, the capacity of every water-supply, consulted the whims and won the support of the tribal chieftains, maintained a high discipline and at the same time gained the entire confidence of the officers and men under his command. If further proof were needed, the disastrous experiences of the Italians many years later give an idea of what would have happened had there been any serious hitch in the conduct of the campaign." But the fact that no such hitch occurred may be attributed also to the unremitting toil of the Royal Engineers and Sappers and Miners whom Napier selected carefully for his great adventure.[1]

The next expedition across the seas in which Sappers and Miners took part was to Perak, a state in the Malay Peninsula south of Penang. The British Resident had been murdered on November 2nd, 1875, and Captain W. Innes, R.E., had been shot in a subsequent skirmish, so troops were requisitioned from India and the Far East and a force of about 1,500 men, under Brig.-General J. Ross, was soon concentrated at Penang.[2] Included in the Indian contingent was "C" Company, Madras S. & M., under Lieutenant A. Howlett, M.I., with Lieutenant H. B. Rich, R.E., attached. The company embarked at Rangoon on November 22nd and reached Penang on the 29th. The assembled force then voyaged down the Malacca Straits to the mouth of the Larut River, 40 miles south-east of Penang, and landing 6 miles upstream, marched 30 miles inland to Kuala Kangsa on the upper reaches of the Perak River. Meanwhile, another column composed of troops from Singapore and Hong Kong had ascended the Perak River and marched eastwards to the capital at Kinta, and by December 17th, the combined forces were in complete control of the country.

"C" Company was occupied at first in clearing a road through the jungle and stockading and improving camps for the force under Ross. It was then sent forward to Kuala Kangsa where, between December 8th and the end of the month, it built 10,000 square feet of hutting for the troops and erected a number of bridges and many palisades, working steadily from sunrise to sunset in all weathers. The unit saw no fighting until January 28th when, being engaged in road-making northwards, it was present during an attack on the village of Kota Lama. It re-embarked for Rangoon on March 22nd, 1876, and returned thence to Madras, arriving at headquarters within a few weeks of the receipt of a Government Order notifying that Her Majesty the Queen had conferred on the Madras Sappers and Miners the distinction of being styled the "Queen's Own."[3] The campaign in Perak was a small affair, but "C" Company did well and gained valuable experience of jungle warfare.[4]

[1] An excellent account of the campaign in Abyssinia, with particular reference to the work of the Madras Sappers and Miners, is given in an essay written in 1926 by Capt. B. F. Whitestone, R.E. (See Case 19, Historical Records, at Bangalore.)

[2] See the *Sketch Map of the Malay Archipelago* in Chapter V.

[3] G.O.G., dated March 10th, 1876.

[4] Further details of the Perak Expedition are given in *The Military History of the Madras Engineers and Pioneers*, by Maj. H. M. Vibart, Vol. II, pp. 479–486, and in *Frontier and Overseas Expeditions from India*, Vol. VI, pp. 347–350.

Two years after the return of " C " Company from the Malay Peninsula, " G " and " H " Companies, Madras S. & M., and the 3rd and 5th Companies, Bombay S. & M., accompanied the first military mission ever sent from India to Europe. A " Malta Expeditionary Force," of about 7,000 men drawn from all three Presidencies, voyaged to the Mediterranean in 1878 under the command of Major-General J. Ross to occupy Cyprus as a warning to Russia against attempting to impose unnecessarily severe terms on Turkey and perhaps to dominate south-eastern Europe. " G " Company was commanded by Lieutenant C. C. Ellis, R.E., with Lieutenants W. D. Lindley and S. C. N. Grant, R.E., and " H " Company by Lieutenant C. B. Wilkieson, R.E., with Lieutenants W. D. Conner and F. W. T. Attree, R.E. The 3rd Company was commanded by Lieutenant G. Turner Jones, R.E., with Lieutenants W. Coles and C. McG. Bate, R.E., and the 5th Company by Captain F. T. Stock, Bo.I., with Lieutenants J. D. Fullerton and E. H. Bethell, R.E. Captain J. H. R. Cruickshank, R.E., was in command of the Bombay Sappers, and Brevet-Colonel H. N. D. Prendergast, V.C., R.E., was Commanding Royal Engineer with Major A. F. Hamilton, R.E., as Adjutant. Madras and Bombay Engineer Parks accompanied the expedition.[1]

The 3rd and 5th Companies left Bombay in the sailing ship *Oreflamme* on April 29th, 1878, and " G " and " H " Companies in the steamship *Canara* on May 2nd, the entire transport fleet consisting of 12 steamships towing 15 sailing ships.[2] The Madras Sappers landed in Malta on May 26th and the Bombay Sappers on the 28th, and all were quartered in the Lazaretto Barracks. There is little to record of their stay in the island. They were issued with Martini-Henry rifles as a temporary measure and spent their time in drilling with their new weapons, handling stores, road-making, bridging, water-supply and fitting tents and huts with additional coverings. On June 17th they were inspected by H.R.H. The Duke of Cambridge. They saw most of the sights of Malta, though not a remarkable notice once erected at a spot on the lofty fortifications, where caper-shrubs from Sicily had been planted. This notice ran as follows :—" No one is allowed to cut capers on the fortifications except the C.R.E."[3]

The Sappers and Miners enjoyed their stay in Malta, for it was a novel experience under pleasant conditions. Their experiences in Cyprus, however, were not so pleasant. Leaving half the 5th Company to follow with the Bombay Park, they left Malta on July 11th, 1878, and arrived off Larnaka five days later. Their first work was to assist in disembarking a siege train. That done, they built landing-stages with timber from ruined houses and prepared a large camp. Road-work, water-supply and signalling arrangements also kept them fully occupied, and many of their

[1] " The Indian Expeditionary Force," appearing in *The R.E. Journal*, Vol. 8, 1878, p. 69.
[2] *Frontier and Overseas Expeditions from India*, Vol. VI, pp. 21–24. The strength of the Madras Sappers (with Park) was 9 B.O.s, 12 B.N.C.O.s, 4 I.O.s, 239 I.O.R.s and 90 followers. The Bombay Sappers numbered 4 B.O.s, 12 B.N.C.O.s, 4 I.O.s, 188 I.O.R.s and 48 followers.
[3] " Occasional Notes, " in *The R.E. Journal*, Vol. XIV, 1884, p. 20.

British officers surveyed the island. Archibald Forbes describes the Madras Sappers and Miners as " dark lissom fellows, stripped to the *dhotie* and streaming at every pore " and contrasts their honest road-work with the slip-shod methods of the local gangs.[1] From the beginning of August, the units were employed chiefly in improving the main road between Larnaka and Nicosia, but progress was slow because they were decimated by fever. Colonel Prendergast left for India on August 25th after handing over charge to Lieut.-Colonel J. P. Maquay, R.E., who was senior to him in the Corps. On September 23rd, huts for a winter encampment began to arrive, and " G " Company laboured daily from sunrise to sunset in disembarking them. The work was hard and exhausting, and all the Sappers and Miners were glad to see the last of Cyprus when they steamed for Port Said on November 2nd. They landed in Bombay on November 22nd without having seen a shot fired; but the 5th Company, Bombay Sappers and Miners, was rewarded soon afterwards by receiving orders to proceed to Baluchistan during the Second Afghan War, whither it was followed by the 3rd Company in October, 1879.

An opportunity for active service overseas was afforded to two companies and a telegraph section of the Madras Sappers when an Indian division under Major-General Sir H. T. Macpherson was mobilized in July, 1882, to join an expeditionary force under Lieut.-General Sir Garnet Wolseley which was sent to Egypt from England, Malta and Cyprus to subdue Arabi Pasha and his insurgent army. " A " and " I " Companies were warned for service, and also the 2nd and 8th Companies of the Bengal Sappers;[2] but after " I " Company had sailed for Aden with the Seaforth Highlanders in the middle of July in anticipation of final orders, the despatch of the Bengal units was countermanded. At the head of the Madras Sappers destined for Egypt was Major A. F. Hamilton, R.E. The officers with " A " Company were Lieutenants C. H. Darling, P. B. Baldwin and H. S. Andrews-Speed, R.E., and with " I " Company, Lieutenants W. D. Lindley and H. E. Goodwyn, R.E. The Commanding Royal Engineer was Colonel James (" Buster ") Browne, late R.E., famous for his exploits on the Indian frontier.[3] There was great enthusiasm at Bangalore when mobilization orders were received, and the men of other companies volunteered in large numbers to fill the vacancies in " A " and " I " Companies caused by men pronounced to be medically unfit. Mobilization was easy because the companies had their complete field equipment except draught animals. Each was brought rapidly to its war strength of 125 officers and men and was then ready to embark.[4] " I " Company, starting for Aden on July 12th, reached Suez on August 8th

[1] *The Military History of the Madras Engineers and Pioneers*, by Maj. H. M. Vibart, Vol. II, p. 491. An account of the experiences of the Madras Sappers in Malta and Cyprus is given in pp. 487–494 of that volume.

[2] *Frontier and Overseas Expeditions from India*, Vol. VI, p. 26.

[3] See *The Military Engineer in India*, by the present author, Vol. I, pp. 375, 382, 387, 425, 428, and 511, and Vol. II, pp. 68, 71, 73, 124, 130, 143–50, 152–55, 243, 328, 339–42, and 349.

[4] " The Sappers of the Indian Contingent for Egypt," appearing in *The R.E. Journal*, Vol. XII, 1882, p. 197. The war strength was 2 B.O.s, 2 B.N.C.O.s, 2 I.O.s, 4 Havildars, 8 Naiks, 2 Buglers and 105 Sappers, with a surgeon and a hospital assistant.

and was the first Indian unit to land. " A " Company left Bangalore on August 1st and did not arrive in Suez until the 23rd. The two units were followed by a telegraph section of " E " Company which disembarked at Suez on September 23rd with mule transport and instruments and cable sufficient for 10 miles of line.[1]

Before " A " Company joined " I " Company in Egypt, Major-General Gerald Graham, V.C., late R.E., in command of the 2nd Brigade of the 1st Division from England, had occupied Ismailia on the Suez Canal and had begun an advance on Tel-el-Kebir by seizing Mifisha on the Sweetwater Canal, the channel supplying the inhabitants of Suez with fresh water from the Nile.[2] Meanwhile, " I " Company had been busily employed near Suez. On August 16th, Goodwyn and a party of Sappers were attacked while surveying along the Sweetwater Canal and had to abandon their boat. Half the unit afterwards accompanied some infantry to Es Shallufa (Chalouf) and destroyed the enemy's cover. On the 20th, a section marched to Es Shallufa with the Seaforths and demolished 80 yards of railway, and during the next two days, the whole company was engaged in repairing a wide breach made by the retreating enemy in the bank of the Sweetwater Canal through which water was escaping into the adjacent Maritime or Suez Canal.[3] " A " Company then arrived and helped " I " Company to strengthen the bank and repair the railway and telegraph lines as far as Gineifa. On August 27th, Darling and half of " A " Company went with Colonel Browne on a trial trip over the railway to Ismailia while the other half-company moved by the canal route. Afterwards, " A " Company was employed at Ismailia until September 8th in building landing-stages, disembarking stores and repairing the railway.

Meanwhile, " I " Company was beginning to move northwards from Es Shallufa. Half the company reached Fayid on August 27th and, after two days' work on the railway and telegraph, marched to Serapeum to entrench a lock on the Sweetwater Canal. It joined " A " Company at Ismailia on the 31st. The other half-company remained at Es Shallufa until September 7th, when it followed the remainder to Ismailia. The Telegraph Section of " E " Company was already in Ismailia. All the Madras Sappers marched westwards on September 10th through El Magfar to El Mahuta, and on the following day through El Mahsama to El Qassasin (Kassassin), where they made arrangements for water-supply. El Qassasin had been occupied by General Graham on August 24th and held against a strong counter-attack by Arabi Pasha on the 28th.[4]

Some interesting comments on the equipment of the Madras Sapper

[1]" I " Company left Bombay in the S.S. *Malda* on July 21st and " A " Company in the S.S. *Bhandara* on Aug. 7th. The section of " E " Company left Bombay in the S.S. *Kerbela* on August 18th.

[2]See the *Sketch Map of Lower Egypt, Communications*, 1882, included in this chapter.

[3]*Historical Record of the Q.V.O. Madras Sappers and Miners*, Vol. I, p. 116.

[4]These military operations are described in greater detail in *The Royal Engineers in Egypt and the Sudan* by the present author (pp. 36–38), and also the Battle of Tel-el-Kebir and the advance on Cairo. The modern spelling of names, as followed in that volume, has been adopted in this narrative.

companies are made in a report by Major Hamilton. "There was a great diversity in clothing," he remarks.[1] "The 'I' Company started on so short a notice that the men took their usual dress with them—blue serge jacket and black drill trousers. Khaki was taken in bulk, but the weather was so stormy between Bombay and Aden that the tailors could not work, so the khaki coats intended for wear were not completed. The 'A' Company wore a full suit of khaki; the section of 'E' Company, khaki coats and black trousers. Opinions differed much as to which was the best kind of dress. When near the sea, the khaki seemed to absorb moisture, and the coat felt damp when first put on in the morning. Blue was doubtless hot, but the 'I' Company was not singular in that dress, for all the troops of the 1st and 2nd Divisions wore red or blue serge frocks, and in the 29th Beloochees all the officers and men wore dark green helmets. The 'I' Company took the ordinary soda-water bottle covered with leather. The 'A' Company had copper water-bottles, but as they seemed to fancy that the copper affected the water, they supplied themselves when possible with Egyptian water-bottles made of block tin, hammered into shape and in form like a flattened teapot. Ammunition boots, blankets and waterproof sheets were issued. The valises, holding the necessary changes of clothes, were useful. A circular tent to hold 12 men was supplied. These tents were just a mule load. The heliostats were not very successful. When used in the desert they were so low that the mirage rendered it difficult to read a message. All the native signallers took kindly to the Roorkee pattern heliograph, and as soon as the R.E. Park with heliographs arrived, the heliostats were put into store."[2]

At dawn on September 13th, 1882, Sir Garnet Wolseley stormed Arabi's entrenched position at Tel-el-Kebir and virtually ended the brief campaign which had begun with the bombardment of Alexandria by the British fleet on July 11th. A former Bengal Sapper officer in the person of Major Bindon Blood, R.E., was present at the battle, but not with the Sappers and Miners, for he was in command of the 26th Field Company, R.E. The Indian contingent under General Macpherson operated on the extreme left with a Naval Brigade advancing south of the Sweetwater Canal, and consequently it was not in the main assault directed against the centre and right. The contingent left camp somewhat later than the remainder of the force, but by 2.30 a.m. it had begun the approach march from El Qassasin under cover of darkness. The Madras Sappers were not called upon to execute any technical work other than laying a telegraph cable, which was done by the section of "E" Company, and they acted, apparently, as

[1] "The Work of the Detachment of the 'Queen's Own' Sappers and Miners in Egypt," by Maj. A. F. Hamilton, R.E., appearing in *The R.E. Journal*, Vol. 13, 1883, pp. 67–70, with reports by Lieut. W. D. Lindley, R.E., on the repair of the breach in the Sweetwater Canal at Es Shallufa, by Lieut. H. E. Goodwyn, R.E., on the defences of Nifisha, and by Lieut. C. H. Darling, R.E., on clearing the Zagazig-Benha section of the railway to Cairo. These reports appear also in Historical File No. 8 at Bangalore.

[2] The heliostat had a fixed mirror. It was superseded by the heliograph, with an oscillating mirror. This instrument was brought to the notice of the Indian Government by Mr. Mance in 1869. It was adopted by the British Army in 1875, and used extensively in the Second Afghan War in 1878–80. Many heliographs were made in the Roorkee workshops.

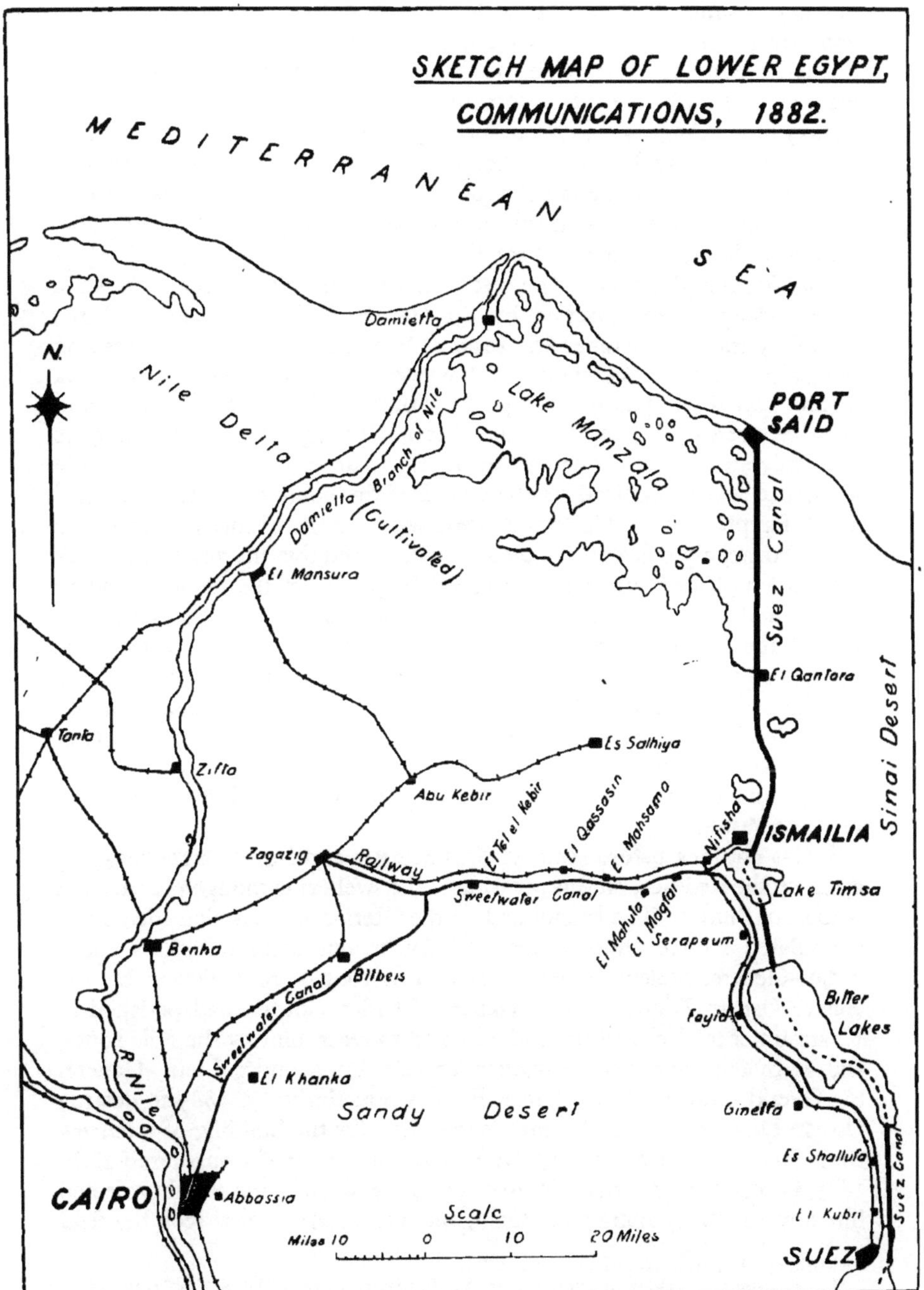
SKETCH MAP OF LOWER EGYPT,
COMMUNICATIONS, 1882.
MEDITERRANEAN SEA
N.
Nile Delta
Damietta
Lake Manzala
PORT SAID
Damietta Branch of Nile
(Cultivated)
El Mansura
Suez Canal
El Qantara
Sinai Desert
Tanta
Es Salhiya
Zifta
Abu Kebir
El Tel el Kebir
El Qassasin
El Mahsama
Nifisha
ISMAILIA
Zagazig
Railway
Sweetwater Canal
Lake Timsa
El Mahuta
El Magfar
El Serapeum
Benha
Bilbeis
Bitter Lakes
Sweetwater Canal
Fayid
El Khanka
Sandy Desert
Ginelfa
R. Nile
Es Shallufa
Suez Canal
CAIRO
Abbassia
Scale
Miles 10 0 10 20 Miles
El Kubri
SUEZ

infantry in support. After the battle, " A " and " I " Companies marched with Macpherson to Zagazig, covering 26 miles in one day. A detachment was left behind at Tel-el-Kebir to remove an obstruction across the railway. On the 14th, the two companies began to clear the Zagazig-Benha railway of wreckage and to repair a bridge, and on the 22nd they entrained for Cairo. It is said that, at Zagazig, a Sapper *bhisti* discovered an Egyptian ammunition box containing gold coins. These he secreted in his *mussack*, and having patiently carried this additional load until his return to India, retired as the richest man in his village.

The Madras Sappers were present in Cairo on September 30th when 18,000 troops were reviewed by Sir Garnet Wolseley. They left the capital by train on October 8th, reached Suez on the 9th, and Bombay on the 28th. Two representatives, however—Subadar Jeyram and Naik Sheikh Ismail—were sent to England with men of other Indian units and were received by Her Majesty the Queen. Though the Madras Sappers took only an inconspicuous part in the Egyptian campaign, their valuable assistance was recognized by the award of the honours " Tel-el-Kebir " and " Egypt, 1882."[1] Colonel Browne wrote of them[2] that he had found them thoroughly efficient, handy and willing, and that the amount of work they accomplished surprised the Royal Engineers of the home establishment; and when Sir Frederick Roberts presented medals to the companies from Afghanistan on parade at Bangalore on February 5th, 1883, he mentioned that he had been so impressed with the usefulness of the Corps that he had recommended that two regiments of Madras Infantry should be formed into Pioneers on the model of the 23rd and 32nd Regiments of Punjab Native Infantry and that his suggestion had been approved.[3] Thus the labours of the Madras Sappers in Afghanistan and Egypt had far reaching results.

It was not long before some Madras Sappers and Miners were voyaging again up the Red Sea, on this occasion to the sweltering though picturesque seaport of Suakin. The Mahdi had set the interior of the Sudan aflame and annihilated a force under Colonel W. Hicks, and some irregulars under Major-General Valentine Baker had been routed near Tokar[4] by the elusive Osman Digna. Major-General Charles Gordon had perished in Khartoum after Lord Wolseley had failed to reach him by the Nile route, and as Suakin was then in danger, an expedition under Lieut.-General Sir Gerald Graham, V.C., late R.E., was sent thither in 1885 to destroy Osman Digna and clear the coast sufficiently for the building of a railway from Suakin to Berber on the Nile. Arriving in Suakin on March 12th, 1885, Graham set his engineers to work on the construction of the projected line towards the mountains at Otao, and shortly afterwards took the field

[1]Military Despatch dated May 17th, 1883.
[2]Letter from Col. James Browne to Gen. Sir Frederick Roberts dated Nov. 15th, 1882.
[3]" Presentation of Medals to the Q.V.O. Sappers and Miners at Bangalore," appearing in *The R.E. Journal*, Vol. XIII, 1883, pp. 76, 77.
[4]The battle took place at Et Teb, 12 miles north of Tokar, on Feb. 4th, 1884. Tokar is 55 miles south-east of Suakin. All places mentioned in this narrative of the Suakin operations are shown in the *Sketch Map of the Suakin District in* 1885 which is included in this chapter.

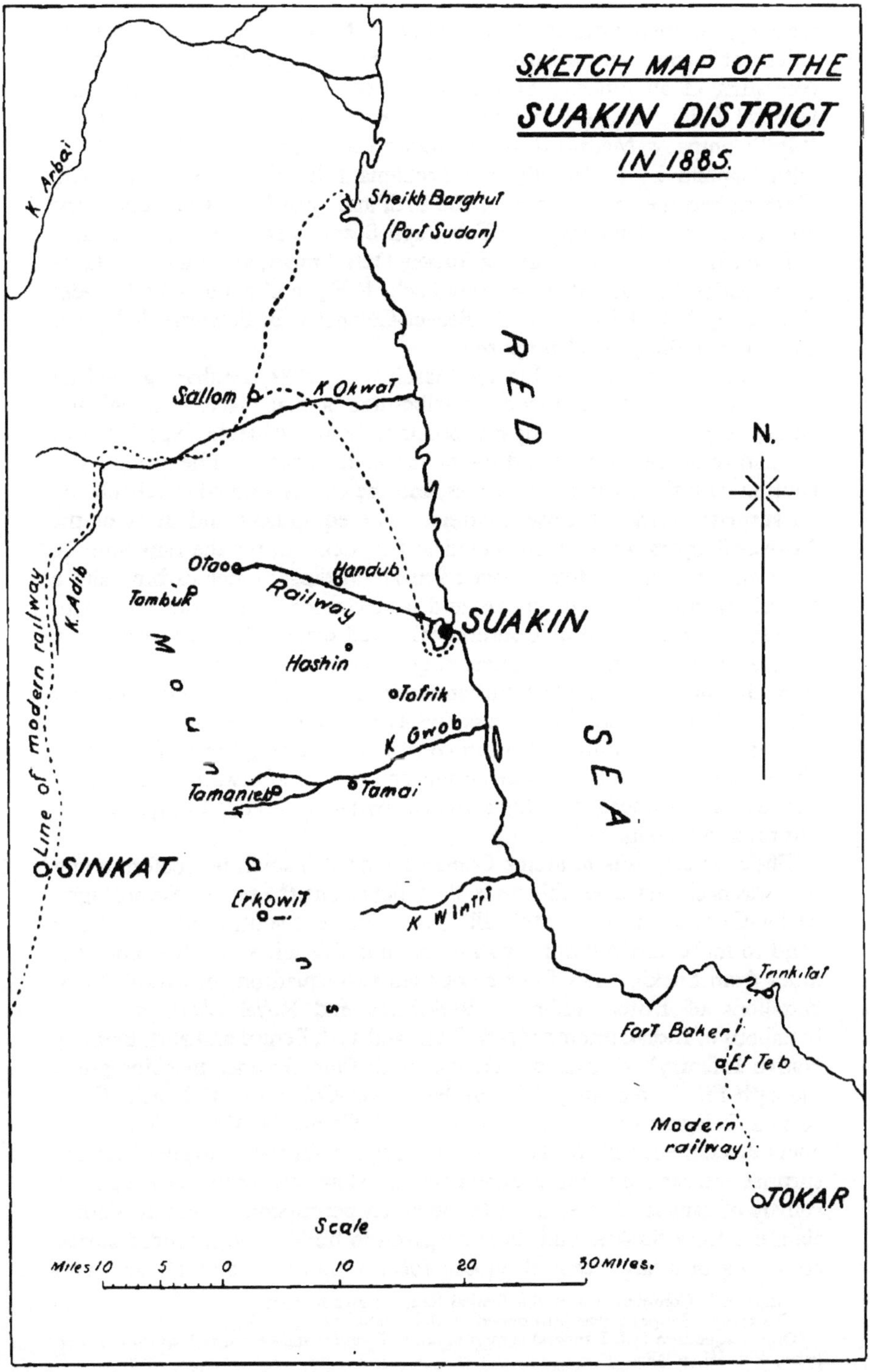
SKETCH MAP OF THE
SUAKIN DISTRICT
IN 1885.
K. Arbai
Sheikh Barghut
(Port Sudan)
RED
SEA
N.
Sallom
K. Okwat
Otao
Handub
Tambuk
Railway
K. Adib
Line of modern railway
SUAKIN
Hashin
Tofrik
Mountains
K. Gwob
Tamaniet
Tamai
SINKAT
Erkowit
K. Wintri
Trinkitat
Fort Baker
Et Teb
Modern
railway
TOKAR
Scale
Miles 10
5
0
10
20
30 Miles.

with 13,000 men against Osman Digna's force of 7,000, concentrated chiefly at Tamai with a further 3,000 at Hashin. An Indian contingent, consisting of an infantry brigade and a cavalry regiment under Brig.-General J. Hudson, was included in Graham's division, and with it was "F" Company, Madras S. & M., under Captain C. B. Wilkieson, R.E., with Captain F. J. Romilly and Lieutenant E. M. B. Newman, R.E. Graham had the services also of the 17th and 24th Field Companies, the 10th (Railway) Company, two Telegraph Sections and a Balloon Section, R.E., an Indian Labour Corps, a Survey Detachment, a Mounted Detachment under Lieutenant A. E. Sandbach, R.E.,[1] and a Field Park under Captain S. A. E. Hickson, R.E. Brevet-Colonel J. B. Edwards, R.E., was the Commanding Royal Engineer.

Advancing towards Hashin on March 20th, 1885, Graham gained an easy victory over the Hadendowa tribesmen at that place. Though not closely engaged, "F" Company obtained some valuable experience of the nature of the country and the tactics of the enemy. The ground was covered with thorny mimosa bushes, and the enemy seemed to rely chiefly on surprise attacks at close quarters. The equipment and dress of the Madras Sappers were hardly suited to the occasion, for the rank and file were armed with the five-grooved muzzle-loading Snider carbine and a "working knife" or a hand-axe, and were clothed in a scarlet tunic with blue facings and dark blue trousers with a red stripe. On their heads, they wore a black turban. It is interesting to observe that this was the first campaign in which the black turban was worn in place of the former dark blue head-dress, and that it was the last in which the men served as "Privates."[2] The work at Hashin consisted in helping the 17th and 24th Field Companies to build four strong points, and afterwards preparing a *zariba* as an advanced post for a British battalion. "F" Company then returned to Suakin.

The next step was to attack Osman Digna at Tamai, but before doing so it was necessary to establish supply depots along the route. Accordingly, Major-General Sir John McNeill, V.C., was sent southwards on March 22nd to make and garrison two zaribas, one five miles and the other ten miles from Suakin. His force comprised two squadrons of cavalry,[3] two battalions of British infantry (Berkshires and Royal Marines), three battalions of Indian infantry (15th Sikhs and 17th Bengal and 28th Bombay Native Infantry), a naval detachment with four Gardner machine-guns, the 24th Field Company, R.E., under Brevet-Colonel E. P. Leach, V.C., R.E., a Telegraph Section, R.E., and "F" Company, Madras S. & M.—about 4,000 men in all. McNeill set out in square formation to guard against surprise attacks; but his progress was so slow, owing to his enormous convoy of camels, that at noon he obtained permission to halt at Tofrik, six miles from Suakin, and there prepared to build a thorn-fenced *zariba* consisting of a large central square for his transport animals and two

[1]Afterwards Commandant of the Bengal Sappers and Miners.
[2]The term "Sapper" was introduced in Dec., 1885.
[3]Only 1 squadron (5th Lancers) is mentioned in *Frontier and Overseas Expeditions from India*, Vol. VI, p. 58.

smaller flanking squares for his troops. Screened by cavalry vedettes in the bush, the Berkshires and Marines were posted to the east of the selected site, while the Indian troops covered the other sides, the 17th Bengal Infantry facing south, the 15th Sikhs west, and the 28th Bombay Infantry north. As the heat was terrific, the infantry and engineers piled arms before setting to work and then proceeded to clear a field of fire and build the defences. When the flanking enclosures began to take shape, some of the Marines occupied the northern one with two Gardner guns and some of the Berkshires the southern one with the other two guns. The bush being thickest on the north and west, the defences on these sides were finished first.

A brief account of what followed has been given in another volume,[1] and as that account was approved by General Sir Reginald Wingate, the distinguished officer who was Governor-General of the Sudan for no less than 17 years, it is reproduced here with a sketch map to explain the situation.[2] At 2 p.m., when many of the troops were at dinner, the central square was still open to the east and south and partly also to the west and north. The camels and mules, having been unloaded in the central square, were collected to the east of it, and near them were two companies of Berkshires. The men were tired and there was yet no proper field of fire around the incomplete defences. At 2.30 p.m., a cavalry soldier reported that the enemy were advancing, and orders were given for the working and covering parties to come in; but before they could be collected, the cavalry galloped towards the *zariba* with the Sudanese swarming at their heels. The attack was delivered mainly against the southern and eastern sides and into the midst of the transport animals and non-combatants. Enveloped in clouds of dust, and filling the air with savage cries, the Sudanese surged onwards in a vast impetuous mass. Our working parties rushed for their arms; some men found them, others did not. Thrown into disorder by the cavalry riding through them, the 17th Bengal Infantry fired a volley, broke their ranks, and rushed towards the central square. The two companies of Berkshires, forming square to the north of the transport animals, stood firm, but the enemy were soon among the camels and mules, and an avalanche of Sudanese, Bengal Infantry, followers and animals burst through the central square in a stabbing and hacking mob and carried away with them some of the Royal Engineers and Madras Sappers. A party of the 24th Field Company managed to fight its way back, and another under Lieutenant C. Godby, R.E., joined the rallying square of the Berkshires outside the *zariba* and helped to repel the assault. "For the next few minutes," writes Godby,[3] "we were infantry pure and simple: targets in plenty: range, three to thirty yards; ammunition, not marksmanship, required." The situation was saved chiefly by the Marines and those of the Berkshires who were securely entrenched with

[1] *The Royal Engineers in Egypt and the Sudan*, by the present author, pp. 72, 73.
[2] *Sketch Map of the Battle of Tofrik* (or *McNeill's Zariba*), 2.30 *p.m.*, *March 22nd*, 1885.
[3] Notes by Brig.-Gen. C. Godby, C.B., C.M.G., D.S.O., late R.E., sent to the author on Oct. 24th, 1934.

their Gardner guns in the flanking squares, although their fire killed hundreds of our stampeding camels.

Both the 24th Field Company, R.E., and "F" Company, Madras S. & M., suffered severely.[1] When the attack began, Captain F. J. Romilly, R.E., was superintending the Madras Sappers who were loading their equipment on mules, and the retreating Bengal Infantry carried these Sappers with them across the unfinished angle of the central square. Captain C. B. Wilkieson, R.E., severely wounded in the leg, saw a Sudanese warrior run alongside Romilly's horse and spear the rider through the side and heart. The man was shot immediately afterwards. It seems that Romilly was attempting to save the life of a brother officer. Lieutenant E. M. B. Newman, R.E., was killed by a swordsman, his left arm being severed and the top of his head sliced clean off. His opponent was soon among the dead. The Battle of Tofrik was finished in twenty minutes. When the smoke cleared away, the place was a shambles. Dead bodies of men and animals lay in heaps on every side. The British lost about 100 men killed and 140 wounded, and no less than 900 camels perished. At least 1,000 of the enemy lay motionless around and within the *zariba*.[2]

It appears that when the Sudanese broke into the central square a party of Madras Sappers under Wilkieson gathered round a pile of stores and biscuit boxes and firing with the greatest steadiness checked the assault and thus helped the Marines and Berkshires in the flanking squares to save the situation. Newman fell when a number of the enemy penetrated the Berkshires' square, where some of the Sappers were building a gun emplacement. In later years, when Commandant at Bangalore, Wilkieson used to describe how a "Fuzzy-Wuzzy," his spear dripping with blood, came rushing at him, and how he shot the man dead with his revolver after missing him twice. As a result, every officer of the Corps was required to fire 24 rounds on the revolver range each Sunday, and the Madras Sappers used to win all the revolver competitions at the Bangalore Rifle Meeting.[3] Brig.-General Evans relates that in 1888 Lance-Naik (afterwards Hon. Captain) Alexander told him many stories of Tofrik, and when asked how he felt when the enemy attacked the *zariba*, replied with a smile "I not fraiding too much, sah!"[4] The comradeship established between the British infantry and the Sappers at Suakin stood the latter in good stead in an emergency, for the Sappers had fraternized much with the British soldiers. They smoked and drank with them in their canteens and claimed that they had even won money from them at cards.

[1] "F" Company lost 2 British officers and 13 Indian other ranks killed, and 1 British officer and 18 Indian other ranks wounded.

[2] For further details of the Battle of Tofrik see *The Egyptian Campaigns*, 1882–1899, by C. Royle, pp. 416–429; an article entitled "Suakin, 1885, Field Operations" in *The R.E. Journal*, Vol. XVI, 1886, pp. 97–101; and a report by Bt. Col. E. P. Leach, V.C., R.E., entitled "Appendix to Diary for March 1885. Action at Zereba (Tofrik), 22nd March, 1885," appearing in the Official Report on the Royal Engineers at Suakin. A good account is given also in an essay by Capt. A. V. Anderson, R.E., written in 1926 and filed in Case 19, Historical Records, at Bangalore.

[3] Notes by Col. P. E. Hodgson, D.S.O., late R.E., sent to the author on Aug. 28th, 1937.

[4] Notes by Brig.-Gen. U. W. Evans, C.B., C.M.G., late R.E., sent to the author on May 29th, 1937.

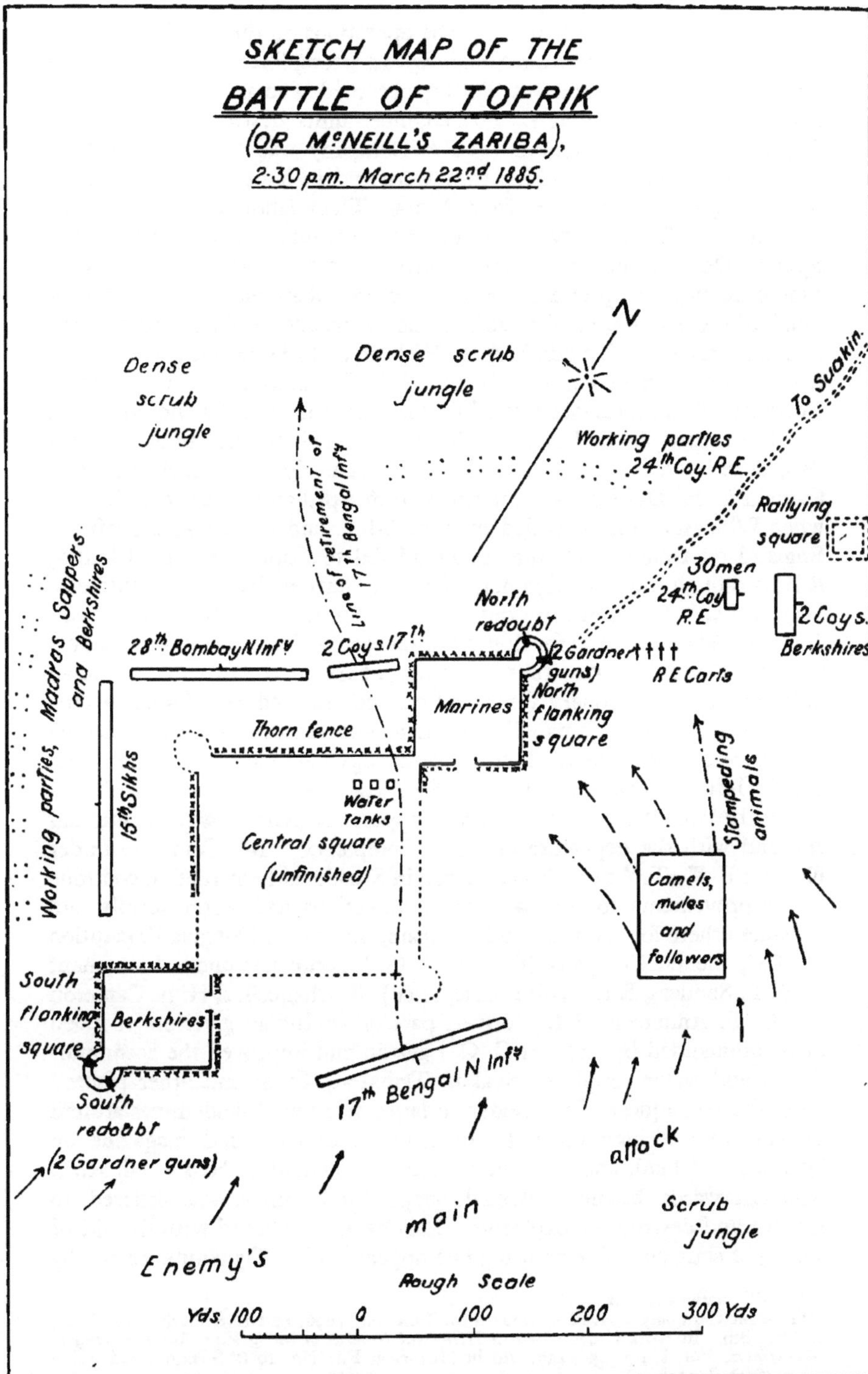
SKETCH MAP OF THE
BATTLE OF TOFRIK
(OR McNEILL'S ZARIBA),
2·30 p.m. March 22nd 1885.
N
Dense scrub jungle
Dense scrub jungle
To Suakin
Working parties 24th Coy. R.E.
Rallying square
30 men
24th Coy R.E
2 Coys. Berkshires
Line of retirement of 17th Bengal Infy
Working parties, Madras Sappers and Berkshires
28th Bombay N Infy
2 Coys 17th
North redoubt
(2 Gardner guns)
R E Carts
North flanking square
Marines
Thorn fence
15th Sikhs
Water tanks
Central square (unfinished)
Stampeding animals
Camels, mules and followers
South flanking square
Berkshires
South redoubt (2 Gardner guns)
17th Bengal N Infy
Enemy's main attack
Scrub jungle
Rough Scale
Yds. 100 0 100 200 300 Yds

Little remains to be recorded of the operations on the Red Sea coast in 1885. Graham marched from Suakin with a strong force on April 2nd, and reinforced by the brigade at Tofrik, occupied Tamai on the 3rd. No resistance was encountered. The engineer units destroyed Tamai, and Graham returned to Suakin. "F" Company was next employed on railway construction, in which they were said to have done more useful work then any other Corps from India. Their labours, however, were thrown away, for the railway was a complete failure. When rail-head had reached Otao at the end of April, orders were received that the force should be broken up and the railway project abandoned, and thereafter much of the material lay for years in the desert and on Quarantine Island in Suakin harbour. Captain S. A. E. Hickson and Lieutenant J. A. Tanner, R.E., were attached temporarily to "F" Company after the Battle of Tofrik to fill the vacancies caused by the deaths of Romilly and Newman, and Lieutenant A. C. MacDonnell, R.E., joined the unit in April from Bangalore but was soon invalided. Malaria and dysentery took their toll. Captain C. H. Darling, R.E., joined also in April and assumed command when Wilkieson was invalided on June 8th; and when Darling left for England on October 1st, the command fell to Captain W. D. Lindley, R.E. Although the campaign may be said to have ended in the middle of May, 1885, "F" Company did not leave Suakin until November 20th. It embarked on that date for Bombay after earning for its Corps the honours "Tofrek" and "Suakin, 1885."[1] By May, 1886, all the British and Indian units of the expeditionary force had quitted the Red Sea. Osman Digna had then reoccupied Tamai, Hashin, Otao and Handub and was besieging Suakin, which was defended mostly by an Egyptian garrison. Once more, the Mahdi's followers overran the Red Sea coast.

Yet the connection of the Madras Sappers and Miners with Suakin did not end with the departure of "F" Company. "B" Company under Captain F. W. T. Attree, R.E., arrived in Suakin early in 1886 to continue the improvements to the harbour, fortifications and water supply and remained there for several months. Again, during the Dongola Expedition of 1896, the 1st Company (formerly "G" Company) under Lieutenant G. A. F. Sanders, R.E., with Lieutenants J. R. Chancellor, H. A. Cameron and C. F. Anderson, R.E., formed part of an Indian garrison of 4,000 men commanded by Colonel C. C. Egerton and improved the accommodation and water supply of Suakin, Trinkitat, Tokar and other places.[2] After the reconquest of the Sudan, a large number of land-mines around Suakin were dismantled and stored in an underground magazine on Quarantine Island, and some years later, Lieutenant S. H. Powell, R.E., who afterwards became a Bengal Sapper and Miner, was ordered to remove and destroy the explosive. This he accomplished with the aid of a gang of convicts. The amusing tale appears as "A Dynamite Yarn" by

[1] G.G.O. dated July 16th, 1885.

[2] The 1st Company arrived in Suakin on June 1st, 1896, and re-embarked for India on Dec. 8th. Its work is described in *Historical Records of the Q.V.O. Madras Sappers and Miners*, Vol. I, pp. 156, 157, and in Historical File No. 10 ("Suakin Field Force Diary") at Bangalore.

"Lens" in *The R.E. Journal* of December, 1937. The Italian conquest of Abyssinia in 1935–36 saved Suakin temporarily from complete eclipse by thriving Port Sudan, and as an outpost of the British Empire it regained some of the importance it possessed in the days of the Mahdi, Osman Digna and the Khalifa when the Madras Sappers and Miners laboured so manfully on its defences, water supply and ill-starred railway. Now it sleeps again on its blue lagoon.

Shortly after the return of "B" Company, Madras S. & M., from Suakin in May, 1885, the conduct of King Thibaw of Burma became so outrageous that the Government of India decided to depose and deport him and for this purpose organized a force of about 9,000 men for an advance up the Irrawaddy to Mandalay under the command of Major-General H. N. D. Prendergast, V.C., C.B.[1] The force was well supplied with engineer units, as was to be expected when an engineer was Commander-in-Chief in the field. From Roorkee came the 4th and 5th Companies, Bengal S. & M.; from Secunderabad and Bangalore, "C," "D" and "H" Companies and a Telegraph Section of "A" Company, Madras S. & M.; and from Kirkee, the 2nd Company, Bombay S. & M., the whole being under Colonel G. E. L. S. Sanford, R.E., as Commanding Royal Engineer, with Brevet-Major C. B. Wilkieson, R.E., as Adjutant. Of the Bengal units, the 4th Company was commanded originally by Lieutenant W. A. Cairnes, R.E., with Lieutenants F. H. Kelly and J. M. Wade, R.E., as Company Officers, but from August 20th, 1886, it came under Lieutenant F. J. Aylmer, R.E.[2] The 5th Company was under Captain M. C. Barton, R.E., with Lieutenants W. A. J. O'Meara and J. W. Pringle, R.E. "C" Company, Madras S. & M., was under Captain A.R. F. Dorward, R.E., with Lieutenant F. J. Anderson, R.E.; "D" Company under Captain H. S. Andrews-Speed, R.E.; "H" Company under Captain J. M. T. Badgley, R.E.; and the Telegraph Section under Lieutenant F. Glanville, R.E. The 2nd Company, Bombay S. & M., was commanded by Captain J. D. Fullerton, R.E., with Lieutenants H. V. Biggs and C. E. Baddeley, R.E. Lieutenants H. H. Barnet, C. D. Learoyd, J. Stewart, T. F. B. Renny-Tailyour and C. N. Beevor, R.E., were attached to the Madras companies from the Military Works Department, but Beevor was soon invalided and replaced by Lieutenant W. R. Morton R.E. Among other Royal Engineers who served with the Sappers and Miners in Burma during or after the major operations were Captain A. W. Cockburn and Lieutenants H. E. Goodwyn, H. G. C. Swayne, G. Palmer, J. A. Dealy, H. B. H. Wright, C. H. Roe, W. Ewbank, L. P. Chapman, J. A. S. Tulloch, U. W. Evans, E. P. Johnson, G. M. Hutton, C. H. Heycock, T. Fraser, C. Ainslie, H. J. M. Marshall, E. D. Bullen, J. R. B. Serjeant and A. E. Sandbach, and with the Burma Company, Captain E. W. Cotter and Lieutenant B. A. James. The large number of officers is accounted for by the unhealthiness of the climate. During or after the

[1]A good description of the country in which the force was required to operate is given in an article entitled "Burmah" which appears in *The R.E. Journal*, Vol. XV, 1885, pp. 268, 269.

[2]Afterwards Lieut.-Gen. Sir Fenton Aylmer, V.C., K.C.B., Col. Commandant, R.E.

war, only Beevor, Palmer and James were killed and Badgley, Glanville and O'Meara seriously wounded; but Anderson, Stewart, Swayne, Dealy, Evans, Hutton and Fraser were invalided, and most of the others suffered from fever or dysentery contracted in the Burmese jungles.

The third Burma War was brief and decisive, though followed by years of unrest during which hundreds of small punitive or police operations were undertaken. The 4th and 5th Bengal Sapper companies started from Roorkee on October 29th, 1885,[1] twelve days before the official declaration of war, and arrived in Rangoon from Calcutta on November 8th. "D" and "H" Companies and the Telegraph Section of the Madras Sappers started for Madras from Bangalore on October 28th, and "C" Company entrained two days later at Secunderabad. These units, with the 2nd Company of the Bombay Sappers, sailed from Madras on November 4th and disembarked at Rangoon on the 10th. There they were joined by the two Bengal companies and a Field Park from Calcutta, and embarking with them on three barges attached to the river-steamer *Shway Myo*, left Rangoon on November 12th as part of the main body under General Prendergast. After an uneventful voyage up the Irrawaddy, the Sapper companies arrived on November 17th at Thayetmyo, within 18 miles of King Thibaw's frontier.[2]

The Burmese army numbered about 20,000 men, concentrated mostly in forts on either bank of the Irrawaddy at Minhla and Gwegyaung, about 50 miles beyond the frontier, and at Ava and Mandalay. In addition, entrenchments existed at Sinbaungwé, downstream of Minhla, and at Pagan and Myingyan. The enemy had a few gunboats and steamers armed, like the forts, with smooth-bore cast-iron guns. Prendergast had no land transport other than coolies, and he knew that, if the enemy were given time to block the river channel, the expedition must fail. Success depended accordingly on the speed at which the advance could be carried out. On November 15th, 1885, the flotilla carrying the expeditionary force crossed the frontier above Thayetmyo. The Madras Sappers were aboard the *Shway Myo*, but the Bengal and Bombay Sappers were left to follow later.

Prendergast carried the works at Sinbaungwé on November 16th and attacked the Minhla and Gwegyaung forts on the 17th. Gwegyaung, on the left bank, was a strong redoubt, 250 feet above the river, with a large ditch revetted with masonry. It mounted 21 guns, and its garrison of 1,700 men lived in casemated barracks. The stockaded village of Minhla on the right bank had at the north end a square stone fort with walls 25 feet high.[3] The defenders of Gwegyaung fled at the approach of the British; but Minhla was not so easily taken, for the troops came under a heavy fire

[1] "The Bengal Sappers and Miners in Burma," appearing in *The R.E. Journal*, Vol. XVII, 1887, p. 171. The strength of each unit was 3 B.O.s, 6 B.N.C.O.s, 2 I.O.s and about 115 I.O.R.s.

[2] See the *Sketch Map of Upper Burma in* 1885–87, included in this chapter.

[3] Usually, the Burmese defences were not so formidable. They are described in an article by Capt. J. D. Fullerton, R.E., entitled "Notes on Burmese Field Fortifications," appearing in *The R.E. Journal*, Vol. XIX, 1889, pp. 154, 155. The Burmese relied mostly on stockades, thorny hedges, and deep pits strewn with sharp bamboo spikes.

while advancing up the right bank from Malun, where they had been landed. However, they entered the village in due course and finally rushed the fort at the point of the bayonet. The Madras Sapper companies took an active part in these operations, but the Bengal and Bombay units were not present, for they did not appear from Thayetmyo until the following morning. On arrival, the 4th (Bengal) Company under Cairnes was detailed to remain temporarily at Minhla as part of the garrison. The 5th (Bengal) Company, the 2nd (Bombay) Company and the Madras Sappers proceeded upstream with the remainder of the force after spending 14 hours ashore repairing the fort. The Burmese casualties at Minhla were so heavy that thereafter there was little resistance and the campaign became a triumphal progress up the river to Mandalay.

The 5th (Bengal) Company under Barton landed at Pagan on November 22nd and remained there as part of the garrison until April 1887.[1] Pakokku was passed on the morning of the 24th, and on the same day 6,000 Burmese deserted their defences at Myingyan and fled. The 2nd (Bombay) Company disembarked with other troops and built huts and fortifications at Myingyan until March 1886. On November 26th, the flotilla reached Yandabo, and Burmese envoys appeared with a proposal for an armistice. The request was refused, however, and the advance was continued past Sagaing to Kyauktalon and next day to Ava, where 8,000 Burmese had assembled in several forts. These men surrendered without resistance, but unfortunately most of them escaped with their arms into the jungle and formed themselves into gangs of dacoits which troubled the country for many years. The ships anchored off Mandalay on November 28th, and on the 29th Prendergast received the submission of King Thibaw, who was then deported with his family to Rangoon and afterwards to Western India.[2] Thus the objectives of the expedition were attained within three weeks of the declaration of war. The Madras Sappers, interested spectators of these dramatic scenes, took up their quarters on December 4th in the enclosure of the Royal Palace, while some of their officers surveyed the surrounding country.

Armed parties scoured the country during December and operated in mobile columns against the dacoits. The 5th Company, Bengal S. & M., stationed at Pagan, took its full share in this work, and the men saw much jungle fighting throughout the following year. They supplied detachments to columns, cut roads, built defensible posts[3] and demolished obstacles with explosives. Information having been received that the Chinese were massing on the north-eastern frontier, General Prendergast started up the Irrawaddy from Mandalay on December 18th, 1885, with a force of 1,000 men including the 4th Company, Bengal S. & M.[4] and, seizing Shwebo

[1]Notes by Col. M. C. Barton, D.S.O., late R.E., sent to the author on Sept. 15th, 1937.

[2]The military operations ending with the occupation of Mandalay are described in the *Official History of the Third Burmese War*, Period I, pp. 1–178, and also in *Frontier and Overseas Expeditions from India*, Vol. V, *Burma*, pp. 133–163. The indices for the various " Periods " dealt with in the three large volumes of the *Official History* give every reference to the activities of the Sappers and Miners during the war and for several years afterwards.

[3]These posts are described in the *Official History*, Period III, pp. 144, 145.

[4]The 4th Company had arrived in Mandalay from Minhla on Dec. 14th.

en route, occupied Bhamo on the 28th. The town stretched for more than a mile along the river bank and was enclosed on three sides by a stockade some 15 feet high. Prendergast announced the annexation of Upper Burma under a proclamation made on January 1st, 1886, and was then invested with the supreme civil as well as military power; but the country was in such a turmoil that the Viceroy and the Commander-in-Chief (General Sir Frederick Roberts) visited it in February to examine the conditions on the spot. Though not a warlike race, the Burmese loved desultory fighting, raiding and robbery and abhorred any settled form of government; and as the dacoit bands usually melted away on the approach of a column, it was most difficult to act effectively against them. The nature of the operations demanded incessant forced marching through swamps or jungles, and the troops suffered accordingly. O'Meara was dangerously wounded near Pagan on January 2nd during one of these small expeditions when he had pushed on ahead of the advanced guard.[1] On January 3rd, Dorward defeated a band of dacoits at Madaya, north of Mandalay, when in command of a column which included two companies of Madras Sappers. As the spring drew on, however, the task of dealing adequately with dacoities and outrages grew so onerous that reinforcements were sent from India. The local dacoit leader was often himself the chief of a village. Socially, he was a hero, and the villagers sympathized with him. On one occasion, when a column had dispersed a gang, the victims asked for military protection against the neighbouring villages because, as they affirmed, their neighbours would now dacoit them instead of being dacoited by them! No young Burman was considered to have won his spurs till he had committed a few dacoities, and a gun hanging idly in his hut was deemed so much unemployed capital.

General Prendergast vacated his command on March 31st, 1886, and was succeeded by Brig.-General G. S. White, V.C.[2] During the next four months, more than one hundred small engagements were fought[3] in most of which detachments of Sappers and Miners took part and in one of which—near Myingyan on April 27th—Badgley was wounded while leading "B" (late "H")[4] Company against the enemy. The columns employed rarely exceeded 200 men, and to attempt to describe their operations would be wearisome. A typical example is furnished by the work of a small body of 148 infantry and 7 Bengal Sappers with two guns which marched from Padein to Napé, west of Minhla, and engaged 500 dacoits on June 19th. The guns opened fire, the infantry charged, two

[1]Lieut. O'Meara was replaced in June by Lieut. H. B. H. Wright, R.E., who took charge of a detachment of the 4th Company at Salin, north of Minbu. There, he was besieged for several days until relieved by a column including another detachment under Lieut. J. C. Rimington, R.E.

[2]Afterwards Gen. Sir George White, the defender of Ladysmith.

[3]Many of these skirmishes are described in *Frontier and Overseas Expeditions from India, Vol. V. Burma*, pp. 195–219.

[4]On Jan. 26th, 1886, the Madras Sapper companies were renumbered. "A" Company remained as such. "I," "K" and "R.D." Companies were broken up, and "B," "C," "D," "E," "F" and "G" Companies became respectively the 2nd, 3rd, 4th, 5th, 6th and 1st Companies.

Sappers were wounded, the dacoits vanished and Napé was occupied. These Sappers belonged to the 5th (Bengal) Company. Meanwhile, a detachment of the 4th Company had been engaged in April in an affair against the Kachins near Karwan, in the Ponkan hills east of Bhamo, and again the Sapper casualties were only two men wounded. The 2nd Company, Bengal S. & M., under Lieutenant R. D. Petrie with Lieutenant J. R. B. Serjeant, R.E., left Roorkee for Burma on September 5th, 1886,[1] and arriving in Mandalay at the end of the month, took part in an expedition eastwards to the Shan Hills. Thence it proceeded to Kyanhnyat, north of Shwebo, and was engaged in operations in the Ruby Mines District, the 4th Company being still at Bhamo and the 5th Company at Pagan.

The army was now so large, and the operations so difficult that Sir Frederick Roberts spent the winter of 1886–87 in Mandalay to direct the movements of the troops. The ravages of disease had been terrible. Lieut.-General Sir H. T. Macpherson, in chief command, had died on October 20th, 1886, and 3,000 out of 13,000 men had been invalided. Nevertheless, the work of restoring order in Upper Burma continued steadily. Columns including Bengal and Bombay Sappers overran the country in the region of Pauk, Kanlé and Myaing, north-west of Pakokku. During operations undertaken in October on the Singaung-Maymyo plateau east of Mandalay to open a way northwards from the capital to the Ruby Mines District of Mogok, Glanville was seriously wounded at Zibingalé while his Madras Sappers and the 2nd Company of Bengal Sappers were assaulting some stockades overlooking a defile. An advance was made later into the Ruby Mines District from Kyanhnyat towards Kyatpin and Kathé, and Mogok was taken on December 27th. As organized resistance was then almost at an end, some of the Sapper and Miner units returned to India. The 4th and 5th Companies of the Bengal Sappers (the former now under Lieutenant F. J. Aylmer, R.E.) reached Roorkee on April 13th, 1887. The 1st,[2] 3rd and 4th (late " G," " C " and " D ") Companies of the Madras Sappers arrived in Bangalore during May, and the 2nd Company of the Bombay Sappers rejoined in Kirkee during May and June. All had done well in the land of swamp and jungle.

The late Lieut.-General Sir Fenton Aylmer had an amusing tale to tell of work in the Ruby Mines District in 1887.[3] It appears that a certain junior officer of the Corps was employed on road-making and had to pay his coolies weekly at the rate of 9 annas a day. As the Treasure Chest Officer would send him only whole rupees, he assembled the coolies and asked them whether they would agree to toss for the odd annas due to them to the nearest rupee up or down the scale. Ever ready to gamble, the coolies agreed to a man ; but the net result was that before he left Mogok the subaltern found that he was Rs. 24 in credit. This being Government

[1]The 2nd Company returned to Roorkee on April 15th, 1888.

[2]The 1st (or " G ") Company, Madras S. & M., under Lieut. H. E. Goodwyn, R.E., which had been in garrison in Rangoon from Jan. to Dec., 1885, had moved later up the Sittang River through Toungoo to Yamethin.

[3]Notes by Lieut.-Gen. Sir Fenton Aylmer, V.C., K.C.B., Col.-Commandant, R.E., sent to the author on June 19th, 1932.

money, though gained in a most unofficial manner, it was necessary that it should be credited in proper form, and the subaltern sought the advice of the more experienced Aylmer. The latter then suggested that the sum should be entered as " won from coolies at tossing," and so it appeared in the accounts and caused a financial storm of unbelievable violence which raged for months.

Though there was little trouble in the interior of Upper Burma after 1888, sporadic operations took place in outlying areas until 1893. They extended up the Chindwin River to Mingin, Kalewa, Kindat and Paungbyin, where military posts were established, and included expeditions against the Chins and Lushais, in the hills between Burma and India, which will be dealt with in a subsequent chapter. Operations based on Myitkyina in the north were undertaken against the Kachins of the Mogaung District, and on the Salween River, east of Toungoo, against the Karens. In 1891, an expedition was sent from Katha, west of Bhamo, to deal with insurgents at Wuntho, Kawlin, Pinlebu, Manlé and other places in the Wuntho District, and the subsequent operations extended northwards to the Jade Mines, north-west of Mogaung. In February, 1892, Lieutenant T. Harrison, R.E., with the Burma Sapper Company and a few infantry and invalids, made a gallant defence of a post at Sadon, near the Chinese frontier east of Myitkyina.[1] These minor operations have been described in many historical works and are beyond the scope of this volume. It must suffice to say that, from 1888 onwards, the Sappers and Miners took part in many small expeditons and maintained in them the excellent reputation which gained for all three Corps the honour " Burma, 1885 " awarded for the capture of Mandalay.[2]

The raising of a Burma Company of Sappers and Miners was authorized on July 9th, 1887, the unit being affiliated to the Madras Corps.[3] The Royal Engineer officers were to be lent in rotation from the three Corps of Sappers and Miners, each being relieved after two years in Burma if he so desired. British non-commissioned officers were to be lent also and were to come in the first instance from the Bengal Corps. Indian officers were to be drawn only from the Madras Corps. Great difficulties were encountered in getting recruits, only fifteen of whom had enlisted by the end of 1887 when the company at Mandalay was commanded by Captain E. W. Cotter, R.E., familiarly known as " Terror-cotta." The original idea was that one-half the unit should be Burmans, one-quarter Kachins and Karens, and one-quarter Shans; but the Kachins and Shans would not come forward, and when the company reached its full strength for the first time in October, 1890, about four-fifths of the men were Burmans and the remainder Karens. In 1893, the Burma Company became an integral part of the Madras Corps and rendered useful service for many years. Two

[1] Lieut. Harrison (afterwards Harrison-Topham) was joined during the siege by Lieut. (now Lieut.-Gen. Sir George) MacMunn, R.A., with a few Gurkhas, and together they resisted all attacks until relieved. The siege lasted from February 7th to 20th, 1892.

[2] G.G.O. dated Jan. 16th, 1891.

[3] The provisions of I.A.C. No. 117, authorizing this measure, are given in the *Historical Record of the Q.V.O. Madras Sappers and Miners*, Vol. I, pp. 135–137.

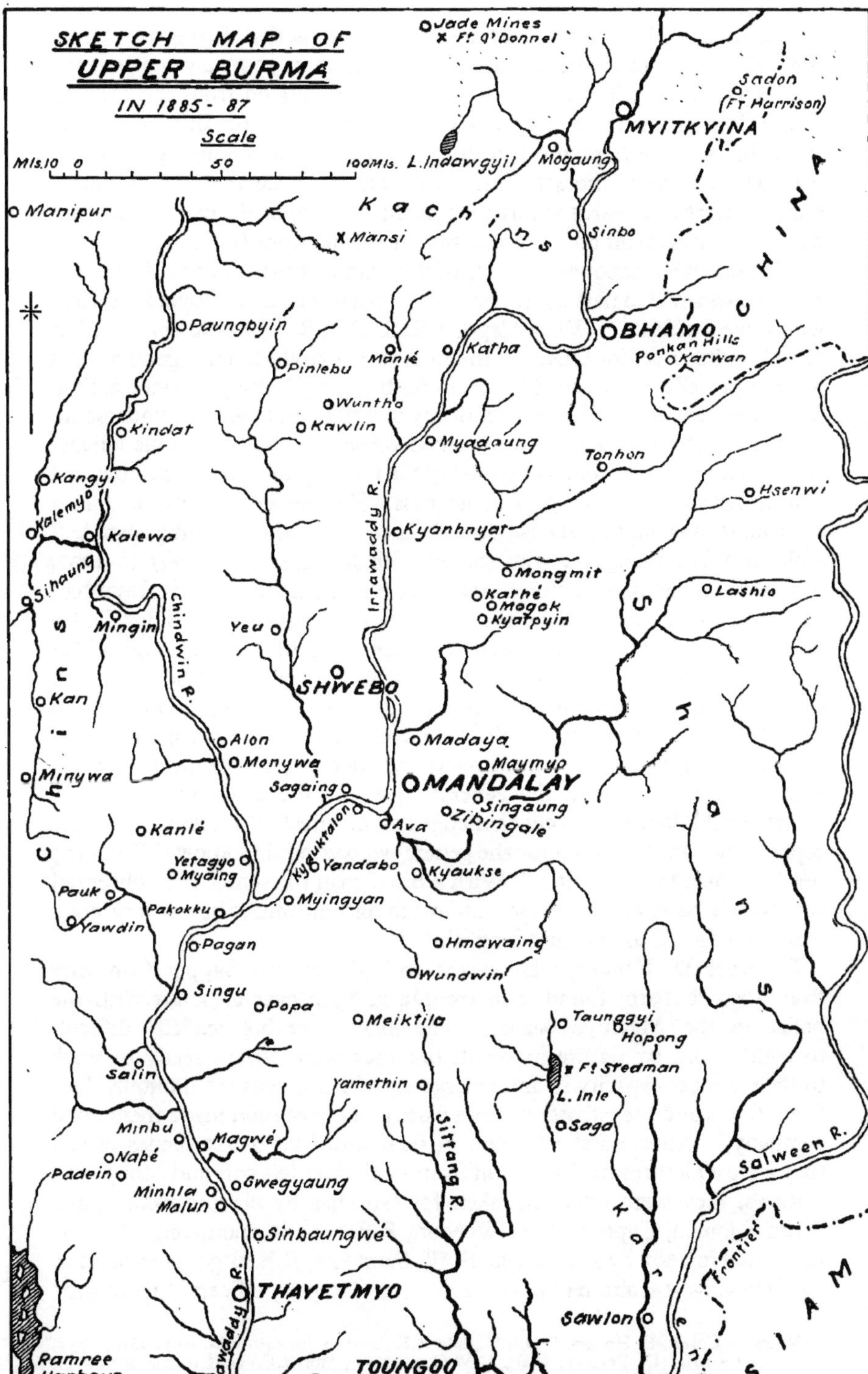
SKETCH MAP OF UPPER BURMA
IN 1885-87
Scale
Mls.10 0 50 100Mls.
Jade Mines
Ft O'Donnel
Sadon
(Ft Harrison)
MYITKYINA
L. Indawgyi
Mogaung
Manipur
Kachins
Mansi
Sinbo
CHINA
Paungbyin
BHAMO
Ponkan Hills
Karwan
Pinlebu
Manlé
Katha
Wuntho
Kawlin
Kindat
Myadaung
Tonhon
Kangyi
Kalemyo
Hsenwi
Irrawaddy R.
Kalewa
Kyanhnyat
Sihaung
Mongmit
Lashio
Kathé
Mogok
Kyatpyin
Mingin
Yeu
Chindwin R.
Chins
SHWEBO
Kan
Shans
Alon
Madaya
Monywa
Maymyo
Minywa
Sagaing
MANDALAY
Singaung
Zibingale
Kanlé
Kyauktalon
Ava
Yetagyo
Myaing
Yandabo
Kyaukse
Pauk
Pakokku
Myingyan
Yawdin
Pagan
Hmawaing
Wundwin
Singu
Popa
Meiktila
Taunggyi
Hopong
Salin
Ft Stedman
Yamethin
L. Inle
Sittang R.
Saga
Minbu
Magwé
Napé
Salween R.
Padein
Minhla
Gwegyaung
Malun
Karen
Sinbaungwé
Frontier
THAYETMYO
SIAM
Sawlon
Irrawaddy R.
Ramree Harbour
TOUNGOO
Pazaung

additional companies (the 62nd and 68th) were added during the Great War of 1914–18 but were disbanded in September, 1921, and on January 10th, 1922, the 15th (Burma) Company was separated from the Madras Corps after a connection of 35 years and became the " 4th Burma Sappers and Miners." On September 30th, 1929, under orders issued previously, the disbandment of the 4th Burma Sappers and Miners was completed, but they were afterwards resurrected as the " Corps of Burma Sappers and Miners " consequent on the separation of Burma from India.

The somewhat chequered career of the original Burma Sapper Company may be explained in part by quoting a few reminiscences of Royal Engineers who served with it. " When Captain E. S. Hill, R.E., was in command in 1889," writes a senior officer, " the men were extraordinarily good at field work, especially in the use of bamboos for bridging, hutting and stockading. They were devoid, however, of military instinct and could not understand discipline. If a man felt ill he returned without permission to his village, and if there was an important cock-fight in the neighbourhood, he attended it as a matter of course, pass or no pass. He seemed to consider that a cock-fight was ample excuse for absence from the morning parade." Colonel P. E. Hodgson, who served with the unit from 1897 to 1902, agrees that in many ways the men were excellent sappers—handy, resourceful, cheerful, athletic, good shots and capable artisans. " They had a keen sense of humour and were no respecters of persons," he adds.[1] " A general once told me to ask a sentry what he would do if he saw a man creeping towards him through the bush." " I would say 'Holl. Oo go dah ' " replied the sentry. " Yes," said the general, " but supposing the man *didn't* halt ? " The sentry answered that he would repeat his challenge. Rather annoyed, the general then told me to enquire what the sentry would do if his second challenge had no effect. " Nothing " was the reply. This was too much for the general who wanted to know " What the devil the man meant by it ? " With a broad grin the sentry then observed that for all he knew the person approaching him might be ' a very good man who didn't understand English ! ' "

Brigadier D. Forster, who served with the Burma Sapper Company from 1902 to 1910, found it in trouble in 1902 over an affair with the police in the Maymyo bazaar. The men were hot-headed, difficult to control and by nature indolent, but they were always ready to work to their utmost capacity in any emergency. "Their sense of humour, their friendliness and their freedom from caste and convention made them good company," writes Forster,[2] " and in their mufti kit of art shades of silk they were a picturesque lot. In uniform, with their felt hats and Mongolian features, they were often mistaken for Gurkhas by visitors from India. When I joined, Captain F. F. Weedon, R.E., was in command. He was succeeded in 1903 by Lieutenant F. W. Saunders, R.E. I got command in the following year and had in succession, as Company officers, Lieutenants

[1]Notes by Col. P. E. Hodgson, D.S.O., late R.E., sent to the author on Aug. 28th, 1937.
[2]Notes by Brig. D. Forster, C.B., C.M.G., D.S.O., late R.E., sent to the author on Oct. 29th, 1937.

E. K. Molesworth, C. W. Bushell and T. B. Harris, R.E." Colonel Bushell adds the following remarks :—[1] " Football (' Soccer ') had a tremendous hold on the men, and in my time it was becoming almost a national game. On one occasion, when a Burma Sapper, my fellow back, was playing barefooted as usual, I saw him wince, stoop down, and remove from the sole of his foot a horse-shoe complete with nails. Then, quite unconcerned, he went on playing ! On another ocasion, after a vigorous purge of animals from the Sapper lines, I went there for a mufti kit inspection. As I approached, I saw a Sapper running up followed by a small pig and furiously demanded an explanation. In reply, the man blandly pointed out that no mention of pigs had been made in the recent order prohibiting animals."

The Burma Sapper of thirty years ago was in fact a child of nature. His strong personal independence and national pride was grafted on to a love of adventure, a devotion to gambling, and a complete recklessness in money matters. He laughed, played, quarrelled, and fought, and, if obliged to do so, worked. That child has now been moulded into a man. The modern Burma Sapper is a good soldier with a reputation founded on gallantry in two world wars and many small affairs in his native jungles.

[1]Notes by Col. C. W. Bushell, O.B.E., late R.E., sent to the author on Dec. 7th, 1937.

CHAPTER XII

FURTHER OVERSEAS EXPEDITIONS INCLUDING THE THIRD CHINA WAR, 1890–1911

WHILE the pacification of Burma was still in progress, trouble began to develop in British Somaliland, where it became necessary in 1889 to punish the Isa tribe near Zeila for killing two French priests during an attack on a caravan at Hensa, and also for raiding the friendly Habr Awal tribe at Bulhar, west of Berbera.[1] Little was known of the country, but that little tended to show that our columns must act as explorers as much as fighting bodies. In the north is a maritime plain, ten miles wide at Berbera, ascending to a range of mountains beyond which is a plateau stretching far to the south with a gradual descent. This plateau, called the Haud, is mostly a forbidding desert covered with scrub and mimosa and dotted here and there with a few wells. The Haud is cut in two by the Nogal Valley, about 280 miles long and 50 miles wide, bounded by steep cliffs and possessing numerous wells. The strategy of any campaign in Somaliland depends largely on the Nogal, because it must be based on the available grazing for animals. Camels can graze always in the Haud ; but sheep and cattle must spend the greater part of the year in the Nogal pastures. Consequently, the occupation of the Nogal at the proper time of the year forces the Somalis to fight or starve, since they depend on meat for food. The same remarks apply in a minor degree to the Mudug District in the Southern Haud, where wells are also plentiful. There are no rivers worthy the name. The wells in the Haud are often five or six days' march apart, and supplies, except meat, are usually unobtainable.

During the operations in Somaliland, it was necessary always to reconnoitre for water before starting on a march. The distances were so great that the transport was liable to fail before touch could be gained with the elusive enemy. The so-called friendly tribes were distrustful and disinclined to help. They refused to submit to discipline and were liable to panic in any emergency. As for the enemy's methods of warfare under their redoubtable leader Haji Muhammad Abdullah, popularly known as the " Mad Mullah," it is interesting to remark that, unlike the Dervishes, the Somalis preferred fire action to shock tactics and, advancing in extended order through the scrub jungle, tried always to envelop their opponents and shoot them down. Each rifleman was mounted and was followed, like a knight of old, by a train of spearmen ready to take and use his rifle if he fell.

To subdue the Isa rebels, a Zeila Field Force under the command of

[1]See *Sketch Map of Somaliland, the Aden Hinterland and Abyssinia in* 1902, included in this chapter.

Captain J. R. C. Domvile, Bo.I., composed of 350 men, including 30 men of the 4th Company, Bombay S. & M., embarked at Aden, and landing at Zeila on January 13th, 1890, marched 30 miles south-eastwards along the coast.[1] Joined by a reinforcement of 40 men of the 4th Company under Captain B. B. Russell, R.E.,[2] Domvile marched into the interior on January 27th and halted at dusk on the 29th at Husain, where the Sappers made a *zariba* near a nullah but had insufficient time to provide it with a thick fence. The result was that, in the early hours of the morning after the moon had set, the camp was rushed by a small party of Somalis, some of whom crept under the thorny barrier while others leapt over it by using their long spears as jumping poles. The intruders caused several casualties before they were killed or driven out, but they taught our men the lesson that a *zariba* fence should be at least as wide as it is high. The column recrossed the maritime plain by a more westerly route and re-embarked at Zeila on February 3rd after burning several encampments. No more trouble was experienced from the Isas, nor was there any in Western Somaliland until 1893, when it became necessary to despatch from Aden a small force under Colonel E. V. Stace, late Bo.I., including 4 men of the 3rd Company, Bombay S. & M., to march south-westwards from Berbera to the region of Hargeisa to deal with the Sultan of Aida Galla.[3] Thereafter, Somaliland remained quiet until 1899, when the Mad Mullah came to power and began to raid the country.

The scene now shifts to another part of Africa, where a few Madras Sappers and Miners were on service from 1898 to 1900 and were the first Indian soldiers to visit the area. On March 14th, 1898, the Government of India called for 20 volunteers from the Madras Corps to form part of a mixed engineer company for attachment to a force in Nigeria under Major F. J. D. Lugard.[4] The men embarked in May at Tuticorin or Bombay and proceeded *via* England to West Africa. There they formed a "half-company" of the new unit, the other half-company being of local Yorubas. The company was commanded for a time by Lieutenant R. L. McClintock, R.E., afterwards a Sapper and Miner.[5] The detachment of Madras Sappers earned high praise from Lieut.-Colonel (later General Sir) James Willcocks, in command of the West African Frontier Force,[6] and on September 19th, 1900, whilst in Great Britain on their return journey to India, they were inspected at Balmoral by H.M. Queen Victoria.[7] On that occasion, they and a detachment of the Yoruba Sappers were under the command of Captain E. A. Molesworth, Royal Dublin Fusiliers. They reached Bangalore in December, less three of their number who had died in West Africa.

[1] *Frontier and Overseas Expeditions from India*, Vol. VI, pp. 96, 97.
[2] *A Short History of the Royal Bombay Sappers and Miners*, p. 19.
[3] *Digest of the Services of the Bombay Sappers and Miners*, by Maj. G. H. W. O'Sullivan, R.E., p. 64. Hargeisa is 90 miles south-west of Berbera.
[4] *Historical Record of the Q.V.O. Madras Sappers and Miners*, Vol. 1, p. 169.
[5] A photograph of the unit on parade is in the Officers' Mess at Bangalore. Lieut. R. L. McClintock, R.E., joined the Corps of Madras Sappers and Miners in India in 1905 after serving in South Africa.
[6] *The R.E. Journal*, Vol. XXX, 1900, pp. 25, 26.
[7] *Ibid.*, pp. 209, 210.

The strip of inhospitable territory known as Makran, lying along the northern shore of the Arabian Sea where Persia meets Baluchistan, has afforded many opportunities for active service to small detachments of the Bombay Sappers and Miners. The country is sparsely populated. Behind a sandy coastal area, ridges of rocky mountains alternate with equally barren valleys, the latter debouching on to bleak and arid plains where camel-tracks wind monotonously through deserts of stone, sand and sun-baked clay. The heat at midday is devastating; the cold at night, bitter. The few streams in the northern valleys lose their muddy and brackish waters in sand-swamps and salt-marshes. Vegetation in most regions is confined to mimosa trees and tamarisk jungle around occasional wells. Yet Makran, like Somaliland, has one or two fertile districts, notably the Kech Valley, where lies the important village of Turbat.[1] Date plantations and irrigated fields make this depression a habitable area. The Kech Valley has many villages, each with its armed garrison and its mud fort or tower for defence against bandits.

On January 21st, 1898, a detachment of the 1st Company, Bombay S. & M., consisting of an Indian officer and 12 other ranks under Lieutenant W. Bovet, R.E., embarked at Bombay for Makran and landed six days later at Pasni. Thence they marched to join a small force under Lieut.-Colonel R. C. G. Mayne, Bo.I., at Turbat, which they reached on February 2nd. Mayne was engaged in subduing an outlaw named Mehrab Khan, who had seized Turbat Fort, but shortly before the Sappers arrived Mehrab escaped and was reported to be making for Churbuk. The Sappers had marched 40 miles on the 2nd; yet they set out with other troops on the 3rd, and after covering a further 30 miles, assisted in the capture and destruction of Churbuk Fort. That they were able to accomplish the feat of marching 70 miles through broken country in 48 hours was due to the determination of their leader, William Bovet, a keen soldier and ardent pigsticker who was killed in the Great War. During the remainder of the expedition to Makran in 1898, Bovet and his men destroyed a number of forts and afterwards proceeded through Kalat to Quetta, where they arrived on April 16th *en route* for Kirkee.[2]

Some three years later, another detachment of the Bombay Sappers and Miners was on service in Makran. An outlaw named Muhammad Ali Khan had raided the Kech Valley from the Persian border on October 18th, 1901, at the head of 100 men, and with the connivance of the owner, had occupied Nodiz Fort, about 23 miles west of Turbat, as a preliminary to further operations against Mirullah Khan, the Nizam of Makran. Mirullah invested Nodiz and asked for assistance from India. Major H. L. Showers, the Political Agent at Kalat, hastened to Makran, and on November 25th, a detachment of the 4th Company, Bombay S. & M., consisting of Jemadar Arjun Powar and 19 other ranks under Lieutenant J. B. Corry, R.E., left Kirkee for Gwadar to join the Agent's escort of 250 men of the 27th Baluchis under Major M. J. Tighe, Bo.I.[3] Corry was not only

[1]See *Sketch Map of Makran*, included in this chapter.
[2]*A Brief History of the Royal Bombay Sappers and Miners*, p. 21.
[3]*Ibid.*, p. 23.

brilliantly clever but a remarkable athlete. So strong was he that if he could get three fingers on to the top of a wall he could pull himself over it with ease. He was also a keen student of native character, and his detachment in Makran was the pick of the 4th Company, selected as carefully as if for an expedition to the South Pole. One man, for instance, owed his inclusion to the fact that he had let himself be dragged along the ground by a bolting mule rather than release the reins and save his skin—a trivial incident, but one which shows the stuff of which the men were made.

The Bombay Sappers and Baluchis embarked at Karachi and landed at Gwadar. Thence they marched with a train of 1,000 camels to Turbat, and a week later through Kalatuk to a camp near Nodiz, where they were reinforced by some Baluchis and Scinde Horse with two mountain guns from Jacobabad. The Nizam had been besieging Nodiz Fort for nearly two months with a force of 1,000 men, but was afraid to attack. The fort was a square enclosure with walls of mud-brick some 10 feet high, raised on a solid plinth of similar height. At three corners were small towers, while at the fourth, a huge inner keep rose about 15 feet above the ramparts.[1] The towers and ramparts were elaborately loopholed, and the solitary gate on the eastern side was blocked with sandbags. The garrison was well armed and had ample ammunition, food and water. Surrounding the fort on three sides were palm groves, but on the fourth side there was an open plain.

Tighe attacked Nodiz on December 20th, 1901. The two mountain guns shelled the ramparts and towers on the south and west sides, though with little apparent effect except against the battlements of the towers. Meanwhile, the infantry made a detour through the palm groves to a nullah within 200 yards of the south-west tower from which they could keep down the fire from the ramparts. When it seemed that the 7-pounders could not make a practicable breach, the task was entrusted to the Bombay Sappers. Carrying charges of guncotton, they were detailed to precede a storming party of 40 Baluchis under Lieutenant J. D. Grant, Bo.I., which was supported by a further 80 rifles under Lieutenant H. Hulseberg, Bo.I., with a similar number in reserve. Corry dashed forward with most of his Sappers, and after passing through some matting huts outside the fort, discovered to his surprise that the shell fire had actually made a narrow breach in the south wall near a tower, so he went back to ask Grant to assault and then charged with the infantry to the breach, racing Grant to be the first through it.[2]

The opening, however, was so narrow that it could be traversed only in single file. " Grant and I," writes Corry,[3] " with Naik Baryam Singh and Sapper Nur Din, got clear away and killed eight of the enemy before they

[1]Article entitled " The Empire's Work in Makran," appearing in *Chambers Journal*, 1902.

[2]Article entitled " The Fighting in Mekran," appearing in *The R.E. Journal*, Vol. XXXII, 1902, pp. 57, 58. See also an article entitled " The Operations in Mekran, " appearing in the same volume, pp. 160, 161.

[3]Letter from Lieut. J. B. Corry, R.E., to Lieut. F. S. Garwood, R.E., quoted in notes sent to the author on Feb. 18th, 1938, by Lieut.-Col. F. S. Garwood.

knew what was up. Nur Din was as cool as a cucumber and took aim, as if he were on a range, at a man rushing at him and only five yards distant. Meanwhile, about 30 Baluchis had got in. A sniper in a tower blazed at them, and Grant and three men were hit. The enemy then made a counter-attack round both flanks. Grant was hit again and dropped, and two of the enemy in front blazed at me and a bullet grazed my right wrist and went through my shoulder. Then they went for Nur Din and me with swords. Guarding one cut with his *pagri* and two with his rifle, Nur Dir sent his bayonet home. I was not so successful but parried three cuts and cut my man three times over the head. The third time, he crumpled. Nur Din bayoneted him, and Baryam Singh, coming up on my left, shot him as he fell.[1] Baryam Singh had previously been engaged with other outlaws in rear, and had killed the man who wounded Grant. When Grant had got on his feet again, we all cleared off. Sahib Singh was the only other Sapper who entered the fort. My assailant took off the top of my right first finger and cut my shoulder-strap. I think he was the chief, Muhammad Ali. Grant and I took no further part in the fight, but the guns were brought up close to the walls and more breaches were made and another charge. The enemy then surrendered. In all, 74 prisoners were taken, including 17 wounded, and they say that 25 were killed, though only 14 were found."

Both Corry and Grant received the D.S.O., and Baryam Singh and Nur Din the I.O.M., for their gallantry at Nodiz.[2] It seems that, when the leading stormers clambered through the narrow breach, they encountered not merely the fire of a solitary sniper, as Corry states, but a heavy fusillade from several towers overlooking the interior, followed by a charge of swordsmen from the damaged south-west tower close to the breach. After Corry and Grant and several men had been hit, the remainder retreated with them to the shelter of the tower. The guns then came into action again at 100 yards range and demolished the western tower and the roofs of some interior works, and Hulseberg, entering with supports, completed the capture of the fort. The whole fight lasted a little over two hours. Both Corry and Grant were seriously wounded; Corry in the shoulder and wrist, and Grant in the shoulder and neck. It was fortunate that Corry was ambidextrous, for his wounds prevented him from using his right hand, in which he held his revolver, and he managed to parry, with his sword held in his left hand, three fierce cuts from Muhammad Ali, though one of these ran down his blade and sliced off the top of a finger of the other hand. The interior of the fort presented a pitiable spectacle. Gunfire had demolished the wooden supports of three elevated blockhouses, burying the defenders in the ruins and setting fire to the debris. The open courtyard was strewn with the bodies of animals. After the wounded had been collected, the remains of Nodiz Fort were blown up with guncotton, and

[1]According to A *Brief History of the Royal Bombay Sappers and Miners*, p. 24, the man was shot also by a Subadar of the 27th Baluchis.

[2]The three Sappers and Miners perished in the Great War—Corry killed at Sailly-sur-Lys, Nur Din killed at Neuve Chapelle, and Baryam Singh mortally wounded in the defence of Kut-al-Amara. Grant won the Victoria Cross in Tibet in 1904 (see Chap. XV).

on the 23rd the troops returned to Turbat, where Lieutenant W. F. Maxwell, R.E., assumed command of the Bombay Sapper detachment. A few days later, the Sappers marched with a column of all arms through Tump and Mand to the Persian border, whence they returned to India after destroying many other forts.

Service in Somaliland, Arabia and Makran seems to have been the prerogative of the Bombay Sappers and Miners; but the next expedition to be described in these pages saw the employment of units of all three Corps. In 1899, an association of brigands, who called themselves the "Fists of Patriotic Union" but were commonly known as "Boxers," gained ascendancy in Northern China and began to murder foreigners. Joined by thousands of other desperadoes, they advanced on Peiping (Peking)[1] and attacked the European legations there on June 13th, 1900. After an international naval brigade had relieved Tientsin but failed to reach the capital, a "China Expeditionary Force" of about 10,000 men, under Brigadier-General (local Lieut.-General) Sir A. Gaselee, was despatched from India and began to arrive at Taku, at the mouth of the Paiho, on July 17th to co-operate with contingents of Japanese, Russian, American, French, German and Italian troops in a general advance.[2] Successful battles were fought at Peitsang on August 5th and Yangtsun on August 6th, and on August 14th the allied forces relieved the besieged legations at Peiping and thus ended the major operations of the Third China War.[3]

Few Sappers and Miners took any part in these events because their embarkation at Calcutta and Bombay was delayed.[4] The units under orders to proceed to China were the 3rd Company, Madras S. & M., under Captain J. A. S. Tulloch, R.E., with Lieutenants E. G. Henderson and R.E. Goldingham and 2nd Lieutenant J. A. Garstin, R.E.; the 4th Company, Bengal S. & M., under Captain H. R. Stockley, R.E., with Lieutenants C. M. Carpenter, H. D. Pearson and M. R. Elles, R.E.; the 2nd Company, Bombay S. & M., under Captain G. H. Boileau, R.E., with Lieutenants G. R. Pridham, J. E. E. Craster and W. H. Chaldecott, R.E.; the Malerkotla Sapper Company;[5] a Telegraph Section of the Madras Sappers under Lieutenant S. G. Loch, R.E., and another of the Bengal Sappers under Lieutenant F. W. Brunner, R.E.; a small Mounted Detachment of Bengal Sappers under Lieutenant E. C. Tylden-Pattenson, R.E., and Photo-Litho and Printing Sections of the Madras and Bombay Corps. Two Engineer Field Parks, a Railway Section and a Survey Section were added, and also a Balloon Section, R.E., from England. The advance on Peiping, however, could not be delayed to await the arrival of the Sapper

[1]Although the city is better known as Peking or Pekin, it is advisable to use the modern name, Peiping.

[2]See the *Sketch Maps of China*, included in this chapter.

[3]The operations are described fully in the official despatches and in *Frontier and Overseas Expeditions from India*, Vol. VI, pp. 454–487.

[4]" The Work of the R.E. in the China or 'Boxer' War of 1900–01," by Col. F. T. N. Spratt-Bowring, C.B., late R.E., appearing in *The R.E. Journal*, Vol. XIII, Jan.–June, 1911, pp. 169–188.

[5]Imperial Service (Indian States) Troops. The Malerkotla Company was commanded by Lieut.-Col. Asuf Ali and was accompanied by Lieut. W. A. Stokes, R.E.

and Miner companies. The rainy season might start at any time and render the country impassable, and the Chinese, who had been driven from Tientsin on June 23rd, were beginning to collect again to bar the road to the capital and were trying to cut the river banks to flood the adjacent territory. The allied commanders decided that immediate action was necessary, and consequently the Sapper companies did not share in the general advance up the Paiho. The only Sapper unit which had that privilege was the Telegraph Section of the Madras Corps, whose experiences may serve to illustrate the difficulties encountered.

The Telegraph Section under Loch, consisting of Sergeant Keenan and 16 Indian other ranks, had been placed under orders in June, 1900, to proceed to China with 20 British telegraphists. With great difficulty, Loch managed to obtain in India sufficient material for a line from Tientsin to Peiping, and it was fortunate that he did so because, on arrival at Taku, he learned that the Chinese had destroyed their telegraph and railway lines most thoroughly.[1] " The units of the expeditionary force were disembarked and railed to Tientsin, " remarks Major-General S. G. Loch,[2] " and there we joined the Japanese, American, French, Russian, German and Italian troops detailed for the relief of the Legations.[3] From Tientsin, since the railway was non-existent and road transport inadequate, the line of advance had to be along a single rough track alongside the Paiho as far as Tungchow in order that river transport might be employed. This consisted of junks of various sizes, and I was allotted two. In Tientsin I made the acquaintance of my opposite number, a " Lootenant " in the American Signal Corps fresh from the campaign in the Philippines, and as his resources in personnel were even smaller than my own, he suggested that we should join forces and use my equipment. This was sanctioned and our two sections worked with the greatest harmony. At last the order for the advance was given, and the motley army of British and Indian troops, Americans white and coloured, French Colonials and Annamites, Germans, Italians and Russians, with the Japs in the van, left Tientsin, each contingent under its own commander. The heat was great, but luckily there had been no rain, so the track through the giant millet, known as *kaoling*, was practicable. This *kaoling* prevented all visual signalling as the country was flat and the villages surrounded by trees. The advance was opposed at Peitsang and again at Yangtsun; but subsequently, until near Peiping, the enemy made little stand. The Telegraph Section was able to keep up with the army until nearing Tungchow; but when the supply of bamboos gave out and poles had to be collected, the rate of construction slowed down. I think we had the hardest and most continuous work of any troops in the force. We reached Peiping a couple of days after the relieving force

[1] " Notes on Engineering Work in Northern China," by Brevet-Col. G. K. Scott-Moncrieff, C.I.E., R.E., appearing in *The R.E. Journal*, Vol. I, Jan.–June, 1905, pp. 20–30. The country and the people are described also in this article.

[2] Notes by Maj.-Gen. S. G. Loch, C.B., C.S.I., D.S.O., late R.E., sent to the author on Oct. 10th, 1937.

[3] The strengths were as follows :—Japanese, 10,000 ; Russians, 4,000 ; British, 3,000 ; Americans, 2,000 ; French, 800 ; Germans, 200 ; Italians, 100. Total, 20,100 men with 70 guns.

WESTERN GATE, PEIPING.

had entered it, and my American friend suggested that we should put up with the American Headquarters in the Temple of Agriculture. General Chaffey and his officers had excellent food but no drink, so I produced my one remaining bottle of whiskey and, possibly on that account, was presented next morning with a bronze bell from the Temple which now reposes in the Bangalore Mess. Our stay at Peiping was short, for the hastily constructed telegraph line was giving trouble. We worked down to Tientsin and the resulting line lasted well until we were required to build a new one along the Tientsin-Peiping Railway, which was being reconstructed by our Sapper Railway Officers. The field line along the river was then dismantled."

The bronze bell referred to was one of many trophies obtained by the allied troops from the palaces of Peiping. When the city was first occupied, there was indiscriminate looting by civilians as well as soldiers in the Summer Palace and other large buildings, but General Gaselee soon checked this practice among his own troops. He issued an order allowing the collection of booty only by organized parties visiting the houses of the Chinese known to be hostile to foreigners or connected with the Boxers. The accumulated loot was afterwards sold by auction and the money credited to a prize fund for distribution among all the British and Indian units present. In the Officers' Mess at Roorkee can be seen some remarkably fine screenwork of gilded wood secured in Peiping by the Mounted Detachment of the Bengal Sappers. It is whispered that this was saved in the nick of time from being broken up for issue to the troops as firewood. Be that as it may, many messes in India benefited by the capture of Peiping.[1]

The first of the three Sapper companies to arrive in China was the 4th Company of the Bengal Corps under Stockley. This unit embarked at Calcutta on July 12th, 1900, reached Taku on August 4th, and landing at Sinho, arrived in Tientsin by rail on the 5th. The allied forces had started for Peiping four days earlier, and the 4th Company was detained in Tientsin until August 9th to improve the defences; then it followed the army up the Paiho in charge of a supply convoy of 14 junks. Tungchow was reached on the 19th, and Peiping on the 20th after a most unpleasant voyage. The work of towing the junks was exhausting, the sun extremely powerful, the flies pestilential, the drinking water highly medicinal, and the air polluted with the stench of burning villages. From August 21st to September 5th, the company was engaged in improving communications in the Legation Quarter and the Temple of Heaven and in tunnelling through the wall (64 feet thick) of the Tartar City.[2] Leaving one section to complete this tunnel, Stockley moved with the remainder of the Company to Fengtai, a railway junction 7 miles south of Peiping, to restore 20

[1]The Bombay Sappers and Miners secured for the Officers' Mess at Kirkee two standards, a fat golden "God of Happiness" and a jingal; for the Sergeants' Mess, a brass Buddha, and for the Guard Room, a fine gong.

[2]"Record of the China Expedition, 1900–01." (Extract from the diary of the 4th Company, Bengal S. & M., appearing in *The R.E. Journal*, Vol. XXXIII, 1903, p. 194.) See also the *History and Digest of Service of the 1st K.G.O. Sappers and Miners*, p. 71.

miles of the Tientsin-Peiping Railway along a section of line adjoining another taken over by the Russians.[1] The Boxers had left only the rails, and it was necessary to search the neighbouring villages for buried fish-plates and bolts and to find timber for sleepers. The Sapper and Miner officers knew little of railway work, and the men had neither tools nor instruments. Consequently, the track was very irregular, and as the temperature ranged from below zero in winter to 180° in the sun in summer, the estimation of the proper expansion joint between rails was a matter of guess work.[2] Nevertheless, the line was completed. The first locomotive to traverse it was one made from a stationary engine discovered by the Sappers in the Summer Palace and mounted on a bogey truck.[3] The next task allotted to the 4th Company was to construct a short line in Peiping itself. Carpenter had once laid a light railway at a practice camp in India, so he was detailed to lay out a complete station yard near the Temple of Heaven; but fortunately, a party of trained railway men was sent from Tientsin by Lieutenant H. E. C. Cowie, R.E., and arrived in the nick of time to undertake this work. Trains were running in Peiping in December over an unballasted line which the Sappers kept open by unceasing labour. The track was often like a switchback, but it served its purpose.[4]

Other work performed in Peiping by the 4th Company, Bengal S. & M., consisted of installing stoves and fireplaces in the very inflammable Chinese houses allotted as winter quarters for the troops. The Sapper units, and the local labour gangs supervised by the staff of Lieut.-Colonel G. K. Scott-Moncrieff, R.E., the Commanding Royal Engineer, provided shelter for no less than 18,000 troops, 14,000 followers and 10,000 animals. They installed 2,000 stoves and 7½ miles of flue piping before the winter set in. So severe was the cold that it was necessary to heat even the sentry boxes and drinking troughs. The 4th Company laboured in Peiping, or on the railway to Tientsin, until August, 1901, when it moved down the Paiho and embarked at Sinho for India. It reached Calcutta on September 15th, and five days later, was back at headquarters in Roorkee.

After the 4th Company, the next Sapper unit to reach China in 1900 was the 3rd Company, Madras S. & M., under Tulloch. This unit left Bangalore on July 6th, embarked at Calcutta on the 13th, arrived at Taku on August 6th and, moving up-country by river and rail, appeared in Tientsin on August 8th, three days after the Bengal Sappers. Like the 4th Company, it was employed at first on the Tientsin defences, but on August 16th it proceeded up the Paiho to strengthen the works at Peitsang, Hosiwu

[1]The Russians were difficult neighbours. They tried to obtain entire control of the railway and were always encroaching on the British section. When Peiping was reached, they occupied the Summer Palace and held it for two months, contrary to agreement, to the exclusion of the other allies.

[2]Notes by Brig.-Gen. C. M. Carpenter, C.M.G., D.S.O., late R.E., sent to the author on July 6th, 1937.

[3]An illustration showing this locomotive accompanies an article entitled " The Grasshopper, " appearing in *The R.E. Journal*, Vol. I, Jan.–June, 1905, p. 59.

[4]One result of the troubles experienced in China was the raising of the Railway Companies of Sappers and Miners which did so well in East Africa and elsewhere during and after the Great War.

and other posts on the line of communication. One half-company reached Peiping on August 27th while the other remained for a time at Tungchow to repair the road.[1] The Peiping half-company moved with a small force to seize and fortify the railway junction at Fengtai and remained there till September 7th, when it returned to the capital. The whole unit was then employed in preparing winter quarters for the troops, Tulloch being appointed Garrison Engineer, Tartar City, and Henderson being given the celestial title of " Garrison Engineer of the Temple of Heaven ! " Tulloch and Garstin, with half the company, marched on October 12th with a column of 3,500 British, French, German and Italian troops towards the important town of Pao-Ting-Fu, on the railway about 100 miles south-west of Peiping, while a detachment of Bombay Sappers advanced with another column from Tientsin. No opposition was encountered. The Madras Sappers blew up two temples at Pao-Ting-Fu and destroyed two more temples and three villages on their return journey. The 3rd Company left Peiping on November 8th, 1900, and entrained at Tientsin for Sinho. There they embarked for Shanghai, which they reached on the 23rd. They were in garrison at Shanghai until April 1901, when they moved to Wei-Hai-Wei and two months later returned to India.

The last of the Sapper companies to land in China was the 2nd Company, Bombay S. & M., under Boileau. This unit sailed from Bombay on July 15th, 1900, and disembarked at Sinho on August 10th, reaching Tientsin on the following day. The men had the .303 rifle in place of the Martini-Henry, and during the voyage, practised with the new weapon by firing at a target mounted on an improvised " otter," a contrivance which worked well in calm weather at 12 knots' speed and was the forerunner of the naval paravane. An amusing incident occurred at Sinho. Twelve barrels of liquid cow-dung had been taken aboard for the purification of the ship's galleys by the Hindu ranks in order that they might cook and eat their food without defilement while at sea, and three barrels remained unopened when the ship berthed at Sinho. As these barrels were being hoisted from the hold, a sling broke and the load fell with a crash on to the fore deck. There was a grand splash, reaching even to the upper deck, where a smart Naval Transport Officer was directing operations. The language and actions of that officer after his immaculate white uniform had received a generous coating are said to have brightened a hard day's work ! On the journey to Tientsin by train, the equipment mules provided some diversion. They took the opportunity to jump off the low-sided trucks in which they were travelling and scattered over the countryside ; and when they had been chased and caught, they tried with the utmost vigour to avoid boarding the train again. However, order was restored eventually and Tientsin reached without further mishap.

The 2nd Company was employed for a time on the Tientsin defences, for the Boxers were threatening the city from the west and south.[2] On

[1] *Historical Record of the Q.V.O. Madras Sappers and Miners*, Vol. I, p. 174.

[2] See " Extracts from Despatches. Tientsin," appearing in *The R.E. Journal*, Vol. XXX, 1900, pp. 249–252.

August 18th, it was decided that the time had come to disperse the enemy, and on the 19th, a column of American and Bengal cavalry and detachments of Japanese infantry, the Hong Kong Regiment, the Chinese Regiment and Indian infantry under Colonel A. R. F. Dorward, late R.E., moved out with half the 2nd Company to attack them.[1] This led to a fight at a place called Ma-Cha-Su, south-west of Tientsin. "Marching at dawn," writes Boileau,[2] "we were soon involved in a belt of *kaoling* about twelve feet high growing in knee-deep mud. The Sappers forced their way through it without losing direction and were the first to emerge on the battlefield. We took the right of the line, the Chinese Regiment forming up on our left. The battlefield was a marshy plain scattered with Boxers in no sort of formation. Huge banners—green, yellow or red—were raised from time to time as some sort of signal. The Boxers were sturdy men, armed mostly with *jingals* (a sort of two-man punt-gun). Others carried rifles of various patterns, and many had pikes with red tassels. The American cavalry, far on our right, opened a heavy fire, and a number of Chinese commanders on white ponies could be seen galloping off the field. The Boxer army soon became a leaderless mob, swaying this way and that. Some of the enemy came on, but a few steady volleys turned them. Keeping well together, we advanced—except the detachment of the Chinese Regiment on our left which remained behind, firing wildly. However, some of our troops came up in support, and the Boxers melted away, leaving many dead. We picked up a number of rifles, *jingals*, drums and blood-stained banners, some of which are now in the Kirkee Mess. After Ma-Cha-Su we had no further fighting, but sections were often sent out with mobile columns."[3] In October, half the 2nd Company marched with the Tientsin Column in the bloodless operations against Pao-Ting-Fu. Afterwards, the whole unit was occupied in bridging and preparing winter quarters. The men stood the severe winter very well and worked hard during the spring at demolishing wrecks in the Paiho.[4] On August 22nd, 1901, the 2nd Company left Tientsin for Kirkee, where it arrived on September 20th after an absence of 14 months.

The Mounted Detachment of the Bengal Sappers and Miners, which served under Tylden-Pattenson in China, consisted of Sergeant Fisher and 24 Indian other ranks from the 2nd and "A" Companies. Leaving Roorkee on August 9th, 1900, it landed at Taku on September 5th, and proceeding to Tientsin, joined the Cavalry Brigade. On September 8th, it accompanied the brigade on an expedition to Tin-Lin, where it built a bridge of junks, 48 yards long, in 1½ hours. After reaching Peiping on September 22nd, it was employed chiefly in building winter quarters, but

[1]Notes by Brig.-Gen. G. H. Boileau, C.B., C.M.G., D.S.O., late R.E., sent to the author on Sept. 15th, 1937.

[2]"The Chinese Expeditionary Force," appearing in *The R.E. Journal*, Vol. XXXI, 1901, pp. 100–103.

[3]For instance, detachments accompanied two columns of a force under Col. Dorward which operated against the Boxers around Tin-Lin, 22 miles from Tientsin, and occupied that place without opposition on Sept. 10th, 1900.

[4]"Hasty Demolitions in China," by Lieut. J. E. E. Craster, R.E., appearing in *The R.E. Journal*, Vol. XXXIII, 1903, p. 123.

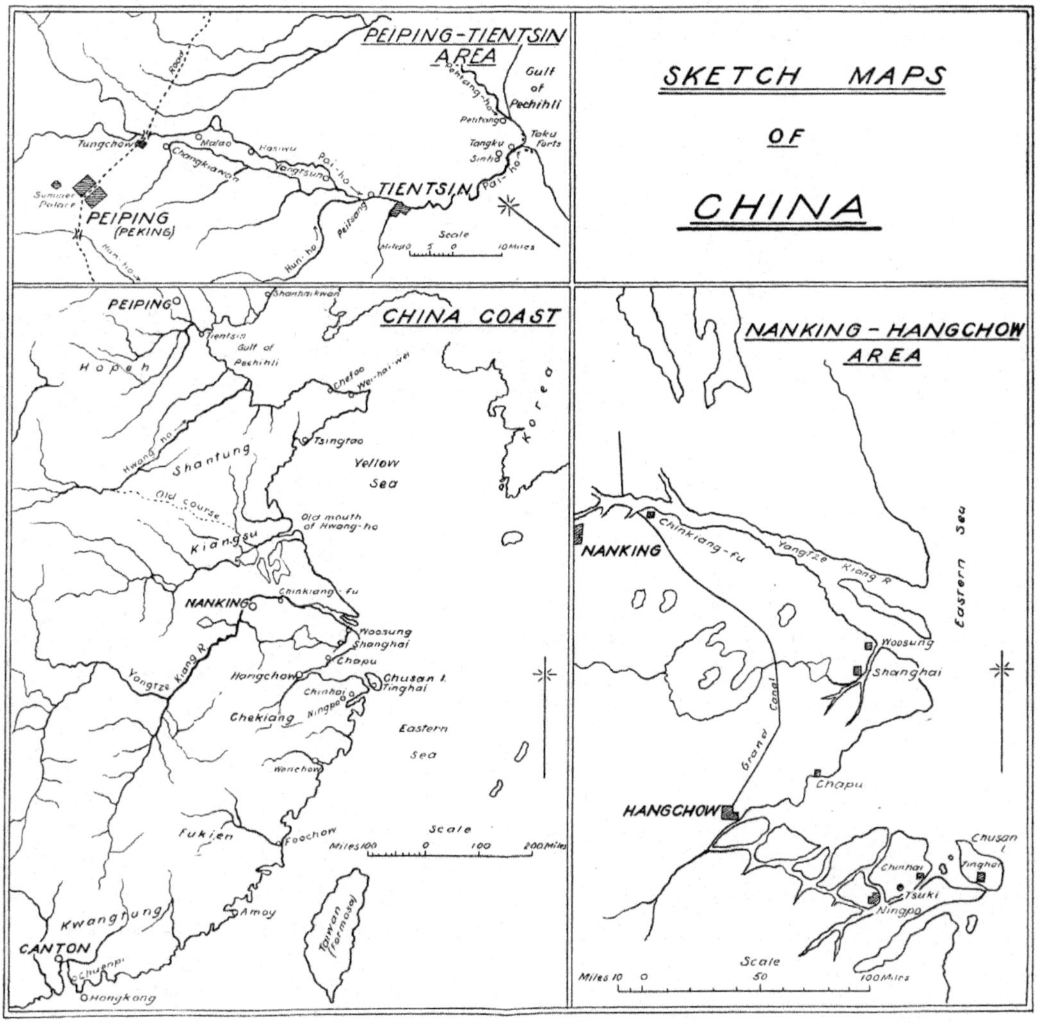

SKETCH MAPS
OF
CHINA
PEIPING-TIENTSIN AREA
Gulf of Pechihli
Pehtang-ho
Pehtang
Taku Forts
Tangku
Sinho
Tungchow
Matao
Hosiwu
Changkiawan
Yangtsun
Pai-ho
Summer Palace
PEIPING (PEKING)
TIENTSIN
Peitsang
Hun-ho
Road
Scale
Miles 10 5 0 10 Miles
CHINA COAST
PEIPING
Shanhaikwan
Tientsin
Gulf of Pechihli
Hopeh
Chefoo
Wei-hai-wei
Korea
Tsingtao
Hwang-ho
Shantung
Yellow Sea
Old Course
Old mouth of Hwang-ho
Kiangsu
NANKING
Chinkiang-fu
Woosung
Shanghai
Chapu
Yangtze Kiang R.
Hangchow
Chusan I.
Chinhai
Tinghai
Ningpo
Chekiang
Eastern Sea
Wenchow
Fukien
Foochow
Scale
Miles 100 0 100 200 Miles
Amoy
Kwangtung
Taiwan (Formosa)
CANTON
Chuanpi
Hongkong
NANKING - HANGCHOW AREA
NANKING
Chinkiang-fu
Yangtze Kiang R.
Eastern Sea
Woosung
Shanghai
Grand Canal
Chapu
HANGCHOW
Chusan I.
Chinhai
Tinghai
Tsuki
Ningpo
Scale
Miles 10 0 50 100 Miles

the tedium of this work was relieved occasionally by small excursions. For instance, the detachment accompanied the Peiping Column to Pao-Ting-Fu on October 12th and encountered the enemy on the 23rd when returning with a German battalion by a westerly route. It remained in Peiping until August, 1901, when it left for India with the 4th Company. It was disbanded at Roorkee on December 1st. Another small unit from Roorkee—the Telegraph Section under Brunner—arrived in China in November 1900 and returned to India in September 1901, with the 4th Company and Mounted Detachment, after operating the line along the Tientsin-Shanhaikwan Railway.

The Railway Section did excellent work, as also did the Survey Section, but these were not Sapper and Miner formations. After the conclusion of the campaign the material and some of the personnel of the Balloon Section were sent to India to form the nucleus of an "Experimental Balloon Section", officered and manned by Bengal Sappers and Miners.

The services of the Sapper and Miner units in China earned for all three Corps the honour "China, 1900", awarded in 1903.[1] The officers and men saw little fighting, but they gathered much valuable experience. Apart from their normal duties, they helped the Railway Section in railway work and the Military Works staff and personnel in building construction. The Railway Section produced the first surveyors for the army, and Major J. R. L. Macdonald, R.E., the officer originally commanding the Balloon Section, became the Director of Railways. "In this way," writes Craster,[2] "all the engineering work was performed without delay, and the British force was ready for further field operations before its European allies had established trustworthy communication with Peiping. In short, the operations in North China resulted in the complete triumph of the 'single corps' over the 'multiple corps' organization." The Germans, in contrast, favoured rigid specialization. Their telegraphists could get no help from their railway personnel, and while their railway men were overworked, their Pioneers were doing physical training to keep fit! Their engineering branches were kept, as it were, in hermetically sealed compartments and there was no co-operation between them.[3]

We return now from the Far East to the inhospitable country bordering the Gulf of Aden. Shortly before the commencement of the Third China War, trouble began to develop in the Aden Hinterland where the Turkish tribe of Humar encroached on the territory of the Haushabi Arabs, who were under British protection. In March, 1900, the Haushabis reported to the Resident at Aden that a certain Sheikh Muhammad Bin Nasir Mukhbil had erected a stone tower on a hill within the limits of their territory about 1½ miles west of Dareja.[4] Representations to the Turkish authorities having proved unavailing, the Resident was instructed to

[1]G.O.C.C., dated April 3rd, 1903.

[2]"The Organization of Engineers," by Maj. J. E. E. Craster, R.E., appearing in *The R.E. Journal*, Vol. XXI, Jan.–June, 1915, pp. 29–30.

[3]"With the Allies in China, 1900–01," by Capt. J. E. E. Craster, R.E., appearing in *The R.E. Journal*, Vol. I, Jan.–June, 1905, pp. 253–259.

[4]See the ***Sketch Map of Somaliland, the Aden Hinterland and Abyssinia in*** **1902, included in this chapter.**

authorize the Haushabi Sultan to demolish the offending tower. The Sultan tried to do so, but his men were driven back and he then asked for ammunition and money from Aden to enable him to undertake a regular siege. Meanwhile, Sheikh Muhammad reinforced the garrison of the tower, and as it was evident that the Haushabis could not capture the place unaided, a force of 400 British and Indian infantry, a Camel Battery and the 4th Company, Bombay S. & M., under Lieutenant F. P. Rundle, R.E., was despatched from Aden on July 15th, 1900, under the command of Major W. E. Rowe, R. West Kent Regiment, with orders to advance through Lahej into the Hinterland to deal with the situation.[1]

Before Rowe could reach D'areja, a contingent of Turkish regulars from Ta'iz joined Sheikh Muhammad, and these soldiers defended the tower when Rowe attacked it on July 25th. Under cover of artillery fire, two companies of the West Kents were directed against the tower and some heights beyond it, while two companies of the 5th Bombay Light Infantry were sent to capture the adjacent village of Dareja. The West Kents took the tower and drove the enemy from the heights, and the Bombay Infantry cleared the village. The Bombay Sappers, who had been in reserve, then came up and joined the West Kents. The position, however, was swept by fire from some hills beyond, and Jemadar Ashad Khan of the 4th Company was mortally wounded; so the Sappers and some of the West Kents were sent to another hill, whence they could enfilade the Turks and Humars. This manœuvre, supported by artillery fire, produced the desired result. The enemy's fire died away, and at nightfall our troops camped in Dareja. Dawn revealed that Sheikh Muhammad had retired. It was estimated that he had with him at least 800 Turkish regulars in addition to 1,200 Humars. The Bombay Sappers under Rundle demolished the tower which had caused so much trouble and afterwards returned to Aden.[2]

The affair at Dareja induced the Turks to propose that a proper frontier should be demarcated between the Aden Hinterland and Yemen, and negotiations were begun with the Porte. A British Commissioner was sent to meet the Turks at Dhali, about 65 miles north of Aden, and discussions proceeded throughout 1902; but in January, 1903, as the Turks still remained in the neighbourhood, a column of 2,000 men was despatched to Dhali to clear up the situation. With it marched the greater part of the 19th (late 3rd) Company, Bombay S. & M., under Captain W. H. Chaldecott, R.E., and also a Telegraph Section of the same Corps.[3] The Turks then withdrew northwards beyond Sanah, whither the British Commissioner followed them. The Arabs, however, continued to give trouble, and punitive operations had to be undertaken in the regions around Ad Dabra and Awabil, where the Sappers were employed in blowing up towers. In the middle of 1903, the 19th Company proceeded to Somaliland on relief by the 23rd (Fortress) Company under Lieutenant G. U.

[1]*Frontier and Overseas Expeditions from India*, Vol. VI, p. 266.
[2]A detailed account of these operations is given in an article entitled "The Aden Expedition," appearing in *The R.E. Journal*, Vol. XXXI, 1901, pp. 165, 166.
[3]*A Brief History of the Royal Bombay Sappers and Miners*, p. 26.

Yule, R.E. The 23rd Company continued on field service in the Hinterland until April, 1904, when it returned to Aden and received the thanks of the General Officer Commanding for the good work it had done, and for the way in which it had maintained the reputation of the Bombay Sappers and Miners.

The raids of the Mad Mullah into British Somaliland from 1899 onwards were so incessant that in May, 1901, a force of levies under Captain (local Lieut.-Colonel) E. J. E. Swayne, Bo.I., was sent from Burao along the caravan route between Berbera and the Nogal Valley and, defeating the Mullah at Eil Dab, forced him to fly southwards to the Mudug District.[1] Swayne followed to Bohotle, and when the Mullah tried to return in June, drove him back again across the Southern Haud. In December, 1901, the Mullah made yet another incursion, raiding the friendly tribes and threatening Burao; but it was not until May, 1902, that Swayne was able to advance from Burao towards Bohotle to engage, with only 1,200 men, the 15,000 horse and foot of his elusive adversary. The Mullah retired to Erigo in the Southern Haud, and Swayne occupied Damot. There he reached his limit owing to lack of water. During July and August, he cleared the Nogal Valley, and on October 2nd, reinforced at Baran by a battalion of the King's African Rifles, marched southwards towards Erigo; but he was heavily attacked at that oasis on October 6th and lost so severely that he was fortunate in being able to extricate his small force and bring it safely back to Bohotle.[2] These were some of the events which preceded the arrival of the Bombay Sappers and Miners in Somaliland.

It was now evident that strong action would be needed to suppress the Mad Mullah, and accordingly a proper expeditionary force was organized. British and Boer mounted infantry were brought from South Africa and considerable reinforcements from Aden and India, while contingents of Sikhs, Yaos and Sudanese were collected from Nyassaland and Uganda.[3] A small detachment of the 19th Company, Bombay S. & M., consisting of Jemadar Poshati Mari and 12 men under Lieutenant A. L. Paris, R.E., was sent from Aden to Berbera in November, 1902, to join the expedition and marched along the caravan route through Burao towards Bohotle, improving the defences of military posts and arranging for water supply.[4] The Sapper equipment was not all that could be desired. Paris remarks[5] that the gun-cotton, drawn from store at Aden in sealed and certified tins, was found to be black and rotten, and that a case supposed to hold 58 lbs. actually contained only 18 lbs. in small pieces. He was told that he would find blasting materials at a spot 150 miles inland from Berbera; but on arrival at the place indicated, all that he could discover was a heap of large gun-cotton primers of naval pattern and a few detonators. Later, he found

[1]See *Sketch Map of Somaliland, The Aden Hinterland and Abyssinia in* 1902, included in this chapter.

[2]The operations under Col. Swayne are described in *Frontier and Overseas Expeditions from India*, Vol. VI, pp. 97–101.

[3]"Somaliland," by Capt. H. Hughes Hallett, appearing in the *Journal of the United Service Institution of India*, Vol. XL, 1911, pp. 55–65.

[4]*A Brief History of the Royal Bombay Sappers and Miners*, p. 25.

[5]Notes by Lieut.-Col. A. L. Paris, R.E. (retd.), sent to the author on Aug. 13th, 1937.

some lengths of fuse; but they were being used as tethering ropes for the transport animals in the local *zariba!*

The hardships endured by the troops in Somaliland were such as they were not likely to forget. "The water," writes Paris, "was largely impregnated with sulphuretted hydrogen and foul in every way, though it did not seem to do us any harm, but cleaning out old wells was always a dangerous job.[1] Rations were poor and scarce, and there was much scurvy. This taught us the value of enlisting meat-eating men. An entry in my diary reads:—'February 22nd, 1904. Fresh vegetables. The first for nearly sixteen months.' The casualties among camels were enormous, and, towards the end of the campaign, I had sometimes to make a new track merely to avoid the stench of the dead animals lying along the original one. Marches were long and tiring. We would set out before dawn one day and receive no issue of water from the camel-tanks until the evening of the following day, and then never more than one gallon per man and often only half a gallon. For 36 hours, and two complete marches, each man had to live on what he carried. In the longest of our series of marches, the Sappers covered 906 miles in 90 consecutive days, including halts. On arrival in camp they had to water the force, and consequently it was usually dark before they got any rest. It is not surprising, therefore, that by the end of the campaign they were thoroughly worn out."

The foulness of the water in Somaliland was not always due to natural conditions. A medical officer once told the author that, when reconnoitring for water ahead of a column, he came to an oasis where an adequate supply was anticipated and found only a solitary and muddy pool in which three dead Somalis had been floating for several days. Instant action was necessary as the thirsty column was due to appear in an hour or two, and accordingly, expediency triumphing over medical training, the doctor and his small escort hurriedly extracted and buried the corpses. The troops arrived and drank deeply and thankfully, and not a man suffered any ill effects; but the total abstinence of the reconnoitring party occasioned some surprise and not a little suspicion.

As the check at Erigo had left our advanced force concentrated at Bohotle with the Mudug oasis still in the possession of the Mullah, it was decided to launch a new campaign to secure a decisive result. Therefore, with the consent of the Italian Government, it was arranged that a force should be landed at Obbia on the Indian Ocean to strike north-westwards at the Mudug region through Italian Somaliland, while another, based on Bohotle, moved down from the north and an Abyssinian army advanced to occupy the line of the Webi Shebeli to prevent the escape of the Mullah westwards. The main expeditionary force of about 2,000 men, under the command of Lieut.-Colonel (local Brig.-General) W. H. Manning, B.I., was landed at Obbia in January, 1903. The Commanding Royal Engineer was Captain W. B. Lesslie, R.E., and included in the force was the 17th

[1]The debris in the wells usually included broken water-vessels, a few Somali corpses and a collection of rotting timber and filth, and the gaseous fumes often rendered the workers insensible.

Company, Bombay S. & M., under Captain W. Bovet, R.E., with Lieutenant E. D. Tillard, R.E. This unit had come direct from Bombay with other Indian troops, the remaining units of the Obbia Force being supplied from Berbera and South Africa. The Berbera Force, operating from the north under the command of Major (local Lieut.-Colonel) J. C. Swann, Bo.I.,[1] included the detachment of the 19th Company, Bombay S. & M., under Lieutenant A. L. Paris, R.E. Its chief duty was to keep open the line of communication between Berbera and Bohotle while the Obbia Force drove the Mullah from Mudug.

General Manning marched from Obbia on February 22nd, 1903, and reached Galkayu on March 5th, but lack of transport and supplies obliged him to halt there. Meanwhile, Colonel Swann had occupied Damot. Manning planned next to advance westwards against the Mad Mullah, who had moved to Galadi, and although his fighting strength had fallen to 800 men he reached that place safely on March 31st only to find that the Mullah had retired still further westwards towards Wardair. On April 17th, a disaster occurred near Gumburru where a column of 223 men under Captain (local Lieut.-Colonel) A. W. V. Plunkett, Central African Rifles, marched out to the attack and was annihilated by a horde of 8,000 Somalis. A few days later, another column had a very hard fight at Daratoleh. On June 26th, Manning established contact with Swann's advanced troops at Bohotle, but he was too late because the Mullah had already slipped through between the converging forces. By a daring march northeastwards, the Somali leader had traversed the Southern Haud from the region of Wardair and Gerlogubi and had reached the Nogal Valley. The British operations had failed through lack of transport. It was decided to close the Obbia line of communication, and Manning moved on towards Berbera, leaving garrisons at Bohotle, Kirrit and Burao. Most of the troops went down to the coast; but the Sappers and Miners remained in the interior to make defensible posts, improve the desert tracks, and arrange for water supply in preparation for a renewed offensive.

For the final campaign against the Mad Mullah, the force in Somaliland was increased to 6,400 men and placed under the command of Major-General Sir C. C. Egerton. Brig.-General Manning commanded the African troops forming the 1st Brigade, and Lieut.-Colonel (local Brig.-General) C. G. M. Fasken, B.I., commanded the 2nd or Indian Brigade. There was also a Mounted Brigade under Major (local Lieut.-Colonel) P. A. Kenna, V.C. An advanced base was established at Kirrit, and strong working parties of Indian infantry assisted the 107th Pioneers in making a cart road over the Sheikh Pass and improving the route through Burao. Thousands of camels were purchased for transport purposes, and depots of supplies laid out. In August, 1903, the greater part of the 19th Company, Bombay S. & M., under Captain W. H. Chaldecott, R.E., landed at Berbera on transfer from the Aden Hinterland and moved into the interior to reinforce the detachment under Paris and the 17th Company under Bovet. Major R. F. Allen, R.E., became Commanding Royal Engineer,

[1]Lieut.-Col. E. J. E. Swayne, Bo.I., had been invalided.

and an Engineer Field Park of Madras Sappers and Miners made its appearance under Major E. P. Johnson, R.E. The 17th Company was attached to the 1st Brigade, and the 19th Company to the 2nd Brigade when acting independently.

By the end of October 1903, all the necessary preparations for a general advance had been completed. The 1st Brigade moved to Bohotle and the 2nd Brigade to Eil Dab, the Mad Mullah being then in the southern part of the Nogal Valley. As it was feared that the Mullah might retreat into the Southern Haud, the Abyssinians were asked to occupy Galadi. This, however, they could not undertake, so the 1st Brigade was sent straight across the Haud to carry out the task. Bovet and a detachment of the 17th Company went with the brigade on this journey of 95 miles across waterless country. Galadi was garrisoned and the 1st Brigade then returned, encountering and defeating a raiding party of the enemy on the way. A certain Royal Engineer, well known in India, once expressed his opinion of the value of Somaliland in the words " When I see a bad egg lying in the gutter, I do not pick it up." A pessimist perhaps ; but Bovet, after his experiences in the Southern Haud, might have felt inclined to agree with him. The Sappers were often reduced to drinking water so foul that no man would wash his hands in it. Rations were always scarce, and the allowance of jam in the officers' mess was one spoonful a day.[1] Each man had to carry 40 lbs. of kit—no small load under the burning rays of a tropical sun. The troops rested during the heat of the day under improvised shelters of blankets and sticks ; but the marching hours—dawn till 11 a.m. and 3 p.m. to sunset—were enough to try the strongest constitution.

Asit was reported, early in December, that the Mad Mullah was moving westwards up the Nogal Valley and concentrating at Jidbali, and as it was hopeless to expect the Abyssinians to reach Galadi in reasonable time, Egerton recalled the Galadi garrison and marched from Eil Dab on January 8th, 1904, with the 2nd Brigade and mounted troops, to meet the 1st Brigade coming up from Bohotle. The Mullah was located with 6,000 men at Jidbali, and on January 10th the two brigades advanced in square formation to attack him, the 17th and 19th Companies of Bombay Sappers being with the infantry in the firing line. The enemy's skirmishers could be discerned lying down in short grass within 700 yards of the square or creeping slowly forward through the scrub, and the crackle of musketry deepened into a deafening roar as the square was attacked on the front and both flanks ; but the extended lines of the Somalis soon melted away under a hail of bullets, and within half an hour, the survivors were in full flight, pursued by our mounted troops. They left 660 dead on the field and many more strewn along the line of retreat.

Egerton now planned to occupy the southern edge of the Nogal Valley to prevent the Mullah from escaping southwards to the Mudug oases, and as the Mullah was believed to be near Hansoga, the two brigades were directed at first on Halin at the east end of the valley. Subsequently, the

[1]Account by Capt. W. Bovet, R.E., as given in notes by Lieut.-Col. F. S. Garwood, R.E. (retd.), sent to the author on Feb. 18th, 1938.

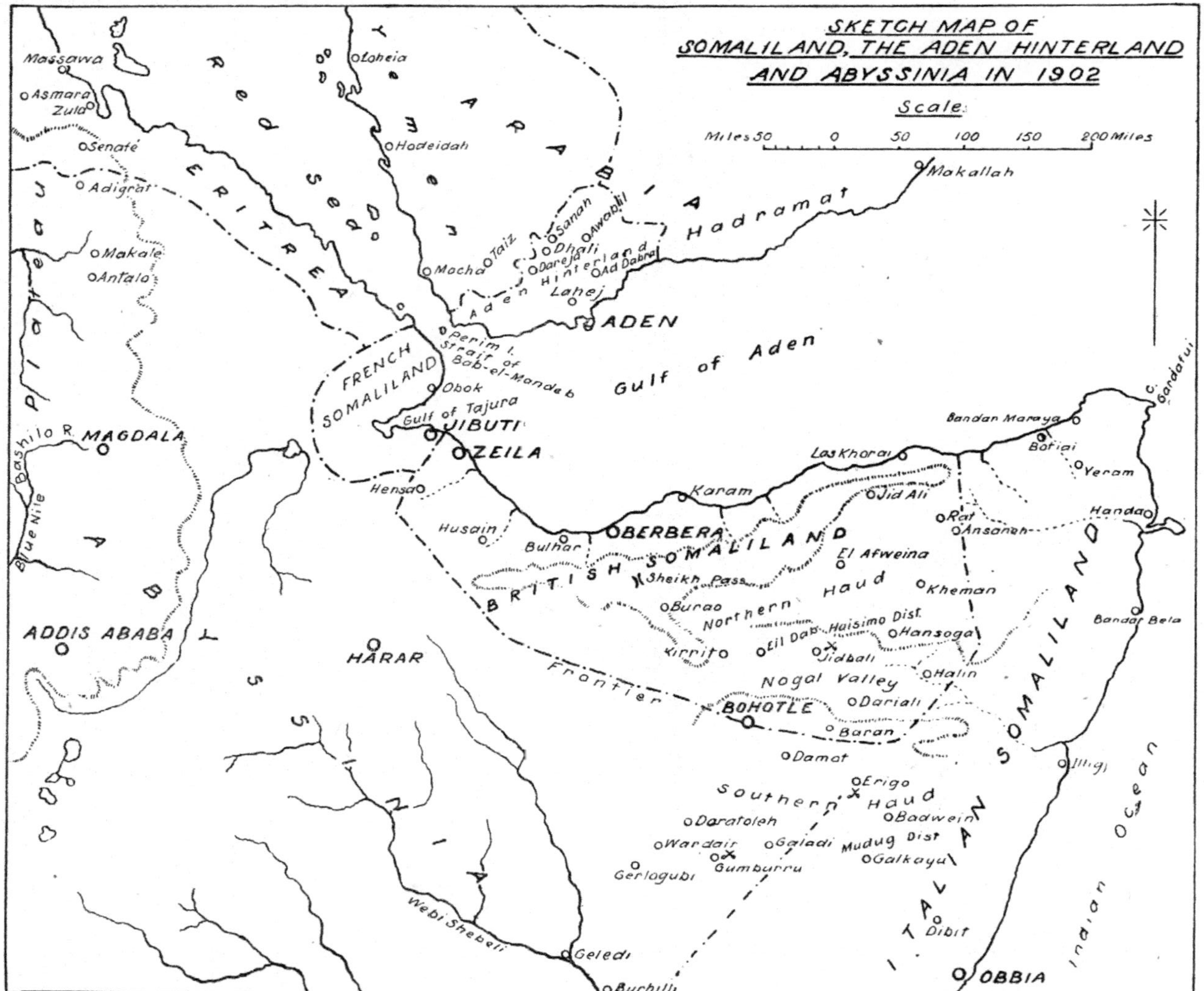
SKETCH MAP OF
SOMALILAND, THE ADEN HINTERLAND
AND ABYSSINIA IN 1902
Scale:
Miles 50 0 50 100 150 200 Miles
Massawa
Asmara
Zula
Senafe
Adigrat
Makale
Antalo
Red Sea
ERITREA
Loheia
Hodeidah
Yemen
ARABIA
Hadramat
Makallah
Macha
Taiz
Sanah
Awabil
Dhali
Darejali
Ad Dabra
Aden Hinterland
Lahej
ADEN
Perim I.
Strait of Bab-el-Mandeb
Gulf of Aden
FRENCH SOMALILAND
Obok
Gulf of Tajura
JIBUTI
ZEILA
Hensa
Husain
Bulhar
BERBERA
Karam
Las Khorai
Bandan Maraya
Bofiai
Yeram
C. Gardafui
Handa
Rat
Ansaneh
Jid Ali
BRITISH SOMALILAND
El Afweina
Sheikh Pass
Burao
Northern Haud
Kheman
Haisimo Dist.
Kirrito
Eil Dab
Jidbali
Hansoga
Nogal Valley
Halin
Frontier
BOHOTLE
Dariali
Baran
Bandar Bela
SOMALILAND
Damat
Illigi
Erigo
Southern Haud
Badwein
Daratoleh
Wardair
Galadi
Mudug Dist
Galkayu
Gumburru
Gerlogubi
ITALIAN
Dibit
OBBIA
Indian Ocean
Geledi
Burhilli
Webi Shebeli
HARAR
ABYSSINIA
ADDIS ABABA
MAGDALA
Bashilo R.
Blue Nile
Plateau

1st Brigade was detailed to hold the Nogal Valley, while the 2nd Brigade and mounted troops reconnoitred the Haisimo District to the north. The 17th Company marched down the Nogal with the 1st Brigade and assisted in the capture of 20,000 camels and 50,000 sheep which formed the Mullah's chief reserves of transport and supply. This brigade also blocked the passes leading from the Nogal into the Sorl or Northern Haud. Meanwhile, the 2nd Brigade marched back with the 19th Company to Eil Dab, and thence towards Berbera, preparatory to taking up the chase of the Mullah in the Northern Haud. A party of the 19th Company was attached to a movable column despatched from Eil Dab, and another of the 17th Company set out with a column under Brig.-General Fasken which assembled east of the Sheikh Pass. The two columns met at Al Afweina on March 15th, 1904, and then advanced to Jid Ali, and later to Las Khorai on the coast, where another detachment of Sappers was at work.[1] The pursuit of the Mullah was resumed to the region of Rat and Ansaneh but without result, and at the Italian frontier it had to be abandoned. Fasken retired to Las Khorai and reached that place on April 10th.

With the escape of the remnants of the Mad Mullah's army into the north-eastern corner of Italian Somaliland, the military operations came to an end and the troops were withdrawn gradually to Berbera, some by land and others by sea from Las Khorai. By the end of May, 1904, the bulk of the expeditionary force had reached the base, and on June 14th, the 17th and 19th Companies of the Bombay Sappers were back in their headquarters at Kirkee. They had found the campaign extremely arduous, but had earned for their Corps the honour "Somaliland, 1901–04." The constant marching on short rations had served to show which classes produced the hardiest men, and as these proved to be the Deccani Marathas, Punjabi Muhammadans and Sikhs, the Bombay Sappers proceeded to remodel their composition in the light of the knowledge gained. Maratha recruiting was restricted to men from the Deccan, and Mussulman recruiting to men from the Punjab, while the enlistment of Hindustanis, other than Rajputs, was stopped and Punjabi Muhammadans enrolled instead.[2]

The Mad Mullah survived for many years; but this was of small consequence because his power had been broken at Jidbali and his following had ceased to exist as a fighting force. The tribes under British protection were relieved from the fear of his devastating raids, and thus tranquillity was restored throughout the length and breadth of Somaliland.

The last two expeditions overseas in which Sappers and Miners were concerned before the Great War were both to Makran. On January 21st, 1910, Lieutenant T. A. S. Swinburne, R.E., with 50 men of the 18th Field Company, Bombay S. & M., sailed from Bombay with two double-companies of the 123rd Rifles and a section of Mountain Artillery, under Lieut.-Colonel (afterwards Lieut.-General Sir) W. S. Delamain, 123rd

[1] *A Brief History of the Royal Bombay Sappers and Miners*, p. 26.
[2] Notes by Lieut.-Col. E. V. Binney, D.S.O., R.E. (retd.), sent to the author on March 26th, 1938.

Rifles, to operate against gun-runners in the Persian Gulf and the Gulf of Oman. The troops were transported up and down the Makran coast in ships, landing where required, and the Sappers were employed chiefly in making arrangements for disembarking and embarking men and animals at Khor Lash, providing defences for the telegraph station at Jask, and surveying the country around Galag and Sirik.[1] With the exception of one small engagement, there was little fighting. A ramp for disembarking mules from boats on a shelving shore was designed by Swinburne and the officers of the R.I.M.S. *Hardinge*, and proved to be so efficient that it became the standard pattern. On April 4th, the force re-embarked for Bombay, and on arrival the Sapper detachment returned to Kirkee.

Makran was revisited in 1911. On this occasion, the combined naval and military operations were conducted by Rear-Admiral Slade, R.N., and Colonel Delamain, and the field force comprised the 104th Rifles, two sections of the 34th Mountain Battery, and two sections of the 19th Field Company, Bombay S. & M. The Sapper sections were under Captain N. W. Webber and Lieutenant M. Rawlence, R.E., and left Kirkee for Bombay on April 4th.[2] The first landing was at Galag. " We were always obliged to disembark with three days' rations and water," writes Rawlence.[3] " The reason was that the surf might get up and the shore party be cut off. On one occasion, my Subadar, Musa Khan, without reference to me, persuaded my section to cook and eat the whole of their three days' ration before disembarkation. He was an old campaigner and assured the men that ' the new General would give them no time to cook for many days.' Unfortunately, there was a tow of five or six miles from the ship to the shore, and the voyage proved too much for the men. I never discovered how they existed for the next three days, but I know they were very hungry at the end. Webber and I surveyed the Rabch River from Galag to the northern end of the Kurandab Pass—a rough triangulation with prismatic compass, but better than the available map. The force was very mobile as kits were reduced to a minimum. One blanket (4 lbs.) was allowed per officer and half a blanket per man. A single Mess mule sufficed for all the officers of the force, and we lived entirely on bully beef and biscuit. All wore beards, and we washed only when pools were discovered in the dry river bed."

Another landing was made at Sarzeh in the Strait of Hormuz, where the troops camped beside a spring-fed pool overflowing into the Gaz River. The pool was marked for drinking and the river for washing, but the water from the pool proved to be more powerful in its effects than the strongest Epsom Salts and the muddy liquid in the river was full of biting minnows. The force moved inland, where it had a brush with gun-runners. On return to Sarzeh, the troops used the river for drinking and the pool

[1] *A Brief History of the Royal Bombay Sappers and Miners*, p. 27. Khor Lash is 7 miles east of Jask. Sirik is 7 miles north of Sarzeh in the Hormuz Strait. See *Sketch Map of Makran* in this chapter.

[2] *A Brief History of the Royal Bombay Sappers and Miners*, p. 27.

[3] Notes by Maj. M. Rawlence, D.S.O., R.E. (retd.), sent to the author on March 3rd, 1938.

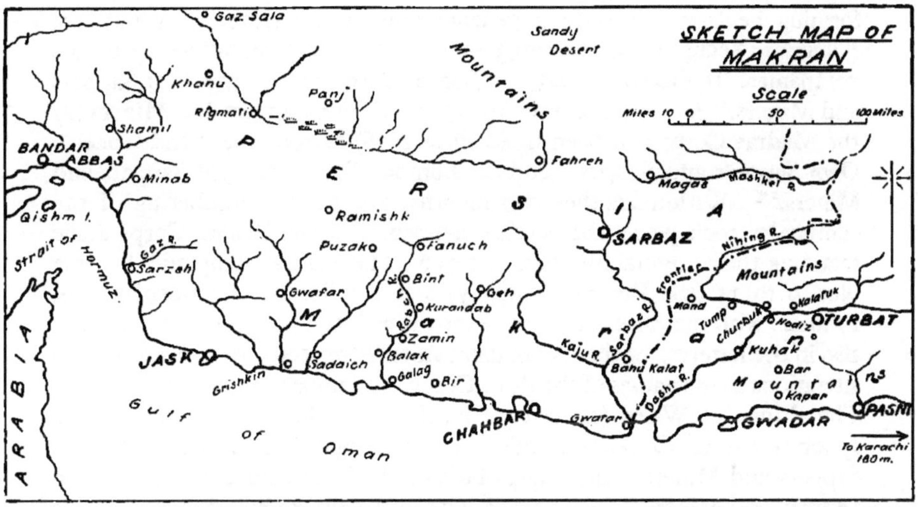
SKETCH MAP OF MAKRAN
Scale
Miles 10 0 50 100 Miles
Gaz Sala
Sandy Desert
Mountains
Khanu
Panj
Rigmati
Shamil
BANDAR ABBAS
Minab
P E R S I A
Fahreh
Magas
Mashkel R.
Qishm I.
Ramishk
SARBAZ
Nihing R.
Strait of Hormuz
Gaz R.
Sarzeh
Puzak
Fanuch
Bint
Gwafar
Geh
Kurandab
Rabch R.
M a k r a n
Zamin
Balak
Galag
Bir
Sadaich
JASK
Grishkin
Mountains
Kalatuk
Mand
Tump
Churbuk
Nodiz
TURBAT
Frontier
Kaju R.
Sarbaz R.
Bahu Kalat
Dasht R.
Kuhak
Bar
Kaper
Mountains
PASNI
GWADAR
Gwatar
CHAHBAR
Gulf of Oman
ARABIA
To Karachi 180 m.

for washing—an advantageous change as the pool was supplied by intensley hot springs and there was little risk of swallowing the aggressive minnows. The expeditionary force was back in Bombay on May 8th, 1911, and with its return the adventures of the Bombay Sappers and Miners in Makran came to an end.

This chapter may be concluded with a description of some of the changes in the three Corps of Sappers and Miners following the abolition of the Indian Staff Corps in January, 1903, and the reorganizations in the Army in India proposed by Lord Kitchener as Commander-in-Chief.

The relative order of precedence of the Corps had been fixed in 1897, the senior being the Madras Sappers, the next the Bengal Sappers, and the junior the Bombay Sappers,[1] but there was still much to be done in forming the Sappers into a homogeneous branch of the Service. As a first step, Kitchener secured the renaming of the Corps and renumbering of the companies. In October, 1903, the Bengal Corps became the " 1st Sappers and Miners." At the same time, the Queen's Own Sappers and Miners (as the Madras Corps had been titled since 1876) became the " 2nd Queen's Own Sappers and Miners," and the Bombay Corps the" 3rd Sappers and Miners."[2] Within another two months, a general renumbering of the companies took place, the service companies of the Bengal Corps alone retaining their original numbers of 1 to 6. The Madras companies became Nos. 9 to 15 (the Burma Company) and the Bombay Companies Nos. 17 to 22, with the Aden Fortress Company as No. 23.[3] Changes were made also in the lettering of the Depot companies. After 1905, there were several alterations in the names of the three Corps. In January, 1906, when H.R.H. The Prince of Wales (afterwards H.M. King George V) accepted the appointment of Colonel-in-Chief of the Bengal Corps, then the " 1st Sappers and Miners," that Corps became the " 1st Prince of Wales' Own Sappers and Miners " with permission to wear the plume of three feathers on its colours and appointments ;[4] and in 1910, when the Prince ascended the throne, the title was altered to the " 1st King George's Own Sappers and Miners." After the Great War of 1914–18, the Bengal Corps became the " King George's Own Bengal Sappers and Miners," and after the death of King George V. it was called the " King George V's Own Bengal Sappers and Miners." The Madras Corps (the " 2nd Queen's Own Sappers and Miners ") became in 1911 the " 2nd Queen Victoria's Own Sappers and Miners "[5], and in 1923 the " Queen Victoria's Own Madras Sappers and Miners." In 1921 the designation of the 3rd Sappers and Miners was altered to the " 3rd Royal Bombay Sappers and Miners " in recognition of the services of the Corps in the Great War.[6] The title became later the " Royal Bombay Sappers and Miners."

In the London Gazette of February 1st, 1946, His Majesty the King

[1]G.G.O. No. 605 of June, 1897.
[2]Indian Army Order No. 181 of Oct., 1903.
[3]Indian Army Order No. 382 of Dec., 1903.
[4]G.G.O. No. 1 of Jan., 1906.
[5]Gazette of India, Dec. 22nd, 1911.
[6]Indian Army Order No. 821 of July, 1921.

conferred the title of " Royal" on the Corps of Indian Engineers, which had been formed during the 1939-45 War. As a sequel to this, the titles of the three S.&.M. Corps became " Q.V.O. Madras Group, R.I.E.," " K.G.V's O. Bengal Group, R.I.E.," and "Royal Bombay Group, R.I.E." respectively.

Other changes made before the Great War of 1914–18, were the abolition in July, 1909, of the title " Service Company " in favour of " Field Company " and the substitution in 1912 of Defence Light Sections for the small Submarine Mining Sections maintained by the three Corps at certain Indian ports.[1] When all the available Sappers and Miners were concentrated in Delhi in 1911 for the magnificent Durbar ceremonies, during which Their Majesties King George and Queen Mary laid the foundation stones of the new capital, no finer body of troops could be desired ; and when called upon, less than three years later, to take their share in the defence of the Empire, they showed the value of training which had been secured, to a considerable extent, by their service in many expeditions overseas.

[1]See the Appendices at the end of this volume.

CHAPTER XIII

EXPEDITIONS ON THE NORTH-WEST FRONTIER, 1849–1891

DURING the latter half of the nineteenth century, the North-West Frontier of India was probably the scene of more internecine warfare than any other tract of country in the world. Its 700 miles of mountainous territory, from the boundary of Russian Turkestan in the north to the borders of Sind in the south, were unproductive, barren and inhospitable, and its inhabitants the fiercest and most warlike and vindictive people that imagination can picture. The struggle for bare existence, where life was almost insupportable, had produced men of wonderful physique, extraordinary hardihood and matchless cunning—desperate characters in desperate surroundings. These were the foes against whom the Sappers and Miners began to take the field after the Sikh Wars and the resulting annexation of the Punjab.

Two great nations, the Pathan and the Baluch (including the Brahui), inhabit the North-West Frontier, the former to the north and the latter mostly to the south of a line drawn from Dera Ghazi Khan westwards to Quetta, though in the trans-Indus valley, and on the Punjab face of the Sulaiman Mountains, the Baluchis have pushed northwards to the neighbourhood of Dera Ismail Khan.[1] The Pathans far outnumber the Baluchis —in 1881 they could muster 190,000 fighting men as compared with 17,000 of the southern nation—and they are beyond comparison the more dangerous fighters. The Brahui of Baluchistan is a smaller man, less turbulent, less treacherous and less bloodthirsty than his northern neighbour. He is a born horseman and an expert thief, but like the Baluchi proper, of no great account in war. Consequently, most of the frontier campaigns having been waged against the Pathan, we are concerned chiefly with him and his country.

Far up in the north, beyond Kashmir, are the little states of Hunza and Nagar, peopled by Kanjutis and Nagaris, and between them and Kashmir proper, Gilgit and Astor. To the west of Hunza and Nagar are Yasin and Chitral, and south of these, Drosh, Dir, Kohistan, Bajaur, Swat, Buner, Hazara and other territories, the home of the Yusufzai Pathans who include among their many clans the Bunerwals, Swatis, Utman Khel, Ranizais, Baizais and Isazais. North of the Kabul River are the Mohmands, and to its south the most powerful of all the Pathan tribes, the Afridis around the Khaibar Pass. The Zakka Khel, an important Afridi clan, occupy the Bazar, Bara and Waran valleys of the Tirah or highlands west of Peshawar. Another large Afridi clan, the Adam Khel (including the Jowakis) live in the region between Peshawar and Kohat. South of the Afridi Tirah and west of Kohat are the Orakzais, Zaimukhts and Turis of

[1]See Map III, *Sketch Map of the North-West Frontier including Afghanistan,* which appears at the end of this volume.

the Miranzai and Kurram valleys. Between the Kurram valley and the Gomal valley south of Bannu is that hotbed of unrest, Waziristan, whose largest clans are the Darwesh Khel, near the Afghan border, and the Mahsuds of the mountainous area around Razmak and Kaniguram. South of the Gomal dwell the Baluchis and Brahuis, including the Shiranis of the Zhob Valley, the Bozdars near Dera Ghazi Khan and others scattered between the Durand Line, marking the boundary of Afghanistan, and the Administrative Boundary Line of British India. Many other tribes or clans inhabit the trans-frontier regions, such as the Hassanzais, Akazais, Mada Khel and Utmanzais adjoining Hazara; the Gaduns, Khudu Kehl and Chamlawals adjoining Peshawar; the Batanis and Dawaris near Kohat, Bannu and Dera Ismail Khan, and the Kasrani, Marri and Bugti Baluchis around Dera Ghazi Khan; but sufficient has been written to show that the peoples of the North-West Frontier present a curious medley united only in one respect in that all are followers of the Prophet.

The Pathan character is most difficult to understand. It touches the heights of valour and self-sacrifice: it plumbs the depths of treachery and villainy. After the annexation of the Punjab, Sir John Lawrence came to visit Major-General Sir Harry Lumsden in the Hazara District, and being a very thorough inspecting officer, harassed Lumsden considerably. This, at least, was the opinion of Lumsden's Pathan soldiers, who had the keenest regard for him. One night, an Afridi of the Guides approached Lumsden and said in a low voice "Since the great Lawrence came, you have been depressed. Many have observed this. Is he interfering with you? He starts for Peshawar tomorrow morning; *but there is no reason why he should ever reach it!*"[1]

In 1855, Mr. Richard Temple, an official of the Punjab Government, gave the following description of the trans-frontier Pathans:—[2] "These tribes are savages—noble savages perhaps—and not without some tincture of virtue and generosity, but absolute barbarians nevertheless. They have nothing approaching to Government. They have, for the most part, no education. In their eyes, the one great commandment is blood for blood and fire and sword for all infidels. They are superstitious and priest-ridden. For gold, they will do almost anything except betray a guest. They are thievish and predatory to the last degree. The Pathan mother often prays that her son may be a successful robber. They are utterly faithless to public engagements. Even when grazing their cattle or tilling the soil, they are armed. They are perpetually at war with each other. Every tribe and section of a tribe has its internecine wars, every family its hereditary blood-feuds and every individual his personal foes. There is hardly a

[1] "The Punjab Frontier Force," appearing in *The R.E. Journal*, Vol. XIV, 1884, pp. 222, 223.

[2] Report by Mr. (afterwards Sir Richard) Temple, Secretary to the Chief Commissioner of the Punjab, quoted in *A Record of the Expeditions against the North-West Frontier Tribes* (1873), by Lieut.-Col. W. H. Paget, 5th Punjab Cavalry, revised by Lieut. A. H. Mason, R.E., in 1884, pp. 9, 10. This volume by Paget and Mason is the most comprehensive work in existence on the subject of the early campaigns on the N.W. Frontier. It forms the foundation of *Frontier and Overseas Expeditions from India*, Vols. I, II and III, which describe, in addition, all the campaigns up to 1908.

man whose hands are unstained. Every person counts up his murders. Each tribe has a debtor and creditor account with its neighbours, life for life. They consider retaliation and revenge to be the strongest of all obligations. They possess gallantry and courage, and men of the same party will stand by one another in danger. To their minds, hospitality is the first of virtues. Any person who can make his way into their dwellings will not only be safe but will be kindly received; but as soon as he has left the roof of his entertainer, he may be robbed or killed. They are fond of trading and cultivating, though too fickle and excitable to be industrious. They will take military service, and though impatient of discipline, will prove faithful unless excited by fanaticism. Such, briefly, is their character, replete with the unaccountable inconsistencies and the mixture of vices and virtues belonging to savages."

Writing in 1873, Colonel Paget adds that the Pathan, though often brave and reckless of his life, would scorn to face an enemy whom he could stab from behind, and in support of his opinion quotes several Pathan proverbs such as "Speak good words to an enemy very softly; gradually destroy him root and branch." Sir Robert Warburton, himself of Afghan extraction, remarks[1] that the Afridi of the Khaibar Pass is forced from his earliest childhood to look upon his nearest relative as his deadliest enemy. Distrust of mankind is therefore almost a religion to him; but once this distrust is removed he is capable of the greatest devotion and may become a staunch friend. If you treat him unfairly or abuse him, or interfere with his customs or his women, he will cut your throat without the slightest compunction.

This brief sketch of the Pathan character—a necessary preliminary to a narrative of frontier warfare—may be amplified by two stories which illustrate the naïvety of the children of the border. The first is by Brig.-General W. E. R. Dickson. "On one occasion," he writes,[2] "when my Sapper company was halted in the Kohat Pass on the march to Peshawar, we noticed that a battle royal was in progress on the hills above us. Presently, a native was seen running down towards us. He proved to be an ex-Sapper, formerly of my company,[3] and after profuse greetings he explained the situation. The inhabitants of a neighbouring village being away on a raid, his own people had seized the opportunity to pay off old scores. Unfortunately, the neighbours had returned unexpectedly and the ex-Sapper implored me to bring the company to the assistance of his side. The opportunity, said he, was unparalleled for some real '*chand mari*' (target practice) instead of firing at those silly paper targets, and he was much disappointed when I had to decline."

General Sir Bindon Blood relates[4] that during the Jowaki Expedition,

[1]Extract from *Eighteen Years in the Khyber*, by Col. Sir Robert Warburton, K.C.I.E., C.S.I., given in "British Relations with the Afridis of the Khyber and Tirah," by Capt. C. D. Davies, published in *The Army Quarterly*, Vol. XXIII, Jan. 1932, pp. 251–267.

[2]Notes by Brig.-Gen. W. E. R. Dickson, C.M.G., C.I.E., late R.E., sent to the author on May 20th, 1937.

[3]Maj.-Gen. Sir Theodore Fraser writes that the man had been discharged from the 4th Company, Bengal Sappers and Miners, in 1891.

[4]*Four Score Years and Ten*, by Gen. Sir Bindon Blood, G.C.B., G.C.V.O., Representative Colonel-Commandant, R.E., p. 161.

AFRIDI VILLAGES IN THE KHAIBAR PASS.

when marching with two Sapper companies near Kohat, he noticed a Muhammadan cemetery with the usual bamboos and flags and also a number of small cairns indicating the spots where men had been killed. His orderly officer, Jemadar Nur Beg, explained the abundance of cairns by remarking " Oh, yes. That is a place where a good deal of money is made by the neighbours. The cemetery is visited by many Mussulman pilgrims, and when these appear to be worth it, they are shot and robbed." Nur Beg added that, to avoid blood-feuds, care was taken to avoid shooting men from neighbouring districts. Then he launched out into a story of his own village far distant from Kohat. A needy relative, he said, was ploughing his field when he saw a prosperous and holy man, obviously a pilgrim, riding towards him and carrying a new breech-loading rifle. " Here is luck," said the relative to himself. " I will speak him fair, and when he is going away I will shoot him, bury him in my field, and plant a bamboo and flag over him. Then other pilgrims will visit his grave, as he is a *Hajji*, and I can shoot them also and so assure my livelihood." Accordingly, he pointed out the best road to the *Hajji*, shot him, annexed his pony and belongings, buried him, planted the flag, and afterwards lived in comfort for several years until slain by a brother of the *Hajji*. The brother was too cunning. He came unarmed except for a dagger under his clothes, and when Nur Beg's relative was off his guard in friendly conversation, suddenly stabbed him to the heart. " My relative," remarked Nur Beg, " was certainly rash in shooting the *Hajji* : but you will understand, Sahib, that he was hard up at the time."

A surprising feature of the early campaigns on the North-West Frontier is the dearth or absence of Sappers and Miners. In most of the expeditions which followed the annexation of the Punjab there was rarely more than a single company of Sappers, and in many none whatever. For instance, no Sappers and Miners took part in the expeditions against the Umarzai Waziris in 1852, the Hindustani Fanatics of the Black Mountain in 1853, the Bizoti Orakzais and the Aka Khel Afridis in 1855, the Mohmands in 1864, the Bizoti Orakzais again in 1868–69, the Dawaris of the Tochi Valley in 1872, the Ranizais and Utman Khel of Swat in 1878, and the Marris of Baluchistan in October 1880; and it is worthy of note that Sir Frederick Roberts took no Sappers and Miners with him on his famous march from Kabul to Kandahar in August, 1880, though plenty were available at Kabul. Some of these expeditions were small affairs, but others comprised 2,000 men or more. In some thirty-seven expeditions across the frontier between 1849 and 1891, excluding the Second Afghan War, only seven included more than one company of Sappers and Miners.[1] After 1890, however, when the armament of the tribesmen began to improve and their tactics changed, almost every expeditionary force was provided with at least one Sapper company. The reorganization of 1885 had taken effect and the value of the Sappers was recognized. Their omission from many of the early expeditions may have been due in part to

[1]Hindustani Fanatics, 1858 ; Ambela, 1863 ; Black Mountain, 1868 ; Zakka Khel Afridis, 1879 ; Mahsuds, 1881, and Zhob Valley, 1884.

the fact that the Punjab Irregular (or Frontier) Force,[1] which was under Provincial control and was employed by the Lieutenant-Governor in small operations acoss the border, had no authorized establishment of Sappers and Miners although one or two companies of so-called " Punjab Sappers and Miners " were maintained on the frontier before the Indian Mutiny and might have been used more frequently. For many years after the Mutiny, the Bengal Sappers and Miners were in the process of recovering from the disorganization in their establishment caused by that disastrous episode and of regaining the confidence of Government, which they had forfeited at Roorkee and Meerut through the misguided actions of some of their number.

We come now to a long record of twenty-eight early expeditions. It is curious that the honour of providing the first engineer unit for an expedition across the North-West Frontier should rest, not with the Bengal Sappers and Miners of Northern India, but with the Bombay Corps of the western littoral. The annexation of the Punjab in 1849 was followed by encounters with most of the frontier tribes, and the earliest of these expeditions was directed against the Baizais of Swat. In October, 1849, the Utman Khel villages of British Baizai refused to pay revenue and prepared for war; so on December 3rd, a mixed force of about 2,300 men including the 1st Company, Bombay S. & M., under Lieutenant W. Kendall, Bo.E., was despatched from Peshawar under Lieut.-Colonel J. Bradshaw, 60th Rifles, to coerce the refractory Baizais. Sharp fighting ensued at Sangau, 15 miles south-east of the Malakand,[2] and around Palai, a few miles from Sangau, and ended in a complete victory over 10,000 Baizais and other Swatis.[3] The Bombay Sappers built a fortified post before returning to Peshawar with the Guides in January, 1850. They were experienced men who had fought in the Siege of Multan and the Battle of Gujarat before marching with the Army of the Punjab to expel the Afghan invaders and garrison Peshawar.[4]

The next expedition was against the Adam Khel Afridis of the Kohat Pass. Eight sepoys of the 2nd Company, Bengal S. & M., having been massacred on February 2nd, 1850, while at work on the road through the pass, a force of about 3,200 men under Brig.-General Sir Colin Campbell was sent from Peshawar to punish the perpetrators of the outrage. The 2nd Company was included,[5] and the Commander-in-Chief, Major-General Sir Charles Napier, was present. Campbell entered the Kohat

[1]The Punjab Irregular Force, known as the " Piffers," developed from the Corps of Guides raised by Lieut. Harry Lumsden in Dec., 1846. After the annexation of the Punjab, a frontier brigade in the Jullundur *Doab* was moved to the Afghan border and, with the Guides and other formations added, became known as the " Punjab Irregular Force " and later the "Punjab Frontier Force." In 1884, the Punjab Frontier Force consisted of 4 Mountain Batteries, 1 Garrison Battery, 5 regiments of Cavalry, the Corps of Guides, 4 regiments of Sikh Infantry, 6 regiments of Punjab Infantry and 1 regiment of Gurkha Infantry. In April, 1903, while Lieut.-Gen. Sir Bindon Blood was G.O.C. in C., Punjab Command, it was distributed among the Peshawar, Kohat and Derajat Districts.

[2]See *Sketch Map of the North-West Frontier: North of the Kabul River*, included in Chapter XIV.

[3]*Frontier and Overseas Expeditions from India*, Vol. I, pp. 333–343.

[4]*A Brief History of the Royal Bombay Sappers and Miners*, p. 12.

[5]*History and Digest of Service of the 1st K.G.O. Sappers and Miners*, p. 15.

Pass on February 10th. The enemy offered a determined resistance, but they were driven from their positions, and the villages of those concerned in the massacre were destroyed by the Sappers. The top of the pass was reached on the 11th, and two days later, after a severe engagement, the force began to withdraw. Though harassed by the Afridis, it reached Peshawar safely on February 14th, having taught the enemy a very necessary lesson.

On October 14th, 1851, a detachment of Sappers and Miners left Kohat with a force of 2,000 men under Captain J. Coke, B.I., to expel Waziri raiders from the Miranzai territory.[1] Coke marched through Hangu, Togh, Kahi, Nariab, Torawari and Darsamand to Thal, and at Biland Khel, south of Thal, repulsed several night attacks. Otherwise, there was little fighting and the force returned to Kohat on November 12th after restoring order. The Miranzai Expedition of 1851, typical of many others, is mentioned only because it included a few Sappers and Miners. There is no record that any engineering work was executed.

During the cold weather of 1851–52, another and larger expedition in which Sappers and Miners were employed was sent against the Mohmands north-west of Peshawar. A mixed force of about 1,600 men, including the 2nd Company, Bengal S. & M.,[2] under 2nd Lieutenant A. Boulnois, B.E., marched from Peshawar on October 25th, 1851, under the command of Brig.-General Sir Colin Campbell, to punish the Mohmands for numerous raids. Campbell crossed the Kabul River by a boat bridge, and having selected the site for a fort at Michni and demolished ten towers in adjacent villages, moved past Shabkadar northwards to Matta, where he defeated 4,000 Mohmands on December 8th. The building of Michni Fort was soon completed by the Sappers and other troops. On January 15th, 1852, Boulnois fell a victim to a sniper while incautiously approaching a tower some three miles from the fort. In March, the Mohmands issued in force from the barren hills to the north-east and a skirmish took place at Shabkadar. They came down again on April 15th, but were repulsed at Panjpao after a stiff fight in which, however, the Sappers were not concerned. The enemy then dispersed and the troops returned to Peshawar on April 18th. The work of the 2nd Company in the Mohmand Expedition of 1851–52 consisted chiefly of building Michni Fort and demolishing village towers under the direction of Captain J. R. Oldfield, B.E., the Field Engineer.

An expedition of about 2,000 men under Campbell was sent, in March 1852, to coerce the Ranizais, a Swat clan which had attacked a British detachment. No Sappers and Miners took part in this operation and there was no fighting. The Ranizais submitted and promised to pay a fine, and Campbell returned to Peshawar. Within the next two months, however, he was obliged to take the field again to punish the Utman Khel tribe for a raid

[1] *A Record of the Expeditions against the North-West Frontier Tribes*, by Lieut.-Col. W. H. Paget and Lieut. A. H. Mason, p. 437. The company from which the detachment came is not stated. Possibly it was the 2nd Company, Bengal S. & M.

[2] As the strength of the Sappers and Miners was only 1 B.O., 2 I.O.s, 1 B.N.C.O. and 34 I.O.R.s, it is possible that the entire 2nd Company was not present. (See Paget and Mason, p. 266.)

on Charsadda, an important village on the Kabul River, north-east of Peshawar. Marching from Abazai on May 11th with a small force including the 2nd Company, Bengal S. & M., he occupied and burnt several villages, and on the 13th, stormed the Utman Khel stronghold at Prang Ghar. No sooner had he returned to Peshawar than he was obliged to resume hostilities against the Ranizais because they refused to pay the fine imposed on them. He marched again on May 15th with 3,270 men including the 2nd Company, and three days later, routed 4,500 Ranizais at Sakhakot, south of the Malakand. The Sappers then destroyed Sakhakot, Dargai and other villages, and on May 24th marched back to Peshawar with the infantry, cavalry and guns. Thus, during the early summer of 1852, the 2nd Company saw a good deal of active service across the border against the Ranizais and Utman Khel.[1]

The next expedition in which Sappers and Miners took part was against the Hassanzais, a section of the Isazai clan of Yusufzai Pathans in the Black Mountain region north of Abbottabad. These people had murdered two British officers and accordingly, on December 20th, 1852, a mixed force of about 5,000 regulars and levies, including the 7th Company, Bengal S. & M., was despatched against them from Shergarh, south of Oghi, in three columns. The right column was commanded by Lieut.-Colonel Robert Napier, B.E., and the whole force by Lieut.-Colonel F. Mackeson, B.I., the Commissioner of Peshawar. After the Sappers had rebuilt a fort at Shanglai, west of Shergarh, two of the columns entered the Hassanzai territory by a difficult march over the heights of the Black Mountain. Several strong positions were carried and the force returned across the frontier on January 2nd, 1853, having destroyed many villages and subdued the tribesmen.[2] The Sappers saw little fighting in the Black Mountain expedition of 1852 and had no casualties, but they suffered much from the extreme cold.

The scene now shifts southwards to the mountains of the Takht-i-Sulaiman, where the Shiranis had long been the terror of the Dera Ismail Khan border and had recently attacked a British reconnoitring party. A force of 2,800 men, including a small detachment of Bengal Sappers and Miners,[3] was organized under Brig.-General J. S. Hodgson, commanding the Punjab Irregular Force, and entered the enemy's country on March 31st, 1853. During the next three days, the troops marched unopposed through the Shirani territory, destroying villages and restoring law and order, and then recrossed the border into British India.[4] Afterwards, Hodgson proceeded to deal with the Kasranis beyond the Dera Ghazi Khan border, and in these operations the same Sapper detachment took part.

In 1853, the raids and outrages committed by the Jowaki Afridis of the

[1]Paget and Mason, pp. 198–201 and 215–219.
[2]*Ibid.* pp. 34–41.
[3]*History and Digest of Service of the 1st K.G.O. Sappers and Miners*, p. 17. The unit is not specified.
[4]Paget and Mason, pp. 582–585. Paget makes no mention of the Sapper detachment.

Bori Valley, north-east of Kohat[1], necessitated an expedition against that clan of the Adam Khel. A force of 1,740 men under Colonel S. B. Boileau, late 22nd Foot, moved on November 4th from a camp 15 miles north-east of Kohat, and marching southwards over the Shergasha Pass, entered the Bori Valley, drove the enemy away and burnt their villages. With this force was the redoubtable 2nd Company, Bengal S. & M., now under Ensign A. U. F. Ruxton, B.I. The Sappers were rather "out of the picture" in these operations. The pass was so steep and narrow that orders were given that an elephant battery should be left behind with the reserve. "The Sappers and the materials for blowing up the towers of the Bori villages had been placed with the 9-pounders," writes Paget,[2] "as, in case the force had met with opposition, the mules of the Sapper park would have encumbered the advance up the pass. By some mistake, the order for detaining the 9-pounders and their elephants was not delivered until they had accomplished part of the ascent, and their return down the pass so obstructed the road that Ensign Ruxton, in spite of every exertion, was unable to come up in time. The Sappers were awaited until 11 o'clock, when it was determined to go on withoutt hem and abandon the idea of blowing up the towers." The villages were accordingly burnt by some Khaibar levies under the direction of Lieutenant J. T. Walker, Bo.E., but little damage could be done to the towers. Later in the day, the force left the Bori Valley by the Taruni Pass further east and returned to camp.

It may be interesting to remark that, although the brief operations against the Jowakis in 1853 were hindered by the use of elephants, the lesson that these animals were unsuitable for mountain warfare was not learnt until many years later. They were valuable carriers, but required an excessive amount of forage and presented too large a target to rifle fire. Nevertheless, they were employed frequently in frontier expeditions until 1879, particularly by Brig.-General Neville Chamberlain, who always embodied in his orders instructions that the elephants were to be females and were to have leather pads on which to kneel, and leather shields for their foreheads so that they could demolish walls or push guns up slopes.[3]

A second expedition against the Mohmands became necessary in 1854—on this occasion against those near Michni—and a force of 1,780 men under Lieut.-Colonel S. J. Cotton, 10th Foot, including the 2nd Company, Bengal S. & M., under Ruxton,[4] assembled at Michni on August 30th and moved up the Kabul River at dawn on the 31st towards Shah Mansur Khel. This village and two others were occupied, and the towers blown up by the Sappers under the direction of Lieutenant H. Hyde, B.E. The timber of the houses was burnt after the walls had been pushed down by elephants. The troops then returned to Peshawar; but notwithstanding

[1]See *Sketch Map of the North-West Frontier : South of the Kabul River*, included in Chapter XIV.

[2]Paget and Mason, p. 333.

[3]Paget and Mason, p. 653.

[4]Strength, 1 B.O., 2 I.O.s and 48 I.O.R.S (see Paget and Mason, p. 268).

the destruction of the villages near Michni, the Mohmands continued to give trouble throughout the following year.[1]

On the Kohat border, the Miranzai villagers had remained hostile to the British in spite of the operations undertaken in 1851, and in 1855, supported by Zaimukhts, Turis and Waziris, they refused to pay revenue. Such defiance could not be permitted, so a force of about 3,760 men, under Brig.-General Neville Chamberlain, was despatched from Kohat on April 4th, 1855, and reached Togh on the 7th. With it was a detachment of Bengal Sappers, probably from the 2nd Company.[2] The column followed the route taken in 1851 and arrived at Darsamand on the 28th. There, on the 30th, it repulsed a furious assault by 1,500 tribesmen; but otherwise there was little fighting, and by May 21st it was back in Kohat having apparently subdued the Zaimukhts and Turis and restored order in the Miranzai territory.[3]

The Zaimukhts and Turis, however, had not actually been brought to order and it became necessary during the following year to send another expedition to the Miranzai country to punish the Turis for raids into British territory and to deal with the Zaimukhts, who had seized the village of Torawari. Accordingly, a force of nearly 5,000 men under Brig.-General Chamberlain, including the 2nd Company, Bengal S. & M., under Lieutenant A. W. Garnett, B.E.[4] was despatched from Kohat on October 21st, 1856, and moved by the usual route through Hangu, Togh and Kahi to Nariab, the Sappers improving the road where required. On the morning of the 25th, Chamberlain took Torawari by surprise and subdued the Zaimukhts. Then he advanced into the Kurram Valley, and marching up the Kurram River through Sadda to Kurram Fort, some 7 miles from the modern station of Parachinar, effected a settlement with the Turis. After a personal reconnaissance into Afghanistan through the Peiwar Pass, Chamberlain led his force southwards from Kurram Fort, and later eastwards to regain the Kurram Valley, and arrived at Thal on November 28th. There he remained for several weeks while detachments were engaged in small punitive operations, and consequently the force did not reach Kohat until the end of December.[5] The Miranzai expeditions of 1855 and 1856 provided little work, but much marching, for the Sappers and Miners.

The last frontier expedition in which Sappers and Miners were engaged before the Indian Mutiny was against the Bozdars, a tribe of the Dera Ghazi Khan border, far down the Indus, who had raided British territory for several years. On March 5th, 1857, a force of 2,750 men under Brig.-General Chamberlain marched from Taunsa, 40 miles north of Dera Ghazi Khan, and entered the Bozdar country by a convenient pass. The enemy held a defile with 1,700 men, but Chamberlain forced their position on March 7th and the Bozdars fled. For the next fortnight, the British force traversed the country in various directions, destroying villages and

[1]Paget and Mason, pp. 240–244.
[2]Strength, 3 I.O.s and 33 I.O.R.s (see Paget and Mason, p. 455).
[3]Paget and Mason, pp. 438–442.
[4]Strength, 1 B.O., 2 I.O.s and 40 I.O.R.s (see Paget and Mason, p. 457).
[5]Paget and Mason, pp. 442–451.

seizing grain, and eventually the Bozdars tendered their submission and the troops were withdrawn to Taunsa on March 23rd.[1] Although this small expedition was of little importance, it has a particular interest because the force included a unit called the "1st Company, Punjab Sappers and Miners," belonging apparently to the Punjab Irregular Force and comprising 58 men. This formation seems to have had no British officers and was commanded during the expedition by Lieutenant J. G. Medley, B.E., the Field Engineer to the force, who was then stationed at Dera Ghazi Khan in charge of the defences of the frontier posts.[2] The Punjab Irregular Force is supposed to have had no Sappers and Miners on its establishment. Here, then, is proof to the contrary, although the Punjab Sappers and Miners—consisting presumably of more than one company—do not appear in the Army Lists of the period.

It will be seen that, from 1849 to 1857, small bodies of Sappers and Miners served in no less than twelve expeditions on the North-West Frontier, the most favoured unit being the 2nd Company of the Bengal Corps; yet in no expedition did the detachments concerned suffer more than one or two casualties and usually none whatever. The inference is that the Sappers were kept always with the reserve. They had received little training in musketry and were still regarded as artisans rather than soldiers. In the official despatches of some expeditions in which they took part—for instance, that against the Shiranis in 1853—they are not even included in the detail of the troops present. Their services were not required in the front line because the tribesmen in those days were poorly armed and relied chiefly on shock tactics with the sword. Hence, the Sappers were kept in the background to prepare the track for elephant and mule transport, and when all was over, they were brought forward with charges of black powder to demolish village towers. Despite an excellent reputation earned in the Afghan and Sikh wars, they were employed in the early frontier expeditions as mere labourers and lictors to the British *Raj* and had small prospect of honour or reward.

There was a lull on most of the North-West Frontier during the Indian Mutiny, the only people who gave any serious trouble being the sect of bigoted Muhammadans known as the "Hindustani Fanatics," founded in 1823 by a saintly adventurer named Said Ahmad. These folk had settled among the Khudu Khel at Sittana, near the Black Mountain region on the Upper Indus, and in 1857 began to instigate a religious war against the Government.[3] Minor operations having failed to subdue them, an expedition was despatched from Nowshera on April 22nd, 1858, the force employed being 4,877 men under Major-General Sir Sydney J. Cotton. Included in this force was the 5th Company and part of the 6th Company, Bengal S. & M.,[4] under Captain H. Hyde, B.E. These Sappers had

[1]Paget and Mason, pp. 604–613.

[2]See Chapter VIII and also *A Year's Campaigning in India*, by Capt. J. G. Medley B.E., p. 6. *et seq.*

[3]The history of the Hindustani Fanatics is given in an article by Capt. A. H. Mason, R.E., appearing in the *Journal of the United Service Institution of India*, Vol. XIX, 1890, pp. 182–200.

[4]100 men and 47 men respectively.

remained loyal to Government and had been employed in strengthening the forts at Peshawar and Attock. A party of 36 Indian ranks of the 5th Company, under Lieutenant P. Murray, B.E., had marched from Attock on May 16th, 1857, to join Nicholson's column *en route* for Delhi,[1] but most of them had been disarmed at Ambala and sent back to Attock. Cotton crossed the frontier on April 26th, and operating in three columns, captured and destroyed the Khudu Khel strongholds at Panjtar, Chingalai and Mangal Thana, west of Sittana.[2] At Mangal Thana, the Sappers were engaged all night in mining the buildings, and the demolition on April 30th was most effective. Sittana itself, where the main colony of the Hindustani Fanatics was located, was taken on May 4th, and after the Sappers had destroyed the towers and buildings, the force returned to Nowshera.

A very strong expeditionary force marched from Kohat on December 15th, 1859, almost destitute of Sappers and Miners. This was on the occasion of operations undertaken by Brig.-General Neville Chamberlain against the Kabul Khel clan of the Darwesh Khel Waziris, located principally on the right bank of the Kurram River, south of Thal. The Kabul Khel tribesmen were to be punished for sheltering the murderers of a British officer. Though Chamberlain took the field with 5,372 regulars and levies and 13 guns, he had only 15 men[3] of the 4th and 5th Companies, Bengal S. & M., under the command of Captain C. Pollard, B.E.—an absurdly weak contingent for such a force. The main body entered Waziristan on December 22nd, and on the same day, a detached column encountered and defeated the Kabul Khel at Maidani, a hill village 9 miles south-west of Thal. The Waziri encampments were then destroyed and their flocks and herds seized. Chamberlain marched southwards to Spinwam on the Kaitu River, and afterwards, moving eastwards, crossed the Kurram River and dealt with the enemy in the mountains beyond. No resistance was encountered, and by January 14th, 1860, the force was back in Thal.

The next expedition was against the Mahsuds, a much more dangerous Waziri clan than the Kabul Khel. The Mahsuds bore the reputation of being among the fiercest and best fighters, and at the same time the most profoundly treacherous and predatory people, throughout the length and breadth of the frontier. It was said with some justification that the only good Mahsud was a dead one. The greater part of the Mahsud country west of the frontier between Bannu and Tank is rugged, bare and most forbidding. It is intersected in all directions by deep ravines flanked by steep hills and has many narrow gorges or *tangis* which offer ideal sites for ambushes. Far up in the mountains are Kaniguram and Makin, the largest and most important of the Mahsud settlements.[4] These were the chief objectives of an expedition led by Brig.-General Chamberlain, who

[1] See Chapter VIII and also the *History and Digest of Service of the 1st K.G.O. Sappers and Miners*, p. 25.
[2] Paget and Mason, pp. 90–97. See *Sketch Map of the North-West Frontier : North of the Kabul River*, included in Chapter XIV.
[3] Paget and Mason, p. 496.
[4] See *Sketch Map of the North-West Frontier : Waziristan*, included in Chapter XIV.

marched from Tank on April 16th, 1860 with 5,196 men including the 5th Company,[1] Bengal S. & M., commanded by Lieutenant James ("Buster") Browne, B.E. On April 17th, Chamberlain entered the Mahsud country by the huge ravine called the Tank (or Takki) Zam, and during the next few days, advanced up it through Khirgi, Jandola and Palosin Kach to Shingi Kot, a village near Kotkai. Then, returning to Palosin, he reconnoitred up another ravine, the Shahur Zam, passing through Haidari Kach and reaching on April 23rd a point within 14 miles of Kaniguram. Again he retraced his steps to Palosin, where the garrison had meanwhile repulsed a furious assault by 3,000 Mahsuds. The Tank Zam was finally selected as the best route to Kaniguram, and the advance began from Palosin on May 2nd. The enemy offered no resistance at the Ahnai Tangi above Shingi Kot, but held the far more difficult Barari Tangi with 5,000 men, and it was only after a very severe contest on May 4th that their positions were carried. Kaniguram, the Mahsud capital, was reached on May 5th and was found to consist of about 800 houses. The buildings were of stone with flat roofs, and the principal street was roofed in as a protection against snow or rain.

Cold and exposure at a height of 6,700 feet soon caused sickness among the troops, so the Sappers and Pioneers busied themselves in making camel-litters out of native beds to transport the invalids. On May 9th, the force marched back to Dwa Toi, where the Tank Zam bifurcates, and then ascended the northern branch of the ravine to Makin, where the houses had solid stone walls and excellent timber roofs. As the Mahsuds still refused to submit, Makin was set on fire, and by the evening of the 11th the place was a roaring furnace. Lack of supplies now obliged Chamberlain to leave the district. He marched to Razmak, over 7,000 feet above sea-level, where the country resembled the English downs and there were wild flowers in abundance, and continuing thence by the Khaisora route through Razani and Asad Khel, he reached Bannu on May 20th. The Sappers and Miners suffered only one casualty in this strenuous expedition, so it is evident that they were not closely engaged; but there can be little doubt that the experience which they gained of the conditions in Waziristan was useful to the Bengal Corps in subsequent operations in that territory.

Three years later, the 4th and 5th Companies, Bengal S. & M.,[2] under Lieutenant L. H. E. Tucker, B.I., were engaged in the Ambela Campaign, which is described in more detail in *The Military Engineer in India.*[3] This was a critical affair, and the "spectre of Ambela" was not laid for many years afterwards. The object of the expedition was to deal once again, and more effectively, with the Hindustani Fanatics of the Black Mountain region, numbers of whom had returned southwards to Sittana from Malka, whither they had fled in 1858 and had kept the Hazara and

[1]According to Paget and Mason (p. 509) the unit was the 1st Company with a strength of 1 B.O. and 59 I.O.R.s (p. 554), but it is stated in the *History and Digest of Service of the 1st K.G.O. Sappers and Miners* (p. 27) that the unit was the 5th Company. The operations are described in Paget and Mason, pp. 505–527.

[2]Paget and Mason, p. 110. The 4th Company is not mentioned in the *History and Digest of Service of the 1st K.G.O. Sappers and Miners*, p. 27.

[3]*The Military Engineer in India*, by the present author, Vol. I, pp. 425–428.

Yusufzai borders in a state of constant unrest. The force employed comprised about 5,000 men. The main body marched northwards from the neighbourhood of Parmulai (Parmali) on October 20th, 1863, under the able leadership of Brig.-General Sir Neville Chamberlain. Soon, it began to enter and ascend the defile leading to the Ambela or Surkhawai Pass, the Sapper companies, under the direction of Lieutenant James Browne, R.(B.)E.,[1] being engaged in improving the track in the bed of a stream encumbered with boulders and overgrown with jungle. So difficult was the path that the guns had to be loaded on to elephants and the men to march in single file. No transport could accompany the force, and when the troops gained the summit, they had to face a night of cold and misery. The Commanding Engineer, Lieut.-Colonel Alexander Taylor, R.(B.)E., did all he could to get the baggage through, but little of it reached the Ambela *kotal* on the 21st. The amount of baggage was stupendous. " Taylor himself," writes Miss A. C. Taylor,[2] " Spartan though he was, had a following of seventeen servants, six mules and three horses."

Chamberlain camped near the top of the pass and piqueted the heights around, the most important posts being named the " Eagle's Nest " and the " Crag." On the morning of the 22nd, as the rearguard was approaching, arrangements were made for a further advance, and details of the 4th and 5th Companies were sent forward with covering troops to prepare the road. The neighbouring Bunerwals having agreed to remain neutral, Taylor went ahead to reconnoitre ; but no sooner did he begin to retire than the Bunerwals rose and were joined by Swati tribesmen, and Chamberlain found himself practically isolated on the pass and threatened by a really formidable gathering. He could neither advance with safety nor retreat with honour. It was essential that he should strengthen his defences and improve his line of communication so that he might be reinforced quickly and easily, and for these extensive undertakings he needed a strong contingent of engineer troops, which unfortunately was not at his disposal. He had only two weak companies of Sappers and a single battalion of Pioneers.[3]

The Fanatics, Bunerwals and Swatis lost no time in taking the offensive. After an abortive attack on October 25th, they made two desperate though unsuccessful assaults on the Eagle's Nest Piquet on the 26th, and on the night of the 29th–30th they carried the Crag Piquet and were ejected only after a hand-to-hand fight. Meanwhile, the Sappers and Pioneers were preparing an alternative line of communication along the southern spurs from Ambela to Parmulai, where Chamberlain wished to establish a new base. This was dangerous work for they were much exposed to attack, but by November 18th the road was practicable and the camp on the *kotal* was moved to a better position. The Crag Piquet changed hands three times, being lost and retaken for the last time on November 19th.

[1]On April 1st, 1862, the Engineers of the East India Company's armies had been amalgamated with the Royal Engineers. Hence the latters " R.(B.)E." instead of " B.E."

[2]*General Sir Alex Taylor*, by A. C. Taylor, Vol. II, p. 174.

[3]The 32nd Punjab Native Infantry. This Pioneer battalion was reinforced, late in November, by another, the 23rd Punjab Native Infantry.

Chamberlain was severely wounded on that occasion and handed over his command to Major-General J. Garvock when the latter arrived, on November 30th, with reinforcements. Garvock, now with 9,000 men, took the offensive on December 15th. He stormed a peak known as Conical Hill and captured the adjacent village of Lalu. The hostile Bunerwals then submitted, the Swatis vanished, and a small party of British set out with some friendly Bunerwals to destroy Malka. This was accomplished successfully. On December 22nd, Malka was burnt to the ground, thus bringing well merited retribution on the Hindustani Fanatics and ending an exceptionally hard struggle.[1]

The Bengal Sappers and Miners were praised for their road work at Ambela. They certainly acquitted themselves well with tools which are said to have been insufficient in number and poor in quality. Nevertheless, the Ambela Expedition was badly conceived and wrongly organized. General Sir Bindon Blood, who marched over the pass with the Buner Field Force in 1898, informed the author in 1932 that in his opinion many of the unfortunate incidents in 1863 might be accounted for by the lack of a proper complement of Sappers.[2] Only two companies were present—perhaps only detachments of two companies, for they mustered only 73 men all told[3]—and though assisted by a battalion of Pioneers, they were quite inadequate for the defence work and road construction. The experience gained at Ambela emphasized the utter folly of sending a large force into the field without a sufficient establishment of engineer troops.

Some two years after the end of the Ambela Expedition, the 1st and 3rd Companies, Bengal S. & M.,[4] were on service against the Baizais of Swat as part of a force of 4,200 men under Brig.-General H. F. Dunsford. As the Baizais had never settled down since the expedition of 1849 and were a perpetual source of annoyance, a punitive expedition was despatched from Nowshera on January 16th, 1866, and proceeding northwards through Mardan, destroyed Sangau, Khui Barmol and other villages in the Baizai territory.[5] It is recorded that, at Khui Barmol, the chastened villagers themselves unroofed their houses so that the Sappers and elephants could demolish the walls more easily ! The force was broken up on January 22nd and the Sappers and Miners returned to Peshawar.

A more spectacular parade of military strength was made in 1868, when an expedition was sent against the Akazais, Hassanzais and other clans of the Black Mountain region who, with the assistance of many of the Swati clans, had raided a number of villages in British territory. It was decided to gather the necessary troops from distant stations in or beyond the Punjab, and consequently most of the units had to make long and forced marches to reach Hazara. The 2nd and 7th Companies, Bengal S. & M., under Lieutenant M. S. Bell, R.E., with Lieutenants H. H. Murphy, R.E.,

[1]The operations are described in detail in Paget and Mason, pp. 102–153.
[2]Notes by Gen. Sir Bindon Blood, G.C.B., Col.-Commandant, R.E., sent to the author on Feb. 17th, 1932.
[3]1 B.O., 1 I.O. and 71 I.O.R.s (see Paget and Mason, p. 166).
[4]1 B.O., 2 I.O.s, 4 B.N.C.O.s and 103 I.O.R.s (see Paget and Mason, p. 209).
[5]Paget and Mason, pp. 192, 193.

and W. B. Holmes, R.(B.)E., were ordered to join, and starting from Chakrata in the hills near Roorkee on August 27th, reached Abbottabad on September 24th after covering nearly 600 miles in 29 days in the damp heat of the monsoon period.[1] A force of no less than 12,544 men was soon concentrated in Hazara under the command of Major-General A. T. Wilde, and the operations began on October 3rd, 1868, with an advance northwards from Oghi, a place some 45 miles north of Abbottabad.[2] Enemy positions were carried on October 4th and 5th against feeble resistance, and after the operations had been extended eastwards and westwards, the Black Mountain tribes made their submission. Fines were imposed, villages burnt and crops destroyed or seized, and by October 22nd, the force was back at its base.[3]

The Black Mountain Expedition of 1868 was made in overwhelming strength, and as a result, the troops suffered only 34 casualties. There was much road-making for the Sappers and Miners, and Bell had a great deal to say afterwards about deficiencies in equipment and personnel. "All tools were carried on mules by means of rope lashings," he writes.[4] "The ordinary mule pad-saddle was used and much delay and inconvenience followed. The two companies in Hazara could furnish a working party of only two or three sections, a number quite inadequate to perform the work they were called upon to do. They would have failed altogether had not the Field Engineer engaged 250 coolies on high rates of pay to work on the lines of communication. . . . A force of even 8,000 men on hill service should be accompanied by not less than *four* Sapper companies." In 1869, the question of Sapper and Miner equipment began to receive some attention, and in 1871 the Government published a book entitled *Sappers and Miners' Siege Trains and Company Equipments* in which tables of tools were given for general service and hill service, and for cases in which there was a scarcity of transport,[5] but it is extremely doubtful whether these scales of equipment were actually provided. India was not given to rapid reform.

Several years elapsed after the Black Mountain Expedition before the Sappers and Miners were again on active service on the North-West Frontier for it was not until 1877 that they were called upon to take the field—on this occasion against the Jowaki Afridis, north-east of Kohat. It is true that a company of the Bengal Corps, either the 1st or the 3rd, marched southwards from Peshawar on April 17th, 1876, with a small force under Lieut.-Colonel R. G. Rogers, 20th P.N.I., to deal with some recalcitrant Gallai Afridis in the hills south of Fort Mackeson,[6] but this was a trivial affair and there was hardly any fighting. The campaign against the Jowakis was a more serious undertaking and was conducted on a lavish scale. The Jowakis had committed a long series of outrages since the

[1] *History and Digest of Service of the 1st K.G.O. Sappers and Miners*, pp. 29, 30.
[2] See Map III at the end of this volume, and the detailed map in Chapter XIV.
[3] Paget and Mason, pp. 42–65.
[4] "Proposed Organization of Sappers and Miners," by Capt. M. S. Bell, V.C., R.E., appearing in *The R.E. Journal*, Vol. IX, 1879, pp. 54, 55.
[5] "Equipment, Bengal Sappers and Miners," by Capt. E. G. Clayton, R.E., appearing in *The R.E. Journal*, Vol. IX, 1879, p. 78.
[6] Paget and Mason, p. 340.

campaign of 1853 and consequently it was decided to carry out a second invasion of their country around the Bori Valley and to occupy it until they submitted. Two strong columns were therefore detailed to enter the Jowaki hills, one from Kohat under Brig.-General C. P. Keyes and the other from Peshawar under Brig.-General G. C. G. Ross, the whole force amounting to 7,400 men.[1] With the 4,000 men under Ross marched the 2nd and 3rd Companies and a detachment of the 4th Company, Bengal S. & M.[2] Lieutenant H. Dove, R.E., commanded the 2nd Company, Lieutenant E. S. Hill, R.E., the 3rd Company, and Lieutenant J. C. Campbell, R.E., the detachment of the 4th Company which carried field telegraph equipment. The Commanding Royal Engineer to this large expedition was Lieutenant G. W. Bartram, R.E., a subaltern of 9 years' service !

Although the column under Keyes was able to enter the southern Jowaki country from Kohat on November 9th, 1877, that under Ross was delayed by rain and could not leave Peshawar until December 4th. On that day, however, it seized the passes in the Shergasha range and debouched into the Bori Valley and for the next three days the Bengal Sappers were fully occupied in destroying the towers of the Jowaki villages. Afterwards, they converted a native track over the Shergasha Range into a road 8 feet wide and constructed new roads elsewhere, being assisted in these operations by working parties of infantry.[3] Ross marched through the Jowaki territory as far eastwards as Pustawanai (Pastaoni) which he captured on December 31st, and was joined at that place by the Kohat column under Keyes. Captain Bindon Blood, R.E., then arrived from Roorkee to take command of the Sapper and Miner units. Little opposition was encountered during the subsequent operations except on January 15th, 1878, by a detached column in a narrow defile. Towards the end of January, having scoured the country thoroughly, the troops began to withdraw, and the movement was followed almost immediately by the submission of the Jowakis.

General Sir Bindon Blood gives some interesting and entertaining reminiscences of the later stages of the Jowaki Campaign in which he took part within a few months of his departure to the Zulu War.[4] "When I joined the expedition," he writes,[5] "it had already attacked and occupied Pastaoni, the chief village. In this first advance, several men were wounded

[1]Paget and Mason, p. 655.

[2]3 B.O.s, 4 I.O.s and 194 I.O.R.s (see Paget and Mason, p. 379).

[3]"Narrative of the Jawaki Campaign," by Capt. J. M. Trotter, appearing in the *Journal of the United Service Institution of India*, Vol. VII, 1879, pp. 47–96. This article gives a full account of the campaign. See also Paget and Mason, pp. 348–370, and a Peshawar Field Force Order dated Jan. 3rd, 1878, in the *Corps Order Book*, 1877–78 (at Roorkee), in which a tribute is paid to the work of the Sapper companies.

[4]On April 17th, 1878, Capt. B. Blood, R.E., was ordered to proceed to Calcutta to "conduct the torpedo defence of the Hughli." He reported his departure from Calcutta for England on July 14th, 1878, and was then struck off the strength of the Bengal Sappers and Miners. (See *Corps Order Book*, 1877–78, at Roorkee.) In Feb., 1879, he proceeded from England to South Africa to join the Zulu Field Force and did not rejoin the Bengal Sappers and Miners until Feb., 1880, when he went to Kabul during the Second Afghan War.

[5]Extract from *Four Score Years and Ten*, by Gen. Sir Bindon Blood, G.C.B., G.C.V.O., Representative Col.-Commandant, R.E., pp. 158–160.

and among them a fine old Sikh havildar. When the General was visiting the wounded he asked the old Sikh if there was any request he wished to make. The old man suggested that he might be granted the medal for the Second Sikh War because he had been present at Chilianwala and badly wounded. The General was rather puzzled at first, but presently it turned out that the old man had served in the Sikh Army *against us!*" The story of a similar claim after the Mohmand Campaign of 1908 comes from Brig.-General W. E. R. Dickson who writes:—[1] "One of our companies took some trouble to look after an old Pathan woman who had been left behind, sick, in a vacated village. She recovered and was restored to her people. Some time later a Pathan came to Peshawar with a young lad and said that he wanted to show his gratitude for the care taken of his mother by enlisting his son in the Sappers. When the medals for the campaign were being distributed, the lad, then a recruit, complained to me that he had not got one although he had taken part in the fighting. It did not seem to occur to him that it mattered which side he was on!"

Sir Bindon Blood continues:—"A day or two after I arrived at Pastaoni we advanced again taking with us, as an experiment, some elephants carrying 7 cwt. horse artillery guns and equipment on their backs. They were taken only a short distance over a road which had been improved and were then sent back as the loads were much too heavy. From Pastaoni we were ordered to march through the hills to Kohat, about 40 miles, and then back to the standing camp (near Fort Mackeson). On the way we halted for several days in a valley with many villages and were ordered to destroy the towers. This we did with black blasting powder and Bickford's fuse. I learnt afterwards that these towers were no part of the defences but merely places of safety in which the owners could sleep comfortably without fear of having their throats cut. We reached Kohat and next day marched some 25 miles to the standing camp and thence a few days later to Peshawar as the Jowakis had sued for peace."

A novel feature of the Jowaki Campaign of 1877–78 was the field telegraph operated by the detachment of the 4th Company, Bengal S. & M. Colonel J. C. Campbell, late R.E., writes:—[2] "I joined from Roorkee bringing with me a 'Receiving and Sending set.' This had been made from wood and zinc by Captain J. W. Savage, R.E., probably from a description in the *Scientific American* by Graham Bell, and we used it between Peshawar and Shergasha prior to the campaign and afterwards. I regard this as the first case of the use of such apparatus in war. Whether the line went on into Jowaki territory I do not know."

This raises the question of the extent to which the Sappers and Miners were connected with and responsible for the general development of military telegraphy and other signalling in India, a matter on which a volume might be written. A brief précis must suffice here. The Sappers and Miners were first employed on line telegraph work in 1869. A year

[1]Notes by Brig.-Gen. W. E. R. Dickson, C.M.G., C.I.E., late R.E., sent to the author on May 20th, 1937.

[2]Notes by Col. J. C. Campbell, late R.E., sent to the author on March 26th, 1934.

later, the Bengal Sappers built a line from Rawalpindi to Kohat and in 1871 another from Dera Ismail Khan to Bannu. Indian Signal personnel were first employed on active service in 1874 when Captain E. W. Begbie, M.I., of the Madras Sappers and Miners, joined the Duffla Expedition[1] with two men for signal duties and established four visual stations. The Bengal Corps, as just related, provided a field telegraph for the Jowaki Expedition of 1877–78. The 6th Company of the same Corps was employed on field telegraphy under Lieutenant W. F. H. Stafford, R.E., during the Second Afghan War of 1878–80, and a Telegraph Section of "E" Company, Madras S. & M., served in the Egyptian Campaign of 1882. In 1885, Telegraph Sections (each of about 45 men) were formed in the "A" Companies of all three Corps, and a Madras section under Lieutenant F. Glanville, R.E., served under Lieut.-Colonel Begbie, Director of Signalling, in the Third Burma War of 1885–87. A Telegraph Section of the Bengal Corps under Lieutenant C. C. Perceval, R.E., formed part of the Hazara Field Force in September, 1888, and in 1889–92 a Section of the Bombay Corps operated in the Chin-Lushai country. In January, 1890 the Indian Telegraph Department assumed responsibility for military telegraphy in India, though the Sappers and Miners retained the necessary personnel for their Telegraph Sections, some of the men being trained by the Telegraph Department. A small Telegraph Section of the Madras Corps under Lieutenant G. D. Close, R.E., was employed with the Hazara Field Force in 1891, and a Section of the Bombay Corps, and part of a Section of the Bengal Corps, served with the Miranzai Expeditions of that year. In 1894–95 a Section of the Bombay Corps was on service in Waziristan, and in 1895 a Section of the Bengal Corps under Lieutenant R. H. Macdonald, R.E., was with the Chitral Relief Force. A section of the Bombay Corps served in the Tirah in 1897, and one of the Madras Corps under Lieutenant W. Robertson, R.E., accompanied the Buner Field Force. During the Third China War, a Madras Section was in the field under Lieutenant S. G. Loch, R.E., and also a Bengal Section under Lieutenant F. W. Brunner, R.E., and from 1902 to 1905 a Section of the Bombay Corps served in the Aden Hinterland and Somaliland. From 1901 to 1911 the Sapper and Miner Telegraph Sections were employed frequently on staff rides and manœuvres. In December, 1908, an improvised "Communication Company" was attached to the Meerut Division on manœuvres.[2] This unit was organized and commanded by Major (later Major-General) S. H. Powell, R.E., of the Bengal Sappers and Miners, to whom much of the credit is due for the subsequent creation of a proper Signal Service in India. The company had an establishment of about 212 officers and men and comprised a Divisional Headquarters Section, three Brigade Sections and a Telegraph Section, the

[1]See Chapter XV.

[2]It may be remarked that a similar unit made a brief appearance in Southern India under the auspices of the Madras Sappers and Miners. Maj. M. Rawlence, D.S.O., R.E. (retd.) wrote as follows on March 3rd, 1938 :—" In the cold weather of 1908–09 an improvised Signal Company was formed for the Bangalore Brigade manœuvres by Capt. R. G. Earle, R.E., and I was attached to it."

last being under Lieutenant H. W. Tomlinson, R.E. In 1911 the Sapper and Miner Telegraph Sections were absorbed into the Indian Signal Corps, and from that date line telegraphy may be said to have passed out of the hands of the Sappers though a slender connection was maintained with wireless telegraphy for another year at Roorkee. This bald recital of the services of the Sappers and Miners as military telegraphists and signallers in war is enough to show that the beginning made by them in the Jowaki Campaign of 1877–78 had far reaching results.[1]

From the beginning of the Second Afghan War the Afridis around the Khaibar Pass began to give trouble, the worst offenders being the Zakka Khel of the Bazar and Bara Valleys, so an expedition was planned against that clan and two columns totalling 2,500 men converged on the Bazar Valley from Jamrud and Dakka on December 19th, 1878. Lieut.-General F. F. Maude, V.C., in chief command, was with the Jamrud column, while the Dakka column was led by Brig.-General J. A. Tytler, V.C. The 8th Company, Bengal S. & M., (only 41 bayonets)[2] under Lieutenant H. P. Leach, R.E., marched with the force from Dakka. On the 20th the columns came into communication between Chora and China in the Bazar Valley west of Jamrud,[3] and on the following day the Jamrud column occupied China, the most important village of the Zakka Khel. Maude then returned to Ali Masjid and Tytler to Dakka after the Sappers had destroyed several village towers. When half way to Dakka, Tytler was hotly assailed in a pass, but the Sappers and some infantry eased the situation by capturing an Afridi position overlooking the road and after further fighting the pass was negotiated successfully and the column reached Dakka on the 22nd.[4]

The Zakka Khel, however, continued to interfere with the traffic to Afghanistan through the Khaibar and consequently a second expedition under Maude was sent against them early in 1879 consisting of 3,750 men in three columns. With a column from Jamrud under Maude himself was a detachment of 55 men of "E" Company, Madras S. & M., under Captain F. H. Winterbotham, M.I.:[5] with another from Ali Masjid under Brig.-General F. E. Appleyard was a detachment of 31 men of "B" Company of the same Corps under Lieutenant W. D. Conner, R.E., and with a third from Basawal under Brig.-General Tytler the 8th Company, Bengal S. & M. (43 men) under Lieutenant H. P. Leach, R.E. The Jamrud column marched on January 24th and the others on the following day. Destroying many village towers on their way, the Jamrud and Ali Masjid columns seized China on the 26th and were joined in the Bazar Valley by the Basawal column on the 27th. A contemplated extension of the operations into the Bara Valley was abandoned in order to avoid complications with other Afridi clans. On January 31st Lieutenant R. C. Hart, R.E., earned the Victoria Cross for saving the life of a wounded

[1]The information given in these pages was supplied to the author by Maj.-Gen. G. H. Addison, C.B., C.M.G., D.S.O., late R.E., Engineer-in-Chief, India, on April 10th, 1934.
[2]Paget and Mason, p. 294.
[3]See Map III at the end of this volume and the area map in Chapter XIV.
[4]Paget and Mason, pp. 293–300.
[5]*Ibid.*, p. 301.

soldier and three days later the Zakka Khel submitted and the columns withdrew from the Bazar Valley.[1] The second expedition against the Zakka Khel Afridis is noteworthy because the Madras Sappers and Miners encountered almost for the first time the tribesmen of the North-West Frontier.[2] It is said that they did well in a novel form of warfare.

Operations were necessary later against the Zaimukhts living in the hills between the Miranzai and Kurram Valleys beyond Thal because these folk had repeatedly attacked the line of communication of the Kurram Valley Field Force under Major-General Sir Frederick Roberts, V.C. They seemed to have forgotten the lesson taught them by Brig.-General Chamberlain in 1855. Consequently, a force of 3,226 men under Brig.-General Tytler was sent down the Kurram Valley from the Peiwar Pass in November, 1879, and concentrated near Sadda. With it was the 8th Company, Bengal S. & M., under Lieutenant H. P. Leach, R.E., which had been transferred recently from the Peshawar Valley Field Force. Tytler advanced south-eastwards into the Zaimukht territory and then northwards to Zawo, which he captured under heavy fire on December 13th. Afterwards he marched through the country, levying fines and destroying villages, and reached Thal on December 23rd.[3]

When the Afghan War had ended,[4] the Government was free to deal with the incorrigible Mahsuds of Waziristan who, incited from Kabul, had raided the borders during the war and had been a constant source of annoyance since the expedition under Brig.-General Chamberlain in 1860. Accordingly, on April 18th, 1881, a force of 3,662 men under Brig.-General T. G. Kennedy, including the 8th Company, Bengal S. & M. (75 bayonets) under Lieutenant R. V. Phillpotts, R.E., was directed into the Mahsud country from Tank. The 8th Company had marched across the Khattak territory from Togh to Bannu and continuing southwards had joined Kennedy's force at Tank on April 7th.[5] Kennedy reached Jandola on April 23rd and reconnoitred up the Shahur Zam while the Sappers improved the track. By this time the submission of most of the Mahsuds had already been received, but the Nana Khel section still held out and it was against them that the subsequent operations were directed. On April 24th Kennedy was at Haidari Kach and on May 5th at Kaniguram having encountered little opposition except on May 3rd when he repulsed a furious attack at Shah Alam Raghza, north of Torwam. A Reserve Brigade of 3,700 men under Brig.-General J. J. H. Gordon, including the 6th Company, Bengal S. & M. (124 bayonets) under Lieutenant W. F. H. Stafford, R.E., with Lieutenant J. A. Tanner, R.E., now started from Bannu *en route* for Razmak by the Khaisora route to co-operate with the column from Tank. The company had left Roorkee on March 20th

[1]Paget and Mason, pp. 300–308.
[2]The only previous occasion was when 30 Indian other ranks marched through Afghanistan in 1842 during the First Afghan War. (See Chapter VI.)
[3]Paget and Mason, pp. 417–427.
[4]Minor expeditions forming part of the operations of the Second Afghan War, such as the expedition against the Mohmands in Jan., 1880, in which a detachment of "C" Company, Madras S. & M., served, are dealt with in Chapter X.
[5]*The Mahsud-Waziri Expedition of* 1881 (official), p. 26.

to join Gordon's brigade.[1] Gordon reached Razmak on May 9th and made contact with the Tank force which was then at Makin. The 8th Company was transferred to Gordon's brigade, and shortly afterwards, as the Nana Khel Mahsuds had submitted, the troops retired to British territory, Kennedy by the Tank Zam route through Dwa Toi and Jandola to Tank and Gordon by the Khaisora route to Bannu.[2] The 6th Company soon marched from Bannu for Roorkee and reached headquarters on June 7th, followed in due course by the 8th Company. The work of these two units in Waziristan in 1881 was mostly road improvement and the demolition of towers. They suffered no casualties because they saw little fighting. The second Waziri expedition was a compromise between the former and objectionable practice of making a mere punitive raid and the modern and more effective procedure of occupying the country until security for good behaviour is forthcoming.

The next expedition in which Sappers and Miners were engaged was a small affair in Baluchistan where certain tribes had perpetrated many outrages. A Zhob Valley Field Force of 4,761 men under Brig.-General Sir O. V. Tanner advanced from the Thal-Chotiali area west of Dera Ghazi Khan early in October, 1884, and camped at Dulai near Loralai.[3] The force then moved on Kila Saifulla near which there was a skirmish on October 24th. On the 26th the towers of Kila Saifulla and of adjacent villages were blown up, and the brief campaign ended in the middle of November with minor operations eastwards to Murgha Kibzai resulting in the complete submission of the offenders.[4] The Sapper units present were the 4th Company, Bengal S. & M., under Captain E. W. Cotter with Lieutenant R. D. Petrie, R.E., and the 10th Company under Lieutenant C. Maxwell with Lieutenant F. H. Horniblow, R.E. Until August these companies had been employed on the Harnai Road, whence they had proceeded to Quetta. They marched together to Thal-Chotiali and onwards to the advanced base at Dulai. There they separated, the 10th Company going to the Zhob Valley to destroy towers and the 4th Company remaining at Dulai to build a fort.[5] At the end of November, 1884, both units marched to Sibi and in December, returned to Roorkee by rail. This was the last expedition in which the rank and file served as " Sepoys." Twelve months later they became " Sappers."[6]

In 1888 Major-General J. W. McQueen led an expedition of 9,400 men against the Hassanzais, Akazais, Pariari Saids and Tikaris of the Black Mountain to punish them for the murder of two British officers. The Hazara Field Force, as it was called, was organized in two brigades, each of two columns, the 1st, 2nd and 3rd Columns assembling at Oghi on October 1st and the 4th Column at Darband. The 3rd Company, Bengal S. & M., under Captain P. T. Buston with Lieutenants J. R. L.

[1] *History and Digest of Service of the 1st K.G.O. Sappers and Miners*, pp. 37, 39.
[2] Paget and Mason, pp. 543–552, gives a detailed account of the operations.
[3] See Map III at the end of this volume.
[4] *Frontier and Overseas Expeditions from India*, Vol. III, pp. 191–202.
[5] " Field Works executed during the Zhob Valley Expedition," by Capt. E. W. Cotter, R.E., appearing in *The R.E. Journal*, Vol. XV, 1885, pp. 73–75.
[6] I.A.C. No. 174 dated Dec. 16th, 1885.

Macdonald and A. J. Huleatt, R.E., and a Telegraph Section of the same Corps under Lieutenant C. C. Perceval, R.E., were detailed to join the force, the former (strength, 155 men) being divided between the 1st and 3rd Columns and the latter posted to the 4th Column. Buston had learnt much from his previous experience in the Second Afghan War. "I took care to see that the mule loads were accurately weighted," he remarks,[1] "and during the whole of the expedition I had hardly any mules with sore backs." On October 2nd, 1888, the 4th Column moved up the left bank of the Indus from Darband and thence to Kotkai which was captured on the 4th after an attack had been repulsed. The advance was resumed later and on the 13th the 4th Column crossed the river and destroyed Maidan, near Palosai (Palosi), a few miles upstream. The other three columns, marching north-westwards from Oghi into mountainous country, began their operations on October 4th. They encountered little resistance and reached the summit of the Black Mountain on the 5th. The Sappers and the infantry working parties assisting them laboured hard to make the mountain tracks passable for the pack artillery and transport and had often to work under fire from tribesmen concealed among the trees. The important village of Siri in the heart of the Black Mountain ranges, and other villages around it, were occupied and burnt, and by October 13th the first phase of the operations had ended. The Akazais submitted on the 19th and soon afterwards the Hassanzais. McQueen then marched northwards and on October 24th entered the territory of the Pariari Saids. This incursion was followed by operations still further north against the Tikaris of the Allai country beyond the Ghorapar Pass, and after these had ended with the occupation of Pokal on November 3rd the troops withdrew to British territory.[2] The Government, however, had no idea of relinquishing its hold on the Black Mountain and in 1890 ordered the construction of several roads in that area. This scheme was opposed by the Hassanzais and Akazais and resulted in further operations which will be described later. The ascent to the Ghorapar Pass on November 2nd, 1888, was so difficult that after the 3rd Company and Pioneers had worked all day to improve the track, the baggage took twelve hours to cover the last mile and fourteen mules fell over the precipice. This will give some idea of the task allotted to the Sappers and Miners.

We return now to the Zhob Valley in Northern Baluchistan, the scene of fighting in 1884, where the 1st Company, Bombay S. & M.,under Lieutenant W. A. Liddell, R.E., with 2nd Lieutenants E. H. de V. Atkinson and R. E. Greer, R.E. (attached), was on service in 1890. The company (123 men) left Quetta on September 28th with a Zhob Valley Field Force of 2,500 men commanded by Major-General Sir George White, V.C., and accompanied by Sir Robert Sandeman, the British Agent in Baluchistan. The force concentrated at Hindubagh,[3] and afterwards, in two

[1]Notes by Brig.-Gen. P. T. Buston, C.B., C.M.G., D.S.O., late R.E., sent to the author on Sept. 2nd, 1937.

[2]The operations are described in *Expedition against the Black Mountain Tribes by a Force under Major-General J. W. McQueen, C.B., A.D.C., in* 1888 (official), by Capt. A. H. Mason, R.E., and in *Frontier and Overseas Expeditions from India*, Vol. I, pp. 145–169.

[3]See Map III at the end of this volume.

columns, each with a detachment of Sappers, explored the almost unknown valleys of the Zoi and Kandar Rivers until it re-assembled at Fort Sandeman (Apozai) on the Zhob River on October 28th. The operations entailed exertions and exposure of an exceptional kind. In co-operation with a column of the Punjab Frontier Force moving down from the Derajat, the Zhob Valley Force next proceeded against the Khidarzai and other sections of the Shiranis inhabiting the slopes of the Takht-i-Sulaiman. These people offered little resistance and the operations ended on December 3rd.[1] The Bombay Sappers were employed continuously on road-making and opened up several difficult passes leading from the Apozai plain into the Punjab.[2] They worked hard and well, as Bombay Sappers always do.

The greater part of the North-West Frontier was in a disturbed state at this time and the early months of 1891 witnessed the despatch of no less than three expeditions, two against the Orakzais west of Kohat and the third against the tribes of the Black Mountain in Hazara, those against the Orakzais being known generally as the "Miranzai Expeditions" because they were largely in the Miranzai country.

The first Miranzai Expedition of 1891 was carried out by a force of about 5,000 men under Brig.-General Sir W. S. A. Lockhart which concentrated at Kohat on January 12th and began its operations in three columns a fortnight later. Included in it was the 5th Company, Bengal S. & M. under Captain H. S. King, R.E., with Lieutenants A. G. Hunter-Weston,[3] G. A. Travers and W. M. Coldstream, R.E., and also a Telegraph Section of the Bombay Corps and part of another of the Bengal Corps.[4] The Commanding Royal Engineer was Major W. T. Shone, R.E. From the neighbourhood of Hangu, the advanced base, the columns traversed the Miranzai country westwards in various directions and crossed the Samana Ridge where posts were established at three points as a protection against further raids. The Orakzais in the Khanki Valley beyond the ridge were punished by the destruction of their village towers, and after the columns had met at Gwada in that valley on January 29th, the troops were withdrawn to Kohat. The opposition encountered was trivial, but the hardships undergone were exceedingly severe for the temperature at night often fell to 20° below freezing point.

A second Miranzai Expedition was soon necessitated by an Orakzai attack on the Samana posts on April 4th, 1891, when most of the ridge fell into the enemy's hands, so Lockhart took the field once more with a powerful force operating from Hangu and Darband, a place to the south of the ridge. The Sapper and Miner units of the first expedition were again

[1]For details of the operations see *Frontier and Overseas Expeditions from India*, Vol. III, pp. 209–228. Though no Bengal Sappers and Miners took part in the expedition, half the 2nd Company marched down the Zhob Valley in April, 1891, with the Commander-in-Chief.

[2]*Digest of the Services of the Bombay Sappers and Miners*, by Maj. G. H. W. O'Sullivan, R.E., p. 60.

[3]Afterwards Lieut.-Gen. Sir Aylmer Hunter-Weston, K.C.B., D.S.O., Col.-Commandant, R.E.

[4]*A Brief History of the Royal Bombay Sappers and Miners*, p. 21, and *History and Digest of Service of the 1st K.G.O. Sappers and Miners*, p. 51.

present. The force advanced against the ridge and after somewhat severe fighting on April 17th and 18th drove the Orakzais away. Further resistance of a spasmodic character was experienced as the columns scoured the country, but by May 16th the tribesmen had been completely subdued and shortly afterwards the Sappers and Miners returned with other troops to Peshawar.[1]

The work of the 5th Company in both the Miranzai expeditions of 1891 was mainly road-making, demolishing towers and fortifying camps and posts. No less than 70 towers were destroyed, and so expert did the Sappers become that on one occasion a small party under Lieutenant E. D. Haggitt, R.E. (Assistant Field Engineer), blew down a tower with 12 lbs. of dynamite within 10 minutes of commencing operations. In the extreme cold of the first expedition the method adopted for thawing the dynamite was to place a cartridge in each hand of every Sapper and make him keep his hands under his opposite armpits until he reached the scene of the proposed demolition.[2] Lieutenant S. H. Powell, R.E. (then an Assistant Field Engineer) states that in the cold of the first expedition the dynamite rarely thawed naturally, but that in the heat of the second it was reduced to a sticky mass, exuding copiously. Despite its dangerous nature in both conditions, it was preferred to guncotton or powder on account of its portability and power. Experience proved that a well tamped charge of 15 lbs. of dynamite or 50 lbs. of powder was sufficient to bring down a tower 15 feet square at the base and 25 to 30 feet high.[3]

The last expedition to be recorded in this chapter was directed in 1891 against the Hassanzais, Akazais and other clans of the Isazai tribe in the Black Mountain territory. Since the expedition of 1888 these people had persistently hindered the construction of roads in their country and had refused to allow British troops to move along the crest of the mountain. Accordingly, an Hazara Field Force of about 7,300 men under Major-General W. K. Elles was concentrated at Darband and Oghi early in March 1891 for the invasion of the district, but mostly at Darband because it was intended that the advance should be up the Indus along which lay the more important Hassanzai and Akazai villages. With the Hazara Field Force was the 4th Company, Bengal S. & M., under Captain F. J. Aylmer, R.E., with Lieutenants T. Fraser, H. R. Stockley and F. F. N. Rees, R.E., and in addition a Pontoon Section of "A" Company of the same Corps under Captain P. T. Buston, R.E., and a small Telegraph detachment (9 men) of the Madras Corps under Lieutenant G. D. Close, R.E., the whole being under Lieut.-Colonel W. L. Greenstreet, R.E., as Commanding

[1]The Miranzai operations in 1891 are described in detail in *Frontier and Overseas Expeditions from India*, Vol. II, pp. 227–247, and in an article entitled "The Miranzai Expeditions, 1891," by Capt. A. H. Mason, D.S.O., R.E., appearing in the *Journal of the Royal United Service Institution*, Vol. XXXVI, 1892, pp. 109–123. See also pp. 124–129 of *Campaigns on the North-West Frontier*, by Capt. H. L. Nevill, D.S.O., R.F.A., a valuable book of reference dealing with all frontier operations from 1849 to 1908 inclusive.

[2]Notes by Lieut.-Col. G. A. Travers, C.M.G., R.E. (retd.), sent to the author on July 25th, 1937.

[3]"The Miranzai Expeditions," by Lieut. S. H. Powell, R.E., appearing in *The R.E. Journal*, Vol. XXI, 1891, pp. 228–230.

Royal Engineer. Though the Engineer Department was assisted by the 32nd Pioneers and a Cooly Corps of 200 men under Lieutenant H. C. I. Birdwood, R.E., it was obviously inadequate for operations conducted by so large a force in extremely mountainous country.

An advance northwards from Darband was made on March 12th, 1891, one column moving up the left bank of the river and another by a route to the east. Road and telegraph construction began at once, but these call for no special notice except to remark that the 4th Company benefited by having proper pack saddles for their equipment mules and consequently did not need to stop frequently to adjust loads. Kotkai was occupied on the evening of the 12th and little opposition was experienced until the 19th when a British outpost a short distance upstream was attacked violently. Small engagements occurred near Palosai (Palosi) on the right bank and later at Kanhar, Diliarai (near Bakrai) and Darbanai on the left bank during a methodical progress up the Indus. In April, after the Second Miranzai Expedition had been launched, the operations were extended eastwards from Bakrai into the heart of the Black Mountain, the base being shifted to Oghi and the river line of communication abandoned. The brief campaign came to an end on April 17th and within the next fortnight the tribesmen made their submission and accepted the terms imposed on them.[1]

Perhaps the most interesting engineering work in the Black Mountain Expedition of 1891 was that performed by Buston on the river and it was also highly important.[2] Brig.-General Buston writes as follows:—[3] "Prior to the expedition, I was sent with a detachment of Bengal Sappers to Attock to get sufficient boats up the Indus to make a bridge above Darband. As there was no road suitable for the transport of pontoons, it was considered that native boats should be employed, so I engaged boats at Attock and hired coolies to tow them up. Several boats were lost in the rapids, and when we arrived at Kotkai on March 12th and the troops came over the mountains and wished to cross, we had only just enough boats for a bridge." The Kotkai bridge, 110 yards in length, was completed on March 16th, and on the 23rd Buston established a flying bridge of two boats at Bakrai, some 3 miles upstream. This resulted in a large gathering of tribesmen at Diliarai on a hill overlooking the bridge and some sharp fighting ensued to gain and retain possession of the hill, but the bridge was well covered and remained in constant use. The Kotkai bridge was dismantled on April 9th and the Bakrai flying bridge a few days later.

Major-General Sir Theodore Fraser records a curious instance of the rapid transmission of news among the natives on the frontier. "While the main body was entrenched on the Palosi plains on the right bank," he

[1]The operations of the Black Mountain Expedition of 1891 are described in *Frontier and Overseas Expeditions from India*, Vol. I, pp. 169–187.

[2]The work of Pontoon Section is described fully in an article by Maj. P. T. Buston, R.E., entitled "Short Account of the Bridging Operations of Bengal Sappers with the Hazara Field Force, 1891," appearing in *Professional Papers of the Corps of Royal Engineers*, Vol. 19, 1893, pp. 147–156.

[3]Notes by Brig.-Gen. P. T. Buston, C.B., C.M.G., D.S.O., late R.E., sent to the author on Sept. 2nd, 1937.

writes,[1] " and Brig.-General Hammond's brigade was in occupation of the heights on the left bank, the 4th Company was working on a road between these heights and the river. One night the company was ordered to camp in a village half way up—a very isolated situation for we had no signalling communication. Aylmer, with his Pathan Jemadar, was considering the best dispositions for the night when the Jemadar suddenly observed some tribesmen on the move a long way off and said ' They will attack us tonight, Sahib.' At dawn a runner arrived with a message from Captain A. H. Mason, R.E., the Intelligence Officer, saying that he hoped that all was well with us but that he had learnt late at night, when he could not communicate with us, that a small *lashkar* had set out to attack us. The attack did not eventuate, possibly owing to Aylmer's skilful dispositions, but some days later our Company Sergeant-Major received a letter from his anxious wife in distant Peshawar, *written on the day after the alarm*, in which she said that there was a rumour in the bazaar that the company, whose peace-time station was Peshawar, had been caught alone and wiped out. So much for ' wireless ' on the frontier in 1891." As Peshawar is 80 miles from the spot where the alarm occurred, the incident is certainly remarkable.

Most of the force was withdrawn from the Black Mountain before the middle of June, 1891, but the 4th Company, which came under Fraser's acting command in September, remained there until November with four battalions of infantry and a battery of artillery although the Pontoon Section had returned to Roorkee on April 22nd. " While we were in summer quarters on the Black Mountain," writes General Fraser, " a certain Pathan sapper got leave to go to his home to settle some family affair. On his return he was asked whether he had had a successful leave. " In truth I did, Sahib," he replied. " I took with me some guncotton, and, having mined under my enemy's house, I blew him up with all his family. A *very* good leave, Sahib ! "

In 1891, the tactics of the tribesmen were changing rapidly. After the Jowaki Expedition of 1877–78 the enemy began to realize that it was certain destruction to stand up against the fire of breech-loading rifles. At Kotkai in 1888 they were literally mown down by the fire of Martini rifles when they tried the old tactics of charging sword in hand, and in the Black Mountain in 1891 they freely announced that it was madness to oppose our troops in the open when exposed to rifle and shell fire. From 1890 onwards the armament of the tribesmen showed a steady improvement and with that improvement they began to prefer long-range fire to shock tactics. This brought about a demand for better protection for British camps and fortified posts, and with that demand a more urgent need for the services of the Sappers and Miners, the experts in such matters. Consequently, it may be said with some justification that after 1890 or 1891 the Sapper and Miner attained at last his rightful position in North-West Frontier warfare ; but it had taken him more than forty years to secure it, years spent in unremitting toil for which others reaped the reward.

[1]Notes by Maj.-Gen. Sir Theodore Fraser, K.C.B., C.S.I., C.M.G., late R.E., sent to the author on Sept. 22nd, 1937.

CHAPTER XIV

FURTHER EXPEDITIONS ON THE NORTH-WEST FRONTIER, 1891–1914

DURING the autumn of 1891, serious disturbances occurred in the remote khanates of Hunza and Nagar in Northern Kashmir which necessitated military operations of an unusual character in a land of glaciers, precipices and raging torrents. A small guard of infantry had been placed at Gilgit, where there was a British Agency, and in September the Government decided to provide a garrison at Chalt on the Hunza River and to improve the road between Gilgit and Chalt.[1] A company of Kashmir State Sappers was stationed at Gilgit, but the men were poorly trained and consequently more expert assistance for an expedition to Hunza and Nagar was sent from India in the form of a small detachment of the 4th Company, Bengal S. & M., under Captain (afterwards Lieut.-General Sir) Fenton J. Aylmer, R.E., who thus started on an adventure which not only made him famous for gallantry in the field but established him as the leading exponent of rapid bridging in the Himalaya. Aylmer was an outstanding personality—courageous, tireless, resourceful and with an intimate understanding of human nature and a ready wit which endeared him to his men. Of Rulya Singh, his fine old Subadar in the 4th Company, he used to say, " He is a good observer with the theodolite or level; but you must know his personal error of the day. I have never known it to be as much as 10 degrees; but whatever it is, it remains constant for the day." There is a good tale of Aylmer and this same Rulya Singh. On one occasion Aylmer showed the Subadar a group photograph of the 4th Company and asked him what he thought of it. The answer " Bahut achha, Sahib! *Bahut* achha!" was so obviously a mere display of politeness that Aylmer enquired what the Subadar thought the picture represented. This, apparently, was a poser. The old man studied the group intently for a long time and at last ventured an opinion. " Perhaps, Sahib," said he, " it may be the sea."[2]

The story of Aylmer's experiences and exploits on the road to Hunza in 1891 is best given in his own words. " The Kashmir Force at Gilgit consisted of three battalions of infantry," he writes,[3] " and the Resident (Lieut.-Colonel A. G. A. Durand) had three or four British officers to help him. There was also a company of Kashmir Sappers, mere coolies of very low caste but with an efficient Kashmiri officer at their head. The mule road to Bunji was being constructed by the firm of Spedding & Co. with half a dozen British assistants and to supervise the work there was an

[1]See Map III at the end of this volume.

[2]Notes by Maj.-Gen. Sir Theodore Fraser, K.C.B., C.S.I., C.M.G., late R.E., sent to the author on Sept. 22nd, 1937.

[3]Notes by Lieut.-Gen. Sir Fenton Aylmer, V.C., K.C.B., Col.-Commandant, R.E., sent to the author on June 17th, 1932.

officer of the Public Works Department. The road was through as far as Bunji and the terrible zigzag ascent from Ramghat to Hattu Pir was being avoided by a new track along the left bank of the Astor River. When I received my orders, there was no time to spare. I hastened to Rawalpindi and got permission to take with me six Sappers from my own company and six from Roorkee who were efficient in boat work. Also, I collected a small amount of equipment, including a long wire rope and traveller for a flying bridge at Bunji and a supply of explosives. After a few days we started for Kashmir, and, joining Colonel Durand and other officers, set out for Gilgit. On arrival at Ramghat after a bad time on the Burzil Pass in heavy snow we found the cantilever bridge in a poor state. It was impossible to repair it as no materials were available, so we dismantled it and used some of the materials to build a winter bridge close to the water. Then we went on to Bunji where I was able to construct a two-boat raft and complete a flying bridge across the 500 feet waterway in ten days.

" On reaching Gilgit," continues Aylmer, " we found the ford dangerously deep and the current very rapid. A trestle bridge was out of the question so I decided to make a stone pier bridge at the ford, where the width was about 500 feet, and for this purpose secured the assistance of one of the Kashmir regiments to carry big stones to the site. Then the work began. From a shore pier a cantilever platform was pushed forward on which two strong men stood as far out as possible. They were kept supplied with boulders which they hurled forward as far as they could, thus gradually forming a second pier. When this appeared above water level, a temporary way was made to it and it was built up to the necessary height and the bay completed. The cantilever platform was then pushed forward again and a third pier made, and by working from both ends the bridge was finished in five days. From Gilgit we marched to Chalt up the Hunza River. The *parri* or precipice below Chalt Fort necessitated a most precarious ascent and descent by a number of zigzags, but by the construction of wooden cradles slung by wire from jumpers driven into the cliff I was able in a couple of days to build a gallery above the stream, thus avoiding the zigzags. A mile above Chalt the track to Nilt crossed the river, and here we built a winter bridge at a spot where there were big rocks in the channel, using timber collected by the local men. The force under Colonel Durand consisted of 3 battalions of Kashmir Infantry, each 500 strong, 2 companies of Gurkhas, 20 men of the 20th Punjab Infantry, 6 men of the Bengal Sappers and Miners and 200 of Spedding's wild Pathans, with two 7-pounder guns of the Hazara Mountain Battery. This force crossed the bridge above Chalt on December 1st and marched next morning towards Nilt, about 10 miles up the left bank, where it halted half a mile from the fort."

The story of the capture of Nilt Fort on December 2nd, 1891, is told in some detail in *The Military Engineer in India*[1] and a more abbreviated version must suffice here. The fort was perched on the top of a high cliff overlooking the river and behind it rose the mountain side. Its stone

[1]*The Military Engineer in India*, by the present author, Vol. I, pp. 436–438.

and timber walls were 14 to 20 feet in height and 8 feet thick. Towers at the angles and in the faces afforded flanking fire. The main gateway was concealed from view in a walled courtyard where it was flanked by a loopholed bastion. A tangle of abattis ran along the edge of a nullah outside the courtyard wall thus blocking the easiest line of approach to the fort. Nilt was reputed to be impregnable, but Aylmer showed that it was not. The troops moved towards the fort, and with three Sappers carrying 12-lb. charges of guncotton and three others with axes, Aylmer advanced at the head of the Gurkha units to blow in the main gate. Accompanied by Sappers Abdulla Khan and Hazara Singh and by Lieutenant G. H. Boisragon with a dozen Gurkhas he climbed out of the nullah under a hot fire and reached the gate of the courtyard. One Gurkha was killed and several wounded; but the others with their *kukris*, and Abdulla Khan with his axe, battered down the gate and the party rushed into the courtyard. While the Gurkhas fired at the loopholes in the covering bastion, Aylmer and the two Sappers dashed across to the main gateway and though subjected to a point blank fusillade from loopholes in the entrance and in the gate itself laid a guncotton charge carried by Hazara Singh. Aylmer was wounded in the leg, but nevertheless he managed to light the fuse before taking cover with the two Sappers. It was soon evident, however, that the fuse had gone out, so he ran back into the entrance, relit the fuse and again took cover though not before one of his hands had been badly crushed by a boulder flung over the wall. The charge exploded and the gate was blown in. This should have been the signal for the storming party to arrive on the scene, but only Lieutenant F. F. Badcock and three of his Gurkhas appeared, so Boisragon went back with a bugler to bring up the remainder and Aylmer and Badcock with their few Sappers and Gurkhas were left before the main gate under a hail of bullets and showers of stones.

The gate was at the outer end of a tunnel or passage through the massive wall, and as it was obvious to Aylmer that the only effective cover was inside the tunnel he determined to enter it although it was still held by the enemy. A Gurkha who looked round the corner of the gateway was shot dead, but by putting his revolver round the corner and emptying it twice down the tunnel Aylmer killed or wounded enough of the defenders to enable him to lead a charge into the dark opening. This he did, and for the next half hour the small party carried on a hand-to-hand fight at the inner end of the tunnel during which two of their number were killed and most of the remainder wounded. Weak from loss of blood, Aylmer at last collapsed. He stated to the author that he had little recollection of what happened afterwards except that Sapper Abdulla Khan carried him back to the nullah outside the Fort and there left him to rejoin the party fighting in the tunnel under Badcock, himself severely wounded. The main body now arrived and the fort was taken. Aylmer and Boisragon were awarded the Victoria Cross and Badcock the Distinguished Service Order though recommended for the higher honour. Sappers Abdulla Khan and Hazara Singh were promoted and awarded the Indian Order of Merit which was granted also to several of the Gurkhas. No decorations could have been better earned.

After the fall of Nilt, the Hunza-Nagar Force rested for nearly three weeks and then advanced and captured the fort at Thol on December 20th, 1891. The flanks of the enemy's position at Thol were protected by glaciers and its front by a steep slope covered with ice. Maiun and Pissan were reached on the 21st, and with the occupation of Hunza and Nagar on the 22nd the " campaign on the roof of the world " came to an end.

Two months elapsed before Aylmer was fit for active work, but meanwhile he tried to solve the problem of maintaining communication by road during the approaching summer when the winter bridges would be washed away. " As all the passes were closed," he writes, " I could obtain no materials from India. Nothing under a clear span of 200 feet seemed to be of the least use and many bridges would have to be much longer. I discovered a few bundles of telegraph wire in Gilgit and a large store of it at Bunji and a solution of my difficulties was thus found though I had to experiment as to the best way to use the wire in making cables for suspension bridges. At first I did not venture to have a span of more than 200 feet, but with the aid of a large rock I was able to construct a suspension bridge at Gilgit with some high crib piers. Fir trees from the mountains formed the uprights. The bridge gave much trouble during the summer because the approaches were not high enough above the flood level which I had been unable to discover. Without Naik Kala Singh of my company, I could not possibly have got through the bridging work. He was the ablest and most ingenious man in the Corps. Once I had chosen a site, made the calculations and started the work, I could leave him to finish any suspension bridge I had to make. From Gilgit I went up to Chalt and threw a suspension bridge of about 200 feet span across the Hunza River near the site of the winter bridge.[1] Meanwhile, the Kashmir Sappers had erected a bridge at Tashot, halfway to Hunza, but as I knew that it could not withstand the floods I selected a site near it for a 250 feet suspension bridge high above the torrent and, materials being very scarce, adopted low uprights and placed the roadway directly on the cables. In April I had to shift the flying bridge at Bunji some five miles upstream to secure smoother water, but the new crossing soon became dangerous and accordingly I decided to bridge the Indus. There was an ideal site for a suspension bridge of about 340 feet span high above flood level and with solid rock at each end. To save materials and weight, the roadway was arranged to rest on the cables for most of the span. In five days we got the materials collected and the cables of telegraph wire constructed and fixed in position, but an attack of fever then laid me low and I was obliged to hand over charge to Kala Singh and spend two months in hospital in Gilgit. Kala Singh completed the bridge within a fortnight of my departure from Bunji. Though due for relief by Lieutenant A. E. Sandbach, R.E., at the end of September, I got leave to start a little earlier to join the

[1]*Winter Bridge.* A temporary structure for use before the melting of the snows and consequent floods.

Isazai Expedition. Captain J. E. Capper, R.E., was then on his way to Gilgit to build permanent bridges at Ramghat and Bunji, which he did with his usual ability."[1]

The Isazai Expedition, which Aylmer joined in 1892, was a brief affair in the Black Mountain region[2] involving little fighting but much sickness. In April of that year the three Isazai clans—the Hassanzais and Akazais and the Madda Khel—had given asylum at Baio to a banished chief and it was necessary to punish them and expel the man. Accordingly, a force of 6,250 men in two brigades with divisional troops was concentrated at Darband on October 1st under the command of Major-General Sir W. S. A. Lockhart and, crossing the Indus at Marer near Kotkai, advanced on Baio during October 5th and 6th, the 1st Brigade from the north-east by Palosai and Walé[3] and the 2nd Brigade from the south-east through Manjakot and Doba. Baio was found to be deserted, so having destroyed its defences the troops withdrew. They reached Darband on the 11th after burning many villages.

The engineer units with the force were the 4th and 6th Companies, Bengal S. & M., under Captains F. J. Aylmer, V.C., and W. A. Cairnes, R.E., and a Pontoon Section of the same Corps under Lieutenant E. H. Bland, R.E. Lieutenant H. R. Stockley, R.E., served under Aylmer in the 4th Company, and others who took part in the expedition, either with the Sappers and Miners or as Field or Assistant Field Engineers, were Lieutenants C. C. Perceval, G. S. Cartwright, A. T. Moore, J. S. Fowler, D. L. Mallaby, A. H. D. Riach and W. M. Coldstream and 2nd Lieutenant R. H. Macdonald. The Commanding Royal Engineer was Major M. C. Barton, R.E., who writes as follows :—[4] " In September, 1892, we were ordered to construct a bridge over the Indus at Marer below Kotkai for operations against the Isazais. The width was stated to be 250 to 300 yards, so the only possible way to make a bridge was to use the boats plying up the Indus and Kabul rivers as had been done in 1888. With the help of Amir Ali of Attock I managed to collect twenty good boats and two hundred boatmen, and the North-Western Railway gave me a number of rails to serve as baulks. Deodar planking for chesses was procured from Peshawar. Cairns brought the materials up with the Pontoon Detachment of 'A' Company, and the bridge was ready when General Lockhart wished to cross the river." Aylmer relates that the 4th Company had some heavy work in making a track towards Baio where Cairnes was ordered to blow up two towers. This he proceeded to do most effectively and economically with small charges of powder, and the first tower subsided with little noise and no spectacular effect. "That is useless," said Sir William Lockhart

[1]Some of the bridges built by Capt. Capper (now Maj.-Gen. Sir John Capper, K.C.B., K.C.V.O., Col.-Commandant, Royal Tank Corps) are described in an article by him entitled " Notes on Suspension Bridges on the Road from Kashmir to Gilgit," appearing in *Professional Papers of the Corps of Royal Engineers*, Vol. 22, 1896, pp. 51–74. These are the Purtap Bridge over the Indus at Bunji (337 feet), the Ramghat Bridge over the Astor River (171 feet) and the Garikot Bridge over the Astor River (162 feet and 81 feet spans).

[2]See *Sketch Map of the North-West Frontier: North of the Kabul River*, included in this chapter.

[3]Walé is a few miles north-east of Baio.

[4]Notes by Col. M. C. Barton, D.S.O., late R.E., sent to the author on Sept. 15th, 1937.

to Aylmer. " The tribesmen are watching for miles around and won't be in the least impressed. Go and blow up the other tower properly." Aylmer did so, using a whole box of guncotton, and a gorgeous explosion followed. Many of the onlookers had narrow escapes, though there were no casualties, but Sir William was delighted and was afterwards always very friendly to Aylmer.

A word must be said here of the character of Major Maurice Barton, the able leader of the engineer contingent in this small expedition. Barton was a strict disciplinarian, a regimental officer of the old school, liked by most and respected by all, whose sayings when Commandant of the Bengal Corps live in the memory of all who knew him. He had little respect for persons or institutions and detested the " boot-slapper." The Staff College, he is reputed to have stated, was " an institution for adding impudence to ignorance ! " " Half the fools in the army," said he, " spend their time in examining the other half," and " A man's knowledge of a language varies inversely with the number of examinations he has passed in it." On a Queen's Birthday parade, after the General had solemnly and dramatically given the caution " The Parade will give three cheers for Her Most Gracious Majesty the Queen Empress of India," Barton passed the following translation to his Bengal Sappers :—" *Jis wakt General Sahib topi uthata, khub shor karo !* " (When the General lifts his hat, make a great noise !)[1] If ever there was a Commandant who lived for his Corps it was Barton. He knew every detail and every man and had little interest in life other than the efficiency, welfare and honour of the Bengal Sappers and Miners.

Within a year of the end of the Isazai Expedition, Aylmer was the victim of a serious accident. Under his command, the 4th Company, with Stockley as subaltern, had been engaged since August, 1893, in making a road from the Kaghan Valley of North-West Kashmir towards Chilas and Gilgit in connection with operations by Sir William Lockhart to suppress a threatened rising. On October 20th a few Sappers were filling a mine with guncotton when the charge exploded. Aylmer, who was sitting on the edge of the cliff within two feet of the mine, had one eye badly damaged and the drum of one ear broken and suffered also a number of minor injuries. One of the Sappers lost a hand and six others were wounded, two of them being blown over the edge of the cliff.[2] Aylmer may have borne a charmed life, but he rarely had a whole skin.

Events at the headquarters of the Bengal Corps at Roorkee late in 1893 are described in *The R.E. Journal*. The Sapper and Miner officers present were Lieut.-Colonel H. P. Leach, Major P. T. Buston, Captains H. E. Tyler, E. St. C. Pemberton and J. R. B. Serjeant and Lieutenants H. J. Sherwood and A. H. Cunningham. Leach had taken over command on June 30th from Colonel Bindon Blood who had been absent for several months in staff employment. Captain G. M. Heath arrived from the Staff

[1]Notes by Brig.-Gen. W. E. R. Dickson, C.M.G., C.I.E., late R.E., sent to the author on May 20th, 1937.

[2]" Station News, Roorkee," appearing in *The R.E. Journal*, Vol. XXIV, 1894, p. 12.

College in December and the Corps had then two Staff College graduates, the other being Pemberton who was also a Russian scholar and a keen explorer of Central Asia and China. The Roorkee Club was said to be flourishing. It had begun an uncertain existence in 1891, moving from bungalow to bungalow and in constant financial straits; but as a Gymkhana Club catering for all amusements, it was at last firmly established and became a fairly popular resort despite a rigid ban on "poodle-faking" in the Sappers and Miners. "The Club House," writes a correspondent,[1] "is a large bungalow which used to be the College Mess, close to the race-course. It has a good dancing-room generally used as a ladies' room, whist and reading rooms, and two or three suites of bedrooms and bathrooms always rented by bachelors. Many of the trees in front have been removed and the jungle cut down, and in their place a broad lawn and rose garden now appear. Major J. Clibborn of the Indian Staff Corps, Principal of the Thomason College, has been the chief mover in all this. The race-course, Buston's hobby, is undergoing improvement." Such was Roorkee more than half a century ago. The race-course was rarely used, and it is sad to relate that the club was closed in May, 1939, after a long and somewhat chequered career. Leach kept the Roorkee Cantonment in apple-pie order, and being determined that the Sappers should be recognized as engineer troops rather than infantry with tools kept them on field works' training throughout the year except when at drill or musketry.[2] They had four elephants, sixty bullocks and scores of mules for their Corps transport. They threw 300 feet suspension bridges across the Ganges Canal at Roorkee and trestle bridges for pilgrims across the Ganges River at Hardwar. They attended an annual Siege Works' Camp at Pur. They dug furiously whenever and wherever possible. The elephants, though maintained nominally to pull the Heavy Artillery guns, were often to be seen in the shafts of huge carts laden with engineer stores and equipment; but when the official eye was shut they were still more often to be found on small game *shikar* in the Ganges *khadir* or "tiger shoots" in the Siwalik Hills. Pig-sticking was the most popular diversion, with duck-shooting a good second. Life at Roorkee, as at Bangalore and Kirkee, was filled to the brim with work and sport, and each Corps had a waiting list of young officers who hoped that some day they might be invited to join.

We return now to the North-West Frontier where, in accordance with a treaty negotiated by Sir Mortimer Durand with the Amir of Afghanistan, the demarcation of the frontier between Afghanistan and India was begun in Southern Waziristan in the autumn of 1894. The Amir had always claimed suzerain rights over Waziristan—an attitude repudiated by the Waziris—but when, with his consent, the marking of a boundary was started by the British from the junction of the Gomal and Kundar rivers, the Mahsud Waziris were so infuriated that they registered their protest against a seeming prelude to annexation by launching a sudden and

[1] "Station News, Roorkee," appearing in *The R.E. Journal*, Vol. XXIV, 1894, p. 30.
[2] Notes by Maj. D. M. Griffith, D.S.O., R.E. (retd.), sent to the author on Nov. 22nd, 1937.

violent assault on the camp of the British Delimitation Commission and its escort near Wana.[1] The assault was made before dawn on November 3rd, 1894, by 3,000 Mahsuds under the Mulla Powindah, a noted firebrand. The escort commanded by Brig.-General A. H. Turner consisted of a squadron of the 1st Punjab Cavalry, the 3rd Mountain Battery, 3 battalions of infantry (3rd Sikhs, 20th Punjab Infantry and 1st Gurkhas) and the 2nd Company, Bengal S. & M., under Captain A. G. Hunter-Weston, R.E., with Lieutenants L. H. Close, W. E. R. Dickson and W. S. Traill, R.E. The Sapper company had come from Rawalpindi after working during the summer on the pipe line of the Murree Water Supply scheme.[2] Political considerations had influenced the selection of the site for the camp which lay below the Inzar Kotal on open ground intersected by nullahs. Its location was a source of great anxiety to Turner who could do no more than strengthen his defences and establish an elaborate cordon of picquets to watch the concealed approaches. The dispositions of this combined civil and military camp amounted in fact to a compromise between the dictates of war and the conveniences of peace and as such were objectionable and even dangerous.

The Mahsuds were quick to seize their opportunity. At 5.30 a.m. on November 3rd the camp was roused by a few shots followed by wild yells and the beating of drums. At the same time, a thousand Mahsuds made a desperate rush from the west on the left flank and left rear of the area held by the Gurkhas. So rapid was this rush that they were into the camp before the Gurkhas could turn out of their tents. The enemy had crept up two nullahs and overwhelming a couple of picquets had charged straight in. Another large body of Mahsuds continued down one of the nullahs and splitting into two parties joined in the main assault on the left flank or broke against the rear-guards further on. Some made their way into the camp behind the hospitals and wrought havoc among the transport animals or freed the cavalry horses in the hope of causing a stampede. All was confusion until the Gurkhas formed a rallying square and fought the Mahsuds hand to hand. Reinforced by other troops, they stemmed the tide, and within half an hour the enemy were in retreat pursued by the cavalry who charged with great effect. The British lost 45 killed including Lieutenant P. J. F. Macaulay, R.E. (a Survey Officer), and in addition, 75 wounded, and the enemy left 350 dead on the field.[3] The Sappers and Miners escaped lightly for they occupied ground near the eastern side of the camp between the Sikhs and the Mountain Battery and consequently did not have to bear the brunt of the first assault from the west.

During the course of a tour of India and Burma in 1936–37, Lieut.-General Sir Aylmer Hunter-Weston revisited the scene of the night-action near Wana and by arrangement with the Chief Political Officer met some nine Mahsuds who had fought against him in 1894. At Kaniguram

[1]See the *Sketch Map of the North-West Frontier : Waziristan*, included in this chapter.
[2]*History and Digest of Service of the 1st K.G.O. Sappers and Miners, p.* 57.
[3]The Mahsud attack at Wana is described in *Frontier and Overseas Expeditions from India*, Vol. II, pp. 416–420, and also in *Campaigns on the North-West Frontier*, by Capt. H. L. Nevill, D.S.O., R.A., pp. 150–154.

the local Waziri chieftains had given a Khattak dance in his honour and had presented him with a couple of knives in gilt scabbards, so he was able to approach his old adversaries in true Mahsud style with one of the knives pushed down inside his collar at the back of his neck.[1] This indicates friendship, for in order to draw the knife a man must raise his hand and thus expose his stomach to a thrust. Friend and foe alike are suspect in Waziristan unless obviously powerless to act treacherously.

The unprovoked outrage near Wana necessitated the despatch of a punitive expedition and accordingly a Waziristan Field Force of three mixed brigades was formed early in December, 1894, under Lieut.-General Sir W. S. A. Lockhart to invade the Mahsud territory simultaneously from three directions. With the 1st Brigade under Brig.-General A. H. Turner at Wana was the 2nd Company, Bengal S. & M., and with the 2nd Brigade under Brig.-General W. Penn Symons at Jandola the 5th Company of the same Corps. Captain Hunter-Weston (O.C. 2nd Company) was in command of all the Sappers and Miners. The 3rd Brigade under Lieut.-Colonel C. C. Egerton near Bannu had no engineer unit. The 5th Company, which joined the force from Peshawar, was commanded by Lieutenant G. A. Travers, R.E., with Lieutenants H. R. Stockley, H. H. Austin and S. H. Sheppard, R.E., as Company Officers. On December 18th the columns were set in motion, the Wana Column on Kaniguram, the Jandola Column on Makin and the Bannu Column on Razmak. Little opposition was encountered. By December 21st all the columns had reached their objectives and on the 22nd the Bannu Column joined the Jandola Column at Makin. During the next few days, small parties scoured the surrounding country and destroyed many villages and towers. On the 31st Egerton led a small force, including a half-company of Sappers, eastwards from Razmak to the Sammal Narai and reached Jandola by a circuitous route on January 8th, 1895. On January 2nd a column under Turner, including a company of Sappers, marched south-eastwards from Kaniguram to Ahmadwam in the Shinkai Valley and after destroying villages around Splitoi joined Egerton at Jandola. Meanwhile, punitive measures had been continued around Kaniguram and the 2nd Brigade with Sir William Lockhart had explored the region near Janjal. Snow now lay thick on the ground and the cold was intense, so the troops withdrew from the higher regions and concentrated at Jandola; but afterwards, as the Mulla Powindah remained defiant in spite of the fact that some 90 towers had been demolished, they resumed their work of scouring the country and seizing cattle, and at length, on January 21st, the Mahsuds submitted. The brief campaign of 1894 in Waziristan is notable as the first in which the Lee-Metford rifle and cordite ammunition were used in frontier warfare.

The Sappers and Miners were required to undertake some exceptionally difficult roadmaking during this expedition in addition to blowing up

[1]Letter from Lieut.-Gen. Sir Aylmer Hunter-Weston, K.C.B., D.S.O., Col.-Commandant, R.E., to Brig.-Gen. Sir James Edmonds, C.B., C.M.G., late R.E., dated March 11th, 1937.

towers and building fortified posts. An interesting account of their experiences is given by Brig.-General H. H. Austin who remarks that guncotton and dynamite were carried for demolitions in preference to gunpowder as being more portable.[1] After the concentration of the whole force at Jandola, the Wana (1st) Brigade was ordered to return to Wana by Tank and the Gomal River route while the Jandola (2nd) Brigade pushed up the Shahur Zam to Kundiwam between Wana and Kaniguram and the Bannu (3rd) Brigade marched to Bannu and thence up the Tochi Valley. As the physical difficulties confronting the Jandola Brigade were known to be great, both the 2nd and 5th Companies were attached to it for road-making and left Jandola for Haidari Kach on January 11th. Much blasting was needed in the cleft of the Shahur Tangi near Jandola, and twenty miles beyond it the road in the bed of the stream narrowed almost to nothing in a gorge where vertical cliffs rose hundreds of feet on either side. An immense rock, firmly jammed between the cliffs, prevented the passage of laden camels, and many of the boulders in the bed of the stream were as big as cottages. The Sappers were obliged to leave the bed and make a diversion up to and across wind-swept heights by which at last they opened a way to Kundiwam, the home of some of the worst *budmashes* in the country.

It was at Kundiwam on January 21st that the final *jirga* was held and the submission of the Mahsud chiefs received, but meanwhile the Sappers had extended the road to Wana, another 13 miles. On January 26th, half the 5th Company returned and began to open up a road down the river bed through the two difficult *tangis* of the Shahur Zam between Kundiwam and Para Khel. The upper one having yielded to extensive blasting, the detachment then proceeded to tackle the lower one in which was the wedged rock. Icy blasts hurtled down the sombre gorge and numbed the Sappers drilling holes in the rock or wading in the frigid water, but in the end the rock was successfully shattered by explosives and when the debris had been cleared away the width between the cliffs was widened to about 8 feet by further blasting so that laden camels could pass up the bed instead of having to use the steep diversion. Both Wana and Kundiwam began to expand into flourishing military stations, but serious trouble in Chitral drew some of the troops away and in February 1895 the 2nd Company, Bengal S. & M., marched to Bannu for work in the Tochi Valley. While the company was at Datta Khel, an officer of the infantry was so ill that the doctors ordered a coffin for him from Miramshah. On its arrival the coffin was placed quietly in readiness under the flap of the sick man's tent. The slight noise awoke the invalid who asked his bearer what was the matter. "*Huzoor ka bokkus agya*" (Your honour's box has come), replied the servant.

The delimitation of the Afghan boundary had already been restarted near Wana by the 5th Company. In April, having been transferred to the

[1] "A Winter in Waziristan," by Brig.-Gen. H. H. Austin, C.B., C.M.G., D.S.O., late R.E., appearing in *The R.E. Journal*, Vol. XLI, 1927, pp. 585–597 and Vol. XLII, 1928, pp. 9–22.

2nd Company, Austin began with the right half-company of that unit the delimitation of the portion of the line up to the Laram Peak north of Miramshah and afterwards built fortified posts at Miramshah, Idak and other places in the Tochi Valley.[1] Meanwhile, the left half of the 2nd Company proceeded to Abbottabad to join an " Immovable Column " for the Chitral Relief Expedition and was sent thence to Murree. The 5th Company was stationed at Wana until the end of 1895 when it returned to Peshawar. Games and sports were started as soon as possible at Wana for the benefit of the troops, and the *mochis* and carpenters of the company were kept busy in making hockey balls and sticks.[2] There were other diversions also. Travers remarks[3] that a number of fighting-cocks were discovered in abandoned villages and that inter-regimental cock-fights became very popular. A novel form of fishing was evolved by the Sappers. A row of men was stationed across a stream using their khaki trousers as eel-pots, the waist portion held open to the current and the ankles tied up. Another party then marched downstream in a row, shouting and splashing, and the fish were driven into the gaping trousers of the trouserless.

As regards the delimitation of the boundary along the Durand Line fixed by Sir Mortimer Durand, Travers writes :—" In the spring of 1895 I was ordered to detail an officer to accompany a party of Waziris to set up temporary boundary pillars of rough stone, so I selected S. H. Sheppard knowing his proclivity for climbing hills. The tribesmen smiled somewhat derisively when they saw a white Sahib, but he walked them off their legs." According to General Sheppard, the Sikh half-company was detailed for the work and the party was led by Major R. A. Wahab, R.E., a Survey officer of immense experience in frontier expeditions, and by a Political officer who was no climber. Wahab was the moving spirit in the undertaking being as active as an ibex and seemingly tireless. The demarcation was begun at Domandi at the junction of the Gomal and Kundar rivers and the pillars or cairns were erected by the Sappers along the crests of the mountain ranges as far northwards as Kwaja Khidr, 25 miles west of Kaniguram. At the end of a fortnight, working 14 hours a day, the men were very fit though very thin. It is presumed that on this occasion even Sheppard, a future Amateur Racquets Champion,[4] had sufficient exercise to satisfy him.

In January, 1895, while the campaign in Waziristan was in progress, an insurrection occurred in Chitral which led to the advance northwards of a large force through Dir and Swat and of a small one from Gilgit. The garrison of Chitral Fort was beset on March 3rd by hostile tribesmen under

[1]The right half of the 2nd Company finally left the Tochi Valley in May, 1896, and proceeded to Rawalpindi.

[2]Notes by Maj.-Gen. S. H. Sheppard, C.B., C.M.G., D.S.O., Col.-Commandant, R.E., sent to the author on Oct. 5th, 1937.

[3]Notes by Lieut.-Col. G. A. Travers, C.M.G., R.E. (retd.), sent to the author on July 25th, 1937.

[4]In 1906, as a Major S. H. Sheppard won the British Amateur Racquets Championship (Singles) in addition to the Army Championship. He had already won the latter in 1903 and proceeded to win it again as a Major-General in 1921 at the age of 51 years.

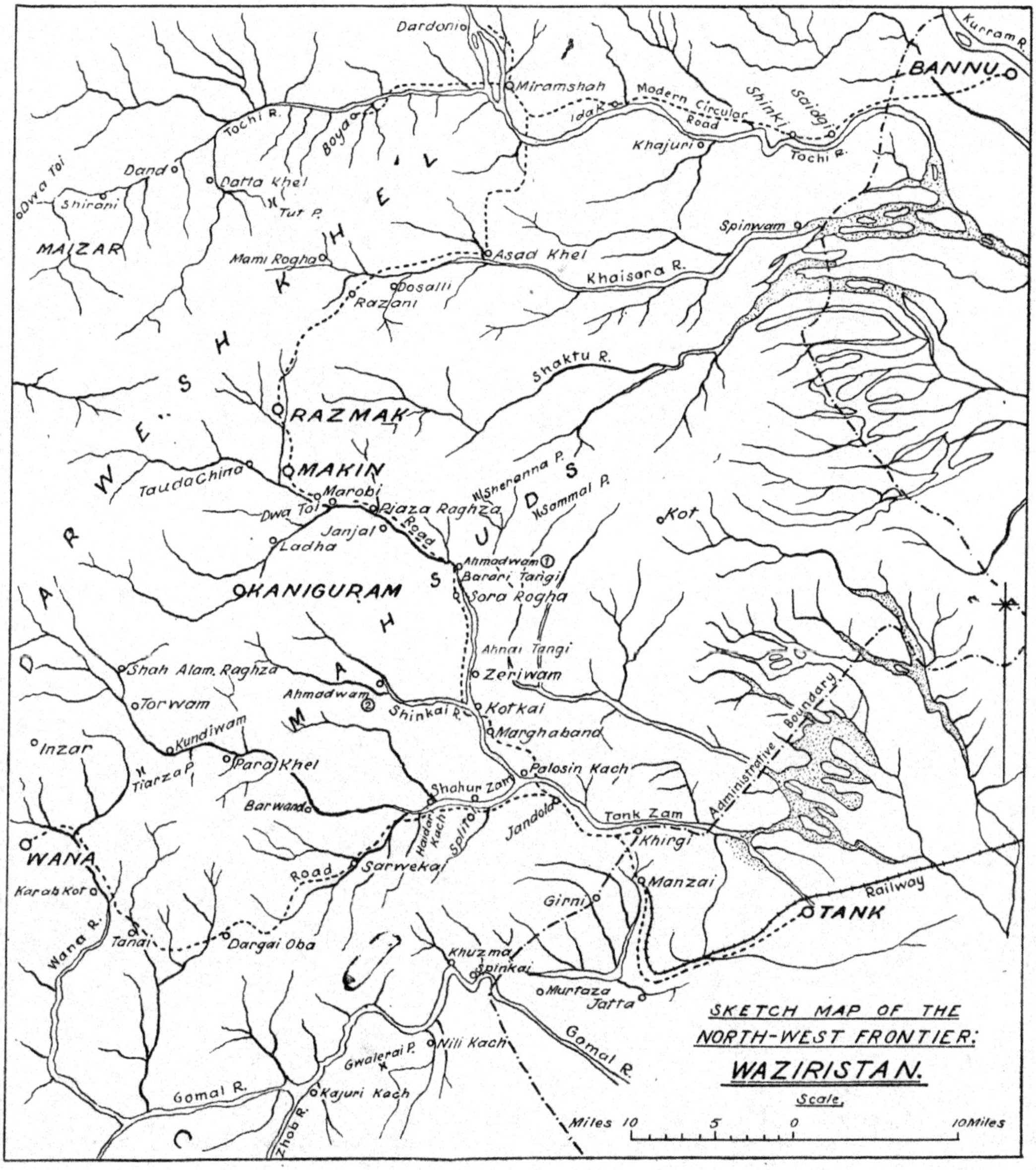
SKETCH MAP OF THE NORTH-WEST FRONTIER:
WAZIRISTAN.
Scale.
Miles 10 5 0 10 Miles
BANNU
Kurram R.
Dardoni
Miramshah
Idak
Modern Circular Road
Shinki
Saidgi
Tochi R.
Khajuri
Spinwam
Khaisora R.
Asad Khel
Boya
Tochi R.
Dand
Datta Khel
Tut P.
Dwa Toi
Shirani
MAIZAR
Mami Rogha
Dosalli
Razani
Shaktu R.
RAZMAK
MAKIN
Tauda China
Marobi
Dwa Toi
Piaza Raghza
Road
Sheranna P.
Sammal P.
Kot
Janjal
Ladha
Ahmadwam ①
Barari Tangi
Sora Rogha
KANIGURAM
Ahnai Tangi
Zeriwam
Shah Alam Raghza
Torwam
Ahmadwam ②
Shinkai R.
Kotkai
Marghaband
Inzar
Kundiwam
Tiarza P.
Para Khel
Palosin Kach
Barwand
Shahur Zam
Haidari Kach
Splitoi
Jandola
Tank Zam
Khirgi
Administrative Boundary
WANA
Karab Kot
Road
Sarwekai
Manzai
Girni
TANK
Railway
Wana R.
Tanai
Dargai Oba
Khuzma
Spinkai
Murtaza
Jatta
Nili Kach
Gomal R.
Gwalerai P.
Kajuri Kach
Gomal R.
Zhob R.
DARWESH KHEL
MAHSUDS

Umra Khan, Chief of Jandol, and the famous siege of Chitral then began. The story of that episode is well known and need not be repeated here for no Sappers and Miners were among the 400 men commanded by Surgeon-Major G. S. Robertson.[1] We are concerned only with the adventures of a detachment of Bengal Sappers and Miners on the march to Chitral from Gilgit, the operations by Lieut.-Colonel J. G. Kelly which resulted in the relief of the beleaguered garrison and those of the main Chitral Relief Force of 15,000 men under Major-General Sir R. C. Low.

A detachment consisting of Jemadar Lal Khan and 19 other ranks of the Bengal Sappers and Miners under Lieutenant J. S. Fowler, R.E., had left Gilgit for Mastuj in February 1895 and passing through that place had joined a party of 42 men of the Kashmir Rifles under Lieutenant S. M. Edwardes at Buni.[2] On March 7th the combined parties were attacked in a defile beyond Reshan and retreated to that village where they occupied and fortified a detached group of houses. On the same day another party, hurrying to their rescue from Mastuj, was nearly overwhelmed in a defile below Koragh and the garrison of Mastuj was besieged. Fowler led a successful sortie at Reshan on March 10th when casualties and sickness had reduced the effective strength to only 34 men. On the 13th the Chitralis became suddenly friendly and on the 15th invited Edwardes and Fowler to witness a polo match close outside the defences, which invitation the British officers decided to accept. " At first," writes Fowler,[3] ' there were few onlookers but by degrees they increased. The game went on for about half an hour and then the players said they proposed to have a dance. Muhammad Issa (in command of the Chitralis) now sat between us on our *charpoy* and the dance began, but men pressed closer and closer to the dancers and to us. Standing up I said to Edwardes that we must go in. Then Muhammad Issa threw himself upon us and a rush of men got us flat on the ground and tied our hands and feet. Our sepoys in the fort fired on the men surrounding us though without effect. A hard fight was going on around our post which the Chitralis had attacked. Gradually the firing grew less and less and men came from the houses carrying dead and wounded and loot. As soon as the fighting was over we were taken up to the village through a crowd of wild Pathans and Chitralis to the headquarters of Muhammad Issa." Twelve Sappers and Miners were killed at or near Reshan and there were three wounded among the party consisting of Fowler, the Jemadar and seven men who were taken prisoners. A quantity of ammunition which the British force had been escorting fell into the enemy's hands. On March 19th the survivors, including Edwardes and some of the Kashmiris, were taken to Chitral where they were well treated. Later they were removed to Drosh and then

[1]The defence of Chitral Fort is described fully in *Chitral. The Story of a Minor Siege*, by Sir G. S. Robertson. See also " Episodes in the defence of Chitral " (anonymous), appearing in *The R.E. Journal*, Vol. XXIX, 1899, pp. 185, 186.

[2]See Map III at the end of this volume.

[3]*Diary of Our Captivity in Chitral*, by Lieut. J. S. Fowler, R.E., pp. 35–37. A copy of this small publication was presented to the author in 1938 by the late Lieut.-Gen. Sir John Fowler, K.C.B., C.M.G., D.S.O., Col.-Commandant, Royal Corps of Signals, the Lieut. J. S. Fowler of 1895.

over the high Lawarai Pass to Dir, arriving there on the 28th. Thence they were moved to Barwa, the stronghold of Umra Khan, and finally to Munda where the Chitralis released Edwardes on April 12th and Fowler on the 16th. Dressed as a Pathan the latter met a party of the 4th Sikhs belonging to the Chitral Relief Force and so his adventures came to an end. Both he and Edwardes were awarded the Distinguished Service Order, and Sappers Nabi Baksh and Chanda Singh and some of Edwardes' men received the Indian Order of Merit. Two other Sappers and Miners—Naik Kala Singh and Sapper Nadir Khan—were to have received the Order of Merit had they not died at Reshan after refusing to surrender. Thus the heroic conduct of a few brave men met with proper recognition.

The operations under Lieut.-Colonel J. G. Kelly, 32nd Pioneers, whose regiment was roadmaking in the Gilgit Agency in March 1895, concern this narrative only because a party of 40 Kashmir Sappers under Lieutenant L. W. S. Oldham, R.E., took part in them. Under orders to attempt the relief of Chitral, Kelly started from Gilgit on March 23rd with about 450 men including the Sappers and after one failure reached with extreme difficulty the top of the Shandur Pass (12,230 feet) and bivouacked there in deep snow on April 3rd. The cold at night was terrible and many of the men were frost-bitten. Nevertheless, Kelly reached Mastuj on April 9th after defeating the enemy at Chokalwat and on the 13th drove them from a formidable position at Nisa Gol. In this action Oldham and a party of his Kashmir Sappers distinguished themselves by some remarkable rock-climbing and contributed greatly to the success of the operations.[1] Marching steadily onwards, Kelly arrived in Chitral on April 20th to find the garrison safe and sound and the besiegers gone. Thus the main expedition under Sir Robert Low was forestalled and its *raison d'être* removed, though its near approach had caused the besiegers of Chitral to withdraw. The operations under Kelly showed that the Kashmir Sappers had courage and daring when properly led. Their attack across a prodigious chasm at Nisa Gol was an exploit which would have done credit to any Alpine regiment.

Soon after Kelly had set out from Gilgit, the main expeditionary force under Major-General Sir Robert Low began to mobilize at Peshawar. It consisted of three infantry brigades with cavalry, artillery and engineers, and Low had as his Chief of Staff Brig.-General Bindon Blood, late R.E., the former Commandant of the Bengal Sappers and Miners. The engineer units under Lieut.-Colonel W. T. Shone, R.E., as Commanding Royal Engineer were the 1st, 4th and 6th Companies of the Bengal Corps, the 1st Company under Captain J. R. B. Serjeant, with Lieutenants W. E. R. Dickson, H. W. Weekes and E. G. Farquharson, R.E., the 4th Company under Captain F. J. Aylmer, V.C., with Lieutenants J. M. C. Colvin, G. Lubbock and H. F. E. Freeland, R.E., and the 6th Company under Captain F. E. G. Skey with Lieutenants G. C. Kemp, R. F. G. Bond and C. O. Halliday, R.E.[2] A Telegraph Section under Lieutenant R. H.

[1] "The Defence and Relief of Chitral," by Lieut. L. W. S. Oldham, R.E., appearing in *The R.E. Journal*, Vol.XXV, 1895, pp. 153–155.
[2] Notes by Col. F. E. G. Skey, late R.E., sent to the author on Nov. 2nd, 1939.

Macdonald, R.E., and Photo-Litho and Printing Sections, were also supplied by the Bengal Corps. In addition, the 6th Company, Madras S. & M., came from Bangalore under Lieutenant C. Ainslie with Lieutenants A. R. Winsloe and W. G. Hibbert and 2nd Lieutenant W. Robertson, R.E.,[1] but it arrived at the front too late to take part in the military operations as did also a Pontoon Detachment of " A " Company, Bengal S. & M., under Captain G. M. Heath, R.E., These late-comers, nevertheless, rendered invaluable service in the engineering work which followed the defeat of the enemy. A very fine Engineer Field Park from Roorkee was of great assistance throughout the operations.[2]

The long road to Chitral was beset with difficulties.[3] Two lofty passes, the Jambatai (7,212 feet) and the Lawarai (10,250 feet) lay on the line of operations and only pack transport was possible. Nearly 31,000 animals were required for that purpose. There were three routes by which Low might advance into Lower Swat—the Malakand, Shakot and Mora passes[4]—all of which were strongly held, and it was decided that the main attack should be on the Malakand assisted by demonstrations against the others. Low advanced from Nowshera on April 1st, 1895, and while the 1st Brigade (Brig.-General A. A. Kinloch) threatened the Shakot Pass and the cavalry the Mora Pass the main body moved from its point of concentration at Jalala to Dargai. On April 3rd, the 2nd Brigade (Brig.-General H. G. Waterfield), supported by the 1st Brigade and with the 3rd Brigade (Brig.-General W. F. Gatacre) in reserve, carried the Malakand position by storm with small loss. This was a most creditable performance for the position was very strong and held by 12,000 Swatis and Bajauris. On the following day the advance was continued down into the Swat Valley, and while the transport streamed up to and over the Malakand Pass by a road opened by the Sappers and Miners the enemy were met and defeated at Khar. During April 5th and 6th, Brig.-General Bindon Blood and other officers reconnoitred for fords across the Swat River so that the cavalry might keep in touch with the retreating enemy. A ford was discovered, and on April 7th, Chakdarra Fort was seized by the infantry after they had waded naked through the river carrying their kits on their heads.

General Sir Bindon Blood writes that no one knew the exact nature of the Malakand Pass prior to the attack.[5] " The effect of the artillery fire," he adds, " was a revelation and our guns prevented any large concentration. The Sappers and Miners were at work pioneering the artillery advance and improving the road behind the infantry attack while it was in progress. The ancient Græco-Buddhists had made a cart road leading through the Malakand, part of which was in existence on the southern side, but it had been overgrown with jungle. Our infantry discovered it in the attack and

[1]*Historical Record of the Q.V.O. Madras Sappers and Miners*, Vol. I, p. 155.
[2]" Station News, Roorkee," appearing in *The R.E. Journal*, Vol. XXV, 1895, p. 270.
[3]A good description of the route appears in *The Story of the Malakand Field Force*, by Winston Churchill, pp. 24, 25.
[4]See *Sketch Map of the North-West Frontier: North of the Kabul River*, included in this chapter.
[5]*Four Score Years and Ten*, by Gen. Sir Bindon Blood, G.C.B., G.C.V.O., Representative Col.-Commandant, R.E., p. 265.

it was quickly put in order." It was at the Malakand that General Bindon Blood first noted the value of concentrated artillery fire in mountain warfare, a lesson which he applied with marked effect in his campaigns across the border in 1897 and 1898.

After the capture of Chakdarra, the Sappers set to work to bridge the Swat River and cavalry patrols were pushed up the Panjkora River which was in flood and impassable for infantry. On the night of April 12th/13th, Aylmer succeeded in getting the Guides across the Panjkora by a footbridge, but this was washed away and the Guides had a hard time in regaining the main body. Aylmer having provided a suspension bridge, the advance was resumed two days later and, except for a show of resistance at Munda, Low encountered no opposition and on May 16th entered Chitral. With this brief outline of the military operations we may turn to the exploits of the Sappers and Miners which did much to bring those operations to a speedy conclusion and earned for the Madras and Bengal Corps the honour " Chitral."[1]

Major H. E. S. Abbott, R.E., a Field Engineer under Colonel Shone, states that owing to heavy rain the advance towards the Malakand over an unmetalled road from Mardan to Dargai was most difficult.[2] The heavy traffic churned up the clay surface into liquid mud so deep that it had to be removed continually to provide even a temporary foothold for the transport camels and draught animals. Describing the attack on the Malakand position, Sir Fenton Aylmer writes :—[3] " I was detailed to find the best path up the mountain. The old Græco-Buddhist road had been most skilfully disguised, but with the aid of one of my Pathans who had been there before I found it and the three Sapper companies were put to work on it. As soon as we had finished the lower half and had started on the upper, two mountain batteries were sent up with the result that the Sappers could not work nor could the batteries get through and consequently there was a delay of many hours. Next day we descended to the Swat Valley and there was some fighting at Khar in which the 4th Company took part as infantry." Abbott records that while the attack was in progress he received many messages from the Sapper companies ahead emphasizing the great difficulties to be overcome before even mule transport could carry up supplies, but he managed to improve the track sufficiently by the liberal use of dynamite. Each explosion loosened masses of rock which, when levered down the *khud*, exposed the remains of the Græco-Buddhist road, and thus within the next three days the ancient thoroughfare was made passable for camel transport. It was improved later, with the aid of the 32nd Pioneers and native labourers, until it was a good road with a ruling gradient of 1 in 12 and a width of 8 feet. Subsequently, Abbott started the construction of a properly graded road over the pass from Dargai to Khar with a width of 10 feet and a ruling gradient of 1 in 20.

[1]G.G.O., No. 397, dated April 16th, 1897.

[2]Notes by Col. H. E. S. Abbott, C.B.E., D.S.O., late R.E., sent to the author on June 11th, 1933.

[3]Notes by Lieut.-Gen. Sir F. J. Aylmer, V.C., K.C.B., Col.-Commandant, R.E., sent to the author on June 17th, 1932.

Lieutenant A. J. H. Swiney, R.E., aligned it, Lieutenant S. D'A. Crookshank, R.E., worked on the northern face and Lieutenant G. H. Boileau, R.E., on the southern face. This road was completed by the middle of July, 1895, under the direction of Captain H. C. Nanton, R.E., and followed approximately the line of the present highway over the Malakand.

The Chitral Relief Force having crossed the Malakand, the Sappers and Miners turned their attention to bridging, though road construction was undertaken also to facilitate the advance northwards. The main engineering feature of the operations before and after Chitral was reached in 1895 is undoubtedly the extensive and ingenious bridge building by the Sapper companies and military or civilian labour under Majors M. C. Barton and F. J. Aylmer, V.C., Captains G. Williams, G. M. Heath, J. R. B. Serjeant, F. E. G. Skey and H. C. Nanton, Lieutenants C. Ainslie, G. C. Kemp, C. O. Halliday, H. F. Thuillier and F. R. F. Boileau and several other junior officers of the Royal Engineers. A list of these bridges, and reports on the construction of the more important ones, are given in *Professional Papers of the Corps of Royal Engineers*.[1] Barton, with the 1st and 6th Companies, Bengal S. & M., under Serjeant and Skey, built a trestle and crate bridge, 1,350 feet in length, over the Swat River at Chakdarra between April 9th and 16th, 1895;[2] and on April 12th, Aylmer, with the 4th Company, made a floating bridge, 92 feet long, of log rafts across the Panjkora River two miles below Sado[3] and between April 14th and 16th, after the log bridge had been washed away, a suspension bridge of 90 feet span two miles further downstream. Serjeant, with the 1st Company, completed a suspension bridge (200 feet) across the Panjkora above Sado between April 20th and May 1st. Between April 19th and May 30th, Williams,[4] with the 6th Company, Madras S. & M., under Ainslie, assisted by 200 civilian artificers and parties of a Pontoon Detachment of the Bengal Corps, erected a very fine structure over the Swat River at Chakdarra consisting of a suspension bridge across the left-bank channel with a central span of 250 feet and two subsidiary spans of 125 feet each, and across the right-bank channel a similar bridge with dimensions 110 feet and 55 feet respectively. Over the intervening island, a trestle bridge of trussed beams was provided giving a total length of bridge of 944 feet.[5] Heath, with Lieutenant G. H. Boileau, R.E., and the Pontoon Detachment before mentioned, bridged the channels of the Swat River at Chakdarra with pontoons on several occasions between April 28th and May 13th

[1] Vol. 22, 1896, pp. 113–170, with 38 plates including many photographs by Sergt. (afterwards Capt.) F. Mayo, R.E.

[2] It may be noted, however, that the 4th Company under Maj. Aylmer started the work on April 8th.

[3] See the *Sketch Map of the North-West Frontier: North of the Kabul River*, included in this chapter.

[4] Capt. G. Williams, R.E., was assisted from April 19th till May 3rd by Lieut. A. Walpole, R.E., and from May 16th by Lieut. F. F. N. Rees, R.E.

[5] The Chakdarra suspension bridge, built in 1895, was nearly wrecked by floods in 1899 and 1900, and consequently the building of a new permanent bridge 100 feet further downstream was begun in Sept., 1901, by Capt. H. Biddulph, R.E. This bridge (the Connaught Bridge) had five 160-feet steel girder spans and was completed in March, 1903, after which the suspension bridge was dismantled. (See *Prof. Papers of the Corps of Royal Engineers*, Vol. 29, 1903, pp. 101–125.)

while Williams was at work on his suspension bridge.[1] Early in May, the 6th Company, Bengal S. & M., with Kemp and Halliday in charge, erected a trestle and crib bridge, 240 feet long, over the Jandol River near its junction with the Panjkora. In June, Serjeant, with the 1st Company, completed a suspension bridge of 78 feet span at Chutiatan below Dir and in July remodelled a cantilever bridge (66 feet span) over the Ushiri River at Darora. The list may be concluded with a mention of a fine suspension bridge of 294 feet span erected by Aylmer and the 4th Company between August 22nd and September 13th over the Chitral River opposite the site selected for a new fort about 1½ miles downstream of the old fort at Chitral, and of two bridges built by Nanton between Mardan and Dargai —one a suspension bridge of 200 feet span at Jalala and the other a large wooden trussed bridge of two spans near Sakhakot. When it is added that some 78 small cantilever or trestle bridges were built also between May and September 1895 along the road to Chitral it will be realized that the Bengal and Madras Sappers and Miners had unique experience in this branch of engineering.

Lieut.-Colonel H. P. Leach, R.E., then a staff officer under General Low, states that when the Relief Force was mobilized the first engineering work was the duplication of the floating bridge across the Kabul (Landai) River at Nowshera by Barton and the Public Works Department. "To supplement the trestle bridge made by Major Barton, R.E., and the 1st and 6th Companies at Chakdarra," he continues,[2] "the pontoon equipment of the Bengal Sappers was ordered up from Roorkee. It was in position over the Ganges at Hardwar but was despatched with commendable rapidity. Captain G. M. Heath and Lieutenant G. H. Boileau, R.E., experienced much difficulty in getting it over the Malakand Pass as the road was narrow and had many sharp corners.[3] As neither of these bridges could be expected to stand the floods in July and August the construction of a permanent suspension bridge was ordered as soon as possible. This was started at once under the direction of Lieut.-Colonel W. T. Shone, R.E., and it will be seen from the report of Captain G. Williams, R.E., who was entrusted with its erection, that it proved an unusually heavy undertaking for a work in the field. The two suspension bridges made by the 1st and 4th Companies over the Panjkora River were excellent of their kind. The extended use of telegraph wire was a noteworthy point in the design of the suspension bridges and the experience gained in its use on former occasions by Major F. J. Aylmer, V.C., proved of great value."

[1]A graphic description of the bridging operations at Chakdarra is given in an article entitled "The Malakand on Three Days' Leave," by Lieut. C. de W. Crookshank, R.E., appearing in *The R.E. Journal*, Vol. XXV, 1895, pp. 223, 224.

[2]*Professional Papers of the Corps of Royal Engineers*, Vol. 22, 1896, pp. 114, 115.

[3]The equipment consisted of 26 pontoons and their stores carried on 38 wagons and 4 carts. Hauled by elephants and often carried by working parties, four pontoons reached Chakdarra on April 27th when a flying bridge was made. Boileau was then sent back to the Malakand to bring up the remainder and had them all at Chakdarra by May 5th. The copper bows of the pontoons proved to be too weak to stand the battering of the current in the Swat River even in May and they gave much trouble. So rapid was the current that the pontoons were secured to a cable stretched across the river instead of being anchored.

SUSPENSION BRIDGE OVER THE PANJKORA RIVER BELOW SADO.

Under construction on April 16th, 1895, by the 4th Company, Bengal Sappers and Miners, under Major F. J. Aylmer, V. C., R. E. Span, 90 feet.

Of all the bridges made by the Sappers and Miners in 1895 perhaps the most interesting and the most important for the uninterrupted progress of the advanced troops were the two frail structures hurriedly thrown by Aylmer across the turbulent Panjkora between April 12th and 16th with any materials which he could find. As regards the first bridge, Sir Fenton Aylmer states that although the log-rafts were terribly unwieldy and had hardly any flotation he could evolve no other design because he had no pontoons nor had he sufficient wire for a suspension bridge. After the Guides had crossed and the log-raft bridge had been washed away, some men of the Telegraph Department arrived with telegraph wire and Aylmer was able to begin the construction of a suspension bridge, two miles below the other, where a span of 90 feet was possible. Again there was a shortage of materials, and wood for the frames had to be brought a long distance to the site; but the bridge was completed on the third day and would have been ready earlier had not Brig.-General Gatacre insisted on marching his brigade across before the bridge was finished and immediately marching it back again, a process which occupied nearly seven hours.[1]

When news was received of the relief of Chitral by Colonel Kelly, General Gatacre was sent ahead with a small force including the 4th Company, Bengal Sappers and Miners, under Aylmer. The 4th Company was the first unit of the Relief Force to cross the Lawarai Pass and arrived in Chitral on May 17th. It remained in or near Chitral until the middle of September when it left for Roorkee after building a suspension bridge of 294 feet span at the site selected for the new Chitral Fort and in addition several smaller bridges on the main road along the river. The unit was employed also on the defences of the fort at Drosh.[2] On October 4th it was back at headquarters, together with the Pontoon Detachment under Heath, its place in the garrison at Chitral having been taken by the 1st Company under Serjeant. This company began the construction of the new fort after detaching one section to Gilgit. Meanwhile, the 6th Company under Skey had reached Roorkee, and the 6th Company, Madras S. & M., had arrived in Bangalore after both companies had worked for some weeks on the road in the Panjkora Valley.[3] Until May 1896 the 1st Company at Chitral continued the building of the new fort, an enclosure 110 yards by 90 yards in size with stone walls nearly 30 feet in height, a large hornwork towards the river and four towers.

On May 17th, 1896, the 1st Company was relieved at Chitral by the 4th Company from Roorkee under Lieutenant H. R. Stockley, R.E., with Lieutenants J. M. C. Colvin, F. W. Brunner and E. G. Henderson, R.E. Colvin went in July to Mastuj and built a stiffened cantilever bridge of 100 feet span in replacement of a recently dismantled bridge erected by Lieutenant L. W. S. Oldham, R.E., during Colonel Kelly's march to

[1]Notes by Lieut.-Gen. Sir Fenton J. Aylmer, V.C., K.C.B., Col.-Commandant, R.E., sent to the author on June 17th, 1932. The crossing may have been made because of a rumour that the garrison of Chitral was *in extremis*.

[2]*History and Digest of Service of the 1st K.G.O. Sappers and Miners*, p. 59.

[3]*Historical Record of the Q.V.O. Madras Sappers and Miners*, Vol. I, p. 155, and notes by Col. F. E. G. Skey, late R.E., sent to the author on Nov. 2nd, 1939.

Chitral.[1] The new fort at Chitral was almost finished by the end of September and in the middle of December the 4th Company marched southwards to Gahirat (Gairat), 8 miles above Droṣh, where a suspension bridge was required across the Chitral River. Stockley began to build it on February 12th, 1897, and completed it on March 24th. The span was 309 feet and the roadway 136 feet above the winter water level. As it was difficult to get long timbers for the frames, and the steel cables were only 550 feet in length, the central third of the roadway was built up on wooden trestles resting on the cables. This type of bridge is most difficult to construct owing to the problems of getting the cables level and the trestles riding true. However, these difficulties were surmounted successfully by part of the 4th Company. In 1899, to secure greater stiffness and steadiness, the bridge was given exceptionally strong handrails by the 2nd Company, then in Chitral under Lieutenant P. Maud, R.E., and it was anchored with four pairs of side-guys to prevent it from swaying in the stormy winds that whistled down the deep gorge. The Gahirat Bridge was an impressive example of its type.[2]

A suspension bridge completed at Drosh by Colvin and a detachment of the 4th Company in February 1897 also deserves notice. This structure had frames 50 feet in height and a span of 290 feet. Afterwards, Colvin built a 42-feet cantilever bridge across the Shishi Kuh tributary three miles above Drosh, and Stockley and Brunner began the construction of a 322 feet suspension bridge at Shishi Kuh which was completed early in May by the 6th Company under Skey, with Macdonald, Brunner and Henderson, after that unit had relieved the 4th Company in the Chitral garrison.[3] It would be hard, indeed, to equal such a record of bridging as that created by the Bengal Sappers and Miners in Chitral between 1895 and 1897.[4]

Until 1903 a Sapper and Miner company always formed part of the Chitral garrison, but in 1904 the detachment was reduced to one section of either the Bengal or Madras Sappers. Chitral was a popular Sapper station for there was ample sport as well as interesting work. Captain C. E. Salvesen, R.E., who was there in 1901–02 with Lieutenant John Charteris, R.E., and the 1st Company, Bengal S. & M., had a novel method of reaching the haunts of big game. To save fatigue, and to mount the heights quickly before dawn, he used to hire two powerful Chitralis to pull him up

[1]The Mastuj Bridge, completed by Lieut. Colvin, R.E., in Aug. 1896, was rebuilt in 1899 by the 2nd Company, Bengal S. & M., under Capt. S. H. Powell, R.E., with Lieuts. P. Maud, E. C. Tylden-Pattenson and B. W. Mainprise, R.E.

[2]The Gahirat bridge was repaired by the 6th Company, Bengal S. & M., under Lieut. J. R. E. Charles, R.E., in the winter of 1902–03, and reconstructed by the Chitral Section of No. 9 Field Company, Madras S. & M., under Lieut. T. P. Bassett, R.E., in 1907.

[3]The 4th Company, Bengal S. & M., arrived in Rawalpindi from Chitral on June 2nd, 1897, and within two months proceeded on service with the Malakand Field Force. The 6th Company reached Chitral on May 11th, 1897, and saw no active service. It left Chitral for Roorkee on May 14th, 1898, and two days later, in the Lawarai Pass, Lieut. R. H. Macdonald, R.E., and three Sappers earned the Albert Medal (2nd Class) for gallantry in rescuing a soldier of the 27th Punjab Infantry who had been buried in an avalanche.

[4]For a detailed description of the work of the 4th Company see the *Diary of No. 4 Company, 1st K.G.O. Sappers and Miners, 19th April, 1896–6th June, 1898*, at Roorkee.

SUSPENSION BRIDGE OVER THE CHITRAL RIVER AT GAHIRAT.

Constructed by the 4th Company, Bengal Sappers and Miners, under Lieut. H. R. Stockley, R. E., during February and March 1896. Span, 309 feet.

the first 3,000 or 4,000 feet by means of an elastic rope passed through a pulley attached to his leather belt and thus arrived fresh and ready to shoot. In the evening the pulley was shifted to the back of his belt and he could then stroll easily down the precipitous mountain side checked by his patient tribesmen.[1] Lieutenant P. E. Prince, R.E., who was in Chitral a few years later with a section of the Madras Sappers, considered the station one of the finest a subaltern could desire. Though cut off from the outside world he found the work most varied and the opportunities for *shikar* almost unlimited.[2] Markhor, oorial, ibex, snow leopard and bear, all were there, and abundant small game in addition. And so, with this digression, we say goodbye to Chitral, the far northern arena of many engineering exploits by Sappers and Miners, and return to the Malakand region where in 1896 the clouds were beginning to gather for the mightiest storm which has ever convulsed the North-West Frontier.

The garrison on the Malakand Pass had little inkling of trouble. The 5th Company, Madras S. & M., was there during the winter of 1895–96 under Captain E. P. Johnson, R.E., with Lieutenants G. A. F. Sanders, A. R. Winsloe and F. W. Watling, R.E., and the letters from some of these officers to headquarters at Bangalore make interesting reading. The chances of active service were considered small because the Utman Khel would give no pretext for an expedition against them. A new use had been found for the company's mule-wrappers of red material—they made excellent tablecloths. The Fort was almost ready for occupation. The Sappers had built a Picquet Tower on Guides' Point, a short distance away, and a road to it. A fine Mess House for the Staff was under construction on the Ridge. The R.E. Mess hut had a stove made out of an iron wheelbarrow with a pipe let into a tin top. The company's carpenters were manufacturing dozens of tables and chairs—and a fishing rod. Polo was played two days a week, Johnson and Sanders being the best Sapper players. There was partridge shooting always on Sundays. The General's wife and daughters were in residence and all officers were expected to call. The cold was biting but the men were standing it well. The letters breathe peace and contentment in every line. There was no thought of war, and even up to the middle of 1897 this happy state of affairs continued.

Then came news of a treacherous assault on a political agent in the distant Tochi Valley of Northern Waziristan and the smouldering Frontier burst into flame. The outbreak in the Tochi was a small affair. It was but the match which kindled the fire. The Madda Khel clan of the Darwesh Khel Waziris attacked a small force in the Maizar territory west of Datta Khel[3] on June 10th, 1897, and nearly overwhelmed it; but reinforcements from Datta Khel, with whom was Lieutenant H. R. Stockley, R.E., saved the situation. To punish the offenders, two brigades under Major-General Corrie Bird were concentrated at Datta Khel on July 19th and marching up the valley occupied Shirani and the Maizar district on the following

[1]Notes by Major C. E. Salvesen, R.E. (retd.), sent to the author on Jan. 31st, 1938.
[2]Notes by Col. P. E. Prince, D.S.O., late R.E., sent to the author on Sept. 20th, 1937.
[3]See *Sketch Map of the North-West Frontier: Waziristan*, included in this chapter.

day. The inhabitants had fled, and the force spent the next sixteen days in destroying without opposition many villages and their towers, a task which devolved chiefly on the 2nd Company, Bengal S. & M., the only engineer unit present.[1] All parts of the Tochi Valley were visited in turn, but the Madda Khel did not submit finally until the middle of November.

Meanwhile, stirring events had occurred further north where the Swatis, Mohmands, Afridis and Orakzais had taken the field. On July 26th, 1897, an army of Swatis assaulted the British defences on the Malakand. The position was somewhat extended. The Malakand Fort had been built about 600 yards west of the pass on a spur overlooking the southern ascent of the old Buddhist road, and a signalling post had been established on Guides' Hill still further west. In or around a hollow or "Crater" north of the Fort lay the camps of the 24th Punjab Infantry, the 45th Sikhs and the 5th Company, Madras S. & M., in addition to the Engineer Park, Commissariat stores and bazaar. In a North Camp some 1,100 yards to the north-west were the 31st Punjab Infantry, No. 8 Mountain Battery, a squadron of the 11th Bengal Lancers and the transport. The Sapper camp, the Engineer Park and the Commissariat godown and office were grouped within a flimsy line of abattis and wire entanglement surrounding a low mound in the centre of the Crater. The 24th Punjab Infantry and 45th Sikhs were camped south and west of the Crater. "It was a polo day," writes Sir Bindon Blood,[2] "and on that evening the usual game was played on a ground near the village of Khar in the Swat Valley, three miles or so from the Fort. It was noticed that an unusual crowd of spectators came to look on at the game, and as a matter of fact these were tribesmen who were passing the time until it was dark enough to begin an attack on the Malakand position. All remained calm at the Malakand until 9.45 p.m. when a telegram came in from Chakdarra reporting that large bodies of tribesmen were moving down the valley to attack the British positions." The Guides were then summoned from Mardan and a movable column of all arms, including the Sapper company, was ordered to be ready to march at midnight; but at 10.15 p.m. a bugle sounded the alarm and the fight began with an attack by 1,000 Swatis who were trying to steal into the camp from the north and east. This was met by the 45th Sikhs and only after several hours of desultory fighting did the enemy withdraw.

The tribesmen met with greater success against the north and centre camps and particularly against the latter in the cup-shaped hollow of the Crater. It so happened that Lieutenants F. W. Watling and E. N. Manley, R.E., were the only British officers with the 5th Company, Madras S. & M., Watling being in temporary command.[3] The enemy broke into the Commissariat and Sapper lines in the Crater and carried off many rifles and a quantity of ammunition, and the lines were not cleared of them until

[1]The 2nd Company had left Roorkee on June 22nd, 1897, to join the Tochi Field Force.

[2]*Four Score Years and Ten*, by Gen. Sir Bindon Blood, G.C.B., G.C.V.O., Representative Col.-Commandant, R.E., p. 290.

[3]Capt. E. P. Johnson and Lieut. A. R. Winsloe, R.E., were on leave. Lieut. E. N. Manley, R.E., had joined the 5th Company on the departure of Lieut. G. A. F. Sanders, R.E., on March 22nd, 1896.

shortly before dawn. "The Sapper camp was practically unprotected," remarks Watling,[1] "the slender abattis of boughs which demarcated it being neither bullet proof nor assault proof. I was put out of action fairly soon.[2] Jemadar Chinnasami was shot through the chest and Sergeant F. Byrne, R.E., was killed. There were other casualties, but Manley and the company carried on staunchly through the night." Manley himself writes :—[3] "There were no orders in case of attack. We extended along the abattis, 250 yards in length, and gained a short respite while the enemy were looting the bazaar. The men were in plain file and many were hit by stones, so I told them to throw away their white puggries and to strip and leave their clothes on the ground. The night was dark and when the devils broke in one could not tell friend from foe at three paces. My sword knot was cut off by a bullet but I was not hit. When Watling was wounded he was, I fancy, at the Quarter Guard and I was near the picquet on the east side. As we had run out of ammunition I told Sergeant Byrne to double to the Quarter Guard to get some while I kept the men steady on the abattis. He ran into the brutes and was killed. Not understanding why he did not return I then went down myself and came across a tribesman whom I challenged and shot. Others chased me and I fell over a tent peg but got away and returned to the picquet. There I found that the enemy had broken in at the south-east corner. We charged them and they scuttled out again. I stalked four devils with a couple of banners, but my revolver ammunition was bad and all the rounds missed fire. It was near dawn when things began to quiet down. My whole time was spent in going from one end of the line to the other talking to the men and controlling their fire. The enemy were never driven out. They went because they thought our 25 rifles and our mules loaded with ammunition were good enough or because they got scared. The loot saved us that night. The enemy cleared out when they had their hands full." This is the story of the hardest fight in which Madras Sappers and Miners have ever been concerned on the North-West Frontier.[4]

On July 27th the Guides marched in from Mardan in time to join in repelling another violent night attack which was repeated within 24 hours. The fighting was often of a desperate character but the troops held their ground. On the night of July 30th/31st the tribesmen made their last effort against the Malakand position and failed. "It was work all day and fight all night," writes Manley. More reinforcements arrived, followed on August 1st by Major-General Sir Bindon Blood who then assumed the chief command. A column was sent on August 2nd to relieve the besieged garrison of Chakdarra, and half the 5th Company under Winsloe marched

[1]Notes by Col. F. W. Watling, C.B.E., D.S.O., late R.E., sent to the author on April 18th, 1934.

[2]Lieut. F. W. Watling, R.E., wounded in the shoulder, neck and leg, was invalided on Aug. 11th and was replaced by Lieut. F. H. C. Burne, R.E.

[3]Extracts from a letter from Lieut. E. N. Manley, R.E., to Lieut.-Col. C. B. Wilkieson, R.E., Commandant, Madras S. & M., dated Aug. 14th, 1897, appearing in *Historical Records*, Case 16, at Bangalore.

[4]For further details see "The Fighting in the Malakand," appearing in *The R.E. Journal*, Vol. XXVII, 1897, p. 195.

with it and afterwards repaired the damaged defences. The losses of the Madras Sappers in the Malakand fighting were considerable and indicate clearly the hand-to-hand nature of the conflict.[1] As for the tribesmen, they themselves computed their losses before the Malakand and Chakdarra as 3,700 in killed alone. For gallantry at the Malakand, Subadar Ramasami, Naik Azhagiri and Dooly-Bearer Nallatambi of the 5th Company were awarded the Indian Order of Merit, and the honour "Malakand" was granted to the Madras Corps.[2]

Lack of space forbids the description in any detail of the intricate operations of the Malakand, Mohmand, Buner and Tirah Field Forces during 1897 and 1898. These are dealt with fully in official publications and despatches and in a number of historical works.[3] It is proposed, accordingly, to confine this narrative to the experiences of the Sappers and Miners supplemented by a brief outline of each campaign.

At the beginning of August 1897 a Malakand Field Force comprising 3 brigades of infantry, 8 squadrons of cavalry, a battery of field artillery, 3 batteries of mountain artillery and 3 companies of Sappers and Miners with the usual medical, transport and supply services was concentrated under the command of Major-General Sir Bindon Blood between the Malakand and Chakdarra with one brigade in reserve at Mardan. With the 1st Brigade (Brig.-General W. H. Meiklejohn) was the 5th Company Madras S. & M., under Captain E. P. Johnson with Lieutenants A. R. Winsloe, E. N. Manley and F. H. C. Burne, R.E.; with the 2nd Brigade (Brig.-General P. D. Jeffreys) the 4th Company, Bengal S. & M., under Lieutenant H. R. Stockley with Lieutenants T. C. Watson, A. H. D. Riach, C. W. Wilkinson and D. M. Griffith, R.E.; and with the 3rd Brigade (Brig.-General J. H. Wodehouse) in reserve the 3rd Company, Bombay S. & M., under Captain C. E. Baddeley with Lieutenants F. P. Rundle, G. R. Hearn, C. R. Tonge[4] and F. R. S. Gervers, R.E. A Telegraph Section of the Madras Corps under Lieutenant W. Robertson, R.E., was also present. The Commanding Royal Engineer was Brevet-Colonel J. E. Broadbent, R.E., with Captain H. J. Sherwood, R.E., as Adjutant. Thus a very considerable establishment of engineer troops was available, as was to be expected when an ex-Royal Engineer and Sapper and Miner was in chief command.

The advance of the Malakand Field Force from Chakdarra into Swat was delayed by rain, but on August 16th Thana was occupied and the road

[1]The casualties were Sergt. F. Byrne and 2 I.O.R.s killed and Lieut. F. W. Watling, Jemadar Chinnasami, 21 I.O.R.s and 3 followers wounded. (See *Historical Record of the Q.V.O. Madras Sappers and Miners*, Vol. I, p. 161.)

[2]G.O. No. 288, dated March 16th, 1900.

[3]For instance, *The Operations of the Mohmand Field Force in* 1897; *The Operations of the Malakand Field Force and the Buner Field Force*, 1897–98; *The Campaign in Tirah*, 1897–98, by Col. H. D. Hutchinson; *The Indian Frontier War*, 1897, by Lionel James; and *The Story of the Malakand Field Force*, by Winston Churchill. Extracts from the official despatches appear in *The R.E. Journal*, Vol. XXVIII, 1898, pp. 27–34, 75–79, 99–107 and 125–126.

[4]Lieut. C. R. Tonge, R.E., soon left the 3rd Company, Bombay S. & M., to join the 4th Company which started from Kirkee for service on the N.W. Frontier on Aug. 14th, 1897.

to Landakai reconnoitred.[1] The next step was to force the "Gate of Swat" below Landakai where a spur from the mountains ends near the river in almost unscalable cliffs. Though the enemy held this spur in strength, Sir Bindon Blood drove them from their position on August 17th and his cavalry pursued them towards Buner. This success was due partly to an outflanking movement by the 1st Brigade to the south which threatened the enemy's line of retreat across swampy ground, but it was secured also by the skilful use of massed artillery including the 12-pounder guns of the 10th Field Battery. "The principle of concentrating artillery has been admitted in Europe," wrote Winston Churchill after the campaign,[2] "but Sir Bindon Blood is the first general who has applied it to mountain warfare in India." On August 18th the force advanced to Barikot and on the next day to Mingaora where it halted for several days to receive the submission of the Swat Valley tribes. Sir Bindon then marched back to Barikot and reconnoitred southwards to the Karakar Pass leading to Buner which he wished to invade. This, however, was forbidden, and so the first phase of the campaign came to an end. Meanwhile the 3rd Brigade, stationed at Rustam, had held in check large gatherings of the Bunerwals on the Malandrai and Ambela Passes, and having thus guarded the right flank and rear, moved to Chakdarra and thence northwards through Wuch to Sado which Wodehouse occupied on September 4th to save the bridge from damage by tribesmen from Dir.

The 4th Company, Bengal S. & M., and the 5th Company, Madras S. & M., were present at Landakai where the latter unit repaired the narrow track on the left bank which was the only passage through the "Gate." Afterwards, both companies were engaged in roadmaking and demolishing towers. The 3rd Company, Bombay S. & M., moved forward to Rustam with the 3rd Brigade on August 15th. Hearn records that the men marched splendidly in the great heat though clad in cloth tunics and trousers with putties; but when one of the British sergeants was asked by Rundle how he liked active service he replied that "it came rather 'ard on a man as is used to 'is seven to fourteen pints a day.[3]" There was some idea of a possible advance into Buner from the south; but later, when the Malandrai Pass was found to be impracticable, the 3rd Company returned with the brigade to Mardan and marched over the Malakand to Chakdarra. As operations against the tribes in the Upper Mohmand country were contemplated, the company then discarded its carts and converted its draught saddles into pack equipment by cutting up the cart-ropes and fitting them with rings.[4] This done, it marched to Sado on the Panjkora

[1]See *Sketch Map of the North-West Frontier: North of the Kabul River*, included in this chapter.

[2]*The Story of the Malakand Field Force*, by Winston L. S. Churchill, p. 290. At the end of Aug., 1897, as a subaltern in the 4th Hussars, Churchill joined Sir Bindon Blood's staff as an A.D.C. Later, he was attached to a Sikh regiment and became very popular with the men.

[3]Notes by Col. Sir Gordon R. Hearn, C.I.E., D.S.O., late R.E., sent to the author on Sept. 21st, 1937.

[4]Notes by Brig. F. R. S. Gervers, C.I.E., C.B.E., late R.E., sent to the author on Dec. 4th, 1937.

where it improved a ford across the river. Soon afterwards, Baddeley was invalided and Rundle assumed command.

The next operation of the Malakand Field Force was an advance westwards into Bajaur to subdue the Mamund clan of the Mohmand tribe. Leaving the 1st Brigade (Meiklejohn) to guard the line of communication, Sir Bindon Blood pushed the 3rd Brigade (Wodehouse) forward to Nawagai and the 2nd Brigade (Jeffreys) towards the Rambat Pass. Then he advanced northwards with the 2nd Brigade to Inayat Qila and working up the Mamund Valley in three small columns attacked Shahi Tangai on September 16th and destroyed it; but in the subsequent retirement a party of the 4th Company, Bengal S. & M., with a few men of the Buffs and four mountain guns, was caught by darkness, and General Jeffreys, who was with it, decided to take shelter in the village of Bilot. He was forestalled by the Mamunds and a bitter struggle followed. This was the occasion on which Lieutenants T. C. Watson and J. M. C. Colvin, R.E., won the Victoria Cross. According to Colvin[1] he was retiring with two sections of Bengal Sappers (about 20 men) towards the camp at Inayat Qila when he was joined by Watson with two more sections escorting the mountain guns. Darkness was falling as Bilot was reached and Jeffreys ordered the guns to halt and come into action outside the east wall of the village. The Gunners made a ditch and parapet around their guns, helped by the Sappers who used their bayonets for digging as apparently they had no tools. Three companies of the 35th Sikhs, which were to have occupied Bilot, failed to appear, so Watson took some men of the Buffs round the corner of the village to drive the enemy from under the walls but had to return after being shot in the thigh. Again he led the men round the corner and again he was hit, this time in the arm and hand. Colvin then went into and through the burning village with eight Sappers, and climbing with two men on to the roof of a house on the west face, fired on the enemy under the wall on that side and drove them away. Under a hail of bullets and showers of stones from other houses he was soon obliged to retire. Nevertheless, he returned to the roof for a time and only left it again because he could see nothing in the darkness. Leading his men back to the gun position, he was told by Lieutenant F. A. Wynter, R.A., that General Jeffreys and another officer had been wounded and that only he and Wynter remained to carry on the defence. Saddles taken from the mules gave some cover, but many men and animals were hit. After 8.30 p.m. the enemy fired both from inside and outside the village, and half an hour later it began to rain. Wynter was shot through both legs, and it was not till midnight, when Colvin was the only British officer unwounded, that the enemy made off on the arrival of four companies of Sikhs and Guides. The Sapper and Miner casualties were heavy—3 Sappers killed, and Watson, Havildar Baryam Singh and 15 Sappers wounded, one of whom afterwards died. The Buffs

[1]Report by Lieut. J. M. C. Colvin, R.E., included in the *Diary of No. 4 Company, 1st K.G.O. Sappers and Miners, 19th April,* 1896, *to 6th June,* 1898, at Roorkee. See also *The Operations of the Malakand Field Force and, the Buner Field Force* 1897–98, p. 56, and *The Story of the Malakand Field Force*, by Winston Churchill, p. 204. The strength of the Sapper party at Bilot was 2 British officers and 43 Indian ranks.

also suffered severely. Watson was incapacitated for months. In addition to the award of the Victoria Cross to Watson, Colvin and Corporal James Smith of the Buffs,[1] Colour-Havildar Mian Khan and Naik Natha Singh of the Bengal Sappers were given the Indian Order of Merit[2] and several of the Buffs received the Distinguished Conduct Medal.

Writing of the experiences of the 4th Company, Bengal S. & M., in Bajaur in 1897 Major D. M. Griffith remarks :—[3] " After crossing the Panjkora we marched towards Khar and Nawagai. On September 13th, the 2nd Brigade camped near Khar and the 1st Brigade near Nawagai, and on the following day the 4th Company proceeded with the Buffs to open up a road over the Rambat Pass as one brigade was to move to Peshawar to join a force proceeding against the Afridis in the Tirah. However, while we were bivouacked that night on the pass, the 2nd Brigade was attacked by Mamunds from the valley running north-west from that place. Casualties were heavy, and we were ordered to return to the brigade which then marched to Inayat Qila to carry out punitive operations. The brigade set out in three columns, two up the centre of the valley and one up the north-eastern side. With the last went half the 4th Company under Stockley with Wilkinson and myself; the remainder, with Watson and Colvin, accompanied the centre columns which were soon merged into a single column. Having cleared and destroyed two small villages, we came to the village of Damadola. Here there was considerable opposition, and as the Column Commander wished to get back to camp before dark we withdrew, sniped all the way. A bullet went through Stockley's helmet and shaved the hair from the top of his head. Arrived in camp we heard heavy firing of mountain guns up the valley where Bilot was being defended most gallantly by Watson and Colvin with a party of Bengal Sappers and Buffs. In the morning the remnants of the party were brought back to Inayat Qila. Poor Watson had his arm badly shattered by a Martini bullet and Colvin had been nearly stunned by a large stone which had crushed his helmet.

" All idea of joining the Peshawar Force was now abandoned " continues Griffith. " We remained at Inayat Qila nearly a month to carry out further punitive operations. Watson was carried away in a *dhooly* to Chakdarra *en route* for Nowshera and we busied ourselves in making *kajawahs* for the transport of the less serious cases on camels. On October 4th we were reinforced by the 5th Company, Madras S. & M., and the 10th Field Battery. The latter, assisted by the Madras Sappers, had crossed the narrow Panjkora bridge, built only for pack transport, by dismantling its guns and carriages and carrying each piece over separately. Damadola was one of the villages destroyed. While preparing a tower for demolition Stockley discovered a Pathan woman with a newly-born baby in a house next door. We carried her—bed, baby and all—up the hillside to a safe place and then blew up the tower and two others before setting fire to the

[1] *London Gazettes*, May 20th, 1898, and (for Corporal Smith) April 21st, 1899.
[2] *History and Digest of Service of the 1st K.G.O. Sappers and Miners*, pp. 65, 69.
[3] Notes by Maj. D. M. Griffith, D.S.O., R.E. (retd.), sent to the author on Nov. 22nd, 1937.

village and removing as much corn as our mules could carry. On another day we went to Agrah and Gat close to the Afghan frontier and destroyed some towers and parts of the villages. There was much firing and fighting and many casualties, and the valley was full of the smoke of burning villages when we returned to camp. We became most expert in blowing up towers and must have destroyed nearly forty of them in the Mamund Valley alone. They were built of rubble stone and mud mortar, usually 15 to 20 feet square and 20 to 30 feet in height, some solid and others hollow, with loopholes, a rough staircase inside, a parapet wall on top, and sometimes a *machicouli* gallery. Dynamite was employed as a rule, and we found that after boring a hole 4 feet to 5 feet deep towards the centre of the tower and tamping the charge well, 5 lbs. would bring down a tower 15 feet square.[1] Having no electric firing apparatus, we used safety fuze. Peace terms were eventually arranged at a great *jirga* and hundreds of old *jezails* and some rifles were handed in by the tribesmen. Among them was a weapon evidently made by a village blacksmith from the odd parts of a condemned Martini-Henry rifle.[2] The Ordnance Department used to destroy old rifles by cutting the barrels into pieces and the blacksmith had welded some pieces together without bothering about making the grooves of the rifling agree ! I remember that a fine old warrior brought his stalwart son to the *jirga* and said that he wanted to see the ' Captain Sahib ' of the ' Suffers and Miners,' so we took him to Stockley to whom he salaamed profoundly and announced that his wife had told him how the ' Suffers and Miners Sahibs ' had carried her out of the village of Damadola and that he was so grateful that he had brought his eldest son to enlist in the Corps. We kept the young man and sent him down to Roorkee by the next convoy. On October 12th we left Inayat Qila and marched eastwards to Jar and later by Chakdarra and the Malakand to Dargai and Jalala."

In connection with the experiences of the 4th Company in Bajaur it may be remarked that Sir Bindon Blood had decided on arrival at Nawagai to remain there with the 3rd Brigade until he came in touch with a " Mohmand Field Force " under Major-General E. R. Elles operating from the direction of Peshawar. He made every preparation against attack, and indeed invited it, and the expected assaults came on the nights of September 19th–20th and 20th–21st. In both actions Sir Bindon repulsed the enemy with severe loss. " In view of the difficulty of inflicting loss on the tribesmen in their own hills," writes Sir George MacMunn,[3] " the

[1]The destruction of frontier villages and towers is discussed in " Demolition of Towers on the N.W. Frontier," by Lieut. J. B. MacGeorge, R.E., appearing in *The R.E. Journal*, Vol. 29, 1899, pp. 29–30, and in " Demolitions in Savage Warfare in India," by Capt. S. H. Sheppard, R.E., appearing in *Prof. Papers of the Corps of Royal Engineers*, Vol. 28, 1902, pp. 86–96. The saving of time in using a central charge was discovered by Sheppard in 1901–02 in Waziristan where he blew up 25 towers. A vertical hole can be dug more rapidly than a horizontal one and the men can work under cover inside the tower. The normal central charge is now 24 lbs. of gun-cotton, or 48 lbs. for a solid-base tower (*The R.E. Journal*, Vol. LIII, 1939, p. 545).

[2]Modern rifle manufacture across the N.W. Frontier is described in " The Kohat Pass Rifle Factory," by Lieut.-Col. E. E. Read, M.C., R.E., appearing in *The R.E. Journal*, Vol. LIII, 1939, pp. 539–541.

[3]*The Romance of the Indian Frontiers*, by Lieut.-Gen. Sir Gèorge MacMunn, K.C.B., K.C.S.I., D.S.O., p. 212.

mere fact of provoking them to attack your defensible camp must be considered a tactical triumph." The 3rd Company, Bombay S. & M., was present in these actions. "The first attack on Nawagai was not a very determined affair," writes Brigadier Gervers,[1] "but the second was a violent one by 4,000 tribesmen and the Sappers and cavalry on the south side got the bullets in reverse. The junction with General Elles was effected on the 21st, and subsequently, Sir Bindon Blood having moved eastwards, the 3rd Brigade joined the Mohmand Field Force. The Bombay Sappers were given the task of blowing up all the towers in the Suran and Mittai valleys and marched to the mouth of the Bedmanai Pass.[2] General Elles then completed the discomforture of the Mohmands by crossing the pass and reaching Jarobi and, the operations being finished, the 3rd Company marched with the 3rd Brigade to Peshawar."

The chief burden of the engineering work with the Mohmand Field Force fell on the 5th Company, Bengal S. & M., under Captain J. S. Fowler, R.E., with Lieutenants S. H. Sheppard, G. T. Scott and J. B. MacGeorge, R.E., which had joined the force at Shabkadar on September 12th. This unit prepared the road for the general advance north-westwards over the Karapa and Nahakki Passes and was in action later at Lakarai, the Bedmanai Pass and Jarobi. With the 28th Bombay Pioneers, it destroyed some 66 towers and 36 fortified enclosures in 6 days.[3] The Mohmand Field Force having been broken up on September 29th, the 5th Company returned to Peshawar and on October 17th joined the Tirah Field Force at Bara.

Before leaving the subject of the military operations north of the Kabul River it may be well to deal briefly with the expedition into Buner conducted by Major-General Sir Bindon Blood after his success in Bajaur. Simple and austere in their habits, religious and truthful in their ways and brave in battle, the Bunerwals were the best of all the Pathan tribes; yet they had to be taught the lesson that it was foolish to defy the Government and in consequence a Buner Field Force of two brigades was concentrated at Sangau on January 6th, 1898, with detachments at Pirsai and Rustam. Sir Bindon had decided that the best line of advance would be by the Tanga Pass, north-east of Sangau, while detachments crossed by the Pirsai Pass further south. The Commanding Royal Engineer, Lieut.-Colonel W. Peacocke, R.E., had at his disposal the 4th Company, Bengal S. & M., under Lieutenant H. R. Stockley, R.E., with Lieutenants J. M. C. Colvin, V.C., C. W. Wilkinson and D. M. Griffith, R.E., and the 5th Company, Madras S. & M., under Captain E. P. Johnson, R.E., with Lieutenants A. R. Winsloe, E. N. Manley and F. H. C. Burne, R.E. A Telegraph Section of the Madras Corps under Lieutenant W. Robertson, R.E., was also present. The forcing of the Tanga Pass was accomplished rapidly and effectively on January 7th. The 4th Company had started work on the

[1]Notes by Brig. F. R. S. Gervers, C.I.E., C.B.E., late R.E., sent to the author on Dec. 4th, 1937.

[2]Between Sept. 23rd and 29th, 70 towers and 20 villages were destroyed.

[3]*The Operations of the Mohmand Field Force in* 1897, p. 79 and *History and Digest of Service, 1st K.G.O. Sappers and Miners*, p. 65.

track on the previous day, and when the attack was launched, two sections under Griffith were with the advanced guard of the 1st Brigade to make the steep path passable for mountain artillery and transport. "The ridge at the top of the pass was crowded with tribesmen waving flags, flourishing swords and shouting defiance," writes Griffith.[1] "It was some 3,000 feet above us and a stiff climb, but the Bunerwals were soon demoralized by the fire of the 12-pounders and by the time our flank attack developed they had cleared off. We worked hard on the pathway and eventually got one section over the pass with its equipment mules. This section went on with the advanced guard to Kingargalai where it bivouacked for the night." The remainder of the 4th Company, less two sections under Colvin at the Pirsai Pass,[2] bivouacked in extreme cold on the Tanga Pass after working till long after darkness had fallen. The 5th Company was more comfortable in a basin below; it had laboured all day on the lower reaches of the track. When the way was open for mule traffic on January 12th, the 4th Company crossed into Buner and the 5th Company went eastwards to work on the Ambela Pass, the scene of desperate fighting in 1863. It is interesting to note that the Bunerwal villages were found to be without any defences. The Ambela road was opened by January 17th and the 5th Company then advanced with the 2nd Brigade into Buner.[3] Meanwhile, the 4th Company had shared in Sir Bindon Blood's rapid sweep eastwards in two columns from Kingargalai through Jowar, Tursak, Pacha, Dagar and Rega and after much roadmaking marched out of the country by the Ambela Pass on the 19th and returned to the Malakand with the 5th Company to keep the road open to Chitral. The Buner Field Force was then broken up. It had been in existence for only fifteen days but had accomplished much in that short period. By selecting the difficult Tanga Pass in preference to the easier Pirsai, Malandrai or Ambela routes, Sir Bindon Blood had outwitted the enemy in this his last campaign on the North-West Frontier; but it should not be forgotten that his outstanding success was secured largely by the unremitting toil of his Sappers and Miners. Without them, the surprise entry through the Tanga Pass would have been impossible.

The rising of the tribes in 1897 was even more serious to the south of the Kabul River than to the north. It had become known in the middle of August that the Afridis and Orakzais were planning simultaneous attacks, the former on the Khaibar Pass defences and the latter on the Samana Ridge defences in the Miranzai country and in the Kurram Valley. The Afridi onslaught was launched on August 23rd against Ali Masjid and Fort Maude, a small work above Jamrud. Both were captured and destroyed. Landi Kotal fell on the 25th and the Khaibar remained closed until the end of December. On August 26th some Orakzais seized the Ublan Pass, north-west of Kohat, and others, combining with the Afridis, threatened

[1]Notes by Maj. D. M. Griffith, D.S.O., R.E. (retd.), sent to the author on Nov. 22nd, 1937.

[2]*Diary of No. 4 Company*, at Roorkee. In 1897–98 a Sapper company had 8 small sections.

[3]*Historical Record of the Q.V.O. Madras Sappers and Miners*, Vol. I, p. 167.

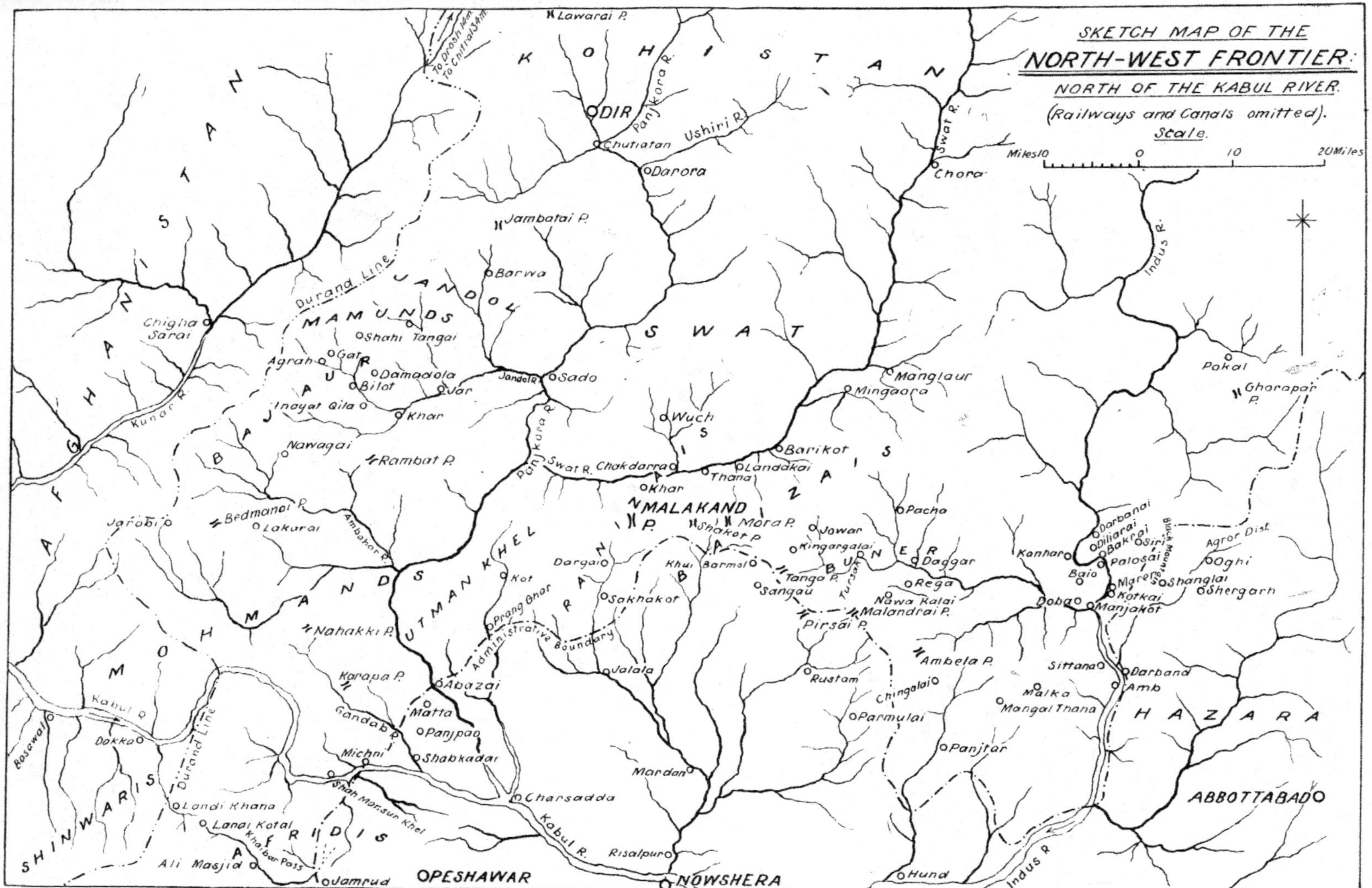
SKETCH MAP OF THE
NORTH-WEST FRONTIER:
NORTH OF THE KABUL RIVER.
(Railways and Canals omitted).
Scale.
Miles 10 0 10 20 Miles
KOHISTAN
AFGHANISTAN
SWAT
JANDOL
MAMUNDS
BAJAUR
MOHMANDS
UTMAN KHEL
RANIZAI
SWAT
AKAZAI
BUNER
HAZARA
SHINWARIS
AFRIDIS
Lawarai P.
To Drosh
To Chitral
DIR
Panjkora R.
Chutiatan
Ushiri R.
Darora
Swat R.
Chora
Indus R.
Jambatai P.
Barwa
Durand Line
Chigha Sarai
Shahi Tangai
Agrah
Gat
Damadola
Bilot
Jandol R.
Sado
Jar
Inayat Qila
Khar
Kunar R.
Nawagai
Rambat P.
Wuch
Manglaur
Mingaora
Barikot
Chakdarra
Landakai
Thana
Khar
MALAKAND P.
Shakot P.
Mora P.
Jowar
Pacha
Pokal
Gharapar P.
Jarobi
Bedmanai P.
Lakarai
Ambahar R.
Kot
Dargai
Khui
Barmal
Kingargalai
Tanga P.
Tursak
Sangau
Daggar
Rega
Nawa Kalai
Malandrai P.
Kanhar
Darbanai
Diliarai
Bakrai
Siri
Black Mountain
Agror Dist.
Palosai
Oghi
Baio
Mareri
Shanglai
Kotkai
Shergarh
Doba
Manjakot
Prang Ghar
Sakhakot
Administrative Boundary
Nahakki P.
Pirsai P.
Ambela P.
Sittana
Darband
Amb
Karapa P.
Abazai
Jalala
Rustam
Chingalai
Malka
Mangal Thana
Matta
Gandab
Panjpao
Parmulai
Kabul R.
Bosawal
Dakka
Durand Line
Michni
Shabkadar
Panjtar
Mardan
Shah Mansur Khel
Charsadda
ABBOTTABAD
Landi Khana
Landi Kotal
Khaibar Pass
Kabul R.
Risalpur
Ali Masjid
Jamrud
PESHAWAR
NOWSHERA
Hund
Indus R.

the British posts on the Samana Ridge and in the Kurram Valley.[1] A small force including the 4th Company, Bombay S. & M., was therefore sent up the Kurram and reinforced the garrison of Sadda on September 5th. Minor operations ensued in the Kurram Valley and desperate fighting on the Samana Ridge where the enemy captured the Saragarhi Post on September 12th and annihilated the defenders. They invested Fort Gulistan but were finally driven from the ridge by troops from Hangu. Preparations were then made to send a powerful force into the Tirah. It was decided that the advance should be on a single line from the south and by October 10th, 1897, two divisions under Lieut.-General Sir W. S. A. Lockhart were concentrated in Kohat.

With the 1st Division under Major-General W. Penn Symons were the 3rd and 4th Companies, Bombay S. & M., under Captains C. E. Baddeley and W. J. D. Dundee, R.E., and a company of Malerkotla Imperial Service Sappers under Lieut.-Colonel Mir Muhammad Khan of the Malerkotla State forces. With the 2nd Division under Major-General A. G. Yeatman-Biggs were the 4th Company, Madras S. & M., under Captain H. B. H. Wright, R.E., and a company of Sirmur Imperial Service Sappers under Lieutenant Bir Bikram Singh of the Sirmur State forces. On the line of communication were the 1st and 5th Companies, Bengal S. & M., under Captains J. R. B. Serjeant and J. S. Fowler, R.E., the former unit being with the Line of Communication troops under Lieut.-General Sir A. P. Palmer and the latter with a "Peshawar Column" under Brig.-General A. G. Hammond, V.C.[2] These seven engineer companies were under the orders of Colonel J. E. Broadbent and later of Colonel J. W. Thurburn, late R.E., as Commanding Royal Engineer to the force with Lieut.-Colonels H. H. Hart and C. B. Wilkieson, R.E., as Commanding Royal Engineers to the 1st and 2nd Divisions. Photo-Litho and Printing Sections were supplied by both the Madras and Bengal Corps and a Telegraph Section by the Bombay Corps. A Field Park of the Madras Corps under Captain U. W. Evans, R.E., was also present.

A compliment was paid to the Madras Sappers and Miners in the constitution of the Tirah Expeditionary Force. Not only was their Commandant (Lieut.-Colonel Wilkieson) selected as Commanding Royal Engineer, 2nd Division,[3] but their Adjutant, Captain T. Fraser, R.E., was appointed Adjutant, R.E., to that division and Captain Weedon and Lieutenants Chancellor and Hemming, R.E., were posted as engineering advisers

[1]See *Sketch Map of the North-West Frontier: South of the Kabul River*, included in this chapter.

[2]The other R.E. officers with the Sapper companies were as follows :—*3rd Company (Bombay)*—Lieuts. F. P. Rundle, F. R. S. Gervers and G. R. Hearn ; *4th Company (Bombay)*—Lieuts. J. B. Corry, F. M. Westropp, G. Dick and C. R. Tonge ; *Malerkotla Company*—Capt. F. F. Weedon and Lieut. N. M. Hemming (attached) ; *4th Company (Madras)*—Lieuts. W. S. Traill, H. G. Joly de Lotbinière and B. H. Rooke ; *Sirmur Company*—Lieut. C. W. Singer and later Lieut. J. R. Chancellor (attached) ; *1st Company (Bengal)*—Lieuts. E. Barnardiston and A. H. Cunningham ; *5th Company (Bengal)*—Lieuts. S. H. Sheppard, G. T. Scott and J. B. MacGeorge. Maj. F. G. Bond took over the command of the 5th Company (Bengal) from Capt. J. S. Fowler at Jamrud on Dec. 20th, 1897, after the main operations had ended.

[3]Lieut.-Col. Wilkieson, R.E., was invalided after a time and succeeded by Maj. F. H. Kelly, R.E.

to the two companies of Imperial Service Sappers. The 2nd Division came in for most of the fighting. "I have never had a more strenuous time than in the Tirah" writes Major-General Sir Theodore Fraser.[1] "The campaign in South Africa was a mere picnic compared with it and the trenches in Flanders were no worse." In this expedition the Madras Sappers and Miners were tried to the limit and stood every test. "Who *are* these Madras Sappers? Are they *soldiers?*" asked a British cavalry officer at a Bangalore polo tournament. The Tirah provides the answer, if answer is needed.

Major-General Yeatman-Biggs, with the 2nd Division and 43,000 transport animals, started from Kohat on October 11th, 1897, and, marching by Hangu and Shinwari, turned northwards, carried the heights of Dargai in a spectacular assault on October 20th and descended on the following day into the Khanki Valley. Both divisions then concentrated at Kharappa and continuing northwards carried the Sampagha Pass on the 29th and entered the Mastura Valley. Two days later, the whole force, less one brigade, surmounted the Arhanga Pass and camped in the fertile Maidan district where most of the villages were found to be deserted. On November 9th an action was fought on the Saran Sar Ridge to the north-east, and afterwards a brigade scoured the Waran Valley and three brigades advanced to Bagh and beyond it to Dwa Toi in the Bara Valley. Punitive operations were next extended westwards, and by the end of November the Orakzais and Chamkannis north of Sadda had been subdued. A general evacuation of the Tirah was begun on December 7th after every part of the country had been visited. Sir William Lockhart moved his two divisions eastwards by separate routes converging at Barkai some 20 miles north-west of Kohat and near the junction of the Bara and Mastura Rivers. The 1st Division had an easy passage down the Waran and Mastura Valleys through Mishti Bazar and Hissar to Barand Khel, followed by a difficult climb over the Tsaprai (Sapri) Pass and a long descent by Khwaja Kidr; but the five days' march of the 2nd Division down the parallel Bara Valley was so arduous and costly that it has been compared with the retreat from Kabul in 1842 though happily it did not end in disaster. The Zakka Khel Afridis launched desperate and repeated assaults against the rearguard, the troops were almost paralysed by the extreme cold, and the casualties were heavy. However, the battered and weary 2nd Division met the 1st Division near Barkai and the main operations of the Tirah Field Force then ended. There remained only to punish the Zakka Khel by visiting their homes in the Bazar Valley further north and to reopen the Khaibar Pass. These operations were accomplished by the 1st Division and the Peshawar Column respectively during the latter half of December, but the last of the Afridi clans did not submit until their country had been blockaded for several months.

As the experiences and achievements of the Sappers and Miners in the Tirah are recorded somewhat meagrely in official despatches and histories,

[1]Notes by Maj.-Gen. Sir Theodore Fraser, K.C.B., C.S.I., C.M.G., late R.E., sent to the author on Sept. 22nd, 1937.

they may be elaborated in these pages by quoting a few extracts from notes by officers who were present. Brigadier Gervers describes as follows the experiences of the 3rd Company, Bombay S. & M., with the 1st Division :—[1] " At Kohat we were supplied with pack transport of the worst description—fifty young ponies which could hardly carry even the regulation pack saddle—and the weary march through Kahi and Hangu to Shinwari began. Hearn and I had our revolvers stolen from under our pillows at the first camp.[2] The company was at Shinwari during the two attacks on Dargai and next day proceeded to the Chagru Kotal[3] on which we bivouacked for the night in bitter cold. In the morning we began to prepare the road down into the Kharappa defile and, by continuous blasting throughout the day, made it passable for transport. We were present at the attacks on the Sampagha and Arhanga Passes and afterwards encamped with the whole force at Maidan. While there, our daily task consisted in converting the track over the Arhanga Pass into a graded road for camels. We moved with the 1st Division to Bagh, where the whole force was soon established. Sir William Lockhart wished to find a way down the Bara Valley so he accompanied a reconnaissance in force to Dwa Toi by a large column including the 3rd Company, Bombay S. & M., and the 4th Company, Madras S. & M. The route taken was the most arduous of the whole campaign and led mostly along a track in the bed of the stream. The temperature was so low that the tails of our Arab ponies became whip-lashes of ice. No baggage got through that night and even Sir William was tentless. We marched back the next day and were detailed with the Madras company and other troops to proceed into the Chamkanni territory. The Chamkannis were punished and we returned to Bagh through the Mishti Bazar and Adam Khel country.[4] Sir William Lockhart decided to leave the Tirah by two routes and we were with the 1st Division which marched over the Arhanga Pass and down to Mastura Valley. No opposition was encountered and we were joined at Tsaprai (Sapri) by a brigade which had marched through the Waran Valley. The Tsaprai Pass was densely wooded and the track very rough and narrow. As it was a matter of single file all the way it was fortunate for us that the Afridis had been drawn away to contend the passage of the 2nd Division down the Bara Valley. Arrived at Mamanai, near Barkai, the 1st Division was ordered to proceed to Bara *en route* for Jamrud. The re-opening of the Khaibar Pass found the 3rd Company on the move. Just before Christmas, the 1st Division marched to Ali Masjid, and on Christmas Day we entered the Bazar Valley and blew up towers at Chora. On December 26th we proceeded up the valley and camped for the night at China where we

[1]Notes by Brig. F. R. S. Gervers, C.I.E., C.B.E., late R.E., sent to the author on Dec. 4th, 1937.

[2]Rifle thieves on the frontier are most enterprising and follow a lucrative trade. On one occasion when a Sapper had halted for a few moments to adjust the load on a transport animal, his rifle was whipped away from behind from under his arm and the thief made good his escape in the darkness. It is rumoured that at Rawalpindi in 1939 a certain unit of Imperial Service Sappers used to bury their rifles each night in camp to safeguard them, and, as a further precaution, made a man sleep on the newly turned earth !

[3]A pass between Dargai and Gulistan.

[4]The Adam Khel inhabit the country north of Khanki Bazar.

demolished all the towers before withdrawing to Ali Masjid. At China, General Methuen, who was with us as a spectator, had the narrowest escape of his life. We had lit our mine-fuzes on the order to march but fortunately Rundle and I happened to return to one tower to see that all was correct and within it we found the General in temporary seclusion. In another minute the tower would have been down and Methuen missing."

Colonel Sir Gordon Hearn, who served also with the 3rd Company, Bombay S. & M., adds that, after the Sampagha and Arhanga Passes had been forced, the company worked until November 14th on the road over the latter. On November 26th, following the reconnaissance to Dwa Toi, it marched, as recorded by Gervers, with the column under Brig.-General A. Gaselee which made a circular tour through the Chamkanni country and returned on December 6th to Bagh. " I remember " writes Hearn,[1] " that on one occasion I was assisted by Sir Pertab Singh of Jodhpur in levering a boulder off the road, my men being frozen stiff. We proceeded to the Mastura and joined the 1st Brigade thus escaping the disastrous march under Brig.-General Kempster down the Bara Valley. Going through Mishti Bazar and Barand Khel and over the Tsaprai Pass we reached Bara on December 15th and Jamrud on the 18th. On Christmas Day we invaded the Bazar Valley and on December 27th blew up 13 towers at China Bazar before returning to Chora and later to Jamrud. I regret to say that Lieutenant C. R. Tonge, R.E., of the 4th (Bombay) Company, was killed on December 28th through the premature explosion of a mine."

Major-General Wright records the following experiences in command of the 4th Company, Madras S. & M.—[2] " On August 14th, 1897, while watching a polo match I received orders that the company should mobilize and proceed to Rawalpindi, and to show the state of efficiency of the Corps I may say that we entrained complete at 6 p.m. on the following day. After a fortnight at Rawalpindi we were sent to Khushalgarh to take charge of the boat bridge over the Indus and to prepare it for the advance of the troops to Kohat. For the next six weeks the company watched the troops march forward, but finally, at 10.30 p.m. on September 21st, we were ordered to advance and were on the march by midnight. Covering 44 miles in the next 24 hours, we joined the 2nd Division at Shinwari. The company was in action at Dargai and I think in every other battle of the Tirah Campaign. The return march down the Bara Valley was very trying. While the troops were pushing forward it was impossible to do anything to improve the evil paths along which they stumbled. I did my best to help them along by leaving detachments of Sappers at the crossings of streams to drag the weary mules through, as the muleteers could not manage their strings of four or five animals apiece.[3] My sword was frozen in its scabbard

[1]Notes by Col. Sir Gordon R. Hearn, C.I.E., D.S.O., late R.E., sent to the author on Sept. 21st, 1937. The 1st Brigade (1st Division) was under Brig.-Gen. Reginald Hart, V.C., late R.E. Brig.-Gen. F. J. Kempster commanded the 3rd Brigade (2nd Division) which bore the brunt of the rearguard work in the retreat down the Bara valley.

[2]Notes by Maj.-Gen. H. B. H. Wright, C.B., C.M.G., late R.E., sent to the author on Oct. 9th, 1937.

[3]From Dec. 10th to 14th the 4th Company, Madras S. & M., formed part of the advanced guard in the march down the Bara Valley.

and my horse's tail was a mass of icicles. Yet the Madras Sappers came through it all cheerfully. Before debouching into India the force halted at Mamanai and the company built an excellent suspension bridge over the Bara River. The cables were attached to their anchorages by railway carriage screw-couplings which enabled us to get an even tension. When we reached Peshawar on April 9th, 1898, we were ordered to join the Swat Movable Column and there we spent the next year."

Captain H. Dawkins relates some of the experiences of the 1st Company, Bengal S. & M., under Serjeant. "The company marched over Dargai from Shinwari to Kharappa Camp," he writes,[1] "and followed the main force to the Sampagha Pass where we worked for several weeks on the road. Afterwards, we worked on the Arhanga Pass until the force retired from the Tirah.[2] On that journey we had to traverse a defile named Dwa Toi where a certain sniper proceeded to take a particularly heavy toll of men and mules—so heavy, indeed, that General Lockhart is said to have asked his Pathan orderly how best to get rid of the marksman. "Leave that to me, Sahib," replied the orderly and proceeded to climb rapidly up the hillside. Some minutes later, a shot was heard and down fell an ancient Pathan, complete with rifle. "*Shabash*, Akbar Khan," exclaimed the General. "How did you manage it?" "Well, Sahib," said the orderly rather shyly, "you know that I belong to these parts; and as the old man was my father, of course I knew his ways."

To complete the picture, a few extracts may be given from notes by Brig.-General U. W. Evans on some of his experiences. Evans came from Bangalore where, he states, the Madras Corps had for several years been very keen on polo. C. H. Roe, T. Fraser, H. J. M. Marshall, E. L. Dunsterville, J. A. S. Tulloch, J. R. Chancellor, W. S. Traill, G. A. F. Sanders, S. G. Loch, N. M. Hemming and Evans himself all played as much as their limited means permitted. The game was very popular also in the Bengal and Bombay Corps and it is regrettable that no account of the victories of Sapper and Miner teams on the polo field can find a place in this narrative of military engineering. The same restriction applies to records of shooting, pigsticking and rowing; but it is to be hoped that these diversions may be dealt with in another volume at some future date for they would make fascinating reading. It must suffice to say that in August 1897 Evans abandoned his polo and, moving first to Calcutta and then to the frontier, began his very diverse duties in charge of the Madras Sapper Field Park at Kohat and Shinwari. The Field Park was expected to supply anything and everything at short notice and on one occasion Evans received a demand for twelve coffins. "Corporal Slade soon produced one," he writes,[3] "but as it looked too small, though he maintained that it was not, I told him to get into it himself. At this he turned rather

[1]Notes by Capt. H. Dawkins, M.B.E., R.E. (I.A.) (retd.), sent to the author on Jan. 6th, 1938.

[2]Both the 1st and 5th Companies, Bengal S. & M., took part later in the Bazar Valley and Khaibar operations. Capt. J. R. B. Serjeant, R.E., died at Landi Kotal on Aug. 1st, 1898, after commanding the 1st Company for 11 years.

[3]Notes by Brig.-Gen. U. W. Evans, C.B., C.M.G., late R.E., sent to the author on May 29th, 1937.

pale, having been none too well of late, but after some objection he lay down in it and proved his point. I suffered much ridicule about these coffins. One of them was commandeered, on its way to the front, by Major R. S. Scallon of the Imperial Service Troops who wanted an arms-chest. It was duly filled with arms and sent to Rawalpindi, and later there was a rumour (fortunately without foundation) that it had been given a military funeral because Scallon's name was on the lid ! "

So much for the lighter side of active service on the North-West Frontier. In the Tirah Campaign there was little that was amusing. It was a grim business ; but as a military achievement, the march of the long column plodding its way down the Bara Valley will live in history as an epic of endurance. That march, as indeed every movement of every force in every area, was helped and accelerated by the labours of the Sappers and Miners and of their redoubtable assistants the Pioneers, and in March 1900 all three Corps were awarded the honours " Tirah " and " Punjab Frontier."[1]

With the submission of the Afridis in 1898, the exhausted frontier settled down gradually to a period of recuperation broken only by sporadic trouble in Waziristan. During the vice-royalty of Lord Curzon, strategic railways were built to Dargai, Jamrud and Thal and Sappers and Miners were often employed on these or other lines. For instance, from December 1900 to March 1901 the 2nd Company of the Bengal Corps was occupied in platelaying on the Ludhiana-Jakhal chord,[2] and from January to July 1901 the 1st Company was at work on the Khushalgarh-Kohat-Thal line. The 1st and 5th Companies, Madras S. & M.,[3] and the 5th and 6th Companies, Bengal S. & M., as well as the Sirmur Sapper Company, also helped to complete this line, and during the winter of 1901–02 and the following spring and summer no less than four Sapper units were employed on it. Regarding the part taken by the 6th Company under Captain W. H. Beach, R.E., Lieut.-General Sir Ronald Charles writes :—[4]
" The idea was to train the Sappers and Miners in railway construction, and during the cold weather the 5th and 6th Companies and Evans' company of Madras Sappers developed a fine competitive spirit which ultimately enabled them together to lay and rough-pack a mile of 2 ft. 6 in. track a day. The length laid was about 20 miles, ending at Kohat station. The Executive Engineer having suggested that the 6th Company should mark in some way its share in the construction I cast about in my mind for a suitable inscription to be cut on a stone memorial. The problem was solved, however, by a Jat Havildar who was superintending the laying of the last few pairs of rails into Kohat and enquired how far he should go. I indicated the last sleeper, on which he at once chalked " *Yahan tak* " (Thus far). So " *Yahan tak* " it was ; and an admirably laconic inscrip-

[1]G.O., No. 288, dated March 16th, 1900.
[2]See " The Ludhiana-Dhuri-Jakhal Railway," by Capt. P. Maud, R.E., appearing in *Prof. Papers of the Corps of Royal Engineers*, Vol. 28, 1902, pp. 99–120.
[3]*Historical Record of the Q.V.O. Madras Sappers and Miners*, Vol. I, pp. 179–181.
[4]Notes by Lieut.-Gen. Sir J. R. E. Charles, K.C.B., C.M.G., D.S.O., Col-Commandant, R.E., sent to the author on Oct. 18th, 1937.

tion too, though I should have liked to add " and no further, thank God," if my knowledge of Hindustani had permitted.

The trouble in Waziristan after the end of the general rising of the frontier tribes took the form of treacherous attacks on convoys and survey parties and the non-payment of fines imposed by the Government, and as a reprisal a Mahsud Blockade was instituted in December, 1900, by means of a chain of police posts supported by movable columns of troops. However, as the outrages still continued, columns were organized at Datta Khel, Jandola, Sarwekai and Wana to execute " counter-raids " into tribal territory. Four series of these operations were undertaken between November 1901 and January, 1902, and proved so effective that order was soon restored, and, with a last flicker of rebellion from the Kabul Khel late in 1902, all serious disturbances ceased. Officers and men of the Sappers and Miners took part in the blockade and counter-raids. For instance, in September 1900 half the 1st Company, Bengal S. & M., under Lieutenant S. H. Sheppard, R.E., left Roorkee for the Tochi Valley to join a column proceeding against the Madda Khel clan of the Darwesh Khel Wazirs and was on service till the beginning of November when it moved to Kohat to rejoin the other half-company then at work on the railway.[1] Sheppard himself returned to Waziristan on special duty in November 1901 and was joined there by Lieutenant E. F. J. Hill, R.E. Lieutenant F. D. Irvine, R.E., was also present with a party of Madras Sappers. Sheppard and Hill, with detachments from the 3rd Company of the Bengal Corps, took part in counter-raids against the Kabul Khel. On January 6th, 1902, when Sheppard was preparing to blow up a tower which was believed to be empty, fire was opened on his demolition party and one man was wounded. Captain C. O. Swanston of the 18th Bengal Lancers then reinforced the party and under a heavy fusillade the two British officers carried the wounded Sapper down a steep slope to a place of safety. Both were subsequently awarded the Distinguished Service Order.[2] Mention must be made also of a gallant action by Lieutenant C. M. Browne, R.E., and four men of the 3rd Company who in November 1902 blew down a tower at the village of Gumatti under close fire from Darwesh Khel outlaws who had taken refuge in it.[3]

Some of the men who served on the North-West Frontier in 1897 and 1898 were selected in May 1902 to accompany an Indian Contingent detailed to proceed to England to attend the coronation of H.M. King Edward VII. The Sappers and Miners so selected were under the command of Captain G. H. Boileau, R.E., of the Bombay Corps, and comprised 3 Indian officers and 48 Indian other ranks drawn from all three Corps.[4] They took part in the various ceremonies and were shown the usual sights, and no doubt they were duly impressed, though less so perhaps

[1] *History and Digest of Service of the 1st K.G.O. Sappers and Miners*, p. 69.

[2] *London Gazette*, Sept. 2nd, 1902. The incident is recorded in an article entitled " The Operations in Waziristan," appearing in *The R.E. Journal*, Vol. XXXII, 1902, p. 161.

[3] " Operations against the Darwesh Khel Wazirs," appearing in *The R.E. Journal*, Vol. XXXIII, 1903, pp. 157, 158.

[4] *Madras Corps*—Subadar Devasahayam and 15 I.O.R.s ; *Bengal Corps*—Subadar-Maj. Hira Singh and 16 I.O.R.s ; *Bombay Corps*—Subadar-Maj. Rup Singh and 17 I.O.R.s.

than a certain Lance-Naik of the Madras Corps who, after gazing in rapture on the ballet at the old Empire Music Hall in 1882, is said to have ejaculated " Sir. This is indeed God's House ! " However, the contingent of 1902 thoroughly enjoyed a novel experience. The officers and men were resplendent in new uniforms and created a very good impression, but a distinctive feature of the Bengal Sapper kit had vanished. This was the necklace of alternate gold and crimson beads as large as walnuts which until 1897 had adorned the neck of every Indian officer in full dress. Jemadars wore one necklace, Subadars two and Subadar-Majors no less than three. The necklaces had been condemned as " effeminate " by a distinguished General and so they had disappeared. The Indian officers naturally deplored a change in an old custom, yet the abolition of necklaces relieved them of considerable expense on promotion.

Some mention must be made of the work of the " balloonatics "—the officers and men of the Bengal Sappers and Miners who composed the personnel of a Balloon Section stationed at Rawalpindi for employment on the North-West Frontier though never actually used in war. In 1900 the Government of India decided to form an " Experimental Balloon Section " and in August, 1901, brought to Rawalpindi 7 men of the 4th Balloon Section under Captain A. H. B. Hume, R.E., who had served in the Third China War. The remainder of the 4th Balloon Section returned to Aldershot under Lieutenant T. E. Martin-Leake, R.E. Captain W. A. Stokes, R.E., took charge of the experimental unit soon after its arrival and was joined by Lieutenant G. C. B. Loch, R.E. A detachment of 28 men of the Bengal Sappers and Miners under Company-Sergeant-Major H. Dawkins, R.E., was sent from Roorkee and, with 8 non-commissioned officers, completed the original establishment.[1] Hydrogen was manufactured in Rawalpindi and carried (compressed) in long steel cylinders loaded on wagons. The first experiment with the balloon *Venus* (11,500 cu. ft.) in the Murree foot-hills showed the risk of damage from trees and rocks though some useful observation was carried out. Lieutenant F. C. Molesworth, R.E., joined the Section in June, 1902, when Stokes handed over command to G. C. B. Loch. November found the unit in Delhi for the Coronation Durbar and afterwards the balloon *Achilles* (13,000 cu. ft.), was used to transport troops across a canal. Larger balloons, made of cotton fabric, were supplied in 1904, but their valves were defective and they gave much trouble. By this time the strength of the unit had mounted to 51 of all ranks. Molesworth left the Section and Lieutenant T. H. L. Spaight, R.E., joined it early in 1905. A demonstration was given in 1907 at Agra for the benefit of the Amir of Afghanistan, and Lieutenant P. W. L. Broke-Smith, R.E., joined the establishment. Experiments by Broke-Smith near Murree at an altitude of 7,000 feet proved that the available balloons were too small for use at such a height and were consequently unsuitable for frontier warfare.[2] In 1908 a death-blow was given to the

[1]Notes by Lieut.-Col. G. C. B. Loch, R.E. (retd.), sent to the author on Nov. 11th, 1937.
[2]Notes by Brig. P. W. L. Broke-Smith, C.I.E., D.S.O., O.B.E., late R.E., sent to the author on Feb. 28th, 1938.

prospects of the Balloon Section by recent developments in aeroplanes. Loch and Broke-Smith having left the unit, Spaight took it to Roorkee as Government was contemplating its abolition. Lieutenant C. E. Colbeck, R.E., assumed charge and afterwards Lieutenant L. Evans, R.E., and at the end of 1910 the Balloon Section ceased to exist. The men rejoined their companies and most of the equipment was sold by auction, the balloon envelopes, which had cost hundreds of pounds, fetching only a few annas.

Many amusing stories might be told of ballooning by the Bengal Sappers. Someone describing an ascent said that he saw the officer in the car " shouting down the telephone with one hand and being dreadfully sick with the other." When the cease-fire was sounded on certain manœuvres in 1902 all units were ordered to march on the balloon which appeared to be stationary at a height of 1,000 feet. Unfortunately, however, it was actually being towed along at a smart pace and the confusion which ensued among the sweating troops may be left to the imagination. The last occasion on which a captive balloon was used in field exercises was in 1909 when the Commandant (Lieut.-Colonel G. M. Heath, R.E.) and his Adjutant (Lieut. E. H. Kelly, R.E.) tried to manœuvre a balloon at night towards some trenches below the Siwaliks and were ignominiously captured by the 4th Company.[1] Some three years later, the next Commandant (Lieut.-Colonel P. G. Twining, R.E.) was ordered to prepare a few small signal balloons[2] for manœuvres and was told that arrangements had been made with the North-Western Railway at Saharanpur to fill them with gas. He replied briefly that coal gas is heavier than air. Nevertheless, he was directed to " experiment " and consequently sent a Warrant Officer to Saharanpur to watch the inflation of a balloon which could never leave the ground and subsequently to prepare a suitable report for transmission to Simla.[3]

Although all was quiet on the North-West Frontier for several years after the counter-raids in Waziristan had taken effect, the Zakka Khel Afridis of the Bazar Valley began in 1907 to raid so persistently across the border that it became necessary to despatch a punitive expedition against them. Accordingly, two brigades with the necessary divisional troops and ancillary services were organized and placed under the command of Major-General Sir James Willcocks, who left Peshawar on February 13th, 1908, and concentrated his force near Ali Masjid in the Khaibar Pass. The Commanding Royal Engineer (Lieut.-Colonel W. J. D. Dundee, R.E.) had under his orders 3 sections of the 9th Company, Madras S. & M., under Captain C. M. Wagstaff, R.E., with Lieutenants T. P. Bassett, E. P. Le Breton and J. A. McQueen, R.E., and the 6th Company, Bengal S. & M., under Captain J. R. E. Charles, R.E., with Lieutenants A. J. G. Bird, G. E. Sopwith and L. V. Bond, R.E. The operations of the Bazar Valley Field Force were models of celerity and efficiency. The entrances

[1]Notes by Col. C. E. Colbeck, M.C., late R.E., sent to the author on Dec. 22nd, 1937.
[2]These signal balloons had been retained when the original equipment was sold.
[3]Notes by Capt. H. Dawkins, M.B.E., R.E. (I.A.) (retd.), sent to the author on Jan. 6th, 1938.

to the valley were taken by surprise. Chora and Walai were seized on February 15th and the work of destroying China and other villages proceeded steadily. On the 21st a combined attack of the two brigades was made on Halwai, and the Zakka Khel having submitted on the 27th the troops withdrew to Jamrud. The entire expedition had occupied less than three weeks.

There is little to record of the work of the Sappers and Miners. Both companies carried out the usual demolitions, road repairs and water supply.[1] As regards his experiences in this brief expedition, Lieut.-General Sir Ronald Charles remarks :—[2] " To pander to the rage for secrecy, the two brigades were ordered to pitch their camp outside Peshawar and spend a night there before starting. The tents were left standing in order to delude the Zakka Khel—who were 30 miles away—that this was a camp for divisional training only ; and it did not seem to have occurred to the responsible strategist at Simla that the tribesmen would guess that a column 8,000 strong, which raised a vast cloud of dust along the Peshawar-Jamrud road, was probably marching for the Khaibar where manœuvres were impossible. However, the leading brigade advanced practically unopposed up the Bazar Valley to the vicinity of Walai where we camped with it in a nullah and afterwards accompanied several expeditions to destroy the adjacent Zakka Khel villages, notably China and Halwai. China had a dozen well-built towers, but Halwai only one ramshackle affair. The 6th Company was with the 1st Brigade and the 9th Company under Wagstaff with the 2nd Brigade, and as Halwai was the objective of a combined attack it was evident that the privilege of destroying its solitary tower would be accorded to whichever company arrived there first. I therefore implored the hotly engaged infantry to cease firing at a non-existent enemy and, bursting through them with a section of Sappers, made straight for the tower while I could see Wagstaff performing the same manœuvre from another direction. The Bengal Sappers won the race, and climbing on to the roof I entered into an argument with Wagstaff down below as to who should have the pleasure of demolishing the tower. I had directed Bond, my junior subaltern, to follow at full speed with explosives and tools, but as these had not yet arrived and Wagstaff had his equipment mules with him I had to carry on the argument until Bond approached at the double, urging a reluctant mule along with a *khud*-stick in one hand while with the other he held up his breeches which had somehow come adrift. Wagstaff then good-naturedly stood down and the 6th Company proceeded with the demolition." The only remark of Major-General Bond on this graphic account is that he believes that he held a sword and not a *khud*-stick in his less responsibly occupied hand and that this was the only occasion on which he was ever called upon to use that weapon in war.[3]

[1]The work of the 9th Company, Madras S. & M. is recorded in the *Historical Record of the Q.V.O. Madras Sappers and Miners*, Vol. I, p. 205. See also the report of the C.R.E. Bazar Valley Field Force appearing in *Frontier and Overseas Expeditions from India*, Vol. II, Supplement A. (1908), p. 41.

[2]Notes by Lieut.-Gen. Sir J. R. E. Charles, K.C.B., C.M.G., D.S.O., Col.-Commandant, R.E., sent to the author on Oct. 18th, 1937.

[3]Letter from Maj.-Gen. L. V. Bond, C.B., late R.E., dated Dec. 5th, 1937.

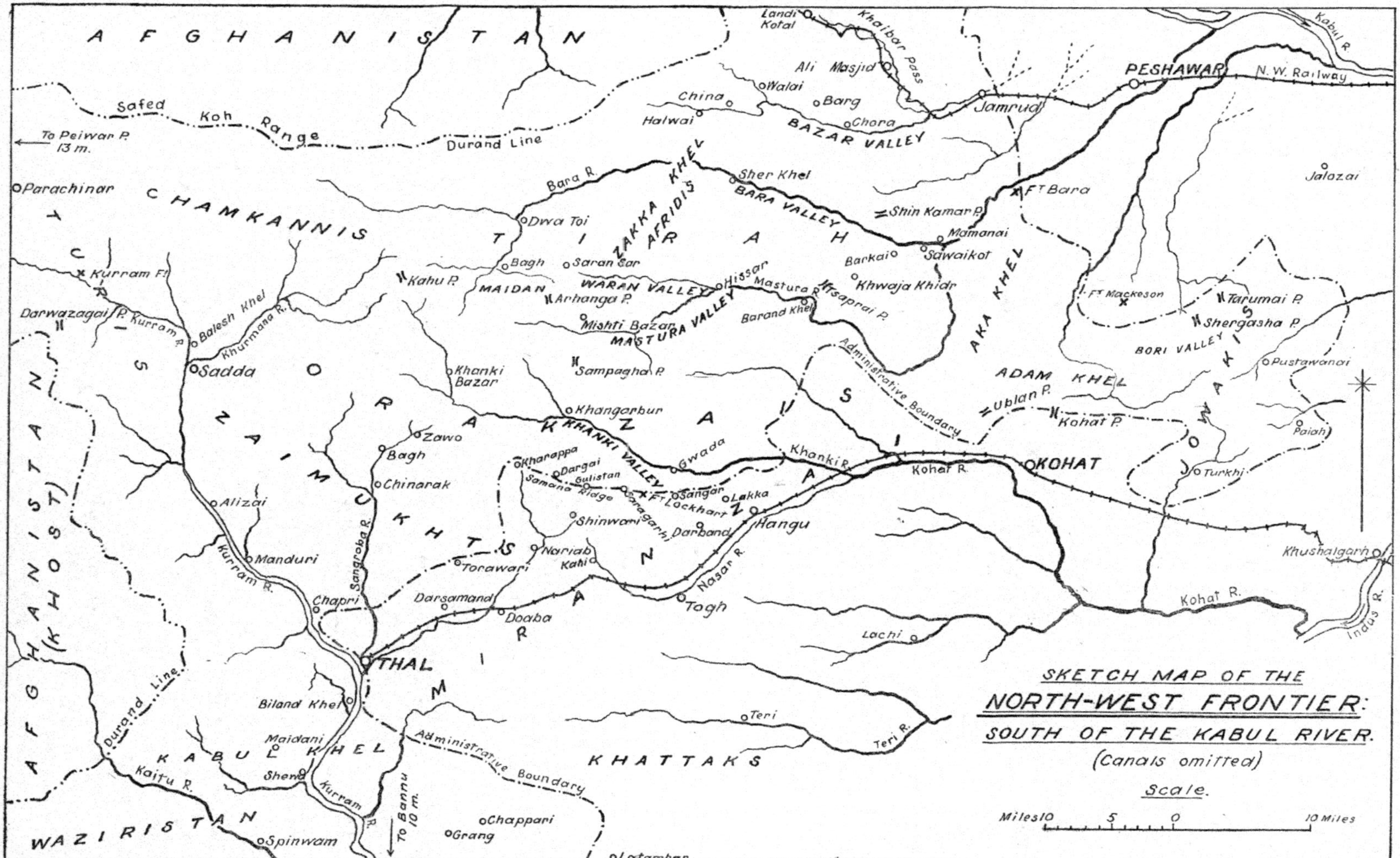

SKETCH MAP OF THE NORTH-WEST FRONTIER: SOUTH OF THE KABUL RIVER.

(Canals omitted)

Scarcely had the Bazar Valley Field Force returned to Peshawar than it was learnt that the Mohmands were rising and it became necessary to move troops to the border beyond Shabkadar and to repel an assault in April 1908. Parties of Afghans joined the Mohmands in attacking Landi Kotal in the Khaibar, but Sir James Willcocks drove them back and made early preparations to invade the Mohmand territory. He did so with three brigades[1] to which were attached the necessary divisional troops and services including several units and detachments of the Bengal Sappers and Miners. These were the 1st Company under Captain A. H. Cunningham, R.E., with Lieutenants E. J. Loring and A. F. Macauley, R.E., the 6th Company under Captain J. R. E. Charles, R.E., with Lieutenants A. J. G. Bird, L. V. Bond and B. H. Fox, R.E., a detachment of the 2nd Company under Lieutenant P. C. S. Hobart, R.E., and two Telephone Sections under Captain T. H. L. Spaight and Lieutenant H. W. Tomlinson, R.E. The Commanding Royal Engineer was Lieut.-Colonel W. J. D. Dundee, R.E. Willcocks crossed the Karapa Pass on May 14th with the 1st Brigade, and two days later the 1st and 2nd Brigades were below the Nahakki Pass. The 1st Brigade then crossed that pass and, except on one occasion, encountered little resistance. On May 18th the 2nd Brigade moved westwards up the Bohai Valley while Willcocks marched northwards with the 1st Brigade and occupied Lakarai on the 21st. Already the Mohmands were beginning to tender their submission. The 1st Brigade next proceeded eastwards against the Utman Khel and defeated them on the Ambahar River on May 23rd, and then, turning southwards, dealt with a rebellious clan to the east of Nahakki. By May 21st, Willcocks had overrun the entire Mohmand country and had subdued all the clans except one near the Afghan border. This was brought to order by the 2nd Brigade, and the Mohmand Field Force returned to India after a campaign lasting only 20 days.

Incessant road-work by day, and restless nights caused by persistent sniping, proved very exhausting to the Sappers and Miners. The companies were expected also to organize and control the supply of water from village tanks. For the first few days the men had no chance of cooking their meals, and as the snipers prevented them from lighting fires at night they had to exist on uncooked *atta*. Nevertheless, they made no complaint and a week elapsed before they asked that at the next camp they might be allotted a section of the perimeter which contained a building so that they might cook under cover. By June 5th the Sapper companies were back in Roorkee after accounting for more than 100 Mohmand towers.

Between 1908 and the outbreak of the Great War there were no disturbances of any importance on the North-West Frontier, though the prevalent calm was broken occasionally by minor insurrections which demanded punitive measures. For instance, in February 1914 the inhabitants of two villages in the Buner country raided Rustam and the 1st and 2nd Brigades from Peshawar and Nowshera were sent to clear up the

[1] 1st, 2nd and 3rd Brigades under Brig.-Gen. C. A. Anderson, Maj.-Gen. A. A. Barrett and Brig.-Gen. J. Ramsay respectively.

situation and secure compensation. Among the troops concentrated at Rustam was the 1st Company, Bengal S. & M., under Captain A. R. C. Sanders, R.E., with Lieutenant W. Cave-Browne, R.E., which had been engaged in field training at Akora east of Nowshera. The force marched to the Malandrai Pass on the night of February 22nd–23rd and reached the summit at daybreak. Nawe Kalai and another village were destroyed by the 1st Company and 82nd Punjabis and by nightfall all the troops were back in Rustam.[1] This raid is typical of others undertaken to police tribal territory, and with it we may conclude the long story of the exploits of the Madras, Bengal and Bombay Sappers and Miners on the North-West Frontier from 1849 to 1914.

The rugged mountains, barren uplands and sombre gorges of the great barrier between India and Afghanistan have been the scene of many heroic deeds, many notable achievements and many disasters. They change little with the passage of time, presenting to the world the same wild and seemingly trackless wilderness of crags and defiles as in the days of the early Afghan wars. Yet roads and railways are creeping steadily through them month by month and year by year, bringing peace and contentment and fostering trade and agriculture. This extension of communications is one of the chief tasks of the engineers of India and much of it has fallen to the lot of the Indian Sappers and Miners, the pioneers of the Frontier.

[1]Notes by Col. W. Cave-Browne, C.B.E., D.S.O., M.C., late R.E., and Major W. E. Coltham, R.E. (I.A.) (retd.), sent to the author on June 22nd and July 23rd, 1937.

CHAPTER XV

EXPEDITIONS ON THE NORTH-EAST FRONTIER, 1860–1913

THE country and people of the North-East Frontier of India are as different from those of the North-West as the proverbial chalk from cheese. Windswept and icy tablelands, or stupendous mountain ridges clad in dense jungle and deluged for months by rain, are substituted for the bare and rocky gorges and defiles of the Afghan border, and men whose features bear the imprint of China replace the semitic Pathan. North of the Himalaya, above Nepal, lie the mysterious and desolate wastes of Tibet stretching eastwards for more than a thousand miles from the region of Simla to the point at which the Tsan-po bursts southwards through the main range to reappear in Assam as the Brahmaputra. On the southern slopes of the Himalaya, east of Nepal, lies Sikkim, and further eastwards, Bhutan. Then come the territories of the Akas, Daflas and Miris, and in the extreme north-east, the land of the Abors and Mishmis. South of the Brahmaputra live the Singphos, Nagas and Manipuris, and the Garos, Khasias and Jaintias near Shillong; and still further south the Lushais and Chins who inhabit a country of precipitous and forest covered ranges running north and south and presenting an effectual barrier to free intercourse between India and Burma.[1] The tactical and strategical problems of warfare on the North-East Frontier are simpler than on the North-West because the tribesmen are less numerous and less formidable though the country is more difficult. Except amid the glaciers of Tibet, jungle fighting is the order of the day. In bygone years the chief weapons were poisoned arrows, bamboo spikes and avalanches of stones. More of our soldiers, however, fell victims to malaria than to the primitive devices of man.

As on the North-West Frontier, unimportant punitive expeditions were often despatched without the inclusion of any engineer troops. For instance, the expeditions to Bhutan in 1772, 1828 and 1835 and to Sikkim in 1814 and 1850, and those against the Singphos in 1825, the Khasias and Jaintias between 1824 and 1829 and in 1862, the Lushais in 1844, 1849 and 1868, the Mishmis in 1855, the Abors in 1858 and 1894, the Nagas in 1875, 1877 and 1880, the Chins in 1887 and the Manipuris in 1891. It is probable that the services of regular Sappers and Miners were too much in demand elsewhere to be available for such minor operations. The first appearance of engineer troops in North-East Frontier warfare was in the third expedition to Sikkim in 1861 when Lieut.-Colonel J. C. Gawler, H.M. 6th Regiment, had two companies of "Sibandi Sappers" (190 men) in his force of 1,800 men. These Sibandis had recently been attacked by the Sikkim Bhutias while roadmaking in a strip

[1]See *Sketch Map of the North-East Frontier* included in this chapter.

of territory occupied by the Government as a reprisal and are said to have fled in all directions because they did not know how to use their firearms; but they deserve some notice because, during the campaign, they bridged the foaming torrent of the Tista River (212 feet wide) in 28 working hours and thus contributed materially to the success of the expedition.[1]

According to *Hobson-Jobson*, "Sibandi" troops were irregulars maintained for revenue or police duties. The Sappers presumably formed one branch of the establishment. Lord Napier of Magdala, who as a Captain commanded the Sibandi Sappers at Darjeeling from 1838 to 1842 before he made his military reputation in the Sikh wars, describes their origin in the following terms :—[2] "When Captain J. Gilmore, Bengal Engineers, was appointed to open the settlement of Darjeeling he was directed to raise two companies of Sebundy Sappers to provide the necessary labour. He obtained some native officers and non-commissioned officers from the Bengal Sappers and enlisted about half of each company. The first season found the little colony quite unprepared for the early commencement of the rains. All the coolies, who did not die, fled, and some of the Sappers deserted. Gilmore got sick and in 1838 I was suddenly ordered from the extreme border of Bengal to relieve him for a month. Just then our relations with Nepaul became strained and it was thought desirable to complete the Sebundy Sappers with men from the border hills unconnected with Nepaul. The necessary number were enlisted and sent to me. When they arrived, I found, instead of the 'fair recruits' announced, a number of most unfit men. It seemed probable that the original recruits had managed to insert substitutes during the journey. I encamped them on the newly opened road; but during the night there was a storm, and in the morning, to my intense relief, they had all disappeared. My month's acting appointment was turned into four years. I completed the Corps with Nepaulese and left them in a satisfactory condition. The men were armed and expected to fight if necessary. Their pay was Rs. 6 a month instead of the sepoy's Rs. 7½. I supplied the native officers and non-commissioned officers with pea-jackets out of my private means and made them smart and happy with a little gold lace." The last official reference to the Sibandis occurs in 1869 when mention is made of "The Sebundy Corps of Sappers and Miners employed at Darjeeling." As the establishment had then been maintained for more than thirty years it must have proved its value in the construction and repair of hill roads as well as in the field.

Three years elapsed after the third expedition to Sikkim before regular companies of Sappers and Miners made their first appearance on the North-East Frontier. This was in December, 1864, on the occasion of the fourth expedition to Bhutan under Brig.-General W. E. Mulcaster, when a "Duar Field Force" of one brigade and attached troops advanced northwards from Bengal in four columns, one from Gauhati on Diwangiri, a

[1] *Frontier and Overseas Expeditions from India*, Vol. IV, pp. 46–49.

[2] Letter from Field-Marshal Lord Napier of Magdala, G.C.B., G.C.S.I., Col.-Commandant, R.E., to Col. Sir Henry Yule, K.C.S.I., C.B., late R.E., quoted by the latter in an article entitled "Sebundy Sappers" appearing in *The R.E. Journal*, Vol. XV, 1885, p. 65.

second from Goalpara on Bissengiri, a third from Cooch Behar on Buxa and a fourth from Jalpaiguri on Chamurtsi. The 6th and 7th Companies, Bengal S. & M., marched with the columns from Cooch Behar and Jalpaiguri, while the two easterly columns had each a company of Sibandi Sappers.[1] One of the regular companies took with it a few pontoons for bridging. A bridge of boats was constructed by a company of Bengal Sappers across the Tista north of Jalpaiguri, and during December all four columns reached their objectives with little opposition. The country was then annexed and the force was about to withdraw when, at the end of January, 1865, the Bhutias suddenly launched a series of violent attacks on the British garrisons at Diwangiri, Bissengiri, Chamurtsi and other places. The Bengal Sappers did well in the fighting which ensued and particularly on January 29th at Diwangiri whither the 7th Company had been transferred. According to General Mulcaster, " the 7th Company covered themselves with glory on the night of the attack and were equally efficient when working with the pick and shovel or fighting with rifle and bayonet."[2] The Sappers counter-attacked with the infantry and Lieutenant J. H. Urquhart, R.E., was struck by a large bullet which severed his femoral artery. Had any of his men known how to apply a tourniquet, his life might have been saved; but unhappily he bled to death before medical aid could reach him. On February 4th, as the water-supply channel had been cut by the enemy, the troops evacuated Diwangiri and began a disastrous retreat to the plains, losing all their baggage and guns and lowering British prestige throughout the length and breadth of Northern India. In other quarters, however, the Bhutias met with little success. There was a tradition in the Bengal Corps that during the operations at Diwangiri a certain powerful Sapper named Dyal Singh picked up and carried on his back for a considerable distance an abandoned mountain gun.[3] This is possible as the mountain gun of those days weighed only 200 lbs.[4]

The campaign was brought to a successful conclusion after the supersession of Brig.-General Mulcaster by Brig.-General Henry Tombs, V.C., and the arrival, early in March, 1865, of large reinforcements including the 2nd Company, Bengal S. & M. Having deceived the Bhutias regarding his probable line of advance, Tombs attacked Diwangiri on April 3rd.[5] Most of the defenders fled, but 150 men took refuge in a loopholed block-house and prepared to fight to the last. The only means of entry was by scaling the wall, 14 feet in height, and squeezing head first through a narrow opening between the top of the wall and the flat roof. Tombs called

[1] *Bhotan and the Story of the Dooar War*, by Surgeon Rennie, pp. 163, 164.

[2] *Lectures on the Regimental History of the K.G.O Bengal Sappers and Miners*, by Lieut.-Col. L. V. Bond, R.E., p. 7.

[3] Sepoy (Sapper) Dyal Singh was awarded the Indian Order of Merit (3rd Class) for gallantry at Diwangiri on April 2nd, 1865.

[4] The 7-pounder guns of the elephant battery commanded by the author's father, Brevet-Col. (then Maj.) H. T. T. Sandes, R.A., in Burma in 1884 weighed 200 lbs. apiece. They were not screw guns.

[5] The operations in Bhutan are described in *Frontier and Overseas Expeditions from India*, Vol. IV, pp. 135–153. Also in *The Services of the Bengal Native Army*, by Lieut. F. G. Cardew, pp. 312–316, and in *Bhotan*, by Surgeon Rennie.

upon the storming party of native infantry to assault the place, but not a man would attempt it. Seeing this, he turned to Captain W. S. Trevor, R.(B.)E., who stood near him, and said "Will *no* officer give the men a lead?" "I will, sir," replied Trevor, and throwing away his scabbard, he took his sword in his teeth. Followed by Lieutenant J. Dundas, R.(B.)E., and a young British officer of the native infantry with a few men, he climbed the wall under a shower of stones, crawled through the opening and dropped among the enemy crowded below. Instantly, he was severely wounded by a spear-thrust but managed nevertheless to keep the Bhutias at bay with his revolver until Dundas and the others dropped alongside him, wounded and bruised.[1] So many Bhutias were crowded within the blockhouse that they could not use their swords with full effect and consequently they were slaughtered almost to a man when the storming party forced an entrance. For this gallant exploit all three officers were awarded the Victoria Cross[2] and the men who followed them received the Indian Order of Merit.

After the re-occupation of Diwangiri, the Bhutias offered little resistance in any part of the country though it was not until the end of February 1866 that they finally laid down their arms. The 7th Company, Bengal S. & M., returned to Roorkee in July 1865 and was replaced in Bhutan (generally known as the "Eastern Frontier") by the 4th, 5th and 8th Companies, so that in January, 1866, there were five regular and two Sibandi companies on service. The 2nd, 6th and 8th Companies returned to headquarters in March 1866 and the 4th and 5th Companies at the end of the year.[3] The campaign in Bhutan was remarkable rather for the fatigue undergone by the troops than for hard fighting, and the climate proved far more deadly than the enemy. The Sappers were employed for weeks at a time in hacking a way through dense jungle for the advance of the troops, but the companies were so weak that they could not perform the task properly and consequently there were many delays and heavy losses in transport animals.[4]

The scene now shifts temporarily from the slopes of the Himalaya to the forest-clad ranges of the frontier between India and Burma where it became necessary in 1871 to restrain the Lushais from raiding British territory. An excellent description of these peculiar people is given by Colonel Woodthorpe.[5] They were active, intelligent and great hunters,

[1]Memoir of Maj.-Gen. W.S. Trevor, V.C., late R.(B.)E., appearing in *The R.E. Journal*, Vol. VII, Jan.–June, 1908, pp. 79–85.

[2]*London Gazette*, Dec. 31st, 1867.

[3]*History and Digest of Service of the 1st K.G.O. Sappers and Miners*, pp. 27, 29. The names of the Company Commanders and Company Officers are not on record, but it may be noted that the following Royal Engineers received the Bhutan medal:—2nd Capts. G. N. Kelsall, F. S. Stanton, Aeneas Perkins, W. S. Trevor and J. L. Watts, and Lieuts. W. H. Collins, M. T. Sale, C. N. Judge, G. S. Hills, J. A. Armstrong, R. de Bourbel, J. H. Urquhart, F. Bailey, K. C. Pye, W. T. Whish, T. B. B. Savi, G. F. O. Boughey, T. H. Holdich, G. Strahan, C. Strahan, F. F. Cotton, W. J. Heaviside, A. J. C. Cunningham and J. Dundas.

[4]See the remarks of Capt. M. S. Bell, V.C., R.E., in "Proposed Organization of Indian Sappers," appearing in *The R.E. Journal*, Vol. IX, 1879, pp. 54, 55.

[5]"The Lushai Country," by Col. R. G. Woodthorpe, C.B., late R.E., appearing in the *Journal of the United Service Institution of India*, Vol. XIX, 1890, pp. 14–48.

but unclean in their habits and given to eating putrid meat. The men were heavy drinkers and both sexes inveterate smokers. Malaria was their only disease, and medicines of any sort were unknown to them. They had few firearms and relied chiefly on the poisoned arrow, the small bamboo stake or *pánji* concealed in the grass, and the long, two-handed Burmese knife or shorter *dao*. For them the whole art of war might be summed up in one word—" surprise "—and any foe reported to be on the alert was left in peace. To subdue these primitive folk, two small columns were formed, one under Brig.-General G. Bourchier at Silchar in the north and the other under Brig.-General C. H. Brownlow at Chittagong in the south, each column comprising 1,500 native infantry, half a mountain battery and a company of Sappers and Miners. The 1st Company of the Bengal Corps under Captain E. Harvey, R.E., with Lieutenant E. P. Leach, R.E., started from Silchar with the Northern Column on November 21st, 1871, and the 3rd Company under Lieutenant R. M. Hyslop, R.E., with the Southern Column from Chittagong at the beginning of December. The Northern Column struck eastwards and, turning southwards, passed through Kungnung and reached Champhai on February 17th, 1872.[1] Very little resistance was encountered and the troops returned to Silchar in March. The Southern Column marched north-eastwards through Demagiri and after a few skirmishes occupied Savanga. During January and February it scoured the surrounding country and finally returned to Chittagong in March after the Lushais had submitted.[2] In the course of these operations some 3,000 square miles of almost unknown territory were surveyed by Captain J. M. T. Badgley and Lieutenant R. G. Woodthorpe, R.E. The Sappers and Miners reached the theatre of war by ship from Calcutta to Chittagong where one company disembarked and the other voyaged up the Surma River to join the Northern Column at Silchar. They were highly praised for their work. The 1st Company was mentioned as indefatigable in going ahead and driving roads through almost impenetrable forests and along rocky mountain sides, and the 3rd Company as having worked with a willingness and intelligence worthy of the distinguished regiment (?) to which it belonged. The casualties in both companies, except from malaria, were negligible.

A detachment of 64 men from the 2nd and 7th Companies, Bengal S. & M., under Lieutenant F. J. Home, R.E.,[3] took part during the winter of 1874–75 in an expedition to the southern slopes of the Himalaya which would hardly be worthy of mention but for the unique fact that it was designed to deal with trouble arising from an outbreak of whooping cough! In 1871 that infantile complaint had attacked the Daflas of the plains north of the Brahmaputra and had spread to their kinsmen in the hills. The

[1] These places are shown in *Sketch Map of the North-East Frontier* included in this chapter.

[2] The operations during the fourth Lushai Expedition are described in *Frontier and Overseas Expeditions from India*, Vol. IV, pp. 244–247, *The Lushai Expedition*, 1871–1872, by Lieut. R. G. Woodthorpe, R.E., and " Narrative of the Cachar Column, Looshai Expeditionary Force," by Maj.-Gen. Frederick Roberts, V.C., C.B., appearing in *Proceedings of the United Service Institution of India*, Vol. VII, 1878, pp. 1–16.

[3] *History and Digest of Service of the 1st K.G.O. Sappers and Miners*, p. 31.

latter whooped their fury and demanded compensation. When that was refused, they raided the villages whence the infection had come and carried off a number of prisoners. The Government tried to secure the release of the captives by blockading the villages of the kidnappers, but this measure was ineffective and an expeditionary force of 800 men, including the Sapper detachment, was despatched into the Dafla hills in December, 1874, under the command of Brig.-General W. J. F. Stafford. The Daflas offered no resistance, and by the beginning of January, 1875, the offending villages had been occupied. The prisoners were then freed, fines were imposed and the troops withdrew.[1] By the middle of March the Sapper detachment was back in Roorkee after what may be described as an interesting trip to the hills. The Dafla Expedition of 1874–75 was organized on an absurdly large and costly scale for it is evident that an efficient body of armed police would have sufficed to restore order.

The Daflas having been subdued, the Government turned its attention to the Nagas south of the Brahmaputra and despatched three expeditions into their territory between 1875 and 1880. No Sappers and Miners were engaged in these operations, but soon after hostilities had ceased they were sent to the Naga Hills to make roads. The 6th Company, Bengal S. & M., under Lieutenant W. F. H. Stafford, R.E., with Lieutenant H. M. Jackson, R.E., came from Roorkee in November, 1881 and worked until the following April on a road from the plains at Nichuguard to the Naga capital at Kohima.[2] In October, 1882, the unit returned to the Naga Hills under Jackson with the 9th Company under Lieutenant A. C. Foley, R.E., and before the two companies left for Roorkee in April, 1883, they had completed the road to Kohima and built a fortified post.[3] The work involved much blasting in a precipitous gorge. According to Jackson, the Nagas had been thoroughly subdued and gave no trouble. Indeed, they assisted the Sappers by making bamboo shelters for them, in which accomplishment they were almost as expert as in cutting off heads.[4] It may be well to add that in later years other Sapper and Miner units were employed in improving the communications from Assam to the Naga Hills and Manipur. For instance, during the winter of 1891–92 the 1st and 4th Companies, Madras S. & M., under Lieutenants C. H. Roe and H. B. H. Wright, R.E., worked on the Manipur Road. The 1st Company undertook much blasting on precipices so treacherous that the men drilling holes had to be suspended from trees by ropes. The 4th Company was occupied chiefly in bridging.[5] During the following winter, the 3rd Company, Madras S. & M., under Lieutenant E. L. Dunsterville, R.E., with Lieutenant T. Fraser, R.E., and

[1]The operations are described in *Frontier and Overseas Expeditions from India*, Vol. IV, pp. 168–170. Visual signalling was carried out successfully by Capt. E. W. Begbie, M.I., and two men of the Madras S. & M., assisted by two volunteers. Such signalling was then in its infancy.

[2]Nichuguard is 20 miles west of Kohima, where the Japanese were repulsed in the recent World War.

[3]*History and Digest of Service of the 1st K.G.O. Sappers and Miners*, pp. 39, 41.

[4]Notes by Col. H. M. Jackson, late R.E., sent to the author on Sept. 8th, 1933.

[5]*Historical Record of the Q.V.O. Madras Sappers and Miners*, Vol. I, p. 148, and notes by Maj.-Gen. H. B. H. Wright, C.B., C.M.G., late R.E., sent to the author on Oct. 9th, 1937.

the 3rd Company, Bengal S. & M., under Captain A. G. Hunter-Weston, R.E., laboured with the 28th Bombay Pioneers on the Manipur Road. " Each unit had its own section " writes General Fraser,[1] " and we controlled large gangs of Kuki and Naga coolies, amusing people though head-hunters at heart. The Chief Engineer was Mr. G. K. Watts, P.W.D. There was much interesting work in the Namba Forest and any amount of shooting. Elephants used to knock down the telegraph poles and uproot the furlong posts along our new road, and one night our postman had to run past a tiger engaged in eating a pony alongside the road. When our two British non-commissioned officers were invalided and had to travel down the line by *tonga* they took the precaution of beating kerosine oil tins all the way to give tigers and elephants time to clear off." It is evident from these remarks that peaceful engineering on the Assam border had its exciting moments.

Some nine years after the subjection of the Daflas, the Government was obliged to adopt punitive measures against their neighbours, the Akas, a people who were divided into two clans known as the " lurkers among the cotton plants " and the " eaters-up of a thousand hearths." These shy and apparently voracious folk inhabited a jungle-covered and mountainous district north of the Brahmaputra and were armed chiefly with bows and arrows, the latter poisoned with aconite obtained from roots found near the Himalayan snows. The cause of the Aka Expedition, undertaken in December 1883 by a force of 1,000 men under Brig.-General R. S. Hill, was almost as ludicrous as that of the Dafla Expedition in 1874 for it arose from a misunderstanding about certain arrangements for the Calcutta Exhibition. The Government had asked that an Aka man and woman should be sent to Calcutta to sit as models, a request construed by the Akas into a demand that their Raja and Rani should be sold to the Calcutta Museum ![2] They seized the Government emissary and other persons and consequently an expedition was organized for the release of the captives. Among the troops detailed was the 2nd Company, Bengal S. & M., under Lieutenant M. C. Barton, R.E.[3] The unit reached the base at Diju Mukh on the Boreli tributary of the Brahmaputra too late to share in the few skirmishes which caused the Akas to submit in the middle of January 1884, but it found time to construct an excellent floating bridge across the Boreli for the passage of the returning troops. No warning having been received of the probable requirements, Barton had arrived without bridging equipment or wire rope and consequently he had to use local boats and ropes made of canes.[4] No doubt he profited by observing the cane ropes used by the Akas in their remarkable single-cable suspension bridges along

[1]Notes by Maj.-Gen. Sir T. Fraser, K.C.B., C.S.I., C.M.G., late R.E., sent to the author on Sept. 22nd, 1937.

[2]*Frontier and Overseas Expeditions from India*, Vol. IV, p. 165.

[3]The 2nd Company was not at full strength for it had left a detachment of 30 men at Calcutta on its return to Roorkee in May, 1883. The detachment was required for work on the submarine mining defences.

[4]" The Aka Expedition," by Col. R. G. Woodthorpe, C.B., late R.E., appearing in the *Journal of the United Service Institution of India*, Vol. XVIII, 1889, pp. 428–450. This article gives full details of the expedition and describes the people and country.

which a man could crawl upside down supported in a cane hoop. The Aka Expeditionary Force was broken up at the end of January, and the 2nd Company returned to Roorkee without suffering any casualties other than those caused by sickness.

At the end of 1887, the Raja of Sikkim having broken the treaty concluded in 1861 and allowed a Tibetan garrison to be established at Lingtu, some 15 miles south-west of Chumbi, a force of 1,500 men under Brig.-General T. Graham was concentrated in February, 1888, on the Sikkim border. Graham captured Lingtu on March 21st and established an entrenched camp at Gnathong on the road from Lingtu to the Jelep La.[1] There, on May 22nd, he repulsed a heavy attack by the Tibetans. On September 24th, after receiving reinforcements, he drove the Tibetans from positions on the Jelep La at a height of over 14,000 feet and, two days later, occupied Chumbi, but as winter was approaching he soon withdrew to Gnathong.[2] Concurrently with the advance to Chumbi, a detachment marched northwards to Gantok and afterwards a small party proceeded to Tumlong, the capital of the country. All resistance was then at an end and the troops began to improve the communications on both sides of the Tibet frontier. In this employment a leading part was taken by a section (50 men) of the 5th Company, Bengal S. & M., under Lieutenant A. E. Sandbach, R.E., which had left Roorkee on September 11th.[3] Sandbach and 10 Sappers accompanied the party which visited Tumlong after the cessation of hostilities.[4] The detachment remained in Sikkim until October 1889 and was employed chiefly on road construction from Gantok towards the Nathu La and on the descent from the Jelep La into the Chumbi Valley.[5] The fourth expedition to Sikkim was a small affair; but the experience gained proved useful, fifteen years later, in the expedition to Tibet.

We revert now to the frontier between India and Burma where the Lushais and Chins, unsettled by the Third Burma War and the lawlessness of the Kachins, Shans and other tribes of the interior, were encroaching on British territory and causing grave concern to the Government. The Chins in particular were incessant in their depredations and consequently were the first to be dealt with. They were an athletic people of Indo-Chinese origin, slow of speech, serious in manner, proud, avaricious, distrustful, dirty and addicted to drunkenness. Flint-lock muskets, *dahs*[6] and spears were their usual weapons, but some carried bows and arrows, the latter poisoned by being dipped in the head of a decomposed fowl. The Chins did not relish an open fight. They preferred to stalk a column for days on the chance of obtaining an easy shot, or to ambush it,

[1]See *Sketch Map of the Route to Lhasa, Tibet Mission*, 1903–04, included in this chapter. (*La*. A pass.)

[2]The operations are described in *Frontier and Overseas Expeditions from India*, Vol. IV, pp. 50–62.

[3]*History and Digest of Service of the 1st K.G.O. Sappers and Miners*, p. 49.

[4]*Report on the Sikhim Expedition, Jan. 1888–Jan. 1890*, by Lieut. C. J. Markham (official), p. 59.

[5]" Sikhim Field Force," by Lieut. A. E. Sandbach, R.E., appearing in *The R.E. Journal*, Vol. XIX, 1889, p. 173, 174.

[6]Burmese swords.

fire at the back of the nearest man on the narrow path and dive down a zigzag run-way prepared through the forest below.

Minor operations conducted from Burma in 1887 having failed to bring the Chins to order, two columns were sent against them in September 1888, one from Pauk and the other from Kalewa. These moved up to the eastern boundary and occupied Kan, Sihaung, Indin, Kalemyo and other villages along the Myittha River.[1] Still the raids continued, and accordingly, in November 1888, a small mixed force under Brig.-General E. Faunce, which included half the 2nd Company, Madras S. & M., under Lieutenant G. Palmer, R.E., entered the Chin country. An encounter occurred near Kambale[2] on December 7th in which Palmer was mortally wounded while the Sappers were preparing to build a stockade, and there were several other skirmishes before the force was strongly posted in this area. Lieutenant J. A. S. Tulloch, R.E., with the remainder of the 2nd Company, and Lieutenant B. A. James, R.E., with a detachment of 14 Burma Sappers, arrived on December 26th and the work of making a mule track into the Chin Hills was pushed on with such vigour that on February 5th, 1889, Brig-General Faunce was able to occupy a place called Tokhlaing, the site selected for Fort White.[3] Meanwhile, Lieutenant H. B. H. Wright, R.E., had assumed command of the 2nd Company. "The conditions at Fort White were indeed strenuous" remarks Major-General Wright.[4] "There were constant night alarms which on most occasions revealed a headless corpse in our post to mark the fact that a Chin had entered and got away with his trophy. At noon one day we received news by heliograph that a column which had been sent to destroy a distant village had had several casualties in attacking the place, so we went out with other troops to assist. The Sappers fortunately provided themselves with torches made from pine branches, for it was midnight before we got back, exhausted, to Fort White, lighted by our torches. I had reminded the men that Madras Sappers never fell out on the march, and during the night I noticed several who could no longer walk being carried on the backs of their comrades."

Until the Chins made their submission in May 1889, roadwork through dense forest, interspersed with occasional sharp skirmishes, was the order of the day. This incessant labour continued long after hostilities had ended, and so unhealthy was the locality that at one time no less than 64 per cent of the 2nd Company were on the sick list. When the unit left the Chin Hills for Mandalay in November 1889, after building Fort White and completing 22½ miles of mule track, it had lost 8 dead and 37 invalided, mostly from malaria. Its services, however, were fully appreciated. Brig.-General Faunce had already acknowledged that it was due to the skill and hard work of Wright and his Sappers that a mule track had

[1]See *Sketch Map of the North-East Frontier*, included in this chapter.
[2]Three miles south of Kalemyo.
[3]The operations are described in *Frontier and Overseas Expeditions from India*, Vol. V, pp. 325–330.
[4]Notes by Maj.-Gen. H. B. H. Wright, C.B., C.M.G., late R.E., sent to the author on Oct. 9th, 1937. Lieut. Wright had joined the force as an Intelligence Officer.

been made from the plains and accommodation provided in Fort White in less than a month for 700 men besides followers, and to this tribute Brig.-General W. Penn Symons added in October, 1889 :— " It is altogether due to the Madras Sappers that the troops have been able to remain at Fort White during the past rains. This result was accomplished by incessant labour on mountain paths, buildings and defensive works under the able direction of Lieutenant Wright, R.E., to whom the greatest credit is due. . . . General Symons has long known and appreciated the Madras Sapper. His capabilities in construction, and his endurance, have been severely tested in the Chin Field Force and all ranks have stood the test right well."[1]

In March, 1889, while General Faunce was dealing with the Chins, an expedition had been sent against the Lushais as a punishment for recent raids. A force of 1,100 men under Colonel V. W. Tregear was concentrated at Demagiri, north-east of Chittagong, and marching into the hills to Lungleh proceeded to improve the road and scour the surrounding country. At Lungleh it was reinforced by other troops, including a section of Sappers and Miners,[2] but at the end of the month it withdrew to Demagiri. The building of a fortified post at Lungleh was completed by the middle of April shortly before the Chins submitted to Faunce. No more need be recorded of the fifth expedition against the Lushais. A few villages were burnt after the inhabitants had fled and there was no bloodshed.

It might be imagined that the operations by Faunce and Tregear in the spring of 1889 would have sufficed to pacify the Chins and Lushais, but this was far from being the case. Throughout the following summer both tribes ambushed convoys, cut telegraph wires and fired into British posts until the Government lost patience and decided to undertake combined operations against them from Burma and Chittagong and at the same time to explore their territories thoroughly. A Burma Field Force was organized under the command of Brig.-General W. Penn Symons consisting of two brigades, one forming a " Northern Column " to advance from Fort White and the other a " Southern Column " to march from Kan. With the Northern Column was the 5th Company, Madras S. & M., under Lieutenant L. P. Chapman, R.E., with Lieutenants C. H. Heycock and T. Fraser, R.E., and with the Southern Column the 6th Company, Madras S. & M., under Captain H. G. C. Swayne, R.E., with Lieutenants U. W. Evans, G. M. Hutton and C. Ainslie, R.E., and also the Burma Company of the same Corps under Lieutenant B. A. James, R.E.[3] A Chittagong Field Force of more than 3,000 Bengal and Bombay troops under Brig.-General V. W. Tregear was also mobilized. This included only one engineer unit—the 2nd Company, Bengal S. & M., under Captain

[1]Chin Field Force Order by Brig.-Gen. Faunce, dated May 6th, 1889, and Order by Brig.-Gen. Symons, dated Oct. 21st, 1889, quoted in *Historical Record of the Q.V.O. Madras Sappers and Miners*, Vol. I, p. 139, and *The Roll of Honour of the " Queen's Own " Madras Sappers and Miners*, p. 43.

[2]*Frontier and Overseas Expeditions from India*, Vol. IV, p. 248. The Corps and company to which the section belonged are not recorded.

[3]*Historical Record of the Q.V.O. Madras Sappers and Miners* Vol. I, p. 144.

R. D. Petrie, R.E., with Lieutenants H. J. Sherwood and E. H. de V. Atkinson and 2nd Lieutenant W. A. Harrison, R.E.[1] The Bombay Sappers and Miners supplied a Telegraph Section,[2] and the Bengal Corps provided the Commanding Royal Engineer in the person of Major H. P. Leach, R.E. The Chittagong Force was directed to march eastwards from Lungleh over a succession of ridges to Haka to join hands with the Southern Column of the Burma Force.

The Northern Column from Burma set out from Fort White at the end of November 1889 and by the close of the year had established ten posts designed to check further raids by the Chins. Rationing of the garrisons was simplified by the fact that during the rains the 2nd Company, Madras S. & M., then at Fort White, had converted the track used by General Faunce into a good mule road.[3] The difficulties confronting the Northern Column were considerable, but those of the Southern Column were far more serious. Before the expedition started it was believed that the Southern Column would be able to cover the 64 miles from Kan to Haka in 10 to 12 days, but the country proved to be so mountainous that with every man engaged in roadmaking it took the head of the column 66 days, and the working parties 77 days, to reach Haka. In one valley the road crossed and recrossed the stream 43 times, and it was not until December 23rd that the Chin Hills were really entered. Meanwhile, the deadly malaria of the misty valleys was decimating the troops. Swayne and Hutton fell ill on December 18th and Evans took command of the 6th Company, assisted by Ainslie. Lieutenants E. P. Johnson and H. J. M. Marshall, R.E., joined the unit with a small reinforcement on February 19th, 1890, three days before it marched into Haka, but the wastage through sickness continued to be devastating. The Sappers were so saturated with malaria that it was quite common for 30 men to report sick in the morning. Between November 15th, 1889 and April 30th, 1890, the company lost 3 officers and 72 men invalided, or half its strength. In the Southern Column as a whole, only 7 British officers out of 69 escaped infection, and of the 62 sick, one died and 27 were invalided. Among the latter was Evans who carried on until the 6th Company (less one section left at Haka under the unfortunate Ainslie) arrived with the Burma Company in Mandalay in June.[4] The two units had done well. They had fortified Haka and improved the line of communication to Burma but had seen little fighting. All the troops of the Southern Column were withdrawn before the rains broke except the garrisons necessary for the defence of Haka and other posts.

As regards the work of the Chittagong Field Force operating against the Lushais, it may be remarked that, apart from punitive measures, the chief objective was to improve the mule road between Demagiri and

[1]The 2nd Company, Bengal S. & M., left Roorkee on Nov. 16th, 1889, and arrived at Chittagong on the 24th and at Lungleh on the 28th.

[2]*A Brief History of the Royal Bombay Sappers and Miners*, p. 21.

[3]*Frontier and Overseas Expeditions from India*, Vol. V, p. 332.

[4]Notes by Brig.-Gen. U. W. Evans, C.B., C.M.G., late R.E., sent to the author on May 29th, 1937.

Lungleh and to prolong it to Haka so that it might connect with the road constructed to that place by the Southern Column of the Burma Field Force and eventually provide a permanent highway from the Chittagong hill tracts to Burma.[1] The problems of roadmaking in the Lushai country were stupendous. Owing to the jungle, vision was limited to a few yards. Great masses of rock had often to be removed by blasting. Huge trees had to be cut or blown down and even then their tangled roots remained. The forest extended for miles and miles without a break and consisted either of a network of trees, creepers and thorny scrub or else of almost impenetrable bamboo or tall elephant grass. So steep were the hillsides that the mule path had sometimes to be given a gradient of 1 in 5. Vapour shrouded the bottoms of the valleys and flowed along the deep gorges with the ponderous movement of molten lava. Such was the country in which the 2nd Company, Bengal S. & M., had to work during the Chin-Lushai Expedition of 1889–90. The unit was engaged chiefly in taking the mule road through to Haka, bridging many streams and building Fort Tregear and two smaller posts on the Kaladan River and its tributary, the Mat, with the assistance of Pioneers and Gurkhas. Work on the mule road was started from Lungleh on December 12th, 1889, and in the middle of the next month, when four miles of difficult alignment had been finished, Petrie and Atkinson moved off with half the company to join the Northern Column from Burma, leaving Sherwood and Harrison with the other half-company to continue the road construction. After the site selected for Fort Tregear had been reached at a height of 5,000 feet above sea level, 30 Sappers were employed until March 20th in building the defences. Those finished, they went with Harrison to build the posts on the Kaladan and Mat Rivers while Sherwood and the remainder of the half-company continued roadmaking towards Haka which they reached on April 13th. The enemy had erected elaborate stockades—notably at Falam to the north—but they did not attempt to hold them and consequently there was little fighting. There was much engineering, however, particularly by the half-company under Petrie which built a number of large trestle or suspension bridges, constructed many rafts for transporting stores and improved the channel of a river.[2] This half-company was back in Roorkee on April 7th, but the other half-company under Sherwood did not reach headquarters until the end of May.[3] Weakened by fever, soaked by torrential rain and bitten by leeches and mosquitoes, the Bengal Sappers must have been glad to see the last of the Chin-Lushai jungles.

For several years after the occupation of their country, the Chins showed signs of rebellion which necessitated small punitive or police operations against them. In the winter of 1890–91, for instance, the Burma Sapper Company under Lieutenant T. Harrison, R.E., with Lieutenant

[1] The officer who laid out the alignment and supervised the work generally was Capt. H. Mullaly, R.E., a Field Engineer under Maj. H. P. Leach, R.E.

[2] "Report on the Engineering work done during the Chin-Lushai Expedition," by Maj. H. P. Leach, R.E., appearing in *Report on the Chittagong Column, Chin-Lushai Expedition of* 1889–90, by Capt. O. A. Chambers (official), pp. 133–135.

[3] *History and Digest of Service of the 1st K.G.O. Sappers and Miners*, p. 51.

B. A. James, R.E., was on service in the Chin Hills with other troops including the 1st Company, Madras S. & M., under Lieutenant C. H. Roe, R.E. The Burma Company reached Haka towards the end of December and a few days later James was killed in an assault on a stockade at Thetta. Again, in January, 1893, a detachment of the 4th Company, Madras S. & M., under Lieutenant G. A. F. Sanders, R.E., was on service with a column whose objective was the village of Kaptial west of the Manipur River. In February 1893, the Burma Company under Lieutenant W. Babington, R.E., was engaged in barrack construction at Tiddim, east of the Manipur River, and during 1894 the 3rd and 4th Companies and most of the Burma Company were working in the region of Tiddim and Falam, so it is clear that the consolidation and development of the frontier between India and Burma was no light task.

The next expedition on the North-East Frontier in which Sappers and Miners were concerned was one despatched in 1899 against the Mishmis who had murdered or kidnapped some people of a neighbouring tribe. The remote area of Mishmiland, north of Burma and adjoining China, was almost unknown in those days for no troops had visited it since 1855 when a small party under Lieutenant F. G. Eden, B.I., went there to round up a gang of murderers. The country is described graphically in some letters written in 1912 by Captain J. B. Corry, R.E., " Imagine trees up to 150 feet in height," he writes.[1] " They are covered with creepers to about 50 feet above the ground and the intervening space is a dense tangle of creepers, palms, canes, wild plantain and elephant grass. The hill-sides are composed of material which will stand naturally at 30° slope but is held up at a slope of 45° or more by roots, so that as soon as you cut a root the mountain begins to fall. There are slopes covered with trees and bushes which actually measure 70° by clinometer and are composed entirely of sandy gravel. The rock is often so rotten that if one dislodges a cubic foot at road level some 50 cubic feet fall from above. In such a case the only way to make a road is for men to climb above the alignment, fix ropes and then work downwards, dislodging all loose pieces with crowbars and swinging clear on the ropes as they fall. Another sort of rock is so hard that it will scratch glass. The streams run in deep gorges and the native tracks ascend or descend in a sort of staircase of roots and rocks. The mountain spurs end in precipices sometimes falling 2,000 feet sheer into the river, and many of the valleys end in waterfalls over precipices. One cannot make a track along the river bed as the bases of the cliffs are below flood level and there are frequent avalanches of stones. It would be like traversing below a hanging glacier. Road reconnaissance is distinctly difficult in a country where one can move along a path at only one mile an hour and off it at perhaps 200 yards an hour. A slip, unless one is caught by a creeper, means a slide down a steep slope and then a sheer drop of 1,000 feet. There are innumerable thorn bushes and one of the plants has leaves that sting like wasps. Animals, except monkeys, are rare, and

[1]Extracts from letters written by Capt. J. B. Corry, D.S.O., R.E., when serving with the Mishmi Survey Expedition of 1912–13.

birds still rarer; but blood-sucking flies and leeches abound. The Mishmis are the ugliest, dirtiest and laziest of people. They smoke all day long and their only conversation is to ask for tobacco or matches."

Into this wild country an expeditionary force of 1,500 men marched from Sadiya on the Upper Brahmaputra on December 1st, 1899, under the command of Lieut.-Colonel E. H. Molesworth, 44th Gurkha Rifles. Included in the force was the left half of the 5th Company, Bengal S. & M., under Lieutenant S. H. Sheppard, R.E., with Lieutenant C. M. Carpenter, R.E.[1] The men of the right half-company (Sikhs) had urged their claim most strongly; but as they had served under Sheppard on the delimitation of the Waziristan boundary in 1895 it was decided that the Punjabi-Muhammadan left half-company should go. The detachment started from Roorkee without mule transport on October 20th and, proceeding by rail through Calcutta to Goalundo, voyaged up the Brahmaputra for seven days in flat-bottomed boats to Dibrugarh and thence in dug-out canoes to Sadiya. Joined by large gangs of Naga and Khasia coolies, it then marched with an escort of Gurkhas north-eastwards into the Mishmi country to prepare the road. The advance of the column was necessarily very slow for the mountain slopes were so steep that the men had often to be hauled up by ropes. However, towards the end of December the main body surmounted a pass 8,900 feet high only to find the Mishmi stockades and principal village deserted. No resistance being offered, the column soon withdrew to Sadiya which it reached on February 8th, 1900.[2] Seventeen days later, the Sapper detachment was back in Roorkee.

"Throughout our two months in Mishmiland," writes Major-General Sheppard,[3] "it hardly ever stopped raining, day or night. The country consisted of more or less parallel knife-ridges, rising to 6,000 feet, with torrents between them. No pack animal could possibly move over it. I left Carpenter to work up from the base camp to meet the returning force, and the first piece of his handiwork we encountered was a fine suspension bridge of rattan cane, spanning a 100 feet ravine, which had a neatly printed notice 'Steam-rollers must cross slowly'!" Brig.-General Carpenter, the author of this witticism, records that the first task was to cut an elephant road for some twelve miles from Sadiya to a supply base at the foot of the mountains, Naga coolies leading with their *daos*, Gurkhas following with *kukris* and finally the Sappers with axes.[4] Several streams were bridged with long tree trunks on crib piers, and trestles were added to prevent sway. Christmas was spent on top of the pass where steps had to be cut in the snow to enable the troops to carry supplies forward. The Mishmis, armed only with bows and arrows, were careful not to appear in force but contented themselves with setting booby traps (hurdles of cane and bamboo loaded with boulders) to sweep the path. The climate

[1] *History and Digest of Service of the 1st K.G.O. Sappers and Miners*, p. 69.
[2] *Frontier and Overseas Expeditions from India*, Vol. IV, p. 185.
[3] Notes by Maj.-Gen. S. H. Sheppard, C.B., C.M.G., D.S.O., Col.-Commandant, R.E., sent to the author on Oct. 5th, 1937.
[4] Notes by Brig.-Gen. C. M. Carpenter, C.M.G., D.S.O., late R.E., sent to the author on July 6th, 1937.

was so damp that advantage had to be taken of every ray of sunlight to dry the guncotton primers in the Sapper equipment. Pools were successfully bombed for fish, but many were infested with leeches and on one occasion a Gurkha pulled Sheppard back in the nick of time when the latter was about to quench his thirst. All accounts agree that the Mishmi country was a land of surprises, and very unpleasant ones too.

Five years after the expedition under Colonel Molesworth to Mishmiland, units of the Bengal and Madras Sappers and Miners took part in the so-called " Military Mission " to Tibet which was in reality a military expedition of considerable magnitude. The northern portion of that vast and mysterious country is a bare, icy, windswept and almost uninhabited plateau, some 15,000 feet above sea-level, merging towards China into a wild tangle of mountains. The southern part, more temperate, fertile and populated though at a great altitude, contains the famous city of Lhasa, the home of the Dalai Lama, and through it, beyond the Himalayan barrier, runs the Tsan-po, afterwards to become the Dihang and finally the Brahmaputra. The Tibet Mission of 1904 was ambitious in scope and masterly in execution. During an advance of nearly 400 miles from the rail-head base at Siliguri to the capital at Lhasa, the troops encountered extreme natural and climatic obstacles. The section of 150 miles from Siliguri to Phari (14,300 feet) was deluged with rain during the monsoon. On two stretches beyond it, each 100 miles in length, food and fuel were unobtainable and the difficulties of supply almost insuperable. During the winter months, gales and snowstorms swept the mountains, and temperatures of many degrees below zero were common. A Tibetan army of 16,000 men, poorly armed but strongly posted in fortified castles and monasteries, was ready to offer a stout resistance to invasion. To gain the Tsan-po Valley, four ranges of mountains had to be crossed by passes between 14,000 and 17,000 feet in height; and the last natural obstacle before Lhasa, the Tsan-po itself, was a dangerous and raging torrent on whose banks no timber could be found.

Serious alarm had been felt since 1899 when the Dalai Lama began to cast off the yoke of China and make overtures to Russia, and in July, 1903, a mission was sent through Sikkim to Khamba Jong[1] under Colonel F. E. Younghusband to negotiate with representatives of China and Tibet; but as the Tibetans refused to attend and began to mass troops in the neighbourhood, the Government directed in November 1903 that the Chumbi Valley should be occupied and negotiations resumed at Gyantse, far towards Lhasa.[2] This gesture should have brought the Dalai Lama to reason, but unfortunately it had no effect and it became evident that hostilities were unavoidable.

The 12th Company,[3] Madras S. & M., under Lieutenant J. A. Garstin, R.E., with Lieutenant E. K. Molesworth, R.E., had arrived in Sikkim in March and had been working with the 23rd and 32nd Sikh Pioneers on the

[1]*Jong.* A fort or castle.
[2]See *Sketch Map of the Route to Lhasa, Tibet Mission,* 1903–04, included in this chapter.
[3]Actually, at that time, the " 4th Company." It was renumbered in Dec., 1903.

Rungpo-Gantok road in the Tista Valley. It had suffered severely from malaria and consequently the decision that it and the two Pioneer regiments should be attached to Younghusband's escort on transfer to the Chumbi Valley must have been very welcome. Captain C. H. Heycock and Lieutenant H. L. Lewis, R.E., joined the unit on November 26th, and Heycock then moved with half the company to Gantok to work on a new road into the Chumbi Valley while Garstin and Lewis marched with the other half-company to Rungpo to join a column which was to enter the Chumbi Valley by Gnathong and the Jelep La. These were some of the engineering preliminaries to the general advance into Tibet.

The composition of Colonel Younghusband's military escort is worthy of remark. It included a section of No. 7 (British) Mountain Battery with two 10 pr. B.L. guns, two 7 pr. R.M.L. guns allotted to the 8th Gurkhas, a Maxim Gun Detachment of the Norfolk Regiment, the 3rd (Bengal) and 12th (Madras) Companies of Sappers and Miners, and the 8th Gurkhas and 23rd and 32nd Sikh Pioneers. Of its 3,000 fighting men, two-thirds were Sappers or Pioneers and it was commanded by a Royal Engineer, Major (temporary Brig.-General) J. R. L. Macdonald. Twenty other Royal Engineer officers served with it,[1] and consequently the expedition to Tibet may be called with some justification an "Engineer War." The Government was fully aware of the hardships to be endured. Every man was issued with a long sheepskin overcoat (*poshtin*), a quilted rug (*rezai*), fur-lined gloves, lambskin vests, extra socks, felt knee-boots, a woollen comforter and, as a precaution against snow-blindness, a pair of goggles. It was well that this was done for so bitter was the cold during the winter months that the machine-gun jackets had to be filled with a mixture of water, rum and kerosene oil to prevent freezing and it was impossible even to lubricate the locks of the rifles.

Before describing the exploits of the Sappers and Miners on the road to Lhasa it may be well to deal briefly with the general course of the operations.[2] The first phase, from October 15th, 1903, to March 24th, 1904, included the occupation of the Chumbi Valley and preparations for the advance to Gyantse. At the end of 1903 the enemy were concentrated around the Mission at Khamba Jong, apparently anticipating an advance from that place, and thus they were outwitted when the Mission withdrew into Sikkim simultaneously with the beginning of the main advance into the Chumbi Valley from the south-west. The Mission crossed the Jelep La on December 13th and occupied Chumbi on the 15th. A flying column was pushed forward on December 20th to Phari Jong where the garrison surrendered, thus completing our hold on the valley. On January 7th,

[1]Capt. S. H. Sheppard and Lieuts. E. F. J. Hill, A. D. Walker, C. H. Haswell and G. F. B. Gough (3rd (Bengal) Company) ; Maj. C. H. Heycock and Lieuts. J. A. Garstin, C. F. Birney, H. L. Lewis and E. K. Molesworth (12th (Madras) Company) ; Capts. C. H. D. Ryder and H. Wood and Lieut. H. McC. Cowie (Survey) ; Capt. C. A. Elliott (Staff) ; Capt. R. St. J. Gillespie and Lieuts. P. E. Hodgson, J. A. McEnery and V. Giles (Works) ; and Lieuts. A. F. S. Hill and L. N. Malan (Cooly Corps). Birney joined on Dec. 28th, 1903, and Wood during the return journey to India.

[2]The operations are described in *Frontier and Overseas Expeditions from India*, Vol. IV, pp. 87–108, and in an article entitled "The Recent Mission to Tibet," by Maj. A. T. Moore, R.E., appearing in *The R.E. Journal*, Vol. I, Jan.–June, 1905, pp. 102–113.

1904, the Mission crossed the Tang La (15,700 feet) to the bare plateau of Tuna (15,300 feet) and remained there throughout the winter with an escort of 4 companies of Pioneers and a detachment of Madras Sappers under Lewis. Macdonald led the rest of the troops back to Chumbi. The collection of supplies at Phari was completed by March 24th and so the first phase came to an end.

The second phase, from March 25th to June 12th, 1904, comprised the advance to Gyantse and preparations for the march to Lhasa. On March 29th the Gyantse column was at Tuna facing 3,000 Tibetans at Guru and 2,000 at Harm. A further 2,000 Tibetans were distributed along the route northwards from the Kala Tso[1] to Gyantse. The Guru force attacked the Gyantse column and was defeated, and as the Harm force then retired to beyond the Kala Tso the advance was resumed on April 4th after reinforcements had arrived. On April 10th Macdonald drove the enemy from their positions in the Zamdang (or Red Idol) Gorge and occupied Gyantse on the following day. The Mission and its escort took up their quarters in an adjacent hamlet called Junglu which Lieut.-Colonel H. R. Brander, 32nd Pioneers, was detailed to hold with a garrison of 500 infantry and sappers with two guns. This having been arranged, the remainder of the force began its return march to Chumbi on April 19th. Brander started out on May 2nd with a Movable Column, and four days later, by flank attacks over almost inaccessible heights, defeated 3,000 Tibetans on the Kharo La (16,600 feet). Meanwhile, an enemy force of 1,600 men from Dongtse had occupied the Gyantse Jong after failing to overwhelm the depleted garrison of the Mission Post. For the next two months the Mission was practically besieged; but a reinforcement of 200 men, including a composite half-company of Sappers and Miners under Captain S. H. Sheppard, R.E., with two 10 pr. guns, having been sent to Brander, the latter was able to maintain an active defence and even to extend his position by the capture of a building called Gurkha Post on May 19th and the village of Palla on May 26th, and thus the Tibetans were kept too busy to interfere seriously with our communications.

The third phase from June 13th to August 3rd, 1904, included an advance in force to Gyantse, the capture of the Gyantse Jong and an advance to Lhasa. By this time the enemy had collected 8,000 men in Gyantse and had established outpost forces at Khangma, Niru, Gabzi and Niani to the south and south-east and a reserve in the Tsechan Monastery on the road to Shigatse. Macdonald arrived from Chumbi with strong reinforcements on June 26th after driving the Tibetans from Niru, the Zamdang Gorge and Niani. On June 28th he took the Tsechan Monastery, and on July 6th, after fruitless negotiations, assaulted and captured the formidable Gyantse Jong. The way to Lhasa was now open and Younghusband and Macdonald set out on July 14th with 2,100 fighting men, 8 guns, 6 maxims, 2,000 followers and 3,900 animals. At Ralung, on the 16th, Macdonald learned that the Kharo La was strongly fortified by *sangars* and by a wall extending to vertical cliffs at the snow line; but

[1]*Tso*. A lake.

nevertheless he forced a passage in an action during which the Gurkhas fought at 18,500 feet above sea-level and ended by pursuing the enemy across a glacier. Nagartse Jong was seized on July 19th and Pede Jong on the 21st. The advance continued steadily and on July 24th the force surmounted the last pass, the Khamba La (16,400 feet), and descended to the Tsan-po at Partsi. Thence, on the 25th, it marched downstream to Chaksam to attempt a crossing at a spot where the river narrowed. This dangerous operation will be described later. It was accomplished in six days and on July 31st the advance was resumed to Lhasa. At length, on August 3rd, Younghusband and Macdonald with only 1,600 men encamped before the holy city whence the Dalai Lama had fled after his representations had been rejected.

The fourth and last phase of the operations included the occupation of Lhasa and the withdrawal to India. The negotiations at Lhasa were protracted, but a treaty was signed on September 7th, 1904, in the Throne Room of the wonderful Potala Palace whose golden roofs towered majestically to the sky. Then, all was haste. Winter was approaching and the passes would soon be blocked by snow. On September 9th the Sappers set out with some infantry for Chaksam to arrange for re-crossing the Tsan-po but decided in favour of an easier site at Partsi as more equipment had arrived. Younghusband and Macdonald evacuated Lhasa on the 23rd and the whole force crossed at Partsi between September 27th and 29th. From Partsi the force marched in two columns to Gyantse where it arrived on October 5th and 6th. A survey party under Captains C. H. D. Ryder and H. Wood, R.E., was sent to reconnoitre Western Tibet[1] and the troops returned to India in small columns. This, briefly, is the record of the Tibet Mission. We turn, now, to the achievements of the Sappers and Miners without which such rapid success could never have been secured.

On November 18th, 1903, the 3rd Company, Bengal S. & M., under Captain S. H. Sheppard, R.E., with Lieutenants E. F. J. Hill, A. D. Walker, C. H. Haswell and G. F. B. Gough, R.E., arrived at Siliguri from Roorkee and was sent to work at once on a new cart-road near Gantok. In December it was engaged with half the 12th Company, Madras S. & M., on roadmaking from Gantok towards the Nathu La; but when the Madras Sappers moved to the Chumbi Valley in January, 1904, the 3rd Company took charge of the entire road construction assisted by 1,100 coolies. Snow fell on February 16th. The men were then working on the Lagyap La (10,700 feet) some 6 miles from Gantok, and from that time till the middle of May they were often in two feet of snow or freezing slush. Huge bonfires were kept burning to thaw them at the end of each hour's work. Some stretches of road were paved in Sikkim fashion with stones on edge, hammered in and covered with gravel: others beyond the Nathu La were "corduroyed" with the trunks of pine trees with a similar top-dressing.

[1]Capt. C. G. Rawling, Somersetshire L.I., and Lieut. F. M. Bailey, 32nd Pioneers, were with the party as Political Officers. (See "Exploration and Survey with the Tibet Frontier Commission," by Maj. C. H. D. Ryder, D.S.O., R.E., appearing in *The R.E. Journal*, Vol. III, Jan–June, 1906, pp. 53–70.)

On May 15th, the 3rd Company was split up; half remained with Hill and Haswell in the Chumbi Valley and the other half joined a composite detachment under Sheppard which was to proceed to Gyantse. This detachment comprised 60 men of the 3rd Company under Walker and 20 men of the 12th Company, Madras S. & M., under Garstin.[1] Hill's half-company laboured for the next five months on road construction and hut building in the Chumbi Valley. The work was most exacting and a length of one mile of road had to be blasted out of a granite cliff.[2] Meanwhile, Sheppard's composite detachment had reached Gyantse with other troops on May 24th and had reinforced the defenders of the Mission Post at Chunglu.

The garrison at Chunglu was subjected to a daily bombardment from the Gyantse Jong which crowned a steep hill 1,000 yards to the north, but there were few casualties owing to the excellent defences contrived by Ryder and Cowie, the Survey officers. Although a fortified house known as " Gurkha Post " formed a strong British outpost, all the other houses and hamlets around Chunglu were held by the enemy who were particularly menacing from the village of Palla, 1,000 yards to the north-east, where they were beginning to mount guns. It was decided, accordingly, that Palla should be stormed without delay and Sheppard was entrusted with the task of opening a way for the infantry. For this purpose he detailed four small explosive parties, each of four men under a British officer. The first he commanded in person. The second, to follow 30 yards in rear, he placed under Captain W. F. T. O'Connor, R.A., a Political Officer who volunteered for this hazardous duty. The third was under Walker; and the fourth, in support of Walker, under Garstin. Two assaulting columns, each of a British officer and 60 men of the 32nd Pioneers, were to follow the explosive parties, and on a mound called " Gun Hill " a reserve was to be stationed consisting of the remainder of the Sappers and two companies of infantry with two mountain guns.

The attack on Palla was planned for May 26th and was to be delivered against the side furthest from the Mission Post where the defences might be expected to be weak. A night march, begun at 2.30 a.m., brought the explosive parties by a circuitous route to within 300 yards of the village before they were discovered and came under fire. They ran forward, and Sheppard collected them under the village wall. Sending Walker towards the first house of the village (the one nearest to the Jong), Sheppard dashed through an open gateway between that house and the second and almost ran into the arms of three Tibetans. Quick as lightning he shot two with

[1] " No. 3 Company, 1st (Bengal) Sappers and Miners, on the Thibet Mission, 1903–1904," by Bt. Maj. S. H. Sheppard, D.S.O., R.E., appearing in *The R.E. Journal*, Vol. II, July–Dec., 1905, pp. 104–113. This article gives a detailed description of the chief exploits of the Sappers and Miners in Tibet.

[2] Subsequent road construction in Chumbi is described in " The Construction of the Nathu La Road, Tibet Mission, 1904," by Capt. R. St. J. Gillespie, R.E., appearing in *The R.E. Journal*, Vol. II, July–Dec., 1905, pp. 289–295. A " Mussoorie Cooly Corps " under Lieut. L. N. Malan, R.E., and a " Peshawar Cooly Corps " under Lieut. A. F. S. Hill, R.E., each of 1,000 men, were engaged on the work from Aug. to Oct., 1904, under Capt. Gillespie assisted by Lieuts. P. E. Hodgson, J. A. McEnery and V. Giles, R.E. The Nathu La road was ready for the returning Mission at the end of Oct., 1904.

his revolver, while the third bolted back into the first house but forgot to shut the door. Sheppard then called up Sapper Chagatta, a soldier who afterwards distinguished himself in France during the Great War. Chagatta appeared with a box of guncotton and, though fired on heavily from all sides, Sheppard laid the charge against the wall of the second house, lit the fuse and retired, the subsequent explosion blowing a good breach in the wall. Walker was successful also in breaching the wall of the first house, and he and Sheppard, back under cover, then looked around for the assaulting columns, but they looked in vain. These columns had been attacked in flank during their advance, and having lost direction, were making their way towards the other end of the village which they entered in due course; so, as Sheppard could find no more than 20 men, he decided that it was possible only to assault the first house in which 60 Tibetans held the upper floor. It seems that Lieutenant G. P. Gurdon of the 32nd Pioneers had already led a few men into this house through the open doorway, and now he re-entered it with O'Connor, and the latter placed a whole box of guncotton in the lower room and lit the fuse; and when the explosion had killed or buried half the garrison, the attackers, rushing in, bayoneted the remainder or shot them as they fled. This gallant exploit, however, entailed many casualties. Only Sheppard, Gurdon, 8 Sappers and 11 Pioneers remained unwounded. Garstin had been mortally wounded, O'Connor and a young Pioneer officer severely wounded, and Walker, one Sapper and four Pioneers slightly wounded. Nearly every man had been hit by stones or bricks, and it was impossible to do more than hold the house. The arrival of the assaulting columns eventually relieved the tension and ended a hard fight. The loss of J. A. Garstin was felt keenly by all ranks for he was very popular. As General Macdonald remarked, he was a most gallant officer who had done excellent work in Sikkim and Tibet. His place in the Sapper detachment was taken by Lieutenant C. F. Birney, R.E.[1]

After the capture of Palla, a fortified post was established there. Many houses were demolished and a covered way was dug to the Mission Post. To safeguard the line of communication it was necessary to bridge the river skirting the Mission Post as the existing Tibetan bridge had been damaged by gunfire from the Jong, so Sheppard selected a site further upstream where the water was shallow and the width about 150 yards, and in three days, with the help of infantry working parties, the Sappers built a crib-pier bridge which lasted until the Jong was captured.[2] The only timber available was from houses in the vicinity and consequently the spans had to be very short. With the arrival on June 26th of General Macdonald with 3,000 men and 8 guns, preparations were made to take the Tsechan Monastery a few miles in rear of the Jong. This miniature city was attacked on May 28th by the 8th Gurkhas operating from a ridge to the south and by the 40th Pathans and a party of about 20 Bengal

[1]*Historical Record of the Q.V.O. Madras Sappers and Miners*, Vol. I, p. 192. A Memoir of Lieut. J. A. Garstin, R.E., appears in *The R.E. Journal*, Vol. XXXIV, 1904, p. 202.

[2]After the capture of the Gyantse Jong another bridge was built two miles below the Mission Post. This consisted of cantilever structures across two deep and narrow channels.

Sappers and Miners under Sheppard making a frontal advance across the plain with artillery support. The enemy kept up a heavy though inaccurate fire and held some outlying *sangars* with considerable tenacity. Sheppard and his men ran forward to the main gate of the monastery, laid a box of guncotton against the gate and lit the fuze, and after the explosion took place they headed the rush into the gateway. Most of the Tibetans fled from the monastery to a fort overlooking it, for their experiences at Palla had inspired them with a wholesome dread of large charges of explosive, and when the Sappers prepared to blow down the gate of the fort, they fled again. Major-General Sheppard records[1] that at this time he had a number of Tibetan prisoners working under him—cheery fellows who greeted him every morning with thumbs upturned and tongues fully extended in polite welcome. One of these prisoners had been blown up at Palla and being an intelligent man was selected to carry a demand for the surrender of the Gyantse Jong and was promised his pardon if he brought back an answer. He went and returned and was then told that he might go. "Go?" said he. "Not I! Why, if I do, *he* (pointing to Sheppard) might blow me up again."

The attack on Gyantse Jong on July 6th, 1904, began with preliminary operations against some fortified houses and enclosures at the foot of the hill, the chief objective being a double-storeyed building known as the "Chinese House" standing in a courtyard. The British force emerged from behind Palla before dawn in three columns, each of two companies of infantry preceded by a small explosive party under a Royal Engineer officer. With the Right Column were 12 Bengal Sappers under Captain C. A. Elliott; with the Centre, a similar party under Captain S. H. Sheppard; and with the Left, 12 Madras Sappers under Lieutenant C. F. Birney.[2] Each party carried several 12-lb. charges of guncotton, ready for instant use, and also a few picks and crowbars. Additional explosive charges and tools were carried by the infantry in rear. The Centre Column was detailed to attack the Chinese House and the other columns to close on it after taking the walled gardens to right and left. The left column encountered little opposition, but the centre and right columns came under heavy fire and took cover in the right-hand gardens until a mountain gun supporting the centre column had planted three shells on the roof of the Chinese House. Then the Sappers made a dash for the entrance gate to the courtyard. Sheppard and Sapper Chagatta laid a charge against the gate while Naik Usman Singh returned the point-blank fire from the enemy's loopholes, and when the charge had been exploded and the gate blown in, the Sappers headed the rush of infantry through the opening. Most of the enemy fled into the house and, after the door had been blown down, jumped from the roof on to the roofs of the adjacent houses and so made their escape. Every house below the Jong was soon empty and the Sappers proceeded to make covered ways through the town to connect the

[1]Notes by Maj.-Gen. S. H. Sheppard, C.B., C.M.G., D.S.O., Col.-Commandant, R.E., sent to the author on Oct. 5th, 1937.

[2]*Report on the Engineer Operations of the Tibet Mission Escort*, 1903–04 (official), p. 25.

picquets established there. The capture of the Chinese House was followed by an assault on the Jong. At 2 p.m., a company of the 8th Gurkhas, led by Lieutenant J. D. Grant and supported by Royal Fusiliers, began to scale the heights under a hail of bullets and stones and entering by a breach made by the guns were soon masters of the place.[1] This defeat broke the enemy's resistance and opened the way to Lhasa. The Sappers took no part in the assault on the Jong; but for their exploits at Palla and the Chinese House Sheppard received brevet promotion and Naik Usman Singh and Sapper Chagatta of the 3rd Company were awarded the Indian Order of Merit.[2] The Sapper detachment spent some days in demolishing the defences of the Jong before marching eastwards on July 14th with the column bound for Lhasa.

The detachment accomplished a fine performance in providing a ferry across the Tsan-po at Chaksam during the final stages of the advance.[3] The width of the main channel from the end of a rocky promontory on the right bank to a large sand-bank near the left bank was 140 yards, and beyond the sand-bank was a subsidiary channel 25 yards wide. In mid-stream, above the promontory, another sand-bank had the effect of making the water pour with terrific force past the promontory, thus creating a backwater and whirlpools below it—a dangerous locality for a ferry, yet lack of bridging material prevented the choice of a better site. The stores available were only four Berthon (collapsible) boats with superstructure for two rafts, two large Tibetan ferry-boats and a few small skin-boats, 200 yards of 1-in. steel cable and a traveller, and 640 lbs. of 2-in. and 1½-in. manilla rope. With this meagre equipment the Sappers had to transport across the torrent a total of 3,500 men and 3,500 animals with 350 tons of stores. The crossing began at midday on July 25th by rowing the ferry-boats and Berthon boats (the latter made up into rafts), but this method was painfully slow. The unwieldy ferry-boats were swept far downstream on each trip and had to be towed up again; and after a Berthon raft had foundered in a whirlpool and Major G. H. Bretherton of the Supply and Transport Corps and two sepoys had been drowned in attempting to swim ashore the use of Berthon boats for rafting was abandoned. On July 26th, several attempts were made to get a line across for the establishment of a flying bridge, but they were unsuccessful and rowing was resumed. The river had risen and only fourteen boatloads made the journey in twelve hours. At such a rate, a fortnight would have been required for the passage of the whole force, and accordingly on July 27th Sheppard resumed his efforts to connect the banks by a line and after two failures succeeded in doing so.

Berthon boats were anchored far out from each bank and the boats connected by a line. Other Berthon boats then brought out lines and the crews threw the ends to the men in the anchored boats who caught them

[1]Lieut. J. D. Grant, 8th Gurkha Rifles, a son of Col. Suene Grant, late R.E., was awarded the Victoria Cross for his gallantry in this assault.

[2]G.G.O.s dated Dec. 10th and 17th, 1904.

[3]These engineering operations are described in detail in the *Report on the Engineer Operations of the Tibet Mission Escort*, 1903–04, pp. 13–16 and 37, 38.

TIBET MILITARY MISSION CROSSING THE TSAN-PO AT CHAKSAM ON JULY 25TH, 1904.

and joined them to the connecting line. The 1-in. steel cable was next hauled across by the now continuous line. It was made fast to the high promontory on the right bank and having been passed over a tripod to an anchorage on the sand-bank, the traveller was slung on it. The large Tibetan boats were employed as ferries by using the traveller to carry across one end of a 2-in. rope and then attaching the end of the rope to a boat and allowing the boat to be swung across the river assisted by rowing and hauling. The boats were then unloaded, towed upstream and rowed back empty. By this method the rate of crossing was increased to forty boat-loads a day and the whole operation was completed in 5½ days. A small flying bridge of skin-boats sufficed for the narrow channel beyond the sand-bank, and thus the Tibet Mission and its escort were landed safely on the northern shore.

During the ferrying operations on the 27th, Sheppard nearly followed Bretherton to a watery grave. He was standing on the high right bank downstream of the steel cable when a towing rope fouled and threw him twenty feet downwards into the rapid backwash below the promontory. His head struck a rock and he was half stunned; but fortunately, as he was being swept upstream, he had just enough strength to cling to a rock at the end of the promontory until a rope was thrown to him. His legs were then almost in the nearest whirlpool, and had he been carried another two yards he would certainly have been drowned. As it happened, he was little the worse for his accident and was able to carry on all day as usual.

The Sapper detachment shared in the triumphal progress from Chaksam to the Tibetan capital. "I think," writes General Sheppard,[1] "that the greatest thrill I have ever experienced was when, on the morning of the last march before reaching Lhasa, I climbed a hill and saw in the far distance the dim outline of the Potala with its golden roofs catching the rays of the rising sun." And so, after many hardships and dangers, the goal was attained and the Forbidden City yielded up its secrets.

The anti-climax came in an uneventful return to India. Sheppard, Walker and Birney, with their Bengal and Madras Sappers and Miners, marched from Lhasa on September 9th and reached Chaksam on the 11th; but as reports had been received that a better place for a crossing existed at Partsi, 11 miles upstream, the boats were towed up to that spot with the help of coolies and preparations made at once to provide ferries. Additional stores had been sent from India, including steel cable and another traveller, and the work at Partsi progressed so rapidly that, when the main body arrived from Lhasa, two cable-ferries, one of 105 yards' and the other of 140 yards' span, were ready for use, supplemented by a rowing ferry of Tibetan skin-boats.[2] The force began to cross on the morning of September 27th, and before midnight on the 28th/29th every man and animal and every ton of stores had been carried to the right bank. The march southwards involved no engineering work of any importance.

[1]Notes by Maj.-Gen. S. H. Sheppard, C.B., C.M.G., D.S.O., Col.-Commandant, R.E., sent to the author on Oct. 5th, 1937.
[2]*Report on the Engineer Operations of the Tibet Mission Escort*, 1903–04, pp. 17–19.

It was a race against the first fall of snow. Chumbi was reached on October 18th, and there the half-company of Bengal Sappers under Sheppard was rejoined by the other half-company under Hill. A week later the 3rd Company marched for Siliguri and arrived in Roorkee on November 7th, 1904, after an absence of nearly one year.[1] The 12th Company, Madras S. & M., less the small party which went to Lhasa, had returned somewhat earlier to Southern India. A detachment under Lewis had proceeded from Phari to Gyantse in July to complete the demolition of the Jong, but otherwise the unit had been fully occupied on the communications in the Chumbi Valley.[2] The company left Chumbi under Heycock on September 19th and arrived at Bangalore on October 6th. The Tibet Mission of 1903–04 is commemorated in the Headquarter Mess at Chatham by a silver model of a *chorten* copied from a miniature in brass inlaid with turquoises which was presented to General Macdonald on his departure from Lhasa.[3] It is safe to say that no more romantic adventure has ever fallen to the lot of Sappers and Miners than this journey into the unknown territory beyond the Himalaya.

After the expedition to Tibet there was no chance of active service on the North-East Frontier until the Abor Expedition of 1911 which started shortly before the Coronation Durbar at Delhi. Units of all three Corps and of the Indian States' Sappers were present at the Delhi Durbar ceremonies from December 7th to the 16th including the State Entry, the Durbar itself, the Royal Review and the State Departure. Those who were privileged to take part in that wonderful pageant will never forget it. The country for miles to the north of the famous Ridge was covered with tents and illumined after dark with a myriad lights. Wide roads had appeared where a few months before the humble villager tilled his field. Light railways threaded their way between great camps and past a huge amphitheatre. This metamorphosis was due in part to the labours of the 1st and 6th Companies, Bengal S. and M., from February to May 1911, and of the 11th Company Madras S. and M., during the autumn. They laid railways, bridged streams and roads, built fire-alarm stations, erected signposts, provided water-supply systems and prepared standing camps in conjunction with the Public Works Department and Military Works Services. Even church furniture came within their orbit. The Bengal Sappers having been asked whether they could make the furniture for a service which the King and Queen were to attend, C.S.M. Dawkins, R.E., delivered it from the Corps Workshops at Roorkee within a week. It consisted of *prie-dieu* for the King, the Queen, the Viceroy and the Vicereine and stalls for the bishops, clergy and choir. The King's *prie-dieu* was brought back to Roorkee after the Durbar and placed in the Commandant's office; but urgent telegrams soon began to fly, and it had to

[1] *History and Digest of Service of the 1st K.G.O. Sappers and Miners*, p. 75.
[2] *Historical Record of the Q.V.O. Madras Sappers and Miners*, Vol. I, pp. 184, 185.
[3] "The R.E. Headquarter Mess," by Lieut.-Col. B. R. Ward, R.E., appearing in *The R.E. Journal*, Vol. IX, Jan.–June, 1909, pp. 455–456. This article describes the trophies of many other campaigns.

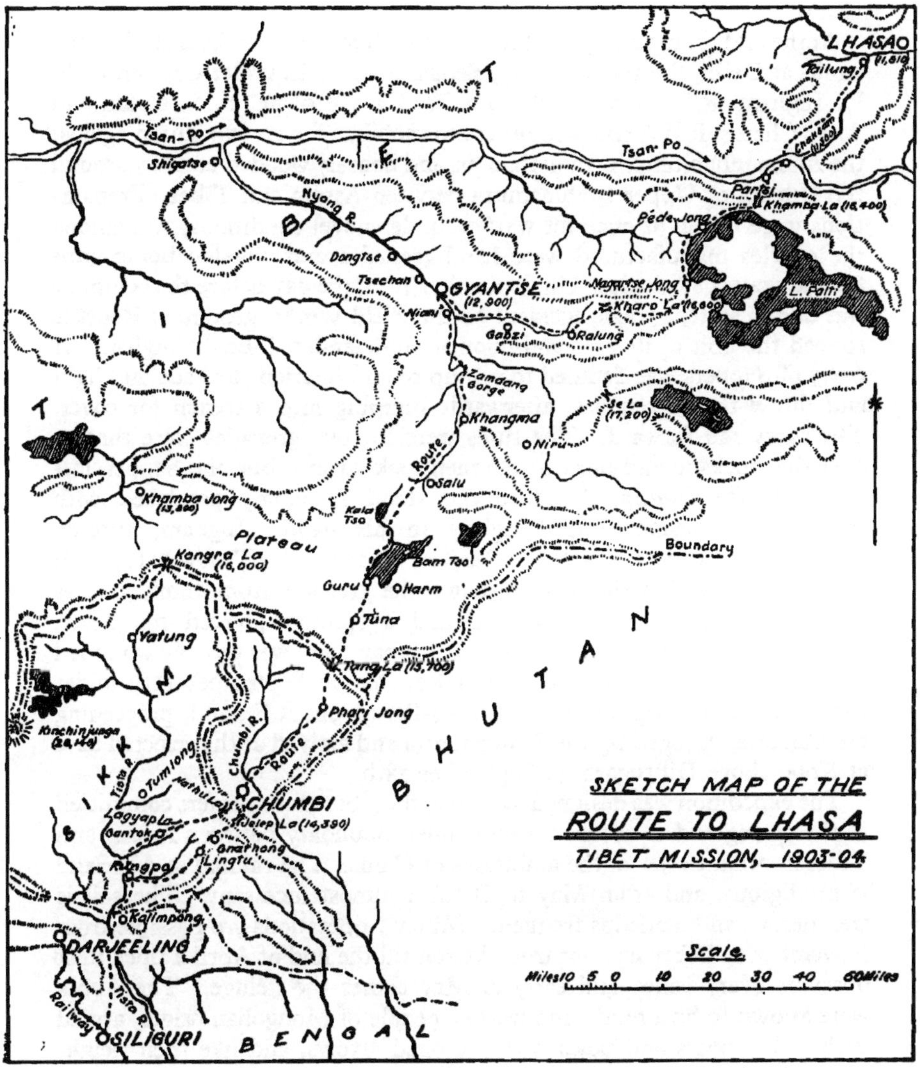
SKETCH MAP OF THE
ROUTE TO LHASA
TIBET MISSION, 1903-04.
LHASA
Tsan-Po
Shigatse
Nyang R.
Dongtse
Tsechan
GYANTSE
(12,900)
Niani
Gobzi
Ralung
Kharo La
Nagartse Jong
Pede Jong
Khamba La (16,400)
Partsi
Chaksam
Tailung
L. Palti
Zamdang Gorge
Khangma
Se La
(17,200)
Niru
Route
Salu
Kala Tso
Bam Tso
Guru
Harm
Tuna
Tang La (15,700)
Phari Jong
Plateau
Kangra La
(16,000)
Khamba Jong
Boundary
Yatung
Kinchinjunga
Tumlong
Tista R.
Chumbi R.
CHUMBI
Jelep La (14,390)
Gnathong
Lingtu
Gantok
Rungpo
Kalimpong
DARJEELING
Railway
SILIGURI
B E N G A L
B H U T A N
S I K K I M
T I B E T
Scale
Miles 10 5 0 10 20 30 40 60 Miles

be delivered to the Bishop of Lahore for use in the Lahore Cathedral.[1] The representative units of all three Corps and the Indian States' Sappers were brigaded for the Royal Review under Colonel O. M. R. Thackwell, late R.E., and the Bengal Sappers provided a King's Guard at the Royal Camp.

At the end of August 1911, three months after its return from the Durbar works at Delhi, the 1st Company, Bengal S. and M., under Captain O. E. U. Ingham, R.E., with Lieutenants W. Cave-Browne, F. S. Collin and A. F. Chater, R.E.,[2] received orders to mobilize for an expedition against the Abors inhabiting the mountainous and densely wooded country around the Dihang or Upper Brahmaputra between Assam and Tibet. Preparations were begun at once for warfare under novel conditions, and among the articles manufactured were hand-grenades and wooden bomb-guns for use against stockades. On September 10th, the day before the company was due to start, a tragic accident on the Field Works' ground at Roorkee robbed the unit of its able and popular commander, "Boy" Ingham. A party of Sappers was detailed to run up to an imitation stockade and light and throw three grenades, afterwards jumping into a trench for cover. The party ran forward. The fuses were lit, two grenades were thrown over the stockade and most of the men took cover; but one Sapper lost his head after lighting his fuse and stood, seemingly paralysed, with the hissing grenade clasped tightly in his hand. Ingham, turning back from the trench, shouted "*Phenko! Phenko!*" (Throw! Throw!) and then jumped at the man to snatch the grenade from him; but as he did so the grenade exploded and a splinter pierced his heart, killing him instantly.[3] The Sapper lost his hand and was terribly wounded in the neck. The 1st Company left Roorkee on September 11th under the command of Captain E. C. Tylden-Pattenson, R.E., and, proceeding *via* Calcutta, voyaged up the Brahmaputra and arrived at the selected base at Kobo above Dibrugarh on September 28th.

The expedition was designed to punish the Abors for murders committed in the spring and to secure a well defined boundary between Assam and Tibet in order to defeat the ambitions of China. The rainfall in Aborland is prodigious, and from May to October almost incessant. The soil is treacherous and landslips frequent. Military operations are possible from November to February, but from March till the end of April a thick mist obscures every valley and early in May comes the deluge. The Abors were known to be a hardy and warlike people of Mongolian origin, armed with *dahs*, spears and bows with poisoned arrows, and like their neighbours the Mishmis they loved to launch avalanches of stones on their enemies from well concealed and easily released bamboo platforms. In 1911 they could put into the field about 3,000 fighting men, so they were no mean foes in their native jungles. To deal with them, a force of about

[1]Notes by Capt. H. Dawkins, M.B.E., R.E. (I.A.) (retd.), sent to the author on Jan. 6th, 1938.

[2]Lieut. Chater, R.E., joined the unit from the Military Works Services.

[3]Notes by Lieut.-Col. E. P. Le Breton, R.E. (retd.), sent to the author on Nov. 19th, 1937.

2,500 men under Major-General H. Bower, consisting of the 32nd Pioneers, 1/2nd and 1/8th Gurkha Rifles, 1st Company, Bengal S. and M., and 400 Military Police, was sent to Kobo and given 3,000 Naga coolies for supply and transport work. The general idea was that the main body should advance up the Dihang through Pasighat while a smaller column operated west of the river. The force was concentrated at Kobo by the middle of October and on the 26th Bower reached Pasighat with the main body. This place, being the limit of navigation up the Dihang, was adopted as the advanced base. Renging, near the junction of the Sirpo tributary,[1] was occupied on November 9th. The Sappers and Pioneers were employed in widening and improving the existing Abor track up the right bank of the Dihang. They worked usually to a ruling gradient of about 1 in 7; but beyond the Sirpo they met a rise of 1,000 feet which the native track ascended at a slope of 1 in 2, and here they were obliged to cut a new path at a gradient of 1 in 5. Their progress was hampered not only by large trees which had to be felled and removed but by heavy rain and the unceasing attacks of voracious leeches. Indeed, the Abor Expedition of 1911–12 has been aptly described as "a nightmare of rain and leeches."

A small engagement was fought on November 19th, and on the following day the force marched to Rotung beyond which the Abors held a large stockade on a high cliff. Bower decided to turn the left of this position after sending a detachment across the Dihang to enfilade it from the right, and accordingly he directed Tylden-Pattenson to establish a ferry for the passage of the enfilading troops.[2] This was the outstanding exploit of the Sappers and Miners during the expedition. The first attempt was made on November 30th at a place where the width was about 350 yards and the current very rapid in certain channels. On the far side was a rocky cliff 30 feet high, and on the near side the bank was covered with immense rocks. The stores available were a number of Wheatley bags,[3] some steel wire cables up to 1½" in circumference, a traveller and a limited supply of rope and line. A raft of 10 bags was made up with bamboo framework, and Cave-Browne and five Sappers tried without success to row across with a line. An attempt was made to run an "otter"[4] across, but the otter refused to go further than half-way and, after overturning in a whirlpool, dived to the bottom and remained there. On December 1st, two larger otters were prepared and launched. One dived and broke loose; the other leapt like a porpoise and capsized. No less than seven attempts with otters failed on December 2nd, but some adjustments and a new procedure brought success at last. A raft was swung out from the far bank by a 1" steel cable until it was 150 yards from shore and a re-designed otter was started on a 200 yards' run from the near bank to meet it. Cave-Browne,

[1]The Sirpo, one of numerous small tributaries on the right bank of the Dihang, is not shown in the *Sketch Map of the North-East Frontier* included in this chapter.

[2]*Frontier and Overseas Expeditions from India. Official Account of the Abor Expedition, 1911–12*, p. 37.

[3]Waterproof canvas bags stuffed with compressed hay or dry grass. They soon became waterlogged and were abandoned in favour of Polyanski (pneumatic) bags.

[4]An apparatus, resembling a paravane, designed to drag a line across by the combined action on it of the current and the tension of its cable.

on the raft, managed to catch the otter's tail and with great difficulty joined the 1″ cables. On the following day, a 1½″ cable was pulled across and tightened clear of the water and the enfilading detachment was ferried over in 19 trips by a flying bridge.[1] The Abor stockade was then assaulted and captured according to plan, and the 1st Company proceeded to demolish it and destroy forty stone chutes overhanging the approaches.

The campaign was soon brought to a successful conclusion. Bower pushed up the Dihang as far as Kebang,[2] the occupation of which on December 12th was followed by the submission of the Abors. Captain O. H. B. Trenchard, R.E., and Lieutenants G. F. T. Oakes and J. A. Field, R.E., (Survey of India officers) then explored northwards.[3] Meanwhile, the Sappers and Pioneers continued to improve roads and build bridges (including two large structures of suspension type) and to strengthen a number of small Abor bridges. The largest Abor suspension bridge, for cooly traffic only, had a span of 700 feet and was composed entirely of cane and bamboo.[4] The Sappers provided a ferry across the Dihang at Yambung after covering their operations by firing two 3½-lb. dynamite bombs across the river from their wooden mortars.[5] In addition, they built defensible posts at Rotung and Pasighat. By the middle of April, however, deluges of rain made further work impossible. The troops were living in extreme discomfort, though there was little sickness. At Tylden-Pattenson's suggestion, each of his British officers had arranged to receive a monthly parcel of delicacies from a firm in Calcutta, and it is whispered that the guncotton boxes of the unit did not always contain explosive. Each officer was allowed only 40 lbs. of kit and there was a similar allowance for the Mess.[6] The Bengal Sappers left Pasighat by half-companies on April 16th and 17th, 1912, and before the end of the month were in Roorkee. According to General Bower the work done by the 1st Company was above all praise and the success of the expedition was largely due to the skill and energy displayed by all ranks. Both Tylden-Pattenson and Cave-Browne were mentioned in despatches, and the former, then a Major, was promoted to Brevet Lieut.-Colonel.

While the Abor Expedition was forcing its way up the Dihang, a peaceful Mishmi Mission of a few hundred men under Major C. Bliss, 1st Gurkha Rifles, was moving eastwards towards the ill-defined frontier of China. Included in this Mission was the 5th Company, Bengal S. & M., under Captain E. P. Le Breton, R.E., with Lieutenants C. H. R. Chesney,

[1] *Frontier and Overseas Expeditions from India. Official Account of the Abor Expedition, 1911–12. Report on Engineering Operations*, pp. 199–200.

[2] About 10 miles upstream of Rotung.

[3] See *The Military Engineer in India*, by the present author, Vol. II, p. 248. In the autumn of 1912, Lieut. P. G. Huddleston, R.E., replaced Lieut. Field, R.E., and the exploration continued until Aug., 1913. In the summer of 1913, Lieut. H. T. Morshead, R.E., and Capt. F. M. Bailey, 32nd Pioneers, journeyed from Mishmiland to the Tsan-po in Tibet and followed that river up to the Lhasa region, while Capts. O. H. B. Trenchard and S. Pemberton, R.E., as related later, explored far up the Dihang.

[4] The bridge is described in " Abor Suspension Bridges," by Lieut. A. F. Chater, R.E., appearing in *The R.E. Journal*, Vol. XVI, July–Dec., 1912, pp. 217, 218.

[5] See the illustration opposite p. 472 of *The Military Engineer in India*, Vol. I, by the present author. Yambung is about 8 miles upstream of Rotung.

[6] Notes by Col. A. F. Chater, late R.E., sent to the author on Oct. 15th, 1937.

J. F. Gray and A. D. de R. Martin, R.E. For a time, during the absence of Major Bliss, Captain Le Betron was in chief command.[1] Captain C. P. Gunter and Lieutenant H. T. Morshead, R.E., accompanied the expedition as Survey officers. The first part of the journey from the base at Sadiya up the valley of the Lohit Brahmaputra led through dense forest interlaced so thickly with creepers that the Sappers could not cut more than two miles of track in a day. Sweltering heat, poisonous plants and still more poisonous and bloodthirsty insects made life a purgatory, but several fortified posts were built along the line of advance and at the end of November 1911 the Mission was ready to strike north-eastwards into Mishmiland proper from a post called Temeimukh. It reached the Del-li tributary of the Lohit[2] on December 19th, and two days later started to march eastwards across enormous and jungle-clad ridges and spurs divided by precipitous gorges which were spanned sometimes by native suspension bridges of bamboo and cane.[3] At last the Mission emerged from the jungle on to bare and wind-swept uplands and on January 4th, 1912, reached a place above the Lohit River where a red flag, with the five-toed dragon of China, fluttered in the breeze and a placard on a wooden post announced that this was the southern limit of the " Great Pure Dynasty." A mile or so on the Chinese side of this arbitrary boundary, the British force, now reduced to 110 rifles of whom 80 were Sappers, camped for a month at a spot called Menil-krai on the bank of a tributary popularly known as the Yepak. The names are unimportant as no place in Mishmiland seems to have any permanent denomination. The Chinese being accustomed to encroach on British territory whenever the monsoon permitted, it was necessary to stake a claim on behalf of the Indian Government, and accordingly Le Breton was directed to construct a length of properly graded road on a ridge near Menil-krai although it never would be, nor could be, used. Chinese emissaries arrived, polite and inscrutable, and returned smiling across the border after being entertained lavishly with *crème-de-menthe*. However, as the rivers in Mishmiland were already rising, the Mission could not afford to delay its departure ; but before it left, the Political Officer found time to erect a placard bearing in Chinese characters a quotation from Confucius. " How pleasant," read the notice, " it is to meet a stranger from a distant country ! " It is to be hoped that the hint was not wasted on the next representatives of the Great Pure Dynasty who visited the spot. The return march was begun on February 3rd, 1912, and fifteen days later the Mission arrived in Sadiya having gathered much information and surveyed wide tracts of almost unknown territory. The work of the 5th Company had been most varied in character, ranging from the construction of a 300 feet bridge to the manufacture of

[1]The story of the Mishmi Mission is told in an interesting article entitled " An Unknown Frontier," by Lieut.-Col. E. P. Le Breton, R.E., appearing in *Blackwood's Magazine*, April, 1922, pp. 427–438.

[2]The Del-li tributary is about 20 miles N.E. of Temeimukh.

[3]These bridges, one of which was 350 feet in length, are described in " Résumé of the Work Done by the 5th Company, 1st K.G.O. Sappers and Miners " included as Appendix F. in the *Brief Narrative of the Mishmi Mission*, 1911–12 (official), by Major C. Bliss.

a new pin for the hinge of an officer's soap-box,[1] but all had been done satisfactorily and the unit had fully maintained the excellent reputation of the Corps.

During the cold weather of 1912–13, several companies or detachments of Sappers and Miners were employed in the Abor and Mishmi countries in connection with Survey operations. Half the 10th Company, Madras S. & M., under Lieutenant S. Pemberton, R.E., with Lieutenant J. C. Wickham, R.E., left Bangalore at the end of November 1912 for road and bridge construction in the Abor Hills to assist a Survey party under Captain O. H. B. Trenchard, R.E., with Lieutenants G. F. T. Oakes and P. G. Huddleston, R.E. A battalion of Military Police acted as an escort from the base at Kobo. The objects of the expedition were to extend the survey of the Dihang valley and to trace the course of the Tsan-po through the Himalayan gorges further north. The Madras Sappers set out from Kobo on December 18th and repaired the bridges constructed in 1911 as far as Rotung. A flying bridge was established at Rotung for an advance up the left bank of the Dihang but was dismantled when the scheme was abandoned in favour of an advance up the right bank. Many tributaries had to be crossed in the slow progress upstream. Some of the native cane suspension bridges were repaired; others rebuilt above flood level.[2] Those repaired were strengthened with 1½" steel cables and provided with a bamboo footway suitable for cooly traffic. In all, 19 tributaries were dealt with, the largest ones by means of flying bridges of Polyanski or Wheatley bags and the smaller ones (up to 340 feet width) by crib-pier, suspension or cantilever structures.[3] Local Abors joined enthusiastically in the work and provided an accompaniment of shouting, wailing and singing. Rain fell incessantly, and leeches, flies and snakes abounded.

It was not until June 1913 that the head of the expedition reached Khapu below the mighty gorges of the Tsan-po. There it halted and two small flying columns were pushed forward. One column under the Political Officer, including four Sappers, continued for a short distance up the main river, while the other, under Trenchard and Pemberton with three Sappers, set out to explore westwards into Tibet. The latter party had a most arduous journey. At one place it had to cross the face of a cliff by a pathway consisting only of two poles with a clear drop of 1,800 feet into the river below. It reached the Tsan-po in Tibet and tried to explore downstream to Gyala but had to abandon the project.[4] A general retirement from Abor territory was begun in the middle of July. The last of the half-company of Madras Sappers arrived in Kobo on August 10th, 1913,

[1]Notes by Lieut.-Col. E. P. Le Breton, R.E., sent to the author on Nov. 19th, 1937.

[2]In notes sent to the author on Dec. 12th, 1937, Col. S. Pemberton, D.S.O., M.C., late R.E., remarks that the largest single-span Abor bridge he saw was one of 1,000 feet length across the Dihang River.

[3]"Report on the Work of Right (Half-Company) Sappers, No. 10 Field Company, 2nd Q.V.O. Sappers and Miners, with the Abor Survey Party, 1912–13," by Capt. S. Pemberton, R.E., included in the Historical Records at Bangalore. See also *Historical Record of the Q.V.O. Madras Sappers and Miners*, Vol. II, p. 37.

[4]"The Abor Expedition Survey Detachment, 1911–12, and the Abor Exploration Survey Detachment, 1912–13," by Capt. O. H. B. Trenchard, R.E., appearing in *The R.E. Journal*, Vol. XXI, Jan.–June, 1915, pp. 221–241 and 268–292.

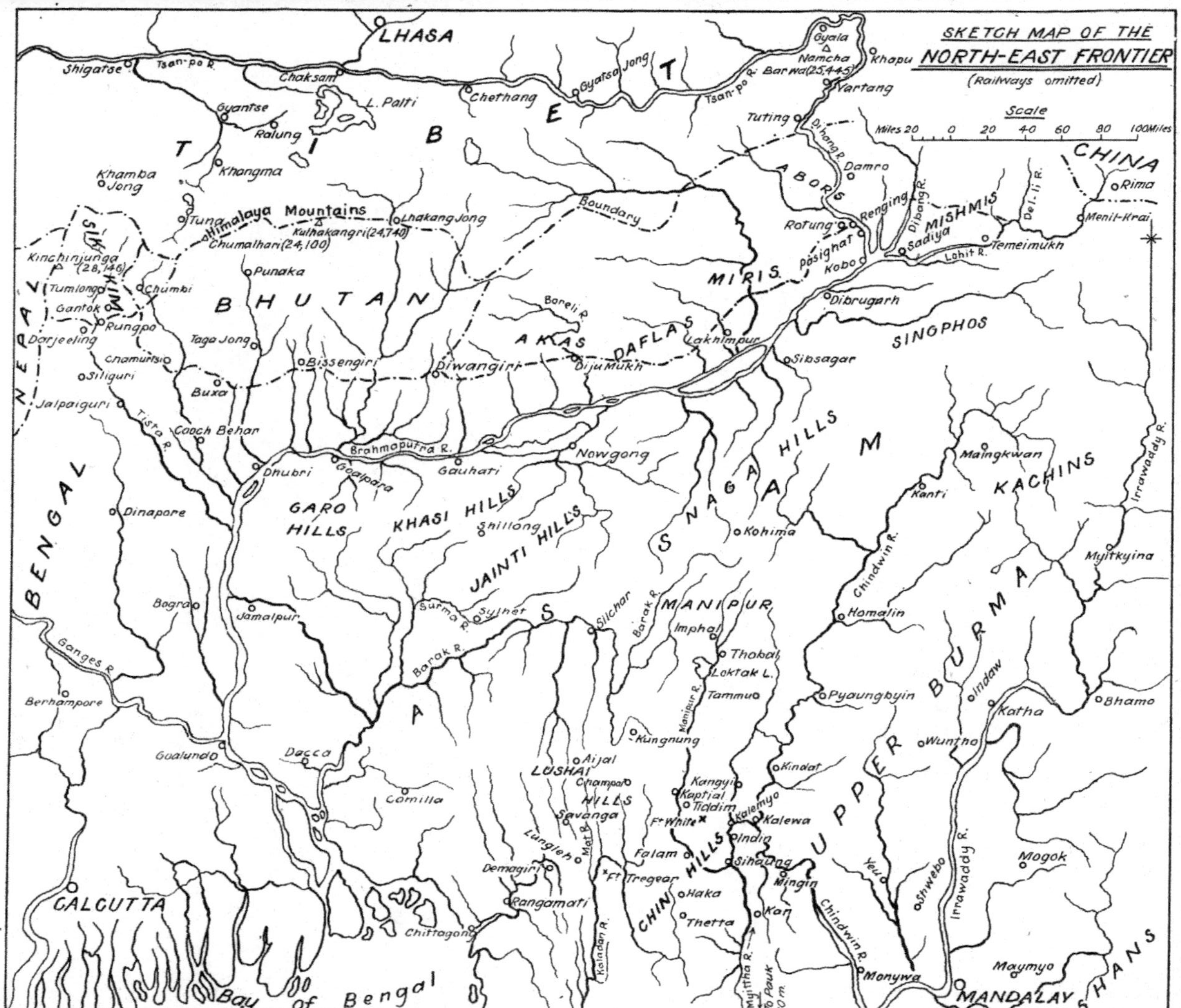
SKETCH MAP OF THE
NORTH-EAST FRONTIER
(Railways omitted)
Scale
Miles 20 0 20 40 60 80 100Miles
LHASA
Shigatse
Tsan-po R.
Chaksam
Gyantse
Ralung
L. Palti
Chethang
Gyatsa Jong
Gyala
Namcha
Barwa (25,445)
Khapu
Vartang
Tuting
Dihang R.
Damro
ABORS
Renging
Rotung
Pasighat
Kobo
Dibang R.
MISHMIS
Sadiya
Lohit R.
Temeimukh
Del. li R.
CHINA
Rima
Menil-Krai
T I B E T
Khangma
Khamba Jong
Tuna
Himalaya Mountains
Kulhakangri (24,740)
Chumalhari (24,100)
Lhakang Jong
Boundary
SIKKIM
NEPAL
Kinchinjunga (28,146)
Tumlong
Gantok
Chumbi
Rungpo
Darjeeling
Chamurtsi
Siliguri
Jalpaiguri
Tista R.
Buxa
Cooch Behar
Taga Jong
Punaka
B H U T A N
Bissengiri
Diwangiri
Boreli R.
AKAS
DAFLAS
Diju Mukh
Lakhimpur
MIRIS
Dibrugarh
Sibsagar
SINGHPOS
Brahmaputra R.
Dhubri
Goalpara
Gauhati
Nowgong
GARO HILLS
KHASI HILLS
Shillong
JAINTI HILLS
NAGA HILLS
Kohima
BENGAL
Dinapore
Bogra
Jamalpur
Ganges R.
Berhampore
Goalundo
Dacca
Comilla
Surma R.
Sylhet
Barak R.
Silchar
A S S A M
MANIPUR
Imphal
Thobal
Loktak L.
Manipur R.
Tammu
Kungnung
Aijal
LUSHAI HILLS
Champai
Savanga
Mat R.
Lungleh
Demagiri
Rangamati
Chittagong
Kaladan R.
Ft Tregear
Kangyi
Kaptial
Tiddim
Ft White
Falam
CHIN HILLS
Haka
Thetta
Myittha R.
To Pauk 10 m.
CALCUTTA
Bay of Bengal
Kanti
Maingkwan
KACHINS
Irrawaddy R.
Myitkyina
Chindwin R.
Homalin
Pyaungbyin
UPPER BURMA
Indaw
Katha
Bhamo
Wuntho
Kindat
Kalemyo
Kalewa
Indin
Sihaung
Mingin
Kan
Yeu
Shwebo
Mogok
Monywa
Maymyo
MANDALAY
SHANS

and eighteen days later the detachment rejoined the headquarters in Bangalore.

While the Madras Sappers under Pemberton were roadmaking and bridging with the Abor Survey Party, three companies from the Bengal and Bombay Corps were working northwards from Sadiya up the Dibang River or eastwards along the Lohit Brahmaputra. These units were the 6th Company, Bengal S. & M., under Lieut.-Colonel E. C. Tylden-Pattenson, R.E., (with Lieutenants R. N. Bocquet and F. P. Nosworthy, R.E.) and the 20th and 21st Companies, Bombay S. & M., under Captains A. L. Paris and J. B. Corry, R.E.[1] They worked in conjunction with a Mishmi Survey Party led by Captain C. P. Gunter and Lieutenant H. T. Morshead, R.E., and their duties were to provide paths for the surveyors and to improve the route towards the Chinese border. " Following Mishmi tracks usually consists in climbing cliffs by roots and creepers " wrote Corry during the expedition.[2] " Our coolies are mostly Nagas. Their usual costume is a bit of rag, and each man, in addition to a 60 lb. bag of rice, carries his kit, a *dah* and always an umbrella ! Dogs are their favourite food and beetle pie their chief delicacy. The scenery is quite beyond description and Gunter has painted some wonderful pictures. We have been building an improved Mishmi bridge of 290 feet span—all from local materials except 700 feet of 1½-inch steel wire rope, a little wire and a dozen nails. We make the roadway first and finish off with the cables. The roadway consists of eight lengths of cane knotted together in long ropes and pulled tight round logs fixed in the rock. We can get cane in lengths up to 210 feet and had one 350 feet rope with only a single knot. The eight ropes are stretched side by side and then bound into a continuous hurdle 300 feet long and one foot wide. This is slung from cane ropes and will carry four men. Wire ropes are added later and pulled tight. The theory is that the cane bridge is capable of supporting itself and a small extra load and that the wire ropes will take any additional strain that comes on it."

Work in the Dibang Valley had to be abandoned in February, 1913, because of torrential rain, and thereafter the three Sapper companies were occupied in constructing 90 miles of graded mule-road from Sadiya up the Lohit Valley. The 6th Company built eight suspension bridges, the largest being one across the Del-li River of 218 feet span,[3] and the 20th and 21st Companies constructed a number of bridges and several aerial ropeways. Tylden-Pattenson was in chief command during the latter part of the expedition. In April, the monsoon put an end to the operations and the troops had the greatest difficulty in reaching Sadiya before the road became impassable.[4]

[1]*A Brief History of the Royal Bombay Sappers and Miners*, p. 28.

[2]Extracts from letters written by Capt. J. B. Corry, D.S.O., R.E., between Nov. 11th, 1912, and Jan. 7th, 1913.

[3]" The Delei River Suspension Bridge, Mishmi Country," by Lieut. F. P. Nosworthy, R.E., appearing in *The R.E. Journal*, Vol. XVIII, July–Dec., 1913, pp. 193–196.

[4]Notes by Maj.-Gen. F. P. Nosworthy, D.S.O., M.C., late R.E., sent to the author on April 8th, 1938.

The experiences of the Sappers and Miners in their numerous expeditions on the North-East Frontier from the uplands of Tibet to the gorges of the Dihang, Dibang and Lohit and the pestilential forests of the Chin-Lushai country were often extremely unpleasant. The work, the climate and the methods of warfare were utterly unlike those to which they were accustomed. Yet the lessons which they learnt were not without value, for native ingenuity can produce wonders of primitive engineering from the natural products of the soil.

CHAPTER XVI

THE GREAT WAR: FRANCE AND BELGIUM, 1914–1915

IN the autumn of 1914, India sent to France and Belgium an expeditionary force of some 45,000 British and Indian soldiers, highly trained and well adapted and equipped for frontier operations, but in no sense designed to fight in Europe. Their equipment was utterly inadequate. For instance, a certain Divisional Cavalry Regiment in France in September, 1914, had no guncotton, though its stores included some steel nails for spiking muzzle-loading guns.[1] The troops had no air support, no regimental mechanical transport, no trench-mortars, hand grenades or periscopes. Their equipment in heavy artillery, machine guns and medical supplies was insufficient and obsolete, their reserve organization unsuitable and unsound, and the first reserves were exhausted before the units reached the front. The entire Indian Corps had to be re-armed, re-equipped and re-clothed at Marseilles. The British officers, whom the Indians knew and trusted, were soon picked off by German snipers and replaced by strangers. As the dark days of winter dragged on, battalions became mere amalgamations of drafts held together by a few of the original officers and men. The freezing cold ate into the bones of the Indians, and they missed the sunshine of their native land, yet they hung on doggedly in their flooded trenches and retaliated effectively in the face of a vastly superior armament. A sombre picture, indeed, but one which adds additional lustre to the records of the Indian Army.

During the Great War, the three Corps of Sappers and Miners underwent prodigious expansion. On August 4th, 1914, apart from subsidiary formations, the Madras Corps under Lieut.-Col. E. P. Johnson, R.E., consisted of only 6 Field Companies, a Burma Company and a Depot Company, with a total strength of 1,930 of all ranks; but at the end of the war it had more than 10,000 men in 16 Field Companies, 3 Field Troops, 3 Burma Companies, a Bridging Train and 16 Depot Companies.[2] Similarly, at the beginning of the war, the Bengal Corps, under Lieut.-Col. P. G. Twining, R.E., had only 6 Field Companies, a Field Troop (Mounted Detachment), a Pontoon Park and a Depot Company, and its strength was 1,491 of all ranks; yet, at the armistice, it included 21 Field Companies, a Field Squadron, 3 Field Troops, 3 Bridging Trains and 14 Depot Companies, and the strength exceeded 8,000 men.[3] So also with the Bombay Corps under Lieut.-Col. U. W. Evans, R.E. This formation started the war with 6 Field Companies, a Fortress Company at Aden, a

[1]Notes by Lieut.-Col. A. L. Paris, D.S.O., R.E., sent to the author on Aug. 13th, 1937.
[2]*Historical Record of the Q.V.O. Madras Sappers and Miners*, Vol. II, 1914–19, pp. 28, 29.
[3]*A Short History of the Corps of K.G.O. Bengal Sappers and Miners during the War, 1914–18*, p. 10.

Pontoon Park and a Depot Company, and had a total establishment of 1,440 officers and men; but it emerged at the end with 16 Field Companies, a Field Squadron, 2 Field Troops, 3 Pontoon Trains and 9 Depot Companies, and during hostilities no less than 250 British officers, 90 British non-commissioned officers and 6,000 Indian ranks passed through the headquarters at Kirkee.[1] Most of the British officers came from the Indian Army Reserve of Officers (I.A.R.O.), which, although only 40 strong in 1914, supplied over 5,300 officers to the Indian Army during the war.[2] It is not too much to say that without the services of these patriotic volunteers the Army would have been crippled by the initial heavy casualties among the regular officers. The Sapper and Miner units in France were reinforced also by young Royal Engineer officers from the Survey of India, the Public Works Department and the Indian Railways. More than 100 of these were sent home in 1914 and soon revived their knowledge of field engineering. They, and the I.A.R.O.s, knew India and could speak Urdu, and consequently they were welcomed by the Indian ranks.

Within a fortnight of the declaration of war, the first transport conveying troops to France sailed from Bombay, and soon the 3rd (Lahore) Division, the 7th (Meerut) Division and the 9th (Secunderabad) Cavalry Brigade were on their way as an Indian Corps under Lieut.-General Sir James Willcocks. With the Lahore Division, under Lieut.-General H. B. B. Watkis, were the 20th and 21st Companies, Bombay S. & M., under Captains A. L. Paris and J. S. Richardson, R.E.; and with the Meerut Division, under Lieut.-General C. A. Anderson, the 3rd and 4th Companies of the Bengal Corps, the 3rd under Captain E. F. J. Hill, R.E. with Lieutenants E. O. Wheeler and A. Mason, R.E., and the 4th (temporarily) under Lieutenant H. S. Trevor, R.E. with Lieutenant E. L. Farley, R.E. The 4th Company was met in Egypt by its proper commander, Captain A. J. G. Bird, R.E., with Lieutenant C. A. Bird, R.E., and Lieutenant F. Mc C. Douie, R.E., rejoined the 3rd Company. These three had been on leave in England. The Secunderabad Cavalry Brigade included a Field Troop of the Bengal Corps under Captain R. C. R. Hill, R.E., with Lieutenant F. S. Collin, R.E., Hill having been recalled from Aden while proceeding on leave to England. That India was indeed surprised by the outbreak of war is shown by the fact that, on August 4th, 1914, the only officers of the Bengal Sappers present at Roorkee were Major A. H. Cunningham, Captains E. F. J. Hill and W. Cave-Browne, R.E., and Lieutenant A. F. Chater, R.E. Brig.-General H. C. Nanton, late R.E., was Chief Engineer of the Indian Corps, and Lieut.-Colonels Campbell Coffin and P. G. Twining, R.E., were the Commanding Royal Engineers of the Lahore and Meerut Divisions respectively.[3] An Indian Cavalry Corps of two divisions, under Lieut.-General M. F. Rimington, followed

[1]*A Brief History of the Royal Bombay Sappers and Miners*, pp. 30, 31.

[2]The first I.A.R.O. to join the Bengal Sappers for training was 2nd Lieut. E. M. Proes, a senior officer of the P.W.D. He reported at Roorkee on Oct. 19th, 1914, and left for France in November. The I.A.R.O. was formed about 1903.

[3]Lieut.-Col. P. G. Twining, R.E., Commandant, Bengal S. & M., handed over charge to Major A. H. Cunningham, R.E., on Aug. 15th, 1914.

the other troops and reached France before the end of 1914. With the 1st Cavalry Division of this Corps was a Field Troop of the Madras Sappers and Miners under Captain E. K. Molesworth, R.E., with Lieutenant T. B. Harris, R.E., as Troop Officer.

The Sappers and Miners who sailed for France were greatly envied, and there was some " pulling of strings " by officers who imagined that the war might end before they could reach the front. The Simla wires hummed a lively tune. And, indeed, the lot of some companies not earmarked for immediate service overseas was a hard one, for they were set the task of assisting the Royal Indian Marine in preparing ships for use as transports and laboured from dawn to dusk in the sweltering heat of the Bombay and Karachi dockyards. The Madras Corps sent 267 carpenters and smiths from Bangalore and Secunderabad, under Captains R. G. Earle, P. E. Prince and S. Pemberton and Lieutenant R. H. Dewing, R.E., to work in the Alexandra Docks at Bombay. There they were joined by 100 artisans of the Bombay Sappers under Lieutenant E. B. Fox, R.E., and by a detachment of Bengal Sappers under Lieutenant A. F. Chater, R.E., coming from Karachi. Lieutenants D. Mc A. Hogg and E. K. Squires, R.E., also reported for duty. The Sappers were issued with rough plans of the alterations and additions required to fit the ships to carry troops and animals. Enormous numbers of stalls for mules and horses, rifle racks, kit racks and other fittings had to be provided, and the remarks of some of the ships' captains when holes were drilled in the wrong places in the steel decks were unprintable. Nevertheless, the work was done, and done well, and the improvised transports left port according to schedule. Similar labours were undertaken at Karachi by detachments of Bombay Sappers under Lieutenant M. Rawlence, R.E., and of Madras Sappers under Lieutenant E. Bradney, R.E. Captain P. E. Prince, R.E., came later from Bombay with artisans of the 10th and 11th Madras Sapper companies and joined those of the 18th and 19th Bombay companies and 1st and 6th Bengal companies already at work. Altogether, between August and October 1914, more than 30 troopships were prepared by Sapper labour, and thus the Sappers and Miners made their first and novel contribution as shipwrights towards the success of the expeditions to France, Iraq and East Africa.

During August and September, 1914, the transports conveying the Meerut Division to France left Karachi, and those carrying the Lahore Division sailed from Bombay, followed later by others with the Secunderabad Cavalry Brigade. Their destination was at first a strictly guarded secret, but some thought it was East Africa as mosquito nets were included in the mens' kits. Lieut.-General Sir Francis Nosworthy, then a subaltern with the Bombay Sappers and Miners, gives some interesting details of the voyage of the two Sapper companies in the S.S. *Taiyibeh*, which sailed from Bombay on August 24th.[1] The ship had been condemned as unfit to take pilgrims going to Mecca, and was about to be broken up

[1]Notes by Maj.-Gen. (now Lieut.-Gen. Sir) F. P. Nosworthy, D.S.O., M.C., late R.E., sent to the author on April 8th, 1938.

when the war started. For the first three days the seas were mountainous, and she lagged far behind the rest of the convoy. Cooking was difficult, and the men were very sea-sick. The lower deck ports could not be closed except by using canvas caulking on the deadlights; but before this could be done, the troop-decks and cabins were flooded. To crown all, the engines broke down. Then came better weather and the Sappers set about the difficult task of exercising the mules. They built ramps to the upper deck so that they were able to give each mule a daily walk, with the result that the animals were in excellent condition on disembarking. The troops were railed from Suez through Cairo to Alexandria, while the mules and equipment continued the journey by ship. It seems that this was due to political tension in Egypt and the recent departure of the British garrison to France. On arrival in Cairo the troops were accommodated in a camp near Heliopolis and made a most exhausting march through the streets of the capital as a display of strength; but a few days later, the Sappers were aboard the *Taiyibeh* again at Alexandria and sailing for France. On September 26th, they disembarked at Marseilles, the 20th Company being the first formed body of Indian troops to land in France. Their march through the streets to a camp on a race-course was marked by scenes of great enthusiasm. The far-famed warriors of India had arrived! The war was as good as won! On the journey northwards by train, the story was the same. At every halt, women and girls crowded the platforms with gifts of cigarettes, fruit and sweets. It was all very amusing, but also most embarrassing, and they were glad on October 1st to reach Orleans where the Lahore Division, less the Sirhind Brigade which had been left temporarily in Egypt, proceeded to concentrate during the next fortnight. Home Service kit was issued to replace khaki drill uniform, and the Sappers got fit by route marching. On October 17th they railed to a village near St. Omar, and marching with the Division through Bailleul and Estaires, reached their billets at La Gorgue, north-west of Neuve Chapelle, on the 23rd.[1] Though they had been peppered once by a German aeroplane with aerial darts—feathered nails about 8 inches long—no one had been hit, and all were jubilant because they had been told that the Germans were retreating.

The 3rd and 4th Companies, Bengal S. & M., under Captains E. F. J. Hill and A. J. G. Bird, R.E., had very similar experiences after landing at Marseilles with the Meerut Division on October 15th, 1914. They railed and marched to billets at Le Touret, 5 miles south of La Gorgue, and there reorganized and trained for work under novel conditions. At this time the British Expeditionary Force under Field Marshal Sir John French was holding the line Ypres–Armentiéres–Givenchy and repulsing strong attacks by the Germans. The Indian Corps, less two brigades of the Lahore Division,[2] came up behind the British 2nd Corps and gradually relieved

[1]See *Sketch Map of Northern France and Belgium*, 1914–15—*Ypres-La Bassée Sector*, included in this chapter. La Gorgue was a small village situated in low-lying fields. It was the fate of the Indian Corps to be posted in the upper valley of the River Lys, once a lake, and in 1914–15 the most swampy sector of the front.

[2]7th (Ferozepore) Brigade lent to the British Cavalry Corps, and 9th (Sirhind) Brigade still in Egypt.

it on the general line Fauquissart–Neuve Chapelle–Givenchy. Already it was gravely depleted in strength. The four Sapper companies dug second-line positions and replenished their equipment. By October 29th the Indian Corps was in occupation, but before that date the Bombay Sappers had fought gallantly and suffered heavily at Neuve Chapelle.

The enemy had gained a footing in Neuve Chapelle on October 26th, and had clung to it in spite of several counter-attacks. These culminated on October 28th in an assault in which the 20th and 21st Companies co-operated with the 47th Sikhs and 9th Bhopals. "Practically only four companies definitely took part in the attack." writes Brig.-General J. E. Edmonds.[1] "The attack of four companies—two of the 47th Sikhs with the 20th and 21st Companies of the Bombay Sappers and Miners on either side of them—was carried out with the greatest gallantry. Their right was to have been protected by the Bhopal Regiment, but as this unit advanced it came under very heavy fire and halted and continued the action by fire from a trench that it had reached. The Sikhs and Sappers went on. Covering the 700 yards of open ground between them and Neuve Chapelle by rushes alternating with fire, as if on a training ground, the four companies reached the ruins of the village and drove out the Germans—reported by prisoners to be three battalions—by close hand-to-hand fighting. They even penetrated to the eastern and northern borders. Here they were met by heavy shell and machine-gun fire, and counter-attack after counter-attack was launched against them. Major S. R. Davidson, commanding the 47th Sikhs, finding that he was unsupported except by the Sappers and Miners, eventually ordered a retreat. This had to be carried out under enemy fire, and so heavy were the losses that of his men he rallied only 68 out of 289, whilst of the Sappers and Miners all the officers were killed or wounded and over a third of the other ranks of each company." So runs the official account of an engagement which exemplified the folly of using engineer units as infantry except in a truly desperate situation. The result of this action was to cripple the Lahore Division for weeks until the Sapper companies could be re-officered and reinforced.

Some incidents in the fight at Neuve Chapelle are described graphically in *The Indian Corps in France*,[2] but the experiences of Lieutenant F. P. Nosworthy, R.E., may throw additional light on the events of a fateful day. Captain A. L. Paris, R.E., commanding the 20th Company, Bombay S. & M., had under him Lieutenants E. J. B. Hayes-Sadler, F. P. Nosworthy and R. S. Rait Kerr, R.E.; and Captain J. S. Richardson, R.E., commanding the 21st Company, had Lieutenants R. L. Almond, J. H. Rohde and M. A. R. G. Fitzmaurice, R.E. On the evening of October 27th, according to Nosworthy,[3] the 20th Company moved southwards from billets at Bout de Ville to Richebourg St. Vaast, west of Neuve

[1]*Military Operations, France and Belgium*, 1914, by Brig.-Gen. J. E. Edmonds, C.B., C.M.G., late R.E., Vol. I, p. 218 (Official Account).

[2]*The Indian Corps in France*, by Lieut.-Col. J. W. B. Merewether, C.I.E. and the Rt. Hon. Sir Frederick Smith (afterwards Lord Birkenhead), p. 54, *et seq.*

[3]Notes by Maj.-Gen. F. P. Nosworthy, D.S.O., M.C., late R.E., sent to the author on May 6th, 1938.

Chapelle. Paris told them that they were to dig a rear line of trenches near Pont Logy on the Estaires-La Bassée road, so they had a hasty meal and set off; but when they started work they found that there were no troops between them and the Germans. Consequently, they threw out their own outposts as the enemy seemed to be digging in within 300 yards of them. Nosworthy reconnoitred after dark and discovered that a company of the 9th Bhopals was on their right rear. On their left, separated by a gap of perhaps 600 yards, was the 21st Company. Nosworthy met Almond, who commanded a section of that company, and discussed the situation with him. They never met again, for Almond was killed soon afterwards. When dawn broke on October 28th, the 20th Company had finished a trench along their sector, and meanwhile the gap between them and the 21st Company had been filled by two companies of the 47th Sikhs. Paris told them later that the artillery would put down a short concentration of fire, after which they were to attack as infantry in conjunction with the Bhopals on their right and the 47th Sikhs and 21st Company on their left, but without supports or reserves as they were already so widely extended.

"I was in command of No. 2 Section," continues Nosworthy, "and we began to move forward about 11 a.m. The ground between us and the village was dead flat plough, devoid of cover, but the advance continued with parade-ground precision in spite of some casualties. Paris was so worried by the exposure of our right flank through the lateness of the Bhopals in starting that he went back to get them on, and that was the last we saw of him. It seems that he collected a few Bhopals and led them towards the village but was soon wounded and afterwards picked up by the enemy.[1] His loss was felt severely, for he had commanded the 20th Company for more than seven years. My section came under heavy fire from the right, and we swung right and charged a German trench with the bayonet. Meanwhile, the Bhopals were heavily engaged on our right rear. After entering Neuve Chapelle there was bitter street fighting. Havildar Muhammad Khan rushed up to me, trying to speak, but he could not do so as he had been shot through the throat and was bleeding profusely. I persuaded him to go back, but his wound proved mortal and so I lost a particular friend. Then Hayes-Sadler appeared with his section and together we worked steadily forward, clearing the main street, house by house. At the cross-roads in the centre of the village, a machine gun opened fire on us at point-blank range, and Hayes-Sadler charged forward against it. He was killed immediately, but we soon got that machine gun and avenged his death. Though now in complete possession of the cross-roads, we could get no further. Less than twenty men remained with Rait Kerr and myself in the centre of the village. Others had joined forces with the 47th Sikhs on our left. We barricaded the main street with furniture and I sent Rait Kerr back to get reinforcements. Sappers posted in windows covered the road block, and three attempts to dislodge us failed with

[1]Capt. A. L. Paris was in a German hospital in France until May, 1915, and afterwards a prisoner-of-war in Germany until 1918, when he was sent to Switzerland.

heavy loss. Rait Kerr never returned, nor did reinforcements arrive. It appears that Rait Kerr made his way to the south-western edge of the village where he saw some Bhopals under Major G. A. Jamieson trying to check a German outflanking attack. With a few Sappers he went to join them, but was wounded in the arm and collapsed. We were now completely isolated and were too weak to send out patrols as only Subadar Ganpat Mahadeo and 13 Sappers remained. About 4 p.m., however, I decided to attempt to find out what had happened and reconnoitred alone down the main street. At the outskirts of the village I met Major Jamieson who was surprised to hear that we were in the middle of the place and advised a withdrawal. This we accomplished successfully, taking with us as many wounded as we could. On the way we came across Rait Kerr sitting in a shell-hole with a shattered arm. Thus ended our fight at Neuve Chapelle. On the day after the battle there was not a single British officer available for duty with either of the two Bombay Sapper companies."

Little is recorded of the exploits of the 21st Company at Neuve Chapelle except that, with the 47th Sikhs, they fought their way into the northern and western outskirts of the village and lost heavily in officers and men. Captain J. S. Richardson, R.E., was killed in a gallant charge, and Lieutenants R. L. Almond and J. H. Rohde, R.E., fell also in close fighting, while Lieutenant M. A. R. G. Fitzmaurice, R.E., was severely wounded.[1] In the two companies combined, Nosworthy and Rait Kerr were the only British officers on their feet after the battle and both were wounded and had to be evacuated to hospital. Out of a total of 6 Indian Officers and about 300 Indian other ranks, the two companies had lost 1 Indian officer and 45 other ranks killed and 2 Indian officers and 71 other ranks wounded, among the wounded being Jemadar Baryam Singh of the 20th Company.[2] The remnants of the units went into billets behind the front where Captains G. H. Stack, H. S. Gaskell and C. D. W. Bamberger, R.E., all Field Engineers, assumed temporary charge of them until other officers could be posted. On November 1st, Captain C. F. Birney, R.E., took command of the 20th Company, with Lieutenant R. G. G. Robson, R.E., as Company Officer, and Lieutenant H. W. R. Hamilton, R.E., joined on the following day.[3] Subadar Ganpat Mahadeo was now the only survivor of the seven British and Indian officers who had left Kirkee with the 20th Company less than three months earlier. Birney left on November 17th to join the Railways, and Robson was transferred to the Bengal Sappers. Major A. R. Winsloe, R.E., then arrived to command the 20th Company with Captains W. P. Pakenham-Walsh and M. Everett and Lieutenant H. G. Greswell, R.E. After Major J. B. Corry, R.E., had held temporary command of the 21st Company for a time, assisted by Lieutenants H. M. McKay and F. E. Buller, R.E., he was killed by a shell and Captain B. C. Battye, R.E., came to take command of the unit with Lieutenants L.

[1]Lieut. M. A. R. G. Fitzmaurice, R.E., was killed in France on Aug. 6th, 1916.

[2]"The Third Sappers and Miners in the War," by Maj. A. L. Paris, D.S.O., R.E., appearing in *The R.E. Journal*, Vol. XXXIII, Jan–June, 1921, pp. 14–20.

[3]*History of the 20th (Field) Company, Royal Bombay Sappers and Miners, Great War, 1914–1915*, by Maj. H. W. R. Hamilton, D.S.O., M.C., R.E., p. 11.

Manton (Fraustadt), F. H. Kisch and F. G. Drew, R.E. Such frequent changes in officer personnel were unavoidable because men with the necessary experience were difficult to find. However, the lesson of Neuve Chapelle was not wasted. Never again were Sappers and Miners used in France as infantry in the attack. They were employed instead on technical work and particularly in the manufacture of trench mortars and hand grenades which the Indian Corps needed so urgently.

The 3rd and 4th Companies, Bengal S. & M., who disembarked at Marseilles on October 15th, 1914, and came into line with the Meerut Division on the 29th, suffered no casualties comparable with those of the Bombay Sappers, though they had their fill of trench warfare. They were billeted in the village of Le Touret, about 4 miles south-west of Neuve Chapelle. On the night of 11th/12th November, part of the 3rd Company under Lieutenant F. Mc C. Douie, R.E., was ordered to blow up some houses standing between our lines and those of the Germans, which were less than 300 yards apart. The enemy were driven out of one house and six houses were demolished before dawn. One remained, however, so Douie led a party of four men to it in daylight and was preparing to lay the charges when the enemy opened a murderous fire. All the party were hit, two being killed outright. Douie, severely wounded, managed to crawl back to our trenches, though hit again on the way. Then, under a hail of bullets, Jemadar Ram Rup Singh headed a rescue party and brought in the remaining dead and wounded. Douie never recovered fully from the effects of his wounds; yet he was back in the line a few months later, and at Festubert, on May 22nd, 1915, he and his orderly, Sapper Jiwa Singh, went out in broad daylight and rescued a wounded man under heavy fire.[1] He was recommended for the V.C. but was awarded the D.S.O., and Jiwa Singh received the I.O.M.

On the night of November 15th/16th, 1914, a detachment of the 3rd Company was in action near Festubert. The Germans had sapped up close to our front line and it was necessary to eject them and fill in the saps. This was accomplished by parties under Captain E. H. Kelly and Lieutenant E. O. Wheeler, R.E., working with a company of the 6th Jats. Advancing under fire, the party under Kelly with Havildar Chagatta, drove the enemy from one sap and filled it in, while Wheeler's men filled in the other sap. Eight nights later, after some British and Indian battalions had retired before a powerful attack, Kelly was sent to ascertain whether a certain trench was occupied by the enemy. Most of it proved to be held thinly by Indian troops, but towards the far end the dead alone were in possession. Picking his way between the corpses, alone and in pitch darkness, Kelly came to a traverse beyond which he heard whispering but was unable to distinguish the language spoken. As he listened, a bomb exploded at his feet and he fell severely wounded in the face, neck, shoulder and hand; but rolling over, he crawled back and, lying on his side, directed the attack till he collapsed. Such lonely reconnaissances require

[1] *Lectures on the Regimental History of the K.G.O. Bengal Sappers and Miners*, by Maj. L. V. Bond, R.E., p. 14.

the utmost courage. Darkness, uncertainty and suspense add to the terrors of the situation, and the stimulus of companionship in danger is lacking.

Many other instances of bravery could be given. How Havildar Nausher Khan of the 4th Company, standing in the open at Picquet House near Festubert in December, 1914, directed the blocking of a trench until severely wounded; and how, at the same place, Havildar Sucha Singh of the same unit extricated buried miners and successfully connected up an explosive charge to blow up a German trench; how Lieutenant R. G. G. Robson, R.E., a leader in clearing trenches with bomb and bayonet, risked his life a dozen times and finally lost it while trying to bring in the body of a German officer; also, how Corporal Dower, a British non-commissioned officer of the unit, ran back under heavy fire for a distance of 300 yards along a road and returned with a load of bombs. These few examples must suffice to show that the Bengal Sappers equalled in devotion to duty their brothers of the Bombay Corps. Their calmness and stoicism in the presence of danger were remarkable. Separated from the enemy by only a double block in a trench, a sapper was observed standing on the top of the barricade and shading his eyes. He explained that he was trying to see where the enemy were shooting from! Another was pulled back into a trench while clambering up the parados over which machine gun bullets were streaming. This man gave, as his excuse, that he wished to recover some matches from his coat which was lying in the open behind the trench. Lieut.-General Sir Clarence Bird relates that a Naik of the 4th Company once remarked to him "Sahib. This is a rotten war," and on being asked his reasons, replied, "Who are the people who get killed? Only the young and newly-joined Sappers. No Subadar or Jemadar is *ever* killed, and so I shall never be a Jemadar."[1]

After Neuve Chapelle, the Sapper and Miner units were employed chiefly in remedying the deplorable deficiency of the troops in equipment for trench warfare. "The Indian Corps," writes Brig.-General Edmonds,[2] "took the lead in the manufacture of trench mortars, grenades, periscopes and other trench appliances, which the troops were driven to improvise. Little of this nature had been received from home. The official returns show that the average number of hand grenades issued in France weekly in November, 1914, was 70, and of rifle grenades, 630. In October, the Commander-in-Chief had asked for a minimum of 4,000 and 2,000 per month, respectively, but even this very moderate total had not been reached by March, 1915." A few periscopes arrived at the end of January. Mills hand grenades made an appearance in small numbers in the latter half of March together with 75 trench mortars. In 1914, however, the favourite patterns of improvised hand grenades were the "jam-pot," the "Battye bomb" and the "hair-brush." The maker of a "jam-pot" secured an empty tin, filled it with shredded guncotton and nails or rivet punchings,

[1]Notes by Brig. C. A. Bird, D.S.O., late R.E., sent to the author on Jan. 2nd, 1938.
[2]*Military Operations, France and Belgium*, by Brig.-Gen. J. E. Edmonds, C.B., C.M.G., late R.E., Vol. III, 1915, p. 7.

inserted a No. 8 Detonator and a short length of Bickford's fuze, and smeared the lid with clay. The "Battye bomb" was named after Captain B. C. Battye, R.E., of the 21st Company, Bombay S. & M. who initiated its manufacture in some ironworks in Bethune. It was based on the design of a rifle grenade made at Bangalore before the war by Major R. L. McClintock, R.E., when Superintendent of Instruction of the Madras Corps, and consisted of a small cast-iron cylinder, closed at one end and with serrations on the outside. After the bomb had been charged, the open end was sealed by a wooden plug with a central hole for the detonator and fuze. In the "hair-brush" grenade, a slab of guncotton was attached by wires to a flat piece of wood of hair-brush shape which afforded a convenient handle for throwing. As in the "jam-pot" variety, the fuse was ignited by a match, cigarette or pipe. Both patterns were very unreliable in action. At a demonstration of the "hair-brush" before some forty Generals and their staffs, only the stick went forward and the charge dropped to the ground. Some spectators fled, others crouched low, but no explosion took place. After an interval a search was made, and the charge was found eventually beneath one of the Generals.

The Indian Corps in France, known as the Indian Expeditionary Force "A," owed much to the pre-war ingenuity shown by Major R. L. McClintock, R.E., in the workshops at Bangalore. About 1907,[1] he began designing his "Bangalore Torpedo," an elongated and portable container of explosive which could be pushed into a barbed wire entanglement and used to destroy it, and during 1911–12 he improved the torpedo and designed a simple hand grenade, and a rifle grenade of the Hales type, which could be manufactured rapidly in the field from materials and explosives carried normally by a Sapper and Miner Company.[2] The "Bangalore Torpedo" of 1912 pattern was made of thin sheet-iron tubes, capable of being used singly or fitted together to produce a torpedo of considerable length.[3] McClintock produced also a hand grenade which had a wooden handle and a charge was composed of two 1 oz. guncotton primers.[4] In addition, he turned his attention to designing a rifle grenade, and in 1913 evolved a simple type called the "Universal," because it could be propelled by a rifle cartridge or thrown by hand.[5] He extended his experiments later to a star-shell in the form of a rifle grenade, and a wire-cutter as an attachment to the bayonet of a rifle,[6] but neither of these met with official approval. Thus, although the Madras Sappers and Miners took little part in the war in France, it is clear that at least one of their

[1]In notes sent to the author on Nov. 17th, 1937, Lieut.-Col. W. D. B. Conran, R.E., states that he fired the first Bangalore Torpedo in 1907 when serving with the 10th Company, Madras S. & M., under Bt. Maj. R. L. McClintock, R.E.

[2]*Historical Record of the Q.V.O. Madras Sappers and Miners*, Vol. II, 1910–14, p. 32.

[3]"The Destruction of Wire Entanglements. A Suggested Method," by Bt. Maj. R. L. McClintock, D.S.O., R.E., appearing in *The R.E. Journal*, Vol. XVII, Jan.-June, 1913, pp. 129–137.

[4]"An Extemporized Hand-Grenade," by Bt. Maj. R. L. McClintock, D.S.O., R.E., appearing in *The R.E. Journal*, Vol. XVII, Jan.–June, 1913, pp. 193–199.

[5]"An Extemporized Rifle-Grenade," by Bt. Maj. R. L. McClintock, D.S.O., R.E., appearing in *The R.E. Journal*, Vol. XX, July–Dec., 1914, pp. 281–294.

[6]"Rifle Attachment Wire Cutter," by Maj. R. L. McClintock, D.S.O., R.E., appearing in *The R.E. Journal*, Vol. XXII, July–Dec., 1915, pp. 273–276.

number contributed largely towards the design of equipment for the Western Front.

"On November 16th, 1914," writes Lieut.-Colonel E. O. Wheeler, R.E.,[1] "while the 3rd Company, Bengal S. & M., with whom I was serving, were filling in saps in front of the Rue du Bois near Richebourg L'Avoué, I was sitting on a nice square seat, smoking a cigarette, when Jemadar Abdul Aziz Khan asked me whether I knew what I was sitting on. Examination showed the seat to be a stack of several hundreds of German 'hair-brush' bombs, fitted with detonators and ready for throwing. We carried them from the enemy's sap to our trench and copied them, using gun-cotton. These were, I believe, the first 'hair-brush' bombs made by the Sappers and Miners, or indeed by any unit in France. On November 17th, the 3rd Company produced 'jam-tin' bombs and afterwards experimented with a cast-iron trench mortar. On December 1st we adopted a trench mortar made by the 4th Company from an 18-in. length of some 2.95-in. steel high-pressure piping found in Bethune. It resembled the Stokes' mortar of later days and was fired through a touch-hole, like any old muzzle-loader, after being given a cupful of gunpowder. A specimen was taken to England by Lieut.-Colonel P. G. Twining, R.E."

While the Bengal Sappers took their share in the manufacture of trench mortars, bombs and hand grenades, it seems that the bulk of the work fell to the Bombay Sappers through the inspiring energy of Captain B. C. Battye, R.E., who assumed command of the 21st Company when it was recovering from the casualties incurred at Neuve Chapelle. With Captain E. K. Squires and Lieutenants L. Manton, F. H. Kisch, F. E. Buller and F. G. Drew, R.E., he set a pace which it was difficult to emulate. The 20th Company followed suit. After a small bomb-factory behind the Givenchy-Festubert sector had been taken over on November 18th from the 4th Company of the Bengal Sappers, Battye worked hard to improve the original products. The "jam-tins" were uncertain in action, and the mortar bombs apt to explode at the muzzle; and the first trench-mortars—hollow, wire-bound pieces of timber—became relics at the 4th Company's billets. The classes of infantry under instruction were anything but enthusiastic in learning to throw "jam-tins" though encouraged by practical demonstrations against German sap-heads given by experts such as Lieutenants R. G. G. Robson and H. G. Greswell, R.E. The 21st Company transport made a daily tour round all billets to collect empty tins. The "Battye" (or Bethune) bomb was a notable improvement on the "jam-tin," and was cheaper and hardly less efficient than the Mills bomb which superseded it. Battye superintended a divisional school for bombing, fieldworks and trench warfare, where the "double-block" system was taught, and also initiated a scheme for providing electric searchlights in the trenches and electric lights and radiators in dugouts, the power being secured from the German supply in La Bassée until the enemy ceased to co-operate. The searchlights were unpopular with the troops in the front

[1]Notes by Lieut.-Col. E. O. Wheeler, M.C., R.E., sent to the author on Feb. 22nd, 1938

line as they drew fire.[1] It seems, also, that some of the Bombay Sappers were inexperienced as electricians. For instance, on one occasion when a transformer had been connected up, Battye noticed a Sapper fingering a high-tension lead and rated him soundly. "*Janta, Sahib*," murmured the culprit. "*Magar, bahut ahista, ahista kya*."[2] The electric scheme was abandoned, but Battye continued his indefatigable labours until he was wounded and evacuated to England in April, 1915. He returned to the Western Front in August, though no longer as a Sapper and Miner, and rendered valuable service on the staff of the 3rd Corps till he reverted, after the war, to his normal hydro-electric work in India.[3]

On November 23rd, 1914, the enemy attacked at Festubert and captured some trenches, and afterwards the Sappers and Miners had to work hard to improve our position. The companies relieved each other frequently in the front line. On December 11th, the Lahore Division took over from the French a new section of line astride the La Bassée Canal and found that there were no loophole plates in the trenches and that the parapets were not even bullet-proof. Accordingly, besides wiring, sapping and making blocks, the Sappers had to do much loopholing. They discovered that, in making machine gun emplacements, it was best to prepare a wooden loophole in advance and to place it quickly in position at night after siting it by looking through it. They improved the communication trenches by introducing 40 yard "straights" to guard against traverse-to-traverse bombing by the enemy. On December 19th, the Indian Corps made several small attacks on the Givenchy front, north of the La Bassée Canal. Some parties reached the enemy's lines and were isolated in the German sapheads, among them being one which included Lieutenant F. G. Drew, R.E., and a few Sappers of the 21st Company, and in trying to run a sap out to their rescue, Lieutenant E. K. Squires, R.E., was severely wounded in the head.[4] The enemy counter-attacked in force on December 20th, concentrating their efforts on the Indian Corps. Givenchy was lost, and although it was retaken later, the Corps suffered such casualties that it was withdrawn into reserve and replaced by the British 1st Corps. The list of Battle Honours for 1914 shows that all four Sapper companies fought at La Bassée (October 10th–November 2nd) and at Festubert (November 23rd–24th), and that all, except the 3rd Company of the Bengal Corps, were present at Givenchy (December 20th–21st).[5] The period of the hardest fighting for the Sappers and Miners in France ended with the replacement of the battered Indian troops in December, 1914.

In January, 1915, Nosworthy rejoined the 20th Company in France and

[1]Experiments with motor-car headlights, conducted by Lieut. F. H. Kisch, R.E., were equally unpopular.

[2]"I know, sir. But I did it very, *very* gently." Notes by Lieut.-Col. F. E. Buller, O.B.E., M.C., R.E., sent to the author on Aug. 22nd, 1937.

[3]Memoir of Col. B. C. Battye, D.S.O., late R.E., appearing in *The R.E. Journal*, Vol. XLVI, Dec., 1932, pp. 699–703.

[4]Notes by Maj.-Gen. E. K. Squires, C.B., D.S.O., M.C., late R.E., sent to the author on Nov. 30th, 1937.

[5]"Battle Honours of R.E. Units, Great War, France and Belgium," appearing in *The R.E. Journal*, Vol. XXXIX, 1925, pp. 241–246.

THE 3RD INDIAN DIVISION IN ESTAIRES, 1915.

received a great welcome from the men, who regarded him as their one remaining link with the India they knew. The unit was at Richebourg St. Vaast under Major A. R. C. Sanders, R.E., a popular Bengal Sapper of pre-war days. It moved to Le Touret on February 11th and took over a section of the line from the 4th Company, Bengal S. & M. Early in March it was helping the 3rd and 4th Companies to construct bridges over a canal in preparation for a second attack on Neuve Chapelle. This was launched on March 10th by the Meerut Division and the British 4th Corps, with the Lahore Division in reserve. All the Sapper companies were present, and a section of the 3rd Company, under Captain P. C. S. Hobart, R.E.,[1] with Havildar Chagatta, was very heavily engaged when under the command of a Field Engineer, Major G. H. Boileau, R.E., an ex-Bombay Sapper and Miner. The exploits of Field Engineers are normally outside the scope of this narrative, for the Field Engineer of the Indian Corps was an understudy of the Commanding Royal Engineer and concerned chiefly with fieldworks executed by civilian labour; but in France the Field Engineer was called upon occasionally to command engineer troops in battle and to share with the Sappers and Miners in the toughest fighting. Majors G. H. Boileau, C. G. W. Hunter and A. Gardiner, R.E., did so, and Gardiner gave his life at Givenchy in December 1914, in trying, single-handed, to defend trenches which he considered his own.

In the second Battle of Neuve Chapelle, Brig.-General H. C. Nanton, the Chief Engineer, wished the Sappers to follow up the infantry attack to establish two strong points, but he insisted that heavy casualties should be avoided. Major Boileau, Field Engineer, and Captain E. F. J. Hill of the 3rd Company were detailed to lead consolidation parties. Boileau's party comprised a section of the 3rd Company under Captain P. C. S. Hobart, R.E., and a company of Pioneers, and it formed up in trenches held by the Leicesters at " Port Arthur," south-west of Neuve Chapelle. The infantry assault was successful, although, owing to some loss of direction, it was not known that a fully occupied section of the enemy's trenches had been left untouched in front of the party. Boileau, with Hobart and the Sappers and Pioneers, advanced in broad daylight, and when within 20 yards of the German wire, came under devastating fire. Casualties were heavy, though the officers were untouched because they were so close to the German parapet that the bullets passed over their heads. An hour later, they were able to crawl back to the Leicesters' trench. Hobart then asked permission to establish a block in an unoccupied section of the German line to the left, and did so with six remaining Bengal Sappers. With the infantry, he held the block until reinforced after dark by the rest of Boileau's party.[2] The other party, under E. F. J. Hill, was more

[1]Capt. P. C. S. Hobart, R.E., Adjutant, Bengal S. & M., was recalled from leave in England in Aug., 1914, and sailing in the S.S. *Ballarat* (a week after the S.S. *Dongola* which carried more than 600 military officers) resumed his duties at Roorkee. On Nov. 17th, 1914, he handed over charge to Capt. W. Cave-Browne, R.E., and proceeded to France with a first reinforcement of Bengal Sappers.

[2]Notes by Maj.-Gen. Sir Percy Hobart, K.B.E., C.B., D.S.O., M.C. and Brig.-Gen. G. H. Boileau, C.B., C.M.G., D.S.O., late R.E., sent to the author on April 22nd and June 1st, 1944.

fortunate, though it suffered heavy casualties through working under fire in daylight. Neuve Chapelle was retaken, and after a strong counter-attack had been repulsed on the 12th, a line was consolidated east of the village. The enemy lost heavily. In some places our parapet rested on a solid line of Bavarians whose boots could be seen in the forward slope. Captain C. A. Bird, R.E., of the 4th Company, was wounded and evacuated to England, and Lieutenant F. V. B. Witts, R.E., was posted to the unit. A newly-arrived reinforcement for the 21st Company, consisting of 34 Indian ranks of the Malerkotla Imperial Service Sappers under Captain M. Rawlence, R.E., came under heavy fire during the German counter-attack and suffered many casualties while moving later into Neuve Chapelle.[1] These Indian States' Sappers were part of a contingent of 3 officers and 194 other ranks generously supplied by the Nawab of Malerkotla to reinforce the Bombay Sappers and Miners in France. They served afterwards in the second Battle of Ypres and at Loos, and earned a high reputation for gallantry and good work.[2]

A curious incident occurred after the recapture of Neuve Chapelle. One night, Sanders and Nosworthy found a desperately wounded German close to the enemy's wire and decided to bring him in. Sanders tried repeatedly to hoist him on to Nosworthy's back, but at each attempt the German shouted something which they did not understand and fire was opened on them by the enemy. Nevertheless, they succeeded eventually in carrying the man back to our lines. A fortnight later they were summoned to Brigade Headquarters, where they were confronted by a civilian of the Geneva Convention who had been sent to enquire into an alleged "atrocity" vouched for by many Germans. It was asserted that a wounded German had been crucified at a certain spot and on a certain night by two Indians, and as Sanders and Nosworthy were indicated, they were required to give evidence on oath. It then appeared that the delirious German had shouted repeatedly to his comrades that he was being crucified. Both officers, of course, were completely exonerated; but after a full account of the incident had appeared in *The Times*, they decided that they would never allow themselves to fall alive into the enemy's hands. It is sad to relate that Sanders died of wounds on January 1st, 1918, while serving as a Lieut.-Colonel on the Staff.

On April 24th, 1915, the 20th and 21st Companies, Bombay S. & M., moved northwards with the Lahore Division to take part in the second Battle of Ypres. Captain A. D. S. Arbuthnot, R.E., had assumed command of the 20th Company from Major A. R. C. Sanders, R.E., with Captains M. Rawlence, K. Mason and F. P. Nosworthy and Lieutenant H. W. R. Hamilton, R.E. Captain B. C. Battye, R.E., having been wounded on the 22nd, Captain E. K. Squires, R.E., had returned to command the 21st Company with Lieutenants F. H. Kisch and M. A. R. G. Fitzmaurice,

[1]Notes by Maj. M. Rawlence, D.S.O., R.E., sent to the author on March 3rd, 1938.

[2]*A Short History of the Services rendered by the Imperial Services Troops during the Great War*, 1914–18, by Maj.-Gen. Sir Harry Watson, K.B.E., C.B., C.M.G., C.I.E., pp. 45, 46. A platoon of the Tehri-Garhwal Imperial Service Sappers served in France, but only as an infantry reinforcement to the 39th Garhwal Rifles.

R.E., and 2nd Lieutenant F. A. Menzies, I.A.R.O. In moving through Ypres on April 26th, however, Squires had his lower jaw shattered by a shell, and on the 28th Rawlence took command of the 21st Company. As the enemy had launched a gas attack, the Sappers were instructed in two primitive methods of "protection," one of which was by chewing tobacco incessantly. The companies took part in heavy fighting in the Potizje Area, north-east of Ypres, and especially in and around localities known as "The Moated Grange" and "Defensible Farm," where positions were dug.[1] They had many casualties in the trenches and suffered from severe headaches caused by lingering chlorine gas. During a reconnaissance with Hamilton on the night of April 28th/29th, Nosworthy was shot, in error, by a Canadian sentry, and apparently through the heart. Happily, he survived; but this accident terminated his service with the Sappers and Miners and he did not return to the front until January, 1916. Captain W. P. Pakenham-Walsh, R.E., rejoined the 20th Company, and, a few days later, Lieutenant A. Mason, R.E., replaced Captain K. Mason, R.E., who had been wounded on April 27th. In six days at Ypres, the Bombay Sapper companies lost 60 men, mostly from shell-fire, and apart from a line dug on the night of the 28th/29th, little useful work was accomplished. If the units had been kept out of the front line during daylight, the casualties would have been much lighter. The companies left the Ypres Area on May 2nd and were back at Bout de Ville, in the Neuve Chapelle Area, on the 5th. With the 3rd and 4th Companies of the Bengal Corps, they were in action at Aubers on May 9th; and all the Sapper units, except the 20th Company, took some part in the fighting near Festubert between May 15th and 25th. Afterwards, they worked for nearly four months on the defences in the Neuve Chapelle and Rue du Bois sectors. Bomb manufacture was no longer part of their duties. Casualties were few, though the Bombay Sappers lost Captain A. G. Glenday, R.E., who was killed on August 8th.

Early in September, 1915, preparations were begun for an offensive near Loos, south of La Bassée, and the Sapper companies built observation posts, buried telephone cables, arranged water supplies and drove mine galleries. On September 25th, as a diversion to assist the main operations, the Meerut Division and the British 19th Division attached at Le Pietre, some 10 miles to the north. They broke through the German line but were counter-attacked and repulsed with heavy loss. The 3rd and 4th Companies, Bengal S. & M., and two sections of the 20th Company, Bombay S. & M.,[2] were present though not heavily engaged. The Bengal Sappers afterwards excelled themselves in wiring, for 140 men erected 2,800 yards of wire in a single night, although the German trenches were in one place only 50 yards from our front line.[3] On October 13th, the 20th Company

[1] *History of the 20th (Field) Company, Royal Bombay Sappers and Miners, Great War, 1914–18*, by Maj. H. W. R. Hamilton, D.S.O., M.C., R.E., pp. 21–26, and letter from Maj. M. Rawlence, D.S.O., R.E., appearing in *The R.E. Journal*, Vol. XLI, Jan.–June, 1927, pp. 380–382.

[2] Under Lieuts. H. W. R. Hamilton, R.E., and A. V. Venables, I.A.R.O.

[3] *Lectures on the Regimental History of the K.G.O. Bengal Sappers and Miners*, by Maj. L. V. Bond, R.E., p. 14.

co-operated with the Lahore Division by lighting phosphorus bombs in our sap-heads during a feint attack at Loos.

Then came rain and storm, and the Indian troops began to view with misgiving the prospect of another winter in the mud. However, they were spared that ordeal. On August 13th, 1915, General Sir John Nixon had asked that an Indian division should be transferred to his command in Iraq, and the Secretary of State for India had informed the Viceroy that he was anxious to get all the Indian infantry withdrawn from France. To this, Lord Kitchener at first objected; but on October 31st, instructions were received that the entire Indian Corps, then under Lieut.-General Sir Charles Anderson,[1] should be transferred to Iraq, while the Indian Cavalry Corps remained in France. Gratified by a royal message of thanks to the Indian troops from H.M. The King-Emperor, which was read by H.R.H. The Prince of Wales on November 25th, the Sappers and Miners left the Neuve Chapelle-La Bassée Area on the 28th, and with little regret although Rawlence marked the occasion by erecting a notice drawing attention to Ecclesiastes ii, 18 and 19, for the benefit of his successor. Marseilles was reached in due course by road and rail. The Bengal Sappers embarked on December 7th and the Bombay Sappers on the 16th; and on December 24th, 1915, the last transport left Marseilles. The Indian Corps was now but a shadow of the powerful force which had sailed westwards in 1914; but it went with honour for it had played its part well and bravely in a most critical period of the war.

Unfortunately, there is little of interest to record regarding the two Field Troops of Sappers and Miners in France. They left India with the Indian cavalry, hoping for exciting adventures when a "break-through" occurred on the Western Front. Instead, they found themselves making bombs or digging positions far behind the line. The 1st Field Troop, composed of Sikhs of the Bengal Sappers and Miners under Captain R. C. R. Hill, R.E., with Lieutenant F. S. Collin, R.E., disembarked at Marseilles with the Secunderabad Cavalry Brigade on September 27th, 1914, and after reaching Orleans on October 7th, worked on field defences in rear of Festubert until the end of December. It was then withdrawn still further, and the Cavalry Brigade was incorporated in the 2nd Indian Cavalry Division of a newly formed Indian Cavalry Corps. In forming this Corps it had been decided to abolish the Indian organization of engineer units with cavalry and to adopt the British system by forming two "Indian" Field Squadrons, equipped from England and manned partly, if not entirely, by British personnel.[2] Accordingly, the 1st Field Troop soon found itself "nobody's child." It carried out a variety of small engineering jobs behind the line, and afterwards, as reinforcements were not available, it dwindled away until, in the summer of 1915, it was abolished and the personnel distributed among the 3rd and 4th Companies.

[1]Gen. Sir James Willcocks had vacated command of the Indian Corps on Sept. 6th, 1915.

[2]*Brief History of the Royal Engineers with the Cavalry in France during the War*, 1914–18, by Col. W. H. Evans, D.S.O., late R.E., p. 5 (see *R.E. Journal*, Vol. XL, 1926, pp. 43–52 and 305–314).

SKETCH MAP OF
NORTHERN FRANCE AND BELGIUM
1914–15, YPRES – LA BASSÉE SECTOR.
BELGIUM
POPERINGHE
Vlamertinghe
YPRES
Zonnebeke
Potijze
Hooge
Voormezeele
Hollebeke
Kemmel
Wytschaete
Messines
R. Lys
Steenvoorde
CASSEL
From Dunkerque 18m.
Caestre
Fletre
Meteren
BAILLEUL
Neuve Eglise
Ploegsteert
HAZEBROUCK
Nieppe
Steenwerck
ARMENTIÉRES
Roquetoire
Wittes
Neuf Berquin
Sailly
AIRE
Lys Canal
MERVILLE
Estaires
Fleurbaix
Bois Grenier
La Gorgue
L'Aventie
LILLE
St Venant
Lestrem
Berguette
Fosse
Fauquissart
Robecq
Aire Canal
Ham
Busnes
Fromelles
Aubers
Fournes
St Hilaire
Pont Logy
Lacouture
NEUVE CHAPELLE
LILLERS
Richebourg St Vaast
Rue du Bois
Richebourg L'Avoué
Hinges
Illies
Le Touret
Chocques
Gorre
Lorgies
Canal
SECLIN
La Bassée
Festubert
BETHUNE
Canal
Givenchy
LA-BASSÉE
Cuinchy
Auchy
Anchel
Fouquières
Sailly
Pernes
Noyelles
Vermelles
Hulluch
CARVIN
Scale
Miles 0 5 10 Miles
Grenay
LOOS
Canal
LENS
Aix

On July 27th, Hill was posted to the 2nd Indian Field Squadron, and in September Collin followed him after serving for a time with the 3rd Company.

The fate of the 2nd Field Troop, Madras S. & M., under Captain E. K. Molesworth, R.E., with Lieutenant T. B. Harris, R.E., was almost as hard as that of the Bengal unit. It landed at Marseilles on November 10th, 1914, equipped with tonga transport[1] provided by the Gwalior Imperial Service Troops, and reached St. Hilaire on December 25th as part of the 1st Indian Cavalry Division. A reinforcement under Captain J. C. Wickham, R.E., with Lieutenant A. H. Morin, I.A.R.O., which arrived in Marseilles on November 26th, was detained for some time at that port to build a hutted camp, though Wickham himself was sent up at once to St. Hilaire to replace Harris who was ill. Morin followed in February 1915 with all available reinforcements. Meanwhile, the unit had lost a popular commander through the death of E. K. Molesworth on December 30th. The work at St. Hilaire was uninspiring for it consisted mainly of manufacturing bombs, conducting bombing classes and making specimen machine gun emplacements.[2] It was now recognized officially that a single Field Troop was insufficient for a Division, but India was unable to produce the additional personnel needed to complete an Indian Field Squadron incorporating the Bengal and Madras Field Troops already in France, so it was decided in February 1915 that an Indian Field Squadron composed mainly of British Sappers should be formed, and that the Madras Field Troop should be part of it and train with it. This was done, and early in March the hybrid formation moved to St. Venant for technical work on a second line some six miles behind the front. It acted as a mobile reserve during the second Battle of Neuve Chapelle and at the operations near Ypres in April 1915. At the end of May, the 2nd Field Troop was detached for work in the Ypres Salient, and was employed for a few days in the trenches at Hooge. Wickham was seriously wounded on June 3rd and Morin took command. The formation of two Field Squadrons—the 1st and 2nd Indian Field Squadrons, R.E.—was now completed rapidly with entirely British personnel. The 1st Squadron was commanded by Major A. G. Bremner, R.E., with Major W. H. Evans, Captain A. A. Chase and Lieutenant H. G. Greswell, R.E., and the 2nd Squadron by Major S. D'A. Crookshank, R.E.,[3] with Captain D. Ogilvy and Lieutenant B. H. Fox, R.E. The 2nd Field Troop, after narrowly escaping conversion into a "mobile workshop," remained for a time with the 1st Field Squadron but was then transferred to the Lahore Division. It was employed on front line work near Bout de Ville in August, and was in reserve at Loos on September 25th. It left the battle front on November

[1]Thirty small 2-wheeled carts, each drawn by 2 ponies. Each cart carried a driver and 3 men, or a driver and about 3 cwt. of equipment. The tonga transport made the unit very mobile.

[2]"The 2nd Field Troop, 2nd Q.V.O. Sappers and Miners, 1914 to 1916," by Maj. A. H. Morin, I.A.R.O., p. 1, forming Part III of *The Q.V.O. Madras Sappers and Miners in France and Iraq*, 1914–1920.

[3]Maj. R. C. R. Hill, R.E., assumed command on July 27th *vice* Maj. S. D'A. Crookshank, R.E.

8th, and embarked on December 21st, 1915, at Marseilles in the last troopship conveying the Lahore Division to Iraq.

This brief story of Sapper and Miner exploits in France ends with the departure of the 2nd Field Troop. With the four Field Companies, the Troop voyaged eastwards to fight the Turk. This was a more congenial task ; a duty to be accomplished under conditions more easily understood and in a climate better suited to the Indian constitution. The men knew that the struggle in Iraq was connected intimately with the defence of India itself. In France they had fought for an ideal. In Iraq they would fight to save their country from the imminent threat of German and Turkish domination. As the sun grew stronger, their hopes rose higher, and the sodden fields of France and Flanders receded into the dim distance till they became only a memory of mist, cold, and hellish bombardment.

CHAPTER XVII

THE GREAT WAR: IRAQ, 1914–1916

POLITICAL expediency, and the need to safeguard British oil supplies at the head of the Persian Gulf, brought about the campaign in Iraq. Dashing leadership, fine troops and poor opposition in the early stages accounted for the initial successes. Rashness, bad management and lack of men and material led to the subsequent disasters. In war, nothing succeeds like success, but no failure is worse than one due to over-confidence. The victories of 1915, under an optimistic commander, gave place in 1916 to reverse after reverse. Plans were changed constantly, and responsibility was shifted from shoulder to shoulder; and when the Imperial General Staff at last assumed control from the Government of India, it was powerless to save much from the wreckage of the politically-inspired and Treasury-ridden operations launched by that Government. Lured to destruction by the lodestar of Baghdad, the small Indian Expeditionary Force "D" moved further and further up the Tigris till the spearhead was halted finally at Ctesiphon. Nothing then remained but to retreat if retreat were possible. Most of the troops reached Kut al Amara, where they surrendered after a long siege, while a greater number died in vain efforts to save them. The complete story of these operations is given in the Official History of the campaign and many other publications and is outside the scope of this narrative.[1] We are concerned only with the part taken by the Sappers and Miners, whose units made no small contribution towards the early victories and maintained in defeat the honour of their Corps.

The 22nd Company, Bombay S. & M., was the first engineer unit to land in Iraq during the Great War. It was commanded by Captain A. M. Twiss, R.E., with Lieutenants C. M. G. Dunhill, E. C. Whiteley and A. B. Matthews, R.E., and after embarking at Bombay on October 16th, 1914, with the 16th Brigade of the 6th (Poona) Division under Brig.-General W. S. Delamain, it spent a fortnight in sweltering heat on a transport at Bahrein in the Persian Gulf awaiting the declaration of war which occurred on November 5th. Delamain immediately entered the Shatt al Arab estuary,

[1]The following general histories are recommended:—*The Campaign in Mesopotamia* 1914–18 (Official History), Vols. I to III, by Brig.-Gen. F. J. Moberly, C.B., C.S.I., D.S.O.; *Report of the Mesopotamia Commission*, 1917 (Official); *A Brief Outline of the Campaign in Mesopotamia* 1914–18, by Maj. R. Evans, M.C., Royal Horse Guards; *In Kut and Captivity*, by the present author; *My Campaign in Mesopotamia*, by Maj.-Gen. Sir C. V. F. Townshend, K.C.B., D.S.O.; *The Long Road to Baghdad*, by Edmund Candler; *A Chapter of Misfortunes*, by Maj.-Gen. W. D. Bird, C.B., C.M.G., D.S.O.; and *Mesopotamia*, 1914–15, by Capt. M. H. Birch-Reynardson, 15th Lancers. The following Sapper and Miner accounts are valuable:—*History of the 20th (Field) Company, Royal Bombay Sappers and Miners. Great War*, 1914–18, by Maj. H. W. R. Hamilton, D.S.O., M.C., R.E.; *The Madras Sappers in the Campaign in Mesopotamia*, 1914–18, by Lieut.-Col. R. Hamilton, O.B.E., R.E.; and *History of the 18th (Field) Company, 3rd Royal Sappers and Miners during the Great War*, 1914–18.

occupied the telegraph station at Fao and by November 10th had disembarked his troops opposite Abadan Island where the Anglo-Persian Oil Company's works were situated.[1] Reinforcements were on the way from India. They consisted of the 18th Brigade under Major-General C. I. Fry with other troops including the 17th Company, Bombay S. & M., under Captain A. D. S. Arbuthnot, R.E., with Lieutenants R. C. Lord, M. G. G. Campbell and K. B. S. Crawford, R.E., which had embarked at Bombay on November 6th.[2] Major-General Sir Arthur Barrett arrived on the 13th as Divisional Commander, and also Lieut.-Colonel U. W. Evans, R.E., as D.E.C. 6th Division[3] with Major H. E. Winsloe, and Captains F. C. Molesworth and H. W. Tomlinson, R.E., Field Engineers. After dislodging the enemy from a position at Saihan on November 15th, General Barrett fought a successful action on the 17th at Sahil against 5,000 Turks and Arabs, but during the course of the battle, the Sappers and Miners, acting as infantry, lost two valuable officers. Twiss was mortally wounded while leading the 22nd Company against enemy trenches amongst the palm groves, and Arbuthnot was dangerously wounded by a large Arab bullet. Colonel Evans and Major Winsloe were also hit. Arbuthnot, a man of iron constitution and indomitable courage, survived and was invalided to England, and, as already related, recovered sufficiently to take command of the 20th Company in France in April 1915. Twiss was a most popular officer and was greatly missed. He had served for twelve years with the Bombay Sappers and had commanded the 22nd Company for four years. He was replaced by Whiteley, as Dunhill was at work further downstream, and under its new commander the 22nd Company entered Basra with the other troops on November 22nd. The 17th Company marched near the head of the main body, and both companies soon found accommodation in tents near a large house on the river front, which remained the R.E. Headquarters throughout the war.

Work in Basra was hard and exhausting. According to an Arab proverb " When Allah made Hell he found it was not bad enough, so he made Iraq and added flies." Basra in 1914 was typical of the country—an insanitary town stretching along the right bank of the river amid palm trees which, as the Arabs say, grow best with their feet in water and their heads in hell.[4] Evil-smelling creeks led from the Tigris to congested areas occupied by a turbulent and cosmopolitan population, and the heaviest work of both the Sapper companies included the bridging of the larger creeks and the building of landing stages for disembarkation. Demands for landing stages followed an inevitable routine. First for a light stage to land only a few men; then for expansion to take stores and animals; and finally for conversion into a full-fledged pier. Indeed, it is said that the exasperated Sappers soon decided to calculate every structure to take a

[1]See *Sketch Map of Lower Iraq*, 1914–16, included in this chapter.

[2]Minor engineer formations such as Printing and Litho Sections, are omitted.

[3]Divisional Engineer Commander, otherwise C.R.E. Lieut.-Col. Evans had been Commandant, Bombay S. & M., at Kirkee.

[4]" Early Days in Mesopot," by Col. F. C. Molesworth, late R.E., appearing in *The R.E. Journal*, Vol. XLVI, 1931, pp. 280–290.

load of " galloping elephants, crowded at a check ! " Local resources were very limited, for Iraq has neither stone nor timber, but a large store of imported German timber was found and Molesworth quickly organized an efficient Field Park. All trestles had to be made of planks bolted together. The 22nd Company built an ingenious trestle bridge across the Robat Creek, and afterwards a lifting-span bridge, known for years as " Whiteley's Bridge," over the Ashar Creek. The Sapper units also undertook flood control, mounted guns on barges, installed electricity, altered ships and even erected gallows, and all in a humid atmosphere infested by mosquitoes which, as one man put it, were " as large as elephants and as ravenous as hyenas ! "

The purgatory of life in Basra, however, was not to continue indefinitely, for soon after the occupation, Colonel Sir Percy Cox, the Political Officer, had wired direct to the Viceroy, with General Barrett's permission, that an advance on Baghdad could hardly be avoided, though it is understood that Barrett himself preferred to consolidate his position at Basra. The political side was already tending to assume control. However, General Sir Edmund Barrow, the Military Secretary to the India Office, advised a limited advance only to Qurna, 40 miles upstream, and this was approved on November 27th as sufficient to secure British interests in Lower Iraq and in Arabistan, the area of the Persian oil-fields. Nevertheless, the fatal seed of ambition had been sown. With the arrival of the 17th Brigade under Brig.-General W. H. Dobbie at the end of November, the 6th Division was at full strength and needed only the stimulus of a dashing Army Commander to urge it on its way.

On December 8th, a detachment of the 17th Company was detailed to assist the 18th Brigade to cross the Tigris above Qurna and capture that place. It was decided to construct a flying bridge where the river was only 130 yards wide, though with a rapid current, and three Bombay Sappers volunteered to swim across with a log-line. This they did, and reinforced by two more men, pulled across a $1\frac{1}{2}$-in. cable. Campbell then swam the river and the party hauled across a 1-in. wire rope and used a captured Arab *mahela*[1] as a ferry boat. A battalion and some guns were ferried to the right bank, and 1,100 Turks in Qurna surrendered.

On January 2nd, 1915, a company of Sirmur Imperial Service Sappers reached Qurna under Lieutenant Jiwan Singh, with Lieutenant F. E. Mayo as 2nd-in-Command and Captain C. E. Colbeck, R.E., as " Special Service Officer." It should be explained here that four small states in India (Faridkot, Malerkotla, Sirmur and Tehri-Garhwal) maintained Sapper companies, and that it was customary to attach the local Inspecting (or Assistant Inspecting) Officer of Imperial Service Troops, a Royal Engineer, to any company proceeding on active service. Officially, this officer was an adviser, but actually he performed most of the duties of a commander. Lieutenant Frank Mayo was an ex-Regimental Q.M.S.,

[1] *Mahela*—a dhow about 70 ft. long and 20 ft. in beam, with a tall mast and lateen sail. Other Arab boats are the *Bellum*, a paddling boat about 30 ft. long of fairly strong planking ; the *Danak*, a flimsy gondola about 40 ft. long of thin planking covered with bitumen ; the *Mashoof*, a miniature *Danak* ; and the *Guffa*, a bitumen-covered coracle.

R.E., of the Bengal Sappers and Miners, who had become a Field Works' Instructor in the Sirmur State after his retirement in 1906 and had been promoted in 1914 to the rank of Lieutenant in the State Forces.[1] As the Sirmur Sappers were not regular troops, they were kept mostly at Basra during the early stages of the campaign. Fate decreed, however, that they should be at Kut al Amara in December 1915, and thus they ended their war service with a long siege. At Qurna, between January and April, 1915, they built reed huts and flood embankments and threw a boom of masts across the river a mile above the town. They earned a high reputation in Iraq, as the Malerkotla Sappers did in France and the Faridkot Sappers in East Africa. The Tehri-Garhwal Sappers sent a platoon under Lieutenant Rana Jodha Jung as an infantry reinforcement to the 39th Garhwal Rifles in France in 1914 and despatched a company to Iraq in 1916. Thus the Imperial Service Sappers were well represented in many theatres of war.[2]

The first Bengal Sapper and Miner unit in Iraq reached Qurna in the middle of February 1915. This was a small Bridging Train of only 22 men under Jemadar Sadar Din which had left Roorkee on January 27th with 18 pontoons and a very complete equipment of stores. Ten of the pontoons were of copper and the remainder of steel, some of the latter being of bipartite pattern. As no wagons or draught animals were sent, the equipment could be moved only by river. Towed by large steamers against rapid currents and around sharp bends, the pontoons were often dashed into the bank and severely damaged. Only 95 yards of floating bridge suitable for infantry or field guns could be made, and the Tigris was usually 200 to 350 yards wide. The ten Weldon trestles in the equipment were too heavy for the slimy ooze of the river bed, and the pontoons were undecked and liable to founder in a gale. In fact, the Bridging Train, while excellently adapted to deal with the narrow and rocky ravines of the North-West Frontier, was quite unsuited to conditions on the Tigris. Enormous expansion was needed and continual improvisation. Nevertheless, the unit acquitted itself with credit under the greatest difficulties.[3] On arrival in Qurna it was placed under the command of Lieutenant M. G. G. Campbell, R.E., of the 17th Company, Bombay S. & M., and bridged the Tigris with 17 pontoons, 8 *mahelas* and 4 trestles. This bridge enabled the garrison of Qurna to keep in touch with an outpost at Mazera on the left bank.

Another small unit of Bengal Sappers in Iraq at this time was a " Wreck Party " under Lieutenant O. Slater, R.E., formed from the Calcutta

[1]Lieut. F. E. Mayo served the Sirmur State for 30 years, for he returned to Nahan in 1919 as O.C. State Forces with the rank of Capt. He retired in 1936 and settled in New Zealand (see Obituary Notice appearing in *The R.E. Journal Supplement*, Vol. LIV, May, 1938, pp. 157–159).

[2]*A Short History of the Services rendered by the Imperial Service Troops during the Great War*, 1914–18, by Maj.-Gen. Sir Harry Watson, K.B.E., C.B., C.M.G., C.I.E., M.V.O., pp. 15, 45, 56 and 63.

[3]" The Adventures of a Bridging Train in Mesopotamia," by the present author appearing in *The R.E. Journal*, Vol. XXXVIII, 1924, pp. 233–248.

Defence Light Section of the Bengal Corps.[1] The Wreck Party raised or demolished sunken ships in remote stretches of the Tigris, cleared the river of floating mines, and assisted in electrical work. Meanwhile, most of its normal defence-light duties were performed in Iraq by a special Searchlight Section under Captain R. E. Stace, R.E., who had been employed in the Bombay Mint.[2] The Searchlight Section operated mostly at Basra, but it erected lights also at Qurna fitted with projectors taken from a captured German ship and cinematograph power-plant. It was not a Sapper and Miner unit, though it worked under the direction of the Divisional Engineer Commander. The men were mostly British or Eurasian volunteers recruited by Stace in Bombay and brought to Iraq at the end of December 1914, and the equipment comprised three electric searchlights and two oxy-acetylene lights. This small unit accompanied the unfortunate advance to Ctesiphon in 1915 to take over and operate the mechanical and electrical plant in captured Baghdad, and it ended its days in Kut al Amara, where Stace and his dozen men were the recognized mechanical experts during the siege.

Throughout February 1915, the 17th Company, Bombay S. & M., worked on the Qurna and Mazera defences, and Lord erected an observation tower, 90 feet high, from which the Turkish island positions were visible over the tops of the river-side palm trees. This tower was the only cool spot in the " Garden of Eden," and many were the excuses made to justify a visit to the top platform. Below, where the troops lived in reed huts, the mid-day heat was already suffocating and was soon to become indescribable—a hell in which men sweated day and night in a temperature rising to 120°. Life at Qurna, however, was uneventful, and interest shifted, early in March, to Basra and the oil-fields of Arabistan.

As a Turkish advance on Basra from Nasariya seemed imminent, the 17th Company, now under Captain E. J. Loring, R.E.,[3] returned to Basra and marched to Shaiba, 10 miles from the city, to prepare defences. On March 7th, it was joined by the 22nd Company under Whiteley. Meanwhile, Matthews and a detachment of the 22nd Company were similarly engaged at Ahwaz on the Karun River in Arabistan, where we had suffered a slight reverse at the hands of the Bawi Arabs. It was decided that reinforcements must be sent at once to Iraq and a 12th Indian Division was formed under Major-General G. F. Gorringe (late R.E.) consisting of the 12th, 33rd and 30th Brigades (the last named coming from Egypt under Brig.-General C. J. Melliss, V.C.). The 12th Division began to concentrate at Basra on April 8th, on which day Lieut.-General Sir John Nixon took over the supreme command from Lieut.-General Sir Arthur Barrett. The engineer troops allotted to the 12th Division were the Sirmur

[1]Before the Great War, 1914–18, there were 5 Defence Light Sections of Sappers and Miners, i.e., Calcutta and Karachi Sections (Bengal Sappers), Rangoon Section (Madras Sappers) and Bombay and Aden Sections (Bombay Sappers).

[2]*The Military Engineer in India*, by the present author, Vol. II, p. 312.

[3]Capt. E. J. Loring, R.E., had assumed command of the 17th Company on arrival from India at the end of Dec., 1914, in replacement of Capt. A. M. Twiss, R.E., mortally wounded at Sahil.

Sapper Company, already in the country, and the 12th Company, Madras S. & M., which was thus the first unit of the Madras Corps to join in the campaign. The 12th Company, under Captain S. Pemberton, R.E., with Lieutenants R. H. Dewing and A. B. Aitken, R.E., disembarked at Basra on March 24th and was employed at first chiefly on road work and building piers and bridges, though Dewing and some Sappers were attached for a time to an "Euphrates Blockade Force" organized to proceed up the Euphrates to harass the enemy's communications.

The expected Turkish attack on Basra developed at Shaiba on April 12th, 1915. The fighting was heavy throughout that day and the next, but on the 14th the impetus lessened and General Melliss, who was in command, was able to gain a decisive victory though at considerable cost. The 17th and 22nd Companies were both in the thick of the fight and the Searchlight Section was present. On the 12th, the 17th Company was holding, with the 48th Pioneers, the southern salient of our position defending Basra, and the 22nd Company was in reserve on the right. The ground between the position and Basra was flooded. Melliss took the offensive on the 13th with the 16th Brigade and improved his position, and on the 14th launched an attack in force. The 22nd Company with the 16th Brigade, and the 17th Company with the 18th Brigade, fought as infantry. The Turks, in trenches near the Barjasiya Wood, were assaulted by the 16th Brigade while the 18th Brigade turned their flank, and in the end they broke and fled towards Nasiriya. In this battle, Whiteley was mortally wounded by machine gun fire and Loring was hit in the thigh, and thus both the Sapper companies again lost their commanding officers. Whiteley was a brave and efficient officer and most popular with all ranks. Fortunately, Loring's wound was not serious and he was able to return to duty at the end of the month. Campbell was recalled at once from Qurna to take command of the 22nd Company at Basra, while Captain E. W. C. Sandes, R.E., who had arrived from India during the battle, was sent to Qurna on April 19th to command the Bridging Train, Bengal S. & M., in place of Campbell. Curiously enough, Sandes had watched with envy the start of this unit by rail from Roorkee on January 27th when he was on the staff of the Thomason College and consequently had no connection with the Sappers and Miners.

After Shaiba, General Nixon decided that he must clear his right flank by driving all enemy forces from Arabistan, for he was already contemplating advances up the Tigris to Amara and up the Euphrates to Nasiriya. Accordingly, in April, he despatched General Gorringe with most of the 12th Division up the Karun River towards Ahwaz. Included in this force was the 12th Company, Madras Sappers and Miners. The column moved up the Karun to Braika, whence Gorringe proposed to cross the desert to Illa on the Karkha River, and the 12th Company went on to Ahwaz to collect land transport and material for crossing the Karkha. Pontoons were improvised from thin planking and tarpaulins and were loaded, with gear for flying bridges, on to Persian carts and oil-pipe carts. The oil-pipe vehicle had a pair of large steel wheels joined by an arched axle from which a platform was slung to carry pipes.[1] Two traction engines served to draw trains of these vehicles, and ponies pulled the carts. With this remarkable equipment the 12th Company arrived at Illa on May 7th, and the crossing of the Karkha was begun. The river was 200 yards wide and in full flood, but ferries were arranged and a flying bridge completed by the 9th and another by the 13th, on which date Gorringe was able to advance and disperse the enemy. The column then returned to Illa to hold Arabistan while the 6th Division operated up the Tigris.

At the beginning of May, 1915, Qurna was a hive of industry in spite of the exhausting heat. Major-General C. V. F. Townshend, of Chitral fame, had recently taken command of the 6th Division and had been ordered to attack the Turkish island positions upstream by an advance across the marshes. The enemy made some attempts to destroy the bridge by floating mines, but these were defeated by a novel type of boom thrown across the river by the Bridging Train under Sandes. The Qurna camp was below water-level and was kept dry only by continual pumping within a perimeter of sandbag breastworks. The 22nd Company at Basra, and the Sirmur Sapper Company at Qurna,[2] experimented with *bellums* fitted with transverse steel shields, overlapping the gunwales and designed to give protection against frontal fire. Crews of infantry could be seen at all hours training in the marshes around Qurna, some men in the boats, others pushing and cursing alongside, while the Sappers were preparing rafts to mount small guns or machine guns. On May 26th, the 22nd Company arrived from Basra, and on the 31st Townshend opened his campaign by attacking the Turkish positions above Qurna in an action known thereafter as "the Regatta." It was a marked success. The 17th Brigade, floundering through the swamps, soon gained its objectives, and the Sirmur Sappers followed to detect and remove mines. The bridge-cut was opened by Sandes; the ships, crowded with troops, steamed through; and an amazing pursuit began which ended only on June 3rd when Townshend, with a handful of men, reached Amara and received the surrender of a garrison of 1,100 Turks. Gradually, the remainder of the force arrived in Amara, and by June 10th, both the 22nd Company and the Sirmur Sappers were there and the Bridging Train had completed a bridge of pontoons, *danaks* and trestles across the 200 yards' width of the Jahalla Creek to enable a column marching from Arabistan to join the 6th Division. Major H. E. Winsloe, R.E., was now Divisional Engineer Commander,[3] with Captain H. W. Tomlinson, R.E., as his Staff Officer. The Bridging Train remodelled the old Arab bridge across the Tigris, and the 22nd Company assisted it, built a hangar, improved the hospital accommodation, wired defences and executed a number of other works. The Sirmur Sapper Company was similarly employed until it returned to Basra at the

[1]Notes by Col. R. H. Dewing, D.S.O., M.C., late R.E., sent to the author on May 26th, 1937.

[2]The Sirmur Sappers had relieved the 17th Company at Qurna on March 13th.

[3]Maj. H. E. Winsloe, R.E. had replaced Lieut.-Col. U. W. Evans, R.E., who had become G.S.O.I. Lt. Col. F. A. Wilson, R.E., was appointed D.E.C. 6th Division early in Sept., 1915, *vice* Major Winsloe.

end of July to deck steel barges and extend jetties for three months in appalling heat. Life at Amara had its compensations, for there was a cool breeze at night although the days were so hot that work was impossible except in the early morning and late afternoon. Captain G. E. Leachman, the Political Officer, scoured the country for *danaks* suitable for bridging, and thus Sandes was able in time to improvise a Bridging Train which, with his pontoons, was capable of bridging the Tigris anywhere. Saddles, baulks, chesses, rack-lashings—everything, in fact—had to be manufactured on the spot, and the Bridging Train earned much unpopularity because of its rapacious demands on all material arriving from Basra. Townshend's strategy, however, was based largely on his ability to transfer troops rapidly across the river, and hence the priority given to bridging.

With Amara and Ahwaz in his hands, General Nixon looked towards his left flank and proposed an advance to Nasiriya to safeguard Basra from an attack down the Euphrates. The General Staff in India opposed this scheme, but Nixon obtained the required permission and, on June 27th, an expedition consisting of the 30th Brigade and other troops under General Gorringe started out from Qurna. With it went most of the 12th Company, Madras S. & M., under Pemberton. The expedition crossed the Hammar Lake, but found the Akaika Channel beyond it blocked by a large earthen dam. After 36 hours' work, however, the dam was demolished by the 12th Company and the 48th Pioneers, and the force advanced to the main Euphrates Channel. The level of the Hammar Lake was falling and men were collapsing daily from heat-stroke, so when Gorringe had reached the Euphrates, after some fighting *en route*, he asked for help and was reinforced by the 12th and 18th Brigades and the 17th Company, Bombay S. & M. Advancing up the Euphrates, Gorringe attacked the Turks on July 24th in an entrenched position in front of which was a creek reported as unfordable; but the 17th Company managed, under very heavy fire, to bridge the creek with trestles after it had been blocked with an armoured *mahela*, and so the crossing was effected. The unfortunate Loring was again slightly wounded; his subaltern, Lord, was shot through the leg and invalided to India, and almost half the party employed on bridging became casualties. The 12th Company, meanwhile, was bridging in rear. After Nasiriya had been occupied, the 17th Company remained there until August 6th, when it returned to Basra, but the 12th Company did not leave the Euphrates until October.

With Nasiriya occupied, General Nixon had little excuse for an advance up the Tigris beyond Amara; yet he pressed for such a move, stating that Kut al Amara, standing at the junction of the Tigris and its effluent, the Hai Channel, was a potential advanced base for a Turkish offensive down either channel and thus caused an unnecessary dispersion of his forces; and further that, by occupying Kut, he could secure the resources of the fertile Hai region and deny them to the enemy. Brushing aside administrative difficulties, and supported on political grounds by the Viceroy, he obtained the sanction of the Secretary of State for India, and accordingly Kut al Amara was fixed as a new objective of the Indian Expeditionary

Force in Iraq. Thus a limited and defensive policy of occupation and consolidation at the head of the Persian Gulf was changed overnight into an ambitious move pointing eventually at Baghdad itself. On August 23rd, 1915, General Townshend received orders to occupy Kut, and on September 1st he began to concentrate forward at Ali Gharbi. He seems to have imagined at this time that he was at liberty, if necessary, to pursue the Turks to Baghdad itself. Nixon, however, was told by the Commander-in-Chief in India on September 6th that Townshend was not to be allowed to advance beyond Kut without permission from India, so he could have been under no illusion about the extent of the operations to be undertaken by his subordinate.

The 17th Company, under Captain E. J. Loring, R.E., with Captain C. M. G. Dunhill, R.E., and Lieutenants A. T. East and W. R. Boyes, I.A.R.O., reached Amara from Basra on August 20th and joined the 16th Brigade under General Delamain at Ali Gharbi on September 10th. With it went the right half of the 22nd Company under Captain M. G. G. Campbell, R.E., with Lieutenant A. B. Matthews, R.E., to join the left half, under Lieutenant K. B. S. Crawford, R.E., with Lieutenant W. O. Garrett, I.A.R.O., which was already at Ali Gharbi. The Bridging Train, under Captain E. W. C. Sandes, R.E., had been towed up a few days earlier and had bridged the river at Ali Gharbi in preparation for a general concentration there on September 12th. On the 14th, Townshend advanced from Ali Gharbi to Shaikh Saad, and on the 16th to Sannaiyat. Sandes then dismantled the Ali Gharbi bridge, and on the 19th, with the assistance of the 17th and 22nd Companies, completed a 280 yards' bridge at Sannaiyat in six hours. Five days later, the Sannaiyat bridge was dismantled and moved a few miles up-stream to Nukhailat, above Bait Isa, where Townshend required a bridge before attacking the enemy holding a powerful position astride the river at Es Sinn below Kut al Amara. During the voyage up to Nukhailat a falling beam crushed Sandes' left foot, but he managed to build the bridge, sitting in a boat. He was unable to wear a boot for the next two months and had to hobble around with a carpet slipper secured to the sole of his foot by a puttee.

The Battle of Es Sinn[1] was fought on the left bank of the Tigris on September 28th, 1915, after General Townshend had made a feint attack up the right bank on the previous day. Half the 17th Company was attached to the 18th Brigade in a holding attack near the river, while the 22nd Company marched with the 17th Brigade and other troops under Major-General Delamain against the enemy's left front and left in the desert. Observation towers, erected by the Sapper companies, proved most useful, as dust-storms and mirage often obscured the view. Delamain's night march was guided by Lieutenant A. B. Matthews, R.E., of the 22nd Company, whose chief problem had been to determine the varying boundaries of several large marshes. He had tried to do this by observing the signals of a spotting aeroplane by day, but as this method gave no reliable results he relinquished the attempt and led the troops by marching on

[1]Known also as the First Battle of Kut.

selected stars, instead of on compass bearings, and so brought Delamain's column to its proper *rendezvous* at the appointed hour. Nevertheless, part of the column afterwards went astray and wandered round an uncharted marsh. However, some hard fighting, and the repulse of a Turkish counterattack, brought Delamain at last to the river on the morning of the 29th, when it was found that the enemy had evacuated all his positions under cover of darkness. The 22nd Company, under Campbell, acted mostly as an escort to the guns during this exhausting detour in the desert, but it fought also as infantry and Crawford was the first man to reach the parapet of a redoubt captured with the bayonet.

At noon on September 29th, General Delamain entered Kut al Amara and, while the remainder of the 6th Division followed to occupy the town, he pursued the retreating Turks for a distance of 60 miles upstream to Aziziya, which he reached in ships on October 5th. Loring and half the 17th Company were with this force. By October 9th, both the Bombay Sapper companies were at Aziziya and were soon engaged on defence or road work or in helping the Bridging Train to bridge the 280 yards' width of the Tigris. Owing to lack of towing facilities, the bridging equipment arrived piecemeal, and when Sandes reached Aziziya on the 15th he could provide no more than a foot-bridge and then only after requisitioning every available boat on the river, including the Political Officer's private *bellum*; but with the advent of his eighteen pontoons on the 17th, he was able to reconstruct the bridge and General Townshend's position at Aziziya was then secure. The 30th Brigade, under Major-General Sir Charles Melliss, V.C., marched in, and thus the forward concentration of the striking force was completed.

General Nixon had already begun to urge an advance on Baghdad itself. On October 3rd, he had telegraphed to the Commander-in-Chief in India that he was strong enough to " open the road to Baghdad " and that consequently he proposed to concentrate at Aziziya. On the 5th, he added that he was confident that he could defeat the Turks and seize Baghdad, though to hold the city he would need another division and a cavalry regiment. It should be noted that at this time he had no general reserve and very inadequate transport and supplies, and that his striking force was already 400 miles from its main base. The Military Secretary at the India Office, and Lord Kitchener and the General Staff at the War Office, advised against the Baghdad venture; but Army Headquarters in India and, for political reasons, the Viceroy himself, favoured it. The Cabinet was inclined to support the Viceroy, though Lord Kitchener deprecated anything more ambitious than a raid. On October 23rd, however, the Viceroy wired to a special War Committee appointed in England that he accepted the risk of advancing and would order General Nixon to march at once on Baghdad, and the Committee approved the scheme and ordered the despatch to Iraq of the 3rd and 7th Indian Divisions from France and a cavalry regiment from India. So the die was cast. That Townshend himself had grave misgivings was apparent in several conversations with Sandes when he inspected the Aziziya bridge. But he hoped that his luck would hold. He knew that Nixon was determined to go forward, and consequently on November 11th, with some 14,000 fighting men of the 6th Division and 30th Brigade, he began his final advance on Baghdad, although he had heard that the enemy might shortly receive powerful reinforcements. He had the trust and confidence of his men and had never known defeat.

The 18th Brigade occupied Kutunia on November 16th, and the Bridging Train, towed up by launches, built a 250 yards' bridge in 5 hours with the help of a section of the 17th Company under Lieutenant W. R. Boyes, I.A.R.O. When General Nixon arrived on the following day he seemed surprised to find only 18 pontoons in the makeshift bridge and telegraphed to India demanding the despatch of 50 more. These, however, were never received by the 6th Division, for India could not supply them.[1] On November 18th, the 17th Brigade, with the remainder of the 17th Company, crossed from the left to the right bank and the bridge was dismantled, but on receipt of news that the Turks were advancing it was reformed after dark in 3½ hours—a record, perhaps, in rapid bridging. Townshend then advanced to Zor, where the river was bridged again on the 20th, though with only two damaged *danak* rafts to spare. A section of the 17th Company, under Lieutenant A. T. East, I.A.R.O., was now attached permanently to the Bridging Train. The 17th Brigade rejoined the main body at Zor, and Townshend advanced to Lajj where, on November 21st, the Bridging Train bridged the river once more at a most difficult site with a very high left bank and a current running at 5 knots. The 17th and 22nd Companies, while on the march, had been engaged chiefly in preparing *nullah* crossings for the troops.

On November 22nd, 1915, General Townshend launched his troops against the Turkish position at Ctesiphon, 6 miles above Lajj, in a converging attack by four columns on the left bank, one against the enemy's front and three against his left flank. Matthews, of the 22nd Company, guided the three columns in a night march to their positions of assault. This he did with extreme accuracy, in control of a party of officers and men marching on compass bearings and selected stars and organized so as to eliminate any small errors in direction or distance. Half the 17th Company, with Loring and Dunhill, was with the frontal or holding attack made by the 17th Brigade under Brig.-General F. A. Hoghton, the remainder being with the Bridging Train or acting as an escort to the heavy artillery. Half the 22nd Company, with Campbell and Garrett (I.A.R.O.), accompanied the main flanking attack of the 16th and 30th Brigades under Major-General W. S. Delamain, and the other half, with Matthews and Crawford, marched with a more northerly column composed chiefly of the 18th Brigade under Brig.-General W. G. Hamilton. On the extreme flank, a "Flying Column"[2] under Major-General Sir C. J. Melliss, V.C., had no Sappers and Miners.

[1] "The Adventures of a Bridging Train in Mesopotamia," by the present author, appearing in *The R.E. Journal*, Vol. XXXVIII, 1924, pp. 233–248. Maj.-Gen. J. C. Rimington, the Chief Engineer, had been trying for months to obtain more pontoons from India, but none arrived at the front until March, 1916.

[2] The 6th Cavalry Brigade with some infantry and artillery.

General Delamain soon captured a powerful redoubt in the Turkish line known as "Vital Point," and General Hoghton took the "Water Redoubt" further south, and both commanders then proceeded to clear the adjacent front line trenches. In some trench fighting near Vital Point, Garrett was killed by a bayonet thrust and Campbell severely wounded by machine gun fire. Matthews, and Crawford with the other half of the 22nd Company, were unwounded, though Matthews was hit by a spent bullet. Crawford's half-company acted as infantry in support of General Hamilton's attack across open ground. In the holding attack near the river, Loring was ordered to assault a redoubt with his Sappers and some infantry. He did so and was shot through both lungs.[1] Thus the first day of the battle again deprived both the Sapper companies of their commanders, and when night fell, no Royal Engineer officer who had served with either company before the war remained with it. A powerful Turkish counter-attack was repulsed on November 23rd and on the following day General Townshend concentrated his reduced and battered force near the river bank. Dunhill now took command of the 17th Company, and Lieutenant H. S. Cheshire, I.A.R.O., was attached for duty with the 22nd Company under Matthews. On the 25th, Townshend decided to retire to Lajj, which he reached on the 26th after the Army Commander had proceeded downstream towards Kut al Amara. The rash attempt on Baghdad had failed, and Townshend had lost nearly half his force.

While the Bombay Sapper companies were fighting at Ctesiphon, the Bridging Train had been working hard at Lajj. During the 22nd the bridge was dismantled and formed into tows in expectation of an early advance to Baghdad; but hardly had the last anchor been raised than Sandes was ordered to re-erect the bridge and did so, with the help of East and his men, before dark. On the 23rd he was required to dismantle the bridge again, and throughout the 24th and most of the 25th, the Bridging Train remained ready to move. Then, at 8.30 p.m., orders came to rebuild the bridge for the third time, and by working all night in the glare of Stace's searchlights, this was accomplished before dawn on the 26th. Wounded were arriving in streams and crowding on to the ships, and Townshend marched in with the main body. A general retreat from Lajj began on November 27th. At 2 p.m. Sandes was ordered to dismantle the bridge and be gone in two hours, and by abandoning his anchors he succeeded. Every craft went at full speed down the river, the captains guessing the right channels as best they could, and the bridging-rafts, towed by launches, following in their wake. On the morning of the 28th, after many adventures, most of the Bridging Train flotilla steamed into Aziziya, where a bridge was required at once, and not until sunset, when the structure had been completed, were the exhausted Bengal Sappers able to get any rest. After evacuating his wounded and stores, and receiving a small reinforcement, Townshend resumed his retreat on the 29th, sending

[1]Campbell and Loring were invalided to India, and Campbell eventually to England. They made the voyage down the Tigris, lying with hundreds of other wounded on the hard deck of a river steamer in conditions of indescribable filth and misery.

the 30th Brigade ahead to clear the way. Again the Bridging Train was ordered to be gone at short notice and got away with the loss of only a few sinking *danaks*. The advancing Turks then occupied Aziziya while Townshend bivouacked at Umm at Tabul, a further 10 miles downstream. A section of the 17th Company under East was still with the Bridging Train, and another under Boyes was with the advanced 30th Brigade.

On December 1st a sharp action developed at Umm at Tabul, where Townshend struck back at the enemy after ordering Melliss to countermarch to reinforce him. The 22nd Company, with Matthews and Crawford, and half the 17th Company under Dunhill, escorted the guns and improved *nullah* crossings. As soon as he was able, Townshend broke off the action and resumed his retreat. Shortly afterwards, Dunhill was killed, and as the half-company was without a British officer, Lieutenant H. M. Spink, I.A.R.O., took command of it until Boyes rejoined with Melliss' column. Matthews and Crawford were now the only regular officers left with the two Bombay Sapper companies and each had less than four years' service.

The remainder of the long retreat to Kut al Amara was a nightmare of forced marches by land and confusion and sniping on the river. The Turks, badly mauled at Umm at Tabul, interfered little with the progress of the tired and hungry troops plodding steadily along the desert track and bivouacking in bitter cold at night. The Bridging Train was given up for lost; but by a miracle it reached Kut, with Stace and his Searchlight Section as passengers,[1] steaming its hardest and taking all chances. It lost several rafts at Umm at Tabul under artillery and infantry fire, and narrowly avoided collision with two stranded and burning gunboats. Without escort, and out-distanced by the other shipping, it was sniped at every bend of the river, and near Shumran it was chased by Arab cavalry and lost its remaining pontoons. When Sandes moored at Kut on December 2nd, after Townshend's advanced guard had entered the place, he had only 12 *danak* rafts out of the 30 pontoon or *danak* rafts with which he had started upstream from Aziziya only 17 days before, and consequently he was unable to bridge the river. The situation was saved, however, by the excellent work done in Kut since October by the Sirmur Sapper Company under Colbeck. This unit had built a defended enclosure, known as "The Fort" on the river bank below the town, and had repaired an old Turkish bridge of boats further downstream. On December 2nd it began to dismantle the Turkish bridge and tow the boats up to the Fort, and the material so collected, together with some new *danaks* and timber and the remaining *danaks* of the Bridging Train, enabled Sandes to build a bridge to a sandbank opposite the Fort on December 6th across which the 6th Cavalry Brigade escaped downstream before Kut was completely invested. The Brigade was extremely lucky for there was no bombardment by the enemy. Every boat was leaking like a sieve and there was not one to spare, and as the last vehicle reached the sandbank, some of the boats sank. The

[1] Lieut. A. T. East, I.A.R.O., and his section had rejoined the 17th Company at Umm at Tabul.

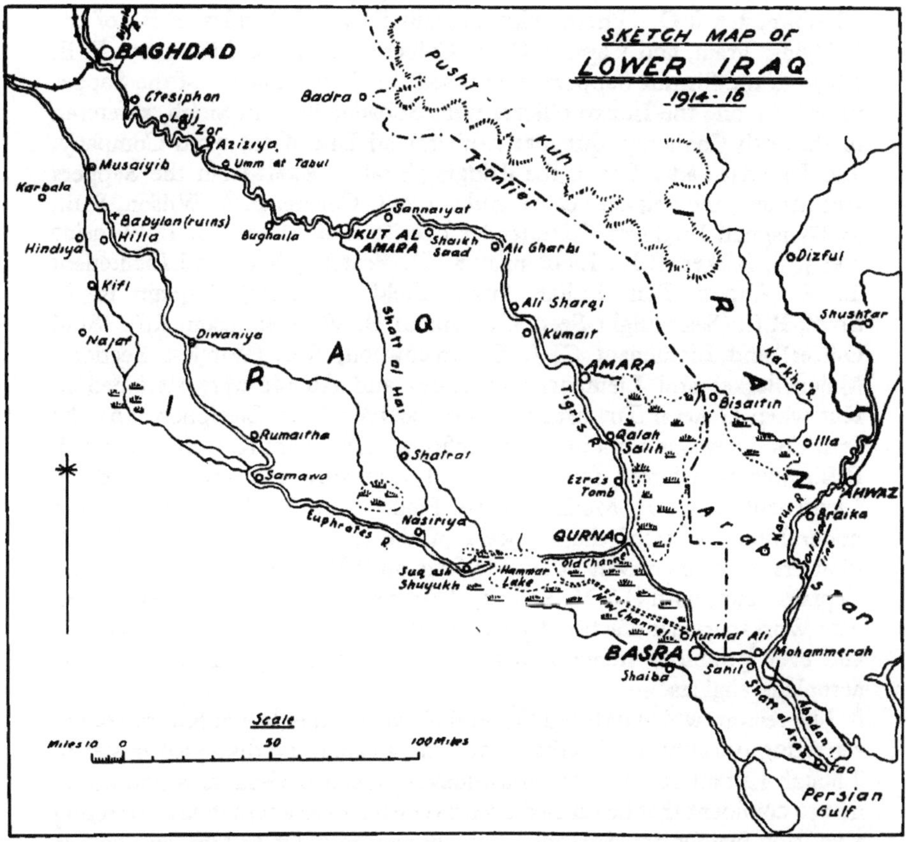
SKETCH MAP OF
LOWER IRAQ
1914-16
BAGHDAD
Ctesiphon
Lajj
Zor
Aziziya
Umm at Tabul
Musaiyib
Karbala
Babylon (ruins)
Hilla
Hindiya
Bughaila
Sannaiyat
KUT AL AMARA
Shaikh Saad
Ali Gharbi
Badra
Pusht-i-Kuh
Frontier
Kifl
Najaf
Diwaniya
IRAQ
Shatt al Hai
Ali Sharqi
Kumait
AMARA
Tigris R.
Qalah Salih
Bisaitin
Illa
Dizful
Shushtar
Karkha R.
IRAN
Rumaitha
Shatra
Samawa
Ezra's Tomb
Nasiriya
Euphrates R.
QURNA
Suq ash Shuyukh
Hammar Lake
Old Channel
New Channel
Arabistan
Karun R.
Oil pipe line
AHWAZ
Braika
Kurmat Ali
BASRA
Mohammerah
Shaiba
Sahil
Shatt al Arab
Abadan I.
Fao
Persian Gulf
Scale
Miles 10 0 50 100 Miles

saving of the 6th Cavalry Brigade was the crowning achievement of the Bridging Train on the Tigris.

On arrival in Kut from Ctesiphon, the 17th Company was commanded by Lieutenant A. T. East, with Lieutenants W. R. Boyes and H. M. Spink, all of the I.A.R.O., and the 22nd Company by Lieutenant A. B. Matthews, R.E., with Lieutenant K. B. S. Crawford, R.E., and Lieutenant H. S. Cheshire, I.A.R.O. These, with Captain E. W. C. Sandes, R.E., of the Bridging Train, and Captain C. E. Colbeck, R.E., and Lieutenant F. E. Mayo of the Sirmur Sappers, comprised the British officers of the Sapper units. Among the Indian officers were Subadar Baryam Singh, a veteran of the 17th Company, Subadar Muhammad Din of the 22nd Company, and Jemadar Sadar Din of the Bridging Train. Apart from the Sappers and Miners, the engineer cadre under Lieut.-Colonel F. A. Wilson, R.E., as Divisional Engineer Commander consisted of Majors H. E. Winsloe and J. S. Barker, R.E., Lieutenant K. D. Yearsley, R.E., and Lieutenant T. W. Abbott, R.E. Indian Army (Field Engineers), Captain R. E. Stace, R.E. (Searchlight Section), Captain H. W. Tomlinson, R.E. (Staff Officer) and Lieutenant C. J. E. Greenwood, R.E. (Wireless Section). Major Barker and Lieutenants Yearsley and Abbott were stationed in Kut when General Townshend's force arrived from Ctesiphon. As the 17th Company was without regular officers, Lieutenant K. B. S. Crawford, R.E., was transferred from the 22nd Company and was assisted by Lieutenant L. W. H. Mathias, 128th Pioneers, who volunteered to serve under him. Most of the artificers of the Sapper companies and 48th Pioneers were taken away at once to form an R.E. Workshop in Kut under Captain Stace, with C.S.M. Bellis and Sergeants Toleman and Baker, R.E. The Workshop manufactured grenades, periscopes and other war material, and even produced trench-mortars made from the cylinders of Gnome aeroplane engines.

The reasons which induced General Townshend to halt at Kut instead of retreating possibly to Ali Gharbi or Amara cannot be discussed in detail. Though Kut offered no strong positions for defence, General Nixon was at first so confident that he refused even to consider the alternative of selecting a position further downstream. The decision rested with him, and he was supported by the Viceroy. Townshend informed Nixon that his troops were too exhausted to move further and was told, on December 4th, that he could entrench at Kut, if he wished, and might expect to be relieved within two months. But Townshend seems to have anticipated relief within one month, so he replied, on December 6th, that he had changed his mind and would retreat to Ali Gharbi. The General Staff in India considered that Kut should be abandoned; but the Commander-in-Chief left the decision to Nixon, and the latter informed Townshend that he did not approve of a withdrawal to Ali Gharbi because he counted on the early arrival at the front of the 3rd and 7th Divisions from France and on some help from the Russians. So Townshend was reassured and telegraphed on December 7th that he would remain in Kut. It is interesting to note that in the opinion of Major-General Rimington, the Chief Engineer, Townshend had a mistaken belief in the strategical importance of Kut and his proper course would have been to retire across the Tigris and hold the Es Sinn position only a few miles downstream.[1] The decision to defend Kut was wrongly left by Nixon to Townshend, and the result of much vacillation was that the latter remained in Kut and thereby signed the death warrant of his force. The Turks closed in, and the 6th Division and 30th Brigade were soon hemmed into a bend of the wide River Tigris.

Every measure was taken at once to strengthen the Kut defences and to prepare equipment. The front line across the peninsula followed roughly the alignment of some existing blockhouses and wire. A second line was dug nearer Kut, and afterwards an intermediate line and communication trenches. Piquets were posted on the river bank, and a detachment occupied and fortified the outpost of Woolpress Village on the right bank.[2] The Sirmur Sappers formed part of the garrison of the Fort, which was situated at the downstream end of the North-East Section of the defences manned by the 17th Brigade, and the 17th and 22nd Companies were camped north of the town and relieved each other in the vulnerable North-West Section held alternately by the 16th and 30th Brigades. The 18th Brigade was in reserve in Kut.

After the escape of the 6th Cavalry Brigade on December 6th, Sandes was ordered to dismantle the bridge at the Fort and rebuild it nearer Kut, and by the evening of the 8th, the Bridging Train and a section of the 17th Company had completed a rickety structure of all the available Turkish and Arab boats. Townshend seems to have been still considering the possibility of evacuating Kut, for he visited the bridge and asked whether it would carry field artillery and transport. He was told that it would not. On the morning of December 9th, the Turks attacked and captured the bridgehead. The Bridging Train kept the bridge under fire and thus prevented an immediate crossing, and with the arrival of Gurkha reinforcements, the situation was saved, but it was decided later that the bridge should be destroyed. The task was undertaken by Matthews and six other volunteers from the 22nd Company. Matthews prepared two large charges of guncotton between planks to be laid across the bridge near each end, the fuze for the more distant charge being lit before the party started out in case all were hit before they could get across. The Sapper party was joined by another consisting of Lieutenant R. T. Sweet and six volunteers from the 7th Gurkhas, who undertook to cut the anchor ropes. After dark, the two parties stole silently across the bridge. Matthews and his Sappers crossed till they were within earshot of the enemy. They laid the distant charge and ran back while the Gurkhas cut the ropes as they passed. Not a shot was fired, and both parties got back safely without using the second charge. The distant charge exploded, and then both banks of

[1] "Kut-ul-Amarah," by Maj.-Gen. J. C. Rimington, C.B., C.S.I., late R.E., appearing in the *Army Quarterly*, Vol. VI, April, 1923, pp. 17–26. See also "The Decision to defend Kut-el-Amarah," by the present author, appearing in *The R.E. Journal*, Vol. XXXVIII, 1924, pp. 423–433.

[2] See the insert entitled *Defences of Kut al Amara, Jan.*, 1916, appearing in *Sketch Map of the River Tigris, Shaikh Saad to Shumran, Jan.*, 1916, in this chapter.

the river blazed with machine gun and rifle fire. The bridge broke into pieces and afterwards the remnants gradually foundered. Both Matthews and Sweet were recommended for the Victoria Cross and both received the D.S.O. The rank and file were also decorated. With this affair, the exploits of the Bridging Train on the Tigris came to an untimely end. The unit was re-named " Town Engineers " and worked chiefly on communications in Kut. It had bridged the Tigris no less than 17 times and had never failed Townshend in his victorious advance or his strategic retreat.

Throughout December, the Turkish artillery was active and the infantry aggressive around Kut. The Bombay Sappers dug and wired trenches and then resorted to mining towards the enemy's sapheads under the direction of Matthews. Colbeck and some of his Sirmur Sappers accompanied a successful sortie from the Fort, which was closely invested. The 17th Company suffered severe casualties in officers. On December 17th, Subadar Baryam Singh was severely wounded, and on the following day East was shot through both lungs. Cheshire was then transferred from the 22nd Company. On the 19th, Crawford was shot through both legs and Jemadar Fateh Khan was also wounded. As Boyes was in hospital, this left Cheshire as the sole British officer, so Lieutenant K. D. Yearsley, R.E., an Assistant Field Engineer, was appointed to command the unit. Crawford remained in hospital till the end of the siege, and it is sad to relate that East died of his wounds. Thus, when the Turks launched a general attack on December 24th and failed to take Kut by storm, the officers on duty with the Sapper companies were Yearsley, Spink and Cheshire (17th), Matthews and Mathias[1] (22nd) and Colbeck and Mayo (Sirmur Sappers). The Sirmur Sappers distinguished themselves in the successful defence of the Fort, where Colbeck was the leading technical expert. After this, the enemy relinquished all attempts to storm Kut and transferred troops downstream to oppose the advance of a Relief Force under Lieut.-General Sir F. J. Aylmer, V.C., late R.E., an ex-Bengal Sapper and Miner and a hero of the Chitral Campaign of 1895.[2] Deluges of rain in January caused the Tigris level to rise, and large areas in Kut were flooded. The Sappers fought desperately against the rush of water. Their mines were put out of action, and long stretches of the first and second line trenches had to be abandoned. The enemy suffered in like manner, and thereafter flood, pestilence and starvation were more dangerous than the Turk.

We turn now to the relief operations of the Tigris Corps concentrating under General Aylmer at Ali Gharbi.[3] At the beginning of December 1915, the only Sapper and Miner unit in Iraq, outside invested Kut, was the 12th Company of the Madras Corps under Captain S. Pemberton, R.E., but this unit was not available for the relief operations because it

[1]Lieut. L. W. H. Mathias, 128th Pioneers, had been transferred from the 17th to the 22nd Company.

[2]Lieut.-Gen. Sir Fenton Aylmer, V.C., assumed command of the Tigris Corps at Amara on Dec. 12th, 1915.

[3]See *Sketch Map of the River Tigris, Shaikh Saad to Shumran, Jan.*, 1916, included in this chapter.

KUT AL AMARA.

was required to build part of a road from Basra to Amara to supplement the river route which could not cope even with the forage needed for the animals. Accordingly, the 13th Company, Madras S. & M., under Captain E. Bradney, R.E., with Lieutenants J. Tate and F. A. Adlard, I.A.R.O., was summoned from India, and, arriving at Basra on December 6th, proceeded to collect bridging material for Aylmer's force. It reached Ali Gharbi on the 19th and bridged the river on the 24th. Generals Nixon and Townshend had expected that the 3rd and 7th Divisions from France would reach Basra early in December, and with them the 3rd and 4th Companies, Bengal S. & M., the 20th and 21st Companies, Bombay S. & M., and the 2nd Field Troop of the Madras Corps; but owing to lack of shipping at Marseilles, the Bengal Sapper units did not leave France until December 7th and the other formations still later. It had been intended originally that the 3rd and 7th Divisions should halt and reorganize in Egypt; but instead, owing to urgent representations by Townshend that his supplies in Kut were insufficient, they were hurried through piecemeal to Basra, where they disembarked without proper transport early in January. Consequently on January 6th, 1916, when General Aylmer, over-estimating the urgency of the relief operations, launched his available forces under Major-General G. J. Younghusband against the Turkish positions at Shaikh Saad far below Kut, he had no Sappers and Miners whatever on the Tigris front.

The 3rd Company, Bengal S. & M., under Captain F. McC. Douie, R.E.,[1] with Captain E. O. Wheeler, R.E., and Lieutenant J. A. Stein, I.A.R.O., and the 4th Company under Captain A. J. G. Bird, R.E., with Captain E. L. Farley and Lieutenant F. V. B. Witts, R.E., and Lieutenant P. J. Roche, I.A.R.O., disembarked at Basra at the beginning of January, 1916, but neither unit was sent at once up the Tigris. Both went to the Euphrates front, the 3rd Company for several weeks and the 4th for many months. The 4th Company, indeed, did not reach the Tigris front until it rejoined the 7th Division at Sannaiyat at the end of 1916 in time for the final advance on Baghdad. Meanwhile, it bridged the Euphrates at Nasiriya and worked on road construction between Basra and Sannaiyat.[2] Another engineer unit at Nasiriya during the summer of 1916 was a company of Malerkotla Imperial Service Sappers under Lieut.-Colonel Quadir Baksh Khan with Captain J. F. Turner, R.E., as Special Service Officer. It reached Nasiriya in July and returned to Basra in January 1917, where it was joined by Captain L. V. Bond, R.E.[3] No doubt there were adequate reasons for diverting the two Bengal Sapper companies up the Euphrates in January, 1916, but they are somewhat difficult to understand in view of the entire lack of engineer units on the Tigris front at that time.

[1]Capt. F. McC. Douie, R.E., had assumed command of the 3rd Company in France on Oct. 5th, 1915, when Capt. E. F. J. Hill, R.E., was appointed Field Engineer, 7th Division.

[2]Notes by Col. A. J. G. Bird, C.I.E., D.S.O., late R.E., sent to the author on June 25th, 1944.

[3]*A Short History of the Services rendered by the Imperial Service Troops during the Great War*, 1914–18, by Maj.-Gen. Sir Harry Watson, K.B.E., C.B., C.M.G., C.I.E., M.V.O., p. 46.

As regards the two Bombay Sapper units from France, the 20th Company, under Captain A. D. S. Arbuthnot, R.E., with Lieutenants H. W. R. Hamilton and A. Mason, R.E., and Lieutenant A. V. Venables, I.A.R.O., and the 21st Company, under Captain M. Rawlence, R.E., with Captains M. Everett and K. Mason, R.E., and Lieutenant C. Tedman, I.A.R.O., began to disembark at Basra on January 7th, 1916, gravely handicapped because their transport had been left in France. They marched up-country in heavy rain and did not reach the Tigris front until February 7th. The 2nd Field Troop, Madras S. & M., under Captain A. H. Morin, I.A.R.O., landed on January 20th and was employed on the Basra–Amara road.

Thus the eagerly awaited Sapper and Miner reinforcements from France were not available during the earliest stages of General Aylmer's attempt to relieve Kut, and everything devolved upon the 13th Company under Bradney. However, the unit excelled itself in circumstances of extraordinary difficulty. It removed the Ali Gharbi bridge, rebuilt it 5 miles below Shaikh Saad on January 7th, and, the Turks having been driven from Shaikh Saad, completed a 275 yards' bridge at that place on January 10th. All this was accomplished in gales of wind and storms of rain, with flimsy Arab *danaks*. The enemy retired to a position at Wadi, where Younghusband attacked them on the 13th and, after incurring heavy losses, drove them back to another position on the left bank at Hanna. The 13th Company dismantled the Shaikh Saad bridge, and having now received a few pontoons from Basra, threw a pontoon bridge across the Wadi influent on the 15th and completed a *danak* bridge, 400 yards long, across the Tigris at Ora, above the Wadi, on the evening of January 17th.[1] Then another gale sprang up. The bridge tossed wildly and many of the *danaks* foundered, and finally half the structure was carried downstream and most of the remaining boats sank. The Wadi pontoon bridge was also destroyed. A battalion commander near the bridge, who received a message " Is the Wadi bridge causing you any anxiety ? " is said to have replied " Bridge causing no anxiety. Was washed away half an hour ago."

These disasters on the river upset General Aylmer's plans, and at this moment he received a message from General Townshend that the rations in Kut would last only until February 7th. In desperation, he attacked the Hanna position on January 21st and failed with heavy casualties. Such was the situation confronting the new Army Commander, General Sir Percy Lake, soon after he had relieved General Sir John Nixon.[2] The country was a sea of mud in which movement was almost impossible. Aylmer had no bridge, little river transport and hardly any supplies, and his men were exhausted. A respite was secured, however, by the receipt of another message from Townshend announcing that he had recently discovered stores of grain in Kut which would enable him to hold out for

[1]*The Madras Sappers in the Campaign in Mesopotamia*, 1914–18, p. 13. (This forms Part I of *Q.V.O. Madras Sappers and Miners in France and Iraq*, 1914–1920.)

[2]Gen. Sir P. H. N. Lake assumed the supreme command in Iraq on Jan. 19th, 1916, *vice* Gen. Sir J. E. Nixon.

no less than 84 days, so the Tigris Corps sat down to reorganize and await the early arrival of reinforcements from the 3rd and 7th Divisions in addition to three brigades from India, and, it was hoped, the 13th British Division from Egypt. Aylmer had been lured into a premature attack by incorrect information regarding the food situation in Kut.

The 13th Company, Madras S. & M., proceeded to collect *mahelas* to replace their lost *danaks*, and by February 11th the Tigris at Ora had been bridged once more. A small Bridging Train of Bengal Sappers, raised in Iraq and commanded by Lieutenant J. M. S. Trelawny, I.A.R.O., now arrived to help the 13th Company. Whenever a storm arose it was necessary to dismantle the superstructure of the bridge and leave the *mahelas* to ride out the gale. No man or animal could keep a footing on the swaying roadway. With the arrival from the Euphrates of the 12th Company, Madras S. & M., under Captain S. Pemberton, R.E., with Captain R. H. Dewing, R.E., and Lieutenants J. M. B. Stuart and A. W. Thomas, I.A.R.O., the critical situation on the river was somewhat eased, and Colonel E. R. B. Stokes-Roberts, the Chief Engineer of the Corps, with Captain E. K. Squires, R.E., as his Staff Officer, could carry out some part, at least, of the engineering work expected of him.

During February 1916, General Aylmer built up his force for a new attempt. Prospects of success seemed brighter, for the Imperial General Staff had taken over control of the campaign from Army Headquarters, India.[1] Aylmer planned to relieve Kut by a *coup de main* by containing the Turks in the Hanna position on the left bank while he marched the bulk of his force up the right bank to cross the Hai Channel, and subsequently, if possible, the Tigris itself above Kut, thus cutting the enemy's communications, or at least covering a withdrawal of the Kut garrison. Townshend, however, again altered his estimate of his available resources and wired on March 4th that he could not hold out beyond March 31st, so Aylmer decided to put his plan into operation at once. During the night of March 7th/8th, a powerful striking force made a long march through the desert towards the Es Sinn position on the right bank, ably guided by Captain K. Mason, R.E.,[2] and dawn found the 3rd Division (less 1 brigade), under Major-General H. D'U. Keary, before the Dujaila Redoubt, which was then empty. Keary asked permission to advance and occupy the redoubt, but was forbidden to do so until adequate artillery preparation had been made. The guns opened fire and the Turks poured into the redoubt. In the early afternoon, Keary was ordered to attack the redoubt with his 8th Brigade, but as this brigade was deployed widely along his front it was not until about 4.30 p.m. that the attack was delivered. Nevertheless, it succeeded, though the brigade was afterwards driven out because there were no proper arrangements for support and consolidation. The 12th Company, Madras S. & M., and the 20th and 21st Companies, Bombay S. & M., accompanied the march to Es Sinn, while the 13th Company, Madras S. & M., and the recently arrived 3rd Company of the Bengal Corps, were

[1]The transfer of control took place on Feb. 16th, 1916.
[2]*Records of the Survey of India, Vol.* XX, *The War Record,* p. 11.

at or below Hanna. In the fiasco at the Dujaila Redoubt on March 8th, 1916, the 20th Company lost its gallant commander, Captain A. D. S. Arbuthnot, R.E., who had accompanied the 8th Brigade with a small detachment of Sappers detailed to help in consolidating the position when won. The circumstances of his death will never be known, but it is believed that he entered the redoubt and perished while trying to hold it with his Sappers and a few remaining British infantry. On March 9th, Aylmer withdrew to Ora, where Captain S. Boyd, R.E., took command of the 20th Company.[1]

Immediately after the failure at Dujaila, the Tigris rose in angry flood. The Ora bridge was damaged by storms, and both the 12th and 13th Companies had to come to the assistance of the small Bridging Train. By March 23rd, however, the bridge had been rebuilt, and before the end of the month the companies received a number of pontoons intended to form an "advanced" Bridging Train. Captain F. V. B. Witts, R.E., arrived from the 4th Company to command the unit with personnel consisting of 80 Bengal Sappers and Miners sent from Roorkee under Lieutenant A. Eastmond, I.A.R.O.[2] This formation, which became known as the 2nd (or No. 2) Mobile Bridging Train,[3] took temporary charge of the Ora bridge. After the retreat from Es Sinn, General Aylmer handed over the command of the Tigris Corps to his Chief of Staff, Lieut.-General Sir G. F. Gorringe, the former leader of the 12th Division and a Royal Engineer with a distinguished record in the Sudan.[4] Confidence was felt that General Gorringe would force a way through the maze of Turkish trenches, and with the gradual arrival at Ora of the 13th British Division from Egypt under Major-General F. S. Maude, the situation looked more hopeful. Gorringe could muster 30,000 rifles and 127 guns against 20,000 Turks with 70 guns; but much depended, of course, on the weather.

On April 5th, the 13th British Division advanced to assault the Hanna position on the left bank, carried it, and captured the Fallahiya position further upstream; but on the following day, the 7th Indian Division failed with heavy casualties before the Sannaiyat position. The 12th and 13th Companies managed with the greatest difficulty to throw a pontoon bridge across the 340 yards' width of the Tigris close below Fallahiya, for the new pontoons were found to be very inferior and liable to founder in a heavy sea.[5] On April 9th, Gorringe made a second assault at Sannaiyat. He suffered heavily, but had no success. On the 17th, he captured the Bait

[1] *History of the 20th (Field) Company, Royal Bombay Sappers and Miners, Great War, 1914–1918*, by Maj. H. W. R. Hamilton, D.S.O., M.C., R.E., p. 33.

[2] *A Short History of the Corps of K.G.O. Bengal Sappers and Miners during the War, 1914–18*, p. 31.

[3] The 1st (or No. 1) Bridging Train, Bengal S. & M., was under Lieut. J. M. S. Trelawny, I.A.R.O., and the original Bridging Train of the same Corps was under Capt. E. W. C. Sandes, R.E., in Kut.

[4] *The Royal Engineers in Egypt and the Sudan*, by the present author. Many references.

[5] "Pontoon Experience in Mesopotamia," and "Light Floating Bridges in Mesopotamia," by Maj. F. V. B. Witts, C.B.E., D.S.O., M.C., R.E., appearing in *The R.E. Journal*, Vol. XXXIV, July–Dec., 1921, pp. 205–208, and Vol. XXXVII, March–Dec., 1923, pp. 627–639, respectively.

Isa position on the right bank, lost part of it to a determined counter-attack, and regained it on the 20th. Then, on April 22nd, he made a third and final attempt on Sannaiyat, and, with its repulse, he had shot his bolt. The Sappers and Miners of the Tigris Corps took little part in these bloody affairs except to support the infantry by hard and consistent labour. While the 13th Company maintained the Fallahiya bridge and the 20th and 21st Companies fought the floods, the 3rd and 12th Companies built strong-points for the 7th Division. Final attempts to supply the Kut garrison by aeroplane, and by running the S.S. *Julnar* through the Turkish positions, having failed, Townshend surrendered on April 29th, 1916, and the curtain fell on a tragedy which had cost England nearly 40,000 soldiers in and below Kut.

We revert now to events in Kut itself. There is little of engineering importance to record regarding the last four months of the long siege. The story is told in *In Kut and Captivity*[1] and in *A Short History of the 17th and 22nd Field Companies in Mesopotamia*, 1914–18. During a cold and wet January the 17th and 22nd Companies worked on flood protection and field defences, and the Bridging Train on making communications in the town and collecting materials for bridging.[2] Aylmer's guns could be heard downstream. Rations were reduced on the 24th and an issue of horse-meat started. During February, the Bombay and Sirmur Sapper Companies worked principally on breastworks which replaced fire trenches in flooded areas. Boyes having returned to the 17th Company from hospital, Cheshire rejoined the 22nd Company. Both Matthews and Mathias were in poor health, and after Mayo had been seriously wounded, the situation as regards officers was very difficult. When the enemy started bombing on February 13th, Matthews provided some anti-aircraft defence by slinging a field gun to a mast erected in a pit. All the companies were ready, on the 22nd, to take part in a sortie from Kut to co-operate with General Aylmer, but the sortie was never made. By the end of the month the men were getting little to eat except coarse barley flour. They tried boiled grass, but it had a bad effect on their health, and scurvy appeared among them because they would not vary their diet by eating horse-flesh. There was much excitement on March 7th when Colbeck, Matthews and Yearsley received orders for co-operation with Aylmer's attack on the Es Sinn position by ferrying Townshend's force, less the 16th Brigade, across the river. After dark, Stace released an ingenious floating mine in an attempt to destroy a Turkish bridge in the Hai Channel. The garrison stood to arms throughout the 8th, but all arrangements were cancelled when Aylmer's failure became known, and rations were promptly reduced. Soon afterwards, the level of the Tigris rose. Flood protection under Matthews claimed prior attention, and towards the end of the month the situation became critical. There was water everywhere, but little to eat. The Indians still refused horse-flesh and received only 10 oz. of

[1] *In Kut and Captivity*, by the present author. Part II.

[2] Every Arab door in Kut was requisitioned to form decking for a possible trestle bridge across the Hai Channel, and material was collected for flying bridges

coarse barley flour ground in mills managed by Captain S. C. Winfield-Smith, R.F.C. The oil engines operating the mills were kept in repair by spares dropped by aeroplanes, which brought also medical supplies, cash and other necessaries in small quantities. At the end of March, everyone was getting weak. Some felt a craving for alcohol: others for sugar. Arab labour had become almost useless, and the Indian soldiers were easily tired.

Rations in Kut were further reduced on April 1st. The British received 12 oz. of coarse bread; the Indians, 10 oz. of barley meal, 4 oz. of barley for parching, and 1/3rd oz. of *ghi*. There was little else except horse-flesh, which the Indians still refused to eat. By April 9th, after General Gorringe had been checked at Sannaiyat, the bread ration for the British had fallen to 5 oz. and the Indian ration to 7 oz. of barley meal. The Sappers were so weak that they could work only a 90-minute relief. Indeed, it was pitiful to see their attempts to dig. On the 10th came news of Gorringe's failure at Sannaiyat, and the rations reached their lowest ebb—a 4 oz. loaf for the British and 5 oz. of barley meal for the Indians. On the 12th, Jemadar Sadar Din of the Bridging Train informed Captain Sandes that, in response to General Townshend's appeals, the Bengal Sappers (all Muhammadans) were prepared to eat horse-flesh. The men drew and consumed their rations, and the news spread at once to the Bombay Sappers who, with the exception of a few Brahmans, followed suit. Thus the Sappers gave a lead to most of the other Indian troops in Kut and, by April 15th, 9,500 Indians were eating horse-flesh, though too late to affect the situation materially. A small supply of flour, dropped in sacks by aeroplanes, was insufficient to feed the garrison and 6,000 Arabs for more than a few days. The civil population was decimated by starvation. Many Arabs, with their families, attempted to leave the town by floating down the river on small rafts at night, but all were machine-gunned by the Turks. Subadar Baryam Singh of the 17th Company died of his wounds on April 18th, and Subadar Muhammad Din of the 22nd Company then became the recognized representative and mouthpiece of the Indian Sapper ranks. After the final repulse of the Relief Force at Sannaiyat, the issue of all reserve and emergency rations, and the failure of the *Julnar* to reach Kut, an armistice was arranged with Halil Pasha, the Turkish commander. The Sappers destroyed their equipment and helped in the destruction of the guns, and on April 29th, 1916, they surrendered with 13,000 other troops and followers under Townshend.

So ended a siege of tragic memory, and with it the careers of the original 17th and 22nd Companies, Bombay S. & M., the original Bridging Train, Bengal S. & M., and the 1st Sirmur Sapper Company. The morale of these men was never shaken and their endurance never failed. Weak and ill, they remembered always the great traditions of their Corps. They passed into a long captivity from which many never returned. But the story of what happened after the surrender cannot be given here. It is a sad tale, unconnected with war. Nevertheless, it is worth reading for it shows how loyalty can survive in the darkest hour and how courage can maintain self-respect under the most terrible conditions.[1]

A long pause followed the fall of Kut. The need for immediate action by the Tigris Corps had gone and reorganization was the order of the day. The enemy on the right bank withdrew to the line of the Hai, and on May 20th the 3rd (Lahore) Division advanced and occupied the Es Sinn position between Maqasis and Dujaila, where the 20th and 21st Bombay Sapper companies worked on water supply. Rawlence was invalided, and Everett took command of the 21st Company. In July, Bradney was also invalided, and Captain D. McA. Hogg, R.E., was appointed to command the 13th (Madras) Company. Hogg remained in command until his transfer in October to the command of the 2nd Field Troop, which he held for two years.[2] He was followed by Major W. D. B. Conran, R.E., with Captain A. J. Cruickshank, R.E., as one of his Company Officers. Everyone was overworked, and changes in appointment were frequent.

On July 11th, 1916, Lieut.-General Sir F. S. Maude succeeded Lieut.-General Sir G. F. Gorringe in command of the Tigris Corps, and on August 28th he took over the supreme command in Iraq from General Sir Percy Lake. Though Maude recognized that by remaining inert on the Tigris he surrendered temporarily every vestige of strategical initiative, he would not move until he had adequate strength for an offensive up the right bank. In October he reorganized the Tigris Corps into two Army Corps, the 1st Corps consisting of the 3rd and 7th Indian Divisions and the 3rd Corps of the 13th British and 14th Indian Divisions. The 14th Division had been formed in June under Major-General Sir R. G. Egerton with engineer troops comprising the 12th and 13th Companies, Madras S. & M., under the orders of Lieut.-Colonel E. C. Ogilvie, R.E., as C.R.E. with Captain P. E. Prince, R.E., as Adjutant. The 12th and 13th Companies were reinforced later by the 15th (Burma) Company of the same Corps. During the period of recovery and reorganization, all the Sapper units on the Tigris were very busy. The 20th and 21st (Bombay) Companies built blockhouses and wire fences to protect a light railway from Shaikh Saad to the Es Sinn position, the 12th and 13th (Madras) Companies continued their water supply operations, and the 3rd (Bengal) Company was employed on defence work and other miscellaneous duties.

An interesting feature of this period was the development of the Mobile Bridging Train under Captain F. V. B. Witts, R.E. From June onwards, Witts was employed in forming and equipping a Bridging Train which could move by land. He abandoned the Indian pattern pontoon of copper or steel and adopted the British type carried on an ordinary Indian two-

[1]The story of the Kut prisoners-of-war is told in many volumes. Among these the following may be mentioned :—*In Kut and Captivity* and *Tales of Turkey*, both by the present author. ; *A Kut Prisoner*, by Maj. H. C. W. Bishop ; *The Secrets of a Kuttite*, by Capt. E. O. Mousley ; 450 *Miles to Freedom*, by Capts. K. D. Yearsley, R.E., and M. A. B. Johnston, R.A. ; *Caught by the Turks*, by Capt. Francis Yeats-Brown ; *Adventures in Turkey and Russia*, by Capt. E. H. Keeling ; and *The Road to Endor*, by Lieut. E. H. Jones.

[2]Capt. Hogg reorganized the 2nd Field Troop into a mounted section and 3 sections with A.T. carts and greatly improved its mobility and efficiency.

wheeled A.T. cart, fitted with a lengthened axle and drawn by mules. The superstructure was loaded on to G.S. wagons. With 200 A.T. carts, 56 G.S. wagons and 900 animals, No. 2 Mobile Bridging Train, Bengal S. & M., occupied two miles of road on the march, but it was independant of river transport and could provide 500 yards of medium bridge.[1] In July, another Bridging Train (No. 3 of the Bombay S. & M.), a non-mobile unit under Captain E. B. Fox, R.E., arrived in Iraq, and after bridging the Euphrates at Kurmat Ali and the Tigris at Ali Gharbi, took charge of the Shaikh Saad bridge.[2] Thus Witts was free for mobile work up the Tigris against the enemy's right flank and rear, a fact which helped eventually to open the way to Baghdad.

In August, 1916, the 1st Company, Bengal S. & M., under Captain J. F. Gray, R.E., with Lieutenants H. A. Joly de Lotbinière, R.E., and W. J. Lyall, R.E. (I.A.) and Lieutenant S. T. H. Munsey, I.A.R.O., arrived at the front. Captain W. Cave-Browne, R.E., who had brought a company of Tehri-Garhwal Sappers to Iraq in May, took command of the 3rd Company, Bengal S. & M., at Sannaiyat on August 12th when Captain F. McC. Douie, R.E., went on leave. Douie was wounded on October 3rd, shortly after his return, and in November, on the abolition of the post of "Field Engineer," Major E. F. J. Hill, R.E., resumed command of the unit which he had led in France. Cave-Browne then became Adjutant to Lieut.-Colonel G. A. J. Leslie, R.E., the C.R.E. 7th (Meerut) Division. In October, Captain R. H. Dewing, R.E., left the 12th Company, Madras S. & M., which was then commanded by Captain S. Pemberton, R.E., with Lieutenants R. B. Woakes, J. A. Goepel and A. W. Thomas, I.A.R.O., as Company Officers.[4] Another Bombay Sapper and Miner unit arrived at Fallahiya on the Tigris front on November 14th. This was the 18th Company under Captain E. V. Binney, R.E., with Lieutenants H. W. Wagstaff, R.E., and J. G. Marshall and G. C. Minnitt, I.A.R.O. It had been working in Basra since June and had reached the front after an arduous march up-country. On December 19th it joined the 9th Brigade of the 5th Division facing the Turks in the Khudhaira (or Abdul Hassan) bend of the Tigris below Kut.[5]

The last Sapper reinforcements to reach the Tigris front in 1916 were the 4th Company, Bengal S. & M., from the Euphrates and the 15th (Burma) Company, Madras S. & M., under Captain C. W. Bushell, R.E., with Lieutenants J. A. Stewart and F. Marshall, R.E. The Burma company (less one section) had sailed from Rangoon on October 9th and joined the 12th and 13th Companies with the 14th Division at Es Sinn on December 11th.[6] Accordingly, when the offensive was resumed on the

[1]Notes by Brig. F. V. B. Witts, C.B.E., D.S.O., M.C., late R.E., sent to the author on Nov. 23rd, 1937.

[2]Notes by Lieut.-Col. E. B. Fox, R.E., sent to the author on Oct. 13th, 1937.

[3]Notes by Col. W. Cave-Browne, C.B.E., D.S.O., M.C., late R.E., sent to the author on June 22nd, 1937.

[4]Notes by Col. S. Pemberton, D.S.O., M.C., late R.E., sent to the author on Dec. 12th, 1937.

[5]*History of the 18th (Field) Company, 3rd Royal Bombay Sappers and Miners during the Great War*, 1914–18, p. 3.

[6]*Historical Record of the Q.V.O. Madras Sappers and Miners*, Vol. II, 1914–19, p. 12.

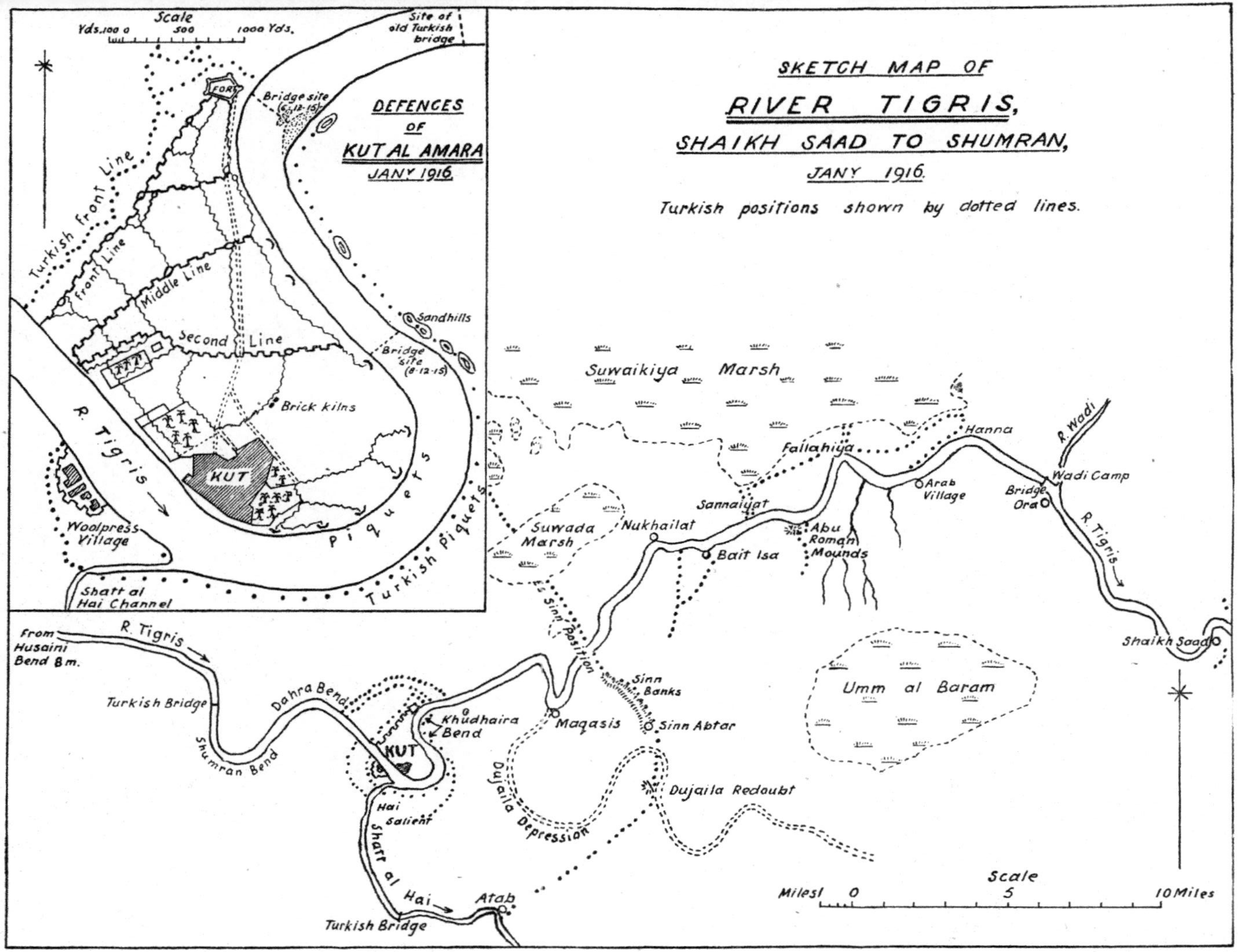
SKETCH MAP OF
RIVER TIGRIS,
SHAIKH SAAD TO SHUMRAN,
JANY 1916.
Turkish positions shown by dotted lines.
DEFENCES
OF
KUT AL AMARA
JANY 1916.
Scale
Yds.100 0
500
1000 Yds.
Site of old Turkish bridge
Bridge site (5.12.15)
FORT
Turkish front Line
Front Line
Middle Line
Second Line
Sandhills
Bridge site (8.12.15)
Brick kilns
KUT
R. Tigris
Woolpress Village
Piquets
Turkish piquets
Shatt al Hai Channel
Suwaikiya Marsh
Hanna
R. Wadi
Wadi Camp
Fallahiya
Arab Village
Bridge
Ora
Sannaiyat
Nukhailat
Suwada Marsh
Abu Roman Mounds
Bait Isa
R. Tigris
Shaikh Saad
Sinn Position
Sinn Banks
Sinn Abtar
Umm al Baram
From Husaini Bend Bm.
R. Tigris
Turkish Bridge
Dahra Bend
Khudhaira Bend
Maqasis
Shumran Bend
KUT
Hai Salient
Dujaila Depression
Dujaila Redoubt
Shatt al Hai
Atab
Turkish Bridge
Scale
Miles1 0
5
10 Miles

Tigris, General Maude had at his disposal the 1st, 3rd and 4th (Bengal) Companies, the 12th, 13th and 15th (Madras) Companies, the 18th, 20th and 21st (Bombay) Companies, the 2nd (Madras) Field Troop, the 1st and 3rd Bridging Trains of Bengal and Bombay Sappers respectively (non-mobile units), and the 2nd Mobile Bridging Train of Bengal Sappers —in all 9 Field Companies, a Field Troop and 3 Bridging Trains, forming a cadre of Indian engineer troops, in addition to R.E. units,[1] which was greatly superior to the 2 Field Companies with which Generals Lake and Aylmer had been obliged to begin the attempt to relieve Kut in January, 1916.

On December 12th, 1916, General Maude made his first advance towards Baghdad at the head of 50,000 men with 174 guns. The 3rd Corps, under Lieut.-General W. R. Marshall, seized a position astride the Hai Channel, and the 1st Corps, under Lieut.-General A. S. Cobbe, moved into the Khudhaira Bend below Kut. Then Maude used his Mobile Bridging Train in an attempt to make a surprise crossing of the Tigris some 15 miles upstream of Kut at the Husaini Bend above Shumran. He had kept the formation of No. 2 Bridging Train a close secret, the pontoons having been towed up to the advanced base and the special A.T. carts employed in carrying supplies. Also, the pontoons and their carts had been parked separately until operations started. A crossing was attempted on December 20th, 1916, by a column of all arms after some slight opposition on the right bank had been brushed aside. The Tigris at the Husaini Bend was 300 yards wide, with flat and bare banks, but a dry irrigation channel afforded a covered approach. Under heavy fire, Captain F. V. B. Witts, R.E., made a personal reconnaissance of the river bank and subsequently led a party of his men, carrying a pontoon, to the water's edge. The pontoon was launched in full view of the enemy and loaded with British troops. Then the Turks opened a heavy fire. Many of the British soldiers were killed and Witts himself was among the wounded. As it was evident that the enemy were on the alert and that a crossing in force was impossible, the attempt was abandoned and the column withdrew.[2] Had the operation succeeded it might have caused the enemy to evacuate both Sannaiyat and Kut. Its failure lulled the Turks into a false sense of security and thereby probably facilitated the successful crossing made, two months later, at Shumran.

At the end of 1916, General Maude was firmly established on the river bank opposite Kut from the Khudhaira Bend almost up to the entrance to the Hai Channel, and much of that channel was also in his possession. An eventful year had shown many things. The heroism and endurance of our soldiers, the parsimony of the Indian Government, the evils of dual control, the dire effects of political paramouncy in war, the futility of ignoring difficulties of transport and supply, and lastly, the impossibility of conducting military operations in a desert country without an adequate engineer

[1] 71st, 72nd and 88th Fd. Coys., R.E., and 7th Fd. Troop, R.E.

[2] *A Short History of the Corps of K.G.O. Bengal Sappers and Miners during the War*, 1914–18, p. 76, and notes by Brig. F. V. B. Witts, C.B.E., D.S.O., M.C., late R.E., sent to the author on Nov. 23rd, 1937.

establishment, suitably, or even lavishly, supplied. Two Royal Engineers, Lord Napier of Magdala and Lord Kitchener of Khartoum, had recognized this last point, and both had succeeded as commanders in desert warfare because they applied their knowledge and experience to good purpose. It seems that the lessons of 1867 and 1898 were disregarded in the planning and conduct of the campaign in Iraq until General Maude assumed control after the disaster at Kut.

CHAPTER XVIII

THE GREAT WAR: IRAQ AND IRAN, 1917–1918

AT the beginning of 1917, General Sir Stanley Maude could view with equanimity the strategical situation on the Tigris below Kut al Amara, where he was opposed by the Turkish 13th and 18th Corps under Halil Pasha. Yet political and military needs in other theatres of the war demanded early action, and so he determined to secure freedom of manœuvre by clearing the enemy from the Khudhaira Bend, the Hai Salient and the Dahra Bend positions on the right bank before attempting to force them from their left bank positions stretching for many miles from Sannaiyat to Shumran.[1] He was prepared to operate slowly and methodically, for he had been instructed to avoid heavy casualties and had clearly in mind the failure of his predecessors.

The Mesopotamia Expeditionary Force was now well supplied with Engineer and Pioneer units. On the Tigris front, with the Cavalry Division, were the 7th Field Troop, R.E., and the 2nd Field Troop, Madras S. & M.; with the 3rd Indian Division (1st Corps), the 18th, 20th and 21st Field Companies, Bombay S. & M., and the 34th Sikh Pioneers; with the 7th Indian Division (1st Corps), the 1st, 3rd and 4th Field Companies, Bengal S. & M., and the 121st Pioneers; with the 13th British Division (3rd Corps), the 71st, 72nd and 88th Field Companies, R.E., and the 8th (Welch) Pioneer Regiment;[2] and with the 14th Indian Division (3rd Corps), the 12th, 13th and 15th (Burma) Field Companies, Madras S. & M., and the 128th Pioneers. The Army Troops on the Tigris front included the 64th Pioneers, several Labour Corps, and Nos. 1 and 2 Bridging Trains, Bengal S. & M., No. 2 being a mobile unit attached to the 3rd Corps. The Tehri-Garhwal Sapper Company and No. 3 Bridging Train, Bombay S. & M., were at Shaikh Saad on the line of communication. Thus General Maude had at his disposal on the Tigris no less than 3 Field Companies and a Field Troop, R.E., 10 Field Companies, a Field Troop and 3 Bridging Trains of Indian Sappers and Miners, 4 battalions of British or Indian Pioneers and a number of subsidiary formations. On the Euphrates front, with the 15th Indian Division guarding his left flank, were the 3/1st and 1/3rd (Northumbrian) Field Companies, R.E., the Malerkotla Sapper Company and the 48th Pioneers.[3]

The first step was to capture the Turkish position in the Khudhaira (or Abdul Hassan) Bend below Kut which was a menace to our communi-

[1]See *Sketch Map of the River Tigris, Shaikh Saad to Shumran, Jan.*, 1916, included in Chapter XVII.

[2]The C.R.E., 13th British Division, was Lieut.-Col. E. C. Tylden-Pattenson, R.E., who had been Offg. Commandant, Bengal S. & M., at Roorkee, from June, 1915, to Nov., 1916.

[3]*The Campaign in Mesopotamia*, 1914–18 (Official History), by Brig.-Gen. F. J. Moberly, C.B., C.S.I., D.S.O., Vol. III, pp. 392–401.

cations because it enabled the enemy to flood parts of our trench system when the Tigris rose. The task was allotted to the 3rd Division, and the Sapper units engaged were the 20th Company, under Major S. Boyd, R.E., with the 8th Brigade on the right, and the 18th Company, under Captain E. V. Binney, R.E., with the 9th Brigade on the left near the river bank. An assault was launched across flat ground on January 9th, 1917, supported by intense artillery fire. Both brigades entered the Turkish front line, but the 8th Brigade was soon driven out by a powerful counter-attack, and half the 20th Company, which was under Major Boyd with the advanced troops, lost 2 British officers and 15 Indian ranks wounded. On the 9th Brigade front, two battalions repulsed a counter-attack and pushed straight on towards the Turkish second line, while the 18th Company dug a firing trench to protect the right flank exposed by the retirement of the 8th Brigade. Both brigades attacked the second line on January 11th and failed with such heavy loss that the Sappers and Pioneers had to act as infantry reserves during the following night. On the 12th, the 9th Brigade was relieved by the 7th Brigade, but the 18th Company was kept at the front to dig and wire trenches.[1] Thereafter, the work of pressing the Turks out of the Khudhaira Bend went on steadily, and a final assault against a position in some sandhills was made on January 19th. The enemy, however, had already evacuated the position and crossed the river; but at the very moment of success, Binney was seriously wounded by shrapnel.[2] and thus the 18th Company lost a popular and unassuming commander with unique knowledge of his men and of the Bombay Sappers in general. He was invalided to India, where he resumed work at Kirkee long before he was fit for duty, having been succeeded in command of the 18th Company by Captain H. W. Wagstaff, R.E. The casualties in the 3rd Division as a whole had amounted to 1,639 killed and wounded, and both Sapper companies had suffered severely.[3] Also, they had been worked to the point of complete exhaustion—their usual lot in trench warfare.

While the 1st Corps, under Lieut.-General A. S. Cobbe, was operating against the Khudhaira Bend, the 3rd Corps, under Lieut.-General W. R. Marshall, was preparing to attack the Hai Salient. The 13th British Division faced the eastern and southern faces of the salient, with the 14th Indian Division prolonging the line to the west beyond the Hai Channel. On January 25th, 1917, the 13th Division advanced astride the Hai to attack the Turkish positions and succeeded on the east bank though it failed on the west. On the following morning, the 14th Division assumed the offensive on the west bank, and by nightfall had made some progress. The 12th Company, Madras S. & M., under Major S. Pemberton, R.E., the 13th Company under Major W. D. B. Conran, R.E., and the 64th and 128th Pioneers had to supervise all the consolidation work and

[1] "Engineer Work in the Khairdari Bend," by Lieut.-Col. E. V. Binney, D.S.O., R.E., appearing in *The R.E. Journal*, Vol. LI, 1937, pp. 408–416.

[2] Capt. E. V. Binney had already been slightly wounded on Jan. 3rd, 1917.

[3] *History of the 18th (Field) Company, 3rd Royal Sappers and Miners during the Great War, 1914–1918*, p. 5.

occasionally to establish forward blocks with the assaulting troops. In one such venture, three small parties of the 13th Company under Lieutenants F. A. Adlard, J. Tate and A. A. Gardiner, I.A.R.O., lost Gardiner and 6 Indian ranks killed and Tate and 16 others wounded.[1] Some of the captured Turkish trenches were found to be full of naked British dead of the 13th Division, stripped by prowling Arabs during the night.[2]

Between January 27th and 30th, the 3rd Corps gained ground slowly along the Hai and, on February 1st, launched a general attack on both banks while the Cavalry Division co-operated on its left flank. Some progress was made, but two Sikh battalions of the 37th Brigade (14th Division) on the west bank were almost annihilated in repelling a fierce counter-attack, losing 1,032 out of 1,227 men. Hardly an officer survived, and a small party of the 13th Company in this sector lost a Jemadar killed and Lieutenant J. H. Johnston, I.A.R.O. wounded. The 13th Company was rapidly becoming crippled by its losses in British officers. However, the assault on the east bank gained its objective and General Marshall transferred the 13th Division to the west bank to help the 14th Division. On February 3rd, under a heavy artillery barrage, the 14th Division again assaulted the Turkish positions west of the Hai and by nightfall had made headway, though at heavy cost. Then, under cover of darkness, the enemy withdrew to the Dahra Bend, holding a line from Woolpress Village[3] opposite Kut westwards towards the southern end of the Shumran Bend. The 15th (Burma) Company, Madras S. & M., under Major C. W. Bushell, R.E., had a section under Lieutenant J. A. Stewart, I.A.R.O., operating with the 36th Brigade on February 3rd, and the Burma Sappers acquitted themselves well in establishing trench blocks behind the assaulting troops.[4]

Having suffered severe casualties in clearing the Khudhaira Bend and Hai Salient, General Maude decided to proceed cautiously in launching the 3rd Corps against the Dahra Bend positions. His plan was to demonstrate against the defenders of Woolpress Village while he assaulted the trench systems further west. His left flank was to be covered by the Corps cavalry, and the Cavalry Division was to move northwards towards the Shumran Bend to intercept any withdrawal to the enemy's bridge of boats, located beyond the apex of the bend. The 12th Company built a sandbagged observation tower within 950 yards of the Turkish front line and dug and wired trenches under fire. It suffered a number of casualties, including Lieutenant A. W. Thomas, I.A.R.O., who was killed on February 7th, and Lieutenant J. A. Goepel, I.A.R.O., who was among the wounded. The attack began on February 9th. Woolpress Village fell on the 10th, and by the 12th the enemy were hemmed into the Dahra Bend. Owing to the casualties already suffered, Sapper parties were no longer attached to the assaulting troops but employed in consolidating positions

[1] *Q.V.O. Madras Sappers and Miners in France and Iraq*, 1914–1920, p. 25.
[2] Notes by Lieut.-Col. W. D. B. Conran, D.S.O., R.E., sent to the author on Nov. 17th, 1937.
[3] Also known as the Liquorice Factory.
[4] Notes by Col. E. H. Clarke, M.C., late R.E., sent to the author on Nov. 10th, 1937.

when won. After a particularly severe struggle on February 12th, the 3rd Corps assaulted the main Turkish position on the 15th and completed the clearance of the Dahra Bend before dawn on the 16th.

General Maude was now able to make the final preparations for his *coup-de-main*—a crossing of the Tigris to sever the enemy's communications on the left bank. Tactically, he had complete freedom of manœuvre, but his ability to use that freedom was restricted because his supply ships could not steam past the Turkish positions far downstream. However, the enemy's attenuated line along the left bank from Shumran to Sannaiyat, though covered by the formidable obstacle of the Tigris, gave Maude the opportunity to mystify the Turks regarding the probable point of crossing.

On February 5th, after the occupation of the Hai Salient, Captain F. V. B. Witts, R.E., commanding No. 2 (Mobile) Bridging Train, Bengal S. & M., had been summoned to a private interview with General Maude and ordered to take soundings around the mouth of the Hai Channel for a crossing at Kut itself. Some motor lighters had arrived at Shaikh Saad from Gallipoli, and Maude intended that they should run the gauntlet of the enemy's positions below Kut, turn into the mouth of the Hai, pick up landing parties, and dash across the river. Witts was sworn to absolute secrecy and was to make his reports in private letters addressed to Maude by name. Even Brig.-General W. H. Beach, late R.E., an ex-Bengal Sapper who was head of the Intelligence Branch, was told nothing of the scheme, although Maude asked him several questions regarding the depth of water at the Hai entrance.[1] "Paddling about in a pontoon for two or three nights, with the Turks on one bank and our troops on the other, was no joke," writes Witts,[2] "and though the river was 400 to 600 yards wide. I was not sorry when I was in a position to report the scheme impracticable." It had been discovered also that the engine-power of the motor lighters was insufficient to enable them to reach the Hai entrance against the rapid current of the Tigris. These preliminary reconnaissances for a crossing at Kut were made while the Turks were still holding the Dahra Bend. No. 2 Bridging Train was close at hand, for it was engaged at the time in bridging the Hai. After the Dahra Bend had been cleared, Witts reconnoitred secretly for a bridge site at Shumran and selected the apex of the bend, but any idea of an immediate crossing had to be abandoned because of the weather, which was vile. Meanwhile, the enemy was encouraged to believe that Kut was still the probable spot, and preparations were made as if for building a pontoon bridge across the river near Woolpress Village. A hostile plane was allowed to observe an apparent withdrawal of our posts from Shumran and the towing of pontoons up the Hai. There was much dumping of timber near Woolpress Village and a forest of artillery observation towers arose.[3] At the Shumran Bend, the

[1] *The Campaign in Mesopotamia*, 1914–18 (Official History), by Brig.-Gen. F. J. Moberly, C.B., C.S.I., D.S.O., Vol. III, p. 129, footnote.

[2] "Light Floating Bridges in Mesopotamia," by Maj. F. V. B. Witts, C.B.E., D.S.O., M.C., R.E., appearing in *The R.E. Journal*, Vol. XXXVII, March–Dec., 1923, pp. 627–639.

[3] *The Long Road to Baghdad*, by Edmund Candler, Vol. II, p. 51.

enemy was made accustomed to the creaking of unoiled wheels after dark and ceased to pay particular attention to it.

The Shumran Crossing was a carefully planned and boldly executed operation which deserves a prominent place in military history. The crossing was to be accomplished by the 3rd Corps, while the 1st Corps pinned the enemy down at Sannaiyat and guarded the river line, and the Cavalry Division screened the movements on the right bank. The preparatory operations opened badly, for when the 7th Division assaulted the Sannaiyat position on February 17th, heavy rain and furious resistance brought about a costly failure. The rain lasted until the 21st, but nevertheless, preparations for a crossing in force at the apex of the Shumran Bend continued steadily. This site had been selected because it could be covered effectively by fire from the right bank, and because the river was estimated to be not more than 340 yards wide and had a shelving beach on the Turkish side. The 1st Corps now began to display abnormal activity downstream, and on February 22nd the 7th Division again attacked at Sannaiyat and entered the enemy's second line.

During the ensuing night, the 3rd Division made a small raid across the river at Maqasis, near the Es Sinn position below Kut. This was a gallant affair which helped to mislead the enemy. A company of the 27th Punjabis under Captain C. R. S. Pitman embarked in 11 pontoons, 6 rowed by men of the 21st Company, Bombay S. & M., and 5 by men of the 34th Sikh Pioneers, the arrangements being in the charge of Captain K. E. L. Pennell, R.E. (S.R.) of the 21st Company. The river was 700 yards wide, and the current up to 5 knots, but the pontoons rowed by the Sappers got across, though the others were swept downstream.[1] The raiding party cleared a small work and returned an hour later, its retirement being assisted and covered by the 18th Company.[2] The raid succeeded in its object, which was to attract the enemy's reserves to the wrong place. Indeed, according to the Turkish historian, Muhammad Amin, the attack at Sannaiyat and the raid at Maqasis caused the despatch downstream of all available troops from Shumran and Kut.[3] During the same night the 13th British Division made a feint at crossing opposite Kut, and this helped also to denude the Shumran peninsula of enemy forces.

All was now ready for the great attempt in the Shumran Bend. Gun positions had been selected, and the troops practised in handling pontoons. The 14th Indian Division, under Major-General R. G. Egerton, was to cross the river by a pontoon bridge after covering detachments had been ferried to the left bank and had occupied a position across the bend. Downstream of the bridge site, at intervals of some 500 yards, three ferries were to be operated, each for one battalion of infantry. Ferrying and bridging were to be distinct operations, the former under Major S. Pemberton, R.E., of the 12th Company, Madras S. & M., and the latter under

[1]Notes by Col. M. Everett, D.S.O., late R.E., sent to the author on Jan. 15th, 1937.

[2]*History of the 18th (Field) Company, 3rd Royal Sappers and Miners during the Great War*, 1914–1918, p. 6.

[3]*Baghdad, and the Story of its Last Fall*, by Capt. Muhammad Amin, Turkish General Staff.

Captain F. V. B. Witts, R.E., of No. 2 (Mobile) Bridging Train, Bengal S. & M. During the night of February 22nd/23rd, the Bridging Train, escorted by a company of Welch Pioneers, marched towards the bridge site and parked about a mile from the right bank. The Welch Pioneers then moved forward, and at about 4 a.m., working as silently as possible, began to dig ramps through the high bank for launching the pontoons and also two motor-boats provided for laying anchors in the flooded river. The 71st Field Company, R.E., under Captain W. H. Roberts, R.E., also moved up to the launching site to complete the preparations for the Bridging Train. Three battalions of the 37th Brigade—the 2nd Norfolks, 1/2nd Gurkhas and 2/9th Gurkhas—were detailed to make the initial crossing by the ferries. Thirteen bi-partite pontoons, of British pattern, made of wood covered with canvas, were allotted to each ferry, each pontoon to have a crew of five and to carry ten armed men or a load of stores and equipment. An additional pontoon, manned by the 14th Divisional Signal Company, was provided for laying signal cable. A total of 735 rowers was needed for the ferrying pontoons, to give three reliefs and a reserve, and 100 rowers at each ferry were detailed to off-load the pontoons. The routes to the ferries, each about 5 miles long, were marked with small heaps of earth. Every man, party and pontoon was numbered, and every man knew his exact duties. Absolute silence was to be maintained on the march. Wheel axles were smothered in grease, and wooden plugs were carried for stopping bullet holes.

The ferrying columns set out after sunset on February 22nd, each preceded by a company of 128th Pioneers to improve the track. No. 1 Column, with Lieutenant J. Tate, I.A.R.O., 13th Company, Madras S. & M., as "Beachmaster," was composed of the 2nd Norfolk Regiment, with 100 men of that unit as rowers and off-loaders, together with a further 100 volunteers from the 71st, 72nd and 88th Field Companies, R.E., and 75 men of the 128th Pioneers as additional or reserve rowers. No. 2 Column, with Lieutenant R. B. Woakes, I.A.R.O., 12th Company, Madras S. & M., as Beachmaster, included the 2/9th Gurkha Rifles, with 100 men of the 12th Company as rowers and off-loaders, and 100 men of the 1/4th Hampshire Regiment and 30 men of the 15th (Burma) Sapper Company as reserve rowers. No. 3 Column, with Lieutenant F. A. Eustace, R.E., of the 13th Company, Madras S. & M., as Beachmaster, included the 1/2nd Gurkha Rifles, with 100 men of the 13th Company, as rowers and off-loaders, and 130 men of the 1/4th Hampshire Regiment as reserve rowers. The three columns halted some distance from the river, and the pontoons for ferrying were carried to the bank. At 1 a.m. all was quiet and the men lay down to rest. In their loopholed trenches on the far bank, the Turkish sentries dozed over their rifles.

The crossing by ferry began before dawn on February 23rd, 1917. By 5.30 a.m. all the pontoons were in the water, and soon the leading crews were rowing across, still undetected by the enemy. Then the storm broke. At No. 1 Ferry, furthest upstream, the Norfolks encountered little resistance and occupied a line some 300 yards inland on the left bank. At

THE SHUMRAN CROSSING, RIVER TIGRIS, FEBRUARY 23RD, 1917.

the other two ferries, however, the fighting was bitter. When the leading pontoons of No. 2 Ferry were in mid-stream, the Turks opened an intense enfilade fire. Only ten pontoons reached the left bank: the other three drifted downstream, full of dead or dying. About 100 men of the 2/9th Gurkhas, under Major G. C. Wheeler,[1] landed and penetrated 150 yards inland. The ten pontoons started to return, but only six got back to reload and attempt another crossing. Of these, five reached the left bank again at 7 a.m. and disembarked a few more men, but owing to heavy casualties among the rowers, none was able to return, and at 8.30 a.m., after three derelict pontoons had been recovered and sent across, it was decided to close No. 2 Ferry and embark the remainder of the 2/9th Gurkhas at No. 1 Ferry. Two more pontoons made the deadly crossing and then all traffic ceased.

At No. 3 Ferry, further downstream, the Hampshire Regiment rowers[2] suffered even more heavily than those of the 12th and 15th Companies and Hampshires at No. 2 Ferry. Although all thirteen pontoons reached the left bank, the casualties among the rowers in the first passage were so heavy that only two pontoons were able to return to the right bank, whence, with 13th Company rowers, they started on a second trip together with two derelict pontoons from No. 2 Ferry. The four pontoons made for the left bank under a hail of fire, but only one reached it, and that contained only one unwounded man. One pontoon sank almost immediately and the other two went to the bottom in midstream, riddled with bullets. All attempts to retrieve the twelve surviving pontoons from the left bank failed because most of the rowers were dead or wounded. Of the 140 Gurkha infantry ferried across the river, only 56 remained to hold a precarious footing on the bank. Gallantry of the highest order was shown by the rowers, as may be gathered from a description given by Captain E. J. Ross, 8th Gurkha Rifles, a Staff Officer at the site.[3] Ross watched a pontoon, manned by only two 13th Company Sapper rowers, which put out from the far bank under devastating fire in a forlorn attempt to make the return journey. About twenty yards from the shore, one of the rowers was hit, and his oar drifted away. The other began sculling with one oar. It was soon broken by machine-gun bullets, so he threw it away, tied a breast-line round his waist, and, diving overboard, tried to tow the pontoon by swimming. For several minutes his head was visible amid the bullet splashes as he struggled against the current. Then it vanished, and the pontoon drifted away with its load of dead, towing behind it the corpse of the brave but unknown swimmer.

At 10 a.m. it was decided to close No. 3 Ferry and to send the remainder of the 1/2nd Gurkhas across by No. 1 Ferry, where additional volunteer rowers from the 13th British Division were available. The net result of the ferrying operations organized by Major Pemberton was complete

[1]Maj. G. C. Wheeler, 2/9th Gurkha Rifles, was awarded the Victoria Cross.

[2]It seems that the Hampshires, detailed as reserve rowers, had replaced the 13th Company rowers for the first passage.

[3]Notes by Lieut.-Col. A. V. Anderson, M.B.E., R.E., sent to the author on Dec. 30th, 1937.

success at No. 1 Ferry and almost complete failure at Nos. 2 and 3 Ferries. Nevertheless, the success at No. 1 Ferry was sufficient to enable bridging to be put in hand, and that was the main object of the undertaking. Major W. D. B. Conran, R.E., and Lieutenant F. A. Adlard, I.A.R.O., of the 13th Company, were wounded during the operations, and Lieutenant G. W. Maunsell, I.A.R.O., of the 12th Company, was killed. Conran was invalided to India, and on February 28th Major P. E. Prince, R.E., took command of the 13th Company.

We turn now to the bridging operations. As already related, No. 2 (Mobile) Bridging Train, under Captain F. V. B. Witts, R.E., with Lieutenant A. Eastmond, I.A.R.O., was parked in the early hours of the morning about a mile from the right bank at Shumran. The bi-partite pontoons were on 200 A.T. carts, the trestles and superstructure on 56 G.S. wagons, and two motor boats were cradled on bullock-drawn pontoon wagons. Before dawn the 71st Field Company, R.E., and 1½ companies of Welch Pioneers did the necessary preliminary work on the river bank. At 6.30 a.m., Witts moved most of his men to the bank, and an hour later he received orders from General Egerton that, as the crossings at Nos. 2 and 3 Ferries had come to a standstill and it was necessary to give moral support to the small covering parties holding out on the left bank, the construction of a bridge should be undertaken forthwith although the bank immediately opposite the bridge site was still in enemy hands. The Norfolk covering party at No. 1 Ferry site had not yet had time to spread upstream to the bridge site and consequently Witts suggested a short postponement, but he was told to proceed with the work at once because of the desperate situation at Nos. 2 and 3 Ferries, of which he was unaware as the sites were some distance downstream.[1] The carts and wagons carrying the bridging material came up at a gallop at 300 yards intervals and unloaded and galloped off practically without loss, for the Turkish gunners were concentrating their fire on a dry irrigation channel which they thought would be the line of approach. By 8.30 a.m. the shore transom was in position and the land anchorage fixed, but attempts to lay anchors by rowing pontoons against the rapid current failed. Accordingly, the two motor boats, the smallest available on the Tigris, were ordered up. Slowly they lumbered forward, each drawn by twelve bullocks and towering eleven feet in the air on its swaying wagon. If they were hit, no anchors could be laid, no bridge built, the 14th Division could not cross in time to secure the left bank against reinforcing Turkish troops, and General Maude's plan would fail. Fortune favoured us, for the motor boats arrived undamaged. Such are the chances of war. The first boat was launched successfully by the 71st Company, R.E., though the unit suffered some casualties from rifle fire. The second followed and anchor laying proceeded at high speed; and by 11.30 a.m., when the Norfolks had cleared the far bank, bridge construction was continuing almost unmolested.

The bridge was made by "forming-up," the rate of construction being

[1]Notes by Brig. F. V. B. Witts, C.B.E., D.S.O., M.C., late R.E., sent to the author on Nov. 23rd, 1937.

governed by the time required to lay each anchor. No downstream anchors were used, for, with a rapid current and a moderate wind, there was little danger of the bridge sailing bodily upstream, as had happened on one occasion to a bridge built by Captain E. W. C. Sandes, R.E., in 1915. Every second pontoon had a 1 cwt. anchor, with a ½-cwt. kedge anchor at the end of 400 feet of rope, and consequently no anchors dragged perceptibly. Luckily the structure was never damaged by shell fire or floating mines. Work continued at high pressure, and at 4.30 p.m., a 295-yards' bridge was ready for traffic. It had been built in 8 hours—a performance which brought a congratulatory message from the Army Commander in which he remarked that to cross a river in flood in the face of an enemy in position was a feat of which the troops might be very proud. By midnight on February 23rd/24th, the entire 14th Division had crossed, and the 13th Division was approaching the right bank bridgehead. The operation had entailed only 350 casualties, of which 200 were among the rowers at the ferries.[1] The 12th, 13th, and 15th Companies, Madras S. & M., lost only 21, 27 and 5 men respectively. Many decorations were awarded for the crossing which was the most spectacular operation of the war in Iraq.

While a crossing was being forced at Shumran, the 7th Division of the 1st Corps attacked at Sannaiyat and took the third and fourth lines of Turkish trenches. At dawn on the 24th it occupied the fifth line, and was preparing to advance to the sixth when air reconnaissance showed that the enemy was in full retreat. The 1st, 3rd and 4th Companies, Bengal S. & M., were engaged in these operations. General Maude now ordered the 1st Corps to press on, and the Cavalry Division to cross at Shumran, pass through the 3rd Corps on the left bank, and pursue the Turks towards Baghdad. The 1st Corps swept rapidly through the Nukhailat and Es Sinn positions downstream, but the Cavalry Division was not so successful. The enemy clung grimly to an entrenched position stretching across the neck of the Shumran peninsula and the cavalry could not get through in pursuit until the afternoon. Then they became involved in a dismounted action and retired later to the Shumran Bend, where the 3rd Corps was still fighting in the area in which so many Kut prisoners had died after the surrender in April, 1916.[2] The Turkish rearguard, having fulfilled its purpose, withdrew during the ensuing night and the 3rd Corps advanced upstream. The pursuit made good progress during February 25th and 26th, especially after our Naval Flotilla had shelled the enemy at close range on the 26th and converted the retreat of the Turkish 18th Corps into a rout. On the 27th, when the Cavalry Division had reached Aziziya, General Maude broke off the pursuit to reorganize his line of communications, as advised by Major-General G. F. MacMunn, his Inspector-

[1]The Hampshires alone lost 98 rowers.

[2]*In Kut and Captivity*, pp. 269–271, and *Tales of Turkey*, pp. 13–14, both by the present author.

[3]H.M. Gunboats *Tarantula*, *Mantis*, *Moth*, *Gadfly* and *Butterfly* under Capt. W. Nunn, R.N. The flotilla afterwards recaptured H.M. Gunboat *Firefly* taken by the enemy at Umm at Tabul on Dec. 1st, 1915, during the retreat from Ctesiphon.

General of Communications. The 2nd Field Troop, Madras S. & M., was busily employed during the cavalry advance, working in close co-operation with the 7th Field Troop, R.E.[1] The 3rd Corps halted between Bughaila and Aziziya,[2] with the 1st Corps further downstream, and the Sapper and Miner units improved roads, arranged water supplies and salvaged abandoned Turkish material.

Political opinion, both in London and Delhi, was now strongly in favour of an immediate attempt to capture Baghdad, and on March 2nd General Maude was given permission to exploit his success to the full extent, consistent with the security of his force and the capacity of his communications. He was told that the strength of the British and Russian forces, which, it was hoped, would soon be operating in Iraq, should enable him to occupy and hold Baghdad with 4 infantry divisions and a cavalry division, provided that he could maintain them in the Baghdad area, and a subsequent exchange of views resulted in definite permission being given to him to occupy Baghdad. Accordingly, on March 5th, after the 3rd Corps, Cavalry Division and Naval Flotilla had been concentrated at Aziziya, he advanced to Lajj. Strong opposition was expected on the line of the Diyala River, where the remnants of the Turkish 18th Corps were entrenched on a front of about 13 miles. The 3rd Corps was ordered to force a crossing of the Diyala, while the Tigris was bridged at Bawi, 10 miles below the mouth of the Diyala, in order that the 1st Corps and Cavalry Division might advance up the right bank on Baghdad.

There was bitter fighting on the Diyala. On the afternoon of March 7th, 1917, the advanced guard of the 3rd Corps, consisting of the 38th Brigade (13th Division), under Brigadier-General J. M. O'Dowda, with other troops including the 71st and 72nd Companies, R.E., the 8th (Welch) Pioneers and a detachment of No. 2 (Mobile) Bridging Train, Bengal S. & M., under Lieutenant A. Eastmond, I.A.R.O., was a few miles south-east of Diyala Village. The 35th Brigade (14th Division), under Brigadier-General W. M. Thomson, with other troops including the 12th Company, Madras S. & M., was preparing to cross the Tigris at Bawi by ferry to advance up the right bank to support the passage of the Diyala by the 38th Brigade. The first attempt to cross the Diyala failed on the night of March 7th/8th. The river was 120 yards wide, with banks 20 feet high, and the crossing was attempted in a few pontoons. These were carried down to the water's edge in bright moonlight, but when three had been launched and manned, all the occupants were killed or wounded by heavy fire and the pontoons were swept downstream. Preparations were then made for a second attempt, and meanwhile a mobile column, under Brig.-General O. G. Gunning, including the 15th (Burma) Company, Madras S. & M., reconnoitred some 7 miles northwards for a crossing higher up the river. The second attempt was made upstream of Diyala Village on the night of March 8th/9th. Three pontoons were lost, but 100 men of the Loyal North Lancashire Regiment were landed on the far bank, where they beat off

[1]Notes by Col. D. McA. Hogg, M.C., late R.E., sent to the author on May 18th, 1939.
[2]See *Sketch Map of Lower Iraq*, 1914–16, included in Chapter XVII.

all counter-attacks and held their precarious position until relieved.[1] On the 9th, General Marshall (G.O.C., 3rd Corps) heard of possible enemy counter-measures from the north, and pushing out a brigade group, including the 13th Company, Madras S. & M., as a right flank guard, withdrew Gunning's column behind it. Assisted by the threat of the 1st Corps and Cavalry Division operating on the right bank of the Tigris, the crossing of the Diyala was finally completed by the 13th British Division by 2.30 p.m. on March 10th, first by ferrying and then over a pontoon bridge built by thedetachment of No. 2 (Mobile) Bridging Train assisted by the 88th Field Company, R.E. The Bengal Sappers have reason to be proud of the exploits of their small detachment on the Diyala.

Meanwhile, the Tigris had been bridged at Bawi on March 8th by No. 1 Bridging Train, Bengal S. & M., under Lieutenant J. M. S. Trelawny, I.A.R.O., which had been towed up from Sannaiyat. This enabled the Cavalry Division, the 7th Division of the 1st Corps under Major-General V. B. Fane and part of the 3rd Division under Major-General H. D'U. Keary to cross the river and operate on the right bank. No. 2 Field Troop, Madras S. & M., was with the cavalry, and the 1st, 3rd and 4th Companies, Bengal S. & M., with the 7th Division. The 18th and 21st Companies, Bombay S. & M., accompanied the 3rd Division.[2] The 12th Company, Madras S. & M., was ahead with Thomson's brigade which had already crossed by ferry. The Cavalry Division failed to outflank the enemy's right on the right bank, and the 7th Division was held up; but on the night of the 9th/10th, while the 13th Division was forcing the crossing of the Diyala, the Turks withdrew to their main position on the right bank, which the 7th Division attacked on the 10th. Finally, during the night of March 10/11th, the enemy gave up the struggle against vastly superior numbers, and withdrawing from all their positions covering Baghdad, retreated northwards. On March 11th, 1917, General Maude's victorious army occupied Baghdad, the first Sapper and Miner unit to enter the city being the 12th Company. The goal which British policy had so long sought to reach had been attained at last, and the defeats of 1915 and 1916 avenged.

The Turkish bridge of boats in Baghdad had been cut by the enemy before evacuating the city, and consequently the most urgent Sapper work after the occupation was to bridge the Tigris. Accordingly, the pontoon bridge at Bawi was dismantled, towed upstream, and re-erected by No. 1 Bridging Train at the Turkish bridge site, where the river was narrow. Meanwhile, No. 2 (Mobile) Bridging Train was moving up from Shumran and, on arrival at Baghdad, bridged the river below the city. These bridges were replaced later by structures known as the North and South Bridges. The South Bridge sank during construction, and afterwards was completely destroyed in a gale; and the Maude Bridge, which replaced it in 1923, met a similar fate.[3] The North Bridge was made of large, open, iron pontoons

[1]Their commander, Capt. O. A. Reid, was awarded the Victoria Cross.

[2]The 20th Company was on the line of communication downstream.

[3]"Light Floating Bridges in Mesopotamia," by Maj. F. V. B. Witts, C.B.E., D.S.O., M.C., R.E., appearing in *The R.E. Journal*, Vol. XXXVII, March–Dec., 1923, pp. 627–637.

sent from India, and the South Bridge of dredger pontoons from the Kurmat Ali bridge above Basra. The South Bridge was built by the Tehri-Garhwal Sapper Company, of which Captain J. R. Davidson, R.E., was the Special Service Officer. This unit had reached Baghdad on April 9th, 1917, after maintaining four bridges over the Hai Channel during the advance from Shumran.[1]

The military situation at Baghdad demanded that General Maude should strike in several directions; westward to the Euphrates, northward up both banks of the Tigris, and north-eastwards towards Khaniqin to co-operate with the Russians in Iran under General Baratoff. He had also to solve urgent problems of supply and transport, to control the civil population, and to protect the Baghdad area from inundations which the Turks could arrange by cutting the banks of the Tigris and Euphrates. The Turkish 18th Corps was on the Tigris north of Baghdad, and the 13th Corps on the Diyala towards the Iran frontier, and Maude proposed to keep them apart while, in conjunction with the Russians, he defeated the 13th Corps. On March 14th, 1917, the 7th Division under General Fane drove the enemyfrom a strong position at Mushahida between the Baghdad-Samarra Railway and the Tigris, north of Baghdad,[2] the 1st, 3rd and 4th Companies, Bengal S. & M., being present on this occasion. Then, between March 18th and 20th, a column which included the 21st Company of the Bombay Corps advanced westwards and occupied Falluja on the Euphrates. Meanwhile, operations were in progress up the Diyala, and a column including the 20th Company and a detachment of No. 2 (Mobile) Bridging Train occupied Baquba on the 18th. The Diyala was bridged, and on the 20th, a mixed force under Major-General Keary, including the 18th and 20th Companies, began to advance from Baquba towards Shahraban *en route* for Khaniqin. The Turks were found to be holding a rearguard position covering Shahraban and commanding the Mahrut Canal, a rapid waterway about 15 yards broad. No pontoons being available at first, the 20th Company bridged the canal with materials taken from mud huts. However, on the 23rd, the company completed a trestle bridge, and this, with two pontoon bridges provided by the 18th Company, enabled the advance of General Keary's column to be resumed. Captain M. Rawlence, R.E., now rejoined from sick leave and took command of the 20th Company, while the 18th Company was commanded by Captain H. W. Wagstaff, R.E.

The enemy withdrew to a position in the Jabal Hamrin, a range of rocky hills running north-westwards to the Fat-ha Gorge, where the Tigris breaks through the range some 20 miles below the confluence of the Little (or Lesser) Zab. The position was covered by the Balad Ruz and Haruniya Canals, both of which had high banks. The canals were bridged by the Bombay Sapper companies on March 24th, but, after the failure of Keary's attack on the 25th, it became necessary to construct another bridge over

[1] *A Short History of the Services rendered by the Imperial Service Troops during the Great War*, 1914–18, by Maj.-Gen. Sir Harry Watson, K.B.E., C.B., C.M.G., C.I.E., M.V.O., p. 65.

[2] See *Sketch Map of Upper Iraq and N.W. Iran*, 1918, included in this chapter.

the Balad Ruz and to breach the Haruniya Canal to enable it to be forded by our retreating troops. It was fortunate that the 20th Company was able to build the bridge in time to meet the emergency. "The retreat was led by a battery at full gallop," writes Rawlence,[1] "and it was lucky that they failed to see the direction-board to our new bridge. There was a right-angled turn on to the old bridge, and the first gun failed to negotiate it and arrived in the stern of the nearest pontoon. The drivers and horses swam ashore, but we had to retrieve both gun and pontoon from 14 feet of water running at 3 knots. When we returned the gun we got a formal receipt, together with a complaint that the dial sight had been carelessly damaged!" Until the 29th, the two Sapper companies were engaged constantly in shifting bridges to meet the requirements of a changing situation.[2] Then the Turks, threatened in rear by Baratoff's Cossacks from Khaniqin, retired across the Diyala, and Keary advanced and met some Russian cavalry at Qizil Ribat. On April 4th, having fulfilled his mission, he withdrew his main body from Shahraban and marched down the Diyala to Baghdad.

During General Maude's final thrust towards Baghdad, a Russian army in the Caucasus had tried to co-operate by moving southwards on Mosul while Baratoff's men approached through the snowy passes of Iran, and it seemed that, although the Russian revolution had begun, a junction of the allied forces might be effected in strength. By the middle of March 1917, when the British had reached Baquba, Baratoff was nearing Kermanshah with 21,000 men and, on the 18th, had passed Karind. Then he was checked and held in the Pai Taq Pass by the Turkish 13th Corps. However, the Turks soon retired westwards towards Kifri, and after Keary had met the Russians at Qizil Ribat it appeared that our allies in the Caucasus and Iran should be able to deal with the 13th Corps while we defeated the 18th Corps on the Tigris. But Russia was in a chaotic state and her troops exhausted. After Maude had started operations against the 18th Corps, he was told that the Russians would not advance on Mosul, nor debouch from Iran into Iraq, and consequently he was left with the entire responsibility for the security of Iraq from Baghdad to the Persian Gulf at a time when rumours were already afloat that the Turks were contemplating the recapture of the country by forces made available through the failure of the Gallipoli campaign and the apparent stalemate in Palestine. The general situation demanded caution, and Maude's strategy during the spring of 1917 was governed by this attitude.

After dealing with the Turkish 13th Corps on the Diyala, Maude planned to hold off that Corps while he pushed up both banks of the Tigris against the 18th Corps, for he was anxious to gain possession of the Baghdad-Samarra Railway and to occupy Samarra. Part of the 7th Division (1st Corps) defeated the enemy at Balad on April 8th, 1917, but on the following

[1]Notes by Maj. M. Rawlence, R.E., sent to the author on March 3rd, 1938.

[2]*History of the 18th (Field) Company, 3rd Royal Sappers and Miners during the Great War, 1914–1918*, p. 7, and *History of the 20th (Field) Company, Royal Bombay Sappers and Miners*, by Maj. H. W. R. Hamilton, D.S.O., M.C., R.E., p. 39.

day the 13th Corps began to threaten trouble on the Diyala and Maude felt bound to strike it another blow. This was effected by detachments from the 13th and 14th Divisions, and by the 6th Cavalry Brigade to which the 2nd Field Troop, Madras S. & M., was attached, and the 13th Corps withdrew again into the Jabal Hamrin. A defensive position was then constructed on the Baghdad-Samarra Railway near Balad and a site selected for a bridge across the Tigris at Sinija, the 1st, 3rd and 4th Companies, Bengal S. & M., being concerned in these projects. The 3rd Corps, under General Marshall, advanced up the Tigris, and, by a well planned operation on April 18th, a crossing of the Shatt al Adhaim tributary on the left bank was forced by the infantry while the cavalry turned the Turkish retreat into a rout. No. 2 (Mobile) Bridging Train, Bengal S. & M., then threw a 275 yards' pontoon bridge across the river at Sinija.

It was now the turn of the 1st Corps, under General Cobbe, on the right bank. On April 21st and 22nd, part of this Corps encountered stubborn opposition near Istabulat, where the enemy was strongly entrenched; but at the cost of 2,228 casualties, Cobbe forced the enemy to withdraw and occupied Samarra on April 24th. No. 2 Bridging Train dismantled the Sinija bridge and re-erected it at Samarra, which was a key position in the Baghdad scheme of defence. The Samarra bridge was 500 yards in length—the longest in Iraq—and during the summer floods it had to be dismantled and replaced by a flying bridge and a steamer ferry.[1] On leaving Samarra, the Turks had tried to render their railway locomotives useless by blowing off all the cylinders on one side of the line, but fortunately they omitted to notice that some locomotives were facing up the line and others down. Consequently, it was easy for our railway engineers to make a number of locomotives serviceable by transferring undamaged cylinders.

While the 1st Corps was advancing to Samarra, the Turkish 13th Corps had shifted to the Shatt al Adhaim, and when the Turks moved down towards the left bank of the Tigris, the 3rd Corps resumed the offensive. On April 30th, detachments from the 13th and 14th Divisions attacked the enemy's main position astride the Adhaim, 6 miles south of Band-i-Adhaim, and with sufficient success to force the 13th Corps to withdraw to the Jabal Hamrin and thus lose touch with the 18th Corps on the Tigris. There is nothing of importance to record regarding the work of the Sappers and Miners in these operations. They prepared positions, bridged rivers, laid out camps, made roads, arranged water supplies and fought floods, but they rarely came under fire because it was recognized that to employ technical troops in the front line, except in an emergency, was the height of folly.

Now firmly established on a line from the Adhaim through Samarra to Falluja on the Euphrates, General Maude called a halt and proceeded to consolidate his gains. His troops were tired and the heat was becoming

[1] "Light Floating Bridges in Mesopotamia," by Maj. F. V. B. Witts, C.B.E., D.S.O., M.C., R.E., appearing in *The R.E. Journal*, Vol. XXXVII, March–Dec., 1923, pp. 627–637.

intense. However, when the situation deteriorated in the early summer owing to the withdrawal of the Russians in Iran, he began to prepare a defensive line from Sindiya on the Tigris to Baquba on the Diyala to cover the northern approaches to Baghdad. The three Madras Sapper companies with the 14th Division were employed at Baquba on work in connection with this scheme, the 12th and 13th Companies chiefly on defences and communications, and the 15th (Burma) Company, under Captain E. H. Clarke, R.E., on building two bridges of Arab boats across the Diyala.[1] Mobile bridging sections were formed in each company and supplied with Weldon trestles and superstructure for a 45-feet bridge.[2] On May 8th the 9th Company, Madras S. & M., under Captain J. C. Pringle, R.E., arrived in Iraq and joined the 15th Division under Major-General H. T. Brooking on the Euphrates, where it improved the defences of Nasiriya and maintained the bridge of boats. During August and September, the Bengal Sapper companies laboured on the defences at Samarra and the Bombay companies on those at Istabulat. The 2nd Sirmur Sapper Company, under Captain P. N. G. Geary, R.E., arrived in Baghdad in October, 1917 and was employed on road and railway construction.[3] At this time General Marshall, having taken Shahraban in August, was preparing to drive the Turkish 13th Corps from the southern end of Jabal Hamrin. The operation succeeded, and he occupied Qizil Ribat and the part of the Jabal Hamrin lying east of the Diyala. The 12th and 13th Companies of the Madras Corps, and a detachment of No. 1 Bridging Train, Bengal S. & M., marched with the 14th Division and bridged many canals.

Meanwhile, there had been fighting on the Euphrates, where a detachment of the 1st Corps had occupied the stretch from Falluja southwards to Hindiya. In July, 1917, half the 21st Company, Bombay S. & M., was engaged in an unsuccessful attempt by Colonel C. L. Haldane to capture Ramadi. The attempt was renewed in September by General Brooking with a strong force including the same half-company and the 2nd Field Troop, Madras S. & M., which accompanied the 6th Cavalry Brigade. In preparation for this operation a second bridge had been built at Falluja by a detachment from No. 1 Bridging Train, Bengal S. & M. The infantry attacked up the right bank of the Euphrates on September 28th while the cavalry got astride the enemy's line of retreat, and with the surrender of the Turks and the occupation of Ramadi, any immediate danger to Baghdad from the west was removed. General Maude was now able to resume his offensive on the Tigris with complete confidence, for it was obvious that General Allenby's operations in Palestine were distracting the enemy's attention from Iraq.

Maude planned first to clear the Jabal Hamrin with the 3rd Corps

[1]Notes by Col. E. H. Clarke, M.C., late R.E., sent to the author on Nov. 10th, 1937.

[2]*Q.V.O. Madras Sappers and Miners in France and Iraq*, 1914–1920, p. 37.

[3]*A Short History of the Services rendered by the Imperial Service Troops during the Great War*, 1914–18, by Maj.-Gen. Sir Harry Watson, K.B.E., C.B., C.M.G., C.I.E., M.V.O., p. 61. The 2nd Sirmur Sapper Company was raised in the Sirmur State in 1916 by Col. R. K. Bir Bikram Singh and reached Iraq on July 25th, 1917. It was in replacement of the original unit lost at Kut.

under General Marshall in order to screen his right flank, and it was decided that Marshall should drive the enemy from Delli Abbas and then hold them in front while he attacked their left flank. This he did on October 20th, 1917, with decisive results, the Sapper units present being half the 15th Company and a detachment of No. 1 Bridging Train. On November 2nd, the 7th and Cavalry Divisions surprised and destroyed an advanced enemy detachment at Daur below Tikrit. On this occasion, the 4th Company, Bengal S. & M., under Major A. J. G. Bird, R.E., operated with the 21st Brigade commanded by Brig.-General G. A. J. Leslie, late R.E., an ex-Bombay Sapper who had been C.R.E., 1st Indian Cavalry Division, in France.[1] The enemy withdrew to Tikrit, which the 7th Division captured with considerable loss on November 5th before returning to Samarra. It is sad to record that, on November 18th, General Maude died of cholera in Baghdad. He was succeeded in the chief command by Lieut.-General Sir W. R. Marshall, while Major-General Sir R. G. Egerton assumed command of the 3rd Corps and Brig.-General W. M. Thomson became G.O.C. 14th Indian Division. Maude was greatly missed by all ranks, for his strong personality pervaded every department of military and civil affairs.

The Sapper and Miner establishment in Iraq now underwent sweeping alterations. General Marshall found himself opposed only by the remnants of the Turkish 6th Army, over which he had marked superiority in numbers, material and morale. The remnants lay inert at Kirkuk and Kifri in Kurdistan, at Tikrit on the Tigris, and at Hit on the Euphrates. However, administrative considerations in Iraq, and the need for reinforcements in Palestine, restricted offensive action. Allenby required replacements for British troops sent to France, and consequently the 7th Indian Division was ordered to Palestine and with it went the 1st, 3rd and 4th Companies, Bengal S. & M. These units, under Captains J. F. Gray and W. Cave-Browne[2] and Major A. J. G. Bird, R.E., with Lieut.-Colonel E. F. J. Hill, R.E., as Commanding Royal Engineer, sailed from Basra on January 4th, 1918, to earn fresh laurels in the advance to Damascus and beyond. A 17th Indian Division had been formed in Iraq during the summer of 1917 and in December it was placed under the command of Major-General G. A. J. Leslie, late R.E. An 18th Division under Major-General H. C. Fanshawe was in process of formation, and also an 11th Cavalry Brigade under Brig.-General R. A. Cassels. The commander of the 53rd Infantry Brigade of the 18th Division was Brig.-General G. A. F. Sanders, late R.E., an ex-Madras Sapper and Miner. In November, 1917, the 2nd Company, Bengal S. & M., under Captain F. G. Drew, R.E., arrived from Roorkee to join the 18th Division and was followed by the 8th Company under Captain E. O. Wheeler, R.E. In December came No. 7 Bridging

[1] *The Campaign in Mesopotamia*, 1914–18 (Official History), by Brig.-Gen. F. J. Moberly, C.B., C.S.I., D.S.O., Vol. IV, p. 75.

[2] Capt. W. Cave-Browne, R.E., did not actually assume command until the 3rd Company reached Egypt, when it was discovered that the Company Commander, Maj. F. Mc. C. Douie, R.E., had been invalided from Iraq to India.

[3] The Company Officers were Lieuts. G. Bartholemew, G. Dixon and R. R. MacFadden, I.A.R.O., with the 2nd Company, and Lieuts. J. D. Shepherd, R.E., and T. F. Carter, D. D. Crawford and A. C. Elton, I.A.R.O., with the 8th Company.

Train, Madras S. & M., under Captain R. Hamilton, R.E.;[1] also, from Aden, the 5th Company, Bengal S. & M., under Major E. P. le Breton, R.E.,[2] to join the 53rd Brigade, and from India, the 19th Company, Bombay S. & M., under Captain C. F. Stoehr, R.E., to join the 15th Division on the Euphrates. The 5th Field Troop, Bengal S. & M., under Captain E. G. Gidley-Kitchin, R.E., was raised in Baghdad. It included the personnel of the original Field Troop in France who had been absorbed into the 3rd and 4th Companies. This reorganization of the engineer establishment was necessary not only because the 7th Division was bound for Palestine but because it was probable that the 3rd Division would follow it shortly to that theatre of operations and consequently the Army in Iraq would lose the services of the 18th, 20th and 21st Companies, Bombay S. & M. But pending the departure of the 3rd Division, General Marshall was well provided with Sappers and Miners and Pioneers, and it was fortunate that this was the case since heavy commitments in Iran were soon to be added to those in Iraq.

On January 27th, 1918, a small mission under Major-General L. C. Dunsterville left Baghdad for Tiflis in Ford cars to raise and train local forces of Armenians and Georgians in the Caucasus in order to hinder Turkish plans for an invasion of Iran. The mission penetrated no further than Enzeli on the Caspian Sea, and by February 25th was back in Hamadan. A column, which included a section of the 13th Company, Madras S. & M., had preceded it, early in January, to make a passable road, and moving from Mirjana through Khaniqin and Qasr-i-Shirin to Pai Taq it accomplished useful work before its return to Mirjana on January 13th. Major P. E. Prince, R.E., who commanded the 13th Company, was then detailed to reconnoitre the road further ahead and left Baghdad with the Dunsterville Mission. "Beyond Pai Taq," he writes,[3] "my escorting armoured car stuck hopelessly and could not be extricated until the mud had frozen during the night. Meanwhile, the "Dunsterforce" troops had pushed on and I saw no more of them. My small party reached Kermanshah, where we were snowed up for a week, but on February 21st we were back in Mirjana." Soon afterwards, the 12th Company, Madras S. & M., began to operate in Iran. A section moved to Qasr-i-Shirin and, with the assistance of some Pioneers, infantry and local labour, re-aligned the road from Khaniqin. The remainder of the unit followed during March and took charge of 50 miles of road between Khaniqin and Pai Taq.

The experiences of the Dunsterville Mission are recorded in General Dunsterville's book, *The Adventures of Dunsterforce*. The Mission was more political than military, and consequently it included no Sappers and

[1]No. 7 Bridging Train went to the Baghdad area in Jan., 1918, to take over the Samarra and Sadiya bridges.

[2]In Feb., 1918, Maj. Le Breton handed over command of the 5th Company to Capt. A. F. Chater, R.E., on his transfer to the Staff.

[3]Notes by Col. P. E. Prince, D.S.O., late R.E., sent to the author on Sept. 20th, 1937. In May, 1918, Maj. Prince handed over command of the 13th Company to Maj. G. H. J. G. Morris, R.E., and returned to Bangalore. In July, 1918, he was transferred to Roorkee to raise a new Corps to be known as the 6th (Artificer) Sappers and Miners, with Capt. H. Dawkins, R.E., as Adjutant. The headquarters were located in the Canal Foundry Workshops, but the scheme was abandoned when the Armistice was signed.

Miners. Gradually reinforced by troops, it continued to operate in North-west Iran; and in August, 1918, when a Turkish army was advancing on Baku, 2,000 men of "Dunsterforce" attempted to hold that town. Some description will be given later of the part taken by Sappers and Miners in the achievements of "Dunsterforce," which developed eventually into "Norperforce," and also of their work with the East Persia Cordon and with "Farsforce" in South-east Iran, but meanwhile it is necessary to revert to events in Iraq.

From January to April 1918, Major-General W. Gillman, Chief of the General Staff in Iraq, was absent in Egypt as a member of a conference on future policy in all theatres; and during his absence, Major-General Theodore Fraser, late R.E., an ex-Madras Sapper who had been Brig.-General, General Staff, 3rd Indian Corps since 1916, acted for him.[1] It was recommended at the conference that an active defence should be pursued by General Marshall in Iraq, but that a further reinforcement of 1 division and 4 batteries should be sent to support General Allenby's offensive in Palestine. This was approved, with the result that in March 1918 the 3rd Indian Division received orders to prepare to leave Iraq. The 17th Division relieved the 3rd Division at Samarra, and during April and May, 1918, the 18th, 20th and 21st Companies, Bombay S. & M., sailed from Basra and thus severed their connection with a country in which they had fought and laboured with fine resolution.

The spring and summer of 1918 saw little fighting but much activity. The enemy was in no shape to attack. Reorganization was the order of the day, and the building of roads, railways, bridges and quarters the chief requisite. No. 2 (Mobile) Bridging Train, Bengal S. & M., had gone to the Euphrates and was bridging the river above Hit and elsewhere. With the 2nd Field Troop, Madras S. & M., and a detachment from No. 1 Bridging Train, Bengal S. & M., it was concerned in March 1918 in General Brooking's successful operations at Khan Baghdadi. On one occasion it gave unwitting tactical assistance when its two-mile column was mistaken by the Turks for artillery and caused a withdrawal of the enemy's advanced posts. In March the 2nd Sirmur Sapper Company was under fire during a reconnaissance with the 34th Brigade north of Tikrit. The 2nd Company, Bengal S. & M., under Captain F. G. Drew, R.E., relieved the Malerkotla Sapper Company, under Major L. V. Bond, R.E., at Akab, where the Adhaim joins the Tigris, and built an elaborate suspension bridge across the Adhaim to replace a pile bridge, constructed by the 20th Company, Bombay S. & M., which had been destroyed by a flood. The unit also did river-training work, using huge brushwood "sausages" for the purpose,

[1]Maj.-Gen. Sir Theodore Fraser served with the Madras Sappers and Miners from 1889 to 1898, and was with the Bengal Corps in Hazara in 1891. After holding Staff appointments in India and England, he served in France (1914–15) as Embarkation Commandant, Marseilles, and A.A. and Q.M.G., 3rd Indian Division. He proceeded to Iraq with the 3rd Division in 1916 and was transferred to the 15th Indian Division as G.S.O.I. in May of that year. In Sept., 1916, he became B.G.G.S. 3rd Indian Corps, and in Sept., 1918, as recorded later, he was appointed G.O.C. 14th Indian Division. After the Great War he commanded the 18th Indian Division at Mosul (1919–21), the S. Kurdistan F.F. (1919), and the Mosul Vilayet Troops (1920). He officiated as C.-in-C., Iraq from Feb. to April, 1921, and was G.O.C. Forces in Iraq, from April to Oct., 1922.

and it improved many tracks in the Ain Nukhaila area of the Jabal Hamrin.[1] In April, the 2nd Field Troop and the 15th (Burma) Company, Madras S. & M., took part in a successful offensive by General Egerton against the depleted Turkish 13th Corps around Kifri, beyond the Jabal Hamrin. In May, the Malerkotla Sapper Company was with a reconnaissance by the 17th Division to Tikrit. The 13th Company, Madras S. & M., and the 2nd Sirmur Sapper Company were employed during the summer on railway construction up the Diyala River Gorge in the Jabal Hamrin, and did much bridging and tunnelling. This was the only extensive railway work carried out in Iraq by the Sappers and Miners since the spring of 1917, when the Tehri-Garhwal Company had built a narrow-gauge line from Shaikh Saad to the Es Sinn position below Kut.[2] The 9th Company, Madras S. & M., bridged the Euphrates during May and June, and a detachment co-operated with the 8th Company of the Bengal Corps in the blockade of Najaf by the 53rd Brigade under Brig.-General G. A. F. Sanders, late R.E. After the capture of the city, Captain E. O. Wheeler, R.E., commanding the 8th Company, was required to carry out extensive demolitions as a reprisal and used nearly 2 tons of guncotton for the purpose.[3]

At the end of the hot weather, preparations were made for a resumption of the general offensive. No. 2 (Mobile) Bridging Train returned in September, 1918, to the Tigris front, where it was reinforced by half No. 3 (Mobile) Bridging Train of the Bombay Corps[4] so that Captain Witts could make 750 yards of bridge. No. 7 Bridging Train, Madras S. & M., replaced it on the Euphrates after handing over charge of the Samarra bridge to the 2nd Company of the Bengal Corps. Sapper reinforcements were on their way both to Iraq and Iran. On September 12th, the 6th and 52nd Companies, Bengal S. & M., under Captains V. E. G. Guinness and H. E. Roome, R.E., left Roorkee for Iraq, and a few days later the 61st and 63rd Companies, Madras S. & M., under Captains A. E. Collier and C. R. Gurney, R.E., sailed from Karachi, the 61st for Basra and the 63rd for Bushire. These Madras units were followed by another—the 65th Company under Captain R. B. Woakes, I.A.R.O.—but it arrived in the Jabal Hamrin area too late to fight the Turks. In September, also the 54th Company, Bengal S. & M., under Captain W. J. Lyall, R.E., proceeded from Roorkee to Bushire, and the 24th, 71st and 73rd Companies, Bombay S. & M., were sent to Eastern Iran. At Ramadi on the Euphrates, where Lieut.-Colonel J. F. Turner, R.E., was C.R.E. 15th Division, the 104th Company, Bombay S. & M., was formed under Captain E. B. Fox, R.E., from the 19th Company, half No. 3 Bridging Train and some men of the 128th Pioneers. But enough of reorganization and expansion. Sufficient

[1]Notes by Lieut.-Col. F. G. Drew, O.B.E., R.E., sent to the author on Dec. 24th, 1937.

[2]Notes by Brig.-Gen. G. Lubbock, C.M.G., D.S.O., late R.E., sent to the author on Nov. 24th, 1937. After the Armistice, the Tehri-Garhwal Sappers worked on the extension of the railway line beyond Samarra.

[3]Notes by Lieut.-Col. E. O. Wheeler, M.C., R.E., sent to the author on Feb. 22nd, 1938.

[4]Both No. 1 and No. 3 Bridging Trains had now been converted to Mobile units.

[5]In April, 1919, the designation of the 104th Company was changed to 22nd Company, and thus the memory of the original 22nd Company of the 6th Indian Division in Kut was revived.

has been written to show that the preparations were thorough and far-reaching.

Early in October, 1918, General Marshall received permission to exploit the effect of General Allenby's victories in Palestine by undertaking an offensive on the Tigris. The remnants of the Turkish 6th Army, under Ali Ihsan Pasha, were holding a formidable position astride the river at the Fat-ha Gorge, in the Jabal Hamrin, which they had prepared for nearly eighteen months to cover the approaches to Mosul. A second position had been dug for several miles along the Little (or Lesser) Zab tributary and prolonged across the Tigris at Humr. Marshall entrusted the offensive to the 1st Corps (17th and 18th Divisions) under General Cobbe, assisted by the 7th and 11th Cavalry Brigades, under Brig.-Generals C. E. G. Norton and R. A. Cassels, and a Light Armoured Motor Brigade (L.A.M.B.), and detailed half the 40th Brigade of the 3rd Corps, under Brig.-General A. C. Lewin, to advance through Kirkuk to Altun Kopri on the Little Zab to prevent enemy forces from moving down that stream. The Sapper and Miner units involved in this scheme were the Malerkotla and Tehri-Garhwal Companies with the 17th Division, and the 2nd, 6th and 8th Companies of the Bengal Corps with the 18th Division. Cobbe planned to attack the Fat-ha position with his main body while he turned its eastern flank with his cavalry. He began his operations on October 23rd. The infantry closed up to the position, the 17th Division on the right bank and the 18th on the left, and the 7th Cavalry Brigade crossed the Jabal Hamrin by the unguarded Ain Nukhaila Pass, north-east of Tikrit. Next morning it was found that the Turks had retired to their Humr position, and the infantry pushed towards it while the 7th Cavalry Brigade advanced across the Little Zab and, swinging left, cleared the area down to the Tigris. North of the Little Zab, the 7th Cavalry Brigade made contact with the 11th, which had been reconnoitring ahead.

On October 26th, 1918, the 17th Division attacked the Humr position, though with little success. Lewin reported that his brigade was held up near Altun Kopri, but Cassels with the 11th Cavalry Brigade was already pushing towards the Tigris, some 13 miles north of Sharqat, where he hoped to cross the river and, in conjunction with the L.A.M.B., to cut the enemy's line of retreat. He reached the Tigris at 1 p.m. and his leading regiment, the Guides Cavalry, forded the river at Hadraniya, upstream of Huwaish. During the night of October 26th/27th, the main body of the enemy evacuated the Humr position and fell back to Sharqat, towards which the 17th Division advanced on the 27th. Meanwhile, Cassels was in a dangerous situation, assailed from front and rear; but encouraged by the approach up the left bank of the 53rd Brigade and other troops under Sanders,[1] he clung grimly to his position astride the Turkish line of communication. At dawn on the 28th, Sanders' force was in sight, and a battalion crossed the river in time to secure the 11th Cavalry Brigade in the line it had held so lightly. The 7th Cavalry Brigade and reinforcements

[1]There were no Sappers and Miners with this column.

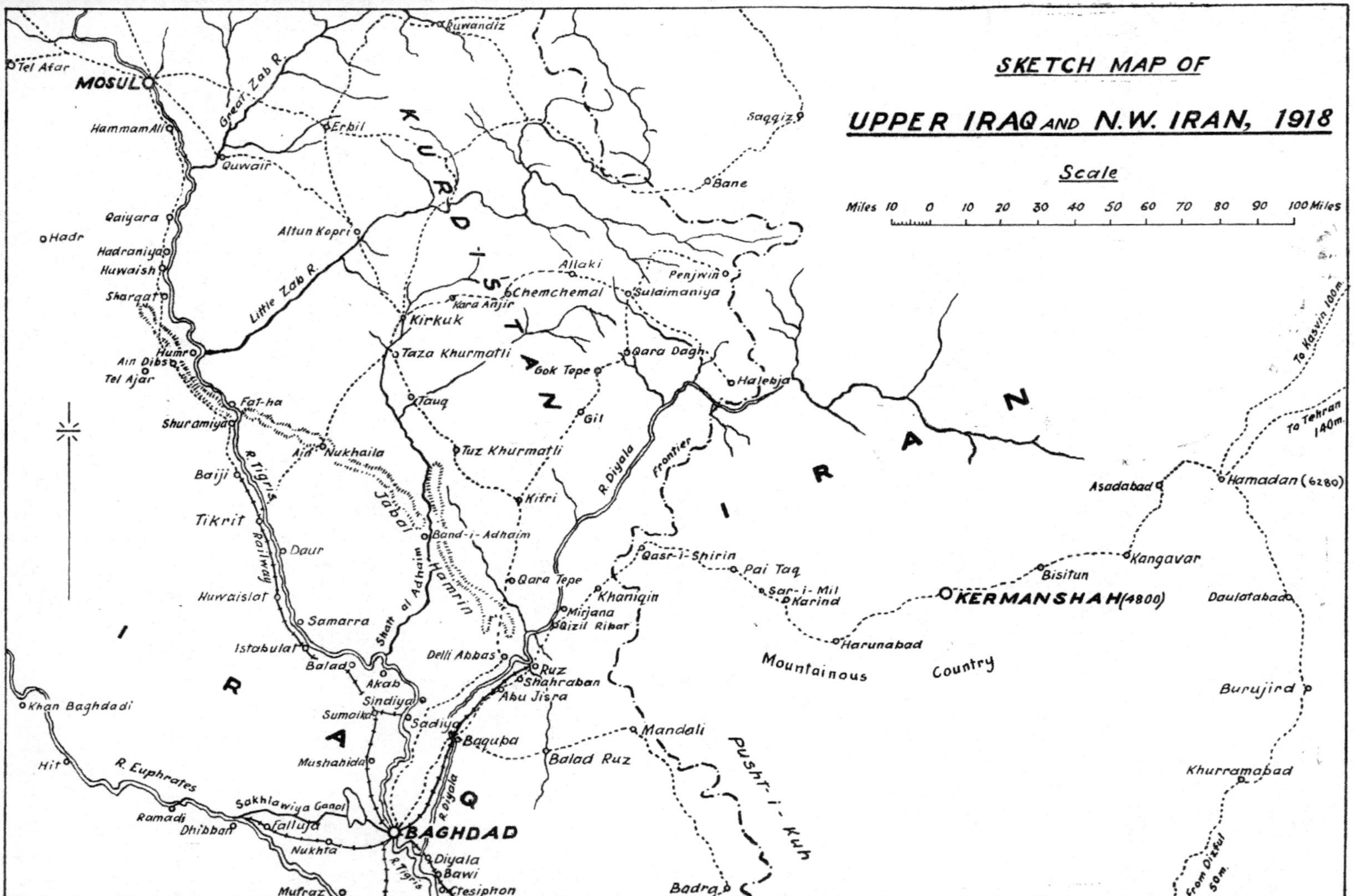
SKETCH MAP OF
UPPER IRAQ AND N.W. IRAN, 1918
Scale
Miles 10 0 10 20 30 40 50 60 70 80 90 100 Miles
KURDISTAN
IRAN
IRAQ
MOSUL
Tel Afar
Hammam Ali
Great Zab R.
Erbil
Ruwandiz
Saqqiz
Bane
Quwair
Qaiyara
Hadr
Hadraniya
Huwaish
Sharqat
Altun Kopri
Little Zab R.
Allaki
Penjwin
Chemchemal
Sulaimaniya
Kara Anjir
Kirkuk
Humr
Ain Dibs
Tel Ajar
Taza Khurmatli
Qara Dagh
Gok Tepe
Halebja
Fat-ha
Tauq
Gil
Shuramiya
Ain Nukhaila
Tuz Khurmatli
Baiji
R. Tigris
R. Diyala
Frontier
Jabal Hamrin
Kifri
Tikrit
Railway
Daur
Band-i-Adhaim
Shatt al Adhaim
Qara Tepe
Huwaislat
Samarra
Khaniqin
Mirjana
Qizil Ribat
Istabulat
Delli Abbas
Balad
Akab
Ruz
Shahraban
Abu Jisra
Sindiya
Sumaika
Sadiya
Baquba
Mandali
Balad Ruz
Khan Baghdadi
Hit
R. Euphrates
Mushahida
Sakhlawiya Canal
Ramadi
Dhibban
Falluja
Nukhta
BAGHDAD
Diyala
Bawi
Ctesiphon
Mufraz
Badra
Pusht-i-Kuh
Qasr-i-Shirin
Pai Taq
Sar-i-Mil
Karind
Harunabad
Mountainous Country
KERMANSHAH (4800)
Bisitun
Kangavar
Asadabad
Hamadan (6280)
To Kasvin 100m.
To Tehran 140m.
Daulatabad
Burujird
Khurramabad
From Dizful 50m.

from the 53rd Brigade followed in due course, and by nightfall the position was satisfactory.

The Turkish 6th Army was now doomed. On October 29th the 17th Division approached rapidly. The Turks withdrew and were brought to action north of Sharqat, while Cassels, Sanders and Norton blocked their retreat to Mosul. At dawn on October 30th, 1918, white flags went up all along the enemy's trenches, and 11,300 Turks under Ismail Hakki Bey laid down their arms. An armistice was signed on October 31st. Bold and vigorous action had brought complete victory, and the war in Iraq was at an end. A force under General Fanshawe, including half the 8th Company, Bengal S. & M., marched into Mosul on November 1st and received the surrender of Ali Ihsan Pasha and the remainder of his 6th Army.

During these decisive and final operations on the Upper Tigris the Sappers and Miners were engaged chiefly in road-making and bridging, particularly in the Fat-ha Gorge, where the 6th Company and detachments of the 2nd and 8th Companies of the Bengal Corps laboured hard to make a track passable for wheeled traffic. The soil consisted of gypsum which disintegrated so rapidly that a road could be maintained only by unceasing shovelling. Captain F. V. B. Witts, R.E., with his expanded No. 2 (Mobile) Bridging Train, bridged the Tigris once at Baiji and twice at Fat-ha, and afterwards established a two-mile crossing of the Little Zab consisting of three bridges with intervening stretches of sand. Captain F. G. Drew, R.E., with a section of the 2nd Company, Bengal S. & M., escorted a Ford van supply convoy of the 11th Cavalry Brigade when Cassels was operating around the Little Zab, and Captain E. G. Gidley-Kitchin, R.E., with the 5th Field Troop of the same Corps, helped Cassels by maintaining a flying bridge across the Tigris. The 8th Company was stationed in Mosul after the Armistice. The 2nd Company remained for some time at Fat-ha and then marched up the Little Zab and opened a road to Altun Kopri and Kirkuk. The 6th Company returned to Samarra.

We turn now to the operations in Iran after the failure of the Dunsterville Mission to Baku. Attempts were made to screen India from enemy infiltration by the despatch of two other missions—one under Major-General Sir Wilfred Malleson, formed in June, 1918, to establish contact at Askhabad with the Russian Provisional Government of Trans-Caspia, and the other, under Sir George Macartney, designed to penetrate to Tashkent in the Pamirs to negotiate with a Bolshevik Commissar known as "Sirul the Baker." No Sappers and Miners served with the Dunsterville, Malleson or Macartney Missions, although a few may have helped the missions on their way. They operated, however, to a small extent with the original East Persia Cordon. In 1915, a British Cordon Force, based on Quetta, had been established in conjunction with the Russians to exclude enemy agents from Afghanistan, and in 1917, after the withdrawal of the Russians, it occupied Meshed in order to assist Malleson and, moving northwards in 1918 into Trans-Caspia, engaged Bolshevik forces based on Merv.[1] This was a most peculiar war, fought out along the Trans-Caspian Central

[1]See *Sketch Map of Iran*, 1918, included in this chapter.

Asian Railway between Merv and Askhabad. Each side lived in trains which carried all their possessions. When one side attacked, the other, if weak, bolted to their trains and steamed away; if strong, they hung on, and the disconcerted attackers retired quietly to their trains, shunted to a safe distance, and considered what they should do next.[1] No Sappers and Miners took part in this railway war, but a small detachment consisting of a Naik and 8 men from the 9th and 14th Companies of the Madras Corps at Quetta helped the British Cordon Force between July 1915 and March 1917 by improving roads and undertaking demolitions and water-supply.[2]

Although the Sappers and Miners had little to do with the East Persia Cordon, it may be remarked that when, early in 1918, it became necessary to increase the military strength of the Cordon because of the collapse of Russia, the task of creating, organizing, administering and defending the line of communication with India was entrusted to an ex-Bengal Sapper and Miner, Brig.-General W. E. R. Dickson, late R.E. whose experiences are recorded in his entertaining book, *East Persia: A Backwater of the Great War*. Railhead was approaching Duzdab, the terminus of the Indian North Western Railway from Quetta through Northern Baluchistan, whence the line of communication ran northwards through Birjand, Turbat and Meshed to Askhabad on the Russian railway. A road had to be made and maintained between Duzdab and Meshed, beyond which the Russians had a metalled highway to Askhabad, and this involved very hard labour, especially in certain tracts between the mountain ranges where a raging wind buried the road unceasingly in drifts of the finest sand.[3] No bridging of any size was attempted. At first, Dickson had only the 107th Pioneers and a Corps of Persian Levies working under Captain Stubbs, R.E.;[4] but a detachment of Bombay Sappers and Miners soon arrived with Lieutenants A. Prain and N. E. V. Patterson, R.E., and also the 104th (Indian) Labour Corps, and a Works cadre was formed consisting of Lieut.-Colonels W. P. Pakenham-Walsh, J. A. Graeme and L. E. Hopkins, Major M. A. H. Scott, and Lieutenants P. A. Bourdillon, M. A. Scott, C. F. A. Bird and T. J. P. Price, R.E. Other units which served in Eastern Iran during the Great War, and consequently had some connection at times with the East Persia Line of Communication, were the 24th, 71st and 73rd Companies and a Seistan Detachment of the Bombay S. & M.[6] and the 6th Field Troop, Bengal S. & M., under Lieutenant F. A. Farquharson, I.A.R.O. The Field Troop joined the Baluchistan Field Force in October, 1918. By November, 1918, the road from railhead near Duzdab to Meshed, a length of about 600 miles, was fit for light

[1]"Operations in Trans-Caspia," by Col. J. K. Tod, C.M.G., appearing in *The Army Quarterly*, Vol. XVI, July, 1928, pp. 280–303.

[2]*Q.V.O. Madras Sappers and Miners in France and Iraq*, 1914–1920, p. 44.

[3]"Royal Engineers in East Persia, 1918–20," appearing in *The R.E. Journal*, Vol. LV, Dec., 1941, pp. 406–410.

[4]Capt. Stubbs was a P.W.D. officer granted a temporary commission in the Royal Engineers.

[5]Lieuts. Bird and Price, R.E., were officers of the Bengal Sappers and Miners.

[6]*A Brief History of the Royal Bombay Sappers and Miners*, p. 30.

motor traffic. The East Persia Line of Communication was maintained until the autumn of 1920 by Brig.-General W. B. Lesslie, late R.E., who succeeded Brig.-General Dickson in December, 1919. During his period of control, Dickson had many curious experiences. For instance, a Russian officer once told him that a new Governor of Turbat, wishing to earn popularity, had recently invited all the prominent residents and many influential visitors to witness the public execution of four robbers. Tea was served to the guests while one robber was shot, another hanged, a third hurled from a cliff on to spikes, and the last killed by having his throat cut, and, in the intervals between the items of entertainment, a band played suitable selections.

The main theatre of engineer operations in Iran during 1918 was undoubtedly in the north-western area, where the 14th Indian Division was based on Qizil Ribat. By the beginning of April, the 12th and 15th Madras Sapper companies, under Lieut.-Colonel H. S. Gaskell, R.E., as C.R.E., 14th Division, had completed a motor track as far as Sar-i-Mil. Gaskell then pushed forward these two units, together with the 5th and 52nd Companies, Bengal S. & M., and the 48th and 128th Pioneers and some Persian labour, to work on the road as far as Kangavar, 60 miles beyond Kermanshah.[1] In September, as the line of communication was operating as far as Hamadan, Gaskell moved his headquarters to Kermanshah. The road between Harunabad and Kermanshah was very hilly, and numerous diversions were needed to avoid bad soil. Beyond Kermanshah, in mountainous country, the road followed roughly the line of a Persian track leading through Kangavar to Asadabad. A diversion was made southwards to avoid a steep climb to the Asadabad Pass (7,200 feet). The original C.R.E. " Dunsterforce," Major B. J. Haslam, R.E., who had been killed in the defence of Baku, had improved the Asadabad Pass track with local labour, and his successor, Lieut.-Colonel E. de L. Young, R.E., had continued the work, but the track was liable to become impassable when snow fell and hence a diversion was needed. Gaskell was required to provide, in nine months, a road extending from Qizil Ribat to Hamadan, a distance of 264 miles, and accordingly, he was obliged to concentrate his attention on the worst portions. The work during the winter was very hard, especially to the men of the 15th (Burma) Company who had never seen snow. Shortly after the Armistice, the 61st and 65th Companies, Madras S. & M., arrived from India and relieved the 12th and 15th Companies. Between Qasr-i-Shirin and Hamadan, seven passes were negotiated, ranging from 4,000 to 7,241 feet in height. The Persian Line of Communication was operating with some success before the end of the Great War, but it was not completed until the close of 1920, when Lieut.-Colonel Gaskell handed over charge to Major W. J. W. Noble, R.E., and it was closed after the withdrawal of " Norperforce " in April, 1921.

In conclusion, some mention may be made of the subsidiary operations

[1]Notes by Maj.-Gen. H. S. Gaskell, C.B., D.S.O., late R.E., sent to Maj.-Gen. Sir Theodore Fraser, K.C.B., C.S.I., C.M.G., late R.E., on July 27th, 1939. The Field Engineers were Majors B. Burgess, C. H. Palmer and R. N. Borton, R.E., and Capts. Crichton, Hull and Lister, R.E. (temp. commissions).

in South-East Iran in which Sappers and Miners figured during 1918. The focal point was Bushire, on the Persian Gulf. From the outbreak of war, a German named Wassmuss had intrigued among the local tribesmen to such purpose that, by the end of 1915, British influence had almost disappeared from Southern Iran and the central part of the country was becoming a corridor for enemy agents proceeding to Afghanistan and India. Accordingly, in March 1916, Brig.-General Sir Percy Sykes was allowed to raise the South Persia Rifles at Bandar Abbas and, marching through Kerman and Yezd, met the Russians at Isfahan in November and afterwards withdrew to Shiraz. His activities had good results; but powerful anti-British elements were still at work, and in March 1918 several tribes rose and attacked our posts. It was then decided to despatch an expedition from India during the following autumn, and meanwhile to leave the Shiraz garrison to fend for itself. The expeditionary force ("Farsforce"), consisting of about two brigades with ancillary troops under Major-General J. A. Douglas, began to assemble in Bushire in September 1918 with orders to establish early contact with Shiraz and to link the two places by a proper road.[1]

The first move was made by a column of brigade strength including the 54th Company, Bengal S. & M., under Captain W. J. Lyall, R.E., with Lieutenant A. M. Cameron, R.E., and Lieutenants H. E. Jeffery and E. C. Watson, I.A.R.O.[2] The column marched from Bushire on October 1st, 1918, and crossed the arid coastal plain through Borazjan and Dalaki to the hilly country beyond, and by December 1st the 54th Company had made a track extending far into the hills. On December 19th, the unit took part in forcing the Kamarij Pass and occupying the village of that name. The native track up to the pass was no more than a cobbled stone stairway, so the Sappers had to spend the next fortnight in making a diversion. Military and engineering operations continued, although the Great War was at an end. On December 26th, against slight opposition, the column reached Rahdar. Again a diversion was needed, and it was not until early in January, 1919, that the column arrived in Kazarun and halted to allow for the completion of the track and the accumulation of supplies. Meanwhile, another Sapper unit had been working on the line of communication. This was the 63rd Company, Madras S. & M., under Captain C. R. Gurney, R.E., with Lieutenant M. Hotine, R.E. The company had landed at Bushire on September 30th and had been improving the track with the assistance of the 81st Pioneers. The work of linking Bushire with Shiraz proceeded steadily during the spring. The track was taken up to a pass 6,700 feet above sea level, and afterwards, in heavy rock cutting, along 200 yards of almost vertical cliff until it joined a track from Shiraz made by a column operating westwards from that place under Colonel E. F. Orton. Fortified posts were then built at strategic points, and both the Sapper companies returned to India in the summer of 1919.

[1] "Engineer Operations in South Persia," by Col. F. C. Molesworth, late R.E., appearing in *The R.E. Journal*, Vol. XLIX, 1935, pp. 237–247.

[2] Notes by Lieut.-Col. W. J. Lyall, O.B.E., R.E. (I.A.), sent to the author on Oct. 6th, 1937.

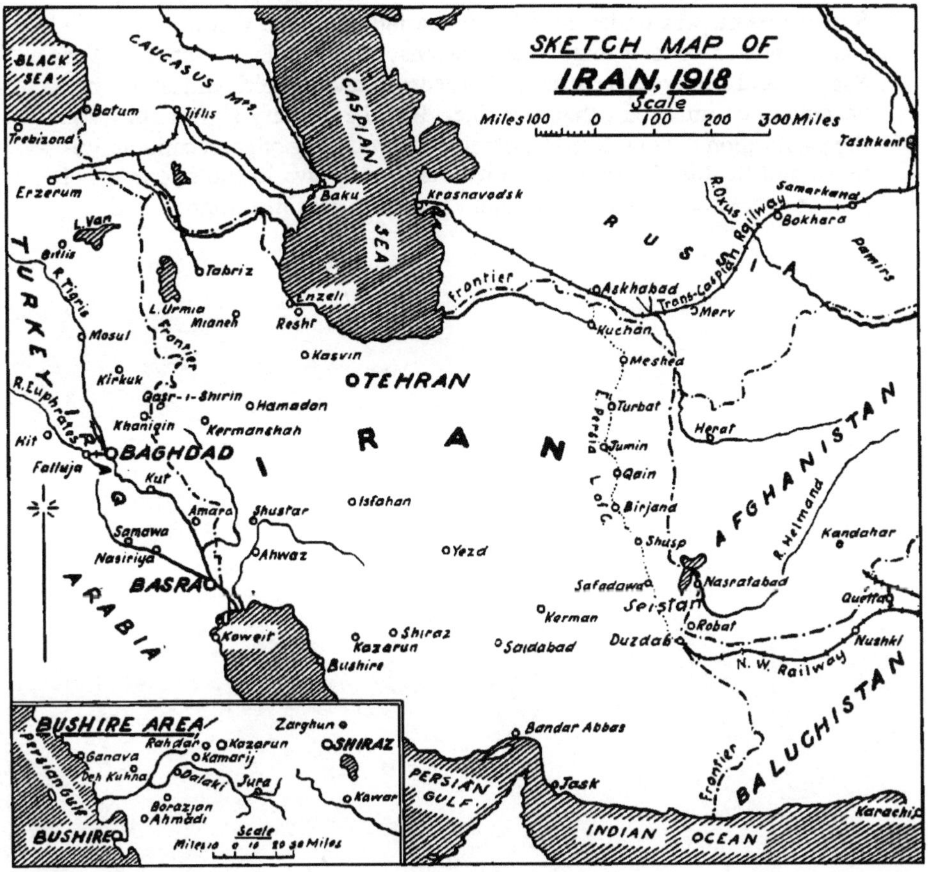
SKETCH MAP OF
IRAN, 1918
Scale
Miles 100 0 100 200 300 Miles
BLACK SEA
CAUCASUS Mts.
CASPIAN SEA
Batum
Tiflis
Trebizond
Erzerum
Baku
Krasnovodsk
L. Van
Bitlis
R. Tigris
Tabriz
L. Urmia
Mianeh
Enzeli
Resht
Mosul
Kasvin
TEHRAN
Kirkuk
Qasr-i-Shirin
Hamadan
R. Euphrates
Khaniqin
Kermanshah
Hit
BAGHDAD
Falluja
Kut
Amara
Shustar
Isfahan
Samawa
Nasiriya
Ahwaz
Yezd
BASRA
Koweit
Shiraz
Kazarun
Bushire
Kerman
Saidabad
TURKEY
ARABIA
IRAN
RUSSIA
R. Oxus
Samarkand
Tashkent
Bokhara
Pamirs
Trans-Caspian Railway
Askhabad
Merv
frontier
Kuchan
Meshed
E. Persia L. of C.
Turbat
Jumin
Qain
Birjand
Herat
AFGHANISTAN
R. Helmand
Kandahar
Shusp
Nasratabad
Safadawa
Seistan
Robat
Quetta
Duzdab
Nushki
N. W. Railway
BALUCHISTAN
Bandar Abbas
Jask
PERSIAN GULF
INDIAN OCEAN
Karachi
Frontier
BUSHIRE AREA
Zarghun
Rahdar
Kazarun
SHIRAZ
Persian Gulf
Ganava
Kamarij
Deh Kuhna
Dalaki
Jura
Kawar
Borazjan
Ahmadi
BUSHIRE
Scale
Miles 10 0 10 20 30 Miles

A volume might be written on the work of the Sappers and Miners in Iran alone, but with this brief record of a small expedition undertaken for political reasons the story of the Great War in Iraq and Iran must come to an end. Much remained to be done in both countries, and, as will be seen in a subsequent chapter, the Sappers and Miners were called upon to labour and fight over the same ground between 1919 and 1922. The operations of 1914–18, however, had produced the desired result. Iraq, from the Persian Gulf to Mosul, and from the Kurdish Mountains to the Syrian Desert, was under British domination, and Iran was held in sufficient strength to safeguard India against political interference. The Sappers and Miners were scattered broadcast, and the pick and shovel had become more important than the rifle. But the primary aim in 1919 was the pacification of conquered territory by the opening of good communications, and in this the engineer units were, as always in the aftermath of war, the necessary adjuncts of a sound system of administration.

CHAPTER XIX

THE GREAT WAR: EGYPT AND PALESTINE, 1914–1918

IN August, 1914, the situation in Egypt was intricate and dangerous, for the British occupation was based only upon an unwritten convention. Nominally, Egypt was still a part of the Turkish Empire, but actually the Turks had little influence in her policy. Yet her importance in a world war was immeasurable because of the Suez Canal; indeed, to German ideas, the Canal was the jugular vein of the British Empire. This was an exaggeration, but the value of the Canal as a means of expediting the concentration of the scattered resources of the Empire during the first year of the war needs no emphasis, and its protection was an important factor in British strategy. Since its opening in 1869, it had exerted a profound influence on our policy in Egypt, and in 1914 it was our chief concern in the Near East. The peace-time British garrison in Egypt was insufficient to guard it, and it was obvious that, should Turkey join forces with Germany, the situation might become critical.

The General Staff had maintained in 1906 that the Sinai Peninsula, east of the Canal, formed no impassable obstacle to an invader from Palestine.[1] They believed that a raiding party of 5,000 rifles, with strong support, could approach to within striking distance of the waterway, and they advocated the posting of a force of Egyptian camelry at Nekhl[2], to observe and harass the enemy. This scheme became unnecessary when the Royal Navy undertook to defend the Canal by gunfire, and in 1914 it was decided to restrict the defensive position to the Canal itself. The intention was to allow the enemy to attempt the passage of the desert so that he would encounter the Canal as a second obstacle, and to strike him only when he reached the Canal—a deplorable example of passive defence. On August 3rd, 1914, Turkey began a leisurely mobilization, and a few days later, received at Constantinople the German warships, *Goeben* and *Breslau*. Her subsequent attitude showed which way the wind was blowing. As for the Germans, they imagined that the mere appearance of a Turkish force on the Suez Canal would be the signal for a wholesale rising in Egypt, which was ruled at that time by a pro-Turkish Khedive, Abbas Hilmi. Events proved that they were wrong; yet even without a hostile population in their rear, the defenders of the Suez Canal were in a difficult position when Turkey entered the war on the side of Germany on November 5th, 1914.

The Commander-in-Chief in Egypt, Lieut.-General Sir John Maxwell, had formed the Canal defences into a separate command under Major-General Alexander Wilson. In September, the 3rd (Lahore) and 7th

[1] *Egypt and the Army*, by Lieut.-Col. P. G. Elgood, C.M.G., p. 120.
[2] See *Sketch Map of the Sinai Desert in* 1917, included in this chapter.

(Meerut) Divisions, which included the 20th and 21st Companies, Bombay S. & M., and the 3rd and 4th Companies, Bengal S. & M., had spent a few days in Egypt while on their way to France;[1] but the Sapper units could take no part in any preparations for the defence of the Canal, for the disembarkation of the two divisions had been ordered chiefly to impress the populace. In November, large contingents of Indian infantry reached Suez and were formed into the 10th and 11th Indian Divisions, which, with an Imperial Service Cavalry Brigade, the Bikaner Camel Corps and some artillery, provided a strength of 30,000 men. The Sirhind Brigade of the 3rd (Lahore) Division remained in Egypt as a precautionary measure until November 23rd, and Sir John Maxwell was then informed that large contingents from Australia and New Zealand would arrive in due course for training and would be available as reserves. One Australian division and a cavalry brigade landed at Suez at the beginning of December, and by the end of the year the garrison of Egypt had risen to more than 70,000 men and the first danger had passed.

During November and part of December, 1914, the only regular engineer officer, whose services were available for the Suez Canal defences, was Captain R. E. M. Russell, R.E., of the Egyptian Intelligence Department, though some Royal Engineers of the Egyptian State Railways were able to give assistance in the emergency.[2] Until the 10th Company, Madras S. & M., arrived from India in the latter half of December there was only one engineer unit available for defence work—No. 1 Field Company, East Lancashire Territorial Engineers—and when that unit was withdrawn on January 6th, 1915, the 10th Company was the sole engineering unit until No. 3 Field Company, Australian Engineers, arrived on January 16th. Excellent work was carried out by the 128th Pioneers from India, and by a Mobile Section on camels raised by the Military Works Department of the Egyptian Army, but it was not until February 6th, 1915, that the Sappers and Miners were reinforced by another company of Territorial Engineers.

The 10th Company, under Captain T. P. Bassett, R.E., with Lieutenants D. McA. Hogg and A. H. B. Papillon, R.E., and A. T. Buchanan, I.A.R.O., had left Bangalore on December 5th, 1914, to join the Indian Expeditionary Force "E." It disembarked at Suez on the 22nd and moved to Esh Shatt and El Kubri near the southern entrance to the Canal.[3] A fortnight later, two sections, under Hogg, were transferred to El Qantara, the important post between Port Said and Ismailia.[4] The first defensive position, designed to guard the Canal from an attack by 70,000 Turks under Djemal Pasha, was simple, almost primitive. Materials and labour were deficient, and the question of water-supply dominated both attack and defence. The target for the Turks was the Sweetwater Canal, about

[1]See Chapter XVI.

[2]The Sudan Government Railways, under the direction of the distinguished Governor-General of the Sudan, Gen. Sir Reginald Wingate, assisted also by supplying rolling-stock and permanent way for railway extensions.

[3]See *Sketch Map of the Suez Canal Defences*, 1915–1916, included in this chapter.

[4]*Historical Record of the Q.V.O. Madras Sappers and Miners*, Vol. II, 1914-19, p. 2.

30 feet wide, which carried fresh water from Cairo to Ismailia, and thence, northwards and southwards, to Port Said and Suez. If the enemy could cut this artery at Ismailia, they could render untenable the entire defensive position along the maritime canal. This, accordingly, was the vital point. The easiest avenue of approach from Palestine was by a coastal road from Rafa through El Arish, El Mazar, Bir el Abd and Qatiya to El Qantara, along which water was procurable from shallow wells. An alternative route was from Beersheba through El Auja, El Quseima, Bir el Hassana and Bir el Jifjafa to Ismailia. This led directly to the main objective, but it could be followed only when recent rain had filled the rock-cisterns and wells in the desert. A southern route existed from Aqaba through Nekhl to Suez, but it traversed broken and waterless country. On the whole, it seemed probable that, weather permitting, the Turks would advance by the central or Beersheba–Ismailia route to their main objective, and would follow the northern route to El Qantara only if no rain had fallen. Accordingly, the defensive position along the Suez Canal was designed on that supposition.

The system consisted of small redoubts along the east bank and trenches at intervals along the west bank. North of Ismailia the posts on the east bank were at Port Said, Ras el Esh, El Tina, El Kab, El Qantara, El Balla, El Firdan and a spot known as "Benchmark." There was an extensive work at Ismailia Ferry. Between Lake Timsa and the Great Bitter Lake, strong posts were established at Tussum, Serapeum and Deversoir to guard this critical sector. Further south, between the Little Bitter Lake and Port Taufiq (Tewfik) near Suez, posts were built at Geneifa, Esh Shallufa, "Gurkha," El Kubri, "Baluchistan" and Esh Shatt.[1] In accordance with pre-war ideas, most of the trenches were made with head cover and some with overhead cover.[2] To reduce the total frontage open to attack from the Sinai Desert, the east bank had been cut near Port Said on November 25th, and the resulting inundation had already spread over the desert as far southwards as El Kab, thus safeguarding 20 miles of the position. Subsequent inundations around El Qantara confined the objective of any serious Turkish offensive to the central portion of the Canal between El Balla and Deversoir. Deducting the length of Lake Timsa, the threatened section was then only 21 miles in extent, and this could be defended adequately by the troops assembled on the Canal. Communications, however, were defective. The Canal Zone was destitute of metalled roads except in the towns,[3] and the only railway was a single line, along the western bank of the maritime waterway, connecting Port Said, Ismailia and Suez and linked with Cairo by a line running westwards from Ismailia through Zagazig.

When the 10th Company arrived on the Suez Canal in December, 1914, the shortage of skilled supervision had already resulted in a lower standard

[1] *The Royal Engineers in Egypt and the Sudan*, by the present author, p. 312.
[2] Notes by Col. D. McA. Hogg, M.C., late R.E., sent to the author on May 18th, 1937.
[3] The existing metalled road connecting Port Said with Ismailia and Suez was built in 1916.

of work on the posts and trenches than was desirable.[1] The Sappers were required to advise the infantry in the design and excavation of trenches, to build bridges, construct aeroplane hangars, store water, lay water-supplies to camps, instal and operate searchlights and perform hosts of other necessary duties. The 10th Company alone could not cope with the volume of work, and as other engineer units arrived they also were taxed to the uttermost. Eight bridges were required over the Sweetwater Canal, and large floating bridges at El Qantara, Ismailia Ferry Post, and El Kubri. These were provided with the assistance of the Suez Canal Company. "The first thing that struck one on arrival," writes Bassett,[2] "was that there were many different ideas as to how, in principle, the Canal was to be defended. The official idea of a passive defence did not appeal to some of the Commanders of Canal Sections. When the scheme was explained to a distinguished General who was taking over a large area, he dismissed it with contempt and, waving his hand towards the desert, said '*I fight out there.*' Egypt was the 'Clapham Junction' for other theatres of war. Units arrived from all directions and, after brief halts, disappeared in all directions. Consequently, it was difficult for Headquarters to impose their ideas, either in the principles or details of defence. Each unit brought with it the ideas current in some other theatre. No two commanders thought alike. As excavations reveal successive prehistoric civilizations, so the Canal posts showed the varying notions of many commanders. The onus of attempting to work to some definite principle fell on the Engineers." However, order came gradually out of confusion, the defences increased and multiplied, and the position became more secure. A simple plan was evolved to discover traces of the approach of Turkish patrols under cover of darkness. Each day, a brush-barrow, made of sandbags, was dragged over the rough sand between the posts on the east bank, leaving a smooth track which showed the smallest mark made during the night.

The work of the 10th Company was varied in nature and sometimes very interesting. "Early in 1915," writes Hogg,[3] "a temporary shortage of barbed wire led us to adopt the *trou de loup* as an obstacle, i.e., a pit with a sharpened stake at the bottom, and our outpost line at El Qantara was mainly covered by such pits until we got more wire. For the defence of the inner perimeter we used wire and land mines. During their first attack by night on El Qantara, the Turks followed the permanent telegraph line from El Arish and outflanked our No. 5 Picquet near the line. On the next day, however, the Brigade Commander ordered me to deflect the line in a gentle curve so that it ran straight through No. 5 Picquet. This I did, and doubled the wire defences of the post. The Turks fell into the trap, and when they attacked again a few days later, they suffered heavily. We bridged the Sweetwater Canal in several places, but our main task was to bridge the Suez Canal, called by our Sappers either the

[1] *Military Operations. Egypt and Palestine* (Official History), by Lieut.-Gen. Sir George MacMunn, K.C.B., K.C.S.I., D.S.O., Vol. I, p. 33.
[2] Notes by Lieut.-Col. T. P. Bassett, D.S.O., R.E., sent to the author on May 28th, 1936.
[3] Notes by Col. D. McA. Hogg, M.C., late R.E., sent to the author on May 18th, 1937.

'Sewage' or 'Suet' Canal! Our first efforts were based on the existing chain ferries, with additional barges added to make a continuous bridge, but these proved unsatisfactory. The barges were of poor quality and liable to founder. At El Qantara we got some excellent steel lighters, rectangular in plan, and made a continuous bridge, mooring the lighters end to end with no waterway between them. While the Canal was open to traffic, the two halves of the bridge lay along the banks; and when a bridge was needed, the halves could be swung easily into position. No decking was required, as the decks of the lighters, and the landing flaps at their ends, made a roadway. Later, we took over some admirable bridges of pontoon type made by the Australian Field Companies. The Australians used the large floats employed by the Suez Canal Company to carry the discharge pipe of a dredger across a wide stretch of water. Each float consisted of a pair of iron cylinders connected by a longitudinal cradle which held the pipe, and by turning the float so that the cylinders were transverse to the line of the bridge, it made a suitable pier. The bridge was stiffened with horizontal diagonal bracing of wire rope. The Turks tried on several occasions to mine the Canal. One mine was lifted by the Royal Indian Marine and given to me to destroy, and as it was of French manufacture, I was told to consult a French Naval Officer who was said to be an expert. Accordingly, we arranged to meet; but he failed to appear, and so I destroyed the mine with guncotton. Shortly afterwards, I received a note of apology from the Frenchman addressed to me as '*Le Commandant des Soumarins et Mines*,' a novel interpretation of the meaning of the letters 'S. & M.'"

The Suez Canal Zone was divided, for defence purposes, into four sections. Before the arrival of the Australians and New Zealanders, the 10th and part of the 11th Indian Divisions furnished garrisons for the posts on the east bank, while the remainder of the 11th Division was retained in reserve at Moascar, near Ismailia, together with the Imperial Service Cavalry Brigade. Early in November, 1914, the enemy began to filter into Sinai, and by the 15th they were believed to have 5,000 infantry and 3,000 Arab auxiliaries at El Arish, which, with Nekhl, had been evacuated according to plan. On the 19th, they reconnoitred Bir el Abd on the northern route, and, on the 20th, skirted the Qatiya Oasis and appeared within 18 miles of El Qantara. Heavy rain during December having filled the rock-cisterns of Sinai, the enemy began to approach also by the more southerly routes. On January 25th, 1915, it was reported that they had occupied Moiya Harab, 25 miles from the Bitter Lakes, and they raided El Qantara. Warships took post in the Canal, and troops were moved to their positions of defence. The Turks closed in on El Qantara and attacked the southern post at El Kubri. Dragging their pontoons and guns with infinite labour across the wastes of Sinai, they camped in large numbers east of El Qantara, Ismailia and Serapeum, and it became obvious that the main attack might be expected shortly in the region of Ismailia.

We had now twelve posts on the west bank in the vital section between

Lake Timsa and the Great Bitter Lake, in addition to those on the east bank at Tussum, Serapeum and Deversoir. This section was held by four battalions of Indian infantry, a company of Territorial engineers, a field battery, a pack battery and some Pioneers. A roaring dust-storm arose on February 2nd and continued throughout the following night and morning. At 3.25 a.m. on February 3rd, 1915, squads of the enemy could be discerned, through the haze south of Tussum, engaged in carrying galvanized-iron pontoons and rafts of kerosine-oil tins down the sandy gullies leading to the water's edge, and, about an hour later, the pack battery opened fire on them. Other parties could be seen approaching on a frontage of about 1½ miles. The wreckage of pontoons and rafts soon strewed the bank. Only three pontoons succeeded in crossing, and their occupants were killed or captured to a man.[1] The first attempt had ended in complete failure. Yet Djemal Pasha did not abandon hope. At 9.30 a.m. he sent fresh troops against Serapeum and renewed the attempt to force a crossing. Traffic in the Canal was suspended. Shipping in Lake Timsa suffered under accurate artillery fire. Two British battleships and two French cruisers joined in the engagement, and finally, at 1.30 p.m., the Turks began to retreat across Sinai with the remnants of other forces which had attacked El Qantara, El Firdan and El Kubri. Unfortunately, they were allowed to withdraw without molestation until the afternoon of February 4th, when the Imperial Service Cavalry Brigade rode eastwards from Ismailia but did not come to grips with them. Difficulties of supply and transport may afford some excuse for this inaction, and it seems that General Maxwell had limited General Wilson to a passive defence, based on the Canal, because he had been warned by Lord Kitchener not to risk a reverse which might have far-reaching effects.[2] Nevertheless, a golden opportunity was lost, and the Turks escaped, though with heavy casualties.

A detachment of the 10th Company, Madras S. & M., was present at Ismailia during the Turkish attempt to cross the Canal in force, though it did not come into action. It had been sent from El Qantara to improve the Ismailia defences. The remainder of the half-company at El Qantara was engaged in defence work and in maintaining and operating the floating bridge over which reinforcements passed continually. The other half-company was busy in the southern sector around El Kubri. A few weeks after the abortive Turkish attempt, most of the half-company at El Qantara moved southwards to Ismailia and Serapeum, where they erected wooden huts and strengthened the defences. A small party distributed water daily by launch to the posts south of Serapeum. The unit, as a whole was occupied chiefly with water-supply and with the supervision of defence work by the infantry and hutting by contractors—uninspiring tasks, but necessary for the safety and well-being of the garrisons of the posts.

During the spring and summer of 1915, the 10th Company was attached to the 29th Indian Infantry Brigade (11th Indian Division) under Brig.-

[1] *L'Attaque du Canal de Suez, 3rd Fevrier*, 1915, by Lieut. de Vaisseau Georges Douin.
[2] *Military Operations. Egypt and Palestine* (Official History), by Lieut.-Gen. Sir George MacMunn, K.C.B., K.C.S.I., D.S.O., Vol. I, pp. 48, 49.

THE SUEZ CANAL AT TUSSUM.

Near the point of the Turkish crossing in February, 1915.

[*Photo by the Author.*]

General P. C. Palin, and was assisted by the 23rd Pioneers.[1] The Turks were occupied so fully by the allied landings in Gallipoli from April 25th onwards,[2] and by General Townshend's advance in Iraq, that they were in no position to resume their attack on Egypt. The last great offensive in Gallipoli—the landing at Suvla Bay—took place on August 6th. It failed, and on October 11th Lord Kitchener began to contemplate evacuation. He visited Mudros in November to discuss the situation with Lieut.-General Sir Charles Monro, who had replaced General Sir Ian Hamilton in command, and having decided on evacuation, issued orders for the preparation of an improved line of defence for Egypt, not on the Suez Canal, but far out in the Sinai Desert. His telegraphic order to Brig.-General H. B. H. Wright, the Chief Engineer, was brief and comprehensive. " The defence of the Canal," it ran, " must be taken up seriously and in depth." Wright immediately drew up plans for three lines of defence in the desert, ordered vast quantities of stores, bought timber to the value of £500,000 and secured the mobilization of the Egyptian Public Works Department under an eminent engineer, Sir Murdoch MacDonald. A strong line of redoubts and entrenchments was planned far east of the Canal, and behind this, other lines with roads, railways and piped water-supply, the whole to be held by 8 infantry divisions, 5 mounted divisions and 19 batteries, with 15 field companies of engineers in addition to those available in Egypt or obtainable from the Dardanelles. On December 20th, 1915, the last soldier left Gallipoli, and two days later, the general line of defence of the Suez Canal was advanced some 6 miles into the Sinai Desert.

The 10th Company, now under Captain D. McA. Hogg, R.E.,[3] was placed in charge of the defence work in the extreme southern section of the new line north of Ayun Musa, its headquarters being at Gebel Murr, a rocky hill in the desert some 6 miles east of Esh Shatt on the Canal. The Sappers had to blast hundreds of yards of trench out of solid rock. In the desert alongside, it was necessary to use double sandbags, one inside the other, because the sand was so fine that it ran through a single bag. Detachments were sent to El Kubri, " Baluchistan," Esh Shatt, " Quarantine " and Ayun Musa. The design of the defences varied according to the ground. At Ayun Musa, between which and " Quarantine " on the sea coast there was a level stretch of 3 miles, some positions were built as breastworks because the soil was mostly waterlogged, while in others, large excavations were needed in the fine sand before revetting hurdles for the trenches could be placed correctly. The company was

[1]The 30th Brigade of the 11th Indian Division, under Brig.-Gen. Sir C. J. Melliss, V.C., was transferred to Iraq in March, 1915, and the 28th Brigade, under Maj.-Gen. Sir G. J. Younghusband, to Aden in July, 1915, leaving only the 29th Brigade in Egypt. The divisional organization of the 10th and 11th Indian Divisions was broken up in June, 1915, and the remaining troops administered by the O.C. Canal Defences.

[2]From July to Oct., 1915, the C.R.E., 1st Australian Division, in Gallipoli was Maj. A. H. Cunningham, R.E., formerly Offg. Commandant, Bengal S. & M., at Roorkee. He was invalided in Oct., 1915. In Nov., 1917, he returned to his appointment at Roorkee as Commandant and held it until June, 1922.

[3]Capt. T. P. Bassett, R.E., was appointed to the Staff in December, 1915. He returned to the command of the 10th Company, Madras S. & M., in May, 1916, when Capt. D. McA. Hogg, R.E., went to Iraq.

engaged also in water-supply, and, with the help of the Egyptian Labour Corps, laid a 3-inch pipe line from Esh Shatt to Gebel Murr. For a short time in December 1915, some Tehri-Garhwal State Sappers worked also on the defences in Sinai. They formed an "infantry" platoon of the 39th Garhwal Rifles, then on its way from France to Iraq. They were, however, mere "birds of passage," and during 1915, and also in 1916 and 1917, the 10th Company was the sole unit in Egypt representing the three Corps of Indian Sappers and Miners.

When Lord Kitchener returned to England in November 1915, he sent Major-General H. S. Horne to Egypt to reconnoitre the contemplated line of defence east of the Suez Canal, and Horne selected a front line roughly 11,000 yards from, and parallel to, the Canal, skirting the main inundation in the north and terminating near Ayun Musa in the south. He proposed that there should be a second line about 4,500 yards in rear, and that a series of mutually supporting works, covering bridgeheads and other vital points on the east bank of the Canal, should form a third line. Unfortunately, no additional engineer units were immediately available for the execution of this scheme, though thirteen Royal Engineer officers arrived in January 1916. The responsibility for the work in its initial stages fell on Brig.-General Wright, but it was fortunate that, when military labour was so scarce, Egypt possessed ample civilian labour and capable civilian engineers. Sir Murdoch MacDonald controlled most of the non-military work, including the provision of roads and landing stages and water-supply to the desert areas. Railway extensions came under Brig.-General G. B. Macauley, late R.E., and Telegraph extensions under Major J. S. Liddell, R.E., Director of Army Signals. Military engineering duties in connection with the new scheme fell to Major (temporary Brig.-General) P. G. Grant, R.E.

Early in January, 1916, Lieut.-General Sir Archibald Murray replaced Lieut.-General Sir Charles Monro in the chief command in Egypt,[1] and Lieut.-General Sir John Maxwell undertook the internal military administration of the country and the control of the operations in the western desert against the Senussi.[2] Some two months later, the Mediterranean Expeditionary Force from Gallipoli and the Force in Egypt were amalgamated to form an "Egyptian Expeditionary Force," strongly reinforced from home and placed under the command of Sir Archibald Murray. This force included 13 infantry and mounted divisions and had a strength of nearly 400,000 men. It was, in fact, the general strategic reserve for the whole Empire.[3] Included in it were 21 British and Dominion field companies of engineers, of which 18 were on or near the Suez Canal;[4] yet India was still represented only by the 10th Company, Madras S. & M.

[1]Lieut.-Gen. Sir Charles Monro had assumed command when he arrived with the Mediterranean Expeditionary Force evacuated from the Dardanelles.

[2]For the operations against the Senussi see *The Royal Engineers in Egypt and the Sudan*, by the present author, pp. 329–333. No Sappers and Miners served in these operations.

[3]*An Outline of the Egyptian and Palestine Campaigns*, 1914 *to* 1918, by Maj.-Gen. Sir M. G. E. Bowman-Manifold, K.B.E., C.B., C.M.G., D.S.O., late R.E., p. 18.

[4]Three Territorial Field Companies, R.E., were with the Western Frontier Force, under Maj.-Gen. W. E. Peyton, fighting against the Senussi beyond Mersa Matruh.

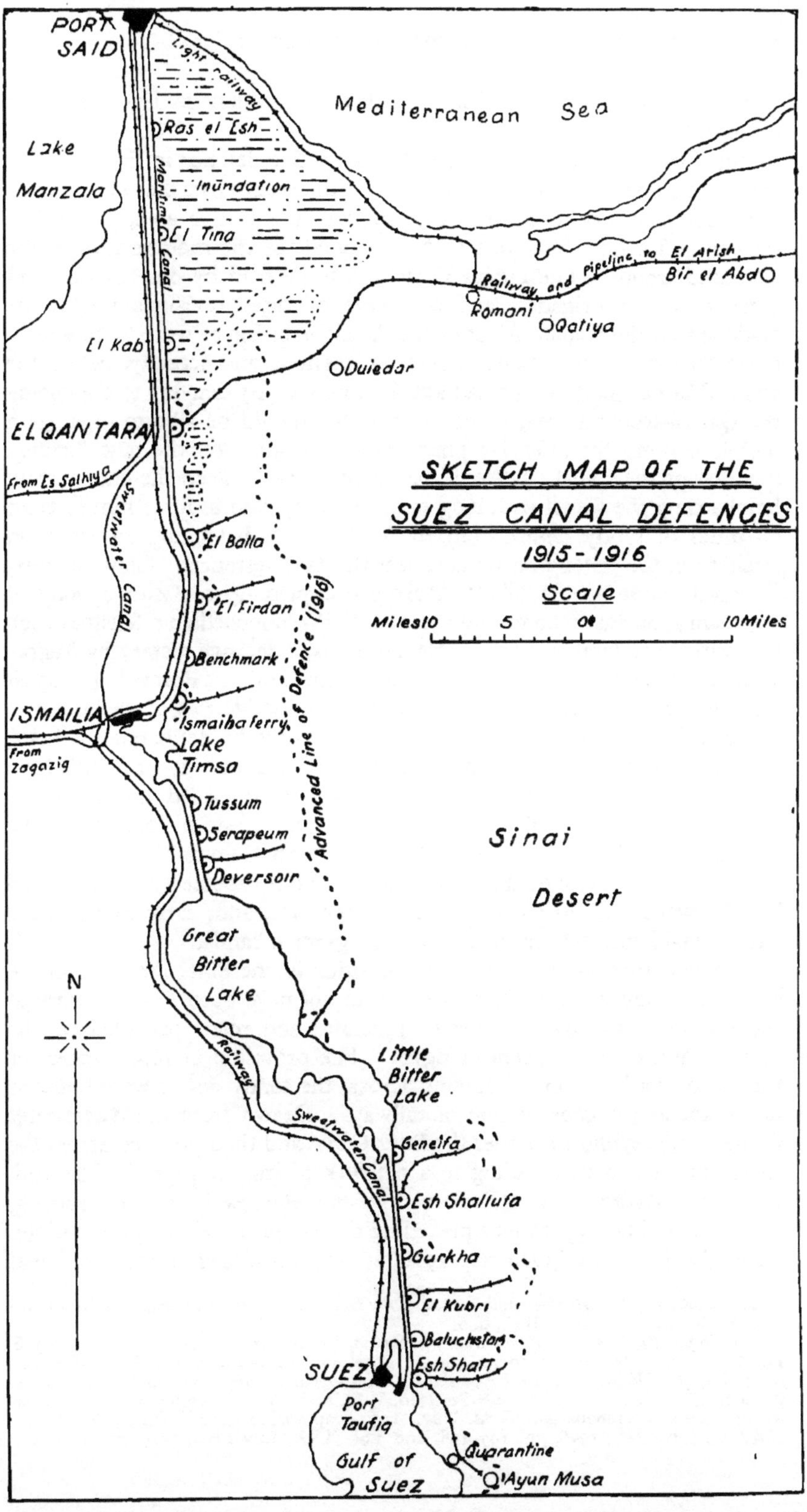
SKETCH MAP OF THE
SUEZ CANAL DEFENCES
1915-1916
Scale
Miles 10 5 0 10 Miles
PORT SAID
Mediterranean Sea
Light railway
Lake Manzala
Ras el Esh
Inundation
Maritime Canal
El Tina
Railway and Pipeline to El Arish
Bir el Abd
Romani
Qatiya
El Kab
Duiedar
EL QANTARA
From Es Salhiya
Sweetwater Canal
El Balla
El Firdan
Advanced Line of Defence (1916)
Benchmark
ISMAILIA
Ismailia Ferry
Lake Timsa
From Zagazig
Tussum
Serapeum
Deversoir
Sinai
Desert
Great Bitter Lake
N
Railway
Little Bitter Lake
Sweetwater Canal
Geneifa
Esh Shallufa
Gurkha
El Kubri
Baluchistan
Esh Shatt
SUEZ
Port Taufiq
Gulf of Suez
Quarantine
Ayun Musa

She was naturally concerned more with the operations in Iraq than with those in Egypt.

Our plans for 1916 were to maintain an active defence in Egypt and to reduce the number of troops required for the security of the Suez Canal.[1] The first step was to be the occupation of the Qatiya area, to which a railway and a pipe-line were to be extended for the maintenance of the advanced troops. The Qatiya Oasis was to be held by one division and three mounted brigades, and a reserve of three divisions was to be stationed on the Canal. Most of the divisions in Egypt were to be sent to other theatres of operations as soon as possible, and actually, before the end of March, six divisions had left the country. By denying to the enemy the Qatiya-Romani area, it seemed that we should be able to organize a mobile column for offensive purposes and to abandon the new fortified line east of the Canal. It would be possible also to keep the enemy from bombarding the Canal with long-range artillery, and to force him to cross 60 miles of sandy desert from El Arish before launching an attack in strength in the water-bearing area near the Mediterranean. Consequently, in April 1916, Sir Archibald Murray occupied Qatiya with a body of Yeomanry, against whom however, the Turks launched an offensive which met with considerable success. Nevertheless, a decisive victory by Major-General the Hon. H. A. Lawrence over 18,000 Turks at Romani on August 4th opened the way to El Arish, and the initiative passed definitely to General Murray, who then proceeded to advance by deliberate methods, accompanied by the requisite extensions of the railway and pipe-line. The troops to the east of the Suez Canal were placed under Lieut.-General Sir Charles Dobell and constituted an " Eastern Force," and the advance to El Arish was entrusted to a " Desert Column " of 4 divisions under Lieut.-General Sir Philip Chetwode. No resistance was encountered by Chetwode. El Arish fell on December 21st, and, early in 1917, the entire Sinai Peninsula was once again in Egyptian hands.

The construction of the defensive position in the Sinai Desert, and the subsequent advance into Palestine, would not have been possible without the excellent systems of railways, pipelines and roads provided by the military and civil engineers in Egypt. The provision of piped water for the troops stationed in, or moving across, the sandy desert was almost as important as the construction of railways. Drawn from the Sweetwater Canal, it was syphoned under the Suez Canal and then pumped across the desert in large mains leading to a network of smaller pipes.[2] The 10th Company, Madras S. & M., however, was not engaged in this undertaking, nor in the military operations preceding the extension of the water-supply. Towards the end of October, 1916, it was withdrawn from the Canal

[1] *A Summary of the Strategy and Tactics of the Egypt and Palestine Campaign*, by Lieut.-Col. A. Kearsey, D.S.O., O.B.E., p. 6.

[2] *The Royal Engineers in Egypt and the Sudan*, by the present author, pp. 325–328. Details of the water-supply operations are given in *The Work of the Royal Engineers in the European War*, 1914–19, *Egypt and Palestine—Water-Supply*, and in " Water-supply in Sinai and Palestine," by Maj. G. Streeten, R.E., and " Water-supply during the Operations against Beersheba and Gaza, Nov., 1917," appearing in *The R.E. Journal*, Vol. XXVIII, July–Dec., 1918, pp. 193–198, and Vol. XXX, July–Dec., 1919, pp. 97–103.

Zone, and, moving through El Qantara, reached Bir el Abd by train on November 7th. There it was employed for a time on defence works, wire-netting roads and water-supply, and afterwards on similar work at El Mazar and El Arish, where it remained until the end of March 1917.

At the beginning of 1917, our policy being still restricted to an active defence, Sir Archibald Murray decided to capture Rafa and Gaza by an advance along the coastal road from El Arish. If he could take Gaza, the Turks would be forced to evacuate Southern Palestine as he would have outflanked their main base at Beersheba. Rafa fell on January 9th after some stiff fighting and a long night-march by the Desert Column. On March 5th, the enemy began to fall back on Gaza and Beersheba, and within the next fortnight the railway reached Rafa. Murray nearly captured the powerful defences at Gaza when he attacked on March 26th. The mounted troops passed between Gaza and Beersheba and operated from the north, while the infantry attacked from the south; but a heavy fog delayed the movements of the infantry, and in the end the assault had to be delivered in broad daylight across open country. The result was a costly failure, and the troops retired to a depression called the Wadi Ghuzzee. The 10th Company took no active part in the affair. On April 1st it marched from El Arish to Khan Yunus, some 6 miles beyond Rafa, leaving a section at Rafa and sending another forward to Deir el Belah, 7 miles north of Khan Yunus. The Sappers supervised the work of 6,000 men of the Egyptian Labour Corps employed on water-supply and defence schemes, but they undertook also the construction of blockhouses for a distance of 80 miles along the railway between Romain and Rafa. Afterwards, the unit sank wells and laid wire-netting roads around El Arish.

In an optimistic telegram to England after the First Battle of Gaza, Sir Archibald Murray reported his advance to the Wadi Ghuzzee but he made no mention of his failure to reach his main objective. The news of this apparent victory, coupled with that of General Maude's occupation of Baghdad on March 11th, induced the War Cabinet to believe that the power of the Turks was crumbling everywhere, and consequently they directed Murray to exploit his success without delay by defeating the enemy in Southern Palestine with a view to the occupation of Jerusalem.[1] This sudden extension of his rôle naturally surprised Murray, who replied that, as he had already stated, he needed two more divisions for an advance into Palestine. These were not available, so he was instructed to follow up his recent success but not to aim at Jerusalem. His troops were ill-equipped for static warfare, and his artillery was inadequate for a frontal assault on an entrenched position held by five divisions.[2] Yet he accepted the risk and began his second attack on Gaza on April 17th. The Eastern Force captured some of the outer defences and, two days later, Dobell

[1] "The Campaigns in Palestine and Egypt, 1914–18," by Maj.-Gen. Sir F. Maurice, K.C.M.G., C.B., appearing in *The Army Quarterly*, Vol. XVIII, No. 1, April, 1929, pp. 14–23.

[2] "Egypt and Sinai, 1914–17," appearing in *The Army Quarterly*, Vol. IV, No. 1, April, 1922, pp. 93–106.

launched the main attack. The two wings made some progress, but the centre was checked and suffered heavy casualties. Murray then decided to suspend the operations, consolidate his gains, and prepare for a more systematic effort in the autumn.

Undoubtedly, the Second Battle of Gaza was a blunder due to misunderstandings between the commander on the spot and the authorities at home. As Lieut.-Colonel (now Field-Marshal Earl) Wavell remarks,[1] it met with the almost inevitable fate of such attacks on strongly entrenched positions with insufficient artillery support. The Egyptian Expeditionary Force had already attained its original objective—the security of our main lines of deployment through the Suez Canal and Egypt—and it held a strong natural position at Rafa. Why, then, was a further advance contemplated? Firstly, because the Allies wished to exert the maximum pressure on all fronts during 1917. Secondly, to prevent powerful reserves of the Turkish "Yilderim" Army at Aleppo from being despatched to Iraq for the recapture of Baghdad; and thirdly, because the Prime Minister, Mr. Lloyd George, sought for some success to compensate the public for the disappointment caused by General Nivelle's failure in France and the imminent collapse of Russia. Although Sir Archibald Murray had cleared Sinai with the utmost energy, it was only natural that, after the second failure at Gaza, there should be changes in the higher commands. Lieut.-General Sir Philip Chetwode succeeded Lieut.-General Sir Charles Dobell in command of the Eastern Force, and, at the end of June 1917, General Sir Edmund Allenby, who had led the 3rd Army with distinction in France, arrived to replace Sir Archibald Murray and initiate the invasion of Palestine.

General Allenby reported that, given a force of 7 infantry divisions and 3 mounted divisions, he could attack Gaza and Beersheba with a good prospect of reaching Jerusalem, but that he required 2 infantry divisions, 11 field batteries, some heavy artillery and cavalry, and 3 squadrons of the Royal Flying Corps to complete his strength. These demands were met by the transfer of the 10th and 60th Divisions from Salonika, some artillery and aeroplanes from the United Kingdom and Italy, and the Indian Cavalry from France. Allenby then reorganized his army into a "Desert Mounted Corps," under Lieut.-General Sir Henry Chauvel, and two Army Corps, the 20th under Lieut.-General Sir Philip Chetwode and the 21st under Lieut.-General Sir Edward Bulfin, and he abolished the Eastern Force.

Gaza had now become a veritable fortress. The enemy had also constructed a chain of entrenched positions extending for 30 miles almost to Beersheba, which was covered by five outlying systems of redoubts. This front was held by the 20th and 22nd Turkish Corps and the 3rd Turkish Cavalry Division, amounting to 50,000 rifles and 1,500 sabres with 300 guns. As Gaza seemed almost impregnable, and the centre very strong,

[1] "The Strategy of the Campaigns of the Egyptian Expeditionary Force," by Lieut.-Col. A. P. Wavell, C.M.G., M.C., The Black Watch, appearing in *The Army Quarterly*, Vol. III, No. 2, Jan., 1922, pp. 235–248.

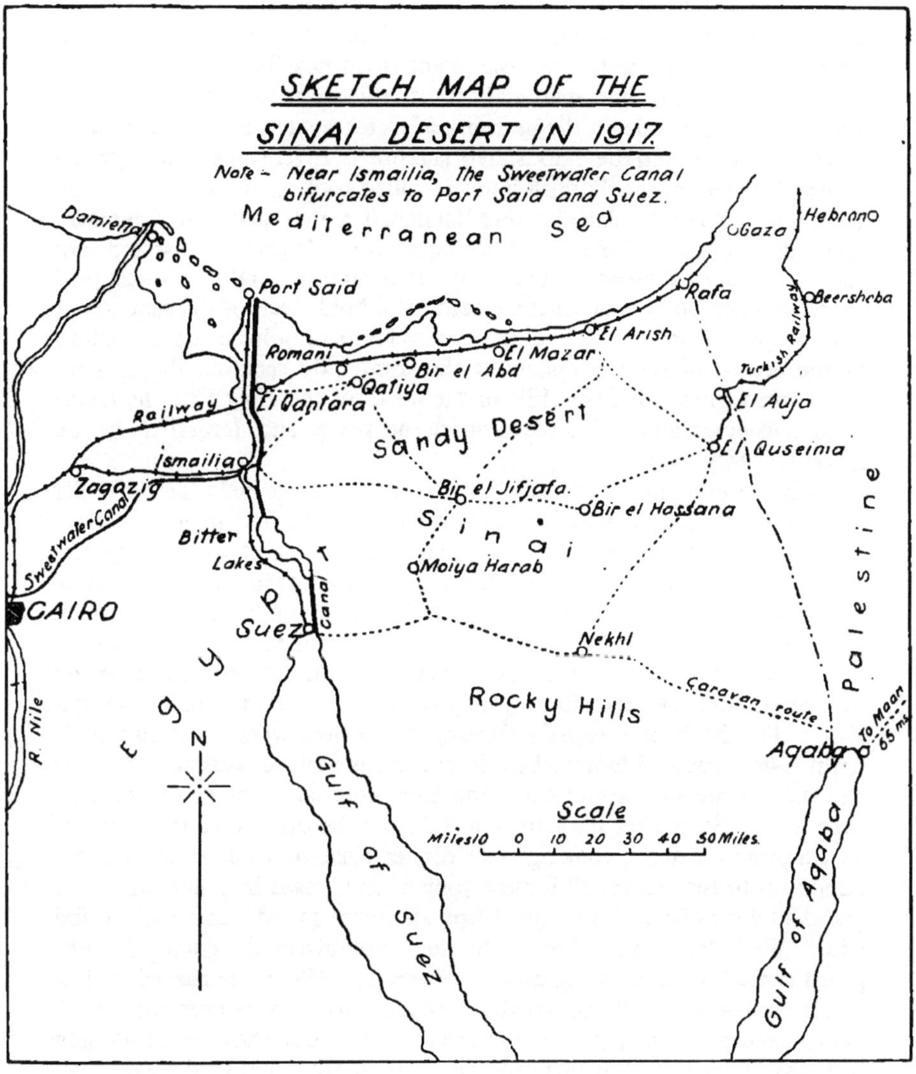
SKETCH MAP OF THE
SINAI DESERT IN 1917
Note – Near Ismailia, the Sweetwater Canal bifurcates to Port Said and Suez.
Mediterranean Sea
Damietta
Port Said
Gaza
Hebron
Rafa
Beersheba
Turkish Railway
El Arish
Romani
El Mazar
Bir el Abd
Qatiya
El Qantara
Railway
El Auja
Sandy Desert
El Quseima
Ismailia
Zagazig
Bir el Jifjafa
Bir el Hassana
Sinai
Sweetwater Canal
Bitter
Lakes
Moiya Harab
Canal
Palestine
CAIRO
Suez
Nekhl
Egypt
Caravan route
Rocky Hills
R. Nile
N
To Maan 65 ms.
Aqaba
Gulf of Suez
Scale
Miles 10 0 10 20 30 40 50 Miles
Gulf of Aqaba

Allenby planned to capture Beersheba with the 20th Corps, thus turning the enemy's left, while the 21st Corps pinned the enemy down by an attack on Gaza.[1] Secrecy was an important factor, but the chief difficulties in carrying out this plan were connected with transport and water-supply, for Allenby had to rely on camel transport in the desert, not only for stores and equipment, but also for water. The Turks feared and expected an attack on Gaza, so the fortress was bombarded heavily on October 27th. Then, after a long night-march, Beersheba was attacked from the south and east by Chetwode on the morning of October 31st, and by nightfall it was in our hands and the Turkish left laid open. After some bitter fighting around Beersheba, the Turkish line was rolled back on November 6th and Gaza fell on the 7th. Allenby then launched 3 mounted and 2 infantry divisions in pursuit of the Turks fleeing northwards up the coast and sent another infantry division eastwards towards Hebron. Jaffa was occupied on November 16th, and Allenby made the bold decision to advance at once on Jerusalem without the proper development of his communications or the arrival of reinforcements at the front. By securing the difficult passes through the Judean Hills to the north of the Holy City, he facilitated a concentration of force around the place, and Jerusalem fell on December 8th, 1917.

With the exception of a detachment formed into a Field Troop under Lieutenant J. A. de Rosse, I.A.R.O., none of the 10th Company, Madras S. & M., shared in the advance to Jerusalem. The unit worked near the Wadi Ghuzzee, south of Gaza, from September 23rd until the end of November, when it rejoined the 75th Division[2] under Major-General P. C. Palin and took part in minor operations until March 31st, 1918.

Allenby's success was due to his courage, versatility, careful planning and iron discipline. His forcefulness may be illustrated by the following episode. The habit of carelessly lighting camp fires where they might do harm always enraged him, so he told one of his Staff to issue an order that any such negligence would entail the court-martial of the officer responsible for it. Soon after his arrival at the front, he discovered the guard of an ammunition dump cooking their dinner close to a pile of shells. He strode up to the sentry. "Repeat your orders," said he; and when the man had got as far as "In case of fire, alarm the guard," interrupted him with "Well, *there's* your fire. Why don't you alarm the guard?" The guard turned out and extinguished the fire, and Allenby remarked "The officer responsible will be tried by court-martial, whatever his rank." On his return to headquarters, however, he found that the original warning had never been issued, which brought about another and louder explosion of wrath.[3] If "Bull" Allenby did not always inspire liking, at least he infused confidence, for he was a brilliant leader in the field. Such was the man who

[1] "Palestine," by Field-Marshal The Viscount Allenby, G.C.B., G.C.M.G., appearing in *The R.E. Journal*, Vol. XLIII, March–Dec., 1929, pp. 41–49.

[2] The 75th Division included the personnel of the former 29th Infantry Brigade, to which the 10th Company had been attached previously.

[3] *Allenby*, by Gen. Sir Archibald Wavell, K.C.B., C.M.G., M.C., pp. 198, 199.

commanded the Egyptian Expeditionary Force in its triumphal progress through Palestine and Syria.

After the fall of Jerusalem, there seemed to be no valid reason for a further advance. The situation on the Western Front was perilous; the campaign in Palestine was a drain on shipping; and Turkey, though exhausted, was prevented by Germany from capitulating. Yet, because of a belief that we could hold the Germans in France until American help turned the scale, it was decided by the Supreme War Council that our policy for 1918 should be defensive in the West and aggressive against Turkey in the East. The year 1917 ended with a crossing of the Auja River, 3 miles north of Jaffa,[1] to render that port more secure for shipping, and the crushing defeat of a Turkish attempt to recapture Jerusalem. Allenby's line then lay in an arc extending from east of Jerusalem to the sea-coast, 10 miles north of Jaffa. The 20th Corps (Chetwode) was on the right, the 21st Corps (Bulfin) on the left, and the Desert Mounted Corps (Chauvel) in reserve. Rail-head was approaching Ludd, near Ramleh. some 15 miles behind the line. Allenby proceeded to improve his communications, replenish supplies and prepare to cross the River Jordan. There was sharp fighting in an advance to Jericho, which was occupied on February 21st, 1918. The Jordan was crossed on March 21st, and Allenby launched a powerful raid against the line of communication which supplied the Turkish troops opposing King Hussein's Arab forces in the Hedjaz led by the Sherif Feisal and Captain T. E. Lawrence (Lawrence of Arabia). The object of the raid was to cut the Hedjaz Railway at Amman and join hands with the Arabs. This was accomplished, and, in April, another force raided Es Salt. Then the German offensives in France necessitated the depletion of the Army in Palestine. As many British units as possible had to be sent to France and replaced by Indian units, and the Palestine front was required to adopt the Indian pattern of division. The 52nd and 74th Divisions left for France. The Yeomanry regiments were withdrawn from the Desert Mounted Corps and replaced by Indian cavalry. The Imperial Camel Corps was disbanded. One division alone, the 54th, was retained on a British establishment. In all, 48 British battalions, 9 Yeomanry regiments and many batteries were lost to the Egyptian Expeditionary Force. It was a crippling blow and forbade any immediate resumption of the offensive. Intensive training and drastic reorganization became the order of the day and lasted throughout the summer.[2]

The stage was now set for the entry in strength of the Sappers and Miners into the war in Egypt and Palestine. A change came over the scene when the Egyptian Expeditionary Force was largely "Indianized" and Sapper and Miner units began to reach it from Iraq. Then, at last, the men of the hardworking and experienced 10th Company, Madras S. & M., were able to welcome their brothers of the Bengal and Bombay Corps, and then, at last, Sappers and Miners began to appear in the forward zone

[1]See *Sketch Map of Palestine and Syria*, 1918, included in this chapter.

[2]*An Outline of the Egyptian and Palestine Campaigns*, 1914 *to* 1918, by Maj.-Gen. Sir M. G. E. Bowman-Manifold, K.B.E., C.B., C.M.G., D.S.O., late R.E., p. 70.

of active military operations. India's entry in force into the war in Palestine opened when the 7th Indian Division, under Major-General V. B. Fane, followed by the 3rd Indian Division, under Major-General A. R. Hoskins, arrived from Iraq, and the Indian Cavalry from France. It is true that Indian States troops, such as the Bikaner Camel Corps and the Imperial Service Infantry and Cavalry Brigades, had served in Egypt since 1914,[1] and that the 10th and part of the 11th Indian Divisions were there in 1915, but this was only a small contribution to the general effort. The 7th Division led the stream of reinforcements from Iraq and reached Suez during January 1918. With it were the 1st Company, Bengal S. & M., under Captain J. F. Gray, R.E., with Lieutenant H. A. Joly de Lotbinière, R.E., the 3rd Company under Captain W. Cave-Browne, R.E.,[2] and the 4th Company under Major A. J. G. Bird, R.E., with Captain E. L. Farley, R.E. There were also a number of I.A.R.O. officers.[3] The 7th Division went into camp at Moascar, near Ismailia, where it remained until the end of March. The 3rd and 4th Companies, however, had moved forward earlier into Palestine to work on roads and water-supply. In April, the 7th Division relieved the 52nd (Lowland) Division at the front and took over the coastal area on the extreme left of the line, the advanced defences being about 7 miles north of the River Auja. The three Bengal Sapper companies remained with the 7th Division until the summer, when the 1st Company was transferred to the 60th (London) Division on the Indianization of that formation.

According to Brigadier E. F. J. Hill, the Bengal Sappers were busily employed from the moment they reached the front. "For some 10 to 20 miles inland from the sea," he writes,[4] "the country consisted of low downs, with occasional villages and orange orchards. East of this plain, the mountains extended to the steep Jordan Valley. The large area occupied by the 7th Division was treeless, and almost waterless except for the Auja River and a few wells, and there were no roads. Our line was very weakly defended. It faced the Turkish trenches across a valley, and was some 2,000 yards from them on the coast and only 700 yards at the eastern end. The first task was to consolidate our position by a defence in depth, and this work continued throughout April and May, 1918. The position having been made secure from attack, the Engineer and Medical Services then combined to fight the mosquito. To protect the troops from the deadly ravages of malaria, it was necessary to drain two marshy lakes in the 7th Divisional area. In three weeks, the water from the first was pumped into the sea, 300 yards away; but the second lake, which was a mile long and ¼ mile wide, presented a more difficult problem. It was in full view of the

[1] *A Short History of the Services rendered by the Imperial Service Troops during the Great War,* 1914–18, by Maj.-Gen. Sir Harry Watson, K.B.E., C.B., C.M.G., C.I.E., M.V.O., pp. 2, 13, 23 and 41.

[2] Actually, Capt. W. Cave-Browne, R.E., assumed command of the 3rd Company after disembarkation, when it was found that Major F. McC. Douie, R.E., had been left behind in hospital in Iraq. Capt. Cave-Browne had been adjutant to Lieut.-Col. E. F. J. Hill, R.E., C.R.E., 7th Division.

[3] The 3rd Company alone had 4 I.A.R.O. officers—Lieuts. R. Trevor-Jones, J. A. Stein, G. D. Baxter and W. B. Haughton.

[4] Notes by Brig. E. F. J. Hill, D.S.O., M.C., late R.E., sent to the author in 1932.

enemy and separated from the sea by a rocky ridge, 200 feet high and 600 feet thick, and by a small valley. Fortunately, an ancient duct, made possibly by the Crusaders, was discovered and was found to lead partly through the ridge. This was cleared and connected by tunnelling with a convenient cavern on the western side, and through these passages, the water from the lake was drained into the sea in three weeks. The 3rd Company began the work, the 4th Company continued it, and the entire project was completed in two months. As regards water-supply, pumps were installed in the existing wells in the area, and a series of square shallow wells, revetted with corrugated iron, were dug along the seashore. Perfectly pure water could be obtained within a few feet of the surface up to high-water mark, though after a time it tended to become brackish and new wells had to be dug. The so-called roads needed constant attention. We covered the principal communications with wire-netting,[1] 12 feet wide and stretched over a grass mat, but the wire soon broke under heavy lorry traffic."

These remarks give some idea of the general nature of Sapper and Miner employment during the period of consolidation north of the Auja before the great offensive which ended the war. The experiences of the 7th Indian Division were unique. It carried out practically the whole of the engineering preparations for the attack, and it was the leading infantry formation in the sweep through Syria. Consequently, the 3rd and 4th Companies, Bengal S. & M., were very much in the limelight during the concluding stages of the campaign. The 1st Company, with the 60th Division, was not so conspicuous, but was often in the thick of the fighting.

While the Bengal Sappers were draining marshes, digging wells and making roads and defences in the coastal area, several units of the Bombay and Madras Corps were hard at work in other sectors. Between April 26th and June 9th, 1918, three companies of Bombay Sappers had reached Suez from Iraq with the 3rd Indian Division. These were the 18th Company under Major M. Rawlence, R.E., the 20th Company, under Major S. Boyd, R.E., with Captain H. W. R. Hamilton, R.E., and the 21st Company, under Captain M. Everett, R.E., each with a number of I.A.R.O. subalterns as Company Officers.[2] They were re-equipped at Moascar and arrived at Ludd before the end of June. There they were employed mostly on roads and water-supply in the 3rd Divisional area pending the resumption of the offensive, but, on July 8th, the 18th Company was transferred to the 10th Division under Major-General J. R. Longley. The 16th Company, Madras S. & M., under Captain T. B. Harris, R.E., arrived in Egypt from Rawalpindi on May 9th and joined the 10th Company already serving with the 75th Division. Another new arrival was the 72nd Company, Bombay S. & M., which joined the 53rd Division. General Allenby then had 9 Sapper and Miner companies at the front, in addition

[1]Wire-netting on roads had been introduced in Gallipoli by Lieut.-Col. E. M. Paul, C.B., R.E., and had been used in 1915 during the operations against the Senussi in the Western Desert.

[2]Those with the 18th Company were Lieuts. J. G. Marshall, T. Pearce, T. I. S. Mackay, G. C. Minnitt, and D. G. L. Pirie, I.A.R.O.

to 12 Field Companies, R.E., two British and one Australian Field Squadrons and 6 battalions of Indian Pioneers,[1] the whole being under Major-General H. B. H. Wright as Chief Engineer. It was well that he had so fine an array of engineer troops, for the campaign in Palestine was in many respects an "Engineer" war since rapidity of movement was dependent on the provision of adequate communications in a peculiarly rugged country.

The engineer units worked so hard and consistently in the coastal area that the enemy failed to regard with suspicion a sudden increase in industry towards the middle of June 1918, when General Allenby began to make his preparations for attack. The C.R.E., 7th Division (Lieut.-Colonel E. F. J. Hill), was summoned to headquarters and ordered to report secretly whether he could water 5 infantry and 3 cavalry divisions in the divisional area. He replied that he could do so if given the necessary apparatus, and Allenby then decided to attack on a large scale from the coastal area.[2] Extreme secrecy was maintained. No civilians were allowed north of the Auja, and only a few senior officers had any idea of what was afoot. Every device which could mislead, not only the enemy, but our own troops and the civilian population, was adopted. All movements pointed to a probable attack through the mountains near the Jordan. For instance, after the 60th Division and the Desert Mounted Corps had been transferred to the coast, the vacated cavalry headquarters were kept lit up every night and wireless messages were sent from them. Allenby required a great concentration of cavalry on his left to exploit a break-through near the coast, and accordingly the marches of the mounted troops from the Jordan were made by night, while any infantry sent eastwards to replace them moved openly by day. Dummy camps sprang up in the Jordan area. The principal hotel in Jerusalem was commandeered as an advanced report depot and fitted with a telephone system. Fifteen thousand dummy horses, made of canvas, filled the empty horse-lines, near the city, and sleighs drawn by mules raised clouds of dust when the horses should have been going to water. Battalions marched ostentatiously down to the Jordan by day, and returned, unobserved, in lorries at night.

A tragedy occurred in the camp of the 1st Company, Bengal S. & M., on July 11th, when the Company Commander, Captain J. F. Gray, R.E., was murdered by one of his own men. A Sikh Sapper, who was in the guard tent awaiting trial by court-martial, managed to escape after dark with a loaded rifle and shot Gray in the back as he was sitting in his tent, reading a letter. The murderer then fired at the Company Subadar and finally committed suicide.[3] Through this foul crime the Bengal Sappers

[1]The units, apart from Sappers and Miners were the 65th, 66th, 85th, 436th, 437th, 484th, 486th, 495th, 496th, 519th, 521st and 522nd Field Companies, R.E. ; the 4th and 5th Field Squadrons, R.E., and an Australian Field Squadron ; and the 2/32nd, 1/34th, 2/107th, 121st, 1/155th and 2/155th Pioneers. (See *Military Operations, Egypt and Palestine* (Official History), by Capt. Cyril Falls, Part II, Appendix 3, pp. 666–673 and *The Military Engineer in India*, by the present author, Vol. I, p. 495.)

[2]Notes by Brig. E. F. J. Hill, D.S.O., M.C., late R.E., sent to the author in 1932.

[3]Notes by Maj.-Gen. W. Cave-Browne, C.B.E., D.S.O., M.C., late R.E., sent to the author on Nov. 18th, 1944.

lost an officer who was the soul of good nature, full of energy, a keen pig-sticker and an ardent musician. The unit then came under the command of Captain H. A. Joly de Lotbinière, R.E., who led it with success in the subsequent operations.

Preparations continued quietly near the sea-coast. Tube wells were sunk, existing wells improved, and pumping plants installed in dug-outs, until twelve large water-supply installations were ready for watering eight divisions. The cavalry, concentrated south of the Auja, were hidden in orchards. As the construction of numerous bridges for the passage of the river might attract unwelcome attention, a clever ruse was adopted to allay suspicion. Some weeks before the attack, a " School of Pontooning " was established on the Auja where parties of engineer troops from all divisions were trained assiduously and with the full knowledge of the enemy. This explained to inquisitive Turkish observers the purpose of the bridging material scattered along the river banks. Assaulting distance was reached by a series of small operations, ostensibly to strengthen the defences. In each case, the new advanced line was marked out at night. The tapes were then removed, but the pegs left in position, and on the following night the infantry stole forward to dig the trenches while the Sappers erected the wire entanglements. Finally, the front line in the coastal sector was within 100 yards of the enemy, who still did not expect a mass attack. By the middle of September, Allenby was ready. He now envisaged an advance to Damascus and beyond and promised the cavalry a haul of 30,000 prisoners, an optimistic view of the situation which was fully justified by the fact that, on the left of his line, he had massed 35,000 infantry and 9,000 cavalry with 400 guns against only 9,000 Turks with 120 guns, while, on the right, his strength was equal to that of the enemy, though he was inferior in artillery.[1]

The fate of Turkey was decided on September 19th, 1918. An irresistible assault by the 60th, 7th, 75th, 3rd and 53rd Divisions on a seven-mile front, with the 4th and 5th Cavalry Divisions and the Australian Mounted Division in rear, tore a huge rent in the Turkish defences near the coast. The task of the engineer units was to prepare two wide tracks through the enemy's positions for the advance of the cavalry, artillery and transport. Each was made by a field company, and a Pioneer company following closely on the infantry; and so rapidly was the work done that, two hours after the assault, the leading cavalry division passed through on its long ride into Syria. The broken Turkish 8th Army was soon streaming northwards towards Tulkeram, and thence eastwards to Nablus, under persistent and heavy bombing. The 3rd and 7th Indian Divisions, being largely on pack transport, were detailed to cross the mountains to Samaria in an attempt to catch the enemy forces retiring from the Jordan area, while the 53rd, 60th and 75th Divisions halted for a time in the captured positions.[2] A section of a field company was attached to each advancing infantry

[1] *Allenby*, by Gen. Sir Archibald Wavell, K.C.B., C.M.G., M.C., p. 269.

[2] *A Brief Record of the Advance of the Egyptian Expeditionary Force, July*, 1917, *to October*, 1918 (Official), pp. 56, 59. This volume contains the Records of Service of all divisions, and also General Allenby's despatches.

brigade to arrange for water-supply. On September 20th, the 21st Corps, having advanced and wheeled eastwards, turned the flank of the Turkish 7th Army which was retreating through the mountains of the Samaria region towards exits already held by the Desert Mounted Corps. The 20th Corps entered Nablus on September 21st, and, by the 23rd, the infantry of both Corps had driven the enemy into the arms of the waiting cavalry, with the result that the entire Turkish 7th and 8th Armies were captured. The 5th Cavalry Division occupied Nazareth, Haifa and Acre. Meanwhile, the Turkish 4th Army, harassed by the Arab forces and the Australian and New Zealand Mounted Division while in full retreat up the Jordan Valley and towards Es Salt and Amman, was gravely compromised by the destruction of the 7th and 8th Armies. Es Salt was taken on the 23rd, and Amman on the 25th. The Desert Mounted Corps was then directed to occupy Damascus to cut off the last remnants of the 4th Army, and on September 30th the 5th Cavalry Division was in the city. By this time, the group of Turkish armies under the supreme command of the German General, Liman von Sanders, had been smashed beyond repair. Rapid pursuit became the order of the day.

In this pursuit, the 3rd and 4th Companies, Bengal S. & M., performed a notable feat. The 21st Corps had been directed to move up the coast to the valuable port of Beirut, and the leading troops of the 7th Indian Division set out accordingly from Acre on October 2nd, 1918. With the second of three columns were the 3rd and 4th Companies under Captains W. Cave-Browne and E. L. Farley, R.E.,[1] which, with the 121st Pioneers and two battalions of infantry, were detailed to prepare the road for the advance of the division and some of the Corps heavy artillery and transport. Speed was essential, so Lieut.-Colonel E. F. J. Hill, R.E., and his Sappers and Pioneers marched near the head of the column to begin any necessary work as soon as possible, and two R.E. officers with the mounted column ahead[2] sent back word daily of the difficulties likely to be encountered. Within twelve miles of Acre, the road bent towards the coast and skirted a promontory called the Ras en Naqura for a distance of seven miles. It was a rocky track, only six feet wide, with several gradients of one in five, and the last mile lay along the face of an almost vertical cliff. This stretch was known as the "Ladder of Tyre," for here the track took the form of a series of great steps, cut in the solid rock and partly covered by debris. General Bulfin, the Corps Commander, came forward to examine the formidable obstacle and was told by Hill that extensive blasting would be needed to make the Ladder fit for wheeled traffic, and that, in the process, there was every possibility that the whole shelf might slip into the sea. There was no other route for many miles inland, and if the Ladder were destroyed, the progress of the 7th Division, and perhaps of the 21st Corps, would be blocked. Bulfin demanded "time for a couple of cigarettes" and then ordered the attempt to be made. It was com-

[1]Capt. E. L. Farley, R.E., had assumed command of the 4th Company *vice* Maj. A. J. G. Bird, R.E., who had become C.R.E., 60th Division, in the middle of September.

[2]*Military Operations. Egypt and Palestine* (Official History), by Capt. Cyril Falls, Part II, p. 602. The first, or mounted, column comprised the Corps Cavalry Regiment, a company of infantry and the 2nd Light Armoured Motor Battery.

pletely successful. The Ladder was demolished to ease the gradient and widen the road, and within three days, the entire length of seven miles around the headland was fit for wheeled traffic, including 60 pr. guns. The credit for this achievement has sometimes been given to the Pioneers, but it was the Bengal Sappers who made the track passable for wheels. The Pioneers came up after the 7th Division had passed, and converted the track into a good road.[1]

Meanwhile, the Corps Cavalry Regiment had entered Tyre. On October 6th the 7th Division was in Sidon, and, on the 8th, in Beirut. The 21st Corps was then ordered to advance on Tripoli, while the Desert Mounted Corps pushed towards Homs on the railway to Aleppo. The 7th Division, followed by the 54th Division, continued its triumphant progress up the coast, and Homs fell to the 5th Cavalry Division on October 15th. The cavalry then rode hard for Aleppo, only 120 miles distant, dispersing with ease the weak Turkish rearguards they encountered. They were forestalled, however, by the Arab Army which broke into Aleppo on October 25th, so the cavalry took up a position beyond the city and astride the railway leading towards Baghdad, thus completing the utter defeat of the Turkish armies, whose commander, Liman von Sanders, had already fled through Anatolia. The power of Turkey was irretrievably broken. An Armistice was granted on October 31st, 1918, and Allenby's remarkable campaign was finished. In twelve days, he had routed the enemy, and, four weeks later, had occupied the whole of Syria. His pursuit of the beaten Turks was certainly one of the most relentless in history. He was a cavalryman, and he used his cavalry in masterly fashion.

The Bombay and Madras Sappers and Miners rendered valuable assistance in the preparations for the advance from the Auja, and during and after the penetration of the Turkish defences. The 18th Company, Bombay S. & M., went into the line with the 3rd Indian Division on June 25th, 1918, taking over the defences of the right sector of the divisional front, held by the 9th Infantry Brigade. This was an important pivot of the defence line, adjoining the main road and railway, and consequently it came in for much attention. Soon, however, the unit was transferred to the 10th Indian Division and joined the 31st Brigade at Nebi Saleh in the rugged area of the Mountains of Ephraim, where it worked on roads, water-supply and defences. On September 19th, the day of the great attack, two sections accompanied the 29th Brigade for water-supply duties, while the remainder of the unit helped the 85th Company, R.E., and some infantry to lay a timber track towards an important ravine. On the following day, a lateral road was built from this ravine to Selfit, where the company concentrated. Urgent orders then arrived that the unit should follow the retreating Turks to Nablus with the 29th and 30th Brigades. This was done, and the 18th Company had the satisfaction of witnessing the surrender of 8,000 Turks and Germans with 120 guns. More water-supply followed, until, in October, the unit moved southwards to Tulkeram.[2]

[1]Notes by Col. W. Cave-Browne, C.B.E., D.S.O., M.C., late R.E., sent to the author on June 22nd, 1937.

[2]*History of the 18th (Field) Company, 3rd Bombay Sappers and Miners, during the Great War*, 1914–18, pp. 11–14.

The 20th and 21st Companies, Bombay S. & M., went to the front on June 24th and worked on water-supply near Ludd until July 8th, when a detachment of the 20th Company moved forward and took over defences in the 9th Brigade area. At the end of July, the 20th Company crossed the Auja in relief of the 3rd Company, Bengal S. & M. There it remained, hard at work on roads, water-supply, bridging and defences until the day of the attack. The weather was delightful, the country pleasantly green, and the Turks inoffensive. Life in the orange groves north of Jaffa afforded a welcome contrast to the dreary plains of Iraq. On the fateful September 19th, the company marched with the 9th Infantry Brigade into the Judean Hills, and, by the 23rd, was close to Nablus. After visiting Messudieh, it returned to the Auja area, where it remained until October 9th, its chief occupations being, as usual, road construction and water-supply.[1] Captain H. W. R. Hamilton, R.E., was now in command as Major S. Boyd, R.E., had been sent to Egypt to form some new Sapper companies. Meanwhile, the 21st Company had been working at Semakh, at the southern end of the Sea of Galilee, and had suffered severely from malaria. It was relieved by the 20th Company after the Armistice and then moved up to Damascus. The 20th Company was transferred later to Nazareth. Another Bombay Sapper unit, present during the attack on September 19th, was the 72nd Company. The unit had reached Palestine recently from Baluchistan and did some useful roadwork under fire while operating with the 53rd Division. The 10th and 16th Companies, Madras S. & M., were with the 75th Division on September 19th, but although the 10th Company was under fire for a time, neither unit saw much fighting. Shortly after the Armistice, several units of Sappers and Miners were raised in Egypt. These were the 94th (Madras), 82nd, 83rd and 84th (Bengal), and 80th and 101st (Bombay) Companies. The 94th Company was formed from drafts from the 10th and 16th Companies: it returned to India in January 1919, as did the 82nd Company, under Captain S. T. H. Munsey, I.A.R.O. The 83rd and 84th (Bengal) Companies were disbanded in Egypt.

After all military operations had ceased, the 3rd and 4th Companies, Bengal S. & M., spent the whole of 1919 in providing winter hutting and water-supplies for the troops in Syria, while the 1st Company worked on the newly opened railway through the Taurus Mountains. Syria was handed over to the French in December, 1919. The 7th Indian Division then returned to Egypt, where the 3rd and 4th Companies were rejoined by the 1st Company. All three units received a great welcome on reaching Roorkee early in 1920. The 3rd and 4th Companies had fought in all the battles of the 7th Division in three theatres of war, and had been absent for more than five years. The 10th Company, Madras S. & M., was welcomed back to Bangalore in December, 1920; but the 16th Company did not arrive until April, 1922, and shortly afterwards it was disbanded. Both Madras units had been employed after the Armistice in building

[1] *History of the 20th (Field) Company, Royal Bombay Sappers and Miners, Great War, 1914–18*, by Maj. H. W. R. Hamilton, D.S.O., M.C., R.E., pp. 47–51.

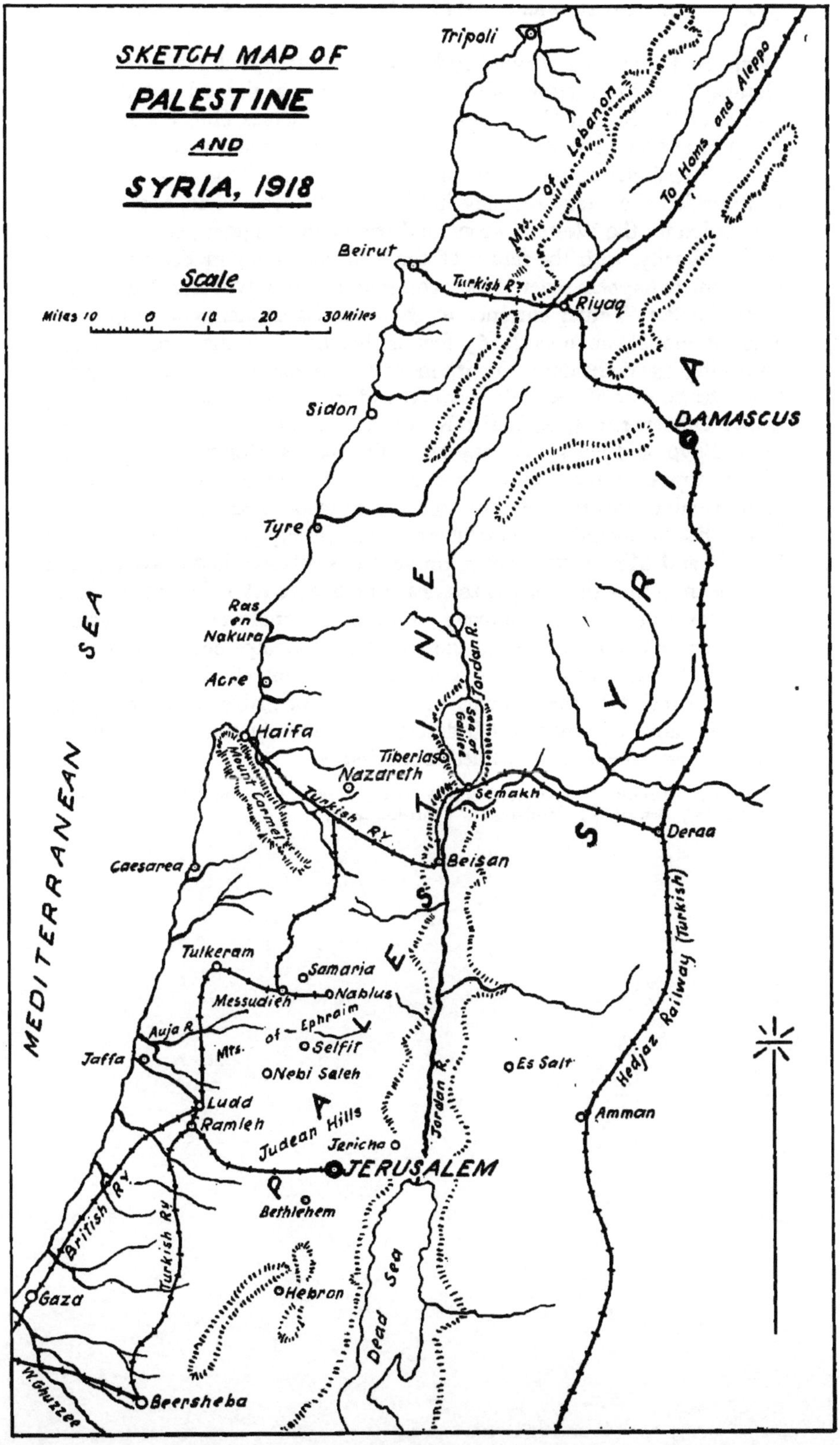
SKETCH MAP OF
PALESTINE
AND
SYRIA, 1918
Scale
Miles 10 0 10 20 30 Miles
Tripoli
Mts. of Lebanon
To Homs and Aleppo
Beirut
Turkish Ry.
Riyaq
Sidon
DAMASCUS
Tyre
Ras en Nakura
Acre
Haifa
Mount Carmel
Jordan R.
Sea of Galilee
Tiberias
Nazareth
Semakh
Turkish Ry.
Deraa
Beisan
Caesarea
MEDITERRANEAN SEA
PALESTINE
SYRIA
Hedjaz Railway (Turkish)
Tulkeram
Samaria
Nablus
Messudieh
Mts. of Ephraim
Selfit
Auja R.
Jaffa
Nebi Saleh
Es Salt
Ludd
Ramleh
Amman
Judean Hills
Jericho
Jordan R.
JERUSALEM
British Ry.
Bethlehem
Turkish Ry.
Dead Sea
Gaza
Hebron
W. Ghuzzee
Beersheba

camps in Egypt. On August 17th, 1920, the 20th and 21st Companies, Bombay S. & M., veterans of as many campaigns as the 3rd and 4th Companies of the Bengal Corps, marched proudly across Holkar's Bridge to the parade ground at Kirkee, where they were received with due honour by the remainder of the Corps under Major A. L. Paris, R.E., who had commanded the 21st Company in France. Six years had elapsed since they sailed for the Western Front, and few of the original personnel came back. Finally, with the return of the 18th Company in February 1921, the Bombay Sappers severed their connection with Egypt and Palestine.

At the Port Taufiq entrance to the Suez Canal stands an impressive War Memorial, an obelisk, 65 feet in height, with the figures of two crouching tigers below. On it, in four languages, is the inscription "To the honour of the Indian Army, and to the enduring memory of 84 Indian Officers and 4,844 Indian Non-commissioned officers and men who fell in Egypt and Palestine, 1914–18." The names of only 36 Sappers and Miners appear on the obelisk[1]—a small contribution, one might say, to the total casualties incurred by the 150,000 men whom India sent to the Near East. But it should be remembered that, in Egypt and Palestine, the Sappers and Miners were never employed as infantry in the assault, and consequently they did not pay the heavy price exacted in France and Iraq. The labours of the 10th Company on the Suez Canal were invaluable at a critical period, and the work of the 3rd and 4th Companies in the advance through Palestine and Syria was spectacular; but all the Sapper units helped to maintain the impetus of Allenby's offensive by enabling the troops to move rapidly through desert and mountain country. That was their primary rôle, and they filled it admirably.

[1]*Historical Records. Q.V.O. Madras Sappers and Miners*, Case 16. The details are:—Madras, 18; Bengal, 8; Bombay, 9; Tehri-Garhwal, 1.

CHAPTER XX

THE GREAT WAR: EAST AFRICA, 1914–1918

IF ever there was a theatre of the Great War in which the services of Sappers and Miners were needed, it was East Africa. Yet, for the first three months, there was not a Sapper unit in the country, and for the next three years, only a single non-regular company, a small Bridging Train, from two to four companies of railway engineers and some subsidiary formations. Not until the final year, after the main operations had ended, did a regular company arrive, for the order had gone forth in 1914 that no unit should be sent to Africa which could be employed in France or Iraq. Consequently, East Africa had to be content with local formations and a small force from India until substantial reinforcements could arrive from South and West Africa. During 1914 and 1915, our commanders had to lead a heterogeneous body of troops, inexperienced in war, and particularly in bush fighting, against an experienced, seasoned and highly mobile enemy, and as Lieut.-Colonel Hordern remarks, they were confronted with problems unlike any elsewhere and often well-nigh insoluble.[1] The campaign was one of gradual attrition and extermination in which the enemy continued the fight until reduced almost to vanishing point. Little was known to the public about this long struggle in dense bush and waterless desert. The operations were extremely intricate. No maps were published and, except in 1916, there were no Press correspondents.[2] The fog of war enshrouded East Africa from start to finish.

As usual, Germany was first in the field. General Von Lettow-Vorbeck, the German commander, was an experienced Staff Officer who had served in China during the Boxer rebellion. He had learned bush warfare in recent expeditions in German South-West Africa and was an energetic and exceedingly capable leader. Landing in German East Africa at the beginning of 1914, he began to prepare the colony to take its part in the scheme of world domination which the Kaiser had in view. He found the local forces organized in 14 African *askari* companies, led by Germans, each with an establishment of about 162 men with two or three machine guns. In addition, there were 2,000 armed native police and 8,000 levies. The *askari* companies were self-contained, mobile, tactical units, each with its own supply and transport organization, including 250 well-trained porters or carriers. As, however, they were insufficient for aggressive action and were armed mostly with old rifles using black powder,[3] Von

[1] *Military Operations, East Africa, Vol I, August,* 1914–*September,* 1916 (Official History), by Lieut.-Col. Charles Hordern, R.E. (retd.), p. 14.

[2] "The East African Campaign, 1914–1916," by Maj.-Gen. S. H. Sheppard C.B., C.M.G., D.S.O., late R.E. (a review of the Official History), appearing in the *Journal of the Royal United Service Institution,* Feb., 1942, pp. 71–76.

[3] *My Reminiscences of East Africa,* by Gen. Von Lettow-Vorbeck, p. 8. The rifles were of 1871 pattern.

Lettow set to work to reorganize, re-equip and expand them, and with such success that by 1916 he had some 60 companies totalling at least 16,000 men. In 1914 he had only two field guns of 1873 pattern, but he soon reinforced these with naval guns taken from disabled German warships and with very effective light howitzers. His troops were specialists trained for one particular form of warfare.[1]

The enormous extent of the country in which our forces had to operate has never been exceeded in a single campaign except in Alexander the Great's march to India. German East Africa alone was nearly twice the size of Germany; and Portuguese East Africa, to which the operations extended in 1918, was almost as large as France. From Mount Kilimanjaro southwards to the Zambezi is as far as from Paris to Leningrad. The distance from Dar es Salaam to Lake Tanganyika equals that from Paris to Naples.[2] There were no roads in German East Africa, for the Germans never used animal draught for wheeled traffic because of the deadly ravages of the *tse-tse* fly. Also, they had few motor vehicles. Two railways formed the principal avenues of traffic. These were the Northern or Usambara line from the port of Tanga to Moshi near Kilimanjaro, and the Central from Dar es Salaam through Morogoro and Tabora to Kigoma on Lake Tanganyika. To the north, in British East Africa, the Uganda Railway, from Mombasa through Nairobi to Kisumu on Lake Victoria, was our main line of communication.[3] During the normal rainy season, from April to June, German East Africa was almost impassable, although for the remainder of the year there was little water except in the largest rivers. In 1917, however, the rains continued from January to May, and rivers normally half a mile wide attained a width of ten miles. Nine-tenths of the country was covered with pathless bush, ranging from giant forests with dense undergrowth to elephant grass twelve feet high, or impenetrable thorn, in which two forces might be quite close and yet completely unaware of each other's existence.

The absence of roads, the loose nature of the soil and the scarcity of water made pioneering and engineering prominent features in the campaign.[4] Sometimes, whole brigades were employed for weeks on road-making. Von Lettow's *askaris* required no roads; but the British, using motor vehicles, had to make them as they advanced. Von Lettow retreated by well-known paths to selected water-supplies, destroying all bridges as he went. The British followed him into strange country, hoping to find water and facing his concealed machine-guns. The machine-gun was the king of weapons in the bush. A man twenty yards from his fellows felt as if he were alone in Africa. He moved, as it were, in a mist, his nerves on edge and with nothing but cold courage to sustain him. Our men in East Africa

[1] "Some Notes on Tactics in the East African Campaign," by Brig.-Gen. S. H. Sheppard, C.B., C.M.G., D.S.O., late R.E., appearing in the *Journal of the United Service Institution of India*, Vol. XLVIII, 1919, pp. 138–157.

[2] For a general description of the country see "East Africa," by Capt. H. L. Woodhouse, M.C., R.E., appearing in the *Journal of the United Service Institution of India*, Vol. XLVI, 1917, pp. 329–336.

[3] See *Sketch Map of East Africa*, 1914–1918, included in this chapter.

[4] *General Smuts' Campaign in East Africa*, by Brig.-Gen. J. H. V. Crowe, C.B., p. 9.

fought as did their sons in later years against the Japanese in the jungles of Burma.

But our troops had to contend also against enemies other than the German *askaris* and the country. Lions, rhinoceroses, hippopotami and crocodiles were encountered, sometimes with unfortunate results, and elephants and giraffes interfered with communications. Lions were dangerous in certain areas. On several occasions they attacked men and carried them away into the bush, and their roaring around our camps often caused a stampede among transport animals. A rhinoceros once charged a column on a night march and threw it into such confusion that it was delayed for an hour.[1] Another charged one of our patrols while it was engaged with a German patrol. First, it scattered our patrol, then the enemy, and finally turned on some Masai tribesmen who were watching the fight and killed one of them.[2] Hippopotami attacked boats at river crossings and had to be repelled with bayonets. Crocodiles took an unceasing toll of unwary porters. Elephants wandered by night along newly made roads and left pot-holes which delayed our motor convoys. Giraffes broke our telephone lines so often that it became necessary to raise the wires to a height of 25 feet. " In 1916," writes General Sheppard,[3] " the Sappers built a Squash court in our camp from aeroplane packing cases. One night there was some firing, followed by a fearful crash. A rhino had been hit and had charged clean through the court. Later, when we were camped near the sandy bank of a river, we had a football match. All went well until a powerful kick sent the ball into the water. There, it was promptly swallowed by a crocodile ! "

So much for the wild beasts and saurians of East Africa. Now for some of its myriad insect pests, whose depredations were even more serious. To man, the worst of these were the *anopheles* mosquito, bearing the germ of malaria, and the species of *tse-tse* fly which carries sleeping sickness. Another *tse-tse* was deadly to animals. Indeed, the attacks of this pest forced us to replace animal by motor transport, with a consequent enormous increase in road-making. Other pests were the *spirillum* tick, causing fever ; the Bott fly, which left a maggot beneath the skin ; the white ant, destructive of almost any material except steel and concrete ; scorpions, centipedes and warrior ants ; and last, but by no means least, the burrowing *jigga* flea. This tiny insect lays a bag of eggs under the skin, preferably beneath a toe-nail, and if the bag is allowed to remain, it bursts, releases its progeny and causes blood-poisoning. The African porters, however, were experts in removing the eggs with a pin. Sometimes, bees interfered with military operations. They did so at Tanga in November, 1914, and on three occasions in 1917 they attacked a column under Lieut.-Colonel G. M. Orr. Once they drove a thousand of his men from camp ; on another

[1]Notes by Maj.-Gen. S. H. Sheppard, C.B., C.M.G., D.S.O., late R.E., sent to the author on July 22nd, 1932.

[2]" At the River's Brink," by " *Batouri* " (Lieut.-Col. R. L. McClintock, D.S.O., R.E.), appearing in *Blackwood's Magazine*, Vol. CCIII, Jan., 1918, p. 10.

[3]Notes by Maj.-Gen. S. H. Sheppard, C.B., C.M.G., D.S.O., late R.E., sent to the author on Oct. 5th, 1937.

occasion, they attacked the advanced guard on the march and forced the main body to make a detour of several miles; and on a third occasion, they prevented the crossing of a river.[1]

The only regular unit in British East Africa before the war was the 3rd Battalion, King's African Rifles, with headquarters at Nairobi and a detachment in Zanzibar. For internal security there was a small force of armed police. Some defence forces were raised in 1914 at Mombasa, Nairobi and Kisumu, and also two European volunteer units, the East African Rifles and the East African Regiment. A corps of Arab Rifles, recruited on the coast, rendered good service until 1916. Some 7,500 carriers were enrolled after the declaration of war, and by 1918 the Carrier Corps had increased to 200,000 men. In Uganda, the only regular unit was the 4th Battalion, King's African Rifles, with headquarters at Entebbe on Lake Victoria, but four additional companies of the 1st Battalion were available from Nyasaland. Nevertheless, owing to operations already in progress, only 11 companies of the King's African Rifles could be detailed in 1914 for defence duties in the whole of British East Africa and Uganda—a fact which shows that these two protectorates were completely unprepared for war.

On August 9th, 1914, a first reinforcement for our garrison in East Africa was despatched from Karachi. This consisted of the 29th Punjabis, forming part of an "Indian Expeditionary Force 'C'" under the command of Brig.-General J. M. Stewart. The battalion landed at Mombasa on September 1st and was sent up-country at once by rail. Half the unit was stationed in the Voi-Tsavo area to guard the vital Uganda Railway from the threat of enemy concentrations around Moshi near Mount Kilimanjaro, and the other half proceeded to Nairobi, where Stewart established his headquarters.[2] The remainder of I.E.F. "C" arrived early in October. It comprised two composite battalions of Imperial Service Infantry (half-battalions from Jind, Kapurthala, Rampur and Bharatpur), the 27th (Indian) Mountain Battery, a Calcutta Volunteer Battery with six ancient 12-pr. guns, and a battery of four Maxim machine-guns manned by British railway volunteers. This was the force which, with the 29th Punjabis and a few companies of the King's African Rifles, was expected to guard nearly 250,000 square miles of British territory and 600 miles of railway! Some of the units were distributed along the railway, but most were concentrated in Nairobi. Several small actions were fought in defence of the coastal section of the railway, and the Germans advanced from Moshi to Taveta, but neither side was strong enough to launch a powerful offensive.

The primary objective of British strategy at the outbreak of war was the capture of the port of Dar es Salaam, the terminus of the German Central Railway, which was bombarded by two of our cruisers on August 8th. The Government of India detailed a force of 8,000 men for the opera-

[1] "Random Recollections of East Africa, 1914–1918," by Col. G. M. Orr, C.B.E., D.S.O., appearing in *The Army Quarterly*, Vol. XI, Jan., 1926, pp. 282–293.

[2] *Military Operations, East Africa, Vol. I, August*, 1914–*September*, 1916 (Official History), by Lieut.-Col. Charles Hordern, R.E. (retd.), p. 37.

tion but included no Sappers and Miners nor Pioneers; later, however, when they realized that much work would be needed on railways and roads, they decided that two Railway companies of Sappers and a battalion of Pioneers should be added. The 16th (Poona) Infantry Brigade, of the 6th Indian Division, was the formation originally selected for the seizure of Dar es Salaam, but at the end of August the project was shelved temporarily because of the urgent need to protect the Suez Canal and the oil supplies at the head of the Persian Gulf. It was revived on September 9th, when the 27th (Bangalore) Infantry Brigade, under Brig.-General R. Wapshare, was substituted for the 16th Brigade, which had meanwhile been assigned to the Persian Gulf. The designation of the force intended for East Africa was now changed to "Indian Expeditionary Force 'B'." The battalions forming the 27th Brigade were the 2nd Loyal North Lancashires, 63rd Palamcottah Light Infantry, 98th Infantry and 101st Grenadiers. An Imperial Service Brigade was added, under Brig.-General M. J. Tighe. It included the 13th Rajputs, 2nd Kashmir Rifles, half-battalions of the 3rd Kashmir Rifles and 3rd Gwalior Infantry, and the 61st Madras Pioneers, a unit lately employed in prolonging the Coonoor Railway to Ootacamund. The Divisional troops included the Faridkot Imperial Service Sapper Company under Lieut.-Colonel Harnam Singh, with Major B. W. Mainprise, R.E. (an ex-Bengal Sapper) as Special Service Officer; the 25th and 26th Railway Companies, S. & M., under Majors C. F. Anderson[1] and C. W. Wilkinson, R.E.; two Railway Construction Companies under Captains L. N. Malan and E. St. G. Kirke, R.E., with Lieutenants H. L. Woodhouse, J. R. Roberts and R. E. Gordon, R.E.; a small Bridging Train (No. 5 Pontoon Park), Bombay S. & M., under Captain E. D. Tillard, R.E.; No. 4 Engineer Field Park, Madras S. & M., afterwards under Major R. L. McClintock, R.E.;[2] and No. 3 Photo-Litho Section and No. 4 Printing Section, Madras S. & M. Major-General A. E. Aitken was appointed in supreme command, and on his staff were Lieut.-Colonel S. H. Sheppard, R.E. (an ex-Bengal Sapper) as G.S.O.I., Lieut.-Colonel C. B. Collins, R.E., as C.R.E., Major G. Lubbock, R.E., as Deputy Assistant Director of Railways under Sir William Johns as Director, and Captain H. C. Hawtrey, R.E., as Assistant Director of Signals. The Artillery was represented by the 28th (Indian) Mountain Battery. It will be noticed that I.E.F. "B" had only one regular British battalion, the North Lancashires. The 13th Rajputs and 101st (Maratha) Grenadiers had seen some active service; but the other regular battalions had seen none, and the Imperial Service troops were inexperienced in the field and, in some cases, imperfectly trained. "The campaign will be either a 'walk-over' or a tragedy," remarked an officer who inspected the troops at Bombay. It certainly started with a tragedy, though it ended in complete victory—which seems to be the British way.

The Faridkot Sapper Company, and the 25th and 26th Railway Com-

[1]Maj. C. F. Anderson, R.E., was invalided early in the campaign, and Lieut. H. L. Woodhouse, R.E., then assumed command of the 25th Company.

[2]Maj. R. L. McClintock, R.E., left Bangalore for East Africa on March 31st, 1915.

panies, sailed with other details from Karachi on October 16th, 1914, and joined a convoy from Bombay in which were the Bridging Train, Bombay S. & M., the Madras Sapper subsidiary formations, and the remainder of the force destined for East Africa, in addition to large contingents bound for Basra, Egypt and Marseilles. The convoy of 45 ships moved in nine columns abreast, led by H.M.S. *Goliath* and followed by H.M.S. *Swiftsure*. The first to part company were the transports bound for the Persian Gulf, then those for East Africa, and the remainder set course for the Red Sea.[1] At a conference in Mombasa on October 31st, General Aitken arranged with the Senior Naval Officer on the coast, the Captain of H.M.S. *Fox*, that this light cruiser should escort the convoy close into Tanga, where the German District Commissioner was to be summoned aboard and given an hour in which to decide to surrender. The *Fox*, however, proceeded alone into the harbour on November 2nd, and the District Commissioner protracted the negotiations until General Von Lettow-Vorbeck was able to rush reinforcements down from Moshi. There is little need to dwell upon the disaster that followed.[2] During the night of November 2nd/3rd, General Tighe landed 1½ battalions about two miles east of Tanga and advanced on it at daybreak but made little headway against concentrated machine-gun fire. The greater part of General Aitken's troops disembarked on November 4th on the southern shore of the harbour entrance about a mile from Tighe's landing place, though all the Sapper and Miner formations remained aboard. Aitken then launched a general attack, was heavily counter-attacked, and finally repulsed with more than 800 casualties. He was fortunate to be able to re-embark successfully on November 5th, though with the loss of much equipment which was valuable to the enemy. The arrangements for this difficult re-embarkation were made by Lieut.-Colonel S. H. Sheppard, R.E. An absurd rumour became current that the Germans had used trained bees to disorganize our assault. The bees were there; but we were repulsed by bullets, not stings, and the insects did not distinguish between the opposing sides. Indeed, Von Lettow himself remarks that, at a decisive moment, all the machine-guns of one of his companies were put out of action by bees.[3] The moral effect of the battle at Tanga was bad. "Tanga," writes Von Lettow, "was the birthday of the soldierly spirit in our troops," and it was that soldierly spirit which prolonged the campaign for four weary years. The War Office now assumed control of the operations, and I.E.F. "B" steamed back to Mombasa, where, on December 4th, Brig.-General Wapshare took over command from Major-General Aitken. For many months thereafter, some of the units were in no condition to fight.

The war in East Africa may be divided for convenience into four phases. During the first phase, after the failure at Tanga, there was a stalemate

[1] "Random Recollections of East Africa, 1914–1918," by Col. G. M. Orr, C.B.E., D.S.O., appearing in *The Army Quarterly*, Vol. XI, Jan., 1926, pp. 282–293.

[2] The operations at Tanga are described fully in *Military Operations, East Africa, Vol. I., August, 1914–September, 1916*, by Lieut.-Col., Charles Hordern, R.E., (retd), pp. 75–107, and also in *My Reminiscences of East Africa*, by Gen. Von Lettow-Vorbeck, pp. 35–48.

[3] *My Reminiscences of East Africa*, by Gen. Von Lettow-Vorbeck, p. 44.

which lasted throughout 1915, a pause which Von Lettow turned to good account by raising and training many new companies. The second phase, during 1916, saw a successful invasion of German East Africa from the north by British, Indian and South African troops under Lieut.-General J. C. Smuts, assisted by an advance southwards by Belgian forces of the interior, and northwards by troops under Brig.-General E. Northey operating from the southern border. During the third phase, in 1917, the occupation of German East Africa was almost completed by a reconstituted army with new African reinforcements, though the dwindling enemy still remained in being and full of fight. The fourth and final phase in 1918 resolved itself into a steady pursuit of Von Lettow, first in Portuguese East Africa and ultimately in Northern Rhodesia, until the remnants of his forces surrendered after the Armistice.

On November 8th, 1914, I.E.F. "B" began to move inland from Mombasa. The North Lancashires and the 28th Mountain Battery were despatched by rail to Nairobi to reinforce the troops under Brig.-General Stewart who had made a demonstration towards Longido while the operations at Tanga were in progress. The Faridkot Sappers and a half-battalion of Kashmir Rifles started for Voi on November 9th. The 25th and 26th Railway Companies, S. & M., also moved up the Uganda Railway to afford additional protection to the line, but most of the other units remained for a time in Mombasa to reorganize. At the end of the month, the Faridkot Sappers were employed in the Voi-Tsavo area and the Railway Companies had their headquarters in Nairobi. Meanwhile, the Germans had begun to advance up the coast north of Tanga, but they were driven back in December with the aid of the Royal Navy, and only at Taveta did they retain any permanent hold beyond their borders. They captured the British frontier post of Jasin on January 12th, 1915, two days after we had occupied their island of Mafia, south of Dar es Salaam. Other minor operations filled the period before the rains broke. In the middle of April, Major-General Tighe relieved Major-General Wapshare in the chief command, Wapshare being under orders for Iraq. With the exception of some raids and skirmishes along the border, and the destruction of the German cruiser *Königsberg* in the Rufiji River in July, there were no operations of any importance during the remainder of the year. We were content to protect British East Africa and the Uganda Railway and were fortunate to be able to do so with the inadequate force at our disposal. The frontier was 900 miles in length, and the only line of communication was a railway parallel to it and about 50 miles from it.

In the Voi-Tsavo area, the Faridkot Sappers were employed until March 1915 on road-making and bridging.[1] Few of the men were skilled in any trade, so the unit worked under a considerable handicap. Conversion of the Voi-Maktau track into a motor road was undertaken with the help of the 61st Pioneers and large gangs of Africans. This road, 37 miles in length,

[1] *A Short History of the Services rendered by the Imperial Service Troops during the Great War*, 1914–18, by Maj.-Gen. Sir Harry Watson, K.B.E., C.B., C.M.G., C.I.E., M.V.O., p. 15.

was taken across the Voi River on a fine suspension bridge, designed to carry 5 tons, and proved of great value during the advance in 1916. A similar road was made later from Tsavo to Mzima through bush country and involved the construction of three bridges over the Tsavo River. The work was severe and the unit suffered much from sickness. As there was a deficiency of stores and equipment, the Faridkot Sappers had always to improvise. Papyrus reeds laid in thick transverse layers were found to wear down in time to form a tough road-surface. At one place a corduroy road was made with scantlings of ebony, and the company equipped itself with boning and measuring rods of the same expensive wood.[1] It equipped itself also with a company pet, a grey parrot which screeched " *Gott Strafe England* " and " *Hoch der Kaiser*," in the best Teutonic style; but when the bird began to imitate the " fall-in " whistle at all hours of the day and night, it had to be suppressed. The unit took part, in June 1915, in a raid on Bukoba on the western shore of Lake Victoria, where it was among the first to land from the S.S. *Nyanza* and had the satisfaction of destroying a German wireless station. At the end of the year, Lieut.-Colonel Harnam Singh was invalided to India and replaced in command by Major Nand Singh.

The Bridging Train, Bombay S. & M., under Captain E. D. Tillard, R.E., with Sergeant W. Smeeth, R.E., landed in Mombasa with a full complement of pontoons and Berthon boats but only 30 men, and consequently, like the small Bengal unit in Iraq under Captain E. W.C. Sandes, R.E., it needed reinforcement by a Sapper or Pioneer company in any emergency. In Africa, the emergency did not arise, for the Bridging Train was never required to execute any rapid bridging. It was employed entirely on ordinary Field Company work and handed over its pontoons to the Royal Navy. The lack of pontoons was felt severely when a raft was required for a flying bridge across the Rufiji River early in 1917, for the necessary pontoons had then to be built in workshops and sent to the site. Fortunately, the unit had retained its collapsible Berthon boats, which could be carried by porters. On one occasion these men transported half-boat loads (120 lbs.) for a distance of 20 miles in a single night, two carrying and two resting, although they had already marched 12 miles during the morning.

The Railway Companies were undoubtedly the most important Indian engineer units in the East African campaign, for railways provided the only reliable means of rapid transit. The origin of these units dates back to 1902 when the 25th Company was raised at Sialkot by Lieutenant C. F. Anderson, R.E., as a result of experience gained during the Third China War. In 1905, the 26th Company was raised by Lieutenant T. Gracey, R.E.[2] Each unit was organized in two branches, one being " Regular " and the other " Traffic and Loco," the strength of the " Regular " branch

[1]Notes by Lieut.-Col. E. D. Tillard, D.S.O., R.E., (retd.), sent to the author on Jan. 4th, 1945.

[2]The formation of 6 companies was authorized, and the 25th and 26th Companies were known originally as the " 1st and 2nd Military Railway Companies " (see *A Brief History of the Royal Bombay Sappers and Miners*, p. 15).

being 198 ranks.[1] The men of this branch had one month's military training annually, with the idea that " they should be able to defend themselves if attacked." The Traffic branch was recruited from civilian railway employees who received reservist pay to join when called up, but these men had no military training whatever. The 25th and 26th Companies were classed officially as " Sappers and Miners " because there was a vague idea that the 25th was under the aegis of the Bengal Corps and the 26th under that of the Bombay Corps, although the connection never existed in practice and in theory it had become extinct long before 1914.[2] The companies were employed normally on the maintenance of two short sections of the North Western Railway—the Sialkot and Nushki branches —but occasionally they gained some constructional experience on new lines. This was rare, because it was simpler to employ a civilian contractor than a Sapper unit, and during the four years which preceded the Great War the only constructional work carried out by the two units was at the Delhi Durbar. On landing in East Africa, the Traffic branch of each company was transferred to a special Railway Traffic organization on the Uganda Railway and had no further contact with the unit. It is evident from the history of the Railway Companies, S. & M., that they had much to learn when they were thrust suddenly into the war ; but they rose nobly to the occasion and soon became most efficient in their technical duties.

At first, the 25th and 26th Railway Companies were employed in guarding the bridges along the Uganda Railway against German raiding parties. " At this time," writes Colonel Wilkinson,[3] " the Germans had occupied Taveta, near Kilimanjaro, and also Gazi, south of Mombasa, and from Taveta they sent parties by night to damage the line. I was ordered to take over the defence of the railway with the two Railway companies, and, as this involved guarding 400 miles of line with only 400 men, I decided to post small parties to protect the more important bridges with the help of native levies armed with spears, and to employ the remainder of the men in patrolling. However, the enemy did not attack the bridges but contented themselves with placing mines under the rails. Fortunately, locomotives leave a trail of oil on the ballast, and when the Germans laid a mine they disturbed the ballast and broke the trail. This was our guide. When constructing a new line we always laid a thin trail of oil and were thus able to defeat the demolition parties. Sometimes, the ballast was whitewashed for the same purpose. As our locomotives were valuable, we took the precaution of varying their position in the trains."

After six weeks as bridge-guards, the Railway Companies were given ox-transport and employed as field companies on improving the road from the Uganda Railway to Longido. They felled trees to make bridges and

[1]One British officer, 1 British N.C.O., 3 Indian officers, 193 Indian other ranks.

[2]Notes by Col. H. L. Woodhouse, M.C., late R.E., sent to the author on Jan. 4th, 1938.

[3]Notes by Col. C. W. Wilkinson, C.M.G., D.S.O., late R.E., sent to the author on Oct. 10th, 1937.

used the broad leaves of the *sisal* plant for revetting slopes.[1] In March, 1915, it was decided that a metre-gauge line should be built from Voi on the Uganda Railway for a distance of 37 miles, through dense thorn jungle infested with the *tse-tse* fly, to Maktau, the advanced post on the Voi-Moshi road, and accordingly the Railway units returned to their proper work. The 61st Pioneers and gangs of African labourers cleared the bush in advance, and the platelaying was carried out on alternate days by the two companies in a keen spirit of rivalry. The line was built with material obtainable from any source. Four types of sleeper and as many types of rail were used in the section to Maktau, which was reached in June.[2] After a further spell of road-making, the units returned to the Uganda Railway to build crossing stations. Captain E. St. G. Kirke, R.E., was sent back to India to organize a depot and recruit men to form two additional Railway companies, the 27th and 28th. Kirke must have had great powers of persuasion for it is said that his last recruit was the *gharry-wallah* who drove him to the railway station in Bombay! Subsequently, the 25th and 26th Companies prolonged the Voi-Maktau line to Njoro, some five miles beyond Mbuyuni, which was reached in January, 1916. They were often at work several miles in advance of our outpost line, covered only by a small party of infantry.

Another branch of the Service, originally recognized as part of the Sappers and Miners, was represented in East Africa by a single unit. This was Army Signalling. In 1914, Army Signalling in India was performed by four Divisional Signal Companies and a Wireless Section, which were affiliated to the Sappers and Miners but were independent as regards administration. The British officers were drawn from the British or the Indian Army, and the Indian ranks were called "Sappers"; but nevertheless the men were not interchangeable with the rank and file of the three Sapper and Miner Corps.[3] Two Brigade Signal Sections accompanied I.E.F. "B" to East Africa in 1914 but were withdrawn in March 1915; consequently, in April 1915, Captain H. C. Hawtrey, R.E., the A.D.A.S. of the force, raised a local Section under Lieutenant G. D. Ozanne, 99th Indian Infantry, who made the necessary signalling preparations for the raid on Bukoba. The local Section was reinforced in July by two Brigade Signal Sections from India under Captain W. E. Beazley, 54th Sikhs, and from these three Sections Hawtrey formed the unit known as "'Z' Divisional Signal Company, Sappers and Miners." It was commanded by Beazley, and the Company Officers were drawn from the Indian Infantry. "Z" Company rendered excellent service until it was disbanded at Dar es Salaam in June 1917. Detachments took part in the action at Salaita on February 12th, 1916, the advance on Taveta and Moshi in March and down the Pangani River and Northern Railway between May and August, the advance on Morogoro, the fighting in the Uluguru

[1] Report by Col. H. L. Woodhouse, M.C., late R.E., prepared in Aug., 1937, for the *R.E. Corps History*.

[2] "Notes on Railway Work in East Africa, 1914–1918," by Capt. H. L. Woodhouse, M.C., R.E., appearing in *The R.E. Journal*, Vol. XXXVII, March–Dec., 1923, pp. 37–46.

[3] *The Army in India and its Evolution*, p. 110.

Mountains, the action at Duthumi and the operations in the Kilwa area before the end of the year, and later it maintained a submarine cable under the Rufiji River.[1] At the outset the men were inexperienced and the equipment poor, but the unit improved rapidly and earned a fine reputation for efficiency. The personnel were absorbed later into other units of the greatly expanded Signal Service, which became in December 1925 the Indian Signal Corps. In 1916 and 1917 they were still classed as Sappers and Miners, and accordingly they find a place in this history.

The second phase of the war opened in 1916 when, with the arrival of strong reinforcements from South Africa and India, it became possible to discard the defensive and invade German territory. The general plan was for simultaneous thrusts from all the Allied frontiers. The main force was under the command of the famous South African leader, Lieut.-General J. C. Smuts, who arrived on February 19th as Commander-in-Chief in place of General Sir Horace Smith-Dorrien, the latter having been invalided from Cape Town while on his voyage from England. The strategical situation was then as follows. North-west of Mount Kilimanjaro, the British were based mainly on Longido. South-east of the mountain, they were based on the new Voi-Maktau railway, which they hoped to extend later to Taveta, the key to the whole front. Taveta blocked the best route to German East Africa, and the enemy had an advanced position at Salaita, which South African troops had failed to take on February 12th.[2] Smuts at once commenced operations designed to occupy the Kilimanjaro area before the rainy season. His striking force, 18,000 men with 57 guns, was organized in two divisions and a flanking force. The 1st East African Division, which included half the Faridkot Sapper Company, was under Major-General J. M. Stewart and the 2nd East African Division, with the other half company, under Major-General M. J. Tighe. Brig.-General J. L. Van Deventer commanded the flanking force of South African troops. Colonel J. A. Dealy, late R.E., was the Chief Engineer, and Lieut.-Colonel C. B. Collins and Major R. L. McClintock, R.E., were the C.s R.E., 1st and 2nd Divisions respectively.[3] The line of communication absorbed another 9,000 men, including the two Railway Companies and the Bridging Train. To oppose Smuts, Von Lettow-Vorbeck had about 6,000 men with 16 guns concentrated south and west of Kilimanjaro.

General Smuts began his advance on March 5th, 1916. The 2nd East African Infantry Brigade, under Brig.-General S. H. Sheppard, late R.E., was with the 1st Division on the Longido-Moshi road, and the 1st East African Infantry Brigade, under Brig.-General W. Malleson, with the 2nd Division on the Mbuyuni-Taveta line. After several sharp engagements south of Kilimanjaro, particularly with Malleson's brigade at the Reata-Latima Pass and with Sheppard's on the Soko Nassai tributary of the Pangani River, the enemy withdrew on March 22nd across the Ruvu

[1] "History of 'Z' Divisional Signal Company, Sappers and Miners," by Col. G. D. Ozanne, M.C., appearing in the *Royal Signals Quarterly Journal*, July, 1937, pp. 123–130.
[2] *The Empire at War*, by Sir Charles Lucas, Vol. IV, p. 161.
[3] In 1917, when Lieut.-Col. R. L. McClintock, R.E., became A.D.W. (E), Lieut.-Col. A. A. McHarg, R.E., became C.R.E., 2nd E.A. Division.

tributary near Kahe and Smuts called a halt. On March 12th, at Reata-Latima, west of Taveta, the Faridkot Sappers had lost their popular Special Service Officer, Major B. W. Mainprise, R.E., who was acting at the time as Brigade-Major to General Malleson. General Tighe was directing in person the forcing of the pass and had ordered the 130th Baluchis to advance in support of the 5th South Africans. The South Africans were checked and compelled to withdraw. Mainprise then put himself at the head of a party of 23 Baluchis and bravely charged at the middle of enemy's position. He fell, riddled with bullets from three machine-guns, and of the party with him, only two survived.[1] The news was received with deep regret in Roorkee, where he had served for several years in the Bengal Sappers.

Smuts now reorganized his command into the 1st Division under Major-General A. R. Hoskins[2] (1st and 2nd E. A. Brigades under Brig.-Generals S. H. Sheppard[3] and J. A. Hannyngton), the 2nd Division under Major-General J. L. Van Deventer (1st S.A. Mounted Brigade and 3rd S. A. Infantry Brigade under Brig.-Generals Manie Botha and C. A. L. Berrangé), and the 3rd Division under Major-General C. J. Brits (2nd S. A. Mounted Brigade and 2nd S. A. Infantry Brigade under Brig.-Generals B. G. L. Enslin and P. S. Beves). The main invasion of German East Africa was on two lines of advance towards the Central Railway. The western approach was from Arusha, through Kondoa Irangi to Dodoma; the eastern, down the Pangani River, through Handeni, towards Morogoro. Von Lettow's main body was south of Mount Kilimanjaro. Smuts' first move was to send a force under Van Deventer towards Kondoa Irangi at the beginning of April, 1916, thus causing Von Lettow to transfer the bulk of his troops south-westwards to meet the threat against the centre of the German protectorate. Van Deventer occupied Kondoa on April 17th and then found his way to the Central Railway barred by ten companies. On May 18th, Smuts began to march down the Pangani in a south-easterly direction in three columns astride the Northern or Usambara Railway, and later, swinging southwards through Handeni, reached the Nguru Mountains at the end of June.[4] " He was a great believer in wide turning move-

[1]*General Smuts' Campaign in East Africa*, by Brig.-Gen. J. H. V. Crowe, C.B., p. 83, and " The Campaign in East Africa," by Maj. F. S. Keen, D.S.O., appearing in the *Journal of the United Service Institution of India*, Vol. XLVI, 1917, pp. 71–90.

[2]The former 2nd Division was renamed the 1st Division, and Maj.-Gen. A. R. Hoskins replaced Maj.-Gen. M. J. Tighe whose services were required in India.

[3]Brig.-Gen. S. H. Sheppard, late R.E., was G.S.O.I., I.E.F. " B " (Sept. 22nd, 1914–Jan. 31st, 1916); Commander, 2nd E.A. Brigade (Feb. 1st–March 18th, 1916); G.O.C., 1st E.A. Division (temp.) (March 19th–31st, 1916), including action on the Soko Nassai, March 21st; and Commander, 1st E.A. Brigade (April 1st, 1916–Jan. 19th, 1917) including actions at Bwiko (May 31st), Mkalamo (June 9th), Lukigura (June 24th), Wami River (August 17th), Mgeta River (Jan. 1st, 1917) and crossing of Rufiji River at Kibambawe (Jan. 5th–15th, 1917). From Jan. 20th, 1917, to the end of hostilities in Dec., 1918 he was B.G.G.S. to the Forces in East Africa. The crossing of the wide Rufiji by Sheppard's brigade was a remarkable feat as only 7 small Berthon boats, each for 3 men, were available. It was effected gradually by night, often under fire and across water infested with crocodiles and hippopotami.

[4]" Smuts *v.* Lettow," by Col. G. M. Orr, C.B.E., D.S.O., appearing in *The Army Quarterly*, Vol. IX, Jan., 1925, pp. 287–299.

ments," writes General Sheppard,[1] "and made use of them, both strategically and tactically. They were very successful, and the enemy was often forced out of almost impregnable positions with losses heavier than ours." This was exemplified in actions at Handeni and elsewhere in which Sheppard's brigade took a prominent part. Von Lettow now transferred his main body eastwards to oppose Smuts; whereupon Van Deventer, seizing his opportunity, resumed his movement southwards and cut the Central Railway at Kilimatindi and Dodoma at the end of July, thus separating Von Lettow, in the area west of Morogoro, from his detachments in the Tabora region, far inland, which were opposed by Belgian and British columns operating from the north-west and Lake Victoria.

At the beginning of August 1916, Van Deventer was directed to move eastwards along the Central Railway towards Smuts. The plan was to corner Von Lettow in the Nguru Mountains, where he was believed to have assembled some 20 companies. On August 5th, Smuts began a drive southwards through the mountains in four columns, and Van Deventer started eastwards on the 9th. Four days later, however, when Smuts had concentrated near Turiani and Van Deventer was at Mpwapwa, it became evident that the bulk of Von Lettow's force had retired further southwards towards the Central Railway, either on Morogoro or Kilosa. Smuts then made for Morogoro, but when he reached it on August 26th, he found it unoccupied. Von Lettow, fearing that an attempt would be made to cut him off by working round the west side of the Uluguru Mountains to the south of Morogoro, had retreated into those mountains and was marching on Kisaki, where he hoped to replenish his supplies. As for Smuts, his troops were becoming exhausted, for his transport could not supply half his needs.

Intricate operations followed in the Uluguru Mountains. Brits, with Enslin's and Nussey's[2] mounted brigades and some infantry, pursued the ennmy along the western flank and reached the vicinity of Kisaki with part of his force on September 5th. Meanwhile, on the eastern flank, Hoskins, with Hannyngton's and Sheppard's brigades, had been advancing steadily against strong opposition, but he was still some 40 miles from Kisaki when Brits attacked the place on September 7th. A wide turning movement by Enslin failed; and on the 8th, Nussey was held up. Von Lettow then evacuated Kisaki and moved further southwards. Hannyngton followed Von Lettow, and fighting continued throughout the 10th and 11th. On the 12th, Von Lettow withdrew again, and by the 14th had concentrated his force to cover his line of retreat to Kibambawe in the unhealthy Rufiji Valley. He would have preferred to move to the Mahenge uplands, further inland, but in that case he would have had to abandon his stores in the coastal region. His strategy was governed by his supplies.

On September 19th, 1916, Belgian forces occupied Tabora on the Central

[1] "Some Notes on Tactics in the East African Campaign," by Brig.-Gen. S. H. Sheppard, C.B., C.M.G., D.S.O., late R.E., appearing in the *Journal of the United Service Institution of India*, Vol. XLVIII, 1919, pp. 138–157.

[2] Brig.-Gen. A. H. M. Nussey had replaced Brig.-Gen. Manie Botha in command of the 1st S.A. Mounted Brigade.

Railway. Portugal had entered the war, and Portuguese troops had already crossed the Ruvuma River into German East Africa, only to be driven out again with the loss of arms and supplies. However, Dar es Salaam had been occupied on September 4th, and the entire coast line, with the exception of the Rufiji delta, was in our hands. In the south-western area, General Northey, advancing from the Nyasaland-Rhodesia border, had penetrated as far as Iringa. Yet the defeat and elimination of the enemy's forces had not been attained. Smuts established a new sea-base at Kilwa, south of Dar es Salaam, and proceeded to reorganize his troops, who had now been marched almost to a standstill. He disbanded the 3rd Division under Brits and decided that most of the South Africans should be sent home to recuperate. So ended the second and most important phase of the campaign in East Africa. Shortly after the operations had been suspended, General Smuts was called to an Imperial Conference in London. He sailed from Dar es Salaam on January 20th, 1917, and the chief command then devolved on General Hoskins.

The foregoing outline of the military operations during 1916 is necessary to explain the activities of the Sapper and Miner units concerned. Before Smuts began his advance down the Pangani in May, the 25th and 26th Railway Companies had prolonged the new link-line from the Uganda Railway as far as Salaita and Taveta and finally joined it to the German Northern Railway at Kahe. This was the most arduous engineering work of the campaign. The line traversed virgin forest and swamp. In the swampy tracts, no stable foundation could be found and the permanent way had to be floated on mattresses of tree-trunks and palm-leaves. The passage of a construction train over these sections was like that of a ship at sea. Nevertheless, the railway was completed to Kahe at the remarkable rate of a mile a day, and in the nick of time to enable Smuts to start his invasion as planned. An additional Railway Company, the 27th, had been formed in March 1916 by Captain R. E. Gordon, R.E., with drafts from the 25th and 26th Companies and from India, and in May a new Railway Company, the 28th, arrived from India under Captain E. St. G. Kirke, R.E. The 27th Company was employed for a time in constructing a new line from Moshi towards Arusha, and then, with the other three companies, followed Smuts down the Northern Railway, repairing the damage done by the retreating Germans. The four companies were grouped as a " Railway Battalion " under Lieut.-Colonel C. W. Wilkinson, R.E.,[1] and with the other Indian and South African engineer formations,[2] made a respectable cadre of specialists. Almost all the bridges and culverts on the Northern Railway had been demolished, and in some cases trains

[1]On the return of the companies to India in 1918 it was decided that no sanction existed for a Battalion Commander because a " battalion " of Sappers and Miners was unknown in the Indian Army. The battalion continued to exist, but there was difficulty in matters of supply. It was commanded for a time by the senior Company Commander.

[2]In addition to the 4 Railway Companies, the Faridkot Sappers, the Bridging Train and the 61st Pioneers from India, General Smuts now had an East African Pioneer Company, and from South Africa a Pioneer Battalion, 2 Field Troops and a Water Supply Corps (*vide*, *Summary of Work of Technical Units*, 1916–1918, by Col. F. P. Rundle, late R.E., dated Nov. 26th, 1918).

DIVERSION BRIDGE ON NORTHERN RAILWAY, GERMAN EAST AFRICA.

25th Railway Company, Sappers and Miners, at work on July 9th, 1916.

had been run into the wreckage, but wherever the girders were not too seriously damaged they were re-erected successfully on sleepers, cribs or trestles.

The Railway Companies halted at Mombo, about 30 miles from the coast, where Smuts had left the Northern Railway to move southwards to the Central Railway. Near Korogwe, in July 1916, the 25th and 26th Companies formed the major part of a column, under Lieut.-Colonel C. W. Wilkinson, R.E., detailed to clear a large body of enemy raiders from our line of communication. Troops were scarce, and accordingly the Railway Sappers had to act as infantry. They marched by night, and at dawn on the second day took the enemy by surprise and captured a field gun, and two days later, charged a position with the bayonet. Fortunately, their casualties were light. Now, according to Field Service Regulations,[1] "Engineer units may be regarded as a reserve of fighting men, but will be used only in an emergency, as a last resource." It is doubtful, in this case, whether such a stage had been reached. Lieut.-Colonel Hordern remarks :—[2] "To take specialist railway troops off their technical work for use as infantry when the fighting troops in front were stationary and short of supplies was a drastic measure, justifiable only by emergency. These units constituted half of the organized military plate-layers and railway-bridge builders in the country, replaceable only by small drafts from India, if at all. . . . Seen in retrospect, the situation hardly seems to have been serious enough to call for such a diversion of highly skilled specialists from their proper technical rôle."

Tanga was occupied on July 7th, 1916, and through railway communication was established with it on August 19th. When news arrived of the capture of Dar es Salaam, the Railway Sappers prepared to move to the Central Railway. The 25th and 28th Companies went to Dar es Salaam, while the 26th and 27th Companies and some South African Pioneers were sent to Bagamoyo, further north, and reached Ruvu on the Central Railway on September 10th.[3] The 26th then worked towards Dar es Salaam, and the 27th westwards. They found that almost every bridge from Morogoro to the sea (108 miles) had been demolished. While the 28th Company repaired wharves and sidings in Dar es Salaam, the 25th worked up the line to meet the 26th. A service of Ford vans, mounted on railway axles and dragging trailers, was maintained while repairs were in progress.[4] On November 17th, the railway was open for normal traffic as far as Morogoro, and by the end of the year to Dodoma, 300 miles from the coast.[5] Dar es Salaam could then relieve the congestion at Mombasa, and

[1] *F.S.R.*, 1935, Vol. II, 75 (4).

[2] *Military Operations, East Africa, Vol I, August*, 1914–*September*, 1916 (Official History), by Lieut.-Col. Charles Hordern, R.E. (retd.), p. 326.

[3] Report by Col. H. L. Woodhouse, M.C., late R.E., entitled "R.E. Railway Work in East Africa, 1914–1918," prepared for the *R.E. Corps History* in Aug., 1937, and notes thereon by Col. L. N. Malan, O.B.E., late R.E.

[4] "Notes on Railway Work in East Africa, 1914–1918," by Capt. H. L. Woodhouse, M.C., R.E., appearing in *The R.E. Journal*, Vol. XXXVII, March–Dec., 1923, pp. 37–46.

[5] Notes by Col. C. W. Wilkinson, C.M.G., D.S.O., late R.E., sent to the author on Oct. 10th, 1937.

the Central Railway replaced the Uganda Railway as the main line of communication with the interior.

There is little to record about the work of the Faridkot Sappers and the Bridging Train during 1916 on the lines of communication. The Faridkot Sappers, with whom Captain E. D. Tillard, R.E., was now serving, were engaged at first on roadmaking for the forces under Generals Stewart and Tighe. From March till May, in ceaseless rain, under the direction of Tillard,[1] they improved communications for the advance of General Van Deventer's South Africans. In July and August they built a bridge at Mkalamo and, with the assistance of the Bridging Train, reconstructed a German trolley-line. Road-work continued during August and September, still in ceaseless rain, and in November the unit was sent to Morogoro to recuperate and refit.[2] "For months," writes Tillard,[3] "the Sappers never got full rations or replacements of kit. Once we drew two days' rations, and, at the end of the period, were asked to make the issue last another two days. Foraging parties went out daily to hunt for bananas, but most of the men became very weak from lack of proper food and the effects of malaria." The Bridging Train fared better. Early in the year the unit was in Nairobi, engaged in making a transportable lattice-girder bridge for the crossing of a small river near Taveta. In July it assisted the Faridkot Sappers, and in August, under Lieutenant W. Smeeth, R.E., it erected bridges in the coastal area south of Dar es Salaam.

During the third phase of the campaign—the year 1917—the retreating enemy moved roughly parallel to the coast, keeping clear of a malarial belt, and it became necessary to maintain contact with him by using new sea-bases south of Dar es Salaam. Kilwa, Lindi and Mikindani had been seized in September 1916 and were coming into operation, but owing to delays caused by military reorganization, and subsequently by heavy rain, the advance southwards could not be resumed until the middle of June 1917. Meanwhile, many small actions were fought against the 1,100 Europeans and 7,300 *askaris* remaining to Von Lettow, in one of which, on January 3rd, Captain F. C. Selous of the 25th Royal Fusiliers (the famous big game hunter) was killed. General Sheppard had relinquished the command of the 1st East African Brigade on January 20th to become Chief of Staff to General Hoskins, and when Hoskins was replaced in the supreme command by Van Deventer at the end of May 1917, Sheppard continued as Chief of Staff and held that appointment under Van Deventer till the end of the war. In June 1917, the principal enemy concentration was in the Lindi area, but other bodies were in the Kilwa area, and there were scattered columns in the south-west which General Northey had failed to round up in an advance in February from Lake Nyasa on Kitanda

[1]Capt. E. D. Tillard, R.E., became Special Service Officer after Maj. B. W. Mainprise, R.E., had been killed at Reata-Latima on March 12th, and Lieut. (ex-Sergt.) W. Smeeth, R.E., then assumed command of the Bridging Train.

[2]*A Short History of the Services rendered by the Imperial Service Troops during the Great War*, 1914–18, by Maj.-Gen. Sir Harry Watson K.B.E., C.B., C.M.G., C.I.E., M.V.O., p. 16.

[3]Notes by Lieut.-Col. E. D. Tillard, D.S.O., R.E. (retd.), sent to the author on Jan. 4th, 1945.

and Ifinga. Von Lettow seemed to be withdrawing his forces southwards in three main groups, one under Colonel Tafel on the Mahenge plateau, another under his personal command east of the Luwega River, and a third under Major Wintgens west of the Upper Ruaha. Van Deventer's plan was to squeeze the enemy gradually south, applying pressure from further and further down the coast by the use of the southern ports. When Lindi had been opened fully, Von Lettow fell back in the Kilwa area to Narungombe where, on July 19th, he gave battle before resuming his retreat. On September 27th, three of our columns captured Nahungu on the Mbemkuru River, after which all our available troops were ordered to the Lindi front. Belgian forces entered Mahenge on October 9th. Six days later there began the last important battle of the campaign. This was near Mahiwa in the area between Masasi and Mtama on the Lukuledi River where, in four days' fighting, the British lost 2,700 out of 4,900 men and the Germans suffered an irreparable blow. Von Lettow then retired to the Makonde plateau from which he was driven southwards on November 15th with his strength reduced to only 300 Europeans and 1,200 *askaris*. Colonel Tafel soon surrendered to Northey and the Belgians, and German sovereignty in East Africa became virtually extinct. Early in December, 1917, the whole province was declared an Allied Protectorate and was later styled "Tanganyika Territory." Von Lettow, however, continued the hopeless struggle. Retreating across the Ruvuma River at Ngomano, he defeated some Portuguese detachments and thus secured arms, ammunition and food; but he was now a fugitive whose wanderings were dictated by the necessity of replenishing his supplies.

Roadmaking in 1917 is well described by Brig.-General R. T. Ridgway. "Generally speaking," he writes,[1] "one moved in the dark, wherever one went. In grass or bush country it was impossible to see more than 50 to 100 yards. The name of a place meant, as a rule, an area covering perhaps 20 square miles. The local method of reckoning distance was by hours, and when still four miles from a locality, a native guide would insist that it was quite close; but a sound rule was to make for water, wherever it might be found. The method of cutting a motor road through the bush was as follows. An advanced guard of a battalion started to blaze the track while, behind it, a company of Pioneers began the roadwork, and by the time the main body had caught up, a mile had been prepared. Passing through the Pioneer company, the column moved on until it had completed 50 minutes' march. Then it halted and every man cut the bush to right and left of him for 3 minutes and rested for 7 minutes. If a column occupied 3 miles of track, the result was the rough making of 3 miles of road in a few minutes; and as the distance normally traversed in 50 minutes was 2 miles, the entire track was covered, so far as cutting was concerned, at each halt. The Pioneers followed to deal with heavy timber or revetments. The result of this rapid method of roadmaking was that food convoys, or heavy artillery drawn by lorries, could keep up with the

[1] "With No. 2 Column, German East Africa, 1917," by Brig.-Gen. R. T. Ridgway, C.B., appearing in *The Army Quarterly*, Vol. V, Oct., 1922, pp. 12–28.

column. Donkeys, with their intolerable braying at night, were a nuisance; but as a donkey cannot bray without cocking his tail, we filled gunny-bags with 7 lbs. of earth and attached them to all tails. This had the desired effect." The facility acquired by the infantry in roadmaking relieved the strain on the engineer units, which were able consequently to devote their energies to more technical work and thus to assist in bringing the long-drawn operations to a more speedy end.

In January, 1917, Major L. N. Malan, R.E., took over the command of the Railway Battalion, S. & M., from Lieut.-Colonel C. W. Wilkinson, R.E. The four companies worked for some months on bridging in the coastal region of the Central Railway and on the Dodoma branch line, but when the enemy retreated in June from the Rufiji area, more important work awaited the units further south. It was decided that some sort of rail communication inland was desirable from the two ports of Kilwa and Lindi, and accordingly the 25th Company was moved to Lindi, and afterwards the 26th and 27th Companies, followed by the 28th, were sent to Kilwa. All four units proceeded to build light tramways to supply the forces advancing towards the Portuguese frontier. The tramway material was collected from local plantations, and traction on the lines was provided by Ford vans mounted on tramway axles. Sixty miles of line were laid from Kilwa and proved invaluable when the local "black cotton" soil became impassable to road traffic during the rains. Progress was slower on the Lindi line, but rail-head was 15 miles inland when the enemy had been driven from the area served by the more northerly Kilwa tramway. Lions, rhinoceroses and elephants delayed the survey parties of both lines and on one occasion a party had to drive off a German patrol with the bayonet. In August, part of the Railway Battalion was present at an action at Mingoyo, near Lindi. By November 1917, the unhealthy climate of the Lindi area had reduced the strength of the 25th Company to only 35 men. Nevertheless, the entire battalion was concentrated there when the maintenance of the Kilwa tramway became no longer necessary.[1] The work of most of the Railway companies in East Africa may be said to have been finished early in 1918. It was decided that the depleted 25th Company should be sent back to India as soon as possible, and accordingly the unit embarked in February 1918 while the 26th and 27th Companies were extending the Lindi tramway to a length of 60 miles. These units sailed in April, but the 28th Company remained until September to improve the harbour works at Lindi. The Railway Battalion established a fine reputation in East Africa and maintained it in Palestine and Syria and on the Indian frontier after the Great War.[2]

[1] *Report on the work done by the Railway Battalion in East Africa, Jan.*, 1917–*April*, 1918, by Col. L. N. Malan, O.B.E., late R.E., dated Oct. 8th, 1937.

[2] In Oct., 1918, the 25th and 29th Companies (the latter formed in May, 1918, in India) were sent to Palestine and worked near Haifa and Tulkeram. In Jan., 1919, the 25th moved northwards and repaired the Amanus line between Mersina and Aleppo. It returned to Palestine in April and, with the 29th Company, was employed between Beersheba and Jaffa. Both units sailed for India in Dec., 1920. Meanwhile, the 26th, 27th and 28th Companies had taken part in the 3rd Afghan War and other trans-frontier operations. As a result of reorganizations in 1921, it was decided to make the 25th and 26th Companies an integral part of the Bombay S. & M. and to disband the 27th, 28th and 29th Companies. This was done, and the Railway Battalion ceased to exist.

The Faridkot Sappers worked in many areas during the third phase of the campaign. In January, 1917, they built two flying bridges, one of which was for the passage of troops across the Rufiji River, and from April to June they maintained a motor-road running from Mikese, on the Central Railway, towards the Uluguru Mountains. In July a detachment joined a Belgian column operating southwards towards Mahenge, while the remainder of the unit was attached to a column dealing with an enemy force which had broken back northwards. In October the company went by sea to Kilwa and joined a Belgian column moving south-westwards to prevent a junction between Von Lettow and Tafel. Marching with these Belgians, the Faridkot Sappers cut and cleared a road for a distance of 163 miles in 27 days.[1] The company was attached to a British column operating on the Ravuma River in January 1918 and constructed and maintained a flying bridge. This ended its active service in East Africa. It embarked at Lindi on February 14th and reached Faridkot, nine days later, after 3½ years' absence, during which it had been the only Sapper and Miner company in a vast theatre of war.[2]

We come now to the last phase of the long-drawn operations. After years of almost continuous fighting, neither side was in a position to bring about a decisive action. The British communications could barely cope with the requirements of many scattered columns: the Germans were short of supplies and munitions. In November, 1917, however, Von Lettow had decided to replenish his stocks by invading Portuguese East Africa. The Portuguese were unable to protect their territory and called for assistance. Von Lettow overwhelmed a Portuguese post at Ngomano and obtained such a haul of munitions that he had an excellent prospect of being able to continue his operations for many months. He might even hope to invade Nyasaland and Rhodesia. Van Deventer was ordered to follow him into Portuguese territory, though with a much reduced force, for almost all the British, Indian and Nigerian troops were to be withdrawn, leaving only the King's African Rifles and, for a time, the Gold Coast Regiment.[3] Von Lettow's aim was to compel us to keep large forces in East Africa by making us extend our lines of communication. He tried to switch his mobile columns continually to areas far from our sea-bases, provided that he could find supplies in those areas for his men. Lindi was obviously too far north to be used as a base for our operations in Portuguese East Africa, and consequently it became necessary to open another base further south from which our columns could be supplied more easily. The best chance of rounding up the remnants of Von Lettow's forces was by a combined movement of converging columns, and this Van Deventer

[1] *A Short History of the Services rendered by the Imperial Service Troops during the Great War*, 1914–18, by Maj.-Gen. Sir Harry Watson, K.B.E., C.B., C.M.G., C.I.E., M.V.O., p. 16.

[2] The Bridging Train, Bombay S. & M., was even longer in East Africa, for it did not return to Kirkee until Aug., 1919, when it was disbanded. (See *A Brief History of the Royal Bombay Sappers and Miners*, p. 30.)

[3] *The East African Force*, 1915–1919, by Brig.-Gen. C. P. Fendall, C.B., C.M.G., D.S.O., p. 113. No. 3 Photo-Litho Section and No. 4 Printing Section, Madras S. & M., had returned to India in July, 1917. No. 4 Engineer Field Park, Madras S. & M., returned in Jan., 1918.

proceeded to do, much as Kitchener had done in the concluding stages of the South African War.

Early in 1918, Von Lettow moved southwards up the Lujenda River from Ngomano, and having occupied Nanguari, split his force into two columns, one marching eastwards through Medo and Mesa towards Porto Amelia, and the other westwards in the direction of Mwembe. Van Deventer then sent the Gold Coast Regiment to guard Porto Amelia, which became our main sea-base for operations in Portuguese territory. The enemy in the Medo-Mesa area were forced back, and during May there were sharp fights at Maketa, on the Msalu River, and also at Nanungu. It was now decided to open a base at Mozambique, still further down the coast, the plan being to confine the enemy columns between lines drawn westwards from Porto Amelia and Mozambique. Von Lettow, however, was not to be caught. Continuing his way south, and mopping up Portuguese posts as he went, he reached Malema and headed for Quelimane near the mouth of the Zambezi. "This is a funny war," remarked one of his men, "we chase the Portuguese and the English chase us." Von Lettow next turned north-eastwards and surprised a detachment of King's African Rifles at Nyamirue, and at the end of July, was moving north-westwards to more fertile country. Then he swung northwards towards Songea beyond the Ruvuma River, which he crossed on September 21st, 1918, with Nyasaland troops to his left and Lindi troops to his right. The garrisons of Mahenge and Iringa were reinforced and arrangements made to meet him south of Tabora on the Central Railway if he got so far. However, he turned north-westwards and then westwards, and passing south of Lake Tanganyika, entered Northern Rhodesia. The end came with his surrender at Abercorn, under the terms of the Armistice, on November 25th, 1918, when he had only 155 Europeans and 1,165 *askaris*, with one field gun and 38 machine-guns.[1] In fairness to Von Lettow-Vorbeck it must be admitted that, unlike many of his countrymen, he was a clean fighter with an honourable record.

The final phase of the war in East Africa was marked by the employment, for the first time, of a regular unit of Sappers and Miners. The 14th Company of the Madras Corps, under Captain W. E. Britten, R.E., with Lieutenants J. Dunn, A. Littlejohn and T. B. Vickers, I.A.R.O., which had left Quetta on January 20th, 1918, landed at Dar es Salaam on February 4th. After spending a month there, and suffering severely from malaria, it was sent to Porto Amelia, whence it marched 70 miles inland to join "Pamforce," a column of King's African Rifles with the 22nd (Indian) Mountain Battery. The unit was required to prepare the track behind the advancing troops for light motor traffic. "The work was hard and monotonous" writes Britten.[2] "Long stretches of swamp had to be corduroyed, and small nullahs ramped and bridged. As camp was moved almost daily and no tents were carried, new grass huts were needed constantly. Local timber provided the material for bridging. The African

[1] *The Empire at War*, by Sir Charles Lucas, K.C.B., K.C.M.G., Vol. IV, p. 305.

[2] "Portuguese East Africa, 1918," by Lieut.-Col. W. E. Britten, O.B.E., R.E., appearing in *The R.E. Journal*, Vol. XLIX, 1935, pp. 430–444.

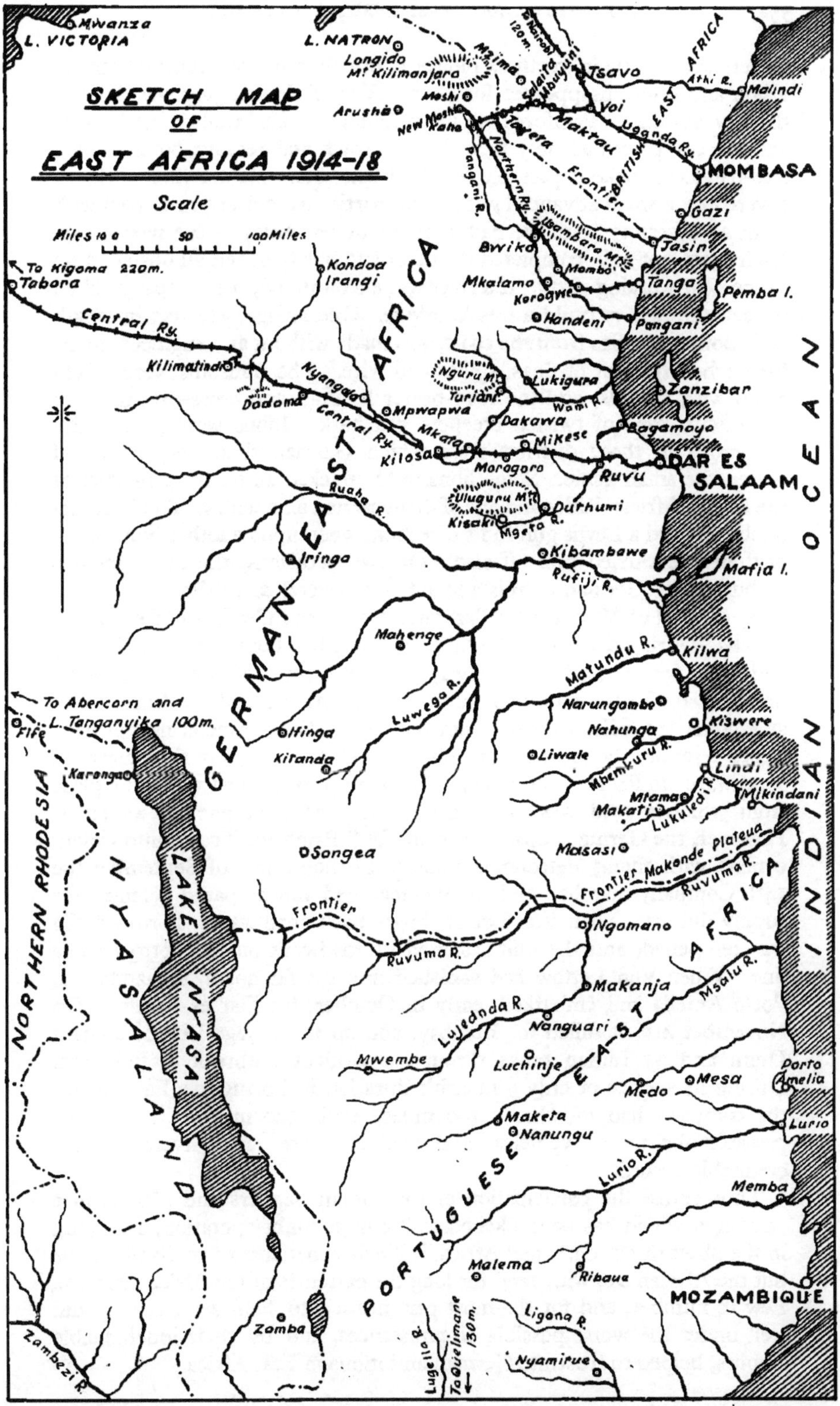
SKETCH MAP OF EAST AFRICA 1914-18
Scale
Miles 10 0 50 100 Miles
Mwanza
L. VICTORIA
L. NATRON
Longido
Mt Kilimanjaro
Moshi
Arusha
New Moshi
Kahe
Mzima
Salaita
Mbuyuni
Tsavo
Voi
Maktau
Taveta
Uganda Ry.
Athi R.
Malindi
BRITISH EAST AFRICA
MOMBASA
Frontier
Northern Ry.
Pangani R.
Gazi
Usambara Mts
Bwiko
Jasin
Mombo
Tanga
Mkalamo
Korogwe
Pemba I.
Handeni
Pangani
To Kigoma 220m.
Tabora
Kondoa Irangi
Central Ry.
Kilimatinde
Nyangala
Dodoma
Nguru Mt
Turiani
Lukigura
Wami R.
Zanzibar
Mpwapwa
Dakawa
Bagamoyo
Mkata
Mikese
Kilosa
Morogoro
Ruvu
DAR ES SALAAM
Uluguru Mt
Duthumi
Kisaki
Mgeta R.
Ruaha R.
Iringa
Kibambawe
Rufiji R.
Mafia I.
GERMAN EAST AFRICA
Mahenge
Kilwa
Matundu R.
Narungombe
Luwega R.
Kiswere
To Abercorn and L. Tanganyika 100m.
Fife
Ifinga
Nahunga
Liwale
Kitanda
Mbemkuru R.
Lindi
Karonga
Mtama
Mikindani
Makati
Lukuledi R.
NORTHERN RHODESIA
LAKE NYASA
Songea
Masasi
Makonde Plateau
Frontier
Ruvuma R.
INDIAN OCEAN
Ngomano
NYASALAND
Makanja
Msalu R.
Lujenda R.
Nanguari
PORTUGUESE EAST AFRICA
Mwembe
Luchinje
Porto Amelia
Medo
Mesa
Maketa
Nanungu
Lurio
Lurio R.
Memba
Malema
Ribaue
MOZAMBIQUE
Zomba
To Quelimane 130m.
Lugella R.
Ligonha R.
Nyamirue
Zambezi R.

porters showed their worth as pioneers, but they needed constant supervision and often disappeared for hours. Very little bridging was done in the dry season. 'Pamforce' usually followed some well-defined track, and the company had only to widen the track and remove boulders and tree-trunks to make it passable for Ford box-cars. We marched at dawn, covered by a small advanced guard, and parties were dropped to deal with work as necessary until we had gone about ten miles to the next camp. Each party not only completed its job at site but removed all obstacles up to the next working party. If a river was encountered, the company halted for several days to build a trestle bridge. One bridge, 312 feet in length and about 200 miles from the coast, was made without any engineer stores, for we had run out of dogs, spikes and wire. The transoms were spiked down with trenails, and the road-bearer lashings and cross-bracing were made with rope of twisted creepers and bark. Lions were particularly dangerous in those districts from which German shooting-parties had driven the small game. Some lions once attacked an outlying picquet of the King's African Rifles and one of them carried off a sentry. The Corporal in charge fired a Lewis gun in its direction, whereupon another lion sprang on him and carried him off also. On two occasions, the company was ambushed by German patrols and suffered several casualties."

By the end of May, 1918, "Pamforce" was 250 miles inland from Porto Amelia. During the month the 14th Company had built 474 feet of bridge, laid 2,430 feet of corduroy roadway, and cut 6 miles of new road through dense bush. In the middle of June, the column reached the Lurio River at a point 315 miles by road from the coast. Porto Amelia having been closed temporarily and Mozambique opened, the company then marched southwards to Ribaue, and afterwards 80 miles south-westwards to a place from which a road was to be made southwards for another 45 miles. However, the Germans upset this plan, for " Pamforce " came into violent contact with enemy detachments and until the middle of September the 14th Company marched and counter-marched and prepared defences for supply dumps. Then Von Lettow broke back northwards, Porto Amelia was re-opened, and the unit resumed its roadwork on the Porto Amelia line. When Von Lettow had vanished into the far north, it marched to Porto Amelia and embarked, early in October, for Dar es Salaam. On November 4th, it sailed for Bombay, and on the voyage lost Lieutenant Dunn and 25 Indian ranks through a virulent outbreak of influenza. During its service of only 9 month's duration in Portuguese East Africa, the company had marched 1,100 miles, made 320 miles of bush-track passable for motor vehicles, and bridged three large rivers—a very creditable record.

Thus ended the participation of the Indian Sappers and Miners in a campaign which has been likened to " a huge night-operation, a groping in the obscurity of darkened Africa." Their experiences proved that none but the African can withstand for long the extremes of the African climate. Few in number, and for the most part unused to field service, they did well under the worst possible circumstances, and by their indefatigable labours, helped to frustrate German ambitions in East Africa.

CHAPTER XXI

THE GREAT WAR: ADEN AND INDIA, 1914–1918

ADEN has had many masters. The Persians were established there before the Christian era. The Romans sent an expedition against it. Afterwards its history is obscure until it was rebuilt and re-armed by the Turks and became an exclusive *entrepot* of Eastern commerce. In 1513, the Portuguese adventurer, Albuquerque, attacked it with a fleet of twenty ships while on his voyage from Malacca and suffered a severe repulse. He sailed on into the Red Sea, and while he was absent the inhabitants strengthened the fortifications so greatly that he did not dare to make another attempt on his return voyage. One of his officers, Lope de Suarez met with no better success in 1516, and tentative efforts by the French and Dutch failed to establish a footing. Aden remained under Turkish control and continued to monopolize the Indian trade until the Portuguese opened a regular route round the Cape during the 16th Century. Then its importance suffered a steady decline. The defences fell to ruin, and by 1835 it was inhabited only by a small population of Jews, Arabs and Somalis. However, the commercial, military and naval possibilities of the place had not escaped the notice of the East India Company, and after various outrages had been perpetrated on British subjects, it was seized in 1839 by a force sent by the Bombay Government.[1] With the annexation of the Island of Perim in 1857, and a subsequent treaty with the Sultan of Sokotra, Great Britain secured strategic control of the Red Sea, and after the opening of the Suez Canal in 1869, Aden became the Gibraltar of the East and a coaling station and port of call of prime importance. This, briefly, is the history of a key point in our chain of Empire communications which we came within an ace of losing in 1915.

A Persian poet once described Aden as " giving to the panting sinner a lively anticipation of his future destiny." If it is warm in Suez, it is hot in Aden: if hot in Suez, unbearable in Aden. The place is an extinct volcano, five miles in length and three in width, connected to the mainland by a narrow isthmus of flat ground. The highest peak of the crater walls is more than 1,700 feet above sea-level. Both the port on the eastern side, and the crater within, are thickly populated, and in a cleft of the crater walls is the famous series of ancient water-tanks which legend ascribes to the Queen of Sheba. These reservoirs were repaired by two Bombay Engineers during and after the Indian Mutiny and can hold 11,000,000 gallons of rainwater;[2] but the rainfall is so brief and uncertain that were it not for a modern system of artesian wells and emergency plant for distilling sea-water, the inhabitants might often go thirsty. In the desert

[1]No Sappers and Miners were included in this force.
[2]*The Military Engineer in India*, by the present author Vol. II, p. 41.

beyond, water is the elixir of life. That sandy waste, stretching along the isthmus through Maala to Khor Maksar, and thence over the mainland through the oases of Sheikh Othman and Lahej[1] to the distant fertile valleys of the Yemen Mountains, had few wells in 1914, and those beyond Sheikh Othman were small and yielded only brackish water. North of Sheikh Othman there was no road and only one good camel track—that through Lahej—so the desert belt between Aden and the mountains presented a formidable barrier, both in attack and defence. Over this desolate region shone a sun whose piercing rays in midsummer could strike men down by the score. It is no exaggeration to say that the lot of the Sappers and Miners who fought in the Aden theatre was not a happy one.

The entry of Turkey into the war on November 5th, 1914, brought her into immediate contact with the British land frontier at the southern end of the Red Sea. For several years, the Turks had been engaged in expeditions of some magnitude in and around the Hedjaz, and in 1914 a Turkish Army Corps under General Said Pasha was stationed in the Yemen, the most fertile part of Arabia, where it constituted a direct threat to the small and isolated garrison of Aden.[2] The garrison comprised only one British and one Indian battalion, 3 companies of Royal Garrison Artillery, an Aden Troop of 100 Indian cavalry *sowars*, and the 23rd (Fortress) Company, Bombay S. & M., under Captain C. F. Stoehr, R.E. It had no field nor mountain artillery, and in this respect resembled the Sudan Defence Force of 1935, which had only one gun and that a saluting gun! As the British Protectorate covered the territories of the Arab tribes of the Aden Hinterland, and as the coast of Arabia from Perim to Muscat was considered to be within the British sphere of influence, it is evident that the situation at Aden was precarious.

Before the declaration of war, Said Pasha's forces were reported to be collecting in strength around the Aden Protectorate, and at a place called Sheikh Said, on the mainland opposite Perim about 100 miles west of Aden, their presence was a serious menace. However, the 29th Indian Infantry Brigade was landed there on November 10th while on its way to Egypt, and having driven the Turks inland, left the 23rd Sikh Pioneers as a reinforcement at Perim. This secured a short respite, but the Turks soon re-entered Sheikh Said and continued to threaten Perim, and with the utmost secrecy Said Pasha brought one of his divisions to within a march of Lahej. The political aspect was as unsatisfactory as the military situation, for although the Abdali Sultan of Lahej was undoubtedly loyal to the Crown, the Arabs in the desert beyond, and in the Yemen generally, were coming increasingly under the influence of Turkish intrigue. At about this time, the 1st Battalion, Middlesex Regiment, which had formed the nucleus of the Aden garrison, was replaced by a Territorial unit, the Brecknockshire Battalion of the South Wales Borderers, and all idea of

[1]See *Sketch Map of Aden*, 1914–18, included in this chapter.
[2]See *Sketch Map of Somaliland, The Aden Hinterland and Abyssinia in* 1902, included in Chapter XII.

ADEN IN 1857.

offensive operations had to be abandoned until the young Territorials had gained experience.

There were no hostilities at Aden during the early part of 1915. A small addition to the strength of the garrison occurred in March when the 30th Indian Infantry Brigade (11th Indian Division), under Brig.-General C. J. Melliss, V.C., disembarked half the 126th Baluchistan Infantry while on its way from Egypt to reinforce the 6th Indian Division in Iraq. As the summer drew on, however, it became clear that the Turks intended to attack the Protectorate, so Major-General D. L. B. Shaw, commanding the Aden Brigade, decided to forestall them at Lahej and thus to support the friendly Sultan.[1] Some obsolete field and mountain guns having become available, Shaw organized a small Movable Column of 1,000 men with six 15-pounder and four 10-pounder guns, drawn or carried by camels and manned by the Garrison Artillery. The Turkish offensive soon materialized in the west. On June 14th, 1915, the enemy attempted to land on Perim and were repulsed by the 23rd Pioneers. The Sultan of Lahej, gravely threatened from the north, appealed for help, and the Aden Troop and some infantry were sent to his assistance. The remainder of the Movable Column with most of the 23rd (Fortress) Company, Bombay S. & M., set out on July 3rd to cover the seven miles to the advanced post at Sheikh Othman. Even this short march caused a number of casualties from heat-stroke, particularly among the Brecknockshire Territorials. At 3 a.m. on July 4th, the column left Sheikh Othman on a twenty miles' march to Lahej. The sun rose, and men began to fall out by the dozen, overcome by the fearful heat, the shortage of water and the heavy going on the sandy track. At midday, brought to a standstill some five miles short of Lahej, the troops composing the main body heard firing in the village where the advanced guard of the 109th Indian Infantry and the 23rd (Fortress) Company, with four 10-pounder guns, was already in action. An effort was made to get the main body forward, and some Brecknocks, 126th Baluchis and 23rd Sikh Pioneers reached Lahej, but many of these were fit only for admission to hospital. The force camped in a walled enclosure which was shelled persistently and attacked at dusk by Turks and Arabs. Meanwhile, the native drivers of the camel transport on the road to Lahej had cut the cords of their loads and fled, and thus all the reserve ammunition, food and water were lost. The 15-pounder guns were stuck hopelessly in the sand four miles from the camp. Every friendly Arab vanished, and, to complete the disaster, the loyal Sultan of Lahej was shot accidentally by some of our infantry who mistook him for one of Said Pasha's irregulars.

The 109th Infantry, a detachment of the 126th Baluchis, and 100 men of the Brecknockshire Battalion who were still capable of holding a rifle, repelled all attacks until dawn on July 5th when a retirement was begun on Bir Nasir, where stragglers had been collected. Fortunately, it was unmolested. Assisted by transport sent out from Aden, the retirement was

[1]*Military Operations. Egypt and Palestine* (Official History), by Lieut.-Gen. Sir George MacMunn, K.C.B., K.C.S.I., D.S.O., Vol. I, p. 22.

resumed at dusk, and before midnight the remnants of the force were in Sheikh Othman. Although this important oasis was essential to the Aden water-supply, it was decided that it must be abandoned and the force retired to the narrow isthmus at Khor Maksar, where naval support could be given on both flanks. The Turks advanced and occupied Sheikh Othman, and some units penetrated through Khor Maksar as far as Maala near the fortifications of Aden. Had the enemy then been aware of the true situation, they might have captured Aden by a powerful assault.

The behaviour of the 23rd (Fortress) Company under Captain C. F. Stoehr, R.E., during these operations was beyond all praise. The unit formed part of the peace-time garrison and was not a field formation, yet it acted most efficiently in the field. " It is difficult," writes Colonel Sir Edward Le Breton,[1] " to convey in words the meaning of a march of nearly 20 miles in midsummer over the worst desert in the world, followed by a defeat and a retreat of the same distance before a victorious enemy. There were no two opinions about the magnificent way in which Stoehr and his Bombay Sappers had acquitted themselves. At one period, when the Turks were on one side of a wall and the handful of Sappers on the other, Stoehr was reaching over the wall from time to time to empty his revolver point-blank into the enemy in an endeavour to slow down their advance." Stoehr records[2] that the 23rd Company marched from Sheikh Othman behind the 109th Infantry but passed them on the road and reached Lahej at full strength at 10 a.m. It made a sortie at sunset with the Aden Troop and some men of the 23rd Pioneers and held an advanced and very exposed position for three hours. At 2 a.m., Stoehr led a bayonet charge of Sappers and infantry and routed an enemy patrol, and at dawn the company marched with the remainder of the force to Bir Nasir.

The loss of the Sheikh Othman water-supply was a shattering blow to Aden, for, though primitive, it was sufficient to meet all ordinary demands. The supply came mainly from a great well which was worked day and night by relays of camel-teams pumping water into a small masonry aqueduct reputed to have been built by Suleiman the Magnificent. It is said that Major-General Shaw met the crisis by ordering the ships in harbour to condense sea-water, which they did by putting their engines at full speed astern while securely anchored by the bows. Sheikh Othman, however, did not remain long in enemy hands. Reinforcements came in the nick of time. Half the 108th Indian Infantry landed on July 8th, and the 4th Buffs relieved the Brecknocks. On July 18th, the 28th (Frontier Force) Indian Infantry Brigade, under Major-General Sir G. J. Younghusband, arrived from Egypt with two non-regular batteries (Berkshire Battery, R.H.A. (T) and " B " Battery, H.A.C.). Younghusband assumed the post of Governor and Commander-in-Chief in Aden and sent his brigade under the command of Lieut.-Colonel A. M. S. Elsmie, 56th Punjab Rifles, to recapture Sheikh Othman. A detachment of the 23rd

[1]Notes by Col. Sir Edward Le Breton, D.L., J.P., late R.E., sent to the author on Feb. 15th, 1945.

[2]Official Report by Capt. C. F. Stoehr, R.E., dated July 14th, 1915.

(Fortress) Company was included. Elsmie took the place on July 21st and pursued the Turks for several miles northwards, and thus secured the safety of Aden and restored the normal water-supply.[1]

Part of the 23rd Company was involved in more hard fighting at the end of August 1915 in an attempt to capture the village of Waht, between Sheikh Othman and Lahej. The Movable Column, which marched from Sheikh Othman at 1 a.m. on August 28th, included two sections of Bombay Sappers with four loads of explosives and grenades. It halted about a mile from Waht, which was then attacked by the 53rd Sikhs. The attack was repulsed, and the retreating firing line and reserve became completely mixed up with the Sappers who had moved to the head of the column. The flat country was intersected by stone walls dividing the fields, and the dust and the walls prevented proper communication and close support. Some of the infantry lost direction, and the Sappers, retreating to a small hillock, found themselves on the extreme left of the line which the enemy was endeavouring to outflank. Stoehr decided to counter-attack. Collecting a few of the 53rd Sikhs and some of his Sappers, he led a bayonet charge round the left side of the hillock; but the impetus of the assault died away under heavy fire some 30 yards from the enemy and the battle resolved itself into a fire fight during which a temporarily attached officer, Lieutenant Durand, I.A.R.O., was wounded.[2] Stoehr then fell back to rejoin the other troops holding a long ridge in rear and, with 150 men of the 53rd Sikhs and his Sapper company, took charge of the left flank. Later, the whole line withdrew steadily for half a mile to a position held by the 51st Sikhs who were in support. There, Stoehr handed over his 53rd Sikhs, collected his Sappers, and marched with the advanced guard to As Sela, where water was obtainable in small quantities. By 1.15 p.m. the column was back in Sheikh Othman. The operation had been a failure, but the 23rd Company had shown once again that it could acquit itself well in the firing line under energetic leadership.

Major-General J. M. Stewart, from East Africa, was now in chief command at Aden. He had suggested in July that the time had arrived for a general advance, for the Arab revolt under the Sherif of Mecca had altered the situation in Arabia and it seemed advisable for political reasons to make an effort to recover lost territory. But the suggestion met with scant approval, and even a limited offensive up to the Waht-Fiyush line was deprecated. It was pointed out that, if serious operations were to be undertaken, they should be carried out in strength in the cooler weather of the autumn, and Stewart stated that for such operations he would require an additional infantry brigade, two batteries of field artillery and more engineers and other services.[3] In the end, the War Committee restricted him to an active defence until troops could be transferred from East Africa, though approval was given to the extension of a projected line of railway

[1] *Forty Years a Soldier*, by Maj.-Gen. Sir George Younghusband, K.C.M.G., K.C.I.E., p.275, and Official Report by the same officer dated July 21st, 1915.
[2] Official Report by Capt. C. F. Stoehr, R.E., dated Aug. 30th, 1915.
[3] *The Empire at War*, by Sir Charles Lucas, K.C.B., K.C.M.G., Vol. V, p. 143.

through Sheikh Othman as far as Robat. It is probable, therefore, that the attack on Waht in August was undertaken merely as a reconnaissance in force in pursuance of the approved policy of active defence and to safeguard the progress of the railway.

Small reinforcements continued to arrive and among them the 5th Company, Bengal S. & M., under Captain E. P. Le Breton, R.E., with Lieutenant R. Boal, R.E. (I.A.), and Lieutenants F. J. Salberg and J. L. Muir, I.A.R.O. The senior British N.C.O. was C.S.M. W. J. Lyall, R.E., who was commissioned in November and left the 5th Company in February, 1916, to join the 1st Company at Roorkee.[1] The 5th Company had started from Roorkee on August 10th, 1915, and reached Aden towards the end of the month. On September 1st it marched out to Khor Maksar to carry out defence works.[2] These included a second line at Maala, running through the Golf Links near that place but tactfully avoiding the Polo Ground—an arrangement due perhaps to the fact that Le Breton, who selected the line, was a polo player but no golfer. However, as soon as the company had begun to dig, an agitated deputation of Aden golfers waited on Le Breton to express the hope that it would not be necessary to cut into the "browns," which had been consolidated by the labour of two generations, so a "brown" which was due for destruction was incorporated in the defence line as possibly the largest traverse ever seen. General Younghusband viewed it with some astonishment on the following day, but he appeared satisfied when assured by Le Breton that traverses were being made very wide in France![3]

Having completed the Maala defences without offending either the local polo players or golfers, the 5th Company concentrated on September 11th at Sheikh Othman for further defence work. Le Breton was the senior R.E. officer with the troops in the desert and in control of both the 5th and 23rd Companies. Official approval was marked by the issue of a blue armlet, to be worn only during an action. One can imagine the wild hunt for the crumpled armlet when the bullets began to fly! Fortunately, they seldom flew, for life at Sheikh Othman was dull and wearisome and consisted mostly in supervising defence work and devising means of reducing the casualties from the climate and the hardships of existence in that God-forsaken part of Southern Arabia. The garrison outside Aden increased with the defences. On September 11th, a Territorial Howitzer Battery disembarked at Maala, followed by a Camel Corps on the 14th and the 26th Indian Light Cavalry on the 20th, so that the defences at Sheikh Othman and Maala were held in sufficient strength. On the other hand, the garrison of the Aden area as a whole

[1]Lieut W. J. Lyall, R.E. (I.A.), went with the 1st Company to Iraq in June, 1916. As a Captain (acting Major) he commnded the 54th Company in the Bushire operations in October, 1918 (See Chapter XVIII), and afterwards commanded the 2nd Company at Roorkee and was Superintendent of Park. When killed in a motor accident in Nov., 1938, he was C.R.E. Peshawar Dist. with the rank of Lieut.-Col. His career exemplifies the capabilities of the B.N.C.O. ranks of the Sappers and Miners.

[2]War Diary of Maj. F. W. Saunders, R.E., A.C.R.E. Aden.

[3]Notes by Col. Sir Edward Le Breton, D.L., J.P., late R.E., sent to the author on Feb. 15th, 1945.

was weakened in the middle of September by the recall to Egypt of the 28th Indian Infantry Brigade, which had been sent to deal with the crisis in July but was now required urgently on the Suez Canal.

From September, 1915, onwards, the situation at Aden underwent little substantial change. Minor operations in this area could not directly affect the course of the war, so it was laid down that although an active defence was still to be maintained, and the Turks harried by reconnaissances and patrolling, no general offensive for the recovery of the portions of the British Protectorate overrun by the enemy should be undertaken. Accordingly, for more than three years the mobile part of the Aden Expeditionary Force, comprising all the troops except a few Garrison formations, remained in Sheikh Othman facing Turkish forces which were much superior in numbers and in the strength and modernity of their artillery. Several reconnaissances led to sharp fighting in which the Sappers and Miners were used as infantry, and on more than one occasion they formed a considerable part of the rearguard covering a retreat. Indeed, in one skirmish, after the Turks had begun to disengage, the 5th Company, although the only field unit of Engineers in the Aden theatre of war, was ordered to advance to clear up the situation by drawing the enemy's fire. Fortunately, it suffered few casualties, but the emergency must have been great to justify such employment of technical troops.

Although no permanent advance to the Waht-Fiyush line was permissible, operations continued against Waht itself, and on September 25th, 1915, a column under Lieut.-Colonel A. M. S. Elsmie was directed to ascertain the situation at that place, which was believed to be held by 700 Turks and 1,000 Arabs with 8 guns.[1] The column, which was of brigade strength and included the 5th Company, Bengal S. & M., and the 23rd (Fortress) Company, Bombay S. & M., started before dawn from Sheikh Othman. In the operations which followed, while acting as escort to the guns, the 5th Company had its baptism of fire in the Great War. The 4th Buffs and Indian infantry plodded onwards through the sand until midday, when the Buffs were immobilized by the appalling heat and lack of water. The desert heat-haze had reduced visibility to 200 yards, and because of the lack of telephones and wireless sets, the units were completely out of touch with headquarters. The British gunners began to collapse from heat-stroke. " In the early afternoon," writes Le Breton, " a message reached us ordering the guns to withdraw and the Sappers to remain in position to cover the retirement of the infantry. Without the Gunners, the 5th Company seemed as isolated as though on a raft in a fog in mid-ocean. The sand was so hot that it was impossible to sit or lie on it for more than a few minutes, and the temperature in the hospital *tonga* was 136°F. The firing died down, but we could not know whether the rest of the brigade had retired, unseen by us. The Senior Medical Officer, who had remained with some light Ambulance transport, urged that the 5th Company should withdraw to escort the transport to the rear, but I felt

[1]Despatch by Gen. Sir Beauchamp Duff, G.C.B., G.C.S.I., K.C.V.O., C.I.E., C.-in.-C., India, dated March 9th, 1916.

bound to act on my original orders and accordingly we held our position. Later, a solitary officer appeared, suffering from incipient heat-stroke and able only to mutter hoarsely "All the Buffs are dead." He vanished into the haze, still repeating his distressing but fortunately inaccurate statement. About 4 p.m. the haze lifted and we saw some exhausted Punjabi infantry carrying or supporting to the rear a number of the Buffs who had collapsed from the incredible heat. With them was Brigade Headquarters, including Colonel Elsmie who was full of energy though speechless from thirst. After he had been restored with some of our Reserve water, he explained that the brigade was retiring to a hillock, a few miles from Sheikh Othman, where he hoped that we should get water, and whence, after a rest, we should fall back to our defence line. The Sappers, as the least exhausted troops, were to cover the retirement. It was now growing perceptibly cooler, and, with a company of Indian Infantry, the Sappers acted as rearguard until the hillock was reached at dusk. The Turks did not press the pursuit. The 26th Light Cavalry brought up water and carried back many of the Buffs on their horses, and by midnight the force was back in Sheikh Othman. The 23rd Company was engaged in the fighting and Stoehr was slightly wounded and had his horse shot under him." On the whole it may be said that although the enemy in Waht were taken by surprise, the results of this reconnaissance in force were unsatisfactory. Many of our men were incapacitated, and the operation proved only that there are climatic conditions under which the range of action of even the best troops is strictly limited.

After this second unfortunate venture to Waht, activity at Sheikh Othman resumed the normal routine of patrolling, strengthening the defences and improving the living conditions. Lieutenant F. J. Salberg, I.A.R.O., of the 5th Company, suggested that bricks might be made from sand mixed with mule and camel droppings and straw. An experiment having proved successful, all units asked for Sapper instructors and started their own brickworks, and buildings of every sort sprang up from a mosque to an observation tower. The work was heavy, and the climate continued to take a severe toll. The Indian troops became accustomed to the brackish drinking water, which they preferred to the distilled variety because, as they said, "it had more strength in it"; but it had such a bad effect on the British troops that small quantities of distilled water had to be brought for them from Aden. The crucial importance of a proper distribution of water led to the formation of a motley-looking but efficient "Water Column," capable of carrying 10,000 gallons and working under the direction of Le Breton. It was commanded by Lieutenant R. Boal, R.E. (I.A.), who had two Infantry officers as assistants. A detachment from each unit in Sheikh Othman was posted to the 5th Company for Water Column duties, and the Sappers were responsible for the distribution of water not only in camp but also during operations in the desert.[1] Yet in spite of all preucations, the health of the garrison

[1]It was found that, during desert operations in the summer, a daily allowance of 1 gallon of drinking water per man was required.

suffered, and frequent relief of the British units became necessary. For instance, the 4th Buffs left Aden at the end of January, 1916, on relief by the 4th D.C.L.I. This unit remained until February, 1917, when it was replaced by the 6th East Surreys, and in January, 1918, the East Surreys were relieved by the 7th Hampshires. There were fewer changes among the Indian units. The 75th Carnatics, who relieved the detachments of the 108th Infantry and 126th Baluchis in January, 1916, were still in Aden when the war ended, as also were the Malay States Guides who had arrived in October, 1915. The record was held by the 109th Infantry who were in Aden from before the declaration of war until October, 1917, a period of more than three years.

Early in January, 1916, information was received that the Turks were despatching troops to coerce the Arabs in the eastern part of the Aden Protectorate, and accordingly the Movable Column was directed to demonstrate in support of the friendly tribes. It marched from Sheikh Othman towards Lahej at 2.15 a.m. on January 12th, the 5th Company, Bengal S. & M., being with the advanced guard. Four hours later, news arrived that the Turks were coming out in strength, and the Malay States Guides were sent ahead, with Captain E. P. Le Breton, R.E., and Lieutenant J. L. Muir, I.A.R.O., to prepare a position in front of a ridge at Dar Ahmad Hatum, generally known as Hatum. At about 7 a.m., the enemy appeared and opened fire on Le Breton, Muir and two officers of the Guides who were reconnoitring for a line of obstacles in advance of the position, and when the 5th Company arrived and began to make the obstacles it came under fairly heavy shrapnel fire. This lasted until 10 a.m., when the Sappers were ordered to come in and man a section of the defences. To their surprise they found that no trenches had been dug for them by the infantry, who were already entrenched to right and left, and consequently they had to lie in the open. However, the infantry soon had to leave their trenches because they found that firing from cover raised so much sand that they could see nothing. Casualties were light as the enemy's rifle fire was aimed too high and his high-explosive shells were smothered in the soft sand. The brass fuzes from his shrapnel did some damage. One of these ricochetted with such force from the water-bottle of a Sapper that it killed a camel. The 5th Company remained in the front line until 2.45 p.m. when it was withdrawn to join the reserve behind the ridge. A desultory fire-fight continued till dusk. Then a retirement was begun, the rearguard being formed of the 5th and 23rd Sapper companies, the Malay States Guides and a company of the Buffs, and Sheikh Othman was reached without further incident. There were no casualties among the Sapper officers, though Le Breton's horse was wounded. This small affair is typical of many excursions undertaken into the desert in pursuance of a policy of active defence, and under the energetic leadership of Le Breton, the 5th Company was usually to the fore.

The 23rd (Fortress) Company, under Captain C. F. Stoehr, R.E., took part in a small clash with the enemy at Imad on March 16th, 1916, when the Turks attacked our advanced post at that place. The unit marched from Sheikh Othman with the Movable Column and shared in repelling the attack.[1] The spring and summer of 1916 brought little fighting for the Bengal and Bombay Sappers who were still occupied chiefly with defence work and improving the conditions of living. Problems of supply had been eased somewhat by the arrival of No. 6 Engineer Field Park, Bengal S. & M., under Lieutenant A. M. R. Montagu, I.A.R.O. The construction of a metalled road was begun across the desert from Sheikh Othman towards Lahej alongside a metre-gauge railway line which was being built by local labour under Captain L. V. Kent, R.E. This work was often interrupted by shell fire, and on one occasion the Turks launched an infantry attack and captured some rolling stock, but Lieutenant F. J. Salberg and a few men of the 5th Company went out on a locomotive and recovered the abandoned wagons.

The rations issued to the troops were sometimes very bad and caused much discontent. Indeed, it is recorded that a certain Commanding Officer was so disgusted with a case of flour that he returned it forthwith to the Supply and Transport Office, where it was found to be full of weevils among which was his indent demanding an equivalent weight in flour ! As the troops began to suffer from scurvy, arrangements were put in hand to import vegetables. Meanwhile, the Sappers came to the rescue by repairing and restarting a number of old, wind-driven irrigation pumps found in the local date-gardens, and thus secured sufficient water to enable all units to grow some wholesome, though unpleasant, green stuff. Sports were organized for the men, and the British officers played tennis on an improvised mud court under the protection of an armed guard.

Reports received early in September, 1916, indicated that the Turks were preparing to retire from Lahej, and consequently it became necessary to ascertain the true situation by increased patrolling and reconnaissance. On September 8th, 120 men of the 5th Company, carrying material for a number of booby-traps, marched from Sheikh Othman to Imad with a company of the 109th Indian Infantry. The small force was ordered to attack a strongly fortified Turkish post in the old town of Jabir (Bir Jabir) and then to retire after placing the booby-traps. At dawn on the 9th it was in position about a mile from Jabir, the 109th on the left, the Sappers on the right, with the 109th machine-guns on the right flank and some mountain and field guns in rear. Advancing at high speed across the open desert in half-company rushes, the troops came under heavy fire, fortunately aimed too high. The 109th were checked by a patch of heavy sand and the Sappers were ordered to push ahead, with the result that Jabir was eventually carried by a bayonet charge of the 5th Company alone, headed by Le Breton. There was a touch of humour in this affair. Le Breton had forgotten to load his revolver and had fastened the ammunition pouch in the centre of the back of his crowded Sam Browne belt,

[1] *Official Report on the action at Imad on March 16th*, 1916. Capt. C. F. Stoehr, R.E., was then in command, but in June, 1916, he was invalided to India and Lieut. J. K. Douglas, R.E., acted as O.C. until the arrival of Lieut. E. F. Johnston, R.E., in July. In India, in October, 1916, Capt. Stoehr became O.C., 19th Company, Bombay S. & M., and took the unit to Iraq in November, 1917.

where it was quite inaccessible. However, a 5th Company bugler, seeing his predicament, grasped the belt from behind and passed the cartridges round as they ran, and so the final charge was headed by a swiftly moving, though somewhat ungainly, combination. Surprised, perhaps, by this novel assault-formation, the Turks fled into the scrub jungle behind the town, and the Sappers, covered by the 109th Infantry, proceeded to lay their booby-traps. They were unhindered except by spasmodic shell-fire from Turkish artillery and from a few British 15-pounder guns which the enemy had captured in the first attempt on Lahej. The force then returned to Imad, and later to Sheikh Othman. Casualties among the Sappers were very light. Lieutenant R. Boal, R.E. (I.A.), was hit on the head by a shrapnel bullet; but since it takes much to damage a hardy ex-R.S.M. of the Sappers and Miners, he was able to ride back to Imad and to return to duty within a few days. Lieutenant A. C. Austin, I.A.R.O., did well in these operations, and Subadar Habibullah Khan, a Colour Havildar, and also the Bengali Assistant Surgeon attached to the unit were rewarded for gallantry under fire. The official record states that the Sappers attacked with great dash, and that, by their rapid advance, they saved the situation.

Owing to sickness, and the demands of other theatres, there were many changes among the British officers of the 5th Company during 1916 and 1917. Lieutenant W. J. Lyall, R.E. (I.A.), returned to India in February, 1916, and Lieutenant A. C. Austin, I.A.R.O., joined the unit in April in replacement of Lieutenant F. J. Salberg, I.A.R.O. In July, Lieutenant J. L. Muir, I.A.R.O., left for Roorkee. Captain E. P. Le Breton, R.E., was invalided in October, 1916, and the command of the unit devolved on Lieutenant R. Boal, R.E. (I.A.), until Le Breton returned in March 1917 after spending some hours in an open boat in the Mediterranean while a German submarine circled his ship. Boal then departed to India to raise the 51st Company. Lieutenant G. Bartholomew, I.A.R.O., joined in November, 1916. Lieutenant A. C. Austin was on sick leave from February to August, 1917, during which period Lieutenants H. S. Crowley and W. S. Tinsley, I.A.R.O., joined the company. It is apparent that, without the invaluable assistance of the Indian Army Reserve of Officers, the Sapper activities at Aden, as elsewhere, would have been impossible. These temporary soldiers filled a gaping breach in our military structure, and with their expert knowledge of civil engineering, filled it to perfection.

Reconnaissance and patrolling from Sheikh Othman continued during the winter of 1916–17. In one of these minor operations, the 75th Carnatics cleared Bir Jabir and the 4th D.C.L.I. entered Hatum after heavy fighting. Yet the need to withdraw subsequently to conform strictly to a defensive policy was discouraging and ignominious, for the local Arabs knew only the war around Aden and judged by what they saw. Nevertheless, small raids afforded a welcome relief from the dreary existence in Sheikh Othman and they were undertaken during 1917 whenever and wherever possible. For instance, after dark on August 2nd, a party of 50 Sappers and 20 Infantry was led by Le Breton for some two miles into No Man's Land to drive a Turkish picquet off a ridge dominating a village. This was accomplished and the village destroyed before withdrawal. A more important operation took place on August 16th, 1917, when Le Breton was ordered to destroy a Muhammadan *Ziarat* (tomb) from which enemy snipers often fired on our cavalry patrols. As this involved crossing a mile of open ground and working for an hour within close range of enemy artillery at Darb, Le Breton suggested that the work should be done after dark, but he was overruled and accordingly set out in broad daylight with half the 5th Company and a squadron of cavalry. By a miracle, the Sappers were saved from annihilation, for a sandstorm arose which screened their advance. They had finished most of the demolition before the swirling clouds subsided, but after the air had cleared they had an unpleasant half-hour during which they worked furiously with pick and shovel in full view of the enemy. Yet they remained unobserved until the work was finished and got back to the shelter of the scrub jungle around As Sela as the Turkish guns opened fire.

Possibly the most important result of the 5th Company's labours in and around Sheikh Othman was the discovery that water could be obtained locally from Artesian wells. After Le Breton had tried in vain to get a geological map of the area, he sank a Norton tube well at a venture and struck a supply of brackish water at about 40 feet below the surface. This induced the authorities to obtain from India an obsolete boring apparatus which, under the skilled supervision of the I.A.R.O. officers, produced another, though still undrinkable, supply from a depth of 90 feet. Le Breton then applied for a proper outfit. This failed to reach Aden while the 5th Company was there, but there is little doubt that the lead given by the unit in sinking Artesian wells helped towards the elaboration of an installation at Sheikh Othman which has transformed life at Aden by yielding a daily supply of more than 100,000 gallons of potable water.

On November 3rd, 1917, the newly-raised 51st Company, Bengal S. & M., under Captain R. Boal, R.E. (I.A.), with Captain A. G. C. Fane, I.A.R.O., and Lieutenants J. S. Lethbridge, R.E., and G. A. MacNiven, I.A.R.O., arrived from Roorkee in relief of the 5th Company, which sailed for Iraq in December to earn fresh laurels in a wider sphere. All ranks of the out-going unit welcomed the change of scene and occupation. Their sentiments were expressed with remarkable aptitude in the following opening verses of a poem by one of their officers which was published anonymously in *The Times* :—

The hot red rocks of Aden
Stand from their burnished sea ;
The bitter sands of Aden
Lie shimmering in their lee.

We have no joy of battle,
No honour here is won ;
Our little fights are nameless
With Turk and sand and sun.

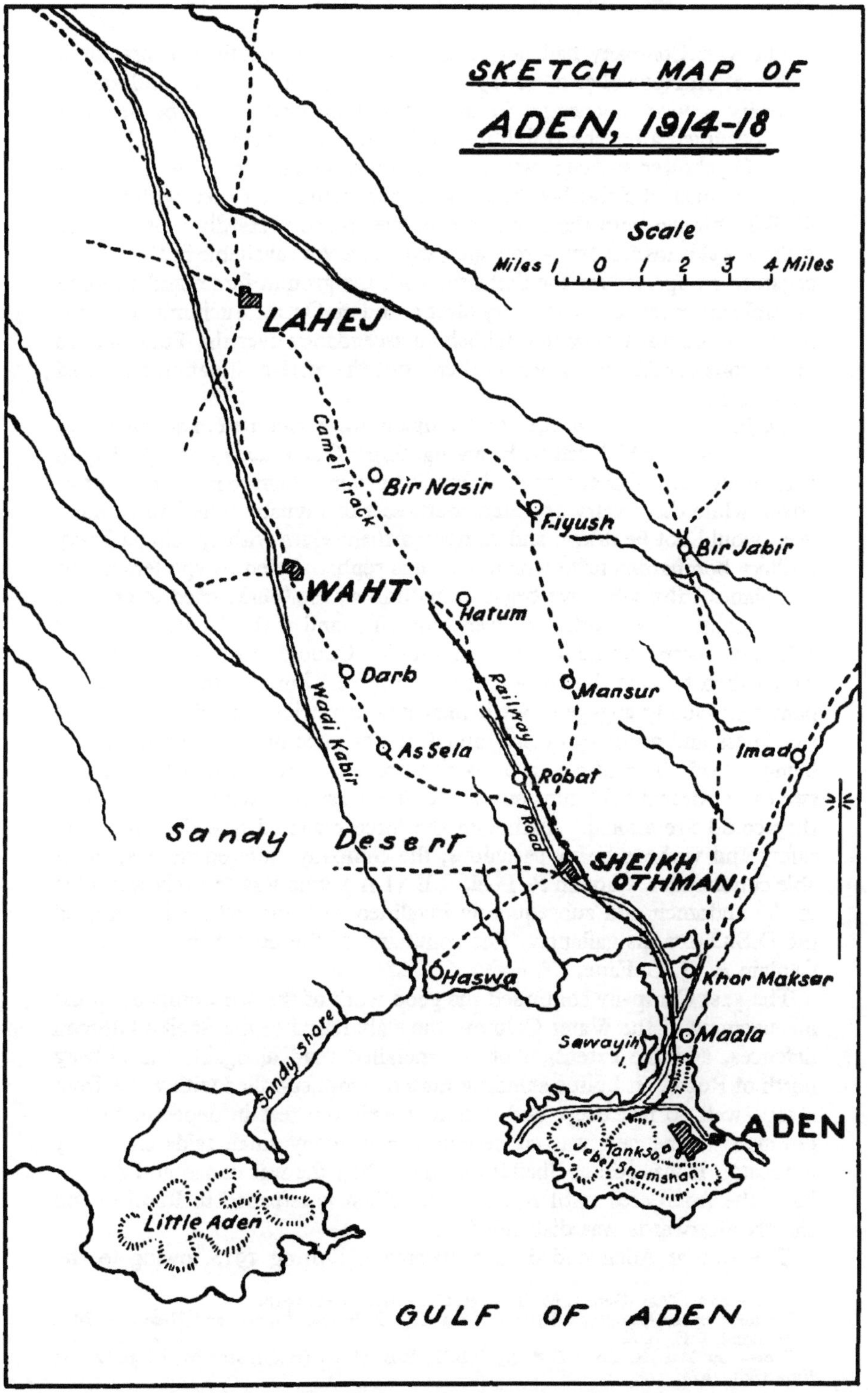
SKETCH MAP OF
ADEN, 1914-18
Scale
Miles 1 0 1 2 3 4 Miles
LAHEJ
Camel track
Bir Nasir
Fiyush
Bir Jabir
WAHT
Hatum
Darb
Mansur
Railway
Wadi Kabir
As Sela
Robat
Imad
Road
Sandy Desert
SHEIKH OTHMAN
Haswa
Khor Maksar
Sandy shore
Maala
Sawayih I.
ADEN
Tanks
Jebel Shamshan
Little Aden
GULF OF ADEN

The 51st Company had not long to wait for its baptism of fire for it took part on November 22nd, 1917, in an attack on Bir Jabir, undertaken to verify reports of changes in the enemy's dispositions. The defences were occupied after sharp fighting during which Captain A. G. C. Fane, I.A.R.O., showed gallantry which brought him a Military Cross. The company demolished a fortified house with gun-cotton and then withdrew to Sheikh Othman with the remainder of the troops.[1] Hardly a day passed without a skirmish. A few aeroplanes, which became available in December, began to co-operate for the first time with the ground forces and afforded valuable air cover to our infantry after a raid on Darb. Such minor operations enabled our troops to establish an ascendancy over the Turks and to inflict considerable casualties on them, but the general situation remained unchanged.

On January 5th, 1918, the 51st Company was concerned in an enterprise against Hatum which led to heavy fighting. Our infantry occupied both Hatum and Bir Jabir and pushed forward beyond them to invite a counter-attack while the cavalry operated south-east of Fiyush. The Turks, however, would not be drawn and contented themselves with opening a heavy artillery bombardment to which our guns replied, aided by spotters in our aeroplanes. But when we began to withdraw, the Turks tried to envelop both flanks. Two battalions were cut off; and a third battalion, after suffering severe casualties, retired rapidly through the 51st Company, which then became the rearguard of the force. For two hours, the company was closely engaged, but it managed to retrieve the situation by its steadiness and accuracy of fire though it was once in imminent danger of being cut off. The efficiency of its rifle fire is shown by the fact that it put two camel-drawn field guns out of action at a range of nearly a mile before they could fire a shell.[2] Although the force regained Sheikh Othman in safety and without heavy casualties, the company suffered the loss of its able commander, Captain R. Boal, R.E. (I.A.), who was severely wounded in the abdomen and subsequently invalided to India, where he received the D.S.O. for his gallantry. The command of the unit then devolved on Captain A. G. C. Fane, I.A.R.O.

The 51st Company continued the good work of the 5th Company in the management of the Water Column, the elaboration of the Sheikh Othman defences, and the extension of the metalled road alongside the railway north of Robat. It built a standing hutted camp, supplied with water from a tube-well 80 feet deep, and it sank a well 250 feet in depth in Sheikh Othman.[3] The unit was concerned also in many small raids on enemy outposts. It was still at Sheikh Othman when the war ended and did not leave the Aden area until April 1921. Then it returned to Roorkee and shortly afterwards was disbanded.

The war at Aden ended in a stalemate. During 1918, owing to the

[1]Despatch by Maj.-Gen. J. M. Stewart, C.B., dated Feb. 1918.

[2]*Lectures on the Regimental History of the K.G.O. Bengal Sappers and Miners*, by Maj. L. V. Bond, R.E., p. 8.

[3]Notes by Maj. R. Boal, D.S.O., O.B.E., R.E. (I.A.) (retd.), sent to the author on June 18th, 1937.

activity of our aeroplanes and the increased efficiency of our artillery, the Turks remained mostly in their defences. In April, the road towards Lahej reached a point a mile beyond Robat. Hatum was raided on May 16th, and a small engagement was fought near it on June 7th and others east of Darb on July 2nd and August 10th.[1] Before the end of the war, the railway had been extended some two miles north of Robat. On October 31st, after the receipt of news of the Armistice, hostilities came gradually to an end. The Turkish commanders in the Yemen seemed reluctant to submit, and accordingly the Movable Column marched in December to Lahej and a landing was made by another force at Hodeida on the Red Sea coast, north of Perim. These operations brought the Turks to reason. A weak but well-equipped enemy division of 2,500 men surrendered forthwith at Lahej, and by March 1919, after the capitulation of a further 4,100 men, the evacuation of the Turkish forces was completed and the demobilization of the Aden Field Force begun. So ended the hostilities at Aden. There were no easy honours and rewards to be picked up in this backwater of the Great War, and there were many hardships and discomforts; but the troops maintained their morale, and their participation in this smallest of "side-shows" had its effect on the course of the struggle in the Middle East.

* * * * *

To complete the picture of Sapper and Miner exploits in the Great War, we return from wanderings in France, Belgium, Iraq, Iran, Egypt, Palestine, East Africa and Aden to India itself where, from the outset, it was necessary to hold the North-West Frontier in an iron grip while the bulk of the country's forces were fighting overseas. Much depended upon the attitude of Afghanistan. The Amir, Habibullah Khan, following the example of his father, Abdur Rahman, had maintained good relations with the British since 1905 and could be relied upon to continue a policy of friendly neutrality. Had he proved hostile in 1914, it would have been impossible to denude India of troops for service overseas. His position, however, was rendered difficult when Turkey entered the war because, in the eyes of all Sunni Muhammadans, the Sultan of Turkey was the successor of the Prophet (Khalifa) and the head of the Islamic world. The fanatical *mullas* of Afghanistan and the North-West Frontier urged the tribesmen to look towards Kabul and prepare for a *jihad* (holy war). The wildest rumours were current, and Afridis serving in regiments near the Tirah began to desert. But Habibullah continued to abide by his treaty engagements. Afghanistan remained neutral and refused to join a *jihad*. The North-West Frontier was held by a covering force of experienced troops, supported by four divisions which had been retained in India for limited offensives. The British units of these divisions, however, were mostly Territorial formations and few of the Indian units had fought on the frontier. The country was garrisoned chiefly by Volunteers, and these continued to function until the Indian Defence Force Act of 1917 gathered

[1]Despatch by Maj.-Gen. J. M. Stewart, C.B., dated Aug. 31st, 1918.

all Europeans into an Indian Auxiliary Force designed for internal security.

On the whole it may be said that the North-West Frontier remained remarkably quiet during the Great War, for none but the Mohmands and Mahsuds gave really serious trouble. Towards the end of 1914, military necessity forced us to overlook some raiding from Khost into the Bannu and Upper Tochi districts, but the Mahsuds were not concerned to any great extent in these forays nor would they listen to an anti-British party led by *Mulla* Fazl Din which urged them to begin hostilities. Turkish and German emissaries were at work along the Indian frontier and in Afghanistan. A Turco-German Mission arrived in Kabul in October 1915 but failed to shake the loyalty of the Amir. Afghanistan remained staunch and the Government of India conciliatory towards the frontier tribes. Gradually, however, the frontier became so unsettled that military operations had to be undertaken across the border in Baluchistan, the Tochi Valley, Swat, Buner and the Black Mountain, and particularly against the Mohmands, on a scale involving the employment of the entire 1st (Peshawar) Division and part of the 2nd (Rawalpindi) Division.[1] These expeditions were forced upon India in self-defence.

In the north, three *mullas* were responsible for raids by the Mohmands in January, April, August and October 1915, when the tribesmen suffered severely and lost 1,400 men in a fight near Shabkadr.[2] A blockade was instituted and the Mohmands submitted in April 1916 and were fined Rs. 30,000; but in September they resumed their raids, so the blockade was re-imposed from a line of defensible posts and barbed wire erected by the Sappers and Miners and Engineers along the Michni-Abazai front. The posts were 400 yards apart and connected by a double apron of barbed wire fence in front of which was a curtain of live wire supplied with electric current from a power-house at Abazai. In May 1917 the defensible posts were replaced by towers and the live wire removed. Meanwhile, on November 7th, 1916, another collision had taken place between the blockading troops and a *lashkar* (army) of 6,000 Mohmands, who were dispersed eventually by artillery fire. The blockade was then handed over to a newly raised Mohmand Militia[3] under British officers and was not raised until the Mohmands submitted once more in July 1917. Thereafter, they gave no more trouble.[4]

Several units of Sappers and Miners served in these operations. The 1st Company, Bengal S. & M., under Captain J. F. Gray, R.E., with Lieutenant H. A. Joly de Lotbinière, R.E., and Lieutenants A. R. Pollard, F. O. Townsend and J. Izat, I.A.R.O., was present from June 1915 to February 1916. The 2nd Company, under Captain H. N. G. Geary, R.E., with Lieutenant F. G. Drew, R.E., and Lieutenants R. R. MacFadden, K. Horton and G. Murray, I.A.R.O., served on the frontier from October 1916 to February 1917. The 6th Company, under Lieutenant

[1] *The Empire at War*, by Sir Charles Lucas, K.C.B., K.C.M.G., Vol. V, p. 185.

[2] See *Sketch Map of the North-West Frontier: North of the Kabul River*, included in Chapter XIV, and General Map I in pocket.

[3] The Mohmand Militia was replaced by Frontier Constabulary in 1922.

[4] *Military Report on the Mohmand Country* (General Staff, India, 1926), p. 8.

A. D. De R. Martin, R.E., with Lieutenants W. S. Tinsley and W. B. Haughton, I.A.R.O., joined the Malakand Movable Column at Chakdarra in June, 1915, and remained there until January, 1916. It remobilized for service against the Mohmands in October, 1916, and did not return to Peshawar until February, 1917. No. 1 Field Troop, of the same Corps, under Captain E. G. Gidley-Kitchin, R.E., with Lieutenant J. L. Muir, I.A.R.O., served against the Mohmands from October, 1916, to March, 1917. No unit of the Madras Corps was present, but the Bombay Corps was represented from October, 1916, to March, 1917, by the 19th Company under Captain C F. Stoehr, R.E., with Captain A. R. P. Price, I.A.R.O. The work of these units consisted as usual of bridging, demolition, water-supply, and the construction of roads and defences.

In the spring of 1917, Waziristan burst into flame. We had received grave provocation but had been obliged by force of circumstances to bide our time, and our conciliatory policy was mistaken for weakness. *Mulla* Fazl Din decided at the end of February that the time for action had come, and moving to Barwand with a *lashkar* of 3,000 men, invested the British post at Sarwekai on March 1st. Waziristan is a barren and inhospitable country with a small population. The chief inhabitants are the Darwesh Khel Wazirs, the Mahsuds, the Daurs and the Bhittanis, but only the Mahsuds took the field in strength during the Great War. The Wazirs are a warlike and nomadic tribe divided into the Utmanzai of the Tochi Valley and the Ahmadzai around Wana. More dangerous are the Mahsuds, whose main branches are the Alizai, Shaman Khel and Bahlozai. The settlements of these sons of Ishmael are so intermingled that internal feuds are rare and accordingly the risk of combined action has to be taken into account. Strongly democratic and independent, the Mahsuds pay little heed to their *maliks* (elders) and eke out a difficult existence chiefly by plundering their more peaceful neighbours. Being less fanatical than many of the frontier tribes, they are not much under the influence of their *mullas* nor liable to join in a *jihad*. Also, they have no love for the Wazirs. In dealing with the Mahsuds, however, it is difficult to ensure the execution of any treaty because their *jirgas*, or assemblies of tribal leaders, have small authority and can produce no reliable guarantee that the terms of an accepted treaty will be carried out. In their own country, both Wazirs and Mahsuds may be classed among the finest fighters in the world, brave, hardy, active, cunning and elusive. They never forget an injury, nor let a tactical error go unpunished.

The military operations in Waziristan in 1917 were under the direction of Lieut.-General Sir Arthur Barrett, G.O.C.-in-C., Northern Army, who promptly ordered the despatch of the Derajat Movable Column, under Brig.-General G. M. Baldwin, to relieve Sarwekai, where heavy fighting was in progress.[1] Marching from Murtaza with 3,000 men by the route through Spinkai on the Gomal,[2] Baldwin reached Sarwekai on March

[1]Despatch by Lieut.-Gen. Sir A. A. Barrett, K.C.B., K.C.S.I., K.C.V.O., on the operations against the Mahsuds, March-Aug., 1917. (General Staff, India.)

[2]See *Sketch Map of the North-West Frontier: Waziristan*, included in Chapter XIV and General Map III in pocket.

9th and drove off the investing *lashkar* of 4,000 Mahsuds. He had no Sappers and Miners under his command. On the 10th he advanced to Barwand in the Shahur Valley, burnt the village, withdrew to Sarwekai, and on the 11th marched to Khajuri Kach in the Zhob Valley. The 44th Infantry Brigade and 23rd Mountain Battery reinforced the Derajat Brigade in Tank and proceeded, on March 12th, to Jatta to support the Movable Column north of the Gomal and the garrison of Jandola on the Tank (or Takki) Zam. Minor raiding, which had been going on for some time, culminated on April 9th in an attack near the Gwalerai Narai (pass) on a convoy returning from Khajuri Kach to Nili Kach.[1] A general rising of the Mahsuds was not anticipated at the moment, and accordingly offensive action was restricted to keeping open the lines of communication to the various British posts. The Derajat Movable Column began an advance up the Gomal on April 17th, 1917, and reached Khajuri Kach on the 18th, Tanai on the 20th and Wana on the 21st with little opposition except in a defile near Karabkot. Three days later, it returned to Tanai, where it halted until May 2nd, being well situated to support either Wana or Sarwekai.

The first unit of Sappers and Miners appeared on the scene when the Derajat Brigade was strengthened by the arrival of the 7th Company, Bengal S. & M., and the 107th Pioneers. The 7th Company, under Captain G. D. Watson, R.E., with Lieutenant G. D. M. Gwynne-Griffith, R.E., and Lieutenants R. R. MacFadden, A. W. Strachan and J. H. Fawcett, I.A.R.O., had left Roorkee on April 24th to join "Wazir Force," and after reaching Tank was employed in improving communications and bridging the Gomal near Murtaza to facilitate transport between Jatta and Nili Kach. The Sappers and Pioneers had to work hard in great heat. Indeed, the British troops in this area had a catchword that "Hell was the hill-station of Tank." The Derajat Brigade now received further reinforcements and was formed into the "Derajat Field Force" under the command of Major-General W. G. L. Beynon. Minor raiding continued. General Baldwin's Movable Column marched to Khajuri Kach on May 2nd and to Nili Kach on the 3rd, for the Mahsuds were particularly troublesome in the difficult section of the road through the Gwalerai Narai. They attacked a post at Tormandu on May 6th and suffered severely in an abortive assault on Palosi, near Sarwekai, on May 10th.

It was now evident that the whole of the Mahsuds were openly against us and that a punitive expedition must be undertaken to restore order. Accordingly, on May 12th, 1917, the Bannu Brigade, under Brig.-General the Hon. C. G. Bruce (of Mount Everest fame) was placed under General Beynon, and the troops in the Derajat and Bannu areas were designated the "Waziristan Field Force."[2] Operations were planned for an entry into the rich Khaisara Valley, the heart of the Mahsud territory, and orders were issued that the Derajat concentration should be reinforced by the 45th Brigade, under Brig.-General C. C. Luard, and other troops including

[1]See *Sketch Map of Southern Waziristan*, 1917–19, included in this chapter.
[2]*Operations in Waziristan*, 1919–1920 (General Staff, India), p. 39.

the 11th Company, Madras S. & M., which had been stationed at Rawalpindi since December 1915. The Mahsuds became more aggressive. On May 16th, a *lashkar* of 2,000 men attacked a convoy on the Gwalerai Narai and there was heavy fighting before a way was opened to Wana. As the Gomal was often in flood at this season and the route along it was dangerous, Beynon proposed to invade Mahsud territory through Jandola and up the Shahur Zam by way of Barwand in preference to the more southerly route. It was hoped that, even at this late hour, the Mahsuds might listen to reason, for their overtures to Afghanistan had been rejected by the Amir Habibullah; but instead, they concentrated in the Tochi Valley to the north, and on May 31st, by a clever stratagem, captured the British post at Tut Narai, a few miles south-east of Datta Khel.[1]

The fall of Tut Narai is a good example of Mahsud cunning. During the morning a party of five men and two girls approached the post and entered into friendly conversation with some of the militia garrison. Three Mahsuds, apparently unarmed, then came closer to the wire and asked a sepoy to buy them some sweets from a stall inside the post, and as he walked towards the main gate they followed him stealthily. Suddenly, one of the Mahsuds whipped out a revolver and shot the sepoy, while the others rushed towards the gate. They then killed the men of the guard before the latter could seize their rifles. At the first shot, the two remaining Mahsuds, who were with the two dressed as girls, had opened fire at a sentry on the wall, and all four immediately joined the leading three in the fray at the gate. A party of thirty men then rushed from the surrounding jungle, charged through the gate and locked the remainder of the garrison into their barrack rooms, where they had no rifles. Other sentries on the walls were soon overpowered and the telegraph clerk murdered, but not before the gallant fellow had managed to despatch a message "Please help. Raiders are plundering." A rescue party arrived in due course and six hundred Mahsuds were driven out of the post, yet the tribesmen managed to decamp with 59 rifles and 120,000 rounds of ammunition—a valuable haul in frontier warfare. Their success may be attributed to the care with which they had laid their plans. Every habit of the garrison had been studied for weeks, and some of the raiders knew our methods well because they had served in the Frontier Militia.

Major-General Beynon having assumed command of the punitive force which was to advance up the Shahur Zam from Jandola, it was decided that the troops in the Bannu area should form a "North Waziristan Field Force" and those in the Derajat area a "South Waziristan Field Force," the whole being under General Sir Arthur Barrett. The northern force, in Bannu and Miramshah under Brig.-General Bruce, contained no Sappers and Miners and made no movement, so it need not be mentioned further. It maintained order in the Tochi Valley. The southern force, however, included the 11th Company, Madras S. & M., in addition to the 7th Company of the Bengal Corps. The 11th Company, under Captain C. J. S. King, R.E., with Lieutenants A. R. Arnell, C. W. Mathews, A. B. Aitken

[1]See *Sketch Map of the North-West Frontier: Waziristan*, included in Chapter XIV.

and E. N. C. Marshall, R.E., and Lieutenant W. E. Bushby, I.A.R.O., had arrived in Tank on June 2nd, 1917,[1] and joined the 45th Brigade. This unit, with the 7th Company attached to the 43rd Brigade and the 107th Pioneers on the line of communication, formed a somewhat inadequate cadre of engineer troops for operations in a country such as Waziristan.[2]

The Mahsuds, encouraged by *Mulla* Fazl Din, had now risen *en masse*, though their neighbours, the Wazirs remained passive. On June 7th they attacked a company of Gurkha Rifles near Khirgi and inflicted very severe casualties. General Beynon began his advance on June 12th, when a column moved from Jandola against a *lashkar* near the junction of the Shahur and Tank Zams. The Mahsuds withdrew, and on the 13th the 43rd Brigade reconnoitred as far as the eastern end of the Shahur Tangi (gorge) while the 7th Company, Bengal S. & M., and the 107th Pioneers, cleared a double camel-track up the river bed. Beynon decided to advance to Haidari Kach in two echelons, the first to occupy the heights commanding the Shahur Tangi and the second to escort the baggage and supplies through the defile. Accordingly, on June 14th, the 45th Brigade moved from Jandola to Chagmalai at the eastern end and seized the heights, and on the following day the second echelon and the convoy marched safely through to Haidari Kach. This success was due largely to the excellent road-work of the Sappers and Pioneers. By June 16th, the greater part of the force was in Haidari Kach, while the Sappers and Pioneers and some infantry continued to improve the camel-track and destroyed a few villages. The rapid advance up to Shahur had taken the enemy by surprise.

Convinced by this time that they would not be attacked in the Tochi Valley area to the north, the Mahsuds planned to oppose Beynon by concentrating a powerful *lashkar* on the Ispana Raghza (plateau) some 3 miles upstream from Barwand. Beynon advanced from Haidari Kach on June 19th against strong resistance. He camped on high ground beyond Barwand and repulsed an attempt to rush an important picquet. On the 20th the camp was moved to the western end of the Ispana plateau, where water could be raised from the river which, at this point, disappeared underground. Spirited action by the 43rd Brigade drove the Mahsuds from a dominating spur and they withdrew northwards. On the 21st, Beynon attacked and destroyed Nanu Village, beyond the Ispana Raghza, which had been used by the enemy as a base, the demolitions being carried out by the 11th Company, and on the 22nd he took a large village in an adjoining valley, where the work of demolition fell to the 7th Company. Sufficient supplies had now been collected to justify an advance into the Khaisara Valley, so Beynon pushed forward on June 23rd to the Narai Raghza, a distance of 7 miles, moving without tents and with only three days' supplies. While the infantry set fire to villages, the 7th and 11th Sapper companies improved the track, blew up towers and destroyed water-

[1] *Historical Record of the Q.V.O. Madras Sappers and Miners*, Vol. II, 1914-19, p. 18.

[2] Subsidiary engineer units in the theatre of operations included No. 7 Photo-Litho Section and No. 9 Printing Section, Bengal S. & M.

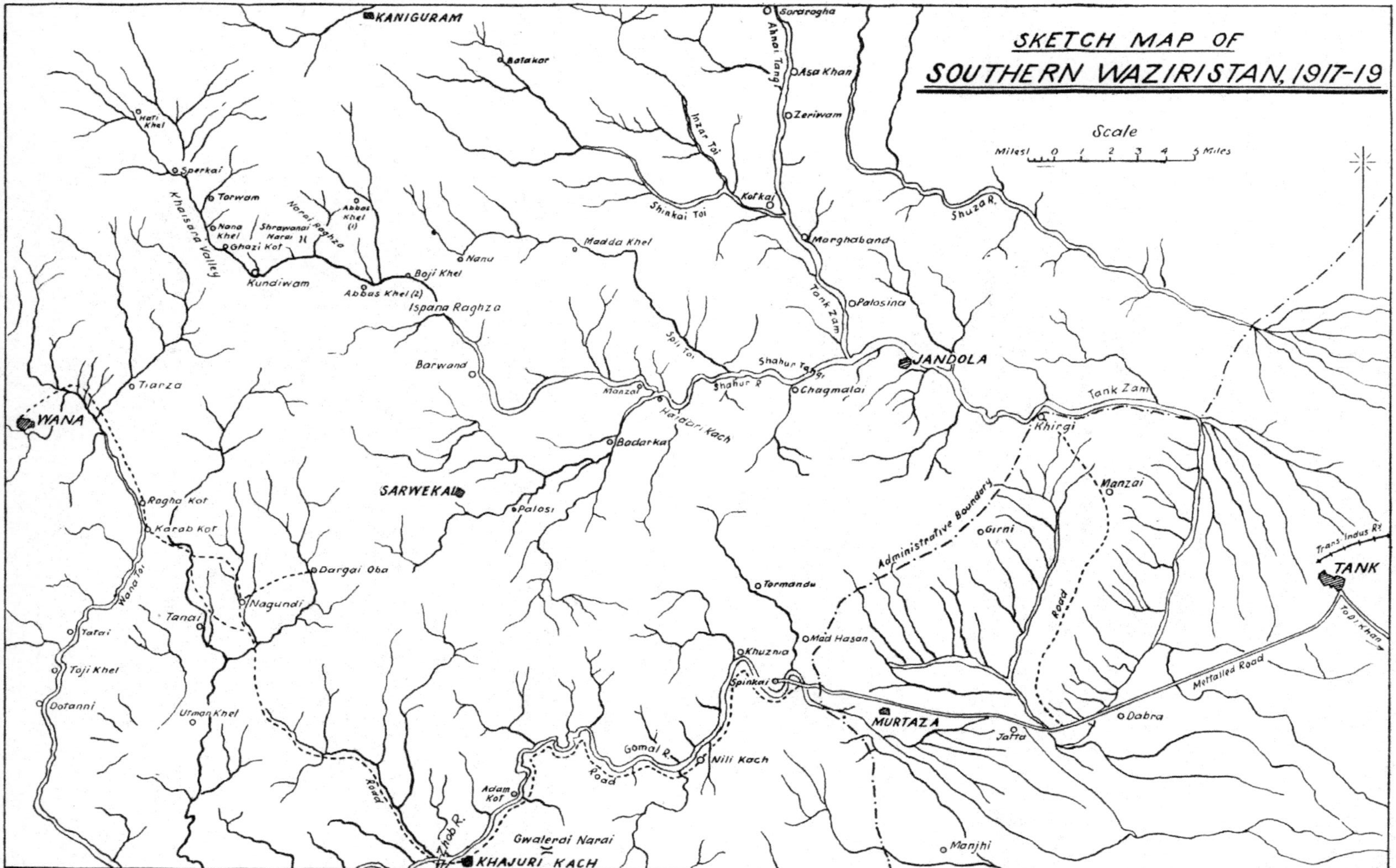
SKETCH MAP OF
SOUTHERN WAZIRISTAN, 1917-19
Scale
Miles 1 0 1 2 3 4 5 Miles
KANIGURAM
Batakar
Sararogha
Ahnai Tangi
Asa Khan
Zeriwam
Inzar Toi
Kotkai
Shinkai Toi
Shuza R.
Marghaband
Tank Zam
Palosina
JANDOLA
Hati Khel
Sperkai
Torwam
Khaisara Valley
Nana Khel
Shrawanai Narai
Narai Raghza
Abbas Khel (1)
Ghazi Kot
Kundiwam
Abbas Khel (2)
Baji Khel
Nanu
Madda Khel
Ispana Raghza
Barwand
Spli Toi
Shahur Tangi
Shahur R.
Chagmalai
Manzai
Haidari Kach
Badarka
Tiarza
WANA
SARWEKAI
Palosi
Ragha Kot
Karab Kot
Wana Toi
Dargai Oba
Nagundi
Tanai
Tatai
Toji Khel
Dotanni
Utman Khel
Tank Zam
Khirgi
Manzai
Administrative Boundary
Girni
Road
Termandu
Mad Hasan
Khuznia
Spinkai
MURTAZA
Jatta
Dabra
Metalled Road
TANK
Trans-Indus Ry.
Tabi Khan
Gomal R.
Nili Kach
Road
Adam Kot
Zhob R.
Road
Gwalerai Narai
KHAJURI KACH
Manjhi

mills. The most formidable obstacle was the *tangi* below the plateau which, for a distance of 40 yards, was only 12 feet wide and was commanded by precipitous heights. However, little opposition was encountered in this cleft, and all the transport was through by 3 p.m. Although the Mahsuds had already begun to ask for an armistice, it was decided that the punitive operations should proceed as planned, and accordingly, on June 24th, the 43rd Brigade was ordered to seize the Shrawanai Pass and hold it to enable the 45th Brigade to pass through and carry out the work of destruction in the Khaisara Valley. This was done, and all the towers in the villages on the eastern slope and north of Kundiwam were demolished by the two Sapper companies and the Pioneers, while the Royal Flying Corps carried out bombing operations.

Having completed his mission, General Beynon began his withdrawal from the Khaisara Valley. Further Mahsud emissaries had arrived, asking for peace, but when our troops retired towards the Ispana Raghza they were followed and attacked by parties of the enemy. A Mahsud *jirga* at Kaniguram was now deliberating on the British terms for surrender, and hostilities were suspended for a time. Beynon moved his camp from the Ispana Raghza to Boji Khel, 3 miles upstream, where he awaited the result of the *jirga*. On July 12th he marched down the valley to Manzai. Groups of the enemy began to surrender their rifles at Sarwekai, and finally, on August 10th, after a full *jirga* of 3,000 Mahsuds had ratified the peace terms, Beynon returned to Jandola and most of his troops dispersed to their normal stations. The 7th Company, Bengal S. & M., entrained for Roorkee in September; but the 11th Company, Madras S. & M., remained for a time in Tank before returning to Rawalpindi, and, between December, 1917, and March, 1918, built a 300-feet pile bridge across the Gomal at Murtaza. The operations against the Mahsuds in 1917 were carried out during the hottest season of the year and in one of the most unhealthy and mountainous areas across the border. Few expeditions had entailed such continuous hardship and fatigue, and as the troops were mostly young and unseasoned, the sick rate was high. Nevertheless, the 7th and 11th Companies did well under adverse circumstances and were gratified that two ex-Sappers and Miners—Brig.-General S. G. Loch, late R.E., and Lieut.-Colonel W. E. R. Dickson, R.E.—were highly praised for their work on the Staff.

Some other Sapper and Miner units served on the North-West Frontier during the Great War. For instance, from May to July, 1915, a section of the 14th Company, Madras S. & M., under Lieutenant P. Pryor, I.A.R.O., was attached to a column operating in Baluchistan to secure the restoration of the Khan of Kelat. In November, 1917, a special Frontier Searchlight Section, independent of the Defence Light Sections at the large ports, was formed at Roorkee for service in frontier garrisons. It had four small detachments, stationed at Malakand, Fort Lockhart on the Samana Ridge west of Kohat, Tank and Jandola respectively, and was equipped with 20 oxy-acetylene portable searchlights.[1] Between February and

[1]The Frontier Searchlight Section, Bengal S. & M., was disbanded in Aug., 1920.

April, 1918, the 52nd Company, Bengal S. & M., under Captain H. E. Roome, R.E., with Lieutenant G. M. Smith, I.A.R.O., and the 72nd Company, Bombay S. & M., under Captain M. G. G. Campbell, R.E., with Lieutenants L. Cleaver and E. W. Evans, R.E., and Lieutenant G. S. Marsh, I.A.R.O., were on service against the Marris in the Quetta region between Sibi and the Indus. Also, shortly before the Armistice, No. 6 Field Troop, Bengal S. & M., under Lieutenant F. A. Farquharson, I.A.R.O., with Lieutenant R. G. Braimbridge, I.A.R.O., was with the Baluchistan Field Force. All were engaged in the usual work of Sapper units employed in minor frontier operations.

This story of Sapper and Miner exploits in many theatres of the Great War may be brought to a close with the remark that each of the three Corps emerged from the struggle with an enhanced reputation and many honours and rewards. The services of the Bombay Sappers and Miners were recognized on February 10th, 1921, by the grant of the title " Royal," the announcement being made by H.R.H. The Duke of Connaught when laying the foundation stone of the All India War Memorial. That magnificent monument in New Delhi bears the names of no less than 251 Indian Officers and other ranks of the Sappers and Miners, selected from among those who gave their lives for the Empire in the Great War.[1] The ceremony of the completion of the War Memorial Arch was attended on February 12th, 1931, by contingents from all three Corps, who were thus able to pay a personal tribute to the memory of some of their many comrades who had fallen in distant lands or in defence of their own country.

[1]Madras 74, Bengal 70, Bombay 90, Burma 7, Faridkot 8, Tehri-Garhwal 2, Total 251.

CHAPTER XXII

THE THIRD AFGHAN WAR, OPERATIONS IN WAZIRISTAN AND THE MALABAR CAMPAIGN, 1919–1921

THE brief war against Afghanistan in the summer of 1919 had few attractions for the Sappers and Miners. Their work was hard and often tedious, and they found themselves stationed mostly on a long and defective line of communication. The heat was terrific, water scarce and sickness rife. Yet never before had so many engineer units been concentrated on the North-West Frontier, for no less than 26 Field Companies and 3 Field Troops were on active service in addition to 3 Railway Companies and a number of subsidiary formations. The lessons of the Afghan campaigns of 1838–42 and 1878–80 had not been forgotten, and the result was a speedy and decisive victory over Afghanistan, though followed, unfortunately, by prolonged hostilities in Waziristan.

The war started with dramatic suddenness. Since 1915, the Amir Habibullah Khan had followed the example of his father, Abdur Rahman Khan, in observing the pledges of friendship exchanged with the Government of India ; but on February 19th, 1919, he was foully murdered. His brother, Nasrullah Khan, then at Jalalabad, immediately proclaimed himself Amir and compelled the heir-apparent, Inayatullah Khan, to acknowledge his accession. He was opposed by Habibullah's third son, a fire-brand named Amanullah Khan, who induced the principal military officers in Kabul to proclaim him Amir and forced Nasrullah and Inayatullah to come to Kabul to admit his right to the throne. Amanullah felt, however, that his hold was none too secure, and consequently he prepared to pander to his warlike supporters by invading India, in which enterprise he hoped for assistance not only from the trans-frontier Pathan tribes but from revolutionary elements in India itself, where demobilization of much of the army was in progress. The primary cause of the Third Afghan War was, in fact, the desire of Amanullah to gain popularity. This he could attain by recovering the lost provinces of Afghanistan west of the Indus, where the inhabitants were allied to his people in race, language and religion.

An opportunity occurred early in April, 1919, when rebellion spread through the Southern Punjab. Excited mobs, guided by extremist leaders, destroyed railway stations, damaged permanent way and set fire to property. Prompt measures were taken against the rioters, notably by Brig.-General R. F. H. Dyer at Amritsar, and a semblance of order was restored, but meanwhile Afghan troops were on the move. They crossed the frontier near Landi Khana, beyond the Khaibar Pass, and strengthened their garrisons in Dakka, the Khost salient and Kandahar.[1] On May 3rd

[1]See General Map III, (*Sketch Map of the North-West Frontier including Afghanistan,*) at the end of this volume, and also *Sketch Map of the North-West Frontier : North of the Kabul River,* included in Chapter XIV and repeated in this chapter.

they occupied Bagh Village and the Kafir Kot Ridge on our side of the border near Landi Khana and proceeded to pour in reinforcements. At Bagh they were in a position to cut the water-supply to the British fortified post at Landi Kotal in the Khaibar, and hence, on May 6th, 1919, we declared war against Afghanistan.

The Field Army available for service on the entire North-West Frontier consisted of the 1st, 2nd, 4th and 16th Indian Divisions, with the 1st, 4th and 10th Indian Cavalry Brigades and the 12th Indian Mounted Brigade. In addition, there were independent brigades in Kohat, Bannu and the Derajat, and small garrisons stationed in posts in Chitral, the Malakand, the Zhob Valley and elsewhere for internal security.[1] But when the Afghan War started, all units were below strength and short of senior officers, and although eight regular battalions were on the frontier they were composed mostly of young soldiers. The duty of policing independent tribal territory beyond the border devolved on Militia units, Frontier Constabulary and Levies such as the Chitral Scouts, Mohmand Militia, Khyber (Khaibar) Rifles, Kurram Militia, North and South Waziristan Militias, Zhob Militia and the Mekran Levy. There was, in fact, a mere screen of irregular formations incapable of dealing with a powerful enemy. Serious operations were left to the regular army far in rear, and consequently initial withdrawals from some areas were unavoidable before that army could make its weight felt at any focal point. The general scheme was one of elastic defence.

In May, 1919, the focal point was the Khaibar Pass. A defensive attitude was necessary in Chitral, and, further south, in Waziristan. The Afghan Army was reported to consist of 78 battalions of infantry and 21 regiments of cavalry with 280 breech-loading guns and many muzzle-loaders. It could muster possibly 38,000 rifles and 8,000 sabres, but most of its equipment was obsolete and it was badly led. Behind it, however, lurked the danger of a general rising of all the frontier tribes from Chitral to the Zhob, and accordingly we had to move swiftly. Events soon proved that little reliance could be placed on the Frontier Militias. Though some fought well, others had to be disbanded after wholesale desertions to the enemy.

On mobilization, the 1st and 2nd Indian Divisions and the 1st and 10th Indian Cavalry Brigades were allotted to the Peshawar Line as a "North-West Frontier Force" under General Sir A. A. Barrett, with the 16th Indian Division and 4th Indian Cavalry Brigade in reserve and the Independent Brigades holding the Kohat, Bannu and Derajat areas. The 4th Indian Division, with the 12th Indian Mounted Brigade, formed a "Baluchistan Force" under Lieut.-General R. Wapshare, based on Quetta. In the centre was a "Waziristan Force" to which the Independent Brigades were transferred in June. This force, whose operations will be described later, was concerned mostly with the Mahsuds and Wazirs. The brunt of the fighting against the Afghans fell on the North-West Frontier Force.

A large concentration of engineer troops assembled gradually in the

[1] *The Third Afghan War*, 1919 (Official Account), pp. 21, 22.

Khaibar region under Brig.-General R. F. Sorsbie, late R.E., as Chief Engineer, with Captain C. C. Phipps, R.E., as Staff Officer. With the 1st Division, under Major-General C. A. Fowler, were the 7th and 56th Companies, Bengal S. & M. (Captains G. D. Watson and R. A. D. Watson, R.E.), and with the 2nd Division, under Major-General Sir C. M. Dobell, the 11th and 64th Companies, Madras S. & M. (Captains C. J. S. King and F. J. B. Gibson, R.E.). With the 16th Division on the line of communication in India were the 53rd Company, Bengal S. & M., and the 76th Company, Bombay S. & M. (Captain G. R. Pim and Major E. V. Binney, R.E.). The Corps Troops included the 58th Company, Bengal S. & M. (Major D. A. Thomson, R.E.), the 14th Company, Madras S. & M. (Captain C. Sleigh, R.E.), and a Railway Battalion, S. & M.,[1] consisting of the 26th, 27th and 28th Railway Companies under Major L. N. Malan, R.E. Subsidiary formations comprised two Pontoon Parks, two Engineer Field Parks and three Printing or Litho-Sections. With the 1st Cavalry Brigade was the 1st Field Troop, Bengal S. & M. (Captain J. L. Muir, I.A.R.O.). A Chitral Section, Madras S. &M. (Captain H. L. Bartholemew, R.E.), was stationed in the far north. The Baluchistan Force included the 17th, 24th, 71st and 73rd Companies, Bombay S. & M. (Captains L. S. Kidd, J. F. B. Harvey and F. E. Buller, R.E., and Major E. K. Squires, R.E.), and the 7th Field Troop, Bombay S. & M. (Lieutenant A. E. Stewart, R.E.), with the 12th Mounted Brigade. Some of these units, however, supplied detachments to the Force in East Persia, where there was a Seistan Section of the Bombay Corps under Lieutenant A. Prain, R.E. In the Bannu Area, with the Waziristan Force, was the 55th Company, Bengal S. & M. (Captain J. G. O. Whitehead, R.E.), and in the Derajat Area at Tank, the 75th Company, Bombay S. & M. (Captain A. Lister-Jackson, I.A.R.O.). The Baluchistan Force had No. 2 Engineer Field Park of the Bombay Corps and the Waziristan Force No. 8 Engineer Field Park of the Bengal Corps. Other Sapper and Miner units in the field were the 57th Company, Bengal S. & M. (Captain J. S. Lethbridge, R.E.), in the Kohat Area, the 8th Field Troop, Madras S. & M. (Captain R. H. B. Longland, R.E.), in Waziristan, the 15th (Burma), 63rd, 66th, 67th, 68th (Burma) and 69th Companies, Madras S. & M. (Captains E. H. Clarke and C. R. Gurney, R.E., A. A. McClelland, I.A.R.O., and W. H. Knox, R.E., Major C. W. Bushell, R.E. and Captain A. B. Cullen, I.A.R.O.), the 74th Company, Bombay S. & M. (Captain M. J. Dolan, R.E.I.A.), the Sirmur, Tehri-Garhwal, Malerkotla and Faridkot Imperial Service Sapper Companies, and No. 9 Works Company (Major F. C. Molesworth, R.E.). Finally, to complete an elaborate display of engineer strength, there were 10 battalions of Pioneers and 10 Labour Corps.

On the evening of May 6th, 1919, the enemy forces at Bagh, on the Afghan side of the Khaibar Pass, amounted to 3 battalions with two guns, and some 350 Afghans were on Tor Tsappar and Spinatsuka, prominent

[1]In the summer of 1921, the Railway Battalion joined the Royal Bombay S. & M.

features about five miles north of Landi Kotal.[1] It was reported that the garrison of Dakka had been increased to 5 battalions, with 200 cavalry and 6 guns. The British post at Landi Kotal was therefore in imminent danger for it was held by only 2 companies of Indian Infantry, 500 men of the Khyber Rifles, a section of Mountain Artillery and a section of the 7th Company, Bengal S. & M. However, the Afghans missed their opportunity and the post was reinforced on May 7th by a battalion of Somersets followed, on the 8th, by the 1st Infantry Brigade and other troops from Peshawar under Brig.-General G. F. Crocker. Meanwhile, the Afghans on Tor Tsappar and Spinatsuka had advanced and seized the Asa (Ash) Khel Ridge, but they were ejected by Crocker who then established a strong line along the high ground through Asa Khel and "Top Point" to cover Landi Kotal from the north. The enemy held an outpost line on a ridge facing north-east between the Tangi *nala* and a ravine running through Khargali, with the bulk of their forces in position on another ridge behind Khargali. They could now deploy 5 battalions of infantry with 6 guns. Crocker camped west of Landi Kotal below two heights known as "Bright's Hill" and "Suffolk Hill," among his troops being the 7th Company, Bengal S. & M. He decided to seize Bright's Hill, which overlooked the vital Tangi springs, and then, advancing westwards, to recover the springs and attack the Afghan position in the rugged country south-west of Landi Khana. On May 9th he took Bright's Hill and the springs. Half the 7th Company was then sent forward to consolidate the position while the remainder repaired the damaged water-supply system to relieve the acute shortage of water at Landi Kotal. It was impossible to proceed to the assault of the main Khargali position because strong reinforcements, which should have reached Landi Kotal, had been detained in Peshawar to deal with serious riots in that city.

Already the lack of an adequate line of communication through the Khaibar Pass was making itself felt. There was only one metalled road and no railway. Mechanical transport was insufficient and water so scarce that animal transport had to be restricted to a minimum. Engineer troops were needed urgently at the front and General Sorsbie took immediate action to obtain them. The War Section at Simla had ordered two battalions of Pioneers to proceed to the Khaibar from Lahore and Sialkot and the 11th and 64th Companies, Madras S. & M., of the 2nd Division to move thither from Rawalpindi for water-supply duties. A Labour Corps was under orders for Jamrud and two Railway Companies for the restoration of the Peshawar-Jamrud Railway, which had been allowed to fall into disrepair. On May 8th General Sorsbie asked for another Labour Corps and for the 53rd Company, Bengal S. & M., and 76th Company, Bombay S. & M., of the 16th Division. The 11th Company reached Ali Masjid on May 11th, and on the same day the 56th Company of the 1st Division moved up to Landi Kotal, using motor transport because of the lack of water for animals. The 1st Field Troop, Bengal S. & M., marched up the Khaibar on the 12th with the 1st Cavalry Brigade to repair the road beyond

[1]See Insert to General Map III at the end of this volume.

BUILDING SANGARS ON SOMERSET HILL NEAR DAKKA, AFGHANISTAN, 1919.

(By kind permission of Maj.-Gen. C. H. Foulkes, C.B., C.M.G., D.S.O., late R.E.)

Landi Kotal and make a landing ground for aeroplanes. The greatest difficulty was experienced in securing transport for engineer stores and particularly for material needed for the water-supply installations at Ali Masjid and Landi Kotal on which so much depended. A Works Directorate was formed under Colonel H. A. D. Fraser, late R.E., assisted by Lieut.-Colonel C. H. H. Nugent and Major J. Young, R.E., and the Sapper units worked from time to time under its control. On May 12th, Lieut.-Colonel A. ff. Garrett, R.E., was appointed C.R.E., 2nd Division, and, three days later, Lieut.-Colonel E. C. Tylden-Pattenson, R.E., an ex-Bengal Sapper and Miner, became C.R.E. 1st Division in the forward area.

General Fowler, G.O.C. 1st Division, had arrived in Landi Kotal on May 9th and, owing to the water situation and increasing signs of unrest among the Afridis in the Khaibar, had decided to attack the Khargali position without awaiting further reinforcements. This he did with marked success on May 11th, driving in the Afghan right and capturing the Khargali and Kafir Kot Ridges. The enemy suffered 400 casualties and were soon in full retreat towards Dakka, some 10 miles distant. The brunt of the fighting in the battle around Bagh fell on the 2nd Infantry Brigade, then under Major-General S. H. Climo. On the 12th, the Royal Air Force bombed Dakka, and the enemy retired towards Jalalabad. Our cavalry, greatly hampered by scarcity of water, started in pursuit. The force detailed to open the road to Dakka was commanded by Major-General A. Skeen. It crossed the frontier at Torkham on May 13th and camped on a stony plain south of Dakka (Loe Dakka). The site was near the river, but it was exposed to long-range sniping which caused much annoyance and not a few casualties. During the advance the 7th and 56th Companies, Bengal S. &. M., were busily employed on road work between Michni Kandao and Landi Khana, and also beyond Landi Khana, where the track was in the bed of a *nala*. Afterwards, the 7th Company began to build a large reservoir at Landi Kotal while the 56th Company laid a 6-inch distribution main. The 64th Company, Madras S. &. M., was now ordered to relieve the 56th Company at Landi Kotal. In the Dakka Camp, the 1st Field Troop was making a small landing ground and collecting material for bridging the Kabul River. Pontoons were not available because of difficulties of transport, and consequently the Field Troop had to requisition country boats. The 7th Company soon moved up to Dakka, where it acted as infantry until directed to road work.

On May 16th, General Fowler visited Dakka and ordered that the camp should be shifted to a better site near Robat Fort, a small work 2 miles upstream, but the operation was delayed by hostilities which occurred when a reconnoitring force became heavily engaged with Afghans and tribesmen concentrating beyond the adjacent Khurd Khaibar Pass for the recapture of Dakka. The enemy, about 3,000 men with 7 guns, took up a position on some hills extending southwards from the Pass, rendering our camp almost untenable. General Crocker, who was in local command, attacked the position on the 18th but was held up on two heights, " Somerset" and "Sikh" Hills. General Skeen then arrived with reinforcements, and having captured both hills, drove the enemy towards Basawal, leaving the road through the Pass free for improvement by the Sappers and Pioneers.

Whilst the 1st Division and the cavalry were thrusting to Dakka, Afridi tribesmen in the Khaibar began to give trouble. They sniped the road and cut telephone wires, and a *malik* named Yar Muhammad sent a defiant letter from his fort at Chora, 7 miles south-west of Ali Masjid. A convoy from Jamrud was attacked near Ali Masjid on May 14th. Piquets of the Khyber Rifles had to be replaced by regular troops because of frequent desertions to the enemy. "Orange Patch Ridge," a prominent feature which overlooked the road, was occupied by the tribesmen and changed hands several times on the 15th and 16th. Forts Maude and Shagai, below Ali Masjid, were under fire at night, and it was not until a brigade had marched up from Jamrud on May 17th that the situation was restored. The same day saw the disbandment of the Khyber Rifles. During this unsettled period the 11th Company, Madras S. & M., was at Ali Masjid and the 64th Company at Jamrud. By May 21st the 11th Company had completed the building of three permanent posts on Orange Patch Ridge and had improved the wire defences at Forts Maude and Shagai.

The Afridi unrest spread to the Mohmands north of the Kabul River. A chain of fortified posts had been erected during the Great War between Abazai, where the Swat River leaves the hills, and Michni on the Kabul River to shut the Mohmands into their own country. On May 20th, 1919, encouraged by the approach of Afghan forces from Chitral,[1] 4,000 Mohmands and Bajauris threatened to invade British territory, and it became necessary to send a brigade from Peshawar to reinforce Shabkadr and Michni. This had the desired effect. The tribesmen dispersed and order was restored. The 58th Company, Bengal S. & M., arrived at Michni before the end of the month and, after strengthening the defences, made the Michni bridge passable for motor transport.

Meanwhile, arrangements had been made for a further advance by the 1st Division from Dakka to Jalalabad; but owing to the disturbances in the Khaibar and on the Michni-Abazai line the necessary transport was lacking, and every available vehicle had to be taken from the 16th Division on the line of communication in order to mass supplies gradually at Landi Kotal and Dakka. On May 18th, "Dakka Force" shifted camp to the new site between Robat Fort and Dakka Fort (otherwise Sherabad Cantonment) where the 7th Company and 1st Field Troop, soon reinforced by the 56th Company, made arrangements for water-supply from the river. The Royal Air Force prepared the way into Afghanistan by bombing Jalalabad, and it is interesting to note that according to the official record they dropped "1 ton 8 cwts. of explosives in a single day"! By May 26th, all was ready for an advance. Yet it never took place because, on that day,

[1]The Chitral Section, Madras S. & M., was attached to one of four mobile columns operating against 6,000 Afghans and tribesmen in the extreme north between May 20th and June 5th, 1919. It erected ropeways across rivers for the transport of stores and was employed also in bridging and roadwork.

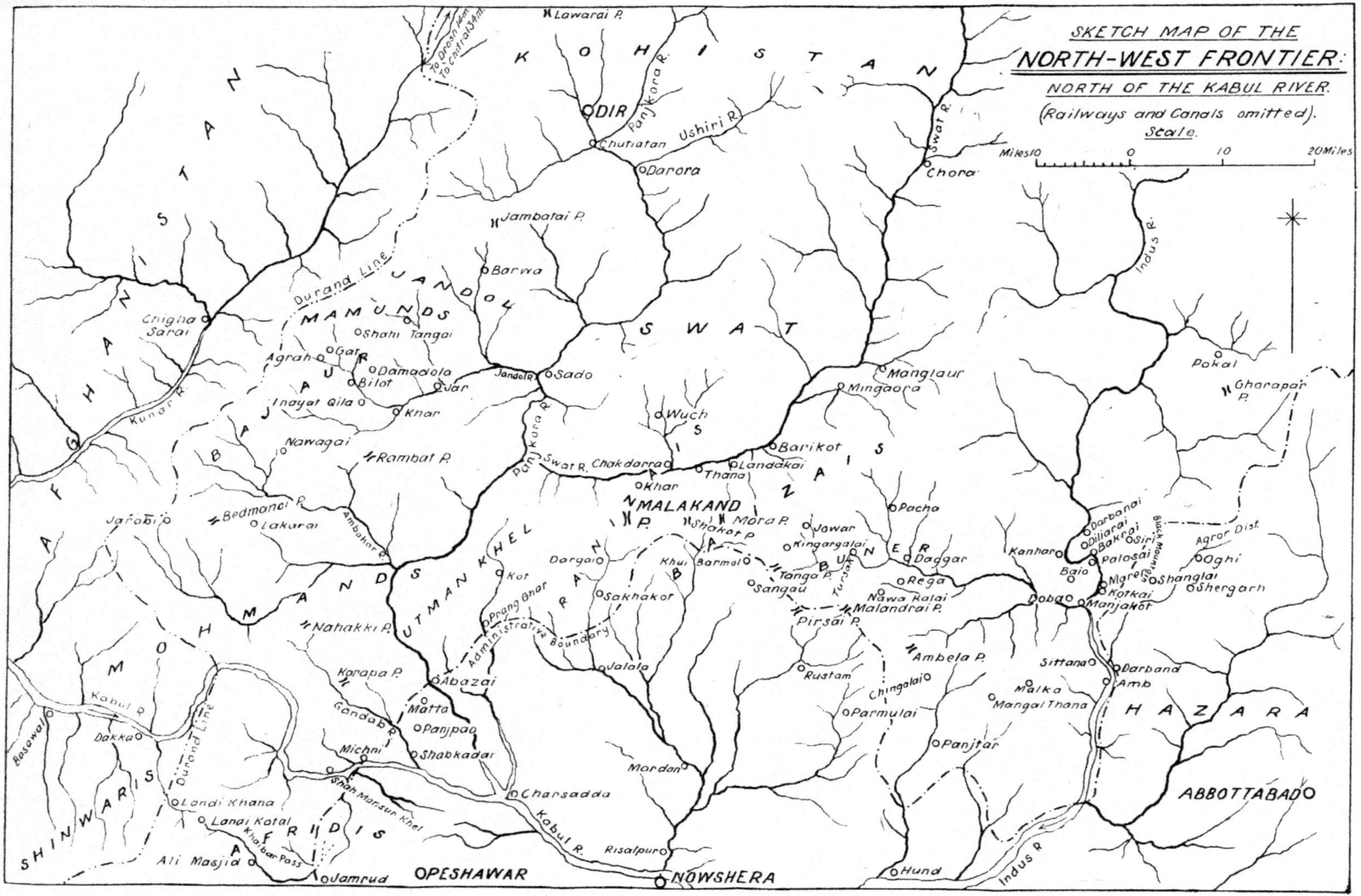
SKETCH MAP OF THE
NORTH-WEST FRONTIER:
NORTH OF THE KABUL RIVER.
(Railways and Canals omitted).
Scale.
Miles 10 0 10 20 Miles
KOHISTAN
AFGHANISTAN
SWAT
JANDOL
MAMUNDS
BAJAUR
MOHMANDS
UTMAN KHEL
RANIZAI
SWAT
AKOZAI
BUNER
HAZARA
SHINWARIS
AFRIDIS
Lawarai P.
To Drosh 14m
To Chitral 34m
DIR
Panjkora R.
Chutiatan
Ushiri R.
Darora
Swat R.
Chora
Indus R.
Jambatai P.
Barwa
Durand Line
Chigha Sarai
Shahi Tangai
Agrah
Gar
Damadola
Bilot
Jandol R.
Sado
Jar
Inayat Qila
Khar
Kunar R.
Nawagai
Rambat P.
Wuch
Manglaur
Mingaora
Pokal
Gharapar P.
Barikot
Chakdarra
Swat R.
Landakai
Thana
Khar
MALAKAND P.
Pacha
Jarobi
Bedmanai P.
Lakarai
Ambahar R.
Shakot P.
Mora P.
Jowar
Kingargalai
Dargai
Kot
Khui
Barmol
Tanga P.
Daggar
Sangau
Sakhakot
Rega
Nawa Kalai
Malandrai P.
Pirsai P.
Kanhar
Darbanai
Diliarai
Bakrai
Siri
Black Mountain
Agror Dist.
Palosai
Oghi
Baio
Mareh
Shanglai
Kotkai
Shergarh
Doba
Manjakot
Prang Ghar
Administrative Boundary
Nahakki P.
Jalala
Ambela P.
Sittana
Darband
Amb
Korapa P.
Abazai
Matta
Rustam
Chingalai
Malka
Mangal Thana
Kabul R.
Gandab R.
Panjpao
Parmulai
Basowal
Dakka
Shabkadar
Panjtar
Michni
Mardan
Shah Mansur Khel
Charsadda
ABBOTTABAD
Landi Khana
Lanai Katal
Khaibar Pass
Ali Masjid
Kabul R.
Risalpur
Jamrud
PESHAWAR
NOWSHERA
Hund
Indus R.

Afghan forces appeared in the Kurram Valley and reinforcements and transport had to be hurried back to Peshawar and thence to Kohat. Five days later, the Amir asked for an armistice which was granted on June 3rd. Nevertheless, under the cloak of the armistice, he continued secretly to incite the tribes to rebellion. The enforced inactivity of the 1st Division at Dakka had an unfortunate effect. The Afridis mistook it for weakness and resumed their sniping throughout the Khaibar region, while the 1st Division, sweltering in extreme heat at Dakka, did not escape the attention of enemy marksmen concealed on the opposite bank of the Kabul River.

With the removal southwards of so much road transport the improvement of the Khaibar line of communication became a matter of increased importance, and, in the absence of a railway, the authorities turned their attention to a scheme for Aerial Ropeways designed to fill the gap until a railway could be built. Meanwhile, surveys were started for alternative railway routes between Jamrud and Landi Khana either up the Khaibar or by way of Kam Shilman.[1] A committee decided that a ropeway from Jamrud to Landi Kotal would be of immediate assistance, and that, if a railway could be got through to Landi Kotal, a temporary ropeway might then be added to carry supplies forward to Dakka. The 26th, 27th and 28th Railway Companies, S. &. M., under Major L. N. Malan, R.E., were repairing the Peshawar-Jamrud Railway,[2] and in Peshawar there happened to be a temporary officer, Captain Limby, R.E., with some experience of Aerial Ropeways. Limby was sent to Simla and given a free hand. He designed ropeway standards in sections for easy transport and placed orders with firms, and in an incredibly short space of time train-loads of material began to pour into Jamrud. Early in July 1919, Malan and his Railway Sappers began the construction of a line surveyed by Limby. At first, everyone had to learn by experience. It was found that the heights of the standards had been calculated incorrectly, and frequent alterations were necessary until a special template was improvised to measure the heights accurately and allow for the catenary. After the first section of ropeway from Jamrud had been erected and the rope mounted on the pulleys, the pulley-bearings wore away quickly under trial loads. This difficulty was overcome when an expert from England discovered that the roller-bearing of the back axle of a Ford car was of the exact size required.[3] Gradually the ropeway crept up the Khaibar Pass, and with occasional assistance from the 67th Company and part of the 15th (Burma) Company, Madras S. & M., the Railway Sappers completed it to Landi Kotal before they left the Khaibar in September, 1919. Eventually it reached Landi Khana, after which it was handed over to the R.I.A.S.C., who maintained a special Ropeway

[1]Kam Shilman is 5 miles north-east of Landi Kotal. These surveys resulted eventually in the design and partial building of the Khaibar Railway by Lieut.-Col. G. R. Hearn, R.E., but although the work was started in 1920 the line was not opened to Landi Khana until 1926. For further details see *The Military Engineer in India*, by the present author, Vol. I, p. 511.

[2]The Railway Companies, when at Sialkot, had previously been supplying detachments to accompany armoured trains to repair bridges and track damaged during the Punjab disturbances.

[3]Notes by Col. L. N. Malan, C.B.E., late R.E., sent to the author on June 4th, 1945.

Company to operate it. Under the supervision of Lieut.-Colonel R. D. B. Perrott, R.E., the Khaibar Ropeway existed until 1927, when it was dismantled after the completion of the railway. It had served its purpose and died a natural death.

The Railway Sappers were attacked on July 18th, 1919, when camped near Ali Masjid and had a sharp fight with some Afridis, but with the assistance of two platoons of the 2/33rd Punjabis they drove the enemy back. The Afridis were mostly deserters from the Khyber Rifles and came marching down the road at dusk in proper formation. When challenged by a sentry they answered " Friend." The sentry then demanded their unit, to which they replied, " Is that a Mussulman or Hindu regiment?" Instantly, the sentry fired and the Afridis scattered among the rocks, and a fire fight ensued which lasted most of the night.[1] It will be seen, accordingly, that no unit of the Sappers and Miners could count on working unmolested, even on the line of communication. The tribesmen interfered also with the operation of the ropeway by hooking off the rope any loads which came within their reach, and they welcomed the frequent breakages of the rope which occurred because the material supplied by the Indian Munitions Board was too weak. The temporary line from Landi Khana onwards to Dakka, planned in May, 1919, was never built, for the sudden end of hostilities rendered it unnecessary.

The scene now shifts to the Kurram and Tochi Valleys further south which were threatened on May 6th, 1919, by an Afghan concentration of 14 battalions and 48 guns under General Nadir Khan at Matun in the Khost salient. It was decided that if Nadir Khan invaded the Tochi, our small posts along that valley above Miramshah should be evacuated forthwith, for the Wazirs might rise against us and the trouble might spread to the Mahsuds of Waziristan. On the other hand, in the Kurram it was necessary to hold our ground up to the Afghan border at the Peiwar Kotal and Kharlachi in order to safeguard the vital region beyond Kohat and Bannu. On May 23rd, Nadir Khan left Matun and marched down the Kaitu River towards Spinwam, the garrison of which was withdrawn to Idak in the Tochi.[2] The Afghans occupied Spinwam and were joined by the local Wazirs and we evacuated the garrisons at Datta Khel, Tut Narai, Boya and elsewhere in the Upper Tochi and brought them down to Dardoni and Miramshah. In Southern Waziristan, as will be related later, Wana was evacuated on May 26th. At Spinwam, with 3,000 regulars, 9 guns and numerous *lashkars* of Wazirs, Nadir Khan was within striking distance of Thal, Bannu and Idak. At Dardoni in the Tochi we had 2,500 men including the 55th Company, Bengal S. & M., under Captain J. G. O. Whitehead, R.E.; and at Thal in the Kurram, a brigade, with most of the 57th Company under Captain J. S. Lethbridge, R.E. On May 27th, Nadir Khan invested Thal, whose defence was directed by Major-General A. H. Eustace, commanding the Kohat District. The Afghans besieged and

[1]Notes by Lieut.-Col. E. V. Binney, D.S.O., R.E. (retd.), sent to the author on March 26th, 1938.

[2]See Sketch Maps of the *N.W. Frontier: South of the Kabul River*, and *Waziristan*, included in this chapter.

shelled the fort until the garrison was relieved on June 1st by a column under Brig.-General R. F. H. Dyer who defeated several *lashkars* of Wazirs in a series of well-planned operations. A detachment of the 57th Company was with Dyer. Eustace returned to Kohat and Dyer assumed command in Thal. On June 2nd, Dyer received a letter from Nadir Khan saying that he had been ordered by the Amir to suspend hostilities and asking for an acknowledgment. " My guns will give an immediate reply," wrote Dyer, and Nadir Khan beat a hasty retreat. Dyer prepared to follow him to Matun, but the plan was interrupted by the armistice on June 3rd. So Nadir Khan marched back to Afghanistan where, after the war, he was made Commander-in-Chief, and to celebrate his " victory " at Thal, a column was erected in Kabul having at its base a chained lion to represent Great Britain. Reinforcements soon reached Kohat consisting of two brigades and other troops including the 66th Company, Madras S. & M., and the situation in the Thal area was then secure.

Nothing remained but to punish the local Wazirs who had supported Nadir Khan, and accordingly on June 5th a small column set out to destroy the village of Biland Khel, 3 miles south of Thal. Half the 57th Company, Bengal S. & M., marched with it. Whilst the village was being cleared, a deep cave was discovered through which ran an underground stream (*karez*). The cave was known to be occupied, and perhaps by armed tribesmen. Yet Bugler Narain Chand of the 57th Company volunteered to enter it alone. He did so unarmed and found only six women. Returning later with a sepoy of the Punjabis, he explored the cave thoroughly but found no enemy. This, says the Official History, affords a good example of the lonely courage required of the rank and file in campaigns on the North-West Frontier.[1]

During the operations around Thal, fighting had begun in the Upper Kurram where the 60th Brigade under Brig.-General A. E. Fagan had its headquarters at Parachinar. The line of the Kurram was held only by small garrisons of militia. On May 28th, 1919, the Afghans attacked our post at Kharlachi, west of Parachinar, but were repulsed. Then, aided by Orakzai tribesmen, they threatened both Sadda and Alizai. The situation was relieved by Dyer's rapid advance on Thal, and the Afghans retreated into Khost, harried by Fagan. No Sappers and Miners were engaged in these operations.

Punitive measures in the Thal region continued for some time. Major-General A. Skeen took command of the Kohat-Kurram Force comprising the 65th Brigade under Brig.-General C. O. O. Tanner at Thal and the 47th Brigade under Brig.-General C. E. F. K. Macquoid at Kohat, and, when Tanner led his brigade on July 16th in operations against some Wazirs south of Biland Khel, half the 57th Company assisted in demolishing Shewa Village and other places in that neighbourhood. No less than 54 villages were burnt, and their towers blown up, in a period of four days. After this, there was no more trouble from the Wazirs or their brethren the Orakzais.

[1]*The Third Afghan War*, 1919 (Official Account), p. 62.

Although the armistice of June 3rd ended hostilities against Afghanistan, the Amir continued secretly to incite rebellion among the Afridis and Mohmands in the north, but engineer work on the Khaibar line of communication never slackened in spite of frequent sniping. The Works Directorate had been reinforced by many officers, among them being Lieut.-Colonel G. H. Boileau, R.E., an ex-Bombay Sapper and Miner, who arrived as Deputy Chief Engineer on May 23rd. Water-supply was the most essential service, followed closely by defence work and road improvement in which the Pioneers and Labour Corps were prominent. The 76th Company, Bombay S. & M., under Major E. V. Binney, R.E., had reached Jamrud from Kirkee on May 31st and was busy realigning the wiring of the fort. Early in June, some Imperial Service Sappers began to appear on the scene. The Faridkot and Malerkotla Companies reached Peshawar on June 7th and the Tehri-Garhwal Company on the 8th. They were followed later by the 2nd Sirmur Sapper Company and were employed mostly on roadwork and water-supply at Ali Masjid. An outbreak of cholera now added to the difficulties of the situation. All troops had to be evacuated from Jamrud on June 7th, and the disease spread to Ali Masjid. A pure and copious supply of water at Ali Masjid then became of vital importance and the responsibility for this fell mainly on the 11th Company, Madras S. & M., stationed at that place. Water-supply fittings and tools were sadly deficient, yet by June 20th a new 3-inch pipe, 5,500 feet in length, had been laid in three working days and was leading water by gravitation from a perennial spring which was capable of yielding 500,000 gallons a day. The spring was then railed off and later supplied water also to Landi Kotal by pumping. At Landi Kotal, only 12,000 gallons a day were obtained for a time by pumping through a 4-inch main from the springs near Bagh. This was quite inadequate for a garrison of 8,000 men with 3,000 animals. Indeed, the animals had to be marched down daily to the springs to be watered. The task of remedying this state of affairs devolved chiefly on the 64th Company, Madras S. & M., and by June 26th the daily supply to Landi Kotal had risen to 28,000 gallons. In July, when a 6-inch main was laid from the Bagh springs and a large reservoir built above Landi Kotal, 60,000 gallons a day were being pumped to the garrison. The Landi Khana supply presented no difficulties as a gravity flow in masonry channels was possible from the Tangi and Bagh springs. These far-reaching improvements in water-supply, in which the Sappers and Miners took a prominent part, helped to arrest, and then to stamp out, the cholera epidemic in the Khaibar.

At Dakka, during July, 1919, the 7th Company and 1st Field Troop, Bengal S. & M., were occupied in bridging the Kabul River. Six pontoons reached them on the 20th, but these were insufficient to span the river and consequently it was decided to build a flying bridge using a country boat. Experiments were made with an " otter," and after a covering party had been ferried across on the 25th, the flying bridge was established on the 29th. This bridgehead made the Dakka Camp secure from sniping. The 14th Company, Madras S. & M., had now arrived, and for a short time it

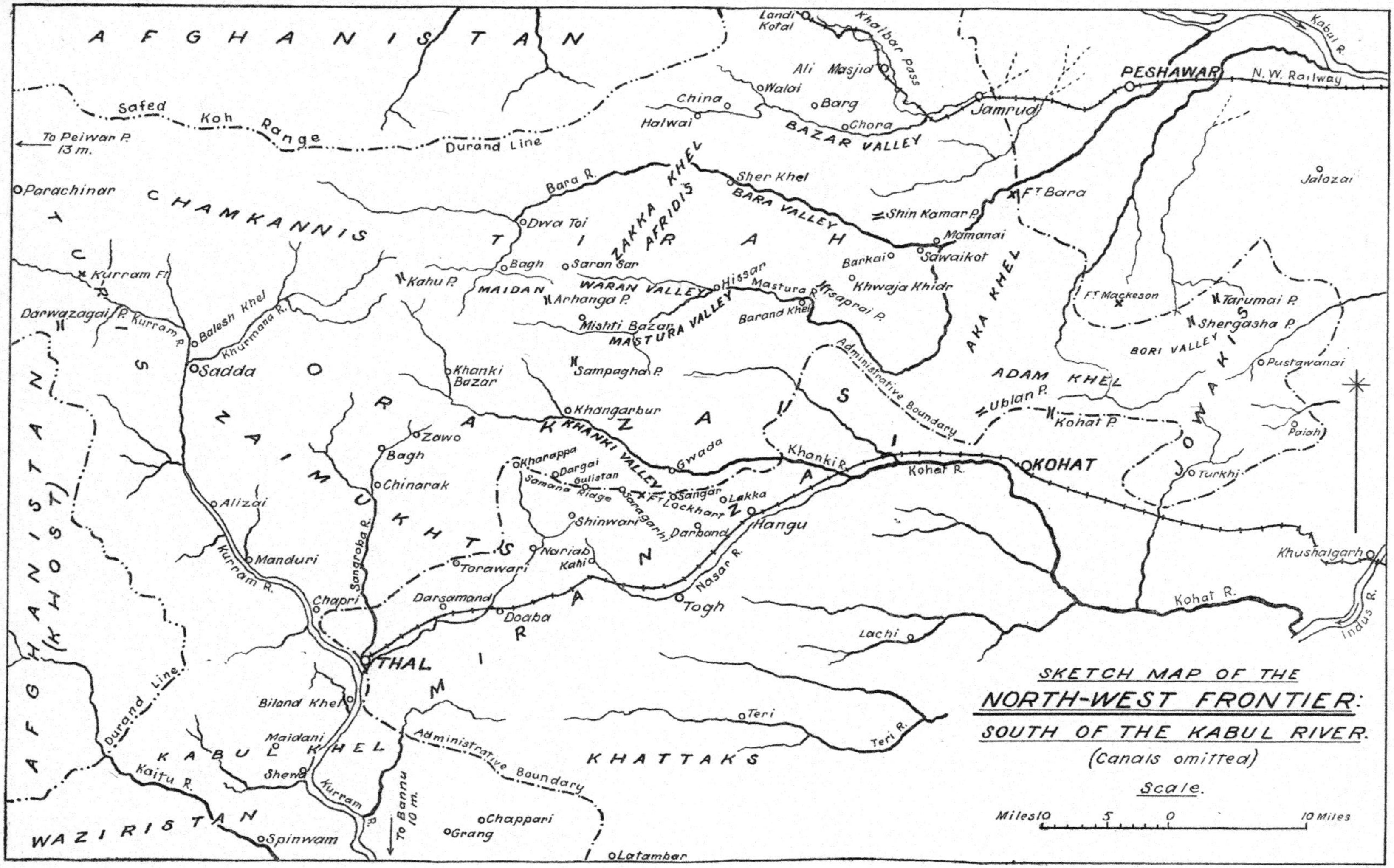
SKETCH MAP OF THE
NORTH-WEST FRONTIER:
SOUTH OF THE KABUL RIVER.
(Canals omitted)
Scale.
Miles 10 5 0 10 Miles
AFGHANISTAN
Safed Koh Range
Durand Line
To Peiwar P. 13 m.
Parachinar
CHAMKANNIS
TURIS
Kurram Ft
Darwazagai P.
Kurram R.
Balesh Khel
Khurmana R.
Sadda
ORAKZAIS
ZAIMUKHTS
Alizai
Manduri
Kurram R.
Chapri
Sangroba R.
THAL
MIRANZAI
Biland Khel
Maidani
Shewa
KABUL KHEL
Kaitu R.
Durand Line
AFGHANISTAN (KHOST)
WAZIRISTAN
Spinwam
Kurram R.
To Bannu 10 m.
Chappari
Grang
Latamber
Administrative Boundary
KHATTAKS
Teri
Teri R.
Lachi
Kohat R.
Indus R.
Khushalgarh
Landi Kotal
Khaibar Pass
Ali Masjid
Walai
China
Halwai
Barg
Chora
BAZAR VALLEY
Jamrud
PESHAWAR
N. W. Railway
Kabul R.
Jalozai
Bara R.
Sher Khel
BARA VALLEY
ZAKKA KHEL AFRIDIS
TIRAH
Dwa Toi
Bagh
Saran Sar
Kahu P.
MAIDAN
Arhanga P.
WARAN VALLEY
Hissar
Mastura R.
Tsaprai P.
Barand Khel
Mishti Bazar
MASTURA VALLEY
Sampagha P.
Khanki Bazar
Khangarbur
KHANKI VALLEY
Zawo
Bagh
Chinarak
Kharappa
Dargai
Gulistan
Samana Ridge
Saragarhi
Ft Lockhart
Sangar
Lakka
Gwada
Khanki R.
Shinwari
Darband
Nariab
Kahi
Torawari
Darsamand
Doaba
Togh
Nasar R.
Hangu
Kohat R.
KOHAT
Shin Kamar P.
Ft Bara
Mamanai
Sawaikot
Barkai
Khwaja Khidr
AKA KHEL
ADAM KHEL
Ublan P.
Kohat P.
Administrative Boundary
Ft Mackeson
Tarumai P.
Shergasha P.
BORI VALLEY
JOWAKIS
Pustawanai
Paiah
Turkhi

worked with the 7th and 56th Companies and two battalions of Pioneers engaged during August and September on the construction of a motor road through the Khurd Khaibar Pass beyond Dakka. In August the 14th Company returned to Landi Khana to erect boundary pillars to demarcate the Indo-Afghan frontier, and, after some of these had been destroyed by tribesmen, it re-erected them with slabs of guncotton inserted as booby traps. This proved very effective, and the wanton destruction of pillars ceased forthwith. Peace was concluded formally with Afghanistan on August 8th, 1919, and all Sapper and Miner units were withdrawn in September when the North-West Frontier Force was demobilized.

There was considerable activity near the Khaibar Pass during July, 1919. About the middle of the month, 6,000 Afridis under Yar Muhammad gathered at Chora in the Bazar Valley south-west of Ali Masjid to attack our line of communication. On July 18th they fired on the piquets around Fort Maude and Fort Shagai, and 400 men, many in the uniform of the Khyber Rifles, overwhelmed a piquet on "Barley Hill," half a mile south of Fort Maude. This was the occasion of the successful defence of the Ropeway Construction Camp by the 26th and 27th Railway Companies. Reinforcements were sent from Peshawar in the form of a small column under Major-General S. H. Sheppard, late R.E., who was then in command of the 5th Infantry Brigade of the 2nd Indian Division.[1] Sheppard reached Fort Maude without difficulty and met detachments which had marched down from Ali Masjid. The road through the Khaibar having been cleared, and peace concluded with Afghanistan, the next step was to deal with Yar Muhammad. This task was allotted to a force under Brig.-General G. A. H. Beatty, commanding the 6th Infantry Brigade, which included the 11th Company, Madras S. & M., and the Tehri-Garhwal Sapper Company. Before dawn on September 13th, 1919, Beatty was on the move from Ali Masjid and by 7.30 a.m. had drawn a net round Chora. There was little resistance. The place was entered by 10 a.m. and the 11th Company and Tehri Sappers began to prepare the fort for demolition under the direction of Major C. J. S. King, R.E., O.C., 11th Company. The fort was a solid masonry building, 100 feet square and with walls 40 feet high. About 3,600 pounds of guncotton were distributed along the perimeter in 24 charges of 150 pounds each, with an extra charge of 200 pounds placed in a tower—an excessive allowance, perhaps, but King wished to take no chances. At the first attempt, 12 charges failed to explode owing to defective fuzes, but at 3.30 p.m. the demolition was completed and the troops returned afterwards to Ali Masjid.

Events on the southern, or Baluchistan, front now claim attention. The operations of the 4th Indian Division in this area are of engineering interest chiefly because they included the reduction of the Afghan stronghold of Spin Baldak lying 6 miles north-west of New Chaman between Quetta and Kandahar.[2] Early in May 1919, the Sapper units available

[1]Gen. Sheppard afterwards officiated in command of the 1st Division from Nov., 1919, to March, 1920, and in command of the 2nd Division from March to Sept., 1920.

[2]See *Sketch Map of Southern Afghanistan and Baluchistan*, included in Chapter X and repeated in this chapter.

comprised the 7th Field Troop and half the 73rd Company, Bombay S. & M., in Quetta, and the 71st Company, with the remainder of the 73rd Company, on the line of communication between Spezand and Meshed in Persia. This small cadre was reinforced on May 20th by the arrival in Quetta of the 24th Company, Bombay S. & M., and half the 17th Company. General Wapshare, G.O.C. 4th Division, knew that if the Afghans took the offensive they would probably invade through Chaman and the Khojak Pass, so he reinforced Chaman and concentrated a large force at Kila Abdullah, 9 miles east of the Khwaja Amran Range. As Spin Baldak was the second strongest fortress in Afghanistan, its reduction would have a great moral effect, and accordingly Wapshare concentrated his division at New Chaman on May 26th for this purpose. The engineer formations present were the 24th Company, half the 73rd Company and a company of the 2/23rd Sikh Pioneers.

The fortress of Spin Baldak lay below the end of a rocky ridge which rose 200 feet above the plain. It was a square work, with inner and outer masonry walls surrounded by a dry ditch 25 feet deep and 25 feet broad. Each face of the outer wall was 250 yards in length and about 25 feet high. The inner wall was reinforced with earth and had casemates for the garrison. Three towers, on the rise to the crest of the ridge, overlooked the fort. General Wapshare decided to storm the ridge and fort with two infantry columns. With the right attack, under Brig.-General J. L. R. Gordon, was half the 73rd Company. The orders for this column were to capture the towers on the ridge and then to assault the northern face of the fort below. With the left attack, under Major-General T. H. Hardy, was half the 24th Company, the remainder of the unit being in reserve. Hardy was ordered to capture the gardens and buildings south and west of the fort and prepare to assault from those directions. The operations met with rapid success. Gordon took the towers, and Spin Baldak was then stormed by the 1/4th Gurkhas and 1/22nd Punjabis, the Gurkhas entering through a breach made by the guns and opening a gate to admit the Punjabis, some of whom were already scaling the walls with ladders. Of the 600 Afghans in the garrison, 200 were killed and the remainder surrendered, and by 4 p.m. the fort was in our hands. The Bombay Sappers were not in the assault but set to work afterwards to arrange for a piped water-supply to replace the dangerous and undrinkable local supply, and by July 10th, they had completed a pipe-line from Chaman. The detachment of the 73rd Company spent the afternoon after the assault in demolishing buildings near the fort and bivouacked at night within it in appallingly filthy surroundings and very short of water. Then, after a few days occupied in demolition work in conjunction with the men of the 24th Company, they began their water-supply operations, during which, however, they met with considerable obstruction from the Afghans who diverted or blocked the underground channels (*karez*) which formed the existing system of supply.[1] The remainder of the 17th Company arrived in Baluchistan on

[1]Notes by Maj.-Gen. Sir E. K. Squires, K.C.B., D.S.O., M.C., late R.E., sent to the author on Nov. 30th, 1937.

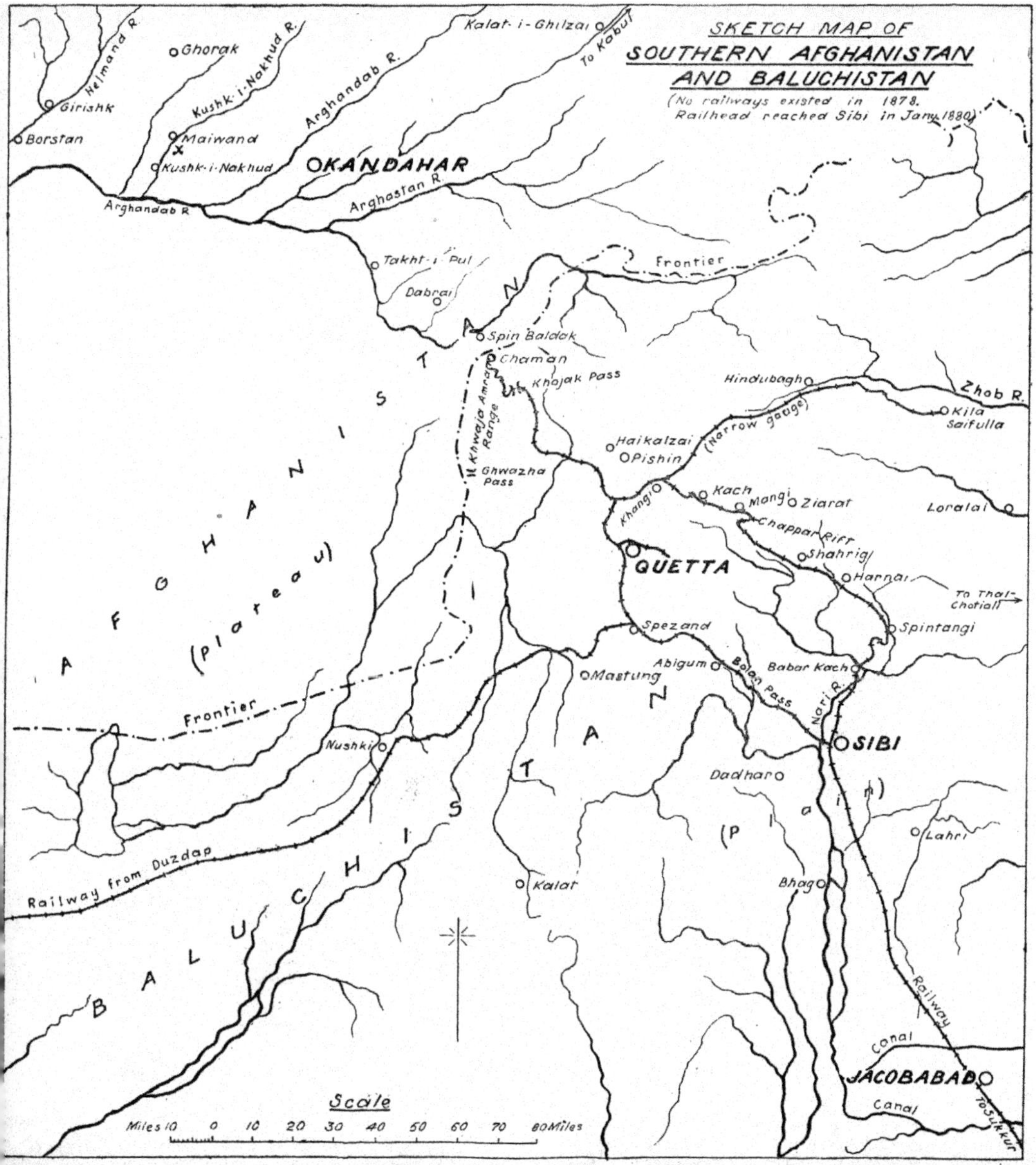

SKETCH MAP OF
SOUTHERN AFGHANISTAN
AND BALUCHISTAN
(No railways existed in 1878. Railhead reached Sibi in Jany 1880)
Helmand R.
Ghorak
Kushk-i-Nakhud R.
Kalat-i-Ghilzai
To Kabul
Girishk
Arghandab R.
Borstan
Maiwand
Kushk-i-Nakhud
KANDAHAR
Arghandab R.
Arghastan R.
Takht-i-Pul
Frontier
Dabrai
Spin Baldak
Chaman
Khojak Pass
Khwaja Amran Range
Hindubagh
Zhob R.
Kila Saifulla
(Narrow gauge)
Haikalzai
Pishin
Ghwazha Pass
Khangi
Kach
Mangi
Ziarat
Loralai
Chappar Rift
Shahrig
QUETTA
Harnai
To Thal-Chotiali
Spezand
Spintangi
AFGHANISTAN
(plateau)
Abigum
Babar Kach
Mastung
Bolan Pass
Nari R.
Frontier
Nushki
SIBI
Dadhar
BALUCHISTAN
(plain)
Lahri
Railway from Duzdap
Kalat
Bhag
Railway
Canal
JACOBABAD
Canal
To Sukkur
Scale
Miles 10 0 10 20 30 40 50 60 70 80 Miles

June 23rd and the 68th (Burma) Company, Madras S. & M., on July 4th, too late to see any fighting. Hostilities ended officially with the signature of a treaty on August 8th, and Spin Baldak was handed back to the Afghans on August 14th. It was a typical fort of the old text-books, well built but quite unsuited to modern conditions of warfare.

We come now to certain repercussions of the Third Afghan War in that cockpit of the North-West Frontier known as Waziristan which had most serious effects on the loyalty of the North and South Waziristan Militias and entailed long and arduous fighting to stamp out rebellion.

Allusion has been made already to the evacuation of the Upper Tochi posts at Datta Khel, Tut Narai, Boya and elsewhere on or after May 23rd, 1919, when the Afghans under Nadir Khan were on the march from Khost. This operation was carried out under the direction of Brig.-General F. G. Lucas, commanding the 67th (Bannu) Brigade, and the troops were concentrated in Miramshah and Dardoni, which, with Idak and Saidgi, further down the Tochi, were soon invested closely by hostile Wazirs.[1] In the south, a loyal remnant of the Wana garrison under Major G. H. Russell, Commandant of the South Waziristan Militia, cut its way through Mughal Kot to Fort Sandeman on the Zhob River, an exploit ranking among the finest in the history of the Indian Frontier.[2] To the Wazirs and Mahsuds, the withdrawal of the Tochi and Gomal garrisons presaged the general collapse of British rule. No Sapper and Miner units took part in the withdrawal, though among those killed in the retreat from Wana was the Garrison Engineer, Lieutenant E. J. MacCrostie, 1/25th London Regiment. The Wazirs in the Tochi were so elated by their success that they believed a statement by one of their *mullas* that he could destroy an aeroplane by casting a spell over it! The situation in the Tochi Valley on May 28th was indeed serious, for the regular troops available in Bannu consisted only of 3 squadrons of cavalry, 2 battalions of infantry, a section of mountain artillery and a section of the 55th Company, Bengal S. & M.[3] Early in June, 1919, the relief was effected of Miramshah, Dardoni and Idak in the Tochi and Jandola near the Derajat border, but heat, cholera and the disorganization caused by the Afghan War prevented any marked change in the situation during the summer months, and it was not until November 8th that Major-General S. H. Climo was able to assemble a powerful force to deal first with the Tochi Wazirs. The defection of the Wazirs and Mahsuds was not due to any particular grievance other than an unfounded suspicion that their country was to be transferred to the Amir. They entered the field because they loved war and were convinced that every true Muhammadan should fight against the unbeliever whenever opportunity offered.

The Waziristan Force which assembled under General Climo in

[1]*Operations in Waziristan*, 1919–1920 (Official Account), p. 64.

[2]"Waziristan," by Maj.-Gen. A. Le G. Jacob, C.B., C.M.G., C.I.E., C.B.E., D.S.O., appearing in *The R.E. Journal*, Vol. XLII, 1928, pp. 219–231. Mughal Kot is on the Zhob River, 15 m. south-west of Khajuri Kach (see Waziristan map).

[3]The 55th Company, Bengal S. & M., was commanded by Capt. J. G. O. Whitehead, R.E., with Capt. M. J. Dolan, R.E. I.A., and Lieuts. A. C. Baillie, O. L. Roberts and W. G. Gibson, R.E., as Section Commanders.

November, 1919, included few British troops but it had 6 brigades of Indian infantry, 4 additional battalions, several batteries, a wing of the Royal Air Force, the 55th Company, Bengal S. & M., and the 74th Company, Bombay S. & M.—altogether, about 29,000 men. Yet the actual striking force at Miramshah for operations in the Tochi amounted to only 2 brigades under Major-General A. Skeen, and the 55th Company was the only engineer unit in it. However, Skeen was able to subdue the Tochi Wazirs after reaching Datta Khel on November 17th. Nine days later his troops were back in Dardoni, and, renamed the "Derajat Column," marched down to Bannu and then southwards to the Tank–Jandola area to deal with the more truculent Mahsuds. Climo planned to send Skeen's column up the defiles of the Tank Zam towards the Mahsud centres at Makin and Kaniguram. He hoped that by advancing along a single line he could economize in defence troops and so bring the enemy quickly to decisive action, but most of his men were inexperienced in frontier warfare and he was impeded by a vast amount of transport.

Piqueting the heights as he went, Skeen reached Jandola with the Derajat Column on December 17th, 1919, and repulsed a fierce attack on his camp. Then he moved a short distance up the Tank Zam to a camp at Palosina,[1] where bitter fighting ensued on December 19th–20th for the establishment of a piquet on a height on the right bank called "Mandanna Hill." Half the 55th Company was engaged in this affair. Another height, "Black Hill" on the left bank, was the scene of a furious struggle on December 21st while a section of the 55th Company and some men of the 3/34th Pioneers were building a *sangar*. Four attacks by 800 Mahsuds were beaten off by the Sappers and Pioneers who did not withdraw to Palosina until their ammunition ran short. Captain J. G. O. Whitehead, R.E., was severely wounded in this fight. The Mahsuds, armed with modern rifles, showed great bravery and marked tactical ability. Black Hill was reoccupied on the 22nd, and Skeen halted for a time while the Sappers and Pioneers consolidated the Palosina position. Casualties on both sides had been heavy. The Mahsuds made some half-hearted overtures for peace, but Skeen knew his enemy and prepared to advance further up the Tank Zam.

On December 29th, the 43rd Brigade and attached troops reached Kotkai, where they were joined by the 67th Brigade on January 6th, 1920. The Mahsuds resumed hostilities, so Skeen prepared to force a passage of the difficult Ahnai Tangi, a gorge about 80 yards long and only 3 yards wide, dominated by precipitous heights. He failed on January 7th, again on the 9th, and yet again on the 10th; but on the 14th, adopting the dangerous expedient of a night march, he passed safely through and, in the face of determined resistance, arrived on the 18th on the Sorarogha Plateau, having fought twenty actions in one month. During the advance, the 55th Company was employed chiefly in improving the track, building

[1]See *Sketch Map of the North-West Frontier: Waziristan*, included in Chapter XIV and repeated in this chapter.

KHIRGI CAMP ON THE TANK ZAM NEAR JANDOLA, WAZIRISTAN, 1919.

(By kind permission of Maj.-Gen. C. H. Foulkes, C.B., C.M.G., D.S.O., late R.E.)

defences and arranging for water-supply. The Derajat Column halted at Sorarogha until the 27th.

About a mile above Sorarogha, in a fantastic wilderness of crag and ravine, the Tank Zam cuts through a ridge to form a gorge known as the Barari Tangi. This is some 300 yards long and 60 yards wide, with precipitous sides 100 feet high, but Skeen forced a passage by a series of operations between January 23rd and 27th while the 55th Company and Pioneers prepared three camel-tracks down to the river bed to facilitate the passage of transport up the defile. Though the enemy's resistance was now waning, the operations were being hindered by extreme cold. Camp was pitched at Ahmadwam and, on February 1st, an advanced force, including half the 55th Company, set out for Aka Khel on the road to the Piaza Raghza (plateau). The Sappers prepared permanent piquets at Aka Khel, and the advance was continued to Janjal (or Janjai) on February 3rd. There was now little resistance but the weather was vile. The temperature fell to 25° below freezing point, and a strong and bitter wind blew unceasingly. The Tank Zam had to be forded many times, and whenever the troops emerged from the water their boots and putties froze hard. The river was ice-covered except in the main channel, and the Sappers on road-work had to wrench up stones frozen fast in the ground. On February 6th the column camped on the bleak Piaza Raghza and awaited reinforcements and supplies. The intense cold continued. As the line of communication lengthened, more and more troops had been sent to Waziristan, but although General Climo had now some 45,000 fighting men in the country, the Derajat Column could muster only 10,000 bayonets for offensive operations in the heart of the Mahsud territory. On February 16th, Skeen marched to the neighbourhood of Makin, and on the 19th, began to devastate the Makin Valley. The 55th Company demolished 17 towers on February 20th, while the infantry burnt 160 houses. Towers which could not be reached were destroyed by gun-fire or bombing.

March 1st, 1920, saw the retirement of the Derajat Column from Makin to Dwa Toi, and on March 3rd Skeen began to ascend the Baddar Toi towards Ladha *en route* for the Mahsud capital of Kaniguram. Half the 55th Company was employed with the advanced guard in building permanent piquets and improving the track. After Ladha had been occupied and fortified, Kaniguram was reached on March 6th. The town, which contained a large bazaar and several rifle factories, was found to consist of about a thousand houses built on steep ground on the left bank of the Baddar. Active operations closed with the occupation of Kaniguram, for the Mahsuds submitted to punitive measures and began to surrender their rifles and pay their fines. After a wide road suitable for mechanical transport had been built from Kaniguram to Ladha, the Derajat Column concentrated at Ladha and began the construction of a permanent camp at that place. On May 7th, 1920, the troops dispersed with the exception of the 67th Brigade, a battery of artillery, a battalion of Pioneers and the 55th Company, Bengal S. & M., who garrisoned Ladha to ensure that the Mahsuds gave no more trouble. The 55th Company returned to Roorkee in August 1920 on relief by the 94th Company, Madras S. & M., and at the same time the 14th Company, Madras, S. & M., relieved the 75th Company, Bombay S. & M., at Sorarogha. Thus ended a campaign which, in severity and hard fighting, equalled or even exceeded any of its predecessors on the North-West Frontier.

After the dispersal of the Derajat Column, the first steps were taken to occupy Waziristan permanently and to open up the country by a system of roads designed for mechanical transport. The 67th Brigade was stationed at Ladha, the 43rd Brigade on the Piaza Raghza, the 68th Brigade at Sorarogha and the 62nd Brigade at Tank. The Tank Zam was held securely by defensible posts, and the Mahsuds remained fairly quiet throughout the remainder of 1920. The situation further south, however, was much less satisfactory, for the Wana Wazirs were still unsubdued and it was imperative to recapture our lost posts and to checkmate the intrigues of Afghan agents. Accordingly, in the autumn of 1920, a " Wana Column " was assembled at Jandola under Major-General W. S. Leslie to deal with the Wana Wazirs and with it was the 14th Company, Madras S. & M., under Captain J. James, R.E., from Sorarogha. Marching from Jandola on November 12th, 1920, the Wana Column reached Sarwekai on the 18th after a successful passage of the formidable Shahur Tangi. Some of the Wazirs submitted forthwith, but others held out, and consequently the column resumed its advance on December 16th. It reached Wana with little difficulty on December 22nd. Yet there were still some recalcitrant sections of the Wazirs in the field, and therefore it was necessary during the next two years to maintain strong garrisons of Indian troops in Wana and the various posts along the Lower Zhob Valley. The 14th Company, Madras S. & M., now under Captain C. Sleigh, R.E., remained in Southern Waziristan throughout most of 1921 in charge of all works at Wana, Rogha Kot, Dargai Oba, Sarwekai, Haidari Kach and Chagmalai,[1] the work at Wana being chiefly water-supply and the improvement of the defences. But the country was still very unsettled and the Sappers were often under fire. For instance, they were involved in a skirmish in the Shahur Tangi on July 16th, 1921, when Lieutenant T. B. Vickers, I.A.R.O., was killed in a gallant attempt to bomb some Mahsuds out of caves. The company left the Wana district in December 1921 to relieve the 94th Company, Madras S. & M., at Ladha.

At the end of 1920, a " Zhob Column " which included the 17th Company, Bombay S. & M., under Major E. B. Fox, R.E., co-operated with the Wana Column against the Wazirs. It left Fort Sandeman on December 13th and reached Mughal Kot on the 19th. Fox records that at Mughal Kot he saw the hole in the wall through which Major Russell and the other British officers of the South Waziristan Militia from Wana had escaped towards Fort Sandeman. Both the Mughal Kot and Mir Ali Khel posts had been wrecked by the Wazirs.[2] The company repaired the defences at

[1]See *Sketch Map of the North-West Frontier : Waziristan*, repeated in this chapter. Wana, Dargai Oba, Sarwekai and Haidari Kach are shown on the road from Jandola. Rogha Kot is 1 m. north of Karab Kot, and Chagmalai is 2 m. west of Jandola.

[2]Notes by Lieut.-Col. E. B. Fox, R.E., sent to the author on Oct. 13th, 1937. Mir Ali Khel is on the Zhob River, 13 m. south-west of Mughal Kot and 30 m. from Fort Sandeman.

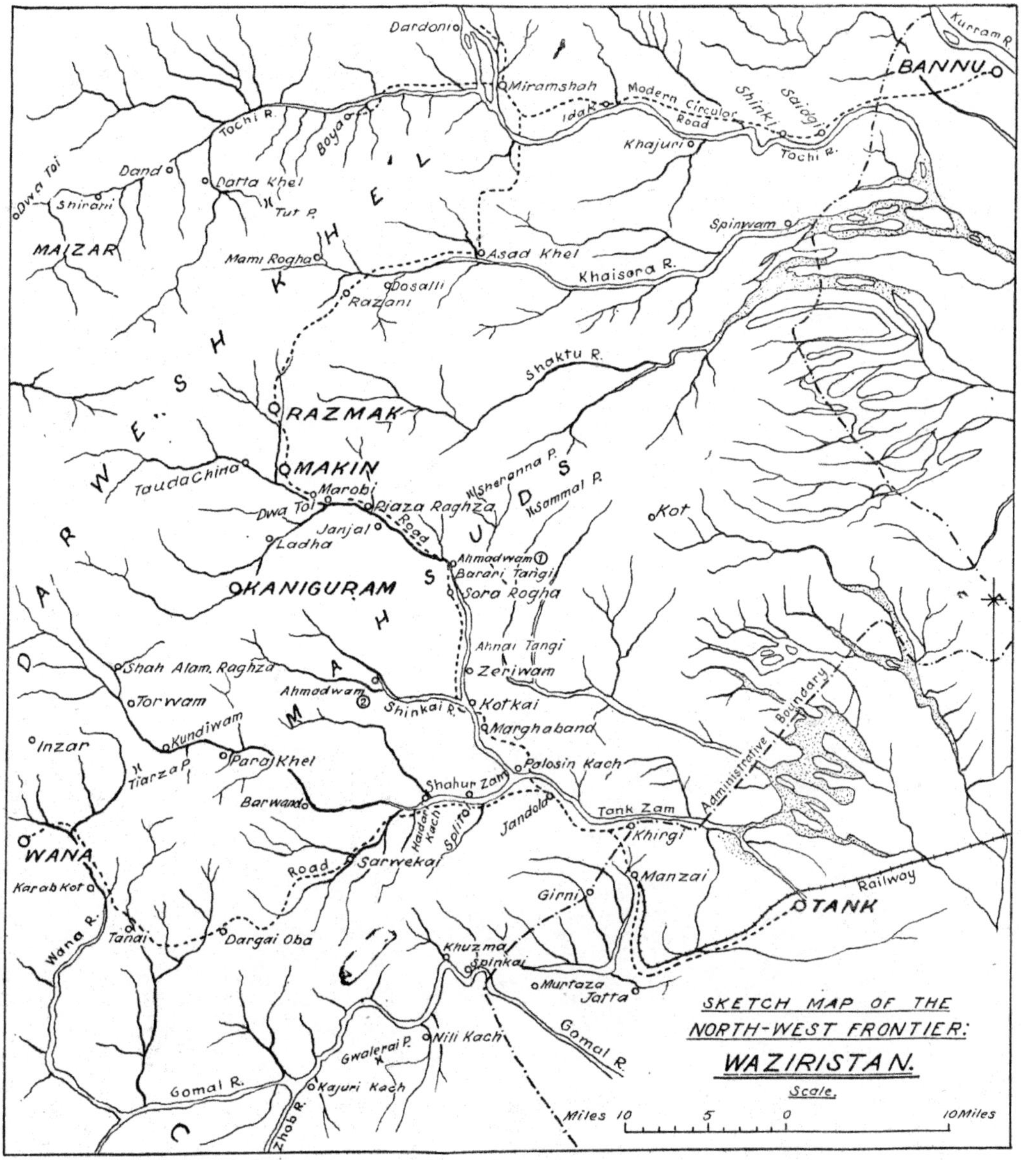

SKETCH MAP OF THE NORTH-WEST FRONTIER:

WAZIRISTAN.

Mir Ali Khel and improved the road to Fort Sandeman. It left a lasting monument at Mir Ali Khel in the form of a tower of Afridi type, 30 feet high, for a permanent piquet on a hill above the post. Fox was in command at Mir Ali Khel for three months during the summer of 1921 when the post was surrounded by 5,000 tribesmen. Afterwards, on return to Quetta, the 17th Company met the 22nd Company under Captain H. E. Horsfield, R.E., and was thus able to renew an association established between the original companies during General Townshend's advance to Ctesiphon and his defence of Kut al Amara in 1915–16.

The Waziristan campaign of 1919–21 was abnormal. As de Watteville remarks,[1] the military and political conditions prevalent in India, the demobilization of the troops, the rawness of the half-trained units, the failure of the Frontier militias, the general war weariness, the improved armament and clever tactics of the enemy and the extremes of heat and cold, rendered the operations formidable beyond expectation. The Mahsuds, impoverished, sullen and exhausted, were ready, nevertheless, to rise again if opportunity offered; and, as will appear in a later chapter, they did so in 1923 before their country was opened up by a great Circular Road to a new fortified camp at Razmak, situated close to the Makin Valley and 7,000 feet above sea-level.

* * * * *

The seditious teaching which was part and parcel of the programme of non-co-operation in India after the Great War had far-reaching and disastrous results. Not only did it encourage Amanullah to invade in the north and incite the Mahsuds, Wazirs and Mohmands to insurrection, but it led to murderous outbreaks in Central India and spread at last to the Moplahs in the extreme south, thus causing the most serious internal disturbance since the Indian Mutiny.

The Moplahs, some 250,000 men, were fanatical and reckless Muhammadans of Arab descent, adepts in jungle warfare and unsurpassed as scouts. For the past 80 years they had revolted from time to time and had always been a thorn in the flesh of the peaceful Hindus amongst whom they lived. They inhabited parts of the Malabar coast from Mangalore southwards to Cochin, an area thick with tidal creeks fringed with palms. Further inland were rice fields and fenced enclosures, and beyond them the dense and malarial jungles of the Nilgiri Hills. The climate of Malabar is hot and steamy throughout the year. The country is well watered by three rivers, the Beypore, Karim Puzha and Ponnani,[2] but during the monsoon period from June to September the rivers are in flood and unfordable. In 1921 the Moplahs had only some 3,000 firearms ranging from elephant guns and old Martini rifles to smooth-bores. Their chief weapon was the sword, which they used with great effect in desperate charges from the jungle against troops held up by road blocks. The numerous mosques, temples and villages were convertible easily into small

[1]*Waziristan*, 1919–1920, by H. de Watteville, p. 222.
[2]See *Sketch Map of Malabar*, 1921, included in this chapter.

fortresses. Any movement of guns or transport, except by road, was impossible, and infantry could advance across country only with the greatest difficulty. Our garrison in Malabar was weak. In fact, in August 1921, the only regular troops actually available for service were 2 platoons of the 2nd Battalion, The Leinster Regiment, at Calicut and most of the 83rd Wallajahbad Light Infantry at Cannanore, 50 miles further north. The South Indian Railway, running down the coast from Cannanore through Calicut to Tirur, and thence inland through Shoranur, Podanur and Erode to Madras was the sole link between Malabar and the rest of India. This was the setting for a small but fiercely contested campaign.

At the outbreak of the Moplah Rebellion on August 20th, 1921, the Madras District had a nominal strength of 4 battalions, 2 batteries and 3 Field Companies and a Field Troop, Madras S. & M., at Bangalore, a battalion (Leinsters) at Wellington in the Nilgiris with detachments in Calicut and Madras, a battalion near Madras, two in Cannanore and one in Trichinopoly.[1] Several of these units, however, were in the process of disbandment, and lack of transport and the demands of internal security forbade the prompt concentration of any large force in Malabar. The two platoons of Leinsters in Calicut were reinforced at once by three others, and a company under Captain P. McEnroy, advancing on the 20th to Tirurangadi to help the civil authorities, detached a platoon to occupy the rebel centre at Malappuram. At Tirurangadi, McEnroy was confronted by a mob of 5,000 Moplahs armed with swords and found the railway station in flames. Martial law had not yet been declared so he dared not take the offensive, having in mind, no doubt, the aftermath of General Dyer's action at Amritsar. Instead, he made a fighting withdrawal to Calicut, where the situation was less threatening. News came that the platoon at Malappuram had been surrounded, their motor transport burnt and the drivers killed. A general rising had begun. The Moplahs cut the railway line in many places, blocked all the roads and demolished the telegraph lines. British planters were murdered and Hindus massacred wholesale or forcibly converted to Islam. Hell was let loose in Malabar.

On August 21st reinforcements were despatched by rail from Bangalore to Podanur in the form of a Movable Column under Lieut.-Colonel F. W. Radcliffe, commanding the 2nd Battalion, The Dorsetshire Regiment. These comprised the Dorsets, a squadron of the Queen's Bays, a section of the 69th Field Battery, a company of the 64th Pioneers and two platoons of Madras Sappers. From Madras came two Auxiliary Force companies and two platoons of the 83rd Wallajahbad Light Infantry. The troops concentrated on the 24th at Tirur, and on the 25th, martial law was declared after H.M.S. *Comus* had steamed into Calicut. McEnroy then led his company of Leinsters from Calicut to the relief of his platoon besieged in Malappuram. He camped for the night at Kondotti, and on the 27th advanced through many road obstacles to Pukkottur, where he was attacked furiously by 2,000 Moplahs. The enemy tried to ambush the little column.

[1] "The Moplah Rebellion, 1921–22," by Capt. W. St. J. Carpendale, appearing in *The Journal of the U.S.I. of India*, Vol. LVI, Jan., 1926, pp. 76–94.

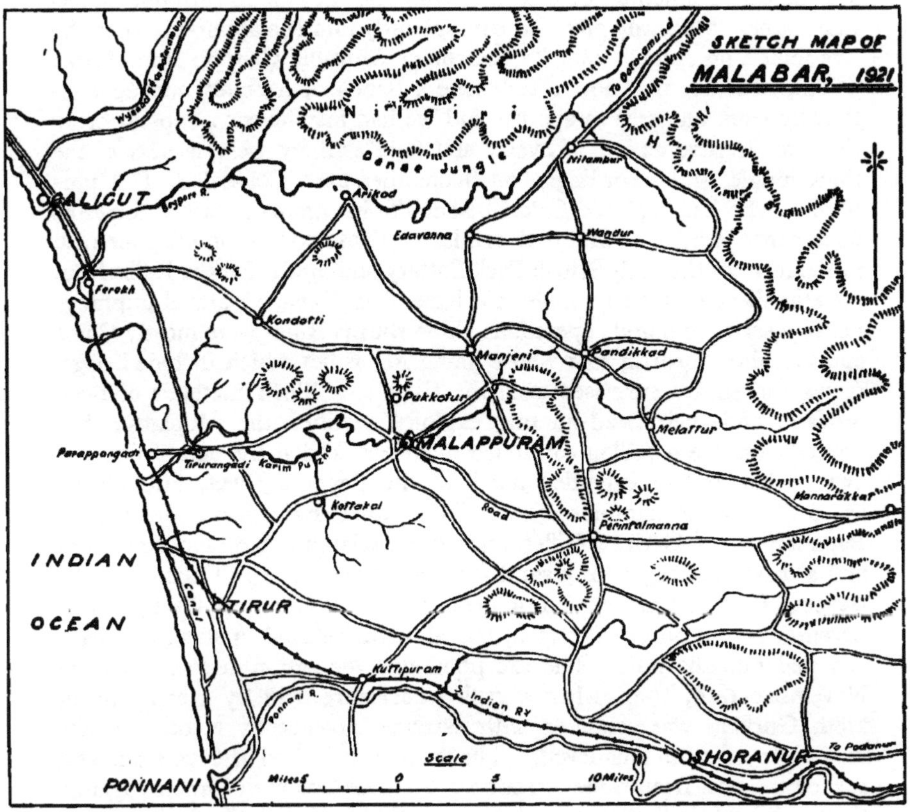
SKETCH MAP OF
MALABAR, 1921
Nilgiri
Hil
Dense Jungle
To Ootacamund
CALICUT
Feroke
Kondotti
Arikod
Edavanna
Nilambur
Wandur
Manjeri
Pandikkad
Pukkotur
MALAPPURAM
Melattur
Parappangadi
Tirurangadi
Kottakal
Road
Perintalmanna
Mannarakkat
INDIAN
OCEAN
Canal
TIRUR
Kuttipuram
Ponnani R.
S. Indian RY
SHORANUR
To Podanur
PONNANI
Scale
Miles 5
0
5
10 Miles

They charged repeatedly, sword in hand and supported by fire from adjoining houses and patches of jungle, and not until after four hours of desperate fighting did they melt away into the jungle, leaving 400 dead on the field. The moral effect of this action was great. Thereafter, the Moplahs had a wholesome respect for our rifle fire and discredited the miraculous powers claimed by their leaders who said they could turn our bullets into water.[1] McEnroy marched triumphantly into Malappuram, where he was joined on August 28th by Radcliffe's Movable Column from Tirur.

The situation was now a stalemate. Bands of Moplahs moved continually from one area to another and we had insufficient troops to bring them to decisive action. Cavalry and field artillery were useless in the thick jungle, and accordingly, on September 21st, Colonel E. T. Humphreys, who had replaced Colonel Radcliffe in command, asked for reinforcements of infantry and pack artillery. These arrived on October 16th in the form of the 10th British Pack Battery and 2/8th Gurkha Rifles from the Himalayas and the 3/70th Burma Rifles from Rangoon, and Humphreys began a series of mobile operations. The Burma Rifles were mostly Chins and Cachins, cheerful folk whose liking for a diet which included dogs, crows and snakes surprised even the Gurkhas. Their methods of bush warfare, and their head-hunting exploits, terrified the Moplahs; but nevertheless the rebellion continued to spread, and at the end of October 1921, when it had extended north of the Beypore River, Humphreys asked for further reinforcements. The 2/9th Gurkha Rifles and the 1st Battalion, Royal Garhwal Rifles, arrived in Malappuram on November 9th and a drive was begun in a south-easterly direction from Calicut and the Beypore River. It made good progress, but the results were disappointing because, except on one occasion, the Moplahs refused to stand and fight and fled into the hills. The exception was the action at Pandikkad on November 14th, 1921, when a walled enclosure held by a company of 2/8th Gurkhas was assaulted with extreme violence by 2,500 Moplahs in a state of mad fanaticism. The enemy surprised the garrison and rushed the post from three directions. So great was their impetus against the northern face that they pushed down the entire length of a high mud wall and, breaking into the enclosure, fought the Gurkhas, hand to hand, for a quarter of an hour. Finally, they were driven out with bomb, bayonet and *kukri*, leaving behind them 237 dead. It was noticed that many of the dead had their heads crushed in. This had been caused by their frantic efforts to push down the wall and by the weight of those pressing on them from behind. The Moplahs never again attempted a massive assault. They dissolved into small bands to carry on a guerilla warfare.

Between November 20th and 23rd the drive progressed from the Edavanna–Manjeri–Malappuram road to the Wandur-Pandikkad road, and it ended on November 25th after a tract of country 15 miles broad and 40 miles in length had been traversed. The theatre of operations was then divided into small areas in which each battalion undertook the task of

[1] "The Moplah Rebellion, 1921–22," by Lieut-Col. A. C. B. Mackinnon, appearing in *The Army Quarterly*, Vol. VII, Jan., 1924, pp. 260–277.

hunting down rebel gangs. The Moplahs who had escaped to the hills were starved into submission by being deprived of all supplies of grain. A rebel leader named Chembrassheri Tangal, whose chief delight had been to flay Hindus alive, surrendered on December 19th and was executed in Malappuram with another villain, Sithi Koya. A third leader surrendered on January 6th, 1922, and the fourth and last submitted in April. The rebellion had been quelled by a force equivalent to two brigades at a cost of only 169 casualties in the field, while the enemy had lost 2,339 killed and 1,652 wounded. More than 40,000 armed Moplahs surrendered during the later stages of the campaign. Such, briefly, is the story of the military operations in Malabar.

Bengal and Bombay Sappers and Miners took no part in the campaign, and the only representatives of the Madras Corps were the 9th Company, under Captain A. V. Anderson, R.E., with Lieutenants E. A. L. Gueterbock and M. Luby, R.E., and a platoon (section) of the 12th Company under Lieutenant Payne, I.A.R.O. One platoon of the 9th Company left Bangalore with the Movable Column on August 22nd, 1921, and the others followed on October 12th. The platoon of the 12th Company left Bangalore also on August 22nd but returned soon after the 9th Company had concentrated in Malabar.[1] The story of the work of the Madras Sappers is told fully in an article by "Assaye Lines" appearing in *The R.E. Journal* of March 1929.[2] The Sappers helped at first to repair the damaged railway and afterwards were attached in small parties to columns traversing affected areas. As each column had to be self-supporting, much of the Sapper work was the repair of small bridges and the removal of road blocks made by felling large trees. The Sapper squads were often absurdly small. For instance, on one occasion a Sapper *Naik* in charge of a dump was ordered by a Post Commander to detail a party to accompany a column. Consequently, as he had only eight men available, he detailed two men who duly reported for duty, one with a felling-axe and the other with a hand-saw! The 9th Company often had very severe labour in clearing road blocks. One block consisted of two large piles of bamboos, each 15 feet thick, reinforced with ten teak logs, each 35 feet long and 2 feet square. Owing to the dense jungle, the bamboos could not be dragged aside, and the logs, which had been hauled into position by elephants, were most difficult to move. Yet a platoon of the 9th Company, with the assistance of another of the Pioneers, cut a way through the block in less than an hour.

Bridges were repaired temporarily with any material obtainable locally and afterwards strengthened to take armoured cars. Much work was necessary on camp defences, for every camp was of the enclosed type to admit of all-round defence. The perimeter was often formed of army transport carts fastened together and interlaced with long bamboos. If carts were not available, the bamboos were anchored to strong posts

[1] *Historical Record of the Q.V.O. Madras S. & M.*, Vol. II (2), pp. 16, 17.

[2] "A Field Company in Malabar," by "Assaye Lines" (Capt. A. V. Anderson, R.E.) appearing in *The R.E. Journal*, Vol. XLIII, 1929, pp. 84–93.

driven into the ground. For permanent camps, large bamboo tripods were erected, connected by wire, and supplied with horizontals at three levels made from spiky bamboos, securely lashed. Sharp bamboo stakes, pointing upwards and outwards and fastened to the horizontals, were then added to complete a barrier reminiscent of the old Burmese wars. While in Malabar, the 9th Company built, repaired or strengthened 25 bridges to take armoured cars. Small blockhouses were erected also for the protection of all isolated bridges of any importance.

The rebellion in Malabar took India unawares, yet it might have been anticipated in view of the inflammable characteristics of the Moplahs, shown so often in the past. The incitement to revolt found a ready field in a peculiarly fanatical tribe, but although the results were deplorable and disastrous, many valuable lessons were learnt in the swamps and jungles of Malabar and some useful experience was gained by a few Sappers and Miners.

CHAPTER XXIII

OPERATIONS IN IRAQ AND IRAN, 1919–1922, INCLUDING THE ARAB REBELLION

THE GREAT WAR ended in Iraq with the signing of an armistice on October 31st, 1918, and the surrender of the remnants of the Turkish 6th Army at Mosul; but although the Turks were defeated, the country actually remained a theatre of warfare until a peace treaty was ratified in 1924. The situation in 1919 was disturbing: in the middle of 1920 it became desperate. "The terms of the armistice," writes General Haldane,[1] "practically left it open to us to take possession of such places as we wished, and in consequence, Mosul, Zakho, Amadiya, Rowandiz, Erbil, Sulaimaniya and Tel Afar were occupied, while on the Euphrates, Ana and Dair ez Zaur were taken under our administration.[2] The communications to most of these places were long and difficult, and the Political Officers enforced their orders largely by relying on the prestige which our troops had won." The truth is that we tried prematurely to apply to Iraq methods of administration based on past experience in India, with the result that a system came into existence which was far too rigid for an Arab population accustomed to the slipshod procedure of Turkish rule.

At the end of April, 1919, Lieut.-General Sir George MacMunn became Commander-in-Chief of our forces in Iraq and North-Western Iran. His troops in Iraq comprised the 17th Indian Division, under Major-General G. A. J. Leslie, late R.E., with headquarters at Baghdad, and the 18th Indian Division, under Major-General Theodore Fraser, late R.E., with headquarters at Mosul.[3] In addition there was a force equivalent to two brigades in North-Western Iran, under Brig.-General H. F. Bateman-Champain, and a number of units stationed on lines of communication. Colonel Sir Percy Cox was acting as British Minister at Tehran and Lieut.-Colonel Sir Arnold Wilson as Civil Commissioner in Baghdad. MacMunn was perturbed by the general position. "We were strong enough along the rivers," he writes,[4] "but I could not reinforce Mosul with rail-head at Baiji and most of the war-time lorries gone. Also, I found existing several of my pet abominations, distant outposts put out for political reasons but hostages to fortune in the event of local trouble. The worst of

[1]*The Insurrection in Mesopotamia*, 1920, by Lieut.-Gen. Sir Aylmer L. Haldane G.C.M.G., K.C.B., D.S.O., pp. 20, 21.

[2]See *Sketch Maps of Operational Areas in Iraq and Iran*, 1919–22, included in this chapter. Also, maps of *Lower Iraq*, 1914–16, in Chapter XVII, and *Upper Iraq and N.W. Iran*, 1918, and *Iran*, 1918, in Chapter XVIII. Ana, on the Upper Euphrates, is about 120 miles upstream of Hit by the river route, and Dair ez Zaur a further 150 miles. No military garrisons were maintained in Rowandiz, Sulaimaniya or Tel Afar.

[3]Both these commanders were ex-Sappers and Miners. Leslie had served in the Bombay Corps and Fraser in the Madras Corps.

[4]*Behind the Scenes in Many Wars*, by Lieut.-Gen. Sir George MacMunn, K.C.B., K.C.S.I., D.S.O., pp. 277, 278.

these was Dair ez Zaur, far up the Euphrates, 400 miles from any support. Nor did I like the garrison at Chemchemal, 200 miles from Baiji in the hills near Sulaimaniya and far ahead of the brigade at Kirkuk, nor another away up in Northern Kurdistan at Amadiya, 100 miles from Mosul.[1] On the other hand, I agreed with Arnold Wilson that for political reasons we must keep them out for a bit, but I warned him that if I saw real trouble I should bring them in quickly and then hit out." Military and civil requirements were opposed. The political heads wanted protection for their young representatives scattered over Iraq and Iran. MacMunn wished to concentrate his limited forces to meet any serious uprising.

The Sapper and Miner companies with the 17th Division were the 9th, 61st and 65th of the Madras Corps (Major E. Bradney and Captain A. E. Collier, R.E., and Captain R. B. Woakes, I.A.R.O.) and the newly formed 104th Company, Bombay S. & M. (Captain E. B. Fox, R.E.). Those with the 18th Division were the 2nd, 6th and 8th Companies, Bengal S. & M. (Captains F. G. Drew and V. E. G. Guinness, R.E., and Lieutenant A. M. Cameron, R.E.). The 2nd Field Troop, Madras S. & M. (Captain D. McA. Hogg, R.E.), and the 5th Field Troop, Bengal S. & M. (Captain E. G. Gidley-Kitchin, R.E.), were attached to the cavalry. No. 2 Bridging Train, Bengal S. & M. (Captain W. S. Wotherspoon, I.A.R.O.),[2] was available for bridging duties, and, until May 1919, No. 1 Bridging Train of the same Corps. The 85th Company, Bengal S. & M. (Captain A. L. Le Merle, R.E.), was also in Iraq, while in North-Western Iran were the 12th and 13th Companies, Madras S. & M. (Majors H. C. Agnew and R. H. Dewing, R.E.), the 5th and 52nd Companies, Bengal S. & M. (Captains A. F. Chater and H. E. Roome, R.E.), and the 19th Company, Bombay S. & M. (Captain C. F. Stoehr, R.E.). The Sapper units in Eastern and South-Eastern Iran, comprising the 24th, 71st and 73rd Companies, Bombay S. & M., and the 54th Company, Bengal S. & M., did not form part of General MacMunn's command.

Trouble started in May, 1919, with a rising in Southern Kurdistan where Major E. B. Soane, the Political Agent at Sulaimaniya, had established such strong influence that he was called by the Kurds " the uncrowned king " of their country.[3] Shaikh Mahmud of Sulaimaniya, a leading Kurdish chief, had been entrusted with the duty of preserving order among the tribes and was well paid for his responsibilities, though Soane knew that he was a scoundrel and would have no personal dealings with him. The only troops in Sulaimaniya were those of the South Kurdistan Militia whose British officers, appointed on the advice of Sir Arnold Wilson, considered themselves as under the orders of Mahmud. The Kurdish officers were, of course, completely Mahmud's creatures. Inspired by a sense of his increased importance, Mahmud schemed to set

[1]On the urgent recommendation of Gen. Fraser, several outlying stations in the Kurdish foothills were abandoned as military outposts, but isolated Political Officers were left in them in spite of his protests.

[2]Capt. W. S. Wotherspoon had succeeded Capt. F. V. B. Witts, R.E., in command of No. 2 Bridging Train on Dec. 14th, 1918.

[3]" The Campaign in South Kurdistan, 1919," by the Rev. J. Cethin Jones, appearing in *The Army Quarterly*, Vol. XI, Oct., 1925, pp. 86–96.

up an independent State in Southern Kurdistan. His personal allowance was reduced twice by Sir Arnold Wilson, and he resented these punishments, which he attributed to Soane's suggestions. Biding his time, he struck in May, 1919, when the British garrison under Lieut.-Colonel A. H. Bridges at Kirkuk, 66 miles from Sulaimaniya, had been reduced to a minimum. The blow was a complete surprise, although the gravity of the situation had been confirmed by Colonel Bridges after a visit to Mahmud's capital, early in May, with Captain F. G. Drew, R.E. Telegraphic communication with Sulaimaniya was interrupted on May 19th, and rumours spread that some of the Political Officers had been murdered. Happily, this was not the case. Soane had escaped, but others had been imprisoned and it became necessary to secure their early release. On May 22nd, the South Kurdistan Militia around Sulaimaniya joined Shaikh Mahmud. Their British officers were interned, and thus the die was cast and the ambitious chief was definitely committed to his military venture.

Under orders from General MacMunn, General Fraser immediately despatched a small mobile column from Kirkuk under Colonel Bridges with instructions to reconnoitre up to the Bazian Pass, some 40 miles from Kirkuk, but no further. Unfortunately, in his eagerness to rescue the Political Officers, Bridges exceeded his instructions and advanced through Chemchemal, the Bazian Pass and Allaki till he reached the Tasluja Pass within 12 miles of Sulaimaniya. The mobile column consisted of only two troops of Indian cavalry with four armoured cars, some Ford vans mounting Lewis guns, and a few men of the 2nd Company, Bengal S. & M., under Lieutenant G. Dixon, I.A.R.O. Behind it came a stronger marching column comprising a company of the 116th Marathas, a section of pack artillery and 2 sections of the 2nd Company. The columns left Kirkuk on May 21st and 22nd, and the remainder of the 2nd Company, coming from Altun Kopri, joined the marching column at Chemchemal on the 23rd.[1] Then came news that the mobile column, far ahead, had met with a severe defeat at the Tasluja Pass, and shortly afterwards the remnants of the cavalry rode into Chemchemal without their armoured cars and most of their Ford vans.[2] Helped by reinforcements from the 55th Brigade at Baiji, the 2nd Company at once started the construction of a perimeter camp south of Chemchemal. A small fort was held as a strong point, and the Sappers guarded the transport in the camp. Bridges having been recalled to Kirkuk, Drew was in command at Chemchemal for two days until relieved by Lieut.-Colonel H. Marr. The reverse at the Tasluja Pass had an unfortunate political effect and increased the danger of a general rising throughout Kurdistan.

On May 29th, 1919, a convoy from Kirkuk was ambushed and destroyed in an attempt to reach the besieged garrison of Chemchemal. A small column marched to Kara Anjir, where it defended itself for three days until relieved, and Kara Anjir then became the headquarters of the 55th Brigade under Brig.-General G. M. Morris. While our aeroplanes bombed

[1]Notes by Lieut.-Col. F. G. Drew, O.B.E., R.E., sent to the author on Dec. 24th, 1937.
[2]Lieut. G. Dixon, I.A.R.O., was wounded during this retreat.

Mahmud's headquarters, a force under Brig.-General G. A. F. Sanders, late R.E. (an ex-Madras Sapper and Miner), won through to Chemchemal and afterwards undertook punitive operations in which the 2nd Company destroyed several hostile villages. Sanders, who commanded the 53rd Infantry Brigade, had been selected to become G.O.C. Line of Communication. The garrison of Chemchemal had made several sorties while besieged, in one of which, on June 3rd, a section of the 2nd Company and some infantry were rescued by troops sent out from Kara Anjir. The relief of Chemchemal, however, was insufficient to remove the general impression that we were no longer able to control events. More was needed, and accordingly General Fraser was directed to assemble at Kirkuk a " South Kurdistan Force," consisting of two brigades of infantry, with cavalry and armoured cars, and to advance at the earliest possible date. The objective of " Fraserforce," as it was called, was Sulaimaniya, and while part of the force, under Brig.-General Sanders, controlled the lines of communication from Kirkuk to Chemchemal and also to Altun Kopri and Erbil, a mixed " Striking Force " of brigade strength, under Brig.-General Morris and including the 2nd Company, was to thrust at Sulaimaniya. By June 16th, Fraser was ready and set out with his Striking Force in sweltering heat to bring Shaikh Mahmud to decisive action.

The Kurds held two strong lines of defence. The first was at the historic Bazian Pass, 12 miles east of Chemchemal. This narrow mountain gorge, 1,000 feet deep, was a veritable Thermopylae which a few resolute men with machine guns might hold against enormous odds. Fraser advanced to within striking distance and before daybreak on June 18th, 1919, sent the 85th Burma Rifles to scale the precipitous heights which flanked the southern side of the defile. Then, at dawn, the attack was launched under a heavy covering fire from artillery and machine guns. On the heights to the right were the Burma Rifles, in the centre the 1/5th East Surreys and on the left the 116th Marathas. The 87th Punjabis were in support. Although the Kurds opened fire with German machine guns, the attack swept forward without appreciable check except on the right, where the Burma Rifles had some hand-to-hand fighting. Walls and *sangars* were surmounted, and soon the Bazian Pass was in Fraser's hands. The cavalry pressed onwards, and, reaching Sulaimaniya at dusk, released the imprisoned Political Officers. Shaikh Mahmud was captured, wounded, in the Pass. He was afterwards court-martialled and sentenced to death, but the sentence was commuted to transportation for life—an act of clemency which was severely criticized in Kurdistan and Baghdad. Finally, on the recommendation of Sir Percy Cox, Mahmud was released in 1922 and was thus able to return to Kurdistan and cause further trouble.

Strenuous work fell to the 2nd Company, Bengal S. & M., on June 19th in the advance to Sulaimaniya. The road was very rough and intersected by watercourses, and since the retreating Kurds had destroyed all timber culverts, every watercourse had to be bridged or ramped for wheeled traffic. The men were thoroughly exhausted when they marched into

Sulaimaniya after dark. The main body arrived on the 20th, and five days later, Fraserforce established contact at Halebja, near the Persian frontier, with a column under Lieut.-Colonel J. Body coming from Qiẓil Ribat. It remained in occupation of Sulaimaniya until October 1919 when it withdrew to Kirkuk after building a fortified post on the Bazian Pass. According to Sir George MacMunn,[1] the Sulaimaniya expedition was perhaps the most instructive and efficiently run small war in our history, teeming with every example of error, correction, and political action.

A section of the 2nd Company, Bengal S. & M., under Lieutenant H. S. White, I.A.R.O., was with the column of Fraserforce which marched towards Halebja, and the 13th Company, Madras S. & M., under Major R. H. Dewing, R.E., accompanied Colonel Body's column. Dewing writes[2] that, although only pack transport could be taken, the 13th Company had to carry material for crossing the wide Shirwan or Upper Diyala River. The problem was solved by loading sufficient tarpaulins, wire rope, cordage and pickets on to mules to make large " sausages " of dried reeds when the Shirwan was reached. While the infantry cut reeds, the Sappers dug " graves " in the ground. These they lined with tarpaulins and filled with reeds, finally folding over the edges of the tarpaulins and lashing and extracting the " sausages " so formed. The " sausages " were afterwards grouped into rafts for a flying bridge.

In June 1919, the unrest in Southern Kurdistan upset the tribes to the north and north-east of the Mosul *Wilayat*. The Political Officer at Amadiya made good his escape, and insurgents occupied that place and also Zakho, from which our garrison had been withdrawn. In the absence of General Fraser at Sulaimaniya, Major-General R. A. Cassels took instant action to prevent the spread of rebellion. A brigade, under Brig.-General M. R. W. Nightingale, was assembled at Suwaira, 25 miles from Amadiya, and another, under Brig.-General H. W. Wooldridge, at Zakho, to traverse all adjacent areas and restore order. This was not accomplished without severe fighting, particularly near Suwaira, but by the middle of September the Northern Kurds had been subdued so effectively that they gave little trouble during the Arab Rebellion in 1920. The 8th Company, Bengal S. & M., then at Mosul, took some part in these operations, but its duties call for no special remark. The outbreak in the north gave a clear indication of the explosive nature of the general atmosphere, a condition fostered by British military weakness and Turkish and Syrian intrigue. Propaganda from Syria soon caused trouble on the Upper Euphrates where, on December 13th, 1919, insurgents occupied distant Dair ez Zaur after the escape of an isolated Political Officer. This *coup* lowered British prestige along the entire Euphrates. The Sapper and Miner units, however, were not affected by political considerations and continued steadily their normal work of road, railway and camp construction. Towards the end of the year they came under the direction of Major-

[1] *Behind the Scenes in Many Wars*, by Lieut.-Gen. Sir George MacMunn, K.C.B., K.C.S.I., D.S.O., p. 294.

[2] Notes by Col. R. H. Dewing, D.S.O., M.C., late R.E., sent to the author on May 26th, 1937.

General E. H. de V. Atkinson, late R.E., who arrived from home to assume charge of all military and civil engineering works in Iraq.

Late in January, 1920, Lieut.-General Sir George MacMunn vacated the supreme command, and on March 24th Lieut.-General Sir Aylmer Haldane arrived as the new Commander-in-Chief. Haldane's position was most difficult. Though a distinguished soldier, he was not young and he lacked experience of Indian troops. His combatant force amounted to less than 35,000 men, and with this he had to maintain order in an enormous country, guard 14,000 Turkish prisoners-of-war and quantities of stores and ammunition, and provide for the safety of 550 British women, the wives of British officers and other ranks, together with their 400 children. MacMunn had agreed that these families should be allowed to come to Iraq, and preparations had already been made to move them to Karind in the Persian Hills before the hot weather. A standing camp at Karind was completed by Lieut.-Colonel H. S. Gaskell, R.E., C.R.E. Persian Line of Communication, on April 19th, the day before the first families arrived.[1] Much of the work at Karind was done in severe cold by the 65th Company, Madras S. & M., under Captain A. H. Morse, R.E., who records that, as most of his men had never seen snow, he had to teach them how to restore the circulation in their fingers by swinging their arms across their bodies.[2] Saddled, against his will, with the responsibility of housing and protecting nearly 1,000 women and children at Karind, Haldane decided that he and his Staff would benefit also by visits to the Persian Hills and established a summer headquarters at Sar-i-Mil, 4 miles from Karind. The two camps cost so much that they inspired a captious critic to pen the following lines :—[3]

Half a lakh, half a lakh,
Half a lakh squandered !
Up to the Persian Hills,
G.H.Q. wandered,
Lured on by Hambro's brains,
Egged on by Julian's pains,
Pushed on by Lubbock's trains,
G.H.Q. wandered.

* * * * *

Honour the brave and bold,
Taxpayer, young and old,
Who, although never told,
Paid by the hundred.

[1]Notes by Maj.-Gen. H. S. Gaskell, C.B., D.S.O., late R.E., sent to Maj.-Gen. Sir Theodore Fraser, K.C.B., C.S.I., C.M.G., late R.E., on July 27th, 1939.

[2]Notes by Lieut.-Col. A. H. Morse, R.E., sent to the author on Sept. 23rd, 1937.

[3]*Truth*, Jan. 19th, 1921, as quoted in *Alarms and Excursions in Arabia*, by Bertram Thomas, pp. 72, 73. Brig.-Gen. P. O. Hambro was B. G. Administration, Col. O. R. A. Julian was P.M.O., and Brig.-Gen. G. Lubbock, late R.E., was Director of Railways.

Think of the camp they made,
Think of the water laid
On, and the golf links made,
Think of the bill we paid.
Oh, the wild charge they made!
Half a lakh squandered!

The families remained in Karind until September, 1920, when they were evacuated with difficulty to Baghdad and so to India. The camps at Karind and Sar-i-Mil gave much extra labour to the Sappers and Miners and entailed a diversion of troops at a critical period.

Late in 1919, a remarkable engineering work was planned in Mosul. In order that the 18th Division should be able to maintain easy control over the trans-Tigris Kurdish tribes and keep in touch with its outposts at Zakho and elsewhere, it was essential that the existing Arab boat bridge at Mosul should be replaced by a pontoon bridge sufficiently strong to survive the heavy floods caused by melting snows. Accordingly, Lieut.-Colonel J. F. Turner, R.E., C.R.E. 18th Division, proceeded to design a structure on most original lines. At the point selected for the bridge, the Tigris was 524 feet in width at low level and 710 feet in flood, with a rise and fall of no less than 30 feet. The probable maximum flood speed was estimated at first as 12 knots, but actually it was found later to reach the almost incredible figure of 25 *knots!* From experience gained on the Gomal River in Waziristan, where the recorded velocity was even greater, Turner knew that under such conditions the unstable bed of the Tigris would be in constant motion and that no upstream anchor would hold. Consequently, he designed the floating portion of his structure as a *suspension bridge on its side* and so earned for it the sobriquet of "*Turner's Folly*."[1] When the first flood came down, the inhabitants of Mosul lined the banks to see the collapse of the bridge, and villagers waited downstream to retrieve the debris; but they were disappointed, for "Turner's Folly" held for seven years until it was washed away in 1928 after being neglected for a long time by the local Municipal authorities.

The erection of the Mosul Bridge was begun on September 24th, 1920, and the roadway was opened to traffic on February 14th, 1921.[2] As three companies of Bengal Sappers and Miners were employed for months in preparing material and building the bridge, some details of the structure may be given. Including the trestled portions, it was 815 feet in length and capable of carrying loaded armoured cars. The floating portion was anchored by horizontal catenary cables, supported on 24 floats and leading to massive concrete shore-anchorages. Three catenaries were provided, each of seven 3-inch wire ropes bound together with wire. Of these, an upstream cable rested normally on cantilevers projecting from the bows of the floats, its purpose being merely to anchor the floats, which were decked-in wooden boats, 24 feet in length, designed to swing easily

[1]Notes by Col. Sir John F. Turner, C.B., D.S.O., late R.E., sent to the author on Aug. 31st, 1945.
[2]Notes by Lieut.-Col. V. E. G. Guinness, R.E., sent to the author on June 18th, 1938.

to any change of direction in the current. Two downstream cables rested normally on the sterns of the floats, and from these, wire cables, adjustable in length, were taken to the bows of the pontoons. All three catenaries were attached to the floats by wire rope slings with sufficient play to rise clear of the floats in periods of very low water. The pontoons were wooden boats, 40 feet long, 10 feet wide and 6 feet high, and were formed into rafts connected by wooden Warren girders which carried transoms, road bearers and decking. The width of the roadway between the girders was only 8 feet, but footways were built outside. In the centre of the bridge, specially long girders allowed adjustment of the total length as the river rose or fell. Nets containing rocks were used as downstream anchors. Unfortunately, most of the available timber was Australian Jarrah wood, badly seasoned and liable to split and warp, and all materials had to be transported by lorries along 80 miles of desert track from rail-head at Sharqat. The pontoons and floats were covered with canvas, painted with crude oil, but nevertheless they were liable to leak and needed constant attention and frequent repair. The pontoons, floats, cables and superstructure were made in Mosul by the 2nd, 6th and 8th Companies, Bengal S. & M., the 6th Company being concerned mostly with the pontoons.[1] The concrete anchorages were built by a contractor. The 6th Company, assisted by a Works Company and Arab labour, was responsible for the erection of the bridge during the early stages and was joined later by the 2nd and 8th Companies. The Mosul Bridge, however, was built after the Arab Rebellion, and it is necessary now to revert to the period before the rebellion when its design was under consideration.

Several changes occurred in the Sapper and Miner establishment in Iraq and Iran during the latter part of 1919 and the spring and early summer of 1920. No. 1 Bridging Train, Bengal S. & M., returned to Roorkee in June, 1919, and the 85th Company in January, 1920. The 5th Company and 5th Field Troop left Iran and Iraq in March, 1920, the former being replaced by the 7th Company (Lieutenant E. A. Crane, R.E.). Of the Madras Corps, the 64th Company (Lieutenant R. E. Wood, R.E.) arrived in March to relieve the 12th Company; in May, the 8th Field Troop (Lieutenant A. M. Cameron, R.E.) relieved the 2nd Field Troop, and in June, the 67th Company (Lieutenant W. H. Knox, R.E.) replaced the 13th Company. Regrouping was the order of the day. The relieved units were under strength and in need of a change of scene. Other companies, such as the 2nd, 6th and 8th (Bengal), the 9th (Madras) and the 19th (Bombay), all with considerable experience to their credit, were destined to see more fighting in the arid plains of Iraq, or the rugged mountains of Iran, before their turn came to say goodbye.

This is no place to deal at length with the causes of the Arab Rebellion. They were many and far reaching. Insufficient and widely dispersed garrisons, loss of prestige through the unfortunate incident at Dair ez Zaur in December, 1919, delay in a final peace settlement with Turkey, the sudden imposition of a system of government foreign to the Arabs,

[1]Notes by Lieut.-Col. F. G. Drew, O.B.E., R.E., sent to the author on Dec. 24th, 1937.

FLOATING BRIDGE UNDER CONSTRUCTION OVER THE RIVER TIGRIS AT MOSUL, JANUARY, 1921.

the premature aspirations of these people towards self-determination, anti-British propaganda from many sources, the inexperience of young Political Officers, a reduction in the controlling power of the Arab Shaikhs, and the effect of the proximity of the holy cities of Karbala and Najaf, overflowing with religious fanatics—all these factors were instrumental in applying the spark to the magazine.

The first outbreak occurred in the north on June 4th, 1920, at Tel Afar, a desert town 40 miles west of Mosul and far from the Euphrates, where a band of 200 Sherifians from Aleppo murdered some British officers and incited the inhabitants to advance with them against Mosul. A small column from Mosul soon restored order, but the incident gave warning of things to come and our troops lost no time in fortifying Tel Afar, which served later as a valuable *point d'appui* during operations in the northern desert.[1] The prompt action taken against this Turkoman centre had an excellent effect throughout the Mosul *Wilayat*. Arab attempts to combine were nipped in the bud by small, but very mobile, columns radiating from Mosul under the orders of General Fraser—a system which differed radically from that adopted in the Baghdad and Basra *Wilayats*. The 2nd Company, Bengal S. & M., under Captain F. G. Drew, R.E., shared in this process of "showing the flag," and very effectively too, especially on one occasion when it was mistaken for a battery of artillery. Drew records that he found several Christian villages and was often addressed in broad Yankee by men who had been to America. A proposal by Sir Arnold Wilson that Zakho should be evacuated was opposed by General Fraser and small garrisons were maintained there and at Tel Afar. Fraser was advised to encircle Mosul with a complete girdle of blockhouses and wire, as planned for Baghdad, but he had other ideas on the subject of protection and was content to place obstacles on only a few main approaches and to build blockhouses to dominate them. This system proved most effective and was so economical in troops that he was able later to send nearly two brigades to Southern Iraq and to agree to the abolition, for six weeks, of his only line of communication with Baghdad while his men lived on local resources. Thus the 18th Division in the north contributed materially towards the ultimate victory of the 17th Division, the "River Area" formations and strong reinforcements from India which fought in the south.

Owing to difficulties of communication, British influence in Iraq, even before the rebellion, was limited practically to the banks of the Tigris from Basra to Samarra, 80 miles north of Baghdad.[2] The single line of metre-gauge railway which, starting from Basra, followed the Euphrates by way of Nasiriya, Samawa, Rumaitha and Diwaniya to Hilla and thence ran due north to Baghdad, was frequently washed away by floods, and a journey over it from Basra to Baghdad occupied at least two days. The alternative was the Tigris River route where transit by ship might occupy

[1]Notes by Maj.-Gen. Sir Theodore Fraser, K.C.B., C.S.I., C.M.G., late R.E., sent to the author on Aug. 10th, 1945.

[2]"The Arab Insurrection of 1920–21," by Capt. C. M. P. Durnford, appearing in *The Journal of the United Service Institution of India*, Vol. LIV, April, 1924, pp. 181–193.

from five to fifteen days, or rather less if the journey were completed by using a narrow-gauge railway on the left bank connecting Kut al Amara with the capital. River transport on the Euphrates was restricted to small country craft. Some areas of Iraq could not be reached from the Tigris, others were inaccessible from the railway, and there were areas which could not be served by either rail or river transport. The railway rolling-stock was inadequate and many of the Indian drivers ill-disciplined. General Haldane describes how the driver of a mail train once refused to leave a wayside station until he had had a hot bath, and this in full view of the fuming passengers ![1] With such defective means of communication, Haldane was responsible not only for the safety of Iraq but also of the British forces in North-Western Iran which were trying to check a Bolshevik infiltration. These forces amounted, at the moment, to an Indian mixed brigade and some line of communication troops with headquarters at Kasvin, and reinforcements took three weeks to reach them from Baghdad over a single line of narrow-gauge railway to Quraitu and thence along hundreds of miles of track through mountainous country. After all necessary reductions had been made in his fighting strength, Haldane had only 4,200 British and 30,000 Indian troops available for duty, and when the Arab Rebellion started, his mobile force amounted to only 500 British and 3,000 Indian soldiers, of which the British alone were in a position to reach the Middle Euphrates promptly.[2] Was there ever a more deplorable state of unreadiness ? But Haldane himself was not to blame. The onus of responsibility must be sought at a much higher level.

On June 30th, 1920, a trivial incident lighted the fire of rebellion on the Euphrates. This occurred at Rumaitha on the Hilla branch of the river about 28 miles upstream from Samawa. Some Arabs fired on the local Political Officer, and others tore up the railway line to the south. The small garrison was besieged, and a relief column, despatched southwards from Diwaniya, was compelled to withdraw. The railway was soon cut in other places, and on July 4th, Samawa also was isolated. General Haldane was still in Iran, but he returned to Baghdad on the 7th and directed General Fraser to send from Tikrit two Indian battalions, a howitzer battery and some details. The garrison of Karind was reduced, and other centres were combed for reinforcements. As the defenders of Rumaitha reported that their rations would be exhausted by July 12th, a strong column under Brig.-General F. E. Coningham, including the 61st Company, Madras S. & M., was despatched by rail from Baghdad to Diwaniya, and, four days later, was within 16 miles of Rumaitha. On the 20th, Coningham relieved Rumaitha, evacuated the garrison, and retired northwards to Diwaniya.[3] The political state of the country, according to Haldane, was now like a sheet of parchment which rises at any point

[1] *The Insurrection in Mesopotamia*, 1920, by Lieut.-Gen. Sir Aylmer L. Haldane, G.C.M.G., K.C.B., D.S.O., p. 71.

[2] *Mesopotamia*, 1917–1920. *A Clash of Loyalties*, by Lieut.-Col. Sir Arnold T. Wilson, K.C.I.E., C.S.I., C.M.G., D.S.O., p. 272.

[3] For details of the part taken by the Madras Sapper units in the operations in Iraq during and after the Arab Rebellion in 1920 see *Q.V.O. Madras Sappers and Miners in France and Iraq*, 1914–1920, Part II.

where a weight is lifted from its surface. Rebellion might occur anywhere, at any time, and there was no knowing to what extent an eruption might spread. Indeed, for the next two months, the British forces in Iraq were faced with complete disaster, and Haldane records that never on the Western Front did he suffer such mental strain as during this period in Baghdad. His meagre strength was spread over an area larger than the United Kingdom, and his elusive enemy could destroy or block almost every line of supply.

At the outbreak of the Arab Rebellion the Sapper and Miner units in Iraq and Iran were located as follows:—With the 17th Division, the 9th 61st, 64th and 67th Companies, Madras S. & M. (Major E. Bradney and Lieutenants A. B. D. Edwards, R. E. Wood and W. H. Knox, R.E.); and, with the 18th Division, the 2nd, 6th and 8th Companies, Bengal S. & M. (Captains F. G. Drew and V. E. G. Guinness and Lieutenant A. M. Cameron, R.E.), and the 8th Field Troop, Madras S. & M. (Captain R. H. B. Longland, R.E.), which was attached to the 7th Cavalry Brigade. No. 2 Bridging Train, Bengal S. & M., was on the Euphrates. In North-Western Iran was the 19th Company, Bombay S. & M. (Captain C. F. Stoehr, R.E.), and behind it, on the Persian line of communication, the 7th and 52nd Companies, Bengal S. & M. (Lieutenants E. A. Crane and H. N. Obbard, R.E.), and the 65th Company, Madras S. & M. (Captain A. H. Morse, R.E.). Reinforcements which arrived in August from India included the 11th, 63rd and 69th Companies, Madras S. & M. (Captain M. Luby, R.E., Lieutenant E. E. G. L. Searight, R.E., and Captain A. B. Cullen, I.A.R.O.), and these were attached to a newly formed 6th Division under Major-General G. N. Cory. The 26th and 28th Railway Companies, S. & M., also made their appearance. Though the reinforcements came after the crisis had passed, they were none the less welcome. Most of the engineering work during the rebellion fell to the Madras Sapper units in the Euphrates Valley. Few Bengal Sappers, and none from the Bombay Corps, were concerned. The work consisted chiefly of building blockhouses along railway lines, providing and operating ferries, improving roads, demolishing villages, arranging water-supplies and constructing defences around important bases. The Sapper companies were often assisted by Pioneer battalions and usually by Arab labour. Their duties were largely of a routine nature, but they were carried out under exceptionally arduous conditions.

After the rescue of the Rumaitha garrison, Haldane began to experience the full weight of conflicting military and civil requirements. "The Political Officer," he writes,[1] "would like to scatter broadcast the forces, often small in number, which are available for the maintenance of order. In fact, he sees no harm in being weak everywhere and strong nowhere." The indictment is perhaps exaggerated, for the Political Officers were mostly ex-soldiers with some experience of war, but Haldane was

[1] *The Insurrection in Mesopotamia*, 1920, by Lieut.-Gen. Sir Aylmer L. Haldane, G.C.M.G., K.C.B., D.S.O., p. 92.

justifiably anxious and could not see altogether eye to eye with Sir Percy Cox and Sir Arnold Wilson. The despatch of troops from Hilla for the relief of Rumaitha was followed by a rising in the Hilla District where a section of the Bani Hasan tribe seized Kifl on July 20th, thus necessitating a display of force in that direction. Some 21 miles south of Hilla lay Kufa, whose garrison kept watch on the fanatical elements in the adjacent holy city of Najaf. Three sections of the 67th Company, Madras S. & M., and a detachment of No. 2 Bridging Train, Bengal S. & M., were in Hilla, but there were no Sappers and Miners at Kufa.

On July 23rd, 1920, a small mixed column consisting mostly of the 2nd Battalion, The Manchester Regiment, moved from Hilla towards Kifl, and on the following day, in extreme heat, reached a position within 5 miles of the place. There, it was heavily attacked, and its commander decided to withdraw after dark. In the course of this movement the transport stampeded, the Manchester battalion lost its way, and only a portion of the column regained Hilla. The immediate effect of this disaster was to bring to a head the trouble brewing on the Middle Euphrates. Sound strategy now dictated a withdrawal from Diwaniya, for the powerful Muntafiq confederation of tribes to the east and south might at any moment take the field against us. General Haldane asked for another division from India, with subsidiary formations including five companies of Sappers and Miners. He began to be concerned seriously about the safety of Baghdad itself, and accompanied by his Chief Engineer, Major-General E. H. de V. Atkinson, selected sites for defensive works around the city. Troops and stores were moved from the Daura and Hinaidi cantonments, 12 miles downstream, and were concentrated in and around Baghdad, and, by the middle of August, the capital was secure behind a formidable wire obstacle and 40 blockhouses on a perimeter of 16 miles. Brig.-General G. A. F. Sanders, late R.E., was concerned in this project which was carried out by the 9th Company, Madras S. & M., and other troops and civilian labour gangs, under the direction of Lieut.-Colonel A. B. Carey, R.E.

After the disaster to the Manchester column, Brig.-General F. E. Coningham prepared to evacuate Diwaniya, for his troops at that place, and a brigade at Hilla, were already threatened by 80,000 armed Arabs. A section of the 67th Company, Madras S. & M., was sent from Hilla with some infantry to reinforce an outpost guarding the Jarbuiya railway bridge across the Euphrates as this would be of vital importance in a withdrawal. Coningham began his retreat on July 30th while the 61st Company, Madras S. & M., repaired small bridges on the line. On the 31st he encountered a breach in the track, 350 yards in length, and beyond it a badly damaged bridge, but under the supervision of Brig.-General G. Lubbock, late R.E., hundreds of sleepers were removed from behind the rearmost of Coningham's two trains and carried forward to repair the gap, and thus, although his progress was painfully slow, and continued to be so during the succeeding days, he reached Hilla on August 9th. " From the date," writes Haldane, "when the news of the disaster to the Manchester column was received at Baghdad until a message came announcing Brig.-General Coningham's arrival at the Jarbuiya bridge, a period of 12 days, I can recall, in my military career, no cycle of quite such tense anxiety. Not only at this period, but for several weeks, the situation of affairs was critical, and visions of the siege and fall of Khartoum sometimes flitted through my mind."[1]

With Hilla securely held, operations were next undertaken in a northerly direction, since the relief of the besieged garrison of Kufa could not be attempted until the Baghdad-Hilla railway had been provided with blockhouses and repaired sufficiently to permit the transit of supplies and of bridging material for crossing the Euphrates. The new objective was the Hindiya Barrage, where the Euphrates bifurcates into the Hilla and Hindiya branches some 40 miles south of Falluja. The rebels had seized the Barrage and were accordingly in a position to cut off the water-supply to Hilla and several stations on the railway. A mixed brigade under Brig.-General H. A. Walker left Hilla by rail on August 10th, bound for Musayib, upstream of the Barrage, and followed by a smaller force to repair the line and cover the construction of blockhouses. The 61st and half the 67th Companies, Madras S. & M., accompanied the columns. Walker occupied Musayib on August 12th and recovered the Hindiya Barrage on the following day. By threatening to cut off the water-supply to Karbala he could then ensure that the fanatical inhabitants of that city gave no trouble. The Baghdad–Hilla railway was already being repaired and defended by an organization under Brig.-General G. A. F. Sanders, late R.E., which, working from both ends, completed the construction of 300 blockhouses by August 19th. The 9th Company worked from the Baghdad end, and half the 67th Company from the Hilla end. Similar work followed on the Baghdad–Baquba and Baghdad–Kut lines, and the advanced base at Hilla was surrounded by a cordon of 32 blockhouses. Nevertheless, the proclamation of a *Jihad*, responsibility for the safety of the families at Karind, and the continued spread of insurrection, prevented any early attempt by Haldane to relieve Kufa and caused him to approve the withdrawal of the outpost guarding the important Jarbuiya Bridge. The rebels were then in complete possession of 200 miles of railway between Samawa and Hilla. They had shattered the Euphrates line of communication, and Haldane had only a haphazard connection between Basra and Baghdad by way of the Tigris.

Meanwhile, on August 6th, 1920, signs of unrest had appeared north-east of Baghdad. These ominous indications spread rapidly among the tribes north of the Diyala River and extended, by the end of the month, to Kirkuk and Erbil. Sporadic attacks were made on our outposts on the Baghdad-Quraitu railway and the branch line to Kingarban, but energetic action by Colonel J. H. F. Lakin, O.C. Persian Line of Communication,

[1] *The Insurrection in Mesopotamia*, 1920, by Lieut.-Gen. Sir Aylmer L. Haldane, G.C.M.G., K.C.B., D.S.O., p. 139. The siege of Khartoum, with special reference to General Gordon's defences, is described in *The Royal Engineers in Egypt and the Sudan*, by the present author, pp. 122–146.

helped to localize the rebellion. In the middle of August Lakin organized a small mixed force near Khaniqin under Lieut.-Colonel H. S. Gaskell, R.E., to restore order, and with it was the 65th Company, Madras S. & M. Gaskell reoccupied Khaniqin, and marching southwards along the railway with some 400 rifles, a troop of irregular cavalry and a couple of mountain guns, relieved a besieged post at Qaraghan on August 24th.[1] Two sections of the 65th Company, under Captain C. F. Scott-Ruffle, I.A.R.O., were attacked on the following day by 300 tribesmen while building a post to cover a railway bridge between Qaraghan and Khaniqin, but Gaskell, who happened to be present, broke through the insurgents on a locomotive under heavy fire and, making for a station near Khaniqin, brought back 130 rifles and relieved the Sappers who had held their own for over two hours.[2] On the 27th, reinforced from Qaraghan, Gaskell reconnoitred southwards and repaired the railway as far as Qizil Ribat. These minor operations were important because they helped to restore in part the interrupted railway communication with Iran, and incidentally they afforded the Madras Sappers an opportunity to use their rifles with good effect.

Further operations on a larger scale were undertaken from Baquba. Two columns advanced northwards, one under Brig.-General F. E. Coningham, which included a detachment of No. 2 Bridging Train, Bengal S. & M., and the other under Brig.-General G. A. H. Beatty with the 9th Company, Madras S. & M. Coningham re-occupied Shahraban on September 8th, and after all railway repairs had been completed, it became possible at last to evacuate the families from Karind. On the 22nd the first trainload of women and children reached Baquba, whence they were sent to Baghdad and afterwards to India. The branch line to Kingarban was re-opened for traffic before the end of the month, and General Haldane was then free to direct his full attention to events on the Euphrates.

No trouble had occurred near Baghdad until August 12th, when Lieut.-Colonel G. E. Leachman, a Political Officer who had served with great distinction since the beginning of Townshend's advance in 1915,[3] was murdered in an Arab encampment between Baghdad and Falluja on the Euphrates. This crime was followed by a series of outbreaks between Falluja and Hit, further up the river. On August 15th, a supply convoy of three steamers set out downstream from Ramadi for Falluja, escorted by a defence vessel in which was a section of the 67th Company, Madras S. & M., under Lieutenant A. W. H. Woods, R.E. After covering some 10 miles it ran into an ambush, and for five hours, Woods and his men put up a stout resistance and suffered 13 casualties, but ammunition then ran short and the ships were boarded and looted by 400 Arabs. Woods and the Muhammadan ranks, stripped of everything, were allowed to make their way back to Ramadi, and the Hindus were marched off as prisoners. It is satisfactory to record that, a fortnight later, the Hindus escaped and

[1] Notes by Maj.-Gen. H. S. Gaskell, C.B., D.S.O., late R.E., sent to Maj.-Gen. Sir Theodore Fraser, K.C.B., C.S.I., C.M.G., late R.E., on July 27th, 1939.

[2] *Historical Record of the Q.V.O. Madras Sappers and Miners*, Vol. II (2), p. 11.

[3] See *In Kut and Captivity*, by the present author.

rejoined the 67th Company. During the fight, after Woods had been incapacitated, Jemadar Krishnasami took command, and, when all ammunition had been exhausted, threw the rifles into the river.[1] The capture of this convoy raised the morale of the insurgents and called for instant action to reopen communication between Baghdad and Falluja. This task was entrusted to Brig.-General Sanders, and on September 3rd, the 11th Company, Madras S. & M., with a suitable escort, began to repair the road and railway and worked so well that an armoured train got through to Falluja three weeks later. Blockhouses were then built along the Baghdad-Falluja line, and with the completion of 173 blockhouses along the Baghdad-Kut line, the railways radiating from the capital were adequately protected.

Operations could now, at last, be undertaken to effect the relief of the small garrison of Kufa on the Lower Euphrates, which had been besieged since July 21st, and also to avenge the loss of the unfortunate defence vessel *Firefly*,[2] which had been sunk there on August 17th. A 55th Brigade Column under Brig.-General H. A. Walker, which included the 61st and 67th Companies, Madras S. & M., was detailed to relieve Kufa and recover some prisoners, and a 53rd Brigade Column under Brig.-General G. A. F. Sanders, late R.E., including the 9th Company, Madras S. & M., was directed to occupy Tuwairij on the Hindiya Branch and to threaten Karbala. Both columns began to advance from Hilla on October 6th, the Sappers being employed chiefly in building blockhouses and erecting wire entanglements. The rebels offered some resistance at Tuwairij and set fire to the boat bridge, but two sections of the 9th Company, under Major E. Bradney, R.E., advanced across the burning bridge with some infantry, extinguished the flames, and took part in the occupation of the town. This action quelled all insurrectionary activities in Karbala and also made bridging material from Hilla available for use by Walker in the operations for the relief of Kufa. The pontoons reached Kifl on the 15th, and after a detachment of No. 2 Bridging Train, Bengal S. & M., had bridged the Euphrates, the 55th Brigade Column crossed and relieved Kufa on October 17th, 1920.

We turn now to the course of the rebellion in the "River Area" of Southern Iraq, where disturbances occurred in June, 1920, chiefly around Samawa on the Euphrates and along the railway to north and south. Small garrisons held Samawa, Nasiriya and the railway junction of Ur, 9 miles from the latter, the garrison of Samawa being commanded by Major A. S. Hay, 31st Lancers. Early in July, a defence vessel, the *Greenfly*, reached Samawa from Nasiriya, but on her return journey she ran aground above Khidhr on August 10th and became a total wreck. The railway between Khidhr and Samawa was damaged daily by insurgents and it was evident that the garrison of Samawa would have to stand a siege, though a

[1] *Historical Record of the Q.V.O. Madras Sappers and Miners*, Vol. II (2), p. 11.

[2] As "H.M. Gunboat *Firefly*," she had had a chequered career. She was the only modern fighting ship with Gen. Townshend in his advance on Baghdad in Nov., 1915. She was captured by the Turks during the retreat from Ctesiphon and recaptured by Gen. Maude in Feb., 1917, shortly before he took Baghdad (see *In Kut and Captivity*, by the present author).

few ships carrying supplies got through on the 26th. An outpost at the Barbuti bridge on the railway was attacked by rebel gangs, and on September 3rd an armoured train was derailed and captured after a gallant defence by two British officers and a few Indian soldiers, most of whom perished. The situation was so grave that General Haldane asked for two additional divisions, each with a cavalry brigade, since a rising of the powerful Muntafiq tribes between Kut al Amara and Nasiriya, which might occur at any moment, would imperil his only remaining line of communication with the sea, that by way of the Tigris, and might necessitate the reconquest of the whole of Iraq north of Basra.[1] In response, the Secretary of State for War, Mr. Winston Churchill, promised all possible aid, and strong reinforcements, though not on the scale demanded, were soon on their way. Meanwhile, Samawa was isolated and the crew of the stranded *Greenfly* beset by hostile Arabs.

Pending the arrival of an experienced Divisional Commander from overseas, Haldane selected his Engineer-in-Chief, Major-General E. H. de V. Atkinson, late R.E., to undertake the relief of Samawa, for he had the fullest confidence in Atkinson's ability and powers of organization. For the actual conduct of the military operations he chose Brig.-General F. E. Coningham, his most successful subordinate. The construction of blockhouses having been begun from Ur towards Samawa, a force under Coningham, comprising 5 battalions, 2 batteries, 2 squadrons and the 69th Company, Madras S. & M., marched on October 1st, 1920, from Nasiriya to Ur, where it was joined by General Atkinson and his Staff. The advance was accompanied by four trains, one armoured, two carrying water and the fourth with blockhouse materials. On October 4th, Atkinson reached Darraji, where he found that 2,500 sleepers and 1,000 yards of track had been removed, but in spite of this check he took Khidhr on the 6th after some stiff fighting and by October 12th was within 5 miles of Samawa. Blockhouse construction by the 69th Company kept pace with the advance, and similar work was undertaken by the 63rd Company which had arrived from the Tigris.[2] The column entered Samawa without serious opposition on October 14th, 1920, although 7,000 rebels were in the vicinity. Between September 8th and October 12th, the 63rd and 69th Companies built no less than 250 blockhouses, some of brick but most of sandbags and gabions.[3] It was responsible work, for the maintenance and defence of the railway were vital to the existence of the force, so the Sappers felt that they had had a considerable share in the success of the relief operations.

Meanwhile, in Mosul *Wilayat*, General Fraser's policy of providing small guards for railway stations and posts on roads and retaining a strong reserve for offensive operations had proved most effective. In June, the

[1] *The Insurrection in Mesopotamia*, 1920, by Lieut.-Gen. Sir Aylmer L. Haldane, G.C.M.G., K.C.B., D.S.O., p. 216.

[2] Since its arrival in Iraq on Aug. 20th, 1920, the 63rd Company, Madras S. & M., had been building blockhouses on the Baghdad-Kut Railway.

[3] The usual type of blockhouse was circular and about 20 ft. in diameter. It was surrounded by an apron of barbed wire. Inside was a 400-gallon water-tank. The roof consisted of a 160-lbs. tent.

BLOCKHOUSE CONSTRUCTION ON THE BASRA–SAMAWA RAILWAY DURING THE ARAB REBELLION IN IRAQ, SEPTEMBER, 1920.

63rd Company; Q.V.O. Madras Sappers and Miners, at work.

(By permission of Brig. E. E. G. L. Searight, O.B.E., M.C., late R.E.)

2nd Company, Bengal S. & M., was stationed at Hadraniya, a few miles up the Tigris from railhead at Sharqat, and was employed for six weeks in escorting road convoys working on the " meeting " system. It suffered 32 casualties on June 20th when the petrol tank of a lorry exploded while the Sappers were trying to extinguish a fire. Fraser rejected a proposal made on July 14th that, to effect an adequate concentration of troops for the defence of Baghdad, he should vacate the entire Mosul *Wilayat*, and subsequent events proved that he was right. Though Samarra was attacked twice, the rebels gained no success along the Tigris, but disturbances in the Diyala region spread during August to the Kurdish tribes around Kifri. A Policial Officer was murdered there, and the safety of the adjacent Kingarban railhead, and of the line of communication to Kirkuk, was endangered. A section of the widely scattered 64th Company, Madras S. & M., under Jemadar Rajagopal, which had moved with some infantry from Kingarban to Tuz, was besieged for 12 days in Tuz by 300 insurgents and had to repel several attacks with the bayonet. However, frequent bombing raids by our aeroplanes assisted the ground forces in restoring order, and after October it was necessary only to send out small columns to traverse doubtful areas. The 2nd, 6th and 8th Companies were then free to resume their work on Turner's bridge at Mosul.

After the relief of Samawa, Major-General G. N. Cory arrived from home and assumed command of the troops on the Lower Euphrates. These were then formed into a 6th Indian Division, and thus the memory of the famous division lost in Kut was revived. At the same time, Brig.-General G. A. F. Sanders replaced Major-General G. A. J. Leslie in command of the 17th Indian Division. Punitive operations, the disarmament of rebellious tribes, and the collection of fines from towns such as Samawa, Rumaitha, Najaf and Karbala, became the order of the day. The Sapper companies destroyed some buildings with guncotton,[1] but as their supply of explosives was limited, the usual method of demolishing walls was to cut them almost through at the base and then get a company of infantry to push them over. During November, a column of the 6th Division, including the 63rd and 69th Companies, Madras S. & M., and the 26th Railway Company, S. & M., advanced northwards from Samawa while another from the 17th Division moved southwards from Hilla to meet it. The 69th Company made a flying bridge at Samawa and a pontoon bridge at Rumaitha, and the 63rd Company ferried troops across the Euphrates at Khidhr. The extreme heat of summer had given place to severe frost, and the Sappers often worked in a cutting wind. By the end of the month, the only considerable area yet unvisited was the triangle Musayib-Falluja-Baghdad, so a column under Brig.-General B. E. C. Dent was despatched northwards from Hilla on December 2nd to meet another moving southwards from above Falluja. The 61st Company, Madras S. & M., was with Dent, and the 67th Company with the other

[1]The 9th Company, Madras S. & M., destroyed houses of prominent rebels in Karbala, and the 67th Company in Najaf and Kufa. At Najaf, the houses had cellars going down two or three storeys below ground level.

column, but they saw no fighting as there was no resistance. All the rebels had now submitted except a few around Diwaniya and these were quickly subdued by a column from Hilla under Brig.-General A. T. Paley which included the 9th Company, Madras S. & M., and a detachment of No. 2 Bridging Train, Bengal S. & M.

The policy of disarmament was difficult to enforce, and during January, 1921, the 17th Division alone had 8 columns in the field. However, by the end of the month it had collected nearly 53,000 rifles. Sheep and goats were often seized as " hostages " until redeemed by rifles. The rebels had removed some 160,000 railway sleepers in the Khidhr-Jarbuiya area and the return of what remained of this material was demanded. The process of " showing the flag " was extended even to the country between Kut al Amara and Nasiriya, usually known as the " Gharraf," where Khayun al Muntafiq, Shaikh of Shattra, had remained loyal throughout the rebellion. Brig.-General F. E. Coningham led a column northwards from Nasiriya and met another under Brig.-General B. E. C. Dent from Kut al Amara. The 63rd Company and half the 69th Company were with Coningham, and the 61st Company with Dent, and a junction was effected at Karradi on the Shatt al Hai. After seven months of marching and fighting the last embers of the Arab Rebellion were extinguished in February 1921 by a descent upon some obstreperous elements in Suq ash Suyukh below Nasiriya. The crushing of this widespread revolt was a fine achievement, a notable retrieval of a critical situation, and painful though it was, it helped Iraq to fit herself for the independence which she secured at a later date.

With order restored throughout the country, the need for a large garrison was removed, and many units, including Sapper and Miner formations, were withdrawn as early as possible to India. The 2nd and 8th Companies, Bengal S. & M., left Mosul at the end of January, 1921, when Major F. G. Drew, R.E., was the only individual in either unit who had served without leave since 1917. Drew had mobilized the 2nd Company in October 1917, taken it overseas, and commanded it for 3½ years, and on April 11th, 1921, he had the satisfaction of marching it back to its lines in Roorkee with the 8th Company. No. 2 Bridging Train did not reach Roorkee until June, 1921, followed by the 6th Company in July, and the 7th Company remained overseas until April, 1922. Of the Madras Sappers, the 61st Company left Iraq in March, 1921, the 9th and 12th Companies in April, the 64th and 67th Companies and No. 8 Field Troop in May, and the 11th and 13th Companies in June. Some of these units had been in Iran and consequently had not been concerned in the operations in Iraq. The 69th Company was retained in Iraq until April, 1922, and the unfortunate 63rd Company was still there in 1923 for it had been allocated permanently to the country.[1] The 26th and 28th Railway Companies, S. & M., left Iraq in May, 1921, the former to join the Bombay Corps and the latter to be disbanded.

Grandiose schemes for new works and thorough reorganization were

[1]This order, however, was not long in force owing to changes in the political situation.

launched in Iraq in 1921–22, but they were abandoned when it was decided that we should leave the country after peace had been concluded with Turkey. Some of these projects were ill-considered. For instance, that for a road from Baiji to Mosul to by-pass Sharqat and the difficult terrain around it. This scheme was proposed by a railway magnate from the Argentine named De Candolle,[1] who was said to be an expert though he had no local experience. The work was started, but as soon as the hard crust of the desert marl was broken, the road degenerated into a sea of dust or mud and the project was abandoned. Nevertheless, much work of a valuable nature was accomplished after the Arab Rebellion by the Works Directorate and the Sapper and Miner units still in the country, notably on communications, bridges, water-supply and housing. In February 1921, the 11th and 63rd Companies, Madras S. & M., were sent to Hinaidi, south of Baghdad, to continue the building of a new cantonment in conjunction with military and civil labour, and they worked there together until June, when the 11th Company returned to India. The 63rd Company continued its labours at Hinaidi where, from October 1921, the work consisted mostly of hangar erection for the Royal Air Force. No less than eight hangars were built in fourteen months, and three of these, completed by June 1922, were of the largest type, 203 feet by 103 feet and 50 feet high to the ridge. It is recorded that the Madras Sappers developed complete indifference to working at great heights and would walk quite unconcernedly along slender steel beams 40 feet above the ground.[2] In January, 1923, the company was transferred to Mosul at the time of a crisis with the Angora Government, and on March 18th it set out with a mixed brigade sent into Southern Kurdistan by Air Vice-Marshal Sir John Salmond to deal with the ubiquitous Shaikh Mahmud, who had reappeared in his old haunts. "Koicol," as it was called, passed through Erbil, and after reaching Koi Sanjak, north-west of Altun Kopri, on April 4th, operated for nearly a month in the mountains about Rowandiz before returning to Mosul.[3] The work of the 63rd Company was mostly of a routine nature, but useful, nevertheless, in improving communications.

* * * * *

In conclusion, we turn to North-Western Iran, where a company of Sappers and Miners was engaged in fighting the Bolsheviks while the units in Iraq were helping to subdue the Arab insurgents. The hostilities south of the Caspian Sea were influenced to some extent by those in Iraq, because the line of communication to Iran ran through Baghdad and Iraq was the sole source of reinforcement. The most advanced Sapper unit in North-Western Iran was the 19th Company, Bombay S. & M., under Captain C. F. Stoehr, R.E., with Lieutenants W. W. Boggs and E. A. L. Gueterbock, R.E., which had joined the headquarters of "Norperforce"

[1]De Candolle held the temporary rank of Maj.-General.

[2]"Hangar Erection in Iraq," by Maj. R. Hamilton, R.E., appearing in *The R.E. Journal*, Vol. XXXVIII, 1924, pp. 13–24.

[3]"The Operations in Southern Kurdistan, March–May, 1923," by Capt. R. G. Thurburn, appearing in *The Army Quarterly*, Vol. XXXI, Jan., 1936, pp. 264–277.

at Kasvin in April, 1919, soon after arrival from India.[1] The force then consisted of the 36th Indian Mixed Brigade and attached troops, under Brig.-General H. F. Bateman-Champain, with detachments to the north at Resht and at Enzeli on the Caspian, to the west at Zinjan, and to the south at Hamadan on the line of communication through Kermanshah to rail-head at Quraitu on the Irak border.[2] All was quiet in Iran during 1919 except for some fighting around Resht between Persian Cossacks and bands of local rebels under Kuchik Khan, in which we remained neutral. Indeed, when General MacMunn visited Enzeli in the summer he found that the only matter which troubled the commander of the Indian battalion stationed there was the insistence of the local Russian girls on indulging in mixed bathing with the troops while in a state of complete nudity! The 19th Company and civilian contractors built barracks at Kasvin, repaired roads and bridges, arranged water supplies, and made all preparations against a severe winter.

After the armistice with Turkey in 1918, we had occupied a line extending westwards from Merv, through Baku on the Caspian, to Batum on the Black Sea; but in August, 1919, when the Bolsheviks began to exert pressure, we withdrew from the Caucasus region. The White Russians under General Denikin, bitter opponents of the Bolsheviks, had a fleet of a dozen ships on the Caspian, but they lost their main sea-base when we evacuated Baku. Intrigue was rampant in Tehran, and we had grave doubts about the loyalty of Colonel Starosselsky, the Russian commander of the friendly Persian Cossacks in the capital. Weak everywhere, and surrounded by uncertain friends and possible foes, we had to resort in February 1920 to a policy of bluff, and when Denikin collapsed, it was decided that Enzeli could not be held against a strong attack and that a retirement to Kasvin might be necessary. Norperforce as a whole was to act as an outpost, though it was hoped that by maintaining for a time an advanced detachment at Enzeli we might postpone a serious attack. The Bolsheviks entered Baku on April 22nd, 1920, and Denikin's ships fled to Enzeli, where they were interned by us. At this time the garrison of Enzeli consisted of two battalions, some artillery and half the 19th Company, Bombay S. & M., under Lieutenant W. W. Boggs, R.E., and was installed in the suburb of Kazian at the harbour entrance. On May 18th, a Bolshevik fleet began to shell Enzeli, and General Bateman-Champain, confused by vague and sometimes conflicting instructions from the War Office, the Foreign Office, Iraq and India, had to decide at once on the best course of action. He chose to arrange an armistice, hand over Denikin's ships, and retire to Resht. From Resht, followed by the Bolsheviks, he retreated towards Manjil (or Menjil), a town on the Safid Rud, and the Bolsheviks installed a Red Government under Kuchik Khan at Resht. The withdrawal to Manjil was a serious blow to British prestige and involved the abandonment of valuable equipment and stocks of petrol.

[1]See *Sketch Maps of Operational Areas in Irak and Iran*, 1919–22, included in this chapter.

[2]At the end of 1918, "Norperforce" (formerly "Dunsterforce") had consisted of 2 brigades, but its strength had been reduced.

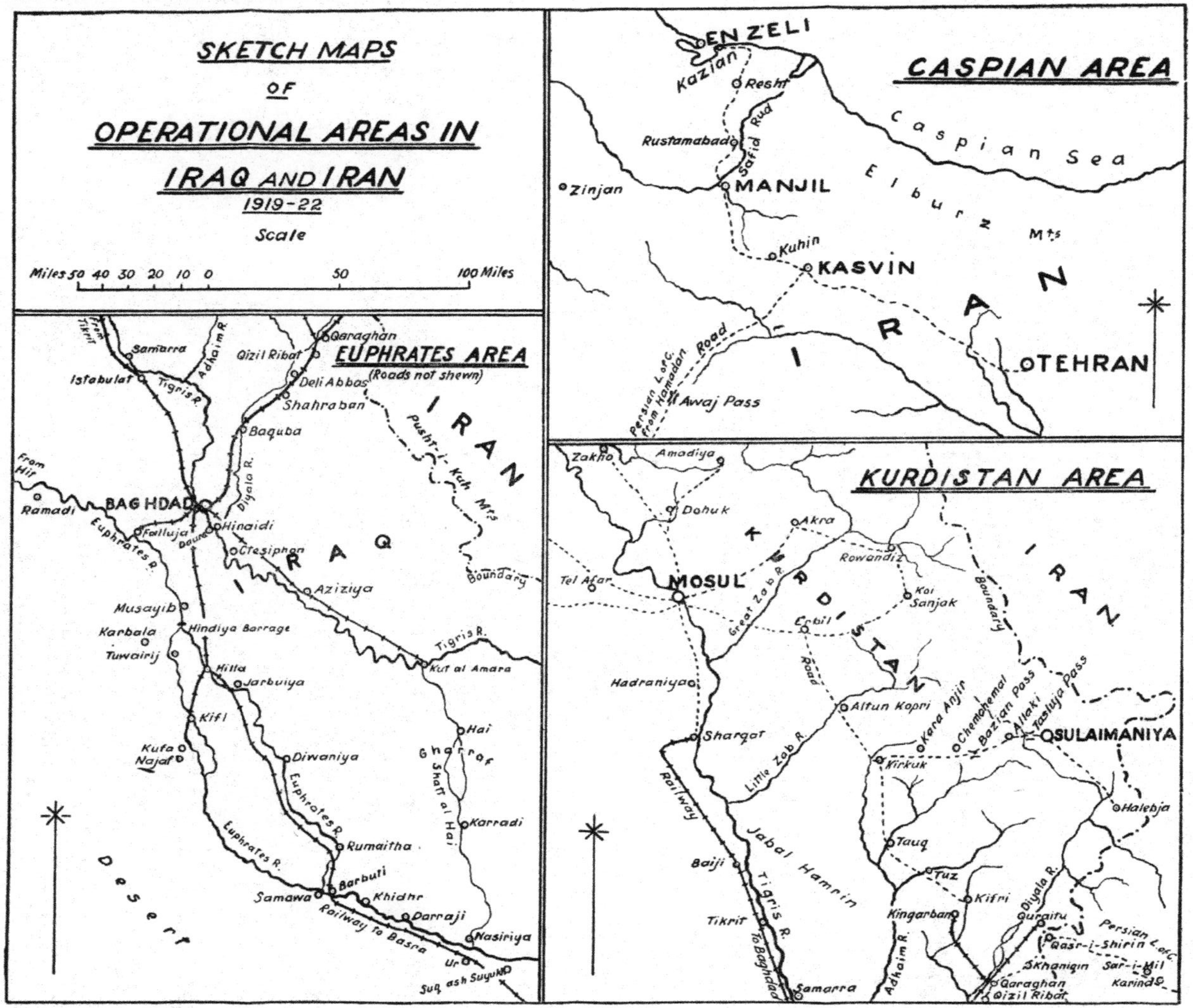
SKETCH MAPS
OF
OPERATIONAL AREAS IN
IRAQ AND IRAN
1919-22
Scale
Miles 50 40 30 20 10 0 50 100 Miles
EUPHRATES AREA
(Roads not shewn)
IRAN
IRAQ
Pusht-i-Kuh Mts
Boundary
From Tikrit
Samarra
Adhaim R.
Istabulat
Tigris R.
Qaraghan
Qizil Ribat
Deli Abbas
Shahraban
Baquba
Diyala R.
From Hit
Ramadi
BAGHDAD
Falluja
Hinaidi
Ctesiphon
Euphrates R.
Aziziya
Musayib
Hindiya Barrage
Karbala
Tuwairij
Hilla
Jarbuiya
Kut al Amara
Kifl
Kufa
Najaf
Diwaniya
Hai
Gharraf
Shatt al Hai
Karradi
Rumaitha
Barbuti
Samawa
Khidhr
Darraji
Railway to Basra
Nasiriya
Ur
Suq ash Suyukh
Desert
ENZELI
Kazian
Resht
CASPIAN AREA
Caspian Sea
Rustamabad
Safid Rud
Zinjan
MANJIL
Elburz Mts
Kuhin
KASVIN
IRAN
TEHRAN
Persian L. of C. from Hamadan
Road
Awaj Pass
Zakho
Amadiya
KURDISTAN AREA
Dohuk
Akra
KURDISTAN
Rowandiz
Tel Afar
MOSUL
Great Zab R.
Koi Sanjak
Boundary
Erbil
Road
Hadraniya
Altun Kopri
Kara Anjir
Chemchemal
Bazian Pass
Allaki
Tasluja Pass
SULAIMANIYA
Sharqat
Little Zab R.
Kirkuk
Railway
Halebja
Jabal Hamrin
Tauq
Baiji
Tigris R.
Tuz
Kifri
Diyala R.
Tikrit
Kingarban
Quraitu
Persian L. of C.
Qasr-i-Shirin
Khaniqin
Sar-i-Mil
To Baghdad
Samarra
Adhaim R.
Qaraghan
Qizil Ribat
Karind

In June, 1920, the rocky gorge of the Safid Rud at Manjil was crossed by an iron bowstring-girder bridge with a central span of 54 feet and three others of 100 feet. Here, under orders from General Haldane, Bateman-Champain formed a defensive position and held it with one battalion and a pack battery while another battalion was posted 10 miles in rear. The 19th Company prepared the 54-feet span for demolition and also an adjacent length of road along the face of a cliff.[1] In July, Norperforce called for reinforcements but could get none owing to the Arab Rebellion. Panic reigned in Tehran where the Persian Government anticipated a general British withdrawal from Iran. Some 2,000 Bolsheviks gradually surrounded Manjil, and on July 26th a party of the 19th Company under Boggs blew up with gunpowder the short length of cliff-road prepared for demolition, but this was ineffective in hindering the enemy because the site was not under fire from our guns. The demolition of the 54-feet span of the bridge produced a better obstacle. Bateman-Champain had decided already to evacuate Manjil and to withdraw the garrison (known as "Menjcol") to Kasvin, 70 miles in rear. The movement was begun, unobserved, on the night of July 30th–31st, and Kasvin was reached unmolested though with the loss of the supplies and tents abandoned at Manjil. The withdrawal was justifiable because Manjil was no longer of any strategic value and the road to it was highly dangerous. Also, Bateman-Champain was restricted to a passive defence for he was under stringent orders not to advance beyond Manjil. But Haldane was not pleased, and Sir Percy Cox viewed with some misgiving the probable political effects in Iran and Iraq. Bateman-Champain established an outpost line around Kasvin with a small advanced force stationed at Kuhin, 20 miles beyond it on the road to Manjil. His line of communication with Baghdad had been cut, and at any moment the Kurds might rise behind him. Yet, for the sake of prestige, he had to stand and fight the Bolsheviks at Kasvin although Great Britain was not at war with Russia and our declared policy was merely to help the Persian Government to keep internal order in Iran. He was told, however, that if the abandonment of Kasvin became inevitable he was to fall back on Hamadan despite the fact that this would render impossible the retention of Zinjan as a western outpost and would uncover Tehran.

After Menjcol had installed itself at Kasvin and Kuhin, the Bolsheviks advanced towards the latter place and were counterattacked on August 17th by Colonel Starosselsky's Persian Cossacks striking towards Resht, with Bateman-Champain co-operating as far as Manjil. The Bolsheviks were soon ambushed by a British column from Kuhin and fled in confusion, hotly pursued by the Cossacks, who occupied Resht on August 25th. Starosselsky now tried to push forward to Enzeli, but his men were repulsed and streamed back in disorder to Manjil, in advance of which Bateman-Champain had posted a force consisting of 2 battalions, some cavalry and artillery and half the 19th Company, Bombay S. & M., under Lieutenant E. A. L. Gueterbock, R.E. The Sappers were engaged at the

[1] "Engineer Work with Norperforce in 1919–20," by Maj. C. F. Stoehr, R.E., appearing in *The R.E. Journal*, Vol. XXXVIII, 1924, pp. 255–266.

time in building a trestle bridge, 100 yards in length, across the Safid Rud, using woodwork obtained from houses and ironwork from the girder bridge. The structure was completed within a week and proved very useful.[1] The trestles were anchored to a chain stretched across the river. By September 2nd, the Cossacks had recovered sufficiently to resume the offensive, and Starosselsky advanced again on Resht, which he reached on the 22nd. Meanwhile, the 19th Company had begun to repair the girder bridge, as the trestle bridge could not be expected to survive the first of the autumn floods. This was heavy work, for it involved the replacement of the demolished 54-feet span and the renewal of the entire roadway, which had been burnt by the Bolsheviks. However, a strutted structure of novel design was erected across the gap and the girder bridge was re-opened for traffic in the middle of October, some three weeks after the trestle bridge had been swept away.

It seemed now that, with our assistance, the Cossacks should be able to expel the Bolsheviks from North-Western Iran, but enforced inaction on our part had the effect of lowering the Cossack morale. The Bolsheviks, heavily reinforced, attacked from Enzeli on October 22nd and the Cossacks repeated their performance of August 25th and fled in disorder. Fortunately, Norperforce now had an exceptionally able commander in the person of Major-General Sir Edmund Ironside, who had arrived at the front early in October. Ironside interpreted so liberally his instructions not to advance far beyond Kasvin that he pushed forward a detachment to a position 12 miles beyond Manjil where, on October 26th, it met the advancing Bolsheviks. But he could go no further, and Menjcol accordingly began to improve its living accommodation in preparation for winter. Barrack accommodation for the remainder of Norperforce at Kasvin and Zinjan was easy to arrange, but half the 19th Company had great difficulty in housing Menjcol at Manjil, though it was accomplished in the end. Winter came, and except for a successful raid in November and a few patrol actions, military operations ceased everywhere and the activities of Norperforce were concentrated on clearing snow from the mountain passes traversed by the 460-mile length of road to the Irak railhead. The policy of the British Government was to withdraw the force entirely during the spring of 1921. Meanwhile, Ironside faced the Bolsheviks with confidence, for in Manjil, Kasvin and Zinjan he had 3 battalions of British infantry, 3 battalions of Indian infantry, a regiment of cavalry, 2 batteries of artillery and the 19th Company, Bombay S. & M., and on the line of communication to Iraq, other troops including three more battalions of Indian infantry, the 7th and 52nd Companies, Bengal S. & M., and the 65th Company, Madras S. & M.

The winter of 1920–21 proved to be exceptionally severe. At Kasvin, the ground was covered with snow from the middle of November and the 170 miles of road through Hamadan to Asadabad were often blocked for weeks on end. A Ford convoy took 52 days to reach Kasvin from Hamadan,

[1]Lecture by Capt. (now Gen. Sir) Miles C. Dempsey, Royal Berks Regt., delivered at the Staff College, Camberley, in 1930.

having been delayed for 32 days at the foot of the Awaj Pass, 70 miles from Kasvin. Thousands of Persian labourers were kept employed constantly in shovelling snow, which was often blown back by a strong wind as quickly as it was removed. A great storm on March 20th, 1921, marked the end of the winter, but it was not until nine days later that the road could be declared open for traffic.[1]

The withdrawal from the Manjil area began on April 9th, 1921, in unprecedented floods caused by melting snow. Gigantic boulders blocked the road, and whole mountain-sides appeared to be slipping. The girder bridge was prepared for demolition, but nature took a hand, and there was no need to use explosives, for the piers collapsed and the wreckage was swept down the gorge. Under Major-General G. N. Cory, who had succeeded General Ironside in command,[2] the withdrawal proceeded slowly but steadily with the 19th Company and gangs of Persian labourers clearing the way. Menjcol reached Kasvin on April 16th and, joined by other troops of Norperforce, withdrew to Hamadan. The 19th Company built or repaired a number of bridges, and finally, after four weeks of marching in good weather, the whole force entrained at Quraitu *en route* for Baghdad, Basra and India, which the 19th Company had not seen for 3½ years. The Persian Cossacks, thoroughly reorganized, undertook the tasks of opposing the Bolsheviks and restoring a semblance of order in Iran. They were led by an able Persian officer, one Reza Khan, who afterwards became King of Persia. No Sappers and Miners, however, served in North-Western Iran after the withdrawal of Norperforce, and accordingly the story of their adventures in that region ends earlier than in Iraq. The Arab in his native deserts was a more formidable foe than the Bolshevik invader of Iran, and the fighting in Iraq was certainly more bitter than that near the Caspian, but the Bombay Sappers were as glad to leave the Persian uplands as the Madras and Bengal Sappers were the dreary plains and swamps of the Tigris and Euphrates, and they received a great welcome when they returned at last to their headquarters in Kirkee.

[1] "Snow and Flood in North-West Persia," by Capt. C. F. Stoehr, R.E., appearing in *The R.E. Journal*, Vol. XXXVI, 1922, pp. 230–235.

[2] Maj.-Gen. Sir Edmund Ironside had been injured in an aeroplane accident in Iraq.

CHAPTER XXIV

PROGRESS IN WAZIRISTAN, OPERATIONS NEAR PESHAWAR AND IN BURMA, AND THE REORGANIZATION OF THE SAPPERS AND MINERS, 1922–1932.

DISCONTENT, the normal accompaniment of any sweeping change in civil administration, was prominent in British India when the Government of India Act of 1919 came into operation early in 1921. This measure had resulted from an enquiry conducted during the winter of 1917–18 by Mr. E. S. Montagu, the Secretary of State, and Lord Chelmsford, who had succeeded Lord Hardinge as Viceroy in 1916. Although it pledged England to set India on the road to self-government, with the ultimate goal of complete independence, the risks were great. A widespread and dangerous revolutionary movement began to spread over the country, and the " dyarchic " system of government showed grave defects. Yet the magnificent deeds of the Indian Army during the Great War demanded recognition, and thus an unique experiment in democracy was launched.

The political disturbances of 1919 and 1920 in Northern and Central India, and the rebellion in Malabar in 1921, indicated the explosive nature of the feeling among the people, and the subsequent operations in Waziristan proved that unrest had affected even the trans-border areas. H.R.H. The Duke of Connaught came to India in 1921 to open the new Provincial Legislative Councils, and, from November, 1921, to March, 1922, H.R.H. The Prince of Wales toured India and Burma. On March 13th, 1922, the Prince opened a Royal Military College at Dehra Dun for training young Indians for entry to Woolwich and Sandhurst with a view to qualifying for King's Commissions in the Indian Army. These praiseworthy gestures of friendship met with a mixed reception. In some places, during the Prince's visit, there was an outward display of enthusiasm : in others, a *hartal* (strike) with empty streets and closed shops. Parts of the Punjab were in disorder through the Akali movement among the Sikhs. The non-co-operative activities of Mr. Gandhi added to the unrest and were checked only by the increasing communal animosity between Hindus and Muhammadans which ultimately split the Congress Party in 1923. Such was the political setting in India and beyond its frontiers at the beginning of 1922 when Lord Reading, the new Viceroy, was given the formidable task of keeping order, reconciling hostile factions and introducing experimental reforms, while effecting, at the same time, the utmost financial retrenchment to offset the ruinous cost of the Great War. The Indian Army, cut to the bone, was required to make up in quality what it lacked in quantity.

The North-West Frontier in 1922 seemed to be returning gradually to the happier conditions which obtained before the 3rd Afghan War. Friendly relations existed with Afghanistan. Some inter-tribal fighting in

Dir, Swat, Bajaur and Buner,[1] though encouraged by Communist agents, was of no great importance. The Mohmands and Afridis were quiet. The Khaibar Railway was making good progress. In the Kurram it became necessary to blockade certain sections of the Orakzais and Wazirs to bring them to reason, but there was no serious trouble. Baluchistan, also, gave no cause for anxiety. The Mahsuds of Waziristan, however, remained sullen and suspicious. They followed their precept " Tell no man where you are going, the time you are starting, or the amount of money you are taking with you." Yet they were sufficiently docile to warrant the withdrawal of all regular garrisons from the Gomal route to Wana and their replacement by *khassadars*, local men who provided their own arms, ammunition and equipment and consequently had little temptation to desert with Government property.

There were two schools of thought regarding the best method of dealing with the problem of Waziristan. One was in favour of complete withdrawal, even to the line of the Indus, leaving the Mahsuds and Wazirs to their own devices unless they raided British territory. The other inclined towards complete occupation because the Mahsuds were intractable folk against whom our troops might have to undertake frequent expeditions under arduous conditions unless the country was garrisoned strongly. A compromise was found in a " half-forward " policy under which the limit of occupation was to be extended from Ladha to Razmak and a network of roads built to link the garrisons of strategic points.

The old main roads from Dera Ismail Khan towards, or skirting, Waziristan were one through Tank to Murtaza and another northwards to Bannu. The latter continued to Kohat and Peshawar, and a transverse road through Kohat connected the Peiwar Kotal, Parachinar and Thal with Khushhalgarh on the Indus.[2] By 1921, the avenues to Waziristan had been prolonged and reinforced by good internal communications. These were the Takki (or Tank) Zam Road, taking off from the Tank–Murtaza Road at Kaur and running through Khirgi and Jandola to Sorarogha near Makin, and the Tochi Valley Road from Bannu through Idak, Isha and Miramshah (near Dardoni) to Datta Khel.[3] They had many river-crossings, some made for engineering reasons, but others to avoid long detours into politically dangerous country, although by these diversions the gradient might have been eased. Road construction in Waziristan has problems not encountered in more civilized areas. Many of the bridges on the Takki Zam and Tochi Valley Roads were provided very cheaply by using obsolete railway bridges from the North Western Railway which was then increasing the size and speed of its locomotives.

After Wana, in the south, had been re-occupied in 1920–21, and Datta Khel, in the Tochi region, in 1921–22, the Government decided to consolidate its hold on Waziristan by establishing a fortified camp at Razmak, 6,500 feet above sea-level and within artillery range of the Mahsud centre

[1]See *General Map III* at the end of this volume.

[2]" Military Roads on the Indian Frontier," by Brig.-Gen. G. P. Campbell, C.I.E., C.B.E., late R.E., appearing in *The R.E. Journal*, Vol. XXXVI, 1922, pp. 257–269.

[3]See *Sketch Map of the North-West Frontier : Waziristan*, included in Chapter XXII.

in the Makin Valley. The occupation of Razmak was calculated to nullify any Mahsud resistance and to provide a healthy advanced base for the regular troops needed to stiffen the irregular formations guarding the roads. But the place could not be garrisoned safely without proper road connection to the existing Tochi and Takki Zam highways, and consequently the Isha-Razmak and Sorarogha-Razmak road schemes were launched to complete a great " Circular Road " through Waziristan. Little was known of the route between Isha and Razmak, for no troops had traversed it since 1860, so it was reconnoitred by Captain L. C. B. Deed, R.E., who, with Lieutenants M. J. Jefferis and J. W. M. Dickson, R.E., subsequently carried out most of the construction. The road had a dual purpose. Not only would it facilitate the concentration of troops at any threatened point but it would encourage trade and give useful employment to numbers of Mahsuds.

Active survey began on June 1st, 1922, from the Isha end. The country consisted at first of bare and stony hills, but later it was covered with scrub jungle and intersected by deep *nullahs*. The route crossed three mountain ranges and reached its highest point at the Razmak Narai (Pass), 7,200 feet above sea-level. Construction began on July 14th and was executed, as far as Razani, mostly by civilian contractors and labour. The road was built in a most unorthodox manner. First came the contractors and labour gangs making it, and with them the Signals units laying a permanent telegraph line. Many miles in rear were the protective troops. A causeway across the Tochi near Isha was built by the 13th Company, Madras S. & M., under Major E. Bradney, R.E., assisted by the 32nd and 34th Sikh Pioneers,[1] and work on the alignment progressed steadily under Major A. Campbell, R.E., as C.R.E., and later under Lieut.-Colonel C. H. Haswell, R.E. By November 16th, the 13th Company, Madras S. & M., the 3rd and 5th Companies, Bengal S. & M., the 20th and 21st Companies, Bombay S. & M., and the two Pioneer battalions were labouring on various portions of the road.[2] They were kept far down the line in order that the Mahsuds should not be tempted to attack them in the hope of acquiring some Government rifles. The duty of protecting the advanced civilian labour gangs fell to the *khassadars* who proved themselves efficient guards; but nevertheless, Lieutenant J. W. M. Dickson, R.E., was ambushed and murdered on December 12th when he and a Pioneer officer had outstripped their small escort.

By the middle of January, 1923, heavy lorries were running as far as Asad Khel, nearly half-way to Razmak, and Ford vans up to Razani. The construction of a passable track up to the Razmak Narai in extremely cold weather was a most difficult undertaking; but three companies of Sappers

[1]This causeway was replaced in 1924 by a girder bridge of six 100-ft. spans, Maj. L. C. B. Deed, R.E., being in charge of the work. (See " The Construction of the Tal (Tochi) Bridge," appearing in *The R.E. Journal*, Vol. XL, 1926, pp. 1–13.)

[2]" The Isha-Razmak Road," appearing in *The R.E. Journal*, Vol. XXXIX, 1925, pp. 361–367. See also " Modern Road Construction and Improvement on the N.W. Frontier of India," by Maj. P. W. L. Broke-Smith, D.S.O., O.B.E., R.E., appearing in *The R.E. Journal*, Vol. XXXVIII, 1924, pp. 651–663.

and a battalion of Pioneers set to work on January 19th and, with a ruling gradient of 1 in 8, reached the crest in three days. On the 23rd they toiled in a blizzard for eleven hours while the 7th Infantry Brigade negotiated the ascent. The track became a sheet of ice, which turned later to freezing slush under the pounding of animal traffic, but by nightfall the entire brigade, with 1,100 mules and 1,450 camels, had surmounted the 1,200 feet rise. Road construction in rear had proceeded so rapidly that when the 7th Brigade marched into Razmak on the evening of the 23rd, the head of the main road was past Razani where the 5th Brigade was encamped. Useful work was done by the Sappers and Miners near Razani. The 20th and 21st Companies completed a 3-span girder bridge, and the 5th Company built a retaining wall at a zigzag bend with boulders so huge that 30 men were required to move them. As soon as Razmak was reached, every hand was turned to preparing a defensible camp, but at the end of March 1923, all the Sapper companies, except the 13th and 20th, were transferred to the Takki Zam. The 13th Company worked on water-supply, and the 20th on road construction, and the road from Isha was opened to motor traffic on August 10th, some 13 months after the first sod had been cut. The construction of the Sorarogha–Razmak Road by the 12th Company, Madras S. & M., the 19th and 23rd Companies, Bombay S. & M., and the Sapper companies, Pioneers and civilian labour transferred from the Isha–Razmak Road was then well in hand, and after its completion in the autumn, attention was turned to building a branch road from Jandola to Sarwekai *en route* for Wana. In all, no less than 8 companies of Sappers and Miners and 8 battalions of Pioneers[1] were concerned in the construction of the section of the Circular Road running from Isha through Razmak to Sorarogha. The cost was nearly a million sterling; but it was a great undertaking, finely accomplished.

The Circular Road was not finished without some fighting, for arrangements for the transfer of the Ladha garrison to Razmak led to rumours that we were about to evacuate Waziristan. Instantly, the Mahsuds opened hostilities which, on December 1st, 1922, involved a suspension of work on the Sorarogha-Razmak line near Dwa Toi. Early in January 1923, it became evident that drastic punitive measures must be taken against Makin to bring the tribes to reason. The 9th Brigade evacuated Ladha on February 1st and moved to Dwa Toi and Marobi to meet the 7th Brigade from Razmak at Tauda China, the 14th Company, Madras S. & M., being with the 9th Brigade and the 13th Company with the 7th Brigade. The task of destroying the villages, towers and crops in the Makin area began on February 6th under the direction of Major M. Everett, R.E., C.R.E. Makin Column, and continued for five days during which the villages were subjected also to bombing and howitzer fire. The incendiary operations required careful timing to prevent smoke from interfering with the withdrawal of the troops. On one occasion, indeed,

[1] "Professional Notes," appearing in *The R.E. Journal*, Vol. XXXVIII, 1924, pp. 298–300. The Pioneer units were the 1/1st and 1/2nd Madras Pioneers, the 1st, 2nd and 3rd Sikh Pioneers, the 4th and 10th Bombay Pioneers, and the 4th Hazara Pioneers.

much confusion was caused through the premature ignition of a house by an Indian transport driver who was feeling the cold ![1] All boundary walls dividing fields were pulled down, and fruit trees killed. The devastation had its effect, for on March 23rd, 1923, the Mahsuds submitted and work was resumed on the Circular Road. Two days later, the 9th Brigade evacuated Tauda China and marched with the 14th Company to Jandola. Thence it proceeded to Wana, dropping the 14th Company at Sarwekai to build a perimeter camp for some South Waziristan Scouts evacuated from Wana.[2]

The military operations of 1922–23 were in marked contrast to those of 1919–20. Although the climatic conditions were even more severe and road-making more difficult, our casualties were light and active resistance by the enemy lasted barely two months. As De Watteville remarks,[3] the control of Waziristan is synonymous with the control of the Mahsuds, for the Tochi and Wana Wazirs hardly count. The operations came as a heartening epilogue to the bloody drama of 1919–20. Our troops were better trained, better armed, better led ; our bombing was more effective, our artillery fire more devastating ; and lastly, our transport could move rapidly along first-class roads. The Mahsuds, however brave, could not stand up to such a combination.

Turning to events outside Waziristan it may be remarked that the year 1922 saw the appearance of a new Sapper and Miner Corps. This was the "4th Burma Sappers and Miners," formed on January 10th from the 15th (Burma) Company, Madras S. & M., and the Rangoon Defence Light Section of the same Corps. This measure had been advocated by Brig.-General W. E. R. Dickson, late R.E., while Inspector of Engineers and Pioneers from 1916 to 1918, for in his opinion there was little real affinity between the Burmese and Madrassis.[4] The Burma Sappers had earned the right to a separate existence by their services during the Great War in Iraq and Iran, especially at the Shumran Crossing in 1917, and more recently, by their work in the Chin Hills during the spring and summer of 1919. The unit concerned in the Chin Hills was the 62nd (Burma) Company, Madras S. & M.,[5] under Captain E. H. Clarke, R.E., with Lieutenants C. R. Cowie, E. W. Hill and F. J. D. Vernon, R.E., and the operations were against a tribe called the Kukis. Although there was little fighting, the Company had to labour hard in a very unhealthy climate, the work consisting mainly of hacking mule-tracks through dense jungle, building defensible posts with few tools except *dahs*, and occasionally despatching patrols to round up rebels. It is unfortunate that the 4th Burma Sappers and Miners had so short an existence. The Corps

[1] "The Destruction of Makin in February, 1923," by Maj. M. Everett, D.S.O., R.E., appearing in *The Journal of the United Service Institution of India*, Vol. LV, 1925, pp. 15–29.

[2] *Notes on the 14th Field Company, Q.V.O. Madras Sappers and Miners in Waziristan, March*, 1921–*May*, 1923, by Capt. C. Sleigh, R.E. (1927).

[3] *Waziristan*, 1919–1920, by H. de Watteville, p. 181.

[4] Notes by Brig.-Gen. W. E. R. Dickson, C.M.G., C.I.E., late R.E., sent to the author on May 25th, 1937.

[5] The 62nd (Burma) Company, Madras, S. & M., was disbanded in Sept., 1921.

deserved a better fate than the disbandment which fell to its lot in 1929 but it is satisfactory to record that it was revived in 1937.

As Inspector of Engineers and Pioneers, Brig.-General Dickson was responsible to the Director-General of Military Works, but it was decided in 1920 that an Inspectorship of Sappers and Miners and Pioneers should be formed instead under the Chief of the General Staff. This was a retrograde step because it abolished unity of control over the Engineer services. Fortunately, it did not remain long in operation. In December 1923, when Lord Rawlinson was Commander-in-Chief, an Engineer-in-Chief was appointed, with a Technical Advisor, R.E., on his staff who dealt with all technical questions affecting the Sappers and Miners and Pioneers. Thus, unification of engineering control was ensured, and the Engineer-in-Chief became responsible that all Engineer units were properly trained and ready for war. The Pioneers formed an important part of his responsibilities. Before the Great War, the Indian Army had 12 Pioneer battalions. The British Army had none; but during the war a British Pioneer Battalion was raised for every division. In 1919, these British Pioneers were absorbed into the Field Companies, R.E. A similar procedure, however, was not adopted in India because the conditions were different and it was considered that the high traditions of the Indian Pioneers should be preserved. In 1923, under the regimental system, the Indian Army had its original 12 battalions of Pioneers of the Sikh, Bombay and Madras Regiments, and in addition a newly-raised independent unit, the 4th Hazara Pioneers. The Pioneer was still recognized as a valuable adjunct to the Sapper and Miner. His training and equipment cost less than that of the Sapper, and he could relieve the latter of much technical work of a simple nature. Road-making was his speciality, and on the North-West Frontier it was still useful to have a road-builder who could also fight. So, for a time, the Indian Pioneer escaped the axe of retrenchment and continued to support the more highly-trained Sapper and Miner.

The year 1923 was marked by a decision of supreme importance, namely, to begin the gradual Indianization of the King's Commissioned ranks of the Indian Army. Two Indian Cavalry regiments, five battalions of Indian Infantry, and the 2/1st Madras Pioneers, were selected for the purpose, but no Sapper and Miner units were named although it was evident that the system would be extended ultimately to the three Corps. The decision to make Indians eligible to hold a King's Commission was a natural consequence of political evolution, an appropriate recognition of gallantry, and a corollary to the admission of Indians to high appointments in civil branches of the public service.

After the destruction of Makin there was little military activity on the North-West Frontier for some months, although there were several "regrettable incidents." On April 14th, 1923, Afridi raiders at Kohat murdered Mrs. Ellis and kidnapped her daughter, Molly, who was rescued later by Mrs. Starr. Again, on July 6th, Lieutenant R. H. F. Webster, R.E., was murdered near Dwa Toi in Waziristan, and on November 7th

Captain and Mrs. Watts were assassinated at Parachinar. The Mahsuds, however, seemed to accept the presence of British and Indian troops as a *fait accompli* and were more interested in earning good money as contractors and labourers on the Circular Road than in organizing raids on the garrisons of the various posts. Only in the Wana area were there any signs of trouble to come. Two officers were murdered in Baluchistan, but otherwise the tribes around Quetta behaved well. The Sapper units in Waziristan continued to work as hard as ever. The 12th Company, Madras S. & M., having arrived with the 19th Company, Bombay S. & M., in Tank in March, 1923, in relief of the 14th Company, moved with the 19th Company to Sorarogha on April 19th to work alongside the 3rd Company, Bengal S. & M., on the construction of a new road through the difficult Barari Tangi. "This *Tangi*," writes Captain B. F. Whitestone, R.E.,[1] "is a typical Waziristan gorge, some 50 yards in width. The road was aligned to follow the right bank which, for nearly half-a-mile, consisted of steep cliffs with vertical strata interspersed with narrow and deep gullies. In the 12th Company's section the whole mass of the hillside had to be blasted down to road level, the road itself being about half-way up the precipitous slope, which was over 200 feet high. So little foothold was obtainable that the men had to be roped to anchors on the crest. Four of them fell, but only one was killed." The three Sapper companies, from the north, centre and south of India, worked until August in perfect harmony. There was an excellent understanding between them, and a combined hockey team of the 3rd and 12th Companies proved a deadly combination. Early in September, the 12th Company was transferred to Razmak to assist the 13th Company in building huts before the onset of winter. In October, the 13th Company left for Bangalore on relief by the 10th Company under Captain G. R. Gilpin, R.E. Building construction at Razmak continued until the end of December by which time the Sappers had erected 70 huts. All work had then to cease until the spring, for the mortar froze as it was laid.

The Royal Bombay Sappers and Miners claimed that they built the first Inglis Bridge ever erected on the North-West Frontier for permanent as opposed to temporary use. This was near Marobi during 1923–24 when the 19th Company under Captain C. de L. Gaussen, R.E., built three Inglis (Mark I) Bridges on the Sorarogha-Razmak Road.[2] The other two were thrown across the Dwa Toi above its confluence with the Baddar Toi to form the Takki Zam. The Marobi ravine was about 80 feet deep and 60 feet wide, but the chief difficulties to be overcome were human rather than engineering for the Mahsuds lived up to their reputation as inveterate thieves. Every fitting had to be guarded closely, night and day, and even so, five large pins disappeared, perhaps because they might be used as weapons. The bridge was erected and launched in two days. A decking of corrugated iron, covered with concrete, was provided

[1]Notes by Capt. B. F. Whitestone, M.B.E., M.C., R.E., O.C. 12th Company, Q.V.O. Madras S. & M., sent to the author on Sept. 13th, 1937.

[2]"The Erection of an Inglis Bridge in Waziristan," by Capt. C. de L. Gaussen, M.C., R.E., appearing in *The R.E. Journal*, Vol. XXXVIII, 1924, pp. 381–383.

instead of timber, because the latter would be too attractive to the Mahsuds.

A graphic description of Razmak at this period comes from the pen of Lieut.-Colonel R. H. R. Neale, Royal Signals.[1] "At the beginning of 1924," he writes, "we were at peace with all sections of the Mahsuds and Wazirs. Contracts for work on the Circular Road were given to Mahsud headmen, who in turn sub-let to down-country experts. A good deal of money, therefore, found its way into the Mahsud villages and had a pacifying effect. Both Mahsuds and Wazirs were enlisted as *khassadars* under their own headmen and were responsible for the protection of the road, and they were even given rifles and ammunition. Brigades were stationed at Bannu, Razani, Razmak and Manzai, but that at Razmak was exceptionally strong for it had 7 battalions, a pack artillery brigade, 2 Sapper companies and ancillary troops, and consequently the camp was very congested. Razmak had to supply the striking force, and when the column of 4 battalions left the place, the remaining three were obliged to take over the defence of the whole perimeter. Razmak in 1924 was a pleasant camp, situated in a valley, about 10 miles long and 2 to 3 miles broad, and guarded by a perimeter wall and belts of barbed wire covered by fire from automatic rifles and machine guns. There were only two stone buildings—Brigade Headquarters and the Signal Office—the remainder of the force being mostly in huts. The floor level in tents was dropped some 4 or 5 feet as a protection against sniping and to provide warmth. The Razmak Club consisted of two marquees joined together, with mud walls instead of canvas. By day, the troops were allowed to walk unarmed within 300 to 600 yards outside the perimeter. Beyond those limits, the recognized escort was four armed soldiers when the road was open. The road from Razani was opened and piqueted every day except Sunday, and a large convoy of supply lorries crawled along it to Razmak and unloaded before returning to Razani." Three years later, Razmak was a very different place. The Mahsuds and Wazirs kept the road inviolate. They had become accustomed to travel by car to sell their produce easily and quickly and at a good price, and so they had fewer hungry folk and less incentive to raid and plunder. The "unarmed" limits of the camp had grown until they were a mile or more from the perimeter. Officers picnicked on the surrounding hills with no more escort than a few armed *badraggas*. On one occasion only was a display of force needed. This was during the Sports held outside Razmak for the benefit of the *khassadars*. While the tugs-of-war were in progress, nothing less than a company of British infantry with fixed bayonets sufficed to keep order. All weapons had been collected in advance from the excited supporters of rival teams, but even so their expressions grew murderous and their fingers sought unconsciously for rifle and dagger when their men lost ground.

Outside Waziristan, there is little to record regarding the Sappers and Miners during 1924 and 1925. Training was the order of the day. On September 10th, 1924, the War Memorial of the Bombay Corps was

[1] "Razmak, Waziristan, 1924–26," by Lieut.-Col. R. H. R. Neale, Royal Signals, appearing in *The Royal Signals Quarterly Journal*, Vol. IV, 1936, pp. 129–197.

unveiled at Kirkee by the Governor of Bombay at the invitation of the Commandant, Lieut.-Colonel E. D. Tillard, R.E., among those present on parade being Colonel B. B. Russell and Colonel-on-the-Staff G. H. Boileau, late R.E., both former Commandants. The Memorial is a stone cenotaph bearing the names of 563 officers and men who fell in the Great War.[1] At the same time, some companies of the Bengal Corps were busily engaged in helping the Railway authorities to cope with a record flood of the Ganges which destroyed miles of line, demolished bridges and dislocated traffic. Between Ghaziabad and Moradabad, a passenger train was marooned for several days at a small station in the Ganges *khadir* and for a time its fate was unknown.[2] All three lines leading into Lakhsar Junction, a few miles from Roorkee, were breached, leaving a number of Indian passengers stranded in the junction without food, so an appeal was made to the Bengal Sappers to provide bridges or ferries across the gaps. A single-plank bridge, thrown across a breach near Lakhsar, enabled most of the marooned people to escape on the second day, but there remained a stout lady, baby in arms, who resolutely refused either to walk or be carried across. Accordingly, the ingenuity of the Sapper and Miner was called into play. The Company Commander (Captain W. J. Lyall, R.E.) consulted his Subadar and they devised a scheme. A wily old Sapper was detailed to enter into conversation with the woman. This he did, and duly admired the baby. Then suddenly, seizing the child, he rushed with it across the swaying bridge. Of course, the furious mother followed, screaming and cursing, and so a difficult problem was solved.[3]

During 1925 and 1926, the North-West Frontier was more peaceful than certain parts of British India. Indeed, between April 1925 and March 1926 there were only 26 raids into British territory as compared with an annual average of nearly 400 raids between 1920 and 1922. A 20-mile stretch of the Khaibar Railway, from Jamrud to Landi Kotal, was opened to traffic on November 2nd, 1925, with beneficial results.[4] The Circular Road in Waziristan had become very popular with the Mahsuds, and a Decauville light railway was in operation alongside the road from Dera Ismail Khan to Tank.[5] In India, however, there were grave riots between Hindus and Muhammadans, notably in Calcutta and further north, and the efforts of Lord Irwin, who became Viceroy in April 1926, met with little success. "Razcol," the striking force from Razmak, made periodical excursions to "show the flag," and on one of these a curious experience befell the 9th Company, Madras S. & M. With a battalion of Punjabis the unit had gone to Sarwekai to establish a temporary advanced base for

[1] "The Royal Bombay Sappers and Miners' Unveiling Ceremony of the War Memorial at Kirkee," appearing in *The R.E. Journal*, Vol. XXXIX, 1925, pp. 23–24.

[2] The "Tale of the Lost Train" appears in *The Military Engineer in India*, by the present author, Vol. II, pp. 141–142.

[3] Notes by Lieut.-Col. W. J. Lyall, O.B.E., R.E. (I.A.), sent to the author on Oct. 6th, 1937.

[4] The history of the Khaibar Railway appears in *The Military Engineer in India*, by the present author, Vol. II, pp. 160–167.

[5] "Waziristan Circular Road," by "Rousseau," appearing in *The Journal of the Royal United Service Institution*, Vol. LXXI, 1926, pp. 569–571.

" Razcol," and having completed the work, had marched back to Jandola with the Punjabis, covering 22 miles in a single day and well earning the customary ration of rum for exceptionally hard labour. After dark it was reported to Captain A. H. Morse, R.E., O.C., 9th Company, that some of his men were in a comatose condition, and on investigation he found that, with the exception of the Guard, every Sapper and follower in the unit was apparently drunk. Actually, they were poisoned. Emetics and injections of strychnine revived the worst cases sufficiently for evacuation to Manzai by lorry on the following morning and a few managed to march the distance. The remains of the " rum " in the rum-jar were analysed and proved to be a mixture of methylated spirit and quinine, a potion too strong even for a hardy Madras Sapper ! The Guard escaped harm because they had received no rum issue, but for 24 hours the 9th Company was practically out of action. It is believed that no explanation of the contents of the rum-jar was ever forthcoming.[1]

During 1927 and 1928 there were few disturbances on the North-West Frontier. Razmak continued to develop, and new roads were built, notably one from Sarwekai to Wana which was constructed by tribal labour under contract.[2] Captain R. E. Wood, R.E., who commanded a Madras Sapper Company at Razmak for 15 months, gives the following description of life in that outpost.[3] " The quarters are now stone huts with corrugated iron roofs, *pukka* doors and windows, concrete floors, bathrooms and verandahs. Service conditions prevail, and the nearest female is at Bannu, 70 miles away, so Razmak is the ideal place for the strong, silent man. Three times a year, the Razmak Column, a mixed brigade of all arms, goes on tour for a week or two. The lot of the Sappers is chiefly the inevitable water-supply which is usually taken direct from the nearest stream. Five thousand men and 1,600 animals drink incredible quantities of water after a hot march. On one occasion, the mules averaged over 6 gallons each. For many of them it was the first drink of the day, for it is usually impossible to water all animals before the march begins. On another day, the brigade drew 16,000 gallons of drinking water in 5 hours. Other Sapper jobs, which occasionally arise, are the roping of fords, when the rivers are in spate, and improvements to roads. We cater for most games at Razmak. Hockey, ' soccer ' and squash are in full swing all the year round. A new pattern of hockey ground of sifted and rammed earth is proving a success, but the problem is to get rid of the stones. The four squash courts are of concrete. In summer we have cricket, tennis and polo, the cricket pitch being of concrete. Polo is played on an aeroplane landing ground which has a transverse slope of 1 in 20 and is full of delightful surprises. There is also a 9-hole golf course, where, as stones seem to grow like daisies, a local rule allows the ball to be ' placed ' for each stroke. Small game shooting is run by the Brigade, but birds are

[1]Notes by Lieut.-Col. A. H. Morse, R.E., sent to the author on Sept. 23rd, 1937.
[2]" Waziristan," by Maj.-Gen. A. le G. Jacob, C.B., C.M.G., C.I.E., D.S.O., appearing in *The R.E. Journal*, Vol. XLII, 1928, pp. 219–231.
[3]" Life on the Indian Frontier," by Capt. R. E. Wood, R.E., appearing in *The R.E. Journal*, Vol. XLII, 1928, pp. 241–243.

not too plentiful. In summer, climbing expeditions are popular, mountains of over 10,000 feet being only a few miles away. Former battle-grounds, such as the Ahnai Tangi, Palosina and Makin are of interest to students of frontier warfare. The Sapper and Miner units work in close touch with the Military Engineer Services and thus get valuable experience in heavy bridging and roadwork."

The Sapper and Miner, like most soldiers of the Indian Army, took little interest in politics, a fact which may be exemplified by the following tale. Towards the end of 1927, a Parliamentary Commission under Sir John Simon visited India to enquire into the system of government and to suggest some means of reducing communal tension. It met with opposition and boycott from certain sections of the populace, and when it visited Burma in 1928 the streets of Mandalay were hung with banners bearing the slogan "Simon. Go back." Thousands of Burmans paraded the bazaars, and the Sapper and Miner company in the garrison was warned to stand by to help the Police if necessary. On the day on which the Commission arrived Major A. V. Anderson, R.E., was delivering a lecture to his Indian officers and men on the period commencing with the Montagu-Chelmsford Reforms, and, as a test, asked the question "What is the Simon Commission?" For a time there was no reply, but finally a worthy Jemadar remarked, "Sahib, I have heard of the King's Commission, and I know about the Viceroy's Commission. But *never* have I heard anything of the Simon's Commission."[1]

In 1928 an addition was made to the Imperial Service Sappers and Miners maintained by Indian States, for in that year the Gwalior Durbar raised 3 Sections of Sappers. The Faridkot, Malerkotla, Sirmur and Tehri-Garhwal Sappers continued to render good service in their own territories where, of course, they saw no fighting. It may be remarked here that in 1930 there was a further addition to the Imperial Service Sappers when the Raja of Mandi converted his infantry into 3 Sections of Mandi Jogindar Sappers and Miners, but there was a corresponding decrease in 1937 when the Gwalior Sappers were disbanded. The total strength of the Imperial Service Sappers then exceeded 1,000 men—a valuable reserve of technical troops in case of war.

As already recorded, the 4th Burma Sappers and Miners, raised in January, 1922, fell to the axe of financial retrenchment in 1929. After the Great War, the 62nd and 68th (Burma) Companies of the Madras Corps were disbanded and only the 15th (Burma) Company (late 63rd Company) remained. From this unit, and the Rangoon Defence Light Section, was formed the 4th Burma Sappers. But by 1927, when Major E. H. Clarke, R.E., was Commandant, it had become apparent that the maintenance of a Depot at Mandalay for a separate Corps of little more than Company strength was too expensive, and accordingly the decision was reached which, in 1929, deprived Burma of her own Sappers. The 15th (Burma) Company had taken its turn of service on the North-West

[1]Notes by Lieut.-Col. A. V. Anderson, M.B.E., R.E., sent to the author on Dec. 30th, 1937.

Frontier at Razmak from 1919 to 1921, and under Captain R. Briggs, R.E., as part of the 4th Burma Sappers, had served again on the Frontier in 1927–28. In both cases, the Burma Sappers were reported to have done well, so it was hard that the financial aspect of the situation should have caused their disbandment. It is pleasant to record that in 1937 they were re-established as a separate Corps under Major J. M. Saegert, R.E.

The North-West Frontier was peaceful in 1929 in the sense that there was little raiding. Some inter-tribal clashes occurred in Dir, Swat, Bajaur and the Tirah, and punitive measures were taken in the Kurram Valley against a section of the Chamkanis. Two British officers were murdered on June 14th within 8 miles of Razmak, but there were no signs of general trouble, and the Mahsuds and Wazirs seemed to have ended their boundary disputes. Nevertheless, affairs in Afghanistan had an unsettling effect, for the Afghans were in revolt against the premature reforms introduced by the headstrong King Amanullah, a rebellion which resulted in Amanullah's deposition in 1930. It was decided that the safety of the Circular Road, some 7 miles north of Razmak, would be enhanced by building a permanent piquet on the Alexandra Ridge, a pivotal point some 8,000 feet above sea-level and overlooking the road where it crosses the Razmak Narai, so the 10th and 13th Companies, Madras S. & M., were set to work on June 10th to build a post for two platoons of infantry on this commanding height. The post, which was typical of modern Frontier fortification, had stone walls 20 feet high enclosing a rectangular space of 170 feet by 100 feet. At diagonally opposed corners were three-storeyed towers to give flanking fire. The Madras Sappers had to work hard to complete the building before the first frosts of winter, but by toiling 9½ hours a day under the protection of regular troops and *khassadars*, they laid the last stone on October 5th.[1]

The story now shifts to Wana which, though established as a militia post in 1895, had not been occupied in strength since the débâcle of 1919 except for short periods in 1920 and 1921. For some two years the Military Engineer Services had been building a road from Sarwekai through Dargai Oba, Tamai and Karab Kot towards Wana,[2] and this was nearly completed, so it was decided that a brigade should advance from Manzai early in November 1929 and with it the 9th Company, Madras S. & M.[3] On November 12th the brigade reoccupied without opposition the ruins of the old Wana Fort, in which Wazir tribesmen had been living for years, and proceeded to establish a temporary camp near it. Naturally, the fort was incredibly filthy, nor could it contain the whole force. The first task was to secure protection for the camp by the erection of a double-apron barbed-wire fence under Sapper supervision. A shallow trench was dug behind the fence in which the perimeter piquets could get some shelter at

[1] "The Construction of Alexandra Ridge Piquet, Waziristan, by Nos. 10 and 13 Field Companies, Q.V.O. Madras Sappers and Miners, in 1929," appearing in *The R.E. Journal*, Vol. XLV, 1931, pp. 100, 101.

[2] See *Sketch Map of the N.W. Frontier : Waziristan*, included in Chapter XXII.

[3] "A Field Company's Two and a Half Years in Wana," by Lieut. E. F. R. Stack, R.E., appearing in *The R.E. Journal*, Vol. XLVI, 1932, pp. 691–698.

night against the chilly wind, and the remainder of the troops were accommodated under canvas. As soon as possible, the trench was replaced by a stone wall. The winter of 1929–30 proved abnormally wet and cold, and accordingly 30 perimeter posts were next built and roofed by the Sappers and infantry working parties. Corrugated iron cookhouses, and brick fireplaces and chimneys for tents, followed in due course. In January 1930, four hockey grounds and three tennis courts were laid out, but the hockey grounds were never satisfactory because of loose stones. The 9th Company designed and manufactured a "Bangalore" pattern of portable oil-cooker which was adopted by all units. Directly the winter frosts had ceased, the entire Brigade started to make mud bricks for walling the tents, and doors and windows for the walls, and thus the permanent camp at Wana soon began to take shape. During the summer of 1930, the 9th Company took in hand the matter of water-supply. Two 4-inch pipes were led from large storage tanks outside the Fort and were connected to a 6-inch main, about 1,000 feet long, from the Fort to the camp. Infantry dug the trenches, and the Sappers and Pioneers laid the piping. Other amenities followed, such as a swimming bath for the Indian troops and Workshops for the Sappers, but as the Workshops building was the only structure with a corrugated iron roof it was often commandeered for use as a church, cinema or lecture hall.

Later, the 9th Company carried out the electrification of the Wana Camp from a distribution station in their lines which drew current from an electrical pump and dynamo in the Fort. As the Company was responsible for distribution, Lieutenant C. B. Boulden, R.E., who was in command, was particularly careful to ensure that no light should fail in the Brigade Commander's camp on the occasion of a visit by the G.O.C.-in-C. who was expected to stay there. The great man duly arrived and inspected the troops. At 8 p.m., however, the pointer in the distribution station went over the red line. Something was wrong, so Boulden pulled out the Bazaar sub-circuit. Who cared about the Bazaar anyway? But, unfortunately, the G.O.C.-in-C. was not staying with the Brigadier but with the Political Agent, whose quarter was in the Bazaar sub-circuit. Also, he happened at the moment to be in his bath!

There was always road-work to be done in and around Wana Camp, varied by occasional small punitive expeditions with the South Waziristan Scouts in one of which the Sappers, in heavy boots, kept pace with the Scouts, in sandals, over 23 miles of broken country. When the 9th Company left Wana in March 1932, the camp was well-equipped and fairly comfortable, though unfortunately infested with malaria. The troops had four improved hockey grounds, a good football ground, a running track, and a swimming bath which was in constant use during the summer. For the officers there were three tennis courts, a 15-hole golf course and a drag. A project to build permanent barracks at a cost of £675,000, was shelved temporarily because of lack of funds and some uncertainty regarding future policy,[1] but it was revived in 1934. The building of Wana,

[1] "Wana," by Lieut.-Col R. L. Bond, D.S.O., M.C., R.E., appearing in *The R.E. Journal*, Vol. LI, 1937, pp. 14–26.

as of Razmak, is a good example of the type of work done by the Sappers and Miners on the North-West Frontier when the tribesmen are not on the warpath.

The re-occupation of Wana in 1929–30 was followed by the construction of a link-road between that place and Razmak by way of the Khaisara Valley. A beginning had been made by Lieutenant E. J. Graham, R.E., in the form of a branch road taking off from the Circular Road near Tauda China, south of Razmak, and running southwards through Ladha to the region of Kaniguram, but the country beyond the Mahsud capital was *terra incognita*. In March, 1931, Captain W. H. Lang-Anderson, R.E., with Lieutenants R. K. Millar and R. I. C. Blenkinsop, R.E., reconnoitred a route northwards from the Wana end under a strong escort, each officer covering many miles a day, mostly on foot.[1] They selected an alignment up the left bank of the Tiarz, and construction was begun from the Kaniguram road-head in June, 1932. It was carried out in a very peculiar manner, for the Mahsuds were extremely suspicious. The reconnaissance party was never allowed to go more than 3 miles from the road-head to decide on the next 2 miles of alignment. No detailed surveying was possible, and the officers were ringed round always by 70 men armed to the teeth. The Mahsud labourers often deserted *en masse* to attend the funeral of a friend killed in a blood-feud, but nevertheless the work went steadily on. By November, 1932, the road-head was some 7 miles beyond Kaniguram and Captain S. G. Hudson, R.E., had begun construction from the Wana end. A junction was effected in December, 1933, some miles north of Torwam, and thus Wana was connected with Razmak by road. No Sappers and Miners were concerned in this project, although several of the officers were ex-Sappers and Miners, but the Razmak-Wana Road deserved some mention because it was one of the most important extensions of the system of internal communication in Waziristan during the years preceding the World War of 1939–45.

Some two years before the construction of the Razmak-Wana Road, the 21st Company, Bombay S. & M., under Captain C. T. Edwards, R.E., was engaged on an interesting road-project in Baluchistan, far to the south. This consisted of a motor-road, 26 miles in length, to connect Maratangi on the Loralai-Fort Sandeman Road with Gwal Haiderzai on the Kila Saifulla–Fort Sandeman Road[2] and thus to open up the difficult country between the Loralai and Zhob valleys. A metalled highway was out of the question because time was scarce, and all that could be done was to prepare a reasonably good track which could be covered later with gravel. The season was the hot weather, when the thermometer showed a maximum temperature of 106° in the shade even at 4,500 feet. The country was a stony and rugged waste, intersected by deep ravines and normally water-

[1] "The Wana-Ladha Road," by Col. C. V. S. Jackson, C.B.E., late R.E., appearing in *The R.E. Journal*, Vol. L, 1936, pp. 27–37.

[2] Maratangi is 25 miles east of Lalai, and Gwal Haiderzai is on the Zhob River 35 miles north-east of Kila Saifulla. (Loralai and Kila Saifulla are shown in General Map III and in the *Sketch Map of Southern Afghanistan and Baluchistan* included in Chapter XXII.)

less; and the soil, though friable in dry weather, became a quagmire after heavy rain. Only pack transport could be used until the road was made. Work began at Maratangi on June 22nd, 1929, and ended at Gwal Haiderzai on August 16th, the last 9 miles from Bharat Khel involving a sharp descent from a watershed and including a difficult stretch among a wilderness of spurs, crags and *nullahs* where much blasting and cutting were necessary. The 21st Company suffered severely from malaria and many of the men had relapses for a long time afterwards; but nevertheless the task was completed before the rains and another link was added to the chain of communications.

Baluchistan, though peaceful in comparison with Waziristan, had its gangs of ruffians, and an unpleasant experience befell Major E. L. Farley, R.E., an ex-Bengal Sapper and Miner, in June 1930 near Chaman. He, and Captain and Mrs. Frere, were ambushed by tribesmen while motoring along the main road and hurried away into the wilderness, where they were held to ransom. For a week they suffered great hardships, though not unkindly treated, and their release was secured only by the payment of Rs. 5,000. Afghan troops from Spin Baldak co-operated in the rescue, thus showing that the unhappy conflict of 1919 had left no lasting resentment.[1]

The year 1930 shared with 1919 the distinction of being the most critical period on the North-West Frontier since 1897.[2] It opened quietly; yet, by the middle of the year, most of the Frontier was smouldering and some of it within an ace of bursting into flame. Common cause among many of the tribes had been secured by Congress agitation and propaganda. Discontent had not reached serious proportions in Chitral, Dir, Swat and Hazara, but it became necessary to bomb some Mohmand *lashkars* during May, and gatherings in Bajaur during June and July. Some sections of the 4th Company, Bengal S. & M., were concerned in the ground operations in these areas. Events took a more ominous turn in the Tirah, where the Afrídis had been deceived by grossly exaggerated reports of rioting in Peshawar. On May 30th, 1930, Afridi *lashkars* began to move down the Bara Valley with the object of looting Peshawar City and Cantonment. They planned to attack Peshawar on the night of June 5th/6th; but being unable to reach the city in strength before dawn, they lay up in villages to the south and west. There they were caught and heavily bombed by our aeroplanes and retreated hastily up the Bara Valley. A few die-hards who reached the outskirts of Peshawar were beaten off by our troops. However, in August they made a second attempt on Peshawar and tried to advance on Nowshera and Attock, only to fail ignominiously and retreat once more. It was then decided that we should occupy permanently the Kajuri and Aka Khel Plains beyond Peshawar, thus denying to the tribesmen their winter grazing-grounds and the caves in which they sheltered their families. The operations were to be in three

[1] "A Journey Enforced—A Border Episode," by Maj. E. L. Farley, M.C., R.E., appearing in *The Journal of the United Service Institution of India*, 1930.
[2] *Summary of the Chief Events in the N.W. Tribal Territory* (Official).

phases. First, the ejection of the Afridis and the establishment of perimeter camps; next, the provision of good communications and water-supply; and finally, the building of permanent camps and defensible posts for a strong garrison.[1] The force available in the Peshawar District comprised the Rawalpindi, Nowshera and Jhansi Brigades, a regiment of cavalry, 4 batteries of artillery, the 2nd, 3rd, 4th, 5th and 41st (D. H. Q.) Companies, Bengal S. & M. (Captains A. H. G. Napier, J. S. Lethbridge, W. M. Broomhall and E. F. E. Armstrong and Lieutenant G. D. S. Adami, R.E.), the 1st Sikh and 2nd Bombay Pioneers and the usual ancillary formations.

The occupation of the Kajuri and Aka Khel Plains proved to be almost entirely an engineering undertaking. There was very little resistance, and the cavalry, artillery and infantry merely held the ring for the Sappers and Miners and Pioneers. The plains lie a few miles south-west of Peshawar and are separated by the deep and precipitous chasm of the Bara River.[2] By October 14th, 1930, the Nowshera Brigade was in position along the "Frontier Road" running southwards from Jamrud through Matanni and covered the water-supply operations of the 4th Company, Bengal S. & M., and a battalion of Pioneers. Three days later, the Jhansi Brigade advanced from Peshawar and crossed the Kajuri Plain to Miri Khel, while the Rawalpindi Brigade marched to Bara. By the 27th, the three brigades had swept the plain clear of Afridis and the Rawalpindi Brigade was ready to advance to a central camp at Karawal Hill. This movement, however, could not be carried out until water was brought to Karawal, for no surface water was obtainable on the arid plains. The task was allotted to the 3rd Company, Bengal S. & M., and a company of the 2nd Bombay Pioneers, and was completed in fifteen days. These units installed a powerful pump on Bara Hill, 2 miles from Bara Fort, and laid a pipe line for more than 5 miles to Karawal where a perimeter camp was occupied by the Rawalpindi Brigade on November 17th. A road was built alongside the pipeline as it progressed. Most of the infantry units were now road-making under the direction of the C.R.E. The roads were 18 feet wide with a foundation of stone overlaid with earth, gravel and sand. *Nullah* crossings were ramped and in some cases covered with wire netting.[3] From November 18th to December 9th, during the second phase of the operations, large gangs of labourers extended the Peshawar-Bara metalled road towards the Kandao Pass, while the engineer units were still busy on water-supply. The 4th Company worked with the Nowshera Brigade along the Frontier Road, the 5th Company with the Jhansi Brigade at Miri Khel, and the 3rd Company with the Rawalpindi Brigade at Karawal. The 41st D.H.Q. Company built workshops at Bara.

Owing to spates in the Bara River, a bridge was needed urgently at

[1] "Operations on the Khajuri and Aka Khel Plains," by Maj. C. W. Toovey, M.C., appearing in *The Journal of the United Service Institution of India*, Vol. LXI, 1931, pp. 286–298.

[2] See *Sketch Map of the Kajuri and Aka Khel Plains* included in this chapter.

[3] *Report on Engineer Work on the N.W. Frontier of India*, 1930–31, *Bara Plain, Peshawar* (Official).

Bara where the Frontier Road crossed the gorge. The 4th Company, Bengal S. & M., and a company of the 1st Sikh Pioneers were detailed for this work. They were faced with a peculiar problem. While the bridge had to be designed to carry a 10-ton steam roller over a span of 144 feet, the Inglis (Mark I) Bridge material available was limited to a span of 120 feet under such loading. However, Captain Broomhall and his Sappers surmounted the difficulty by prolonging the bridge over its supports so that the projecting ends remained as cantilevers. Each end consisted of three bays (36 feet), and the last bay at each end was loaded with 6 tons of concrete to reduce the stress in the centre of the bridge. It was a very ingenious solution. Work began at the site on October 29th, the launching of the girders from both banks was accomplished in 7 hours on November 13th, and the bridge was opened to traffic on November 15th. The 4th Company received a suitable acknowledgment of this feat of engineering, and praise was accorded also to the Sikh Pioneers and infantry working parties who cut the deep approaches in the hardest conglomerate soil.

The third and final phase of the operations, from December 10th, 1930, to March 31st, 1931, began when it was decided that the Kajuri Plain, and the Aka Khel Plain further south, should be garrisoned by two Indian Infantry battalions firmly established in defended camps and with their communications guarded by permanent piquets. Water being the deciding factor in the location of the camps, and no surface supply being available, tube wells were needed. The 2nd Company was detailed to make a piquet post at Samghakai and afterwards to work at Bara Camp; the 3rd Company to prepare a defended camp at Fort Salop and a post at Karawal; the 4th Company to build Nowshera Post; the 5th Company to build Jhansi Post and afterwards construct a second bridge over the Bara River; the 41st D.H.Q. Company to work at Bara Camp; and the Pioneers to make roads and help some of the Sapper units. Many demands were made on the 41st Company which was in charge of engineer stores. It is recorded that on one occasion, the long-suffering unit was called upon to produce several dozen goldfish and duly did so ! [1]

The 5th Company, Bengal S. & M., assisted by a company of the 1st Sikh Pioneers, accomplished a notable feat in constructing in 50 days a second bridge across the Bara River. Lateral communication was required further forward than the first Bara Bridge because operations were to be extended to the Aka Khel Plain, so a site was selected at Mazarai. The banks were of hard gravel conglomerate and the gap 83 feet in width measured from a ledge on the left bank to a sheer cliff on the right bank which was 46 feet above the ledge.[2] It was decided to build a 30 feet pier of concrete and rubble on this ledge and to cut an approach in the right bank down to the level of the pier-top. This approach alone involved the removal of 250,000 cu. ft. of hard soil, a task which fell to the Pioneers and infantry working parties. The Inglis (Mark I) Bridge material avail-

[1] *Adjutant's News Letters, K.G.V.'s O. Bengal Sappers and Miners*, Nov., 1930.

[2] "The Construction of the Mazarai Bridge, Kajuri Plain Operations, 1930–31," by Capt. E. F. E. Armstrong, R.E., appearing in *The R.E. Journal*, Vol. XLVI, 1932, pp. 71–79.

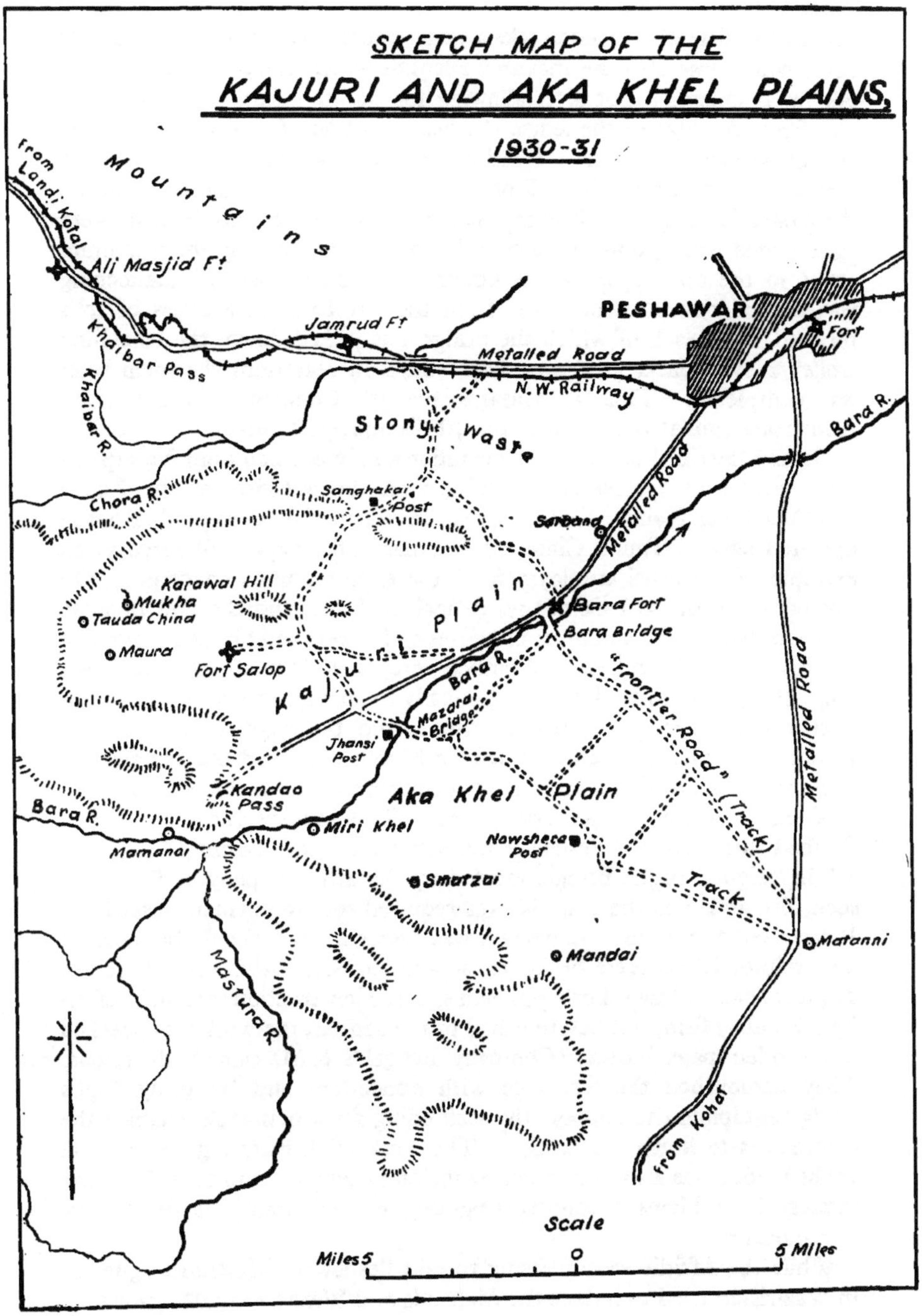
SKETCH MAP OF THE
KAJURI AND AKA KHEL PLAINS,
1930-31
from Landi Kotal
Mountains
Ali Masjid Ft
Khaibar Pass
Khaibar R.
Jamrud Ft
Metalled Road
N.W. Railway
PESHAWAR
Fort
Bara R.
Stony Waste
Chora R.
Samghakai Post
Metalled Road
Karawal Hill
Mukha
Tauda China
Maura
Fort Salop
Kajuri Plain
Bara Fort
Bara Bridge
Bara R.
Mazarai Bridge
Jhansi Post
"Frontier Road" (Track)
Metalled Road
Kandao Pass
Aka Khel Plain
Bara R.
Mamanai
Miri Khel
Nowshera Post
Smatzai
Track
Matanni
Mandai
Mastura R.
from Kohat
Scale
Miles 5
0
5 Miles

able was sufficiently strong to take a steam-roller over a span of ten 12 feet bays, which was also the maximum length which could be cantilevered out for launching; but after allowing for the necessary set-back of the pier from the edge of the ledge, the main span was found to be 11 bays, and consequently counter-weighting had to be adopted, as in the Bara bridge, though at the left bank only. The last two bays, therefore, of the three bays forming the subsidiary span between the pier and the bank were each loaded with 5 tons of concrete flooring, thus reducing the maximum stress in the main span to the limiting amount for safety. Launching was carried out by man-power from the left bank in a series of rolls forward, after each of which the bridge was jacked down, the launching trolley moved back, and more bays added in rear until the main span was completed. Thus at Mazarai, the 5th Company under Captain Armstrong emulated the feat of the 4th Company at Bara.

During the third phase of the operations, several small punitive expeditions were sent against Afridi villages on the outskirts of the Kajuri and Aka Khel Plains. One of these, in which the Rawalpindi Brigade operated against Tauda China on February 8th, 1931, will serve as an example of the usual employment of the engineer units concerned. On this occasion, the 3rd Company, Bengal S. & M., and the 2nd Bombay Pioneers demolished a number of houses and towers and blocked more than 100 caves with thorn trees and barbed wire, cleverly booby-trapped. Not long afterwards, hostilities came gradually to an end, the posts and camps were occupied by permanent garrisons, and the engineer troops were withdrawn. The 4th Company left on March 20th, and the 3rd and 5th Companies on April 1st, and only two sections of the 2nd Company were retained for a time in the forward area. The Sappers and Pioneers had finished their task and Peshawar was safe from Afridi raiding.

The original Inglis Bridge, erected by the 4th Company at Bara, was soon dismantled as the material was required for employment elsewhere. It was used only until 1932 when it was decided that it should be replaced by a reinforced concrete bridge on an adjacent site with a central arch of 114 feet span and two short approach spans. Construction was undertaken by a Bombay firm, but before it had proceeded far, the work was wrecked by a sudden spate. The 2nd Company, Bengal S. & M., came to the rescue. They demolished the wreckage with guncotton, and by using Inglis Bridge equipment to support the scaffolding for a new arch, enabled the contractors to finish the bridge.[1] The work of dismantling the original Inglis Bridge was also carried out by the 2nd Company and provided some interesting problems in counter-weighting to avoid damage in the process of removal.[2]

While the Afridis were massing to raid Peshawar, Khilafatist agitators in Waziristan tried to induce the Mahsuds and Wazirs to unite against us. They persuaded 4,000 Tochi Wazirs to attack Datta Khel on May 11th,

[1] "Bara Bridge Reconstruction," by Lieut. M. C. A. Henniker, R.E., appearing in *The R.E. Journal*, Vol. XLVI, 1932, pp. 678–685.

[2] "Dismantling the Inglis Bridge at Bara," by Lieut. M. C. A. Henniker, R.E., appearing in *The R.E. Journal*, Vol. XLVII, 1933, pp. 473–479.

1930, but the tribesmen were driven off by the Razmak Column which included the 10th Company, Madras S. & M. Sorarogha was invested by the Mahsuds, and the post at Ahnai attacked on July 6th, but both attempts were defeated by bombing. Nevertheless, the Circular Road between Razmak and Jandola was closed for some time. On July 10th the Razmak Column advanced to Tauda China[1] and afterwards through Dwa Toi to Ladha. This ended the hostilities in Waziristan. By December, the new Tauda China-Wana road had been extended almost to Ladha and troops could be moved easily and quickly to the Kaniguram area. Happily, the unrest in Waziristan did not spread to Baluchistan, which remained astonishingly quiet.

In December, 1930, the Madras Sappers and Miners held a notable "Reunion" at Bangalore to celebrate the 150th anniversary of the raising of the Corps. No less than 1,631 pensioners attended, the oldest being Sapper Muttusami who had enlisted in 1863. An object of general interest was a pensioned mule, aged about 44 years, which had joined the Corps in 1891 and had served in many expeditions on both frontiers of India and in Egypt and Palestine during the Great War.[2] The celebrations began with a Corps Parade on December 9th, and ended, three days later, with Sports, a March Past of pensioners, and a dance in the Officers' Mess at which 300 guests were present. A similar Reunion of the Bombay Sappers and Miners took place at Kirkee in February, 1931, when 331 pensioners attended;[3] and the Bengal Sappers and Miners held a successful Reunion of pensioned Indian Officers in March, 1933. These gatherings were greatly appreciated and revived happy memories of past comradeship in arms.

From 1930 onwards, the social and other amenities provided in the three headquarter stations at Roorkee, Kirkee and Bangalore showed a rapid increase. At Roorkee, in October, 1930, work began on a small Indian Family Hospital, which was opened in November 1931. A similar hospital was built at Kirkee in 1930–31 by Bombay Sappers under instruction. For some time it remained almost empty, and then, suddenly, its value was realized and within a year a dozen babies were born in it and it was dealing with 1,000 out-patients a month.[4] At Bangalore, the Madras Sappers and Miners established a Family Hospital with beneficial results. The Roorkee Cantonment was electrified at Corps expense, the system being afterwards taken over by Government. The water-supply was improved by sinking a 300-feet tube well, and the Corps Workshops were enlarged. A valuable addition to the Bengal Corps Headquarters was a Vocational Training School to hold more than 100 boys destined to become artificers. It is recorded that the Superintendent of Instruction took delivery of a consignment of 10,000 marbles from home for a "graining" machine in the Photo-Litho School, and received with them a heavy demand for duty. Naturally, he protested, and then it appeared that the Customs officials at Bombay had classed the marbles as "amusements"!

[1]Not to be confused with the Tauda China on the Kajuri Plain near Peshawar.
[2]The mule survived until June, 1933.
[3]*R.E. Journal Supplements*, Aug., 1931, and April, 1932.
[4]Notes by Col. M. Everett, D.S.O., late R.E., sent to the author on June 15th, 1937.

The mechanization of all three Corps made rapid progress in 1931, when a number of 6-wheeler 30-cwt. lorries were received. Most of the bullocks at Roorkee were sold; but the Bengal Sappers were allowed to keep "Sonepat"—their one remaining elephant and, incidentally, the last in the Indian Army—until the trailers for the lorries arrived. In October, the following advertisement appeared in the Press under the curious title of "Animals and Birds." "*For Sale.* One Elephant, female, 65 years old, 8 feet 9 inches, healthy and staunch on *shikar*. Price Rs. 3,000 or near offer," and "Sonepat" soon disappeared from Roorkee. She fetched only Rs. 500. Her former companions, "Tuni" and "Raghnathpur" had died in 1914, and "Ghazipur" in 1930. The four elephants had been transferred from the Royal Artillery in 1900 "for Field Telegraph purposes," and later were kept "for the transport of heavy stores over difficult ground." Perhaps distinguished visitors and tigers are "heavy stores," and it is obvious that the Siwalik jungles are "difficult ground." Accordingly, until 1931, the official eye remained discreetly closed, or at least half shut, and Roorkee maintained its reputation for *shikar*, big and small. The training of the lorry drivers was not without excitement. "Lately," writes the Adjutant at Roorkee[1] "the chief amusement has been hauling 6-wheelers out of the Ganges Canal. One of the rafts, anchored to the bank, pulled its holdfasts as a lorry left it to climb the steep slope, and the vehicle slid quietly backwards into 14 feet of water. A minute or so elapsed before the driver appeared on the surface. Another driver, whose lorry was on a raft, was ordered to move it forward a foot or so. Instead, he jerked it forward quite 4 feet, and it went head foremost into 20 feet of water." So much for some aspects of life at Corps Headquarters. Expansion, reorganization and mechanization were in full swing so far as funds permitted. Unfortunately, that was no great distance, but the Sappers and Miners were adepts at finding a means to an end. They had proved it with their elephants.

Some Bombay Sappers and Miners had a strenuous time near Quetta in August 1931 when the country was shaken by a series of earthquakes. The units concerned were the 19th, 20th and 42nd D.H.Q. Companies. The first shock occurred before dawn on August 25th and was followed by others during the next two days. At 9 p.m. on the 27th there was a severe shock, lasting about a minute, and afterwards, minor tremors at intervals for the next 7 weeks. Quetta itself suffered little damage, but the road and railway through the Bolan Pass were blocked by landslides and several villages destroyed. The Sappers did salvage work and helped the Railway authorities to clear the line by removing the loose sides of cuttings and reducing the height of an overhanging cliff which threatened to fall on to the metals.[2] A much more serious earthquake struck Quetta in 1935, but an account of that catastrophe must be postponed to another chapter.

While the Kajuri Plain operations were engrossing the attention of the

[1] *Adjutant's News Letters, K.G.V.'s O. Bengal Sappers and Miners*, Nov., 1931.

[2] "The Quetta Earthquake, 1931," by Capt. H. B. Harrison, R.E., O.C., 19th Field Company, Royal Bombay Sappers and Miners, appearing in *The R.E. Journal*, Vol. XLVIII, 1934, pp. 45–54.

BUILDING A CAUSEWAY ACROSS THE PANI RIVER ON THE THAYETMYO–MINDON ROAD DURING THE BURMA REBELLION, 1931.

14th Field Company, Q.V.O. Madras Sappers and Miners, at work.

(By permission of Brig. E. E. G. L. Searight, O.B.E., M.C., late R E.)

Bengal Sappers, some Madras Sappers were engaged in military operations in far-distant Burma, where a rebellion had broken out along the banks of the Irrawaddy. At the end of 1930, troops were sent up to Tharrawaddy, 80 miles above Rangoon, and others to Henzada; but further outbreaks during the spring of 1931 at Thayetmyo and Prome necessitated more extended action and the despatch of strong reinforcements. The operations which ensued had to be carried out in the wet zone of Burma, south of a line through Toungoo, and mostly during the monsoon. Communications were very defective. The railway from Rangoon through Tharrawaddy ran northwards only to Prome, with a branch line westwards to Henzada where it bifurcated northwards to Myanaung and southwards to Bassein.[1] The only continuous metalled and bridged road in the area of operations was that from Rangoon through Prome to Allanmyo opposite Thayetmyo on the Irrawaddy; and although short lengths radiated from all large civil headquarters, these were usually unbridged and the river crossings were consequently impassable in floods. Cart tracks, unmetalled and unbridged, traversed the country in many directions, and though suitable for mechanical transport in dry weather, needed " corduroying " with timber during the rains.

The engineering work fell mostly to the 14th Company, Madras S. & M., under Captain E. E. G. L. Searight, R.E., which, with the 1st Madras Pioneers, was under the direction of Lieut.-Colonel C. Preedy, R.E., as C.R.E. Until the end of July 1931, gangs of dacoits roamed through the districts of Thayetmyo, Prome, Henzada, Tharrawaddy and Insein, and our troops were concentrated in posts from which they could operate quickly against any gang within reach. The first essentials were weatherproof accommodation and a supply of pure water, and these were soon arranged by the Public Works Department; but when it was decided to continue active operations during the monsoon, the 14th Company and the Pioneers were brought into action to make the Thayetmyo-Mindon Road fit for mechanical transport.[2] Three sections of the 14th Company left Mandalay on August 2nd and reached Thayetmyo on the 4th. The place had old associations for the Madras Sappers as the 14th Company had built defences there from 1879 to 1882 and the 11th and 12th Companies had been stationed there during the rainy seasons from 1894 to 1896. Assisted by a company of Pioneers, the 14th Company began to make the road westwards to Mindon passable for 30-cwt. lorries as far as Yegyansin, a distance of 31 miles. The existing metalled portion ended at Kyaukkyi, 9 miles short of Yegyansin, and at Taungbat, between these two places, the track crossed the Pani Chaung (River). Other work consisted of providing accommodation and water-supply for outposts and for small columns operating in the field. Each column was accompanied by 12 Sappers with canvas water-tanks, troughs and lift-and-force pumps. Work on the Mindon Road commenced on August 10th and the road was open to Yegyansin on September 12th. The

[1]See *Sketch Map of Burma in* 1931, included in this chapter.
[2]Notes by Lieut.-Col. C. Preedy, O.B.E., R.E., sent to the author on Jan. 18th, 1933.

Sappers built five timber bridges across *chaungs* while the Pioneers did the earthwork and laid 5,000 yards of corduroy.[1]

The most interesting feature of the Mindon Road was the crossing of the Pani Chaung. The river was 220 feet wide with a normal depth of 3½ feet in August and September, but it was liable to flood to a depth of 17 feet and actually rose 14 feet on September 22nd. During floods the normal velocity of 3½ knots was doubled and the river became choked with floating timber. For these reasons, a trestle bridge being out of the question, it was decided to build a flood-proof causeway for use except in the heaviest spates. A road formation was first made across the river between parallel revetments 20 feet apart, the revetment walls being of split-bamboo hurdling, reinforced with sandbags containing shingle and held in position by timber stakes. A roadway of corduroy timber mats, 12 feet wide, was then laid below water on the prepared formation, the mats being held down by stakes and attached by wires to upstream anchors. The causeway was finished on August 31st after 17 days' work and was in daily use until the middle of September when the floods came and a flying bridge had to be employed instead. During the following winter, the operations in Burma extended to the Henzada area, where two sections of the 14th Company and some Pioneers did useful road-work. Another section was employed in the Prome area, but all were back in Mandalay soon after New Year's Day having been absent on service for five months in very unhealthy surroundings.

In 1932 the Indian Army was deep in the process of Indianization and mechanization. The first King's Commissioned Indian Officer (K.C.I.O.), trained at the Royal Military Academy, Woolwich and the School of Military Engineering, Chatham, had reached India in 1931, and others were on the way. It was then decided that some of the Indian youths admitted as cadets to an Indian Military Academy at Dehra Dun should receive King's Commissions in a branch to be known as the " Corps of Indian Engineers." The Indian officers trained in England became the first officers of the new Corps, but afterwards it was officered from Dehra Dun. The Academy at Dehra Dun was opened early in 1932 under Brigadier L. P. Collins, late 4th Gurkha Rifles, as Commandant, the Assistant Commandant being Colonel A. J. G. Bird, late R.E., a former Commandant of the Bengal Sappers and Miners.[2] The course was of 2½ years' duration, and cadets destined for the Artillery, Engineers or Signals were grouped in a " Woolwich Wing " as distinct from a " Sandhurst Wing." The Prince of Wales' Indian Military College at Dehra Dun then proceeded to train boys for entry to the Indian Military Academy instead of to Woolwich and Sandhurst. The formation of the Corps of Indian Engineers affected also the " other ranks " of the Engineer services. From October 1st, 1933, all Sapper recruits were enrolled into it instead

[1] " A Field Company in Burma, 1931," by " Anon " (Capt. E. E. G. L. Searight, M.C., R.E.), appearing in *The R.E. Journal*, Vol. XLVII, 1933, pp. 89–103.

[2] Col. A. J. G. Bird held the post of Assist. Commandant until 1935, and the institution became the " Royal Indian Military Academy."

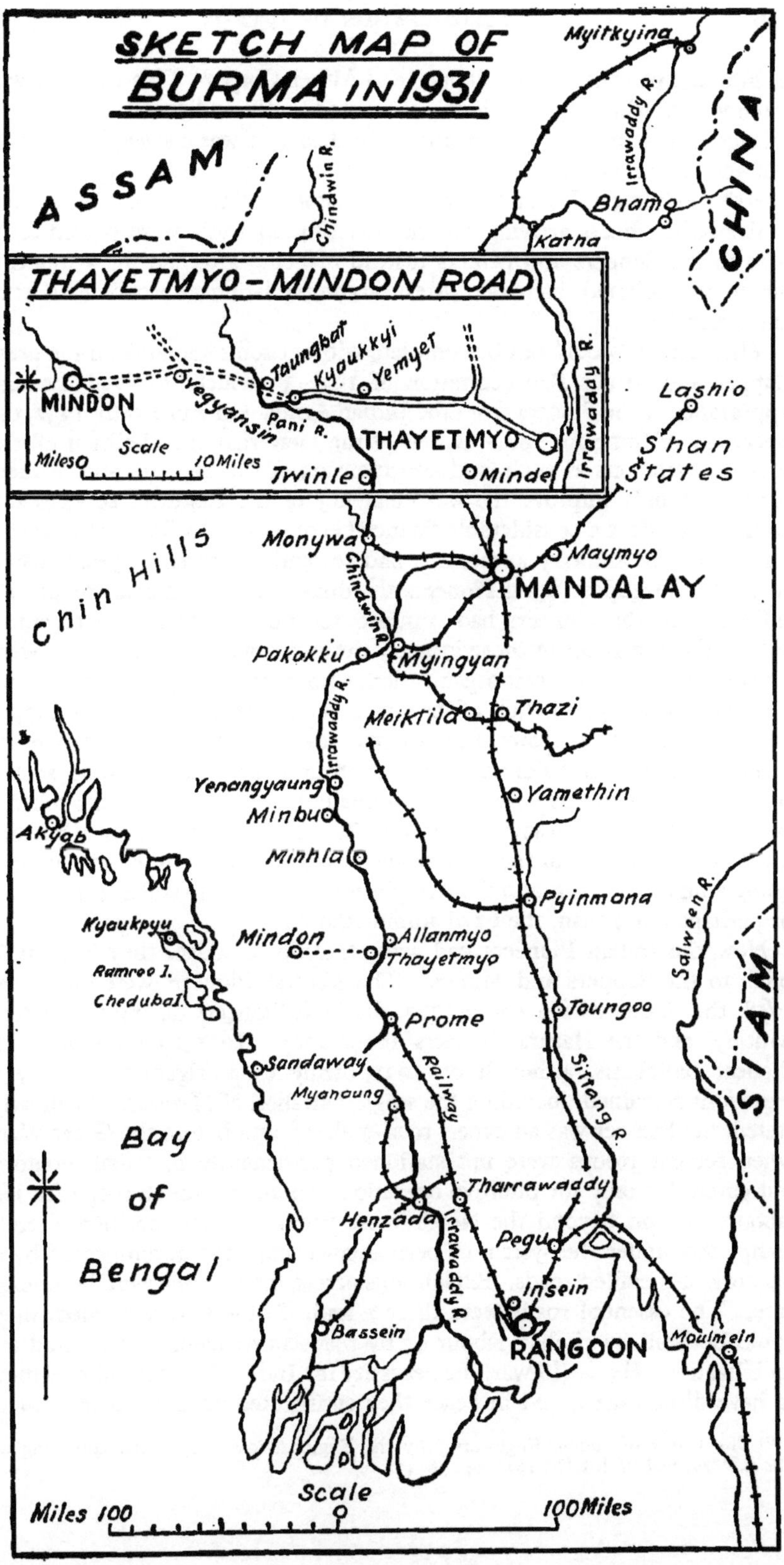
SKETCH MAP OF BURMA IN 1931
ASSAM
Chindwin R.
Myitkyina
Irrawaddy R.
CHINA
Bhamo
Katha
THAYETMYO-MINDON ROAD
Taungbat
Kyaukkyi
Yemyet
MINDON
Yegyansin
Pani R.
THAYETMYO
Irrawaddy R.
Miles 0
Scale
10 Miles
Twinle
Minde
Lashio
Shan States
Chin Hills
Monywa
Chindwin R.
Maymyo
MANDALAY
Pakokku
Myingyan
Irrawaddy R.
Meiktila
Thazi
Yenangyaung
Yamethin
Minbu
Akyab
Minhla
Pyinmana
Salween R.
Kyaukpyu
Mindon
Allanmyo
Thayetmyo
Ramree I.
Cheduba I.
Toungoo
SIAM
Prome
Sandaway
Railway
Myanaung
Sittang R.
Bay of Bengal
Tharrawaddy
Henzada
Irrawaddy R.
Pegu
Insein
Bassein
RANGOON
Moulmein
Scale
Miles 100
100 Miles

of into one or other of the Sapper and Miner Corps.[1] This measure was intended to simplify problems connected with Indianization and the raising of new units on mobilization. In theory, it was a sweeping change, but actually it did not affect a man's choice of a particular Sapper Corps nor the existing titles and distinctive customs of the three Corps. All junior R.E. officers arriving for the first time in India were posted for a year to the Sappers and Miners instead of being attached for 3 months, which necessitated increased Mess accommodation at Roorkee, Kirkee and Bangalore.

This chapter would not be complete without some remarks on the great Sapper and Miner Reorganization of 1932–33 which involved the disappearance of the Pioneer from the Indian Army. On April 18th, 1932, the Secretary of State for India expressed the view that the abolition of the Pioneer battalions as such, and an expansion of the Sappers and Miners would not only improve the war efficiency of the Engineer services but would also effect a considerable financial economy. On September 1st he wrote that the military authorities had recognized for some years that it was futile to impose upon Pioneers the dual rôle of technical troops and infantry, for the Pioneers had concentrated on developing the technical side to the detriment of those infantry duties for which, in fact, they were unsuited by reason of their organization, equipment and system of training. He proceeded to give details of the new organization proposed for a Sapper and Miner Field Company, a Divisional Headquarter Company and other Engineer units; also the number of such units and other matters shown in Appendix H to this volume; and finally he estimated that the scheme would effect an annual saving of at least Rs. 20 lakhs in the military budget. This last point was, in fact, the prime consideration. India was undergoing a financial crisis, and the Army was called upon to suffer as much as, or perhaps more than, the Civil administration.

Now the Indian Pioneers had great traditions. Also, they had given birth to the Sappers and Miners. The Madras Pioneers were formed in 1758, the Bombay Pioneers in 1777, the Sikh Pioneers during the Indian Mutiny, and the Hazara Pioneers about 1905. In 1923 there were 13 Pioneer battalions, although by 1931, owing to amalgamations, only 7 battalions remained, including the single battalion of Hazaras. As already stated, the Pioneer was an expert road-maker; and before the Great War, when regular troops were not stationed permanently in tribal territory but entered it only for punitive operations, there was much scope for his labours on and beyond the North-West Frontier. The position altered completely under the system of permanent occupation accompanied by a network of metalled roads. Expeditions across the frontier were becoming rare. The essential roads were there; and, if others were needed, they could be built by civilian labour or by road-construction units raised on mobilization. Hence, in war, the necessity for Indian Pioneer units seemed to have disappeared, and in peace they constituted an unjustifiable drain

[1] "The Corps of Indian Engineers," by the Engineer-in-Chief, India, appearing in *The R.E. Journal*, Vol. LIX, 1945, pp. 36–43.

on the Exchequer. It was desirable, also, that the Engineer troops of a division should be homogeneous in composition. The Sappers and Miners could execute or supervise any work which might normally fall to the Pioneers, whereas the latter were unable to carry out some of the more technical duties of the Sappers and Miners. The end was inevitable. Economy and utility over-rode tradition, and the establishment of Pioneers received its death sentence on October 21st, 1932.

The abolition of the Pioneers raised two questions. Firstly, to what extent should the Sappers and Miners be increased? And secondly, how could the Pioneers be absorbed?[1] Briefly, the first question was answered by changing every Field Company of Sappers and Miners from a 3-Section to a 4-Section basis both in peace and war, with the addition of one British Officer and a small increase in the strength of each Section. Also, the Section was designed to be a self-contained unit capable of independent action. The Company strength was raised from 234 to 320, and the number of artificers from 24 to 56. The Divisional Headquarter Companies were also strengthened. One Field Company of the Bengal Corps (the 6th Company) was converted into an Army Troops Company, so that the Bengal and Madras Corps should each have 2 A.T. Companies. The Chitral Section was abolished as a separate formation and was to be furnished in future by a conveniently situated Field Company.[2] The Headquarters and Depots of all three Corps were reorganized completely, each being formed into a Training Battalion of 3 Training Companies and a Depot Company. The battalion was to be commanded by a Lieut.-Colonel, R.E., with an adequate Staff.[3] It was expected that, after reorganization, the strengths of the three Corps, including recruits, would be increased to 3,518 for the Madras Sappers, 3,365 for the Bengal Sappers and 2,925 for the Bombay Sappers, or roughly 12 additional British Officers and 600 Indian ranks for each Corps. Whence could these reinforcements come? Obviously, from the Pioneers who were to be abolished.

It was a sound proposition to make use of a part, at least, of the engineering talent thrown suddenly on the market through the abolition of the Pioneers; but in dealing with the second question, that of the best way in which the necessary number of Pioneers could be absorbed, the Government made a regrettable error of judgment. They were justified in ordering the disbandment of the Hazara Pioneers because these men were mostly Afghans enlisted somewhat irregularly in the Indian Army. They made no mistake in directing the absorption of about 940 men of the Madras Pioneers into the Madras Sappers and Miners, for no class or caste objections were involved. But they erred in dealing with the Sikhs. To the Bengal Sappers and Miners they allotted not only 160 Meos (Muhammadans) from the Bombay Pioneers, but also 320 Ramdasia

[1] "Engineer Reorganization in India," by Capt. H. B. Harrison, R.E., appearing in *The R.E. Journal*, Vol. XLVI, 1932, pp. 654–657.

[2] It was decided later that a Field Company of the Royal Bombay S. & M. at Kohat should furnish the Chitral Section.

[3] For further details of the Sapper and Miner Reorganization of 1932–33, see Appendix H.

and Mazbhi Sikhs from the Sikh Pioneers; and to the Bombay Sappers and Miners, 133 Marathas (Hindus) and 160 Lobana Sikhs from the Bombay Pioneers, and a further 160 Lobana Sikhs and 320 Ramdasia and Mazbhi Sikhs from the Sikh Pioneers.

Now, there are Sikhs and Sikhs. The Gurus who founded Sikhism intended that entrance to it should be free from all religious, caste or class discrimination, and that anyone who took the vows might be admitted. For instance, many Muhammadans became Sikhs, though the Hindus supplied most of the converts. But the caste feelings of the Hindu entrants persisted under the surface, and thus there arose Sikhs of many social grades. At the top, the Katris and Jats, traders and cultivators; in the middle, the Lobanas, Ramdasias and others, who were carriers and such like; and at the bottom, the Mazbhis, or sweepers, whose name means "faithful" or "men with a religion" and who had justified that title when they marched under Lieutenant H. W. Gulliver, B.E., to the relief of Delhi during the Indian Mutiny and later formed the famous "Punjab Sappers."[1] The general opinion at Army Headquarters among officers with regimental experience in India was that it would be impracticable to mix Jat Sikhs with Mazbhi Sikhs in the same unit, a view shared by most officers of Sikh regiments and by the Commandants of the Sappers and Miners. The Sikhs already enrolled in the Bengal Sappers and Miners were exclusively Jats, and accordingly the Reorganization Committee at Simla proposed that the Bengal Corps should be allotted only Jats and the Bombay Corps only Lobanas, Ramdasias and Mazbhis. Any Jats already in the Bombay Corps could be transferred. This segregation, however, ran counter to the approved policy of Indianization which stipulated that any Sikh should be eligible to command any other Sikh, and therefore the Committee's proposal was rejected and it was decided that, while the Lobanas should go to the Bombay Corps, *both* the Bengal and Bombay Corps should absorb their quotas of Ramdasias and Mazbhis.[2]

The reorganization of the three Sapper and Miner Corps came into force on November 18th, 1932, and parties of Meos and Mazbhi Sikhs began to arrive in Roorkee. The Meos were distributed among the Musulman Sections of all companies; and the Mazbhi Sikhs, mostly from the 32nd Sikh Pioneers, were formed into new 4th Sections of the 2nd, 3rd and 5th Companies. Everything possible was done by the Commandant, Lieut.-Colonel C. A. Bird, R.E., to ease the situation. A Ceremonial Parade was held to welcome the new-comers. The Mazbhis were given separate messes and seemed at first to be settling down, but difficulties were encountered in the procedure in the *Gurdwara* (Temple). The ex-Pioneers were commanded by some of their own officers, 21 of whom had volunteered to be seconded to the three Corps of Sappers and Miners for two years, and six of these came to Roorkee from Sialkot. The difficulties at Roorkee, however, were less than those at Kirkee, where

[1]See Chapter VIII.
[2]Notes by Col. P. E. Prince, D.S.O., late R.E., sent to the author on Sept. 20th, 1937.

there was a shooting incident. Government then recognized that the scheme was doomed to failure. A Conference was held at Simla at which the Commandants of the Bengal and Bombay Sappers and Miners were present, and early in 1933 it was decided that all Jat Sikhs of the Sappers or Pioneers should be given the option of transfer to the Bengal Sappers and' Miners and all Lobana, Ramdasia and Mazbhi Sikhs to the Bombay Corps. The alternative to acceptance was discharge without the usual concessions, so there were few refusals. Subsequently, the Lobana Sikhs were allocated to the Indian Machine Gun platoons of British Infantry regiments and the general redistribution of Sikhs began in June 1933. It was completed during the next few months, and all classes settled down in their new surroundings. Thus ended a premature and most unfortunate experiment in socialization. India is a conservative country, and her manners and customs cannot be altered in a day.

CHAPTER XXV

PRELUDE TO THE WORLD WAR, 1933–1939

REORGANIZATION, modernization and Indianization were the most prominent features in the history of the Sappers and Miners before Germany launched her war of aggression in 1939. It is true that there was occasional trouble on the North-West Frontier and considerable unrest in Bengal, but these rarely necessitated the use of large forces and consequently the Sappers and Miners saw little fighting. They were employed chiefly as engineers, and Nature added to their commitments by providing earthquakes which did untold damage. At Razmak and Wana in Waziristan there was never an idle moment. Military labour was cheap, and the construction of buildings and roads gave useful employment. The exchange of Sikh personnel between the Bengal and Bombay Corps, and the absorption of the Pioneers, were soon concluded, and the men settled down satisfactorily in their new surroundings although some difficulty was experienced in training the ex-Pioneer Indian officers and N.C.O.s to the standard needed for Instructors.[1]

In 1933 a few Sapper and Miner units were in the field during operations directed from the Peshawar District against a section of the Mohmands living between the administrative border and the Durand line. The Lower Mohmands, close to the border, received allowances from the Government of India and were consequently under control; but the Upper Mohmands, who inhabited the mountains along the Durand line, were unpaid and therefore intensely jealous of their more fortunate brethren. Inter-tribal disputes culminated in an unprovoked attack by the Upper Mohmands on the " assured " tribes of Lower Mohmands who had refused to allow the Upper Mohmands to pass through their territory in order to raid across the border. The Lower Mohmands then asked for assistance and it was decided that an expedition should be sent to bring the Upper Mohmands to reason and to cover the construction of a road through Lower Mohmand territory along which troops could move quickly to the borders of the Upper Mohmand country. Little was known of the Mohmand region, for the last expedition into it had been in 1908, and the operations in 1915 had consisted chiefly in repelling attacks and consolidating behind a line of frontier blockhouses. The ground had been reconnoitred as far as Dand, some 3 miles over the border north of Peshawar, but information was meagre about the country beyond that point. Such was the general situation towards the end of July 1933 when the Peshawar Brigade, supported by the Nowshera Brigade, began to move up the Gandab Valley to help the Lower Mohmands and cover the

[1]Notes by Lieut.-Col. G. de C. E. Findlay, V.C., M.C., R.E., sent to the author on Oct. 25th, 1937.

building of a motor road from Pir Kala, 3 miles south-west of Shabkadar, through Dand to Ghalanai in the heart of the Lower Mohmand territory.[1] The general alignment was fixed after aerial reconnaissance and followed roughly the line of an existing track. In one stretch, however, an old Buddhist trade-route was used which must have been built 2,000 years before and was invisible from the air.

Two Bengal Sapper units were engaged in the construction of the Gandab Road. These were the 2nd Company (Major G. R. Pim, R.E.) and the 3rd Company (Captain R. St C. Davidson, R.E.). In addition, a detachment of the 31st Field Troop (Lieutenant E. W. H. Clarke, R.E.) was employed on watering duties with the Nowshera Brigade.[2] The 2nd Company had been summoned at short notice from the Kajuri Plain, and the 3rd Company from Roorkee. On July 29th, 1933, the 2nd Company began work on the most difficult rock-cutting portions of the 7 miles' length of alignment between Pir Kala and Dand, while road-grading machines operated in the flat country near Pir Kala and civilian gangs laboured towards Dand. In the easier stretches, traffic was carried temporarily on thick wire-netting tracks pending the consolidation of the permanent road-surface. The road-head reached Dand on July 31st, and the Nowshera Brigade camped there while the Peshawar Brigade moved forward a further 7 miles to Ghalanai. This marked the end of the first stage of the road construction. The second stage, to Ghalanai, was a more formidable undertaking. Near Dand the Sappers were faced with cliffs and steep slopes of rock up which the motor road would have to climb. Then followed 4 miles of tangled hills and *nullahs*, culminating in the lofty Karappa Pass, beyond which, however, the route led along an open valley and presented no difficulty. The 3rd Company arrived from Roorkee on August 6th, and with the 2nd Company and large gangs of labourers set to work on the most troublesome sections. The 2nd Company supervised the rock-cutting and blasting operations of the labourers in a ¼-mile length on the Karappa, and the 3rd Company performed the same duty in a ½-mile length of the steep ascent from Dand.[3] Steady progress was maintained although there was some interference by snipers. The rock-drilling compressors used by the 3rd Company in the ascent from Dand caused much consternation among the Tarakzai labourers, most of whom had never seen even a motor-car. On August 28th the road was opened to Ghalanai. The Sappers and road gangs, assisted latterly by infantry working parties, had constructed 14 miles of motor-road in 4 weeks through difficult country and over a high pass, and troops from Peshawar could now reach the heart of the Mohmand territory in a few hours.

The third stage of the Gandab Road project consisted in extending the road through easy country to Yusuf Khel, a village some 6 miles beyond

[1]See *Sketch Map of the N.W. Frontier : North of the Kabul River*, included in Chapter XXII, and also General Map III.

[2]*Annual Records, K.G.V.'s O. Bengal S. & M.*, 1933–34, p. 16.

[3]"The Gandab Road," by Lieut.-Col. A. V. T. Wakely, D.S.O., M.C., R.E., appearing in *The R.E. Journal*, Vol. XLIX, 1935, pp. 1–24.

Ghalanai and close below the Nahakki Pass. This was accomplished in three days. Machines made the road formation, infantry collected gravel, and the Sappers supervised the rock-cutting. The 2nd Company then began to build bridges north of Ghalanai and the 3rd Company between the Karappa and Ghalanai. Tribal jealousy interfered at times with the work and gave rise on one occasion to a free fight between the Tarakzai and Halimzai coolies. Nevertheless, on September 29th, 1933, the 20-mile stretch of road from Pir Kala to Yusuf Khel was opened to traffic. It was probably the first two-way motor highway constructed through independent territory on the North-West Frontier under cover of troops. One half of its length was built by machines, and although permanent road construction was a novel employment for the Sappers and Miners they soon grasped the main principles. Lieut.-Colonel A. V. T. Wakely, R.E., C.R.E. Peshawar District, who was in charge of the engineer operations, states that the lack of Pioneers was found to be no drawback because sufficient unskilled labour could be supplied by the contractors' men and infantry. A battalion or two of Pioneers could not have coped with the work unless reinforced by civilian labour. The opposition also was slight, and consequently the armed worker was not needed. *Khassadars* guarded the nine labour camps and protected the gangs on the road. The chief lesson learnt by the Sappers and Miners was the desirability of having some British and Indian officers who could talk Pushtu and were accustomed to dealing with tribal labour. Lieutenant M. C. A. Henniker, R.E., of the 2nd Company, could speak the language with some fluency and was able to go in person to the local villages and engage daily labour so quickly and cheaply that at one time the company had some 2,000 tribesmen working for it.[1]

Under the peculiar title of " special conditions arising in peace-time," preparations were next made to extend the Mohmand operations into Bajaur, whither the 1st Company, Bengal S. & M. (Captain G. D. S. Adami, R.E.) was sent from the Kajuri Plain in August to build an Inglis bridge over the Panjkora River at Balambat above Sado. This structure was in replacement of a suspension bridge which had been washed away. It took the form of two cantilevers on the old suspension-bridge piers, supported in the middle by a timber trestle. Work began on August 8th and ended on September 1st when, the proposed advance into Bajaur having been abandoned, the 1st Company returned to Fort Salop in the Kajuri Plain to help the 5th and 6th Companies. The Inglis bridge at Balambat was dismantled during the summer of 1934 by a detachment of the 3rd Company under Lieutenant T. Burrowes, R.E.

Political agitation in Bengal during the autumn of 1932 had led to the formation of a special " Bengal Additional Garrison " in which some detachments of Sappers and Miners were included. The Additional Garrison was composed of the 7th and 8th Infantry Brigades, the 7th Brigade being located in Dacca, Mymensing, Comilla and Chittagong to the east of Calcutta, and the 8th Brigade in Midnapore, Bankura and Saidpore

[1] *Adjutant's News Letters, K.G.V.'s O. Bengal S. & M.*, Oct., 1933.

to the west. A special " Bengal Section," Bengal S. & M., was attached to the 7th Brigade, and a " Bombay Section " from the Bombay Corps served with the 8th Brigade. Each had a large proportion of artificers capable of running machinery. Early in 1933, these two sections were still employed on minor defence works, water-supply to camps and other normal duties in the Presidency and Assam District, where the troops were assisting the police to maintain order, but in October they returned to their headquarters at Roorkee and Kirkee and were replaced by the 11th A.T. Company, Madras S. & M. (Major W. H. Knox, R.E.) which remained in Bengal until October 1935.

It was fortunate that the 11th Company happened to be in Bengal when India began to suffer from a series of earthquakes, for within three days of the first severe shock in North Bihar at 2 p.m. on January 15th, 1934, a detachment from Midnapore was busily engaged in clearing up the damage at Monghyr on the Ganges. The first warning was a noise like distant thunder. This was followed by a heavy shock when, for two minutes, the ground swayed so violently that it was difficult for a man to remain standing. As the shock died away, gaping fissures opened through which black slime oozed to the surface. Widespread damage was done throughout North Bihar between the Ganges and the Nepal border, and particularly in Bettiah, Motihari, Muzaffarpur, Darbhanga and Monghyr.[1] Some 10,000 people are believed to have been killed and a far greater number injured. One man fell into a fissure which closed immediately over his head. Then it re-opened and he was ejected unhurt by an eruption of slime and water. Although most of the larger buildings withstood the shock, the bazaars collapsed on all sides. Many road and railway bridges were rendered unusable, and some were completely destroyed. Those least affected were of the screw-pile type. The shock was not confined to North Bihar, for it was felt throughout Nepal and Sikkim and even in distant Roorkee. Such was the catastrophe which brought an urgent call to the Sappers and Miners for assistance.

A telegram reached Roorkee at 11 p.m. on January 18th and within five hours a section of the 2nd Company, with Lieutenants E. H. Ievers, M. C. A. Henniker and L. T. Grove, R.E., was in the Calcutta mail-train *en route* for Patna for employment in the Tirhut Division while the Madras Sappers dealt with Monghyr. Patna itself had suffered little, but Monghyr, Muzaffarpur and Darbhanga were in a shocking condition. The most urgent work at Muzaffarpur having been completed by January 31st, the section went to Darbhanga and demolished the ruins of a hospital with 370 lbs. of guncotton. Meanwhile, reinforcements had been summoned from Roorkee, and two more sections of the 2nd Company under Major G. R. Pim, R.E., with Lieutenant J. M. Guyon, R.E., left headquarters on the 30th while the remaining section under Lieutenant

[1] " Earthquake Relief," by Lieut. L. T. Grove, R.E., appearing in *The R.E. Journal*, Vol. LXIX, 1935, pp. 57–66. Muzaffarpur is 40 miles north of Patna, and Darbhanga 30 miles east of Muzaffarpur. Bettiah and Motihari are 80 miles and 50 miles north-west of Muzaffarpur. Monghyr, south-west of Muzaffarpur, is 90 miles down the Ganges from Patna.

C. R. Wright (Pioneers) came from Jhansi. By February 11th, the entire 2nd Company was scattered over the Tirhut Division. Two sections were repairing bridges on the Muzaffarpur–Darbhanga road, another was building a bridge 30 miles from Motihari, and the fourth was clearing Muzaffarpur. Six days later, the unit concentrated in Muzaffarpur and entrained for Roorkee, leaving the 11th A.T. Company, Madras S. & M., to complete the clearance of wreckage.

In 1935, several units of the Sappers and Miners were called upon to cope with the damage caused by an earthquake more violent even than those about Quetta in 1931 or in Bihar in 1934. Quetta itself was the victim on this occasion. At about 3 a.m. on May 31st, a terrific shock laid the city, civil lines and cantonment in utter ruin. So universal was the devastation that subsequent shocks could do little more harm. The noise of thousands of buildings collapsing in the city was followed by an extraordinary silence. About one-third of the inhabitants lay dead or injured under the debris and most of the remainder were too dazed even to cry out. In the civil lines, many bungalows were razed to the ground: the roofs of others had fallen on the occupants. The Civil Hospital was a pile of rubble, and 300 police were buried in their barracks. In the cantonment, the intensity of the shock seems to have varied; and at the Staff College, which lies some distance from the city, the magnitude of the catastrophe was not at first realized. In the Royal Air Force Camp, however, hardly a building remained and casualties were very heavy. Fate was kind in sparing the Cantonment Hospitals which were expanded immediately to cope with the influx of injured from the city and civil lines. Ladies volunteered to work as nurses and laboured day and night with the regular hospital staffs. Many curious incidents are recorded of the first effects of the shock, but perhaps the most remarkable is the experience of a battalion of infantry which happened to be returning from a night exercise. At one moment, the men were marching smartly in formation. At the next, they were struggling in a confused mass on the ground, and there they lay until it became possible to stand.

The Sapper units in Quetta at the time were the 16th A.T. Company, Madras S. & M. (Captain Sir John S. Forbes, Bt., R.E.) and the 21st and 42nd D.H.Q. Companies, Bombay S. & M. (Captains W. G. Irvine-Fortescue and J. P. C. Mackinlay, R.E.) They were quartered in the Napier and Kabul Lines, almost the only barracks within two miles of the centre of Quetta. The Napier Lines escaped lightly, but many buildings collapsed in the Kabul Lines though only eleven Sapper ranks were injured. From their central position the Sappers were among the first to reach the scene of chaos and destruction in the city, the civil lines and the R.A.F. Camp. They and their tools were in great demand, and their motor transport proved invaluable. Unfortunately, tools were deficient at first because most of them lay buried under the ruins of a fieldworks store, but these were recovered as quickly as possible and brought into use. The bulk of the engineer tasks devolved on the Sappers and Miners because the civilian element of the Military Engineer Services had suffered heavy casualties in the city.[1] A telegram asking for reinforcements was despatched to Roorkee where a rapid mobilization of the 1st and 2nd Companies, Bengal S. & M. (Majors R. H. Perry and G. R. Pim, R.E.) took place on the night of May 31st–June 1st. Both units entrained soon after dawn, but the 2nd Company got no further than Saharanpur where its orders were countermanded and it returned to headquarters. The 1st Company continued to Quetta and began work on June 4th. Reports on the situation then led to the despatch of the 2nd Company, and that unit reached Quetta on the 7th.

During the first few days after the earthquake, all the Sapper units were employed chiefly on rescue work and fire fighting, but later they undertook more technical duties. The 16th A.T. Company, Madras S. & M., restored the City Water-supply main, shored up the roof of the Power Station, and repaired buildings in the Arsenal. The 1st and 2nd Companies, Bengal S. & M., and the 21st Company, Bombay S. & M., demolished unsafe buildings, ringed the city with a barbed wire fence, provided water-supply for numerous tented camps for refugees, built or repaired bridges, and made road and rail diversions. Meanwhile, the 42nd D.H.Q. Company, Bombay S. & M., maintained a workshop for the production of all necessities. The demolition of St. Mary's Church and the Sandeman Hall was undertaken by the 21st Company. When the most urgent work had been finished, the units turned their attention to the provision of hot weather accommodation in the form of steel-framed huts and to the improvement of existing barracks by lowering the roofs and supporting the trusses on stanchions so that the walls carried no load. The work of clearing and repairing devastated Quetta continued steadily throughout the summer of 1935. In the middle of August, two additional units arrived from Kirkee, the 17th and 19th Companies, Bombay S. & M. (Majors A. Prain and H. S. Anderson, R.E.), but by the middle of November most of the urgent work had been finished and all the Sapper units left Quetta with the exception of the 21st and 42nd D.H.Q. Companies. Never was an ample supply of Sapper and Miner labour more welcome than in the catastrophe of 1935.

We must revert now to the situation in the Mohmand territory north of Peshawar where, it will be remembered, the 2nd and 3rd Companies, Bengal S. & M., had carried the Gandab Road to Yusuf Khel in September, 1933. Disputes occurred over the rates of pay for the repair of the road, and military operations against the Upper Mohmands had to be resumed in 1935 after a *lashkar* had moved down the road and severely damaged it. In the middle of August, the Peshawar and Nowshera Brigades were concentrated at Pir Kala, where the road begins, and on the 23rd the Nowshera Brigade advanced to Dand against determined opposition. With it was the 3rd Company, Bengal S. & M., under Major E. E. Nott-Bower, R.E. Two days later, the Peshawar Brigade marched through to Ghalanai without difficulty, but as the Upper Mohmands continued to show signs of

[1] "The Quetta Earthquake, 1935," by Lieut. B. M. Archibald, R.E., appearing in *The R.E. Journal*, Vol. L, 1936, pp. 485–497.

hostility it was decided that the road should be extended into their territory beyond the Nahakki Pass. Reinforcements were sent from Rawalpindi in the form of two infantry brigades, a cavalry regiment, additional artillery and light tanks, and the 5th Company, Bengal S. & M., under Captain S. A. H. Batten, R.E. During the ensuing operations the chief tasks of the Sapper and Miner units and the Military Engineer Services were supplying water to camps, building a road extension over the Nahakki Pass (3,124 feet), and maintaining the road from Pir Kala to Yusuf Khel which had been completed in 1933.[1] The local sources of water were at their lowest and it was necessary to tap underground streams in the bed of the Gandab *nullah* in order to supply projected forward camps at Katsai on the road to Yusuf Khel and at Wucha Jowar to the west of it. The 3rd Company started excavating in the *nullah* bed, but the well yielded only 3,000 gallons an hour. Under cover of darkness, the enemy stole some lengths of 4-in. Victaulic pipe, and later, when the line was "booby-trapped," they removed lengths on each side of the trap. On the evening of September 3rd, a detachment under Captain E. E. Stenhouse, R.E., had an unpleasant experience while trying to retrieve an abandoned Merryweather pump. They were greeted with close range fire from Mohmands who were following up a retreating column, and had to postpone their project till the following day. Meanwhile, a Field Engineer, who was also a water-diviner, had discovered a subterranean source of water in the *nullah* which yielded about 8,000 gallons an hour and was sufficient to meet the needs of Katsai and Wucha Jowar camps, and thus one problem of water-supply was solved.

The first phase of the advance to Nahakki Village, which lies in the plain beyond the Nahakki Pass, was the establishment of a brigade at Katsai, and for this the Sappers had to lay 3½ miles of 4-in. Victaulic pipe-line from Ghalanai to Katsai in a single day. Both field companies and a battalion of infantry were detailed for this work on September 11th and completed it before nightfall. The brigade moved to Katsai and on September 19th occupied the Nahakki Pass without opposition and debouched on to the Nahakki Plain while the Sappers and infantry laid a further 2 miles of pipe-line beyond Katsai. It was then decided to extend the line over the Nahakki Pass, using camels to transport the material. This was accomplished successfully and when the work had been completed the advanced troops at Nahakki were supplied by an 8-mile length of pipe-line from Ghalanai along which water was pumped in four stages against a total head of 1,100 feet. As so often in war, the rapid success of the military operations had depended on the work of the technical troops.

The essential demand for water having been met, the Sappers turned to the improvement of the line of communication. The additional length of motor road to be built from Yusuf Khel to the Brigade Camp at Nahakki was 5 miles, and most of it was on the slopes of the Nahakki ridge. Preliminary work had been begun at Yusuf Khel on September 19th, and by

[1] "Engineer Work in the Mohmand Operations, 1935," by "Comenger," appearing in *The R.E. Journal*, Vol. LI, 1937, pp. 507–522.

the end of the month some 3,000 labourers were extending the road under Sapper supervision. The 3rd Company operated from the Nahakki camp, and the 5th Company from the Wucha Jowar camp further down the line, but occasionally the units worked together as, for instance, in a re-entrant north of the Nahakki Pass. Here, the two companies blasted towards each other, while, higher up the rocky slope, civilian labour blew the hillside down on top of them! During blasting hours the place was so filled with dust and flying stones and the thunder of explosions that it was known as the "Valley of the Shadow of Death."[1] The road had many zigzags and was surfaced only with well-rolled gravel, but it served its purpose. By October 8th, it was open to the summit of the Pass, and by the 28th, to Nahakki Camp. Three days later, after the 3rd Company had demolished a village tower, the advanced brigade at Nahakki withdrew, followed in succession by the other three brigades on the line of communication. The Mohmands made their submission, the pipe-line and pumping plant were dismantled, packed and returned to Peshawar, and, early in November, "Mohforce" was broken up.

Since no Pioneer battalions were available for road work in the Mohmand operations of 1933 and 1935, it was necessary to employ a large amount of contract labour at considerable expense. Such labour on a grand scale was required also in the Waziristan operations of 1936–37, when four Road Construction Battalions had to be raised in addition to cope with the manual work. It is questionable, therefore, whether the abolition of the Pioneer from the Indian Army really effected much economy in the military budget. Such economy pre-supposed a peaceful frontier. But was it correct to assume that intensive road development in Waziristan and elsewhere would change overnight the hereditary instincts of the Mahsud and Mohmand? History indicates that, from a financial point of view the abolition of the Pioneer in 1932 was somewhat premature.

Turning now to events in other parts of India it may be remarked that in January 1935 many retired Indian Officers and other ranks of the former Madras Pioneers were welcome guests at a successful "Re-union" of the Madras Sappers and Miners in Bangalore. The oldest soldier of the 1,100 Pioneers present was Subadar Rahim Khan who had enlisted in 1872, and the Sapper and Miner pensioners included four men who had joined the Madras Corps more than 60 years before.[2] The programme, during six days of festivities, followed the lines of those of earlier Re-unions, and the Sapper pensioners returned to their homes with a vivid picture of the modern activities of the Corps. The inclusion of the Pioneer pensioners was a friendly gesture which showed that the Madras Pioneers were accepted as fully incorporated in the Sappers and Miners.

In the summer of 1934, a new chapter was opened in the history of the three Corps when responsibility began to pass from the British officers of the Royal Engineers to Indian officers of the Corps of Indian Engineers.[3]

[1] *Adjutant's News Letters, K.G.V.'s O. Bengal S. & M.*, Oct., 1935.
[2] "Re-union of Pensioners at Bangalore," appearing in *The R.E. Journal Supplement*, May, 1935, pp. 133, 134.
[3] *Annual Records, K.G.V.'s O. Bengal S. & M.*, 1934–35, p. 3.

This occurred through the selection of three Field Companies, one in each Corps, for gradual Indianization of the King's Commissioned ranks. The units chosen were the 5th Company, Bengal S. & M., the 15th Company, Madras S. & M., and the 22nd Company, Bombay S. & M.[1] Training at the Indian Military Academy in Dehra Dun was extended to selected Indian N.C.O.s, and in August 1934 the Madras and Bengal Sappers each had one N.C.O. at Dehra Dun under instruction as a Gentleman Cadet. Major H. Williams, R.E., an ex-Bengal Sapper and Miner, had joined the Staff of the Academy, and Colonel A. J. G. Bird, late R.E., was still the Assistant Commandant. Accordingly, the Sappers and Miners were well represented. The programme announced for the Indianization of the 5th Company envisaged the appointment of two King's Commissioned Indian Officers (K.C.I.O.s) from England in August 1936, followed by two Indian Commissioned Officers (I.C.O.s) from Dehra Dun, and it was anticipated that the unit would come on to the full Indianized establishment in 1939.[2] Early in 1935, however, the Indianization of the 5th Company was postponed to accelerate that of the 15th and 22nd Companies. Fully trained K.C.I.O.s arriving from England were to be sent to Bangalore or Kirkee, and I.C.O.s from Dehra Dun were to undergo a course of 2½ years' training in civil engineering at the Thomason College, Roorkee, before being posted to one of the three Sapper Corps, though while at Roorkee they would be attached to the Bengal Corps. Under this scheme, 2nd Lieutenants P. S. Bhagat and A. N. Kashyap, I.E., arrived from Dehra Dun in February 1935, and 2nd Lieutenant Anant Singh, I.E., in August 1935, and all were attached to the Bengal Corps to await the re-opening of the Thomason College in October after the vacation. They were followed in February 1936 by 2nd Lieutenants J. S. Dhillon and A. D. Verma, I.E., and later by other I.C.O.s, and in October 1936, Major H. Williams, R.E., was transferred from the Indian Military Academy to take charge of the I.C.O.s at the Thomason College. But the system of training I.C.O.s at the College was soon abandoned, and no more were sent there after the first three had qualified in July 1938. Of these three, one joined the Madras Sappers and two the Bombay Sappers, and it is noteworthy that one of the latter, 2nd Lieutenant P. S. Bhagat, I.E., was awarded the Victoria Cross for conspicuous gallantry in Eritrea in February 1941.[3] The process of Indianization cannot be traced further in these pages.[4] It must suffice to remark that it justified its inception and has provided many trained officers for the new Dominion armies of India and Pakistan.

All Sappers and Miners were greatly pleased by an announcement in the *London Gazette* of October 16th, 1936, that H.M. The King, having approved the creation of the office of Chief Royal Engineer, had appointed thereto General Sir Bindon Blood. This distinguished Royal Engineer,

[1] *The R.E. Journal Supplement*, Feb., 1935.
[2] *Adjutant's News Letters, K.G.V.'s O. Bengal S. & M.*, June, 1934.
[3] *The R.E. Journal Supplement*, July, 1941.
[4] Some details are given in " Sappers and Indianization," by " Anonymous " appearing in *The R.E. Journal*, Vol. LII, 1938, pp. 269–272.

who joined the Bengal Corps in 1871, had spent no less than 17 years of his regimental soldiering with it, serving in the Jowaki campaign of 1877–78 and in Afghanistan in 1880. He left India in 1882 but returned in 1885 and was Commandant of the Bengal S. & M. for 7 years. A fine soldier, a great slayer of tigers and a thorough sportsman, he was idolized by all ranks of the Corps whose Colonel he became on March 6th, 1918. As already recorded, he died on May 16th, 1940, at the great age of 97 years, shortly after resigning the appointment of Chief Royal Engineer in which he was succeeded by another ex-Bengal Sapper and Miner in the person of Lieut.-General Sir J. R. E. Charles, Colonel-Commandant, R.E.[1] General Charles became also Colonel of the Bengal Corps, the Colonel of the Madras Corps being Major-General S. G. Loch (from January 18th, 1935), and of the Bombay Corps, Brig.-General G. H. Boileau (from December 18th, 1936).

The year 1936 was marked also by the arrival in India of the first Colonel-Commandant, R.E., to visit the country in an unofficial capacity. The visitor was Lieut.-General Sir Aylmer Hunter-Weston, an ex-Bengal Sapper and Miner, who, with Lady Hunter-Weston, made a most comprehensive tour of India and parts of Burma between October, 1936, and March, 1937. He omitted no station in which there was any considerable gathering of Royal Engineers or Sappers and Miners, and everywhere he was received with open arms. At Wana, where he had commanded the 2nd Company, Bengal S. & M., in 1894, when the camp was attacked by Mahsuds, he attended a parade of 700 men drawn from all three Sapper Corps and afterwards met in friendly fashion some of his former enemies.[2] At Roorkee he dined in the R.E. Mess, famous not only for traditions dating back to Indian Mutiny days but also for its wonderful collection of sporting trophies.[3] His visit to Roorkee was the occasion for a round of festivities, and the same may be said of his subsequent visits to the headquarters of the Madras and Bombay Corps at Bangalore and Kirkee. On his return to England he was able to give his brother Colonels-Commandant a glowing account of the welfare of the Indian Sappers and Miners and of their technical advancement under modern conditions.[4]

Among other happenings in 1936 it is sad to record a tragic accident at Gulmarg in Kashmir on February 29th in which two young Bengal Sappers, Lieutenants A. R. Hingston and J. L. Nolan, R.E., lost their lives. An avalanche struck the hut in which they were living and lifted off the roof. Snow then poured in and buried them. They were promising

[1]For further details of the career of Gen. Sir Bindon Blood, G.C.B., G.C.V.O., see footnote in Chapter X. See also an Obituary Notice appearing in *The R.E. Journal*, Vol. LIV, 1940, pp. 321–331. A portrait of Sir Bindon Blood forms the frontispiece to this volume.

[2]See Chapter XIV.

[3]These included the following:—*Bara Singh*, 49 in. (Capt. C. L. B. Duke, R.E., 1925); *Bison*, 39 in. (Lieut. A. H. G. Napier, R.E., 1929); *Black Buck*, 27¾ in. (Capt. B. Blood, R.E., 1877); *Buffalo*, 59½ in. (Capt. W. A. G. Wallace, R.E., 1875); *Chital*, 37¾ in. (Maj. F. G. Drew, R.E., 1928); *Ibex*, 49 in. (Lieut. G. C. Clark, R.E., 1930); *Markhor*, 52½ in. (Capt. R. I. C. Blenkinsop, R.E., 1932, and two others); *Ovis Ammon*, 45½ in. (Lieut. R. H. Reynolds, R.E., 1934); *Oorial*, 37 in. (Capt. A. G. Hunter-Weston, R.E., 1894); and *Sambhar*, 41½ in. (Capt. G. D. Watson, R.E., 1919).

[4]*The R.E. Journal Supplements*, Jan. and July, 1937.

youngsters who had gone to Gulmarg for winter sports. During the summer, Brigadier Philip Neame, V.C., late R.E., an ex-Bengal Sapper and Miner, had the unusual experience of accompanying a mission to Lhasa in Tibet. It seems that he had recovered sufficiently from a severe mauling received from a wounded tigress in April, 1933, which nearly cost him his right arm. His escape from Italy during the World War, after his capture in North Africa, and his post-war appointment as Lieut.-Governor of Guernsey, are matters of common knowledge.

In April, 1937, a contingent representing the Sappers and Miners left India to attend the Coronation of H.M. King George VI and returned in the middle of June. It was commanded by Lieutenant W. H. D. Wakely, R.E., of the 8th A. T. Company, Bengal S. & M., stationed at Wana and included two Subadar-Majors and a Subadar from each of the three Corps. While in England, the contingent was quartered at Hampton Court for three weeks, and it is said that, apart from official pageantry, the V.C.O.s were impressed mainly by the system of fixed prices in the London shops, the underground railways, the traffic control by lights, the fat cows of the countryside and the thick cream from their milk.

A few months earlier, the situation on the North-West Frontier, which had been quiet for some time, had begun to cause anxiety in official circles. On this occasion the area was Northern Waziristan and the offenders the Tochi Wazirs. The Mahsuds, further south, were not affected, and indeed were extremely angry with their neighbours who had shown an inclination to encroach into their territory. In the autumn of 1936, there lived in the small village of Ipi, close to Mir Ali, a red-bearded and fanatical *faqir* much venerated by the local inhabitants. It so happened that a Muhammadan in Bannu abducted a Hindu girl and the parents brought a civil action against him. The case dragged on for weeks, and communal feeling mounted steadily. Then the Faqir of Ipi intervened. He moved southwards into the Khaisora Valley at the head of a rabble of Daur tribesmen and, joined by a number of hot-headed young Wazirs, announced his intention of marching on Bannu to enforce his own ideas of justice. The tribal elders were informed that the Hindu girl must be returned at once, and to this they agreed; but they were overruled by the young hot-heads under the influence of the Faqir, who was still in the Khaisora Valley with a small following although many of his adherents had gone home. Lest this open defiance should in time inflame the whole frontier, the Government then arranged to despatch columns into the Khaisora from both Razmak and Mir Ali. The movement began on November 23rd, 1936, and was strongly opposed in the narrow gorges of the Khaisora and on the plain to the north, but the columns concentrated finally in Mir Ali where they were joined by the 2nd Infantry Brigade from Peshawar and other troops. It was decided in the end that the best method of maintaining order would be to build a loop road running through the disaffected areas from Mir Ali, on the Tochi Valley road, southwards to the Khaisora near Biche Kashkai, thence eastwards down the left bank of that river and through a defile called the Sein Gorge, and finally north-

DINING-ROOM, R.E. MESS, ROORKEE.

The Headquarters Mess of the K.G.V's O. Bengal Sappers and Miners.

eastwards to rejoin the Tochi road some 8 miles from Bannu.[1] The surface was to be of shingle, well consolidated to stand motor traffic.

At the outset, only the 15th Company, Madras S. & M. (Captain E. H. T. Gayer, R.E.), was available; but on November 30th, the 18th Company Bombay S. & M. (Major E. N. Clifton, R.E.), arrived from Kohat, and on December 2nd, the 4th Company, Bengal S. & M. (Captain R. D. Ross, R.E.), from Rawalpindi. These units were reinforced at the end of the month by the 22nd Company, Bombay S. & M. (Captain M. R. H. Z. Swinhoe, R.E.), from Kirkee. The four companies worked in friendly rivalry and produced admirable results. The normal procedure was as follows. The fighting column moved from camp at about 7.30 a.m.—protective troops, cavalry, tanks and infantry, with an engineer reconnaissance party ahead. Next came the engineer column with an ungainly circus of auto-patrols looking like enormous spiders against the dawn sky, trail builders and traction engines following close on the heels of the Sappers and Miners, and finally the infantry battalions detailed as working parties.[2] The troops returned to camp on the conclusion of each day's work so that it was frequently necessary to "down tools" at 2 p.m. although work had been started only at 10 a.m. The Sappers laid out the line for a distance of anything up to a mile a day, while infantry road-making parties removed big stones and boulders, prepared the formation and excavated side-drains. Two or three days' work in rear, the remainder of the infantry laid and consolidated a width of 18 ft. of shingle, 2-in. deep. No serious difficulty was encountered until the Sein Gorge was reached. Here the 4th Company threw itself with immense energy at a long side-cut where the size of the boulders made the use of machines impracticable, and the air resounded with the noise of compressors and explosions. Ten-ton boulders were split in all directions, and the place was more dangerous than the piquet line. The chief problem was the removal of large quantities of rock from above the road level, necessitated by the perpendicular strata in the gorge. The 18th Company did excellent work in this section. As the road construction progressed, the troops moved forward to new camps; but meanwhile, on December 21st, work had been begun by contract from the Bannu end, and a race for Rucha Camp, to the east of the Gorge, developed between the Sappers and infantry from the west and the labour gangs from the east. It was won by the labour gangs after a very close finish, and on January 15th, 1937, a car completed for the first time the 33 miles' circuit of the Khaisora Road. The Sapper companies concerned in this project were employed occasionally as infantry, but they shared also in the congenial task of demolishing towers, houses and caves. In all, they dealt with about 16 towers and 50 houses. The outstanding features of the Khaisora Road project were the extensive employment of modern mechanical apparatus and the careful organization of labour for rapid work.[3]

[1]See *Sketch Map of the Waziristan Road System in* 1937, included in this chapter.

[2]"Khaisora Road," by Col. R. L. Bond, C.B.E., D.S.O., M.C., late R.E., appearing in *The R.E. Journal*, Vol. LII, 1938, pp. 190–203.

[3]"The Day's Work on the North-West Frontier," by Maj. E. H. T. Gayer, O.B.E., R.E., appearing in *The R.E. Journal*, Vol. LII, 1938, pp. 341–350.

The military and engineering operations in 1936 were but the prelude to further adventures in Northern Waziristan. The Faqir of Ipi intensified his propaganda against the Government, and in spite of political pressure and some bombing by our aeroplanes, the tribes under his influence continued to raid administered territory. The only remedy was to resume operations on a larger scale. To this end, the Bannu, Razmak and Wana Brigades were organized as a Division, known as "Wazdiv," although the Wana Brigade remained isolated since road communication with Wana had been interrupted. Wazdiv and the 1st Indian Division, which concentrated at Mir Ali at the end of April 1937, were then formed into a single command called "Wazirforce." The Faqir of Ipi was in the Lower Khaisora region; but as the hot weather approached he moved southwestwards, and establishing his headquarters in some caves at Arsal Kot on the Shaktu *nullah* south of the Khaisora, continued to harangue his followers, distribute money and supplies, and send forth his emissaries to preach the gospel of hate.

The operations undertaken in the summer of 1937 took place in the area enclosed roughly by the old Circular Road, a rugged country in which water could be obtained only from the Tochi, Khaisora, Shaktu and Tank Zam streams and from a few springs. Fortunately, the services of no less than 6 Field Companies and a D.H.Q. Company of Sappers and Miners were immediately available. The 15th Company, Madras S. & M. (Captain E. H. T. Gayer, R.E.), which was due to return to Bangalore from Razmak, was detained in Waziristan, and with the 12th Company (Captain H. E. M. Newman, R.E.), which had arrived in relief, was flung at once into the battle. The 4th Company (Captain R. C. P. James, R.E.) and the 43rd D.H.Q. Company (Captain J. H. Blundell, R.E.), both of the Bengal S. & M., came from Rawalpindi with the 1st Division. The 2nd Company, Bengal S. & M. (Captain G. C. Clark, R.E.), was sent from Wana to join them, and in May the 3rd Company (Major W. F. Hasted, R.E.) and the 5th Company (Captain W. L. D. Veitch, R.E.) arrived from Roorkee. This imposing display of engineering talent was increased in July by the advent of the 14th Company, Madras S. & M. (Captain Ll. Wansbrough-Jones, R.E.), and the 19th Company, Bombay S. & M. (Captain A. R. S. Lucas, R.E.), from Wana, and in August by the addition of 4 Road Construction Battalions specially raised for the occasion. The Sapper units were called upon to perform most varied tasks. They repaired bridges and culverts, built blockhouses, supplied camps with water, and even erected ice-factories to provide ice for armoured cars and tanks. Operating with columns on the march, they demolished towers, made tracks, and built piquet posts covered with wire screens as a protection against bombs. All this in addition to never-ending road making, the supervision of working parties, and the building of two large defensible posts for garrisons of the Waziristan Scouts. Their labours found a counterpart in those of the Military Engineer Services, and together the two branches catered successfully for the needs of Wazirforce.[1]

[1] "More Roads (Waziristan, 1937)," by Maj. A. E. Armstrong, M.C., R.E., appearing in *The R.E. Journal*, Vol. LIII, 1939, pp. 1–16.

On May 10th, 1937, the Bannu and Razmak Brigades of "Wazdiv" were concentrated at Dosalli near the Circular Road between Razani and Asad Khel, and after a night march of 6 miles southwards over a precipitous range, the Bannu Brigade established itself on May 12th in Coronation Camp on the stony Sham Plain. Successive bounds forward over easier country brought the troops to Ghariom and Pasal Camps, whence issued the column which, on May 28th, wrecked the Faqir of Ipi's lair at Arsal Kot. The Faqir and his followers had decamped some days earlier, leaving behind them little but masses of literature and legions of fleas; but the 3rd and 12th Companies had the satisfaction of blowing in the Faqir's caves and completing the destruction already wrought in the village by the Royal Air Force. The 3rd Company was detailed to demolish the Faqir's personal cave and others to the south, while the 12th Company destroyed the few remaining buildings of Arsal Kot and some caves to the north. Accompanied by Lieutenant A. F. M. Jack, R.E. (Field Engineer), Major W. F. Hasted, R.E. (O.C. 3rd Company), approached the mouth of the Faqir's cave. Smoke was pouring from it, so they threw in a bomb and waited for the smoke to clear. Then, with revolvers cocked and torches held well away from their bodies, they dashed through the entrance only to discover that the Faqir had fled. The 3rd Company placed 400 lbs. of guncotton in the largest of the four chambers composing the cave and smaller amounts in the other three, and the subsequent detonation of about 1,000 lbs. of explosive completely obliterated the place. Lieutenant R. C. Orgill, R.E., of the 3rd Company, blew in another cave with 400 lbs. of gunpowder, while the 12th Company demolished three more caves and flattened the remains of Arsal Kot.

The destruction of his headquarters lowered the Faqir's prestige and ended the first phase of the operations. The firebrand of Ipi was temporarily a fugitive. The second phase, that of roadmaking, lasted without intermission until October 15th, 1937. There were occasional clashes with hostile gangs, but no organized resistance was encountered. On June 1st, the 1st Division relieved the Bannu and Razmak Brigades in the Sham Plain and the two brigades concentrated in the Razmak area. Meanwhile, the Circular Road, which had been damaged between Dosalli and Razmak, had been re-opened by the combined efforts of the Sappers and Miners and the Military Engineer Services. The third and final phase of the operations took the form of an invasion of the Bhittani country further south by the 1st Division and more roadmaking by the Sappers and Miners and civilian labour in one of the most fantastically rugged regions on the North-West Frontier. This, briefly, was the general trend of events after the downfall of the notorious Faqir.

From an engineering point of view, the second phase, that from the end of May to the middle of October, 1937, may be regarded as the most interesting, for it involved the greater part of the construction of 115 miles of motor road at a cost of £232,500. The scheme was to open up the country by a north-and-south road from Dosalli to Ahmadwam, near Sorarogha, and an east-and-west road from Razmak to Biche Kashkai on the Khaisora loop-road built in 1936. These highways would cross at Ghariom. Work was started from Dosalli by the 1st Division on June 7th, and from Ahmadwam by contract labour three weeks later, and on July 10th the 12th Company, Madras S. & M., turned the first stone on the Razmak-Ghariom section undertaken by "Wazdiv." The 4th Company, Bengal S. & M., and the 14th Company, Madras S. & M., also worked on this section. On November 20th, the Army Commander was able to motor from Ahmadwam through Ghariom to Razmak and "Wazdiv's" immediate task was finished. Meanwhile, the eastern branch from Ghariom to Biche Kashkai, some 21 miles in length, was receiving attention. The 3rd Company and a Road Construction Battalion started work from Ghariom on August 14th, and a fortnight later, work was begun further ahead by contract labour. All the new roads in Northern Waziristan were run, so far as possible, along watersheds instead of up valleys, a procedure which, apart from tactical advantages, reduced cross-water drainage. Water was pumped to the camps along the Ghariom-Biche Kashkai section by a 4-in. Victaulic pipe-line, 12,000 yards in length.[1] This section was completed by November 17th, when the main "Sapper" part of the operations ended. Roadmaking, nevertheless, continued in Waziristan, and in some of these projects a few Sappers were concerned. A 20-mile stretch of motor road from Tajori in administered territory to Kot in the Bhittani country was completed by December 2nd, 1937, a short length was built to Arsal Kot, and a branch from the Khaisora loop-road of 1936 was laid by a Road Construction Battalion from Rucha to Karkanwam. Early in November, some of the Sappers and Miners were detailed to assist in the construction of two semi-permanent posts for the Waziristan Scouts, one at Ghariom and the other at Biche Kashkai. They supplied the skilled labour, and the Road Construction Battalions and infantry furnished the working parties. Each post was designed for 12 platoons of Scouts and held a 3-days' reserve of supplies for a brigade. Each had 1,200 yards of perimeter wall, 6 ft. high, with two belts of barbed wire outside. Within were water-tanks to hold a total of 48,000 gallons, and also barracks and other buildings for the garrison.[2] No risk could be taken of a shortage of water, for water-supply had proved to be the chief problem throughout the campaign.

The situation in the Wana area was becoming tense even before the operations against the Faqir of Ipi were started in the Sham Plain, and since the end of February, 1937, it had been necessary to run convoys from Manzai under escort by armoured cars because the road could not be piqueted adequately. Early in April, a number of Wazirs from the north were seen watching a motor convoy on its way through the 3-miles' length of the Shahur Tangi. Suspicions were aroused, and they were soon shown to be fully justified for a convoy was ambushed in the *tangi* on April 9th and seven British officers lost their lives. Among these was

[1] *Annual Records, K.G.V.'s O. Bengal S. & M.*, 1937–38, p. 28.

[2] A plan of the Biche Kashkai Post is given in "Field Engineering (India)," appearing in *The R.E. Journal*, Vol. LIII, 1939, pp. 542–546.

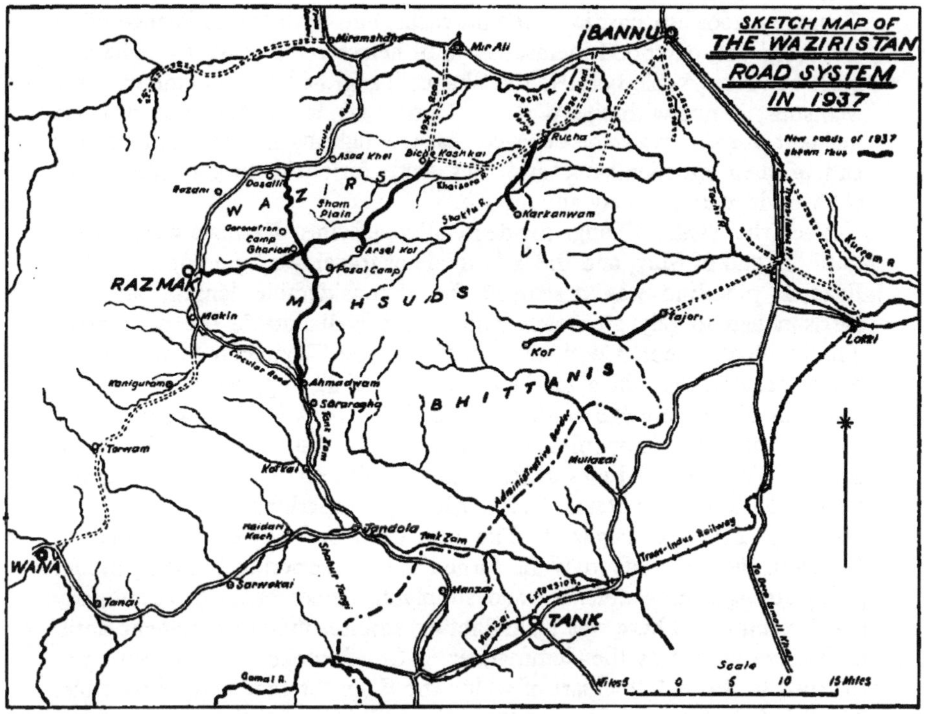
SKETCH MAP OF
THE WAZIRISTAN
ROAD SYSTEM
IN 1937
New roads of 1937 shown thus
BANNU
Miramshah
Mir Ali
Tochi R.
1936 Road
Rucha
Asad Khel
Circular Road
Bich Kashkai
Khaisora R.
Dosalli
Razani
W A Z I R S
Sham Plain
Shaktu R.
Karkanwam
Coronation Camp
Gharion
Arsal Kot
Pasal Camp
RAZMAK
M A H S U D S
Makin
Tajori
Kot
Lakki
Kurram R.
Tochi R.
Kaniguram
Ahmadwam
Sararogha
B H I T T A N I S
Tarwam
Kotkai
Administrative Border
Mullazai
Haidari Kach
Jandola
Tank Zam
WANA
Tanai
Sarwekai
Shahur Tangi
Manzai
Trans-Indus Railway
Extension
TANK
To Dera Ismail Khan
Gomal R.
Scale
Miles 5
0
5
10
15 Miles

Lieutenant E. C. L. Hinde, R.E., who was on his way to rejoin the 19th Company, Bombay S. & M., at Wana. It appears that as the head of the convoy reached a point well inside the narrowest part of the deep gorge it was met by a long string of camels led by unarmed men. The first three lorries got past the camels. Then, on a pre-arranged signal, the camel-drivers drove their camels into the middle of the road, leapt behind some rocks to retrieve their hidden rifles, and opened fire at point-blank range, concentrating on the British officers, lorry-drivers and machine-gun crews. Those who survived, including a leave party of Sappers from the 19th Company, took up positions behind rocks, and with the assistance of an armoured car, defended themselves until help arrived at dusk.[1] The ambush was remarkable because the Shahur Tangi had a bad name with the Mahsuds, if not with the Wazirs. Until 1921 it had never seen a like incident, for the Mahsuds believed that any fighting in it would mark the end of their independence and they were furious with the Wazirs for entering it in 1937 to lay an ambush.

After the Shahur Tangi incident, all roads into Razmak were closed until the end of May, and the only mode of travel was by aeroplane. The Razmak pipe-line was destroyed for a considerable length, and the garrison had to rely on water from a tube well outside the perimeter.[2] The incident, coupled with the transfer of the Waziristan Scouts to the north, resulted also in a gradual cessation of all supplies to Wana and consequently a stoppage of all work on the New Wana Project on which the 9th and 14th Companies, Madras S. & M. (Captains L. A. B. Patten and Ll. Wansbrough-Jones, R.E.), and the 6th and 8th A.T. Companies, Bengal S. & M. (Captains G. D. Mc. K. Sutherland and Hon. R. L. Napier, R.E.), were engaged. The 14th Company moved to Razmak in July, and the units left in Wana turned their attention to building piquet posts, strengthening defences and supplying detachments to accompany small columns. There was little fighting and not much excitement until, in October, a visit by the Commander-in-Chief entailed the re-opening of the road to Razmak, for part of which the Wana Brigade was responsible. The 8th A.T. Company then went out to build *sangars* to guard the road, and the Commander-in-Chief was escorted safely into Wana. During his visit he decided that the camp and its garrison should be expanded still more and that greater attention should be paid to protecting the buildings from sniping than giving them southerly aspects. As the Garrison Engineer was on leave, this decision threw the burden of much re-designing on the Sapper and Miner officers ; but they did their best to meet the emergency, and when materials began to arrive once more from Manzai, the Wana Project took a new lease of life. No serious interruptions followed, although for a time there were occasional skirmishes with small *lashkars*. Then peace returned to Waziristan, and the garrisons of Wana and Razmak resumed their normal life.

[1]Obituary Notice of Lieut. E. C. L. Hinde, R.E., appearing in *The R.E. Journal Supplement*, June, 1937, p. 189.
[2]*Annual Records, Q.V.O. Madras S. & M.*, 1937–38, pp. 42, 43.

There is little to record of the Indian Sappers and Miners in 1938. The threat of Nazi Germany was spreading like a dark cloud over Europe, and the atmosphere in most of India was that of a calm before the storm. Intensive but secret preparation was the order of the day. Mechanization was accelerated, anti-gas training elaborated, and arrangements made for expansion in case of war. All hoped, but few believed in their heart of hearts, that war could be averted, and India was no more ready than England. Yet preparations for war were not allowed at first to interfere seriously with other work. For instance, many Sapper and Miner companies were still employed on the New Wana Project, and the accommodation at Razmak was improved. Also, the 1st and 5th Companies, Bengal S. & M. (Captains T. L. Lloyd and I. G. Loch, R.E.), began to build a road north-west of Landi Kotal leading to the Bens Ridge which overlooks Afghanistan.[1] While so employed, they were under the direction of Lieut.-Colonel W. J. Lyall, R.E. (I.A.), who, it is sad to relate, was killed in a motor accident on November 28th while driving from Nowshera to Peshawar.

Two young officers of the Bengal Corps, Lieutenants J. K. Shepheard and A. F. M. Jack, R.E., who had been sent to Gyantse in Tibet during the summer of 1938 to inspect some buildings, received permission to visit the " forbidden " city of Lhasa and spent ten days there. They called on the Regent and other celebrities and had tea in several of the colleges in the Sera Monastery. They visited also the Mint, the Security Printing Press and the Summer Palace of the Dalai Lama. In the autumn, the 9th and 12th Companies, Madras S. & M., shared in a few small operations by columns from Razmak and Wana against Mahsud gangs in the Torwam-Sharawangi and Kotkai-Ahmadwam areas of Waziristan, and they were engaged also in road-making on the Inzar Narai, but these activities call for no special comment. Already, the shadow of impending war made normal peace-time employment seem unimportant and even incongruous.

The fateful year 1939 opened with the New Wana Construction progressing steadily. The Bengal Sappers had the 2nd and 6th A.T. Companies at work and these were joined by the 3rd Company in February. The Madras Sappers were represented by the 9th and 16th A.T. Companies, and the Bombay Sappers by the 19th Company until it was relieved by the 17th Company in March, and within the next few months, the project seemed to be nearing completion so far as concerned the Sappers and Miners. Elsewhere, most Sapper units were carrying out their usual hot-weather programme of training and preparing for further modernization in the form of increased motor transport and mechanical tools. It is remarkable that the Bengal Sappers' News Letter of September 3rd, 1939, the day of the declaration of war against Germany, opens with the following words :—" We have received no warning orders of any impending mobilization, and it is not clear what effort the Corps will be expected to produce in any war. Cipher wires have been arriving fairly

[1]The Bens Road was completed in July, 1939.

frequently and everyone likely to be mobilized has been medically examined. All leave has been stopped and all ranks have been recalled from leave." But at the foot of the printed sheet is a momentous postscript. " Since writing this News Letter, war has broken out with Germany. V.C.O.s and N.C.O.s listened to the King's broadcast on 3rd September, 1939, in the V.C.O.'s Club." No clearer proof could be given that the sudden declaration took India by surprise. Every Sapper and Miner headquarters then became the scene of rapid mobilization, and within a few days the 4th Company, Bengal S. & M., under Major A. H. G. Napier, R.E., left for an " unknown destination," being among the first to go overseas as in the war of 1914–18.

The story of the Sappers and Miners in the World War of 1939–45 must be told in another volume. The three Corps were expanded to incredible dimensions. In 1944, for instance, the Bengal Corps reached a strength of 23,850 officers and men, which was seven times its total in 1938, and at the close of the war it had no less than 25 Field Companies.[1] The headquarters in Bangalore, Roorkee and Kirkee were more than doubled in size to deal with the flood of new units.[2] The Sappers and Miners were represented in almost every theatre of war in Europe, Asia and Africa, and in each they maintained their fine traditions. By the end of 1941 they had been reconstituted as " Groups " of the Corps of Indian Engineers and operated with new Transportation Services of many kinds.[3] The history of their exploits up to the surrender of Japan should make fine reading.

The Indian Engineer soldier of the present day—formerly the Sapper and Miner—living as he does in a highly mechanized age, must have not only a wide experience of military engineering in general but a specialized knowledge of some of its branches. He bears far more responsibility and requires much greater initiative than the Pioneer of the 18th Century from whom he is descended. Also, he must receive a better education and more elaborate training. These he gets in full measure, and through them he is enabled to attain in modern war the results which have helped towards victory over every enemy in every part of the globe. Changes in government and in the system of recruitment have made the various Corps no longer the " family affairs " of thirty years ago; but heredity still counts for much, and the men would be the first to admit that those of their forebears who served in the early campaigns of the East India Company, or on the Indian frontiers and overseas, set them an example of gallantry and fortitude which they might emulate but never surpass. Battle honours such as " Seringapatam," " Assaye," " Meeanee," " Goojerat," " Afghanistan," " Delhi " and " Lucknow " were not lightly won, nor were " Abyssinia," " Tofrek," " Chitral," " China," " Somali-

[1] *Adjutant's News Letter, K.G.V.'s O. Bengal S. & M.*, Jan., 1946.

[2] " India. Important Changes in the Engineer Organization, etc., during 1940," appearing in *The R.E. Journal Supplement*, March, 1941, pp. 45–47.

[3] " The Corps of Indian Engineers," by the E.-in-C., India, appearing in *The R.E. Journal*, Vol. LIX, 1945, pp. 36–43.

land," " Neuve Chapelle " and " Mesopotamia." From the days of the Indian Mutiny till recent times, it has been the privilege of Royal Engineer officers to lead and command the Engineer field units of India; and as, in the process of political evolution, that honour has now passed to men of Indian blood, they trust that the high standards of this branch of the Dominion forces of India and Pakistan will be maintained as fully as in the late World War.

THE END

APPENDIX A

QUEEN VICTORIA'S OWN MADRAS SAPPERS AND MINERS

The Madras Sappers originated in two companies of Pioneers raised at Madras in 1780 by Lieutenant Joseph Moorhouse of the Madras Artillery. Each company consisted of 110 Indian Ranks and 5 British N.C.O.s under the command of British Officers. Half the men were armed with pistols and half with pikes. A third company was raised in 1783 to take part in the first war against Tipu Sultan.

In 1790 the Pioneers were increased to 5 companies, each of about 100 Indian ranks. Their Engineer equipment consisted mainly of cutting and digging tools. In 1793 they were formed into a Corps with an establishment of 1 Lieut.-Commandant, 3 Lieutenants, 1 Assistant Surgeon, and 6 Companies, each of 1 Sergeant, 1 Jemadar and 106 I.O.R.s. In 1798 and 1799, 4 more companies were added; and in 1803 the Corps was re-organized as 2 battalions each of 8 companies.

In 1831, the 1st Battalion of Pioneers was converted into a Corps of Sappers and Miners officered by the Madras Engineers. The Corps consisted of 8 companies, numbered "A" to "H" and was entitled to the honours and distinctions won as Pioneers from the capture of Seringapatam in 1799 to the 1st Burma War, 1824–26. In 1834, the 2nd Battalion of Pioneers was absorbed into the Corps of Sappers and Miners, but the establishment of the Corps was not permanently increased. The distribution of the Corps was then as follows :—

H.Q. and 3 Coys.	Bangalore.
2 Coys.	Nilgiris.
1 Coy.	Madras.
2 Coys.	Hyderabad.

In 1837, the establishment was changed to 6 companies and a full scale of Engineer tools and equipment was laid down for each. The Corps was reorganized again in 1846 and the Headquarters moved to Mercara, where they stayed until they moved to Dowlaishweram in 1854. The strength of the Corps was then increased to 9 companies and a Depot Company. In 1857, 3 additional companies were added and the scale of equipment was revised. In 1862, "L" and "M" Coys. were disbanded and the Headquarters of the Corps moved to Bangalore. In 1876, the title "Queen's Own" was conferred on the Corps. The three Corps of Sappers and Miners were re-organized in 1885, each to consist of 6 Service and 2 Depot Companies, and the duties of officers, rates of pay, and scales of engineer equipment were revised. In 1887, a company called the "Burma Sappers and Miners" was raised and affiliated to the Corps.[1]

In 1900, there were six Service Companies (Nos. 1 to 6), the Burma Service Company, and "A" and "B" Depot Companies. Each Service Company was organized in two half-companies, each of which was composed of two sections which were further divided into two sub-sections. The establishment of a Service Company was 2 British officers, 2 British other ranks, 3 Indian

[1]See Appendix D.

officers and 168 Indian other ranks.[1] "A" Company consisted of four small Telegraph Sections, two Field Printing Sections and two Field Litho Sections. A reserve of 60 men had been formed in 1899, but it was still 23 under strength in 1901. Four Service Companies, and "A" and "B" Depot Companies, were stationed normally in Bangalore; one Service Company was at Secunderabad, another on the North-West Frontier, and the Burma Company at Mandalay.

The Corps was composed of various classes of Madrassis in proportions which were fixed by the Commandant, and the units and sub-units consisted, like the Corps, of mixed classes. In 1900 the proportions of the various castes and classes were as follows:—

Indian Christians and Paraiyans (or Pariahs, later called Adi-Dravidians), 50 per cent; Tamil Hindus, 21 per cent; Telegu Hindus, 12½ per cent; Muhammadans, 12½ per cent; other castes 4 per cent. It was always a tradition of the Madras Sappers that, in Service matters, caste should not be recognized. In this respect, the Madras Sapper and Miner differed not only from his brethren of Bengal and Bombay, but from the remainder of the Indian Army.

In 1903 the Service Companies were renumbered, Nos. 1 to 6 becoming Nos. 9 to 14 respectively. The Burma Company became No. 15 and "A" and "B" Depot Companies reappeared as "C" and "D." The establishment of the reserve was raised to 274 in 1904, and to 304 in 1908. The year 1909 was remarkable chiefly for the change of the title "Service Company" to "Field Company," and for the cessation of the enlistment of Recruit or Pension boys. The establishment of Recruit boys, which had existed since 1813,[2] provided the Corps with a valuable supply of recruits whose upbringing, nutrition and training had been closely supervised. It had the further advantage that recruits joined the Corps well drilled and with an elementary knowledge of some trade. Four Divisional Signal Companies, classed as Sappers and Miners, were formed by Army Headquarters in 1910, and the result was the end of "C" Company at Bangalore, for the Telegraph Section of that unit was then removed from the Corps[3] and the remaining Sections (Printing and Litho) were transferred to "D" Company. The military training of recruits for Nos. 33 and 34 Divisional Signal Companies began in Bangalore in 1911. The only other change prior to the Great War which calls for special remark occurred in 1912 when the Indian Submarine Mining Section at Rangoon, which had been affiliated to the Corps in 1910, was abolished and replaced by a Defence Light Section.[4]

The Great War caused an enormous increase in the strength of the Madras Sappers. While on March 31st, 1914, there were 21 British officers, 25 Indian officers, 31 British Warrant and non-commissioned officers (R.E.) and 1509 Indian other ranks, on March 3rd, 1919, the corresponding numbers were 144, 60, 85 and 7,019.[5]

On August 4th, 1914, the Corps consisted of only 7 Field Companies, 1 Field Park, 2 Photo-Litho Sections, 2 Printing Sections, 1 Depot Company and a Defence Light Section; but on November 11th, 1918, it had 3 Field Troops, 19 Field Companies, 1 Bridging Train, a Chitral Section, and no less than 16 Depot Companies in addition to a Field Park and Specialist and Defence Light

[1]Four of the Service Companies had 18 first-line equipment mules and the necessary drivers, and by 1902 the two remaining Service Companies, and the Burma Company, were similarly equipped.

[2]The establishment was finally abolished in 1911.

[3]See Appendix I.

[4]See Appendix G.

[5]In 1914, 149 recruits passed to the ranks; in 1918 the number was 3,494.

Sections as before.[1] Of 295 officers who served with the Corps during the war, 59 were Royal Engineers (regulars), 56 held R.E. Territorial or Temporary Commissions, 14 were Indian Army Officers, and 166 came from the Indian Army Reserve of Officers (I.A.R.O.). As an indication of the improvisation necessary in 1914 it may be mentioned that both the Sappers and the equipment of No. 2 Field Troop, which was formed on September 10th of that year, were carried in 30 *tongas*[2] obtained from the Gwalior Imperial Service troops, and it was not until 1917 that the unit was provided with horses.

During 1915, separate establishments of Indian other ranks were laid down for field service and for India; and 3 Depot Companies, which were expanded finally to 16, were formed at Bangalore, each of the strength of a Field Company and organized as such. Steps were taken also to augment the establishment of British Warrant and non-commissioned officers by enlisting skilled men in India for service in the Royal Engineers.

No. 15 (Burma) Company was mobilized in Mandalay for service overseas in 1916, and three sections embarked at Rangoon for Iraq on October 9th, leaving one section in Mandalay as a depot.[3] In 1917 a Bridging Train[4] was formed at Bangalore; it embarked for Basra in December and received its equipment after its arrival in Iraq. During the Great War, recruits came forward in such large numbers that the demands of each successive increase in establishment were met easily; but there were always difficulties in producing efficient training staffs and proper equipment for the new units which were raised. These units were usually raised in Bangalore[5] and sent overseas—mostly to Iraq—after a short period of training.

After the Great War, the reduction of the Corps and its reorganization on a new peace establishment were much delayed by the campaigns in Afghanistan, Waziristan, Iraq and Malabar, and by some punitive expeditions in Burma, to all of which the Corps had to despatch units which in some cases were due for disbandment. As a result of the findings of several committees which assembled at Army Headquarters during 1920 and 1921, some new units were authorized for all three Corps of Sappers and Miners to bring their organization into closer agreement with that of the Royal Engineers at home. Army Troops Companies were formed in the Madras Sappers from existing Field Companies, reduced to about half-strength, and Divisional Headquarter Companies were added. No. 15 (Burma) Company, the Mandalay Depot and the Rangoon Defence Light Section were removed from the Corps and became the "4th Burma Sappers and Miners."[6]

There were other changes between 1920 and 1923—the year in which the "2nd Q.V.O. Sappers and Miners" became the "Q.V.O. Madras Sappers and Miners."[7] The Chitral Section having been handed over to the Bengal Corps in 1920, the section posted there returned to Bangalore and was disbanded. Two Field Companies were allotted as covering troops in Waziristan,

[1]The Field Troops were Nos. 2, 3 and 8. The Field Companies were Nos. 9, 10, 11, 12, 13, 14, 15, 16, 61, 62, 63, 64, 65, 66, 67, 68, 69, 70 and 94. The Bridging Train was No. 7 and from it No. 96 Field Company was raised in Iraq. The units raised during the War were disbanded or abolished between 1919 and 1922 with the exception of Nos. 2 and 3 Field Troops and No. 63 Field Company.

[2]Two-wheeled pony-carriages.

[3]The three sections took part in the advance on, and capture of, Baghdad in 1917. The depot was used subsequently to raise reinforcements and extra companies.

[4]No. 7 Bridging Train, with an establishment of 118 Indian ranks and 6 followers.

[5]They were raised from drafts from Depot Companies. An extra Depot Company ("C") was formed in 1917 to accommodate men returning from service overseas.

[6]The 4th Burma Sappers and Miners came into existence on Jan. 10th, 1922, under A.I.I. 20 of that year. See Appendix D.

[7]*Gazette of India*, No. 367, dated March 9th, 1923.

and Rawalpindi and Secunderabad were abolished as out-stations of the Corps. A Field Troop was allotted to Sialkot and posted to the 2nd Indian Cavalry Brigade. A Field Company (No. 63) was maintained in Iraq, surplus to the establishment of the Corps and working under the Royal Air Force, its *personnel* being relieved by yearly drafts from Bangalore of about half the strength of the unit. As a result of these various reorganizations the units included in the Corps on April 1st, 1923, were 2 Field Troops, 5 Field Companies, 2 A. Tps. Companies, 1 Divisional H.Q. Company, 2 Photo-Litho and Printing Sections and 3 Depot Companies, together with the extra Field Company in Iraq. The strength of the Corps was then 36 British officers, 56 R.E. Warrant and non-commissioned officers and 2,167 Indian ranks—an immense reduction from the total of 7,308 of all ranks in March, 1919. The distribution in peace stations was as follows :— Bangalore, 3 Field and 3 Depot Companies, 1 Field Troop and the Army Troops and D.H.Q. Companies and Photo-Litho and Printing Sections ; Waziristan, 2 Field Companies ; Sialkot, 1 Field Troop ; Iraq, 1 (extra) Field Company. Each Field Troop had 2 British officers, a small H.Q. Section (administrative) and 2 mounted half-troops, each of about 40 Indian ranks including drivers. Tool-carts had replaced pack mules as 1st Line transport, and the 2nd and 3rd Line transport was carried in A.T. carts instead of on pack mules or camels. Some motor vehicles had been provided for Army Troops and D.H.Q. Companies to carry part of the unit equipment. The organization of 4 Sections in a Field Company had been altered to 3 Sections and an H.Q. Section, with 2 British officers in peace-time and 5 in war.[1]

After 1923, although there were some changes in the terms of service and other matters, no major alterations occurred in the organization or strength of the Madras Sappers until those introduced in 1932–33 in connection with the abolition of Pioneers from the Indian Army. In 1925, Indian ranks were required to enrol for 7 years with the colours and 8 years with the reserve. A new reserve of two classes (A. and B.) was introduced. Class A. consisted of reservists with a total service of under 10 years, and Class B. of those with a total of under 15 years. In 1928, Mandalay became an out-station of the Corps, and No. 15 Company, Burma Sappers and Miners, took over one of the Corps out-stations in Waziristan. In the following year, on the disbandment of the 4th Burma Sappers and Miners, No. 63 Field Company, which had returned from service in Iraq, was renumbered No. 15, and thenceforward 3 Field Companies were stationed in Bangalore and 3 more in out-stations. Mechanization began in 1930, during which year and 1931 the Field Troops were reorganized, the tool-carts and limbered and G.S. wagons removed, and mechanical transport substituted. One half-troop was dismounted and carried in six-wheeled vehicles. A beginning was made also in the work of mechanizing the Field Companies. In 1932 came the proposal to abolish the Pioneers, a scheme which produced important reorganizations in the Madras Sappers as described in Appendix H.

In March 1933 Quetta became a Corps out-station for an A. Tps. or D.H.Q. Company, the first unit to be sent there being No. 16 A. Tps. Company. In October, 1933 No. 11 A. Tps. Company was sent to Bengal as part of the additional garrison of that province, being relieved in October 1935 by No. 44 Div. H.Q. Company. The latter Company returned to Bangalore in April 1937 when the Corps ceased to find a detachment in Bengal.

In 1938 one Field Troop (No. 33) was disbanded when the Sialkot Cavalry Brigade was broken up, and the remaining troop (No. 32) was stationed in Bangalore.

[1]These numbers were increased respectively to 3 and 6 in 1928.

APPENDIX B

KING GEORGE THE FIFTH'S OWN BENGAL SAPPERS AND MINERS

In September 1776, four companies of artificers were raised and added to the Bengal Army which had hitherto had only a few artificers and pioneers on the establishment of each regiment of infantry. About 1800, two of these companies of artificers were serving in the forts of the East India Company about Calcutta. They were officered by Engineer officers but seem to have been garrison troops.

In 1803 a Corps of Pioneers, officered from the Infantry, was raised by Captain T. Wood, B.E., at Cawnpore and existed as a separate arm until 1834 when it was merged into the Sappers and Miners. It appeared frequently in General Orders as " Pioneers or Sappers " and acquired a number of battle honours. In 1808, a company of " Miners," commanded by an Engineer officer, was raised for field service and continued to exist until it was merged into the Sappers and Miners in 1819.

In 1818 the formation of a Corps of Sappers and Miners was decided upon, and a draft of European soldiers, trained at Chatham, was sent out for Engineer service in India. The Corps was formed at Allahabad under Major Thomas Anburey, B.E. Its uniform was at first that of the Pioneers raised in 1803, but in 1819 the uniform was altered to that of the Royal Sappers and Miners in England. The Corps moved northwards to Cawnpore and Fatehgarh, and in 1825 took part in the siege of Bhurtpore (now Bharatpur). Lieutenant R. Napier, B.E. (afterwards Lord Napier of Magdala) joined it in March 1829. By 1830, its headquarters had reached Delhi, where, in 1834, it received most of the Indian ranks of the disbanded Pioneers.

In 1843, Broadfoot's Sappers, raised by Captain George Broadfoot, M.I., in 1840, were merged into the Bengal Sappers and Miners as the 7th and 8th Companies. Corps Headquarters remained at Delhi until 1845, and then moved to Meerut. At the time of the 1st Sikh War, the Corps appears to have consisted of 10 companies, all of whom, except the 9th and 10th, took part in that campaign.

In September 1847, the Corps was remodelled into 3 companies of Sappers and 7 companies of Pioneers. The Pioneers were officered from the Infantry and received lower pay. Their uniform was dark green. About 1847, Corps Headquarters moved to Ludhiana and the Corps title became " Sappers and Pioneers."

In 1851, while H.Q. were still at Ludhiana, the Corps was re-organized once more and became known officially as " The Corps of Bengal Sappers and Miners." It was officered from the Engineers ; but Infantry officers could be attached if required. The authorized strength was 12 companies, and the uniform was red with blue facings.

The first mention of campaigns against the North-West Frontier tribes in which the Corps took part occurs in 1852, and, in the following year, the first mention of Roorkee as Headquarters, to which the 3rd, 11th and 12th Companies moved. In March 1854 the H.Q. and companies moved to Meerut, but they returned to Roorkee in December. In 1854, the rates of working pay of all classes were revised and new rules laid down.

After the Indian Mutiny, the Headquarters did not return to Roorkee until February 1859. Once again Infantry officers became eligible for appointment to the Sappers and Miners. In 1863, the establishment of a Company, of which there were then 10, was fixed at 2 Indian officers, 12 Indian N.C.O.s and 80 Privates. "Delhi" and "Lucknow" were added as Battle Honours in 1864, and in 1865, after the recapture of Dewangiri, the 6th and 7th Companies were ordered to take the right of all Native Infantry. Corps H.Q. was organized for the first time on lines resembling modern practice and an Instructional Staff was provided. The strength of a company was increased to 100.

The years up to the 2nd Afghan War passed with H.Q. still at Roorkee, though moving occasionally and temporarily to Camps of Exercise at Delhi and once (in 1873) to Hassan Abdal. The units had varied employment in frontier expeditions, archaeological survey, laying telegraph lines and even "torpedo" work in Calcutta.

In 1878, the whole Corps, excluding H.Q., went on service with the Khaibar, Kurram and Kandahar Columns in the 2nd Afghan War. H.Q. followed, but with the 5th Company it returned to Roorkee in June, 1879. In October 1879, H.Q. went to the frontier again, and not until September 1880 did it and four companies under the command of Major Bindon Blood, R.E., return to Roorkee.

In 1882, H.Q. and three companies were at Roorkee; two companies were at Gwalior, two in Peshawar, one in Rawalpindi, one in the Naga Hills and one in Calcutta, and this or a similar distribution, varied with employment at Quetta, continued for some years.

In 1885, in common with the other two Corps, the Bengal Sappers were re-organized into 6 Service and 2 Depot Companies. The men were to be styled "Sappers" and each company was to have 2 British officers. "A" Depot Company consisted of 2 Pontoon Sections, 2 Telegraph Sections, 2 Field Printing Sections, and 1 Submarine Mining Section. "B" Depot Company was for training recruits. As a result, the former 1st and 2nd Companies became "B" and "A" Companies; the 3rd, 4th, 5th and 6th Companies retained their identity, the 7th and 9th were absorbed, and the 8th and 10th became the 2nd and 1st Companies. The formation of "H" Company, R.E., appears to have occurred at the same time.

In 1891, the Submarine Mining Section was transferred from the Corps[1] and one Printing Section was formed into a Photo-Litho Section for service. In 1897 the gold necklaces worn by Indian Officers were discontinued. An active reserve of 250 men was sanctioned for the Corps in 1899.

In July 1900, Lieutenant E. C. Tylden-Pattenson, R.E., raised a mounted detachment consisting of 1 B.N.C.O. and 24 Indian ranks from the 2nd and "A" Companies for service in China where it joined the Cavalry Brigade at Tientsin. It returned and was disbanded in December, 1901.

In July, 1901, an Experimental Balloon Section was raised at Rawalpindi and went on manœuvres in October. It attended the Yusufzai and Delhi manœuvres, and the Durbar Camp in the following year.

In October 1903, the title of the Corps was changed to "1st Sappers and Miners." In this year also, 15 miles of light railway and 100 yds. of light bridging material were added to the Corps equipment. A permanent Mounted Detachment was authorized as an increase to "A" Company, and the Corps was re-armed with L.E. Magazine rifles and bandoliers. In 1904, Drivers were issued

[1]See Appendix G.

with rifles, and the red *kullah* and fringe and blue puttees were introduced. The strength of the active reserve was increased to 274, and early in 1905 it was called up for training.

On January 1st, 1906, H.R.H. The Prince of Wales was appointed Colonel-in-Chief of the Corps and its designation was changed to "1st Prince of Wales' Own Sappers and Miners" with permission to wear the Prince of Wales' plume on colours and appointments. New buttons, with the Prince of Wales' plume, were adopted also.

In 1907, the caste composition of the Corps was laid down as :—

No. 1 Coy.	½ Sikhs, ½ Punjabi Mussalmans.
2 Coy.	½ Sikhs, ½ Punjabi Mussalmans.
3 Coy	Hindustanis.
4 Coy.	½ Sikhs, ½ Pathans.
5 Coy.	½ Sikhs, ½ Punjabi Mussalmans.
6 Coy.	Hindustanis.
Balloon Sec.	Punjabi Mussalmans.
"A" & "B" Coys.	Mixed.
Mounted Dett.	Sikhs.

In this year, Centenary Celebrations were held. The C.-in-C., Lord Kitchener, inspected the Corps on parade, held at Durbar, and laid the foundation stone of the Corps Memorial Column.

In 1910, on the accession of H.M. King George the Fifth, the designation of the Corps was changed to "1st K.G.O. Sappers and Miners."

The enormous increase in the strength of the Indian ranks during the Great War, 1914–18, is shown below, the British ranks being reinforced correspondingly.

	1st Aug., 1914	*15th Nov.*, 1918
I.O.s	25	90
I.O.R.s	1396	8303
The units were expanded as follows :—		
Field Companies	6	21
Field Troops	1	3
Field Squadrons	—	1
Bridging Trains	—	3

and numerous smaller units. The Training Companies reached "B 14" and four more Field Companies were in the process of formation when the war ended.

Demobilization after the Great War extended over a period of three years, the first of the units formed during the war being disbanded on April 15th, 1919, and the last on August 5th, 1922. Between January 1919 and August 1922, 7,824 Indian ranks were demobilized.

In 1920 the Corps took over the Chitral Platoon from the Madras Sappers; and in 1921, A. Tps. Companies and D.H.Q. Companies were added to the establishment.

In March 1923, the designation of the Corps was changed from "1st K.G.O. Sappers and Miners" to "K.G.O. Bengal Sappers and Miners." At the same time, some of the units were re-numbered. The units then in the Corps were :—

	Class Composition
No. 31 Fd. Troop (previously No. 1 Fd. Tp.)	Punjabi Mussalmans.
No. 35 Fd. Troop (previously No. 5 Fd. Tp.)	Punjabi Mussalmans.
No. 36 Fd. Troop (previously No. 6 Fd. Tp.)	disbanded 1923.
No. 1 Fd. Coy. No. 2 Fd. Coy. No. 3 Fd. Coy. No. 4 Fd. Coy. No. 5 Fd. Coy. No. 6 Fd. Coy. No. 8 A. Tps. Coy. " A," " B-1 " and " B-2 " Depot Coys.	1/3rd Sikhs, 1/3rd Mussalmans (incl. Pathans, P.M.s and H.M.s) and 1/3rd H. Hindus.
No. 41 Div. Coy. (previously " W " D.H.Q. Coy.)	ditto
No. 43 Div. Coy. (previously " X " D.H.Q. Coy.)	ditto
No. 7 Bridging Train (previously No. 2 Bridging Train)	½ Mussalmans ½ Hindus
Chitral Platoon	Mussalmans.
Karachi and Calcutta Defence Light Secs.	Mussalmans.
No. 51 Printing Sec. (previously No. 2 Printing Sec.)	Hindus, Sikhs and Mussalmans.
No. 52 Photo Litho Sec. (previously No. 7 Photo Litho Sec.)	..ditto.

The " three-class " basis of Field Companies enabled them in war to receive reinforcements of any class. The units were normally allotted to peace stations as follows :—

Roorkee	One Fd. Tp. Three Fd. Coys. One A. Tps. Coy. One Div. Coy. No. 7 Bridging Train. " A," " B-1 " and " B-2 " Depot Coys. No. 51 Printing Sec. No. 52 Photo Litho Section.
Rawalpindi ..	Two Fd. Coys. One Div. Coy.
Peshawar	One Fd. Coy.
Risalpur	One Fd. Tp.
Karachi	Karachi Defence Light Section.
Calcutta	Calcutta Defence Light Section.

No further important changes occurred until 1928. In this year the establishment of Field Companies was increased from 2 to 3 British Officers. Mechanization was begun, A. Tps. and D.H.Q. Companies receiving a few M.T. vehicles, and Sappers, trained in M.T. duties, appearing in the establishment for the first time. Further mechanization occurred in 1930 when No. 31 Field

Troop had its tool carts and wagons replaced by lorries, one half-Troop being dismounted and carried in lorries.

In 1931, the three Field Companies and D.H.Q. Company allotted to the 1st Division received a derrick-lorry and lorries for their water supply-gear. The transport at Headquarters was also mechanized, and in 1932, No. 35 Field Troop was half mechanized and units allotted to the 3rd Division received the same lorries as those of the 1st Division. These changes led to an increase of Sappers (M.T. Drivers) at the expense of A.T. Drivers. It led also to the departure of the last elephant from Corps H.Q.

The major reorganization which took place in 1932 owing to the abolition of the Pioneers is dealt with in Appendix H.

In 1938 the Field Company allotted to " Covering Troops " in Peshawar received lorries for its water-supply equipment and all Field Companies exchanged a lorry for a motor van, a type of vehicle which was already held by Divisional Companies and which had proved extremely useful for reconnaissance.

APPENDIX C

ROYAL BOMBAY SAPPERS AND MINERS

The Corps of Royal Bombay Sappers and Miners had its origin in some Pioneer Lascars raised by Major Lawrence Nilson, the first Chief Engineer of the Bombay Presidency, at the end of 1777, and a Corps of Engineer Lascars and Pontoon Train, raised by Major-General Robert Nicholson, Engineer-in-Chief and Commander-in-Chief, Bombay, in 1799.

The Pioneer Lascars were commanded by officers of the Bombay Engineers and took part in all the Mysore and Maratha wars. In 1781 they were called the "Pioneer Corps" and were commanded by a certain Captain Theobald, a temporary Engineer. The establishment was increased to four companies in 1797, including the original Pioneer Lascars. The first connection with Poona was in 1805, when one company formed part of the Poona Subsidiary Force.

In 1821, the units of the Corps were distributed as follows :—

One Company at Khaira.
Two Companies at Bombay.
One Company at Sholapur.
One Company at Baroda.
One Company in the Konkan.

Meanwhile, the "Engineer Lascars" had been reorganized in 1820 as a company of "Sappers and Miners" under the command of Captain Thomas Dickinson, Bombay Engineers. This was the first unit of the Corps to serve overseas. It went to the Arabian Coast (Beni-Boo-Ali) in 1821.

The amalgamation of the Sappers and Miners with the Pioneer Corps had been ordered in 1824 but was not put into effect until 1830. The whole was then designated the "Engineer Corps," though during 1837 and 1838 it was referred to officially as the "Corps of Bombay Sappers and Miners." The latter title was confirmed in 1840.

Corps Headquarters moved from Ahmednagar to Sirur in 1830 and to Poona in 1837, where it remained except for a period in Karachi from 1843 to 1848. In 1868, it moved to its present location at Kirkee.

From 1838 onwards, units of the Corps were constantly on service in Afghanistan and Sind, on the Arabian and Persian coasts, and in Africa. It was natural, therefore, that Quetta and Aden should become permanent outstations. Four out of the five companies took part in the suppression of the Indian Mutiny and the campaign in Central India in 1859.

In 1900, the Corps of Bombay Sappers and Miners included four Service Companies (Nos. 1 to 4), "A" and "B" Depot Companies, and the equipment for one Bridging Train. Pontoon, Telegraph, Bridging, and Photo-Litho and Printing Sections were grouped in "A" Company, and "B" Company was for recruits. The establishment of the Corps consisted of a Commandant, a "Superintendent of Instruction, Park and Train," an Adjutant, a Medical Officer, 6 Company Commanders (British), 5 Company Officers (British), 22 British Warrant and non-commissioned officers, 15 Indian Officers, 849 Indian other ranks, 40 Indian driver ranks and 12 recruit boys. The class composition was settled by the Commandant. The peace distribution of units provided for Headquarters, two Service Companies and "A" and "B" Companies at Kirkee, one Service Company at Aden, and another at Quetta. In 1902, two more Service Companies (Nos. 5 and 6), and also a Fortress Company, were added to the establishment.

The year 1903 saw important changes in the Corps. Not only was its title altered to "3rd Sappers and Miners," but all the companies were renumbered and an official class composition was issued for the first time. Nos. 1, 2 and 3 Companies became Nos. 17, 18 and 19 Companies respectively, and each was composed of one-quarter Rajputs, one-quarter Marathas, one-quarter Mussalmans and one-quarter Mixed. Similarly, Nos. 4, 5 and 6 Companies became Nos. 20, 21 and 22 Companies with the same authorized composition but substituting Sikhs for Rajputs. The Fortress and "A" Companies were changed into No. 23 (Fortress) and "E" Companies respectively with a mixed class composition, and "B" Company emerged as "F" Company composed of all classes.[1] Of these units, one Service Company was normally at Quetta, the Fortress Company at Aden, and the remainder at Kirkee. The appointment of Superintendent of Instruction, Park and Train, was abolished in 1903 and replaced by separate appointments of Superintendent of Instruction and Superintendent of Park and Train. Beyond an expansion of "F" (Depot) Company and an increase in the Reserve, nothing of much importance occurred subsequently until the Service Companies were renamed "Field Companies" in 1909, as in the Madras and Bengal Corps.

In 1910, a new class composition was authorized; one-half of the men were to be Mussalmans (Punjabis), one-quarter Sikhs and one-quarter Marathas. The Telegraph Section of "A" Company was absorbed into the newly-raised Signal Companies,[2] and the Pontoon Section was reduced to cadre; the Printing and Photo-Litho Sections, and the cadre Pontoon Section, were then transferred to "F" Company, and "E" Company vanished. In the same year an additional Field Company was transferred to Quetta from Kirkee, and the Bombay and Aden Defence Light Sections joined the Corps. They were formerly part of the Indian Submarine Mining Corps, but since 1909 their duties had been confined to defence lights, telephones and pumping installations.[3]

The Great War caused a very large expansion of the Corps. In addition to the pre-war strength of 20 British officers, 20 British Warrant and non-commissioned officers, and 1,400 Indian ranks, there passed through the Corps, between August, 1914, and November, 1918, approximately 250 British officers, 90 British Warrant and non-commissioned officers, and 6,000 Indian ranks. In the same period the original 6 Field Companies, 1 Fortress Company, 1 Depot Company and 1 Pontoon Park (cadre only) developed into 16 Field Companies, 1 Field Squadron, 2 Field Troops, 1 Fortress Company, 3 Pontoon Parks, a Seistan Detachment, a Karun Section, and 9 Depot Companies including "E" Company which was reformed. Reinforcements of officers came chiefly from the Indian Army Reserve and were mostly men in civil engineering employment in India. The earliest reinforcements were R.E. officers from the Military Works Services and the Public Works and Survey Departments, followed in 1915 and later by officers of the Indian Army Reserve, officers holding Temporary

[1]The class composition of the Corps as a whole was $\frac{1}{4}$ Marathas, $\frac{1}{4}$ Mussalmans, $\frac{1}{4}$ Mixed, $\frac{1}{8}$ Sikhs and $\frac{1}{8}$ Rajputs. The term "Mixed" included Brahmans, Ahirs, Telegus, etc. From 1907, Mussalman recruiting was, in practice, confined to the Punjab.

[2]See Appendix I.

[3]See Appendix G.

R.E. commissions and officers of the Territorial Force (R.E.). British non-commissioned officers were obtained from England and also by transfer from British units in India. The establishment of Indian ranks was maintained by increased recruiting. The losses in the 20th and 21st Companies during 1914–15 were so heavy that the Malerkotla Imperial Service Sappers and Miners were absorbed into the Corps as reinforcements for these units and so remained until early in 1916, when they were replaced by recruits from Kirkee.[1] A further loss occurred when the 17th and 22nd Companies surrendered to the Turks at Kut al Amara in April, 1916. Altogether, the supply of men to replace casualties was most difficult. The great increase of strength in 1917 and 1918 necessitated the enrolment of Rajputs, Hindu Jats and other Hindus; but in general it may be said that newly-raised companies were composed of two sections of Punjabi Mussalmans and two sections of Hindus who might be either Marathas, Hindustani Hindus, or Jats. At one time during 1915 the single Depot Company ("F") contained over 1,000 men; but it was soon expanded into 4 companies, and in 1917 to 6 companies ("F.1" to "F.6") together with a new "E" Company. In 1918, the Depot had 8 "F" Companies and an "E" Company. In addition to training and supplying recruits, the Corps manufactured at Kirkee an enormous amount of equipment for new units and for the Indian Munitions Board.

As a reward for services during the Great War, His Majesty the King Emperor was pleased to bestow on the Corps the title of "Royal," and in 1921 the full name became "3rd Royal Bombay Sappers and Miners." In 1923, this was altered, by the omission of the number, to "Royal Bombay Sappers and Miners."

From 1919 to 1922 the Corps was in the process of reduction and reorganization. The establishment was fixed in 1920 at a Headquarters, 6 Field Companies, 2 Railway Companies,[2] 1 Fortress Company, 1 D.H.Q. Company, 3 Depot Companies, 2 Defence Light Sections (Bombay and Aden) and Printing and Photo-Litho Sections. Of these the Headquarters, 3 Field Companies, 1 Railway Company, the Depot Companies and the Printing and Photo-Litho Sections were stationed at Kirkee, 2 Field Companies were at Quetta and one at Kohat, 1 Railway Company was on railway work, 1 Defence Light Section was at Bombay, and the other and No. 23 (Fortress) Company at Aden. The strength of the Corps in 1920 was 32 British officers, 49 British Warrant and non-commissioned officers, 49 Indian officers and 2,323 Indian other ranks. Nos. 17 and 22 Field Companies, which till then had each consisted of 4 sections (192 Indian other ranks), were reorganized in 1921 into units each with 3 sections and a headquarter section and a strength of 2 British officers, 3 British Warrant and non-commissioned officers, 4 Indian officers and 224 Indian other ranks. The equipment was also adapted to make each section self-contained. On mobilization, a Field Company was to receive 3 additional British officers so that it would then have an Officer Commanding, a Second-in-Command and 3 Section Commanders. The class composition at this time in all Field Companies was one-third Marathas and one-third Punjabi Mussalmans, while the remaining one-third was of Hindustani Hindus in Nos. 17, 18 and 19 Field Companies and of Sikhs in Nos. 20, 21 and 22. The Fortress and D.H.Q. Companies were of "mixed" composition.

[1]See Appendix E.

[2]In 1921, 2 Railway Companies of Sappers and Miners (Nos. 25 and 26) joined the Bombay Corps after rendering good service in E. Africa during the Great War. (See Appendix F.)

When Nos. 25 and 26 Railway Companies were disbanded in 1931, and No. 42 D.H.Q. Company was increased in strength, the last Hindustani Hindus disappeared from the Corps. At the end of the year, the class composition was two sections of Punjabi Mussalmans and one of Marathas in Nos. 17, 18 and 19 Field Companies, and one section each of Punjabi Mussalmans, Marathas and Sikhs in Nos. 20, 21 and 22. The strength of the Corps was then 32 British officers, 42 British Warrant and non-commissioned officers, 40 Indian officers, 1,853 Indian other ranks, and 149 Indian driver ranks, and the Reserve had reached a total of 704 Indian other ranks. Important changes in the establishment and organization of the Corps were initiated in 1932 in connection with the scheme for the abolition of Pioneers from the Indian Army. These are alluded to in Appendix H. The peace distribution of units remained unchanged except that the Field Company at Kohat provided the Chitral Section.

Mechanization developed steadily from 1930 onwards and by 1938 all units included M.T. vehicles in their transport. Training in power plant increased although no such plant was included in unit equipment, other than for the D.H.Q. Company, until 1939.

On April 1st, 1939, No. 22 Field Company (stationed at Kohat) started its career as an Indianized unit.

APPENDIX D

BURMA SAPPERS AND MINERS

A company of Burma Sappers and Miners was raised in July, 1887, and affiliated to the Madras Corps. Its establishment was identical with that of a Service Company of the Madras Corps except that it had a third British N.C.O., 4 cooks and, when necessary, 2 extra *bhisties*. The officers were lent by the three Corps in rotation without replacement and were relieved after 2 years' service if they so desired.[1] Some Indian officers were appointed in August and September 1887 and the first Sapper was enlisted in October, but during November and December only 15 recruits were obtained although, as a concession, the families of men were allowed to live in the lines. The minimum standard of height for Burmans was fixed at 5 ft. 4 in., and recruits were accepted up to 30 years of age.[2]

In October, 1888, orders were issued that the Burma Sappers should consist of Burmans, Shans, Kachins and Karens, and that at least 50 per cent of the recruits should be fairly skilled artificers.[3] Such men were to receive the same rates of working pay as artificers of the Bengal Corps. By the end of 1888, 108 recruits had been obtained. An interpreter was sanctioned in February 1889.[4] The company reached full strength in October 1890 after the standard of height had been reduced to 5 ft. 3 in., or, for exceptionally good artificers, 5 ft. 2 in. Nevertheless, it was found that Shans and Kachins would not enlist, and in May 1892 the composition of the unit was 125 Burmans and 31 Karens.

In June 1893, the Burma Company was placed on a permanent footing as an integral part of the Madras Corps, two R.E. officers being added on that account to the Corps establishment.[5] British N.C.O.s were appointed similarly, and, except that they received extra pay for service in Burma, were on the same footing as others of the Madras Corps. No British N.C.O.s were required normally to serve for more than 2 years with the Burma Company. Those first appointed under the new scheme were selected from the Bengal Corps and transferred at once to the Madras establishment. Indian officers and N.C.O.s were supplied only by the Madras Corps, receiving a step in rank on appointment and thereafter 50 per cent extra working pay for every day's effective service in Burma. They were seconded in their own Corps and, if they elected later to revert to it, they remained supernumerary till absorbed. While seconded, however, they were eligible for promotion in their Corps. Any vacancies were filled normally by promotions within the Burma Company, but the C.-in-C., Madras, could sanction further transfers from the Madras Corps if necessary. The authorized class composition was ½ Burmans, ¼ Kachins and Karens, and ¼ Shans. All had to be fairly skilled artificers and were paid on the same scale as artificers of the Bengal Corps. The term of enlistment was for 5 years, but men could extend their service to 7 years or 12 years and received appropriate small increases of pay during such extension. Indian officers and N.C.O.s were eligible for

[1] I.A.C. No. 117 dated 9.7.1887.
[2] Govt. of India letters Nos. 1668 dated 26.10.1887 and 283 A. dated 4.2.1888.
[3] I.A.C. No. 164 dated 31.10.1888.
[4] Govt. of India letter No. 416 A. dated 11.2. 1889.
[5] I.A.C. No. 91 dated 15.6.1893.

pensions as paid in the Madras Corps, but the rank and file received no pensions on discharge. Free rations were supplied only when the Burma Sappers were serving with other troops receiving this concession. Altogether, the terms were not very attractive. In February, 1894, the O.C. Burma Sappers was given additional powers of promotion and discharge, but it is worthy of note that until May, 1903, the Government of India refused to allow the Commandant, Madras S. & M., to inspect the Burma company of his own Corps situated in Mandalay.

In October, 1903, the Burma Sappers became the 15th (Burma) Company, Madras S. & M., and as such rendered useful service in Burma for many years until, in October 1916, three sections under Captain C. W. Bushell, R.E., embarked for Iraq during the Great War. The 62nd (Burma) Company was raised in Mandalay during the summer of 1917, and the 68th (Burma) Company in August 1918. Under Captain J. M. B. Stuart, R.E., the depot at Mandalay carried on intensive training and recruiting during the war and reached a total of 1,400 men though handicapped by lack of staff, equipment and funds. No. 15 (or 15th) Company mobilized at Mandalay in May, 1919, for the 3rd Afghan War and returned in July, 1921, when it was reorganized in accordance with A.I.I. 429 of 1920. No. 68 (Burma) Company had been disbanded in February 1920, and in September 1921, No. 62 (Burma) Company suffered a like fate.

On January 10th, 1922, under A.I.I. 20 of 1922, No. 15 (Burma) Company, together with its depot at Mandalay and the Rangoon Defence Light Section, was cut adrift from the Madras S. & M., after a connection of 35 years, and became the "4th Burma Sappers and Miners." The peace establishment of the new Corps was then fixed as follows :—

H.Q. and Depot	Commandant (Major)	1
	Adjt. and Q.M.	1
	Subadar-Major	1
	Jemadar Adjt. and Q.M.	1
	Burma N.C.O.s and O.R.s	72
No. 15 Field Company	O.C. (Capt.)	1
	Coy. Officer	1
	Subadar	1
	Jemadars	3
	Burma N.C.O.s and O.R.s	224
Rangoon D.L.S.	O.C. (Lieut.)	1
	Jemadar	1
	Burma N.C.O.s and O.R.s	55
Reservists		45

The first Commandant was Major (Bt. Lieut.-Col.) J. C. Pringle, R.E., who was succeeded in 1926 by Major E. H. Clark, R.E.

The *personnel* of the disbanded Rangoon Defence Light Section were absorbed into No. 15 Field Company during 1926–27. The company left Mandalay for the North-West Frontier of India in January, 1928, its place being taken by No. 12 Field Company, Madras S. & M. Early in 1929, No. 64 Field Company, Madras S. & M., returned to India from Iraq without relief, and this brought the total of Field Companies on the Indian Establishment to one in excess of the authorized number. It was proposed accordingly that the necessary reduction should be effected by disbanding the 4th Burma Sappers and Miners, but before a decision was taken the Government of Burma was informed that the Burma Sappers could be retained if Burma would meet the annual financial commitment involved. However, the Government refused the offer, and consequently, in April, 1929, No. 15 Field Company, then on the North-West Frontier, was ordered back to Burma. It was met at Mandalay by instructions for disbandment, and these were carried out by Major R. Briggs, R.E., then Commandant of the 4th Burma S. & M. A farewell parade was held early in July, after which only a cadre remained until the middle of September to dispose of equipment and records.[1]

No. 15 (Burma) Company had existed, in one form or another, for a period of 42 years and had rendered good service. It was the only unit in the Indian Army, apart from the Burma Rifles between 1917 and 1925, into which Burmans, as distinct from Karens, Shans, Kachins and Chins, could be enlisted. No. 12 Field Company, Madras S. & M., remained in Burma until January 1931. Afterwards, until the separation of Burma from India, the country had no Sappers and Miners, but in 1937 the Burma Sappers and Miners were reformed as a separate Corps under Major J. M. Saegert, R.E.

[1]On the disbandment of No. 15 (Burma) Company, No. 63 Field Company, Madras S. & M., returning from service in Iraq, was renumbered No. 15 Field Company.

APPENDIX E

INDIAN STATE SAPPERS AND MINERS

Contingents of troops, voluntarily supplied by the Rulers of Indian States, have served alongside the regular forces of the Crown in most campaigns during the past century. In 1885, when war threatened between Great Britain and Russia, many of the Indian States placed their services immediately at the disposal of Government and afterwards offered financial assistance towards the defence of the Indian Empire.[1] The Government considered, however, that assistance in the form of man-power was preferable, and consequently certain units of the small armies maintained by the Ruling Princes were detailed specially for Empire defence. A few British officers were appointed to tour the Indian States and act as advisers and inspectors, and subsequently a number of instructors were lent from the regular forces to supervise training. By 1889, the scheme was well in hand, and a force known as the " Imperial Service Troops " came into being. The selected units were designed to be organized and equipped on the same lines as corresponding units of the Indian Army, though at the expense of the Indian States, and they were supplied gradually with the necessary transport. Their equipment, rifles and ammunition were provided by Government on the understanding that the Indian States would agree to supervision of the units by British " Inspecting Officers."

The Imperial Service Troops soon began to include a few Sapper and Miner formations. In 1890, the Sirmur Durbar converted their Infantry into 2 Sapper companies, each of 75 men, and in 1894, the Malerkotla Durbar raised a Sapper double-company of 150 men. The Faridkot State followed with a double-company raised in 1900, and the Tehri-Garhwal State with a company raised in 1907. The first appearance of the Imperial Service Sappers in the field occurred when the Sirmur and Malerkotla units took part in the Tirah Campaign in 1897. The Malerkotla Sappers served also in China in 1900–01.

Before the Great War of 1914–18, many retired Indian officers of the regular Sappers and Miners took service in the State Forces and rose to senior posts. Their experience, knowledge and high standard of training proved invaluable in the Sapper companies. It was difficult to find, in the States themselves, suitable officers for the higher ranks and to ensure their proper training. This was the case particularly in the smaller States, whose resources were strictly limited, and it was these that maintained Sapper companies. Therefore, when a company was accepted for active service, a British officer, usually one of the Inspecting officers or Assistant Inspecting Officers,[2] was appointed as a " Special Service Officer " to accompany it.

Active service was always most welcome to the Indian State Forces, for apart from the attractions of adventure in war, all ranks became eligible for Indian Army rates of pay and allowances which were considerably in excess of their normal scales. Peace-time training for the Sapper units was never easy to arrange. Theoretically, a Sapper company should be useful in a small State

[1] *A Short History of the Services rendered by the Imperial Service Troops during the Great War*, 1914–18, by Major-Gen. Sir Harry Watson, K.B.E., C.B., C.M.G., C.I.E., M.V.O., Preface, p. (i).

[2] In 1919, the Inspecting Officers became known as " Military Advisers."

because of its potential capacity for engineering work and workshop production; but in practice it proved difficult to find a happy mean between excessive work for the State and too many guard and ceremonial duties, and training varied in different States according to the views of their Rulers. On active service, the units came into their own and improved enormously, though it was difficult to keep them supplied with trained men to replace casualties.

Early in 1914, 29 Indian States maintained Imperial Service Troops and the total strength of all ranks was as follows :—[1]

Cavalry	7,673
Artillery	373
Sappers	741
Infantry	10,298
Signals	34
Camel Corps	637
Transport Corps	2,723
Total	22,479

It will be seen that the Sappers formed a very small part of the establishment; also, as already mentioned, they were maintained by only four States. Although the original intention had been that the strength of an Imperial Service Sapper Company should be indentical with that of a regular Sapper and Miner Company, it was found that this would be too great a financial liability for a small State and consequently a reduced strength was accepted.

The first Imperial Service Sappers to proceed overseas on active service in the Great War were from the Faridkot State. The Faridkot Company embarked at Karachi for East Africa on October 14th, 1914, and did not return until February 21st, 1918, after an absence of nearly 3½ years. From June to December, 1919, the unit served in the 3rd Afghan War. In December 1914, contingents of the Malerkotla and Tehri-Garhwal Companies went to France. H.H. the Nawab of Malerkotla had agreed to provide reinforcements for the 20th and 21st Companies, Bombay S. & M., and the first took the form of a draft of 2 officers and 94 other ranks. It was followed later by other drafts until practically the entire strength was in France. The company was not reconstituted as a separate unit until it was transferred to Iraq in 1916 and reinforced from India from a 2nd Company formed by the Nawab. No. 1 Company returned to Malerkotla in April 1919, and soon afterwards No. 2 Company proceeded to the 3rd Afghan War. The Tehri-Garhwal Company, with the consent of H.H. the Maharaja of Tehri-Garhwal, was used in 1914–15 to supply reinforcements to the 39th Garhwal Rifles in France. The first draft was formed into a platoon of infantry and as such took part in heavy fighting. The survivors were sent to Basra at the beginning of 1916 to join a reformed Tehri-Garhwal Sapper Company in Iraq. This unit returned to India in April, 1919, and aftewards served in the 3rd Afghan War. The Sirmur Company went as a complete unit to Iraq in December, 1914. In 1916 H.H. the Maharaja of Sirmur heard that it was in the besieged garrison of Kut al Amara and undertook to raise a 2nd Company in replacement. Colonel Bir Bikram Singh arranged for the necessary recruitment. No. 2 Company reached Iraq at the end of July, 1917, after a period of training at Roorkee and remained in Iraq until April, 1919, when it returned to India and afterwards served in the 3rd Afghan War. This brief summary indicates the praiseworthy

[1]*The Army in India and its Evolution*, p. 156.

co-operation of the Indian States. Their Rulers were ready to approve the employment of their Sapper units in any theatre or in any capacity which might help the Allied cause.

During the Great War, the dissimilarity in peace and war establishments between Imperial Service Troops and Indian Army units proved a source of weakness. The standards of efficiency were also different. Accordingly, after the war, the Indian States undertook a military reorganization which secured greater homogeneity and improvement in armament and training, and the forces which they were prepared to place at the disposal of Government were designated "Indian State Forces" instead of "Imperial Service Troops." The reorganization, however, caused little increase in total strength, for in 1923 the Indian State Forces numbered only 27,030 men, including 831 in the State Sappers and Miners.

In 1928, the Gwalior Durbar raised 3 sections of Sappers and Miners, and in 1930 H. H. the Raja of Mandi converted his Infantry into 3 sections of Sappers and Miners. The Gwalior Sappers were disbanded in 1937. The strength of the Indian State Sappers and Miners in 1939 was as follows :—

Faridkot	233 (*plus* Depot of 30)
Malerkotla	233 (*plus* Depot of 62)
Mandi	156
Sirmur	232
Tehri-Garhwal	129
Total	983 (*plus* Depots of 92)

APPENDIX F

RAILWAY SAPPERS AND MINERS

The first Railway Companies of Indian Sappers and Miners were raised as a result of experience gained during the 3rd China War of 1900–01. Each of the nationalities composing the Peking Relief Force was supposed to operate a section of the railway system in or near the Chinese capital, but owing to the absence of any British railway troops, the British section was worked temporarily by the Russians. When, at length, a British railway detachment was improvised, the Russians tried to avoid handing back the British section, and although they eventually did so, removed most of the rolling stock. This episode showed the need for properly organized and equipped Railway units, and measures were put in hand to provide them. Meanwhile, a few Sapper and Miner units in India were employed on railway construction to give them some experience. For instance, No. 1 Company, Bengal S. & M., worked on the strategic line from Kushhalgarh through Kohat to Thal on the North-West Frontier from January to July, 1901, and No. 6 Company until April, 1902. No. 5 Company, Bengal S. & M., also worked on this project for five months up to April, 1902,[1] together with Nos. 1 and 5 Companies of the Madras Corps.[2]

The original proposal was to raise six Railway companies, and a beginning was made with the formation of the 1st Military Railway Company by Lieutenant C. F. Anderson, R.E., at Sialkot in 1902. This was followed by the raising of the 2nd Military Railway Company by Lieutenant T. Gracey, R.E., at Sialkot in 1905.[3] The units were soon re-named Nos. 25 and 26 Railway Companies, each having 3 sections of Punjabi Mussalmans and 1 section of Mazbhi Sikhs and an authorized establishment of 1 British officer, 1 British N.C.O., 3 Indian officers and 193 Indian other ranks. Occasionally, a third British officer was posted to the two companies combined. This establishment was known as the " Regular " branch, and the rank and file were " Ways and Works " tradesmen. Attached to it was a " Traffic and Loco " branch of about 150 men for each company, recruited from the civilian staff of various railways, who could be called up for service when required and drew reservist pay. Little attention was paid to military training. The men of the Regular branch were given one month's training annually so that " they should be able to defend themselves if attacked " : those of the Traffic branch had no military training whatever. The chief defect in No. 25 Company was the indifferent military knowledge of the N.C.O.s. No. 26 Company was better off in this respect as it had a number of experienced N.C.O.s with previous service in Sapper units. There was a vague idea that No. 25 Company was under the wing of the Bengal S. & M., and No. 26 Company under that of the Bombay S. & M., but these connections, if they ever existed officially, soon became a dead letter.[4]

The normal employment of the two Railway companies was routine maintenance of the Sialkot and Nushki sections of the North Western Railway. Occasionally, the units were allowed to undertake the platelaying of new lines

[1] *History and Digest of Service of the 1st K.G.O. S. & M.*, p. 71.
[2] *Historical Record of the Q.V.O. Madras S. & M.*, Vol. I, p. 181.
[3] *A Brief History of the Royal Bombay S. & M.*, p. 35.
[4] Notes by Col. H. L. Woodhouse, M.C., late R.E., dated Jan. 4th, 1938.

under contract, but such constructional training was secured only through the initiative of the Company Commanders, supported by the recommendations of other R.E. officers who were serving as engineers on the North Western Railway before the Great War and were interested in the Railway Sappers. The assistance given by these officers was greatly to their credit, for it was simpler to give a contract for platelaying to a civilian contractor, working directly under their orders, than to a military unit working under its own officers.

In 1911, Nos. 25 and 26 Railway Companies, S. & M., were sent to Delhi under contract with the North Western Railway to build a portion of the Delhi Durbar Railway. The terms were so favourable that the units could afford to take with them from Sialkot a number of would-be recruits (*umedwars*) who proved most useful. As in the three Sapper and Miner Corps, the Railway companies had long waiting-lists for recruits and could pick and choose their men. No. 25 Company worked on the light railway around the Durbar camps, and No. 26 Company on a broad-gauge section. The constructional experience so gained was exceptionally valuable, for the units had no more work of this nature before the Great War.

In November, 1914, Nos. 25 and 26 Companies proceeded on active service to East Africa under Major C. W. Wilkinson, R.E., their combined strength being 475 ranks, including reservists but apart from the Traffic and Loco branches. There was also a Coolie Corps of about 300 men which was absorbed later into the Loco Department. Six civilian engineers and ten Upper Subordinates from the Indian State Railways were added to the cadre, and five additional R.E. officers were posted to it to reinforce the three already serving with the companies. The whole contingent was under Colonel Sir William Johns of the Indian State Railways as Director. Yet no Depot was formed in India to supply reinforcements to this considerable body of men, and consequently details had to be sent at first to the 19th Lancers' Depot at Sialkot and later to Kirkee. On landing in East Africa the Traffic and Loco branch of each company was transferred to a special Railway Traffic organization and had no further contact with it. The Traffic men were added to the Indian Traffic *personnel* on the Uganda Railway, and later, reinforced from India, supplied staff for working the captured German railways. Nos. 25 and 26 Companies were employed for a time as Field Companies on road repair work and the defence of the Uganda Railway, after which they began to undertake railway construction and repair. Their exploits, and those of other Railway companies, have been described in Chapter XX. War experience brought changes in establishments. For instance, the original Company strength of 193 other ranks was raised to 216. The strength of a platelaying organization is based on the number of rail-carrying squads, and experience showed that, after allowing for guards, sick and duty men, 193 was too small a number to get full advantage from four rail-carrying squads.

During the summer of 1915, the need for additional Railway Sappers and Miners in East Africa became so pressing that an officer was sent back to India to recruit men for two new companies, Nos. 27 and 28. In November, a Railway Sappers' Depot was established for this purpose in Roorkee and remained under the Commandant, Bengal S. & M., until February 1918 when it was separated from the Bengal Corps.[1] No. 27 Company was formed in East Africa in March 1916 from drafts from the two existing companies and reinforcements from

[1] *A Short History of the K.G.O. Bengal S. & M. during the War*, 1914–18, p. 13. The Depot left Roorkee on Sept. 7th, 1918.

India, and No. 28 Company arrived from India in May, 1916. The four companies were then grouped as a " Railway Battalion " with an adequate headquarter staff, and operated as such under Lieut.-Colonel C. W. Wilkinson, R.E., until Major L. N. Malan, R.E., assumed command in January 1917.[1]

By the beginning of 1918, the work of the Railway Battalion, S. & M., in East Africa was practically completed. No. 25 Company, reduced by sickness to 35 men, embarked for India in February, and early in March it was decided that the further retention of Nos. 26 and 27 Companies was unnecessary. Accordingly, these units left East Africa in April. No. 28 Company, reinforced by fit men from Nos. 26 and 27 and by a draft from India, remained in East Africa until September 1918 when it also left the country. On reassembling in India, the Railway Battalion found itself in an anomalous position, for officially it did not exist. There was no sanction for any Railway formation higher than a company, and accordingly the senior Company Commander had to act as Commanding Officer for all the active companies and for three training companies. The units still functioned as a battalion, but great difficulties were experienced in matters of supply until the position was regularized in 1919.

In May, 1918, after the remnants of Nos. 25, 26 and 27 Railway Companies had reached India, No. 29 Company was raised in that country, bringing the establishment of the Railway Battalion up to 5 companies. In October, 1918, Nos. 25 and 29 Companies, exclusive of Traffic and Loco Sections, were ordered to Salonica but were diverted to Palestine in consequence of the Armistice. They worked in Palestine and Syria until they returned to India in December, 1920. While these units were in the Middle East, Nos. 26 and 27 Companies helped to quell internal disturbances in India in 1919, and later, with No. 28 Company, served in the Khaibar Pass and elsewhere during the 3rd Afghan War and its aftermath. Nos. 26 and 28 Companies were on service overseas during the Arab Rebellion in Iraq in 1920–21. On return from Iraq, No. 26 Company was absorbed by No. 27 Company and the latter was renumbered " No. 26."

As a result of post-war reorganization it was decided in 1921 to abolish the title " Railway Battalion " and to reduce the Railway Sappers and Miners to their pre-war strength of two companies. Experience had shown that the semi-military training of pre-war days had been inadequate and that the companies had been left too much to their own resources. The units selected for retention were Nos. 25 and 26 (late 27) Companies, and consequently Nos. 28 and 29 Companies were disbanded during the summer. The Railway Battalion, as such, then ceased to exist. In August 1921, Nos. 25 and 26 Companies joined the 3rd Royal Bombay S. & M. It was intended that the two companies should spend alternate years carrying out military training at Kirkee and construction on new railways, and for some years this procedure was followed so far as circumstances permitted; but in 1931 the programme was upset by a financial upheaval which caused the cessation of all railway construction in India and a general retrenchment in military expenditure. Orders were issued for the disbandment of Nos. 25 and 26 Railway Companies of the Bombay Corps. Their opportunities for gaining experience in construction had vanished, and their organization, which differed somewhat from that of a Field Company, prevented them from becoming fully efficient in field engineering. A newly raised Railway Reserve Regiment, recruited from North Western Railway employees, was available to cope with any trans-frontier railway construction,

[1] *Official Report on the Work done by the Railway Battalion, Jan.*, 1917 *to April*, 1918, *in East Africa*, by Lieut.-Col. L. N. Malan, O.B.E., R.E.

and the importance of railways in expeditions overseas had been lessened by the development of motor road-transport. Accordingly, No. 26 Railway Company was disbanded in September, 1931, and No. 25 Railway Company on October 16th of the same year. Some of the men were discharged and the remainder transferred to other units of the Royal Bombay S. & M. These two Railway companies had had an honourable, if somewhat chequered, career extending through nearly three decades.

APPENDIX G

INDIAN SUBMARINE MINING AND DEFENCE LIGHT UNITS, SAPPERS AND MINERS

Submarine Mining in India originated in February, 1868, from a report by Major-General Sir H. M. Durand (late Bengal Engineers) recommending the appointment of a Select Committee of scientific officers to conduct experiments so that, in case of war, systems of "torpedo" defence should be available for Calcutta and Rangoon. This body assembled in April, 1868, under the presidency of Lieut.-Colonel H. Hyde, Royal (Bengal) Engineers, then Mint Master at Calcutta, to advise on the applicability of "torpedo" defences to the Hugli and Rangoon rivers and submitted a preliminary report on August 31st, 1870, when the outbreak of the Franco-Prussian War had drawn official attention to the inadequate protection afforded to the Indian ports. The Committee reported again on July 21st, 1871, and recommended that the Hugli should be defended by "torpedoes" and booms; but nothing was done because the war scare had passed, and in 1875 the Committee was dissolved after spending more than a *lakh* of rupees on experiments. The members had other and more important duties, and the experience which they gathered was wasted because a Torpedo Committee in England, working on similar lines, had much greater resources at its disposal.[1]

The Government of India then asked that an expert should be sent out from England to prepare projects for "torpedo" defences in their ports and harbours. Captain G. M. Collings, R.E., arrived in 1877, but he was soon invalided and was replaced by Captain A. Featherstonhaugh, R.E., in 1878. A war scare in that year caused the Government to decide to lay twelve mines ("torpedoes") in each of three waterways, the Hugli and Rangoon Rivers and Karachi Harbour. It was thought to be unnecessary to mine Aden Harbour, and mine-laying at Madras and Bombay was considered as beyond the powers of an untrained establishment. Early in 1879, some officers and men of the Sappers and Miners received elementary training in Submarine Mining, for it is on record that "A" Company, Madras S. & M., and a company of the Bombay Corps, were instructed for a time by some N.C.O.s who had arrived in Bombay from England in charge of stores. This training ceased, however, during the 2nd Afghan War, and no further attention was devoted to Submarine Mining for several years.

In September, 1882, Captain Featherstonhaugh was appointed "Inspector of Submarine Mining Defences" and began to revive interest in his Department.[2] As in the case of Railways, it was natural that his attempts to obtain *personnel* should be directed once again to training Sappers and Miners for the work; but it was soon recognized that a permanent establishment of specialists was needed, and consequently cadres consisting of 1 R.E. officer, 1 Storekeeper and 8 other ranks, R.E., and 10 Indian lascars, borne on the strength of the appropriate Corps of Sappers and Miners, were authorized in 1883 for each of the four major ports, Bombay, Karachi, Calcutta and Rangoon. These permanent detachments, of Europeans and Indians mixed, were to be supplemented, for

[1] *History of Submarine Mining in the British Army*, by Lieut.-Col. W. Baker Brown, R.E., pp. 189–191.

[2] Capt. A. Featherstonhaugh, R.E., was succeeded in April, 1884, by Capt. C. C. Carter, R.E.

practice and war purposes, by trained Sappers and Miners and coolie labour. The detachments were formed in due course, but without the Indian lascars, and in October, 1884," A " Depot Company, Madras S. & M., furnished a detachment of 30 men for Submarine Mining at Rangoon under this arrangement. The men were due for relief after two years, and the system was continued until 1891.[1]

The general reorganization of the Sappers and Miners, which took place in December 1885, provided for a special Submarine Mining Section in the " A " Depot Company of each Corps with an establishment of 8 British N.C.O.s, 1 Indian officer, 1 Havildar, 3 Naiks, 30 Sappers, 1 Bugler and 10 Lascars.[2] However, some months before the order was promulgated, the Sappers and Miners were maintaining " Torpedo Sections " at the various ports. For instance, " A " Depot Company, Madras S. & M., had a Section of 8 British N.C.O.s, 1 Indian officer, 1 Havildar, 2 Naiks, 38 Sappers and 1 Bugler at Rangoon,[3] and the 2nd Company, Bengal S. & M., had a Section at Calcutta.[4] The new Submarine Mining Sections were commanded by R.E. officers, appointed for a term of 3 years. The appointment was not popular as there was no chance of active service.[5]

Although evidence accumulated that Indian Sappers and Miners, enlisted from men of shore-going occupations, made indifferent Submarine Miners, a Special Committee, which assembled in September 1888, made recommendations adhering to this unsatisfactory system of recruitment. It remained for Major P. Von Donop, R.E., who became " Inspector of Submarine Defences " in February, 1889, to elaborate the details of a scheme for forming an Indian Submarine Mining cadre without the inclusion of Sappers and Miners. On October 15th, 1891, Government agreed to the formation of an "Indian Submarine Mining Company " with an establishment of 1 Major, R.E. (the Inspector), 4 Lieutenants, R.E., and 74 N.C.O.s, R.E.[4] Associated with this unit was a Corps of 140 Indian lascars, authorized in April 1891. The company was to maintain a section in each of the four ports, Calcutta, Bombay, Karachi and Rangoon. Thus, at the end of 1891, the special Submarine Mining Sections of the " A " Companies of the three Sapper Corps were no longer required and were dissolved. An attempt to assist the Indian Submarine Mining Company by means of Volunteer Submarine Mining Companies, raised in 1894 at Calcutta and Rangoon, ended in failure. The Europeans of these units could not spare the time to make themselves efficient, and consequently the Rangoon Company was disbanded in 1904 and the Calcutta Company about 1910.

In 1899, under Major A. M. Stuart, R.E., a beginning was made in developing a system of electric light defence for the Indian ports which eventually supplanted Submarine Mining as a Sapper and Miner activity; and in June 1900, a Section consisting of 1 British officer, 2 Mechanists and 6 other ranks (R.E.), with 4 Indian mechanics, was authorized for the maintenance of the electric defence lights, telegraphs and telephones at Aden.

A reorganization was effected in 1902 under which the R.E. *personnel* of the

[1] *Historical Record of the Q.V.O. Madras S. & M.*, Vol. I, p. 121.

[2] Special I.A.C. 174, dated Dec. 16th, 1885.

[3] I.A.C. 97 dated July 31st, 1885 (see *Historical Record of the Q.V.O. Madras S. & M.*, Vol. I, p. 124).

[4] *History and Digest of Service of the 1st K.G.O. S. & M.*, p. 43.

[5] In 1889, two R.E. officers were allowed for each Section, and in 1890 a roster was introduced for active service.

[6] I.A.C. 173 of 1891.

Indian Submarine Mining Company and the Indian *personnel* of the Corps of Submarine Mining Lascars were amalgamated into an "Indian Submarine Mining Corps," the lascars receiving the privileges of fighting men. A further reorganization of this Corps in October 1903 brought it more into line with the organization of the submarine mining companies of the Home Establishment. The new Corps maintained companies at the major Indian ports, and the Calcutta Company, in addition to its normal duties, was employed in raising or demolishing wrecks in the Hugli.[1] In 1906 came the decision to abolish submarine mining defences on the Hugli, and in 1907 to cease this form of defence at all Indian ports. All mines were withdrawn in 1907. The Indian Submarine Mining Corps vanished as such and the companies were reduced to mere sections, whose duties, from 1909 onwards, were concerned chiefly with the maintenance of defence lighting, telephones and pumping installations. These sections were assisted by some very efficient companies of Electrical Engineer Volunteers which had existed for several years in Calcutta, Rangoon, Bombay and Karachi.

In January, 1910, the Indian Submarine Mining Sections at all ports were affiliated to appropriate Corps of the Sappers and Miners—the Bombay and Aden Sections to the Bombay Corps, the Karachi and Calcutta Sections to the Bengal Corps, and the Rangoon Section to the Madras Corps. Submarine mining, nevertheless, was on the wane, and in 1912, orders were issued for the abolition of the Submarine Mining Sections and their replacement by Defence Light Sections.[2] The change came into effect on April 1st, 1912. The Rangoon D.L. Section was allotted an establishment of 1 R.E. officer, 1 Storekeeper and Pay Sergeant (from the Madras Corps), 20 R.E. other ranks (from England) and 32 Indian other ranks (from the Madras Corps), together with 18 Indian followers. It did not reach Rangoon, however, until April 7th, 1913, when the Indian ranks replaced the Submarine Mining lascars in that port. Similar Defence Light Sections from the Bengal and Bombay Corps replaced the Submarine Mining Sections at Calcutta, Karachi, Bombay and Aden. The sections were usually below strength. For instance, in 1914 both the Calcutta and Karachi Sections had only 1 British officer, 9 British other ranks and from 15 to 20 Indian other ranks. In November, 1920, the Madrassi ranks of the Rangoon Section were withdrawn and replaced by Burmans.[3] The section then became part of the Burma Detachment of the Madras Corps and drew its men from the headquarters at Mandalay. On the formation of the 4th (Burma) Sappers and Miners on January 10th, 1922,[4] the Rangoon Section was removed from the Madras Corps and incorporated in the new Corps. Its strength in 1923 was 1 British officer, 1 Indian officer and 55 Burmese other ranks.

Between 1923 and 1925, all the D.L. Sections began to suffer in strength and were reduced gradually to mere cadres. In 1927, the Rangoon D.L. Section was disbanded and absorbed into No. 15 Company, which constituted the major part of the 4th (Burma) S. & M. In the same year, the Aden D.L. Section was amalgamated with No. 23 (Fortress) Company, Bombay S. & M. D.L. Sections,

[1] "Salvage and Destruction of Shipwrecks," by Lieut. P. G. H. Hogg, R.E., appearing in *R.E. Professional Papers*, Vol. 30, 1904, pp. 158–168.

[2] I.A.O. 373 dated Jan. 24th, 1912. (See *Historical Record of the Q.V.O. Madras S. & M.*, Vol. II, Part I, pp. 28, 29.)

[3] *Historical Record of the Q.V.O. Madras S. & M.*, Vol. II (2) p. 13.

[4] A.I.I. 20 of 1922.

in cadre form, still existed in 1932 at Calcutta, Karachi and Bombay, but early in 1933 the Calcutta Section was represented only by 1 British officer and the Karachi Section by 1 British officer and 15 Indian other ranks. The end came in June, 1933, when the D.L. Sections were abolished and their duties taken over by Fortress Companies, R.E., of the Indian Auxiliary Force, assisted by a nucleus of regular R.E. *personnel.*[1]

[1]A.H.Q. letter No. 35667/1/M.O.I., dated June 26th, 1933.

APPENDIX H

THE REORGANIZATION OF 1932–33 AND THE ABSORPTION OF THE PIONEERS

Consequent upon the abolition of all Pioneer units of the Indian Army in October, 1932,[1] an extensive reorganization was effected in the three Corps of Indian Sappers and Miners both in the interests of economy and efficiency and to absorb as many Pioneers as possible.

Briefly, the changes in the Sappers and Miners were as follows. Every Field Company was expanded from a 3-section to a 4-section basis with the addition of one British officer (B.O.) in peace and two in war. Headquarters were to consist of the O.C., 2nd-in-Command, and 2 Subadars, and each section was to be commanded by a Jemadar. The addition of 2 Indian officers (I.O.s) and 86 Indian other ranks (I.O.R.s) raised the company peace establishment from 234 to about 320, the number of artificers being increased from 24 to 56. Each Divisional Headquarter (D.H.Q.) Company was raised to 145 ranks and reorganized in Headquarters(H.Q.), a Field Works Section and a Workshop (E. & M.) Section. The Bengal Corps converted No. 6 Field Company into No. 6 Army Troops (A.T.) Company, thus reducing the total number of Field Companies in India from 18 to 17. The Bengal and Madras Corps then had 2 A.T. Companies each, while the Bombay Corps had none. Each A.T. Company was organized in H.Q. and 2 sections. Each Field Troop was reorganized into H.Q. and 2 half-troops with a small increase in strength. The H.Q. and Depot of each of the three Corps was reorganized completely into a Training Battalion consisting of an " A " Depot Company and " B," " C," and " D " Training or Recruit Companies, a Records unit, and Workshops, the whole being commanded by a Lieut.-Colonel or Major.R.E., with an adequate H.Q. staff. As regards British ranks, the changes involved increases of 7 B.O.s and 3 B.N.C.O.s at Bangalore, and 7 B.O.s and 2 B.N.C.O.s at both Roorkee and Kirkee. The reorganization came into effect on November 18th, 1932.[2]

Two major problems were involved in the decision to abolish the Pioneers and increase the Sappers and Miners. The first was that, although the actual strengths of the Sapper Corps could be augmented rapidly by recruitment and transfers from other sources, qualified Indian officers and N.C.O.s were obtainable only by the promotion of serving *personnel* and by training such men as could be transferred from the disbanding Pioneers. No appreciable lowering of standards was permissible. The second problem arose from the decision that the three Sapper Corps should absorb as many ex-Pioneers as possible to avoid wholesale discharges. However, with a complete disregard of the difference in status between Sikhs of various classes, the absorption of the Pioneers was originally ordered as follows :—The Madras S. & M. to absorb 940 Madrassis from the Madras Pioneers ; the Bengal S. & M., 160 Meos (Mussalmans) from the Bombay Pioneers and 320 Ramdasia and Mazbhi Sikhs from the Sikh Pioneers ; and the Bombay S. & M., 133 Marathas (Hindus) and 160 Lobana Sikhs from the Bombay Pioneers and 160 Lobana Sikhs and 320 Ramdasia and Mazbhi Sikhs from the Sikh Pioneers. Now the Sikhs already serving in the

[1]Army Department letter No. B/22941/1 A.G.3, dated Oct. 21st, 1932.

[2]Army Department letter No. 22942/4/A.G.3, dated Nov. 18th, 1932.

Bengal Corps were mostly Jats of high status, and the allocation as first ordered caused such friction in the Bengal and Bombay Corps that it was altered in May, 1933, so that all Jat Sikhs, both Sappers and ex-Pioneers, were congregated in the Bengal Corps and all Ramdasia and Mazbhi Sikhs in the Bombay Corps. The Lobana Sikhs were transferred from the Bombay Corps to the Infantry. No trouble arose in the case of the Madras Pioneers allotted to the Madras Corps.

For convenience, further details of the reorganization will be given separately for each Corps.

Q.V.O. MADRAS SAPPERS AND MINERS

The absorption of the selected Madras Pioneers[1] into the Madras Sappers and Miners was easy because of their similar class composition and the fact that their headquarters were in Bangalore; but their regimental traditions differed somewhat from those of the Sappers, and as they numbered about 40 per cent of the Sapper strength, there was a risk that a non-homogeneous Corps might result. It was decided, accordingly, that the ex-Pioneers should undergo a preliminary course of training at Corps H.Q. and should not join their field units until fitted to do so as trained Sappers eligible to draw engineer pay. The rank and file were to be posted to " Provisional " Companies for 3 months' training in field engineering and a further 3 months' instruction in a Sapper trade, and the Indian officers and N.C.O.s were to undergo a special 3 months' course in field engineering. All the Sapper field units were required to lend officers and men as additional instructors and administrative staff. The entire preliminary training was to be carried out in the Meeanee and Assaye Lines where the Corps Workshops were situated. In spite of the fact, therefore, that the new Training Battalion was eventually to take over the Clive and Nilsandra Lines, previously occupied by the Madras Pioneers, it was decided that the battalion should come into being in the Meeanee Lines and should remain there while Provisional Companies were needed. This arrangement had the advantage that the ex-Pioneers were separated at once from their former surroundings and started their training in " the Battery " where all Sapper recruits had been trained for the last 60 or 70 years. It emphasized the fact that they were now Sappers and Miners and no longer Pioneers.

On November 18th, 1932, H.Q. with "A" Depot Company and " B ", " C " and " D " Recruit Companies of the Training Battalion were formed in the Meeanee Lines, the *personnel* being found from the former "C," " D.1 " and " D.2 " Depot Companies, from 112 ex-Pioneer recruits, and from men drawn from field units. On the same date, 5 I.O.s and 30 N.C.O.s, 2nd Battalion, Madras Pioneers, were posted to the Training Battalion and began their course under the Superintendent of Instruction (S. of I.). On December 6th, 350 men arrived from the same battalion and were formed into " E " and " F " Provisional Companies, attached to the Training Battalion, the staffs of these companies being supplied by Sapper field units stationed in Bangalore. On January 17th, 1933, 25 I.O.s and N.C.O.s and 326 men arrived from the 1st Battalion, Madras Pioneers, and " G " and " H " Provisional Companies were formed. The Training Battalion then numbered about 1,500 men with a staff of 184. There were 492 recruits, and 736 ex-Pioneers were serving in the four Provisional Companies or undergoing cadre courses at headquarters. Their

[1]The Madras Pioneers comprised the 1st K.G.O. Battalion (formerly 61st K.G.O. Pioneers), the 2nd Battalion (formerly 64th Pioneers), and Corps H.Q. (formerly 81st Pioneers).

training having been completed, the ex-Pioneer I.O.s, N.C.O.s and men were posted to field units, great care being taken that the I.O.s and N.C.O.s were given a seniority in the Madras S. & M. which was fair to the corresponding Sapper ranks. " E " and " F " Provisional Companies were abolished on June 19th and 26th respectively, and " G " and " H " Companies on August 16th. The Training Battalion, at full establishment, then moved into its permanent quarters in the Clive and Nilsandra Lines and the field units returned to the Meeanee Lines. This completed the process of reorganization, and within a short time of their arrival in field units the ex-Pioneers were indistinguishable from their brother Sappers. The difficulties of the transition period were eased by the fact that 9 British and King's Commissioned Indian Officers were attached for two years pending transfer to Indian Infantry units when additional R.E. officers were available in replacement. The colours of the disbanded Madras Pioneers were housed in the Madras Sapper and Miner Officers' Mess in Bangalore, and sufficient funds were handed over to enable assistance to be given to necessitous ex-Pioneers and their dependents and to finance triennial reunions of Sapper and ex-Pioneer pensioners at Bangalore.

A summary of the old and new organizations and establishments of the Q.V.O. Madras Sappers and Miners is given below :—

(*a*) Old Organization

Corps Headquarters and Depot

Commandant.
S. of I. and staff.
S. of P. and staff.
Adjutant and staff.
Q.M. and staff.
" C " Depot Company.
" D.1 " Depot Company.
" D.2 " Depot Company.

Field Units

Two Fd. Tps., horsed.
Six Field Coys., each :—
3 B.O.s.
3 B.N.C.O.s.
4 I.O.s.
H.Q. Section and 3 Sections. (Total strength—234.)
Two Army Troops Coys.
(Not organized into Sections.)
One D.H.Q. Coy. (Cadre only.)

(*b*) New Organization

Corps Headquarters

Commandant.
S. of I. and staff.
O. i/c Workshops and staff.
Adjutant and staff.
O. i/c Records and staff.
" A " Depot Company.

Training Battalion

C.O.
2nd in Command.
Adjutant.
Q.M.
H.Q. Wing.
" B " Recruit Company.
" C " Recruit Company.
" D " Recruit Company.

Field Units

Two Fd. Tps., half horsed, half mechanized.
Six Field Coys., each :—
4 B.O.s.
3 B.N.C.O.s.
6 I.O.s.
H.Q. and 4 Sections. (Total strength—320.)
Two Army Troops Coys., each :—
H.Q.
2 Sections.
One D.H.Q. Coy. :—
H.Q.
1 Field Engineering Section.
1 Workshop Section.

(*c*) ESTABLISHMENTS BY RANKS

	British Officers	B.W. & N.C.O.s	Indian Officers	Indian Other Ranks	Total
Old Establishment	39	58	51	2,337	2,485
New Establishment	53	60	74	3,442	3,629
Increase ..	14	2	23	1,105	1,144

The main advantage under the new organization was the provision of a Training Battalion within the Corps for recruiting and for recruit training. These functions had devolved previously on " D.1 " and " D.2 " Depot Companies, the former being a holding unit for 2nd year recruits undergoing trades' instruction, and the latter being responsible for recruiting and for instruction in drill, weapon training and field engineering. Unlike " D.1 " and " D.2 " Companies, the Training Battalion was well staffed and the training of recruits was under unified control.

K.G.V.'S O. BENGAL SAPPERS AND MINERS

In the Bengal Sappers and Miners the reorganization of 1932–33 involved the conversion of No. 6 Field Company into an Army Troops Company, the expansion of each of the remaining five Field Companies by one section, an increase in the establishment of the two existing Divisional Headquarters Companies and one A.T. Company, the movement of one Field Company and one A.T. Company to Nowshera, the disbandment of the Chitral Section which was to be replaced by a Section from a Field Company of the Bombay Corps stationed at Kohat, and the formation of a Training Battalion at Roorkee. Corps Headquarters was strengthened by the appointment of three Quartermasters (Special List, I.A.), one from the Sikh Pioneers and the others by promotion within the B.N.C.O.s of the Corps.

The reorganization caused an initial expansion of 12 B.O.s, 21 V.C.O.s[1] and 673 I.O.R.s in the establishment of the Corps, absorptions from the disbanded Pioneers being as follows :—

	V.C.O.s	Havildars	I.O.R.s
Sikh Pioneers	5	8	340 (Ramdasia and Mazbhi Sikhs).
Bombay Pioneers ..	2	5	180 (Meos).
Hazara Pioneers ..	—	—	11 (Punjabi Mussalmans).

Hitherto the Bengal S. & M. had recruited no Meos, and strong, though ineffective, representations were made against mixing Ramdasia and Mazbhi Sikhs with the Jat Sikhs already in the Corps. Five B.O.s from the Pioneers were posted to the Corps, including one as Corps Quartermaster, and all rendered invaluable service in the absorption of the ex-Pioneer *personnel.*

The scheme came into force officially on November 18th, 1932. The Ramdasia and Mazbhi Sikhs were formed into three self-contained sections and sent direct to Nos. 2, 3 and 5 Field Companies, while the Meos were distributed throughout the Punjabi Mussalman sections in the Corps. Some Pathans were enlisted and trained by No. 4 Field Company. In order that the ex-Pioneers should be assimilated as quickly as possible, it was arranged that they should be trained up to the necessary Corps standards by the companies themselves and not by Corps H.Q. The class composition of the units was fixed as follows :—

Nos. 31 and 35 Field Troops	Mussalmans.
Nos. 2, 3 and 5 Field Companies ..	¼ P.M.s and Meos. ¼ Jat Sikhs. ¼ Ramdasia and Mazbhi Sikhs. ¼ Hindus.
No. 1 Field Company	¼ P.Ms and Meos. ¼ Jat Sikhs. ½ Hindus.
No. 4 Field Company	½ Pathans. ¼ Jat Sikhs. ¼ Hindus.
Nos. 41 and 43 D.H.Q. Companies ..	½ P.Ms and Meos. ½ Jat Sikhs.
Nos. 6 and 8 A.T. Companies	½ P.Ms and Meos. ½ Hindus.

[1]Viceroy's Commissioned (Indian) Officers, formerly known as Indian Officers (I.O.s). The designation was introduced to differentiate these officers from King's Commissioned Indian Officers (K.C.I.O.s).

Although the Ramdasia and Mazbhi Sikhs formed separate sections in three companies, it became obvious at a very early date that they could not mix freely with the Jat Sikhs. There was considerable friction and many difficulties were experienced, particularly in the *Gurdwara* (temple). These seemed on the point of settlement when more serious trouble of a similar nature was reported in the Bombay Corps. Army Headquarters then decided to transfer all Jat Sikhs to the Bengal Corps and to concentrate all other classes of Sikhs in the Bombay Corps, measures which were carried into effect during the latter half of 1933. The Bengal Corps was given the custody of the records of the Bombay Pioneers and the care of their pensioners, and several handsome pieces of silver plate were presented by the Pioneer officers to the R.E. Mess in Roorkee.

ROYAL BOMBAY SAPPERS AND MINERS

Shortly after the reorganization was sanctioned in November 1932, the Bombay Corps received Lobana, Ramdasia and Mazbhi Sikhs from the Sikh Pioneers, and Marathas and Lobana Sikhs from Bombay Pioneers. The inclusion of Sikhs of different classes in one Corps soon resulted in very serious trouble. Orders were received in May 1933 that all Jat Sikhs and similar classes should be transferred to the K.G.V.'s O. Bengal S. & M., all Ramdasia and Mazbhi Sikhs collected in the Royal Bombay S. & M., and the Lobana Sikhs allocated to the Indian Machine Gun Platoons of British Infantry regiments. Action was taken accordingly, and by the end of August 1933, all Jat and Lobana Sikhs, except a few clerks, had left the Bombay Corps. The Ramdasia and Mazbhi Sikhs from Roorkee were splendid material, but their arrival placed the Bombay Corps in the curious position that one-third of its total strength was untrained in trades and only partially trained in field works. This necessitated the subordination of other activities to training in trades, and for many years the training of men in the Reserve was defective. Another result of the reorganization was that the Corps lost more men than it received, and consequently the total strength fell below establishment. Recruiting had therefore to be increased for several years.

On disbandment, the Bombay and Sikh Pioneers presented some fine Mess plate, historical books and trophies to the Officers' Mess of the Bombay Corps. The Sikh Pioneers sent their Brass Band, complete with instruments and music, and also a Band Fund for upkeep, and they transferred to the Corps a Charitable Fund for the benefit of Ramdasia and Mazbhi Sikhs.

The establishments of the Royal Bombay Sappers and Miners before and after the reorganization and the absorption of the Pioneers are shown below :—

	B.O.s	B.W. and N.C.O.s	I.O.s	I.O.R.s	Total
Old Establishment	32	42	41	2,001	2,116
New Establishment	43	44	62	2,852	3,001
Increase	11	2	21	851	885

Seven British officers of the Bombay and Sikh Pioneers were attached to the Corps for two years to tide over the shortage of R.E. officers, and three Quartermasters (Special List, I.A.) were provided by promoting selected B.N.C.O.s of the Corps.

The change in establishment necessitated an adjustment in the class composition of units. The new composition was as follows :—

Nos. 17 and 18 Field Companies ..	½ P.M.s. ¼ Ramdasia and Mazbhi Sikhs. ¼ Marathas.
Nos. 19 and 20 Field Companies ..	¼ P.M.s. ½ Ramdasia and Mazbhi Sikhs. ¼ Marathas.
Nos. 21 and 22 Field Companies ..	¼ P.M.s. ¼ Ramdasia and Mazbhi Sikhs. ½ Marathas.
No. 42 D.H.Q. Company	P.M.s.

Corps Headquarters was reorganized under a Commandant with four Staff Officers—Superintendent of Instruction (S. of I.) with an Assistant, Officer in charge of Workshops (O.W.) with two assistants and a Quartermaster, Corps Adjutant (C.A.) with a Company Officer, and Officer in charge of Records (O.R.). The O.W. replaced the former Superintendent of Park (S. of P.), his duties being very similar. The C.A. dealt chiefly with " A " and " Q " matters, the S. of I. with " G " work, and the O.R. with Records, including the past records of the Pioneers. All recruit training and most of the Corps institutional work was undertaken by the newly formed Training Battalion. There was little alteration in the location of units, but in May, 1933, the training of outstation units became the responsibility of local Cs. R.E. in liaison with the Commandant. For administration, such units were attached to local formations, although the Commandant remained responsible for promotions, postings, transfers and leave.

APPENDIX I

INDIAN SIGNAL UNITS, SAPPERS AND MINERS

Signal Companies of Sappers and Miners made their first appearance in 1911, although, prior to that year, the Bengal Corps had occasionally detailed Field Companies for communication work when an emergency arose, and all three Corps had maintained small Telegraph Sections.

The earliest record of Telegraphy as a Sapper and Miner concern occurs in June 1869, when the 9th Company of the Bengal Corps was employed on telegraph work.[1] In the following year, the 5th Company built a field telegraph line from Rawalpindi to Kohat, while in 1871 the 6th Company erected a line from Dera Ismail Khan to Bannu. These activities in the north seem to have borne fruit in the south, for in 1872, the Madras Sappers and Miners began to be connected with telegraphy and signalling. Courses of instruction were started at their headquarters in Bangalore, and the Commandant was empowered to grant certificates of proficiency in both Army Signalling and the construction and operation of Field Telegraphs to British officers who qualified in those subjects.[2]

The Madras S. & M. provided a detachment of 2 I.O.R.s under Captain E. W. Begbie, I.A., for visual signalling with the Dafla Expedition in 1874.[3] This appears to be the first instance of the employment of Indian Signal *personnel* on active service. A detachment of the 4th Company, Bengal S. & M., operated a primitive "Receiving and Sending Set" in the Jowaki Campaign of 1877–78,[4] and in the 2nd Afghan War of 1878–80, first the 4th Company, and then the 6th Company, was classified as a Field Telegraph unit. The 4th Company, which accompanied General Sir Donald Stewart from Quetta to Kabul, did little telegraph construction work; but the 6th Company, with General Sir Sam Browne, V.C., erected a line from Landi Kotal to Pezwan near Jagdalak. There is no evidence that the Sappers worked this line.

By 1881 the courses started in Bangalore had developed into a recognized "School of Army Signalling" at which officers and other ranks of both the British and Indian Services were instructed by a British officer assisted by a British N.C.O. Visual Signalling seems to have been the main subject. The instructor was attached to the headquarters of the Madras Corps and was under the orders of the Commandant. This system continued until 1888 when two Instructors in Army Signalling were appointed and Central Signalling Schools were formed elsewhere.[5] In 1882, a Telegraph Section of "E" Company, Madras S. & M., served in the Egyptian Campaign and laid a cable in rear of the troops to maintain communication during the advance from El Qassasin to Tel el Kebir. It consisted of telegraphists and had the necessary instruments and cable for 10 miles of line, carried on mules.[6] "Heliostats"

[1] *History and Digest of Service of the 1st K.G.O. S. & M.*, p. 31.
[2] G.O.C.C. India, letter No. 173 dated July 5th, 1872 (see *Historical Record of the Q.V.O. Madras S. & M.*, Vol. I, p. 99).
[3] See Chapter XV.
[4] See Chapter XIII.
[5] I.A.C. 141 of 1888.
[6] *Historical Record of the Q.V.O. Madras S. & M.*, Vol. I, pp. 117, 118.

were used by the Madras Sappers for visual signalling in Egypt until replaced by the more satisfactory heliographs made by the Bengal Sappers at Roorkee.[1] It is probable that in all military expeditions up to 1890 the Sapper and Miner Telegraph Sections were concerned mainly with constructional work and that the actual operation of the lines was done by men attached temporarily from the Indian Civil Telegraph Department.

In 1890, the telegraph equipment of the Madras Sappers and Miners, other than instructional, was handed over to the Telegraph Department as it was decided that, in future expeditions, that Department should make all arrangements for Army telegraphs, using either civilian telegraphists or Sapper *personnel* who had been attached for training.[2] As a means of training, two subdivisions of the telegraph system north of the Ravi were to be worked entirely by Madras Sappers under the orders of the Director General of Telegraphs. The non-instructional equipment of the Bengal and Bombay Corps was handed over also to the Telegraph Department, as in the case of the Madras Corps. To supply reliefs and keep up a reserve for their Telegraph Sections, the three Sapper Corps were required to maintain at headquarters a total of ten " Instructional Squads," four of which were allotted to the Madras Corps and grouped in " A " Company. Each squad had 1 B.N.C.O. and 8 I.O.R.s. A small Telegraph Detachment, formed from these men, served under Lieut. G. D. Glose, R.E., with the Hazara Field Force in the Black Mountain operations in 1891. British officers, such as Close, were trained in telegraphy during an 18 months' attachment to the Telegraph Department.

From 1889 to 1898, Telegraph Sections, S. & M., accompanied most trans-frontier expeditions. For instance, the Bombay Corps had sections with the Chin–Lushai Expedition (1889–92), in Miranzai (1891), Waziristan (1894–95) and the Tirah (1897).[3] The Bengal Corps had a section with the Chitral Relief Force in 1895, and the Madras Corps supplied sections for the Malakand and Buner Field Forces in 1897–98. It seems that, until 1897, visual signalling was still part of the duties of Telegraph Sections, S. & M., but early in that year, the equipment was withdrawn from all the Sapper Corps.[4]

A Telegraph Section of the Madras Corps, under Lieutenant S. G. Loch, R.E., served in the 3rd China War (1900–01) and erected a temporary line from Tientsin to Peking and a permanent line, 200 miles long, from Taku to Peking. A Section of the Bengal Corps, under Lieutenant F. W. Brunner, R.E., also operated in China. In 1903, the Bombay Corps had a Telegraph Section on service in Somaliland, and in 1908 the Bengal Corps had two " Telephone Sections," under Captain T. H. L. Spaight and Lieutenant H. W. Tomlinson, R.E., with the Mohmand Field Force. Until 1898, communication forward of Force Headquarters in trans-frontier expeditions depended mostly on visual signalling carried out by the regimental signallers of units, some of whom were formed temporarily into Divisional or Brigade Signal Sections. Up to Force Headquarters, telegraph lines were maintained and operated by the Civil Telegraph Department. The opening of the 20th Century saw the gradual replacement of visual signalling in the field by the field telegraph and telephone.

After the end of the South African War in 1902 the Corps of Royal Engineers

[1]See Chapter XI. Heliostats had been used extensively in the 2nd Afghan War.
[2]I.A.C. 16 dated Jan. 21st, 1890 (see *Historical Record of the Q.V.O. Madras S. & M.*, Vol. I, p. 145).
[3]*A Brief History of the Royal Bombay S. & M.*, p. 21. See also *résumé* of the history of Telegraph Sections of all Corps appearing in Chapter XIII.
[4]I.A.C. 3 of 1897.

began to form specialized Corps and Divisional Signal Companies in England, but Army Headquarters in India did not follow suit and until 1910 it had no Signal organization beyond that supplied by the regimental signallers of units. However, early in that year Lieut.-Colonel S. H. Powell, R.E., an ex-Bengal Sapper and Miner, was sent to India by the War Office for attachment to Army Headquarters to organize specialist Signal units and, by the autumn, had obtained sanction for raising 4 Divisional Signal Companies, to be followed later by a Wireless Signal Squadron. These units were to be known as " Sappers and Miners," although independent of the three existing Corps, and were to include both British and Indian other ranks. The only connection between them and the Sappers and Miners was that a few British officers, Warrant Officers and Staff Sergeants, R.E., were seconded from the Sapper Corps to their British ranks, and a few Indian officers and artificers to their Indian ranks. Volunteers from the Regimental Signallers of British and Indian units formed the bulk of the *personnel*. The British officers of each company—1 Captain and 3 Lieutenants—were seconded for four years and were drawn from any branch of the Service. The other ranks were posted till the end of their period of engagement but could be returned to their units if inefficient, or could return voluntarily up to a limit of 6 months. By November, 1910, the units had been designated Nos. 31 to 34 Divisional Signal Companies, S. & M., and the Commanding Officers appointed. These were as follows :—No. 31 Company, Captain H. S. E. Franklin, 15th Sikhs ; No. 32 Company, Captain W. F. Maxwell, R.E., Bombay S. & M. ; No. 33 Company, Captain L. H. Queripel, R.F.A. ; and No. 34 Company, Captain R. G. Earle, R.E., Madras S. & M. Thus every arm except the Cavalry was represented. At the same time came a death blow for the Telegraph Sections, S. & M., for on November 16th, 1910, orders were issued for their abolition and the transfer of their *personnel* to the Divisional Signal Companies.[1]

At a conference held in Simla in January, 1911, between Lieut.-Colonel Powell and the Company Commanders it was recommended that Nos. 31 and 32 Companies should be located at Fatehgarh and Nos. 33 and 34 Companies at Ahmednagar. This was approved, and the officers and men for the Fatehgarh units soon arrived, the companies being formed on February 15th, 1911. The Ahmednagar companies came into existence on March 1st. In June, 1911, No. 41 Wireless Signal Squadron was formed at Saugor under Captain D. A. Thomson, R.E., Bengal S. & M.[2] Men who failed to reach a high standard of training were returned as soon as possible to their units. The Indian ranks were called " Sappers," and in the British ranks, the use of the rank " 2nd Corporal " supplied another link with the Sappers and Miners.

The four Divisional Signal Companies, S. & M., were sent to Delhi in December 1911 for the King Emperor's Durbar and carried out communication duties between the camps and on the route of the State Entry. They took part in the Durbar and the Review, which they were obliged to attend in khaki instead of full dress because their full dress was so variegated. Shortly after the Durbar No. 31 Company provided a detachment for the Abor Expeditionary Force. The first test of general efficiency came in the great manœuvres held at the end of 1912 between Meerut and Ambala when Nos. 31, 32 and 34 Companies were attached respectively to the 7th and 3rd Divisions and the Directing Staff. They

[1]Govt. of India, Army Department, letter No. 188/1/A.G.3 dated Nov. 16th, 1910. The change came into force on March 1st, 1911, under a Special I.A.O. dated Feb. 3rd, 1911.

[2]The unit became known later as No. 41 (Wireless) Signal Company.

passed the ordeal with flying colours and were complimented by the Director, General Sir James Willcocks.

In February, 1913, No. 31 Company was moved to Rawalpindi and No. 32 Company to Ambala, while Nos. 33 and 34 Companies remained at Ahmednagar. During the ensuing summer, consequent upon the abolition of the Central Signalling Schools at Kasauli and Ahmednagar, the companies ran signalling courses to train regimental officers and men as instructors. On August 18th, 1914, a fortnight after the outbreak of the Great War, a fifth Divisional Signalling Company, No. 35, was formed at Meerut by Major R. G. Earle, R.E., who had been transferred from No. 34 Company. A nucleus of officers and other ranks was provided by Nos. 31 and 32 Companies. When it was decided to send the 3rd and 7th Indian Divisions to France, Nos. 32 and 35 Companies were mobilized to accompany them; and later, when the two Divisions became an Indian Corps, No. 31 Company was mobilized as a Corps Signal unit. This company also detached a Brigade Signal Section for service in East Africa; another Section followed, but both returned to India in March 1915. Captain H. C. Hawtrey, R.E., then raised a local Signal Section in East Africa, and in August 1915, when two additional Sections arrived from India, he raised a complete "Z" Divisional Signal Company, S. & M.[1] Each of the three Signal Companies which went to France had 12 motorcyclist despatch riders, volunteers from the young business men of Calcutta and Bombay. The companies had also some military telegraph operators recalled from service with the Indian Telegraph Department. On arrival in France they received reinforcements of General Post Office operators and linesmen to raise their establishment to that of a British Signal Company, and they were provided with British pattern equipment. After the departure of the Indian Corps to France, the 6th Indian Division was mobilized for service in Iraq and sailed with No. 34 Company as its Signal unit. This company served with distinction until it surrendered with General Townshend's force at Kut al Amara in April, 1916.

No. 36 Divisional Signal Company, S. & M., was raised on April 1st, 1916, and Nos. 37, 38, 39 and 40 between January and June, 1917. The highest number reached by the end of the Great War was No. 45, and many of the new units served in 1919 in the 3rd Afghan War. All retained their designation of "Sappers and Miners" until December, 1925, when they became part of the Indian Signal Corps and ceased to have even a nominal connection with the Madras, Bengal and Bombay Corps from which Army Signalling in India had originated.

[1]See Chapter XX.

INDEX

NOTE

The rank shown against a person's name is usually the highest mentioned in this book, not necessarily the highest attained.

z*

D

I

N

S

T

U

V

W

Y

Z

MAP I.

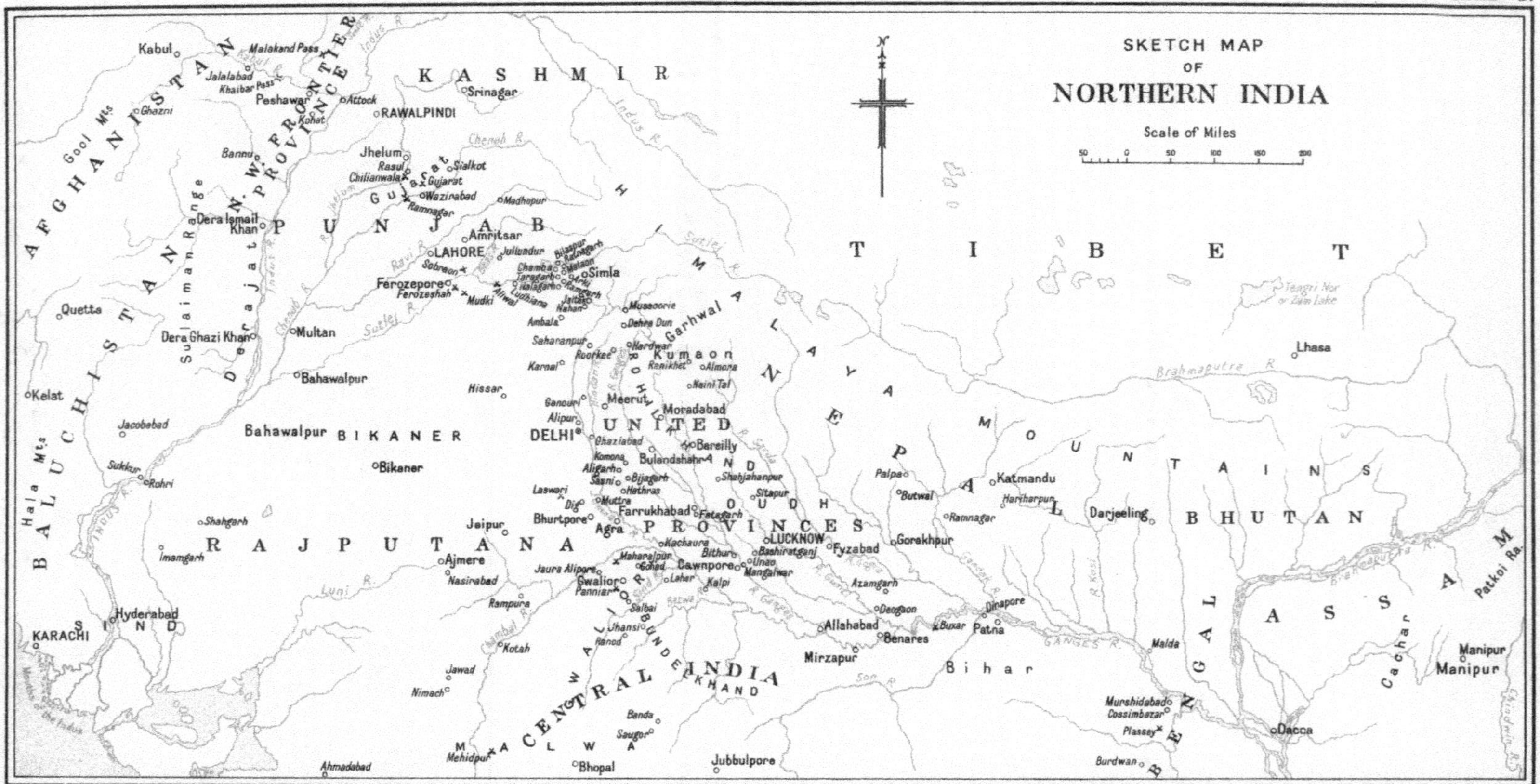

Stanford's Geographical Establishment, London.

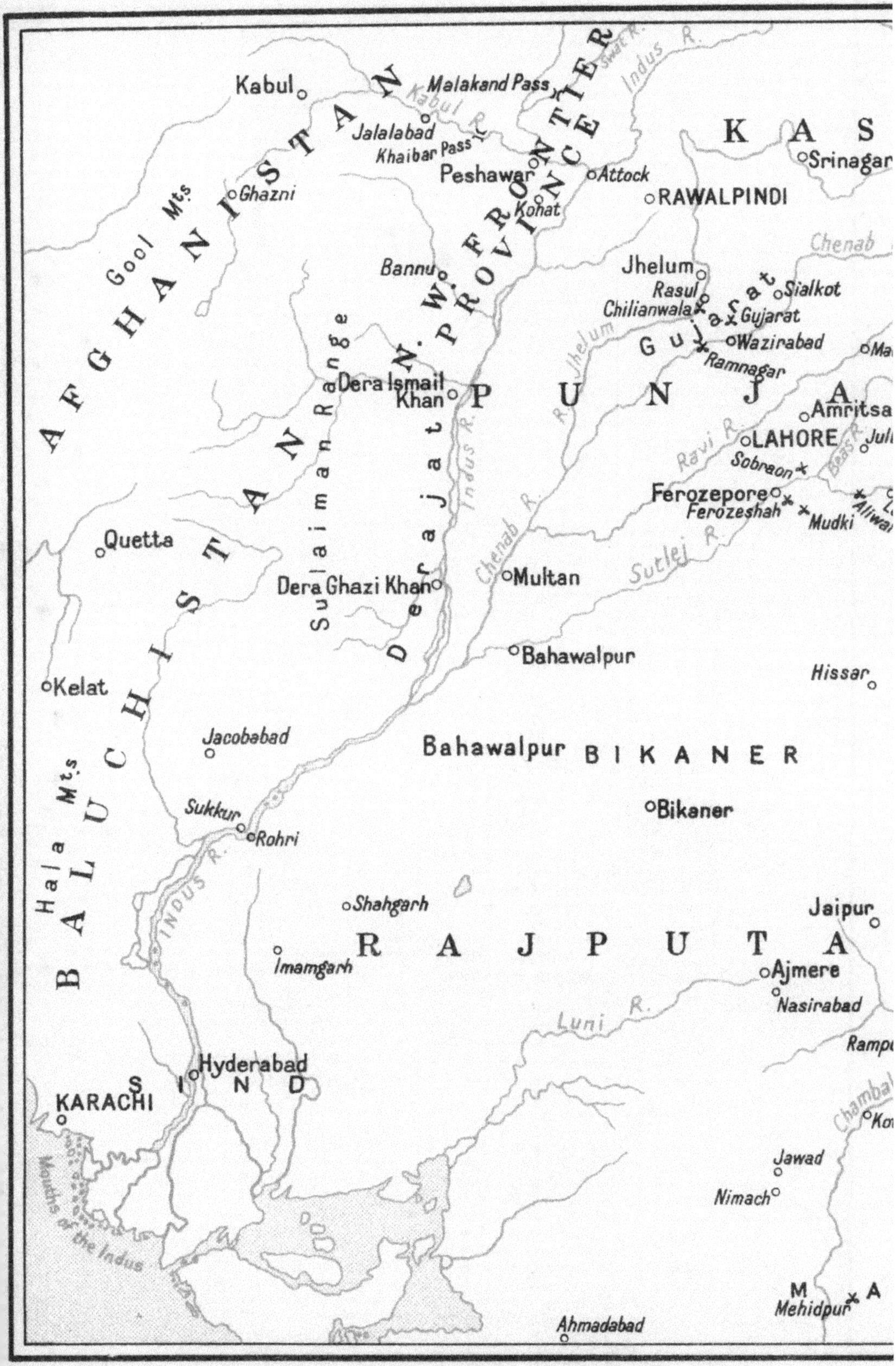

Kabul
Malakand Pass
Swat R.
Indus R.
Kabul R.
Jalalabad
Khaibar Pass
Peshawar
Attock
Kohat
RAWALPINDI
Srinagar
Ghazni
Gool Mts.
A F G H A N I S T A N
N. W. FRONTIER PROVINCE
Bannu
Jhelum
Rasul
Chilianwala
Gujarat
Sialkot
Wazirabad
Ramnagar
Chenab
Jhelum R.
Dera Ismail Khan
Sulaiman Range
P U N J A
Derajat
Indus R.
LAHORE
Ravi R.
Beas R.
Sobraon
Ferozepore
Ferozeshah
Mudki
Chenab R.
Sutlej R.
Quetta
Dera Ghazi Khan
Multan
Bahawalpur
Hissar
Kelat
B A L U C H I S T A N
Jacobabad
Bahawalpur
B I K A N E R
Bikaner
Hala Mts.
Sukkur
Rohri
INDUS R.
Shahgarh
Jaipur
Imamgarh
R A J P U T A
Ajmere
Nasirabad
Luni R.
Hyderabad
S I N D
KARACHI
Mouths of the Indus
Jawad
Nimach
Mehidpur
Ahmadabad

H M I R
Indus R.
Sutlej R.
T I
B
Bilaspur
Ratnagarh
Chamba
Malaon
Simla
Arki
Ramgarh
Nalagarh
Jaitak
Nahan
Mussoorie
Dehra Dun
Garhwal
Ambala
Saharanpur
Hardwar
Roorkee
Kumaon
Karnal
Ranikhet
Almora
Naini Tal
R. Ganges
Hindan R.
Ganouri
Meerut
Moradabad
Alipur
UNITED
DELHI
Ghaziabad
Bareilly
R. Sarda
Komona
Bulandshahr
Aligarh
Sasni
Bijagarh
Hathras
Shahjahanpur
Laswari
Dig
Muttra
Sitapur
Farrukhabad
Fategarh
Bhurtpore
Agra
PROVINCES
LUCKNOW
Fyzabad
Gorakhpur
Palpa
Butwal
Katma
Hariha
Ramnagar
Kachaura
Bithur
Bashiratganj
Maharajpur
Gohad
Cawnpore
Unao
Mangalwar
Jaura Alipore
Gwalior
Lahar
Kalpi
R. Gogra
R. Gumti
Azamgarh
Gandak R.
Panniar
Sind R.
Betwa R.
R. Ganges
Salbai
Deogaon
Dinapore
Jhansi
Allahabad
Buxar
Patna
Ranod
Benares
Mirzapur
Bihar
CENTRAL INDIA
KHAND
Son R.
Banda
Saugor
Bhopal
Jubbulpore
N

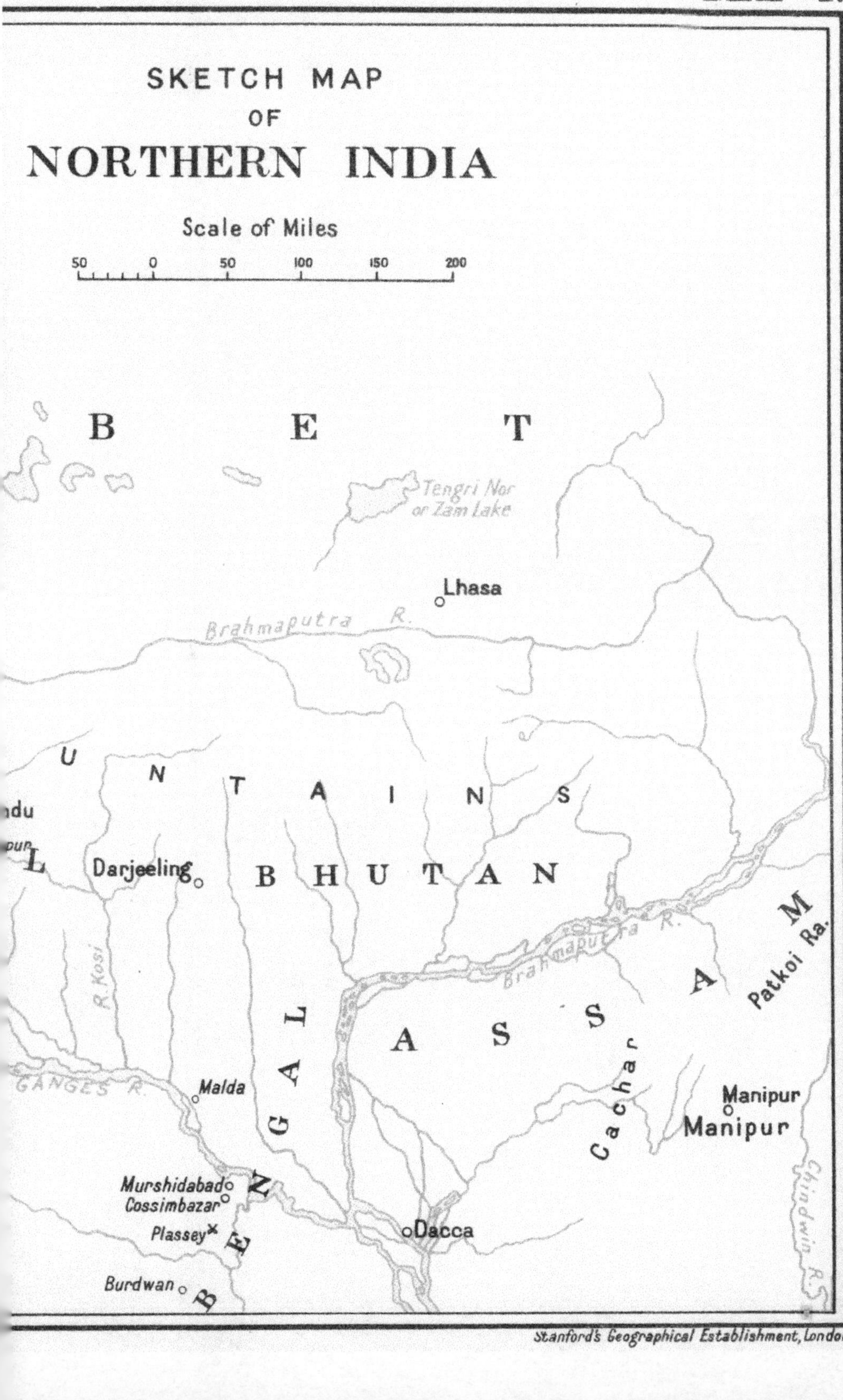

Stanford's Geographical Establishment, London.

MAP II.

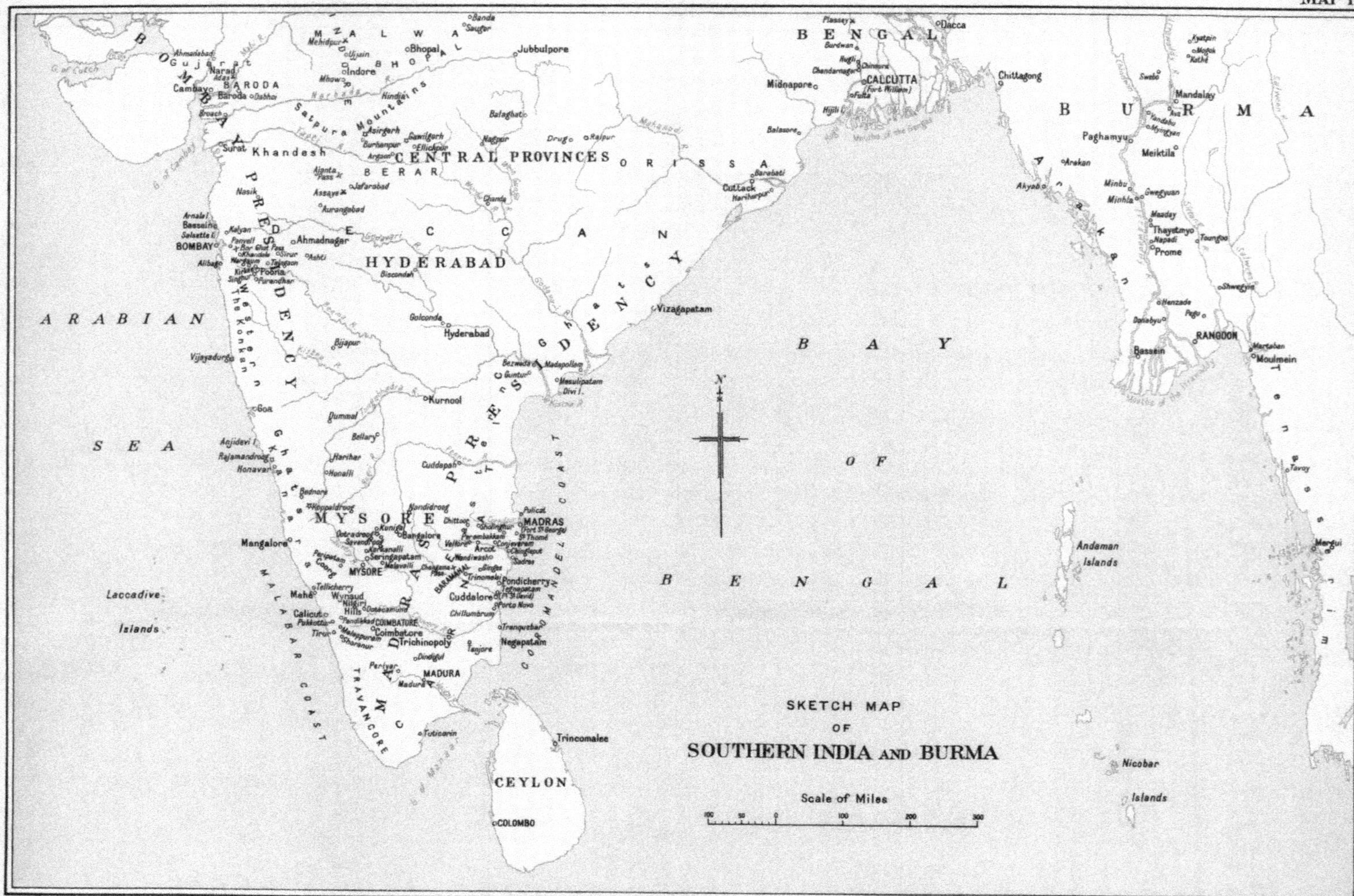
SKETCH MAP
OF
SOUTHERN INDIA AND BURMA
Scale of Miles
100
50
0
100
200
300
BAY
OF
BENGAL
ARABIAN
SEA
BOMBAY PRESIDENCY
MADRAS PRESIDENCY
CENTRAL PROVINCES
ORISSA
BERAR
HYDERABAD
DECCAN
MYSORE
BENGAL
BURMA
ARAKAN
TENASSERIM
MALWA
BHOPAL
BARODA
Gujarat
Khandesh
Satpura Mountains
Western Ghats
The Konkan
MALABAR COAST
COROMANDEL COAST
TRAVANCORE
CEYLON
COLOMBO
Trincomalee
BOMBAY
MADRAS
CALCUTTA
RANGOON
MYSORE
COIMBATORE
MADURA
Hyderabad
Golconda
Kurnool
Vizagapatam
Masulipatam
Pondicherry
Cuddalore
Trichinopoly
Negapatam
Tanjore
Bangalore
Seringapatam
Mangalore
Calicut
Goa
Poona
Ahmadnagar
Surat
Cambay
Indore
Ujjain
Bhopal
Jubbulpore
Nagpur
Cuttack
Balasore
Midnapore
Chittagong
Dacca
Akyab
Mandalay
Meiktila
Pagahmyu
Prome
Thayetmyo
Bassein
Moulmein
Tavoy
Mergui
Andaman Islands
Nicobar Islands
Laccadive Islands
Stanford's Geographical Establishment, London

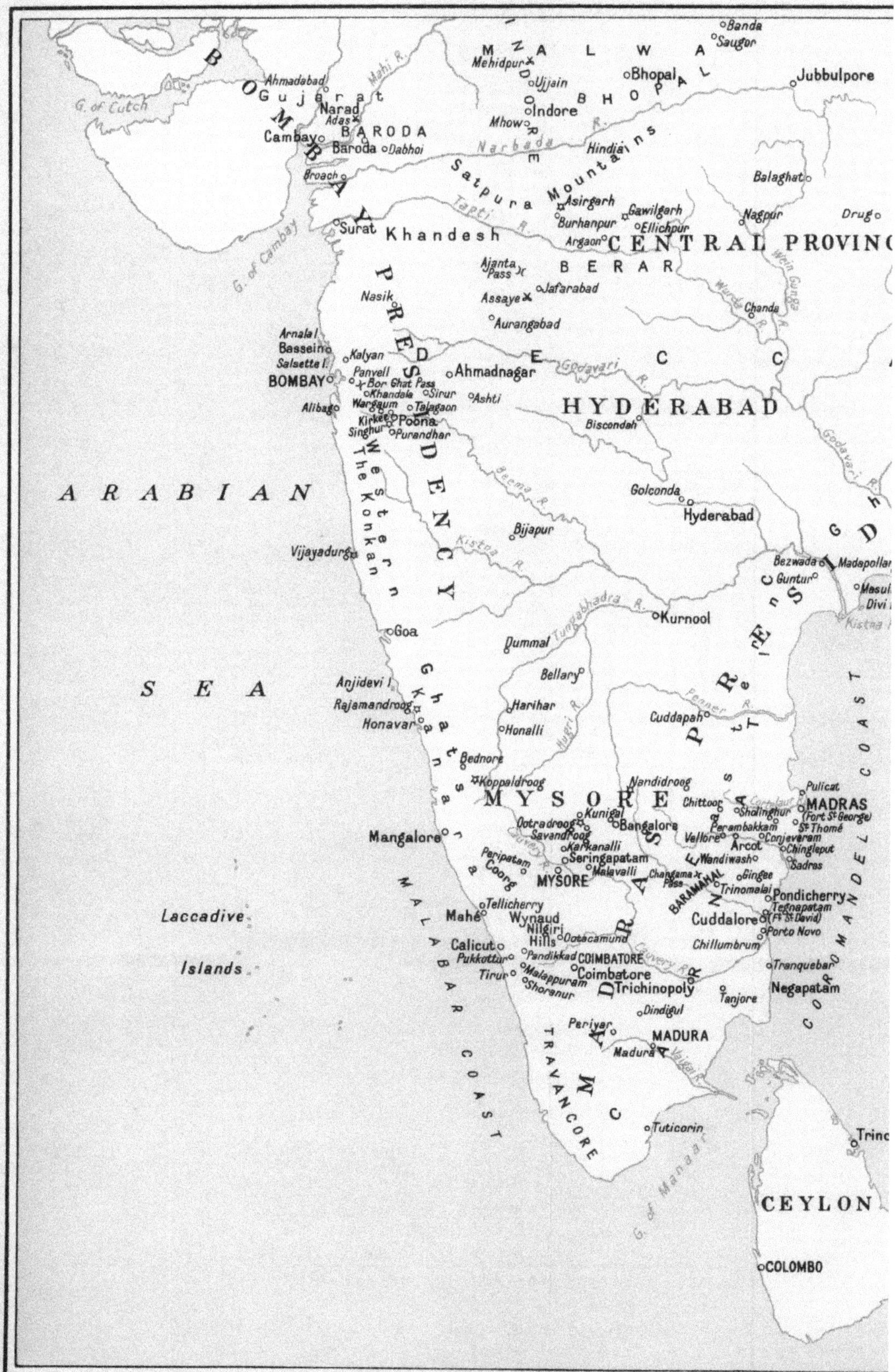
BOMBAY PRESIDENCY
Ahmadabad
Gujarat
G. of Cutch
Mahi R.
Narad
Adas
BARODA
Cambay
Baroda
Dabhoi
Broach
G. of Cambay
Surat
Khandesh
MALWA
Mehidpur
INDORE
Ujjain
Indore
Mhow
Bhopal
BHOPAL
Banda
Saugor
Jubbulpore
Narbada R.
Hindia
Satpura Mountains
Balaghat
Tapti R.
Asirgarh
Burhanpur
Gawilgarh
Ellichpur
Nagpur
Drug
Argaon
CENTRAL PROVINC
Ajanta Pass
BERAR
Jafarabad
Assaye
Wein Gunga
Wardha R.
Chanda
Nasik
Aurangabad
Arnala I.
Bassein
Salsette I.
Kalyan
BOMBAY
Panvell
Bor Ghat Pass
Khandala
Wargaum
Sirur
Talagaon
Ashti
Ahmadnagar
Alibag
Kirkee
Poona
Singhur
Purandhar
DECCAN
Godavari R.
HYDERABAD
Biscondah
ARABIAN SEA
Western Ghats
The Konkan
Beema R.
Golconda
Hyderabad
Bijapur
Kistna R.
Vijayadurg
Bezwada
Madapollam
Guntur
Masuli
Divi I.
Kistna R.
Tungabhadra R.
Kurnool
Goa
Dummal
Bellary
Anjidevi I.
Rajamandroog
Honavar
Kanara
Harihar
Honalli
Hugri R.
Penner R.
Cuddapah
MADRAS PRESIDENCY
Bednore
Koppaldroog
Nandidroog
MYSORE
Chittoor
Pulicat
MADRAS (Fort St George)
Sholinghur
St Thomé
Kunigal
Ootradroog
Bangalore
Perambakkam
Savandroog
Vellore
Arcot
Conjeveram
Mangalore
Kankanalli
Chingleput
Cauvery R.
Seringapatam
Wandiwash
Sadras
Peripatam
Coorg
MYSORE
Malavalli
Changama Pass
BARAMAHAL
Gingee
Trinomalai
Pondicherry
Tegnapatam (Ft St David)
Tellicherry
Mahé
Wynaud
Cuddalore
Nilgiri Hills
Ootacamund
Porto Novo
Calicut
Chillumbrum
Pukkottur
Pandikkad
COIMBATORE
Cauvery R.
Tranquebar
Tirur
Malappuram
Coimbatore
Shoranur
Trichinopoly
Tanjore
Negapatam
COROMANDEL COAST
MALABAR COAST
Laccadive Islands
Dindigul
Periyar
MADURA
Madura
Vaigai R.
TRAVANCORE
Tuticorin
G. of Manaar
Trinc
CEYLON
COLOMBO

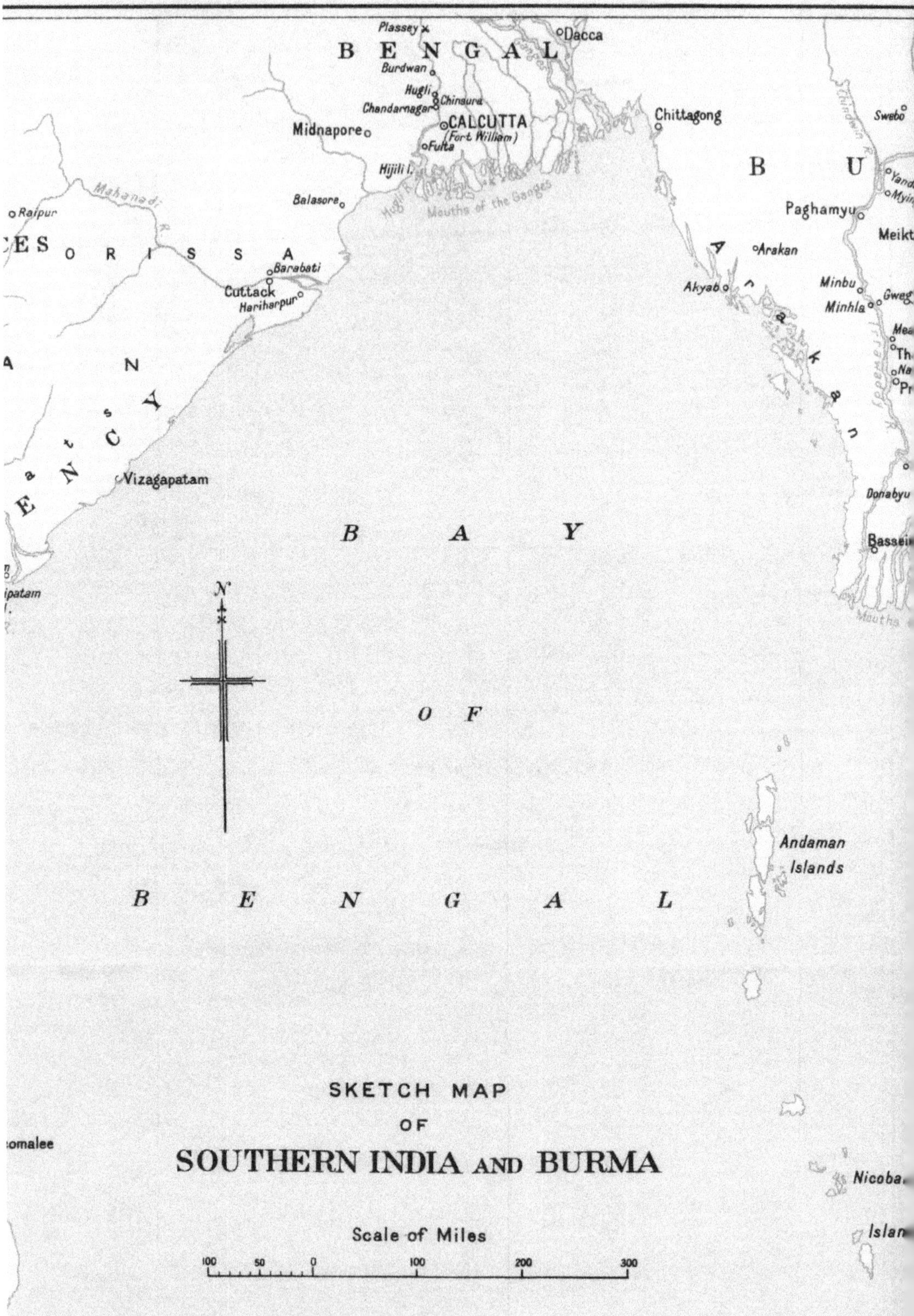
Plassey
BENGAL
Dacca
Burdwan
Hugli
Chinsura
Chandarnagar
CALCUTTA
(Fort William)
Midnapore
Fulta
Hijili I.
Chittagong
Swebo
Chindwin R.
Balasore
Mouths of the Ganges
Mahanadi R.
Raipur
ORISSA
Barabati
Cuttack
Hariharpur
Arakan
Akyab
Paghamyu
Minbu
Minhla
Irrawaddy R.
Donabyu
Vizagapatam
BAY OF BENGAL
N
Andaman Islands
SKETCH MAP
OF
SOUTHERN INDIA AND BURMA
Scale of Miles
100 50 0 100 200 300

MAP II.

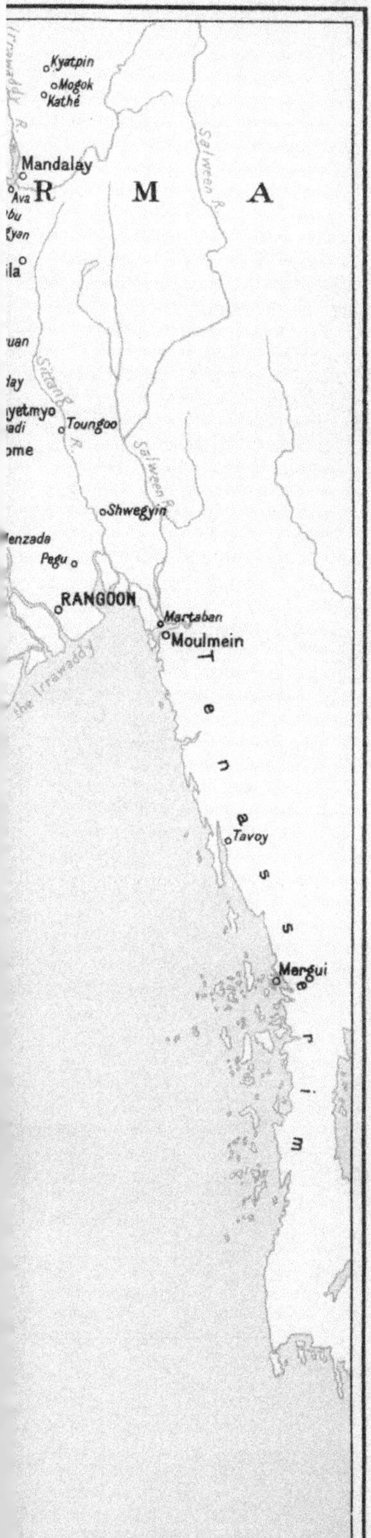

Stanford's Geographical Establishment, London

Map III.

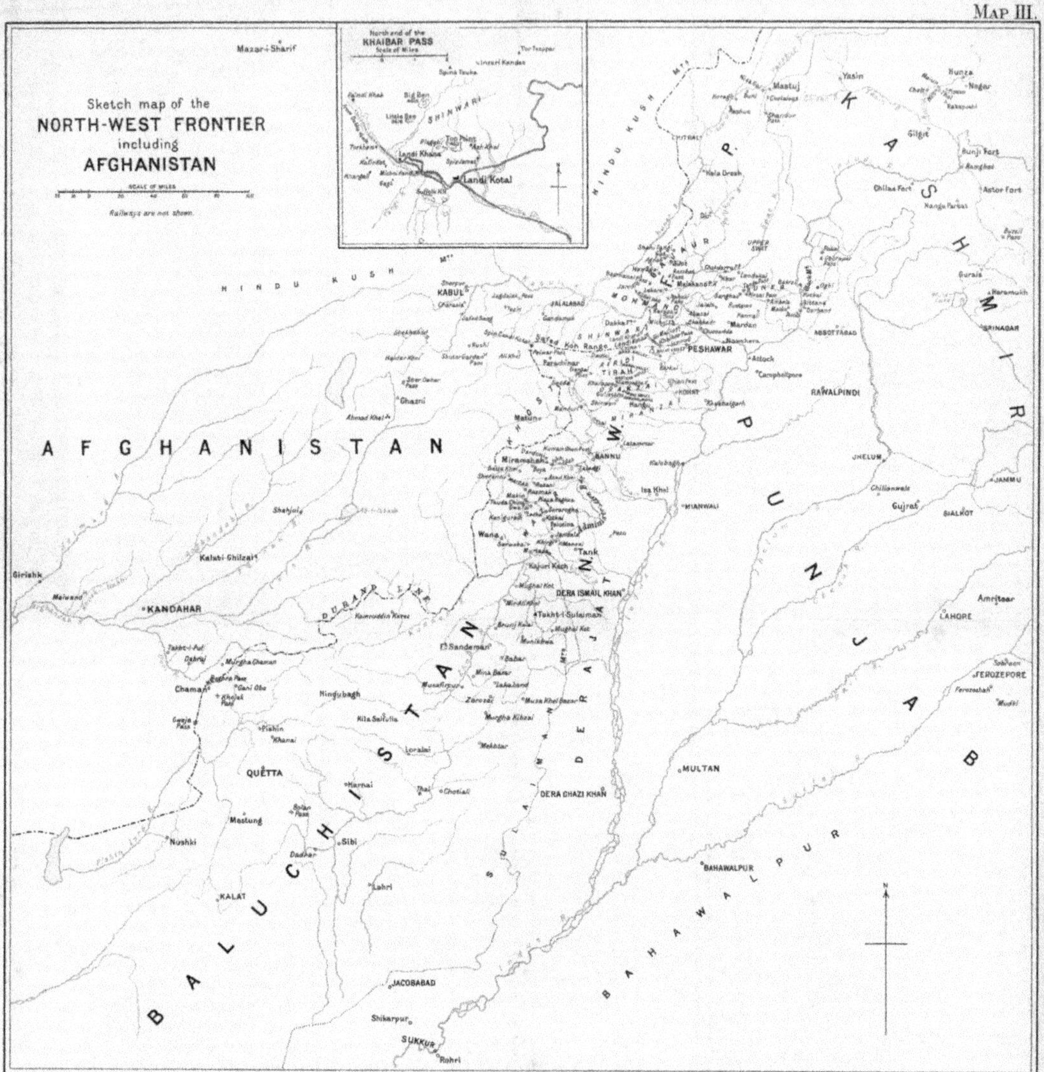
Sketch map of the
NORTH-WEST FRONTIER
including
AFGHANISTAN
Railways are not shown.
North end of the
KHAIBAR PASS
Landi Kotal
Landi Khana
SHINWARI
Mazar-i-Sharif
HINDU KUSH MTS
AFGHANISTAN
KABUL
Ghazni
Kalat-i-Ghilzai
KANDAHAR
Girishk
Maiwand
DURAND LINE
Chaman
Pishin
QUETTA
Mastung
Nushki
KALAT
Sibi
Dadhar
Lahri
JACOBABAD
Shikarpur
SUKKUR
Rohri
BALUCHISTAN
Hindubagh
Fort Sandeman
Loralai
Harnai
Chotiali
DERA GHAZI KHAN
DERA ISMAIL KHAN
Tank
Wana
Miramshah
BANNU
KOHAT
PESHAWAR
Mardan
Nowshera
Attock
Campbellpore
RAWALPINDI
ABBOTTABAD
Chitral
Mastuj
Yasin
Gilgit
Hunza
Nagar
Bunji Fort
Chilas Fort
Astor Fort
SRINAGAR
KASHMIR
JHELUM
Gujrat
SIALKOT
JAMMU
Amritsar
LAHORE
FEROZEPORE
MIANWALI
MULTAN
BAHAWALPUR
PUNJAB
Jalalabad
Parachinar
TIRAH
Safed Koh Range
N.W. F. P.
DERA JAT
SULAIMAN MTS
Takht-i-Sulaiman

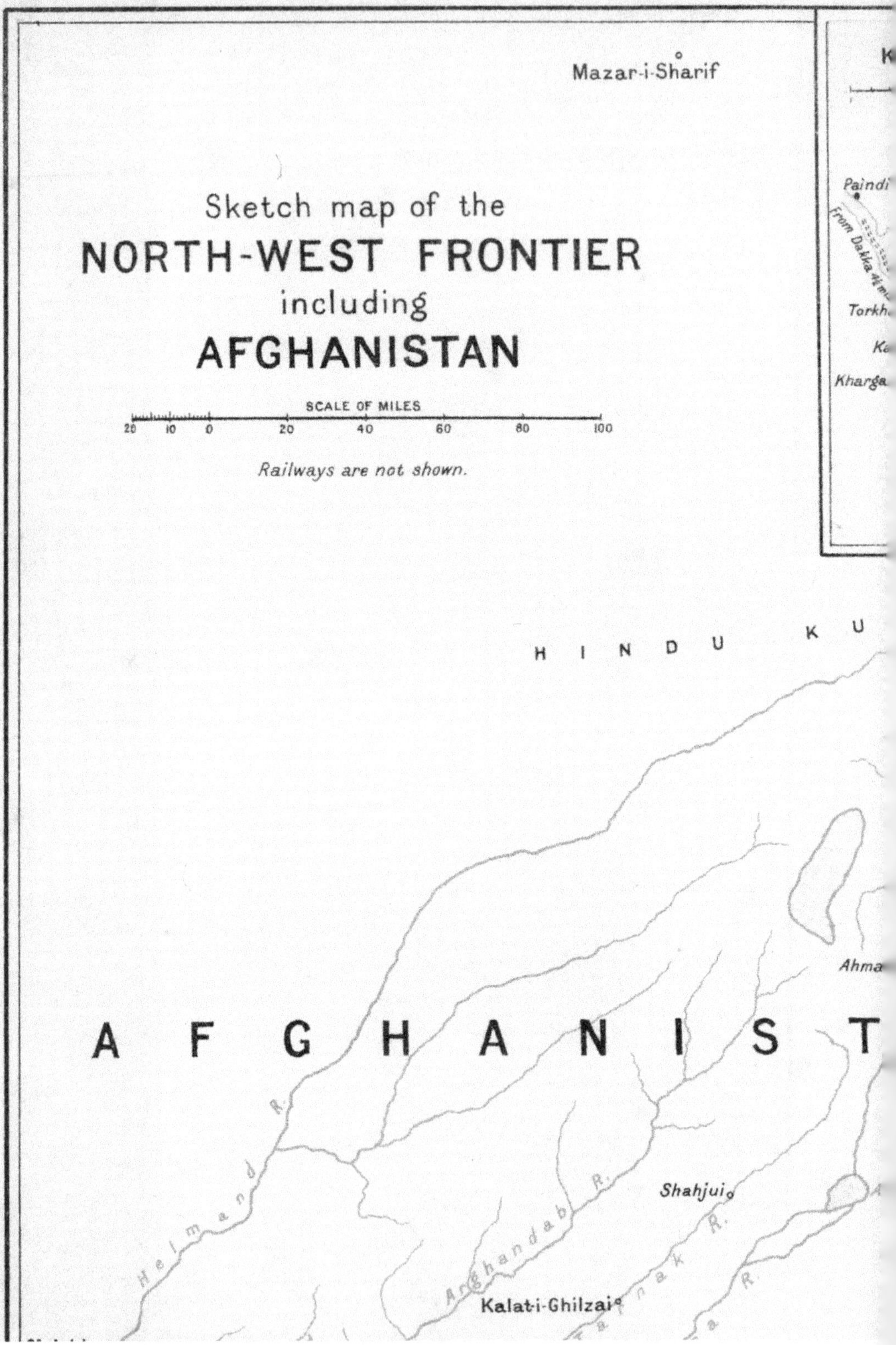
Mazar-i-Sharif
Sketch map of the
NORTH-WEST FRONTIER
including
AFGHANISTAN
SCALE OF MILES
20 10 0 20 40 60 80 100
Railways are not shown.
Paindi
Helmand R.
Arghandab R.
Shahjui
Kalat-i-Ghilzai

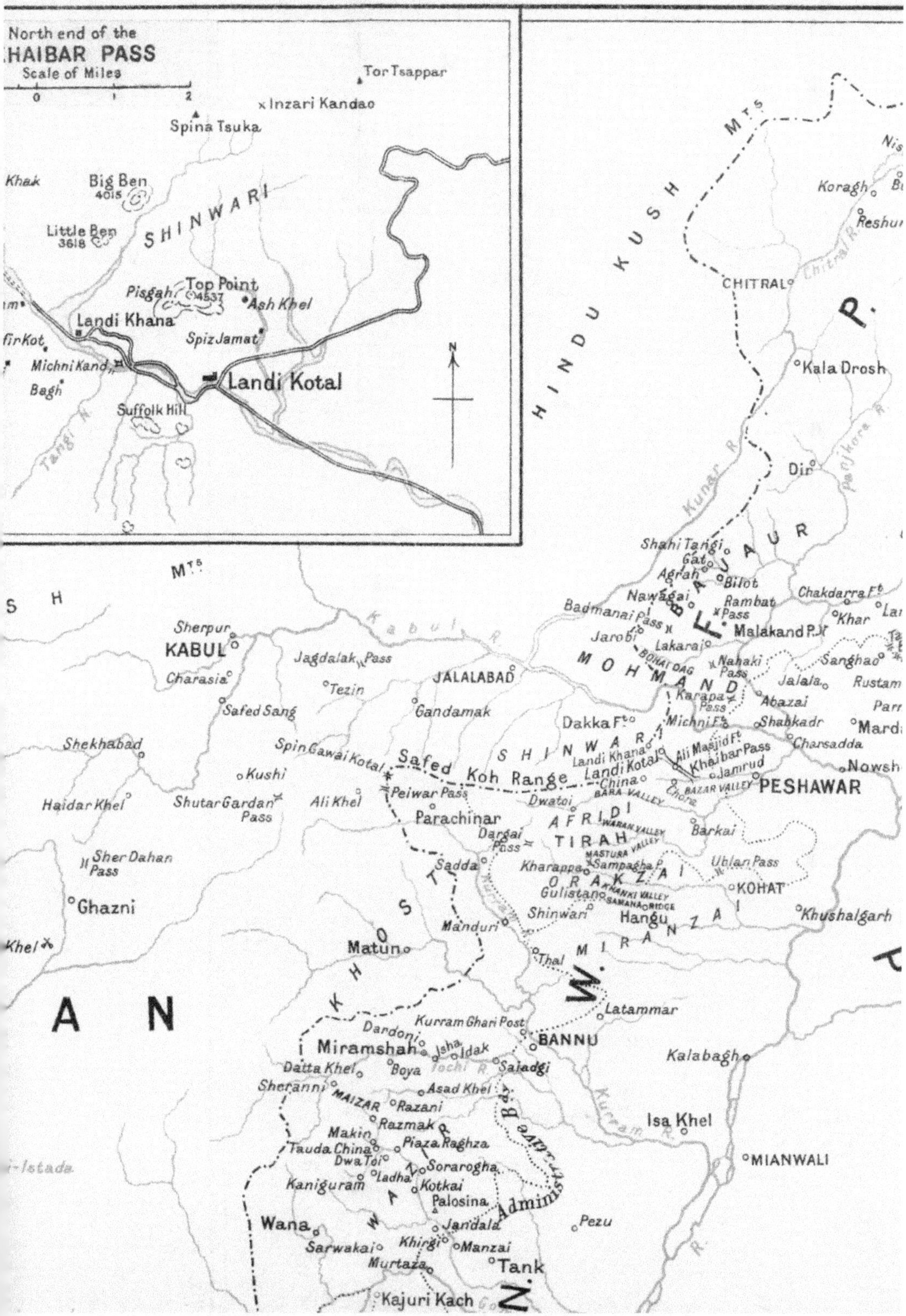

North end of the
HAIBAR PASS
Scale of Miles
0
1
2
Tor Tsappar
Inzari Kandao
Spina Tsuka
Khak
Big Ben
4015
Little Ben
3618
SHINWARI
Top Point
4537
Pisgah
Ash Khel
Landi Khana
Spiz Jamat
Michni Kand
Bagh
Landi Kotal
Suffolk Hill
Tangi R.
N
HINDU KUSH MTS
CHITRAL
Koragh
Reshun
Chitral R.
Kala Drosh
Dir
Kunar R.
Panjkora R.
BAJAUR
Shahi Tangi
Gat
Agrah
Bilot
Nawagai
Rambat Pass
Chakdarra Ft.
Khar
Badmanai Pass
Malakand P.
Jarobi
Lakarai
BOHAI DAG
Nahaki Pass
Sanghao
MOHMAND
Jalala
Rustam
Karapa Pass
Abazai
Michni Ft.
Shabkadr
Mardan
Dakka Ft.
Charsadda
SHINWARI
Landi Khana
Ali Masjid Ft.
Khaibar Pass
Nowshera
Landi Kotal
Jamrud
China
PESHAWAR
BAZAR VALLEY
BARA VALLEY
Dwatoi
AFRIDI
WARAN VALLEY
TIRAH
Barkai
MASTURA VALLEY
Sampagha P.
Ublan Pass
ORAKZAI
KHANKI VALLEY
KOHAT
Gulistan
SAMANA RIDGE
Kharappa
Shinwari
Hangu
Khushalgarh
MIRANZAI
Thal
Latammar
MTS
S H
Kabul R.
Sherpur
KABUL
Charasia
Jagdalak Pass
Tezin
JALALABAD
Gandamak
Safed Sang
Shekhabad
Spin Gawai Kotal
Safed Koh Range
Kushi
Haidar Khel
Shutar Gardan Pass
Ali Khel
Peiwar Pass
Parachinar
Dargai Pass
Sadda
Kurram R.
Sher Dahan Pass
Ghazni
Khel
KHOST
Manduri
Matun
AN
W.
Kurram Ghari Post
Dandoni
BANNU
Miramshah
Isha
Idak
Datta Khel
Boya
Tochi R.
Saiadgi
Kalabagh
Sheranni
MAIZAR
Asad Khel
Razani
Razmak
Kurram R.
Isa Khel
Makin
Piaza Raghza
Tauda China
Dwa Toi
Sorarogha
MIANWALI
Istada
Ladha
Kaniguram
Kotkai
Palosina
Administrative Bdy.
WAZIR
Wana
Jandala
Pezu
Sarwakai
Khirgi
Manzai
Murtaza
Tank
Kajuri Kach
N.

Map III.

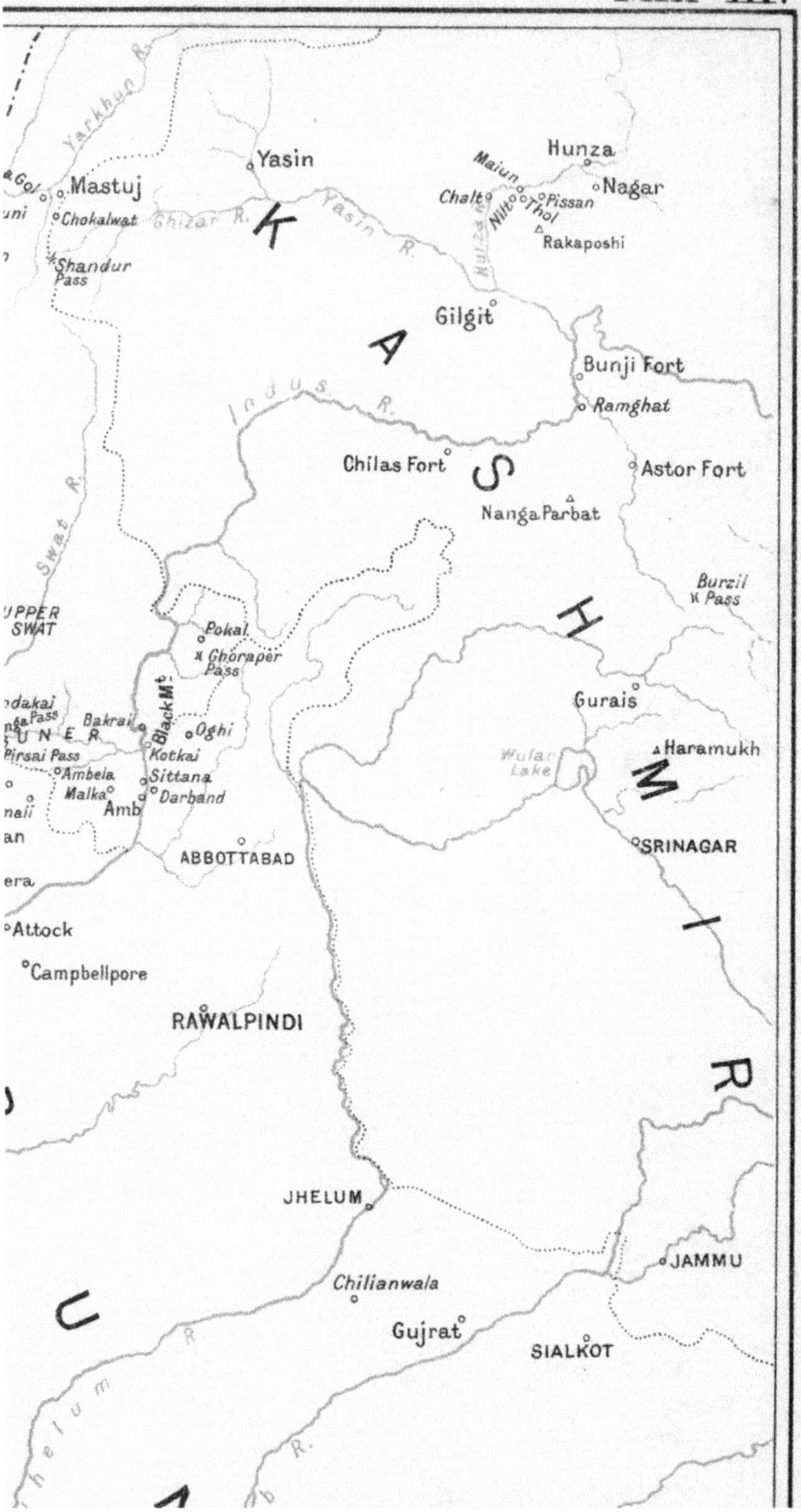

KASHMIR
Yarkhun R.
Yasin
Mastuj
Chokalwat
Ghizar R.
Shandur Pass
Yasin R.
Hunza
Maiun
Nagar
Chalt
Nilt
Thol
Pissan
Hunza R.
Rakaposhi
Gilgit
Bunji Fort
Ramghat
Indus R.
Chilas Fort
Astor Fort
Nanga Parbat
Swat R.
Burzil Pass
UPPER SWAT
Pokal
Ghoraper Pass
Black Mt.
Bakrai
Oghi
Kotkai
Pirsai Pass
Ambela
Sittana
Malka
Darband
Amb
Gurais
Haramukh
Wular Lake
SRINAGAR
ABBOTTABAD
Attock
Campbellpore
RAWALPINDI
JHELUM
JAMMU
Chilianwala
Gujrat
SIALKOT
Jhelum R.

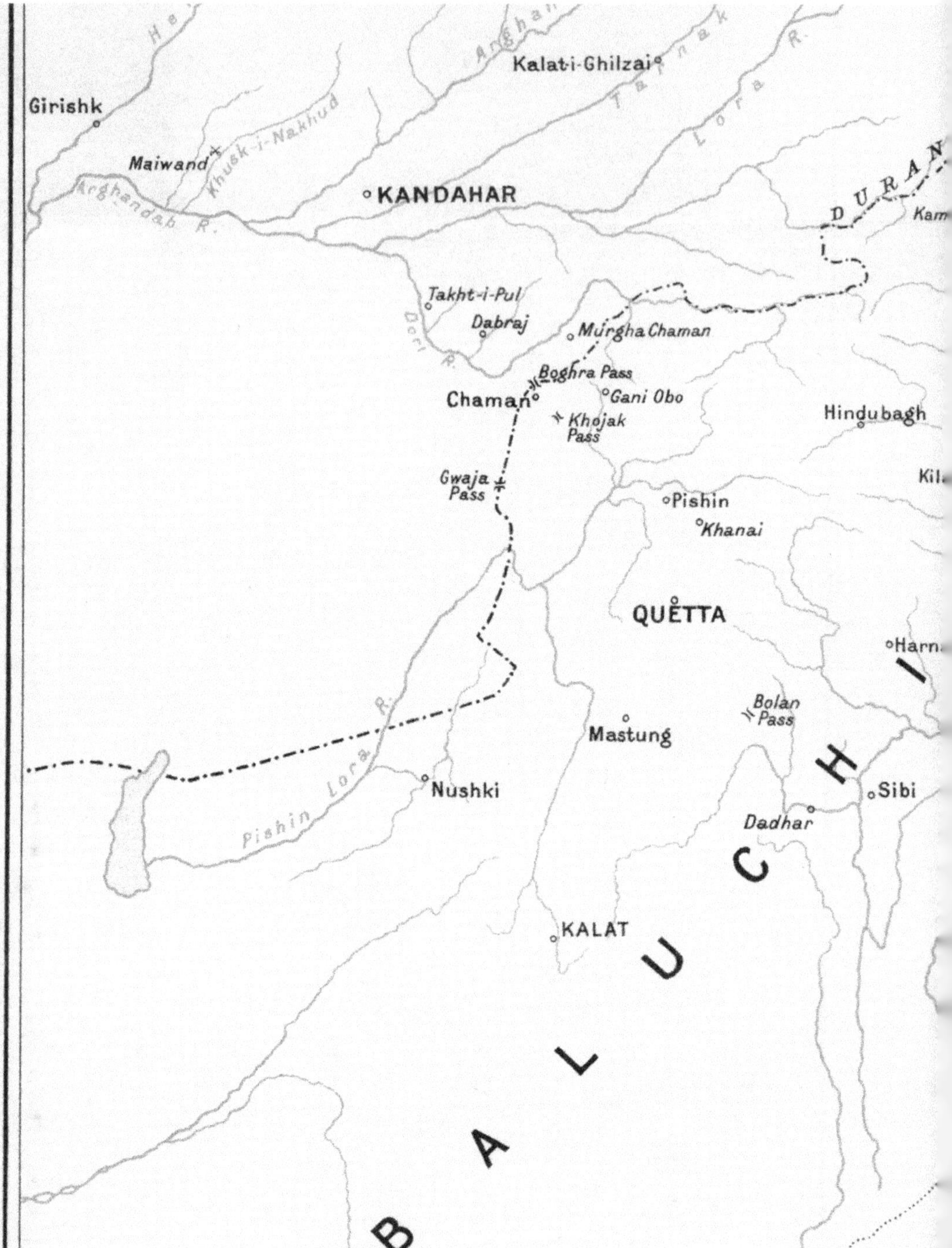
Girishk
Maiwand
Khusk-i-Nakhud
Arghandab R.
KANDAHAR
Kalat-i-Ghilzai
Tarnak
Lora R.
DURAN
Takht-i-Pul
Dabraj
Dori R.
Murgha Chaman
Boghra Pass
Chaman
Gani Obo
Khojak Pass
Hindubagh
Gwaja Pass
Pishin
Khanai
QUETTA
Bolan Pass
Mastung
Nushki
Pishin Lora R.
Sibi
Dadhar
KALAT
BALUCHI

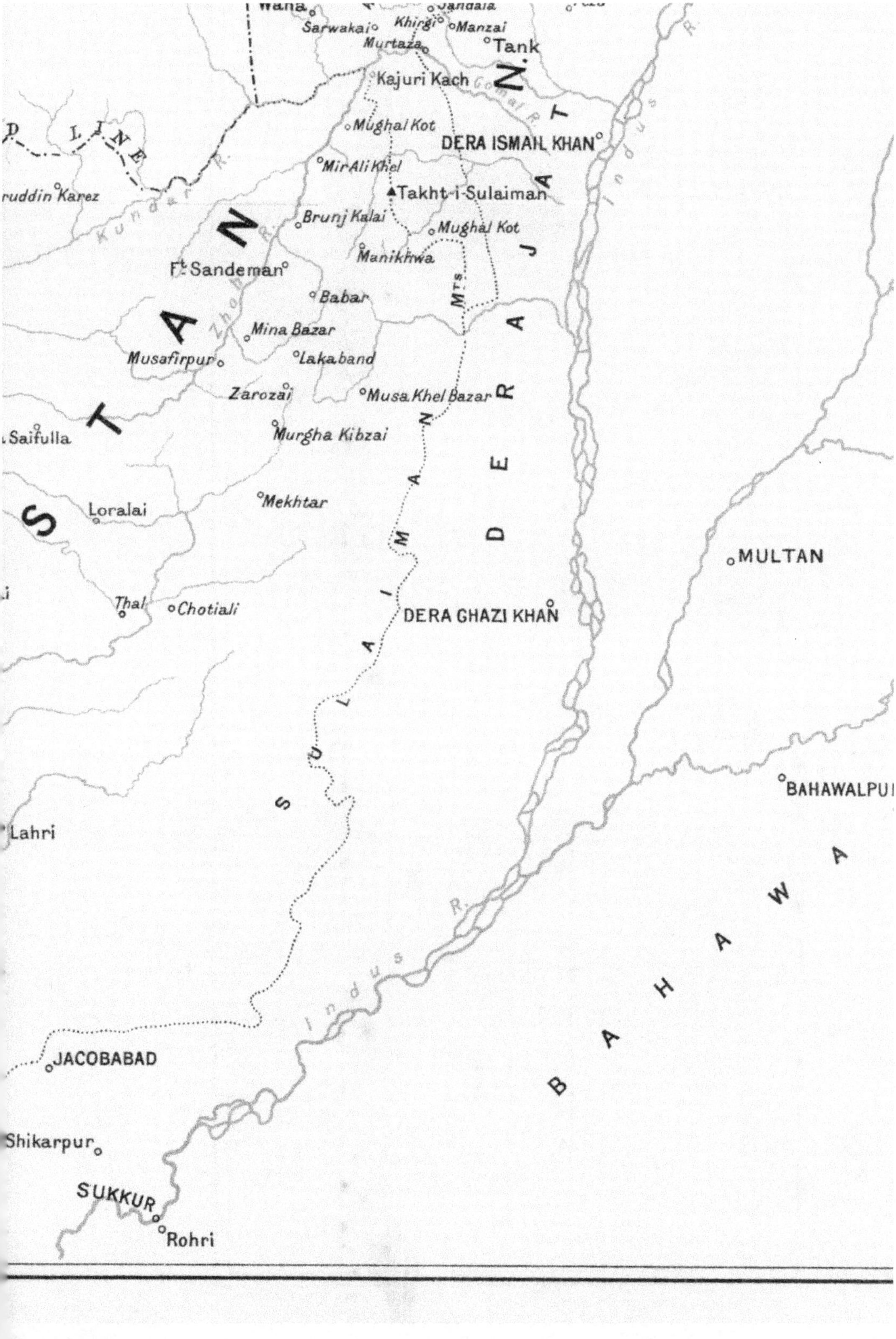
Wana
Jandala
Sarwakai
Khirgi
Manzai
Murtaza
Tank
Kajuri Kach
Gomal R.
D LINE
Mughal Kot
DERA ISMAIL KHAN
Mir Ali Khel
ruddin Karez
Takht-i-Sulaiman
Kundar R.
Brunj Kalai
Mughal Kot
Manikhwa
Ft. Sandeman
Zhob R.
Babar
Mts.
Mina Bazar
Musafirpur
Lakaband
Zarozai
Musa Khel Bazar
Saifulla
Murgha Kibzai
Mekhtar
Loralai
MULTAN
Thal
Chotiali
DERA GHAZI KHAN
SULAIMAN
DERA JAT
STAN
Indus R.
BAHAWALPU
Lahri
JACOBABAD
BAHAWA
Shikarpur
SUKKUR
Rohri

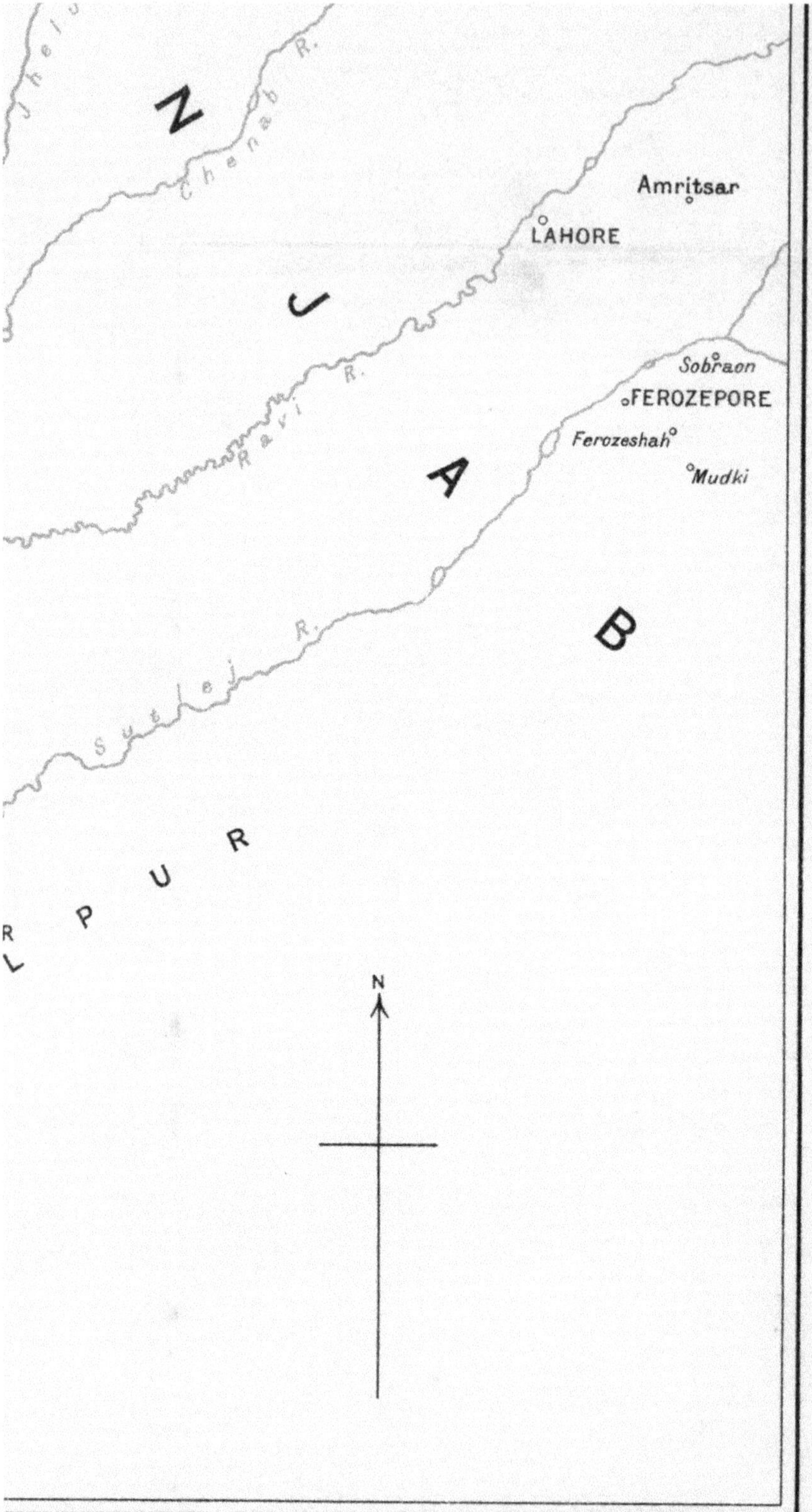

Stanford's Geographical Establishment, London.

Lightning Source UK Ltd.
Milton Keynes UK
UKHW050729120223
416524UK00026B/150

9 781474 537704